USA TODAY SPORTS

RON SHANDLER'S 2022

BASEBALL FORECASTER

AND ENCYCLOPEDIA OF FANALYTICS

TRIUMPH
BOOKS

Triumph Books and colophon are registered trademarks of Random House, Inc.

This book is available in quantity at special discounts for your group or organization. For further information, contact:

Triumph Books LLC
814 North Franklin Street
Chicago, Illinois 60610
(312) 337-0747
www.triumphbooks.com

Printed in U.S.A.
ISBN: 978-1-62937-973-9

Rotisserie League Baseball is a registered trademark of the Rotisserie League Baseball Association, Inc.

Statistics provided by Baseball Info Solutions

Cover design and photo illustration by Brent Hershey
Front cover photographs (2) by Gary A. Vasquez-USA TODAY Sports
Author photograph by Kevin Hurley

Ron Shandler's
BASEBALL FORECASTER

Editors
Ray Murphy
Brent Hershey

Associate Editors
Brandon Kruse
Ryan Bloomfield

• • • • • •

Tech/Data/Charts
Matt Cederholm
Mike Krebs

Graphic Design
Brent Hershey

Player Commentaries
Ryan Bloomfield
Alain de Leonardis
Arik Florimonte
Brent Hershey
Brandon Kruse
Dan Marcus
Ray Murphy
Stephen Nickrand
Kristopher Olson
Greg Pyron
Brian Rudd
Paul Sporer
Jock Thompson
Rod Truesdell

Research and Articles
Bob Berger
Patrick Davitt
Ed DeCaria
Arik Florimonte
Dave Martin
Dan Marcus
Todd Zola

Prospects
Chris Blessing
Jeremy Deloney
Rob Gordon
Tom Mulhall

Injury Chart
Rick Wilton

Acknowledgments

Producing the *Baseball Forecaster* has been a team effort for a number of years now; the list of credits to the left is where the heavy lifting gets done. On behalf of Ron, Brent, and Ray, our most sincere thanks to each of those key contributors.

We are just as grateful to the rest of the BaseballHQ.com staff, who do the yeoman's work in populating the website with 12 months of incredible content: Dave Adler, Andy Andres, Matt Beagle, Alex Beckey, Derrick Boyd, Brian Brickley, Brant Chesser, Doug Dennis, Matt Dodge, Jim Ferretti, Adam Feldman, Greg Fishwick, Neil FitzGerald, Rick Green, Phil Hertz, Ed Hubbard, Tom Kephart, Brad Kullman, Chris Lee, Bill McKnight, Matthew Mougalian, Harold Nichols, Josh Paley, Nick Richards, Peter Sheridan, Andy Smith, Tanner Smith, Skip Snow, Matthew St-Germain, Jeffrey Tomich, Michael Weddell, Mike Werner, and Jeff Zimmerman.

Thank you to all our industry colleagues, a truly impressive group. They are competitors, but they are also colleagues working to grow this industry, which is never more evident than at our First Pitch Forums live events. Maybe we'll even get to plan two of 'em in 2022!

Thank you to Chris Pirrone, Ryan Bonini, and the team at USA Today Sports Media Group.

Thank you for all the support from the folks at Triumph Books and Action Printing.

And of course, thank *you*, readers, for your interest in what we all have to say. Your kind words, support and (respectful) criticism move us forward on the fanalytic continuum more than you know. We are grateful for your readership.

•

From Brent Hershey Multi-tasking is a given in today's world. While not everyone can excel at two things quite to the extent of our coverboy Mr. Ohtani, the Forecaster team listed to the left demonstrates the value and immersing oneself in a singular endeavor. The intense six-week sprint we go through makes this book stand out, as the information, perspectives and analysis deepens with each season. Thanks to you all. Specific kudos to Ryan and Brandon for their behind-the-scenes preparation and execution; to Ron for allowing all of us to share in this little 36-year-old project; and of course to Ray for the co-editor partnership that we've been able to sustain and refine for the past 10 (!) editions. At home, thanks to Lorie, Dillon and Eden for your individual examples of excelling at one task, while being responsible for the completion of many. Finding that balance is not easy, but in the end, is very rewarding.

From Ray Murphy This book goes from vapor in August to your hands in December, and the only way that happens is thanks to the dedication of those people listed at left. A tip of the cap to each of them. Even with those many hands contributing, sometimes real-life events seep into these pages. In my case, see Freddy Galvis' commentary for details.

Collaborating with Ron and Brent remains as much of a joy today as it was the first time Ron asked for help. We've all migrated to somewhat different life stages over the intervening years. I was reminded of that this cycle, as it was 10 years ago that I missed the final week of editing due to the birth of my twin daughters. A decade later, they're thriving in school, and my All-Star wife Jennifer is immersed in her now-resumed career. Happily, the Forecaster continues to thrive as well. Here's to another decade of growth and progress ahead.

From Ron Shandler I lost my Dad a few weeks after last year's Forecaster came out. We had a complicated relationship; he was the type who'd proudly show off this book to friends while never reading a word in it. My career arc was bewildering to him, and although he finally came around, one of the last things he said to me was that I was a disappointment.

As a parent myself, I know that your kids will find their path, because of—or despite—all you do. Either way can lead to their success. So, however I've gotten to 36 years in this business, my Dad somehow drove me towards it. Thanks, I guess.

Now that I'm here, it's all of you readers who keep me coming back each year, and I appreciate that beyond words. Thanks also to Ray, Brent and the gang, and my amazing female support system at home, who all help to build the Forecaster legacy. That legacy includes so many stories, and so I am writing an historical memoir that you'll be able to read soon. Details at RonShandler.com.

TABLE OF CONTENTS

Healing

by Ron Shandler

Back around Memorial Day, in the League of Alternative Baseball Reality (LABR) national experts competition, my team was pacing the field in hitting but lagging in saves. Jake Ciely of *The Athletic* had the opposite problem and reached out to me, offering one of his closers and a lesser bat for one of my big power guys.

Let's attach some names. He was offering closer Matt Barnes; I was willing to discuss outfielder Austin Meadows. Don't judge; remember, this was back in May.

By noon on May 26, we had the basis of a deal in place and were nearly ready to lock it in. He'd send me Barnes and outfielder David Peralta for Meadows.

Then things got funky.

Here are the time-stamped emails:

Jake (2:03 pm): I am leaning towards another deal in which I'd get both Marcell Ozuna and Spencer Howard for the same duo. Just wanted to let you know in case you wanted to offer a bit more. If you're out and too pricey, I understand.

I didn't want to increase my offer when there were other fish in the sea. So I scoped out the standings for another team awash in saves. The category leader was Ray Murphy and he also could use a bat, so I sent him a note:

Me (2:20 pm): Hey, do you have any interest in Austin Meadows for one of your closers as part of a larger deal?

Ray and I bounced around a bunch of ideas over the next few hours until we had the basis of an agreement.

Me (5:06 pm): Okay, I'll agree to do Meadows and Luke Voit for Alex Reyes, Kenta Maeda and Mike Yastrzemski. Confirm?

Again, don't judge. Hindsight makes these offers look silly. So, with that deal in place...

Me, to Jake (5:07 pm): I'm out on Barnes. Working on another deal.

As I waited for Ray's final thumbs up, I received this email:

Jake (5:11 pm): I was about to email you. I just saw Ozuna's injury. I'm back in on a Meadows deal.

Me (5:12 pm): I just accepted the other offer. Sorry.

And then, of course:

Ray (5:26 pm): So it turns out Voit is broken. No-go on this.

And that deal collapsed.

In a span of 20 minutes, two injuries scuttled a pair of trades that had been pretty much nailed down. Within a few months, nearly every player in these deals would spend time on the IL.

For many of us, that was the story of 2021, a season in which your roster was never more than a few hours away from the next injury.

My story was frustrating, but not as bad as one poor guy in my local league. At our July 4 get-together, he sold off a massive trove of prized prospects for his only legitimate shot at a title, landing both Ronald Acuña and Jacob deGrom. Six days later, Acuña tore his ACL. A week after that, deGrom hit the IL. In a span of 15 days, his team effectively lost its present *and* its future.

The flow of constant injuries this year has been unlike any we've ever seen.

Year	IL Players	3 yr Avg	IL Days	3 yr Avg
2010	393	408	22,911	25,783
2011	422	408	25,610	24,924
2012	409	408	30,408	27,038
2013	442	419	29,551	28,523
2014	422	424	25,839	28,599
2015	454	439	28,982	28,124
2016	478	451	31,329	28,717
2017	533	488	30,913	30,408
2018	574	528	34,284	32,175
2019	563	557	36,394	33,864
*2020	393		22,911	
2021	835	657	47,693	39,457

*2020 data not included in 3-year averages.

The 2021 data looks insane, but it is artificially inflated. COVID-19 quarantines accounted for at least 103 players and 1,467 days. There were 78 more players who lost COVID time, but those stints were combined with "actual" injuries so it is tough to tease out the COVID-only time lost.

Also, this was the first full season without 40-man roster expansion in September. Prior to 2020, the larger rosters mostly eliminated the need for using the IL. There were 52 IL stints recorded during the first three weeks of September (beyond that doesn't really matter). Makes you wonder how many injury replacements our fantasy teams were cheated out of in past years.

Even with those adjustments, 2021 was still a year of big hurt. The COVID-shortened 2020 season wreaked havoc with players' conditioning, forcing them to ramp up, then ramp down, then ramp up again. That disruption carried over into the winter as players attempted to get back onto their usual 12-month routines. The injury fallout led to a record-high 265 players making their big league debuts in 2021, many of them to fill the spots of IL denizens. And fantasy leaguers faced similar roster challenges all year long, up and down the draft board.

Since 2009, I've kept an annual Attrition Chart. This is essentially a record of players who began each season in the Top 300 (according to the Average Draft Position rankings from the National Fantasy Baseball Championship) and at some point were placed on the Injured List, optioned to the minors, or designated for assignment (the vast majority—93%—were IL stints). These are the players who represent the core of our teams each year. The attrition percentage hit a new all-time high in 2021, and it wasn't even close:

2009	51%
2010	44%
2011	49%
2012	45%
2013	51%
2014	53%
2015	47%
2016	47%
2017	58%
2018	60%
2019	59%
2020	62%
2021	71%

Imagine! Seven out of every 10 players drafted in the Top 300 amassed less playing time than we expected, or hoped. Roster management required a perpetual effort in 2021. It was crazy.

Not a Doctor

For many years, I've joked that "IL days" should be a Rotisserie category, but really, that's not entirely a bad idea. Many consider that "staying healthy" is a skill, and being forced to consider the impact of health on our fantasy rosters has become a challenge worth tracking. I suspect that if IL days were a standard element in stat data feeds that this would have been incorporated by commissioner services a long time ago.

But why stop there? This past fall, a Tank McNamara comic strip suggests that we could do more:

> TANK (a reporter): "The NFL Injury Fantasy League is based on the instances and severity of player damage each week."

> LEAGUE COMMISH: "Tank, before the season starts, we draft types of injuries, the teams that will be affected most, and for maximum points, we pick individual players."

That sounds like the beginnings of a viable competition, or if nothing else, a pretty cool side bet.

The Commish adds, "This league is almost exclusively made up of orthopedic surgeons," which is presumably the comic's punch line. But we know better—this could be real. We may not be doctors but we could do this.

When it comes to MLB teams, we know that some are better at managing injuries than others and we probably should be incorporating that into our analysis. Below is a chart of team-by-team days lost in 2021. It shows the number of players who were placed on the IL (players who went on the IL multiple times are counted once), the total days lost and the average number of days lost per player.

We can draw rough conclusions from these charts, with the emphasis on "rough." In general, the counting stats of players and IL days might reflect a team's proficiency at *conditioning and*

injury prevention. The averages of days lost per injured player might reflect a team's proficiency at *treatment and rehabilitation.*

We don't know what goes on behind closed doors of major league training rooms, so maybe we're not ready to pass judgment on medical proficiency outright. At minimum, maybe we can just say that some teams were particularly lucky or unlucky.

Teams are sorted by average number of days lost per injured player, least to most.

	— — —2021— — —		
	Players	Days	Avg
BAL	23	1126	49.0
OAK	18	918	51.0
MIL	30	1561	52.0
DET	23	1203	52.3
SF	36	1946	54.1
PHI	23	1244	54.1
KC	21	1140	54.3
BOS	14	764	54.6
WAS	24	1331	55.5
PIT	29	1609	55.5
CHC	29	1629	56.2
CHW	22	1236	56.2
COL	21	1183	56.3
CLE	14	819	58.5
LAA	21	1273	60.6
ARI	21	1288	61.3
MIA	24	1490	62.1
NYY	26	1658	63.8
STL	21	1374	65.4
MIN	26	1704	65.5
TOR	27	1780	65.9
NYM	34	2354	69.2
CIN	21	1464	69.7
ATL	18	1271	70.6
LAD	28	2022	72.2
HOU	21	1520	72.4
TEX	25	1837	73.5
TAM	31	2352	75.9
SEA	21	1973	94.0
SD	24	2578	107.4

The Best: The Indians, Red Sox and Athletics lost the fewest players to injury in 2021, and were the only teams with fewer than 20 players and fewer than 1,000 days lost. Players on Baltimore, Oakland, Milwaukee and Detroit lost the least amount of time per injury.

The Worst: The Giants, Brewers, Mets and Rays were the only teams to lose 30 or more players to injury. Those poor Mariners and Padres! Their average IL stint lasted at least three months.

This is interesting data, but 2021 was just one year. We can look at a three-year scan (2018, 2019 and 2021) to see if there were any patterns or consistency. I have excluded 2020 data because even the worst injury that year did not cost a player more than 60 days. What appear here are annual averages, sorted by average number of days lost per hurt player.

| | —Avg 2018, 2019, 2021— | | |
	Players	Days	Avg
COL	15	708	48.8
CIN	14	697	50.7
MIN	16	840	54.2
SF	18	950	54.3
CHC	17	930	54.7
BAL	13	718	56.3
DET	14	789	56.4
MIL	17	964	57.5
PIT	18	1050	58.3
PHI	16	908	58.6
OAK	14	825	58.9
LAD	19	1124	59.2
CHW	13	752	60.2
WAS	16	960	60.9
ATL	16	948	61.1
HOU	12	752	61.4
STL	15	946	63.1
LAA	18	1123	63.2
MIA	16	1012	63.3
BOS	13	833	65.3
TAM	18	1169	65.8
KC	12	792	66.0
TOR	16	1040	66.0
ARI	13	848	67.9
NYM	19	1314	68.2
CLE	12	840	68.6
TEX	18	1260	69.1
NYY	19	1373	72.3
SEA	15	1089	73.8
SD	16	1531	95.7

The Best: The Astros, Royals and Indians averaged the fewest players lost to injury during those three years, each averaging 12 per year. The Orioles, White Sox, Red Sox and Diamondbacks were right behind, with 13. Players on the Rockies, Reds, Twins and Giants lost the least amount of time per injury.

The Worst: The Dodgers, Yankees and Mets averaged the most players lost, each with 19 per year. The Giants, Pirates, Angels, Rays and Rangers were next with 18.

Players on the Padres, Mariners and Yankees lost the most days per injury.

While this is interesting on a macro level, it's useful to dig a little deeper. We can look at a few common injury types and see if some teams have been better at handling them than others. However, there are two problems with this approach using the data at hand.

First, there are injuries that affect multiple parts of the body or migrate from one area to another. If someone goes down with an elbow injury and has his IL stint extended because of a biceps issue, or oblique, or back, it's tough to parse the IL days and attach them to specific ailments. So the data is a bit muddy. But I think it still feeds back to how the injuries were diagnosed, treated and rehabbed by each team.

The second problem is sample size. Most injuries didn't generate a three-year sample large enough to be worth viewing on a team-by-team basis. So we'll only look at the three injury types with the largest samples and only the most notable teams.

Let's start with hamstrings…

During the three years studied, 10 teams had only 3-5 players going down with hamstring injuries, but they experienced a wide range of days lost. At the top were the Pirates (4 hamstring IL stints) and Orioles (5), the only teams whose players lost less than a month on the IL. Next were the Rockies (4 injuries, average 33 days on the IL), Astros (5, 39), Blue Jays (3, 44), Padres (4, 47) and Reds (3, 49). Losing about twice as much time per injury as the leaders were the Indians (5, 56), Tigers (5, 62), and D'backs (5, 63)—were those hammy injuries more severe or did those teams have subpar rehab programs?

The White Sox (14) and Mets (13) had the most players sustain hamstring injuries, with both teams averaging about six weeks on the IL. The Rays (12), Giants (12), Brewers (11), Red Sox (10), Yankees (10) and Braves (10) were the only other teams incurring double-digit IL stints, with average time lost ranging from 30 days (Red Sox) to 53 days (Braves).

Next, the shoulders…

The Orioles top this list again, leading all teams with only seven players hitting the IL with shoulder injuries. Their average time lost of only 32 days also paced the field. The Rockies, Twins, Padres, Red Sox and Rangers each had eight players lose time, with the Rockies (34 days) on the low end of average time lost and the Red Sox (96) and Rangers (100) at the high end.

Check this out… these were the only teams that averaged 50 or fewer days lost per shoulder injury: Baltimore, Colorado, Pittsburgh, Kansas City, Cincinnati, Chicago Cubs and Minnesota. Aside from the Reds, not a winning team in the bunch. But the Pirates (16) and Royals (14) were also among the teams with the most IL stints. The Cardinals (15), Braves (14) and Brewers (14) were the others, all three averaging around 75 days lost.

The Indians amassed the most days lost to shoulder injuries— over 1,200—with Danny Salazar accounting for 30 percent of them.

Finally, the elbows.

There's something about those Orioles. During the three years studied, they had only three players sustain elbow injuries and were the only organization that avoided even one Tommy John surgery. (Considering that their best team ERA over those three years was 5.18, maybe their pitchers are just not throwing hard enough.) The Reds, Indians and Cubs each had five players with elbow woes and one TJS recipient apiece.

The only teams to average less than three months lost per elbow injury were the Reds (5 elbow injuries, including 1 TJS), Red Sox (8,1), Nats (9,1), D'backs (10,3), Tigers (11,1) and Blue Jays (12,2).

On the flipside, the Padres had 19 players with elbow injuries, seven of them went under the knife for TJS and lost over 2,700 days to the IL. Their average time lost was 145 days, worst of all teams.

Next were the Rangers (17,1) and Mets (16,4). The Rays (10,6) tied San Diego with the most days lost per IL stint (145). The Giants (14,8) had the most TJ surgeries of any team.

How should we use this information in 2022?

There are several teams that appear consistently near the top or bottom of these lists. Is that predictive for 2022? Tough to say. But whether or not we'd choose to create a fantasy competition around this information (thanks, Tank!), I would still approach these tidbits as added color to your overall risk analysis effort.

For instance, if you have to decide between an Orioles or Padres pitcher—assuming they are both of moderately equivalent value (don't judge, just follow the logic)—you might look at the above data and take a chance on the Orioles arm. Am I really recommending that you draft an Oriole over a Padre? Targeting poor players who rarely get hurt seems like a terrible idea; who needs more bad innings? But maybe if you're faced with a choice between John Means and Yu Darvish, or Trey Mancini and Trent Grisham, you opt for the O.

Here are the rough options:

Relatively healthy teams to target: Baltimore, Boston, Cleveland, Colorado

Relatively unhealthy teams to avoid: San Diego, New York Mets, Tampa Bay, San Francisco, Texas

I am not necessarily recommending that you shun playoff contenders, only that this is yet another data point in your fana-lytic arsenal. And as an avowed Mets fan (empathetic tweets always welcome), reminders like these help me separate my fandom from my fantasy.

Risk, "Ish" and the Mayberry List

Ugh, lazy rhymes. Indulge me.

When it comes to all these injuries, was 2021 a one-off or is this going to become a chronic condition? And for fantasy leaguers, is there any cure for our roster distress?

At a panel discussion I moderated at First Pitch Arizona back in October, I asked the speakers whether they thought this frequency of IL moves would continue. The consensus was that it would. Teams will continue to use the IL not only to manage injuries but also to manage workloads. (It's not like they need to provide a doctor's note to put someone on the IL.) So, barring any changes to the IL rules, we can look forward to navigating more playing time challenges in 2022.

How should we handle this uncertainty?

The player forecasting process tends to focus primarily on skills maximization with a dash of risk avoidance. We project the numbers each player should put up and adjust downward for injury risks. Despite this process, there are always a few players who rise in the rankings for no other reason than the hope they will do better. (Look up "The Hope Hypothesis" in the Fanalytic Encyclopedia, page 66, for a more formal definition.)

You will see this *a lot* in 2022. Right up top, Ronald Acuña, Jacob deGrom and Mike Trout will likely still be in or close to the first round of ADPs despite the fact that we really don't know how much they will play next season. The draft value of star players coming off injury, like Clayton Kershaw and Justin Verlander, will also likely get boosted with a healthy dose of Hope.

The sharp rise in injuries begs for a shift in the relative weights we give each part of this analysis. There is a fairly simple, logical draft planning process I like to use to deal with this, and the tools are in your hands right now. However, it is going to require a slight mindset adjustment. Here it is:

1. Stop using ADPs. We have an obsession with ADPs and projected dollar values, which forces us to rank players, one against the other. A $25 player is better than a $24 player who is better than a $23 player. ADP 24 is better than ADP 27 is better than ADP 29.

But it is nearly impossible to project each player's numbers with enough precision for us to assign value at that granular a level.

If you look at the numbers with a slightly more objective lens, you'd see that players are more alike than they are different. There are batters who might hit 25ish homers, or be .270ish hitters, or pitchers with 3.50ish ERAs. It's really all about the "ish"—we can't expect much more precision than that.

That truth makes ADPs nearly pointless. The proof is in the track record—the marketplace does a crappy job of evaluating talent (see "The Ineptitude of ADPs" in the Encyclopedia, page 57). So stop it, especially at the granular level of individual ADP ranks.

That goes for this book too. Our focus is more about projecting general tendencies than hard numbers anyway. Embrace the imprecision. Read the Consumer Advisory a few pages from here.

2. Create your own groups. Since players are just muddled masses of skills—again, all about the "ish"—I prefer to consider each draft round or auction dollar tier as a single entity that describes *a group of comparably-skilled players,* more or less.

In the first round, for instance, Trea Turner will give you more stolen bases and Vlad Guerrero will hit more homers, but they will roughly have the same impact on your team's season, depending upon how you structure your roster. Assess the skills profiles, then toss all potential first-rounders, or $35-plus players, together into Group 1. Toss all potential 5th rounders, or $18-$20 players, together into Group 5. ("Average Player Value by Draft Round" appears in the Encyclopedia, page 60.) That means, Jared Walsh, Jonathan India and Justin Turner are pretty much inter-changeable from a draft perspective.

ADPs and projected dollar values have some value here in that they will tell you roughly how much you'd have to pay to roster each player. But you need to create these groups on your own, using the tools in this book and determining each player's value to the roster you want to construct.

3. Bring in Mayberry. The Mayberry Method is fully described in the Encyclopedia (by now you should know that there is a lot of really cool stuff in there), but here is the 25-cent summary: Mayberry reduces each player's profile to a seven-character code. The first four numeric characters rate skill on a 0 to 5 scale. The final three-character Reliability Grade measures each player's health history, MLB experience/playing time and skills consis-tency on an "A" to "F" scale. Health is probably the more impor-tant variable for our purposes here, but you should evaluate each player using all three. The Random Variance indicator is also useful to identify players whose stats may naturally regress from last year due to, well, random variance (hence, the name).

4. Assemble by injury risk. Okay, you've created your groups of comparably-skilled players, and you know that they are mostly interchangeable (because, again, of the "ish"). Now we can rank the players within those groups based on risk profile.

Let's run through an exercise.

Below is a group of 15 players who I believe are worthy of a first round pick. This is purely speculative as I sit here writing this in November. You might quibble with a few who should not be here, perhaps add a few who you consider blatant oversights. This is my personal list, in alphabetical order.

ROUND 1	MM	Rel	Rand Var
Ronald Acuña	5335	DAA	0
Mookie Betts	4445	BAB	+2
Bo Bichette	3455	AAA	-2
Corbin Burnes	5503	BBF	-2
Gerrit Cole	5505	BAB	0
Jacob deGrom	5503	FAB	-5
Freddie Freeman	4255	AAF	0
Vlad Guerrero, Jr.	4155	AAC	-2
Bryce Harper	5355	BAC	-4
Shohei Ohtani (B/P)	5435/4403	BAD/CDF	0/0
José Ramírez	4455	AAD	+1
Juan Soto	4255	AAF	-1
Fernando Tatis, Jr.	5445	CAB	+1
Mike Trout	5355	FCD	-5
Trea Turner	3555	AAC	-5

Mayberry Score (MM): Batters (power, speed, batting average, plate appearances), Pitchers (ERA, strikeouts, saves, innings)
Reliability: Health, Experience/playing time, consistency
Random Variance: Values over 0 indicate potential for positive regression. Values below 0 indicate potential for negative regression

With a particular focus on injury avoidance, let's rank my speculative first round players by risk and toss them into three buckets:

Rnk	ROUND 1	MM	Rel	Rand Var
Lower risk				
1	Trea Turner	3555	AAC	-5
2	José Ramírez	4455	AAD	+1
3	Bo Bichette	3455	AAA	-2
4	Juan Soto	4255	AAF	-1
5	Vlad Guerrero, Jr.	4155	AAC	-2
6	Freddie Freeman	4255	AAF	0
Moderate risk				
7	Gerrit Cole	5505	BAB	0
8	Mookie Betts	4445	BAB	+2
9	Bryce Harper	5355	BAC	-4
10	Shohei Ohtani (B/P)	5435/4403	BAD/CDF	0/0
11	Corbin Burnes	5503	BBF	-2
12	Fernando Tatis, Jr.	5445	CAB	+1
Higher risk				
13	Ronald Acuña	5335	DAA	0
14	Mike Trout	5355	FCD	-5
15	Jacob deGrom	5503	FAB	-5

In auction leagues, you can assign a dollar value to each slot and then use the above rankings to align each player to a salary range. These are all $30-plus players.

5. Analyze, select, repeat. In viewing this list, all the lower risk players in slots 1-6 are pretty much interchangeable. All have "A" grade health; you can use the Experience or Consistency grade, or Random Variance indicator to color the rankings. I've ordered them here based on my own perceived value, elevating the base-stealers in our speed-starved environment. But really, depending upon how I planned to structure my roster, I could justify listing Freeman at the top as much as Turner.

Acuña, Trout and deGrom all have poor injury grades and are significantly discounted within the round. Yes, any or all of the three *might* be healthy by Opening Day but is that a risk we should be taking this early in the draft? For me, none of them should be anywhere near the top of the first round. Admittedly, it

would not take much arm-twisting to get me to push them into Round 2.

Shohei Ohtani is difficult to peg. His batter and pitcher ratings are different, and with a "C" health grade on the mound, there's more risk of those numbers going south. Seriously, we've been so blinded by his glittering 2021 performance that we often forget about the injury history. I'll talk more about him later.

It may be tough to see Fernando Tatis, Jr. listed so low. The difference between this ranking and his presumably higher ADP might be considered "Hope Inflation." Sure, we'd like to see Tatis put up monster numbers as a Top 3 pick next year, but his balky shoulder might have other ideas. This exercise suggests a discount while still placing him in his target round. Yes, this means the odds are against you getting him, but it also means that someone else has to shoulder the risk. Pun definitely intended.

For each subsequent round, the process is the same. Wash, rinse, repeat.

Do these health grades really work? Well, last year, 28 percent of the players with health grades of A or B went on the IL. Those players with grades of D or F hit the IL at a rate of 53 percent. So there is merit to the system.

Of course, there is no such thing as a risk-free player, but the top six on this list have minimal risk exposure. If they are all gone by the time your pick is up, you might opt to draw a low-risk name from the second round instead of incurring excess risk up front.

This is not to say that there is no place to embrace risk. The further down the draft board, the more that taking chances can provide great benefit. I like to have a risk budget, allocating perhaps 3-4 roster spots for risky acquisitions. In the end, risk tolerance is a personal decision, but current conditions do beg for a more conservative approach.

The View from Section 340, Row Z
All of the above lives within our ever-changing statistical environment so it's always good to have an annual reality check from the cheap seats. There have been plenty of distractions over the past two years, which make it difficult to determine whether the trends are facts or flukes.

Even still, we can tease out some insights. Some trends have continued. Some have regressed. If you ignore 2020, some regressions are actually trends, some trends are actually regressions, or vice versa. Or not. It's all about how you choose to look at the data.

Power

		Players with		
Year	Tot HR	20+ HR	30+ HR	HR/FB%
2012	4934	79	27	11.3%
2013	4661	70	14	10.5%
2014	4186	57	11	9.5%
2015	4909	64	20	11.4%
2016	5610	111	35	12.8%
2017	6105	118	41	13.7%
2018	5585	100	27	12.7%
2019	6776	130	58	15.3%
*2020	6221	119	53	14.8%
2021	5944	102	43	13.6%
* Pro-rated to full season				

It's possible that the 2019 power outburst was an isolated peak event. Whether 2021 was a natural regression or the result of the ever-changing baseball construction, this power data does show some tempering of the recent trends.

Our projections here always assume regression on a macro level, so none of the above is much of a surprise. Whether power plunges or plateaus, or the previous progression persists is unpredictable.

Year	Singles%	Three True Outcomes%	K%
2012	66.4%	30.4%	18.7%
2013	67.6%	30.3%	18.9%
2014	68.3%	30.3%	19.4%
2015	66.5%	30.7%	19.5%
2016	65.1%	32.3%	20.2%
2017	63.8%	33.5%	20.6%
2018	64.2%	33.7%	21.6%
2019	61.7%	35.1%	22.3%
2020	62.8%	36.1%	22.9%
2021	63.3%	35.1%	23.2%

We worry that the game is being reduced to walks, strikeouts and home runs—Three True Outcomes (TTO)—with the decline of singles further dampening the action on the field. The results in 2021 may be cause for some cautious optimism. Maybe.

Two months of singles data may not be enough from which to draw conclusions, but if we include 2020 in our analysis, then singles have been on a two-year upward trend. If not, then 2021 becomes a sharper positive regression. That's potentially good news in either case.

Given that walks and strikeouts stabilize fairly quickly, perhaps we can view 2020's TTO% as real. This is mostly driven by strikeout rates, which continue to soar. Still, TTO% appears to have regressed slightly in 2021 after peaking in 2020. Maybe this is a plateau—who knows? With MLB threatening to futz with the rules, can we place much faith that anything has stabilized?

I'm going to go out on a limb and say—no.

Stolen Bases

Year	Tot SB	Players with 20+	30+
2012	3229	48	23
2013	2693	40	16
2014	2764	39	15
2015	2505	30	7
2016	2537	28	14
2017	2527	29	6
2018	2474	28	11
2019	2280	21	8
*2020	2387	29	9
2021	2213	19	6

* Pro-rated to full season

One trend that did not regress at all was stolen bases. The pro-rated 2020 data appears to be an outlier and I have no problem ignoring it (omnipotence has its perks). Bags continue to get scarcer, so the players who contribute even at the 20-SB level are becoming increasingly more valuable.

Let's look at the 19 speedsters who swiped at least 20 bases in 2021, which will likely inflate their draft cost in March:

20+ SB	Age	SB	Career 20+	*Last 3 yrs avg
Starling Marte	32	47	8	35
Whit Merrifield	32	40	4	35
Trea Turner	28	32	5	37
Cedric Mullins III	26	30	First full season	
Myles Straw	26	30	First full season	
Tommy Edman	26	30	First full season	
José Ramírez	28	27	4	28
Shohei Ohtani	26	26	1	16
Fernando Tatis, Jr.	22	25	1	21
Bo Bichette	23	25	First full season	
Jazz Chisolm	23	23	First full season	
Nicky Lopez	26	22	First full season	
Dylan Moore	28	21	1	15
Robert Grossman	31	20	1	15
Trevor Story	28	20	3	23
Randy Arozarena	26	20	First full season	
Isiah Kiner-Felefa	26	20	1	10
Raimel Tapia	27	20	1	15
Ozzie Albies	24	20	1	16

*2018, 2019, 2021

If we are looking for established track records to minimize our risk, the pickings are slim. For nearly 75 percent of these players, 2021 was either their first full season in the majors or the first time stealing 20 in their career. We can speculate, but we really have no idea about the repeatability of 20-plus SB for this group. Of the established speedsters, it's even possible that Marte and Merrifield could be at risk of aging out of that skill.

So there is going to be a lot of dart-throwing this March; expect to open your wallet in a big way no matter where those darts land.

Starting Pitching

	Number of Pitchers with			
Year	200 IP	200 K	15 W	**10 W
2012	31	13	27	84
2013	36	12	16	82
2014	34	13	25	83
2015	28	18	13	70
2016	15	12	23	70
2017	15	16	17	74
2018	13	18	19	59
2019	15	24	16	74
*2020	6	20	19	70
2021	4	17	5	54

*Prorated to full season
**Includes relief pitchers

This data is a stark recognition of 2021's management of workloads. Only four pitchers with 200-plus innings? As recently as 2010, there were *50 pitchers* who threw over 200!

We took heavy losses on seven of the 11 pitchers drafted in the first two rounds last year. That might suppress pitcher pricing a bit in 2022, but there will still be some owners who will dig deep for some 200-inning Hope. Recency bias will put upward pressure on 2021's top earners, but most of those performances were outliers and likely to regress. There are warts attached to all of 2021's top eight earners:

Top 2021 earners	R$	Wart(s)
Max Scherzer	$39	Age 37, post-season dead arm
Walker Buehler	$39	2021 xERA more than a run higher than ERA
Zack Wheeler	$35	First time over $17. Repeatable?
Julio Urías	$32	185 IP, but first time >80 and >$10. Repeatable?
Corbin Burnes	$32	167 IP, but first time over 60. Repeatable?
Kevin Gausman	$31	First time over $13. Repeatable?
Robbie Ray	$31	7-year career high and only 2nd time over $12
Jacob deGrom	$28	Injury with unknown ETA

I'm no Debby-Downer but I can't help but see major across-the-board regression here. It makes me hesitant to push any of them into first round/$30 consideration. (Yes, I had Burnes in my earlier first round exercise. I confess my perception is infected with an acute case of Hope. Terrible malady.)

So who's left? In these risk-averse days, you have to look for longer track records. For me, Gerrit Cole should still be the first pitcher off the board and the only arm I would consider paying $30 for. Last year's 64 percent bust rate in the first two rounds should advise caution against investing in the hot hands.

These are also the pitchers who are more likely to go deeper into games. That pool is seriously drying up. In 2014, there were 2,114 outings of 100 pitches or more. That dropped to 1,170 in 2019, and in 2021 it plummeted to 694.

Of course, those innings had to go somewhere…

	INNINGS		WINS	
Year	Starters	Relievers	Starters	Relievers
2016	63.3%	36.7%	67.1%	32.9%
2017	61.9	38.1	67.5	32.5
2018	59.9	40.1	62.3	37.7
2019	57.9	42.1	59.7	40.3
2020	55.5	44.5	52.2	47.8
2021	57.3	42.7	55.4	44.6

It looks like the shift of innings from starters into bullpens actually regressed a bit. However, if we say that 2020 was a small-sample anomaly, then the trend is more consistent and we're still on the path to a 50-50 split one day.

Last year, I described a speculative reality in which these trends continued until the starting pitcher became extinct. To some, this may sound like a fictional dystopian universe. But the seeds are here, from the current multi-flavored bullpen management to once-and-future-closer Corey Knebel *starting* important playoff games. MLB would probably prefer that starting pitchers were restored to their days of past glory, but I think the game is better if they allow themselves to be gleefully carried away by these trends.

Pitching roles are arbitrary. The flexibility allows for better management of everything from in-game strategy to injuries. It *would* be gleeful. As long as more teams embrace Opener/Bulk Man games, I don't see this conversation as even remotely over yet.

Relief Pitching

		Number of pitchers with		
Year	Saves	30+	20+	5+
2012	1261	15	27	49
2013	1266	19	28	41
2014	1264	17	25	46
2015	1292	19	28	44
2016	1276	15	22	52
2017	1179	10	23	51
2018	1244	8	20	50
2019	1180	11	22	53
*2020	1139	9	17	67
2021	1191	9	19	62

*Prorated to full season

Yeah, this too. The shift in distribution of saves, from 20- and 30-save closers down to 5-plus has been pretty consistent. I've written this 379 times before, but it begs for a move from a Saves category to Saves-plus-Holds. Yes, holds are incredibly faulty; so are saves these days. But together they provide a reasonable proxy for the value of bullpen arms.

In Tout Wars, we added a 12-team mixed league that implemented Saves-plus-Holds and also replaced Wins with Innings Pitched. The participants really liked the reliever category as there was more standings movement, and more players to target and manage. Here are the comparative standings with the Saves-only 12-team LABR mixed league.

LABR		Tout Wars	
Team	Saves	Team	Svs+Hld
Jeff	88	Jennifer	103
Jake	84	Andy	98
Ray	84	Alex	93
Brian	83	Brian	92
Ariel	65	Doug	92
Ron	61	Ray	86
Nick	47	Jake	80
Ryan	42	Ron	64
Andrea	39	Jim	62
Craig	29	Al	53
Adam	15	Chris	52
Doug	14	Jeff	39

The teams with multiple 30-save closers surged to the top in LABR, creating a cliff in the standings. In Tout, the addition of holds created more competition and a lower cliff. Of course, these are just two leagues, but you can see the potential effect of adding holds.

Yes, I was pretty crappy in both leagues. Holds are tough to project until you see how managers are using their bullpens, but the larger pool of relievers makes it much easier to recover with some aggressive in-season management. Usually, but not for me.

20/20 Hindsight

In last year's book, I wrote: *"In trying to figure out what is going to happen in 2021, the most prudent path might be to make believe 2020 never happened."*

Perhaps that was a bit of hyperbole, but the underlying thought was real. 2020 was too small of a sample to be taken seriously, and maybe even dangerous to the analytical process. It made some sense to leave those 60 games in the past and take forward the promise of a return to sweet normality into 2021.

Sort of like "Leave the gun. Take the cannoli." Because some of you have been waiting for this year's random food metaphor.

Did this turn out to be true? It depended upon the player. For some, like Max Fried, Chris Bassitt and Brandon Crawford, 2020 turned out to be very prescient about what we could expect in 2021. For others, like Bryan Reynolds, Steve Matz and Robbie Ray, removing 2020 from their record was the only way they would have been draftable last March.

And then there was J.D. Martinez, last year's poster boy for navigating 2020.

One of the biggest challenges we had last winter was trying to figure out *how much weight* to give the short 60-game season. So I ran a comparison study using Martinez, a player who had demonstrated consistent 35-100-.300 productivity in the past but whose 2020 was an extreme outlier (19-73-.214 as prorated to 162 games).

I tested three weighting options. The first used a standard three-year .50/.30/.20 weighting. The second gave 2020 a slightly lesser weight. The third hardly weighted 2020 at all.

Weights			Projection						
2020	2019	2018	AB	H	R	HR	RBI	SB	AVG
0.50	0.30	0.20	570	150	81	29	94	3	.264
0.30	0.40	0.30	570	162	90	33	103	3	.284
0.166	0.533	0.30	570	169	95	35	107	3	.296
2021 actual			570	163	92	28	99	0	.286

Nailed the ABs! (Now this blind squirrel will never win the lottery.) Fact is, Martinez posted a line that was almost dead on with a normal .50/.30/.20 weight for his counting stats. His batting average worked best with the middle option. So, in this case, 2020 was a fully valid data point needed to accurately project 2021. Without it, we would have grossly over-projected his stats.

But was that just a lucky guess on one player? Really, 2020 was valid when it worked; invalid when it didn't. Sadly, we couldn't leave the gun *or* the cannoli.

For this year's book, we're suppressing 2020 to a weight of 0.20 and redistributing the other 0.80 around it. That may seem like too much of a discount, but for some players it will be 0.20 too much.

The Elephant in the Room

It's big, it's grey and we don't know how we'll get past it. This pachyderm is spelled C.B.A.

The Collective Bargaining Agreement between Major League owners and the Major League Baseball Players Association (MLBPA) expired on December 1. Even though this book went to press two weeks before that date, I am going to take a leap of faith and say that you are reading these words during an owner lockout.

The CBA negotiations are likely going to frame much of our off-season analysis. While most of the economic issues won't affect fantasy leaguers directly, there are some things that might. And the overarching threat of a work stoppage that extends into the 2022 baseball season is a real danger for us. However, we can take another nosebleed-section view of some of the variables that might affect our fantasy decision-making. Early drafts can leverage the uncertainty to their advantage with some educated speculations.

Universal DH: This has to happen, right? While the owners still claim this is a bargaining topic, both sides want it, it tested successfully in 2020 and the only thing stopping it is thinly veiled posturing. There is no real debate here.

Still, can we forge bravely ahead and start mapping out who the NL designated hitters might be? Logically, you'd think this is safe. But we've come to expect the unexpected when these two sides negotiate, so as of this writing, it's premature and not reflected in the projections here. Ugh.

But this book is more about skills than playing time. For fantasy planning, I'd still tuck away names you might find interesting. Go ahead and add some plate appearances to poor-fielding hitters who might fit nicely into a new DH slot. You can try to use 2020's NL DHs as your guide, but it will be hit or miss. Kyle Schwarber spent 2021 in the already-DHing AL and is a free agent. Marcell Ozuna is a man without a clear future. Dominic Smith may have played himself out of any role. I suppose there's still Adam Duvall. Maybe Seth Beer will prove that DHs can be grown. Many NL teams didn't use a single fixed DH in 2020 anyway.

You also might consider bumping up NL pitcher ERAs by a few tenths of a run. But most of this will wash out in normal statistical variability. Whether a pitcher is projected for a 3.55 ERA or a 3.75 ERA should not wholly change your valuation—that's just four extra earned runs over 180 IP, one ER every six weeks—so don't sweat it.

Different roster sizes: It is possible that the MLBPA will negotiate for larger rosters to give jobs to more players. When rosters expanded to 26 this year, the additional body was invariably a pitcher. But there is talk that any additional changes would limit the number of pitchers, most likely to 13.

The structure of MLB rosters has already broken the traditional 14/9 batter/pitcher split in fantasy leagues. That structure hasn't reflected reality in awhile. AL/NL-only league free agent batter pools are usually bereft of talent and pitcher pools are teeming with middle relievers whose lack of saves suppress their value.

This is an old conversation, but it potentially could get worse. Leagues should have serious rules discussions this off-season to address roster structure and perhaps move to Saves-plus-Holds.

Defensive shift limitations: This rule would force all four infielders to be positioned on the infield dirt with two on each side of second base. The intent of this is to goose offense. Early results from this experiment in Double-A showed little effect on scoring, but more testing was needed.

At its core, defensive shifting just seems to be part of the natural batter versus pitcher meta-game. As such, the common argument we keep hearing is, "Well, batters just need to learn to hit the other way," which is obviously as easy as teaching a frog to croak Puccini. If it was that simple, then this wouldn't even be an issue, but 100 mph fastballs test the limits of human reaction time. It's tough enough for hitters to make *any* contact these days, just like it's tough enough to train frogs to even stay on key.

Defensive shift limitations are a response to a symptom—decline in safe hits and overall offense—but that's not the core issue. Here is the source of the problem, a not-so-subtle change over the past 20 years:

Avg Fastball velocity 95+ mph (min. 30 IP)

Year	# pitchers
2002	5
2003	10
2004	12
2005	12
2006	17
2007	11
2008	16
2009	24
2010	29
2011	35
2012	33
2013	36
2014	41
2015	62
2016	64
2017	100
2018	100
2019	103
2020	112 (min. 10 IP)
2021	128

(Source: FanGraphs)

At this pace, how long will it be before batters need the reflexes to handle 100 mph *curve balls?* If this is what's breaking the game's competitive balance, then something probably does need to be done to level the playing field.

Shift limitations are a side-door option that artificially hamstring the defense without addressing the real problem. An option like moving the pitcher's mound back begins to look at the issue more honestly. But there is a much bigger conversation here.

As you scan the pitchers in this book, you are going to see a whole bunch of commentaries that read something like these:

- "Spent most of year throwing harder than ever, but September rotator cuff strain…"
- "Early skills spike showed massive breakout potential, but mid-May TJ surgery…"
- "Showed his best half season velocity in years, but elbow injury in July…"

Throws harder, hurts more, Health grade: F. What part of this logical causation am I missing? And why isn't it raising a huge red flag??

That all said, if restrictions *are* placed on defensive shifts, it could potentially have a big impact on the numbers. Batting averages could spike for some players; ERAs for most pitchers could

follow. Of all the changes being discussed, I'd think this is the one that scares forecasters the most.

Sticky balls: Last June's crackdown on grip enhancers resulted in a drop in spin rates, but they pretty much reverted back to normal by the end of the season. So MLB decided to experiment with pre-tacked baseballs in the Arizona Fall League. By time you read this, the results of that experiment may be out. This, too, could potentially impact 2022 projections as some previously "clean" pitchers may suddenly discover the newly legal wonders of extreme spin rates.

Larger bases: Standard bases are 15 inches on each side. In Triple-A, they tested bases that were 18 inches. This was intended to reduce player collisions and provide modest increases in stolen base success and infield hits. I can't imagine that three inches makes that big of a difference, especially since we've always been told that size doesn't matter.

At this writing, I do not know the results of this experiment, but there was enough interest to continue testing in the AFL. For us, it's probably premature to be prospecting for speedsters with 67 percent success rates in the Hope that an 18-inch base will boost that percentage to 75. But in the event that it does happen, here are the players projected for 10 or more steals but with SB% rates under 70 percent: Anthony Alford, Randy Arozarena, Harrison Bader, Andrew Benintendi, Adolis García, Yonny Hernandez, Jarred Kelenic, Ramon Laureano, Jorge Mateo, Edward Olivares, Rafael Ortega, Roman Quinn, Brendan Rodgers, Josh Rojas, Juan Soto, Michael A. Taylor, Lane Thomas, Gleyber Torres, Taylor Walls, Bobby Witt, Jr., Kolton Wong. Go nuts.

Those are the rule changes that will potentially have the most impact on the fantasy game. This year it's more important than ever to remember that you get updated projections with the purchase of this book. That typically happens in March, but it will be later if the season is delayed. And a subscription to BaseballHQ.com will always keep you fully linked to any ongoing changes, 24/7/365. Just a reminder.

Revolution

Okay, let's say we are in a lockout. We can already expect that there will be no player movement as long as it continues. No trades. No free agent signings. Since each player's landing spot affects the projections, that effort takes a hit. As we get closer to March, the situation becomes more critical.

But you may not be aware of the extended aftereffects from a work stoppage pushing into March, especially if you don't have the 9th edition of this book on your shelf. As it turns out, when planning for our 2022 leagues, we do have some precedent as to what other types of fallout to expect.

The last time there was a major work stoppage was 1995, which for some of you might seem as far back as the Black Sox scandal. For me, it was almost yesterday. I am in the process of writing an historical memoir about the early days of fantasy baseball, called *Fantasy Expert* (ETA late 2022), and I devote an entire chapter to the 1994-1995 player strike. Here is an excerpt:

> *The strike ended when Sonia Sotomayor, Judge of the United States District Court for the Southern District of*

New York, issued a preliminary injunction against the owners on March 31. On Sunday, April 2, 1995, the day before the season was scheduled to start with the replacement players, the strike came to an official end at 232 days.

Major League Baseball then attempted to crunch five months of activity into the subsequent three weeks, which broke the back of many fantasy support services. More than 100 players switched teams before the delayed Opening Day. Most were inconsequential but fantasy leaguers had to take note of others, like Larry Walker moving from Montreal to Coors Field. Andre Dawson, Marquis Grissom, Terry Pendleton, Benito Santiago, Kevin Brown, David Cone, Orel Hershiser and John Wetteland were also among the dozens who changed uniforms during those 21 days.

This type of frenzy could still happen now. Players would show up for three weeks of spring training, during which time dozens could be swapping uniforms. This would force us to adjust many of our player valuations on the fly, which would affect our rankings. Odds are there would not be enough time for all these moves to filter into the ADPs. Reacting to this activity will be potentially onerous, but at least we all own computers and have access to the internet, something that was not true in 1995.

In addition, dozens of fantasy businesses folded back then and those that survived incurred at least a 20 percent hit on their bottom line. Since most fantasy leagues drafted live, many were unable to get their owners together on such short notice, so they sat out the season; some never came back, including my home league. I suspect that today there will be less devastation, especially since the 2020 COVID experience already prepared surviving businesses for navigating life without baseball.

Still, there will be some tremors.

Evolution

When Shohei Ohtani was first threatening to become a legitimate two-way player, fantasy leagues scrambled to try to figure out how to handle his stats. Then, for several years, he battled injuries that made the issue almost moot. So, coming into 2021, many of us were dubious that he would ever become a player worth worrying about.

Silly us.

We first mentioned Ohtani nine years ago, in the 2013 edition of this book. He was in high school back then, and while we had a preliminary scouting report, it was too soon to know who he'd even take to his prom. Tom Mulhall wrote:

Shohei Otani (RHP, Hanamaki Higashi High School) is still a high school student and is the longest of long shots. However, if your league has an extended farm system, he could be an interesting final selection. Allegedly, he has hit 100 mph, and though normally we regard a report like that as noise, Dodgers' Assistant GM Logan White compared him to Clayton Kershaw and called Otani one of the best prospects in the world. If the Dodgers are that interested, maybe we should be, too. Possible ETA in MLB minors: 2013

Since then, he gained an "h"—presumably, for "hitter"—that forced us to take a more serious look at how to fit him into our system.

Most leagues have been handling Ohtani in one of these manners:

- Drafted as a hitter only.
- Drafted as a pitcher only.
- Drafted as both hitter and pitcher, but can only be active as one or the other in a given week.
- Drafted as both hitter and pitcher but must take up two active roster spots.

There are other variations, and in leagues with daily transactions, Ohtani can be moved around more freely. But in weekly transaction leagues, he is a problem child.

Those leagues where he can only be a hitter or pitcher end up with only half his production. In leagues where he has to take up two roster spots—aside from the fact that Ohtani is allegedly one person, not two, as depicted on this book cover—his team would lose a spot that could be used for another player.

(Hmm…. does the book cover confuse things? He really is one player. That image was Photoshopped.)

Writer Trace Wood drafted Ohtani in the XFL dynasty league (fantasyxperts.com) back in 2015, and when his arrival seemed imminent, began a conversation on handling the oddity. Wood's perspective is that it's just an issue of position eligibility. He wrote:

Essentially, Ohtani is just like any other multi-position eligible player. As long as he has fulfilled the games required criteria, then he should accumulate all the statistics in every category in which he contributes. (It would be like) Marwin Gonzalez, in a given week plays a couple games at 1B, a few in the outfield and maybe during an extra inning game plays catcher for an inning. For the fantasy owner, it does not matter what position they have him on the roster. They get all the stats he produced that week, even the ones where he played a position he did not qualify for (catcher). So why shouldn't Ohtani be afforded the same respect?

On its surface, this seems to make sense, but it's more complicated than that. The problem relates to the taxonomy of baseball players.

If we consider Humans our own Domain, from there we have Athletes (Kingdom) and then Baseball Players (Phylum). Then we have two distinct Classes of Baseball Players—Batters and Pitchers—and then their Roles (Order). The Batter Roles include each of the defensive positions; the Pitcher Roles include the various types of Starters and Relievers.

Similar to the comparative taxonomy of human beings and frogs, a great divergence occurs at the Class level. The Batter Class and Pitcher Class are evaluated with two different sets of statistics. If you are a Hitter, all Roles within that class use one set of stats. If you are a Pitcher, all Roles within that class use a different set of stats. The fact that we use the same terminology within each Class to describe those Roles—"positions"—does not mean they are the same. Humans and frogs both have "hearts" but they are not constructed the same either. From that perspective, Ohtani cannot be described as having multi-position eligibility because his contributions are in two different Classes of Baseball Player.

As much as we want Ohtani to fit into our fantasy game's well-defined structure, this is where the system breaks down. In order for Ohtani to conform to our 14/9 roster on the days he pitches, would he become the 15th hitter or the 10th pitcher? Would our 23-man active roster effectively increase to 24? If so, is that fair? Should fairness even be a consideration? He's just one of 26 on the Angels, but they don't have to adhere to a hitter/pitcher split, so should we?

Even in this book, Ohtani has two player boxes, just as he has two images on the cover. This effectively forced us to omit an analysis for some other deserving hitter or pitcher. It is the structure that we have had to live with.

For now.

Ohtani's success as a cross-Class hybrid could spawn imitators, or at least players who attempt to similarly evolve. The existence of seemingly outlandish hybrids in nature—Heqet and Fiona, for instance—shows that anything is possible.

So, too, might fantasy leagues have to start looking at ways to accept this evolution as an alternative to the intelligent design of Rotisserie's Founding Fathers. That would require us to modify the current system by somehow integrating the Batter and Pitcher classes, or at minimum, finding—or creating—the missing link between the two. For us here, we might need to give Ohtani and his ilk their own page, in their own section, after Hitters, after Pitchers, and perhaps call it "Lucy."

LABR Leader Lament

Oh, and I won the LABR 12-team mixed auction this year (sorry for burying the lede). I did manage to salvage the Austin Meadows trade with Ray, landing Alex Reyes and Amed Rosario in return.

Then I "expertly" timed Rosario's presence on my active roster to coincide with the 259 AB when he batted .313.

I beat out a group of the fantasy industry's rising talents, which was particularly gratifying for this nearly four-decade Roto-vet. But I've been thinking that this victory needs to be savored, and as a perpetually senior member of these leagues, battling constant 100 mph fastballs, you never know when the next hit will fall.

Or if.

So it may be time to take a cue from Buster Posey. I'd go out with the win and put a power cap to 28 years of experts league play. Many others have ended their public competitive careers on a high note, like George Brett, Chipper Jones, Mike Mussina, Mariano Rivera and Big Papi. Such good company. Then maybe I'll go into consulting, do the lecture circuit, kiss a few babies, yada, yada, yada.

Then again…

Maybe this is just a case of COVID fatigue. For me, fantasy baseball is not just about competition, but also camaraderie and community. Two years without an in-person draft has made for an empty, sterile experience that is only exacerbated by each additional hour in front of a computer screen. The LABR victory was satisfying but did not bring me the joy I thought it would. Live, warm-blooded humans recapping the festivities over wings at Virgil's, pub-crawling down in the Village, maybe turning over a few tables… that is what's been missing.

Maybe when it returns, so will my hunger.

But I get it—we're still healing. It hasn't felt normal in a long time. Hopefully, with any luck, we'll enter March with a fully suppressed pandemic, a fully signed C.B.A. and a player pool fully cleansed of off-field septicity.

Sigh.

But that would be like kissing a frog and hoping for a princess, right?

CONSUMER ADVISORY

AN IMPORTANT MESSAGE FOR FANTASY LEAGUERS
REGARDING PROPER USAGE OF THE *BASEBALL FORECASTER*

This document is provided in compliance with authorities to outline the prospective risks and hazards possible in the event that the Baseball Forecaster is used incorrectly. Please be aware of these potentially dangerous situations and avoid them. The publisher assumes no risk related to any financial loss or stress-induced illnesses caused by ignoring the items as described below.

1. The statistical projections in this book are intended as general guidelines, not as gospel. It is highly dangerous to use the projected statistics alone, and then live and die by them. That's like going to a ballgame, being given a choice of any seat in the park, and deliberately choosing the last row in the right field corner with an obstructed view. The projections are there, you can look at them, but there are so many better places to sit.

We have to publish those numbers, but they are stagnant, inert pieces of data. This book focuses on a live forecasting process that provides the tools so that you can understand the leading indicators and draw your own conclusions. If you at least attempt your own analyses of the data, and enhance them with the player commentaries, you can paint more robust, colorful pictures of the future.

In other words...

If you bought this book purely for the projected statistics and do not intend to spend at least some time learning about the process, then you might as well just buy an $8 magazine.

2. The player commentaries in this book are written by humans, just like you. These commentaries provide an overall evaluation of performance and likely future direction, but 70-word capsules cannot capture everything. Your greatest value will be to use these as a springboard to your own analysis of the data. Odds are, if you take the time, you'll find hidden indicators that we might have missed. Forecaster veterans say that this self-guided excursion is the best part of owning the book.

3. This book does not attempt to tackle playing time. Rather than making arbitrary decisions about how roles will shake out, the focus is on performance. The playing time projections presented here are merely to help you better evaluate each player's talent. Our online preseason projections update provides more current AB and IP expectations based on how roles are being assigned.

4. The dollar values in this book are intended solely for player-to-player comparisons. They are not driven by a finite pool of playing time—which is required for valuation systems to work properly—so they cannot be used for bid values to be used in your own draft.

There are two reasons for this:

a. The finite pool of players that will generate the finite pool of playing time will not be determined until much closer to Opening Day. And, if we are to be brutally honest, there is really no such thing as a finite pool of players.

b. Your particular league's construction will drive the values; a $10 player in a 10-team mixed league will not be the same as a $10 player in a 12-team NL-only league.

Note that book dollar values also cannot be compared to those published at BaseballHQ.com as the online values are generated by a more finite player pool.

5. Do not pass judgment on the effectiveness of this book based on the performance of a few individual players. The test, rather, is on the collective predictive value of the book's methods. Are players with better base skills more likely to produce good results than bad ones? Years of research suggest that the answer is "yes." Does that mean that every high skilled player will do well? No. But many more of them will perform well than will the average low-skilled player. You should always side with the better percentage plays, but recognize that there are factors we cannot predict. Good decisions that beget bad outcomes do not invalidate the methods.

6. If your copy of this book is not marked up and dog-eared by Draft Day, you probably did not get as much value out of it as you might have.

7. This edition of the Forecaster is not intended to provide absorbency for spills of more than 7.5 ounces.

8. This edition is not intended to provide stabilizing weight for more than 18 sheets of 20 lb. paper in winds of more than 45 mph.

9. The pages of this book are not recommended for avian waste collection. In independent laboratory studies, 87% of migratory water fowl refused to excrete on interior pages, even when coaxed.

10. This book, when rolled into a cylindrical shape, is not intended to be used as a weapon for any purpose, including but not limited to insect extermination, canine training or to influence bidding behavior at a fantasy draft.

Welcome to the 36th Edition

If you are new to the *Baseball Forecaster*, the sheer volume of information in this book—this is our largest page-count in years—may seem a bit daunting. We don't recommend you assess its contents over a single commute to work, particularly if you drive. But do set aside some time this winter; instead of staring out the window, waiting for baseball to begin again, try immersing yourself in all the wisdom contained in this tome. There's a ton of it, and the payoff—Yoo-Hoo or otherwise—is worth it.

But where to begin?

The best place to start is with the Encyclopedia of Fanalytics, which provides the foundation concepts for everything else that appears in these pages. It's our research archive and collective memory, just as valuable for veterans as it is for rookies. Take a cursory read-through, lingering at any section that looks interesting. You'll keep coming back here frequently.

Then just jump in. Close your eyes, flip to a random page, and put your finger down anywhere. Oh, look—Amed Rosario. Still just 26; we know he doesn't walk ... but look at those Spd scores! With a solid contact rate and a bit of a power rebound from 2020 ... maybe there's another level lurking here. See, you've learned something already!

What's New in 2022?

Our team has hit the ground running after the COVID-shortened 2020 and a full 162-game schedule in 2021:

New draft prep charts: The back of the book has been beefed up with more timely draft tools at your disposal:

- 2021 Actual Stats vs. Expected Stats leaderboards for both batters and pitchers to help you identify players who may be due for an upswing or downturn in 2022.
- A Positional Eligibility chart for those in leagues with 10-game and 5-game position qualification rules.
- Two new head-to-head tools—2021 Usable Weeks for hitters and Aggregate Consistency Score for pitchers.

Take control of FAAB: A research article digs into how to submit more precise bids in what can be a confounding process. Details on page 76.

Also, answers to questions, such as: What happens if we replace ADP with draft-level analytics? Is QBaB relevant over small samples? Should we treat hard-hit fly balls as a skill? And much, much more.

Updates

The Baseball Forecaster page at BaseballHQ.com is at www.baseballhq.com/bf2022. This is your headquarters for all information and updates regarding this book. Here you will find links to the following:

Content Updates: In a project of this magnitude, there are occasionally items that need clarification or correction. You can find them here.

Free Projections Update: As a buyer of this book, you get one free 2022 projections update. This is a set of Excel spreadsheet files that will be posted on or about March 1, 2022. Remember

to keep the book handy when you visit as the access codes are hidden within these pages.

Electronic book: The complete PDF version of the *Forecaster*—plus Excel versions of most key charts—is available free to those who bought the book directly through the BaseballHQ.com website. These files will be available in January 2022 for most of you; those who have an annual standing order should have received the PDF just before Thanksgiving. Contact us if you do not receive information via e-mail about access. Information about the e-book version can be found through the website.

If you purchased the book through an online vendor or bookstore, or would like these files earlier, you can purchase them from us for $9.95. Contact us at support@baseballhq.com for more information.

Beyond the Forecaster

The *Baseball Forecaster* is just the beginning. The following companion products and services are described in more detail in the back of the book.

BaseballHQ.com is our home website. It provides regular updates to everything in this book, including daily updated statistics and projections. A subscription to BHQ gets you more than 1,000 articles over the course of a year updated daily from spring training through the end of the regular season, customized tools, access to data going back over a decade, plus much more. For a free peek, sign up for our BaseballHQFriday newsletter at www.baseballhq.com/friday.

We take this show on the road twice a year via our *First Pitch Forums* weekend conferences. In the fall of 2021, we were able to regather after a year away for *First Pitch Arizona*, our Arizona Fall League weekend. It's the ultimate fantasy baseball getaway, where you can meet top industry analysts and network with fellow fantasy leaguers. There are also plans in place for First Pitch Florida in 2022, with three days of baseball talk, spring training games and the legendary LABR expert league drafts. Find out more about these events on page 284 and at BaseballHQ.com.

The 17th edition of the *Minor League Baseball Analyst* is the *Forecaster's* prospect companion, with stat boxes for 900-plus prospects, essays on prospects, lists upon lists, and more. In an era where rookies matter, it's an essential resource and available in January.

RotoLab is the best draft software on the market and comes pre-loaded with our projections. Learn more at www.rotolab.com.

Even further beyond the Forecaster

Visit us on *Facebook* at www.facebook.com/baseballhq. "Like" the BaseballHQ page for updates, photos from events and links to other important stuff.

Follow us on *Twitter*. Site updates are tweeted from @BaseballHQ and many of our writers share their insights from their own personal accounts. We even have a list to follow: www.twitter.com/BaseballHQ/lists/hq-staff.

But back to baseball. Your winter comfort awaits.

—Brent Hershey and Ray Murphy

ENCYCLOPEDIA OF FANALYTICS

For new readers...

Everything begins here. The information in the following pages represents the foundation that powers everything we do.

You'll learn about the underlying concepts for our unique mode of analysis. You'll find answers to long-asked questions, interesting insights into what makes players tick, and innovative applications for all this newfound knowledge.

This Encyclopedia is organized into several logical sections:

1. Fundamentals
2. Batters
3. Pitchers
4. Prospects
5. Gaming

Enough talking. Jump in. Remember to breathe.

For veteran readers...

As we do in each edition, this year's ever-expanding Encyclopedia includes relevant research results we've published over the past year. We've added some of the essays from the Research Abstracts section in the 2021 *Forecaster* as well as some other essays from BaseballHQ.com.

And we continue to mold the content to best fit how fantasy leaguers use their information. Many readers consider this their fantasy information bible.

Okay, time to jump-start the analytical process for 2022. Remember to breathe—it's always good advice.

Abbreviations

Fundamentals

What is Fanalytics?

Fanalytics is the scientific approach to fantasy baseball analysis. A contraction of "fantasy" and "analytics," fanalytic gaming might be considered a mode of play that requires a more strategic and quantitative approach to player analysis and game decisions.

The three key elements of fanalytics are:

1. Performance analysis
2. Performance forecasting
3. Gaming analysis

For performance analysis, we tap into the vast knowledge of the sabermetric community. Founded by Bill James, this area of study provides objective and progressive new ways to assess skill. What we do in this book is called "component skills analysis." We break down performance into its component parts, then reverse-engineer it back into the traditional measures with which we are more familiar.

Our forecasting methodology is one part science and one part art. We start with a computer-generated baseline for each player, driven by the performance analysis and a contextual assessment of the player's role and expected playing time. We then make subjective adjustments based on a variety of factors, such as discrepancies in skills indicators and historical guidelines gleaned from more than 30 years of research. We don't rely on a rigid model; our method forces us to get our hands dirty.

You might say that our brand of forecasting is more about finding logical journeys than blind destinations.

Gaming analysis is an integrated approach designed to help us win our fantasy leagues. It takes the knowledge gained from the first two elements and adds the strategic and tactical aspect of each specific fantasy game format.

Component Skills Analysis

Familiar gauges like HR and ERA have long been used to measure skill. In fact, these gauges only measure the outcome of an individual event, or series of events. They represent statistical output. They are "surface stats."

Raw skill is the talent beneath the stats. Players use these skills to create the individual events, or components, that are the building blocks of measures like HR and ERA. Our approach:

1. It's not about batting average; it's about seeing the ball and making contact. We target hitters based on elements such as their batting eye (walks to strikeouts ratio), how often they make contact and the type of contact they make. We then combine these components into an "expected batting average." By comparing each hitter's actual BA to how he should be performing, we can draw conclusions about the future.

2. It's not about home runs; it's about power. From the perspective of a round bat meeting a round ball, it may be only a fraction of an inch at the point of contact that makes the difference between a HR and a long foul ball. When a ball is hit safely, often it is only a few inches that separate a HR from a double or long fly out. We can now measure elements like swing speed, exit velocity and launch angle to provide a more granular perspective.

We must incorporate all these components to paint a complete picture of power.

3. It's not about ERA; it's about getting the ball over the plate and minimizing the damage of contact. Forget ERA. You want to draft pitchers who walk few batters (Control), strike out many (Dominance) and succeed at both in tandem (Command). You generally want pitchers who keep the ball on the ground (because home runs are bad), though some fly ball pitchers can succeed under the right conditions. All of this translates into an "expected ERA" that you can use to validate a pitcher's actual performance.

4. It's never about wins. For pitchers, winning ballgames is less about skill than it is about offensive support. As such, projecting wins is a high-risk exercise and valuing hurlers based on their win history is dangerous. Current trends in pitching usage—which fragment roles and spread innings to more pitchers—dilute our ability to project wins even more. Target skill; wins may or may not come, but it's your best hope. Many leagues are switching to tracking innings instead.

5. It's not about saves; it's about opportunity first and skills second. While the highest-skilled pitchers have the best potential to succeed as closers, they still have to be given the ball with the game on the line in the 9th inning, and that is a decision left to others. Over the past 10 years, about 55% of relievers drafted for saves failed to hold the role for the entire season (that percentage is over 63% since 2018). The lesson: Don't take chances on draft day. There will always be saves in the free agent pool. Or toss out a wider net over the bullpen pool and switch to Saves-plus-Holds.

Accounting for "luck"

Luck has been used as a catch-all term to describe random chance. When we use the term here, we're talking about unexplained variances that shape the statistics. While these variances may be random, they are also often measurable and projectable. To get a better read on "luck," we use formulas that capture the external variability of the data.

Through our research and the work of others, we have learned that when raw skill is separated from statistical output, what's remaining is often unexplained variance. The aggregate totals of many of these variances, for all players, is often a constant. For instance, while a pitcher's ERA might fluctuate, the rate at which his opposition's batted balls fall for hits will tend towards roughly 30%. Large variances can be expected to regress towards 30%.

Why is all this important? Analysts complain about the lack of predictability of many traditional statistical metrics. The reason they find it difficult is that they are trying to project performance using metrics that are loaded with external noise. Raw skills metrics follow better-defined trends during a player's career. Then, as we get a better handle on the variances—explained and unexplained—we can construct a more complete picture of what a player's statistics really mean.

Baseball Forecasting

Forecasting in perspective

The crystal ball aura of "predicting the future" conceals the fact that forecasting is a process. We might define it as "the systematic process of determining likely end results." At its core, it's scientific.

However, the *outcomes* of forecasted events are what are most closely scrutinized, and are used to judge the success or failure of the forecast. That said, as long as the process is sound, the forecast has done the best job it can do. *In the end, forecasting is about analysis, not prophecy.*

Baseball performance forecasting is inherently a high-risk exercise with a very modest accuracy rate. This is because the process involves not only statistics, but also unscientific elements, from random chance to human volatility. And even from within the statistical aspect there are multiple elements that need to be evaluated, from skill to playing time to a host of external variables.

Every system is comprised of the same core elements:

- Players will tend to perform within the framework of past history and/or trends.
- Skills will develop and decline according to age.
- Statistics will be shaped by a player's health, expected role and venue.

While all systems are built from these same elements, they also are constrained by the same limitations. We are all still trying to project a bunch of human beings, each one...

- with his own individual skill set
- with his own rate of growth and decline
- with his own ability to resist and recover from injury
- limited to opportunities determined by other people
- generating a group of statistics largely affected by external noise.

Research has shown that the best accuracy rate that can be attained by any system is about 70%. In fact, a simple system that uses three-year averages adjusted for age ("Marcel") can attain a success rate of 65%. This means all the advanced systems are fighting for occupation of the remaining 5%.

But there is a bigger question… *what exactly are we measuring?* When we search for accuracy, what does that mean? In fact, any quest for accuracy is going to run into a brick wall of paradoxes:

- If a slugging average projection is dead on, but the player hits 10 fewer HRs than expected (and likely, 20 more doubles), is that a success or a failure?
- If a projection of hits and walks allowed by a pitcher is on the mark, but the bullpen and defense implodes, and inflates his ERA by a run, is that a success or a failure?
- If the projection of a speedster's rate of stolen base success is perfect, but his team replaces the manager with one that doesn't run, and the player ends up with half as many SBs as expected, is that a success or a failure?
- If a batter is traded to a hitters' ballpark and all the touts project an increase in production, but he posts a statistical line exactly what would have been projected had he not been traded to that park, is that a success or a failure?
- If the projection for a bullpen closer's ERA, WHIP and peripheral numbers is perfect, but he saves 20 games instead of 40 because the GM decided to bring in a high-priced free agent at the trading deadline, is that a success or a failure?
- If a player is projected to hit .272 in 550 AB and only hits .249, is that a success or failure? Most will say "failure." But wait a minute! The real difference is only two hits per month. That shortfall of 23 points in batting average

is because a fielder might have made a spectacular play, or a screaming liner might have been hit right at someone, or a long shot to the outfield might have been held up by the wind... once every 14 games. Does that constitute "failure"?

Even if we were to isolate a single statistic that measures "overall performance" and run our accuracy tests on it, the results will still be inconclusive.

According to OPS, these players were virtually identical in 2021:

BATTER	HR	RBI	SB	BA	OBA	SLG	OPS
Harrison,J	8	60	9	.279	.341	.400	.741
García,A	31	90	16	.243	.286	.454	.741

If I projected Adolis García-caliber stats and ended up with Josh Harrison's numbers, I'd hardly call that an accurate projection. According to Rotisserie dollars, these players were also dead-on in 2021:

BATTER	HR	RBI	Runs	SB	BA	R$
Grossman,R	23	67	88	20	.239	$16
Frazier,A	5	43	83	10	.305	$16

It's not so simple for someone to claim they have accurate projections. And so, it is best to focus on the bigger picture, especially when it comes to winning at fantasy baseball.

More on this: "The Great Myths of Projective Accuracy"

http://www.baseballhq.com/great-myths-projective-accuracy

Baseball Forecaster's forecasting process

Our approach is to assemble component skills in such a way that they can be used to validate our observations, analyze their relevance and project a likely future direction.

In a perfect world, if a player's raw skills improve, then so should his surface stats. If his skills decline, then his stats should follow. But, sometimes a player's skill indicators increase while his surface stats decline. These variances may be due to a variety of factors.

Our forecasting process is based on the expectation that events tend to move towards universal order. Surface stats will eventually approach their skill levels. Unexplained variances will regress to a mean. And from this, we can identify players whose performance may potentially change.

For most of us, this process begins with the previous year's numbers. Last season provides us with a point of reference, so it's a natural way to begin the process of looking at the future. Component skills analysis allows us to validate those numbers. A batter with few HRs but elevated power metrics has a good probability of improving his future HR output. A pitcher whose ERA was poor while his pitching support metrics were solid might be a good bet for ERA improvement.

Of course, these leading indicators do not always follow the rules. There are more shades of grey than blacks and whites. When indicators are in conflict—for instance, a pitcher who is displaying both a rising strikeout rate and a rising walk rate—then we have to find ways to sort out what these indicators might be saying.

It is often helpful to look at leading indicators in a hierarchy. A rank of the most important pitching indicators might be: K-BB%, K%, BB% and GB/FB rate. For batters, contact rate tops the list, followed by power, walk rate and speed.

Assimilating additional research

Once we've painted the statistical picture of a player's potential, we then use additional criteria and research results to help us add some color to the analysis. These other criteria include the player's health, age, changes in role, ballpark and a variety of other factors. We also use the research results described in the following pages. This research looks at things like traditional periods of peak performance and breakout profiles.

The final element of the process is assimilating the news into the forecast. This is the element that many fantasy leaguers tend to rely on most since it is the most accessible. However, it is also the element that provides the most noise. Players, management and the media have absolute control over what we are allowed to know. Factors such as hidden injuries, messy divorces and clubhouse unrest are routinely kept from us, while we are fed red herrings and media spam. *We will never know the entire truth.*

Quite often, all you are reading is just other people's opinions... a manager who believes that a player has what it takes to be a regular or a team physician whose diagnosis is that a player is healthy enough to play. These words from experts have some element of truth, but cannot be wholly relied upon to provide an accurate expectation of future events. As such, it is often helpful to develop an appropriate cynicism for what you read.

For instance, if a player is struggling for no apparent reason and there are denials about health issues, don't dismiss the possibility that an injury does exist. There are often motives for such news to be withheld from the public.

And so, as long as we do not know all the facts, we cannot dismiss the possibility that any one fact is true, no matter how often the media assures it, deplores it, or ignores it. Don't believe everything you read; use your own judgment. If your observations conflict with what is being reported, that's powerful insight that should not be ignored.

Also remember that nothing lasts forever in major league baseball. *Reality is fluid.* One decision begets a series of events that lead to other decisions. Any reported action can easily be reversed based on subsequent events. My favorite examples are announcements of a team's new bullpen closer. Those are about the shortest realities known to man.

We need the media to provide us with context for our analyses, and the real news they provide is valuable intelligence. But separating the news from the noise is difficult. In most cases, the only thing you can trust is how that player actually performs.

Embracing imprecision

Precision in baseball prognosticating is a fool's quest. There are far too many unexpected variables and noise that can render our projections useless. The truth is, the best we can ever hope for is to accurately forecast general tendencies and percentage plays.

However, even when you follow an 80 percent play, for instance, you will still lose 20 percent of the time. That 20 percent is what skeptics use as justification to dismiss prognosticators; they conveniently ignore the more prevalent 80 percent. The paradox, of course, is that fantasy league titles are often won or lost by those exceptions. Still, long-term success dictates that you always chase the 80 percent and accept the fact that you will be wrong 20 percent of the time. Or, whatever that percentage play happens to be.

For fantasy purposes, playing the percentages can take on an even less precise spin. The best projections are often the ones that are just far enough away from the field of expectation to alter decision-making. In other words, it doesn't matter if I project Player X to bat .320 and he only bats .295; it matters that I project .320 and everyone else projects .280. Those who follow my less-accurate projection will go the extra dollar to acquire him in their draft.

Or, perhaps we should evaluate the projections based upon their intrinsic value. For instance, coming into 2021 would it have been more important for me to tell you that Trea Turner was going to hit .325 or that Adam Frazier would rebound from a .230 average to hit .275? By season's end, the Turner projection would have been more accurate, but the Frazier projection—even though it was off by 30 points—would have been far more valuable. The Frazier projection might have persuaded you to go an extra buck on Draft Day, yielding far more profit.

And that has to be enough. Any tout who projects a player's statistics dead-on will have just been lucky with his dart throws that day.

Perpetuity

Forecasting is not an exercise that produces a single set of numbers. It is dynamic, cyclical and ongoing. Conditions are constantly changing and we must react to those changes by adjusting our expectations. A pre-season projection is just a snapshot in time. Once the first batter steps to the plate on Opening Day, that projection has become obsolete. Its value is merely to provide a starting point, a baseline for what is about to occur.

During the season, if a projection appears to have been invalidated by current performance, the process continues. It is then that we need to ask... What went wrong? What conditions have changed? In fact, has *anything* changed? We need to analyze the situation and revise our expectation, if necessary. This process must be ongoing.

When good projections go bad

All we can control is the process. We simply can't control outcomes. However, one thing we *can* do is analyze the misses to see *why* they occurred. This is always a valuable exercise each year. It puts a proper focus on the variables that were out of our control as well as providing perspective on those players with whom we might have done a better job.

In general, we can organize these forecasting missesinto several categories. To demonstrate, here are players whose 2021 Rotisserie earnings varied from our projections.

Performances that exceeded expectation

Development beyond the growth trend: These are young players for whom we knew there was skill. Some of them were prized prospects in the past who have taken their time ascending the growth curve. Others were a surprise only because their performance spike arrived sooner than anyone anticipated... Vladimir Guerrero Jr., Cedric Mullins, Austin Riley, Jesse Winker, Jonathan India, Willy Adames, Julio Urías, Luis Garcia (P), Logan Webb

Skilled players who just had big years: We knew these guys were good too; we just didn't anticipate they'd be this good... Marcus Semien, Salvador Perez, Jorge Polanco, Starling Marte, Zack Wheeler, Shohei Ohtani

Unexpected health: We knew these players had the goods; we just didn't know whether they'd be healthy or would stay healthy all year... Yordan Alvarez, Giancarlo Stanton, Mitch Haniger, Carlos Rodón, Anthony DeSclafani

Unexpected playing time: These players had the skills—and may have even displayed them at some time in the past—but had questionable playing time potential coming into this season. Some benefited from another player's injury, a rookie who didn't pan out or leveraged a short streak into a regular gig... Tyler O'Neill, Chris Taylor, Patrick Wisdom, Frank Schwindel, Akil Baddoo, Freddy Peralta

Unexpected role: This category is reserved for players who played their way into, or backed into, a larger role than anticipated. For most, there was already some previously demonstrated skill: Nicky Lopez, Kyle Farmer, Jake McGee, Yimi Garcia, Giovanny Gallegos, Dylan Floro

Unexpected discovery of the Fountain of Youth: These players should have been done, or nearly done, or at least headed down the far side of the bell curve. That's what the trends were pointing to. The trends were wrong... Paul Goldschmidt, Yuli Gurriel, Joey Votto, Robbie Grossman, Josh Harrison, Adam Wainwright

Surprise, yes, but not as good as it looked: These are players whose numbers were pretty, but unsupported by their skills metrics. Enjoy them now, but be wary of next year ... Isiah Kiner-Falefa, Jazz Chisholm, Adolís Garcia, Cal Quantrill

Who the heck knows? Maybe there are reasonable explanations, but this year was so far off the charts for... Brandon Crawford (heck, insert just about any SF batter here), Robbie Ray

Performances that fell short of expectation

The IL inhabitants: These are players who got hurt, may not have returned fully healthy, or may have never been fully healthy (whether they'd admit it or not)... Ronald Acuña, Mookie Betts, Mike Trout, Christian Yelich, Cody Bellinger, Adalberto Mondesi, Corey Seager, Anthony Rendon, Luis Robert, Ke'Bryan Hayes, Alex Bregman, George Springer, Ketel Marte, Luke Voit, Byron Buxton, Mike Moustakas, Yasmani Grandal, Shane Bieber, Jack Flaherty, Tyler Glasnow, Kenta Maeda, Zac Gallen, Stephen Strasburg, Sonny Gray, Dinelson Lamet, Carlos Carrasco, Zach Eflin, Jordan Hicks

Accelerated skills erosion: These are players who we knew were on the downside of their careers or had soft peripherals but who we did not think would plummet so quickly. In some cases, there were injuries involved, but all in all, 2021 might be the beginning of the end for... Charlie Blackmon, Anthony Rizzo, Yu Darvish, Hyun-jin Ryu, Kyle Hendricks, Zack Greinke, Dylan Bundy, Brad Hand

Inflated expectations: Here are players who we really should not have expected much more than what they produced. Some had short or spotty track records, others had soft peripherals

coming into 2021, and still others were inflated by media hype. Yes, for some of these, it was "What the heck was I thinking?" For others, we've almost come to expect players to ascend the growth curve faster these days. (You're 23 and you haven't broken out yet? What's the problem??) The bottom line is that player performance trends simply don't progress or regress in a straight line; still, the skills trends were intriguing enough to take a leap of faith. We were wrong... Cavan Biggio, Eugenio Suárez, Keston Hiura, Trent Grisham, Austin Meadows, Jeff McNeil, Eddie Rosario, Alec Bohm, Dom Smith, Wil Myers, Mike Yastrzemski, Ian Anderson, Jesús Luzardo, Chris Paddack, Zach Plesac

Unexpected loss of role: This category is reserved for would-be closers who lost the job before they could return profit... Alex Colomé, Rafael Montero, Taylor Rogers, Greg Holland, Héctor Neris, Anthony Bass, Emilio Pagan, Amir Garrett, Daniel Bard, Stefan Crichton

Surprise, yes, but not as bad as it looked: These are players whose numbers were disappointing, but supported by better skills metrics. Diss them now, but keep an open mind for next year... Trevor Story, Francisco Lindor, DJ LeMahieu, Michael Conforto, Jorge Soler, Luis Castillo, Blake Snell, Aaron Nola

Who the heck knows? Maybe any one of these players could have been slotted into another category, but they still remain head-scratchers... Gleyber Torres, Victor Robles, James Karinchak (sticky stuff?)

About fantasy baseball touts

As a group, there is a strong tendency for all pundits to provide numbers that are publicly palatable, often at the expense of potential accuracy. That's because committing to either end of the range of expectation poses a high risk. Few touts will put their credibility on the line like that, even though we all know that those outliers are inevitable. Among our projections, you will find no .350 hitters or 70-steal speedsters. *Someone* is going to post a sub-2.50 ERA next year, but damned if any of us will commit to that. So we take an easier road. We'll hedge our numbers or split the difference between two equally possible outcomes.

In the world of prognosticating, this is called the *comfort zone.* This represents the outer tolerances for the public acceptability of a set of numbers. In most circumstances, even if the evidence is outstanding, prognosticators will not stray from within the comfort zone.

As for this book, occasionally we do commit to outlying numbers when we feel the data support it. But on the whole, most of the numbers here can be nearly as cowardly as everyone else's. We get around this by providing "color" to the projections in the capsule commentaries, often listing UPside or DOWNside projections. That is where you will find the players whose projection has the best potential to stray beyond the limits of the comfort zone.

As analyst John Burnson once wrote: "The issue is not the success rate for one player, but the success rate for all players. No system is 100% reliable, and in trying to capture the outliers, you weaken the middle and thereby lose more predictive pull than you gain. At some level, everyone is an exception!"

Validating Performance

Performance validation criteria

The following is a set of support variables that helps determine whether a player's statistical output is an accurate reflection of his skills. From this we can validate or refute stats that vary from expectation, essentially asking, is this performance "fact or fluke?"

1. **Age:** Is the player at the stage of development when we might expect a change in performance?

2. **Health:** Is he coming off an injury, reconditioned and healthy for the first time in years, or a habitual resident of the injured list?

3. **Minor league performance:** Has he shown the potential for greater things at some level of the minors? Or does his minor league history show a poor skill set that might indicate a lower ceiling?

4. **Historical trends:** Have his skill levels over time been on an upswing or downswing?

5. **Component skills indicators:** Looking beyond batting averages and ERAs, what do his support metrics look like?

6. **Ballpark, team, league:** Pitchers going to Colorado will see their ERA spike. Pitchers going to Oakland will see their ERA improve.

7. **Team performance:** Has a player's performance been affected by overall team chemistry or the environment fostered by a winning or losing club?

8. **Batting stance, pitching style/mastery:** Has a change in performance been due to a mechanical adjustment?

9. **Usage pattern, lineup position, role:** Has a change in RBI opportunities been a result of moving further up or down in the batting order? Has pitching effectiveness been impacted by moving from the bullpen to the rotation?

10. **Coaching effects:** Has the coaching staff changed the way a player approaches his conditioning, or how he approaches the game itself?

11. **Off-season activity:** Has the player spent the winter frequenting workout rooms or banquet tables?

12. **Personal factors:** Has the player undergone a family crisis? Experienced spiritual rebirth? Given up red meat? Taken up testosterone?

Skills ownership

Once a player displays a skill, he owns it. That display could occur at any time—earlier in his career, back in the minors, or even in winter ball play. And while that skill may lie dormant after its initial display, the potential is always there for him to tap back into that skill at some point, barring injury or age. That dormant skill can reappear at any time given the right set of circumstances.

Caveats:

1. The initial display of skill must have occurred over an extended period of time. An isolated 1-hit shutout in Single-A ball amidst a 5.00 ERA season is not enough. The shorter the display of skill in the past, the more likely it can be attributed to random chance. The longer the display, the more likely that any reemergence could be for real.

2. If a player has been suspected of using performance enhancing drugs at any time, all bets are off.

Corollaries:

1. Once a player displays a vulnerability or skills deficiency, he owns that as well. That vulnerability could be an old injury problem, an inability to hit breaking pitches, or just a tendency to go into prolonged slumps.

2. The probability of a player correcting a skills deficiency declines with each year that deficiency continues to exist.

Contract year performance *(Tom Mullooly)*

There is a contention that players step up their game when they are playing for a contract. Research looked at contract year players and their performance during that year as compared to career levels. Of the batters and pitchers studied, 53% of the batters performed as if they were on a salary drive, while only 15% of the pitchers exhibited some level of contract year behavior.

How do players fare *after* signing a large contract (minimum $4M per year)? Research from 2005-2008 revealed that only 30% of pitchers and 22% of hitters exhibited an increase of more than 15% in BPV after signing a large deal either with their new team, or re-signing with the previous team. But nearly half of the pitchers (49%) and nearly half of the hitters (47%) saw a drop in BPV of more than 15% in the year after signing.

Risk Analysis

Risk management and reliability grades

Forecasts are constructed with the best data available, but there are factors that can impact the variability. One way we manage this risk is to assign each player Reliability Grades. The more certainty we see in a data set, the higher the reliability grades assigned to that player. The following variables are evaluated:

Health: Players with a history of staying healthy and off the IL are valuable to own. Unfortunately, while the ability to stay healthy can be considered skill, it is not very projectable. We can track the number of days spent on the injured list and draw rough conclusions. The grades in the player boxes also include an adjustment for older players, who have a higher likelihood of getting hurt. That is the only forward-looking element of the grade.

"A" level players would have accumulated fewer than 30 days on the major league IL over the past five years. "F" grades go to those who've spent more than 120 days on the IL. Recent IL stays are given a heavier weight in the calculation.

Playing Time and Experience (PT/Exp): The greater the pool of MLB history to draw from, the greater our ability to construct a viable forecast. Length of service—and consistent service—is important. So players who bounce up and down from the majors to the minors are higher risk players. And rookies are all high risk.

For batters, we simply track plate appearances. Major league PAs have greater weight than minor league PAs. "A" level players would have averaged at least 550 major league PAs per year over the past three years. "F" graded players averaged fewer than 250 major league PA per year.

For pitchers, workload can be a double-edged sword. On one hand, small IP samples are deceptive in providing a read on a pitcher's true potential. Even a consistent 65-inning reliever can be considered higher risk since it would take just one bad outing to skew an entire season's work.

On the flipside, high workload levels also need to be monitored, especially in the formative years of a pitcher's career. Exceeding those levels elevates the risk of injury, burnout, or breakdown. So, tracking workload must be done within a range of innings. The grades capture this.

Consistency: Consistent performers are easier to project and garner higher reliability grades. Players that mix mediocrity with occasional flashes of brilliance or badness generate higher risk projections. Even those who exhibit a consistent upward or downward trend cannot be considered truly consistent as we do not know whether those trends will continue. Typically, they don't. *(See next: Using 3-year trends as leading indicators)*

"A" level players are those whose runs created per game level (xERA for pitchers) has fluctuated by less than half a run during each of the past three years. "F" grades go to those whose RC/G or xERA has fluctuated by two runs or more.

Remember that these grades have nothing to do with quality of performance; they strictly refer to confidence in our expectations. So a grade of AAA for a bad player only means that there is a high probability he will perform as poorly as we've projected.

Using 3-year trends as leading indicators *(Ed DeCaria)*

It is almost irresistibly tempting to look at three numbers moving in one direction and expect that the fourth will continue that progression. However, for both hitters and pitchers riding positive trends over any consecutive three-year period, not only do most players not continue their positive trend into a fourth year, their Year 4 performance usually regresses significantly. This is true for every metric tested (whether related to playing time, batting skills, pitching skills, running skills, luck indicators, or valuation). Negative trends show similar reversals, but tend to be more "sticky," meaning that rebounds are neither as frequent nor as strong as positive trend regressions.

Reliability and age

Peak batting reliability occurs at ages 29 and 30, followed by a minor decline for four years. So, to draft the most reliable batters, and maximize the odds of returning at least par value on your investments, you should target the age range of 28-34.

The most reliable age range for pitchers is 29-34. While we are forever looking for "sleepers" and hot prospects, it is very risky to draft any pitcher under 27 or over 35.

Evaluating Reliability *(Bill Macey)*

When you head into an upcoming auction or draft, consider the following with regard to risk and reliability:

- Reliability grades do help identify more stable investments: players with "B" grades in both Health and PT/Experience are more likely to return a higher percentage of their projected value.
- While top-end starting pitching may be more reliable than ever, the overall pool of pitchers is fraught with uncertainty and they represent a less reliable investment than batters.

- There does not appear to be a significant market premium for reliability, at least according to the criteria measured by BaseballHQ.com.
- There are only two types of players: risky and riskier. So while it may be worth going the extra buck for a more reliable player, be warned that even the most reliable player can falter—don't go overboard bidding up a AAA-rated player simply due to his Reliability grades.

Normal production variance *(Patrick Davitt)*

Even if we have a perfectly accurate understanding of a player's "normal" performance level, his actual performance can and does vary widely over any particular 150-game span—including the 150-game span we call "a season." A .300 career hitter can perform in a range of .250-.350, a 40-HR hitter from 30-50, and a 3.70/1.15 pitcher from 2.60/0.95 to 6.00/1.55. And all of these results must be considered "normal."

Health Analysis

Injury Primer *(James C. Ferretti, DO)*

Every player injury and recovery process is unique. Still, you can gain a sizable advantage with a better understanding of both injuries and the corresponding medical terms. An overview of the human musculoskeletal system:

- *Bones:* The rigid support framework which is also a foundation for the other moving parts.
- *Cartilage:* Soft tissue that acts as a cushion and prevents wear—usually in areas where bones are close to each other.
- *Muscles:* Bundles of fibers that bend and stretch to perform work.
- *Tendons:* Bundles of (less bendy/stretchy) fibers that attach muscles to bones.
- *Ligaments:* Bundles of (even less bendy/stretchy) fibers that attach bones to other bones.

Some common ailments:

A **fracture** is simply a break in a bone, which means it isn't able to act as a stabilizer or absorb/distribute forces. Time to heal and/or long-term effects? Usually 4-6 weeks, though sometimes longer, though once the new bone has matured, it's as good as new.

Strains/sprains are tears of the fibers of muscles/tendons (strains) and ligaments (sprains). Most doctors categorize them on a Grade 1, 2, 3, scale, from less severe to most.

Time to heal and/or long-term effects? A rough estimate is 2-4 weeks for a Grade 1, 4-8 weeks for a Grade 2, and at least 8 weeks for a Grade 3. There can be long-term effects, notably that the repaired areas contain fibrous ("scar") tissue, which is neither as strong nor as flexible as the original tissue, and is more prone to re-injury.

Inflammation is an irritation of soft tissues, often from overuse or repetitive motion and the structures affected get "angry." Even if they occur for different reasons, inflammation and a Grade 1 strain can behave similarly—and both can keep a player out for weeks. Long-term effects? Injury/pain can recur, or even worsen without adequate time to heal. (So, maybe your player coming back early isn't such good news after all.)

Some widely-used injury terms:

"No structural damage" sounds reassuring, but it's often misleading. When medical imagers unaffiliated with MLB clubs make an injury diagnosis, they might term it a fracture, dislocation, soft tissue tear, or inflammation; all of which are bad news. Or they may call it "normal," or "negative," which is good news. But rarely would they describe an injury in terms of "no structural damage," because it's not an actual diagnosis. Rather, it's a way of saying that whatever body part being imaged is intact, with no broken bone or soft tissue tear. This is not the same as a "normal" or "negative" diagnosis. When you hear "no structural damage", continue to keep a close eye on the situation.

Similarly, **"day-to-day"** sounds reassuring—but really doesn't tell you anything other than "We aren't sure," which can be far more worrisome.

"X-Rays are negative": Imaging a player is usually prompted by sudden or increasing onset of pain. Most baseball injuries, though, are to soft tissue, which is never diagnosed with an X-ray alone. Unless there's suspicion of a broken bone or joint injury, an X-ray probably isn't going to tell you much. We often see writers and analysts use a "negative" X-ray report to justify that the injury is "not believed to be serious." Don't make that mistake—await the results of more definitive imaging/tests, like a CAT scan or MRI.

Injured list statistics

Year	#Players	3yr Avg	IL Days	3yr Avg
2011	422	408	25,610	24,924
2012	409	408	30,408	27,038
2013	442	419	29,551	28,523
2014	422	424	25,839	28,599
2015	454	439	28,982	28,124
2016	478	451	31,329	28,717
2017	533	488	30,913	30,408
2018	574	528	34,284	32,175
2019	563	557	36,394	33,864
2020*	456	-	13,518	-
2021**	835	657	47,693	39,457

*Due to the 60-game season, 2020 data is not included in 3-year averages.
** The 2021 data includes 103 players/1,467 days whose only "injury" loss was due to a COVID-19 quarantine, and another 78 players who had other injuries in addition to a COVID quarantine.

IL days as a leading indicator *(Bill Macey)*

Players who are injured in one year are likely to be injured in a subsequent year:

% IL batters in Year 1 who are also DL in year 2	38%
Under age 30	36%
Age 30 and older	41%
% IL batters in Year 1 and 2 who are also DL in year 3	54%
% IL pitchers in Year 1 who are also DL in year 2	43%
Under age 30	45%
Age 30 and older	41%
% IL pitchers in Yr 1 and 2 who are also DL in year 3	41%

Previously injured players also tend to spend a longer time on the IL. The average number of days on the IL was 51 days for batters and 73 days for pitchers. For the subset of these players who get hurt again the following year, the average number of days on the IL was 58 days for batters and 88 days for pitchers.

How a batter's age affects IL stays *(Jeff Zimmerman)*

Some players seem to get more than their fair share of injuries, but for those hitters with the "injury-prone" tag, it only takes one healthy season to make a difference. After breaking up hitters into three age groups (25 and younger; 26-29; 30 and older), a study examined length and frequency of IL stints. Among the findings:

1. If someone in the youngest group goes on the IL once, they aren't as likely to again the next season. The probability increases after two IL seasons, however, from 33% to 43%.
2. The best health is exhibited by the middle group. It seems this age is the sweet spot for avoiding injuries. The hitters have shown they can hold up to a full season, but their bodies have not started to break down.
3. Not surprisingly, the oldest group takes longer to heal. The IL-related stats hover above the league average, but the IL rate doesn't increase as a player racks up previous injuries.

Do overworked hitters wear down? *(Jeff Zimmerman)*

A study compared the first- and second-half statistics for batters who played the most games over the entire season from 2002-16. These players were continually run out on the field, and one figures that fatigue would show up in their statistics. In actuality, their output improves the more they play. Though this concept goes against conventional wisdom, it is true: If a hitter plays more, the more likely he is healthy and not wearing down.

Spring training spin *(Dave Adler)*

Spring training sound bites raise expectations among fantasy leaguers, but how much of that "news" is really "noise"? A study reported a verdict of: Noise.

BATTERS	No.	IMPROVED	DECLINED
Weight change	30	33%	30%
Fitness program	3	0%	67%
Eye surgery	6	50%	33%
Plans more SB	6	17%	33%
PITCHERS	No.	IMPROVED	DECLINED
Weight change	18	44%	44%
Fitness program	4	50%	50%
Eye surgery	2	0%	50%
New pitch	5	60%	40%

In-Season Analysis

The weight of early season numbers

Early season strugglers who surge later in the year often get little respect because they have to live with the weight of their early numbers all season long. Conversely, quick starters who fade late get far more accolades than they deserve.

For instance, take Max Fried's month-by-month ERA in 2021. The perception is that his 3.04 ERA was a solid follow-up to his 2020 short-season breakout doesn't nearly show how well he performed in May and down the stretch. Fried had two really bad starts in April (6 IP, 12 ER), which inflated his ERA for the rest of the year. From August on, his ERA was only 1.46:

Month	ERA	Cum ERA
Mar-Apr	11.45	11.45
May	1.50	4.63
June	3.58	4.16
July	4.66	4.32
August	1.36	3.54
Sept-Oct	1.54	3.04

Courtship period

Any time a player is put into a new situation, he enters into a courtship period. This period might occur when a player switches leagues, or switches teams. It could be the first few games when a minor leaguer is called up. It could occur when a reliever moves into the rotation, or when a lead-off hitter is moved to another spot in the lineup. There is a team-wide courtship period when a manager is replaced. Any external situation that could affect a player's performance sets off a new decision point in evaluating that performance.

During this period, it is difficult to get a true read on how a player is going to ultimately perform. He is adjusting to the new situation. Things could be volatile during this time. For instance, a role change that doesn't work could spur other moves. A rookie hurler might buy himself a few extra starts with a solid debut, even if he has questionable skills.

It is best not to make a roster decision on a player who is going through a courtship period. Wait until his stats stabilize. Don't cut a struggling pitcher in his first few starts after a managerial change. Don't pick up a hitter who smacks a pair of HRs in his first game after having been traded. Unless, of course, talent and track record say otherwise.

Half-season fallacies

A popular exercise at the midpoint of each season is to analyze those players who are consistent first half to second half surgers or faders. There are several fallacies with this analytical approach.

1. It's arbitrary. The season's midpoint is an arbitrary delineator of performance swings. Some players are slow starters and might be more appropriately evaluated as pre-May 1 and post-May 1. Others bring their game up a notch with a pennant chase and might see a performance swing with August 15 as the cut-off. Each player has his own individual tendency, if, in fact, one exists at all. There's nothing magical about mid-season as the break point, and certainly not over a multi-year period.

2. Analysts often use false indicators. Situational statistics provide us with tools that can be misused. Several sources offer up 3- and 5-year stats intended to paint a picture of a long-term performance. Some analysts look at a player's half-season swing over that multi-year period and conclude that he is demonstrating consistent performance.

The fallacy is that those multi-year scans may not show any consistency at all. They are not individual season performances but *aggregate* performances. A player whose 5-year batting average shows a 15-point rise in the 2nd half, for instance, may actually have experienced a BA decline in several of those years, a fact that might have been offset by a huge BA rise in one of the years.

3. Half-season consistency is rare. There are very few players who show consistent changes in performance from one half of the season to the other even over a three-year span. As such, it's impossible to prove whether or not it's predictive.

Half-season tendencies

Despite the above, it stands to reason logically that there might be some underlying tendencies on a more global scale, first half to second half. In fact, one would think that the player population as a whole might decline in performance as the season drones on. There are many variables that might contribute to a player wearing down—workload, weather, boredom—and the longer a player is on the field, the higher the likelihood that he is going to get hurt. A recent 5-year study uncovered the following tendencies:

Batting

Overall, batting skills held up pretty well, half to half. There was a 5% erosion of playing time, likely due, in part, to September roster expansion.

Power: First half power studs (20 HRs in 1H) saw a 10% drop-off in the second half. 34% of first half 20+ HR hitters hit 15 or fewer in the second half and only 27% were able to improve on their first half output.

Speed: Second half speed waned as well. About 26% of the 20+ SB speedsters stole *at least 10 fewer bases* in the second half. Only 26% increased their second half SB output at all.

Batting average: 60% of first half .300 hitters failed to hit .300 in the second half. Only 20% showed any second half improvement at all. As for 1H strugglers, managers tended to stick with their full-timers despite poor starts. Nearly one in five of the sub-.250 1H hitters managed to hit *more than* .300 in the second half.

Pitching

Overall, there was some slight erosion in innings and ERA despite marginal improvement in skills metrics.

ERA: For those who pitched at least 100 innings in the first half, ERAs rose an average of 0.40 runs in the 2H. Of those with first half ERAs less than 4.00, only 49% were able to maintain a sub-4.00 ERA in the second half.

Wins: Pitchers who won 18 or more games in a season tended to pitch *more* innings in the 2H and had slightly better skills metrics.

Saves: Of those closers who saved 20 or more games in the first half, only 39% were able to post 20 or more saves in the 2H, and 26% posted fewer than 15 saves. Aggregate ERAs of these pitchers rose from 2.45 to 3.17, half to half.

In-season trends in hitting and pitching *(Bob Berger)*

A study of monthly trends in traditional statistical categories found:

- Batting average, HR/game and RBI/game rise from April through August, then fall in September/October.
- Stolen bases decline in July and August before rebounding in September.
- ERA worsens in July/August and improves in September.
- WHIP gets worse in July/August.
- K/9 rate improves all season.

The statement that hitters perform better in warmer weather seems to be true broadly.

Can in-season deficiencies in ratio categories be overcome?
(Patrick Davitt)

Many fantasy players think that later in the season, we can't move the decimals (BA, ERA, WHIP) because with the majority of AB/IP in the books, the ratio's large denominators make it too hard. While it's true we can't move as much late as early, we can still gain points. We tested this idea at the two-thirds mark in the season. Using teams and stats in a 15-team mixed expert's league, we built tables to see how much an owner could gain—first just by dropping a poor performer, and then by replacing a poor performer with a good performer.

From a study of a 15-team mixed expert's league, we found that it's still possible to gain points in the ratio categories by replacing a poor performer with a good performer, even at the two-thirds mark of the season. (Obviously, stratification of league standings will vary.)

Batting Average

The BA test projected a team to finish with a .257 BA. With 190 remaining projected AB per batter, we found that by dropping a players and not replacing him:

- Drop a .235 hitter: Team BA .25756
- .225 hitter: .25783
- .215 hitter: .25810

The gains are amplified when the poor hitter is replaced with a high projected BA hitter. Dropping a .215 pBA hitter and adding a .305 guy jumps team pBA to .25927. Dropping a .245 and adding a .265 still gains 57 baseline points. Again, depending on how close your league standings are, this matters.

ERA

Gains in pitching decimals can be greater because the denominator is smaller than BA. This study used a team with a 4.00 final pERA in 1,325 IP. Let's start again by just dropping a poor performer with 55 pIP:

- Dropping a 4.50 pERA pitcher, finished at 3.976
- 5.00 pitcher: 3.954
- 5.50 pitcher: 3.933

And now, by adding a low-pERA replacement: Dropping a 5.50 disaster for a 2.75 stud means a final pERA of 3.885, an improvement of .115.

Again, much depends on how each category is stratified.

Surprisingly Productive Years *(Ed DeCaria)*

Here's a skills-based method of finding productive in-season roster additions:

1. Consider all batters projected for 50% or less playing time, all starting pitchers projected for 10% or less of his team's innings pitched (about 140 IP), and all relief pitchers projected for less than 4% of his team's innings pitched (about 50 IP)
2. Using each player's projected skills—not stats—in the form of his Mayberry scores, include only batters whose sum of three Mayberry skills (power, speed, and hitting) was 7 or higher (8 or higher for mixed leagues).

For pitchers, only consider players whose sum of two Mayberry skills (xERA and strikeout rate) was 4 or higher (5 or higher for mixed leagues). For relievers, we also counted Mayberry's saves potential score, so we included only relievers whose sum of three scores was 7 or higher (8 or higher for mixed leagues).

3. Examine the specific situation of each player that met our first two criteria and assign a realistic playing time upside given his skills and injury, consistency, and forecast risk, and that of the player(s) ahead of him on his team's depth chart.
4. Calculate a single number that measured their "projected skill" over their "potential playing time" to arrive at their "potential value."
   a. For hitters, take his Mayberry sum and multiply it by his potential playing time (pPT). Then rank batters by this metric and subtract the minimum value of the group from all players, so that the least valuable batter had a marginal score (mSCORE) of zero. Then use mSCORE to calculate each player's "share" of the total, and multiply that by the league's total wasted dollars (using a 65/35 batter/pitcher split) to determine each batter's potential value (pR$).
   b. Similarly for pitchers, take the Mayberry sum multiplied by potential innings percentage (pPT) and rank pitchers by this metric. Subtract the minimum value of the group from all pitchers, then use mSCORE to calculate each pitcher's "share" of the total, and multiply that by the league's total wasted dollars (using a 65/35 batter/pitcher split) to determine each pitcher's potential value (pR$).

Use these rankings to produce lists of players who are projected for far less than full playing time despite good or even great skills. A well-timed pick-up of any one of these players could be a boon to most teams' chances of winning their league.

Teams

Johnson Effect *(Bryan Johnson)*: Teams whose actual won/loss record exceeds or falls short of their statistically projected record in one season will tend to revert to the level of their projection in the following season.

Law of Competitive Balance *(Bill James)*: The level at which a team (or player) will address its problems is inversely related to its current level of success. Low performers will tend to make changes to improve; high performers will not. This law explains the existence of the Plexiglass and Whirlpool Principles.

Plexiglass Principle *(Bill James)*: If a player or team improves markedly in one season, it will likely decline in the next. The opposite is true but not as often (because a poor performer gets fewer opportunities to rebound).

Whirlpool Principle *(Bill James)*: All team and player performances are forcefully drawn to the center. For teams, that center is a .500 record. For players, it represents their career average level of performance.

Other Diamonds

The Fanalytic Fundamentals

1. This is not a game of accuracy or precision. It is a game of human beings and tendencies.
2. This is not a game of projections. It is a game of market value versus real value.
3. Draft skills, not stats. Draft skills, not roles.
4. A player's ability to post acceptable stats despite lousy support metrics will eventually run out.
5. Once you display a skill, you own it.
6. Virtually every player is vulnerable to a month of aberrant performance. Or a year.
7. Exercise excruciating patience.

Aging Axioms

1. Age is the only variable for which we can project a rising trend with 100% accuracy. (Or, age never regresses.)
2. The aging process slows down for those who maintain a firm grasp on the strike zone. Plate patience and pitching command can preserve any waning skill they have left.
3. Negatives tend to snowball as you age.

Steve Avery List

Players who hang onto MLB rosters for six years searching for a skill level they only had for three.

Bylaws of Badness

1. Some players are better than an open roster spot, but not by much.
2. Some players have bad years because they are unlucky. Others have *many* bad years because they are bad... and lucky.

Christie Brinkley Law of Statistical Analysis

Never get married to the model.

Employment Standards

1. If you are right-brain dominant, own a catcher's mitt and are under 40, you will always be gainfully employed.
2. Some teams believe that it is better to employ a player with any experience because it has to be better than the devil they don't know.
3. It's not so good to go *pffft* in a contract year.

Brad Fullmer List

Players whose leading indicators indicate upside potential, year after year, but consistently fail to reach that full potential. Players like Byron Buxton, Andrew Heaney and Chris Paddack are on the list right now.

Good Luck Truism

Good luck is rare and everyone has more of it than you do. That's the law.

The Gravity Principles

1. It is easier to be crappy than it is to be good.
2. All performance starts at zero, ends at zero and can drop to zero at any time.

3. The odds of a good performer slumping are far greater than the odds of a poor performer surging.
4. Once a player is in a slump, it takes several 3-for-5 days to get out of it. Once he is on a streak, it takes a single 0-for-4 day to begin the downward spiral. *Corollary:* Once a player is in a slump, not only does it take several 3-for-5 days to get out of it, but he also has to get his name back on the lineup card.
5. Eventually all performance comes down to earth. It may take a week, or a month, or may not happen until he's 45, but eventually it's going to happen.

Health Homilies

1. Staying healthy is a skill.
2. A $40 player can get hurt just as easily as a $5 player but is eight times tougher to replace.
3. Chronically injured players never suddenly get healthy.
4. There are two kinds of pitchers: those that are hurt and those that are not hurt... yet.
5. Players with back problems are always worth $10 less.
6. "Opting out of surgery" usually means it's coming anyway, just later.

The Health Hush

Players get hurt and potentially have a lot to lose, so there is an incentive for them to hide injuries. HIPAA laws restrict the disclosure of health information. Team doctors and trainers have been instructed not to talk with the media. So, when it comes to information on a player's health status, we're all pretty much in the dark.

The Livan Level

The point when a player's career Runs Above Replacement level has dropped so far below zero that he has effectively cancelled out any possible remaining future value. (Similarly, the Dontrelle Demarcation.)

The Momentum Maxims

1. A player will post a pattern of positive results until the day you add him to your roster.
2. Patterns of negative results are more likely to snowball than correct.
3. When an unstoppable force meets an immovable object, the wall always wins.

Noise

Irrelevant or meaningless pieces of information that can distort the results of an analysis. In news, this is opinion or rumor. In forecasting, this is random variance or irrelevant data. In ballparks, this is a screaming crowd cheering for a team down 12-3 with two outs and bases empty in the bottom of the ninth.

Paradoxes and Conundrums

1. Is a player's improvement in performance from one year to the next a point in a growth trend, an isolated outlier or a complete anomaly?
2. A player can play through an injury, post rotten numbers and put his job at risk... or... he can admit that he can't play through an injury, allow himself to be taken out of the lineup/rotation, and put his job at risk.

3. Did irregular playing time take its toll on the player's performance or did poor performance force a reduction in his playing time?

4. Is a player only in the game versus right-handers because he has a true skills deficiency versus left-handers? Or is his poor performance versus left-handers because he's never given a chance to face them?

5. The problem with stockpiling bench players in the hope that one pans out is that you end up evaluating performance using data sets that are too small to be reliable.

6. There are players who could give you 20 stolen bases if they got 400 AB. But if they got 400 AB, they would likely be on a bad team that wouldn't let them steal.

Paths to Retirement

1. **The George Brett Path:** Get out while you're still putting up good numbers and the public perception of you is favorable. Like Chipper Jones, Mariano Rivera and David Ortiz.

2. **The Steve Carlton Path:** Hang around the majors long enough for your numbers to become so wretched that people begin to forget your past successes. Recently retired players who took this path include Jose Bautista, James Shields and Bartolo Colón. Current players who could be on a similar course include Miguel Cabrera and Albert Pujols, and perhaps Jon Lester and Jake Arrieta.

3. **The Johan Santana Path:** Stay on the disabled list for so long that nobody realizes you've officially retired until your name shows up on a Hall of Fame ballot. Perhaps like Carl Crawford and Jacoby Ellsbury.

Process-Outcome Matrix *(Russo and Schoemaker)*

	Good Outcome	Bad Outcome
Good Process	Deserved Success	Bad Break
Bad Process	Dumb Luck	Poetic Justice

Quack!

An exclamation in response to the educated speculation that a player has used performance enhancing drugs. While it is rare to have absolute proof, there is often enough information to suggest that, "if it looks like a duck and quacks like a duck, then odds are it's a duck."

Rules of Regression

1. The two strongest forces on Earth are regression and gravity.
2. The most accurate forecast is often just a regression to a player's career average.
3. Regression doesn't punch a time clock. *(Todd Zola)*

Surface Stats

All those wonderful statistics we grew up with that those mean bean counters are telling us don't matter anymore. Home runs, RBIs, batting average, won-loss record. Let's go back to the 1960s and make baseball great again! [EDITOR: No.]

Tenets of Optimal Timing

1. If a second half fader had put up his second half stats in the first half and his first half stats in the second half, then he probably wouldn't even have had a second half.

2. Fast starters can often buy six months of playing time out of one month of productivity.

3. Poor 2nd halves don't get recognized until it's too late.

4. "Baseball is like this. Have one good year and you can fool them for five more, because for five more years they expect you to have another good one." — Frankie Frisch

The Three True Outcomes

1. Strikeouts
2. Walks
3. Home runs

The Three True Handicaps

1. Has power but can't make contact.
2. Has speed but can't hit safely.
3. Has potential but is too old.

Zombie

A player who is indestructible, continuing to get work, year-after-year, no matter how dead his skills metrics have become. Players like Ervin Santana, Josh Tomlin and Wade LeBlanc are among the walking dead now.

Batters

Batting Eye, Contact and Batting Average

Batting average (BA, or Avg)

This is where it starts. BA is a grand old nugget that has long outgrown its usefulness. We revere .300 hitting superstars and think of .250 hitters as slightly below average, yet the difference between the two is one hit every five games. BA is a poor evaluator of performance in that it neglects the offensive value of the base on balls and assumes that all hits are created equal.

Walk rate (bb%)

(BB / (AB + BB))

A measure of a batter's plate patience. BENCHMARKS: The best batters will have levels more than 10%. Those with poor plate patience will have levels of 5% or less.

On base average (OB)

(H + BB + HBP) / (AB + BB + HBP + Sac Flies)

Addressing a key deficiency with BA, OB gives value to events that get batters on base, but are not hits. An OB of .350 can be read as "this batter gets on base 35% of the time." When a run is scored, there is no distinction made as to how that runner reached base. So, two-thirds of the time—about how often a batter comes to the plate with the bases empty—a walk really is as good as a hit. BENCHMARKS: We know what a .300 hitter is, but what represents "good" for OB? That comparable level would likely be .340, with .290 representing the comparable level of futility.

Ground ball, line drive, fly ball percentages (G/L/F)

See updated research on page 69.

Line drives and luck *(Patrick Davitt)*

Given that each individual batter's hit rate sets its own baseline, and that line drives (LD) are the most productive type of batted ball, a study looked at the relationship between the two. Among the findings were that hit rates on LDs are much higher than on FBs or GBs, with individual batters consistently falling into the 72-73% range. Ninety-five percent of all batters fall between the range of 60%-86%; batters outside this range regress very quickly, often within the season.

Note that batters' BAs did not always follow their LD% up or down, because some of them enjoyed higher hit rates on other batted balls, improved their contact rates, or both. Still, it's justifiable to bet that players hitting the ball with authority but getting fewer hits than they should will correct over time.

Batting eye (Eye)

(Walks / Strikeouts)

A measure of a player's strike zone judgment. BENCHMARKS: The best hitters have Eye ratios more than 1.00 (indicating more walks than strikeouts) and are the most likely to be among a league's .300 hitters. Ratios less than 0.30 represent batters who likely also have lower BAs.

Batting eye as a leading indicator

There is a correlation between strike zone judgment and batting average but research shows that this is more descriptive than predictive.

However, we can create percentage plays for the different levels:

For Eye	Pct who bat	
Levels of	.300+	.250-
0.00 - 0.25	7%	39%
0.26 - 0.50	14%	26%
0.51 - 0.75	18%	17%
0.76 - 1.00	32%	14%
1.01 - 1.50	51%	9%
1.51 +	59%	4%

Any batter with an eye ratio more than 1.50 has about a 4% chance of hitting less than .250 over 500 at bats.

Of all .300 hitters, those with ratios of at least 1.00 have a 65% chance of repeating as .300 hitters. Those with ratios less than 1.00 have less than a 50% chance of repeating.

Only 4% of sub-.250 hitters with ratios less than 0.50 will mature into .300 hitters the following year.

In this study, only 37 batters hit .300-plus with a sub-0.50 eye ratio over at least 300 AB in a season. Of this group, 30% were able to accomplish this feat on a consistent basis. For the other 70%, this was a short-term aberration.

Contact rate (ct%)

((AB - K) / AB)

Measures a batter's ability to get wood on the ball and hit it into the field of play. BENCHMARKS: Those batters with the best contact skill will have levels of 80% or better. The hackers will have levels of 70% or less.

Contact rate as a leading indicator

The more often a batter makes contact with the ball, the higher the likelihood that he will hit safely.

	Batting Average				
Contact Rate	2017	2018	2019	2020	2021
0% - 60%	.206	.196	.179	.184	.188
61% - 65%	.226	.223	.223	.212	.222
66% - 70%	.244	.237	.241	.224	.225
71% - 75%	.248	.245	.252	.248	.245
76% - 80%	.268	.258	.264	.261	.261
81% - 85%	.270	.268	.277	.269	.268
Over 85%	.285	.277	.282	.284	.273

Contact rate and walk rate as leading indicators

See updated research on page 70.

HCt and HctX *(Patrick Davitt)*

HCt= hard hit ball rate x contact rate

HctX= Player HCt divided by league average Hct, normalized to 100

The combination of making contact and hitting the ball hard might be the most important skills for a batter. HctX correlates very strongly with BA, and at higher BA levels often does so with high accuracy. Its success with HR was somewhat limited, probably due to GB/FB differences. BENCHMARKS: The average major-leaguer in a given year has a HctX of 100. Elite batters have an HctX of 135 or above; weakest batters have HctX of 55 or below.

Balls in play (BIP)

(AB – K)

The total number of batted balls that are hit fair, both hits and outs. An analysis of how these balls are hit—on the ground, in the air, hits, outs, etc.—can provide analytical insight, from player skill levels to the impact of luck on statistical output.

Batting average on balls in play *(Voros McCracken)*

(H – HR) / (AB – HR – K)

Or, BABIP. Also called hit rate (h%). The percent of balls hit into the field of play that fall for hits. **BENCHMARK:** Every hitter establishes his own individual hit rate that stabilizes over time. A batter whose seasonal hit rate varies significantly from the h% he has established over the preceding three seasons (variance of at least +/- 3%) is likely to improve or regress to his individual h% mean (with over-performer declines more likely and sharper than under-performer recoveries). Three-year h% levels strongly predict a player's h% the following year.

Pitches/Plate Appearance as a leading indicator for BA *(Paul Petera)*

The deeper a batter works a count (via pitches per plate appearance, or P/PA), the more likely his batting average will fall (e.g., more strikeouts) but his OBA will rise (e.g., more walks):

P/PA	OBA	BA
4.00+	.360	.264
3.75-3.99	.347	.271
3.50-3.74	.334	.274
Under 3.50	.321	.276

Players with an unusually high or low BA for their P/PA in one year tend to regress heavily the next:

	YEAR TWO	
YEAR ONE	BA Improved	BA Declined
Low P/PA and Low BA	77%	23%
High P/PA and High BA	21%	79%

Expected batting average *(John Burnson)*

$xCT\% * [xH1\% + xH2\%]$

where

$xH1\% = GB\% \times [0.0004\ PX + 0.062\ ln(SX)]$
$\qquad + LD\% \times [0.93 - 0.086\ ln(SX)]$
$\qquad + FB\% \times 0.12$

and

$xH2\% = FB\% \times [0.0013\ PX - 0.0002\ SX - 0.057]$
$\qquad + GB\% \times [0.0006\ PX]$

A hitter's expected batting average as calculated by multiplying the percentage of balls put in play (contact rate) by the chance that a ball in play falls for a hit. The likelihood that a ball in play falls for a hit is a product of the speed of the ball and distance it is hit (PX), the speed of the batter (SX), and distribution of ground balls, fly balls, and line drives. We further split it out by non-homerun hit rate (xH1%) and homerun hit rate (xH2%). **BENCHMARKS:** In general, xBA should approximate batting average fairly closely. Those hitters who have large variances between the two gauges are candidates for further analysis. **LIMITATION:** xBA tends to understate a batter's true value if he is an extreme ground ball hitter (G/F ratio over 3.0) with a low PX. These players are not inherently weak, but choose to take safe singles rather than swing for the fences.

Expected batting average variance

xBA – BA

The variance between a batter's BA and his xBA is a measure of over- or under-achievement. A positive variance indicates the potential for a batter's BA to rise. A negative variance indicates the potential for BA to decline. **BENCHMARK:** Discount variances that are less than 20 points. Any variance more than 30 points is regarded as a strong indicator of future change.

Power

Slugging average (Slg)

(Singles + (2 x Doubles) + (3 x Triples) + (4 x HR)) / AB

A measure of the total number of bases accumulated (or the minimum number of runners' bases advanced) per at bat. It is a misnomer; it is not a true measure of a batter's slugging ability because it includes singles. Slg also assumes that each type of hit has proportionally increasing value (i.e. a double is twice as valuable as a single, etc.) which is not true. For instance, with the bases loaded, a HR always scores four runs, a triple always scores three, but a double could score two or three and a single could score one, or two, or even three. **BENCHMARKS:** Top batters will have levels over .450. The bottom batters will have levels less than .350.

Home runs to fly ball rate (HR/F)

The percent of fly balls that are hit for HRs.

HR/F rate as a leading indicator *(Joshua Randall)*

Each batter establishes an individual home run to fly ball rate that stabilizes over rolling three-year periods; those levels strongly predict the HR/F in the subsequent year. A batter who varies significantly from his HR/F is likely to regress toward his individual HR/F mean, with over-performance decline more likely and more severe than under-performance recovery.

Estimating HR rate for young hitters *(Matt Cederholm)*

Over time, hitters establish a baseline HR/F, but how do we measure the HR output of young hitters with little track record? Since power is a key indicator of HR output, we can look at typical HR/F for various levels of power, as measures by xPX:

	HR/F percentiles				
xPX	10	25	50	75	90
<=70	0.9%	2.0%	3.8%	5.5%	7.4%
71-80	3.3%	5.1%	6.4%	8.1%	10.0%
81-90	3.8%	5.4%	7.4%	9.0%	11.0%
91-100	4.7%	6.6%	8.9%	11.3%	13.0%
101-110	6.6%	8.3%	10.9%	13.0%	16.2%
111-120	7.4%	9.8%	11.9%	14.7%	17.1%
121-130	8.5%	10.9%	12.8%	15.5%	17.4%
131-140	9.7%	11.9%	14.6%	17.1%	20.4%
141-160	11.3%	13.1%	16.5%	19.2%	21.5%
161+	14.4%	16.5%	19.4%	22.0%	25.8%

To predict changes in HR output, look at a player and project his HR as if his HR/F was at the median for his xPX level. For example, if a player with a 125 xPX exceeds a 12.8% HR/F, we would expect a decline in the following season. The greater the deviation from the mean, the greater the probability of an increase or decline.

Expected home run total (xHR) *(Arik Florimonte)*
A study assessing all baseball conditions from 2015-2019 created a model for expected home run rate (xHR) given exit velocity (EV) and launch angle (LA) found in MLB's Statcast system. The model was applied to the entire database of batted balls to calculate the likelihood of each batted ball becoming a home run.

The xHR metric is not a measure of whether a specific batted ball should have been a home run. Rather, it is a measure of how often a ball struck in the way it was turns out to be a home run. By comparing a hitter's actual home run total to xHR over a given year, we can estimate how much of that performance was earned or unearned, and adjust home run expectations for the following season.

Expected home runs to fly ball rate (xHR/F) *(Arik Florimonte)*
A player's xHR divided by his fly balls in a given season. While previous years' HR/F results do have some useful correlation to current year's result, xHR/F does even better in that it has added benefit for shorter periods of time. In predicting the next month's results, xHR/F from one month does as well as two months of HR/F. And for equal samples, a batter's xHR/F is about 15-25% better correlated to the upcoming result over a similar time period. This additional predictive value persists for up to about two years, at which time xHR/F and HR/F are roughly equally valuable.

Is fly ball carry a skill? *(Arik Florimonte)*
Using Statcast data from 2015-17, we determined that "Carry"—how much a fly ball travels compared to its projected distance based on Launch Angle and Exit Velocity—is a repeatable skill for batters. Specific findings from this study include:

- Carry is well-correlated from year-to-year, with Prior Year Carry explaining 47% of Current Year Carry.
- On average, a batter will retain two-thirds of his fly ball Carry from year-to-year.
- Batters with unlucky HR totals in Year 0 tend to see an improvement in Year 1. Of those with high Carry in Year 0, 88% saw improvement in the difference between HR/F and xHR/F (expected HR/F), and the average gain is +0.059 (including non-gainers).

Hard-hit flies as a sustainable skill *(Patrick Davitt)*
A study of data from 2009-2011 found that we should seek batters with a high Hard-Hit Fly Ball percentage (HHFB%). Among the findings:

- Avoiding pop-ups and hitting HHFBs are sustainable core power skills.
- Consistent HHFB% performance marks batters with power potential.
- When looking for candidates to regress, we should look at individual past levels of HR/HHFB, perhaps using a three-year rolling average.

Launch angle (LA)
A Statcast metric defined by MLB.com as the vertical angle at which the ball leaves a player's bat after being struck. In other words, it's a precise measure for how high (or low) a ball is hit.

BENCHMARKS: The league-wide average launch angle in 2021 was 12.6 degrees. We can convert launch angle ranges into traditional batted ball trajectories as follows:

Batted ball type	Launch angle
Groundball	Less than 10 degrees
Line drive	10-25 degrees
Flyball	25-50 degrees
Pop-up	Greater than 50 degrees

Exit velocity (EV)
A Statcast metric defined by MLB.com as the speed of the baseball as it comes off the bat, immediately after a batter makes contact. In other words, it's a precise measure for how hard a ball is hit. Batters with higher average exit velocities make harder contact and are more likely to see favorable outcomes than those with lower exit velocities. **BENCHMARKS:** The league-wide average exit velocity in 2021 was 88.8 miles per hour. Top batters will average above 90 mph with bottom batters struggling to reach 87 mph.

Barrel rate (Brl%)
A "barrel" is a Statcast metric defined by MLB.com as a well-struck ball where the combination of exit velocity and launch angle generally leads to a minimum .500 batting average and 1.500 slugging percentage. Barrel rate (Brl% in hitter boxes) is simply the number of barrels divided by the number of batted balls for a given hitter. **BENCHMARKS:** The league-wide barrel rate in 2021 was 7.9%. A rate of >12% is generally considered top tier.

Quality of batted ball score (QBaB) *(Arik Florimonte)*
For batters, greater exit velocity and greater mean launch angle are better. In addition, we've shown elsewhere that reduced launch angle variability is correlated with better batted ball results. The Quality of Batted Ball score (QBaB) assigns A-F grades for exit velocity, launch angle, and launch angle variability based on percentile groups with the thresholds below:

Percentile	Grade	Exit Velocity (mph)	Launch Angle	Launch Angle Variability
90+	A	> 90.8	> 17.6°	< 23.95°
70-90	B	89.2 – 90.8	14.1° – 17.6°	23.95° – 25.64°
30-70	C	88.6 – 89.2	9.2° – 14.1°	25.64° – 27.91°
10-30	D	84.1 – 88.6	5.7° – 9.2°	27.91° – 29.45°
10-	F	< 84.1	< 5.7°	> 29.45°

These scores can be useful in several ways:

- QBaB is very well correlated with batter output.
- Higher EV grades are always desirable.
- Higher LA grades are good for power, but do not help batting average.
- Smaller Launch Angle Variation is good for batting average, but impact on power is murky.
- QBaB scores are very sticky. It is extremely rare for a great hitter to become terrible and vice versa.
- Batters who have great QBaB scores but underperform tend to recover; the converse is true for those with poor scores.

QBaB appears in our hitter boxes, giving readers and analysts another tool to evaluate hitters, and to know whether appearances are to be believed.

Linear weighted power (LWPwr)

((Doubles x .8) + (Triples x .8) + (HR x 1.4)) / (At bats- K) x 100

A variation of Pete Palmer's linear weights formula that considers only events that are measures of a batter's pure power. **BENCHMARKS:** Top sluggers typically top the 17 mark. Weak hitters will have a LWPwr level of less than 10.

Linear weighted power index (PX)

(Batter's LWPwr / League LWPwr) x 100

LWPwr is presented in this book in its normalized form to get a better read on a batter's accomplishment in each year. For instance, a 30-HR season today is much less of an accomplishment than 30 HRs hit in a lower offense year like 2014. **BENCHMARKS:** A level of 100 equals league average power skills. Any player with a value more than 100 has above average power skills, and those more than 150 are the Slugging Elite.

Expected LW power index (xPX) *(Bill Macey)*

2.6 + 269*HHLD% + 724*HHFB%

Previous research has shown that hard-hit balls are more likely to result in hits and hard-hit fly balls are more likely to end up as HRs. As such, we can use hard-hit ball data to calculate an expected skills-based power index. This metric starts with hard-hit ball data, which measures a player's fundamental skill of making solid contact, and then places it on the same scale as PX (xPX). In the above formula, HHLD% is calculated as the number of hard hit-line drives divided by the total number of balls put in play. HHFB% is similarly calculated for fly balls. The variance between PX and xPX can be viewed as a leading indicator for other power metrics.

Pitches/Plate Appearance as a leading indicator for PX *(Paul Petera)*

Batters that work deeper into the count (via pitches per plate appearance, or P/PA) tend to display more power (as measured by PX) than batters who don't:

P/PA	PX
4.00+	123
3.75-3.99	108
3.50-3.74	96
Under 3.50	84

Players with an unusually high or low PX for their P/PA in one year tend to regress heavily the next:

	YEAR TWO	
YEAR ONE	PX Improved	PX Declined
Low P/PA and High PX	11%	89%
High P/PA and Low PX	70%	30%

Doubles as a leading indicator for home runs *(Bill Macey)*

There is little support for the theory that hitting many doubles in year x leads to an increase in HR in year x+1. However, it was shown that batters with high doubles rates (2B/AB) also tend to hit more HR/AB than the league average; oddly, they are unable to sustain the high 2B/AB rate but do sustain their higher HR/AB rates. Batters with high 2B/AB rates and low HR/AB rates are more likely to see HR gains in the following year, but those rates will still typically trail the league average. And, batters who experience a surge in 2B/AB typically give back most of those gains in the following year without any corresponding gain in HR.

Opposite field home runs *(Ed DeCaria)*

Opposite field HRs serve as a strong indicator of overall home run power (AB/HR). Power hitters (smaller AB/HR rates) hit a far higher percentage of their HR to the opposite field or straight away (over 30%). Conversely, non-power hitters hit almost 90% of their home runs to their pull field.

	Performance in Y2-Y4 (% of Group)		
Y1 Trigger	<=30 AB/HR	5.5+ RC/G	$16+ R$
2+ OppHR	69%	46%	33%
<2 OppHR	29%	13%	12%

Players who hit just two or more OppHR in one season were 2-3 times as likely as those who hit zero or one OppHR to sustain strong AB/HR rates, RC/G levels, or R$ values over the following three seasons.

	Y2-Y4 Breakout Performance (% Breakout by Group, Age <=26 Only)		
	AB/HR	RC/G	R$
Y1 Trigger	>35 to <=30	<4.5 to 5.5+	<$8 to $16+
2+ OppHR	32%	21%	30%
<2 OppHR	23%	12%	10%

Roughly one of every 3-4 batters age 26 or younger experiences a *sustained three-year breakout* in AB/HR, RC/G or R$ after a season in which they hit 2+ OppHR, far better odds than the one in 8-10 batters who experience a breakout without the 2+ OppHR trigger.

A 2015 Brad Kullman study that examined hard hit balls of all types (flies, liners, and grounders) by hitters with 100 or more plate appearances offered a broader conclusion. His research found that hitters who can effectively use the whole field are more productive in virtually every facet of hitting than those with an exclusively pull-oriented approach.

Home runs in bunches or droughts *(Patrick Davitt)*

A study from on HR data showed that batters hit HRs in a random manner, with game-gaps between HRs that correspond roughly to their average days per HR. Hitters do sometimes hit HRs with greater or lesser frequency in short periods, but these periods are not predictive. It appears pointless to try to "time the market" by predicting the beginning or end of a drought or a bunch, or by assuming the end of one presages the beginning of the other, despite what the ex-player in the broadcast booth tells you.

Power breakout profile

It is not easy to predict which batters will experience a power spike. We can categorize power breakouts to determine the likelihood of a player taking a step up or of a surprise performer repeating his feat. Possibilities:

- Increase in playing time
- History of power skills at some time in the past
- Redistribution of already demonstrated extra base hit power
- Normal skills growth
- Situational breakouts, particularly in hitter-friendly venues
- Increased fly ball tendency
- Use of illegal performance-enhancing substances
- Miscellaneous unexplained variables

Speed

Wasted talent on the base paths

We refer to some players as having "wasted talent," a high level skill that is negated by a deficiency in another skill. Among these types are players who have blazing speed that is negated by a sub-.300 on base average.

These players can have short-term value. However, their stolen base totals are tied so tightly to their "green light" that any change in managerial strategy could completely erase that value. A higher OB mitigates that downside; the good news is that plate patience can be taught.

In the past, there were always a handful of players who had at least 20 SBs with an OBP less than .300, putting their future SBs at risk. That number has declined in recent years with the drop in SB attempts in general. In 2019, only Adalberto Mondesi (43 SB, .291 OBP) and Billy Hamilton (22 SB, .289 OBP) fit this profile. In 2021, only Dylan Moore (21 SB, .276 OBP).

Stolen base attempt rate (SBA%)

(SB + CS) / (BB + Singles + HBP)

A rough approximation of how often a baserunner attempts a stolen base. Provides a comparative measure for players on a given team and, as a team measure, the propensity of a manager to give a "green light" to his runners.

Stolen base success rate (SB%)

SB / (SB + CS)

The rate at which baserunners are successful in their stolen base attempts. **BENCHMARK:** It is generally accepted that an 80% rate is the minimum required for a runner to be providing value to his team.

Speed score *(Bill James)*

A measure of the various elements that comprise a runner's speed skills. Although this formula (a variation of James' original version) may be used as a leading indicator for stolen base output, SB attempts are controlled by managerial strategy which makes speed score somewhat less valuable.

Speed score is calculated as the mean value of the following four elements:

1. Stolen base efficiency = *(((SB + 3)/(SB + CS + 7)) - .4) x 20*

2. Stolen base freq. = *Square root of ((SB + CS)/(Singles + BB)) / .07*

3. Triples rating = *(3B / (AB - HR - K))* and the result assigned a value based on the following chart:

< 0.001	0	0.0105	6
0.001	1	0.013	7
0.0023	2	0.0158	8
0.0039	3	0.0189	9
0.0058	4	0.0223+	10
0.008	5		

4. Runs scored as a percentage of times on base = *(((R - HR) / (H + BB - HR)) - .1) / .04*

Speed score index (SX)

(Batter's speed score / League speed score) x 100

Normalized speed scores get a better read on a runner's accomplishment in context. A level of 100 equals league average speed skill. Values more than 100 indicate above average skill, more than 200 represent the Fleet of Feet Elite.

Statistically scouted speed (Spd) *(Ed DeCaria)*

(104 + {[(Runs-HR+10*age_wt)/(RBI-HR+10)]/lg_av*100} / 5
+ {[(3B+5*age_wt)/(2B+3B+5)]/lg_av*100} / 5
+ {[(SoftMedGBhits+25*age_wt)/(SoftMedGB+25)]/lg_av*100} / 2
- {[Weight (Lbs)/Height (In)^2 * 703]/lg_av*100}

A skills-based gauge that measures speed without relying on stolen bases. Its components are:

- *(Runs – HR) / (RBI – HR)*: This metric aims to minimize the influence of extra base hit power and team run-scoring rates on perceived speed.

- *3B / (2B + 3B)*: No one can deny that triples are a fast runner's stat; dividing them by 2B+3B instead of all balls in play dampens the power aspect of extra base hits.

- *(Soft + Medium Ground Ball Hits) / (Soft + Medium Ground Balls)*: Faster runners are more likely than slower runners to beat out routine grounders. Hard hit balls are excluded from numerator and denominator.

- *Body Mass Index (BMI)*: Calculated as *Weight (lbs) / Height (in)2 * 703*. All other factors considered, leaner players run faster than heavier ones.

In this book, the formula is scaled with a midpoint of 100.

Expected stolen bases (xSB) *(Ed DeCaria)*

Stolen bases are an unusual fantasy baseball statistic. While most statistics are largely a reflection of skill, context, and luck, stolen bases involve a unique fourth factor: WILL.

Expected stolen bases (xSB) attempts to predict stolen bases given a player's playing time and ability to get on base. To this end, we focus on estimating a player's expected stolen base attempt rate (xSBA%) and success rate (xSBS%), and then apply those to his projected times on base (TOF) to arrive at an expected stolen base total.

xSB = TOF * xSBA% * xSBS%, where:
xSBA% = 0.027 + (Spd - 100) * 0.000545 + y0SBA% * 0.5645 + y0SBA%^2 * 0.23
xSBS% = 0.6664 + (y0SBS% * 0.1127)

Note that xSBA% is largely driven by last year's actual attempt rate, i.e., the player's demonstrated willingness to run. So to isolate how much of xSB comes from skill vs. will, we created a separate version of xSBA% (xSBA%-Skill) that is unaware of the player's past SB attempt rate. The difference between the version with attempt rate and without attempt rate then represents the player's will (xSBA%-Will):

xSBA%-Skill = 0.049 + y0SBS% * 0.04 + (Spd - 100) * 0.001 + (Spd - 100)^2 * sign (Spd - 100) * 0.000009576
xSBA%-Will = -0.022 + (Spd - 100) * -0.000455 + y0SBA% * 0.5645 + y0SBA%^2 * 0.23 - y0SBS% * 0.04 - (Spd - 100)^2 * sign (Spd - 100) * 0.000009576

Fantasy owners may well choose to continue to invest in high-will players, and those players may make good on their willingness to run for yet another season. But always remember: stolen bases come from players' minds as much as they come from their legs.

Roto Speed (RSpd)
(Spd x (SBO + SB%))
An adjustment to the measure for raw speed that takes into account a runner's opportunities to steal and his success rate. This stat is intended to provide a more accurate predictive measure of stolen bases for the Mayberry Method.

Stolen base breakout profile *(Bob Berger)*
To find stolen base breakouts (first 30+ steal season in the majors), look for players that:
- are between 22-27 years old
- have 3-7 years of professional (minors and MLB) experience
- have previous steals at the MLB level
- have averaged 20+ SB in previous three seasons (majors and minors combined)
- have at least one professional season of 30+ SB

Overall Performance Analysis

On base plus slugging average (OPS)
A simple sum of the two gauges, it is considered one of the better evaluators of overall performance. OPS combines the two basic elements of offensive production—the ability to get on base (OB) and the ability to advance baserunners (Slg). **BENCHMARKS:** The game's top batters will have OPS levels more than .850. The worst batters will have levels less than .660.

Adjusted on base plus slugging average (OPS+)
OPS scaled to league average to account for year-to-year fluctuations in league-wide statistical performance. It's a snapshot of a player's overall skills compared to an average player; also used in platoon situations (vL+; vR+). **BENCHMARK:** A level of 100 means a player had a league-average OPS in that given season.

Base Performance Value (BPV)
(Walk rate - 5) x 2) + ((Contact rate - 75) x 4)
+ ((Power Index - 80) x 0.8) + ((Spd - 80) x 0.3)
A single value that describes a player's overall raw skill level. This formula combines the individual raw skills of batting eye, contact rate, power and speed.

Base Performance Index (BPX)
BPV scaled to league average to account for year-to-year fluctuations in league-wide statistical performance. It's a snapshot of a player's overall skills compared to an average player. **BENCHMARK:** A level of 100 means a player had a league-average BPV in that given season.

Linear weights *(Pete Palmer)*
((Singles x .46) + (Doubles x .8) + (Triples x 1.02)
+ (Home runs x 1.4) + (Walks x .33) + (Stolen Bases x .3)
- (Caught Stealing x .6) - ((At bats - Hits) x Normalizing Factor)

(Also referred to as Batting Runs.) Formula whose premise is that all events in baseball are linear; that is, the output (runs) is directly proportional to the input (offensive events). Each of these events is then weighted according to its relative value in producing runs. Positive events—hits, walks, stolen bases—have positive values. Negative events—outs, caught stealing—have negative values.

The normalizing factor, representing the value of an out, is an offset to the level of offense in a given year. It changes every season, growing larger in high offense years and smaller in low offense years. The value is about .26 and varies by league.

LW is not included in the player boxes, but the LW concept is used with the linear weighted power gauge.

Runs above replacement (RAR)
An estimate of the number of runs a player contributes above a "replacement level" player. "Replacement" is defined as the level of performance at which another player can easily be found at little or no cost to a team. What constitutes replacement level is a topic that is hotly debated. There are a variety of formulas and rules of thumb used to determine this level for each position (replacement level for a catcher will be very different from replacement level for an outfielder). Our estimates appear below.

One of the major values of RAR for fantasy applications is that it can be used to assemble an integrated ranking of batters and pitchers for drafting purposes.

To calculate RAR for batters:
- Start with a batter's runs created per game (RC/G).
- Subtract his position's replacement level RC/G.
- Multiply by number of games played: (AB - H + CS) / 25.5.

Replacement levels used in this book:

POS	AL	NL
CA	3.40	3.69
1B	4.27	4.64
2B	4.06	4.05
3B	4.13	4.41
SS	4.24	4.19
LF	4.25	4.40
CF	4.00	3.94
RF	4.24	4.56
DH	4.66	

RAR can also be used to calculate rough projected team won-loss records. *(Roger Miller)* Total the RAR levels for all the players on a team, divide by 10 and add to 53 wins.

Runs created *(Bill James)*
(H + BB – CS) x (Total bases + (.55 x SB)) / (AB + BB)
A formula that converts all offensive events into a total of runs scored. As calculated for individual teams, the result approximates a club's actual run total with great accuracy.

Runs created per game (RC/G)
Runs Created / ((AB - H + CS) / 25.5)
RC expressed on a per-game basis might be considered the hypothetical ERA compiled against a particular batter. Another way to look at it: A batter with a RC/G of 7.00 would be expected to score 7 runs per game if he were cloned nine times and faced an average pitcher in every at bat. Cloning batters is not a practice we recommend. **BENCHMARKS:** Few players surpass the level of a

10.00 RC/G, but any level more than 7.50 can still be considered very good. At the bottom are levels less than 3.00.

Plate Appearances as a leading indicator *(Patrick Davitt)*
While targeting players "age 26 with experience" as potential breakout candidates has become a commonly accepted concept, a study has found that cumulative plate appearances, especially during the first two years of a young player's career, can also have predictive value in assessing a coming spike in production. Three main conclusions:

- When projecting players, MLB experience is more important than age.
- Players who amass 800+ PAs in their first two seasons are highly likely to have double-digit Rotisserie dollar value in Year 3.
- Also target young players in the season where they attain 400 PAs, as they are twice as likely as other players to grow significantly in value.

When do hitters get platooned? *(Jeff Zimmerman)*
We created a talent baseline to determine when a hitter might get platooned by examining 24 actual platoon pairs from the 2017 season. We compared the more extreme hitter's projected OPS splits entering the year. Among the main findings:

- Normally, a spread of ~200 points of OPS is needed to start a platoon. In only two instances did a platoon happen with a projected split under 130 points.
- For most teams to implement a platoon, they need at least one player to have a projected platoon OPS around .830.
- The minimum projected OPS in which teams begin using platoons is around .590. A player could have a 200-point spread, but if the low projected OPS is over .700, teams aren't likely to add another player to make up the difference.

The simple rule of an ".800-.600 OPS spread" works great for an average platoon benchmark. Owners may want to relax the values to snare a few more players with a .775-.625 OPS spread, or an ".800-.600 OPS spread with shrinkage".

Skill-specific aging patterns for batters *(Ed DeCaria)*
Most published aging analyses are done using composite estimates of value such as OPS or linear weights. By contrast, fantasy GMs are typically more concerned with category-specific player value (HR, SB, AVG, etc.). We can better forecast what matters most by analyzing peak age of individual baseball skills rather than overall player value.

For batters, recognized peak age for overall batting value is a player's late 20s. But individual skills do not peak uniformly at the same time:

Contact rate (ct%): Ascends modestly by about a half point of contact per year from age 22 to 26, then holds steady within a half point of peak until age 35, after which players lose a half point of contact per year.

Walk rate (bb%): Trends the opposite way with age compared to contact rate, as batters tend to peak at age 30 and largely remain there until they turn 38.

Stolen Base Opportunity (SBO): Typically, players maintain their SBO through age 27, but then reduce their attempts steadily in each remaining year of their careers.

Stolen base success rate (SB%): Aggressive runners (>14% SBO) tend to lose about 2 points per year as they age. However, less aggressive runners (<=14% SBO) actually improve their SB% by about 2 points per year until age 28, after which they reverse course and give back 1-2 pts every year as they age.

GB%/LD%/FB%: Both GB% and LD% peak at the start of a player's career and then decline as many hitters seemingly learn to elevate the ball more. But at about age 30, hitter GB% ascends toward a second late-career peak while LD% continues to plummet and FB% continues to rise through age 38.

Hit rate (h%): Declines linearly with age. This is a natural result of a loss of speed and change in batted ball trajectory.

Isolated Power (ISO): Typically peaks from age 24-26. Similarly, home runs per fly ball, opposite field HR %, and Hard Hit % all peak by age 25 and decline somewhat linearly from that point on.

Catchers and late-career performance spikes *(Ed Spaulding)*
Many catchers—particularly second line catchers—have their best seasons late in their careers. Some possible reasons why:

1. Catchers often get to the big leagues for defensive reasons and not their offensive skills. These skills take longer to develop.
2. The heavy emphasis on learning the catching/ defense/ pitching side of the game detracts from their time to learn about, and practice, hitting.
3. Injuries often curtail their ability to show offensive skills, though these injuries (typically jammed fingers, bruises on the arms, rib injuries from collisions) often don't lead to time on the disabled list.
4. The time spent behind the plate has to impact the ability to recognize, and eventually hit, all kinds of pitches.

Spring training Slg as leading indicator *(John Dewan)*
A hitter's spring training Slg .200 or more above his lifetime Slg is a leading indicator for a better than normal season.

In-Season Analysis

Sample size reliability *(Russell Carleton)*
At what sample size do skill and luck each represent 50 percent contributors to a specific metric?

Measured in plate appearances	
60:	Contact rate
120:	Walk rate
160:	ISO (Isolated power)
170:	HR rate
320:	Slg
460:	OBP

Measured via balls in play:	
50:	HR/F
80:	GB%; FB%
600:	LD%
820:	Hit rate (BABIP)

Unlisted metrics did not stabilize over a full season of play.

How to read: "After 60 plate appearances, the luck-to-skill ratio for contact rate has evened out. If a player with a career 70 percent contact rate has an 85 percent contact rate after 60 PA, we can attribute 50% of that new rate to a new skill and the other 50% to random chance." These levels represent the point at which these metrics become useful, though not as direct predictors. Their value is as another data point in the forecasting process.

Can we trust in-season sample size? *(Arik Florimonte)*

When a batter's performance deviates from their established history, when can you trust the change? And are there any metrics that are better in short periods than long? Using data from 2010-2017 and filtering for full-time players (≥ 350 PA in a season, or ≥ 75 PA in a month), we were able to answer these questions.

Not surprisingly, there is no magic date for believing the current season's results more than the previous season's; rather, it's more of a continuum. We were able to estimate the point in the season current year-to-date results are more predictive than the prior year's results, noted in the table below by the change from white blocks to black. We also note at which point the previous month alone offers better predictive value than the entire previous year ("PM>PY").

		Months of the Season					PM>PY starting…
Hard%	A	M	J	J	A	S	June
Soft%	A	M	J	J	A	S	May
HR/FB	A	M	J	J	A	S	Never
GB%	A	M	J	J	A	S	Never
LD%	A	M	J	J	A	S	Never
FB%	A	M	J	J	A	S	Never
IFFB%	A	M	J	J	A	S	Never
K%	A	M	J	J	A	S	Never
BB%	A	M	J	J	A	S	Never

Prior Year is Better
Year-to-date is Better

Note that due to the data filters used, a month in the chart above can be equated to roughly 90 plate appearances.

Key takeaways:

- Don't buy hard into early changes in batter plate skills until at least June
- Changes in ground ball and fly ball rates take a while to become firm; true "swing changers" can't really be discerned until mid-summer.
- In both of the above, it might pay to speculate earlier if you can stash a player on reserve.
- Don't expect the prior year's Soft% to continue, but pay attention to the current year's Soft contact rates.
- Generally, projections based on prior years' skills should remain your fallback position but keep moving the needle toward the current year's results as the year goes on.

Batting order facts *(Ed DeCaria)*

Eighty-eight percent of today's leadoff hitters bat leadoff again in their next game, 78% still bat leadoff 10 games later, and 68% still bat leadoff 50 games later. Despite this level of turnover after 50 games, leadoff hitters have the best chance of retaining their role over time. After leadoff, #3 and #4 hitters are the next most likely to retain their lineup slots.

On a season-to-season basis, leadoff hitters are again the most stable, with 69% of last year's primary leadoff hitters retaining the #1 slot next year.

Plate appearances decline linearly by lineup slot. Leadoff batters receive 10-12% more PAs than when batting lower in the lineup. AL #9 batters and NL #8 batters get 9-10% fewer PAs. These results mirror play-by-play data showing a 15-20 PA drop by lineup slot over a full season.

Walk rate is largely unaffected by lineup slot in the AL. Beware strong walk rates by NL #8 hitters, as much of this "skill" will disappear if ever moved from the #8 slot.

Batting order has no discernable effect on contact rate.

Hit rate slopes gently upward as hitters are slotted deeper in the lineup.

As expected, the #3-4-5 slots are ideal for non-HR RBIs, at the expense of #6 hitters. RBIs are worst for players in the #1-2 slots. Batting atop the order sharply increases the probability of scoring runs, especially in the NL.

The leadoff slot easily has the highest stolen base attempt rate. #4-5-6 hitters attempt steals more often when batting out of those slots than they do batting elsewhere. The NL #8 hitter is a SB attempt sinkhole. A change in batting order from #8 to #1 in the NL could nearly double a player's SB output due to lineup slot alone.

DOMination and DISaster rates

Week-to-week consistency is measured using a batter's BPV compiled in each week. A player earns a DOMinant week if his BPV was greater or equal to 50 for that week. A player registers a DISaster if his BPV was less than 0 for that week. The percentage of Dominant weeks, DOM%, is simply calculated as the number of DOM weeks divided by the total number of weeks played.

Is week-to-week consistency a repeatable skill? *(Bill Macey)*

To test whether consistent performance is a repeatable skill for batters, we examined how closely related a player's DOM% was from year to year.

YR1 DOM%	AVG YR2 DOM%
< 35%	37%
35%–45%	40%
46%–55%	45%
56%+	56%

Quality/consistency score (QC)
(DOM% – (2 x DIS%)) x 2)

Using the DOM/DIS percentages, this score measures both the quality of performance as well as week–to-week consistency.

	Sample configurations		
DOM%	Neutral	DIS%	QC
100	0	0	200
70	20	10	100
60	30	10	80
50	30	20	20
50	25	25	0
40	30	30	-40
30	20	50	-140
20	20	60	-200
0	100	0	-400

Projecting RBI *(Patrick Davitt)*

Evaluating players in-season for RBI potential is a function of the interplay among four factors:

- Teammates' ability to reach base ahead of him and to run the bases efficiently
- His own ability to drive them in by hitting, especially XBH
- Number of Games Played
- Place in the batting order

  3-4-5 Hitters:
  (0.69 x GP x TOB) + (0.30 x ITB) + (0.275 x HR) – (.191 x GP)
  6-7-8 Hitters:
  (0.63 x GP x TOB) + (0.27 x ITB) + (0.250 x HR) – (.191 x GP)
  9-1-2 Hitters:
  (0.57 x GP x TOB) + (0.24 x ITB) + (0.225 x HR) – (.191 x GP)

  ...where GP = games played, TOB = team on-base pct. and ITB = individual total bases (ITB).

Apply this pRBI formula after 70 games played or so (to reduce the variation from small sample size) to find players more than 9 RBIs over or under their projected RBI. There could be a correction coming.

You should also consider other factors, like injury or trade (involving the player or a top-of-the-order speedster) or team SB philosophy and success rate.

Remember: the player himself has an impact on his TOB. When we first did this study, we excluded the player from his TOB and got better results. The formula overestimates projected RBI for players with high OBP who skew his teams' OBP but can't benefit in RBI from that effect.

Ten-Game hitting streaks as a leading indicator *(Bob Berger)*

Research of hitting streaks from 2011 and 2012 showed that a 10-game streak can reliably predict improved longer-term BA performance during the season. A player who has put together a hitting streak of at least 10 games will improve his BA for the remainder of the season about 60% of the time. This improvement can be significant, on average as much as .020 of BA.

What can foul balls tell us? *(Nick Trojanowski)*

Foul balls, because of their relatively meager influence on in-game outcomes, have been examined far less often than balls in play. Using 2008-17 data for every 500+ pitch season, we found that hitting foul balls is a skill, in that it's repeatable from year to year. Other findings:

1. Hitters who swing at more pitches, regardless of location, hit more foul balls, regardless of contact rate.
2. Routinely fouling off pitches doesn't regularly lead to better outcomes, and in fact tends to make walks less likely.

Other Diamonds

It's a Busy World Shortcut

For marginal utility-type players, scan their PX and Spd history to see if there's anything to mine for. If you see triple digits anywhere, stop and look further. If not, move on.

Errant Gust of Wind

A unit of measure used to describe the difference between your home run projection and mine.

Mendoza Line

Named for Mario Mendoza, it represents the benchmark for batting futility. Usually refers to a .200 batting average, but can also be used for low levels of other statistical categories. Note that Mendoza's lifetime batting average was actually a much more robust .215.

Old Player Skills

Power, low batting average, no speed and usually good plate patience. Young players, often those with a larger frame, who possess these "old player skills" tend to decline faster than normal, often in their early 30s.

Esix Snead List

Players with excellent speed and sub-.300 on base averages who get a lot of practice running down the line to first base, and then back to the dugout.

Pitchers

Strikeouts and Walks

Fundamental skills

The contention that pitching performance is unreliable is a fallacy driven by the practice of attempting to project pitching stats using gauges that are poor evaluators of skill.

How can we better evaluate pitching skill? We can start with the statistical categories that are generally unaffected by external factors. These stats capture the outcome of an individual pitcher versus batter match-up without regard to supporting offense, defense or bullpen:

Walks Allowed, Strikeouts and Ground/Fly Balls

Even with only these stats to observe, there is a wealth of insight that these measures can provide.

Control rate (Ctl, bb/9), or opposition walks per game
BB allowed x 9 / IP

Measures how many walks a pitcher allows per game equivalent. BENCHMARK: The best pitchers will have bb/9 of 2.5 or less.

Walk rate (BB%)
(BB / TBF)

Measures how many walks a pitcher allows as a percentage of total batters faced. BB% replaces Control rate (Ctl, or bb/9) in our pitcher boxes as a more precise leading indicator of a pitcher's control.

	Approximate Conversions	
Ctl	Ball%	BB%
1.5	<31	4.1
1.7	31	4.8
1.8	32	5.0
2.2	33	5.9
2.3	34	6.1
2.7	35	7.2
2.9	36	7.6
3.2	37	8.3
3.4	38	8.7
3.8	39	9.6
4.1	40	10.5
4.7	41	11.6
5.4	>41	12.8

BENCHMARK: For those who used a Ctl rate of 2.5 or less as a benchmark for potential skills upside, the comparable level on the BB% scale would be about 6.6%. Better (and easier to remember): target pitchers with a rate of 6% or lower. The league-wide BB% in 2021 was 8.7%.

Dominance rate (Dom, k/9), or opposition strikeouts/game
Strikeouts recorded x 9 / IP

Measures how many strikeouts a pitcher allows per game equivalent. BENCHMARK: The best pitchers will have k/9 levels of 9.0 or higher.

Swinging strike rate as leading indicator *(Stephen Nickrand)*
Swinging strike rate (SwK%) measures the percentage of total pitches against which a batter swings and misses. SwK% can help

us validate and forecast a SP's Dominance (K/9) rate, which in turn allows us to identify surgers and faders with greater accuracy. An expected Dominance rate can be estimated from SwK%; and a pitcher's individual SwK% does not regress to league norms.

BENCHMARKS: The few starters per year who have a 12.0% or higher SwK% are near-locks to have a 9.0 Dom or 25% K%. In contrast, starters with a 7.0% or lower SwK% have nearly no chance at posting even an average Dom. Finally, use an 9.5% SwK% as an acceptable threshold when searching for SP based on this metric; raise it to 10.5% to begin to find SwK% difference-makers.

Strikeout rate (K%)
(K / TBF)

Measures how many strikeouts a pitcher produces as a percentage of total batters faced. K% replaces Dominance rate (Dom, or k/9) in our pitcher boxes as a more precise leading indicator of a pitcher's ability to rack up Ks.

	Approximate Conversions	
K/9	SwK%	K%
5.4	<6.0	13.2
5.6	6.0	14.1
6.1	7.0	15.2
6.6	8.0	17.5
7.3	9.0	19.1
7.8	10.0	20.5
8.5	11.0	22.2
9.3	12.0	24.8
9.9	13.0	27.1
10.7	14.0	29.2
11.3	15.0	31.6
12.0	16.0	33.5
12.9	>16.0	36.0

BENCHMARK: For those who used a Dominance rate of 9.5 as a benchmark for potential skills upside, the comparable level on the K% scale would be about 25%. The league-wide K% in 2021 was 23.2%.

Command ratio (Cmd)
(Strikeouts / Walks)

A measure of a pitcher's ability to get the ball over the plate. There is no more fundamental a skill than this, and so it is used as a leading indicator to project future rises and falls in other gauges, such as ERA. BENCHMARKS: Baseball's best pitchers will have ratios in excess of 3.0. Pitchers with ratios less than 1.0—indicating that they walk more batters than they strike out—have virtually no potential for long-term success. If you make no other changes in your approach to drafting pitchers, limiting your focus to only pitchers with a command ratio of 2.5 or better will substantially improve your odds of success.

Strikeout rate minus walk rate (K-BB%)
(K% – BB%)

Measures a pitchers' strikeout rate (K%) minus walk rate (BB%) and is a leading indicator for future performance. K-BB% replaces Command ratio (Cmd, or K/BB) in our pitcher boxes as a more precise measurement of a pitcher's command, as it's better correlated to both ERA and xERA, and is stickier year-to-year.

Approx Conversions		Correlated
K/BB	K-BB%	ERA
<1.0	-4%	8.43
1.0-2.0	7%	5.44
2.1-3.0	15%	4.26
3.1-4.0	19%	4.00
4.1-5.0	23%	3.73
>5.0	26%	3.13

BENCHMARK: For those who used a Command ratio of 3.0 as a benchmark for potential skills upside, the comparable level on the K-BB% scale would be about 18%. Better (and easier to remember): target pitchers with a rate of 20% or higher. The league-wide K-BB% in 2021 was 14.5%.

Fastball velocity and Dominance rate *(Stephen Nickrand)*
It is intuitive that an increase in fastball velocity for starting pitchers leads to more strikeouts. But how much?

Research shows that the vast majority of SP with significant fastball velocity gains follow this three-step process:

1. They experience a significant Dom gain during the same season.
2. Most often, they give back those Dom gains during the following season.
3. They are likely to increase their Dom the following season, but the magnitude of the Dom increase usually is small.

By contrast, the vast majority of SP with significant fastball velocity losses are likely to experience a significant Dom decrease during the same season.

Those SP with significant fastball velocity losses from one season to the next are just as likely to experience a fastball velocity or Dom increase as they are to experience a fastball or Dom decrease, and the amounts of the increase/decrease are nearly identical.

How aging affects fastball velocity, swinging strikes and strikeout rate *(Ed DeCaria)*
On average, pitchers lose about 0.2 mph per season off their fastballs. Over time, this coincides with decreases in swinging strike rate (SwK%) and overall strikeout rate (K/PA)—the inevitable effects of aging. But one thing that pitchers can do to delay these effects is to throw more first pitch strikes.

Power/contact rating
(BB + K) / IP
Measures the level by which a pitcher allows balls to be put into play. In general, extreme power pitchers can be successful even with poor defensive teams. Power pitchers tend to have greater longevity in the game. Contact pitchers with poor defenses behind them are high risks to have poor W-L records and ERA. **BENCHMARKS:** A level of 1.13+ describes pure throwers. A level of .93 or less describes high contact pitchers.

Balls in Play

Balls in play (BIP)
(Batters faced – (BB + HBP + SAC)) + H – K
The total number of batted balls that are hit fair, both hits and outs. An analysis of how these balls are hit—on the ground, in the air, hits, outs, etc.—can provide analytical insight, from player skill levels to the impact of luck on statistical output.

Batting average on balls in play *(Voros McCracken)*
(H – HR) / (Batters faced – (BB + HBP + SAC)) + H – K – HR
Abbreviated as BABIP; also called hit rate (H%), this is the percent of balls hit into the field of play that fall for hits. In 2000, Voros McCracken published a study that concluded "there is little if any difference among major league pitchers in their ability to prevent hits on balls hit in the field of play." His assertion was that, while a Johan Santana would have a better ability to prevent a batter from getting wood on a ball, or perhaps keeping the ball in the park, once that ball was hit in the field of play, the probability of it falling for a hit was virtually no different than for any other pitcher.

Among the findings in his study were:

- There is little correlation between what a pitcher does one year in the stat and what he will do the next. This is not true with other significant stats (BB, K, HR).
- You can better predict a pitcher's hits per balls in play from the rate of the rest of the pitcher's team than from the pitcher's own rate.

This last point brings a team's defense into the picture. It begs the question, when a batter gets a hit, is it because the pitcher made a bad pitch, the batter took a good swing, or the defense was not positioned correctly?

BABIP as a leading indicator *(Voros McCracken)*
The league average is 30%, which is also the level that individual performances will regress to on a year to year basis. Any +/- variance of 3% or more can affect a pitcher's ERA.

Pitchers will often post hit rates per balls-in-play that are far off from the league average, but then revert to the mean the following year. As such, we can use that mean to project the direction of a pitcher's ERA.

Subsequent research has shown that ground ball or fly ball propensity has some impact on this rate.

Hit rate *(See Batting average on balls in play)*

Opposition batting average (OBA)
Hits allowed / (Batters faced – (BB + HBP + SAC))
The batting average achieved by opposing batters against a pitcher. **BENCHMARKS:** The best pitchers will have levels less than .235; the worst pitchers levels more than .280.

Opposition on base average (OOB)
(Hits allowed + BB) / ((Batters faced – (BB + HBP + SAC)) + Hits allowed + BB)
The on base average achieved by opposing batters against a pitcher. **BENCHMARK:** The best pitchers will have levels less than .290; the worst pitchers levels more than .350.

Walks plus hits divided by innings pitched (WHIP)

Essentially the same measure as opposition on base average, but used for Rotisserie purposes. **BENCHMARKS:** A WHIP of less than 1.15 is considered top level; more than 1.50 indicative of poor performance. Levels less than 1.00—allowing fewer runners than IP—represent extraordinary performance and are rarely maintained over time.

Expected walks plus hits divided by innings pitched (xWHIP) *(Arik Florimonte)*

Hit rate luck makes an amplified contribution to WHIP, due to its impact on both the numerator (hits) and denominator (outs). To neutralize the effect, Expected WHIP (xWHIP) assumes that a pitcher's walk rate, strikeout rate, rate of hit batters, and ground-ball-to-flyball ratio reflect their true skill, but assigns league average rates of line drives, hits per batted ball type (xH%), and double plays per ground ball (xDP%). xWHIP better captures a pitcher's true skill, and is therefore more useful for predicting future results.

Ground ball, line drive, fly ball percentage (G/L/F)

See updated research on page 69.

Ground ball tendencies *(John Burnson)*

Ground ball pitchers tend to give up fewer HRs than do fly ball pitchers. There is also evidence that GB pitchers have higher hit rates. In other words, a ground ball has a higher chance of being a hit than does a fly ball that is not out of the park.

GB pitchers have lower strikeout rates. We should be more forgiving of a low strikeout rate if it belongs to an extreme ground ball pitcher.

GB pitchers have a lower ERA but a higher WHIP than do fly ball pitchers. On balance, GB pitchers come out ahead, even when considering strikeouts, because a lower ERA also leads to more wins.

Extreme GB/FB pitchers *(Patrick Davitt)*

Among pitchers with normal strikeout levels, extreme GB pitchers (>37% of all batters faced) have ERAs about 0.4 runs lower than normal-GB% pitchers but only slight WHIP advantages. Extreme FB% pitchers (>32% FB) show no ERA benefits.

Among High-K (>=24% of BF), however, extreme GBers have ERAs about 0.5 runs lower than normal-GB pitchers, and WHIPs about five points lower. Extreme FB% pitchers have ERAs about 0.2 runs lower than normal-FB pitchers, and WHIPs about 10 points lower.

Revisiting fly balls *(Jason Collette)*

The increased emphasis on defensive positioning is often associated with infield shifting, but the same data also influences how outfielders are positioned. Some managers are positioning OFs more aggressively than just the customary few steps per a right- or left-handed swinging batter. Five of the top 10 defensive efficiency teams in 2013 —OAK, STL, MIA, LAA and KC—also had parks among the top 10 in HR suppression.

Before dismissing flyball pitchers as toxic assets, pay more attention to park factors and OF defensive talent. In particular,

be a little more willing to roster fly ball pitchers who pitch both in front of good defensive OFs and in good pitchers' parks.

Line drive percentage as a leading indicator *(Seth Samuels)*

The percentage of balls-in-play that are line drives is beyond a pitcher's control. Line drives do the most damage; from 1994-2003, here were the expected hit rates and number of total bases per type of BIP.

| | ┌─────── Type of BIP ───────┐ | | |
	GB	FB	LD
H%	26%	23%	56%
Total bases	0.29	0.57	0.80

Despite the damage done by LDs, pitchers do not have any innate skill to avoid them. There is little relationship between a pitcher's LD% one year and his rate the next year. All rates tend to regress towards a mean of 22.6%.

However, GB pitchers do have a slight ability to prevent LDs (21.7%) and extreme GB hurlers even moreso (18.5%). Extreme FB pitchers have a slight ability to prevent LDs (21.1%) as well.

Home run to fly ball rate (HR/F)

The percent of fly balls that are hit for home runs.

HR/F as a leading indicator *(John Burnson)*

McCracken's work focused on "balls in play," omitting home runs from the study. However, pitchers also do not have much control over the percentage of fly balls that turn into HR. Research shows that there is an underlying rate of HR as a percentage of fly balls which in 2021 was 13.6%. A pitcher's HR/F rate will vary each year but always tends to regress to that mean. The element that pitchers do have control over is the number of fly balls they allow. That is the underlying skill or deficiency that controls their HR rate.

Exit velocity, barrel rate and launch angle for pitchers *(Stephen Nickrand)*

Though primarily used to evaluate batter performance and skill, Statcast metrics such as exit velocity, barrel rate, and launch angle have moderate-to-strong correlations to several pitching indicators:

- There is a modest correlation between the average exit velocity and barrel rate allowed by starting pitchers to both their ERA and HR/9.
- As a pitchers' exit velocity and barrel rate go up, so does their ERA and HR/9; and vice-versa.
- A significant deviation from a pitcher's average exit velocity baseline usually results in a regression towards that prior baseline during the following season.
- Starting pitchers experience a lot of volatility in their Barrel%. There is not a pattern of them regressing to their prior barrel rate baseline, partly because launch angle has been increasing in the game steadily over the past four seasons.

Expected home run total (xHR) *(Arik Florimonte)*

A study assessing all baseball conditions from 2015-2019 created a model for expected home run rate (xHR) given exit velocity (EV) and launch angle (LA) found in MLB's Statcast system. The model was applied to the entire database of batted balls to calculate the likelihood of each batted ball becoming a home run.

The xHR metric is not a measure of whether a specific batted ball should have been a home run. Rather, it is a measure of how often a ball struck in the way it was turns out to be a home run. By comparing a pitcher's actual home runs allowed total to xHR over a given year, we can estimate how much of that performance was earned or unearned, and adjust home runs allowed expectations for the following season.

Expected home runs to fly ball rate (xHR/F) *(Arik Florimonte)*

A pitcher's xHR allowed divided by his fly balls given up in a season. It is well-established that a pitcher's HR/F in one season is not a valid predictor for the pitcher's following year's HR/F. Despite this, biases may linger against pitchers who have "proven" to have acute gopheritis, or in favor of pitchers who managed to avoid surrendering HR. Unfortunately, knowing a pitcher's xHR/F history provides negligible improvement to predictive models. If a pitcher's xHR/F is high, it means that he was hit hard, but it does not mean he will be hit hard again. Once park factors are considered, regression to league average HR/F is still the best predictor.

"Just Enough" home runs as a leading indicator *(Brian Slack)*

Using ESPN's Home Run Tracker data, we analyzed year-to-year consistency of "Just Enough" home runs (those that clear the fence by less than 10 vertical feet or land less than one fence height past the fence). For the 528 starting pitchers who logged enough innings to qualify for the ERA title in consecutive years from 2006 through 2016 season, research showed:

- The percentage of Just Enough home runs that a pitcher gives up gravitates towards league average (32%) the following year.
- There is only a tenuous connection between a pitcher's ability to limit the percentage of Just Enough home runs and a pitcher's HR/FB rate. So we should avoid the assumption that a pitcher with a high percentage of Just Enough home runs will necessarily improve his HR/FB rate (and presumably ERA) the following year, or vice versa.
- This means be careful not to over-draft a pitcher based solely on the idea of HR/FB improvement in the coming year. Conversely, one should not automatically avoid pitchers with perceived HR/FB downside.

What can foul balls tell us? *(Nick Tojanowski)*

Foul balls, because of their relatively meager influence on in-game outcomes, have been examined far less often than balls in play. Using 2008-17 data for every 500+ pitch season, we found that inducing foul balls is a skill, in that it's repeatable from year to year. Other findings:

1. Pitchers who induce more swings at strikes allow more fouls, but pitchers who induce more chases do not.
2. Groundball pitchers tend to give up fewer foul balls than flyball pitchers.

Runs

Expected earned run average (xERA)

Gill and Reeve version: $(.575 \times H\ [per\ 9\ IP]) + (.94 \times HR\ [per\ 9\ IP]) + (.28 \times BB\ [per\ 9\ IP]) - (.01 \times K\ [per\ 9\ IP]) - Normalizing\ Factor$

John Burnson version (used in this book):
$(xER \times 9)/IP$, where xER is defined as
$xER\% \times (FB/10) + (1-xS\%) \times [0.3 \times (BIP - FB/10) + BB]$
where $xER\% = 0.96 - (0.0284 \times (GB/FB))$
and
$xS\% = (64.5 + (K/9 \times 1.2) - (BB/9 \times (BB/9 + 1))) / 20$
$+ ((0.0012 \times (GB\%^2)) - (0.001 \times GB\%) - 2.4)$

xERA represents the an equivalent of what a pitcher's real ERA might be, calculated solely with skills-based measures. It is not influenced by situation-dependent factors.

Expected ERA variance

$xERA - ERA$

The variance between a pitcher's ERA and his xERA is a measure of over or underachievement. A positive variance indicates the potential for a pitcher's ERA to rise. A negative variance indicates the potential for ERA improvement. BENCHMARK: Discount variances that are less than 0.50. Any variance more than 1.00 (one run per game) is regarded as a strong indicator of future change.

Projected xERA or projected ERA?

Which should we be using to forecast a pitcher's ERA? Projected xERA is more accurate for looking ahead on a purely skills basis. Projected ERA includes *situation-dependent* events—bullpen support, park factors, etc.—which are reflected better by ERA. The optimal approach is to use both gauges as *a range of expectation* for forecasting purposes.

Strand rate (S%)

$(H + BB - ER) / (H + BB - HR)$

Measures the percentage of allowed runners a pitcher strands (earned runs only), which incorporates both individual pitcher skill and bullpen effectiveness. BENCHMARKS: The most adept at stranding runners will have S% levels over 75%. Those with rates over 80% will have artificially low ERAs which will be prone to relapse. Levels below 65% will inflate ERA but have a high probability of regression.

Expected strand rate *(Michael Weddell)*

$73.935 + K/9 - 0.116 * (BB/9*(BB/9+1))$
$+ (0.0047 * GB\%^2 - 0.3385 * GB\%)$
$+ (MAX(2,MIN(4,IP/G))/2-1)$
$+ (0.82\ if\ left-handed)$

This formula is based on three core skills: strikeouts per nine innings, walks per nine innings, and ground balls per balls in play, with adjustments for whether the pitcher is a starter or reliever (measured by IP/G), and his handedness.

Strand rate as a leading indicator *(Ed DeCaria)*

Strand rate often regresses/rebounds toward past rates (usually 69-74%), resulting in Year 2 ERA changes:

% of Pitchers with Year 2 Regression/Rebound

Y1 S%	RP	SP	LR
<60%	100%	94%	94%
65	81%	74%	88%
70	53%	48%	65%
75	55%	85%	100%
80	80%	100%	100%
85	100%	100%	100%

Typical ERA Regression/Rebound in Year 2

Y1 S% .	RP	SP	LR
<60%	-2.54	-2.03	-2.79
65	-1.00	-0.64	-0.93
70	-0.10	-0.05	-0,44
75	0.24	0.54	0.75
80	1.15	1.36	2.29
85	1.71	2.21	n/a

Starting pitchers (SP) have a narrower range of strand rate outcomes than do relievers (RP) or swingmen/long relievers (LR). **Relief pitchers** with Y1 strand rates of <=67% or >=78% are likely to experience a +/- ERA regression in Y2. **Starters and swingmen/long relievers** with Y1 strand rates of <=65% or >=75% are likely to experience a +/- ERA regression in Y2. Pitchers with strand rates that deviate more than a few points off of their individual expected strand rates are likely to experience some degree of ERA regression in Y2. Over-performing (or "lucky") pitchers are more likely than underperforming (or "unlucky") pitchers to see such a correction.

Wins

Expected Wins (xW) *(Matt Cederholm)*

$$[(Team\ runs\ per\ game)^{1.8}]/[(Pitcher\ ERA)^{1.8} + (Team\ runs\ per\ game)^{1.8}] \times 0.72 \times GS$$

Starting pitchers' win totals are often at odds with their ERA. Attempts to find a strictly skill-based analysis of this phenomenon haven't worked, but there is a powerful tool in the toolbox: Bill James' Pythagorean Theorem. While usually applied to team outcomes, recent research has shown that its validity holds up when applied to individual starting pitchers.

One key to applying the Pythagorean Theorem is factoring in no-decisions. Research shows that the average no-decision rate is 28% of starts, regardless of the type or quality of the pitcher or his team, with no correlation in ND% from one season to the next.

Overall, 70% of pitchers whose expected wins varied from actual wins showed regression in wins per start in the following year, making variation from Expected Wins a good leading indicator.

Projecting/chasing wins

There are five events that need to occur in order for a pitcher to post a single win...

1. He must pitch well, allowing few runs.
2. The offense must score enough runs.
3. The defense must successfully field all batted balls.
4. The bullpen must hold the lead.

5. The manager must leave the pitcher in for 5 innings, and not remove him if the team is still behind.

Of these five events, only one is within the control of the pitcher. As such, projecting or chasing wins based on skills alone can be an exercise in futility.

Home field advantage

See updated study on page 73.

Usage

Batters faced per game *(Craig Wright)*

$$((Batters\ faced - (BB + HBP + SAC)) + H + BB) / G$$

A measure of pitcher usage and one of the leading indicators for potential pitcher burnout.

Workload

Research suggests that there is a finite number of innings in a pitcher's arm. This number varies by pitcher, by development cycle, and by pitching style and repertoire. We can measure a pitcher's potential for future arm problems and/or reduced effectiveness (burnout):

Sharp increases in usage from one year to the next. Common wisdom has suggested that pitchers who significantly increase their workload from one year to the next are candidates for burnout symptoms. This has often been called the Verducci Effect, after writer Tom Verducci. BaseballHQ.com analyst Michael Weddell tested pitchers with sharp workload increases during the period 1988-2008 and found that no such effect exists.

Starters' overuse. Consistent "batters faced per game" (BF/G) levels of 28.0 or higher, combined with consistent seasonal IP totals of 200 or more may indicate burnout potential, especially with pitchers younger than 25. Within a season, a BF/G of more than 30.0 with a projected IP total of 200 may indicate a late season fade.

Relievers' overuse. Warning flags should be up for relievers who post in excess of 100 IP in a season, while averaging fewer than 2 IP per outing.

When focusing solely on minor league pitchers, research results are striking:

Stamina: Virtually every minor league pitcher who had a BF/G of 28.5 or more in one season experienced a drop-off in BF/G the following year. Many were unable to ever duplicate that previous level of durability.

Performance: Most pitchers experienced an associated drop-off in their BPVs in the years following the 28.5 BF/G season. Some were able to salvage their effectiveness later on by moving to the bullpen.

Effects of short-term workloads on relief pitcher value *(Arik Florimonte)*

Using game logs from 2002-17, we studied the effects of recent workload on relief pitcher performance. After accounting for factors such as selection and usage bias—good pitchers get used on short rest more often—we discovered there is almost no measurable performance impact. Pitchers used heavily for several days, including the day before, show perhaps a 5-10% reduction in BPV.

Pitchers who have thrown often in the recent past are less likely to be used, which can significantly reduce their value, with a 36% reduction in saves and a 64% reduction in games pitched when "worn out".

In leagues with daily lineup changes, monitoring RP workloads can help owners decide to start rested closers of lesser quality, and therefore lower cost, over more expensive closers who may be worn out.

Protecting young pitchers *(Craig Wright)*

There is a link between some degree of eventual arm trouble and a history of heavy workloads in a pitcher's formative years. Some recommendations from this research:

Teenagers (A-ball): No 200 IP seasons and no BF/G over 28.5 in any 150 IP span. No starts on three days rest.

Ages 20-22: Average no more than 105 pitches per start with a single game ceiling of 130 pitches.

Ages 23-24: Average no more than 110 pitches per start with a single game ceiling of 140 pitches.

When possible, a young starter should be introduced to the majors in long relief before he goes into the rotation.

Overall Performance Analysis

Base Performance Value (BPV)

((K/9 - 5.0) x 18)
+ ((4.0 - bb/9) x 27))
+ (Ground ball rate as a whole number - 40%)

A single value that describes a player's overall raw skill level. The formula combines the individual raw skills of dominance, control and the ability to keep the ball down in the zone, all characteristics that are unaffected by most external factors. In tandem with a pitcher's strand rate, it provides a more complete picture of the elements that contribute to ERA, and therefore serves as an accurate tool to project likely changes in ERA. Note that the league-normalized version (BPX) is what appears in this book.

Base Performance Index (BPX)

BPV scaled to league average to account for year-to-year fluctuations in league-wide statistical performance. It's a snapshot of a player's overall skills compared to an average player. **BENCHMARK:** A level of 100 means a player had a league-average BPV in that given season.

Runs above replacement (RAR)

An estimate of the number of runs a player contributes above a "replacement level" player.

Batters create runs; pitchers save runs. But are batters and pitchers who have comparable RAR levels truly equal in value? Pitchers might be considered to have higher value. Saving an additional run is more important than producing an additional run. A pitcher who throws a shutout is guaranteed to win that game, whereas no matter how many runs a batter produces, his team can still lose given poor pitching support.

To calculate RAR for pitchers:

1. Start with the replacement level league ERA.
2. Subtract the pitcher's ERA. (To calculate projected RAR, use the pitcher's xERA.)
3. Multiply by number of games played, calculated as plate appearances (IP x 4.34) divided by 38.
4. Multiply the resulting RAR level by 1.08 to account for the variance between earned runs and total runs.

Skill-specific aging patterns for pitchers *(Ed DeCaria)*

Baseball forecasters obsess over "peak age" of player performance because we must understand player ascent toward and decline from that peak to predict future value. Most published aging analyses are done using composite estimates of value such as OPS or linear weights. By contrast, fantasy GMs are typically more concerned with category-specific player value (K, ERA, WHIP, etc.). We can better forecast what matters most by analyzing peak age of individual baseball skills rather than overall player value.

For pitchers, prior research has shown that pitcher value peaks somewhere in the late 20s to early 30s. But how does aging affect each demonstrable pitching skill?

Strikeout rate (k/9): Declines fairly linearly beginning at age 25.

Walk rate (bb/9): Improves until age 25 and holds somewhat steady until age 29, at which point it begins to steadily worsen. Deteriorating k/9 and bb/9 rates result in inefficiency, as it requires far more pitches to get an out. For starting pitchers, this affects the ability to pitch deep into games.

Innings Pitched per game (IP/G): Among starters, it improves slightly until age 27, then tails off considerably with age, costing pitchers nearly one full IP/G by age 33 and one more by age 39.

Hit rate (H%): Among pitchers, H% appears to increase slowly but steadily as pitchers age, to the tune of .002-.003 points per year.

Strand rate (S%): Very similar to hit rate, except strand rate decreases with age rather than increasing. GB%/LD%/FB%: Line drives increase steadily from age 24 onward, and outfield flies increase beginning at age 31. Because 70%+ of line drives fall for hits, and 10%+ of fly balls become home runs, this spells trouble for aging pitchers.

Home runs per fly ball (HR/F): As each year passes, a higher percentage of a pitcher's fly balls become home runs allowed increases with age.

Catchers' effect on pitching *(Thomas Hanrahan)*

A typical catcher handles a pitching staff better after having been with a club for a few years. Research has shown that there is an improvement in team ERA of approximately 0.37 runs from a catcher's rookie season to his prime years with a club. Expect a pitcher's ERA to be higher than expected if he is throwing to a rookie backstop.

First productive season *(Michael Weddell)*

To find those starting pitchers who are about to post their first productive season in the majors (10 wins, 150 IP, ERA of 4.00 or less), look for:

- Pitchers entering their age 23-26 seasons, especially those about to pitch their age 25 season.
- Pitchers who already have good skills, shown by an xERA in the prior year of 4.25 or less.

- Pitchers coming off of at least a partial season in the majors without a major health problem.
- To the extent that one speculates on pitchers who are one skill away, look for pitchers who only need to improve their control (bb/9).

Bounceback fallacy *(Patrick Davitt)*

It is conventional wisdom that a pitcher often follows a bad year (value decline of more than 50%) with a significant "bounceback" that offers profit opportunity for the canny owner. But research showed the owner is extremely unlikely to get a full bounceback, and in fact, is more likely to suffer a further decline or uselessly small recovery than even a partial bounceback. The safest bet is a $30+ pitcher who has a collapse—but even then, bid to only about half of the previous premium value.

Closers

Saves

There are six events that need to occur in order for a relief pitcher to post a single save:

1. The starting pitcher and middle relievers must pitch well.
2. The offense must score enough runs.
3. It must be a reasonably close game.
4. The manager must put the pitcher in for a save opportunity.
5. The pitcher must pitch well and hold the lead.
6. The manager must let him finish the game.

Of these six events, only one is within the control of the relief pitcher. As such, projecting saves for a reliever has less to do with skills than opportunity. However, pitchers with excellent skills may create opportunity for themselves.

Saves conversion rate (Sv%)

Saves / Save Opportunities

The percentage of save opportunities that are successfully converted. **BENCHMARK:** We look for a minimum 80% for long-term success.

Leverage index (LI) *(Tom Tango)*

Leverage index measures the amount of swing in win probability indexed against an average value of 1.00. Thus, relievers who come into games in various situations create a composite score and if that average score is higher than 1.00, then their manager is showing enough confidence in them to try to win games with them. If the average score is below 1.00, then the manager is using them, but not showing nearly as much confidence that they can win games.

Saves chances and wins *(Patrick Davitt)*

Do good teams get more saves because they generate more wins, or do poor teams get more saves because more of their wins are by narrow margins? The "good-team" side is probably on firmer ground, though there are enough exceptions that we should be cautious about drawing broad inferences.

The 2014 study confirmed what Craig Neuman found years earlier: The argument "more wins leads to more saves" is generally correct. Over five studied seasons, the percentage of wins that were saved (Sv%W) was about 50%, and half of all team-seasons fell in the Sv%W range of 48%-56%. As a result, high-saves seasons were more common for high-win teams.

That wins-saves connection for individual team-seasons was much less solid, however, and we observed many outliers. Data for individual team-seasons showed wide ranges of both Sv%W and actual saves.

Finally, higher-win teams do indeed get more blowout wins, but while poorer teams had a higher percentage (73%) of close wins (three runs or fewer) than better teams (56%), good teams' higher number of wins meant they still had more close wins, more save opportunities and more saves, again with many outliers among individual team-seasons.

Origin of closers

History has long maintained that ace closers are not easily recognizable early on in their careers, so that every season does see its share of the unexpected. Dylan Floro, Paul Sewald, Gregory Soto, Lou Trivino…who would have thought it a year ago?

Accepted facts, all of which have some element of truth:

- You cannot find major league closers from pitchers who were closers in the minors.
- Closers begin their careers as starters.
- Closers are converted set-up men.
- Closers are pitchers who were unable to develop a third effective pitch.

More simply, closers are a product of circumstance.

Are the minor leagues a place to look at all?

From 1990-2004, there were 280 twenty-save seasons in Double-A and Triple-A. Over that period, only 13 pitchers ever saved 20 games in the majors and only five who ever posted more than one 20-save season: John Wetteland, Mark Wohlers, Ricky Bottalico, Braden Looper and Francisco Cordero.

More recent data is even more pessimistic:

Year	# with 20 Svs	MLB closers
2006	25	none
2007	22	none
2008	19	none
2009	17	none
2010	14	Craig Kimbrel
2011	16	none
2012	16	A.J. Ramos
2013	16	Kirby Yates
2014	12	none
2015	17	none
2016	10	*
2017	10	*
2018	9	none
2019	7	none
2021	2	none

Ed Mujica saved 20+ games in the minors in 2016 and 2017, but the 37 saves he posted for St. Louis came in 2013. I'm not counting him in the data.

That's 210 twenty-save seasons and only three major league closers.

One of the reasons that minor league closers rarely become major league closers is because, in general, they do not get enough innings in the minors to sufficiently develop their arms into big-league caliber.

In fact, organizations do not look at minor league closing performance seriously, assigning that role to pitchers who they do not see as legitimate prospects. The trend of 20-save relievers since 2006 reflects that evolving bullpen usage. The average age of minor league closers over the past decade has been 27.5.

Elements of saves success

The task of finding future closing potential comes down to looking at two elements:

Talent: The raw skills to mow down hitters for short periods of time.

Opportunity: The more important element, yet the one that pitchers have no control over.

There are pitchers that have Talent, but not Opportunity. These pitchers are not given a chance to close for a variety of reasons (e.g. being blocked by a solid front-liner in the pen, being left-handed, etc.), but are good to own because they will not likely hurt your pitching staff. You just can't count on them for saves, at least not in the near term.

There are pitchers that have Opportunity, but not Talent. MLB managers decide who to give the ball to in the 9th inning based on their own perceptions about what skills are required to succeed, even if those perceived "skills" don't translate into acceptable metrics.

Those pitchers without the metrics may have some initial short-term success, but their long-term prognosis is poor and they are high risks to your roster. Classic examples of the short life span of these types of pitchers include Matt Karchner, Heath Slocumb, Ryan Kohlmeier, Dan Miceli, Joe Borowski and Danny Kolb. More recent examples include Sam Dyson, Brad Ziegler and Jeanmar Gómez.

Closers' job retention *(Michael Weddell)*

Of pitchers with 20 or more saves in one year, only 67.5% of these closers earned 20 or more saves the following year. The variables that best predicted whether a closer would avoid this attrition:

- *Saves history:* Career saves was the most important factor.
- *Age:* Closers are most likely to keep their jobs at age 27. For long-time closers, their growing career saves totals more than offset the negative impact of their advanced ages. Older closers without a long history of racking up saves tend to be bad candidates for retaining their roles.
- *Performance:* Actual performance, measured by ERA+, was of only minor importance.
- *Being right-handed:* Increased the odds of retaining the closer's role by 9% over left-handers.

Closer volatility history

Year	Closers Drafted	Avg R$	Closers Failed	Failure %	New Sources
2012	29	$15.28	19	66%	18
2013	29	$15.55	9	31%	13
2014	28	$15.54	11	39%	15
2015	29	$14.79	13	45%	16
2016	33	$13.30	19	58%	17
2017	32	$13.63	17	53%	15
2018	27	$13.22	17	63%	20
2019	31	$13.29	18	58%	14
2020*	27	$14.30	19	70%	26
2021	33	$11.79	21	64%	22

*The 2020 data should be mostly ignored due to the vagaries of the short season.

Drafted refers to the number of saves sources purchased in both LABR and Tout Wars experts leagues each year. These only include relievers drafted specifically for saves speculation. *Avg R$* refers to the average purchase price of these pitchers in the AL-only and NL-only leagues. *Failed* is the number (and percentage) of saves sources drafted that did not return at least 50% of their value that year. The failures include those that lost their value due to ineffectiveness, injury or managerial decision. *New Sources* are arms that were drafted for less than $5 (if drafted at all) but finished with at least 10 saves.

There was a time when we could identify the players drafted specifically for saves by draft price alone – $10 or more. In 2021, of the 33 we identified as saves investments for the above chart, 14 of them were rostered for less than $10 (and as little as $5). Only three of those earned enough to cover their cost. Even then, we chose to filter out relievers like Héctor Neris, Daniel Bard, Jordan Romano and Mark Melancon – each drafted for $4 – and another five speculations drafted for $3. With all the unsettled bullpens and uncertain expectations for bullpen usage, the experts were more risk-averse on Draft Day than ever before. The average salary of $11.79 was an all-time low. It's questionable whether we will see much improvement in 2022.

Closers and multi-year performance *(Patrick Davitt)*

A team having an "established closer"—even a successful one—in a given year does not affect how many of that team's wins are saved in the next year. However, a top closer (40-plus saves) in a given year has a significantly greater chance to retain his role in the subsequent season.

Research of saves and wins data over several seasons found that the percentage of wins that are saved is consistently 50%-54%, irrespective of whether the saves were concentrated in the hands of a "top closer" or passed around to the dreaded "committee" of lesser closers. But it also found that about two-thirds of high-save closers reprised their roles the next season, while three-quarters of low-save closers did not. Moreover, closers who held the role for two or three straight seasons averaged 34 saves per season while closers new to the role averaged 27.

Other Relievers

Reliever efficiency percent (REff%)
(Wins + Saves + Holds) / (Wins + Losses + SaveOpps + Holds)
This is a measure of how often a reliever contributes positively to the outcome of a game. A record of consistent, positive impact on game outcomes breeds managerial confidence, and that confidence could pave the way to save opportunities. For those pitchers suddenly thrust into a closer's role, this formula helps gauge their potential to succeed based on past successes in similar roles. BENCHMARK: Minimum of 80%.

Vulture
A pitcher, typically a middle reliever, who accumulates an unusually high number of wins by preying on other pitchers' misfortunes. More accurately, this is a pitcher typically brought into a game after a starting pitcher has put his team behind, and then pitches well enough and long enough to allow his offense to take the lead, thereby "vulturing" a win from the starter. This concept has been losing its relevance with the rising use of Openers. Today's "vulture" is the bulk inning relief pitcher who follows the one-inning Opener and does not have to pitch five innings to qualify for a Win.

In-Season Analysis

Sample size reliability *(Russell Carleton)*
At what sample size do skill and luck each represent 50 percent contributors to a specific metric?

*Measured in batters faced

60:	K/PA
120:	BB/PA

Note that 120 batters faced is roughly equivalent to just shy of five outings for a starting pitcher.

*Measured via balls in play:

50:	HR/F
80:	GB%; FB%
600:	LD%
820:	Hit rate (BABIP)

*Unlisted metrics did not stabilize over a full season of play.

How to read: "After 50 balls in play, the luck-to-skill ratio for home run to fly ball rate has evened out. If a player with a career HR/F rate of 12 percent has an 8 percent rate after 50 balls in play, we can attribute 50% of that new rate to a new skill and the other 50% to random chance." These levels represent the point at which these metrics become useful, though not as direct predictors. Their value is as another data point in the forecasting process.

Can we trust in-season sample size? *(Arik Florimonte)*
When a pitcher's performance deviates significantly from their established history, when can you trust the change? And are there any metrics that are better in short periods than long? Using data from 2010-2017 and filtering for full-time players ($\geq$ 120 IP in a season, or $\geq$ 25 IP in a month), we were able to answer these questions.

Not surprisingly, there is no magic date for believing the current season's results more than the previous season's; rather, it's more of a continuum. We were able to estimate the point in the season current year-to-date results are more predictive than the prior year's results, noted in the table below by the change from white blocks to black. We also note at which point the previous month alone offers better predictive value than the entire previous year ("PM>PY").

	Months of the Season						PM>PY starting...
K%	A	M	**J**	**J**	**A**	**S**	July
BB%	A	M	**J**	**J**	**A**	**S**	Never
GB%	A	M	**J**	**J**	**A**	**S**	Never
FB%	A	M	**J**	**J**	**A**	**S**	Never
Soft%	A	**M**	**J**	**J**	**A**	**S**	Always
Hard%	A	**M**	**J**	**J**	**A**	**S**	May

Prior Year is Better
Year-to-date is Better

Note that due to the date filters used, a month here is roughly equivalent to 25-35 IP, or around 125 batters faced.

Key takeaways:

- Don't fully buy into a change in GB/FB mix or K/BB until June (although you may still want to speculate earlier if you can stash a player on reserve)
- Don't expect last year's hard and soft contact tendencies to continue into the current year.
- Pay some attention to the current year's Soft% and Hard%— there is useful information there—but remember that at best, future outcomes are still 80% noise and regression.
- There is essentially no month-to-month or year-to-year correlation for HR/FB for pitchers. There may be pitchers with a "homer problem," but it is not possible to identify them by looking at home run rates.
- Generally, projections based on prior years' skills should remain your fallback position but keep moving the needle toward the current year's results as the year goes on.

Pure Quality Starts
Pure Quality Starts (PQS) says that the smallest unit of measure should not be the "event" but instead be the "game." Within that game, we can accumulate all the strikeouts, hits and walks, and evaluate that outing as a whole. After all, when a pitcher takes the mound, he is either "on" or "off" his game; he is either dominant or struggling, or somewhere in between.

In PQS, we give a starting pitcher credit for exhibiting certain skills in each of his starts. Then by tracking his "PQS Score" over time, we can follow his progress. A starter earns one point for each of the following criteria:

1. *The pitcher must go more than 6 innings (record at least one out in the 7th).* This measures stamina.
2. *He must allow fewer hits than innings pitched.* This measures hit prevention.

3. *His number of strikeouts must equal to or more than 5. This measures dominance.*

4. *He must strike out at least three times as many batters as he walks (or have a minimum of three strikeouts if he hasn't walked a batter). This measures command.*

5. *He must not allow a home run. This measures his ability to keep the ball in the park.*

A perfect PQS score is 5. Any pitcher who averages 3 or more over the course of the season is probably performing admirably. The nice thing about PQS is it allows you to approach each start as more than an all-or-nothing event.

Note the absence of earned runs. No matter how many runs a pitcher allows, if he scores high on the PQS scale, he has hurled a good game in terms of his base skills. The number of runs allowed—a function of not only the pitcher's ability but that of his bullpen and defense—will tend to even out over time.

It doesn't matter if a few extra balls got through the infield, or the pitcher was given the hook in the fourth or sixth inning, or the bullpen was able to strand their inherited baserunners. When we look at performance in the aggregate, those events do matter, and will affect a pitcher's skills metrics and ERA. But with PQS, the minutia is less relevant than the overall performance.

In the end, a dominating performance is a dominating performance, whether Max Scherzer hurls six innings of score-less baseball or gives up two runs while striking out 10 in 6 IP. And a disaster is still a disaster, whether Kris Bubic gets pulled in the second inning after allowing 7 runs, or gets a hook after four innings after giving up 6 runs.

Skill versus consistency

Two pitchers have identical 4.50 ERAs and identical 3.0 PQS averages. Their PQS logs look like this:

```
PITCHER A:    3    3    3    3    3
PITCHER B:    5    0    5    0    5
```

Which pitcher would you rather have on your team? The risk-averse manager would choose Pitcher A as he represents the perfectly known commodity. Many fantasy leaguers might opt for Pitcher B because his occasional dominating starts show that there is an upside. His Achilles Heel is inconsistency—he is unable to sustain that high level. Is there any hope for Pitcher B?

- If a pitcher's inconsistency is characterized by more poor starts than good starts, his upside is limited.
- Pitchers with extreme inconsistency rarely get a full season of starts.
- However, inconsistency is neither chronic nor fatal.

The outlook for Pitcher A is actually worse. Disaster avoidance might buy these pitchers more starts, but history shows that the lack of dominating outings is more telling of future potential. In short, consistent mediocrity is bad.

PQS DOMination and DISaster rates *(Gene McCaffrey)*

DOM% is the percentage of a starting pitcher's outings that rate as a PQS-4 or PQS-5. DIS% is the percentage that rate as a PQS-0 or PQS-1.

DOM/DIS percentages open up a new perspective, providing us with two separate scales of performance. In tandem, they measure consistency.

Quality/consistency score (QC)
(DOM% – (2 x DIS%)) x 2

Using PQS and DOM/DIS percentages, this score measures both the quality of performance as well as start-to-start consistency.

	Sample configurations		
DOM%	Neutral	DIS%	QC
100	0	0	200
70	20	10	100
60	30	10	80
50	30	20	20
50	25	25	0
40	30	30	-40
30	20	50	-140
20	20	60	-200
0	100	0	-400

The Predictive value of PQS *(Arik Florimonte)*

Using data from 2010-2015, research showed that PQS values can be used to project future starts. A pitcher who even threw only one PQS-DOM start had a slightly better chance of throwing another DOM in his subsequent start. For a pitcher who posts two, three, or even four PQS-DOMs in a row, the streak does portend better results to come. The longer the streak, the better the results.

Fantasy owners best positioned to take advantage are those who can frequently choose from multiple similar SP options, such as in a DFS league, or streaming in traditional leagues. In either case, make your evaluations as you normally would (e.g. talent first, then matchups, ballpark or by using BaseballHQ. com's Pitcher Matchups Tool)—and then give a value bump to the pitcher with the hot streak.

PQS correlation with Quality Starts *(Paul Petera)*

PQS	QS%
0	8%
1	18%
2	38%
3	63%
4	87%
5	99%

High pitch counts and PQS *(Paul Petera)*

A 2017 study found that high-scoring PQS starters who also ran up high pitch counts continued to thrive in their next start (and beyond). Taking three seasons of PQS and pitch-count data, starts were grouped by pitch count into five cohorts and averaged by PQS. The study then calculated the average PQS scores in the subsequent starts, and found that pitchers with higher pitch counts are safer bets to throw well in their next start (and beyond) than those who throw fewer pitches. Near-term fatigue or other negative symptoms do not appear to be worthy of concern; so do not shy away from these pitchers solely for that reason.

In-season ERA/xERA variance as a leading indicator
(Matt Cederholm)

Pitchers with large first-half ERA/xERA variances will see regression towards their xERA in the second half, if they are allowed (and are able) to finish out the season. Starters have a stronger regression tendency than relievers, which we would expect to see given the larger sample size. In addition, there is substantial attrition among all types of pitchers, but those who are "unlucky" have a much higher rate.

An important corollary: While a pitcher underperforming his xERA is very likely to rebound in the second half, such regression hinges on his ability to hold onto his job long enough to see that regression come to fruition. Healthy veteran pitchers with an established role are more likely to experience the second half boost than a rookie starter trying to make his mark.

Pure Quality Relief *(Patrick Davitt)*

A system for evaluating reliever outings. The scoring :

1. Two points for the first out, and one point for each subsequent out, to a maximum of four points.
2. One point for having at least one strikeout for every four full outs (one K for 1-4 outs, two Ks for 5-8 outs, etc.).
3. One point for zero baserunners, minus one point for each baserunner, though allowing the pitcher one unpenalized runner for each three full outs (one baserunner for 3-5 outs, two for 6-8 outs, three for nine outs)
4. Minus one point for each earned run, though allowing one ER for 8– or 9-out appearances.
5. An automatic PQR-0 for allowing a home run.

Avoiding relief disasters *(Ed DeCaria)*

Relief disasters (defined as ER>=3 and IP<=3), occur in 5%+ of all appearances. The chance of a disaster exceeds 13% in any 7-day period. To minimize the odds of a disaster, we created a model that produced the following list of factors, in order of influence:

1. Strength of opposing offense
2. Park factor of home stadium
3. BB/9 over latest 31 days (more walks is bad)
4. Pitch count over previous 7 days (more pitches is bad)
5. Latest 31 Days ERA>xERA (recent bad luck continues)

Daily league owners who can slot relievers by individual game should also pay attention to days of rest: pitching on less rest than one is accustomed to increases disaster risk.

April ERA as a leading indicator *(Stephen Nickrand)*

A starting pitcher's April ERA can act as a leading indicator for how his ERA is likely to fare during the balance of the season. A study looked at extreme April ERA results to see what kind of in-season forecasting power they may have. From 2010-2012, 42 SP posted an ERA in April that was at least 2.00 ER better than their career ERA. The findings:

- Pitchers who come out of the gates quickly have an excellent chance at finishing the season with an ERA much better than their career ERA.

- While April ERA gems see their in-season ERA regresses towards their career ERA, their May-Sept ERA is still significantly better than their career ERA.
- Those who stumble out of the gates have a strong chance at posting an ERA worse than their career average, but their in-season ERA improves towards their career ERA.
- April ERA disasters tend to have a May-Sept ERA that closely resembles their career ERA.

Using K–BB% to find SP buying opportunities *(Arik Florimonte)*

Research showed that finding pitchers who have seen an uptick in K–BB% over the past 30 days is one way to search for mid-season replacements from the waiver wire. Using 2014-2016 player-seasons and filtering for starting pitchers with ≥ 100 IP, the K–BB% mean is about 13%. The overall MLB mean is approximately 12%, and the top 50 SP tend to be 14% or higher.
The findings:

- Last 30 days K–BB% is useful as a gauge of next 30 days performance.
- Pitchers on the upswing are more likely to climb into the elite ranks than other pitchers of similar YTD numbers; pitchers with a larger uptick show a greater likelihood.
- Last-30 K–BB% surgers could be good mid-season pickups if they are being overlooked by other owners in your league.

Second-half ERA reduction drivers *(Stephen Nickrand)*

It's easy to dismiss first-half-to-second-half improvement among starting pitchers as an unpredictable event. After all, the midpoint of the season is an arbitrary cutoff. Performance swings occur throughout the season.

A study of SP who experienced significant 1H-2H ERA improvement from 2010-2012 examined what indicators drove second-half ERA improvement. Among the findings for those 79 SP with a > 1.00 ERA 1H-2H reduction:

- 97% saw their WHIP decrease, with an average decrease of 0.26
- 97% saw their strand (S%) rate improve, with an average increase of 9%
- 87% saw their BABIP (H%) improve, with an average reduction of 5%
- 75% saw their control (bb/9) rate improve, with an average reduction of 0.8
- 70% saw their HR/9 rate improve, with an average decrease of 0.5
- 68% saw their swinging strike (SwK%) rate improve, with an average increase of 1.4%
- 68% saw their BPV improve, with an average increase of 37
- 67% saw their HR per fly ball rate (HR/F) improve, with an average decrease of 4%
- 53% saw their ground ball (GB%) rate improve, with an average increase of 5%
- 52% saw their dominance (k/9) rate improve, with an average increase of 1.3

These findings highlight the power of H% and S% regression as it relates to ERA and WHIP improvement. In fact, H% and S% are more often correlated with ERA improvement than are improved skills. They also suggest that improved control has a bigger impact on ERA reduction than does increased strikeouts.

Pitcher home/road splits *(Stephen Nickrand)*

One overlooked strategy in leagues that allow frequent transactions is to bench pitchers when they are on the road. Research reveals that several pitching stats and indicators are significantly and consistently worse on the road than at home.

Some home/road rules of thumb for SP:

- If you want to gain significant ground in ERA and WHIP, bench all your average or worse SP on the road.
- A pitcher's win percentage drops by 15% on the road, so don't bank on road starts as a means to catch up in wins.
- Control erodes by 10% on the road, so be especially careful with keeping wild SP in your active lineups when they are away from home.
- NL pitchers at home produce significantly more strikeouts than their AL counterparts and vs. all pitchers on the road.
- HR/9, groundball rate, hit rate, strand rate, and HR/F do not show significant home vs. road variances.

Other Diamonds

The Pitching Postulates

1. Never sign a soft-tosser to a long-term contract.
2. Right-brain dominance has a very long shelf life.
3. A fly ball pitcher who gives up many HRs is expected. A GB pitcher who gives up many HRs is making mistakes.
4. Never draft a contact fly ball pitcher who plays in a hitter's park.
5. Only bad teams ever have a need for an inning-eater.
6. Never chase wins.

Dontrelle Willis List

Pitchers with skills metrics so horrible that you have to wonder how they can possibly draw a major league paycheck year after year.

Chaconian

Having the ability to post many saves despite sub-Mendoza metrics and an ERA in the stratosphere. (See: Shawn Chacón, 2004.)

ERA Benchmark

A half run of ERA over 200 innings comes out to just one earned run every four starts.

The Knuckleballers Rule

Knuckleballers don't follow no stinkin' rules.

Brad Lidge Lament

When a closer posts a 62% strand rate, he has nobody to blame but himself.

Vin Mazzaro Vindication

Occasional nightmares (2.1 innings, 14 ER) are just a part of the game.

PQS Benchmark

Generally, a single DISaster outing requires two DOMinant outings just to get back to par.

The Five Saves Certainties

1. On every team, there will be save opportunities and someone will get them. At a bare minimum, there will be at least 30 saves to go around, and not unlikely more than 45.

2. Any pitcher could end up being the chief beneficiary. Bullpen management is a fickle endeavor.

3. Relief pitchers are often the ones that require the most time at the start of the season to find a groove. The weather is cold, the schedule is sparse and their usage is erratic.

4. Despite the talk about "bullpens by committee," managers prefer a go-to guy. It makes their job easier.

5. As many as 50% of the saves in any year will come from pitchers who are undrafted.

Soft-tosser land

The place where feebler arms leave their fortunes in the hands of the defense, variable hit and strand rates, and park dimensions. It's a place where many live, but few survive.

Prospects

General

Minor league prospecting in perspective

In our perpetual quest to be the genius who uncovers the next Mike Trout when he's still in high school, there is an obsessive fascination with minor league prospects. That's not to say that prospecting is not important. The issue is perspective:

1. During the 10 year period of 1996 to 2005, only 8% of players selected in the first round of the Major League Baseball First Year Player Draft went on to become stars.

2. Some prospects are going to hit the ground running (Jonathan India) and some are going to immediately struggle (Vidal Bruján), no matter what level of hype follows them.

3. Some prospects are going to start fast (since the league is unfamiliar with them) and then fade (as the league figures them out). Others will start slow (since they are unfamiliar with the opposition) and then improve (as they adjust to the competition). So if you make your free agent and roster decisions based on small early samples sizes, you are just as likely to be an idiot as a genius.

4. How any individual player will perform relative to his talent is largely unknown because there is a psychological element that is vastly unexplored. Some make the transition to the majors seamlessly, some not, completely regardless of how talented they are.

5. Still, talent is the best predictor of future success, so major league equivalent base performance indicators still have a valuable role in the process. As do scouting reports, carefully filtered.

6. Follow the player's path to the majors. Did he have to repeat certain levels? Was he allowed to stay at a level long enough to learn how to adjust to the level of competition? A player with only two great months at Double-A is a good bet to struggle if promoted directly to the majors because he was never fully tested at Double-A, let alone Triple-A.

7. Younger players holding their own against older competition is a good thing. Older players reaching their physical peak, regardless of their current address, can be a good thing too. The Adolis Garcías and Patrick Wisdoms can have some very profitable years.

8. Remember team context. A prospect with superior potential often will not unseat a steady but unspectacular incumbent, especially one with a large contract.

9. Don't try to anticipate how a team is going to manage their talent, both at the major and minor league level. You might think it's time to promote Spencer Torkelson and give him an everyday role. You are not running the Tigers.

10. Those who play in shallow, one-year leagues should have little cause to be looking at the minors at all. The risk versus reward is so skewed against you, and there is so much talent available with a track record, that taking a chance on an unproven commodity makes little sense.

11. Decide where your priorities really are. If your goal is to win, prospect analysis is just a *part* of the process, not the entire process.

Factors affecting minor league stats *(Terry Linhart)*

1. Often, there is an exaggerated emphasis on short-term performance in an environment that is supposed to focus on the long-term. Two poor outings don't mean a 21-year-old pitcher is washed up.

2. Ballpark dimensions and altitude create hitters parks and pitchers parks, and many parks in the lower minors are inconsistent in their field quality. Minor league clubs have limited resources to maintain field conditions, and this can artificially depress defensive statistics while inflating stats like batting average.

3. Some players' skills are so superior to the competition at their level that you can't get a true picture of what they're going to do from their stats alone.

4. Many pitchers are told to work on secondary pitches in unorthodox situations just to gain confidence in the pitch. The result is an artificially increased number of walks.

5. The #3, #4, and #5 pitchers in the lower minors are truly longshots to make the majors. They often possess only two pitches and are unable to disguise the off-speed offerings. Hitters can see inflated statistics in these leagues.

Minor league level versus age

When evaluating minor leaguers, look at the age of the prospect in relation to the median age of the league he is in:

Low level A	*Between 19-20*
Upper level A	*Around 20*
Double-A	*21*
Triple-A	*22*

These are the ideal ages for prospects at the particular level. If a prospect is younger than most and holds his own against older and more experienced players, elevate his status. If he is older than the median, reduce his status.

Triple-A experience as a leading indicator

The probability that a minor leaguer will immediately succeed in the majors can vary depending upon the level of Triple-A experience he has amassed at the time of call-up.

	BATTERS		PITCHERS	
	< 1 Yr	Full	< 1 Yr	Full
Performed well	57%	56%	16%	56%
Performed poorly	21%	38%	77%	33%
2nd half drop-off	21%	7%	6%	10%

The odds of a batter achieving immediate MLB success was slightly more than 50/50. More than 80% of all pitchers promoted with less than a full year at Triple-A struggled in their first year in the majors. Those pitchers with a year in Triple-A succeeded at a level equal to that of batters.

When do Top 100 prospects get promoted? *(Jeff Zimmerman)*

We created a simple procedure to determine if—and when—a player will make it to the majors in the season after being ranked in BaseballHQ.com's HQ100 prospect list (2010-17). We examined only the prospects who had not yet played in the majors, and found that the chances of a major league call-up for a healthy hitter or pitcher who last played in each level to be as follows:

- As a veteran in a foreign league: 100%
- In Triple-A: 90%
- In Double-A: 50%
- In A-ball: 20%
- Other: 0%

Additionally, to increase the odds of a call-up, take the (1) higher-ranked player; (2) the older player; and (3) the player on a contending team.

Major League Equivalency (MLE) *(Bill James)*

A formula that converts a player's minor or foreign league statistics into a comparable performance in the major leagues. These are not projections, but conversions of current performance. MLEs contain adjustments for the level of play in individual leagues and teams. They work best with Triple-A stats, not quite as well with Double-A stats, and hardly at all with the lower levels. Foreign conversions are still a work in process. James' original formula only addressed batting. Our research has devised conversion formulas for pitchers, however, their best use comes when looking at skills metrics, not traditional stats.

Adjusting to the competition

All players must "adjust to the competition" at every level of professional play. Players often get off to fast or slow starts. During their second tour at that level is when we get to see whether the slow starters have caught up or whether the league has figured out the fast starters. That second half "adjustment" period is a good baseline for projecting the subsequent season, in the majors or minors.

Premature major league call-ups often negate the ability for us to accurately evaluate a player due to the lack of this adjustment period. For instance, a hotshot Double-A player might open the season in Triple-A. After putting up solid numbers for a month, he gets a call to the bigs, and struggles. The fact is, we do not have enough evidence that the player has mastered the Triple-A level. We don't know whether the rest of the league would have caught up to him during his second tour of the league. But now he's labeled as an underperformer in the bigs when in fact he has never truly proven his skills at the lower levels.

Bull Durham prospects

There is some potential talent in older players—age 26, 27 or higher—who, for many reasons (untimely injury, circumstance, bad luck, etc.), don't reach the majors until they have already been downgraded from prospect to suspect. Equating potential with age is an economic reality for major league clubs, but not necessarily a skills reality.

Skills growth and decline is universal, whether it occurs at the major league level or in the minors. So a high-skills journeyman in Triple-A is just as likely to peak at age 27 as a major leaguer of the same age. The question becomes one of opportunity—will the parent club see fit to reap the benefits of that peak performance?

Prospecting these players for your fantasy team is, admittedly, a high risk endeavor, though there are some criteria you can use. Look for a player who is/has:

- Optimally, age 27-28 for overall peak skills, age 30-31 for power skills, or age 28-31 for pitchers.
- At least two seasons of experience at Triple-A. Career Double-A players are generally not good picks.
- Solid base skills levels.
- Shallow organizational depth at their position.
- Notable winter league or spring training performance.

Players who meet these conditions are not typically draftable players, but worthwhile reserve or FAAB picks.

Deep-league prospecting primer *(Jock Thompson)*

There's no substitute for having a philosophy, objective, and plan for your fantasy farm system. Here's a prospecting process checklist:

Commit to some prospecting time. Sounds intuitive, but some owners either don't have the time or won't take the time to learn about their league's available prospects.

Have a prospecting framework/philosophy. Such as TINSTAPP—there is no such thing as a pitching prospect. The non-linear rise and development of prospects can be frustrating in general, but much more so with pitchers. Unlike with hitters, you're usually safe in forgoing low-minors pitching, and are better off speculating on near-ready pitching names.

Have objectives. Upside vs. MLB proximity is an ongoing dilemma, but rebuilders will always need to take on some faraway high-ceiling flyers.

Devise a strategy and stick with it. You'll need an idea as to how you'll 1) acquire available talent; and 2) upgrade your roster deficiencies. Above all, play out the year. Your team will improve by making good free agent assessments all season—not by taking off in August and September.

Always account for defense. A plus glove is a real advantage in finding MLB opportunity. Versatility and athleticism are even better, and often feed multi-position eligibility.

Consider all the variables. Things like age, opportunity, organization, venue, and club positional needs should all be factors.

Exercise excruciating patience – with legit hitting prospects. Even the most highly-regarded prospects do not grow to the moon in linear fashion.

Speculate readily and be nimble with your in-season pitching moves. If you see something that looks more promising than what you have, grab it fast. If you don't, someone else will.

Pay attention and dig into in-season minor league developments. All of these lights can flicker on and turn into big edges if you can identify them. For example: a plus hit tool guy suddenly begins tapping into power, a pitcher makes in-season mechanical changes, a hitter makes across-the-board improvement following a position change.

Don't dismiss late bloomers with extended MLB opportunity. Like the more publicized names, plenty of lesser prospects have playable talent, and are just late figuring out how to unlock it.

Batters

MLE PX as a leading indicator *(Bill Macey)*

Looking at minor league performance (as MLE) in one year and the corresponding MLB performance the subsequent year:

	Year 1 MLE	Year 2 MLB
Observations	496	496
Median PX	95	96
Percent PX > 100	43%	46%

In addition, 53% of the players had a MLB PX in year 2 that exceeded their MLE PX in year 1. A slight bias towards improved performance in year 2 is consistent with general career trajectories.

Year 1 MLE PX	Year 2 MLB PX	Pct. Incr	Pct. MLB PX > 100
<= 50	61	70.3%	5.4%
51-75	85	69.6%	29.4%
76-100	93	55.2%	39.9%
101-125	111	47.4%	62.0%
126-150	119	32.1%	66.1%
> 150	142	28.6%	76.2%

Slicing the numbers by performance level, there is a good amount of regression to the mean.

Players rarely suddenly develop power at the MLB level if they didn't previously display that skill in the minors. However, the relatively large gap between the median MLE PX and MLB PX for these players, 125 to 110, confirms the notion that the best players continue to improve once they reach the major leagues.

MLE contact rate as a leading indicator *(Bill Macey)*

There is a strong positive correlation (0.63) between a player's MLE ct% in Year 1 and his actual ct% at the MLB level in Year 2.

MLE ct%	Year 1 MLE ct%	Year 2 MLB ct%
< 70%	69%	68%
70% - 74%	73%	72%
75% - 79%	77%	75%
80% - 84%	82%	77%
85% - 89%	87%	82%
90% +	91%	86%
TOTAL	**84%**	**79%**

There is very little difference between the median MLE BA in Year 1 and the median MLB BA in Year 2:

MLE ct%	Year 1 MLE BA	Year 2 MLB BA
< 70%	.230	.270
70% - 74%	.257	.248
75% - 79%	.248	.255
80% - 84%	.257	.255
85% - 89%	.266	.270
90% +	.282	.273
TOTAL	.261	.262

Excluding the <70% cohort (which was a tiny sample size), there is a positive relationship between MLE ct% and MLB BA.

Pitchers

Skills metrics as a leading indicator for pitching success

The percentage of hurlers that were good investments in the year that they were called up varied by the level of their historical minor league skills metrics prior to that year.

Pitchers who had:	Fared well	Fared poorly
Good indicators	79%	21%
Marginal or poor indicators	18%	82%

The data used here were MLE levels from the previous two years, not the season in which they were called up. The significance? Solid current performance is what merits a call-up, but this is not a good indicator of short-term MLB success, because a) the performance data set is too small, typically just a few month's worth of statistics, and b) for those putting up good numbers at a new minor league level, there has typically not been enough time for the scouting reports to make their rounds.

East Asia Baseball *(Tom Mulhall)*

There has been a slow but steady influx of MLB-ready players from East Asian professional leagues to Major League Baseball, which is especially important in dynasty leagues with larger reserve or farm clubs. The Japanese major leagues (Nippon Professional Baseball) is generally considered to be equivalent to Triple-A ball, though the pitching is possibly better. The Korean league (Korean Baseball Organization) is considered slightly less competitive with less depth, and is roughly comparable to Double-A ball.

When evaluating the potential of Asian League prospects, the key is not to just identify the best players—the key is to identify impact players who have the desire and opportunity to sign with a MLB team. Opportunity is crucial, since players must have a certain number years of professional experience in order to qualify for international free agency, or hope that their team "posts" them early for full free agency. With the success of players like Ichiro, Darvish and Ohtani, it is easy to overestimate the value of drafting these players. Most don't have that impact. Still, for owners who are allowed to carry a large reserve or farm team at reduced salaries, rostering these players before they sign with a MLB club could be a real windfall, especially if your competitors do not do their homework.

When doing your own research, note that in both Japan and Korea, the family name may be listed first, followed by the given name. The *Forecaster* will "westernize" those names for familiarity and ease of use. Names are sometimes difficult to translate into English so the official NPB or KBO designation will be used.

Japan

Baseball was first introduced in 1872 with professional leagues founded in the 1920s. It reached widespread popularity in the 1930s, partially due to exhibition games against American barnstorming teams that included Babe Ruth, Lou Gehrig, and Jimmie Foxx. Baseball is now considered the most popular spectator and participatory sport in Japan. The Nippon Professional Baseball (NPB) has two leagues, the Central League and Pacific League, each consisting of six teams. The Pacific League is currently considered superior to the more conservative Central League. There is also a strong amateur Industrial League, where players like Hideo Nomo and Kosuke Fukudome were discovered.

Statistics are difficult to compare due to differences in the way the game is played in Japan:

1. While strong on fundamentals, Japanese baseball's guiding philosophy remains risk avoidance. Runners rarely take extra bases, batters focus on making contact rather than driving the ball, and managers play for one run at a time. Bunts are more common. As a result, offenses score fewer runs per number of hits, and pitching stats tend to look better.

2. Stadiums in Japan usually have smaller dimensions and shorter fences. This should mean more HRs, but given the style of play, it is the foreign born players who make up much of Japan's power elite. While a few Japanese power hitters such as Shohei Ohtani and Hideki Matsui made a full equivalent transition to MLB, it is still rare for the power to be duplicated.

3. There are more artificial turf fields, which increases the number of ground ball singles. A few stadiums still use all dirt infields.

4. Teams are limited to having four foreign players on an active roster, and they cannot all be hitters or pitchers.

5. Teams have smaller pitching staffs and use a six-man rotation. Starters usually pitch once a week, typically on the same day since Monday is an off-day for the entire league. Some starters will also occasionally pitch in relief between starts. Managers push for complete games, no matter what the score or situation. Because of the style of offense, higher pitch counts are common. Despite superior conditioning, Japanese pitchers tend to burn out early due to overuse.

6. The ball is smaller and lighter, and the strike zone is slightly closer to the batter. Their ball also has more tack than the current MLB ball, which allows for a better spin rate.

7. There is an automatic ejection for hitting a batter in the area of the head and for arguing a call for more than three minutes.

8. Travel is less exhausting, with much shorter distances between teams.

9. If the score remains even after 12 innings, the game goes into the books as a tie.

10. There are 144 games in a season, as opposed to 162 in MLB.

Players may sign with a MLB team out of high school, but this is a rare occurrence and most players sign with a NPB team. Player movement between players signed to a Japanese team and MLB teams is severely restricted by their "posting" system. Japanese teams have far greater control over player contracts than MLB teams. While domestic free agency usually comes a year sooner, players must have nine years of experience before they obtain international free agency. If a player wishes to play in the ML sooner than that, his team must agree to "post" him for free agency. Posting usually comes in the penultimate year of the player's contract but can come sooner if the club agrees. Some

teams are more willing to do that than others, usually those with financial problems. Unfortunately, since not all time spent on Injured Reserve counts towards free agency, some teams manipulate the system to delay the required service time. (For example, the SoftBank Hawks are notorious for manipulated the IR to delay the required service time towards free agency.)

The good news is that under the new posting system, a player may now negotiate with all interested MLB teams, rather than be restricted to the team with the highest posting bid. The Japanese team then receives a "release fee" from the MLB club based on a percentage of the total guaranteed value of the contract, usually around 15-20%. This release fee is received if and only if the player signs with a MLB team.

Korea

Baseball was probably introduced in Korean around 1900. Professional leagues developed long after they did in Japan, with the Korean Baseball Organization (KBO) being founded in 1981. The KBO currently has ten teams in one league with no divisions. While many solid players have come from Korea, their professional league is considered a rung lower than Japan, mostly because of less depth in players.

When comparing statistics, consider:

1. Stadiums were very hitter friendly. For example, Jung-ho Park had 40 HR the year before joining the Pirates, and just 15 in his first ML season. To address this issue, a "dejuiced" ball was introduced in 2019 which has decreased the number of home runs.

2. Since there is just one League, the designated hitter rule is universal.

3. Again, there are much shorter travel times in a smaller country.

4. Like Japan, tie games are allowed.

5. The KBO also uses a "pre-tacked" baseball, like Japan.

6. Ejections are rare, as players and managers seldom argue with calls.

7. Korea also plays fewer games, currently 144 in a season.

The KBO has a very similar posting system to Japan, although a Korean team is allowed to post only one player per off-season while a Japanese team has no limits. However, the requisite experience time is "just" seven years.

China/Taiwan

As with other Asian countries, baseball was introduced long ago to China, possibly in the mid-nineteenth century. Professional baseball is in its infancy, although MLB signed an agreement with the Chinese Baseball Association (CBA) in 2019 to help with development. Baseball in Taiwan is more advanced, with the Chinese Professional Baseball League (CPBL) beginning play in 1990. The best players usually sign with a Japanese team but some players have played MLB ball. Coverage on the Chinese leagues will expand as their impact grows.

A list of Asian League players who could move to the majors appears in the Prospects section of the Forecaster, beginning on page 243.

Other Diamonds

Age 26 Paradox

Age 26 is when a player begins to reach his peak skill, no matter what his address is. If circumstances have him celebrating that birthday in the majors, he is a breakout candidate. If circumstances have him celebrating that birthday in the minors, he is washed up.

A-Rod 10-Step Path to Stardom

Not all well-hyped prospects hit the ground running. More often they follow an alternative path:

1. Prospect puts up phenomenal minor league numbers.
2. The media machine gets oiled up.
3. Prospect gets called up, but struggles, Year 1.
4. Prospect gets demoted.
5. Prospect tears it up in the minors, Year 2.
6. Prospect gets called up, but struggles, Year 2.
7. Prospect gets demoted.
8. The media turns their backs. Fantasy leaguers reduce their expectations.
9. Prospect tears it up in the minors, Year 3. The public shrugs its collective shoulders.
10. Prospect is promoted in Year 3 and explodes. Some lucky fantasy leaguer lands a franchise player for under $5.

Some players that are currently stuck at one of the interim steps, and may or may not ever reach Step 10, include Jared Kelenic, Lewis Brinson, and Bobby Bradley.

Bull Durham Gardening Tip

Late bloomers have fewer flowering seasons.

Developmental Dogmata

1. Defense is what gets a minor league prospect to the majors; offense is what keeps him there. *(Deric McKamey)*
2. The reason why rapidly promoted minor leaguers often fail is that they are never given the opportunity to master the skill of "adjusting to the competition."
3. Rookies who are promoted in-season often perform better than those that make the club out of spring training. Inferior March competition can inflate the latter group's perceived talent level.
4. Young players rarely lose their inherent skills. Pitchers may uncover weaknesses and the players may have difficulty adjusting. These are bumps along the growth curve, but they do not reflect a loss of skill.
5. Late bloomers have smaller windows of opportunity and much less chance for forgiveness.
6. The greatest risk in this game is to pay for performance that a player has never achieved.

Quad-A Player

Some outwardly talented prospects simply have a ceiling that's spelled "A-A-A." They may be highly rated prospects – even minor league stars – but are never able to succeed in the majors. They have names like Franklin Barreto, Danny Hultzen, Andy Marte and Brandon Wood.

Rule 5 Reminder

Don't ignore the Rule 5 draft lest you ignore the possibility of players like Jose Bautista, Johan Santana, and Jayson Werth. All were Rule 5 draftees.

The following are players were acquired in the first two rounds of the Rule 5 Draft who became at least serviceable Major Leaguers:

Year	Players who eventually stuck
2006	Joakim Soria, Josh Hamilton
2007	R.A. Dickey
2008	Everth Cabrera, Darren O'Day, Iván Nova
2011	Ryan Flaherty, Marwin Gonzalez
2012	Héctor Rondón, Ryan Pressly, Ender Inciarte
2014	Mark Canha, Delino Deshields, Odúbel Herrera
2015	Joey Rickard, Jake Cave, Ji-Man Choi
2016	Caleb Smith, Anthony Santander
2017	Victor Reyes, Brad Keller, Elieser Hernandez
2018	Jordan Romano, Connor Joe
2020	Akil Baddoo, Garrett Whitlock

Trout Inflation

The tendency for rookies to go for exorbitant draft prices following a year when there was a very good rookie crop.

Gaming

Standard Rules and Variations

Rotisserie Baseball was invented as an elegant confluence of baseball and economics. Whether by design or accident, the result has lasted for more than four decades. But what would Rotisserie and fantasy have been like if the Founding Fathers knew then what we know now about statistical analysis and game design? You can be sure things would be different.

The world has changed since the original game was introduced yet many leagues use the same rules today. New technologies have opened up opportunities to improve elements of the game that might have been limited by the capabilities of the 1980s. New analytical approaches have revealed areas where the original game falls short.

As such, there are good reasons to tinker and experiment; to find ways to enhance the experience.

Following are the basic elements of fantasy competition, those that provide opportunities for alternative rules and experimentation. This is by no means an exhaustive list, but at minimum provides some interesting food-for-thought.

Player pool

Standard: American League-only, National League-only or Mixed League.

AL/NL-only typically drafts 8-12 teams (pool penetration of 49% to 74%). Mixed leagues draft 10-18 teams (31% to 55% penetration), though 15 teams (46%) is a common number.

Drafting of reserve players will increase the penetration percentages. A 12-team AL/NL-only league adding six reserves onto 23-man rosters would draft 93% of the available pool of players on all teams' 25-man rosters.

The draft penetration level determines which fantasy management skills are most important to your league. The higher the penetration, the more important it is to draft a good team. The lower the penetration, the greater the availability of free agents and the more important in-season roster management becomes.

There is no generally-accepted optimal penetration level, but we have often suggested that 75% (including reserves) provides a good balance between the skills required for both draft prep and in-season management.

Alternative pools: There are many options here. Certain leagues draft from within a small group of major league divisions or teams. Some competitions, like home run leagues, only draft batters.

Bottom-tier pool: Draft only players who posted a Rotisserie dollar value of $5 or less in the previous season. Intended as a test of an owner's ability to identify talent with upside. Best used as a pick-a-player contest with any number of teams participating.

Positional structure

Standard: 23 players. One at each defensive position (though three outfielders may be from any of LF, CF or RF), plus one additional catcher, one middle infielder (2B or SS), one corner infielder (1B or 3B), two additional outfielders and a utility player/designated hitter (which often can be a batter who qualifies anywhere). Nine pitchers, typically holding any starting or relief role.

Open: 25 players. One at each defensive position (plus DH), 5-man starting rotation and two relief pitchers. Nine additional players at any position, which may be a part of the active roster or constitute a reserve list.

40-man: Standard 23 plus 17 reserves. Used in many keeper and dynasty leagues.

Reapportioned: In recent years, new obstacles are being faced by 12-team AL/NL-only leagues thanks to changes in the real game. The 14/9 split between batters and pitchers no longer reflects how MLB teams structure their rosters. Of the 30 teams, each with 26-man rosters, not one contained 14 batters for any length of time. In fact, many spent a good part of the season with only 12 batters, which meant that teams often had more pitchers than hitters.

For fantasy purposes in AL/NL-only leagues, that left a disproportionate draft penetration into the batter and pitcher pools. Assuming MLB teams rostering 13 batters and 13 pitchers:

	BATTERS	PITCHERS
On all MLB rosters	195	195
Players drafted	168	108
Pct.	86%	55%

These drafts are depleting 31% more batters out of the pool than pitchers. Add in those leagues with reserve lists—perhaps an additional six players per team removing another 72 players—and post-draft free agent pools are very thin, especially on the batting side.

The impact is less in 15-team mixed leagues, though the FA pitching pool is still disproportionately deep.

	BATTERS	PITCHERS
On all rosters	390	390
Drafted	210	135
Pct.	54%	35%

One solution is to reapportion the number of batters and pitchers that are rostered. Adding one pitcher slot and eliminating one batter slot may be enough to provide better balance. The batting slot most often removed is the second catcher, since it is the position with the least depth. However, that only serves to populate the free agent pool with a dozen or more worthless catchers.

Beginning in the 2012 season, the Tout Wars AL/NL-only experts leagues opted to eliminate one of the outfield slots and replace it with a "swingman" position. This position could be any batter or pitcher, depending upon the owner's needs at any given time during the season.

Selecting players

Standard: The three most prevalent methods for stocking fantasy rosters are:

Snake/Straight/Serpentine draft: Players are selected in order with seeds reversed in alternating rounds. This method has become the most popular due to its speed, ease of implementation and ease of automation.

In these drafts, the underlying assumption is that value can be ranked relative to a linear baseline. Pick #1 is better than pick #2, which is better than pick #3, and the difference between each pick is assumed to be somewhat equivalent. While a faulty assumption, we must believe in it to assume a level playing field.

Auction: Players are sold to the highest bidder from a fixed budget, typically $260. Auctions provide the team owner with more control over which players will be on his team, but can take twice as long as snake drafts.

The baseline is $0 at the beginning of each player put up for bid. The final purchase price for each player is shaped by many wildly variable factors, from roster need to geographic location of the draft. A $30 player can mean different things to different drafters.

One option that can help reduce the time commitment of auctions is to force minimum bids at each hour mark. You could mandate $15 openers in hour #1; $10 openers in hour #2, etc. This removes some nominating strategy, however.

Pick-a-player / Salary cap: Players are assigned fixed dollar values and owners assemble their roster within a fixed cap. This type of roster-stocking is an individual exercise which results in teams typically having some of the same players.

In these leagues, "value assessment" is taken out of the hands of the owners. Each player has a fixed cost, pre-assigned based on past season performance and/or future expectation.

Stat categories

Standard: The standard statistical categories for Rotisserie leagues are:

4x4: HR, RBI, SB, BA, W, Sv, ERA, WHIP

5x5: HR, R, RBI, SB, BA, W, Sv, K, ERA, WHIP

6x6: Categories typically added are Holds and OPS.

7x7, etc.: Any number of categories may be added.

In general, the more categories you add, the more complicated it is to isolate individual performance and manage the categorical impact on your roster. There is also the danger of redundancy; with multiple categories measuring like stats, certain skills can get over-valued. For instance, home runs are double-counted when using the categories of both HR and slugging average. (Though note that HRs are actually already triple-counted in standard 5x5—HRs, runs, and RBIs)

If the goal is to have categories that create a more encompassing picture of player performance, it is actually possible to accomplish more with less:

Modified 4x4: HR, (R+RBI-HR), SB, OBA, (W+QS), (Sv+Hld), K, ERA

This provides a better balance between batting and pitching in that each has three counting categories and one ratio category. In fact, the balance is shown to be even more notable here:

	BATTING	PITCHING
Pure skill counting stat	HR	K
Ratio category	OBA	ERA
Dependent upon managerial decision	SB	(Sv+Hold)
Dependent upon team support	(R+RBI-HR)	(W+QS)
Alternative or addition to team support:		
Usage/stamina/health	Plate app	Innings

Replacing saves: The problem with the Saves statistic is that we have a scarce commodity that is centered on a small group of players, thereby creating inflated demand for those players. With the rising failure rate for closers these days, the incentive to pay full value for the commodity decreases. The higher the risk, the lower the prices.

We can increase the value of the commodity by reducing the risk. We might do this by increasing the number of players that contribute to that category, thereby spreading the risk around. One way we can accomplish this is by changing the category to Saves + Holds.

Holds are not perfect, but the typical argument about them being random and arbitrary can apply to saves as well. In fact, many of the pitchers who record holds are far more skilled and valuable than closers; they are often called to the mound in much higher leverage situations (a fact backed up by a scan of each pitcher's Leverage Index).

Neither stat is perfect, but together they form a reasonable proxy for overall bullpen performance.

In tandem, they effectively double the player pool of draftable relievers while also flattening the values allotted to those pitchers. The more players around which we spread the risk, the more control we have in managing our pitching staffs.

Replacing wins: Some have argued for replacing the Wins statistic with W + QS (quality starts). This method of scoring gives value to a starting pitcher who pitches well, but fails to receive the win due to his team's poor offense or poor luck. However, with the decline in the average length of starts, the number of QS outings has dropped sharply. W+QS was a good idea a few years ago; less so now. A replacement stat gaining in popularity is Innings Pitched. Pitchers left on the mound for more innings are more likely to be helping your team, regardless of whether they are in line for a win or quality start.

Keeping score

Standard: These are the most common scoring methods:

Rotisserie: Players are evaluated in several statistical categories. Totals of these statistics are ranked by team. The winner is the team with the highest cumulative ranking.

Points: Players receive points for events that they contribute to in each game. Points are totaled for each team and teams are then ranked.

Head-to-Head (H2H): Using Rotisserie or points scoring, teams are scheduled in daily or weekly matchups. The winner of each matchup is the team that finishes higher in more categories (Rotisserie) or scores the most points.

Free agent acquisition

Standard: Three methods are the most common for acquiring free agent players during the season.

First come first served: Free agents are awarded to the first owner who claims them.

Reverse order of standings: Access to the free agent pool is typically in a snake draft fashion with the last place team getting the first pick, and each successive team higher in the standings picking afterwards.

Free agent acquisition budget (FAAB): Teams are given a set budget at the beginning of the season (typically, $100 or $1000) from which they bid on free agents in a closed auction process.

Vickrey FAAB: Research has shown that more than 50% of FAAB dollars are lost via overbid on an annual basis. Given that this is a scarce commodity, one would think that a system to better manage these dollars might be desirable. The Vickrey system conducts a closed auction in the same way as standard FAAB, but the price of the winning bid is set at the amount of the second highest bid, plus $1. In some cases, gross overbids (at least $10 over) are reduced to the second highest bid plus $5.

This method was designed by William Vickrey, a Professor of Economics at Columbia University. His theory was that this process reveals the true value of the commodity. For his work, Vickrey was awarded the Nobel Prize for Economics (and $1.2 million) in 1996.

The season

Standard: Leagues are played out during the course of the entire Major League Baseball season.

Split-season: Leagues are conducted from Opening Day through the All-Star break, then re-drafted to play from the All-Star break through the end of the season.

50-game split-season: Leagues are divided into three 50-game seasons with one-week break in between.

Monthly: Leagues are divided into six seasons or rolling four-week seasons.

The advantages of these shorter time frames:

- They can help to maintain interest. There would be fewer abandoned teams.
- There would be more shots at a title each year.
- Given that drafting is considered the most fun aspect of the game, these splits multiply the opportunities to participate in some type of draft. Leagues may choose to do complete re-drafts and treat the year as distinct mini-seasons. Or, leagues might allow teams to drop their five worst players and conduct a restocking draft at each break.

Daily games: Participants select a roster of players from one day's MLB schedule. Scoring is based on an aggregate points-based system rather than categories, with cash prizes awarded based on the day's results. The structure and distribution of that prize pool varies across different types of events, and those differences can affect roster construction strategies. Although scoring and prizes are based on one day's play, the season-long element of bankroll management provides a proxy for overall standings.

In terms of projecting outcomes, daily games are drastically different than full-season leagues. Playing time is one key element of any projection, and daily games offer near-100% accuracy in projecting playing time: you can check pre-game lineups to see exactly which players are in the lineup that night. The other key component of any projection is performance, but that is plagued by variance in daily competitions. Even if you roster a team full of the most advantageous matchups, the best hitters can still go 0-for-4 on a given night.

Draft Process

Draft-day cheat sheet *(Patrick Davitt)*

1. Know what players are available, right to the bottom of the pool.
2. Know what every player is worth in your league format.
3. Know why you think each player is worth what you think he's worth.
4. Identify players you believe you value differently from the other owners.
5. Know each player's risks.
6. Know your opponents' patterns.
7. For sure, know the league rules and its history, and what it takes to win.

Draft preparation with a full-season mindset *(Matt Dodge)*

Each of the dimensions of your league setup—player pool, reserve list depth; type and frequency of transactions, scoring categories, etc.—should impact your draft day plan. But it may also be helpful to look at them in combination.

Sources of additional stats after draft day

League Player Pool		
Reserve List	Mixed 15 team	AL- or NL-only 12 team
Short	free agents	trades, free agents
Long	free agents, trades	trades

Review the prior season's transactions for your league and analyze the successful teams' category contributions from trade acquisitions and free agent pickups. Trades are often necessary to add specific stats in AL/NL-only leagues as the player pool penetration is generally much deeper, and the size of a reserve roster further reduces the help possible from the free agent pool.

Draft strategies related to in-season player acquisition

Trade Activity		
FA Pool	Low	High
Shallow	solid foundation (STR)	tradable commodoties surplus counting stats
Deep	gamble on upside (S&S)	ultimate flexibility

Trading activity is a function of multiple factors. Keeper leagues provide opportunities for owners to contend this year or play for next year. However, those increased opportunities are often controlled by rules to prevent "dump trading." Stratification of the standings in redraft leagues can cause lower ranked owners to lose interest, reducing the number of effective trading partners as the season goes on.

When deep rosters create a shallow free agent pool in a league with little trading, draft day success becomes paramount. In this case, a Spread the Risk strategy designed to accumulate at bats, innings, and saves is recommended. If the free agent pool is deep, the drafter can take more risks with a Stars and Scrubs approach, acquiring "lottery ticket" players with upside, knowing that replacements are readily available if the upside plays don't hit.

In leagues where trading is prevalent, a shallow free agent pool means you should acquire players on draft day with the intent of trading them. This could mean a traditional strategy of acquiring a category surplus (frequently saves and/or steals), and then trading them in-season to shore up other categories. In a keeper league, this includes grabbing a few bargains (to interest those who are rebuilding) or grabbing top performers to flip in trade (if you are already on "the two year plan").

Draft Day Considerations for In-season Roster Management

Reserve List Txn Freq	4 x 4 League Format	5 x 5 League Format
Daily	careful SP management batting platoons positional flexibility	RP (K, ERA, WHIP) batting platoons positional flexibility
Weekly	SP (2 start weeks) cover risky starters	SP (2 start weeks) cover risky starters

Owners must be careful with pitching, due to the negative impact potential of ERA and WHIP. Blindly streaming pitchers on a daily basis can be counter-productive, particularly in 4x4 leagues. In 5x5, the Strikeouts category can make a foundation of high Dom relievers a useful source of mitigation for the invariable starting pitching disappointments.

The degree that these recommendations can be implemented is also dependent on the depth of the reserve list. Those with more reserves can do more than those with fewer, obviously, but the key is deciding up front how you plan to use your reserves, and then tailoring your draft strategy toward that usage.

The value of mock drafts (*Todd Zola*)

Most assume the purpose of a mock draft is to get to know the market value of the player pool. But even more important, mock drafting is general preparation for the environment and process, thereby allowing the drafter to completely focus on the draft when it counts. Mock drafting is more about fine-tuning your strategy than player value. Here are some tips to maximize your mock drafting experience.

1. Make sure you can seamlessly use an on-line drafting room, draft software or your own lists to track your draft or auction. The less time you spend looking, adding and adjusting names, the more time you can spend on thinking about what player is best for your team. This also gives you the opportunity to make sure your draft lists are complete, and assures all the players are listed at the correct position(s).

2. Alter the draft slots from which you mock. The flow of each mock will be different, but if you do a few mocks with an early initial pick, a few in the middle and a few with a late first pick, you may learn you prefer one of the spots more than the others. If you're in a league where you can choose your draft spot, this helps you decide where to select. Once you know your spot, a few mocks from that spot will help you decide how to deal with positional runs.

3. Use non-typical strategies and consider players you rarely target. We all have our favorite players. Intentionally passing on those players not only gives you an idea when others may draft them but it also forces you to research players you normally don't consider. The more players you have researched, the more prepared you'll be for any series of events that occurs during your real draft.

Snake Drafting

Snake draft first round history

The following tables record the comparison between pre-season projected player rankings (using Average Draft Position data from Mock Draft Central and National Fantasy Baseball Championship) and actual end-of-season results. The 18-year success rate of identifying each season's top talent is only 33.7%. Even if we extend the study to the top two rounds, the hit rate is only around 50%.

2014	ADP		ACTUAL = 4
1	Mike Trout	1	Jose Altuve
2	Miguel Cabrera	2	Clayton Kershaw (6)
3	Paul Goldschmidt	3	Michael Brantley
4	Andrew McCutchen	4	Mike Trout (1)
5	Carlos Gonzalez	5	Johnny Cueto
6	Clayton Kershaw	6	Felix Hernandez
7	Chris Davis	7	Victor Martinez
8	Ryan Braun	8	Jose Abreu
9	Adam Jones	9	Giancarlo Stanton
10	Bryce Harper	10	Andrew McCutchen (4)
11	Robinson Cano	11	Miguel Cabrera (2)
12	Hanley Ramirez	12	Carlos Gomez
13	Jacoby Ellsbury	13	Jose Bautista
14	Prince Fielder	14	Dee Gordon
15	Troy Tulowitzki	15	Anthony Rendon

2015	ADP		ACTUAL = 4
1	Mike Trout	1	Jake Arrieta
2	Andrew McCutchen	2	Zack Greinke
3	Clayton Kershaw	3	Clayton Kershaw (3)
4	Giancarlo Stanton	4	Paul Goldschmidt (5)
5	Paul Goldschmidt	5	A.J. Pollock
6	Miguel Cabrera	6	Dee Gordon
7	Jose Abreu	7	Bryce Harper
8	Carlos Gomez	8	Josh Donaldson
9	Jose Bautista	9	Jose Altuve (12)
10	Edwin Encarnacion	10	Mike Trout (1)
11	Felix Hernandez	11	Nolan Arenado
12	Jose Altuve	12	Manny Machado
13	Anthony Rizzo	13	Dallas Keuchel
14	Adam Jones	14	Max Scherzer
15	Troy Tulowitzki	15	Nelson Cruz

2016	ADP		ACTUAL = 7
1	Mike Trout	1	Mookie Betts
2	Paul Goldschmidt	2	Jose Altuve (11)
3	Bryce Harper	3	Mike Trout (1)
4	Clayton Kershaw	4	Jonathan Villar
5	Josh Donaldson	5	Jean Segura
6	Carlos Correa	6	Max Scherzer (15)
7	Nolan Arenado	7	Paul Goldschmidt (2)
8	Manny Machado	8	Charlie Blackmon
9	Anthony Rizzo	9	Clayton Kershaw (4)
10	Giancarlo Stanton	10	Nolan Arenado (7)
11	Jose Altuve	11	Daniel Murphy
12	Kris Bryant	12	Kris Bryant (12)
13	Miguel Cabrera	13	Joey Votto
14	Andrew McCutchen	14	Jon Lester
15	Max Scherzer	15	Madison Bumgarner

2017	ADP		ACTUAL = 5
1	Mike Trout	1	Charlie Blackmon
2	Mookie Betts	2	Jose Altuve (4)
3	Clayton Kershaw	3	Corey Kluber
4	Jose Altuve	4	Max Scherzer (12)
5	Kris Bryant	5	Paul Goldschmidt (7)
6	Nolan Arenado	6	Giancarlo Stanton
7	Paul Goldschmidt	7	Chris Sale
8	Manny Machado	8	Aaron Judge
9	Bryce Harper	9	Dee Gordon
10	Trea Turner	10	Clayton Kershaw (3)
11	Josh Donaldson	11	Nolan Arenado (6)
12	Max Scherzer	12	Jose Ramirez
13	Anthony Rizzo	13	Joey Votto
14	Madison Bumgarner	14	Marcell Ozuna
15	Carlos Correa	15	Elvis Andrus

2018	ADP		ACTUAL = 3*
1	Mike Trout	1	Mookie Betts (7)
2	Jose Altuve	2	Christian Yelich
3	Nolan Arenado	3	J.D. Martinez
4	Trea Turner	4	Max Scherzer (11)
5	Clayton Kershaw	5	Jacob deGrom
6	Paul Goldschmidt	6	Jose Ramirez
7	Mookie Betts	7	Francisco Lindor
8	Giancarlo Stanton	8	Trevor Story
9	Charlie Blackmon	9	Justin Verlander
10	Bryce Harper	10	Mike Trout (1)
11	Max Scherzer	11	Blake Snell
12	Chris Sale	12	Javier Baez
13	Corey Kluber	13	Whit Merrifield
14	Carlos Correa	14	Aaron Nola
15	Kris Bryant	15	Manny Machado

*2018 represents the lowest first round hit rate in the 15 years. However, the next four players on the list would be: 16) Trea Turner (4); 17) Chris Sale (12); 18) Nolan Arenado (3); 19) Corey Kluber (13)

2019	ADP		ACTUAL = 4
1	Mike Trout	1	Justin Verlander
2	Mookie Betts	2	Gerrit Cole
3	Jose Ramirez	3	Christian Yelich (6)
4	Max Scherzer	4	Ronald Acuna (8)
5	J.D. Martinez	5	Cody Bellinger
6	Christian Yelich	6	Rafael Devers
7	Nolan Arenado	7	Anthony Rendon
8	Ronald Acuna	8	Jacob deGrom (10)
9	Trea Turner	9	Jonathan Villar
10	Jacob deGrom	10	Trevor Story
11	Alex Bregman	11	Nolan Arenado (7)
12	Chris Sale	12	Ketel Marte
13	Francisco Lindor	13	D.J. LeMahieu
14	Aaron Judge	14	Zack Greinke
15	Jose Altuve	15	Xander Bogaerts

Similar to 2018, the next players on the 2019 list would be: 16) Alex Bregman (11); 17) Mookie Betts (2); 18) Mike Trout (1); 19) Trea Turner (9)

2020	ADP		ACTUAL = 5
1	Ronald Acuna	1	Shane Bieber
2	Christian Yelich	2	Trea Turner (8)
3	Cody Bellinger	3	Fernando Tatis, Jr.
4	Gerrit Cole	4	Jose Ramirez (11)
5	Mookie Betts	5	Trevor Bauer
6	Mike Trout	6	Mookie Betts (5)
7	Francisco Lindor	7	Freddie Freeman
8	Trea Turner	8	Jose Abreu
9	Jacob deGrom	9	Manny Machado
10	Trevor Story	10	Marcell Ozuna
11	Jose Ramirez	11	Yu Darvish
12	Juan Soto	12	Trevor Story (10)
13	Justin Verlander	13	Adalberto Mondesi
14	Nolan Arenado	14	Juan Soto (12)
15	Max Scherzer	15	Kenta Maeda

2021	ADP		ACTUAL = 3
1	Ronald Acuna	1	Trea Turner (8)
2	Fernando Tatis, Jr.	2	Shohei Ohtani*
3	Juan Soto	3	Bo Bichette
4	Mookie Betts	4	Vladimir Guerrero, Jr.
5	Jacob deGrom	5	Starling Marte
6	Mike Trout	6	Max Scherzer
7	Gerrit Cole	7	Fernando Tatis, Jr. (2)
8	Trea Turner	8	Jose Ramirez (10)
9	Shane Bieber	9	Walker Buehler
10	Jose Ramirez	10	Cedric Mullins III
11	Christian Yelich	11	Marcus Semien
12	Trevor Story	12	Whit Merrifield
13	Freddie Freeman	13	Teoscar Hernandez
14	Trevor Bauer	14	Bryce Harper
15	Cody Bellinger	15	Zack Wheeler

* Includes earnings as both hitter and pitcher. Ohtani ranked 9th overall on his hitting stats alone.

ADP attrition

Why is our success rate so low in identifying what should be the most easy-to-project players each year? We rank and draft players based on the expectation that those ranked higher will return greater value in terms of productivity and playing time, as well as being the safest investments. However, there are many variables affecting where players finish.

Earlier, it was shown that players spend an inordinate number of days on the disabled list. In fact, of the players projected to finish in the top 300, the number who were placed on the injury list, demoted or designated for assignment has been extreme:

Year	Pct. of top-ranked 300 players who lost PT
2011	49%
2012	45%
2013	51%
2014	53%
2015	47%
2016	47%
2017	58%
2018	60%
2019	59%
2020*	43%
2021	71%

*In 60 games.

When you consider that well over half of each season's very best players had fewer at-bats or innings pitched than we projected, it shows how tough it is to rank players each year.

The Ineptitude of ADPs

What is our true aptitude in accurately ranking players each year? It's very, very bad. Using the ADPs from a 15-team mixed league (2018 and 2019), we looked at each player, round by round and tagged each one:

- PROFIT: Turned a profit on the round he was drafted in
- PAR: Earned back the exact value of the round he was drafted in
- LOSS: Took a 1-3 round loss on his draft round
- BUST: Took a 4-plus round loss on his draft round
- DISASTER: Returned earnings outside the top 750 players, essentially undraftable in a league with 50-man rosters. Disasters are subsets of Busts.

2018					
Rds	**Profit**	**Par**	**Loss**	**Bust**	**Dis**
1-5	21%	8%	27%	44%	4%
6-10	24%	7%	24%	45%	4%
11-15	27%	3%	9%	61%	27%
16-20	37%	1%	8%	53%	25%
21-25	41%	1%	4%	53%	21%
26-30	40%	0%	0%	60%	35%
31-35	15%	0%	0%	85%	76%
36-40	15%	1%	0%	84%	79%
41-45	19%	3%	1%	77%	76%
46-50	28%	0%	3%	69%	68%

2019					
Rds	**Profit**	**Par**	**Loss**	**Bust**	**Dis**
1-5	20%	13%	21%	45%	4%
6-10	28%	8%	12%	52%	5%
11-15	35%	0%	5%	60%	15%
16-20	31%	3%	7%	60%	27%
21-25	37%	3%	4%	56%	39%
26-30	39%	4%	7%	51%	33%
31-35	35%	0%	1%	64%	49%
36-40	32%	0%	3%	65%	55%
41-45	37%	0%	3%	60%	57%
46-50	33%	0%	3%	64%	64%

For starters, there is no such thing as "Player-X is a Y-rounder." We had virtually no ability to identify exactly where a player should be drafted. Over the first five rounds, we got about 90 percent of them wrong and nearly half our picks were full-out busts. Over the rest of the draft, the right answers were blind dart throws.

Our percentage of profitable picks increased as we progressed through the active draft rounds. However, much of that is just probability; the deeper into a draft, the more room for picks to finish higher. In most cases the draft round was random. Rounds 21-30 were the sweet spot for profitable picks. We fared best after the active part of the draft was mostly over.

2018					
Rds	**Profit**	**Par**	**Loss**	**Bust**	**Dis**
1-23	30%	4%	16%	50%	15%
24-50	24%	1%	1%	75%	64%

2019					
Rds	**Profit**	**Par**	**Loss**	**Bust**	**Dis**
1-23	30%	5%	10%	55%	16%
24-50	35%	1%	3%	60%	51%

In the active roster draft, a third of our picks performed at par or better; two thirds performed worse than where we drafted them. Fully half of them could have been considered busts. In other words, *every player we drafted had, at best, only a one-in-three chance of being a good pick.*

Importance of the early rounds *(Bill Macey)*
It's long been said that you can't win your league in the first round, but you can lose it there. An analysis of data from actual drafts reveals that this holds true—those who spend an early round pick on a player that severely under-performs expectations rarely win their league and seldom even finish in the top 3.

At the same time, drafting a player in the first round that actually returns first-round value is no guarantee of success. In fact, those that draft some of the best values still only win their league about a quarter of the time and finish in the top 3 less than half the time. Research also shows that drafting pitchers in the first round is a risky proposition. Even if the pitchers deliver first-round value, the opportunity cost of passing up on an elite batter makes you less likely to win your league.

The Impact of the draft on final statistics *(Todd Zola)*
Which has more impact on your team's final standings—your draft or in-season roster management? The standings correlation based on draft-to-final results ranges from 0.42 to 0.94, with the mean around 0.73. The top hitting counting stat drafted is home runs; the fewest is stolen bases. The top pitching counting stat drafted is saves; the fewest is wins. More hitting is acquired at the draft or auction than pitching. The in-season influx of stats is greatest in Mixed Leagues, suggesting that owners should practice patience with in-season free agents in AL/NL formats while being cautiously aggressive in Mixed formats.

Top teams almost always improve ratio categories from their drafted rosters, despite available free agents sporting poorer aggregate ratios. This is most applicable to improving your pitching staff as the year progresses, but it's easier said than done.

Being top-three in saves is far more important in Mixed leagues than in AL/NL. Most Mixed champions draft the majority of saves while AL/NL winners often acquire saves in season.

What is the best seed to draft from?
Most drafters like mid-round so they never have to wait too long for their next player. Some like the swing pick, suggesting that getting two players at 15 and 16 is better than a 1 and a 30. Many drafters assume that the swing pick means you'd be getting something like two $30 players instead of a $40 and $20.

Equivalent auction dollar values reveal the following facts about the first two snake draft rounds:

In an AL/NL-only league, the top seed would get a $44 player (at #1) and a $24 player (at #24) for a total of $68; the 12th seed would get two $29s (at #12 and #13) for $58.

In a mixed league, the top seed would get a $47 and a $24 ($71); the 15th seed would get two $28s ($56).

Since the talent level flattens out after the 2nd round, low seeds never get a chance to catch up:

$ difference between first player/last player selected		
Round	12-team	15-team
1	$15	$19
2	$7	$8
3	$5	$4
4	$3	$3
5	$2	$2
6	$2	$1
7-17	$1	$1
18-23	$0	$0

The total value each seed accumulates at the end of the draft is hardly equitable:

Seed	Mixed	AL/NL-only
1	$266	$273
2	$264	$269
3	$263	$261
4	$262	$262
5	$259	$260
6	$261	$260
7	$260	$260
8	$261	$260
9	$261	$258
10	$257	$260
11	$257	$257
12	$258	$257
13	$254	
14	$255	
15	$256	

The counter-argument to this focuses on whether we can reasonably expect "accurate projections" at the top of the draft. Given the snake draft first round history, a case could be made that any seed might potentially do well. In fact, an argument can be made that the last seed is the best spot because it essentially provides two picks from the top 13 players (in a 12-team league) during the part of the draft with the steepest talent decline.

Using ADPs to determine when to select players *(Bill Macey)*

Although average draft position (ADP) data provides a good idea of where in the draft each player is selected, it can be misleading when trying to determine how early to target a player. This chart summarizes the percentage of players drafted within 15 picks of his ADP as well as the average standard deviation by grouping of players.

ADP Rank	% within 15 picks	Standard Deviation
1-25	100%	2.5
26-50	97%	6.1
51-100	87%	9.6
100-150	72%	14.0
150-200	61%	17.4
200-250	53%	20.9

As the draft progresses, the picks for each player become more widely dispersed and less clustered around the average. Most top 100 players will go within one round of their ADP-converted round. However, as you reach the mid-to-late rounds, there is much more uncertainty as to when a player will be selected. Pitchers have slightly smaller standard deviations than do batters (i.e. they tend to be drafted in a narrower range). This suggests that drafters may be more likely to reach for a batter than for a pitcher.

Using the ADP and corresponding standard deviation, we can to estimate the likelihood that a given player will be available at a certain draft pick. We estimate the predicted standard deviation for each player as follows:

Stdev = -0.42 + 0.42*(ADP - Earliest Pick)

(That the figure 0.42 appears twice is pure coincidence; the numbers are not equal past two decimal points.)

If we assume that the picks are normally distributed, we can use a player's ADP and estimated standard deviation to estimate the likelihood that the player is available with a certain pick (MS Excel formula):

=1-normdist(x,ADP,Standard Deviation,True)
where «x» represents the pick number to be evaluated.

We can use this information to prepare for a snake draft by determining how early we may need to reach in order to roster a player. Suppose you had the 8th pick in a 15-team league draft and your target was a player with an ADP of 128.9 and an earliest selection at pick 94. This would yield an estimated standard deviation of 14.2. You could have then entered these values into the formula above to estimate the likelihood that this player was still available at each of the following picks:

Likelihood	
Pick	Available
83	100%
98	99%
113	87%
128	53%
143	16%
158	2%

ADPs and scarcity *(Bill Macey)*

Most players are selected within a round or two of their ADP with tight clustering around the average. But every draft is unique and every pick in the draft seemingly affects the ordering of subsequent picks. In fact, deviations from "expected" sequences can sometimes start a chain reaction at that position. This is most often seen in runs at scarce positions such as the closer; once the first one goes, the next seems sure to closely follow.

Research also suggests that within each position, there is a correlation within tiers of players. The sooner players within a generally accepted tier are selected, the sooner other players within the same tier will be taken. However, once that tier is exhausted, draft order reverts to normal.

How can we use this information? If you notice a reach pick, you can expect that other drafters may follow suit. If your draft plan is to get a similar player within that tier, you'll need to adjust your picks accordingly.

Mapping ADPs to auction value *(Bill Macey)*

Reliable average auction values (AAV) are often tougher to come by than ADP data for snake drafts. However, we can estimate predicted auction prices as a function of ADP, arriving at the following equation:

y = -9.8ln(x) + 57.8
where ln(x) is the natural log function, x represents the actual ADP, and y represents the predicted AAV.

This equation does an excellent job estimating auction prices (r2=0.93), though deviations are unavoidable. The asymptotic nature of the logarithmic function, however, causes the model to predict overly high prices for the top players. So be aware of that, and adjust.

Auction Value Analysis

Auction values (R$) in perspective

R$ is the dollar value placed on a player's statistical performance in a Rotisserie league, and designed to measure the impact that player has on the standings.

There are several methods to calculate a player's value from his projected (or actual) statistics.

One method is Standings Gain Points, described in the book, *How to Value Players for Rotisserie Baseball*, by Art McGee. SGP converts a player's statistics in each Rotisserie category into the number of points those stats will allow you to gain in the standings. These are then converted back into dollars.

Another popular method is the Percentage Valuation Method. In PVM, a least valuable, or replacement performance level is set for each category (in a given league size) and then values are calculated representing the incremental improvement from that base. A player is then awarded value in direct proportion to the level he contributes to each category.

As much as these methods serve to attach a firm number to projected performance, the winning bid for any player is still highly variable depending upon many factors:

- the salary cap limit
- the number of teams in the league
- each team's roster size
- the impact of any protected players
- each team's positional demands at the time of bidding
- the statistical category demands at the time of bidding
- external factors, e.g. media inflation or deflation of value

In other words, a $30 player is only a $30 player if someone in your draft pays $30 for him.

Roster slot valuation *(John Burnson)*

When you draft a player, what have you bought?

"You have bought the stats generated by this player."

No. You have bought the stats generated by his slot. Initially, the drafted player fills the slot, but he need not fill the slot for the season, and he need not contribute from Day One. If you trade the player during the season, then your bid on Draft Day paid for the stats of the original player plus the stats of the new player. If the player misses time due to injury or demotion, then you bought the stats of whoever fills the time while the drafted player is missing. At season's end, there will be more players providing positive value than there are roster slots.

Before the season, the number of players projected for positive value has to equal the total number of roster slots. However, the projected productivity should be adjusted by the potential to capture extra value in the slot. This is especially important for injury-rehab cases and late-season call-ups. For example, if we think that a player will miss half the season, then we would augment his projected stats with a half-year of stats from a replacement-level player at his position. Only then would we calculate prices. Essentially, we want to apportion $260 per team among the slots, not the players.

Average player value by draft round

Rd	AL/NL	Mxd
1	$34	$34
2	$26	$26
3	$23	$23
4	$20	$20
5	$18	$18
6	$17	$16
7	$16	$15
8	$15	$13
9	$13	$12
10	$12	$11
11	$11	$10
12	$10	$9
13	$9	$8
14	$8	$8
15	$7	$7
16	$6	$6
17	$5	$5
18	$4	$4
19	$3	$3
20	$2	$2
21	$1	$2
22	$1	$1
23	$1	$1

Benchmarks for auction players:

- All $30 players will go in the first round.
- All $20-plus players will go in the first four rounds.
- Double-digit value ends pretty much after Round 11.
- The $1 end game starts at about Round 21.

How likely is it that a $30 player will repeat? *(Matt Cederholm)*

From 2003-2008, there were 205 players who earned $30 or more (using single-league 5x5 values). Only 70 of them (34%) earned $30 or more in the next season.

In fact, the odds of repeating a $30 season aren't good. As seen below, the best odds during that period were 42%. And as we would expect, pitchers fare far worse than hitters.

	Total>$30	# Repeat	% Repeat
Hitters	167	64	38%
Pitchers	38	6	16%
Total	205	70	34%
High-Reliability*			
Hitters	42	16	38%
Pitchers	7	0	0%
Total	49	16	33%
100+ BPV			
Hitters	60	25	42%
Pitchers	31	6	19%
Total	91	31	19%
High-Reliability and 100+ BPV*			
Hitters	12	5	42%
Pitchers	6	0	0%
Total	18	5	28%

*Reliability figures are from 2006-2008

For players with multiple seasons of $30 or more, the numbers get better. Players with consecutive $30 seasons, 2003-2008:

	Total>$30	# Repeat	% Repeat
Two Years	62	29	55%
Three+ Years	29	19	66%

Still, a player with two consecutive seasons at $30 in value is barely a 50/50 proposition. And three consecutive seasons is only a 2/3 shot. Small sample sizes aside, this does illustrate the nature of the beast. Even the most consistent, reliable players fail 1/3 of the time. Of course, this is true whether they are kept or drafted anew, so this alone shouldn't prevent you from keeping a player.

Dollar values: expected projective accuracy
There is a 65% chance that a player projected for a certain dollar value will finish the season with a value within plus-or-minus $5 of that projection. Therefore, if you value a player at $25, you only have about a 2-in-3 shot of him finishing between $20 and $30.

If you want to raise your odds to 80%, the range becomes +/- $9, so your $25 player has to finish somewhere between $16 and $34.

Predicting player value from year 1 performance *(Patrick Davitt)*
Year-1 (Y1, first season >=100AB) batter results predict some—but not all—subsequent-year performance. About half of all Y1 players have positive value. Players with higher Y1 value were likelier to get playing time in subsequent seasons. Players with –$6 to –$10 in Y1 got more chances than players +$5 to –$5 and performed better. Batters with Y1 value of $16 or more are excellent bets to at least provide positive value in subsequent seasons, and those above $21 in Y1 value play in all subsequent seasons and return an average of $26. But even a $21 batter is only a 50-50 bet to do better in Y2.

How well do elite pitchers retain their value? *(Michael Weddell)*
An elite pitcher (one who earns at least $24 in a season) on average keeps 80% of his R$ value from year 1 to year 2. This compares to the baseline case of only 52%.

Historically, 36% of elite pitchers improve, returning a greater R$ in the second year than they did the first year. That is an impressive performance considering they already were at an elite level. 17% collapse, returning less than a third of their R$ in the second year. The remaining 47% experience a middling outcome, keeping more than a third but less than all of their R$ from one year to the next.

Valuing closers
Given the high risk associated with the closer's role, it is difficult to determine a fair draft value. Typically, those who have successfully held the role for several seasons will earn the highest draft price, but valuing less stable commodities is troublesome.

A rough rule of thumb is to start by paying $10 for the role alone. Any pitcher tagged the closer on draft day should merit at least $10. Those without a firm appointment may start at less than $10. Then add anywhere from $0 to $15 for support skills.

In this way, the top level talents will draw upwards of $20-$25. Those with moderate skill will draw $15-$20, and those with more questionable skill in the $10-$15 range.

Realistic expectations of $1 end-gamers *(Patrick Davitt)*
Many fantasy articles insist leagues are won or lost with $1 batters, because "that's where the profits are." But are they?

A 2011 analysis showed that when considering $1 players in deep leagues, managing $1 end-gamers should be more about minimizing losses than fishing for profit. In the cohort of batters projected $0 to -$5, 82% returned losses, based on a $1 bid. Two-thirds of the projected $1 cohort returned losses. In addition, when considering $1 players, speculate on speed.

Advanced Drafting Concepts

Stars & Scrubs v. Spread the Risk
Stars & Scrubs (S&S): A Rotisserie auction strategy in which a roster is anchored by a core of high priced stars and the remaining positions filled with low-cost players.

Spread the Risk (STR): An auction strategy in which available dollars are spread evenly among all roster slots.

Both approaches have benefits and risks. An experiment was conducted in 2004 whereby a league was stocked with four teams assembled as S&S, four as STR and four as a control group. Rosters were then frozen for the season.

The Stars & Scrubs teams won all three ratio categories. Those deep investments ensured stability in the categories that are typically most difficult to manage. On the batting side, however, S&S teams amassed the least amount of playing time, which in turn led to bottom-rung finishes in HRs, RBIs and Runs.

One of the arguments for the S&S approach is that it is easier to replace end-game losers (which, in turn, may help resolve the playing time issues). Not only is this true, but the results of this experiment show that replacing those bottom players is critical to success.

The Spread the Risk teams stockpiled playing time, which led to strong finishes in many counting stats, including clear victories in RBIs, wins and strikeouts. This is a key tenet in drafting philosophy; we often say that the team that compiles the most ABs will be among the top teams in RBI and Runs.

The danger is on the pitching side. More innings did yield more wins and Ks, but also destroyed ERA/WHIP.

So, what approach makes the most sense? **The optimal strategy might be to STR on offense and go S&S with your pitching staff.** STR buys more ABs, so you immediately position yourself well in four of the five batting categories. On pitching, it might be more advisable to roster a few core arms, though that immediately elevates your risk exposure. Admittedly, it's a balancing act, which is why we need to pay more attention to risk analysis.

The LIMA Plan
The LIMA Plan is a strategy for Rotisserie leagues (though the underlying concept can be used in other formats) that allows you to target high skills pitchers at very low cost, thereby freeing up dollars for offense. LIMA is an acronym for Low Investment Mound Aces, and also pays tribute to Jose Lima, a $1 pitcher whose 1998 breakout exemplified the power of the strategy. In a $260 league:

1. Budget a maximum of $60 for your pitching staff.
2. Allot no more than $30 of that budget for acquiring saves.
3. Ignore ERA. Draft only pitchers with:
   - Command ratio (K/BB) of 2.5 or better.
   - Strikeout rate of 7.0 or better.
   - Expected home run rate of 1.0 or less.
4. Draft as few innings as your league rules will allow. This is intended to manage risk. For some game formats, this should be a secondary consideration.
5. Maximize your batting slots. Spend $200 on batters who have:
   - Contact rate of at least 80%
   - Walk rate of at least 10%
   - PX or Spd level of at least 100

Spend no more than $29 for any player and try to keep the $1 picks to a minimum.

The goal is to ace the batting categories and carefully pick your pitching staff so that it will finish in the upper third in ERA, WHIP and saves (and Ks in 5x5), and an upside of perhaps 9th in wins. In a competitive league, that should be enough to win, and definitely enough to finish in the money. Worst case, you should have an excess of offense available that you can deal for pitching.

The strategy works because it better allocates resources. Fantasy leaguers who spend a lot for pitching are not only paying for expected performance, they are also paying for better defined roles—#1 and #2 rotation starters, ace closers, etc.—which are expected to translate into more IP, wins and saves. But roles are highly variable. A pitcher's role will usually come down to his skill and performance; if he doesn't perform, he'll lose the role.

The LIMA Plan says, let's invest in skill and let the roles fall where they may. In the long run, better skills should translate into more innings, wins and saves. And as it turns out, pitching skill costs less than pitching roles do.

In *snake draft leagues,* you may be able to delay drafting starting pitchers until Round 10. In *shallow mixed leagues,* the LIMA Plan may not be necessary; just focus on the support metrics. In *simulation leagues,* build your staff around those metrics.

Variations on the LIMA Plan

LIMA Extrema: Limit your total pitching budget to only $30, or less. This can be particularly effective in shallow leagues where LIMA-caliber starting pitcher free agents are plentiful during the season.

SANTANA Plan: Instead of spending $30 on saves, you spend it on a starting pitcher anchor. In 5x5 leagues, allocating those dollars to a high-end LIMA-caliber starting pitcher can work well as long as you pick the right anchor and can acquire saves during the season.

Total Control Drafting (TCD)

On Draft Day, we make every effort to control as many elements as possible. In reality, the players that end up on our teams are largely controlled by the other owners. Their bidding affects your ability to roster the players you want. In a snake draft, the other owners control your roster even more. We are really only able to get the players we want within the limitations set by others.

However, an optimal roster can be constructed from a fanalytic assessment of skill and risk combined with more assertive draft day demeanor.

Why this makes sense

1. Our obsession with projected player values is holding us back. If a player on your draft list is valued at $20 and you agonize when the bidding hits $23, odds are about two chances in three that he could really earn anywhere from $15 to $25. What this means is, in some cases, and within reason, you should just pay what it takes to get the players you want.

2. There is no such thing as a bargain. Most of us *don't* just pay what it takes because we are always on the lookout for players who go under value. But we really don't know which players will cost less than they will earn because prices are still driven by the draft table. The concept of "bargain" assumes that we even know what a player's true value is.

3. "Control" is there for the taking. Most owners are so focused on their own team that they really don't pay much attention to what you're doing. There are some exceptions, and bidding wars do happen, but in general, other owners will not provide that much resistance.

How it's done

1. Create your optimal draft pool.

2. Get those players.

Start by identifying which players will be draftable based on the LIMA or Mayberry criteria. Then, at the draft, focus solely on your roster. When it's your bid opener, toss a player you need at about 50%-75% of your projected value. Bid aggressively and just pay what you need to pay. Of course, don't spend $40 for a player with $25 market value, but it's okay to exceed your projected value within reason.

From a tactical perspective, mix up the caliber of openers. Drop out early on some bids to prevent other owners from catching on to you.

In the end, it's okay to pay a slight premium to make sure you get the players with the highest potential to provide a good return on your investment. It's no different than the premium you might pay for a player with position flexibility or to get the last valuable shortstop. With TCD, you're just spending those extra dollars up front to ensure you are rostering your targets. As a side benefit, TCD almost assures that you don't leave money on the table.

Mayberry Method

The Mayberry Method (MM) asserts that we really can't project player performance with the level of precision that advanced metrics and modeling systems would like us to believe.

MM is named after the fictional TV village where life was simpler. MM evaluates skill by embracing the imprecision of the forecasting process and projecting performance in broad strokes rather than with hard statistics.

MM reduces every player to a 7-character code. The format of the code is 5555 AAA, where the first four characters describe elements of a player's skill on a scale of 0 to 5. These skills are indexed to the league average so that players are evaluated within the context of the level of offense or pitching in a given year.

The three alpha characters are our reliability grades (Health, Experience and Consistency) on the standard A-to-F scale. The skills numerics are forward-looking; the alpha characters grade reliability based on past history.

Batting

The first character in the MM code measures a batter's power skills. It is assigned using the following table:

Power Index	MM
0 - 49	0
50 - 79	1
80 - 99	2
100 - 119	3
120 - 159	4
160+	5

The second character measures a batter's speed skills. RSpd takes our Statistically Scouted Speed metric (Spd) and adds the elements of opportunity and success rate, to construct the formula of RSpd = Spd x (SBO + SB%).

RSpd	MM
0 - 39	0
40 - 59	1
60 - 79	2
80 - 99	3
100 - 119	4
120+	5

The third character measures expected batting average.

xBA Index	MM
0-87	0
88-92	1
93-97	2
98-102	3
103-107	4
108+	5

The fourth character measures playing time.

Role	PA	MM
Potential full-timers	450+	5
Mid-timers	250-449	3
Fringe/bench	100-249	1
Non-factors	0-99	0

Pitching

The first character in the pitching MM code measures xERA, which captures a pitcher's overall ability and is a proxy for ERA, and even WHIP.

xERA Index	MM
0-80	0
81-90	1
91-100	2
101-110	3
111-120	4
121+	5

The second character measures strikeout ability.

K/9 Index	MM
0-76	0
77-88	1
89-100	2
101-112	3
113-124	4
125+	5

The third character measures saves potential.

Description	Saves est.	MM
No hope for saves; starting pitchers	0	0
Speculative closer	1-9	1
Closer in a pen with alternatives	10-24	2
Frontline closer with firm bullpen role	25+	3

The fourth character measures **playing time**.

Role	IP	MM
Potential #1-2 starters	180+	5
Potential #3-4 starters	130-179	3
#5 starters/swingmen	70-129	1
Relievers	0-69	0

Overall Mayberry Scores

The real value of Mayberry is to provide a skills profile on a player-by-player basis. I want to be able to see this...

Player A	4455 AAB
Player B	5245 BBD
Player C	5255 BAB
Player D	5155 BAF

...and make an objective, unbiased determination about these four players without being swayed by preconceived notions and baggage. But there is a calculation that provides a single, overall value for each player.

This is the calculation for the overall MM batting score:

MM Score =
(PX score + Spd score + xBA score + PA score)
x PA score

An overall MM pitching score is calculated as:

MM Score =
((xERA score x 2) + K/9 score + Saves score + IP score)
x (IP score + Saves score)

The highest score you can get for either is 100. That makes the result of the formula easy to assess.

Adding Reliability Grades to Mayberry *(Patrick Davitt)*

Research shows that players with higher reliability grades met their Mayberry targets more often than their lower-reliability counterparts. Players with all "D" or "F" reliability scores underperform Mayberry projections far more often. Those results can be reflected by multiplying a player's MM Score by each of three reliability bonuses or penalties:"

	Health	Experience	Consistency
A	x 1.10	x 1.10	x 1.10
B	x 1.05	x 1.05	x 1.05
C	x 1.00	x 1.00	x 1.00
D	x 0.90	x 0.95	x 0.95
F	x 0.80	x 0.90	x 0.90

Let's perform the overall calculations for Player A (4455 AAB), using these Reliability adjustments.

Player A: 4455 AAB
= (4+4+5+5) x 5
= 90 x 1.10 x 1.10 x 1.05
= 114.3

Portfolio3 Plan concepts

When it comes to profitability, all players are not created equal. Every player has a different role on your team by virtue of his skill set, dollar value/draft round, position and risk profile. When it comes to a strategy for how to approach a specific player, one size does not fit all.

We need some players to return fair value more than others. A $40/first round player going belly-up is going to hurt you far more than a $1/23rd round bust. End-gamers are easily replaceable.

We rely on some players for profit more than others. First-rounders do not provide the most profit potential; that comes from players further down the value rankings.

We can afford to weather more risk with some players than with others. Since high-priced early-rounders need to return at least fair value, we cannot afford to take on excessive risk. Our risk tolerance opens up with later-round/lower cost picks.

Players have different risk profiles based solely on what roster spot they are going to fill. Catchers are more injury prone. A closer's value is highly dependent on managerial decision. These types of players are high risk even if they have great skills. That needs to affect their draft price or draft round.

For some players, the promise of providing a scarce skill, or productivity at a scarce position, may trump risk. Not always, but sometimes. The determining factor is usually price.

Previously, we created a model that integrated these types of players into a roster planning tool, called the Portfolio3 Plan. However, over time, variables like baseball's changing statistical environment and the shifting MLB roster construction affected the utility of the model. The rigid player allocation framework of the tiers began to erode, and no fudging could retain the integrity of the model. So we have retired it. The Mayberry Method includes the relevant player evaluators that Portfolio3 used; you can rely on those to create your own roster plan that balances skill and risk.

Head-to-Head Leagues

Consistency in Head-to-Head leagues *(Dylan Hedges)*

Few things are as valuable to H2H league success as filling your roster with players who can produce a solid baseline of stats, week in and week out. In traditional leagues, while consistency is not as important—all we care about are aggregate numbers—filling your team with consistent players can make roster management easier.

Consistent batters have good plate discipline, walk rates and on base percentages. These are foundation skills. Those who add power to the mix are obviously more valuable, however, the ability to hit home runs consistently is rare.

Consistent pitchers demonstrate similar skills in each outing; if they also produce similar results, they are even more valuable.

We can track consistency but predicting it is difficult. Many fantasy leaguers try to predict a batter's hot or cold streaks, or individual pitcher starts, but that is typically a fool's errand. The best we can do is find players who demonstrate seasonal consistency; in-season, we must manage players and consistency tactically.

Building a consistent Head-to-Head team *(David Martin)*

Teams in head-to-head leagues need batters who are consistent. Focusing on certain metrics helps build consistency, which is the roster holy grail for H2H players. Our filters for such success are:

- Contact rate = minimum 80%
- xBA = minimum .280
- PX (or Spd) = minimum 120
- RC/G = minimum 5.00

Ratio insulation in Head-to-Head leagues *(David Martin)*

On a week-to-week basis, inequities are inherent in the head-to-head game. One way to eliminate your competitor's advantage in the pure numbers game is to build your team's pitching foundation around the ratio categories.

One should normally insulate at the end of a draft, once your hitters are in place. To obtain several ratio insulators, target pitchers that have:

- K-BB% greater than 19%
- K% greater than 20%
- xERA less than 3.30

While adopting this strategy may compromise wins, research has shown that wins come at a cost to ERA and WHIP. Roster space permitting, adding two to four insulators to your team will improve your team's weekly ERA and WHIP.

A Head-to-Head approach to the Mayberry Method *(David Martin)*

Though the Mayberry Method was designed for use in Rotisserie leagues, a skill set analysis about whether a player is head-to-head league material is built into each seven-digit Mayberry code. By "decoding" Mayberry and incorporating quality-consistency (QC) scores, one can assemble a team that has the characteristics of a successful H2H squad.

In reviewing the MM skills scores, we can correlate the power and contact skills as follows:

- PX > 4 or 5 = PX of 120 or higher
- xBA > 4 or 5 = xBA index of 103 or higher

Only full-time players will have an opportunity to produce the counting statistics required, so to create a top tier of players, we need to limit our search to those who earn a 5 for playing time. This top tier should be sorted by QC scores so that the more consistent players are ranked higher.

To create the second tier of players, lower the power index to 3, but keep all other skill requirements intact:

PWR	SPD	BA	PT	HLTH
3	N/A	4/5	5	A/B

The interplay between tiers is important; use Tier 2 in conjunction with Tier 1 and not simply after the top tier options are exhausted. For example, it might make sense to dip into Tier 2 if there is a player available with a higher QC score.

Additionally, while the H2H MM codes do not target players based on their speed skills, the second column of the MM codes contains this information. Though you are de-prioritizing the speed skill, you do not need to punt the steals category. You will typically find that the tiers nonetheless contain multiple players with a MM speed score of 3 or higher, so you can still be competitive in the steal category most weeks applying this approach.

Consistency in points leagues *(Bill Macey)*

Previous research has demonstrated that week-to-week statistical consistency is important for Rotisserie-based head-to-head play. But one can use the same foundation in points-based games. A study showed that not only do players with better skills post more overall points in this format, but that the format caters to consistent performances on a week-to-week basis, even after accounting for differences in total points scored and playing-time.

Therefore, when drafting your batters in points-based head-to-head leagues, ct% and bb% make excellent tiebreakers if you are having trouble deciding between two players with similarly projected point totals. Likewise, when rostering pitchers, favor those who tend not to give up home runs.

In-Season Roster Management

Rotisserie category management tips *(Todd Zola)*

1. Disregard whether you are near the top or the bottom of a category; focus instead on the gaps directly above and below your squad.
2. Prorate the difference in stats between teams.
3. ERA tends to move towards WHIP.
4. As the season progresses, the number of AB/IP do not preclude a gain/loss in the ratio categories.
5. An opponent's point lost is your point gained.
6. *Most important!* Come crunch time, forget value, forget names, and forget reputation. It's all about stats and where you are situated within each category.

Sitting stars and starting scrubs *(Ed DeCaria)*

In setting your pitching rotation, conventional wisdom suggests sticking with trusted stars despite difficult matchups. But does this hold up? And can you carefully start inferior pitchers against weaker opponents? Here are the ERAs posted by varying skilled pitchers facing a range of different strength offenses:

	OPPOSING OFFENSE (RC/G)				
Pitcher (ERA)	5.25+	5.00	4.25	4.00	<4.00
3.00-	3.46	3.04	3.04	2.50	2.20
3.50	3.98	3.94	3.44	3.17	2.87
4.00	4.72	4.57	3.96	3.66	3.24
4.50	5.37	4.92	4.47	4.07	3.66
5.00+	6.02	5.41	5.15	4.94	4.42

Recommendations:

1. Never start below replacement-level pitchers.
2. Always start elite pitchers.
3. Other than that, never say never or always.

Playing matchups can pay off when the difference in opposing offense is severe.

Two-start pitcher weeks *(Ed DeCaria)*

A two-start pitcher is a prized possession. But those starts can mean two DOMinant outings, two DISasters, or anything else in between, as shown by these results:

PQS Pair	% Weeks	ERA	WHIP	Win/Wk	K/Wk
DOM-DOM	20%	2.53	1.02	1.1	12.0
DOM-AVG	28%	3.60	1.25	0.8	9.2
AVG-AVG	14%	4.44	1.45	0.7	6.8
DOM-DIS	15%	5.24	1.48	0.6	7.9
AVG-DIS	17%	6.58	1.74	0.5	5.7
DIS-DIS	6%	8.85	2.07	0.3	5.0

Weeks that include even one DISaster start produce terrible results. Unfortunately, avoiding such disasters is much easier in hindsight. But what is the actual impact of this decision on the stat categories?

ERA and WHIP: When the difference between opponents is extreme, inferior pitchers can be a better percentage play. This is true both for 1-start pitchers and 2-start pitchers, and for choosing inferior one-start pitchers over superior two-start pitchers.

Strikeouts per Week: Unlike the two rate stats, there is a massive shift in the balance of power between one-start and two-start pitchers in the strikeout category. Even stars with easy one-start matchups can only barely keep pace with two-start replacement-level arms in strikeouts per week.

Wins per week are also dominated by the two-start pitchers. Even the very worst two-start pitchers will earn a half of a win on average, which is the same rate as the very best one-start pitchers.

The bottom line: If strikeouts and wins are the strategic priority, use as many two-start weeks as the rules allow, even if it means using a replacement-level pitcher with two tough starts instead of a mid-level arm with a single easy start. But if ERA and/or WHIP management are the priority, two-start pitchers can be very powerful, as a single week might impact the standings by over 1.5 points in ERA/WHIP, positively or negatively.

Top 12 trading tips *(Fred Zinkie)*

We all need to make trades to win our leagues. And while every negotiation is unique, here are some quick tips that should make anyone more effective on the trade market.

1. Learn how the other owner wishes to communicate. Some owners prefer email, others like the league website, some prefer a Twitter DM, and texting is often a desirable option. And there are even some who still want a phone call. The easy way to figure this out is to send your initial contact in multiple ways. Generally, the other owner's preferred method is the one they use to send their initial reply.

2. All negotiations start with an offer. Don't beat around the bush—give the other owner something concrete to work with. You can start with your best deal or merely a respectable proposal, but you should get the ball rolling with a firm offer.

3. Check your ego at the door. You should enter trade talks with low expectations and a willingness to accept a different point of view. The other owner is not necessarily wrong when they disagree with your opinions on player values or what makes sense for their roster.

4. Be willing to unbalance your roster. Owners who draft a balanced team and then only seek out deals that maintain that balance are going to miss out on buying opportunities. To improve your roster—especially during the first half—you should be willing to have stretches with weak hitting, poor starting pitching, or a lack of saves. The goal is to acquire value.

5. Proofread. Always take the extra minute to proofread your communication and ensure your thoughts are clear. Beyond looking for typos, be sure that all players mentioned are the ones you intend to mention. Keep your initial communication to a couple sentences.

6. Be prompt. Trading can be inconvenient, but an active trader makes time when the opportunity arises. Don't get yourself fired or abandon your children in search of the perfect trade, but in general, you should be willing to work around your competitor's schedule.

7. Send multiple offers. Submitting multiple offers lets the other owner pick the proposal they like best. If you don't want to take the time to send multiple offers, you can at least mention that you would be willing to trade Player X, Y, or Z to get your desired return.

8. Be clear about all the players who interest you on the other team. An easy way to start negotiations is to mention all players who interest you on the other team. Again, this gives some control to the other owner, who can now tell you which players are most available.

9. The message board is your last resort. Trade messages can make you appear desperate. This is especially true when trying to unload a certain player. Like a house that sits on the market, the asking price on your player tends to drop once a couple days have passed.

10. Look for owners who may be desperate. Because most owners seek to achieve roster balance, you can find value by helping those who have an immediate need. And you can always help since you are the rare owner willing to unbalance their roster to obtain value. Look at the standings, as owners who are low in a roto category are likely to trade away value in order to address their weakness.

11. Look for owners who have a surplus. On the opposite end of the spectrum, owners can be willing to make deals when they have a surplus of a position or skill. Targeting the owner who is running away with the steals category could get you SB at a reasonable price.

12. Have the guts to trade away overachievers. This is one of the hardest tips to put into practice, but experience tells us that most players who have surprising stretches return to normal at some point. If it sometimes seems too good to be true, it probably is.

Other Diamonds

The Universal Tenets of Fantasy Economics

- The marketplace is generally wrong, so we don't have to buy into anything it tells us.
- We don't need precisely accurate projections. All we need are projections accurate enough to tell us when the marketplace is wrong.

- The variance between market cost and real value (in dollars or draft rounds) is far more important than the accuracy of any player projection.
- The market cost of a veteran player is driven more by the certainty of past performance than the uncertainty of future potential.
- The market cost of a young player is driven more by the promise of future potential than the questionable validity of past performance.
- Your greatest competitive advantage is to leverage the variance between market cost and real value.

Cellar value
The dollar value at which a player cannot help but earn more than he costs. Always profit here.

Crickets
The sound heard when someone's opening draft bid on a player is also the only bid.

End-game wasteland
Home for players undraftable in the deepest of leagues, who stay in the free agent pool all year. It's the place where even crickets keep quiet when a name is called at the draft.

FAAB Forewarnings
1. Spend early and often.
2. Emptying your budget for one prime league-crosser is a tactic that should be reserved for the desperate.
3. If you chase two rabbits, you will lose them both.

The Hope Hypothesis
- Hope can keep you interested, but will have no effect on how a player performs.
- Hope is sometimes referred to as "wishcasting" and may sound more scientific, but really it's just plain old hope with a random number attached.
- In the end, hope has virtually no intrinsic value and you can't win with it alone.
- Yet, hope will cost you about $5 over market value at the draft table.

Professional Free Agent (PFA)
Player whose name will never come up on draft day but will always end up on a roster at some point during the season as an injury replacement.

Seasonal Assessment Standard
If you still have reason to be reading the boxscores during the last weekend of the season, then your year has to be considered a success.

The Three Cardinal Rules for Winners
If you cherish this hobby, you will live by them or die by them...
1. Revel in your success; fame is fleeting.
2. Exercise excruciating humility.
3. 100% of winnings must be spent on significant others.

Daily Fantasy Baseball

Daily Fantasy Sports (DFS) is an offshoot of traditional fantasy sports. Many of the same analytic methods that are integral to seasonal fantasy baseball are just as relevant for DFS.

General Format

1. The overwhelming majority of DFS contests are pay-for-play where the winners are compensated a percentage of their entry fee, in accordance with the rules of that game.

2. DFS baseball contests are generally based on a single day's slate of games, or a subset of the day's games (i.e., all afternoon games or all evening games)

3. Most DFS formats are points-based salary cap games.

Most Popular Contests

1. Cash Games: Three variants (50/50, Multipliers, and Head-to-Head) all pay out a flat prize to a portion of the entries.

2. GPP (Guaranteed prize pool) Tournaments: The overall winner earns the largest prize and prizes scale downward.

3. Survivor: A survivor contest is a multiple-slate format where a portion of the entries survives to play the following day. '

4. Qualifiers/Satellites: Tournaments where the prize(s) consist of entry tickets to a larger tournament.

DFS Analysis

1. Predicting single-day performance entails adjusting a baseline projection based on that day's match-up. This adjusted expectation is considered in context with a player's salary to determine his potential contributions relative to the other players.

2. Weighted on base average (wOBA) is a souped-up version of OBP, and is a favorite metric to help evaluate both hitters and pitchers. (For more useful DFS metrics, see next section)

3. Pitching: In DFS, innings and strikeouts are the two chief means of accruing points, so they need to be weighed heavily in pitching evaluation.

Tips for Players New to DFS

1. Start slow and be prepared to lose: While cogent analysis can increase your chances of winning, the variance associated with a single day's worth of outcomes doesn't assure success. Short-term losing streaks are inevitable, so start with low cost cash games before embarking on tournament play.

2. Minimize the number of sites you play: The DFS space is dominated by two sites but there are other options. At the beginning, stick to one or two. Once you're comfortable, consider expanding to others.

3. Bankroll management: The recommended means to manage your bankroll is to risk no more than 10% on a given day in cash games, or 2% in tournaments.

4. General Strategies

    A. Cash Games: Conventional wisdom preaches to be conservative in cash games. Upper level starting pitchers make excellent cash game options. For hitters, it's best to spread your choices among several teams. In general, you're looking for players with a high floor rather than a high ceiling.

    B: GPP Tournaments: In tournaments (with a larger number of entrants), a common ploy is to select a lesser priced, though risky, pitcher with a favorable match-up. It's also very common to overload—or stack—several batters from the same team, hoping that squad scores a bunch of runs.

5. Miscellaneous Tips

    A. Pay extra attention to games threatened by weather, as well as players who are not a lock to be in the lineup.

    B. Avoid playing head-to-head against strangers until you're comfortable and have enjoyed some success.

    C. Stay disciplined. The worst thing you can do is eat up your bankroll quickly by entering into tournaments.

    D. Most importantly, have fun. Obviously, you want to win, but hopefully you're also in it for the challenge of mastering the unique skills intrinsic to DFS.

Using BaseballHQ Tools in DFS

Here are some of the additional skill metrics to consider:

Cash Game Metrics

bb%: This simple indicator may receive only a quick glance when building lineups, but it is imperative in providing insight on a batter's underlying approach and plate discipline. Walks also equal points in all DFS scoring structures.

ct%: Another byproduct of good plate discipline, reflecting the percentage of balls put in play. Players with strong contact rates tend to provide a higher floor, and less chance of a negative score from a free swinger with a high strikeout rate.

xBA: Measures a hitter's BA by multiplying his contact rate by the chance that a ball in play falls for a hit. Hitters whose BA is far below their xBA may be "due" for some hits.

Tournament / GPP Metrics

PX / xPX: Home runs are the single greatest multi-point event. Using PX (power index) and xPX (expected power index) together can help identify underperformers who are due in the power category.

Choosing Pitchers in DFS

The criteria for choosing a pitcher(s) may be more narrow than for full-season league, but the skills focus should remain.

Major Considerations

• Overall skills. Look for the following minimums: BB% under 7%, K% over 24%, K-BB% over 17%, and max 1.2 hr/9.

• Home/Away. In 2021, MLB pitchers logged a 4.09 ERA, 8.3% BB%, 23.5% K% (15.6% K-BB%) at home; 4.46 ERA, 9.0% BB%, 22.7% K% (13.7% K-BB%) on the road.

• Is he pitching at Coors Field? (Even the best pitchers are a risky start there.)

Moderate Considerations

• Recent performance. Examine Ks and BBs over last 4-5 starts.

• Strength of opponent. Refer to opposing team's OPS for the season, as well as more recent performance.

Minor Considerations

• L/R issues. Does the pitcher/opponent have wide platoon splits?

• Park. Is the game at a hitter's/pitcher's/neutral park?

• Previous outings. Has he faced this team already this season? If so, how did he fare? (Skills; not just his ERA.)

You should be left with a tiered list of pitching options, ripe for comparing individual risk/reward level against their price point.

Ground ball, line drive, fly ball percentages (G/L/F): Rates, persistence, outcomes

by Patrick Davitt

Some years ago, BaseballHQ.com did studies on ground ball/line drive/flyball splits (G/L/F) and how they affected our assessments of hitters and pitchers. It's time to update that study, especially in light of changes in the approach to the game, which have put a premium on hitters' "launch angles" in pursuit of the more ballistic lofted trajectories that lead to extra-base hits.

This abstract will look at these aspects of G/L/F for batters:

- Game-wide G/L/F levels from 2017-21 for batters with at least 150 PA in the season
- Aggregated individual ranges over seasons within G/L/F categories.
- Correlations between batted-ball trajectories and on-field outcomes

The abstract further categorizes infield and outfield flyballs for batters with at least 150 PA in a season and pitchers with at least 50 Batters Faced (BF), using Statcast data acquired through baseball-savant.com, and using Statcast definitions of trajectories:

- Ground ball (GB): Less than 10 degrees
- Line drive (LD): 10-25 degrees
- Outfield flyball (OFB): 25-50 degrees
- Infield flyball (IFB): Greater than 50 degrees

The addition of separate OFB and IFB is a welcome advance. Treating FBs that head for the fences as being in any way congruent with FBs that barely get past the infield dirt seems ludicrous, especially when assessing players' HR/FB rates.

That said, there is no OFB/IFB distinction in some of the savant Statcast stats for pitchers, so when we discuss pitchers, we will usually be obliged to stay with the admittedly coarser G/L/F model.

Game-wide general rates

Batters

The first thing to update is the game-wide levels. We'll start with batters' G/L/F/[OFB/IFB] over time. In our earlier report, these rates were very stable, and Statcast says they still are stable:

Season	GB%	LD%	FB%	[OFB%	IFB%]
2017	46%	25%	29%	[22%	7%]
2018	45%	25%	30%	[23%	7%]
2019	43%	25%	31%	[24%	7%]
2020	43%	29%	28%	[21%	7%]
2021	43%	24%	33%	[26%	7%]
TOTAL	44%	25%	31%	[24%	7%]

The system detected a bit of a wobble in LD/FB in 2020, but that was a weird year in a lot of ways, with smaller sample sizes, elevated HR rates, and the transition to the Hawk-Eye measuring system from previous systems. Nonetheless, in general, the pattern was quite stable, as was the pattern of hit rates on the various trajectories (note that hit rates on OFB include HR, which passes through to the FB category):

Season	GBH%	LDH%	FBH%	[OFBH%	IFBH%]
2017	24%	63%	22%	[28%	2%]
2018	24%	62%	21%	[27%	2%]
2019	24%	63%	24%	[30%	2%]
2020	24%	66%	18%	[22%	3%]
2021	24%	64%	22%	[28%	2%]
TOTAL	24%	63%	22%	[28%	2%]

Pitchers

As we saw with the hitters, pitchers' trajectory rates were very stable in the earlier BHQ report, and stable they remain:

Season	GB%	LD%	FB%
2017	49%	27%	24%
2018	48%	27%	25%
2019	48%	27%	25%
2020	49%	30%	21%
2021	48%	25%	27%
TOTAL	48%	27%	25%

These rates are a few points higher on GB% and lower on FB% than the comparable stats for batters. This difference is likely due to how the pitchers were selected: the 50-BF requirement eliminated a lot of less-accomplished pitchers who would have been included in the batter data, and a big reason they're less accomplished is that their GB rates are lower.

Nonetheless, in general, the pattern itself was quite stable, as was the pattern of hit rates on the various trajectories (hit rates on FB include HR):

Season	GBH%	LDH%	FBH%
2017	24%	63%	22%
2018	24%	62%	21%
2019	24%	63%	24%
2020	23%	66%	18%
2021	24%	64%	22%
TOTAL	24%	63%	22%

These rates track the batters' h% rates very closely.

Persistence

Batters

The persistence or "stickiness" of trajectory rates for individual batters across multiple seasons was quite strong on GB% and FB%, but much less so in LD%:

Year-over-year correlation by batted-ball trajectory

Years	GB	LD	OFB	IFB
2017-18	0.73	0.25	0.71	0.62
2018-19	0.67	0.34	0.69	0.64

As a reminder, correlation rates run on a scale from -1 (perfect negative correlation: one variable rises, the other falls in perfect proportion), to +1 (variables rise together in perfect proportion); the closer the rate gets to zero, the less the two variables are connected.

Again, 2019-20 and 2020-21 weren't considered because of 2020's shorter samples and resulting higher variability within season. Except for LDs, the correlations YoY were strong, and can therefore be considered to be at least somewhat effective in a predictive model. A quick examination of the data tables shows that in a given year, changes in GB and/or FB tended to affect LD more than GB affected FB, or vice-versa. This stands to reason given that LD sits between the two in terms of launch angle. So a GB that ticks up a degree or two can become an LD, but can't become a FB. That means quite a few more LDs, creating slightly wider variance in that percentage, which could be reflected in the YoY correlation differences.

Pitchers

Using the adjacent-year pairs of 2017-18 and 2018-19, we found the persistence of trajectory rates for individual pitchers across multiple seasons was even more solid than with hitters, at least for GB% and FB%, with year-over-year (YoY) correlations of 0.70 and higher in both GB% and FB%. As with batters, however, the LD% correlations were medium-weak, at 0.30 and 0.24, respectively.

Connection to outcomes

Batters

Finally, the expectation that batted-ball *trajectories* are connected to (or, especially, predictive of) batted-ball *outcomes* was not especially well born out, as we see in this brief table of correlations between trajectory groups and Batting Average (BA) and Slugging Percentage (Slg):

Correlation	BA	Slg
GB%	0.08	-0.34
LD%	0.39	0.21
FB%	-0.30	0.23
OFB%	-0.21	0.30
IFB%	-0.30	-0.01

In this table, the LD correlation with BA is the strongest—BAs rise as LD rates rise, but with 60% of BA explained by other factors. This research didn't get into those other possible influential variables, but it seems obvious that hardness-of-hit (exit velocity) would be an important factor in both BA and Slg. The negative correlation between FB% and BA was expected, as past BHQ and other research has shown that while a medium- or soft-hit GB can "sneak through," a can o' corn flyball rarely does. Similarly, we would expect opposing correlations between GB% and FB% when it comes to Slg. Not too many GBs become extra-base hits.

Pitchers

The connection between batted-ball trajectories and relevant on-field outcomes for pitchers was even more muted than for hitters, as we see in this brief table summarizing correlations between trajectory groups versus ERA and WHIP:

Correlation	ERA	WHIP
GB%	-0.20	-0.03
LD%	0.22	0.20
FB%	0.10	-0.09

In this table, LD% are again weakly implicated with both ERA and WHIP, which we would probably expect, given that we know more LDs become hits. The weak correlation between GBs and ERA shows that as GBs increase, ERA decreases, probably an

artifact of fewer extra-base hits and sac-flies, but also because other factors bear on ERA more heavily, such as sequence of batted-ball events (homer-single-single is one run, single-single-homer is three). The other three correlations showed no notable connections to outcomes.

Conclusion

In sum, we can say that overall trajectory rates remained very consistent game-wide from 2017-21, at about 45/25/30 G/L/F (23 OFB/7 IFB) for hitters with 150+ PAs and 48/27/25 for pitchers above 50 BF, with more variation in the 2020 outlier season. Year-one GB and FB rates were strongly correlated with year-two rates for both hitters and pitchers, but LDs weren't. There were weak-to-no correlations between batted-ball trajectories and on-field outcomes for either hitters or pitchers.

Hitters' K% and BB% rates as leading indicators

by Patrick Davitt

Introduction

For quite some time, baseball analysts believed that we could use strikeout rates and walk rates to validate hitter performance measures like batting average (BA). The idea was that striking out less meant more balls in play, and even by luck, a few more hits that could raise a BA:

AB	K%	K	BIP	H%	H	BA
500	30%	150	350	30%	105	.210
500	20%	100	400	30%	120	.240
500	10%	50	450	30%	135	.270

The connection with walks, however, was more abstract and required imposing a narrative—an anathema these days in baseball research. The story was that a batter who drew a lot of walks was demonstrating "good patience" or "command of the zone," and was thereby able to "wait for a pitch he could drive" and drive it. But it doesn't take much expertise or imagination to formulate alternative stories: pitchers who couldn't find the plate, banjo hitter trying to "work a walk" because he wasn't otherwise likely to reach, ump with a tight zone... you get the idea.

To see how this conventional wisdom holds up, we ran a study to look briefly at:

- Strikeout rates (K% or K/PA) and walk rates (BB% or BB/PA) over the last five seasons.
- How K% relates somewhat to BA—and BB% doesn't.
- How both K% and BB% relate to isolated power (ISO, Slugging percentage minus BA).
- How a combined metric also relates to BA, but only because of one component.

Some of the research used data from 2000-21, and some only the last five seasons (2017-21). All references to batter data in the following discussion included batters with 150+ PA in a season to qualify for that season, and to be included in any aggregated results.

Discussion

The first factor to keep in mind is that both K% and BB% were extremely stable throughout all five seasons in the study, and therefore no season was affected by a significant swing in either metric.

An earlier research article at BaseballHQ.com had already stated that walk rate was pretty much completely divorced from BA, and that analysis hasn't changed. We looked at how well both BB% and K% correlate with BA in all seasons from 2000-21, looking at the overall and at seasons along the way:

Year	BB%	K%
All	0.01	-0.47
2000	0.14	-0.39
2007	0.00	-0.41
2014	-0.07	-0.53
2021	-0.06	-0.55

A correlation of zero literally means zero correlation, and that's what we see right down the line with walk rate: It doesn't matter to batting average. As we expected, though, strikeouts have quite solid negative correlations: as Ks go up, BA goes down, and vice versa.

But what of the batter with, say a high BB rate and a high K rate? Or vice versa? Or some other combination? We created a matrix chart that shows the average BA at all the intersections of BB% and K% from 2017-21. The BA values are too small to reproduce clearly, so the chart uses gradations of grey, with light grey at the bottom of the BA scale (.127) mid-grey in the middle (.245), and black at the top (.346):

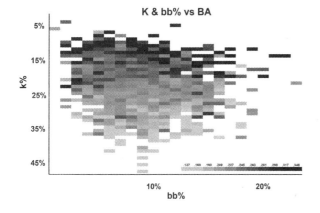

The darker band at the top of the chart indicates higher BAs at lower K% levels and across all walk rates, as expected. The lighter greys as we move down the chart show BA falling as Ks increase, again spread across the range of walk rates. And the bottom of the chart is full of low BAs at the highest K rates. Some of the shaded rectangles represent a single batter-season: way up in the top left, we see a strikeout rate of just 4%—and a walk rate of 2%! Plate command, indeed. But in 2019, Willians Astudillo of MIN

hung up a respectable .268 BA with those plate metrics. And way down there at bottom right, we have a batter with an 18% walk rate a 35% K rate— and batted .199. You don't win any prize for guessing that was Joey Gallo, in the year just completed.

Now you might think, "If Joey Gallo takes a ton of walks and mashes HRs by the bushel, could it be that walks actually correlate more to power than to average?" Excellent question, and the answer we see in this table of BB% and K% vs ISO correlations from 2000-21 is "Yes":

Year	BB%	K%
All	0.37	0.27
2000	0.31	0.27
2007	0.42	0.34
2014	0.25	0.22
2021	0.27	0.20

The table shows that walk rate is actually more potent than strikeouts in explaining power, although the distinction has declined over the last few seasons. This could be the result of strikeout rates climbing to 23% in 2021 from 17% in 2000, while walk rates have been pretty stable. Any ratio with Ks in the denominator is going to fall.

Finally, since K-BB% is a simple and reliable yardstick for pitchers, we tested its inverse, BB-K%, as an explanation for BA and ISO for 2000-21 and every seventh year:

Year	BA	ISO
All	0.45	-0.08
2000	0.44	-0.05
2007	0.40	-0.10
2014	0.47	-0.10
2021	0.50	-0.07

The BB-K% correlations to BA are quite strong, but this seems due to the strong correlation with K% alone, and indeed including BB% has actually made the correlations mostly worse—as we'd expect given the very weak or completely absent correlations of BB% to BA. On ISO, the correlations are just very weak to almost non-existent, even though we saw the two metrics separately correlate pretty well. Apparently batters who strike out a lot or walk a lot hit for power, but hitters who strike out a lot and walk a lot don't! Joey Gallo notwithstanding.

Conclusion

In sum, this small research study reinforces what we learned at BaseballHQ those many years ago: walk rates don't figure into BA, but they do figure into power, while strikeout rates matter quite a lot to power and somewhat to BA. Also, BB-K% rate explains about one-fifth of BA differences, albeit with a significant margin of error. If you need to shore up BA at your draft or in-season, and the choice is between a low-K hitter and a high-bb hitter, grab the contact guy.

Hard-hit fly balls as a skill

by Arik Florimonte

Introduction

In the batter boxes of this book, we have metrics for line drive rate (LD%), fly ball rate (FB%), hard contact (HctX), and xPX (which relies on hard-hit line drives and hard-hit fly balls). Sometimes, the metrics paint a conflicting story. A batter could have above-average hard contact, an above-average fly ball rate, and line drives that are just fine, but their xPX is below 100. Or, the opposite could be true. One might assume they are a candidate for regression. Let's test that hypothesis.

Methodology

Using data from full batter seasons from 2002-2020, we include only batters with 100 or more batted balls (BaB) in a season. In addition, since we'll be examining year-to-year changes, we'll also filter out any batter who didn't achieve 100 or more BaB the following season. Using xPX as our governing metric, we'll check what happens to xPX over- and under-achievers.

"Expected" Expected Power

Recall the formula for xPX:

$$xPX = 2.6 + 269 \cdot HHLD\% + 724 \cdot HHFB\%$$

Now we define a prospective "expected" version of this, which for lack of creativity we'll call xxPX:

$$xxPX = 2.6 + 269 \cdot xHHLD\% + 724 \cdot xHHFB\%$$

And the new terms will be defined thus:

$$xHHLD\% \equiv Hard\% \cdot LD\%$$

$$xHHFB\% \equiv Hard\% \cdot FB\%$$

Now, let's look at the resulting scatter plot, xPX vs. xxPX:

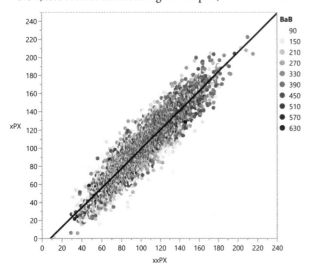

In this chart, the fit is weighted by total number BaB, with the darker points indicating a larger number of batted balls. The equation of fit is:

$$xPX = 3.8 + 1.08 \cdot xxPX$$

The R^2 value is very good at 0.84. Note that the slope is greater than one, which suggests that good hitters can fuse hard contact

with fly balls and liners more often than if it were purely luck. We'll dig in further, moving ahead with our new, clumsily named metric in hand.

Hard-Hit Fly Balls as a skill

Batters' fly ball rates have good correlation year to year. Hard-hit rates also have good correlation year to year. We understand this to mean that each of these is a skill, since good players generally manage to repeat it, while poor hitters generally fail to do it year after year. Each batter has a "true" skill level that is gradually revealed over a large sample of batted balls.

Our hypothesis is that a hard-hit fly ball (HHFB) is simply a happy coincidence of two skills, a hard hit ball happening to occur at the same time as a fly ball. If this is true, then "xxPX" will be an improvement. If not, then we should stop expecting HHFB to regress.

First, let's look at which is better correlated to next year's xPX:

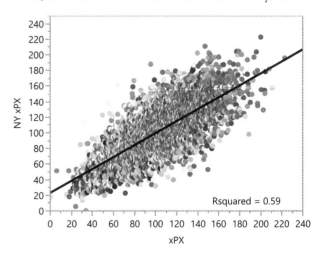

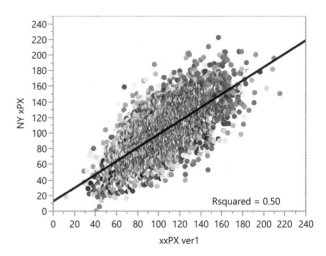

In both graphs, the points are weighted by the geometric mean of the number of batted balls across two years. Darker points are weighted more heavily.

Though similar, this set of graphs reveals that xPX actually is better than xxPX as a predictor of next year's xPX. About 18% better in fact.

Next, let's look at batters whose xxPX varied significantly from their xPX, and see what happened the next season. We'll tabulate xPX-xxPX for each season (min. 100 BaB), and then divide it into 5 quantiles.

xPX-xxPX Quantile	Mean xPX	Mean xxPX	xPX -xxPX	Mean NY xPX	Mean NY xxPX	NY xPX Chg	NY xPX -xxPX	NY xPX Inc. 10+
0-19	77	96	-19	87	96	+10	-9	44%
20-39	93	101	-8	96	101	+3	-5	36%
40-59	103	104	-1	103	105	0	-2	32%
60-79	111	106	+5	108	107	-4	+1	25%
80-99	126	109	+17	116	109	-10	+7	17%

NY= "Next Year"
NY xPX Inc. 10+ = Percent of hitters who saw xPX increase by 10+ pts the following year (overall average 36%)

From this table, we can see that those whose xPX deviated most from xxPX tend to give back about half of that difference the following year. But, they do keep some of those trends, which is consistent with the early implication: some batters are better at finding that sweet spot.

Conclusions

What we have learned is that while the ability to hit the ball hard is good, and the ability to hit fly balls and line drives is also good, the ability to do both at once is a skill in itself. Batters whose xPX exceeds xxPX—what we might expect given HctX and FB%—manage to preserve nearly half of that advantage.

When evaluating batters whose xPX seems out of line with hard hit rate and FB% or LD%, we should expect some regression, and the real talent level probably lies somewhere in the middle.

Home field advantage and Wins

by Ed DeCaria

Starting pitchers have been earning fewer and fewer Wins in recent years. The percent of games started in which the SP earns a Win consistently hovered at about 35% from 2002-2014 before turning downward by an average of 1% per year from 2015-2021, to the point that the average SP won only 28% of their starts in 2021:

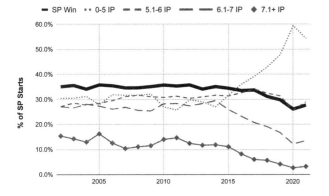

This drop in SP Wins coincided with a steep drop in innings pitched by the game's starter, as shown by both the skyrocketing increase in games in which the starter pitches <=5 IP (inflated by the "Opener" trend) and a steep drop in games in which the starter pitches into the 7th inning (6.1-7 IP) or further (7.1+ IP).

Earning a Win, of course, requires the SP to pitch at least 5 full IP, but that itself is rarely enough. To really increase their chances, a starter typically has to pitch deeper into the game:

Win % by Starter IP (2015-2021)

Starter IP	Starter Win %	% of Starts
0-5	10.8%	43.0%
5.1-6	38.3%	31.5%
6.1-7	53.5%	19.4%
7.1-8	64.7%	4.8%
8.1+	90.9%	1.3%
All	31.4%	100.0%

Most starters who even semi-regularly pitch into the seventh inning are premium arms, or otherwise 100% rostered. But in leagues where the most Win-worthy pitchers are gone, another way to pick up extra Wins is by looking in the right places.

Specifically, pitchers starting at home are 7% more likely to earn a Win than when they start on the road. This extra Win potential comes from two sources: 1) home SPs tend to go deeper than away SPs, and 2) even when home SPs only last 5-6 IP, they are more likely to get the Win:

Start % and Win % by Starter IP, Home vs. Away (2015-2021)

Starter IP	%/Home Starts	%/Away Starts	H/A Index	Home Win%	Away Win%	H/A Index
0-5	40.2%	45.8%	88	10.9%	10.8%	101
5.1-6	31.8%	31.2%	102	38.9%	37.6%	103
6.1-7	21.3%	17.5%	122	52.4%	54.8%	96
7.1-8	5.2%	4.4%	119	62.2%	67.7%	92
8.1+	1.5%	1.2%	124	90.0%	91.9%	98
All	32.9%	32.9%	100	32.5%	30.3%	107

Only a very small part of this advantage seems due to whether or not there is a DH present (home starters being able to complete one more inning before being removed for a pinch hitter), so we would expect this home field Win advantage to stick even if MLB moves to a universal DH in the future.

Practically-speaking, for a typical fantasy team, maybe 2-3 of their pitcher slots for a given week are flexible/streamable (vs. relievers or locked-in starters). This equates to about 65 sit/start decisions per year in which home field advantage might be a realistic consideration. Choosing a home starter every time would equate to 65 * (32.5% - 30.3%) = +1.4 Wins. Not a huge seasonal boost, but still something to think about when setting one's lineup each week.

QBaB over short samples—Exit Velocity

by Arik Florimonte

Introduction

In the *2021 Baseball Forecaster*, we introduced QBaB (Quality of Batted Balls), a score comprised of three letter grades, one each to rate a batter's Exit Velocity, mean Launch Angle, and Launch Angle Variation (standard deviation of Launch Angle). A summary of the research can be found on page 29.

QBaB scores are well-correlated with positive outcomes, they don't change much from season to season, and batters whose results exceed or fall short of their QBaB tend to regress strongly toward the mean that is consistent with their score. In this article, we focus on the Exit Velocity (EV) score to find out what QBaB can tell us in-season.

Methodology

We use data from 2015-2020, then exclude player-seasons with fewer than 100 batted balls. Using the next 25 batted balls as a test, we evaluate hitters who are hot or cold over a recent sample between 1 and 100 batted balls. But first, a caveat about distributions and sample size…

The original study on QBaB scores was based on full-season distributions of player-seasons of more than 100 batted balls. As the sample size shrinks, the distribution of outcomes widens, which for us means that the smaller the sample gets, the more common As and Fs will become, and the more unusual Bs, Cs, and Ds will be. Just how rare? Here is how the distribution of Exit Velocity scores changes with sample size:

EV Score	Baseline	Sample Size						
		100	75	50	25	10	5	1
A	10%	17%	18%	20%	24%	32%	37%	48%
B	20%	22%	21%	20%	17%	13%	10%	5%
C	40%	39%	38%	35%	30%	22%	16%	7%
D	20%	17%	18%	18%	18%	16%	13%	5%
F	10%	4%	5%	7%	11%	18%	24%	36%

Over a full season, an average EV of 90.81 earns an A score. But nearly half the individual batted balls exceed that EV. Still, that's okay, we just need to recalibrate mentally.

Average Hitters on Hot and Cold Streaks

First, we'll examine hitters who were average for exit velocity over the last 100 batted balls, i.e., they are in the C group. Then we'll look at input samples of varying sizes and evaluate what the batter did over the subsequent sample of 25 batted balls. That's roughly 1-2 weeks for most players; just the kind of look ahead we'd like when making weekly roster decisions.

First, we need to establish a baseline: what grade for EV does an average hitter—a C hitter—produce in the next 25 batted balls?

QBaB-EV for next 25 Batted Balls – Baseline

A	B	C	D	F
18.3%	18.1%	34.1%	20.2%	9.1%

How do those outcomes change if the hitter is coming off a hot streak? We studied those distributions and found that a hot streak does indicate better exit velocity to come. The chances of ending up with an A over the next 25 batted balls increases as the body of good work increases in duration. The trend is easy to see

graphically. Note the y-axis is a percentage of the starting rate, not a change in percentage points:

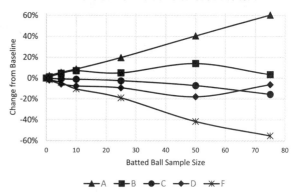

100 BaB are C; Last *n* batted balls are an A
Next 25 BaB relative to baseline is...

The converse is also true:

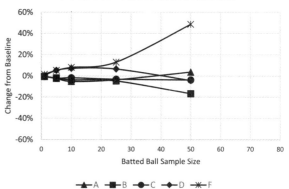

100 BaB are C; Last *n* batted balls are an F
Next 25 BaB relative to baseline is...

Even a few batted balls are enough to move the needle, but the more we have, the better the chances. As beget As. Fs beget Fs.

Single Batted Ball, Revisited

Recall that 48% of individual batted balls would earn an A score using the full-season bin thresholds, and that's what we used above. But what if we instead let's look for a single batted ball that is in the upper 10% of all single batted ball velocities, i.e. ≥ 103.9 mph? Again, filtering only hitters who would earn a C over their last 100 batted balls:

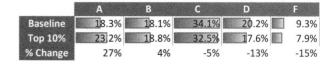

	A	B	C	D	F
Baseline	18.3%	18.1%	34.1%	20.2%	9.3%
Top 10%	23.2%	18.8%	32.5%	17.6%	7.9%
% Change	27%	4%	-5%	-13%	-15%

Extraordinary! Two batters with a C grade over 100 batted balls earns them a C grade. One launched his 100th batted ball at 104+ mph, the other didn't. The former is 27% more likely to earn an A grade over the next 25 balls than the latter.

Which Hitters Should You Start?

We've focused on differentiating better options among average hitters. But what if you have a slumping star or a scrub who's been crushing the ball for a week? To answer that, here are the odds that a batter posts an A in the coming 25 batted balls, based on the grade they earned in their last 100 and last 25.

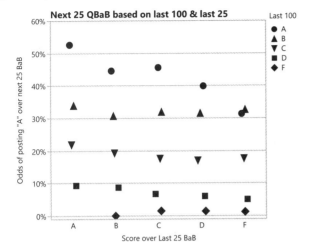

It's clear that you will always want to keep a great hitter in the lineup, and the worst hitters hopefully won't be anywhere near your team. But if you must choose among similar hitters, the one coming off a hot week is a better bet.

Conclusions

Using batted balls from 2015-2020, we determined how quickly QBaB scores for Exit Velocity became meaningful. When looking at upcoming 25-BaB samples, we found in general that there is validity in the intuitive idea that recent results can be a sign of results to come.

Specifically:

- Over any sample size, a QBaB "A" for Exit Velocity is correlated with improved QBaB scores over the next 25 batted balls (1-2 weeks), and "F" scores portended worse results.

- The magnitude of the differences in outcomes changes steadily and dramatically as sample size increases, even when controlled for hitter quality by limiting to batters in the middle 40%.

- The most recent 25 batted balls should move expectations up (or down) for batters within the 100-BaB tiers, but not elevate them above (or drop them below) hitters in the next tier.

- A single batted ball in the top 10% of all batted balls is a surprisingly good indicator of upcoming exit velocity goodness.

As you make roster decisions throughout the year, be sure to check in on the rolling 100- and 25- batted ball exit velocity trends.

A New framework for FAAB bidding

by Ed DeCaria

Great fantasy managers are constantly looking to improve their teams in-season through Free Agent Acquisition Budget (FAAB) pickups. Deciding who to add, who to hold, and who to drop each week is a core part of fantasy strategy. But within that strategic world of who and when—and the why behind each—there's another fundamental question that seems to frustrate just about every fantasy manager on the planet, including us experts, and that is simply: How much?

How much is a player "worth" in FAAB? How much is he going to go for? How much should you bid if you want to make sure you get him, or if you're less desperate how much should you bid otherwise? The simple truth is that most fantasy managers are massively overpaying for every free agent they pick up.

Taking a random sample of 100 National Fantasy Baseball Championship (NFBC) FAAB player-weeks—representing 14,075 total pickups and $475,890 in FAAB spent—the average "overbid" was 120%, where overbid is calculated as the winning bid divided by the bid required to win (e.g., backup bid + $1). To be opinionated about it, we'll call the overbid amount "Wasted FAAB".

To put 120% Wasted FAAB in context, imagine that instead of spending all $1000 of your FAAB—we're using the NFBC's $1000 annual budget with weekly transactions and $1 minimum bids in this analysis—you could have only spent $455, and have $545 left to spend. An extra $545 in 2021 would have bought you Alek Manoah on May 30. Or Eloy Jiménez on July 11. Or any number of newly anointed closers. Or maybe all of the above.

It's pretty easy to tap into this well of extra FAAB. Just take whatever amount you were planning to bid (however high, and however you arrived at that number) and cut it in half—on average, you will still win your target player 70% of the time.

Okay, perhaps "take whatever amount you were planning to bid and cut it in half" isn't the most precise advice. In our sample, the higher the bid, the less the average overbid:

Bid Range	Wasted FAAB %	Win% if bid reduced by Wasted %
$200+	102%	47%
$100-199	98%	51%
$50-99	112%	54%
$10-49	151%	67%
$2-9	154%	82%

Not comfortable with those ~50% win percentages at the $50+ bid levels? Rather than cutting your bids in half, cut them by one-third instead. Then your Win% jumps right back up to 70%, and you still save a ton of FAAB for future bids.

You might ask, though: What's the point of "reducing" whatever you were going to bid by half or one-third if you're not sure what you were bidding in the first place?

It's time to explore a new, more systematic way of thinking about FAAB bids. We will attempt to consolidate the many haphazard thoughts that spin around fantasy managers' heads on Sunday evenings and systematize them into a framework that generates well-reasoned bid suggestions based on the array of facts, assumptions, and opinions in play.

Our new framework has four major components:

1. **Bid context:** How much money is out there to be spent and over what range of time?
2. **Player caliber:** Is the player really worth spending money on in the first place?
3. **Competitor interest:** How likely are others in the league to bid on the player?
4. **Personal need:** How badly do you need or want the player?

We go through these in stepwise fashion below, describing all of the inputs that we will use to generate a suggested league-specific FAAB bid for any player for any week. Come March 2022 on BaseballHQ.com, we'll release a downloadable Excel model that you can use to calculate your own FAAB bids all season long.

Bid Context

The first thing we need to understand is how much money is really in play and how much of it could/should be expected to be spent in the current week. Here's how we do it:

1. Start with the total number of teams in the league and the total FAAB dollars remaining across all teams.
2. Next, look for abandoned teams (those who haven't made a FAAB bid in 6 weeks, or who have not made any transaction (e.g., start/sit) in 4 weeks) and subtract their FAAB from the available total. What remains is what we'll call "Active FAAB".
3. Divide the total Active FAAB by the total number of active teams to arrive at the Average Active FAAB remaining per (active) team.
4. Determine the percentage of FAAB that owners are willing to spend this period. Some fantasy managers like to spread their FAAB evenly over the season, some frontload their spending somewhat but keep plenty in reserve, and some are willing to spend it all in any given week. We'll call these the conservative strategy, the assertive strategy, and the aggressive strategy, respectively. Within a league, strategy can differ from manager to manager, and can differ for a given manager over the course of the season (e.g., start conservative, then get aggressive in mid-May). But for simplicity, just estimate the overall FAAB environment for the league.
5. Calculate this week's FAAB spending target by multiplying the average total active FAAB remaining per team by the percentage of FAAB in play.

Player Caliber

Unlike draft season, when we can easily value all players relative to their full-season projected statistics, valuation for FAAB purposes isn't quite that simple because the player pool in a given week is completely dynamic. To approximate what a player might be worth in the vacuum that is this week's FAAB run, we need to get creative. We'll instead ask these five simple questions about the player, and use the answers to calibrate any player's potential FAAB value:

- *What is the player's current % owned entering this FAAB period?* This measures how established the player is. To answer, look up the player's % owned in similar leagues such as on NFBC, Yahoo, or other services.

- *In what round would the player be taken if you did a full snake draft today?* This measures how talented the player is. No need to get overly precise, just a guess as to whether you think this is a Round 1-4 kind of player vs. a Round 5-8, Round 9-12, Round 13-16, Round 17-23, or a Reserve kind of player.

- *How many comparable players are available?* This measures how unique the player is. Don't just pick a number; think specifically about who else out there is similar to the player in which you're interested.

- *How much playing time is the player expected to get?* This measures how much opportunity the player has. This should be relative to what a "full time equivalent" player at their position would get. You can find specific percentages for each player on BaseballHQ.com's team-level playing time charts.

- *How old is the player?* This is a rough proxy for how much upside the player has. You can find player age here in theis book as well as on BaseballHQ.com PlayerLink pages.

Put all those together and what you get is that the more established, talented, and unique the player is, and the more opportunity and upside he has, the higher his baseline FAAB value.

Competitor Interest

Generating a baseline player value is a good start, but we can (and must) do even better by taking into account some competitive dynamics, which can serve to either depress our suggested bid further or increase it. This is highly subjective, but the big questions we want to answer here are:

- *How many other teams in the league do we expect to bid?* Ideally, you could go through each active competitor's team and decide who is likely to bid or not. Or as a shortcut, just guess. We bucket it into 0 or 1, 2-3, 4-5, or 6+ other bidders.

- *Among those expected to bid, what is their most likely reason for trying to acquire the player?* We break this up into four classifications:
  1. The player is likely seen as an *imminent upgrade* over an existing player at the same position
  2. The player will likely be *in the mix* to be used from week to week
  3. The player will be *stashed* for later
  4. The player will be used for one week and then *flipped*

- *What is the active "hammer" bid, and how much will it impact the bidding?* The "hammer" is the highest re-maining FAAB amount of any active team. Its impact depends on the quality of the player and the other competitive dynamics.

We use the first two to represent "Bid competitiveness."

We then combine that bid competitiveness score with the player caliber score (giving extra weight to the number of competitors and player talent components of each) to determine the "hammer impact" on our bid. For most players, this will be a very small value, but not necessarily zero, as the presence of a big active FAAB budget can still serve to inflate prices a bit.

From all of these components, we can then generate a player's "Likely FAAB cost." While this is impossible to perfectly, empirically calibrate, it is designed to give fantasy managers a high (50%+) chance of placing the winning bid for that player in that week in that league.

Personal Need

Finally, there is one more fact, and one more completely subjective factor, that cannot be ignored. How much FAAB money do you have remaining, and how badly do you need the player?

For the former, we divide our FAAB amount by the league spending target to get a multiplier (which could be greater than or less than 1). So if you have less than average FAAB to spend, you would reduce your bids accordingly; and if you have more than average FAAB to spend, you would increase them accordingly.

For the latter, we apply a simple multiplier based on the following need scale:

- I'm desperate: 2.0x
- Really want him: 1.5x
- Same as anyone: 1.0x
- Slight preference: 0.75x
- Just a guy: 0.5x

This multiplier still gives fantasy managers "the final say" in how much you ultimately bid, but as with every other input, frames things in a systematic way to keep your emotions from overly impacting your bids.

Putting it all together

With this framework, you can stop agonizing—okay, agonize less—over what to bid on the players you want. Instead, methodically work through the facts along with your assumptions and opinions, and then make your bids with this new data-driven guidance in mind.

This should help you save money each week so you'll have the ability to improve your team all season long, including making competitive but smart bids on the biggest difference-makers when the opportunity arises.

More to come on this topic in 2022 on BaseballHQ.com.

A Contrarian roster strategy

by Bob Berger

Many roster construction strategies advocate building a balanced roster between pitching and hitting. There are exceptions, such as punting saves or steals, but these strategies have extreme risk embedded in them, as a team that gets one point (last place) in a category has little room for error in the others. A contrarian roster construction strategy builds a roster focused on either hitting or pitching, but without punting any categories.

The example in this abstract uses a 12-team, 50-round draft-and-hold format with standard 5x5 scoring from the National Fantasy Baseball Championship (NFBC), but it can be adapted to other formats. There are 23 active roster slots (14 hitters and 9 pitchers) and no free agent pickups, so managers lock their rosters all season with the 50 players acquired during the draft.

The strategy can be implemented with either a hitting-focused approach with the goal of getting 90% of the hitting points; or with a pitching-focused team with the goal of getting 90% of the pitching points. A secondary goal is to draft a team that will be at least competitive in all categories of the non-focus area—in other words, no punting of any categories.

League results from 2019 were used to select 30 leagues at random to estimate how many points are typically needed to finish first or second ("in the money" in a 12-team NFBC league). In the random sample:

- A median of 94.0 total points (out of a possible 120) were needed to win a league
- A median of 87.5 points were needed to finish in second.

With the overall point target set at 94 (based on the median of first-place teams), 90% of the hitting or pitching points in a 12-team league would be 54 points. A team that finishes second (or an average of second) in all five hitting or pitching categories would collect 55 points, so to finish with 94 points, the de-emphasized half of the team would need to get 40 points (i.e. an average finish of fifth) in the other categories. To execute this strategy successfully, a team does not have to win all of the emphasized hitting or pitching categories. An average of second place is sufficient.

Also in the 30-team sample:

- 15 first-place teams collected more hitting than pitching points.
- 13 teams had more pitching than hitting points.
- Two teams had equal hitting and pitching points.

This suggests that teams can win these leagues with a variety of roster construction strategies.

The 94-point target breakdown (54 points for the focus area; 40 points for the remaining categories) means we plan to construct a roster with 14 more points in either the hitting or pitching categories than in the opposite category. In our sample, four first-place teams had 14 or more points from hitting than pitching and two had 14 or more points from pitching than hitting, showing that

either a hitting-focused or a pitching-focused strategy can be successful.

We looked at which individual categories were the lowest scoring for the winning teams to check for any important patterns:

Lowest Category Finish For Each 1st Place Team

R	HR	RBI	SB	BA	Hitting Total
0	3	4	5	5	17
K	W	Sv	ERA	WHIP	Pitching Total
3	2	10	3	3	21

Note: The total (38) is more than 30 because some teams had more than one category tied for their lowest finish.

Nine of the 10 scoring categories were represented among the lowest-scoring categories. The one outlier was Saves, which appeared 10 times among the 30 teams as their lowest category. Contrary to intuition, the 10 teams that had Saves as their lowest category were equally split between the hitting-focused and pitching-focused teams. This implies that Saves was the least important category in both strategies.

We'll next look at how many points each of the lowest scoring categories captured.

Lowest Number of Points for Lowest Category

1pt	2pt	3pt	4pt	5pt	6pt	7pt	8pt	9pt	10pt	11pt	12pt
1	2	5	5	7	7	2	0	0	1	0	0

Only one first-place team finished last in any category in the 30-league sample, providing evidence that punting a category while fielding a championship team is an unlikely outcome. Seventeen of the 30 teams had a low-category finish of 5 points or higher (at least 8th place or better in a 12-team league) in their worst category. This implies team construction should not be too extreme between hitting and pitching.

Let's look at how the six first-place teams in the sample with the biggest gap between hitting and pitching points drafted their hitters and pitchers. How many hitters were drafted in the first 10 picks? The first 15?

- The four teams whose results leaned most heavily towards hitting drafted either six or seven hitters in the first 10 picks. Each drafted nine or 10 hitters among the first 15 picks.
- The two teams whose results tilted most heavily towards pitching drafted six and four pitchers in the first 10 rounds, and six and seven pitchers in the first 15.

The contrarian strategy calls for drafting (in terms of when to draft hitters or pitchers) hitting-focused or pitching-focused teams as aggressively as these teams did.

In summary, our contrarian strategy is to target capturing 90% of the points available from either the pitching or hitting categories. Additionally, the strategy calls for finishing an average of fifth in the less-emphasized categories, and not punting any category. To execute the strategy, a team must draft hitters (7-8 in the first 10 rounds, or 10-11 in the first 15 rounds) or pitchers (5-6 in the first 10 rounds, or 7-8 in the first 15 rounds) more aggressively than their competitors.

The Benefits of multiple-position eligibility

by Todd Zola

There was a time when rostering a player or two with multiple position eligibility was a luxury. With the current inventory, it's a necessity. Using the rulebook designation requiring 20 games at the spot the previous year, approximately 15% of the draft-worthy pool in any given league size and format will be multiple-eligibility players. Further, assuming an in-season five-game requirement to add more positions, by midseason, at least 30% and up to half of those occupying active roster spots can be moved to another position.

The stats generated by the players themselves aren't worth any more than anyone else. However, the flexibility they provide adds stats to your roster, so it makes sense to pay a premium for the roster maneuverability.

To maximize the profit, it's best to have an eligibility circle such that every position is covered. One way to do this so there's ample mobility is with five players forming a circle. An example is 1BOF-OF3B-3BSS-SS2B-2B1B. Another is 3B2B-2BSS-SSOF-OF1B-1B3B. Note: both begin and end with the same position, closing the circle. A player eligible at three spots could reduce the number needed to four.

There are two benefits to multiple eligibility players. The first is during the draft, especially if you've filled your utility spot. Flexibility keeps more options in play. This is especially relevant in auction/salary cap formats where it's frustrating to be locked from bidding on a player. The other advantage is in-season roster management, allowing the activation of the best reserve as well as opening more pathways to acquire a player by trade or via free agency/waivers.

The challenge is quantifying the added profit yielded by the multiple-eligibility players. It's virtually impossible to do so with respect to the draft as each one is different. Sometimes, depending on the flow, it isn't necessary to move a player to another position. Other times it seems you're spending half your time playing musical chairs with roster spots. That said, motility is crucial towards the end of a draft when you can usually roster a player priced higher on your list relative to the expectation of the draft spot or bid. Let's say on average, a sage drafter can add $10 of profit with freedom to add a player at any position.

It's a bit easier to do the math in-season, though the process is tedious, requiring reverse-engineering the moves performed in a few leagues to get a reasonable average. The idea is identifying moves doable because of roster flexibility and estimating the volume of extra stats added as compared to what would have been added without the ability to free up any spot. Doing so renders around $20 in profit in mixed leagues, dropping to $10 in single league formats as the players available to add to the active roster are of lesser quality.

This rough math totals $30 in profit in mixed league and $20 extra in AL- and NL-only formats. If this is divided among the five players needed to complete the eligibility circle, you should be willing to pay up to a $6 premium in mixed leagues and $4

in -only. Keep in mind, paying the premium for all five players means you've canceled out the expected profit. Obviously, the objective is minimizing the prices, hence maximizing profit.

These calculations are based on rostering five players with multiple position eligibility. Of course, this will not always be possible. Having fewer may reduce the profit, but it's still beneficial. The algebra works out the same with fewer multiple-eligibility players. That is, regardless of the number, each adds $6 of profit in mixed leagues and $4 in -only leagues.

The principle applies to drafts as well as auctions/salary cap drafts. The best way to convert draft spots to auction prices is using Bill Macey's "Mapping ADPs to auction value" and "Auction Value Analysis", both available in the Gaming section of this book.

While it's helpful to have a numerical guide when deciding how many multiple-eligibility players to draft and their price, it isn't a one-size-fits-all application. Multiple-eligibility players are more beneficial in some leagues, less so in others.

Best Ball

Multiple eligibility players are most useful in best ball formats, since they maximize permutations for your optimal lineup, assuming the rules allow. Beware, some services designate one position per player. In leagues capable of slotting a player where he contributes most to the optimal lineup, having several hitters with roster flexibility allows more pitchers to be drafted. This revolves around one's personal approach, but with pitcher injuries being so prevalent, it helps to have more options to make the weekly optimal lineup.

Draft and Hold

Roster flexibility is crucial in draft-and-hold formats since there is no opportunity to remove and replace injured or underproducing players from your roster. A player legal at more than one spot essentially lengthens the reserve list, increasing the odds of having a healthy and productive batter occupy an active roster spot. Plus, the same notion applies as with best ball as more hitter flexibility allows rostering more pitchers.

Leagues with Limited Reserves

This is an example of a scenario where it's difficult to maximize the deployment of multiple-eligibility players. The explanation may seem counter-intuitive, but it's a reality. In a league with six or seven reserves and no separate IL, there may only be two or three healthy reserve hitters to slot into your active lineup. The other spots are used for injured players, pitchers to stream, speculative closers, and prospects.

Often, the healthy hitters can be moved to the active lineup without needing to clear a spot. These moves don't contribute to the profit generated by multiple-eligibility players. That is, you may end up having paid a premium for some players without the opportunity to take advantage. This doesn't mean you should avoid paying up for some flexibility, as there will be some chances to gain the benefit, not to mention they also may help in the initial drafting process.

Replacing ADP with draft-level analytics

by Ed DeCaria

Despite its ubiquity, average draft position (ADP)—including min/earliest draft position (EDP) and max/latest draft position (LDP)—simply isn't very useful or accurate for guiding fantasy managers as to when a player is actually likely to be drafted.

So this past season, we did something a little crazy: We downloaded ADP data from the National Fantasy Baseball Championship (NFBC) for each individual *day*, used it to impute data for each individual *draft*, and then created a slew of new metrics that will forever change the way we look at "market value" and make all the difference between drafts that go exactly as we hope vs. those where nothing seems to break our way.

Median Draft Position and Mode Draft Position

Median draft position (MeDP) tells us the midpoint of all draft positions (DPs) where 50% of the time the player was drafted earlier and 50% of the time the player was drafted later. Whereas ADP is the answer to a math question ("What is the sum of all of the positions this player has been drafted divided by the count?") that no fantasy manager is really asking, MeDP lines up every draft and points to the one in the middle as the one most likely to be the player's true market value.

As a supplement to MeDP, mode draft position (MoDP) tells us in which specific draft position a player was most often drafted. Again, no calculation required—we just count how many times the player was picked at each DP and find the one with the highest number.

Draft Position Variation (DPV)

It seems like some players always get drafted right around the same draft position, while for others, the market is a little harder to pin down. We can now calculate this phenomenon directly using a simple statistic called the coefficient of variation, which we'll redub Draft Position Variation (DPV).

A player's DPV is calculated as the standard deviation of his draft positions divided by his average draft position. Players with lower variation can more reliably be expected to be drafted right around their ADP, while players with higher variation tend to be under- or over-drafted more often. (Note: It's best to only compare DPV of players with similar ADPs, as variation tends to get smaller as ADP gets higher.) Players with similar ADP, MeDP, and MoDP can have drastically different DPVs.

Knowing whether or not the market is fuzzy about a given player can make the difference in how aggressive or passive we might want to be in a snake draft or how much we might consider "price enforcing" in an auction.

Outliers/Kurtosis (OK)

Related to variance, some players have a higher tendency than others to be drafted much earlier or later than ADP would suggest. Rather than looking at their one-off EDP and LDP, draft-level data measures the presence of all outlier DPs (where the combined tails of a player's DP distribution are bigger or smaller than normal) using a statistic called excess kurtosis, or what we'll call Outliers/Kurtosis, or OK for short. Higher OKs mean fantasy managers sometimes get a little silly with this player (either one manager drafts him way too early or an entire league lets him slip way too late), and lower OKs mean they don't.

Skew

Related to DPV and OK, skew tells us whether the player's DP distribution has a longer/thicker high-side tail or low-side tail relative to their MeDP. Players with significant positive skew (longer/thicker right tail) are more likely to slip a few picks/rounds in the draft. Players with a significant negative skew (longer/thicker left tail) are more likely to be reached for by a few picks/rounds.

These new statistics help us make sense of the hundreds of thousands of individual player DP data points that accumulate throughout draft season. But why stop there? With raw draft-level data, we can calculate the *exact* probability that a target player will be available at any specific point in the draft. This enables us to think through each pick strategically as follows:

1. Make a list of target players at each DP, focused on players with 25-75% availability. In the 25-50% range, this opens up our eyes to players who really might fall despite their earlier ADP. In the 50-75% range, it reminds us to not be afraid to draft players with slightly later ADP. A 75% availability means that in a full quarter of all drafts that player would already have been taken by this point, so considering that player here "before his ADP" isn't a radical idea—it's his normal range! Fantasy managers shouldn't let ADP make them feel bad about drafting the players they want.

2. Make a list of players to reach for early, focused on players with 75-90% availability. This is a really good way to eye our most important targets, knowing that there is a 10-25% chance an opponent might also be willing to jump up to get them. Depending on how our roster is shaping up, we can reach without being blind or foolish about it (which we would be if all we have to go on is ADP and EDP).

3. Make a list of players we hope might fall past their ADP, focused on players with 10-25% availability (it's okay to look at players with <10% availability who might fall, too). These are players we like, but not at their ADP. This helps us be ready to snap up "bargains" even if it means risking that our original target player(s) might then be taken before our next pick.

But because it isn't practical to calculate player-by-player, position-by-position availability percentages and keep them up-to-date all draft season, we instead capture all of these thoughts, feelings, and moments in five new handy metrics that we hope fantasy managers will find intuitive:

The Five S's of Snake Drafts

The Spring: That moment when a fantasy manager springs for a player much earlier than expected. This moment is represented by the player's 90th percentile DP. This is a much more useful metric than min/earliest draft position (EDP), because it gives us a sense of where a player might reasonably get taken but where it wouldn't be a total shock to anyone.

The Snipe: That infamous moment when a player you were targeting "early" gets taken just 1-2 picks before you. This probably happens often to people beholden to that trickster known as ADP, and intuitively likely happens near a player's 75th percentile DP. (If a player you wanted gets taken by a competitor at/after his ADP, you didn't get "sniped." You waited too long!)

The Settle: That feeling you get when no one quite seems right for your team and you don't want to reach for a player you hoped to get later so you settle for a guy right around his 50th percentile DP. This is the same as Median DP (MeDP).

The Steal: That thought that pops into your head as the draft wraps back to you and a player you didn't think would still be on the board is still on the board but you know he won't make it back … but he might make it back … now he probably will make it back … and he does make it back to you! This thinking tends to happen with players around their 25th percentile DP.

¯_(ツ)_/¯ *a.k.a. The Shrug* — One of two feelings you have when you draft a player around his 10th percentile DP or lower. Similar to the Spring, this is much more useful than max/latest draft position (LDP), because it gives us a sense of where a player might reasonably fall. Sometimes there's a reason he fell so far (often new uncertainty), so your shrug means "Sure, why not? He's cheap." But sometimes a guy just slips and slips and no one can believe it yet they too keep passing and finally he falls into your lap three rounds past his ADP and you shrug and say "Hey, you coulda had him!"

It's impossible to overstate how much ADP, EDP, LDP hide these insights. If you dissect any projected round of an upcoming draft using ADP, you will find players with drastically different draft profiles that make them more or less likely to be available "at their ADP," so depending on your specific targets and draft position, your entire plan could either be right on point or be an illusion waiting to blow up in your face. By knowing and playing these critical percentages, you are more likely to game out your snake draft the right way, and walk away with a superior roster than by playing hunches and ADPs alone.

Draft-level data can be used for two other interesting types of insights.

Trend and Break

Often during draft season, we hear touts say that a player has a lot of "helium" this year (rising draft price) or in some cases a lot of "lead" (falling draft price), referring to his current price vs. what it was at some undefined point earlier in the draft season. We can use draft-level data to do much the same, but break it into a few specific metrics for clarity and completeness:

Trend calculates the slope of the player's draft position over time, specifically the % +/- daily movement in draft position. This metric assumes linear movement, which is not true for all players, but it's useful in picking up even modest trends that might otherwise be tough to spot, and makes it easy to identify risers/fallers at any point during draft season.

Break calculates each player's ADP for the latest week minus his ADP for the prior week. This metric reads like a list of recent headlines—a who's who of draft season news. Unlike Trend, we present Break as an absolute number, not as a percentage relative to ADP. This helps surface the most significant changes in the market up and down the draft board. Players with high positive Break are those for whom something good has happened (e.g., won a job, performed well in spring training). Players with high negative Break are those for whom something bad has happened (e.g., lost a job, got injured).

Combination Probabilities

Perhaps the most unique and useful benefit of using draft-level data is being able to estimate the % likelihood of getting any one of a set of target players at a certain draft position. With draft-level data, we can now calculate this directly to help our in-draft decision-making. The math works like this: Take the product of the likelihood of each target player NOT falling, and subtract it from 1 to arrive at the chance of one of them falling.

Let's use an example from the 2021 draft season. Say you were drafting 9th in a 15-team draft and wanted José Ramírez, but only if you knew you could still get an ace on the way back. Individually, the odds that Darvish would make it back were only 11%, Giolito 9%, Buehler 36%, and Nola 43%, but combined you could calculate that the chance of one of them making it back were 1 - 89%*91%*64%*57% = 71%. Any one of them on their own didn't seem likely to make it back, but one of the group? It might be worth taking José Ramírez plus those odds.

With draft-level data in hand, ADP is now nothing more than a quick-and-dirty way to assess market value, and may soon officially be relegated to the trash heap. Look for these new draft-level metrics on BaseballHQ.com this draft season.

Predicting usable weeks in H2H category leagues

by Dan Marcus

Introduction/Method

We set out to identify the BaseballHQ indicators most closely correlated to weeks of "usable" category production in head-to-head leagues. To do so, we pulled data from both the 2019 and 2021 seasons to determine what the fourth-place team in each category averaged per player-slot on a weekly basis. That became the threshold for a usable week. The sample used 12-team leagues with 13 active hitter slots (one C, five OF, MI and CI). Players used were the top 24 at each infield position, top 18 at catcher, and top 60 in the outfield, which led to 130 total players after accounting for players with multi-position eligibility:

Category	2019	2021
HR	1.7	1.15
RBI	4.15	3.7
R	4.3	3.95
SB	0.5	0.5
AVG	.280	.264

Findings

Home Runs and Stolen Bases

Usable HR production was significantly correlated to PX (.702 R^2), HR/F (.678), and xPX (.552). The highest rate of usable scoring periods in 2019 was 65%, which three players reached. Nineteen players posted usable production in 50% of scoring periods:

65% usable scoring periods		50% usable scoring periods	
Median/Min PX	155/139	Median/Min PX	146/118
Median/Min HR/F	28%/25%	Median/Min HR/F	26%/16%
Median/Min xPX	141/129	Median/Min xPX	129/113

RSpd (.814 R^2) and Spd (.547) were the most closely correlated indicators to usable stolen base production. Nine players logged usable weeks in 75% of scoring periods; 27 players logged usable production in 50% of scoring periods:

75% usable scoring periods		50% usable scoring periods	
Median/Min Rspd	144/102	Median/Min RSpd	125/74
Median/Min Spd	137/93	Median/Min Spd	124/76
Median/Min SBO%	25%/19%	Median/Min SBO%	20%/11%

Batting Average, Runs, and RBI

In the remaining three categories, there is significantly less correlation between leading indicators and a player's usable production. RBI production was correlated to PX (.392 R^2), xPX (.383), HctX (.361), and Eye (.313). In 2019, five players posted usable production in 75% of scoring periods; 42 players managed at least 50% usable production:

75% usable scoring periods (RBI)		50% usable scoring periods (RBI)	
Median/Min PX	130/126	Median/Min PX	131/92
Median/Min xPX	133/93	Median/Min xPX	132.5/79
Median/Min HctX	124/107	Median/Min HctX	114/91
Median/Min Eye	0.62/0.40	Median/Min Eye	0.54/0.18

Runs were most closely correlated to PX (.314 R^2), Eye (.305), BB% (.274), Rspd (.256), and Spd (.248). Six players posted usable production in 75% of scoring periods; 61 posted usable production in 50% of scoring periods:

75% usable scoring periods (R)		50% usable scoring periods (R)	
Median/Min PX	97/74	Median/Min PX	118.5/60
Median/Min Eye	0.44/0.14	Median/Min Eye	0.41/0.14
Median/Min BB%	10%/4%	Median/Min BB%	9%/4%
Median/Min Rspd	114/56	Median/Min RSpd	78.5/0
Median/Min Spd	134.5/88	Median/Min Spd	102.5/45

Batting average had the lowest level of correlation, H% (.294 R^2), ct% (.286), Eye (.174), and LD% (.168). Four players managed usable production in 75% of scoring periods; 57 posted usable production in 50% of scoring periods:

75% usable scoring periods (BA)		50% usable scoring periods (BA)	
Median/Min h%	33%/29%	Median/Min h%	34%/25%
Median/Min ct%	85%/75%	Median/Min ct%	79%/63%
Median/Min Eye	0.62/0.38	Median/Min Eye	0.39/0.37
Median/Min LD%	24%/22%	Median/Min LD%	22%/16%

Conclusion

While these results only offer a glimpse of the player pool, they suggest that we should be searching for skills over role or team context (where have we heard that before?) when looking for players who consistently produce in head-to-head leagues. You can find our player list of 2021 Usable Weeks on page 273 of this book.

Creating a new SP consistency metric for H2H

by David Martin

Introduction

In head-to-head play, it is critical to avoid rostering starting pitching that is inconsistent. This abstract quantifies consistency in a single metric using a four-step process that focuses on: (i) pitchers who are dominant from start to start; (ii) pitchers who avoid disaster outings; and (iii) pitchers who stay healthy.

Step 1: Finding Pitchers Who Are Consistently DOMinant

Our beginning point for this analysis to review those pitchers who achieve a high percentage of dominant Pure Quality Starts (PQS). A start is considered PQS-DOMinant (DOM%) if it rates as a PQS-4 or PQS-5.

Step 2: Taking Note of Pitchers Susceptible to DISasters

A start is considered a PQS-DISaster if it rates as a PQS-0 or PQS-1. By accounting for PQS-DISasters (DIS%), we minimize week-to-week volatility in ERA and WHIP. We view PQS-DISasters in two ways. First, we use quality-consistency scores (QC scores) to provide us with a measurement of how consistent a player was on a week-to-week basis. The formula is as follows: (DOM% - (2 x DIS%)) x 2.

We then analyze PQS-DISasters in isolation, which allows us to determine if it was a bumpy ride to get there. If you are investing a mid-to-high-round pick on a starter, be sure to review their DIS% to understand the frequency of their pitching DISasters.

Step 3: Factoring in Health

We also incorporate health by measuring the number of days a pitcher spent on the Injured List over the last three years.

Step 4: Putting It All Together into a Single Consistency Metric

There is an element of each component that is important in insolation, but if we combine these variables into one score, we get a much more complete picture. We have created an aggregate consistency score (ACS) that combines these factors and rates each pitcher. For each of (1) DOM%, (2) DIS%, (3) QC Score, and (4) IL days, each player is assigned a score of 1 to 5 points based on percentiles. That score is then multiplied by a factor of 5 in order to curve the scores to 100:

DOM%	DIS%	QC Score	IL Days
Top 20% = 5 pts	Lowest 20% = 5 pts	Top 20% = 5 pts	Top 20% = 5 pts
2nd 20% = 4 pts	2nd lowest = 4 pts	2nd 20% = 4 pts	2nd 20% = 4 pts
3rd 20% = 3 pts	3rd lowest = 3 pts	3rd 20% = 3 pts	3rd 20% = 3 pts
4th 20% = 2 pts	4th lowest = 2 pts	4th 20% = 2 pts	4th 20% = 2 pts
5th 20% = 1 pt	5th lowest = 1 pt	5th 20% = 1 pt	5th 20% = 1 pt

Note: for IL days, the "Top 20%" refers to those pitchers with the fewest number of IL days across the past 3 years.

We stress that these are not intended to be used as straight rankings. Instead, they should form a component of your own rankings.

Conclusion

The result is an ACS score from 20-100. For more consistent starting pitching, target those pitchers who score 80 or higher. A full list of 2021 ACS scores (min. 100 IP) can be found on page 273 of this book.

The following section contains player boxes for every batter who had significant playing time in 2021 and/or is expected to get fantasy roster-worthy plate appearances in 2022. You will find some prospects here, specifically the most impactful names who we project to play in 2022. For more complete prospect coverage, see our Prospects section.

Snapshot Section

The top band of each player box contains the following information:

Age as of Opening Day 2022.

Bats shows which side of the plate he bats from—(L)eft, (R)ight or (B)oth.

Positions: Up to three defensive positions are listed and represent those for which he appeared a minimum of 20 games in 2021. Note that an additional multiposition chart (with 20-, 10- and 5-game eligibility minimums) can be found on page 282.

Ht/Wt: Each batter's height and weight.

Reliability Grades analyze each batter's forecast risk, on an A-F scale. High grades go to those who have accumulated few disabled list days (Health), have a history of substantial and regular major league playing time (PT/Exp) and have displayed consistent performance over the past three years, using RC/G (Consist).

LIMA Plan Grade evaluates how well a batter would fit into a team using the LIMA Plan draft strategy. Best grades go to batters who have excellent base skills, are expected to see regular playing time, and are in the $10-$30 Rotisserie dollar range. Lowest grades will go to poor skills, few AB and values less than $5 or more than $30.

Random Variance Score (Rand Var) measures the impact random variance had on the batter's 2021 stats and the probability that his 2022 performance will exceed or fall short of 2021. The variables tracked are those prone to regression—h%, HR/F and xBA to BA variance. Players are rated on a scale of −5 to +5 with positive scores indicating rebounds and negative scores indicating corrections. Note that this score is computer-generated and the projections will override it on occasion.

Mayberry Method (MM) acknowledges the imprecision of the forecasting process by projecting player performance in broad strokes. The four digits of MM each represent a fantasy-relevant skill—power, speed, batting average and playing time (PA)—and are all on a scale of 0 to 5.

Commentaries provide a brief analysis of his skills and the potential impact on 2022 performance. MLB statistics are listed first for those who played only a portion of 2021 at the major league level. Note that these commentaries generally look at

performance related issues only. Role and playing time expectations may impact these analyses, so you will have to adjust accordingly. Upside (UP) and downside (DN) statistical potential appears for some players; these are less grounded in hard data and more speculative of skills potential.

Player Stat Section

The past five years' statistics represent the total accumulated in the majors as well as in Triple-A, Double-A ball and various foreign leagues during each year. All non-major league stats have been converted to a major league equivalent (MLE) performance level. Minor league levels below Double-A are not included.

Nearly all baseball publications separate a player's statistical experiences in the major leagues from the minor leagues and outside leagues. While this may be appropriate for official record-keeping purposes, it is not an easy-to-analyze snapshot of a player's complete performance for a given year.

Bill James has proven that minor league statistics (converted to MLEs), at Double-A level or above, provide as accurate a record of a player's performance as major league statistics. Other researchers have also devised conversion factors for foreign leagues. Since these are adequate barometers, we include them in the pool of historical data for each year.

Team designations: An asterisk (*) appearing with a team name means that Triple-A and/or Double-A numbers are included in that year's stat line. Any stints of less than 20 AB are not included (to screen out most rehab appearances). A designation of "a/a" means the stats were accumulated at both AA and AAA levels that year. "for" represents a foreign or independent league. The designation "2TM" appears whenever a player was on more than one major league team, crossing leagues, in a season. "2AL" and "2NL" represent more than one team in the same league. Players who were cut during the season and finished 2021 as a free agent are designated as FAA (Free agent, AL) and FAN (Free agent, NL).

Stats: Descriptions of all the categories appear in the Encyclopedia.

- The leading decimal point has been suppressed on some categories to conserve space.
- Data for platoons (vL+, vR+), xHR and xHR/F, balls-in-play (G/L/F) and batted ball characteristics (HctX, QBaB, Brl%) are for major league performance only.
- Formulas that use BIP data, like xBA and xPX, only appear for years in which G/L/F data is available.

After the traditional five rotisserie stat categories, expected HR, expected SB, and expected BA are presented for comparison. On base average and slugging average appear next, and then OPS+, which is adjusted to league average, for both OPS itself, and OPS splits vs. left-handed and right-handed pitchers.

Batting eye and contact skill are measured with walk rate (bb%), contact rate (ct%). Eye is the ratio of walks to strikeouts.

Once the ball leaves the bat, it will either be a (G)round ball, (L)ine drive or (F)ly ball. Hit rate (h%), also referred to as batting average on balls-in-play (BABIP), measures how often a ball put into play results in a base hit. Hard contact index (HctX) measures the frequency of hard contact, compared to overall league levels. QBaB is a quality-of-contact metric that encapsulates average exit velocity, average launch angle, and launch angle variability, and Brl% is a percentage of batted balls hit with the optimal exit velocity and launch angle combination.

Linear weighted power index (PX) measures a batter's skill at hitting extra base hits as compared to overall league levels. xPX measures power by assessing how hard the ball is being hit (rather than the outcomes of those hits). And the ratio of home runs to fly balls shows the results of those hits. Expected home runs to fly balls give a sense of whether the player over or underperformed in the power department.

To assess speed, first look at on-base average (does he get on base?), then Spd (is he fast enough to steal bases?), then SBA (how often is he attempting to steal bases?) and finally, SB% (when he attempts, what is his rate of success?).

The final section includes two overall performance measures: runs above replacement (RAR) and base performance index (BPX, which is BPV indexed to each year's league average) and the Rotisserie value (R$).

2022 Projections

Forecasts are computed from a player's trends over the past five years. Adjustments were made for leading indicators and variances between skill and statistical output. After reviewing the leading indicators, you might opt to make further adjustments.

Although each year's numbers include all playing time at the Double-A level or above, the 2022 forecast only represents potential playing time at the major league level, and again is highly preliminary.

Note that the projected Rotisserie values in this book will not necessarily align with each player's historical actuals. Since we currently have no idea who is going to play shortstop for the Astros, or whether Adley Rutschman is going to break camp with the Orioles, it is impossible to create a finite pool of playing time, something which is required for valuation. So the projections are roughly based on a 12-team AL/NL league, and include an inflated number of plate appearances, league-wide. This serves to flatten the spread of values and depress individual player dollar projections. In truth, a $25 player in this book might actually be worth $21, or $28. This level of precision is irrelevant in a process that is driven by market forces anyway. So, don't obsess over it.

Be aware of other sources that publish perfectly calibrated Rotisserie values over the winter. They are likely making arbitrary decisions as to where free agents are going to sign and who is going to land jobs in the spring. We do not make those leaps of faith here.

Bottom line… It is far too early to be making definitive projections for 2022, especially on playing time. Focus on the skill levels and trends, then consult BaseballHQ.com for playing time revisions as players change teams and roles become more defined. A free projections update will be available online in March.

Do-it-yourself analysis

Here are some data points you can look at in doing your own player analysis:

- Variance between vL+ and vR+ OPS+
- Growth or decline in walk rate (bb%)
- Growth or decline in contact rate (ct%)
- Growth or decline in G/L/F individually, or concurrent shifts
- Variance in 2021 hit rate (h%) to 2018-2020 three-year average
- Variance between BA and xBA each year
- Variance between 2021 HR and 2021 xHR
- Growth or decline in HctX level
- Growth or decline in QBaB scores
- Growth or decline in Brl%
- Growth or decline in power index (PX) rate
- Variance between PX and xPX each year
- Variance in 2021 HR/F rate to 2018-2020 three-year average
- Variance in 2021 HR/F rate to 2021 xHR/F rate
- Growth or decline in statistically scouted speed (Spd) score
- Concurrent growth/decline of gauges like ct%, FB, PX, xPX, HR/F
- Concurrent growth/decline of gauges like OB, Spd, SBA, SB%

Abrams,CJ

Age: 21	Pos: SS	Health: B	LIMA Plan: D
Bats: L	Ht: 6' 2" Wt: 185	PT/Exp: F	Rand Var:
		Consist: F	MM: 2431

This doesn't look like the stat line of a top-10 prospect, but the context matters: 2019 SD draftee, lit up rookie ball in his draft year. Then spent 2020 at alt site, looked good as a 20-yr old in Double-A until broken leg ended his season. He'll need to reset, but for now you need to know that his speed will play right away when he arrives.

Yr	Tm	PA	R	HR	RBI	SB	BA	xHR	xSB	xBA	OBP	SLG	OPS+	vL+	vR+	bb%	ct%	Eye	G	L	F	h%	HctX	QBaB	Brl%	PX	xPX	HR/F	xHR/F	Spd	SBA%	SB%	RAR	BPX	R$
17																																			
18																																			
19																																			
20																																			
21	aa	174	20	1	18	10	259		2		311	364	93			7	76	0.31				34				78				87	30%	82%		27	$6
1st Half		174	20	1	18	10	259		2		311	364	94			7	76	0.31				34				78				101	30%	82%		42	$8
2nd Half																																			
22	**Proj**	**175**	**18**	**3**	**16**	**9**	**233**	**3**	**6**	**254**	**282**	**367**	**88**	**87**	**88**	**6**	**78**	**0.30**	**44**	**23**	**33**	**28**	**92**		**5%**	**88**		**8%**	**8%**	**102**	**22%**	**83%**	**-3.4**	**85**	**$4**

Abreu,José

Age: 35	Pos: 1B	Health: A	LIMA Plan: B
Bats: R	Ht: 6' 3" Wt: 250	PT/Exp: A	Rand Var: +1
		Consist: D	MM: 4145

2020 MVP started off slowly, with a concerning flood of strikeouts and groundballs. Second half snapped just about all the way back to 2020 form, minus some h% and hr/f help... and of course, 2020 was just a second half, right? At this age, we're on alert for signs of decline, but for now the road ahead looks flat.

Yr	Tm	PA	R	HR	RBI	SB	BA	xHR	xSB	xBA	OBP	SLG	OPS+	vL+	vR+	bb%	ct%	Eye	G	L	F	h%	HctX	QBaB	Brl%	PX	xPX	HR/F	xHR/F	Spd	SBA%	SB%	RAR	BPX	R$
17	CHW	675	95	33	102	3	304	30	9	293	354	552	123	140	116	5	81	0.29	45	18	36	33	133	BCb	10%	134	123	18%	16%	103	2%	100%	26.5	224	$28
18	CHW	553	68	22	78	2	265	26	2	276	325	473	107	121	102	7	78	0.34	44	21	35	30	109	ACc	9%	127	103	16%	19%	73	2%	100%	11.1	170	$16
19	CHW	693	85	33	123	2	284	37	3	272	330	503	115	140	106	5	76	0.24	46	22	32	33	107	ACb	13%	117	104	21%	24%	76	3%	50%	14.3	122	$24
20	CHW	262	43	19	60	0	317	17	1	295	370	617	131	114	136	7	75	0.31	45	24	32	35	122	ACb	14%	163	127	33%	29%	68	0%	0%	19.3	272	$38
21	CHW	659	86	30	117	1	261	32	1	261	351	481	114	132	109	9	75	0.43	46	19	35	30	114	ACc	10%	126	99	20%	21%	66	1%	100%	2.7	154	$22
1st Half		322	40	13	57	1	244	17	1	245	326	434	106	112	103	9	72	0.36	51	17	32	29	111	ACd	11%	113	88	20%	26%	77	1%	100%	-8.7	85	$20
2nd Half		337	46	17	60	0	279	15	1	276	374	526	122	157	113	10	77	0.51	42	20	38	31	118	ACc	10%	139	109	20%	18%	58	1%	0%	7.5	235	$25
22	**Proj**	**630**	**89**	**32**	**108**	**1**	**268**	**34**	**1**	**270**	**339**	**497**	**114**	**126**	**109**	**8**	**76**	**0.36**	**45**	**20**	**34**	**30**	**116**		**11%**	**132**	**108**	**21%**	**23%**	**66**	**1%**	**79%**	**19.7**	**166**	**$25**

Acuña,Ronald

Age: 24	Pos: RF	Health: D	LIMA Plan: B+
Bats: R	Ht: 6' 0" Wt: 205	PT/Exp: A	Rand Var: 0
		Consist: A	MM: 5335

Was well on his way to at least a repeat of monster 2019 season when July ACL tear ended season. Initial estimates on recovery time were 9-10 months, which makes his April readiness questionable. Lingering impact on running game has to be questioned as well. Capping your bid below $30 for 2022 seems prudent based on current info.

Yr	Tm	PA	R	HR	RBI	SB	BA	xHR	xSB	xBA	OBP	SLG	OPS+	vL+	vR+	bb%	ct%	Eye	G	L	F	h%	HctX	QBaB	Brl%	PX	xPX	HR/F	xHR/F	Spd	SBA%	SB%	RAR	BPX	R$
17	a/a	478	66	16	62	29	306		8		358	468	112			8	73	0.30				39				94				107	35%	62%		55	$28
18	ATL *	586	86	27	67	20	276	31	29	252	344	499	113	132	117	9	71	0.36	42	18	39	34	117	ACc	13%	139	140	21%	25%	129	18%	77%	24.3	187	$27
19	ATL	712	127	41	101	37	280	49	22	254	365	518	122	125	120	11	70	0.40	38	24	38	34	111	BBb	15%	128	139	25%	30%	129	24%	80%	21.5	163	$42
20	ATL	202	46	14	29	8	250	16	7	263	406	581	131	111	136	19	63	0.63	35	22	43	30	129	AAc	16%	217	186	33%	37%	90	16%	89%	13.3	360	$29
21	ATL	360	72	24	52	17	283	29	9	277	394	596	136	145	134	14	71	0.58	31	23	46	32	113	AAc	20%	185	139	24%	29%	102	23%	74%	23.8	358	$23
1st Half		332	65	22	48	16	276	27	8	274	389	589	136	150	132	14	71	0.57	32	21	48	31	114	AAc	20%	186	141	23%	28%	106	23%	73%	20.7	369	$44
2nd Half		28	7	2	4	1	364	2	1	324	464	682	155	101	167	15	73	0.67	29	47	24	43	105	ACb	23%	178	125	50%	50%	101	23%	100%	4.4	369	-$5
22	**Proj**	**490**	**93**	**32**	**69**	**16**	**275**	**38**	**17**	**264**	**377**	**565**	**128**	**130**	**127**	**13**	**70**	**0.48**	**36**	**21**	**43**	**32**	**118**		**17%**	**174**	**152**	**25%**	**30%**	**103**	**17%**	**75%**	**36.3**	**302**	**$30**

Adames,Willy

Age: 26	Pos: SS	Health: A	LIMA Plan: B
Bats: R	Ht: 6' 0" Wt: 210	PT/Exp: A	Rand Var: 0
		Consist: A	MM: 4225

Quad injury cost him a chunk of September, but by then his breakout year was already assured. QBaB captures the improvement in exit velocity and launch angle, reduced GB% also provides support for growing power. Add in a few more walks, and erasure of short-season ct% dip, and this now looks like a solid launchpad for his prime years. UP: 30 HR.

Yr	Tm	PA	R	HR	RBI	SB	BA	xHR	xSB	xBA	OBP	SLG	OPS+	vL+	vR+	bb%	ct%	Eye	G	L	F	h%	HctX	QBaB	Brl%	PX	xPX	HR/F	xHR/F	Spd	SBA%	SB%	RAR	BPX	R$
17	aaa	568	69	9	58	10	258		9		339	383	98			11	71	0.42				35				84				109	10%	66%		21	$12
18	TAM *	591	74	13	63	9	268	10	14	212	335	386	97	89	104	9	68	0.32	52	18	30	37	87	CDc	7%	77	89	17%	17%	160	10%	51%	7.9	3	$17
19	TAM	584	69	20	52	4	254	22	9	246	317	418	102	80	112	8	71	0.30	47	23	30	32	104	CCb	8%	94	91	18%	19%	105	4%	67%	-4.6	33	$11
20	TAM	205	29	8	23	2	259	7	2	240	332	481	108	129	100	10	60	0.27	43	25	32	39	90	CCf	10%	165	111	23%	20%	122	7%	67%	5.0	120	$16
21	2 TM	555	77	25	73	5	262	28	7	248	337	481	112	105	116	10	69	0.37	37	23	41	33	106	BBc	11%	142	132	18%	20%	105	7%	56%	14.1	162	$18
1st Half		305	40	13	44	3	246	16	3	246	318	460	108	98	113	10	68	0.33	36	23	41	31	117	BAc	13%	141	150	17%	21%	110	7%	50%	1.8	150	$19
2nd Half		250	37	12	29	2	281	13	3	252	360	507	117	113	119	11	69	0.41	38	22	40	35	92	CBc	10%	145	110	19%	21%	97	7%	67%	11.7	181	$15
22	**Proj**	**595**	**81**	**26**	**69**	**6**	**263**	**27**	**7**	**246**	**336**	**479**	**111**	**105**	**113**	**10**	**67**	**0.34**	**41**	**23**	**37**	**34**	**99**		**10%**	**141**	**112**	**20%**	**20%**	**107**	**7%**	**60%**	**19.7**	**100**	**$22**

Adams,Riley

Age: 26	Pos: CA	Health: A	LIMA Plan: D
Bats: R	Ht: 6' 4" Wt: 225	PT/Exp: D	Rand Var: +2
		Consist: B	MM: 3303

2-10-.222 in 120 PA at TOR/WAS. Traded on July 31, got a brief look with Nats down the stretch and gave a representative sample of his wares: has some pop, and some truck-sized holes in his swing. Catchers take longer to bake, but he's not super-young, so Occam's Razor says he likely settles in as a backup.

Yr	Tm	PA	R	HR	RBI	SB	BA	xHR	xSB	xBA	OBP	SLG	OPS+	vL+	vR+	bb%	ct%	Eye	G	L	F	h%	HctX	QBaB	Brl%	PX	xPX	HR/F	xHR/F	Spd	SBA%	SB%	RAR	BPX	R$
17																																			
18																																			
19	aa	317	44	11	37	3	252		4		323	431	104			10	61	0.27				38				122				109	5%	73%		-19	$6
20																																			
21	2 TM *	253	28	7	22	0	211	5	3	212	301	390	95	96	106	11	58	0.31	46	20	34	33	80	CCb	14%	140	105	10%	25%	114	0%	0%	-1.7	8	$0
1st Half		98	12	5	7	0	182	1	1	214	266	391	92	61	23	10	57	0.26	38	25	38	25	72	DBd	19%	150	119	0%	17%	127	0%	0%	-2.4	27	-$5
2nd Half		155	15	3	16	0	231	4	2	211	324	390	97	116	122	12	59	0.34	49	19	33	37	84	CCa	12%	134	100	14%	29%	105	0%	0%	0.4	0	-$3
22	**Proj**	**280**	**33**	**4**	**28**	**1**	**220**	**12**	**2**	**197**	**335**	**348**	**93**	**87**	**96**	**11**	**59**	**0.29**	**44**	**21**	**35**	**36**	**79**		**14%**	**105**	**108**	**9%**	**24%**	**108**	**3%**	**75%**	**-0.6**	**-126**	**$3**

Adell,Jo

Age: 23	Pos: LF	Health: B	LIMA Plan: C+
Bats: R	Ht: 6' 3" Wt: 215	PT/Exp: B	Rand Var: 0
		Consist: D	MM: 3305

4-26-.246 with 2 SB in 140 PA at LAA. Spent four months gathering himself at Triple-A after 2020's nightmare MLB debut. Got five weeks in majors before abdominal strain ended his year, and looked like he was figuring it out. Contact was rising week-over-week, had hits in final 8 games and 3 HR in last 23 AB. High ceiling remains, may be ready to take off.

Yr	Tm	PA	R	HR	RBI	SB	BA	xHR	xSB	xBA	OBP	SLG	OPS+	vL+	vR+	bb%	ct%	Eye	G	L	F	h%	HctX	QBaB	Brl%	PX	xPX	HR/F	xHR/F	Spd	SBA%	SB%	RAR	BPX	R$
17																																			
18	aa	68	13	2	6	2	225		1		285	402	92			8	63	0.23				32				146				104	18%	100%		60	-$1
19	a/a	303	40	7	25	6	257		7		315	415	101			8	67	0.25				36				110				97	9%	100%		11	$5
20	LAA	132	9	3	7	0	161	3	1	167	212	266	63	74	58	5	56	0.13	43	19	38	26	72	BCf	4%	82	60	12%	12%	114	5%	0%	-13.7	-256	-$4
21	LAA *	465	53	18	70	7	234	5	4	235	271	419	95	104	92	5	67	0.15	47	20	33	31	88	DCd	9%	118	83	13%	16%	127	12%	68%	-16.1	38	$11
1st Half		226	25	10	29	3	206		2	219	240	402	89	0	0	4	61	0.11	44	20	36	28	0		0%	133	-22	0%		122	12%	53%	-14.3	-8	$7
2nd Half		239	28	8	41	5	262	5	2	247	301	437	100	103	91	5	72	0.20	47	20	33	33	95	DCd	9%	106	83	13%	16%	127	12%	82%	-3.3	88	$14
22	**Proj**	**525**	**64**	**16**	**70**	**12**	**248**	**16**	**9**	**222**	**293**	**408**	**95**	**105**	**90**	**5**	**66**	**0.17**	**46**	**20**	**35**	**34**	**86**		**7%**	**108**	**74**	**14%**	**14%**	**114**	**10%**	**71%**	**-5.8**	**-20**	**$18**

Aguilar,Jesús

Age: 32	Pos: 1B	Health: B	LIMA Plan: B
Bats: R	Ht: 6' 3" Wt: 277	PT/Exp: A	Rand Var: 0
		Consist: B	MM: 3025

Knee inflammation, eventually requiring surgery, ended season in early Sept. Held short-season contact gains over 500 PA, and even spiked his FB for good measure. While that sounds really promising, those FB came mostly at the expense of LD, which muted the power gains and dragged his BA a bit. This, not 2018, is his true level. Pay for a repeat.

Yr	Tm	PA	R	HR	RBI	SB	BA	xHR	xSB	xBA	OBP	SLG	OPS+	vL+	vR+	bb%	ct%	Eye	G	L	F	h%	HctX	QBaB	Brl%	PX	xPX	HR/F	xHR/F	Spd	SBA%	SB%	RAR	BPX	R$
17	MIL	311	40	16	52	0	265	14	4	252	331	505	114	120	108	8	66	0.27	41	21	38	34	121	CCc	11%	154	165	23%	20%	68	0%	0%	-1.5	82	$8
18	MIL	566	80	35	108	0	274	33	0	269	352	539	119	123	116	10	71	0.41	35	24	41	32	115	BBc	11%	163	158	24%	22%	34	0%	0%	21.5	157	$23
19	2 TM	366	39	12	50	0	236	14	0	230	325	389	99	97	100	12	74	0.53	42	20	38	28	107	BCc	8%	83	106	13%	15%	60	0%	0%	-10.8	26	$4
20	MIA	216	31	8	34	0	277	8	0	265	352	457	107	125	100	11	79	0.58	36	26	38	31	113	BBb	7%	99	121	14%	14%	62	2%	0%	-1.5	144	$18
21	MIA	505	49	22	93	0	261	22	1	253	329	459	108	109	108	9	79	0.49	33	20	47	28	116	BAc	9%	109	132	13%	13%	46	0%	0%	-9.0	146	$14
1st Half		309	25	12	53	0	259	12	0	255	320	445	107	111	105	9	80	0.46	32	22	46	29	117	BAc	8%	104	129	12%	12%	43	0%	0%	-5.5	131	$16
2nd Half		196	24	10	40	0	263	10	0	251	342	480	111	107	113	10	79	0.54	35	18	47	28	114	CAc	9%	117	136	15%	15%	58	0%	0%	-0.1	188	$10
22	**Proj**	**525**	**63**	**23**	**94**	**0**	**262**	**24**	**0**	**251**	**336**	**461**	**108**	**111**	**107**	**10**	**77**	**0.49**	**36**	**21**	**43**	**30**	**114**		**9%**	**112**	**131**	**15%**	**15%**	**52**	**0%**	**0%**	**12.1**	**99**	**$19**

RAY MURPHY

Ahmed,Nick

Age: 32	Pos: SS	Health B	LIMA Plan C
Bats: R	Ht: 6' 2" Wt: 200	PT/Exp A	Rand Var +3
		Consist B	MM 2325

Spring patellar tendinitis prompted changes in swing mechanics and Sept right shoulder inflammation ended season. Fair to assume those played a part in struggles; but consistently poor QBaB caps BA/HR, and only once has he come close to double-digit steals. Expect partial rebound, but 2019-20 values aren't coming back.

Yr	Tm	PA	R	HR	RBI	SB	BA	xHR	xSB	xBA	OBP	SLG	OPS+	vL+	vR+	bb%	ct%	Eye	G	L	F	h%	HctX	QBaB	Brl%	PX	xPX	HR/F	xHR/F	Spd	SBA%	SB%	RAR	BPX	R$
17	ARI	178	24	6	21	3	251	3	2	261	298	419	98	146	76	6	77	0.26	48	20	32	30	99	DCd	2%	96	91	15%	7%	121	18%	43%	-3.3	100	$
18	ARI	564	61	16	70	5	234	13	11	270	290	411	94	102	88	7	79	0.37	41	24	35	27	113	CCc	5%	107	124	11%	9%	95	8%	56%	0.9	153	$1
19	ARI	625	79	19	82	8	254	19	9	272	316	437	104	130	95	8	80	0.46	48	20	32	29	104	CDd	7%	95	99	13%	13%	122	7%	80%	0.0	185	$1
20	ARI	217	29	5	29	4	266	5	3	249	327	402	97	100	95	8	77	0.39	52	19	29	32	92	CDd	5%	79	66	11%	11%	109	7%	100%	1.0	88	$1
21	ARI	473	46	5	38	7	221	6	6	238	280	339	85	106	75	7	76	0.33	48	18	34	28	80	DCf	2%	80	67	5%	5%	118	10%	78%	-18.9	77	$
1st Half		256	24	2	14	3	224	3	3	224	294	332	87	127	70	8	74	0.34	46	18	36	30	72	DCf	2%	76	51	3%	5%	138	10%	60%	-10.6	62	$
2nd Half		217	22	3	24	4	218	4	2	254	264	347	83	87	80	6	79	0.30	49	19	32	26	90	DDf	3%	85	84	6%	8%	95	10%	100%	-9.2	96	$
22	**Proj**	**525**	**60**	**10**	**58**	**8**	**238**	**11**	**7**	**250**	**294**	**379**	**91**	**106**	**84**	**7**	**77**	**0.35**	**48**	**20**	**32**	**29**	**92**		**4%**	**88**	**80**	**9%**	**9%**	**99**	**8%**	**80%**	**-7.0**	**100**	**$1**

Akiyama,Shogo

Age: 34	Pos: CF	Health C	LIMA Plan D
Bats: L	Ht: 6' 0" Wt: 190	PT/Exp C	Rand Var +5
		Consist C	MM 0231

Sported lifetime .301 BA and averaged 14 HR/13 SB in his last three seasons in Japan, but hasn't parlayed decent plate skills into MLB production. Owns no pop whatsoever, as QBaB and Brl% illustrate. Age and SB% history say SB surge is unlikely, too. Even the positive regression foretold by RandVar would only lift him to passable reserve OF.

Yr	Tm	PA	R	HR	RBI	SB	BA	xHR	xSB	xBA	OBP	SLG	OPS+	vL+	vR+	bb%	ct%	Eye	G	L	F	h%	HctX	QBaB	Brl%	PX	xPX	HR/F	xHR/F	Spd	SBA%	SB%	RAR	BPX	R$
17	for	633	103	15	87	14	300		10		364	471	114			9	84	0.63				34	0			93				118	12%	72%	20.5	200	$2
18	for	665	104	14	80	14	301		15		367	479	113			9	85	0.68				34	0			98				129	14%	55%	33.4	260	$2
19	for	653	109	12	60	11	283		17		352	417	106			10	83	0.61				33	0			69				132	11%	55%	10.9	174	$2
20	CIN	182	16	0	9	7	245	2	4	244	357	297	87	65	90	14	78	0.74	55	24	21	31	78	DFc	1%	35	70	0%	8%	102	17%	70%	-7.1	0	$1
21	CIN	182	16	0	12	2	204	2	4	237	282	253	73	91	70	8	75	0.35	57	24	20	27	79	DFd	1%	41	43	0%	8%	97	12%	40%	-15.6	-73	-$
1st Half		85	7	0	6	1	218	1	2	241	282	256	75	109	70	6	79	0.31	58	23	19	27	73	DFf	2%	31	51	0%	8%	95	12%	50%	-6.7	-58	-$
2nd Half		97	9	0	6	1	190	1	2	234	281	250	72	80	70	10	71	0.38	56	25	20	27	85	DFc	0%	53	36	0%	8%	101	12%	33%	-8.1	-77	-$
22	**Proj**	**210**	**24**	**1**	**16**	**4**	**237**	**2**	**4**	**252**	**324**	**309**	**86**	**94**	**84**	**10**	**78**	**0.49**	**56**	**24**	**20**	**30**	**80**		**1%**	**50**	**49**	**2%**	**8%**	**107**	**10%**	**54%**	**-5.1**	**-8**	**$**

Alberto,Hanser

Age: 29	Pos: 3B 2B	Health B	LIMA Plan D+
Bats: R	Ht: 5' 11" Wt: 215	PT/Exp B	Rand Var +1
		Consist A	MM 1341

Utilityman owns lifetime .333 BA vL, aided by 38% h%, but woes vR persist. Elite ct% forms a solid BA floor, and small-sample HctX gain is interesting, but still-terrible QBaB and low Brl% temper any optimism. Maybe 10 HR and a .280 BA is his absolute ceiling at this point, but only with PAs, which he's not likely to get. Damn those Catch-22s.

Yr	Tm	PA	R	HR	RBI	SB	BA	xHR	xSB	xBA	OBP	SLG	OPS+	vL+	vR+	bb%	ct%	Eye	G	L	F	h%	HctX	QBaB	Brl%	PX	xPX	HR/F	xHR/F	Spd	SBA%	SB%	RAR	BPX	R$
17																																			
18	TEX *	398	32	5	42	0	273	1	5	157	289	369	88	101	45	2	91	0.24	35	0	65	29	84	FAd	0%	53	103	0%	7%	95	5%	0%	-6.0	133	$
19	BAL	550	62	12	51	4	305	9	6	273	329	422	104	132	83	3	90	0.32	47	21	32	32	77	DCb	3%	54	49	8%	6%	110	6%	50%	2.3	170	$1
20	BAL	231	35	3	22	3	283	2	2	275	306	393	93	120	85	2	86	0.17	44	25	31	32	74	FCf	1%	66	37	5%	4%	102	6%	100%	-2.2	140	$1
21	KC	255	25	2	24	3	270	6	2	273	291	402	95	105	85	2	89	0.15	38	22	40	30	114	FCf	5%	78	101	2%	7%	106	8%	75%	-4.7	215	$
1st Half		148	15	1	11	0	270	3	1	275	288	404	96	90	101	1	89	0.13	35	24	41	30	110	FCf	3%	79	87	2%	6%	105	8%	0%	-4.1	219	-$
2nd Half		107	10	1	13	3	270	3	1	272	295	400	94	122	59	2	89	0.18	41	21	38	30	119	DCd	7%	76	122	3%	9%	103	8%	100%	-2.0	208	-$
22	**Proj**	**210**	**24**	**3**	**22**	**3**	**275**	**4**	**3**	**270**	**298**	**397**	**94**	**112**	**79**	**2**	**89**	**0.19**	**41**	**22**	**36**	**30**	**99**		**4%**	**70**	**82**	**4%**	**6%**	**100**	**8%**	**76%**	**-1.4**	**171**	**$**

Albies,Ozzie

Age: 25	Pos: 2B	Health A	LIMA Plan D+
Bats: B	Ht: 5' 8" Wt: 165	PT/Exp A	Rand Var +1
		Consist B	MM 4535

One of just five players in MLB to amass 30 HR/20 SB in 2021, backed by nearly across-the-board skills support. Uptick in FB% plus improved launch angle drove the power spike; xHR says there's additional upside. Above-average ct%, HctX and xBA back the BA. Though xSB casts doubt on a full SB repeat, he remains a prime early round target.

Yr	Tm	PA	R	HR	RBI	SB	BA	xHR	xSB	xBA	OBP	SLG	OPS+	vL+	vR+	bb%	ct%	Eye	G	L	F	h%	HctX	QBaB	Brl%	PX	xPX	HR/F	xHR/F	Spd	SBA%	SB%	RAR	BPX	R$
17	ATL *	682	95	14	66	27	265	7	10	233	317	401	98	125	103	7	78	0.35	41	19	40	32	105	CBa	5%	73	113	8%	10%	175	18%	90%	-8.0	118	$2
18	ATL	684	105	24	72	14	261	21	16	268	305	452	101	120	92	5	82	0.31	39	21	40	29	104	CBc	5%	109	100	12%	10%	123	12%	82%	8.4	213	$2
19	ATL	702	102	24	86	15	295	26	15	284	352	500	118	153	107	8	83	0.48	38	25	37	33	121	CBb	7%	103	114	12%	13%	133	11%	79%	32.0	259	$2
20	ATL	124	21	6	19	3	271	5	2	231	306	466	103	64	114	4	75	0.17	41	14	45	32	82	DBd	9%	108	83	15%	13%	131	15%	75%	-0.4	136	$1
21	ATL	686	103	30	106	20	259	35	13	259	310	488	110	128	103	7	80	0.37	31	20	49	28	113	BAc	9%	126	129	12%	14%	116	18%	83%	4.4	269	$3
1st Half		342	50	15	59	13	269	18	7	273	330	521	119	139	112	8	81	0.46	28	24	48	29	115	BAb	10%	137	131	12%	15%	118	18%	87%	10.9	335	$3
2nd Half		344	53	15	47	7	250	16	6	244	291	456	101	118	95	6	78	0.29	35	17	49	28	112	BAc	8%	114	127	12%	13%	113	18%	78%	-2.6	200	$2
22	**Proj**	**665**	**103**	**31**	**94**	**16**	**267**	**30**	**16**	**256**	**314**	**492**	**109**	**118**	**106**	**6**	**79**	**0.32**	**34**	**19**	**47**	**29**	**107**		**8%**	**123**	**114**	**14%**	**13%**	**130**	**15%**	**80%**	**23.4**	**255**	**$3**

Alcantara,Sergio

Age: 25	Pos: SS 2B	Health A	LIMA Plan D
Bats: B	Ht: 5' 9" Wt: 151	PT/Exp C	Rand Var -2
		Consist B	MM 1503

5-17-.205 with 3 SB in 255 PA at CHC. Strong defender has shown on-base skills and elite speed in minors, but that's where the good news ends. His ct% has lagged thus far in MLB, as have Brl% and HctX. Prior to 2021, he'd never hit more than 3 HR or logged more than 11 SB in a season. Glove could earn him PT, but offense is (charitably) a work in progress.

Yr	Tm	PA	R	HR	RBI	SB	BA	xHR	xSB	xBA	OBP	SLG	OPS+	vL+	vR+	bb%	ct%	Eye	G	L	F	h%	HctX	QBaB	Brl%	PX	xPX	HR/F	xHR/F	Spd	SBA%	SB%	RAR	BPX	R$
17																																			
18	aa	476	45	1	31	7	252		8		307	310	83			7	78	0.36				32				41				115	10%	56%		-13	$
19	aa	369	44	2	26	7	237		7		329	285	85			12	77	0.61				30				31				102	12%	51%		-30	$
20	DET	23	2	1	1	0	143	0	0	227	217	381	79	217	56	9	81	0.50	35	12	53	13	96	DAb		99	106	11%	0%	155	0%	0%	-1.4	276	-$
21	CHC *	352	43	7	23	5	217	4	4	207	318	334	90	59	99	13	67	0.44	46	20	34	30	97	CCd	3%	75	99	10%	8%	154	5%	100%	-8.9	0	$
1st Half		153	19	3	8	3	222	2	2	219	334	384	100	68	108	14	67	0.50	50	16	34	31	85	CFf	4%	100	98	13%	13%	156	5%	100%	-0.9	92	-$
2nd Half		199	24	4	15	2	213	2	2	197	305	298	82	55	95	12	67	0.40	45	21	34	30	102	CCc	3%	56	100	9%	6%	128	5%	100%	-8.4	-96	$
22	**Proj**	**280**	**33**	**6**	**24**	**4**	**227**	**5**	**5**	**217**	**320**	**349**	**91**	**61**	**104**	**12**	**71**	**0.45**	**47**	**19**	**34**	**29**	**95**		**4%**	**74**	**99**	**10%**	**9%**	**146**	**8%**	**74%**	**-4.2**	**-15**	**$**

Alfaro,Jorge

Age: 29	Pos: CA LF	Health B	LIMA Plan D
Bats: R	Ht: 6' 3" Wt: 2?0	PT/Exp B	Rand Var 0
		Consist A	MM 2303

Injuries (hamstring, knee, calf) plagued him all year. In between, it was more of the same: poor ct%, puny bb%, and when he did hit the ball, abundant GBs strangled his decent raw power. xHR indicates some bad HR/F luck, however. Career-high SB salvaged a little value, but history and xSB say it's not repeatable. 2nd CA option with BA downside.

Yr	Tm	PA	R	HR	RBI	SB	BA	xHR	xSB	xBA	OBP	SLG	OPS+	vL+	vR+	bb%	ct%	Eye	G	L	F	h%	HctX	QBaB	Brl%	PX	xPX	HR/F	xHR/F	Spd	SBA%	SB%	RAR	BPX	R$
17	PHI *	452	41	11	51	1	239	5	5	200	267	365	86	68	141	4	62	0.10	53	16	31	36	61	CDa	10%	92	68	22%	22%	108	2%	43%	-10.6	-112	$
18	PHI	377	35	10	37	3	262	16	4	213	324	407	98	96	97	5	60	0.13	48	23	29	41	83	ADb	11%	113	102	17%	27%	132	3%	100%	7.2	-60	$
19	MIA	465	44	18	57	4	262	22	3	227	312	425	102	113	97	5	64	0.14	53	22	25	37	97	BFb	12%	98	102	25%	31%	89	7%	50%	-1.3	-93	$1
20	MIA	100	12	3	16	2	226	4	1	198	280	344	83	83	82	4	61	0.11	49	21	30	33	113	CFf	7%	78	140	18%	24%	90	9%	100%	-2.8	-220	$
21	MIA	311	22	4	30	8	244	9	4	222	283	342	86	100	80	4	66	0.11	57	20	22	35	98	AFd	8%	74	82	9%	20%	93	13%	89%	-7.3	-142	$
1st Half		145	9	2	9	4	221	4	2	201	269	294	78	88	75	4	64	0.10	54	22	24	33	99	ADc	8%	55	79	10%	19%	89	13%	100%	-6.6	-246	-$
2nd Half		166	13	2	21	4	264	6	2	239	295	384	92	110	84	4	69	0.12	60	19	21	37	98	BFd	8%	90	84	9%	26%	97	13%	80%	-1.0	-58	$
22	**Proj**	**315**	**28**	**7**	**37**	**6**	**246**	**12**	**6**	**216**	**293**	**366**	**89**	**95**	**87**	**4**	**64**	**0.12**	**54**	**21**	**25**	**36**	**98**		**9%**	**86**	**98**	**15%**	**25%**	**90**	**10%**	**86%**	**-0.6**	**-153**	**$**

Alford,Anthony

Age: 27	Pos: LF	Health B	LIMA Plan D+
Bats: R	Ht: 6' 1" Wt: 210	PT/Exp D	Rand Var -5
		Consist A	MM 4403

5-11-.233 with 5 SB in 148 PA at PIT. Post-hype prospect's power/speed combo is evident (lifetime 8 HR/11 SB in 236 MLB PA), but ct% issues and injuries have held him back. The ct% hit rock bottom in 2021, even as power soared. Intriguing 71% ct%, 8% bb%, 4 HR/3 SB in 85 PA over final month warrants some deep league speculation.

Yr	Tm	PA	R	HR	RBI	SB	BA	xHR	xSB	xBA	OBP	SLG	OPS+	vL+	vR+	bb%	ct%	Eye	G	L	F	h%	HctX	QBaB	Brl%	PX	xPX	HR/F	xHR/F	Spd	SBA%	SB%	RAR	BPX	R$
17	TOR *	298	38	5	22	16	292	0	5	274	370	407	106	0	100	11	79	0.60	60	20	20	35	64	AFa	20%	74	124	0%	0%	89	21%	83%	4.1	82	$1
18	TOR *	422	48	4	30	16	216	0	11	198	268	309	77	43	33	7	66	0.21	40	20	40	31	24	DAa	0%	76	-2	0%	0%	113	28%	67%	-20.1	-77	$
19	TOR *	337	41	7	31	20	227	1	12	186	287	358	89	0	130	8	62	0.22	53	6	41	34	50	DCd	6%	90	52	14%	14%	127	40%	69%	-9.9	-89	$
20	2 TM	29	5	2	7	3	214	1	1	260	241	500	98	52	124	3	71	0.13	55	10	35	22	29	FFf	5%	138	48	29%	14%	169	75%	100%	-0.5	224	$
21	PIT *	360	39	14	39	11	238	7	39	192	313	424	101	84	106	10	53	0.23	36	20	44	40	75	CCd	11%	154	138	15%	21%	125	26%	50%	-10.5	-19	$1
1st Half		161	16	4	15	6	201	0	21	148	325	317	89	46	44	15	46	0.34	25	25	50	40	23	DAa	0%	112	-22	0%	0%	91	26%	52%	-8.6	-258	$
2nd Half		199	23	10	24	5	265	7	18	224	303	502	109	86	122	5	58	0.13	37	19	43	40	89	BCf	12%	178	157	17%	24%	131	26%	48%	-0.6	104	$1
22	**Proj**	**315**	**36**	**12**	**30**	**13**	**238**	**8**	**11**	**205**	**313**	**418**	**99**	**80**	**110**	**8**	**60**	**0.23**	**37**	**19**	**43**	**35**	**80**		**11%**	**133**	**141**	**16%**	**10%**	**134**	**21%**	**61%**	**-3.4**	**-25**	**$1**

GREG PYRON

Alonso,Pete

Age: 27 Pos: 1B | Bats: R Ht: 6' 3" Wt: 245
Health A | PT/Exp A | Consist B
LIMA Plan B+ | Rand Var +1 | MM 4235

Played through May hand sprain that sent him to IL; came back with a vengeance (.270 BA, 31 HR after 5/31 return). Post-IL power skills (PX/xPX, xHR/F) snapped right back to rookie-season levels, while ct% uptick fueled 2nd half xBA gains. The ceiling is already sky-high (think 2019 plus a few more hits); the floor is catching up as track record grows.

Yr	Tm	PA	R	HR	RBI	SB	BA	xHR	xSB	xBA	OBP	SLG	OPS+	vL+	vR+	bb%	ct%	Eye	G	L	F	h%	HctX	QBaB	Brl%	PX	xPX	HR/F	xHR/F	Spd	SBA%	SB%	RAR	BPX	R$
17	aa	47	7	2	5	0	290		0		322	543	118			5	82	0.27				31				138				114	0%	0%		252	$0
18	a/a	534	66	25	85	0	229		1		311	443	101			11	68	0.37				28				142				82	3%	0%		110	$12
19	NYM	693	103	53	120	1	260	49	4	271	358	583	130	131	129	10	69	0.39	41	18	41	28	101	BBc	16%	176	153	31%	28%	91	1%	100%	24.5	252	$26
20	NYM	239	31	16	35	1	231	15	1	243	326	490	108	93	115	10	71	0.39	39	17	44	24	91	BBd	13%	142	100	25%	23%	72	2%	100%	-5.2	160	$18
21	NYM	637	81	37	94	3	262	44	4	269	344	519	118	123	117	9	77	0.47	39	18	43	28	120	ABd	15%	138	129	20%	23%	87	2%	100%	1.6	258	$22
1st Half		280	34	13	40	1	254	17	2	238	339	455	111	121	106	10	75	0.46	38	17	45	29	114	ABc	15%	113	109	16%	20%	70	2%	100%	-3.4	131	$16
2nd Half		357	47	24	54	2	268	27	2	291	347	568	124	123	124	9	79	0.48	39	19	42	27	125	BCd	15%	156	145	23%	26%	99	2%	100%	9.4	350	$28
22	Proj	665	90	44	105	2	264	47	3	263	350	535	120	119	120	10	74	0.42	39	18	43	29	111		15%	151	129	23%	25%	75	2%	86%	31.1	217	$25

Altuve,Jose

Age: 32 Pos: 2B | Bats: R Ht: 5' 6" Wt: 166
Health B | PT/Exp A | Consist D
LIMA Plan B+ | Rand Var +1 | MM 2245

Vintage PA total, BA rebound made last year's "buy in at a discounted rate" pay off as ct% snapped back to normal. But xHR, subpar Brl% question HR repeat; flyball spike capped h% and BA ceiling; age, recent SB% baseline say red light is here to stay. Outlook depends on loft: a legit .300 threat if FB% regresses; 2021 repeat (minus a few HR) if it sticks.

Yr	Tm	PA	R	HR	RBI	SB	BA	xHR	xSB	xBA	OBP	SLG	OPS+	vL+	vR+	bb%	ct%	Eye	G	L	F	h%	HctX	QBaB	Brl%	PX	xPX	HR/F	xHR/F	Spd	SBA%	SB%	RAR	BPX	R$
17	HOU	662	112	24	81	32	346	23	12	299	410	547	130	132	127	9	86	0.69	47	20	33	37	98	DCc	7%	106	87	15%	14%	133	19%	84%	63.4	264	$45
18	HOU	599	84	13	61	17	316	18	22	278	386	451	112	102	114	9	85	0.70	46	24	30	35	105	CCc	6%	78	96	10%	13%	122	11%	81%	34.5	200	$27
19	HOU *	570	91	31	74	6	291	25	11	291	345	535	122	147	116	7	83	0.46	50	18	33	30	116	CCd	8%	115	85	23%	19%	126	8%	55%	24.8	285	$23
20	HOU	210	32	5	18	2	219	5	3	252	286	344	84	66	89	8	80	0.44	49	21	30	25	99	DDf	5%	71	68	11%	11%	105	11%	40%	-9.7	100	$9
21	HOU	678	117	31	83	5	278	24	11	284	350	489	115	107	119	10	85	0.73	39	22	39	28	107	CBf	6%	108	90	16%	12%	97	5%	63%	23.0	296	$27
1st Half		337	61	18	47	4	286	13	6	280	374	505	122	116	126	13	82	0.82	42	22	36	29	108	CCf	8%	109	95	21%	15%	93	5%	80%	16.1	273	$32
2nd Half		341	56	13	36	1	271	11	5	288	326	475	108	96	113	7	87	0.60	37	22	41	28	105	DBf	5%	108	87	12%	10%	100	5%	33%	3.6	315	$21
22	Proj	595	103	22	73	6	280	22	6	271	346	463	110	104	112	9	84	0.59	42	21	37	30	106		6%	97	85	13%	13%	105	6%	58%	22.7	216	$26

Alvarez,Yordan

Age: 25 Pos: DH LF | Bats: L Ht: 6' 5" Wt: 225
Health A | PT/Exp A | Consist D
LIMA Plan B+ | Rand Var +1 | MM 5145

Quickly brushed aside pre-season knee concerns with .310 BA, 7 HR by Memorial Day; even logged 41 games in the outfield. Impressive 2nd half skill growth featured plate skill gains (ct%, xBA), surge in raw power (PX/xPX, Brl%), and best of all: it was somewhat muted by low h%. Already a four-category stud, and he's just getting started... UP: 50 HR

Yr	Tm	PA	R	HR	RBI	SB	BA	xHR	xSB	xBA	OBP	SLG	OPS+	vL+	vR+	bb%	ct%	Eye	G	L	F	h%	HctX	QBaB	Brl%	PX	xPX	HR/F	xHR/F	Spd	SBA%	SB%	RAR	BPX	R$
17																																			
18	a/a	369	51	17	60	5	261		4		328	469	107			9	70	0.33				32				136				83	8%	69%		110	$13
19	HOU *	610	95	44	130	1	305	27	7	295	396	632	142	144	148	13	71	0.53	38	25	37	35	126	ACa	17%	183	155	33%	33%	71	1%	56%	55.8	300	$30
20	HOU	9	2	1	4	0	250	0	0	338	333	625	127	183	33	0	88	0.00	57	14	29	17	202	ADf		153	116	50%	0%	106	0%	0%	0.1	424	-$1
21	HOU	598	92	33	104	1	277	46	2	272	346	531	120	120	121	8	73	0.34	38	23	39	32	118	ACc	16%	151	153	21%	30%	88	1%	100%	22.7	223	$25
1st Half		292	50	14	51	1	300	18	1	266	370	531	125	121	129	8	71	0.31	40	25	35	37	95	ACb	14%	142	134	21%	27%	103	1%	100%	14.7	181	$27
2nd Half		306	42	19	53	0	256	28	1	279	324	531	116	119	114	9	75	0.39	36	22	42	28	140	ABc	18%	160	170	22%	32%	77	1%	0%	8.0	269	$21
22	Proj	595	90	38	108	2	277	46	2	277	352	558	123	122	124	10	72	0.38	38	23	39	32	123		16%	167	155	25%	31%	77	2%	73%	32.9	226	$29

Anderson,Brian

Age: 29 Pos: 3B | Bats: R Ht: 6' 3" Wt: 185
Health C | PT/Exp B | Consist A
LIMA Plan B | Rand Var -1 | MM 2415

Mostly a lost season given April oblique strain, May shoulder issue that led to Sept surgery. Power dip was likely injury-related—and even xPX, xHR/F say it wasn't that bad—as plate skills held firm and modest running game resurfaced. An unlikely breakout candidate, but R$ baseline says there's modest profit potential if health checks out next spring.

Yr	Tm	PA	R	HR	RBI	SB	BA	xHR	xSB	xBA	OBP	SLG	OPS+	vL+	vR+	bb%	ct%	Eye	G	L	F	h%	HctX	QBaB	Brl%	PX	xPX	HR/F	xHR/F	Spd	SBA%	SB%	RAR	BPX	R$
17	MIA *	567	77	18	80	1	246	2	8	273	317	418	100	73	105	9	72	0.38	49	28	23	31	87	CDb	5%	105	83	0%	15%	119	2%	28%	-13.6	91	$10
18	MIA	670	87	11	65	2	273	19	7	252	357	400	101	100	100	9	78	0.48	52	20	29	33	110	BDc	6%	82	78	8%	14%	125	3%	33%	0.3	120	$16
19	MIA	520	57	20	66	5	261	20	4	263	342	468	112	103	114	8	75	0.39	45	19	35	31	115	BCc	9%	117	108	16%	16%	98	5%	83%	-1.7	159	$13
20	MIA	229	27	11	38	0	255	11	3	239	345	465	108	103	109	10	67	0.33	49	21	30	33	96	CCc	10%	125	120	27%	27%	127	0%	0%	-0.3	108	$17
21	MIA	264	24	7	28	5	249	10	2	214	337	378	98	58	111	10	72	0.40	49	15	36	32	86	CCc	8%	80	93	11%	16%	108	7%	100%	-6.9	27	$5
1st Half		141	13	3	11	3	258	5	1	210	326	375	98	68	107	9	71	0.32	51	14	35	34	96	CCd	9%	78	94	9%	16%	105	7%	100%	-3.0	-12	$1
2nd Half		123	11	4	17	2	238	4	1	216	350	381	99	48	116	12	73	0.50	47	16	38	29	74	CCc	6%	82	92	14%	14%	119	7%	100%	-2.5	77	-$1
22	Proj	560	60	18	73	6	253	21	9	233	342	409	102	78	110	10	72	0.40	48	18	34	32	93		8%	95	99	15%	17%	112	7%	91%	5.2	37	$17

Anderson,Tim

Age: 29 Pos: SS | Bats: R Ht: 6' 1" Wt: 185
Health B | PT/Exp A | Consist A
LIMA Plan D+ | Rand Var -3 | MM 3545

Two IL stints (hamstring) bookended more stat-stuffing goodness. Leads majors with .322 BA since 2019 (min. 600 PA) as lofty h% remains entrenched, and while FB% limits HR ceiling, xHR says there's plenty of pop. Red light in 2nd half likely related to leg issues, but Spd says the wheels are fine. One of the sturdier five-category foundations in the game.

Yr	Tm	PA	R	HR	RBI	SB	BA	xHR	xSB	xBA	OBP	SLG	OPS+	vL+	vR+	bb%	ct%	Eye	G	L	F	h%	HctX	QBaB	Brl%	PX	xPX	HR/F	xHR/F	Spd	SBA%	SB%	RAR	BPX	R$
17	CHW	606	72	17	56	15	257	16	7	248	276	402	92	110	84	2	72	0.08	53	19	28	33	83	DDb	5%	89	68	14%	14%	143	13%	94%	-12.9	30	$15
18	CHW	606	77	20	64	26	240	17	11	248	281	406	92	104	86	5	74	0.20	47	20	33	29	82	DCc	5%	104	83	14%	12%	124	29%	76%	-5.9	90	$21
19	CHW *	541	83	19	59	17	333	16	23	279	352	505	119	117	120	3	79	0.13	49	24	28	40	88	CDa	5%	94	84	17%	15%	115	16%	77%	22.2	119	$28
20	CHW	221	45	10	21	5	322	11	7	274	357	529	118	197	92	5	76	0.20	55	19	26	39	101	CDa	10%	114	101	24%	26%	156	12%	71%	12.8	212	$31
21	CHW	551	94	17	61	18	309	21	12	278	338	469	111	113	110	4	77	0.18	55	23	22	37	107	BFa	8%	94	85	19%	23%	137	18%	72%	15.9	138	$31
1st Half		300	46	6	28	14	292	10	7	260	327	408	102	95	105	5	76	0.20	58	21	20	37	100	BFa	6%	75	78	14%	23%	120	18%	70%	0.6	38	$27
2nd Half		251	48	11	33	4	329	11	5	298	351	539	120	135	116	3	79	0.16	52	24	24	38	114	BDa	10%	116	94	24%	24%	147	18%	80%	16.7	242	$24
22	Proj	560	96	20	61	21	301	22	15	273	330	478	110	128	103	4	77	0.17	53	22	25	36	100		8%	103	88	19%	21%	132	15%	79%	22.5	141	$34

Andrus,Elvis

Age: 33 Pos: SS | Bats: R Ht: 6' 0" Wt: 210
Health B | PT/Exp A | Consist B
LIMA Plan C+ | Rand Var 0 | MM 1333

Posted the second-lowest OPS of any hitter with 500+ PA—how's that for job security? Put bat on ball with ease, but PX/xPX says it was all soft contact; xBA confirms he's no longer a BA asset. Successful enough on basepaths to stay deep-league relevant, but wheels can get squeaky at this age... DN: 250 PA, and not because of injury.

Yr	Tm	PA	R	HR	RBI	SB	BA	xHR	xSB	xBA	OBP	SLG	OPS+	vL+	vR+	bb%	ct%	Eye	G	L	F	h%	HctX	QBaB	Brl%	PX	xPX	HR/F	xHR/F	Spd	SBA%	SB%	RAR	BPX	R$
17	TEX	689	100	20	88	25	297	17	9	289	337	471	110	114	107	6	84	0.38	49	20	32	33	104	DDc	4%	97	80	12%	10%	111	21%	71%	18.0	185	$33
18	TEX *	454	54	6	33	5	243	8	14	252	294	348	86	96	86	7	83	0.43	50	19	31	28	104	CDc	4%	63	59	6%	8%	127	8%	54%	-9.4	123	$6
19	TEX	648	81	12	72	31	275	14	10	271	313	393	98	102	95	5	84	0.35	51	21	28	31	112	CDc	4%	60	72	8%	10%	115	24%	79%	-13.0	115	$26
20	TEX	111	11	3	7	3	194	4	3	249	252	330	77	76	77	7	85	0.53	49	15	36	20	118	CDf	6%	71	120	10%	13%	81	20%	75%	-6.5	156	$3
21	OAK	541	60	3	37	12	243	9	14	257	294	320	84	65	94	6	84	0.38	46	24	30	29	93	CDf	2%	49	71	2%	7%	101	11%	86%	-21.5	69	$10
1st Half		298	25	1	19	7	231	4	7	256	275	307	81	55	96	6	83	0.35	41	27	32	28	95	CDf	2%	52	80	1%	5%	81	11%	78%	-14.7	38	$5
2nd Half		243	35	2	18	5	259	5	7	260	317	336	88	81	91	6	85	0.42	52	22	27	30	91	DDf	2%	46	60	4%	10%	119	11%	100%	-6.0	100	$8
22	Proj	420	50	6	33	11	243	10	7	257	294	345	87	79	90	6	84	0.42	49	21	30	28	102		3%	59	79	6%	9%	101	9%	80%	-9.5	107	$12

Andújar,Miguel

Age: 27 Pos: LF | Bats: R Ht: 6' 0" Wt: 211
Health F | PT/Exp F | Consist C
LIMA Plan D+ | Rand Var -3 | MM 2231

6-12-.253 in 162 PA at NYY. March hand injury gave way to season-ending wrist strain in July. Bat-to-ball skills persist, but the rest of this package—from the PX/xPX baseline, 2021 GB% spike, and xBA/bb% combo that stifles OBP—remains lacking. Deficiencies with glove, reliability grades cloud playing time outlook as 2018 breakout fades further up this box.

Yr	Tm	PA	R	HR	RBI	SB	BA	xHR	xSB	xBA	OBP	SLG	OPS+	vL+	vR+	bb%	ct%	Eye	G	L	F	h%	HctX	QBaB	Brl%	PX	xPX	HR/F	xHR/F	Spd	SBA%	SB%	RAR	BPX	R$
17	NYY *	516	62	18	81	6	306	0	7	284	343	492	114	180	214	5	84	0.36	57	14	29	34	97	AFa	29%	104	81	0%	0%	75	7%	64%	9.0	164	$21
18	NYY	606	83	27	92	2	297	21	6	295	328	527	115	109	115	4	83	0.26	44	20	36	32	110	CCc	6%	133	99	16%	12%	96	2%	67%	25.7	260	$25
19	NYY	49	1	0	1	0	128	1	0	114	143	128	37	0	48	2	77	0.09	49	8	43	17	86	FCf	0%	0	65	0%	6%	93	0%	0%	-7.3	-219	-$5
20	NYY	65	5	1	5	0	242	2	0	222	277	355	84	104	68	5	85	0.33	45	13	42	27	85	DCf	4%	55	68	5%	9%	132	0%	0%	-3.9	148	$0
21	NYY *	221	29	10	22	0	260	6	1	247	302	417	99	80	99	6	83	0.35	53	17	31	27	94	CDf	6%	74	69	15%	15%	94	2%	0%	-7.3	127	$4
1st Half		176	23	8	17	0	255	6	1	242	284	417	98	82	99	4	82	0.22	54	16	31	27	94	CDf	6%	77	67	16%	16%	97	2%	0%	-6.4	108	$5
2nd Half		46	6	2	5	0	279	0	0	297	367	417	106	67	159	12	88	1.15	33	33	33	29	60	FCf	0%	64	103	0%	0%	97	2%	0%	-0.5	223	-$6
22	Proj	245	32	9	32	1	251	7	1	253	284	412	94	95	93	4	83	0.27	49	16	35	27	95		5%	87	75	13%	11%	90	3%	67%	-2.5	112	$7

RYAN BLOOMFIELD

Aquino,Aristides

Age: 28	Pos: LF RF	Health	B	LIMA Plan	D
Bats: R	Ht: 6' 4" Wt: 220	PT/Exp	D	Rand Var	0
		Consist	D	MM	5301

Missed two months with a wrist fracture; came back with some bombs but little else. PRO: History of level platoon splits; has developed plate patience quickly; massive xPX supports HR. CON: Sharply declining contact rate gives credence to su Mendoza BA; HctX and exit velocity surprisingly tepid. This version punishes fly balls only, and his shelf life is expiring.

Yr	Tm	PA	R	HR	RBI	SB	BA	xHR	xSB	xBA	OBP	SLG	OPS+	vL+	vR+	bb%	ct%	Eye	G	L	F	h%	HctX	QBaB	Brl%	PX	xPX	HR/F	xHR/F	Spd	SBA%	SB%	RAR	BPX
17	aa	501	56	19	58	9	215		6		281	408	94			8	65	0.26				29				125				119	12%	74%		42
18	CIN *	435	41	18	46	3	216		6	234	270	403	90	0	0	7	68	0.23	44	20	36	27	0			123	-27	0%		100	11%	37%	-13.3	53
19	CIN *	539	77	44	91	11	264	14	7	262	313	574	123	126	122	7	68	0.23	35	20	45	29	92	CAf	14%	169	110	29%	21%	91	11%	91%	13.2	189
20	CIN	56	7	2	8	1	170	2	1	218	304	319	83	85	80	11	62	0.33	52	24	24	22	52	FCd	7%	95	34	29%	29%	102	7%	100%	-3.7	-88
21	CIN	204	25	10	23	2	190	11	3	197	299	408	97	104	91	13	57	0.36	29	18	53	26	85	CAf	15%	157	151	19%	20%	133	9%	50%	-8.2	85
1st Half		39	5	4	7	1	212	4	0	272	333	636	135	136	133	15	58	0.43	26	11	63	20	87	CAf	28%	300	188	33%	33%	91	9%	50%	1.3	500
2nd Half		165	20	6	16	1	184	7	2	182	291	355	87	92	83	13	57	0.34	29	20	51	27	85	BAf	12%	123	143	14%	17%	149	9%	50%	-8.7	-8
22	Proj	210	25	13	27	3	217	11	3	219	290	463	102	104	100	9	62	0.27	32	17	51	27	87		14%	161	148	21%	19%	118	9%	65%	-0.2	83

Arenado,Nolan

Age: 31	Pos: 3B	Health	A	LIMA Plan	B+
Bats: R	Ht: 6' 2" Wt: 215	PT/Exp	A	Rand Var	+3
		Consist	D	MM	3245

Without the outfield expanse in Coors allowing a few more balls to drop, this departing player's BA took more of a hit thar his power. Still, an incredibly stable skill set—HctX, xPX, and pristine launch angle point to continued 30+ HR pop, and xB and ct% say some BA should return. No longer the centerpiece, but an anchor.

Yr	Tm	PA	R	HR	RBI	SB	BA	xHR	xSB	xBA	OBP	SLG	OPS+	vL+	vR+	bb%	ct%	Eye	G	L	F	h%	HctX	QBaB	Brl%	PX	xPX	HR/F	xHR/F	Spd	SBA%	SB%	RAR	BPX
17	COL	679	100	37	130	3	309	32	10	297	373	586	131	177	113	9	83	0.58	34	21	45	32	123	CBc	9%	145	149	16%	14%	114	3%	60%	44.2	303
18	COL	673	104	38	110	2	297	30	5	291	374	561	125	159	109	11	79	0.60	40	21	39	32	126	BBc	7%	150	138	21%	16%	85	2%	50%	46.8	290
19	COL	662	102	41	118	3	315	27	6	287	379	583	133	143	129	9	84	0.67	36	19	45	32	123	BAd	8%	124	139	18%	12%	111	3%	60%	43.7	333
20	COL	201	23	8	26	0	253	6	1	251	303	434	98	89	101	7	89	0.75	37	16	47	25	126	CAf	5%	87	103	10%	8%	80	0%	0%	-3.8	264
21	STL	653	81	34	105	2	255	27	2	271	312	494	111	127	107	8	84	0.52	31	19	50	25	116	CAf	7%	123	127	14%	11%	88	2%	100%	0.0	296
1st Half		341	38	16	52	0	265	12	1	284	323	506	115	134	111	8	85	0.58	30	20	50	27	104	CAf	7%	129	106	12%	9%	79	2%	0%	5.0	331
2nd Half		312	43	18	53	2	244	15	1	257	301	481	106	118	103	8	82	0.47	33	17	50	24	128	BAf	6%	116	152	15%	13%	110	2%	100%	-1.1	273
22	Proj	665	86	33	106	2	262	27	3	266	323	487	110	122	106	8	84	0.58	34	18	47	26	122		7%	115	130	14%	11%	85	3%	77%	21.0	252

Arozarena,Randy

Age: 27	Pos: LF RF	Health	A	LIMA Plan	B
Bats: R	Ht: 5' 11" Wt: 185	PT/Exp	A	Rand Var	-1
		Consist	D	MM	4425

xHR and xSB confirm that his 20/20 season was legit, but what about 5-category sustainability? PRO: Above avg production vs both LHP and RHP; stable exit velocity; three 125+ Spd scores in this box. CON: FB% and HctX trends question power; h% will regress; SB% could dictate fewer green lights. Valuable profile, but this could be his ceiling.

Yr	Tm	PA	R	HR	RBI	SB	BA	xHR	xSB	xBA	OBP	SLG	OPS+	vL+	vR+	bb%	ct%	Eye	G	L	F	h%	HctX	QBaB	Brl%	PX	xPX	HR/F	xHR/F	Spd	SBA%	SB%	RAR	BPX
17	aa	187	30	3	8	7	236		3		332	352	93			13	78	0.67				29				73				127	21%	69%		115
18	a/a	384	49	9	38	20	237		9		288	361	87			7	74	0.28				30				83				92	35%	69%		20
19	STL *	395	56	13	45	16	299	1	20	259	354	481	116	162	115	8	77	0.37	56	13	31	36	100	BFf	6%	100	42	20%	20%	130	30%	51%	1.1	163
20	TAM	76	15	7	11	4	281	4	3	280	382	641	136	193	109	8	66	0.27	47	19	35	31	99	BDf	14%	208	113	47%	27%	113	20%	100%	5.9	320
21	TAM	604	94	20	69	20	274	21	22	240	356	459	112	125	103	9	68	0.33	49	18	33	37	89	BDf	8%	123	89	17%	18%	145	19%	67%	6.8	131
1st Half		337	50	10	40	11	255	10	12	225	335	4[illegible]	104	110	100	9	69	0.34	50	15	35	34	86	BDf	7%	99	73	14%	14%	137	19%	73%	-4.8	73
2nd Half		267	44	10	29	9	299	11	10	258	382	524	123	144	108	10	66	0.32	48	22	30	42	94	CDf	10%	156	110	21%	23%	144	19%	60%	10.0	204
22	Proj	560	85	22	59	21	266	23	18	250	352	465	111	132	98	9	70	0.33	48	19	33	34	93		8%	127	100	18%	20%	129	16%	64%	11.6	132

Arraez,Luis

Age: 25	Pos: 3B 2B LF	Health	B	LIMA Plan	B
Bats: L	Ht: 5' 10" Wt: 175	PT/Exp	A	Rand Var	-1
		Consist	A	MM	1255

QBaB's Mr. Average. When he puts the ball in play, it comes off his bat at an average exit velocity, at an average launch angle—every single time. In reality, the combination of elite ct%/LD% keeps the h% high and supports a plus BA. And though xHR says there's more pop in here somewhere, it's certainly no more than (surprise!) average.

Yr	Tm	PA	R	HR	RBI	SB	BA	xHR	xSB	xBA	OBP	SLG	OPS+	vL+	vR+	bb%	ct%	Eye	G	L	F	h%	HctX	QBaB	Brl%	PX	xPX	HR/F	xHR/F	Spd	SBA%	SB%	RAR	BPX
17																																		
18	aa	189	21	2	13	2	277		3		317	337	88			6	91	0.63				30				35				100	4%	100%		113
19	MIN *	600	77	4	48	6	333	5	9	297	398	418	113	97	122	10	92	1.29	41	29	29	36	110	CCa	3%	46	73	5%	6%	110	5%	52%	20.6	215
20	MIN	121	16	0	13	0	321	3	1	293	364	402	102	74	110	7	90	0.73	41	29	29	36	104	CCa	3%	55	88	0%	10%	100	0%	0%	2.7	200
21	MIN	479	58	2	42	2	294	9	5	275	357	376	101	89	104	9	89	0.90	46	26	28	33	103	CCa	2%	44	63	2%	8%	136	3%	50%	2.3	196
1st Half		222	29	1	21	0	276	5	2	269	347	362	99	83	104	10	88	0.91	45	26	30	31	111	BCc	4%	43	71	2%	10%	148	3%	0%	-2.8	204
2nd Half		257	29	1	21	2	310	4	3	281	366	388	102	96	104	9	89	0.88	47	27	27	34	96	CCa	1%	45	57	2%	7%	120	3%	67%	2.9	185
22	Proj	455	57	3	40	2	302	9	5	283	359	391	102	85	107	9	90	0.91	44	27	28	33	104		3%	51	70	3%	8%	117	5%	59%	9.6	161

Arroyo,Christian

Age: 27	Pos: 2B	Health	F	LIMA Plan	D
Bats: R	Ht: 6' 1" Wt: 210	PT/Exp	F	Rand Var	0
		Consist	B	MM	3231

6-25-.262 in 181 PA at BOS. Hand, hamstring, knee and COVID led to only 117 PA after a solid April. He's young enough that we'd still like to see what an injury-free season would produce; but old enough that we know the Health grade has teeth. Miniscule 2nd half sample says he's got at least a hint of league-avg pop, but not enough to pony up for.

Yr	Tm	PA	R	HR	RBI	SB	BA	xHR	xSB	xBA	OBP	SLG	OPS+	vL+	vR+	bb%	ct%	Eye	G	L	F	h%	HctX	QBaB	Brl%	PX	xPX	HR/F	xHR/F	Spd	SBA%	SB%	RAR	BPX
17	SF *	231	24	6	28	3	264	2	3	264	306	398	96	76	72	6	79	0.29	61	18	21	31	88	CFa	3%	81	61	15%	10%	65	9%	58%	-5.6	42
18	TAM *	236	21	3	23	2	220	1	3	245	263	321	78	97	98	5	76	0.24	70	14	16	28	144	AFa	8%	70	81	17%	17%	100	11%	34%	-10.2	10
19	TAM *	188	25	8	31	1	255	1	3	268	316	467	108	84	105	8	71	0.30	47	25	28	31	67	DFf	6%	120	65	22%	11%	112	2%	100%	1.5	119
20	2 AL	54	7	3	8	0	240	2	0	209	296	440	98	62	118	7	78	0.36	56	5	38	25	113	BDc	8%	98	121	20%	13%	98	0%	0%	-0.3	148
21	BOS *	214	25	6	26	2	231	7	1	242	266	388	90	120	94	4	71	0.16	49	20	31	30	86	DDd	7%	107	84	16%	19%	84	5%	100%	-6.8	15
1st Half		153	18	4	20	1	248	5	0	242	278	405	95	101	108	4	68	0.13	48	23	29	34	76	DCf	7%	113	79	16%	20%	86	5%	100%	-4.0	-8
2nd Half		62	6	2	6	1	190	2	0	234	240	348	79	189	55	6	77	0.29	52	12	36	21	115	DDd	9%	93	99	17%	17%	94	5%	100%	-3.9	100
22	Proj	245	27	10	30	3	247	8	2	253	305	434	100	114	89	6	74	0.24	50	18	31	29	101		8%	113	91	18%	16%	85	5%	75%	1.5	73

Astudillo,Williams

Age: 30	Pos: 3B 1B	Health	B	LIMA Plan	D+
Bats: R	Ht: 5' 9" Wt: 225	PT/Exp	D	Rand Var	+3
		Consist	B	MM	1041

7-21-.236 in 216 PA at MIN. In theory, a great bench player—plays multiple positions and that unicorn ct% rate! But his league-average HctX means there's no oomph behind that contact, which QBaB, Brl% and xPX all confirm. And now you can't even count on BA. Should rebound some but not enough to matter... unless you want him to pitch! (4 IP, 2.25 ERA)

Yr	Tm	PA	R	HR	RBI	SB	BA	xHR	xSB	xBA	OBP	SLG	OPS+	vL+	vR+	bb%	ct%	Eye	G	L	F	h%	HctX	QBaB	Brl%	PX	xPX	HR/F	xHR/F	Spd	SBA%	SB%	RAR	BPX
17	aaa	122	14	3	14	0	274		1		289	436	99			2	95	0.41				27				90				86	5%	0%		255
18	MIN *	391	34	13	53	6	270	3	2	299	289	435	97	118	117	3	95	0.54	41	23	36	26	112	CCc	6%	81	91	9%	9%	83	14%	55%	9.3	257
19	MIN *	301	46	10	39	1	295	4	5	286	313	434	103	83	97	2	96	0.71	40	22	38	28	100	DBc	3%	59	55	6%	6%	64	4%	24%	9.0	219
20	MIN	16	4	1	3	0	250	0	0	280	250	500	100	0	106	0	88	0.00	7	36	57	23	101	CAa	7%	120	63	13%	0%	77	0%	0%	0.1	284
21	MIN *	307	26	8	27	2	231	5	0	255	244	350	82	90	85	2	94	0.30	41	17	42	22	94	DBf	4%	57	68	8%	6%	46	3%	100%	-11.4	162
1st Half		176	12	4	13	1	242	3	0	244	254	341	83	89	93	2	93	0.22	39	19	42	24	87	DAf	4%	48	69	8%	6%	55	3%	100%	-5.8	115
2nd Half		131	14	4	14	1	215	2	0	268	230	363	80	90	66	2	96	0.53	43	15	42	19	103	CBd	4%	69	68	9%	6%	51	3%	100%	-5.3	238
22	Proj	210	22	6	24	2	252	5	1	272	280	394	92	91	91	2	95	0.46	41	19	40	24	100		4%	68	70	8%	7%	57	2%	60%	-4.3	216

Baddoo,Akil

Age: 23	Pos: CF LF	Health	A	LIMA Plan	B
Bats: L	Ht: 6' 1" Wt: 210	PT/Exp	C	Rand Var	-2
		Consist	F	MM	3515

A player at his age with just 131 PA in A-ball put up these MLB numbers? That's beyond intriguing, and the profile bulges with things to like: Patient plate approach; balanced batted ball trajectory; foundation for plus power; developed speed skills. If 2nd half vL/vR leveling and ct% gains stick, the next step could be ... UP: 25 HR/25 SB

Yr	Tm	PA	R	HR	RBI	SB	BA	xHR	xSB	xBA	OBP	SLG	OPS+	vL+	vR+	bb%	ct%	Eye	G	L	F	h%	HctX	QBaB	Brl%	PX	xPX	HR/F	xHR/F	Spd	SBA%	SB%	RAR	BPX
17																																		
18																																		
19																																		
20																																		
21	DET	461	60	13	55	18	259	20	7	233	330	436	105	71	116	10	70	0.37	40	21	39	34	90	DCd	9%	108	118	11%	17%	136	20%	82%	3.6	119
1st Half		210	25	5	23	12	276	11	4	239	367	475	117	51	131	13	67	0.45	40	22	38	39	91	DCc	10%	135	147	11%	23%	136	20%	86%	7.8	169
2nd Half		251	35	8	32	6	246	9	4	228	299	405	95	80	102	7	73	0.29	40	20	40	30	89	DCd	8%	89	98	12%	13%	131	20%	75%	-5.6	77
22	Proj	595	79	17	72	23	258	26	18	230	326	432	103	71	113	9	71	0.35	40	21	39	34	90		9%	106	118	11%	17%	131	16%	81%	15.2	116

BRENT HERSHEY

Bader,Harrison

Age: 28	Pos: CF	Health	C	LIMA Plan	B+
Bats: R	Ht: 6' 0" Wt: 210	PT/Exp	B	Rand Var	-1
		Consist	A	MM	3315

Forearm flexor strain plus hairline rib fracture limited first half; raked afterwards. Can he deliver full season of joy? PRO: Hugely improved ct% (attributed to nasal surgery that alleviated chronic allergy symptoms); above-average history of xPX, Spd; elite CF defense. CON: Poor history of LD%, QBaB cap BA potential. Intriguing later-round power/speed bet.

Yr	Tm	PA	R	HR	RBI	SB	BA	xHR	xSB	xBA	OBP	SLG	OPS+	vL+	vR+	bb%	ct%	Eye	G	L	F	h%	HctX	QBaB	Brl%	PX	xPX	HR/F	xHR/F	Spd	SBA%	SB%	RAR	BPX	R$
17	STL *	551	71	19	55	14	251	3	7	223	295	401	95	162	66	6	71	0.22	44	16	39	32	97	DDc	10%	92	109	13%	13%	105	20%	57%	-19.6	9	$14
18	STL	427	61	12	37	15	264	11	14	234	334	422	101	117	92	7	67	0.25	40	27	33	36	93	CCc	7%	111	95	14%	13%	141	17%	83%	5.6	53	$15
19	STL *	475	72	17	50	13	214	15	12	214	302	394	96	89	95	11	67	0.38	38	17	44	27	89	CBd	10%	105	141	12%	15%	133	14%	82%	-4.5	59	$11
20	STL	125	21	4	11	3	226	7	3	219	336	443	103	160	86	10	62	0.33	41	15	44	32	90	DBf	12%	148	147	14%	24%	156	14%	75%	-1.7	148	$8
21	STL	401	45	16	50	9	267	16	8	248	324	460	108	104	109	7	77	0.32	43	16	41	31	96	DCf	7%	112	106	14%	14%	106	14%	69%	-0.7	169	$14
1st Half		96	9	5	13	3	212	3	2	245	292	412	98	184	88	11	81	0.63	43	14	43	20	90	DBd	7%	99	85	17%	10%	93	14%	60%	-3.2	212	-$1
2nd Half		305	36	11	37	6	284	12	6	249	334	475	110	91	115	6	76	0.25	43	16	41	34	98	DCf	7%	117	113	13%	14%	112	14%	75%	4.4	165	$20
22	Proj	**560**	**76**	**21**	**63**	**13**	**248**	**23**	**13**	**233**	**325**	**435**	**103**	**124**	**97**	**9**	**72**	**0.34**	**42**	**17**	**41**	**31**	**93**		**9%**	**114**	**116**	**14%**	**15%**	**123**	**12%**	**68%**	**8.7**	**107**	**$17**

Báez,Javier

Age: 29	Pos: SS 2B	Health	B	LIMA Plan	B
Bats: R	Ht: 6' 0" Wt: 190	PT/Exp	A	Rand Var	-4
		Consist	D	MM	4425

Swing and miss a lot, hit it hard sometimes, run like heck--that profile doesn't work for everyone, but for "El Mago" it does the trick. Outperformed expected stats yet again despite historically scary plate discipline while playing through nagging injuries. Just know a girl and her dog will peek behind the curtain before long.

Yr	Tm	PA	R	HR	RBI	SB	BA	xHR	xSB	xBA	OBP	SLG	OPS+	vL+	vR+	bb%	ct%	Eye	G	L	F	h%	HctX	QBaB	Brl%	PX	xPX	HR/F	xHR/F	Spd	SBA%	SB%	RAR	BPX	R$
17	CHC	508	75	23	75	10	273	21	6	247	317	480	108	126	100	6	69	0.21	49	15	36	35	91	CCc	8%	129	104	20%	18%	119	12%	77%	3.9	91	$19
18	CHC	645	101	34	111	21	290	37	12	283	326	554	118	124	114	4	72	0.17	46	22	32	35	96	BCc	13%	163	110	24%	26%	155	24%	70%	33.7	260	$37
19	CHC	561	89	29	85	11	281	31	15	272	316	531	117	134	112	5	71	0.18	50	18	32	35	91	ADa	13%	145	108	24%	26%	125	17%	61%	18.3	178	$24
20	CHC	235	27	8	24	3	203	9	4	222	238	360	79	85	77	3	66	0.09	50	18	32	27	97	CCf	8%	100	87	17%	19%	112	8%	100%	-16.2	-52	$9
21	2 NL	542	79	30	86	18	265	32	9	237	319	490	111	127	106	5	64	0.15	47	19	34	36	95	BCd	13%	145	117	28%	29%	131	19%	78%	1.8	85	$27
1st Half		290	38	17	49	9	224	17	4	220	276	451	101	111	99	5	60	0.12	48	16	37	30	80	BCd	13%	149	104	29%	29%	153	19%	82%	-7.9	58	$24
2nd Half		252	41	13	37	9	313	15	5	255	369	535	122	137	115	6	68	0.21	46	22	32	41	113	BCd	14%	140	131	26%	30%	110	19%	75%	13.4	123	$27
22	Proj	**560**	**83**	**28**	**84**	**15**	**264**	**31**	**14**	**245**	**310**	**482**	**108**	**121**	**103**	**5**	**67**	**0.16**	**48**	**19**	**33**	**34**	**97**		**12%**	**138**	**110**	**24%**	**26%**	**116**	**15%**	**76%**	**11.7**	**93**	**$28**

Barnhart,Tucker

Age: 31	Pos: CA	Health	A	LIMA Plan	D+
Bats: B	Ht: 5' 11" Wt: 192	PT/Exp	B	Rand Var	-2
		Consist	A	MM	2013

Did just enough to put up another decent season--for a catcher, of course. Favorable hit rate and harder contact offset dip in BB%, but low fly ball rate, HR/F, xHR/F kept him from capitalizing on passable xPX. Should continue to be a source of modest profit from the $1 catcher bin.

Yr	Tm	PA	R	HR	RBI	SB	BA	xHR	xSB	xBA	OBP	SLG	OPS+	vL+	vR+	bb%	ct%	Eye	G	L	F	h%	HctX	QBaB	Brl%	PX	xPX	HR/F	xHR/F	Spd	SBA%	SB%	RAR	BPX	R$
17	CIN	423	26	7	44	4	270	7	6	281	347	403	102	90	103	10	82	0.62	46	26	28	32	110	DCb	2%	80	90	8%	8%	82	4%	100%	9.1	112	$7
18	CIN	522	50	10	46	0	248	9	4	254	328	372	94	99	90	10	79	0.56	45	24	31	29	112	CCb	4%	75	82	9%	8%	89	3%	0%	6.3	87	$6
19	CIN	364	32	11	40	1	231	5	1	241	328	380	98	54	104	12	74	0.53	45	22	32	28	86	DCc	3%	83	71	15%	7%	62	1%	100%	-2.2	22	$3
20	CIN	110	10	5	13	0	204	4	0	236	291	388	90	37	103	11	71	0.43	33	24	43	23	78	FBf	7%	103	85	17%	14%	73	0%	0%	-1.3	56	$2
21	CIN	388	41	7	48	0	247	8	1	233	317	368	94	91	95	7	71	0.29	40	25	35	33	98	CBb	4%	85	102	8%	9%	71	0%	0%	-2.6	-31	$5
1st Half		209	29	4	25	0	262	5	0	245	349	410	106	64	112	10	66	0.33	42	30	29	38	93	CCa	5%	116	107	12%	15%	74	0%	0%	3.7	0	$6
2nd Half		179	12	3	23	0	230	3	0	215	279	321	81	110	75	5	78	0.22	38	21	42	28	102	DAc	3%	56	97	6%	6%	80	0%	0%	-6.3	-38	-$2
22	Proj	**420**	**40**	**11**	**50**	**0**	**235**	**10**	**1**	**236**	**311**	**373**	**93**	**78**	**96**	**9**	**74**	**0.38**	**40**	**24**	**36**	**29**	**94**		**4%**	**86**	**91**	**11%**	**10%**	**67**	**1%**	**54%**	**2.6**	**-25**	**$7**

Barrero,Jose

Age: 24	Pos: SS	Health	A	LIMA Plan	C
Bats: R	Ht: 6' 2" Wt: 175	PT/Exp	D	Rand Var	-3
		Consist	F	MM	3503

0-3-.200 in 56 PA with CIN. Promising SS prospect dominated two MiLB levels before running into small-sample brick wall with the big club. Rushed into service in 2020, so don't put too much stock into that line. Tantalizing power/speed skills, solid plate discipline in the minors make for a good dart to throw late.

Yr	Tm	PA	R	HR	RBI	SB	BA	xHR	xSB	xBA	OBP	SLG	OPS+	vL+	vR+	bb%	ct%	Eye	G	L	F	h%	HctX	QBaB	Brl%	PX	xPX	HR/F	xHR/F	Spd	SBA%	SB%	RAR	BPX	R$
17																																			
18																																			
19																																			
20	CIN	68	4	0	2	1	194	1	1	185	206	194	53	78	42	1	61	0.04	39	34	27	32	36	CDd	2%	0	10	0%	9%	135	14%	50%	-7.1	-436	-$3
21	CIN *	416	54	17	57	14	264	1	9	217	324	462	108	79	86	8	69	0.29	36	12	52	34	69	BAb	9%	126	62	0%	6%	143	19%	76%	7.0	154	$18
1st Half		197	28	7	28	6	253		5	229	314	424	103	0	0	8	68	0.27	44	20	36	34	0		0%	111	-22	0%		124	19%	66%	-0.9	54	$12
2nd Half		219	27	10	28	8	274	1	5	232	332	497	112	78	85	8	71	0.30	36	12	52	34	71	BAb	9%	139	62	0%	6%	142	19%	87%	7.5	219	$15
22	Proj	**350**	**46**	**9**	**47**	**12**	**264**	**8**	**11**	**222**	**345**	**419**	**104**	**121**	**93**	**8**	**70**	**0.29**	**37**	**21**	**42**	**35**	**57**		**6%**	**102**	**41**	**10%**	**9%**	**129**	**16%**	**79%**	**4.8**	**40**	**$16**

Bart,Joey

Age: 25	Pos: CA	Health	A	LIMA Plan	D
Bats: R	Ht: 6' 2" Wt: 238	PT/Exp	F	Rand Var	+3
		Consist	C	MM	2013

0-1-.333 in 6 PA with SF. One of the top catching prospects in baseball bided his time in 2021 behind an aging former MVP who discovered the fountain of youth. But now is his moment. Consistently above-average MiLB production, though contact rate has dropped sharply while climbing the rungs. May take a bit of time to make MLB adjustments.

Yr	Tm	PA	R	HR	RBI	SB	BA	xHR	xSB	xBA	OBP	SLG	OPS+	vL+	vR+	bb%	ct%	Eye	G	L	F	h%	HctX	QBaB	Brl%	PX	xPX	HR/F	xHR/F	Spd	SBA%	SB%	RAR	BPX	R$
17																																			
18																																			
19	aa	86	9	3	11	0	302		1		358	505	119			8	72	0.31				39				112				118	9%	0%		111	$0
20	SF	111	15	0	7	0	233	2	2	183	288	320	81	67	85	3	60	0.07	52	16	32	39	98	CCb	5%	69	78	0%	10%	142	0%	0%	-4.1	-212	$1
21	SF *	272	26	6	32	0	233	0	1	263	273	349	85	181	0	5	61	0.14	25	50	25	36	0	CAf	0%	91	-22	0%	0%	78	0%	0%	-6.8	-177	$2
1st Half		135	16	5	21	0	270	0	0	127	303	432	103	0	0	5	61	0.12	0	0	100	40	0	AA	0%	120	-22	0%	0%	76	0%	0%	1.8	-92	$3
2nd Half		137	10	1	12	0	197	0	0	312	244	268	69	268	0	6	61	0.16	33	67	0	31	0	DCa	0%	62	-22	0%	0%	86	0%	0%	-8.2	-258	-$7
22	Proj	**399**	**41**	**5**	**41**	**0**	**245**	**3**	**2**	**227**	**311**	**346**	**89**	**82**	**91**	**5**	**61**	**0.13**	**52**	**16**	**32**	**39**	**88**		**4%**	**81**	**70**	**7%**	**5%**	**89**	**2%**	**0%**	**-2.8**	**-229**	**$7**

Baty,Brett

Age: 22	Pos: 3B	Health	A	LIMA Plan	F
Bats: L	Ht: 6' 3" Wt: 210	PT/Exp	F	Rand Var	
		Consist	F	MM	1301

Former first-round NYM pick topped out at AA in 2021. Showed off an all-fields approach along with solid plate skills and developing power. Could get a taste of MLB in 2022 but will most likely make his full-season mark in 2023. A rising favorite of prospect hounds.

Yr	Tm	PA	R	HR	RBI	SB	BA	xHR	xSB	xBA	OBP	SLG	OPS+	vL+	vR+	bb%	ct%	Eye	G	L	F	h%	HctX	QBaB	Brl%	PX	xPX	HR/F	xHR/F	Spd	SBA%	SB%	RAR	BPX	R$
17																																			
18																																			
19																																			
20																																			
21	aa	169	12	4	16	1	219		2		293	331	86			9	65	0.30				32				81				86	3%	100%		-112	-$1
1st Half																																			
2nd Half		169	12	4	16	1	219		2	198	293	331	0			9	65	0.30	44	20	36	32	0			81	-22	0%		91	3%	100%	-8.7	-112	-$3
22	Proj	**210**	**14**	**4**	**18**	**1**	**226**	**4**	**1**	**198**	**289**	**320**	**83**	**82**	**83**	**8**	**68**	**0.28**	**44**	**20**	**36**	**31**	**94**		**5%**	**65**		**8%**	**8%**	**92**	**4%**	**100%**	**-9.3**	**-182**	**$2**

Bauers,Jake

Age: 26	Pos: 1B RF LF	Health	A	LIMA Plan	D
Bats: L	Ht: 6' 1" Wt: 195	PT/Exp	C	Rand Var	+1
		Consist	B	MM	1301

DFA'd by CLE in June; SEA rolled the dice and came up snake eyes as well. Former promise receding in the distance as decent walk rate and launch angle can't make up for poor contact, xPX, HctX. Improved defense, age, touch of speed may lead to another shot; let someone else roll them bones.

Yr	Tm	PA	R	HR	RBI	SB	BA	xHR	xSB	xBA	OBP	SLG	OPS+	vL+	vR+	bb%	ct%	Eye	G	L	F	h%	HctX	QBaB	Brl%	PX	xPX	HR/F	xHR/F	Spd	SBA%	SB%	RAR	BPX	R$
17	aaa	560	74	12	59	19	245		9		345	379	99			13	74	0.59				31				87				91	15%	85%		67	$15
18	TAM *	605	75	15	69	15	219	11	11	236	316	380	93	79	98	12	69	0.46	43	21	36	28	104	CCc	7%	114	132	14%	14%	77	20%	54%	-12.1	60	$13
19	CLE *	524	57	15	55	10	226	10	14	227	310	373	95	95	94	11	69	0.39	39	24	38	30	74	CBc	5%	90	65	12%	10%	100	12%	64%	-16.6	4	$9
20																																			
21	2 AL	314	27	4	19	6	209	8	4	203	290	277	78	73	79	10	72	0.38	33	25	42	28	75	CAf	5%	43	74	5%	10%	107	9%	86%	-24.2	-85	$1
1st Half		195	16	3	13	1	226	5	3	228	297	305	84	106	78	9	75	0.40	37	28	35	29	88	CBf	5%	49	78	7%	11%	106	9%	50%	-14.6	-38	-$2
2nd Half		119	11	1	6	5	181	4	2	162	277	229	68	29	82	10	69	0.36	26	21	53	25	55	CAc	6%	33	65	3%	11%	112	9%	100%	-12.0	-165	-$5
22	Proj	**245**	**26**	**5**	**21**	**6**	**213**	**7**	**4**	**210**	**302**	**325**	**85**	**73**	**89**	**11**	**71**	**0.41**	**35**	**23**	**42**	**28**	**77**		**6%**	**74**	**82**	**8%**	**11%**	**99**	**8%**	**77%**	**-8.8**	**-55**	**$5**

ALAIN DE LEONARDIS

Beaty,Matt

Age: 29 Pos: LF 1B RF | Bats: L Ht: 6' 0" Wt: 215
Health A | PT/Exp D | Consist C | LIMA Plan D | Rand Var -5 | MM 2131

7-40-.270 in 234 PA at LA. Normally, a collection of 50-grade skills would be enough to carve out a 400 PA/year role, but he is still waiting. Be skeptical of 2020-21 "improvement" vL; was just 29 PA. Strong ct% remains the foundational skill, but PX and HctX sank and xPX suggests it could've been worse. Time is ticking on getting a full-time shot.

Yr	Tm	PA	R	HR	RBI	SB	BA	xHR	xSB	xBA	OBP	SLG	OPS+	vL+	vR+	bb%	ct%	Eye	G	L	F	h%	HctX	QBaB	Brl%	PX	xPX	HR/F	xHR/F	Spd	SBA%	SB%	RAR	BPX
17	aa	465	50	13	57	2	288		6		328	444	105			6	86	0.42				31				87				82	5%	42%		152
18	aaa	110	10	1	9	0	231		1		291	338	84			8	80	0.42				28				81				91	0%	0%		97
19	LA *	396	48	11	59	5	258	6	1	283	303	424	100	46	115	6	87	0.49	48	19	33	27	121	BCc	5%	83	93	13%	8%	89	7%	80%	-10.6	204
20	LA	54	8	2	5	0	220	1	1	240	278	360	85	121	79	4	72	0.14	47	25	28	26	121	BDb	3%	77	98	20%	10%	99	0%	0%	-4.4	-40
21	LA *	263	38	7	43	2	270	5	2	226	331	396	100	124	103	8	77	0.39	44	18	38	33	86	CCf	4%	70	61	12%	8%	105	5%	50%	-9.6	46
1st Half		146	18	3	27	0	250	2	1	231	342	359	98	48	102	7	79	0.37	46	20	35	30	89	CDf	2%	58	62	9%	6%	108	5%	0%	-7.8	42
2nd Half		117	20	4	16	2	294	3	1	216	362	441	109	201	106	10	74	0.41	42	15	42	37	82	DAf	6%	85	59	16%	12%	97	5%	67%	0.1	50
22	**Proj**	**210**	**28**	**8**	**29**	**2**	**265**	**5**	**2**	**258**	**343**	**443**	**107**	**128**	**104**	**8**	**80**	**0.42**	**45**	**19**	**36**	**30**	**99**		**4%**	**99**	**74**	**14%**	**9%**	**89**	**5%**	**61%**	**3.2**	**134**

Beer,Seth

Age: 25 Pos: DH | Bats: L Ht: 6' 3" Wt: 195
Health B | PT/Exp C | Consist C | LIMA Plan D | Rand Var +5 | MM 3021

1-3-.444 in 10 PA at ARI. Shoulder surgery ended season in mid-Sept and could affect 2022. Before that, couldn't find MLB time on a last-place team despite AAA success (.909 OPS), confirming that future role is probably DH. Until then, we're left to wonder if MiLB contact rates will translate to MLB—and now, if the shoulder will impact his plus-power profile

Yr	Tm	PA	R	HR	RBI	SB	BA	xHR	xSB	xBA	OBP	SLG	OPS+	vL+	vR+	bb%	ct%	Eye	G	L	F	h%	HctX	QBaB	Brl%	PX	xPX	HR/F	xHR/F	Spd	SBA%	SB%	RAR	BPX
17																																		
18																																		
19	aa	353	45	16	65	0	258		4		324	450	107			9	72	0.35				31				106				82	1%	0%		67
20																																		
21	ARI *	393	44	9	35	0	215	0	3	290	259	358	85	150	241	6	74	0.23	0	50	50	27	152	CAa	0%	96	269	33%	0%	97	0%	0%	-33.0	62
1st Half		192	21	3	15	0	205		1	240	250	342	82	0	0	6	74	0.23	44	20	36	26	0		0%	98	-22	0%		100	0%	0%	-16.4	73
2nd Half		201	22	6	20	0	225	0	2	291	268	374	87	147	238	6	74	0.23	0	50	50	27	151	CAa	0%	93	269	33%	0%	100	0%	0%	-13.5	50
22	**Proj**	**245**	**28**	**10**	**28**	**0**	**228**	**10**	**1**	**243**	**279**	**418**	**95**	**94**	**95**	**7**	**74**	**0.27**	**38**	**20**	**42**	**26**	**96**		**7%**	**117**		**14%**	**14%**	**96**	**3%**	**0%**	**-5.6**	**60**

Bell,Josh

Age: 29 Pos: 1B | Bats: B Ht: 6' 4" Wt: 250
Health A | PT/Exp A | Consist D | LIMA Plan B | Rand Var 0 | MM 3145

A closer look after 2020 gave reasons to remain interested (HctX, HR/F, exit velocity) and he delivered in 2021. Overcame a slow start (.140 BA in mid-May) and replicated a lot of 2019, save the flyball boost. Summer surge vL likely too small to bet on (109 PA), but firm Eye, h%, HctX, and xHR/F skills offer stability. UP: 2019 is still in play

Yr	Tm	PA	R	HR	RBI	SB	BA	xHR	xSB	xBA	OBP	SLG	OPS+	vL+	vR+	bb%	ct%	Eye	G	L	F	h%	HctX	QBaB	Brl%	PX	xPX	HR/F	xHR/F	Spd	SBA%	SB%	RAR	BPX
17	PIT	620	75	26	90	2	255	19	9	275	334	466	109	102	109	11	79	0.56	51	18	31	28	104	CDc	6%	113	95	19%	14%	94	4%	33%	-11.2	173
18	PIT	583	74	12	62	2	261	18	5	256	357	411	103	97	103	13	79	0.74	49	19	33	31	99	BCc	7%	93	88	9%	14%	97	4%	29%	-2.3	163
19	PIT	613	94	37	116	0	277	38	4	291	367	569	130	106	137	12	78	0.63	44	19	37	29	122	ACc	13%	150	135	24%	25%	67	1%	0%	28.3	285
20	PIT	223	22	8	22	0	226	8	1	212	305	364	89	77	93	10	70	0.37	56	19	26	28	117	ADd	9%	77	57	22%	22%	85	0%	0%	-13.3	-44
21	WAS	568	75	27	88	0	261	28	1	278	347	476	113	114	112	11	80	0.64	54	20	27	28	122	AFc	9%	115	101	25%	26%	70	0%	0%	-3.1	219
1st Half		237	36	11	37	0	237	11	0	266	304	447	104	78	113	9	74	0.36	50	21	29	27	117	ADc	10%	124	114	24%	24%	58	0%	0%	-7.3	119
2nd Half		331	39	16	51	0	279	17	1	287	378	498	119	130	112	14	84	1.00	56	19	25	28	126	AFb	8%	109	92	27%	28%	84	0%	0%	8.1	300
22	**Proj**	**630**	**81**	**29**	**92**	**1**	**266**	**29**	**2**	**269**	**351**	**477**	**112**	**107**	**114**	**12**	**77**	**0.58**	**52**	**19**	**29**	**29**	**118**		**9%**	**116**	**96**	**24%**	**23%**	**79**	**2%**	**59%**	**21.5**	**165**

Bellinger,Cody

Age: 26 Pos: CF | Bats: L Ht: 6' 4" Wt: 203
Health C | PT/Exp A | Consist F | LIMA Plan C+ | Rand Var +5 | MM 4425

Entered with a bum shoulder and added IL stints for calf, leg, hamstring, and rib ... no wonder he was so bad. We can't know if he will be healthy in 2022 so is the discount worth a track record which includes elite PX, good HctX and Eye, solid xBA, bankable Spd, and an MVP in his mid-20s? Great playoff run was just 39 PA, but fuels rebound hope.

Yr	Tm	PA	R	HR	RBI	SB	BA	xHR	xSB	xBA	OBP	SLG	OPS+	vL+	vR+	bb%	ct%	Eye	G	L	F	h%	HctX	QBaB	Brl%	PX	xPX	HR/F	xHR/F	Spd	SBA%	SB%	RAR	BPX
17	LA *	622	99	43	109	16	272	36	8	267	356	579	127	122	127	11	69	0.42	35	18	47	32	120	AAc	12%	184	178	25%	23%	126	13%	84%	34.5	258
18	LA	632	84	25	76	14	260	28	15	250	343	470	109	90	116	11	73	0.46	40	20	40	31	108	BBd	9%	128	130	15%	17%	143	10%	93%	23.1	203
19	LA	660	121	47	115	15	305	45	13	306	406	629	143	137	145	14	81	0.88	31	26	42	31	137	AAb	13%	155	165	25%	24%	121	11%	75%	77.1	422
20	LA	243	33	12	30	6	239	11	4	267	333	455	105	87	114	12	80	0.71	38	22	41	25	124	CBd	9%	111	120	17%	16%	94	12%	86%	0.7	260
21	LA	350	39	10	36	3	165	12	5	205	240	302	74	52	83	9	70	0.33	31	22	48	20	88	CAd	7%	82	110	9%	11%	111	6%	75%	-29.4	0
1st Half		108	18	3	14	2	200	2	2	207	324	333	92	63	103	16	67	0.57	30	30	41	26	80	CAc	6%	76	93	12%	8%	136	6%	100%	-3.7	8
2nd Half		242	21	7	22	1	151	10	3	204	202	289	66	47	74	6	72	0.22	31	19	50	18	92	BAf	8%	84	117	9%	12%	99	6%	50%	-24.0	-12
22	**Proj**	**525**	**78**	**26**	**73**	**9**	**255**	**24**	**7**	**245**	**339**	**471**	**110**	**92**	**117**	**11**	**74**	**0.48**	**33**	**23**	**44**	**29**	**111**		**9%**	**121**	**124**	**17%**	**16%**	**113**	**7%**	**83%**	**21.0**	**178**

Belt,Brandon

Age: 34 Pos: 1B | Bats: L Ht: 6' 3" Wt: 231
Health D | PT/Exp A | Consist F | LIMA Plan B | Rand Var -2 | MM 5143

Career-high in HR despite just 97 games (oblique, knee, thumb injuries) as power skills (xPX) came to the fore with an infusion of FB and HR/F. Surge vL is sample size noise (75 PA), not a skill boost. Age and inconsistent health will tamp down draft price while old man skills of power and patience are worth buying even if he sits vL.

Yr	Tm	PA	R	HR	RBI	SB	BA	xHR	xSB	xBA	OBP	SLG	OPS+	vL+	vR+	bb%	ct%	Eye	G	L	F	h%	HctX	QBaB	Brl%	PX	xPX	HR/F	xHR/F	Spd	SBA%	SB%	RAR	BPX
17	SF	451	63	18	51	3	241	23	6	258	355	469	112	96	117	15	73	0.63	30	23	47	28	113	BAa	11%	140	154	14%	18%	86	4%	60%	-4.7	182
18	SF	456	50	14	46	4	253	24	5	235	342	414	101	83	109	11	73	0.46	24	29	47	31	112	CAa	11%	100	146	10%	18%	102	3%	100%	-3.6	90
19	SF	616	76	17	57	4	234	27	5	238	339	403	103	92	105	13	76	0.65	28	23	49	28	107	CAa	9%	95	139	9%	14%	89	4%	57%	-14.6	130
20	SF	179	25	9	30	0	309	12	2	292	425	591	135	72	148	17	76	0.83	31	27	42	36	125	BBc	17%	161	160	19%	26%	78	0%	0%	13.5	364
21	SF	381	65	29	59	3	274	28	2	265	378	597	134	113	139	13	68	0.47	27	23	50	31	108	CAc	17%	190	166	27%	26%	96	5%	60%	15.7	312
1st Half		201	30	11	28	3	253	11	1	235	363	512	122	138	118	14	62	0.43	32	25	43	34	102	CAd	15%	170	150	25%	25%	111	5%	75%	3.0	181
2nd Half		180	35	18	31	0	297	17	1	302	394	690	147	84	161	11	75	0.53	23	21	56	28	113	CAc	19%	208	180	28%	27%	75	5%	0%	15.4	446
22	**Proj**	**420**	**65**	**26**	**61**	**2**	**279**	**29**	**4**	**265**	**382**	**560**	**128**	**95**	**137**	**13**	**73**	**0.56**	**28**	**24**	**48**	**32**	**112**		**15%**	**163**	**159**	**20%**	**23%**	**83**	**5%**	**59%**	**30.1**	**270**

Benintendi,Andrew

Age: 27 Pos: LF | Bats: L Ht: 5' 9" Wt: 180
Health B | PT/Exp A | Consist F | LIMA Plan B | Rand Var -3 | MM 2235

Solid bounceback after lost 2020. Rib injury returned and ate up 3 weeks. Excellent xPX could've delivered new HR high (see xHR), but Kauffman Stadium stifled that, as it's wont to do vL. Spd dip alone doesn't account for horrid SB% leaving hope for SB rebound. League average power and speed skills, along with firm roles, are fantasy savings bonds.

Yr	Tm	PA	R	HR	RBI	SB	BA	xHR	xSB	xBA	OBP	SLG	OPS+	vL+	vR+	bb%	ct%	Eye	G	L	F	h%	HctX	QBaB	Brl%	PX	xPX	HR/F	xHR/F	Spd	SBA%	SB%	RAR	BPX
17	BOS	658	84	20	90	20	271	19	11	257	352	424	106	84	109	11	80	0.63	40	21	38	31	112	CBc	6%	85	100	11%	11%	103	14%	80%	-3.4	133
18	BOS	661	103	16	87	21	290	22	15	274	366	465	111	92	116	11	82	0.67	41	24	35	33	84	CCb	6%	104	81	9%	13%	108	13%	88%	27.4	220
19	BOS	615	72	13	68	10	266	22	13	243	343	431	107	111	105	10	74	0.42	38	21	41	34	98	CBa	8%	99	107	8%	13%	114	9%	77%	-0.7	115
20	BOS	52	4	0	1	1	103	1	1	120	314	128	59	47	61	21	56	0.65	57	5	38	18	60	FFf	4%	28	57	0%	13%	114	20%	33%	-6.4	-288
21	KC	538	63	17	73	8	276	26	14	254	324	442	105	108	104	7	80	0.37	39	21	41	31	115	CBc	9%	94	133	10%	16%	103	13%	47%	-9.6	165
1st Half		241	31	8	31	7	283	11	7	245	340	429	107	81	118	8	79	0.42	41	22	37	33	102	CCd	9%	76	107	12%	17%	122	13%	54%	-3.4	127
2nd Half		297	32	9	42	1	270	15	6	262	311	453	103	129	93	6	81	0.33	37	20	43	31	126	BBb	9%	108	153	9%	15%	92	13%	25%	-5.0	200
22	**Proj**	**560**	**72**	**16**	**74**	**11**	**276**	**23**	**11**	**254**	**338**	**442**	**106**	**104**	**106**	**9**	**79**	**0.45**	**39**	**22**	**39**	**32**	**106**		**8%**	**97**	**115**	**10%**	**14%**	**102**	**11%**	**65%**	**12.2**	**156**

Berti,Jon

Age: 32 Pos: 3B 2B | Bats: R Ht: 5' 10" Wt: 190
Health F | PT/Exp C | Consist B | LIMA Plan D+ | Rand Var +5 | MM 1413

Concussion ended season in late July. Ugly BA is primarily driven by h% erosion; xBA tells us it's standard variance. BB%, K%, HctX, and PX were in line with 2019-20 run when he hit .269 in 436 PA. Small-sample volatility comes with part-time roles, but he remains a viable late-round SB target in deep formats or as a short-term roster fill-in.

Yr	Tm	PA	R	HR	RBI	SB	BA	xHR	xSB	xBA	OBP	SLG	OPS+	vL+	vR+	bb%	ct%	Eye	G	L	F	h%	HctX	QBaB	Brl%	PX	xPX	HR/F	xHR/F	Spd	SBA%	SB%	RAR	BPX
17	aaa	233	23	3	18	20	186		2		248	296	74			8	71	0.28				25				67				138	58%	81%		-9
18	TOR *	389	53	6	38	23	250	0	33	285	306	375	91	83	113	8	78	0.37	45	36	18	30	183	AFa	9%	73	177	0%	0%	160	38%	66%	-10.9	120
19	MIA *	361	63	9	30	21	264	6	22	264	339	400	102	123	99	10	73	0.41	53	26	21	34	92	CFc	4%	79	59	16%	16%	134	24%	87%	-4.5	59
20	MIA	149	21	2	14	9	258	2	7	219	388	350	98	88	102	15	69	0.62	53	20	27	36	62	DFd	3%	63	40	9%	9%	100	22%	82%	-1.8	-36
21	MIA	271	35	4	19	8	210	4	9	245	311	313	86	75	92	12	74	0.52	59	20	21	27	76	CFc	2%	66	49	11%	11%	108	17%	67%	-16.6	23
1st Half		230	32	4	18	7	227	4	8	260	323	343	93	72	105	12	77	0.61	56	22	21	28	83	CFb	3%	71	56	12%	12%	109	17%	64%	-9.4	88
2nd Half		41	3	0	1	1	114	0	1	149	244	143	52	91	19	10	57	0.27	75	5	20	20	35	FFf	0%	32	-9	0%	0%	95	17%	100%	-5.0	-365
22	**Proj**	**280**	**41**	**3**	**25**	**15**	**241**	**4**	**9**	**238**	**341**	**338**	**92**	**99**	**88**	**11**	**74**	**0.48**	**62**	**17**	**22**	**31**	**64**		**2%**	**62**	**31**	**8%**	**10%**	**113**	**14%**	**75%**	**-4.2**	**19**

PAUL SPORER

Betts,Mookie

Age: 29 Pos: RF CF
Bats: R Ht: 5' 9" Wt: 180

Health	B	LIMA Plan	C
PT/Exp	A	Rand Var	+2
Consist	B	MM	4445

Nagging physical woes (back, forearm, shoulder) factored into slow start. Post-ASB hip injury shelved him for 28 days, cutting into PA as well as the running game and counting stats we've come to expect. But plate skills, HctX remain stellar and power is still intact. Some "youngs" may be drafted earlier, but health rebound will return solid 1st round value.

Yr	Tm	PA	R	HR	RBI	SB	BA	xHR	xSB	xBA	OBP	SLG	OPS+	vL+	vR+	bb%	ct%	Eye	G	L	F	h%	HctX	QBaB	Brl%	PX	xPX	HR/F	xHR/F	Spd	SBA%	SB%	RAR	BPX	R$
17	BOS	712	101	24	102	26	264	17	10	279	344	459	109	125	103	11	87	0.97	40	17	43	27	126	CBd	5%	103	110	10%	7%	95	17%	90%	8.3	255	$28
18	BOS	614	129	32	80	30	346	43	21	302	438	640	145	160	137	13	83	0.89	34	21	45	37	135	AAb	14%	166	151	16%	22%	141	19%	83%	88.6	447	$46
19	BOS	706	135	29	80	16	295	37	25	279	391	524	127	117	130	14	83	0.96	31	25	44	31	124	AAb	10%	113	134	13%	17%	133	9%	84%	35.6	341	$31
20	LA	246	47	16	39	10	292	10	5	277	366	562	123	69	141	10	83	0.63	32	21	46	29	149	BAb	8%	129	179	19%	12%	145	19%	83%	13.5	396	$40
21	LA	550	93	23	58	10	264	22	18	272	367	487	117	117	118	12	82	0.79	35	22	43	28	137	BAc	8%	120	140	14%	13%	138	10%	67%	10.2	346	$21
1st Half		327	49	10	31	7	248	10	10	270	361	456	114	100	119	13	81	0.81	36	22	43	27	133	BAd	7%	118	119	10%	10%	139	10%	70%	2.2	342	$20
2nd Half		223	44	13	27	3	286	12	8	277	377	531	123	142	116	12	82	0.76	34	21	44	29	143	AAc	9%	123	169	18%	17%	116	10%	60%	10.0	338	$17
22	Proj	595	112	30	75	16	286	28	13	276	377	526	123	115	125	12	83	0.78	34	22	44	30	138		9%	125	151	16%	15%	128	10%	77%	38.1	343	$30

Bichette,Bo

Age: 24 Pos: SS
Bats: R Ht: 6' 0" Wt: 185

Health	A	LIMA Plan	D+
PT/Exp	A	Rand Var	-2
Consist	A	MM	3455

Health, skills, age coalesced for breakout season. GB% spiked and he's still not the most selective hitter—but contact skills, h% history, exit velocity and HR/F make the warts less consequential. Impeccable running game capable of more with more green lights. Likely to give back some of this, but monster skills set a high floor and several profit paths.

Yr	Tm	PA	R	HR	RBI	SB	BA	xHR	xSB	xBA	OBP	SLG	OPS+	vL+	vR+	bb%	ct%	Eye	G	L	F	h%	HctX	QBaB	Brl%	PX	xPX	HR/F	xHR/F	Spd	SBA%	SB%	RAR	BPX	R$
17																																			
18	aa	582	84	10	66	28	281		8		333	442	104			7	81	0.41				33				104				108	29%	71%		183	$26
19	TOR *	451	62	18	49	17	287	10	16	279	335	508	117	150	119	7	76	0.30	44	23	34	34	86	BCc	9%	125	97	22%	20%	122	27%	65%	7.8	207	$19
20	TOR	128	18	5	23	4	301	6	4	281	328	512	112	112	111	4	78	0.19	41	26	33	35	102	BCc	13%	120	111	16%	19%	120	19%	80%	5.1	216	$16
21	TOR	690	121	29	102	25	298	34	19	272	343	484	114	129	109	6	79	0.29	49	21	30	34	117	ADd	10%	103	92	19%	22%	105	15%	96%	27.8	162	$42
1st Half		361	68	15	54	12	287	19	10	271	338	479	114	143	105	6	76	0.29	50	21	29	34	106	AFd	11%	110	94	20%	26%	109	15%	100%	12.8	158	$41
2nd Half		329	53	14	48	13	310	15	9	272	350	490	114	116	113	5	81	0.29	48	20	32	35	128	ACc	8%	96	89	18%	19%	104	15%	93%	16.0	173	$37
22	Proj	665	105	29	96	23	288	32	14	279	331	500	113	124	108	6	78	0.27	46	22	32	33	109		10%	120	96	19%	21%	111	16%	83%	30.1	223	$39

Biggio,Cavan

Age: 27 Pos: 3B
Bats: L Ht: 6' 2" Wt: 200

Health	C	LIMA Plan	D
PT/Exp	B	Rand Var	+2
Consist	B	MM	3303

7-27-.224 with 3 SB in 294 PA at TOR. Injuries dogged him out of the gate (finger, hand), in mid-May (chronic neck/back issues) and in late Aug (UCL strain). Plus patience, xPX, SB% still tease; age, handedness buy him time. But contact woes look chronic. Legacy name on a team with Guerrero/Bichette stardom sets a higher bar, unfortunately.

Yr	Tm	PA	R	HR	RBI	SB	BA	xHR	xSB	xBA	OBP	SLG	OPS+	vL+	vR+	bb%	ct%	Eye	G	L	F	h%	HctX	QBaB	Brl%	PX	xPX	HR/F	xHR/F	Spd	SBA%	SB%	RAR	BPX	R$
17																																			
18	aa	533	68	22	84	17	233		8		355	450	108			16	64	0.53				31				150				104	19%	66%		140	$19
19	TOR *	595	85	21	71	18	249	14	18	228	375	439	113	103	112	17	69	0.64	25	28	47	32	94	CAa	9%	112	151	15%	13%	106	11%	94%	11.2	115	$19
20	TOR	264	41	8	28	6	250	6	6	242	375	432	107	118	101	16	72	0.67	38	21	41	31	88	CBd	5%	116	110	13%	9%	108	8%	100%	4.7	188	$23
21	TOR *	379	40	10	36	3	209	7	5	210	307	340	89	73	99	12	67	0.43	38	22	40	28	84	CBc	6%	86	111	10%	10%	97	4%	75%	-15.1	-27	$2
1st Half		239	24	7	22	2	227	6	4	217	335	379	99	80	108	14	68	0.50	39	21	40	30	94	BCd	7%	98	124	12%	12%	106	4%	67%	-5.6	42	$5
2nd Half		140	16	3	14	1	179	1	2	203	258	277	72	54	74	10	66	0.31	33	27	40	25	54	DAc	2%	67	73	6%	6%	90	4%	100%	-11.4	-131	-$5
22	Proj	315	40	9	35	6	240	7	3	221	343	397	100	93	103	14	68	0.50	34	24	42	32	79		5%	103	109	12%	9%	98	5%	86%	3.2	30	$9

Blackmon,Charlie

Age: 36 Pos: RF
Bats: L Ht: 6' 3" Wt: 221

Health	A	LIMA Plan	B
PT/Exp	A	Rand Var	+1
Consist	B	MM	2245

GB% spiked as aging OF's 2020 power collapse now looks entrenched. With running game also gone, elite production is in the rearview. But plate skills, HctX still offer superior BA, OBP support and counting stats. A mild HR uptick and final hurrah wouldn't surprise; just don't pay for it. Free agent likely to exercise player option; his 2022 venue will matter.

Yr	Tm	PA	R	HR	RBI	SB	BA	xHR	xSB	xBA	OBP	SLG	OPS+	vL+	vR+	bb%	ct%	Eye	G	L	F	h%	HctX	QBaB	Brl%	PX	xPX	HR/F	xHR/F	Spd	SBA%	SB%	RAR	BPX	R$
17	COL	725	137	37	104	14	331	32	12	294	399	601	136	129	137	9	79	0.48	41	22	37	37	125	CCb	9%	141	141	20%	17%	161	12%	58%	59.4	294	$42
18	COL	696	119	29	70	12	291	24	14	277	358	502	115	108	117	8	79	0.44	43	23	33	33	104	CCb	7%	119	97	18%	15%	121	9%	75%	33.6	217	$30
19	COL	634	112	32	86	2	314	30	10	298	364	576	130	131	129	6	82	0.38	39	23	38	34	114	CBb	8%	129	132	18%	17%	121	5%	29%	32.1	304	$27
20	COL	247	31	6	42	2	303	7	2	265	356	448	107	121	98	8	80	0.43	36	28	35	36	100	DCf	5%	81	92	10%	11%	90	4%	67%	3.9	116	$25
21	COL	582	76	13	78	3	270	19	6	266	351	411	105	105	105	9	82	0.59	47	22	31	31	112	CCd	7%	77	91	10%	15%	100	2%	100%	-4.0	158	$17
1st Half		301	33	4	38	0	259	8	3	252	359	371	102	95	105	12	84	0.81	50	19	31	30	123	CDd	6%	64	91	6%	12%	99	2%	0%	-5.0	158	$10
2nd Half		281	43	9	40	3	282	12	3	275	342	451	107	118	104	7	81	0.41	44	25	31	32	102	CCd	8%	91	91	14%	19%	98	2%	100%	2.7	162	$19
22	Proj	560	84	18	80	5	290	21	5	271	355	464	111	115	109	8	81	0.48	43	24	33	33	109		7%	96	100	13%	15%	103	4%	71%	19.9	181	$24

Bogaerts,Xander

Age: 29 Pos: SS
Bats: R Ht: 6' 2" Wt: 218

Health	A	LIMA Plan	B+
PT/Exp	A	Rand Var	-2
Consist	A	MM	3345

2nd half h% regression, July wrist injury, Sept COVID IL stint removed some luster from a banner start. But plate skills, HctX held up throughout, and final tally was within hailing distance of previous efforts. Short-season 2020 SBA% looks like a blip though SB% is still worthy. Age, floor say continue to bid with confidence.

Yr	Tm	PA	R	HR	RBI	SB	BA	xHR	xSB	xBA	OBP	SLG	OPS+	vL+	vR+	bb%	ct%	Eye	G	L	F	h%	HctX	QBaB	Brl%	PX	xPX	HR/F	xHR/F	Spd	SBA%	SB%	RAR	BPX	R$
17	BOS	635	94	10	62	15	273	7	10	262	343	403	102	105	99	9	80	0.48	49	21	30	33	101	CDd	1%	77	54	7%	5%	134	9%	94%	4.6	121	$19
18	BOS	580	72	23	103	8	288	27	9	292	360	522	118	107	119	9	80	0.54	43	21	36	32	112	BCd	10%	141	101	16%	18%	102	7%	80%	37.3	283	$25
19	BOS	698	110	33	117	4	309	28	9	283	384	555	130	127	130	11	80	0.62	41	19	40	34	108	BCc	8%	130	116	17%	14%	88	3%	67%	45.4	278	$30
20	BOS	225	36	11	28	8	300	11	2	261	364	502	115	132	106	9	80	0.51	46	18	36	33	117	CDf	9%	103	116	19%	19%	95	13%	100%	13.2	204	$31
21	BOS	603	90	23	79	5	295	26	13	270	370	493	119	111	122	10	79	0.55	40	23	37	34	113	BCd	10%	114	104	15%	16%	96	4%	83%	28.9	219	$25
1st Half		335	52	13	48	5	326	14	7	285	388	540	129	136	126	9	80	0.50	41	23	36	37	115	CCf	10%	127	104	15%	16%	99	4%	83%	26.7	273	$34
2nd Half		268	38	10	31	0	255	12	6	250	347	433	106	87	118	12	77	0.60	39	22	39	29	111	BBc	9%	98	103	14%	17%	98	4%	0%	3.7	162	$11
22	Proj	630	95	26	87	7	291	27	5	267	364	492	116	112	118	10	79	0.55	42	21	37	33	112		9%	114	105	15%	16%	87	4%	88%	35.6	206	$29

Bohm,Alec

Age: 25 Pos: 3B
Bats: R Ht: 6' 5" Wt: 218

Health	A	LIMA Plan	C
PT/Exp	B	Rand Var	0
Consist	D	MM	2223

7-47-.247 in 411 PA at PHI. July COVID IL stint, August demotion ended the disappointment. But 4+ months of playing time exposed once-touted prospect's biggest obstacle: ingrained GB%, reinforced by QBaB. Deterioration of once-sturdy ct%, bb% added to his woes. HctX, HR/F, exit velocity, age all pluses, but needs reset and swing re-tool.

Yr	Tm	PA	R	HR	RBI	SB	BA	xHR	xSB	xBA	OBP	SLG	OPS+	vL+	vR+	bb%	ct%	Eye	G	L	F	h%	HctX	QBaB	Brl%	PX	xPX	HR/F	xHR/F	Spd	SBA%	SB%	RAR	BPX	R$
17																																			
18																																			
19	aa	263	34	14	38	2	252		3		323	478	111			10	82	0.57				25				107				100	7%	45%		233	$6
20	PHI	180	24	4	23	1	338	7	3	259	400	481	117	113	118	9	78	0.44	53	21	25	42	87	BFb	10%	89	73	13%	22%	104	4%	50%	8.1	128	$18
21	PHI *	481	52	8	51	6	245	11	3	235	302	342	88	108	79	7	71	0.28	53	25	23	33	110	AFb	7%	66	78	11%	18%	87	6%	84%	-23.1	-81	$9
1st Half		301	33	4	35	4	238	8	2	243	286	321	85	113	71	6	71	0.24	53	27	20	32	116	AFb	7%	58	79	10%	20%	83	6%	100%	-15.9	-108	$10
2nd Half		180	19	4	16	2	258	3	1	214	328	376	95	100	103	9	69	0.34	52	17	31	35	96	BDc	5%	82	77	14%	14%	107	6%	64%	-4.3	-19	$2
22	Proj	420	50	10	49	4	268	13	5	243	332	396	99	105	96	8	74	0.35	53	21	26	34	100		7%	81	77	13%	18%	105	6%	68%	2.7	-8	$13

Bote,David

Age: 29 Pos: 2B 3B
Bats: R Ht: 6' 1" Wt: 205

Health	C	LIMA Plan	D
PT/Exp	B	Rand Var	+5
Consist	B	MM	2213

Dislocated shoulder cost him a month, likely played into power outage and struggles vR. More aggressive plate approach yielded improved ct% but nothing else. BA, h% woes carried over from 2020 fueled by stagnant GB%, LD%. HctX, xPX, Brl% offer rebound hope. Marginally-skilled bench utility will be on your league's FA list if you need him.

Yr	Tm	PA	R	HR	RBI	SB	BA	xHR	xSB	xBA	OBP	SLG	OPS+	vL+	vR+	bb%	ct%	Eye	G	L	F	h%	HctX	QBaB	Brl%	PX	xPX	HR/F	xHR/F	Spd	SBA%	SB%	RAR	BPX	R$
17	aa	515	58	12	53	4	247		7		313	396	96			9	75	0.39				30				92				100	5%	67%		76	$7
18	CHC *	465	48	15	63	5	230	11	5	242	295	399	93	115	88	8	68	0.29	57	18	24	30	97	AFa	11%	111	101	19%	35%	122	10%	50%	-6.7	57	$9
19	CHC	356	47	11	41	5	257	8	6	249	362	422	109	95	112	12	69	0.47	50	23	27	34	87	BDa	6%	101	78	19%	14%	100	6%	83%	5.4	56	$8
20	CHC	145	15	7	29	2	200	6	2	232	303	408	94	69	107	12	68	0.43	50	16	34	23	99	ACf	10%	117	107	24%	21%	110	6%	100%	-4.2	96	$9
21	CHC	327	32	8	35	0	199	13	4	213	276	330	83	96	78	8	75	0.37	48	14	39	24	121	BCf	10%	75	117	9%	15%	126	1%	0%	-20.6	62	-$1
1st Half		162	16	5	23	0	201	9	2	220	280	340	86	82	88	8	75	0.36	49	16	36	23	120	BDf	14%	81	134	13%	23%	88	1%	0%	-9.2	38	-$1
2nd Half		165	16	3	12	0	197	4	2	203	273	320	80	107	67	9	75	0.38	46	12	42	24	123	BCf	6%	70	101	6%	9%	151	1%	0%	-9.8	77	-$5
22	Proj	280	30	9	36	2	221	11	2	229	306	384	94	95	93	10	72	0.39	49	16	34	27	108		9%	96	104	15%	18%	106	4%	69%	-2.5	29	$6

JOCK THOMPSON

Bradley,Bobby

Age: 26 Pos: 1B | Bats: L Ht: 6' 1" Wt: 225
Health A | PT/Exp C | Consist C
LIMA Plan D+ | Rand Var +1 | MM 4015

16-41-.208 in 279 PA at CLE. Steady erosion of ct% as he's moved up the ladder is a concern, and 2nd half shows it didn' take long for MLB pitchers to find holes in his swing. And while xPX, xHR/F suggest power skills are the real deal, QBaB is decidedly average, and elite Brl% will be tough to repeat. Could get you 30 HR, or... DN: 300 PA, more time in AAA.

Yr	Tm	PA	R	HR	RBI	SB	BA	xHR	xSB	xBA	OBP	SLG	OPS+	vL+	vR+	bb%	ct%	Eye	G	L	F	h%	HctX	QBaB	Brl%	PX	xPX	HR/F	xHR/F	Spd	SBA%	SB%	RAR	BPX
17	aa	515	55	20	75	3	241		6		311	434	101			9	75	0.41				28				114				89	5%	44%		118
18	a/a	530	50	23	69	1	212		4		282	423	95			9	67	0.30				26				142				95	1%	100%		103
19	CLE *	490	58	29	66	0	237	1	1	239	304	495	111	78	84	9	58	0.23	44	24	32	33	88	ACc	8%	177	94	13%	13%	64	0%	0%	1.6	44
20																																		
21	CLE *	381	47	22	54	0	194	18	2	222	258	420	93	95	104	8	59	0.21	40	22	38	25	94	CCc	17%	156	143	29%	32%	62	0%	0%	-20.9	-8
1st Half		193	28	14	30	0	197	8	1	237	255	462	100	107	134	7	62	0.20	52	16	32	22	96	BDd	24%	168	125	44%	44%	75	0%	0%	-10.8	85
2nd Half		188	19	8	24	0	190	10	1	205	282	374	89	88	89	9	55	0.22	33	26	41	28	90	CBc	13%	141	153	21%	26%	67	0%	0%	-13.2	-100
22	**Proj**	**455**	**52**	**25**	**63**	**0**	**210**	**26**	**0**	**231**	**289**	**441**	**99**	**91**	**102**	**9**	**62**	**0.24**	**41**	**22**	**37**	**27**	**92**		**17%**	**158**	**142**	**26%**	**28%**	**62**	**1%**	**62%**	**-6.6**	**15**

Bradley,Jackie

Age: 32 Pos: CF | Bats: L Ht: 5' 10" Wt: 196
Health A | PT/Exp A | Consist D
LIMA Plan D | Rand Var +5 | MM 2301

Yikes. Even our most pessimistic projection wouldn't have spit out a season this bad, with career-worst ct% and nary a plus skill in sight. Didn't spend a day on IL, though did battle spring training soreness from 2020 surgery to remove right wrist cyst, and had Sept plantar fasciitis. Rebound to 2020-21 middle ground is the safe bet, but also... DN: Done

Yr	Tm	PA	R	HR	RBI	SB	BA	xHR	xSB	xBA	OBP	SLG	OPS+	vL+	vR+	bb%	ct%	Eye	G	L	F	h%	HctX	QBaB	Brl%	PX	xPX	HR/F	xHR/F	Spd	SBA%	SB%	RAR	BPX
17	BOS	541	58	17	63	8	245	18	8	246	323	402	99	103	95	9	74	0.39	49	18	33	30	100	CCd	7%	91	89	15%	15%	99	8%	73%	-11.7	58
18	BOS	535	76	13	59	17	234	23	6	243	314	403	96	75	101	9	71	0.34	43	21	36	30	108	ACc	10%	117	130	11%	19%	96	15%	94%	-0.3	87
19	BOS	567	69	21	62	8	225	22	12	242	317	421	102	89	108	10	69	0.36	50	17	33	28	85	BCd	10%	117	99	18%	19%	104	11%	57%	-3.0	78
20	BOS	217	32	7	22	5	283	6	4	255	364	450	108	117	103	11	75	0.48	53	19	28	35	82	CFf	8%	100	57	18%	15%	98	11%	71%	3.5	128
21	MIL	428	39	6	29	7	163	8	5	206	236	261	68	72	68	7	66	0.21	50	19	31	23	92	BCf	5%	68	78	8%	10%	91	10%	88%	-41.7	-150
1st Half		273	24	6	23	5	173	6	4	209	253	296	76	73	77	8	65	0.23	49	19	31	24	102	BCf	5%	83	77	12%	12%	90	10%	83%	-21.5	-119
2nd Half		155	15	0	6	2	146	3	2	199	206	201	55	71	51	5	68	0.17	52	18	30	21	74	BDf	5%	45	78	0%	10%	93	10%	100%	-17.9	-196
22	**Proj**	**245**	**29**	**5**	**21**	**5**	**226**	**7**	**4**	**223**	**300**	**354**	**89**	**95**	**86**	**8**	**69**	**0.28**	**50**	**19**	**31**	**30**	**88**		**7%**	**85**	**83**	**10%**	**14%**	**96**	**8%**	**79%**	**-4.0**	**-30**

Brantley,Michael

Age: 35 Pos: LF DH | Bats: L Ht: 6' 2" Wt: 209
Health B | PT/Exp A | Consist A
LIMA Plan B | Rand Var -1 | MM 1355

One thing you can count on is him putting bat on ball and roping line drives to a .300 BA. xHR says double-digit HR are still in play, but age, injuries have conspired to kill his running game. Series of ailments ruined his 2nd half, so there's profit to be had at the right price—one that factors in PA risks of advancing age and shaky platoon splits.

Yr	Tm	PA	R	HR	RBI	SB	BA	xHR	xSB	xBA	OBP	SLG	OPS+	vL+	vR+	bb%	ct%	Eye	G	L	F	h%	HctX	QBaB	Brl%	PX	xPX	HR/F	xHR/F	Spd	SBA%	SB%	RAR	BPX
17	CLE	375	47	9	52	11	299	8	6	288	357	444	109	94	114	8	85	0.62	49	22	28	33	117	CCb	4%	81	74	11%	10%	93	12%	92%	4.5	158
18	CLE	630	89	17	76	12	309	15	12	299	364	468	112	91	117	8	89	0.80	45	25	30	32	122	BCa	4%	87	79	11%	10%	83	9%	80%	26.4	233
19	HOU	637	88	22	90	3	311	19	8	306	372	503	121	103	127	8	89	0.77	45	24	31	32	128	CCa	6%	92	89	14%	12%	75	3%	60%	25.9	252
20	HOU	187	24	5	22	2	300	5	1	284	364	476	112	83	123	9	84	0.61	47	22	31	34	126	CCc	5%	102	104	11%	11%	85	4%	100%	4.4	244
21	HOU	508	68	8	47	1	311	15	7	293	362	437	110	78	127	6	89	0.62	46	26	28	34	125	BCb	6%	70	80	7%	13%	113	1%	100%	4.3	231
1st Half		279	41	5	31	0	340	9	3	320	384	502	123	100	138	6	88	0.55	45	30	25	37	140	BCa	7%	94	91	9%	16%	96	1%	0%	13.5	269
2nd Half		229	27	3	16	1	276	6	3	257	336	357	94	49	116	7	90	0.73	47	21	31	30	107	CCb	5%	41	66	5%	10%	129	1%	100%	-7.2	177
22	**Proj**	**490**	**65**	**11**	**53**	**4**	**303**	**14**	**3**	**287**	**360**	**448**	**110**	**80**	**123**	**7**	**88**	**0.66**	**46**	**24**	**30**	**33**	**123**		**5%**	**79**	**84**	**9%**	**12%**	**101**	**3%**	**87%**	**19.0**	**206**

Bregman,Alex

Age: 28 Pos: 3B | Bats: R Ht: 6' 0" Wt: 192
Health C | PT/Exp A | Consist C
LIMA Plan B+ | Rand Var 0 | MM 3245

12-55-.270 in 400 PA at HOU Our prior skepticism of power skills (HR/xHR gap, low Brl%, declining QBaB) got borne out, and then there's this—vs. breaking balls, 2017-19: .279 BA, 82% ct, .250 Isolated Power; 2020-21: .198 BA, 76% ct, .153 ISO. Maybe it's the leg injuries, maybe not. But it's clear you can't bid expecting that $30 player to come back.

Yr	Tm	PA	R	HR	RBI	SB	BA	xHR	xSB	xBA	OBP	SLG	OPS+	vL+	vR+	bb%	ct%	Eye	G	L	F	h%	HctX	QBaB	Brl%	PX	xPX	HR/F	xHR/F	Spd	SBA%	SB%	RAR	BPX
17	HOU	626	88	19	71	17	284	15	9	276	352	475	113	132	104	9	83	0.57	38	22	40	32	110	CBc	5%	106	102	10%	8%	119	14%	77%	16.2	212
18	HOU	705	105	31	103	10	286	26	16	298	394	532	124	129	120	14	86	1.13	35	22	43	29	112	BBc	8%	137	127	14%	12%	97	7%	71%	49.3	370
19	HOU	690	122	41	112	5	296	20	11	303	423	592	141	165	130	17	85	1.43	32	23	46	29	131	BAc	5%	138	135	19%	9%	96	3%	83%	61.5	430
20	HOU	180	19	6	22	0	242	4	1	284	350	451	106	129	96	13	83	0.92	34	25	41	26	123	CBc	4%	113	92	11%	8%	87	0%	0%	1.7	308
21	HOU *	440	58	13	58	1	262	13	2	253	345	411	104	114	103	11	86	0.87	41	18	41	28	110	CBd	6%	80	94	10%	11%	88	1%	100%	0.6	215
1st Half		262	37	7	34	1	275	8	1	249	359	428	110	129	97	11	82	0.69	45	17	38	31	111	CBd	6%	89	80	10%	11%	89	1%	100%	2.0	188
2nd Half		178	21	6	24	0	243	6	1	260	327	386	96	76	113	11	91	1.43	34	21	45	24	105	BAc	7%	67	117	10%	12%	98	1%	0%	-3.8	277
22	**Proj**	**595**	**81**	**23**	**83**	**3**	**264**	**20**	**3**	**273**	**361**	**460**	**111**	**118**	**108**	**13**	**86**	**1.00**	**36**	**21**	**43**	**27**	**115**		**6%**	**102**	**108**	**12%**	**10%**	**87**	**2%**	**80%**	**21.3**	**269**

Brinson,Lewis

Age: 28 Pos: LF CF | Bats: R Ht: 6' 5" Wt: 212
Health B | PT/Exp C | Consist A
LIMA Plan D+ | Rand Var 0 | MM 2313

9-33-.226 in 290 PA at MIA. We keep waiting and waiting (and waiting) for any sign that he's finally living up to his top prospect potential, but growth is nowhere to be found. Even if a team holds its nose and gives him full-time PA, which could lead to 20 HR/10 SB, his career .217 xBA means you'll pay for it elsewhere. A deep league flyer at best.

Yr	Tm	PA	R	HR	RBI	SB	BA	xHR	xSB	xBA	OBP	SLG	OPS+	vL+	vR+	bb%	ct%	Eye	G	L	F	h%	HctX	QBaB	Brl%	PX	xPX	HR/F	xHR/F	Spd	SBA%	SB%	RAR	BPX
17	MIL *	377	49	13	37	9	260	2	5	267	319	446	104	126	42	8	74	0.33	57	17	27	32	100	ADa	7%	110	99	25%	25%	119	18%	61%	-3.6	115
18	MIA *	457	32	12	45	3	194	18	9	218	228	327	74	84	73	4	69	0.15	52	17	31	25	99	BDc	9%	82	109	13%	22%	157	5%	74%	-25.7	3
19	MIA *	572	63	12	63	15	205	4	6	206	263	333	83	74	59	7	63	0.21	49	17	34	30	88	CCd	4%	84	72	0%	8%	118	19%	68%	-25.0	-96
20	MIA	112	14	3	12	4	226	3	2	240	268	368	84	104	65	5	72	0.20	49	21	30	29	84	CDf	8%	91	56	13%	13%	108	19%	100%	-5.1	20
21	MIA *	338	26	10	35	3	227	9	7	232	260	369	86	102	81	4	73	0.17	42	21	37	28	81	CCf	6%	88	62	12%	12%	103	6%	72%	-18.5	19
1st Half		109	5	2	7	2	218	1	2	211	236	325	78	74	86	2	71	0.08	45	19	36	29	86	BCf	6%	68	47	12%	6%	122	6%	100%	-7.6	-69
2nd Half		229	22	8	29	1	231	7	5	241	272	391	90	111	79	5	74	0.22	42	21	37	28	79	CCf	6%	97	66	12%	12%	95	6%	50%	-9.3	62
22	**Proj**	**385**	**36**	**11**	**40**	**7**	**231**	**11**	**4**	**227**	**274**	**374**	**88**	**103**	**80**	**5**	**71**	**0.18**	**46**	**19**	**34**	**30**	**85**		**6%**	**91**	**66**	**12%**	**12%**	**107**	**7%**	**81%**	**-10.7**	**-28**

Brosseau,Mike

Age: 28 Pos: 2B 3B | Bats: R Ht: 5' 10" Wt: 205
Health A | PT/Exp C | Consist F
LIMA Plan D | Rand Var +5 | MM 3301

5-18-.187 in 169 PA at TAM. That 2019-20 run of MLB success was fun while it lasted (.284 BA, 11 HR in 240 PA), but xB never bought the high BA, and xHR, xHR/F didn't believe the power. 2021 showed what happens when those expected stats turn into expected regression. He's a good option vL (career .851 OPS, 150 PX), and that's about it.

Yr	Tm	PA	R	HR	RBI	SB	BA	xHR	xSB	xBA	OBP	SLG	OPS+	vL+	vR+	bb%	ct%	Eye	G	L	F	h%	HctX	QBaB	Brl%	PX	xPX	HR/F	xHR/F	Spd	SBA%	SB%	RAR	BPX
17																																		
18	aa	394	44	10	51	9	226		4		273	379	87			6	76	0.27				27				96				98	18%	67%		83
19	TAM *	440	60	18	64	3	261	3	9	240	320	462	108	115	100	8	73	0.32	40	17	43	32	104	DBf	4%	115	149	15%	8%	80	7%	43%	2.0	89
20	TAM	98	12	5	12	2	302	4	2	244	378	558	124	146	101	8	64	0.26	45	18	38	42	120	ABb	9%	164	143	24%	19%	132	8%	100%	6.9	180
21	TAM *	357	41	11	35	4	183	5	4	198	260	326	81	102	53	9	64	0.29	37	19	43	24	90	BAf	7%	96	104	12%	12%	108	6%	100%	-19.7	-50
1st Half		171	20	4	16	3	186	4	2	192	265	311	80	95	57	10	61	0.28	34	22	44	27	77	BAd	7%	95	95	10%	10%	89	6%	100%	-10.4	-115
2nd Half		186	21	7	19	1	180	1	2	190	254	340	81	188	0	9	66	0.30	64	0	36	22	172	AFf	8%	97	182	25%	25%	128	6%	100%	-11.4	4
22	**Proj**	**245**	**28**	**8**	**26**	**3**	**228**	**10**	**3**	**215**	**305**	**386**	**94**	**104**	**79**	**8**	**68**	**0.29**	**39**	**19**	**42**	**30**	**97**		**7%**	**101**	**123**	**13%**	**16%**	**105**	**6%**	**74%**	**-2.2**	**-23**

Brown,Seth

Age: 29 Pos: RF | Bats: L Ht: 6' 1" Wt: 223
Health A | PT/Exp C | Consist F
LIMA Plan C+ | Rand Var -1 | MM 4213

Enjoyed 2019 power breakout in minors thanks to switch to fly-ball-heavy approach (48% FB% in AAA), and successfully carried those skills over to MLB. Low h% hurt his BA, and heavy FB tilt could make that sticky, too. 2nd half gains in QBa xHR/F, SBA% make him a nice end-game speculation in case he can find the good side of a platoon.

Yr	Tm	PA	R	HR	RBI	SB	BA	xHR	xSB	xBA	OBP	SLG	OPS+	vL+	vR+	bb%	ct%	Eye	G	L	F	h%	HctX	QBaB	Brl%	PX	xPX	HR/F	xHR/F	Spd	SBA%	SB%	RAR	BPX
17																																		
18	aa	536	49	10	67	4	233		5		282	366	87			6	67	0.21				33				102				90	4%	100%		-27
19	OAK *	561	84	25	88	7	245	2	4	246	291	473	106	60	123	6	66	0.19	33	29	38	32	92	CBd	12%	139	93	0%	10%	99	8%	85%	-6.9	70
20	OAK	5	0	0	0	0	0	1	0	0	0	0	0	0	0	0	60	0.00	33	0	67	0	81	CAf	33%	0	223	0%	50%	95	7%	0%	-1.0	-512
21	OAK	307	43	20	48	4	214	19	2	243	274	480	104	69	107	7	68	0.26	31	19	50	23	95	CAf	14%	161	144	21%	20%	75	10%	80%	-10.3	158
1st Half		176	22	9	27	0	196	10	1	232	273	418	96	96	96	9	70	0.34	34	18	48	22	90	CAf	11%	130	141	17%	19%	82	10%	0%	-8.8	115
2nd Half		131	21	11	21	4	236	10	1	259	275	561	113	28	120	5	66	0.17	28	20	52	26	102	AAd	17%	205	149	26%	23%	78	10%	80%	-0.8	246
22	**Proj**	**350**	**48**	**18**	**53**	**5**	**230**	**19**	**4**	**235**	**282**	**464**	**101**	**55**	**107**	**6**	**67**	**0.21**	**31**	**21**	**48**	**28**	**96**		**14%**	**149**	**133**	**18%**	**18%**	**85**	**8%**	**83%**	**-0.8**	**124**

BRANDON KRUSE

Bruján,Vidal

Age: 24 Pos: 2B OF
Bats: R Ht: 5' 9" Wt: 155

Health	A	LIMA Plan	C
PT/Exp	C	Rand Var	+2
Consist	A	MM	2523

0-2-.077 with 1 SB in 26 PA at TAM. Didn't get much of a chance in brief MLB cameo, and small sample struggles quickly landed him back in AAA. Has game-changing speed, but can he get on base enough to maximize it? Prospect pedigree and plate discipline skills suggest he can, and perhaps quickly, making him intriguing late-round target.

Yr	Tm	PA	R	HR	RBI	SB	BA	xHR	xSB	xBA	OBP	SLG	OPS+	vL+	vR+	bb%	ct%	Eye	G	L	F	h%	HctX	QBaB	Brl%	PX	xPX	HR/F	xHR/F	Spd	SBA%	SB%	RAR	BPX	R$
17																																			
18																																			
19	aa	227	27	3	24	22	256		4		321	377	97			9	81	0.51				30				61				141	52%	73%		130	$10
20																																			
21	TAM *	458	70	10	51	39	224	0	5	236	297	369	91	16	31	9	79	0.49	56	6	39	26	90	FFf	0%	89	34	0%	0%	104	49%	82%	-13.1	154	$23
1st Half		211	32	8	25	13	232		2	263	311	416	101	0	0	10	79	0.55	44	20	36	26	0		0%	102	-22	0%		128	49%	75%	-3.9	231	$17
2nd Half		247	38	3	25	26	218	0	3	228	284	330	83	16	30	8	79	0.44	56	6	39	26	90	FFf	0%	79	34	0%	0%	97	49%	86%	-11.2	108	$23
22	**Proj**	**280**	**41**	**6**	**30**	**23**	**247**	**6**	**18**	**249**	**313**	**392**	**96**	**73**	**136**	**9**	**80**	**0.48**	**45**	**19**	**37**	**29**	**81**		**8%**	**86**	**31**	**8%**	**8%**	**110**	**37%**	**79%**	**1.3**	**188**	**$14**

Bryant,Kris

Age: 30 Pos: 3B LF RF
Bats: R Ht: 6' 5" Wt: 230

Health	A	LIMA Plan	B
PT/Exp	A	Rand Var	0
Consist	D	MM	4425

Quickly put to rest any concern surrounding injury-riddled 2020 season with 12 HR in first two months. That level of power proved unsustainable as HR/F dipped, but overall, skills sure looked a lot like those from 2019. The floor looks relatively safe again, and other than double-digit SB, a repeat performance is a pretty good bet.

Yr	Tm	PA	R	HR	RBI	SB	BA	xHR	xSB	xBA	OBP	SLG	OPS+	vL+	vR+	bb%	ct%	Eye	G	L	F	h%	HctX	QBaB	Brl%	PX	xPX	HR/F	xHR/F	Spd	SBA%	SB%	RAR	BPX	R$
17	CHC	665	111	29	73	7	295	31	12	274	409	537	129	129	126	14	77	0.74	38	20	42	34	102	CBc	10%	139	111	16%	17%	124	6%	58%	36.1	261	$25
18	CHC	457	59	13	52	2	272	20	7	252	374	460	112	151	99	11	72	0.45	34	25	41	35	83	DAb	10%	125	119	11%	17%	121	5%	33%	10.0	163	$12
19	CHC	634	108	31	77	4	282	28	8	259	382	521	125	147	119	12	73	0.51	36	21	43	33	91	CAb	9%	133	105	18%	16%	116	2%	100%	25.6	222	$22
20	CHC	147	20	4	11	0	206	5	2	205	293	351	85	107	78	8	69	0.30	37	18	45	26	87	DAb	5%	87	111	10%	12%	141	0%	0%	-8.8	32	$3
21	2 NL	586	86	25	73	10	265	26	3	261	353	481	115	124	111	11	74	0.46	37	23	39	31	109	CBc	10%	130	133	17%	17%	102	8%	83%	7.9	200	$22
1st Half		309	47	16	42	4	271	15	2	269	353	513	121	163	108	10	73	0.41	39	24	37	32	98	CCd	11%	144	121	22%	20%	91	8%	67%	6.0	212	$25
2nd Half		277	39	9	31	6	258	11	2	252	354	446	108	92	116	11	75	0.52	35	23	41	31	120	CBb	10%	115	145	12%	15%	113	8%	100%	0.5	196	$16
22	**Proj**	**595**	**89**	**24**	**68**	**7**	**263**	**26**	**10**	**250**	**357**	**466**	**112**	**123**	**108**	**11**	**74**	**0.47**	**37**	**22**	**42**	**31**	**100**		**9%**	**122**	**123**	**15%**	**16%**	**117**	**8%**	**81%**	**19.8**	**175**	**$22**

Burger,Jake

Age: 26 Pos: 3B
Bats: R Ht: 6' 2" Wt: 210

Health	B	LIMA Plan	F
PT/Exp	F	Rand Var	0
Consist	F	MM	3001

1-3-.263 in 42 PA at CHW. Didn't have many opportunities in previous three seasons, thanks to multiple major heel injuries and COVID. Showed off above-average power, but wasn't enough to offset all the whiffs and low bb%. Could eventually emerge as viable power source, but this is probably going to take some time.

Yr	Tm	PA	R	HR	RBI	SB	BA	xHR	xSB	xBA	OBP	SLG	OPS+	vL+	vR+	bb%	ct%	Eye	G	L	F	h%	HctX	QBaB	Brl%	PX	xPX	HR/F	xHR/F	Spd	SBA%	SB%	RAR	BPX	R$
17																																			
18																																			
19																																			
20																																			
21	CHW *	369	37	13	41	0	223	3	4	232	267	395	91	44	139	6	64	0.17	43	26	30	31	102	ACc	13%	117	109	14%	43%	133	0%	0%	-14.7	8	$3
1st Half		188	22	7	26	0	257		2	237	291	452	103	0	175	5	68	0.15	50	17	33	34	46		0%	133	-22	0%		99	0%	0%	-3.0	73	$6
2nd Half		181	16	6	15	0	188	3	2	213	243	337	78	64	132	7	60	0.18	41	29	29	27	115	ACc	13%	98	155	20%	60%	165	0%	0%	-13.5	-69	-$4
22	**Proj**	**175**	**17**	**5**	**18**	**0**	**235**	**5**	**1**	**216**	**282**	**391**	**91**	**48**	**104**	**6**	**63**	**0.18**	**44**	**23**	**32**	**34**	**104**		**12%**	**107**	**140**	**16%**	**15%**	**129**	**4%**	**0%**	**-2.9**	**-104**	**$3**

Buxton,Byron

Age: 28 Pos: CF
Bats: R Ht: 6' 2" Wt: 190

Health	F	LIMA Plan	B
PT/Exp	D	Rand Var	-4
Consist	C	MM	5445

19-50-.306 with 9 SB in 254 PA at MIN. Injuries continue to prevent full breakout—this time hip injury and hand fracture led to extended absences. Speed is never in question, and ct% has settled at respectable level while power has spiked. Ceiling is among the game's best, but IL discount will be severe. Hopeful projection comes with DN: 250 AB, again.

Yr	Tm	PA	R	HR	RBI	SB	BA	xHR	xSB	xBA	OBP	SLG	OPS+	vL+	vR+	bb%	ct%	Eye	G	L	F	h%	HctX	QBaB	Brl%	PX	xPX	HR/F	xHR/F	Spd	SBA%	SB%	RAR	BPX	R$
17	MIN	511	69	16	51	29	253	16	7	223	314	413	99	107	94	7	68	0.25	39	23	38	34	75	CBd	6%	97	85	14%	14%	182	24%	97%	-0.6	58	$20
18	MIN *	238	27	4	16	9	212	0	6	222	248	330	77	29	56	5	67	0.14	43	23	33	30	75	CCd	2%	92	48	0%	0%	124	25%	88%	-9.0	-27	$2
19	MIN	295	48	10	46	14	262	11	7	263	314	513	114	128	109	6	75	0.28	29	22	49	32	92	BAf	8%	148	92	10%	11%	121	35%	82%	8.3	256	$12
20	MIN	135	19	13	27	2	254	12	4	255	267	577	112	100	115	1	72	0.06	36	13	51	25	104	AAf	14%	168	116	27%	24%	124	15%	67%	1.3	264	$16
21	MIN *	277	54	21	38	9	309	21	5	313	346	658	138	136	139	5	74	0.22	40	22	38	34	130	ACd	18%	207	141	29%	32%	122	19%	90%	26.3	431	$18
1st Half		121	24	11	24	5	377	10	3	355	406	803	168	142	176	5	77	0.21	49	21	31	41	140	ADc	21%	241	142	42%	42%	130	19%	100%	24.2	577	$17
2nd Half		157	30	10	14	4	257	11	2	280	300	546	115	130	112	6	73	0.23	33	22	45	29	122	AAd	16%	179	140	21%	26%	111	19%	80%	3.0	312	$8
22	**Proj**	**455**	**78**	**27**	**66**	**15**	**276**	**31**	**10**	**272**	**320**	**547**	**118**	**120**	**116**	**5**	**73**	**0.19**	**39**	**20**	**41**	**32**	**110**		**13%**	**164**	**116**	**20%**	**23%**	**115**	**15%**	**86%**	**25.7**	**277**	**$27**

Cabrera,Miguel

Age: 39 Pos: DH 1B
Bats: R Ht: 6' 4" Wt: 249

Health	C	LIMA Plan	C+
PT/Exp	A	Rand Var	-1
Consist	A	MM	1125

A .542 OPS in mid-June seemed to hint that the end may be near, but he at least returned to respectability the rest of the way. 2020 small sample xHR/F jump did carry over, showing he still has some pop left in his bat. But late BA surge didn't come with support from xBA, and there are plenty of end game 1Bmen who can do what he does at this point.

Yr	Tm	PA	R	HR	RBI	SB	BA	xHR	xSB	xBA	OBP	SLG	OPS+	vL+	vR+	bb%	ct%	Eye	G	L	F	h%	HctX	QBaB	Brl%	PX	xPX	HR/F	xHR/F	Spd	SBA%	SB%	RAR	BPX	R$
17	DET	529	50	16	60	0	249	24	8	265	329	399	99	125	90	10	77	0.49	40	27	33	29	132	ACa	11%	88	125	13%	20%	65	1%	0%	-6.5	58	$7
18	DET	157	17	3	22	0	299	3	0	279	395	448	113	100	116	14	80	0.81	55	25	20	36	136	ADa	5%	100	59	14%	14%	53	0%	0%	7.2	150	$2
19	DET	549	41	12	59	0	282	15	1	245	346	398	103	135	94	9	78	0.44	44	24	32	34	119	BCa	6%	64	93	10%	12%	61	0%	0%	-5.2	4	$10
20	DET	231	28	10	35	1	250	12	0	253	329	417	99	146	89	10	75	0.47	42	26	32	29	92	ACb	10%	86	81	20%	24%	59	2%	100%	-1.0	36	$17
21	DET	526	48	15	75	0	256	24	2	224	316	386	96	95	97	8	75	0.34	48	20	32	31	114	ACc	8%	76	107	13%	21%	65	0%	0%	-9.7	-8	$11
1st Half		250	25	7	31	0	241	10	1	209	300	360	92	98	90	7	71	0.26	48	19	34	31	106	BCc	9%	71	111	13%	18%	69	0%	0%	-8.9	-85	$6
2nd Half		276	23	8	44	0	270	14	1	237	330	410	100	92	103	9	79	0.44	49	20	31	32	121	ACc	8%	79	104	13%	23%	67	0%	0%	-0.7	65	$11
22	**Proj**	**525**	**51**	**16**	**74**	**0**	**251**	**22**	**0**	**242**	**322**	**389**	**96**	**105**	**93**	**9**	**76**	**0.44**	**47**	**23**	**31**	**30**	**114**		**8%**	**80**	**96**	**14%**	**19%**	**58**	**0%**	**90%**	**-5.5**	**-8**	**$13**

Cain,Lorenzo

Age: 36 Pos: CF
Bats: R Ht: 6' 2" Wt: 214

Health	D	LIMA Plan	C+
PT/Exp	C	Rand Var	+1
Consist	D	MM	1433

8-36-.257 with 13 SB in 286 PA at MIL. Missed time with hamstring and quad issues, and seemed a little rusty early on after opting out 21 PA into 2020. Looked like usual self in 2nd half, with ct% and SBA% even exceeding typical levels. At his age, speed could fall off at any time, but most signs point to continued production on a per-PA basis.

Yr	Tm	PA	R	HR	RBI	SB	BA	xHR	xSB	xBA	OBP	SLG	OPS+	vL+	vR+	bb%	ct%	Eye	G	L	F	h%	HctX	QBaB	Brl%	PX	xPX	HR/F	xHR/F	Spd	SBA%	SB%	RAR	BPX	R$
17	KC	645	86	15	49	26	300	11	11	269	363	440	109	111	106	8	83	0.54	44	23	33	34	104	CCb	4%	76	84	9%	7%	147	15%	93%	15.0	167	$28
18	MIL	620	90	10	38	30	308	9	22	273	395	417	109	130	99	11	83	0.76	55	22	23	36	116	CFb	3%	66	72	10%	9%	140	18%	81%	27.9	167	$29
19	MIL	622	75	11	48	18	260	12	16	275	325	372	96	104	93	8	81	0.47	50	26	24	30	103	BDb	4%	63	65	10%	11%	92	16%	69%	-3.8	78	$16
20	MIL	21	4	0	2	0	333	0	1	325	429	389	109	152	92	14	89	1.50	50	38	13	38	112	CFc		38	98	0%	0%	83	0%	0%	0.6	168	-$1
21	MIL *	316	41	8	36	14	248	8	2	246	313	380	95	84	106	9	79	0.46	51	16	33	29	96	CDf	4%	77	71	12%	12%	108	21%	87%	-7.3	119	$11
1st Half		118	17	3	9	4	223	4	1	228	322	350	94	85	97	12	77	0.58	47	16	37	26	119	CDd	6%	74	127	10%	14%	101	21%	80%	-3.8	85	$0
2nd Half		198	24	5	27	10	262	3	1	255	312	397	96	82	112	7	81	0.38	53	16	31	30	81	CDf	3%	79	38	13%	8%	109	21%	91%	-2.3	135	$13
22	**Proj**	**420**	**56**	**10**	**39**	**18**	**267**	**9**	**14**	**256**	**339**	**394**	**100**	**97**	**100**	**9**	**81**	**0.53**	**51**	**20**	**29**	**31**	**102**		**4%**	**74**	**73**	**11%**	**10%**	**112**	**16%**	**83%**	**8.1**	**119**	**$19**

Calhoun,Kole

Age: 34 Pos: RF
Bats: L Ht: 5' 10" Wt: 210

Health	F	LIMA Plan	B
PT/Exp	B	Rand Var	0
Consist	B	MM	3125

Started season on IL with knee issue, and landed there a couple more times with hamstring woes. Not surprisingly, the 2020 power leap proved unsustainable and HR/F luck even flipped in the other direction. But he shouldn't be dismissed following injury-filled season, as rock solid xPX suggests he can provide value as a late power source.

Yr	Tm	PA	R	HR	RBI	SB	BA	xHR	xSB	xBA	OBP	SLG	OPS+	vL+	vR+	bb%	ct%	Eye	G	L	F	h%	HctX	QBaB	Brl%	PX	xPX	HR/F	xHR/F	Spd	SBA%	SB%	RAR	BPX	R$
17	LAA	654	77	19	71	5	244	18	10	248	333	392	99	93	99	11	76	0.53	44	21	35	29	98	CCc	5%	85	91	12%	12%	81	3%	83%	-13.9	67	$11
18	LAA	551	71	19	57	6	208	25	3	240	283	369	87	80	89	10	73	0.40	43	21	35	24	120	BCb	9%	98	132	15%	20%	74	7%	75%	-15.5	43	$8
19	LAA	631	92	33	74	4	232	30	5	259	325	467	110	102	112	11	71	0.43	41	22	37	27	104	BBc	11%	132	121	23%	21%	66	4%	80%	-7.3	119	$15
20	ARI	228	35	16	40	1	226	12	1	283	338	526	115	107	117	12	74	0.56	38	24	39	22	120	BBc	12%	162	154	29%	21%	59	4%	50%	2.2	276	$20
21	ARI	182	17	5	17	1	235	7	1	234	297	373	92	45	107	8	75	0.37	37	22	41	28	112	CBd	6%	85	145	10%	13%	85	2%	100%	-7.1	50	$1
1st Half		51	6	2	5	1	292	3	0	258	333	479	113	109	115	6	73	0.23	37	26	37	36	111	BBc	9%	118	150	15%	23%	106	2%	100%	1.1	123	-$4
2nd Half		131	11	3	12	0	212	4	1	222	282	331	83	22	103	9	76	0.43	36	21	43	25	113	CAd	5%	72	143	8%	10%	69	2%	0%	-7.4	15	-$5
22	**Proj**	**455**	**56**	**20**	**54**	**3**	**235**	**21**	**2**	**249**	**311**	**428**	**100**	**78**	**108**	**10**	**74**	**0.40**	**38**	**23**	**39**	**27**	**113**		**9%**	**114**	**140**	**17%**	**18%**	**61**	**2%**	**81%**	**0.0**	**94**	**$12**

BRIAN RUDD

Calhoun,Willie

Age: 27 Pos: LF DH | Bats: L Ht: 5' 8" Wt: 200
Health: D | PT/Exp: C | Consist: D
LIMA Plan: D+ | Rand Var: 0 | MM: 2033

Groin injury caused late start, then fractured forearm gobbled up another 2+ month chunk of season. In between, flashed power (4 HR in 99 AB in May), sustained great contact rate, but embers of hope for 2019 redux are flickering, need stretc[illegible] of good health for oxygen. At least he's at right age to provide end game pop... if he can stay on field.

Yr	Tm	PA	R	HR	RBI	SB	BA	xHR	xSB	xBA	OBP	SLG	OPS+	vL+	vR+	bb%	ct%	Eye	G	L	F	h%	HctX	QBaB	Brl%	PX	xPX	HR/F	xHR/F	Spd	SBA%	SB%	RAR	BPX	R$
17	TEX *	556	64	25	75	3	267	0	7	316	313	479	108	82	95	6	86	0.48	56	22	22	27	90	BFc	0%	103	57	17%	0%	126	4%	58%	4.3	239	[illegible]
18	TEX *	565	57	9	46	3	252	2	4	248	293	366	88	59	88	6	86	0.41	39	19	42	28	78	CCd	3%	72	77	6%	6%	82	2%	100%	-12.6	127	[illegible]
19	TEX *	499	67	27	68	1	265	11	3	270	335	499	115	108	121	9	82	0.59	36	19	44	27	116	BBd	6%	111	104	18%	10%	79	2%	38%	6.3	230	[illegible]
20	TEX	108	3	1	13	0	190	1	1	192	231	260	65	101	56	5	83	0.29	46	13	41	22	126	BBf	1%	35	97	3%	3%	106	0%	0%	-9.4	12	[illegible]
21	TEX	284	26	6	25	0	250	7	2	256	310	381	95	93	96	7	87	0.62	40	21	39	27	121	BBd	4%	66	81	7%	8%	108	3%	0%	-7.9	192	[illegible]
1st Half		226	23	5	19	0	254	6	1	255	323	385	99	88	102	8	87	0.70	35	22	42	27	114	BBc	3%	67	78	7%	8%	103	3%	0%	-5.3	196	[illegible]
2nd Half		58	3	1	6	0	236	1	0	259	259	364	84	128	77	4	87	0.29	55	16	29	26	146	BDd	4%	63	90	7%	7%	109	3%	0%	-2.8	158	[illegible]
22	**Proj**	**420**	**39**	**16**	**52**	**0**	**261**	**24**	**3**	**261**	**306**	**441**	**101**	**112**	**98**	**6**	**85**	**0.44**	**44**	**18**	**38**	**27**	**123**		**14%**	**88**	**91**	**12%**	**18%**	**104**	**5%**	**32%**	**3.2**	**167**	[illegible]

Cameron,Daz

Age: 25 Pos: OF | Bats: R Ht: 6' 2" Wt: 185
Health: B | PT/Exp: C | Consist: C
LIMA Plan: C | Rand Var: 0 | MM: 3513

4-13-.194 with 6 SB in 115 PA at DET. Hot AAA start (.338/.400/.558 in 85 PA) got him back to bigs, but Ks (63% MLB ct%) still a major issue. Ditch the DNA test—this was Dad's profile, too—but by 24, Mike's walk rate was further along, helping speed not go to waste. Still, son made progress, too, if you squint (bb%, PX/xPX), so don't give up on him yet.

Yr	Tm	PA	R	HR	RBI	SB	BA	xHR	xSB	xBA	OBP	SLG	OPS+	vL+	vR+	bb%	ct%	Eye	G	L	F	h%	HctX	QBaB	Brl%	PX	xPX	HR/F	xHR/F	Spd	SBA%	SB%	RAR	BPX	R$
17																																			
18	a/a	280	35	4	36	12	259		4		321	420	99			8	73	0.34				34				103				129	29%	66%		107	[illegible]
19	aaa	501	60	12	38	15	204		18		288	358	89			11	65	0.34				28				95				139	23%	64%		7	[illegible]
20	DET	59	4	0	3	1	193	0	1	189	220	263	64	75	63	3	67	0.11	42	21	37	29	78	CCf	3%	48	72	0%	0%	156	10%	100%	-5.4	-152	[illegible]
21	DET *	289	43	9	32	12	240	4	5	232	298	413	98	76	95	8	70	0.28	38	22	40	31	88	CCf	8%	111	109	15%	15%	138	24%	78%	-6.2	104	[illegible]
1st Half		141	21	5	20	5	264	3	2	249	310	464	108	36	119	6	74	0.26	41	19	41	32	90	CCf	11%	119	100	20%	20%	155	24%	62%	-1.5	204	[illegible]
2nd Half		148	22	4	12	6	216	1	3	218	287	362	88	108	64	9	66	0.29	36	25	39	29	86	BCf	3%	102	121	9%	9%	109	24%	100%	-5.9	-12	[illegible]
22	**Proj**	**280**	**39**	**8**	**29**	**12**	**235**	**10**	**9**	**229**	**311**	**404**	**97**	**105**	**93**	**8**	**69**	**0.30**	**39**	**22**	**39**	**31**	**85**		**6%**	**109**	**102**	**11%**	**15%**	**133**	**19%**	**76%**	**-1.7**	**86**	[illegible]

Campusano,Luis

Age: 23 Pos: CA | Bats: R Ht: 5' 11" Wt: 232
Health: B | PT/Exp: F | Consist: F
LIMA Plan: D | Rand Var: +2 | MM: 1301

0-1-.088 in 38 PA at SD. Broke camp at MLB level, and while he couldn't capitalize, AAA work suggests he may seize next chance (.906 OPS, 15 HR in 326 PA). Had really turned it up in August (.373, 6 HR in 15 games) before oblique issue brought things to screeching halt. Assuming a full recovery, he's about ready for a true test.

Yr	Tm	PA	R	HR	RBI	SB	BA	xHR	xSB	xBA	OBP	SLG	OPS+	vL+	vR+	bb%	ct%	Eye	G	L	F	h%	HctX	QBaB	Brl%	PX	xPX	HR/F	xHR/F	Spd	SBA%	SB%	RAR	BPX	R$
17																																			
18																																			
19																																			
20	SD	4	2	1	1	0	333	0	0	471	500	1333	243	348	0	0	33	0.00	0	0	100	0	135	AA		1071	722	100%	0%	97	0%	0%	1.0	2484	[illegible]
21	SD *	348	29	9	29	1	215	0	1	244	263	357	85	0	41	6	73	0.25	39	26	35	27	104	ABf	0%	90	54	0%	0%	89	2%	100%	-9.9	19	[illegible]
1st Half		216	14	2	13	0	194	0	1	234	252	299	77	0	42	7	72	0.28	39	26	35	26	103	ABf	0%	75	54	0%	0%	88	2%	0%	-10.8	-27	[illegible]
2nd Half		132	16	6	16	1	248		0	250	282	449	99	0	0	4	74	0.18	44	20	36	29	0		0%	113	-22	0%		93	2%	100%	0.8	96	[illegible]
22	**Proj**	**245**	**24**	**4**	**24**	**1**	**243**	**3**	**1**	**224**	**282**	**361**	**87**	**90**	**87**	**5**	**73**	**0.21**	**42**	**21**	**37**	**31**	**93**		**5%**	**76**	**49**	**7%**	**5%**	**87**	**3%**	**100%**	**-0.6**	**-48**	[illegible]

Candelario,Jeimer

Age: 28 Pos: 3B | Bats: B Ht: 6' 1" Wt: 221
Health: B | PT/Exp: A | Consist: C
LIMA Plan: B+ | Rand Var: 0 | MM: 3135

At first glance, a step back, but this is what happens when 2020 skills meet h%, HR/F regression. Yes, power flourished in 2nd half, but QBaB still counsels caution. Nonetheless, if this is where LD rate is settling, there's a nice BA floor. No substitute for 600+ PA these days, even if it takes that much to get to 20 HR. Call it boring profit, but with UP: 30 HR.

Yr	Tm	PA	R	HR	RBI	SB	BA	xHR	xSB	xBA	OBP	SLG	OPS+	vL+	vR+	bb%	ct%	Eye	G	L	F	h%	HctX	QBaB	Brl%	PX	xPX	HR/F	xHR/F	Spd	SBA%	SB%	RAR	BPX	R$
17	2 TM *	591	65	17	80	1	253	3	7	256	323	442	104	124	101	9	73	0.39	45	19	36	32	86	CCb	4%	121	77	9%	9%	108	1%	100%	0.5	130	[illegible]
18	DET	619	78	19	54	3	224	19	3	228	317	393	95	112	87	11	70	0.41	42	18	41	28	91	CBc	6%	112	88	12%	12%	95	3%	60%	-6.0	77	[illegible]
19	DET *	556	57	15	59	3	227	9	4	236	313	392	97	80	91	11	72	0.44	37	23	40	29	93	CBc	6%	95	86	9%	10%	82	3%	75%	-14.5	41	[illegible]
20	DET	206	30	7	29	1	297	8	2	262	369	503	116	144	107	10	74	0.41	40	26	34	37	107	BCc	10%	118	118	15%	17%	116	4%	50%	8.8	180	[illegible]
21	DET	626	75	16	67	0	271	26	5	267	351	443	109	102	112	10	76	0.48	39	26	34	33	104	CCc	9%	109	108	11%	18%	94	0%	0%	8.4	158	[illegible]
1st Half		310	31	4	22	0	258	8	3	240	342	360	98	100	97	11	73	0.46	40	28	33	34	85	CCc	8%	72	78	6%	12%	90	0%	0%	-7.0	4	[illegible]
2nd Half		316	44	12	45	0	284	18	2	294	361	525	120	103	128	10	78	0.51	39	25	35	33	122	CCc	10%	143	135	15%	23%	95	0%	0%	12.2	300	[illegible]
22	**Proj**	**630**	**79**	**20**	**74**	**1**	**265**	**23**	**3**	**261**	**347**	**458**	**109**	**110**	**109**	**10**	**74**	**0.45**	**41**	**24**	**35**	**32**	**102**		**8%**	**119**	**105**	**14%**	**16%**	**95**	**2%**	**60%**	**18.5**	**140**	[illegible]

Canha,Mark

Age: 33 Pos: LF RF CF | Bats: R Ht: 6' 2" Wt: 209
Health: B | PT/Exp: A | Consist: B
LIMA Plan: B | Rand Var: +2 | MM: 3425

Thanks to strong on-base history, started year atop lineup and struck mother lode of runs. Then power, speed skills fell off cliff, suggesting late June hip injury that forced three-week IL stint dogged him for rest of year. 1st half was more in line with established skill level, so rebound is possible, but he's reaching age where health woes can be tougher to shake.

Yr	Tm	PA	R	HR	RBI	SB	BA	xHR	xSB	xBA	OBP	SLG	OPS+	vL+	vR+	bb%	ct%	Eye	G	L	F	h%	HctX	QBaB	Brl%	PX	xPX	HR/F	xHR/F	Spd	SBA%	SB%	RAR	BPX	R$
17	OAK *	483	53	13	50	5	218	5	5	234	269	395	90	79	92	6	71	0.24	33	20	47	28	80	CAf	6%	119	75	9%	9%	98	6%	100%	-19.3	70	[illegible]
18	OAK	411	60	17	52	1	249	19	5	259	328	449	104	125	88	8	76	0.39	38	22	40	28	104	CBd	9%	123	114	15%	17%	99	3%	33%	1.9	167	[illegible]
19	OAK	497	80	26	58	3	273	22	7	256	396	517	126	111	132	13	74	0.63	41	18	41	31	101	CBd	10%	124	100	21%	18%	140	3%	60%	20.1	244	[illegible]
20	OAK	243	32	5	33	4	246	8	3	225	387	408	106	128	99	15	72	0.69	35	20	44	32	108	BAb	8%	102	126	8%	13%	130	5%	100%	1.7	160	[illegible]
21	OAK	625	93	17	61	12	231	18	12	245	358	387	102	99	104	12	75	0.60	41	23	36	28	97	CCd	7%	90	96	12%	13%	146	8%	86%	-9.5	169	[illegible]
1st Half		325	55	11	33	7	255	13	6	254	375	450	115	113	116	13	75	0.59	38	25	38	30	107	CBc	10%	110	123	14%	17%	157	8%	88%	3.4	238	[illegible]
2nd Half		300	38	6	28	5	206	5	6	233	340	319	89	83	92	13	76	0.62	45	21	34	25	87	DCd	4%	69	67	9%	8%	108	8%	83%	-14.3	73	$7
22	**Proj**	**525**	**79**	**16**	**61**	**8**	**243**	**17**	**10**	**240**	**363**	**413**	**105**	**106**	**105**	**13**	**74**	**0.57**	**40**	**21**	**39**	**29**	**99**		**7%**	**101**	**100**	**12%**	**13%**	**124**	**9%**	**84%**	**6.1**	**141**	**$17**

Canó,Robinson

Age: 39 Pos: 2B | Bats: L Ht: 6' 0" Wt: 212
Health: C | PT/Exp: F | Consist: D
LIMA Plan: D | Rand Var: | MM: 2051

Hard to know where he goes from here, given age and yearlong PED exile, though winter ball may offer some clues. When last seen, plentiful HctX fueled strong xBA, while GB% tempered HR expectations. He's not Chris Davis, but steady PT may prove elusive even if skills reemerge (though DH coming to NL might help). Still, only guarantee is $48M he's owed.

Yr	Tm	PA	R	HR	RBI	SB	BA	xHR	xSB	xBA	OBP	SLG	OPS+	vL+	vR+	bb%	ct%	Eye	G	L	F	h%	HctX	QBaB	Brl%	PX	xPX	HR/F	xHR/F	Spd	SBA%	SB%	RAR	BPX	R$
17	SEA	648	79	23	97	1	280	21	9	281	338	453	108	75	119	8	86	0.58	50	19	31	30	128	BDb	6%	91	111	15%	13%	66	1%	100%	6.2	158	$19
18	SEA	348	44	10	50	0	303	14	1	284	374	471	113	118	108	9	85	0.68	48	23	29	33	130	ADa	9%	99	110	13%	18%	75	0%	0%	17.6	203	$11
19	NYM	423	46	13	39	0	256	12	1	270	307	428	102	80	110	6	82	0.36	49	20	31	28	108	ADc	7%	92	97	13%	12%	75	0%	0%	-1.2	144	$6
20	NYM	182	23	10	30	0	316	7	0	302	352	544	119	115	120	5	86	0.38	50	24	26	32	127	BDd	7%	110	84	26%	18%	69	0%	0%	9.5	256	$20
21																																			
1st Half																																			
2nd Half																																			
22	**Proj**	**210**	**26**	**8**	**30**	**0**	**286**	**6**	**2**	**280**	**337**	**465**	**109**	**98**	**113**	**7**	**85**	**0.46**	**49**	**22**	**29**	**31**	**123**		**7%**	**97**	**98**	**16%**	**12%**	**69**	**0%**	**0%**	**8.1**	**153**	**$8**

Caratini,Victor

Age: 28 Pos: CA | Bats: B Ht: 6' 1" Wt: 215
Health: A | PT/Exp: B | Consist: B
LIMA Plan: D | Rand Var: 0 | MM: 1101

Name sounds like Bugs Bunny's bar order after tough day at the office. Gets bat to ball just fine, but between lack of hard contact and ground balls, little happens when he does. And while power often comes late for backstops, there are scant signs here. Until further notice, he's a barely-rosterable second catcher in deep leagues—but that's all, folks.

Yr	Tm	PA	R	HR	RBI	SB	BA	xHR	xSB	xBA	OBP	SLG	OPS+	vL+	vR+	bb%	ct%	Eye	G	L	F	h%	HctX	QBaB	Brl%	PX	xPX	HR/F	xHR/F	Spd	SBA%	SB%	RAR	BPX	R$
17	CHC *	379	44	9	49	1	286	2	5	281	335	449	107	160	74	7	80	0.36	65	15	20	34	99	DFa	4%	98	61	11%	22%	84	1%	100%	12.9	[illegible]	$10
18	CHC *	329	31	5	37	0	243	4	2	236	303	336	86	59	85	8	76	0.36	53	23	24	30	79	CDb	4%	63	62	6%	12%	90	0%	0%	-0.6	-3	$3
19	CHC	279	31	11	34	1	266	10	1	267	348	447	110	108	109	10	76	0.49	49	24	27	31	88	BDb	9%	96	83	22%	20%	79	1%	100%	7.2	96	$5
20	CHC	132	10	1	16	0	241	2	1	212	333	328	88	116	79	9	73	0.39	49	19	32	32	91	CDd	4%	63	73	4%	7%	86	3%	0%	-2.5	-40	$3
21	SD	356	33	7	39	2	227	9	2	215	309	323	87	88	87	10	74	0.43	51	18	31	29	94	BDc	7%	58	74	10%	12%	74	2%	100%	-7.3	-54	$3
1st Half		210	20	6	28	2	211	7	1	215	310	344	91	94	90	12	69	0.43	45	20	35	27	89	ACc	11%	84	106	13%	16%	73	2%	100%	-3.7	-38	$3
2nd Half		146	13	1	11	0	248	2	1	207	308	293	81	75	83	8	80	0.42	57	17	26	30	101	CDc	3%	28	36	4%	7%	90	2%	0%	-4.2	-46	-$4
22	**Proj**	**245**	**23**	**4**	**28**	**1**	**244**	**6**	**2**	**224**	**323**	**342**	**90**	**96**	**89**	**9**	**76**	**0.42**	**52**	**19**	**29**	**30**	**92**		**6%**	**62**	**68**	**9%**	**12%**	**81**	**3%**	**63%**	**0.5**	**-63**	**$4**

KRIS OLSON

Carlson,Dylan	Health	A	LIMA Plan	B+
Age: 23 Pos: RF CF	PT/Exp	A	Rand Var	-3
Bats: B Ht: 6' 2" Wt: 205	Consist	D	MM	3225

Top prospect's solid first full season was built on high volume and modest skills. Strong 2nd half was encouraging with gains in PX/xPX and HctX. That said, BA was likely h%-boosted; plate skills, xBA were merely average; and he didn't run enough to capitalize on speed. Age, pedigree suggest patience is needed while he finds that next gear.

Yr Tm	PA	R	HR	RBI	SB	BA	xHR	xSB	xBA	OBP	SLG	OPS+	vL+	vR+	bb%	ct%	Eye	G	L	F	h%	HctX	QBaB	Brl%	PX	xPX	HR/F	xHR/F	Spd	SBA%	SB%	RAR	BPX	R$
17																																		
18																																		
19 a/a	536	80	21	57	17	265		8		330	470	111			9	75	0.38				32				109				128	21%	66%		163	$20
20 STL	119	11	3	16	1	200	5	2	239	252	364	82	73	83	7	68	0.23	45	24	32	26	98	CCd	9%	108	131	13%	21%	99	11%	50%	-8.3	16	$2
21 STL	619	79	18	65	2	266	22	11	245	343	437	107	126	102	9	72	0.38	38	25	38	34	84	CBc	7%	108	103	12%	15%	110	2%	67%	-2.7	108	$16
1st Half	342	42	7	31	0	261	11	6	237	342	401	103	113	101	10	73	0.42	39	24	37	34	75	CCb	7%	88	83	9%	14%	112	2%	0%	-6.0	69	$13
2nd Half	277	37	11	34	2	272	11	5	255	344	481	112	143	103	9	71	0.32	36	25	39	34	95	CBc	7%	133	127	16%	16%	112	2%	67%	1.7	162	$15
22 Proj	**595**	**79**	**20**	**69**	**6**	**257**	**23**	**5**	**248**	**328**	**443**	**105**	**125**	**99**	**9**	**72**	**0.34**	**39**	**24**	**36**	**32**	**90**		**8%**	**116**	**115**	**14%**	**17%**	**113**	**4%**	**63%**	**6.7**	**96**	**$16**

Carpenter,Matt	Health	B	LIMA Plan	D
Age: 36 Pos: 2B	PT/Exp	C	Rand Var	+4
Bats: L Ht: 6' 4" Wt: 210	Consist	A	MM	3301

Utter futility on the surface as BA, HR continued their free-fall. Some may write him off, but there are reasons not to: bb% provides OBP floor while Brl%, xPX, and xHR/FB all reveal persistent power. Contact woes and h% history mean BA drag is a given, but power rebound could yield end-game value... if he can find more playing time.

Yr Tm	PA	R	HR	RBI	SB	BA	xHR	xSB	xBA	OBP	SLG	OPS+	vL+	vR+	bb%	ct%	Eye	G	L	F	h%	HctX	QBaB	Brl%	PX	xPX	HR/F	xHR/F	Spd	SBA%	SB%	RAR	BPX	R$
17 STL	622	91	23	69	2	241	25	10	250	384	451	114	90	118	18	75	0.87	27	22	51	28	128	BAa	8%	124	169	12%	13%	98	2%	67%	-2.8	197	$11
18 STL	676	111	36	81	4	257	42	3	273	374	523	120	108	123	15	72	0.65	26	27	47	29	130	BAa	14%	170	189	19%	22%	78	3%	80%	25.6	267	$23
19 STL *	523	60	15	48	6	216	19	5	224	320	374	96	95	101	13	69	0.49	32	25	43	28	99	CAb	7%	95	138	12%	15%	105	5%	86%	-20.0	37	$6
20 STL	169	22	4	24	0	186	7	2	206	325	314	85	79	86	14	66	0.48	38	22	40	25	107	CBa	10%	87	146	11%	19%	92	0%	0%	-13.1	-40	$4
21 STL	249	18	3	21	2	169	12	1	187	305	275	80	37	84	14	63	0.45	27	23	49	25	94	CAb	11%	84	162	5%	19%	81	3%	100%	-23.0	-100	-$4
1st Half	152	11	3	17	1	167	8	0	191	303	286	82	41	84	14	65	0.45	27	21	52	23	106	BAb	15%	87	169	7%	19%	66	3%	100%	-13.0	-81	-$5
2nd Half	97	7	0	4	1	173	4	0	182	309	259	77	32	85	16	59	0.45	28	28	45	29	76	CAa	6%	79	148	0%	19%	109	3%	100%	-8.3	-131	-$9
22 Proj	**210**	**22**	**6**	**20**	**1**	**209**	**10**	**2**	**217**	**338**	**379**	**97**	**79**	**100**	**15**	**65**	**0.49**	**30**	**24**	**45**	**28**	**100**		**10%**	**117**	**155**	**12%**	**19%**	**97**	**4%**	**93%**	**-0.3**	**21**	**$3**

Casas,Triston	Health	A	LIMA Plan	D
Age: 22 Pos: 1B	PT/Exp	D	Rand Var	
Bats: L Ht: 6' 4" Wt: 238	Consist	F	MM	3211

2018 BOS first-rounder slashed .284/.394/.484 in 329 PA at AA, earned September AAA look. Hit tool has improved significantly during ascent, and 2nd half ct%/PX combination a sign of long-term potential. Should be playable from the start (especially in OBP leagues), but power stroke might take time. Worthy of your keeper league investment.

Yr Tm	PA	R	HR	RBI	SB	BA	xHR	xSB	xBA	OBP	SLG	OPS+	vL+	vR+	bb%	ct%	Eye	G	L	F	h%	HctX	QBaB	Brl%	PX	xPX	HR/F	xHR/F	Spd	SBA%	SB%	RAR	BPX	R$
17																																		
18																																		
19																																		
20																																		
21 a/a	355	50	10	47	6	257		5		351	424	106			13	75	0.58				31				99				106	9%	63%		146	$10
1st Half	162	21	3	18	2	247		2		311	355	93			9	72	0.33				33				65				118	9%	68%		-27	$2
2nd Half	193	29	7	29	3	263		3	275	381	482	117			16	78	0.87	44	20	36	30	0			127	-22	0%		90	9%	60%	2.6	288	$10
22 Proj	**210**	**30**	**6**	**28**	**3**	**257**	**6**	**4**	**238**	**355**	**431**	**107**	**106**	**107**	**13**	**75**	**0.62**	**38**	**20**	**42**	**31**	**95**		**8%**	**102**		**11%**	**11%**	**104**	**8%**	**62%**	**2.6**	**147**	**$7**

Castellanos,Nick	Health	A	LIMA Plan	D+
Age: 30 Pos: RF	PT/Exp	A	Rand Var	-3
Bats: R Ht: 6' 4" Wt: 203	Consist	D	MM	4155

Finally! After perennially falling short of perceived potential, BA and HR spiked together to yield the long-prophesied monster season. Under the hood, he reversed 2020's ct% scare while QBaB, xPX, xHR all supported the breakout. Line-drive prowess gives firm BA foundation, making a repeat completely plausible, so roster with confidence.

Yr Tm	PA	R	HR	RBI	SB	BA	xHR	xSB	xBA	OBP	SLG	OPS+	vL+	vR+	bb%	ct%	Eye	G	L	F	h%	HctX	QBaB	Brl%	PX	xPX	HR/F	xHR/F	Spd	SBA%	SB%	RAR	BPX	R$
17 DET	665	73	26	101	4	272	34	8	274	320	490	110	126	104	6	77	0.29	37	25	38	32	135	CCa	11%	122	142	14%	19%	128	6%	44%	2.0	176	$19
18 DET	678	88	23	89	2	298	35	9	276	354	500	114	133	107	7	76	0.32	35	29	36	36	133	BBa	11%	128	139	14%	21%	116	2%	67%	33.1	187	$25
19 2 TM	664	100	27	73	2	289	39	5	280	337	525	119	158	110	6	77	0.29	38	23	40	34	114	CCa	11%	134	131	14%	21%	124	3%	50%	14.4	244	$21
20 CIN	242	37	14	34	0	225	15	2	258	298	486	104	100	105	8	68	0.28	35	26	39	26	101	ABa	16%	154	161	24%	25%	125	4%	0%	-5.2	208	$16
21 CIN	585	95	34	100	3	309	34	4	297	362	576	129	129	129	7	77	0.34	38	27	36	35	127	BCb	11%	152	146	23%	23%	90	3%	75%	34.8	285	$31
1st Half	335	54	16	53	2	340	17	3	304	394	592	137	132	139	8	77	0.37	37	31	32	40	128	BBb	10%	150	135	21%	22%	101	3%	67%	30.5	292	$37
2nd Half	250	41	18	47	1	267	17	2	287	320	556	119	125	116	6	77	0.29	39	21	40	27	127	CCb	11%	155	160	25%	24%	81	3%	100%	6.5	277	$21
22 Proj	**651**	**102**	**36**	**102**	**2**	**288**	**39**	**5**	**279**	**343**	**541**	**120**	**128**	**117**	**7**	**75**	**0.30**	**37**	**25**	**38**	**33**	**121**		**12%**	**147**	**148**	**21%**	**23%**	**97**	**4%**	**52%**	**35.1**	**214**	**$31**

Castro,Harold	Health	A	LIMA Plan	D
Age: 28 Pos: SS 2B	PT/Exp	C	Rand Var	-1
Bats: L Ht: 5' 10" Wt: 151	Consist	D	MM	0133

Part-timer got first long look (predominantly vR) but didn't stand out as contact quality was mediocre, PX/xPX were non-existent, and poor bb% kept him off base. He does have two things going: plus speed, which has yet to translate to SB success; and an LD% stroke that should lead to decent BA. Back-ender in an -only league.

Yr Tm	PA	R	HR	RBI	SB	BA	xHR	xSB	xBA	OBP	SLG	OPS+	vL+	vR+	bb%	ct%	Eye	G	L	F	h%	HctX	QBaB	Brl%	PX	xPX	HR/F	xHR/F	Spd	SBA%	SB%	RAR	BPX	R$
17 aa	429	42	1	25	17	258		6		284	318	82			4	86	0.26				30				35				134	26%	62%		64	$9
18 DET *	368	30	2	24	5	234	0	11	210	249	280	71	0	79	2	79	0.10	63	13	25	29	145	DFa	0%	34	66	0%	0%	108	13%	53%	-20.6	-63	$2
19 DET *	498	46	8	58	5	290	7	12	254	313	394	98	62	102	3	76	0.14	52	25	22	37	104	CDa	4%	55	67	8%	12%	147	9%	47%	-11.8	0	$12
20 DET	54	6	0	3	0	347	1	1	262	407	429	111	109	111	9	78	0.45	47	29	24	45	66	CCa	3%	64	59	0%	11%	127	0%	0%	2.7	80	$2
21 DET	339	35	3	37	1	283	7	2	262	310	359	92	62	97	4	77	0.19	41	34	26	36	90	CCa	3%	50	77	5%	11%	112	2%	50%	-5.9	-27	$7
1st Half	159	14	1	17	0	262	3	1	258	318	303	87	29	95	8	75	0.33	43	36	21	34	97	CDb	4%	28	78	4%	13%	110	2%	0%	-5.2	-104	-$1
2nd Half	180	21	2	20	1	300	4	1	268	303	406	96	87	98	1	79	0.06	39	32	29	37	85	CCa	3%	68	76	5%	10%	116	2%	50%	-0.5	35	$4
22 Proj	**315**	**31**	**3**	**31**	**2**	**273**	**4**	**3**	**257**	**294**	**347**	**87**	**60**	**92**	**3**	**78**	**0.16**	**43**	**31**	**25**	**34**	**93**		**3%**	**47**	**74**	**5%**	**7%**	**120**	**5%**	**44%**	**-6.3**	**-83**	**$8**

Castro,Willi	Health	A	LIMA Plan	C
Age: 25 Pos: 2B SS	PT/Exp	B	Rand Var	+5
Bats: B Ht: 6' 1" Wt: 170	Consist	F	MM	2523

9-38-.220 with 9 SB in 450 PA at DET. Couldn't hold full-time role out of the gate, as expected BA regression struck. Cratering xPX and HctX explain the power outage, while h% correction and poor Eye sunk OBP. He ran a lot anyway, and that makes him worth a dart throw. Just don't dream on anything else seen from 2020's small sample.

Yr Tm	PA	R	HR	RBI	SB	BA	xHR	xSB	xBA	OBP	SLG	OPS+	vL+	vR+	bb%	ct%	Eye	G	L	F	h%	HctX	QBaB	Brl%	PX	xPX	HR/F	xHR/F	Spd	SBA%	SB%	RAR	BPX	R$
17																																		
18 a/a	527	59	8	48	16	250		7		292	372	89			6	77	0.25				31				80				110	18%	75%		53	$13
19 DET *	607	76	11	63	15	279	2	18	238	324	431	105	107	81	6	74	0.26	36	24	39	36	64	DAb	2%	87	43	4%	8%	155	14%	74%	2.2	96	$19
20 DET	140	21	6	24	0	349	7	5	253	381	550	124	131	122	5	71	0.18	42	27	31	46	82	DCc	10%	111	78	21%	24%	173	2%	0%	11.2	140	$17
21 DET *	473	62	10	40	11	227	12	4	238	266	361	86	94	82	5	75	0.21	46	21	33	28	67	DCd	5%	78	56	9%	12%	151	15%	73%	-19.7	65	$9
1st Half	263	33	6	27	4	220	6	3	227	287	352	89	86	90	7	72	0.27	47	19	34	28	61	DCf	4%	80	45	11%	11%	132	15%	80%	-11.9	23	$8
2nd Half	210	29	4	13	7	236	6	2	250	254	372	85	102	69	2	78	0.11	46	22	32	29	74	DCc	7%	75	70	7%	14%	163	15%	69%	-10.7	104	$6
22 Proj	**350**	**48**	**8**	**37**	**7**	**244**	**12**	**9**	**240**	**289**	**393**	**93**	**102**	**89**	**5**	**74**	**0.20**	**45**	**21**	**34**	**31**	**70**		**6%**	**87**	**60**	**10%**	**14%**	**155**	**15%**	**77%**	**-3.4**	**71**	**$11**

Chang,Yu	Health	A	LIMA Plan	D
Age: 26 Pos: 1B 3B	PT/Exp	D	Rand Var	-1
Bats: R Ht: 6' 1" Wt: 180	Consist	C	MM	3211

9-39-.228 in 251 PA at CLE. Marginal prospect delivered marginal value in first substantial look. Poor plate skills offer little hope for BA, and weak HctX and xPX negate benefit of strong launch angle ("A" in QBaB). Likeliest case for this skillset is low power and poor BA/OBP in a utility role... meaning there are better late dice rolls out there.

Yr Tm	PA	R	HR	RBI	SB	BA	xHR	xSB	xBA	OBP	SLG	OPS+	vL+	vR+	bb%	ct%	Eye	G	L	F	h%	HctX	QBaB	Brl%	PX	xPX	HR/F	xHR/F	Spd	SBA%	SB%	RAR	BPX	R$
17 aa	483	60	21	55	9	210		5		282	422	96			9	71	0.34				25				131				106	15%	68%		118	$6
18 aaa	492	44	10	49	3	236		9		291	371	89			7	65	0.22				34				105				89	6%	49%		-33	$6
19 CLE *	359	45	9	38	3	218	3	4	224	289	356	89	55	89	9	70	0.34	51	16	33	28	91	CCb	6%	84	52	6%	18%	122	5%	74%	-14.1	19	$3
20 CLE	13	1	0	1	0	182	0	0	148	308	182	65	95	0	15	64	0.50	71	14	14	29	37	FFb		0	-26	0%	0%	124	0%	0%	-0.9	-296	-$3
21 CLE *	313	38	12	48	2	234	8	1	236	270	435	97	91	99	5	69	0.16	36	21	43	30	82	CAd	7%	130	82	12%	11%	119	8%	41%	-7.5	100	$6
1st Half	114	12	2	14	1	176	3	0	197	211	287	69	53	98	4	72	0.17	30	18	52	22	71	DAf	8%	77	73	5%	7%	98	8%	100%	-10.1	-35	-$5
2nd Half	199	26	10	34	1	268	5	1	260	303	520	111	139	99	5	67	0.15	40	24	36	35	91	CCc	6%	162	89	22%	16%	132	8%	22%	2.0	185	$10
22 Proj	**210**	**24**	**7**	**27**	**2**	**227**	**7**	**2**	**229**	**281**	**404**	**93**	**88**	**97**	**6**	**69**	**0.22**	**40**	**20**	**40**	**29**	**85**		**7%**	**117**	**75**	**13%**	**14%**	**108**	**8%**	**59%**	**-4.9**	**33**	**$5**

ERIK FLORIMONTE

Chapman,Matt

Age: 29 Pos: 3B	Health	B	LIMA Plan	B+
Bats: R Ht: 6' 0" Wt: 215	PT/Exp	A	Rand Var	0
	Consist	B	MM	4105

After 2020 season was ended prematurely by hip surgery, improved health didn't bring a ct% rebound in 2021. Power potential is enticing thanks to high FB%, quality of contact and xPX, but lack of consistent line drives is contributing to a discouraging BA/xBA trend. His plate patience is a virtue, but our player patience is being tested.

Yr Tm	PA	R	HR	RBI	SB	BA	xHR	xSB	xBA	OBP	SLG	OPS+	vL+	vR+	bb%	ct%	Eye	G	L	F	h%	HctX	QBaB	Brl%	PX	xPX	HR/F	xHR/F	Spd	SBA%	SB%	RAR	BPX
17 OAK *	520	63	25	64	4	228	15	6	233	305	469	105	106	105	10	65	0.32	34	16	51	29	95	BAf	12%	159	134	14%	15%	111	12%	34%	-5.8	133
18 OAK	616	100	24	68	1	278	23	11	266	356	508	116	107	117	9	73	0.40	40	20	39	34	117	ABd	9%	148	114	15%	15%	117	2%	33%	28.2	227
19 OAK	670	102	36	91	1	249	36	4	261	342	506	117	118	116	11	75	0.50	41	15	43	27	117	ABf	12%	137	107	19%	19%	102	1%	50%	11.2	233
20 OAK	152	22	10	25	0	232	12	1	244	276	535	108	84	112	5	62	0.15	26	24	51	29	104	AAf	18%	198	150	22%	27%	110	0%	0%	0.0	208
21 OAK	622	75	27	72	3	210	33	5	195	314	403	98	110	92	13	62	0.40	34	15	52	28	76	BAf	14%	126	130	16%	19%	131	3%	60%	-13.3	58
1st Half	342	40	11	42	1	229	14	3	199	327	399	101	109	96	13	65	0.43	34	17	49	31	80	BBf	11%	110	126	11%	15%	139	3%	100%	-6.0	62
2nd Half	280	35	16	30	2	187	18	2	190	296	407	95	111	88	13	59	0.36	34	11	55	23	71	BAf	16%	148	135	21%	23%	100	3%	50%	-11.2	38
22 Proj	**595**	**82**	**31**	**82**	**2**	**225**	**34**	**5**	**222**	**311**	**457**	**104**	**107**	**103**	**11**	**65**	**0.34**	**34**	**17**	**49**	**28**	**92**		**14%**	**150**	**130**	**18%**	**20%**	**104**	**5%**	**51%**	**4.8**	**99**

Chavis,Michael

Age: 26 Pos: 2B	Health	C	LIMA Plan	F
Bats: R Ht: 5' 10" Wt: 210	PT/Exp	C	Rand Var	+2
	Consist	B	MM	3201

3-11-.248 in 124 PA at BOS/PIT. Got fresh start in PIT after being dealt at trade deadline, but consistent run of playing time was interrupted by elbow injury. Poor ct%, exceptionally low eye (0.02 in MLB) continue to torpedo BA and put entir skill set at risk. Add in high GB%, uninspiring QBaB, and below-average xPX, and you've got little reason for optimism.

Yr Tm	PA	R	HR	RBI	SB	BA	xHR	xSB	xBA	OBP	SLG	OPS+	vL+	vR+	bb%	ct%	Eye	G	L	F	h%	HctX	QBaB	Brl%	PX	xPX	HR/F	xHR/F	Spd	SBA%	SB%	RAR	BPX
17 aa	264	32	11	32	1	239		3		287	450	100			6	77	0.28				27				128				83	2%	100%		145
18 a/a	166	26	6	20	2	279		1		327	468	107			7	68	0.23				37				134				94	8%	69%		73
19 BOS *	458	55	24	67	2	251	15	5	228	312	459	107	103	106	8	64	0.25	45	20	35	33	75	CCc	11%	123	90	23%	19%	92	3%	67%	-6.7	4
20 BOS	158	16	5	19	3	212	6	1	227	259	377	84	80	87	5	66	0.16	46	23	31	29	90	CCb	7%	100	80	17%	20%	123	10%	100%	-12.2	-28
21 2 TM *	326	42	12	36	2	228	3	4	230	254	394	89	109	75	3	66	0.10	50	20	30	31	67	BDc	5%	111	66	13%	13%	113	9%	43%	-26.1	-19
1st Half	159	24	5	16	2	212	1	2	214	246	348	83	97	73	4	64	0.12	46	22	32	30	57	CDa	3%	94	46	8%	8%	98	9%	63%	-13.7	-112
2nd Half	167	18	7	21	1	243	3	2	243	262	437	95	117	78	3	67	0.08	53	19	28	32	77	BCf	7%	125	83	17%	25%	115	9%	24%	-10.0	42
22 Proj	**210**	**26**	**7**	**26**	**2**	**236**	**8**	**2**	**225**	**278**	**389**	**91**	**101**	**83**	**5**	**66**	**0.15**	**48**	**21**	**31**	**32**	**74**		**7%**	**102**	**75**	**16%**	**20%**	**96**	**8%**	**64%**	**-3.3**	**-61**

Chisholm Jr.,Jazz

Age: 24 Pos: 2B SS	Health	B	LIMA Plan	C+
Bats: L Ht: 5' 11" Wt: 184	PT/Exp	A	Rand Var	-3
	Consist	D	MM	3515

Sidelined 38 days due to shoulder, hamstring, and COVID protocols, but he's a player still adjusting. PRO: xHR/xHR/F backs power output; Spd/SBA% stands out; real strides making better contact. CON: Could benefit from better SB% efficiency; still a lot of swing/miss; current GB% caps power. Buy the speed; hope for a power/BA spike.

Yr Tm	PA	R	HR	RBI	SB	BA	xHR	xSB	xBA	OBP	SLG	OPS+	vL+	vR+	bb%	ct%	Eye	G	L	F	h%	HctX	QBaB	Brl%	PX	xPX	HR/F	xHR/F	Spd	SBA%	SB%	RAR	BPX
17																																	
18																																	
19 aa	455	63	21	61	18	220		8		320	442	106			13	61	0.38				30				133				153	21%	81%		85
20 MIA	62	8	2	6	2	161	3	1	183	242	321	75	121	59	8	66	0.26	37	11	51	20	72	DBf	11%	91	145	11%	17%	141	36%	50%	-5.8	-4
21 MIA	507	70	18	53	23	248	20	23	241	303	425	100	91	104	7	69	0.23	49	20	31	32	87	BDf	9%	110	88	18%	20%	144	28%	74%	-10.8	85
1st Half	250	33	9	30	12	260	10	12	237	324	449	108	94	114	8	65	0.24	50	19	30	36	81	BDd	10%	123	106	20%	22%	149	28%	80%	0.8	81
2nd Half	257	37	9	23	11	236	10	11	245	282	401	92	88	94	6	72	0.23	47	21	32	29	93	CDf	8%	99	72	17%	19%	131	28%	69%	-8.7	81
22 Proj	**560**	**79**	**19**	**63**	**28**	**251**	**23**	**23**	**227**	**318**	**422**	**101**	**106**	**98**	**8**	**67**	**0.28**	**48**	**18**	**34**	**34**	**84**		**9%**	**108**	**100**	**16%**	**20%**	**139**	**22%**	**77%**	**6.8**	**56**

Choi,Ji-Man

Age: 31 Pos: 1B	Health	C	LIMA Plan	D+
Bats: L Ht: 6' 1" Wt: 260	PT/Exp	C	Rand Var	0
	Consist	A	MM	4023

11-45-.229 in 305 PA at TAM. Already limited by strict platoon split, spent an additional 73 days on injured list with varie of issues in 2021. Ongoing slide in ct% is concerning, especially considering power is only slightly above-average—despit good QBaB—due to moderate FB%. Appeal seems likely to remain limited to deep mixed or only-league formats.

Yr Tm	PA	R	HR	RBI	SB	BA	xHR	xSB	xBA	OBP	SLG	OPS+	vL+	vR+	bb%	ct%	Eye	G	L	F	h%	HctX	QBaB	Brl%	PX	xPX	HR/F	xHR/F	Spd	SBA%	SB%	RAR	BPX
17 NYY *	339	37	17	63	3	254	2	4	230	330	496	112	0	163	10	65	0.32	64	0	36	34	119	ADa	18%	167	178	50%	50%	45	6%	68%	1.6	85
18 2 TM *	458	46	15	61	3	250	12	3	245	349	434	105	68	120	13	70	0.51	43	21	35	32	113	BCc	12%	125	116	21%	25%	54	2%	100%	9.0	83
19 TAM	487	54	19	63	2	261	23	3	258	363	459	114	88	119	13	74	0.59	42	24	35	31	109	ACb	11%	107	120	18%	21%	73	4%	40%	8.0	115
20 TAM	145	16	3	16	0	230	3	1	242	331	410	98	66	104	14	70	0.56	39	20	40	30	99	CBf	3%	130	100	8%	8%	61	0%	0%	-2.8	136
21 TAM *	330	39	11	47	0	226	12	0	234	338	399	101	72	116	14	66	0.49	40	25	35	30	104	ABc	9%	119	111	19%	20%	52	0%	0%	-7.9	15
1st Half	140	16	3	18	0	249	5	0	222	358	380	103	115	108	15	66	0.50	35	26	38	35	104	ABc	15%	95	109	12%	20%	67	0%	0%	-3.6	-31
2nd Half	190	23	8	29	0	210	7	0	243	326	414	100	44	120	14	65	0.48	43	25	32	27	103	BCc	6%	137	112	24%	21%	49	0%	0%	-6.7	62
22 Proj	**350**	**40**	**12**	**48**	**1**	**239**	**15**	**0**	**243**	**346**	**432**	**106**	**74**	**114**	**14**	**68**	**0.50**	**40**	**24**	**36**	**31**	**105**		**9%**	**130**	**111**	**17%**	**20%**	**52**	**0%**	**61%**	**4.7**	**61**

Clement,Ernie

Age: 26 Pos: 2B	Health	A	LIMA Plan	D
Bats: R Ht: 6' 0" Wt: 170	PT/Exp	D	Rand Var	+3
	Consist	A	MM	1233

3-9-.231 in 133 PA at CLE. Contact-heavy prospect lived up to that billing in first taste of majors. The rest of the profile i limited, as both minor-league track record and small big-league sample show no power. Hints of speed exist based on Sp and SBA%, though lack of success calls potential SB production into question.

Yr Tm	PA	R	HR	RBI	SB	BA	xHR	xSB	xBA	OBP	SLG	OPS+	vL+	vR+	bb%	ct%	Eye	G	L	F	h%	HctX	QBaB	Brl%	PX	xPX	HR/F	xHR/F	Spd	SBA%	SB%	RAR	BPX
17																																	
18 aa	68	8	0	4	1	238		1		268	340	81			4	89	0.35				27				68				109	17%	45%		170
19 a/a	430	43	1	24	15	254		11		297	311	84			6	91	0.68				28				31				118	24%	58%		137
20																																	
21 CLE *	271	24	4	16	1	217	2	3	249	257	326	80	99	79	5	81	0.28	37	25	38	25	72	FCc	4%	69	46	8%	5%	119	6%	40%	-15.5	100
1st Half	116	13	0	6	1	237	0	1	269	264	326	82	72	81	4	83	0.22	41	28	31	28	45	BCa	5%	63	13	0%	0%	111	6%	100%	-6.2	104
2nd Half	154	11	4	10	0	199	2	2	241	248	322	77	106	77	6	79	0.31	35	24	41	23	81	FBd	4%	73	59	10%	7%	123	6%	0%	-11.2	92
22 Proj	**280**	**26**	**4**	**17**	**3**	**223**	**3**	**3**	**255**	**278**	**333**	**83**	**88**	**80**	**5**	**83**	**0.34**	**38**	**25**	**37**	**25**	**67**		**4%**	**65**	**41**	**5%**	**4%**	**136**	**8%**	**48%**	**-10.6**	**66**

Collins,Zack

Age: 27 Pos: CA	Health	A	LIMA Plan	F
Bats: L Ht: 6' 3" Wt: 230	PT/Exp	D	Rand Var	0
	Consist	F	MM	2101

4-26-.210 in 231 PA at CHW. Finally got full major-league season under his belt, albeit with uninspiring results. Skills do suggest some power upside, particularly based on QBaB and xPX. Inability to make consistent contact may mean he nev unlocks that thump, but could be worth late speculation in two-catcher formats.

Yr Tm	PA	R	HR	RBI	SB	BA	xHR	xSB	xBA	OBP	SLG	OPS+	vL+	vR+	bb%	ct%	Eye	G	L	F	h%	HctX	QBaB	Brl%	PX	xPX	HR/F	xHR/F	Spd	SBA%	SB%	RAR	BPX
17 aa	45	7	2	5	0	229		1		421	465	121			25	64	0.93				29				159				103	0%	0%		203
18 aa	515	54	15	63	5	218		2		366	382	100			19	58	0.55				34				134				88	3%	100%		10
19 CHW *	443	54	19	70	0	230	5	4	216	339	438	107	52	103	14	59	0.40	32	23	45	33	83	BBc	15%	139	171	14%	24%	95	0%	0%	14.9	30
20 CHW	18	1	0	0	0	63	1	0	173	167	125	39	0	41	11	69	0.40	27	18	55	9	101	AAb	9%	56	200	0%	17%	97	0%	0%	-2.0	-104
21 CHW *	268	28	6	29	1	195	8	1	207	304	329	87	74	98	13	63	0.43	29	26	46	28	96	BAc	10%	102	130	7%	14%	70	3%	50%	-7.2	-58
1st Half	134	14	3	19	1	224	5	0	217	323	379	98	65	112	13	63	0.40	33	24	43	33	97	CBd	10%	124	131	10%	16%	72	3%	50%	-0.6	0
2nd Half	134	14	3	10	0	165	4	0	201	284	278	76	90	81	14	63	0.46	23	28	49	23	93	AAc	10%	80	129	4%	15%	87	3%	0%	-6.3	-100
22 Proj	**210**	**23**	**4**	**25**	**1**	**204**	**7**	**1**	**200**	**326**	**330**	**89**	**72**	**95**	**15**	**63**	**0.47**	**28**	**26**	**46**	**30**	**92**		**11%**	**96**	**140**	**8%**	**14%**	**80**	**3%**	**68%**	**-0.8**	**-94**

Conforto,Michael

Age: 29 Pos: RF	Health	B	LIMA Plan	B
Bats: L Ht: 6' 1" Wt: 215	PT/Exp	A	Rand Var	+4
	Consist	D	MM	4135

Missed significant time with hamstring injury in May/June, which likely contributed to abysmal 1st half. Once fully healthy, brought skills back in line with career norms in 2nd half. 2020 BA looks likely to remain an outlier, though solid Eye ensures it won't dip to extreme. Gaps between PX/xPX and HR/F, xHR/F suggest power could return to... UP: 30 HR

Yr Tm	PA	R	HR	RBI	SB	BA	xHR	xSB	xBA	OBP	SLG	OPS+	vL+	vR+	bb%	ct%	Eye	G	L	F	h%	HctX	QBaB	Brl%	PX	xPX	HR/F	xHR/F	Spd	SBA%	SB%	RAR	BPX
17 NYM	440	72	27	68	2	279	24	7	276	384	555	128	98	135	13	70	0.50	38	24	38	33	117	CCf	13%	166	142	27%	24%	86	2%	100%	23.2	197
18 NYM	638	78	28	82	3	243	26	4	245	350	448	107	106	105	13	71	0.53	44	20	37	29	93	CCc	10%	128	130	20%	18%	86	4%	43%	11.1	130
19 NYM	648	90	33	92	7	257	33	5	262	363	494	119	98	127	13	73	0.56	36	24	40	29	92	BBc	12%	128	120	20%	20%	87	5%	78%	10.2	178
20 NYM	233	40	9	31	3	322	10	3	270	412	515	123	114	128	10	72	0.42	41	30	28	41	106	CCc	11%	117	108	22%	24%	84	8%	50%	11.7	116
21 NYM	479	52	14	55	1	232	19	6	241	344	384	100	79	109	12	74	0.57	45	21	34	28	112	CCc	9%	93	111	13%	18%	73	1%	100%	-11.9	77
1st Half	177	12	2	16	0	209	6	2	222	333	297	88	70	95	13	72	0.56	47	24	29	28	104	CCc	9%	62	69	6%	19%	73	1%	0%	-9.3	-38
2nd Half	302	40	12	39	1	244	14	3	250	351	434	106	83	116	12	76	0.57	43	19	37	28	117	CCc	9%	110	134	16%	19%	79	1%	100%	-0.8	158
22 Proj	**595**	**79**	**27**	**87**	**4**	**256**	**28**	**2**	**255**	**360**	**463**	**112**	**95**	**119**	**12**	**73**	**0.51**	**42**	**22**	**35**	**30**	**106**		**10%**	**123**	**114**	**20%**	**21%**	**76**	**2%**	**62%**	**16.2**	**115**

DANIEL MARCUS

Contreras,William

Age: 24 Pos: CA
Bats: R Ht: 6' 0" Wt: 180

Health	A	LIMA Plan	D
PT/Exp	D	Rand Var	+5
Consist	F	MM	3011

8-23-.215 in 185 PA at ATL. Predictably, given MiLB profile and long swing, struggled with contact and batting average in first extended time in majors. But enough power skills in place to be interesting as a future long-ball threat. Still raw, and catchers notoriously take their own sweet time. But still worth watching.

Yr Tm	PA	R	HR	RBI	SB	BA	xHR	xSB	xBA	OBP	SLG	OPS+	vL+	vR+	bb%	ct%	Eye	G	L	F	h%	HctX	QBaB	Brl%	PX	xPX	HR/F	xHR/F	Spd	SBA%	SB%	RAR	BPX	R$
17																																		
18																																		
19 aa	207	26	3	19	0	253		3		311	351	92			8	79	0.39				31				58				98	0%	0%		30	$0
20 ATL	10	0	0	1	0	400	0	0	391	400	500	119	0	150	0	60	0.00	17	67	17	67	81	DAa	17%	102	140	0%	0%	115	0%	0%	1.0	-164	-$2
21 ATL *	350	40	15	46	0	235	9	2	237	299	419	99	91	98	8	70	0.31	49	19	32	29	94	ADd	11%	110	91	23%	26%	106	0%	0%	1.1	77	$6
1st Half	151	16	7	21	0	215	8	1	229	291	407	97	103	96	9	66	0.28	48	20	31	27	93	ADd	12%	116	105	25%	29%	133	0%	0%	-1.4	62	$1
2nd Half	199	24	8	25	0	250	1	1	229	311	427	100	45	111	8	74	0.34	50	15	35	30	75	ABc	5%	106	28	14%	14%	97	0%	0%	2.2	100	$5
22 Proj	**210**	**25**	**9**	**26**	**0**	**240**	**9**	**1**	**235**	**306**	**419**	**98**	**87**	**101**	**8**	**73**	**0.33**	**49**	**17**	**34**	**29**	**82**		**8%**	**104**	**59**	**19%**	**20%**	**104**	**3%**	**0%**	**4.1**	**26**	**$2**

Contreras,Willson

Age: 30 Pos: CA
Bats: R Ht: 6' 1" Wt: 225

Health	B	LIMA Plan	C+
PT/Exp	A	Rand Var	0
Consist	B	MM	4125

Missed a month with a knee sprain. Otherwise, some small variability aside, he's settling into a relatively predictable range of skills—though QBaB growth suggests he could still tap into a bit more power. So bid on the consistency, but lack of plate skills growth says the "future star" many saw a few seasons ago is increasingly less likely to arrive.

Yr Tm	PA	R	HR	RBI	SB	BA	xHR	xSB	xBA	OBP	SLG	OPS+	vL+	vR+	bb%	ct%	Eye	G	L	F	h%	HctX	QBaB	Brl%	PX	xPX	HR/F	xHR/F	Spd	SBA%	SB%	RAR	BPX	R$
17 CHC	428	50	21	74	5	276	19	6	268	356	499	116	124	111	11	74	0.46	53	17	29	32	106	CDc	10%	131	101	26%	23%	71	8%	56%	21.4	136	$14
18 CHC	544	50	10	54	4	249	15	8	242	339	390	98	109	93	10	74	0.44	52	17	31	31	79	CDc	7%	92	71	9%	14%	110	4%	80%	11.1	87	$9
19 CHC	409	57	24	64	1	272	20	4	263	355	533	123	143	117	9	72	0.37	50	16	34	32	92	CDc	12%	141	128	27%	23%	99	3%	33%	19.8	185	$13
20 CHC	225	37	7	26	1	243	10	1	234	356	407	101	71	110	9	70	0.35	47	20	33	31	99	BDd	10%	103	125	16%	23%	80	5%	33%	0.7	20	$15
21 CHC	483	61	21	57	5	237	26	4	233	340	438	107	121	101	11	67	0.38	50	16	34	30	106	ACc	11%	131	127	22%	28%	79	7%	56%	6.9	69	$11
1st Half	286	35	13	30	3	235	13	2	226	343	432	108	133	98	12	67	0.43	50	15	35	29	93	BCc	9%	123	104	22%	22%	84	7%	50%	3.5	69	$13
2nd Half	197	26	8	27	2	241	12	1	241	335	447	106	105	106	10	66	0.31	51	18	32	32	125	ADc	13%	141	160	22%	33%	79	7%	67%	2.9	81	$7
22 Proj	**490**	**68**	**21**	**65**	**4**	**247**	**25**	**6**	**240**	**344**	**445**	**107**	**110**	**106**	**10**	**69**	**0.36**	**50**	**17**	**33**	**31**	**103**		**11%**	**126**	**125**	**21%**	**25%**	**81**	**6%**	**53%**	**16.1**	**70**	**$16**

Cooper,Garrett

Age: 31 Pos: RF
Bats: R Ht: 6' 5" Wt: 235

Health	F	LIMA Plan	D+
PT/Exp	C	Rand Var	-5
Consist	A	MM	3043

Elbow surgery ended season in July, keeping string alive of IL time in each of his five MLB seasons. Productive when healthy once again, though xBA continues to have doubts. In fact, at 31, skills have likely plateaued—and they really aren't exceptional. Given that and injury risk, there's little reason to go the extra buck here.

Yr Tm	PA	R	HR	RBI	SB	BA	xHR	xSB	xBA	OBP	SLG	OPS+	vL+	vR+	bb%	ct%	Eye	G	L	F	h%	HctX	QBaB	Brl%	PX	xPX	HR/F	xHR/F	Spd	SBA%	SB%	RAR	BPX	R$
17 NYY *	381	61	18	77	0	315	1	5	325	372	560	127	132	93	8	77	0.40	34	38	28	36	118	CCc	3%	145	60	0%	11%	87	0%	0%	17.2	212	$17
18 MIA *	70	4	1	6	0	223	0	0	209	293	284	77	114	64	9	71	0.34	67	24	10	30	37	CFc	0%	44	-27	0%	0%	82	0%	0%	-4.5	-120	-$2
19 MIA	421	52	15	50	0	281	18	2	255	344	446	109	89	116	8	71	0.30	52	25	23	36	100	CFb	10%	93	93	24%	29%	97	0%	0%	-0.5	22	$10
20 MIA	133	20	6	20	0	283	6	0	276	353	500	113	153	93	8	74	0.35	46	26	28	34	94	BCa	10%	127	72	24%	24%	74	0%	0%	0.7	156	$11
21 MIA	250	30	9	33	1	284	11	2	244	380	465	116	132	109	12	68	0.44	51	22	27	38	94	ADa	11%	115	102	23%	28%	100	3%	50%	1.0	81	$7
1st Half	209	23	7	28	0	277	7	1	237	364	451	114	132	105	11	68	0.38	51	20	29	37	93	BCa	9%	112	101	19%	19%	99	3%	0%	-0.7	65	$8
2nd Half	41	7	2	5	1	323	4	0	281	463	548	137	141	136	21	68	0.80	55	32	14	42	101	AFa	19%	136	103	67%	133%	99	3%	100%	3.5	200	-$5
22 Proj	**280**	**38**	**9**	**42**	**0**	**279**	**8**	**2**	**265**	**354**	**449**	**109**	**119**	**104**	**9**	**72**	**0.36**	**51**	**26**	**22**	**36**	**97**		**13%**	**108**	**94**	**22%**	**21%**	**85**	**3%**	**0%**	**7.5**	**46**	**$10**

Cordero,Franchy

Age: 27 Pos: LF
Bats: L Ht: 6' 3" Wt: 226

Health	F	LIMA Plan	F
PT/Exp	D	Rand Var	-1
Consist	A	MM	3301

1-9-.189 in 136 PA at BOS. After yo-yo'ing for a while, finally exiled to minors for good in early September after an awful MLB season. Did hit well in AAA—but he's done that before. Sure, all those past injuries may have just delayed his arrival, and he still owns all those flashy tools. But he's no kid anymore, and our collective patience is running thin.

Yr Tm	PA	R	HR	RBI	SB	BA	xHR	xSB	xBA	OBP	SLG	OPS+	vL+	vR+	bb%	ct%	Eye	G	L	F	h%	HctX	QBaB	Brl%	PX	xPX	HR/F	xHR/F	Spd	SBA%	SB%	RAR	BPX	R$
17 SD *	504	62	14	53	11	264	5	6	229	295	453	102	82	96	4	63	0.12	48	19	33	39	99	ACb	14%	123	125	19%	31%	166	17%	67%	-10.4	36	$13
18 SD *	183	21	8	20	7	234	9	4	227	305	421	97	78	108	9	60	0.25	46	25	29	34	107	ADc	13%	134	144	29%	38%	101	22%	78%	-1.6	0	$4
19 SD *	69	7	2	6	1	209	0	2	196	287	362	90	0	117	10	52	0.23	25	38	38	36	101	AAa	0%	118	276	0%	0%	119	7%	100%	-3.2	-141	-$2
20 KC	42	7	2	7	1	211	3	0	312	286	447	97	43	107	10	89	1.00	62	12	26	19	117	AFb	12%	117	120	22%	33%	86	14%	100%	-1.3	392	$1
21 BOS *	453	51	10	50	10	233	3	8	224	298	381	93	58	70	8	60	0.23	45	27	28	36	64	CDf	5%	120	38	5%	14%	90	13%	82%	-20.4	-58	$9
1st Half	233	27	5	27	4	260	2	4	235	324	417	103	55	72	9	62	0.25	47	26	26	40	64	CFf	5%	126	35	7%	13%	96	13%	100%	-3.6	-12	$10
2nd Half	221	24	5	23	6	205	1	3	210	272	343	83	67	65	8	59	0.22	39	28	33	32	67	FAc	6%	113	48	0%	17%	83	13%	73%	-15.2	-119	$4
22 Proj	**210**	**24**	**4**	**23**	**5**	**236**	**6**	**4**	**213**	**295**	**374**	**91**	**80**	**93**	**8**	**61**	**0.21**	**44**	**25**	**31**	**37**	**81**		**9%**	**107**	**79**	**11%**	**18%**	**101**	**10%**	**77%**	**-3.7**	**-81**	**$6**

Correa,Carlos

Age: 27 Pos: SS
Bats: R Ht: 6' 4" Wt: 220

Health	C	LIMA Plan	B
PT/Exp	A	Rand Var	0
Consist	D	MM	3335

Posted best plate skills since 2017—and not coincidentally his best season since then. Power metrics don't point to any untapped upside, so this is probably about his peak. On the other hand, these numbers are well supported by skills. At 27, if he can keep dodging his old injury bug nemesis, should be good for several more seasons like this.

Yr Tm	PA	R	HR	RBI	SB	BA	xHR	xSB	xBA	OBP	SLG	OPS+	vL+	vR+	bb%	ct%	Eye	G	L	F	h%	HctX	QBaB	Brl%	PX	xPX	HR/F	xHR/F	Spd	SBA%	SB%	RAR	BPX	R$
17 HOU *	506	84	24	88	2	312	21	8	283	386	535	125	145	121	11	78	0.55	48	20	32	35	125	BDb	9%	125	108	23%	20%	92	2%	67%	36.1	191	$23
18 HOU	468	60	15	65	3	239	14	3	241	323	405	98	106	93	11	72	0.48	44	20	36	29	77	CCd	7%	107	83	14%	13%	94	3%	100%	4.7	93	$10
19 HOU *	344	43	21	60	1	277	18	3	274	357	554	126	134	125	11	73	0.46	39	21	40	31	114	CCd	13%	149	133	26%	22%	96	1%	100%	15.9	237	$11
20 HOU	221	22	5	25	0	264	6	1	231	326	383	94	101	91	11	76	0.33	50	21	29	33	110	CCf	6%	71	86	11%	13%	86	0%	0%	-2.3	8	$11
21 HOU	640	104	26	92	0	279	26	3	277	366	485	117	115	118	12	79	0.65	42	24	35	31	118	BCd	9%	116	102	17%	17%	92	0%	0%	25.6	238	$23
1st Half	342	60	16	52	0	300	12	2	284	401	534	130	124	134	14	80	0.81	42	21	36	33	122	BCd	9%	131	95	19%	14%	92	0%	0%	25.2	315	$31
2nd Half	298	44	10	40	0	257	14	1	269	326	430	102	104	101	10	78	0.48	41	26	33	29	115	BCd	10%	99	110	14%	20%	96	0%	0%	2.0	162	$14
22 Proj	**595**	**85**	**23**	**86**	**1**	**271**	**24**	**2**	**262**	**349**	**461**	**110**	**112**	**108**	**11**	**77**	**0.50**	**43**	**23**	**34**	**31**	**112**		**9%**	**110**	**103**	**17%**	**17%**	**85**	**2%**	**93%**	**21.4**	**134**	**$22**

Crawford,Brandon

Age: 35 Pos: SS
Bats: L Ht: 6' 1" Wt: 223

Health	A	LIMA Plan	C+
PT/Exp	A	Rand Var	-4
Consist	C	MM	3235

Well, well—that 2020 power-skills spike was the real deal. A no-doubt career year, even under-performed xHR, and at 34? Yes indeed, and added double-digit SB just for fun. That said, there's no stronger pull than that of regression, and xBA assures us BA will do just that. And yeah, forget about the steals. But another 20+ HR? Why not?

Yr Tm	PA	R	HR	RBI	SB	BA	xHR	xSB	xBA	OBP	SLG	OPS+	vL+	vR+	bb%	ct%	Eye	G	L	F	h%	HctX	QBaB	Brl%	PX	xPX	HR/F	xHR/F	Spd	SBA%	SB%	RAR	BPX	R$
17 SF	570	58	14	77	3	253	18	7	255	305	403	96	89	97	7	76	0.37	46	19	34	30	103	CCc	6%	93	102	10%	13%	65	6%	38%	-6.2	73	$10
18 SF	594	63	14	54	4	254	13	5	258	325	394	96	101	91	8	77	0.41	44	25	31	31	103	CCb	4%	88	91	11%	10%	77	6%	44%	5.3	70	$11
19 SF	560	58	11	59	3	228	15	5	252	304	350	90	83	92	9	77	0.45	48	23	28	28	104	CDb	5%	69	106	10%	14%	78	4%	60%	-19.6	22	$5
20 SF	193	26	8	28	1	256	7	1	259	326	465	105	84	110	8	73	0.32	42	23	35	31	102	CCd	9%	127	123	18%	16%	72	7%	33%	1.5	124	$14
21 SF	549	79	24	90	11	298	33	7	266	373	522	123	98	133	10	78	0.53	40	19	41	34	101	CBd	11%	126	137	15%	21%	103	9%	79%	33.7	258	$28
1st Half	276	46	17	52	6	264	21	3	263	348	537	123	98	133	11	74	0.48	38	17	46	29	107	BBd	17%	155	174	20%	25%	93	9%	100%	14.1	277	$28
2nd Half	273	33	7	38	5	332	12	4	270	399	506	122	98	132	10	83	0.62	42	21	37	38	95	CBc	7%	99	104	9%	16%	107	9%	63%	18.7	242	$21
22 Proj	**525**	**69**	**20**	**75**	**7**	**276**	**20**	**8**	**261**	**348**	**469**	**111**	**94**	**117**	**9**	**77**	**0.45**	**42**	**21**	**37**	**32**	**101**		**9%**	**113**	**121**	**15%**	**15%**	**86**	**7%**	**64%**	**18.9**	**167**	**$22**

Crawford,J.P.

Age: 27 Pos: SS
Bats: L Ht: 6' 2" Wt: 199

Health	B	LIMA Plan	B
PT/Exp	A	Rand Var	-2
Consist	A	MM	1225

A conscious effort to hit to all fields and *not* swing for the fences has improved his offense to... a palatable level. But what's happened to the wheels? Granted, he's never taken advantage of clearly superior speed skills, but 3 steals in 9 attempts is just silly—and xSB agrees. Given that and perhaps a slightly higher OBP floor... UP: 20 SB, still

Yr Tm	PA	R	HR	RBI	SB	BA	xHR	xSB	xBA	OBP	SLG	OPS+	vL+	vR+	bb%	ct%	Eye	G	L	F	h%	HctX	QBaB	Brl%	PX	xPX	HR/F	xHR/F	Spd	SBA%	SB%	RAR	BPX	R$
17 PHI *	631	75	14	62	5	223	0	9	240	329	364	94	51	105	14	76	0.66	31	27	43	27	44	FAc	0%	81	20	0%	0%	134	5%	56%	-10.8	115	$5
18 PHI *	199	22	4	18	3	220	3	2	220	289	374	89	66	99	9	68	0.30	38	23	39	30	64	CBb	5%	102	74	10%	10%	128	7%	100%	-1.0	33	$1
19 SEA *	527	58	9	57	7	236	5	7	242	321	371	96	62	108	11	75	0.51	45	20	35	29	74	DCc	3%	79	69	8%	5%	111	8%	71%	-16.3	81	$8
20 SEA	232	33	2	24	6	255	3	5	240	336	338	90	86	91	10	81	0.59	44	23	33	31	96	DCd	2%	46	83	4%	6%	141	13%	67%	-5.1	96	$18
21 SEA	687	89	9	54	3	273	8	15	256	338	376	98	95	100	8	82	0.51	46	24	31	32	75	DCd	2%	66	42	6%	5%	100	5%	33%	-6.1	108	$16
1st Half	335	42	5	31	3	289	5	7	267	349	408	105	117	98	8	82	0.51	45	24	30	34	77	DDd	4%	76	49	7%	7%	98	5%	50%	3.5	142	$18
2nd Half	352	47	4	23	0	257	3	8	247	328	346	91	78	101	9	81	0.51	46	23	31	31	73	DCd	1%	57	35	5%	4%	104	5%	0%	-8.4	81	$9
22 Proj	**630**	**82**	**8**	**57**	**9**	**261**	**8**	**8**	**244**	**337**	**369**	**96**	**85**	**101**	**9**	**79**	**0.49**	**44**	**23**	**33**	**32**	**76**		**2%**	**67**	**56**	**6%**	**5%**	**114**	**6%**	**63%**	**-0.8**	**58**	**$18**

ROD TRUESDELL

Cron,C.J.

Age: 32 Pos: 1B	Health B	LIMA Plan B+	
Bats: R Ht: 6' 4" Wt: 235	PT/Exp A	Rand Var -2	
	Consist B	MM 4135	

After slow start, big second half drove him to career season as predicted by last year's Forecaster. 'Twas a near 30-point gain in batting average that drove it, and xBA says it will regress. So best to rely on comfy 30-HR baseline as reflected by xHR in last three full seasons. Health, consistency make him a good value once the top 1Bs are gone.

Yr	Tm	PA	R	HR	RBI	SB	BA	xHR	xSB	xBA	OBP	SLG	OPS+	vL+	vR+	bb%	ct%	Eye	G	L	F	h%	HctX	QBaB	Brl%	PX	xPX	HR/F	xHR/F	Spd	SBA%	SB%	RAR	BPX
17	LAA *	457	46	19	71	4	239	17	5	240	284	419	96	107	97	6	73	0.23	33	23	45	29	105	CAc	10%	107	129	15%	15%	78	6%	65%	-24.8	39
18	TAM	560	68	30	74	1	253	33	5	260	323	493	109	123	101	7	71	0.26	40	21	39	30	104	CBd	12%	151	115	21%	24%	85	2%	33%	-0.7	153
19	MIN	499	51	25	78	0	253	33	1	262	311	469	108	142	94	6	77	0.27	42	22	36	28	109	ACc	15%	113	114	20%	26%	60	0%	0%	-8.4	107
20	DET	52	9	4	8	0	190	4	0	264	346	548	119	80	133	17	62	0.56	38	15	46	18	106	DAf	19%	235	194	33%	33%	92	0%	0%	-0.1	400
21	COL	547	70	28	92	1	281	30	1	267	375	530	124	133	121	11	75	0.51	39	19	42	32	111	CBd	11%	145	115	19%	20%	72	1%	100%	12.1	238
1st Half		250	32	11	32	0	252	11	1	248	356	463	114	136	104	12	72	0.51	40	21	40	30	106	CBd	10%	123	116	18%	18%	87	1%	0%	-1.3	158
2nd Half		297	38	17	60	1	305	19	1	282	391	586	132	130	133	10	77	0.52	38	18	44	34	115	CBd	12%	162	114	19%	22%	69	1%	100%	17.4	319
22	**Proj**	**560**	**69**	**32**	**93**	**1**	**267**	**34**	**2**	**263**	**343**	**516**	**117**	**130**	**111**	**8**	**74**	**0.36**	**39**	**19**	**42**	**30**	**109**		**12%**	**144**	**116**	**20%**	**21%**	**71**	**2%**	**66%**	**21.1**	**175**

Cronenworth,Jake

Age: 28 Pos: 2B SS 1B	Health A	LIMA Plan B+	
Bats: L Ht: 6' 0" Wt: 187	PT/Exp A	Rand Var +2	
	Consist A	MM 2345	

Strong sophomore campaign backed by multi-skilled toolbox. Expected metrics point to double-digit homers and steals as a realistic next step, and if hit rate normalizes, a return to .280 average is in play. Best to use 15 HR as baseline though, since late Brl% and xPX fades suggest possibility for some pullback.

Yr	Tm	PA	R	HR	RBI	SB	BA	xHR	xSB	xBA	OBP	SLG	OPS+	vL+	vR+	bb%	ct%	Eye	G	L	F	h%	HctX	QBaB	Brl%	PX	xPX	HR/F	xHR/F	Spd	SBA%	SB%	RAR	BPX
17	aa	175	13	1	17	1	255		3		326	304	86			10	86	0.76				29				31				90	4%	44%		52
18	a/a	480	66	3	43	18	219		5		279	296	77			8	80	0.42				27				49				115	19%	84%		40
19	aaa	384	60	8	36	10	283		12		358	433	109			10	78	0.53				35				84				121	15%	62%		137
20	SD	192	26	4	20	3	285	9	4	295	354	477	110	72	128	9	83	0.60	45	25	29	33	122	BCb	10%	108	104	10%	21%	107	9%	75%	4.6	280
21	SD	638	94	21	71	4	266	23	11	281	340	460	110	105	112	9	84	0.61	42	22	36	29	102	CCd	7%	102	96	12%	13%	125	5%	57%	3.4	288
1st Half		352	56	12	34	3	275	14	6	272	347	457	112	101	116	9	84	0.61	41	20	38	29	107	CCd	9%	96	105	12%	14%	118	5%	75%	5.4	265
2nd Half		286	38	9	37	1	256	9	4	291	332	465	108	108	108	9	84	0.61	43	23	33	27	96	CCc	6%	109	84	13%	13%	128	5%	33%	1.3	312
22	**Proj**	**595**	**84**	**16**	**65**	**8**	**275**	**23**	**7**	**275**	**349**	**451**	**109**	**97**	**114**	**9**	**82**	**0.58**	**43**	**23**	**34**	**31**	**106**		**8%**	**97**	**95**	**11%**	**15%**	**116**	**6%**	**66%**	**20.1**	**230**

Cruz,Nelson

Age: 42 Pos: DH	Health A	LIMA Plan B	
Bats: R Ht: 6' 2" Wt: 230	PT/Exp A	Rand Var +3	
	Consist C	MM 4225	

One of the most amazing streaks you'll see: since age 34, has posted >$20 in eight straight seasons after having only one prior to that. Rock-steady QBaB and ace health both say he can continue, even with slight cracks in power foundation last two years. But this was his deepest 2nd half fade in his entire career, so if there is a reason to hedge on a 42 year-old...

Yr	Tm	PA	R	HR	RBI	SB	BA	xHR	xSB	xBA	OBP	SLG	OPS+	vL+	vR+	bb%	ct%	Eye	G	L	F	h%	HctX	QBaB	Brl%	PX	xPX	HR/F	xHR/F	Spd	SBA%	SB%	RAR	BPX
17	SEA	645	91	39	119	1	288	43	10	268	375	549	126	113	127	11	75	0.50	40	18	42	32	123	ACc	14%	146	150	22%	24%	61	1%	50%	36.0	176
18	SEA	591	70	37	97	1	256	41	1	266	342	509	114	124	108	9	76	0.45	44	18	39	27	119	ACc	14%	139	123	24%	27%	56	1%	100%	18.4	183
19	MIN	520	81	41	108	0	311	44	2	281	392	639	143	168	133	11	71	0.43	40	20	40	35	129	ACc	20%	177	156	31%	34%	74	1%	0%	46.7	267
20	MIN	214	33	16	33	0	303	14	1	267	397	595	132	190	113	12	69	0.43	46	23	31	36	107	ACc	15%	164	113	41%	36%	78	0%	0%	17.8	220
21	2 AL	580	79	32	86	3	265	38	1	260	334	497	114	124	109	9	75	0.40	43	18	39	29	118	ACf	14%	128	113	21%	25%	72	2%	100%	13.1	173
1st Half		289	37	18	45	1	306	22	1	279	381	571	133	151	122	10	78	0.53	44	19	37	33	121	ACf	16%	140	114	24%	29%	77	2%	100%	21.1	269
2nd Half		291	42	14	41	2	226	16	1	241	289	425	97	96	97	8	73	0.31	42	18	40	26	114	ACd	11%	115	113	18%	21%	69	2%	100%	-6.5	85
22	**Proj**	**560**	**79**	**29**	**90**	**2**	**268**	**38**	**3**	**251**	**347**	**485**	**113**	**128**	**106**	**10**	**73**	**0.41**	**44**	**19**	**37**	**31**	**117**		**15%**	**124**	**123**	**22%**	**28%**	**69**	**2%**	**89%**	**16.0**	**114**

Cruz,Oneil

Age: 23 Pos: SS	Health A	LIMA Plan D	
Bats: L Ht: 6' 6" Wt: 175	PT/Exp F	Rand Var +2	
	Consist A	MM 3521	

1-3-.333 in 9 PA at PIT. Long-limbed, toolsy shortstop put up near 20/20 season in minors prior to final-week recall. Like many youngsters, holes in swing will leave him prone to ups and downs. Fortunately, his aren't too big to address, and 2nd half growth is encouraging. At age 23, time is on his side. A premium stash in keeper leagues.

Yr	Tm	PA	R	HR	RBI	SB	BA	xHR	xSB	xBA	OBP	SLG	OPS+	vL+	vR+	bb%	ct%	Eye	G	L	F	h%	HctX	QBaB	Brl%	PX	xPX	HR/F	xHR/F	Spd	SBA%	SB%	RAR	BPX
17																																		
18																																		
19	aa	134	14	1	17	3	269		2		349	409	105			11	70	0.42				38				89				125	11%	74%		48
20																																		
21	PIT *	301	48	13	38	14	269	1	4	280	320	482	110	0	248	7	71	0.27	60	20	20	33	234	AFa	40%	128	178	100%	100%	142	26%	80%	7.2	181
1st Half		184	25	6	21	7	248		3	247	295	432	101	0	0	6	73	0.24	44	20	36	31	0		0%	111	-22	0%		140	26%	76%	-1.5	138
2nd Half		117	23	7	16	7	303	1	2	289	362	564	125	0	245	8	69	0.30	60	20	20	38	227	AFa	40%	157	178	100%	100%	143	26%	85%	9.0	250
22	**Proj**	**175**	**27**	**6**	**22**	**6**	**245**	**5**	**6**	**239**	**307**	**435**	**101**	**100**	**101**	**8**	**70**	**0.30**	**42**	**20**	**38**	**31**	**91**		**9%**	**119**		**13%**	**12%**	**144**	**21%**	**78%**	**1.5**	**142**

D Arnaud,Travis

Age: 33 Pos: CA	Health F	LIMA Plan D	
Bats: R Ht: 6' 2" Wt: 210	PT/Exp C	Rand Var +5	
	Consist F	MM 3123	

Turns out his 2020 leap was a hit rate-fueled mirage. Still, you'll buy him for his flashes of pop and use him as your second catcher. Before you do so again, note that his sporadic 15-HR output is firmly at risk given three straight years of dwindling launch angle. Add flunking health to mix, and maybe it's best to look for other caddies.

Yr	Tm	PA	R	HR	RBI	SB	BA	xHR	xSB	xBA	OBP	SLG	OPS+	vL+	vR+	bb%	ct%	Eye	G	L	F	h%	HctX	QBaB	Brl%	PX	xPX	HR/F	xHR/F	Spd	SBA%	SB%	RAR	BPX
17	NYM	376	39	16	57	0	244	12	4	263	293	443	100	121	91	6	83	0.39	42	17	41	25	109	CCd	7%	105	114	13%	10%	74	0%	0%	3.0	161
18	NYM	16	1	1	3	0	200	2	0	316	250	400	87	66	93	6	67	0.20	10	40	50	22	123	AAa	20%	115	222	20%	40%	92	0%	0%	-0.1	3
19	3 TM	391	52	16	69	0	251	15	1	248	312	433	103	123	90	8	76	0.38	41	21	39	29	109	BBf	8%	97	100	15%	14%	70	1%	0%	2.2	74
20	ATL	184	19	9	34	1	321	10	1	259	386	533	122	66	136	9	70	0.32	43	27	30	42	129	ADb	11%	126	122	26%	29%	83	2%	100%	15.9	96
21	ATL	229	21	7	26	0	220	8	1	252	284	388	92	113	87	7	75	0.32	46	22	31	26	95	BDd	8%	106	80	14%	16%	65	0%	0%	-3.3	77
1st Half		87	5	2	11	0	220	4	0	250	253	341	83	111	77	5	76	0.20	41	27	32	27	83	BDd	10%	77	81	10%	20%	75	0%	0%	-3.1	-8
2nd Half		142	16	5	15	0	220	4	0	258	303	417	97	113	93	9	74	0.39	50	19	31	26	103	BFc	6%	126	79	17%	14%	69	0%	0%	-0.4	146
22	**Proj**	**280**	**29**	**9**	**41**	**0**	**249**	**11**	**0**	**249**	**310**	**414**	**98**	**105**	**96**	**8**	**75**	**0.33**	**45**	**22**	**32**	**30**	**106**		**8%**	**102**	**96**	**15%**	**18%**	**69**	**1%**	**68%**	**5.8**	**28**

Dahl,David

Age: 28 Pos: LF	Health D	LIMA Plan D	
Bats: L Ht: 6' 2" Wt: 197	PT/Exp C	Rand Var +2	
	Consist D	MM 2221	

4-18-.210 in 220 PA at TEX. Once a growth stock with multi-category potential, he's nothing more than end-game fodder now. And sliding xPX, so-so Spd prove those tools are waning. Subpar Statcast metrics don't point at lingering latent talent, either. MLB teams are running out of patience; yours should be long gone.

Yr	Tm	PA	R	HR	RBI	SB	BA	xHR	xSB	xBA	OBP	SLG	OPS+	vL+	vR+	bb%	ct%	Eye	G	L	F	h%	HctX	QBaB	Brl%	PX	xPX	HR/F	xHR/F	Spd	SBA%	SB%	RAR	BPX
17	aaa	72	9	2	10	1	229		1		252	376	85			3	76	0.13				28				77				140	17%	39%		42
18	COL *	349	35	17	54	6	267	12	7	264	308	498	108	92	121	6	73	0.22	39	23	38	32	101	CBc	9%	140	124	23%	17%	102	13%	65%	5.8	157
19	COL	413	67	15	61	4	302	18	8	267	353	524	121	125	119	7	71	0.25	41	26	32	39	89	CCa	10%	131	129	17%	21%	124	8%	50%	13.6	148
20	COL	99	9	0	9	1	183	1	1	184	222	247	62	44	72	4	70	0.14	39	20	41	26	81	DBd	3%	38	94	0%	4%	149	6%	100%	-10.5	-136
21	TEX *	371	37	7	34	3	237	8	3	242	272	364	87	40	94	5	75	0.19	48	21	32	30	98	CCd	7%	84	91	9%	17%	105	6%	73%	-20.5	31
1st Half		198	22	5	18	3	226	7	2	222	255	350	84	47	93	4	72	0.14	47	18	35	29	92	CCf	8%	78	100	10%	18%	113	6%	73%	-13.9	-19
2nd Half		172	15	2	16	0	249	1	2	281	291	381	91	11	98	6	77	0.26	50	29	21	31	108	CFd	2%	91	64	0%	13%	97	6%	0%	-7.6	92
22	**Proj**	**245**	**28**	**4**	**29**	**2**	**256**	**9**	**-3**	**246**	**298**	**394**	**94**	**63**	**106**	**6**	**74**	**0.23**	**44**	**24**	**32**	**33**	**95**		**6%**	**91**	**96**	**8%**	**16%**	**106**	**6%**	**65%**	**-2.3**	**27**

Dalbec,Bobby

Age: 27 Pos: 1B	Health A	LIMA Plan B+	
Bats: R Ht: 6' 4" Wt: 227	PT/Exp A	Rand Var +1	
	Consist D	MM 5235	

Three reasons a breakout is coming: 1) Plate skills improved as season went along; 2) Stepped it up vR in 2nd half; 3) 98th-percentile barrel rate. Contact rate improved as year progressed—and against all pitch types, so it can stick. Even that late xBA hints his average should head north. With 550+ PAs, don't rule out... UP: 50 HR

Yr	Tm	PA	R	HR	RBI	SB	BA	xHR	xSB	xBA	OBP	SLG	OPS+	vL+	vR+	bb%	ct%	Eye	G	L	F	h%	HctX	QBaB	Brl%	PX	xPX	HR/F	xHR/F	Spd	SBA%	SB%	RAR	BPX
17																																		
18	aa	116	11	4	19	0	240		1		269	447	96			4	56	0.09				39				176				95	0%	0%		10
19	a/a	533	59	22	63	5	224		2		313	416	101			11	68	0.41				28				110				99	10%	44%		59
20	BOS	92	13	8	16	0	263	8	1	230	359	600	127	139	120	11	51	0.26	37	20	44	39	86	BBf	22%	254	205	44%	44%	95	0%	0%	4.1	240
21	BOS	453	50	25	78	2	240	38	2	236	298	494	109	119	101	6	63	0.18	37	19	43	32	97	ABb	20%	169	137	22%	34%	114	2%	100%	-7.2	131
1st Half		235	22	10	34	1	215	18	1	213	264	420	95	114	84	5	60	0.14	39	20	41	31	83	ABb	19%	142	126	19%	33%	130	2%	100%	-14.4	15
2nd Half		218	28	15	44	1	268	20	1	261	335	576	123	123	122	7	66	0.24	35	19	45	33	112	AAc	21%	196	149	25%	34%	97	2%	100%	4.8	254
22	**Proj**	**490**	**70**	**35**	**87**	**2**	**241**	**42**	**3**	**252**	**304**	**546**	**115**	**124**	**109**	**7**	**63**	**0.19**	**37**	**19**	**44**	**30**	**97**		**21%**	**200**	**156**	**28%**	**34%**	**94**	**4%**	**63%**	**11.7**	**206**

STEPHEN NICKRAND

Davis,Brennen

Age: 22	Pos: OF	Health	A	LIMA Plan	F
Bats: R	Ht: 6' 4" Wt: 175	PT/Exp	D	Rand Var	
		Consist	F	MM	4201

Promising Cubs prospect started late after being beaned in spring training. But he successfully navigated AA (.841 OPS over 316 PA) into Futures Game MVP performance, then posted a .933 OPS in 68 PA at AAA. Power, patience and speed offer growth foundation; contact and running game clearly need work. Has time, MLB debut could be bumpy.

Yr Tm	PA	R	HR	RBI	SB	BA	xHR	xSB	xBA	OBP	SLG	OPS+	vL+	vR+	bb%	ct%	Eye	G	L	F	h%	HctX	QBaB	Brl%	PX	xPX	HR/F	xHR/F	Spd	SBA%	SB%	RAR	BPX	R$
17																																		
18																																		
19																																		
20																																		
21 a/a	358	44	12	35	4	221		3		298	398	96			10	62	0.29				31				132				88	11%	50%		12	$5
1st Half	105	13	2	6	2	218		1		305	357	92			11	57	0.29				36				122				124	11%	58%		-50	-$4
2nd Half	254	32	10	29	3	223		2	231	297	417	97			10	64	0.30	44	20	36	30	0			136	-22	0%		109	11%	47%	-7.3	81	$8
22 Proj	**175**	**22**	**5**	**19**	**3**	**219**	**5**	**3**	**210**	**300**	**374**	**92**	**91**	**92**	**10**	**61**	**0.30**	**44**	**20**	**36**	**32**	**98**		**8%**	**120**		**14%**	**14%**	**113**	**10%**	**58%**	**-3.2**	**-66**	**$1**

Davis,J.D.

Age: 29	Pos: 3B	Health	D	LIMA Plan	D+
Bats: R	Ht: 6' 3" Wt: 218	PT/Exp	C	Rand Var	-5
		Consist	C	MM	4313

5-23-.285 in 203 PA at NYM. Hand injury sustained in April morphed into year-long problem that kept him shelved more often than not. Plus patience, another lofty h% and unsustainable LD% kept him afloat when active. But ongoing launch angle woes, sub-par ct% kept a lid on HR. Defensive issues add to inconsistency. Still tough to bet on.

Yr Tm	PA	R	HR	RBI	SB	BA	xHR	xSB	xBA	OBP	SLG	OPS+	vL+	vR+	bb%	ct%	Eye	G	L	F	h%	HctX	QBaB	Brl%	PX	xPX	HR/F	xHR/F	Spd	SBA%	SB%	RAR	BPX	R$
17 HOU *	509	51	23	64	5	233	4	6	248	283	430	97	130	86	6	68	0.22	60	16	23	29	109	CFb	14%	125	125	40%	40%	76	8%	59%	-19.3	33	$8
18 HOU *	470	48	13	61	2	250	4	5	248	304	396	94	75	55	7	74	0.30	50	22	28	31	88	CDc	8%	94	71	5%	19%	89	2%	100%	-6.9	50	$9
19 NYM	453	65	22	57	3	307	23	4	278	369	527	124	127	122	8	76	0.39	47	23	30	36	110	ACa	11%	115	111	23%	24%	107	2%	100%	19.2	178	$17
20 NYM	229	26	6	19	0	247	8	2	229	371	389	101	101	100	14	71	0.55	56	20	24	32	101	BFc	9%	89	73	19%	25%	107	0%	0%	-3.6	60	$10
21 NYM *	255	23	7	27	1	274	8	2	234	363	445	111	93	121	12	60	0.35	39	31	30	43	76	BCb	12%	135	95	15%	24%	101	1%	100%	2.5	12	$5
1st Half	70	6	3	8	0	319	3	0	268	372	503	122	217	146	8	63	0.23	33	37	30	47	114	ABa	19%	133	145	25%	38%	97	1%	0%	3.2	19	-$3
2nd Half	185	18	5	19	1	258	5	1	227	361	424	106	79	110	14	58	0.39	41	29	30	41	64	CCc	10%	138	80	12%	19%	101	1%	100%	1.0	19	$2
22 Proj	**350**	**38**	**12**	**39**	**1**	**258**	**16**	**3**	**236**	**354**	**434**	**107**	**103**	**108**	**11**	**67**	**0.36**	**47**	**23**	**30**	**35**	**93**		**12%**	**121**	**98**	**19%**	**26%**	**98**	**3%**	**93%**	**7.3**	**-4**	**$10**

Daza,Yonathan

Age: 28	Pos: CF RF	Health	B	LIMA Plan	D
Bats: R	Ht: 6' 2" Wt: 210	PT/Exp	C	Rand Var	-4
		Consist	A	MM	0211

2-30-.282 in 322 PA at COL. July COVID IL stint then a thumb injury cut into his 2nd half playing time. But torrid 1st half was built on ct%, inflated h%, plus speed and Coors Field (.325 home BA, .236 road BA). Zero power and unimpressive running game leave BABIP-fueled BA as his only possible plus. 2021 is his always uncertain upside.

Yr Tm	PA	R	HR	RBI	SB	BA	xHR	xSB	xBA	OBP	SLG	OPS+	vL+	vR+	bb%	ct%	Eye	G	L	F	h%	HctX	QBaB	Brl%	PX	xPX	HR/F	xHR/F	Spd	SBA%	SB%	RAR	BPX	R$
17																																		
18 aa	225	21	3	23	3	289		3		307	435	100			2	89	0.22				31				86				100	19%	36%		200	$4
19 COL *	508	50	8	34	9	294	0	14	275	327	421	103	61	72	5	84	0.30	59	18	23	34	72	DFc	1%	68	28	0%	0%	132	16%	45%	4.7	148	$13
20																																		
21 COL *	357	28	2	31	3	279	4	6	244	323	347	92	99	92	6	80	0.32	54	22	24	34	82	FDc	2%	42	51	3%	7%	123	4%	72%	-10.1	19	$7
1st Half	244	21	2	25	2	308	3	4	262	350	397	104	110	101	6	80	0.32	53	25	22	38	85	FFb	3%	54	66	5%	8%	125	4%	67%	1.0	62	$10
2nd Half	113	7	0	6	1	217	0	2	186	267	237	68	73	68	6	80	0.34	57	13	30	27	73	FDc	0%	15	7	0%	0%	108	4%	100%	-8.9	-81	-$8
22 Proj	**245**	**20**	**1**	**19**	**3**	**268**	**1**	**3**	**238**	**308**	**335**	**87**	**88**	**86**	**5**	**82**	**0.30**	**56**	**18**	**26**	**32**	**76**		**1%**	**44**	**30**	**2%**	**2%**	**110**	**6%**	**52%**	**-5.6**	**-17**	**$5**

De La Cruz,Bryan

Age: 25	Pos: CF RF	Health	A	LIMA Plan	C
Bats: R	Ht: 6' 2" Wt: 175	PT/Exp	C	Rand Var	-3
		Consist	A	MM	1213

5-19-.296 in 217 PA at MIA. Rookie debuted fast in August (.384 BA, 52% h%) before falling back to earth in September (.239 BA, 30% h%). HctX, Spd, ownership vL offer building blocks; plate skills, QBaB, sub-par running game say he has work to do. An end-game flyer whose progress, playing time path needs a look-see in March.

Yr Tm	PA	R	HR	RBI	SB	BA	xHR	xSB	xBA	OBP	SLG	OPS+	vL+	vR+	bb%	ct%	Eye	G	L	F	h%	HctX	QBaB	Brl%	PX	xPX	HR/F	xHR/F	Spd	SBA%	SB%	RAR	BPX	R$
17 aa	30	4	1	4	0	164		0		212	325	73			6	72	0.22				19				107				100	0%	0%		52	-$2
18																																		
19 aa	290	40	4	21	6	256		5		311	366	94			7	75	0.32				33				64				133	17%	53%		26	$4
20																																		
21 MIA *	502	49	14	52	2	274	5	8	240	316	411	100	129	101	6	73	0.23	48	22	30	35	98	CCc	5%	84	75	11%	11%	141	7%	29%	-12.4	65	$13
1st Half	212	26	6	26	1	268		3	262	308	410	100	0	117	5	69	0.19	0	50	50	36	0		0%	93	-22	0%		105	7%	22%	-8.2	-15	$8
2nd Half	291	23	7	26	1	278	5	5	244	322	411	99	127	99	6	76	0.28	49	21	30	34	103	CCc	6%	77	77	12%	12%	156	7%	50%	-5.6	108	$8
22 Proj	**350**	**38**	**8**	**33**	**3**	**270**	**8**	**5**	**236**	**315**	**394**	**96**	**117**	**89**	**6**	**74**	**0.25**	**49**	**21**	**30**	**34**	**93**		**5%**	**76**	**69**	**10%**	**12%**	**144**	**9%**	**37%**	**1.2**	**-33**	**$10**

DeJong,Paul

Age: 28	Pos: SS	Health	B	LIMA Plan	C
Bats: R	Ht: 6' 0" Wt: 205	PT/Exp	A	Rand Var	+4
		Consist	B	MM	3203

Power rebounded along with HR/F, but what 2020 h% giveth, 2021 h% taketh away. Lost a month of PA due to a rib fracture in mid-May, but it was the season-long BA woes that eventually cost him an everyday lineup spot. This too will rebound some, but stagnant ct%, xBA say a lid is in place. These HR now come with an elevated playing time risk.

Yr Tm	PA	R	HR	RBI	SB	BA	xHR	xSB	xBA	OBP	SLG	OPS+	vL+	vR+	bb%	ct%	Eye	G	L	F	h%	HctX	QBaB	Brl%	PX	xPX	HR/F	xHR/F	Spd	SBA%	SB%	RAR	BPX	R$
17 STL *	627	77	35	92	1	279	20	7	261	311	517	113	129	111	4	71	0.16	34	23	43	34	104	DAb	9%	145	133	20%	16%	82	2%	31%	18.2	103	$20
18 STL	489	68	19	68	1	241	24	3	245	313	433	100	86	103	7	72	0.29	32	24	44	29	102	BAc	9%	125	134	14%	17%	101	2%	50%	6.5	113	$11
19 STL	664	97	30	78	9	233	30	4	245	318	444	105	94	107	9	74	0.42	38	18	44	26	107	CAc	9%	114	123	15%	15%	100	9%	64%	-5.3	148	$17
20 STL	174	17	3	25	1	250	6	3	208	322	349	89	52	96	10	67	0.34	27	28	44	35	105	CAc	8%	68	152	6%	13%	90	2%	100%	-2.7	-112	$9
21 STL	402	44	19	45	4	197	21	2	221	284	390	93	82	96	9	71	0.34	38	16	47	22	100	DBf	11%	111	152	16%	18%	97	6%	80%	-13.2	85	$4
1st Half	216	23	10	24	3	175	11	1	222	278	354	88	77	91	11	72	0.43	40	17	43	18	93	DCf	12%	100	138	17%	19%	87	6%	100%	-9.9	69	$3
2nd Half	186	21	9	21	1	222	10	1	220	290	431	98	88	101	7	70	0.24	35	14	50	26	108	CAd	10%	123	167	15%	17%	108	6%	50%	-4.0	100	$3
22 Proj	**420**	**50**	**17**	**54**	**3**	**230**	**20**	**4**	**222**	**306**	**408**	**97**	**83**	**100**	**9**	**71**	**0.32**	**34**	**20**	**46**	**28**	**103**		**9%**	**108**	**147**	**14%**	**16%**	**88**	**6%**	**72%**	**-2.6**	**31**	**$11**

Devers,Rafael

Age: 25	Pos: 3B	Health	A	LIMA Plan	D+
Bats: L	Ht: 6' 0" Wt: 240	PT/Exp	A	Rand Var	0
		Consist	C	MM	4155

Emphatically answered doubts about sustainability of 2019 breakout vs. 2020 short-season pullback. Mashing peripherals have never looked better. Brl%, HctX and xPX eclipsed previous highs, fueling career-best HR output as exit velocity remained rock-solid. Tough to get better from here, but xHR says we haven't seen his peak yet... UP: 45 HR

Yr Tm	PA	R	HR	RBI	SB	BA	xHR	xSB	xBA	OBP	SLG	OPS+	vL+	vR+	bb%	ct%	Eye	G	L	F	h%	HctX	QBaB	Brl%	PX	xPX	HR/F	xHR/F	Spd	SBA%	SB%	RAR	BPX	R$
17 BOS *	592	81	27	83	3	298	9	8	273	355	523	119	145	99	8	78	0.40	49	15	36	34	109	BDd	9%	129	98	17%	16%	82	5%	42%	25.7	173	$22
18 BOS *	512	62	22	68	5	244	19	3	242	302	439	99	82	102	8	73	0.31	46	15	39	29	93	ACf	9%	123	95	17%	15%	62	7%	71%	1.4	87	$14
19 BOS	702	129	32	115	8	311	32	7	298	361	555	127	103	137	7	82	0.40	44	21	34	34	107	ACc	9%	126	93	18%	18%	84	10%	50%	36.5	252	$34
20 BOS	248	32	11	43	0	263	13	3	255	310	483	105	80	118	5	71	0.19	45	20	35	32	120	ACc	12%	135	78	19%	23%	75	0%	0%	1.2	108	$20
21 BOS	664	101	38	113	5	279	47	1	278	352	538	122	102	135	9	76	0.43	41	20	38	31	124	ACd	15%	148	124	22%	27%	63	6%	50%	26.9	235	$30
1st Half	338	57	20	68	3	286	24	0	288	355	571	129	99	144	9	73	0.36	44	20	36	33	129	ACf	17%	173	137	25%	30%	65	6%	38%	14.0	269	$37
2nd Half	326	44	18	45	2	272	23	0	268	350	503	115	104	124	10	79	0.53	38	21	41	29	119	ABd	13%	123	111	19%	25%	66	6%	100%	8.9	212	$23
22 Proj	**637**	**97**	**39**	**107**	**4**	**277**	**39**	**5**	**279**	**340**	**546**	**120**	**100**	**131**	**8**	**76**	**0.36**	**42**	**20**	**38**	**30**	**116**		**13%**	**153**	**105**	**23%**	**23%**	**68**	**5%**	**55%**	**34.8**	**245**	**$30**

Diaz,Aledmys

Age: 31	Pos: 3B	Health	D	LIMA Plan	D+
Bats: R	Ht: 6' 1" Wt: 195	PT/Exp	C	Rand Var	0
		Consist	A	MM	2133

Health has long been an issue, and fractured hand cost him seven weeks beginning in June. 9-for-73 finish (18% h%) dragged his numbers at the end. But a representative year from a sum-of-the-parts bench utility with no glaring weaknesses, no plus skills, no big splits. A useful fill-in for our game, though single-position eligibility hurts.

Yr Tm	PA	R	HR	RBI	SB	BA	xHR	xSB	xBA	OBP	SLG	OPS+	vL+	vR+	bb%	ct%	Eye	G	L	F	h%	HctX	QBaB	Brl%	PX	xPX	HR/F	xHR/F	Spd	SBA%	SB%	RAR	BPX	R$
17 STL *	478	45	10	40	6	240	5	5	246	273	362	86	81	93	4	83	0.27	46	17	38	27	79	DCd	3%	71	69	8%	5%	113	12%	58%	-24.7	103	$5
18 TOR	452	55	18	55	3	263	18	6	269	303	453	101	94	102	5	85	0.37	41	18	41	27	100	CCc	7%	105	105	12%	12%	95	8%	43%	5.9	220	$12
19 HOU *	270	37	9	40	2	253	7	4	265	334	431	106	105	117	10	84	0.76	46	17	37	27	94	CCf	6%	87	70	13%	10%	111	3%	100%	1.3	230	$5
20 HOU	59	8	3	6	0	241	1	0	287	254	483	98	59	118	2	79	0.08	43	22	35	26	91	CCd	2%	136	77	19%	6%	92	0%	0%	-0.8	236	$1
21 HOU	319	28	8	45	0	259	9	1	258	317	405	99	107	95	5	79	0.26	42	24	34	30	111	CCd	6%	90	89	10%	11%	77	1%	0%	-4.7	88	$5
1st Half	126	14	3	18	0	278	6	0	283	341	435	108	106	109	4	83	0.26	43	25	32	31	121	CCc	10%	94	98	10%	19%	89	1%	0%	-0.9	177	$1
2nd Half	193	14	5	27	0	246	4	0	241	301	385	93	107	85	6	76	0.26	42	23	35	30	105	CCf	4%	87	83	10%	8%	77	1%	0%	-5.6	38	$1
22 Proj	**315**	**34**	**10**	**43**	**1**	**256**	**10**	**1**	**261**	**313**	**418**	**99**	**93**	**102**	**6**	**82**	**0.36**	**43**	**21**	**36**	**28**	**102**		**5%**	**92**	**84**	**11%**	**11%**	**83**	**3%**	**49%**	**-0.1**	**107**	**$9**

OCK THOMPSON

Díaz,Elias

Age: 31	Pos: CA	Health: A	LIMA Plan: D+
Bats: R	Ht: 6' 1" Wt: 220	PT/Exp: C	Rand Var: +2
		Consist: A	MM: 3033

Plate skills have long pointed to better despite slowness afoot, and unfortunate h% slowed him down early. But solid Hct carried over from 2021, and power stepped forward all season aided by improved 2nd half launch angle, FB% uptick. L/R splits look healthy; defense is a plus. Now very rosterable in two-catcher leagues, perhaps better.

Yr Tm	PA	R	HR	RBI	SB	BA	xHR	xSB	xBA	OBP	SLG	OPS+	vL+	vR+	bb%	ct%	Eye	G	L	F	h%	HctX	QBaB	Brl%	PX	xPX	HR/F	xHR/F	Spd	SBA%	SB%	RAR	BPX
17 PIT *	426	34	3	41	3	225	2	5	238	260	300	76	87	74	5	80	0.24	52	18	30	27	84	DDc	2%	52	70	2%	4%	64	4%	100%	-17.8	-15
18 PIT	277	33	10	34	0	286	8	2	263	339	452	106	123	96	8	84	0.53	45	20	35	31	112	BCd	7%	92	104	13%	11%	82	1%	0%	13.4	173
19 PIT *	362	35	2	31	0	249	4	1	235	299	317	85	90	80	7	81	0.38	47	21	31	30	89	CDf	2%	43	46	3%	5%	75	0%	0%	-10.9	-7
20 COL	73	4	2	9	0	235	2	0	235	288	353	85	87	83	7	78	0.33	40	25	36	27	125	CCf	11%	64	119	11%	11%	78	0%	0%	-1.3	8
21 COL	371	52	18	44	0	246	15	1	272	310	464	106	104	107	8	82	0.50	41	19	40	25	118	CBf	8%	115	105	16%	13%	76	0%	0%	7.6	238
1st Half	158	17	6	15	0	197	4	0	253	272	366	89	72	101	10	79	0.50	43	21	35	21	111	BCf	6%	93	91	15%	10%	60	0%	0%	-4.1	112
2nd Half	213	35	12	29	0	281	10	0	286	338	536	118	134	110	7	85	0.50	39	17	43	28	123	DBf	9%	130	114	17%	14%	93	0%	0%	12.2	335
22 Proj	**385**	**47**	**16**	**43**	**0**	**262**	**11**	**1**	**264**	**318**	**451**	**104**	**108**	**102**	**7**	**82**	**0.45**	**41**	**20**	**39**	**28**	**113**		**7%**	**101**	**97**	**14%**	**10%**	**76**	**1%**	**48%**	**14.1**	**151**

Díaz,Isan

Age: 26	Pos: 3B 2B	Health: A	LIMA Plan: F
Bats: L	Ht: 5' 11" Wt: 201	PT/Exp: C	Rand Var: +1
		Consist: D	MM: 1101

4-17-.193 in 272 PA at MIA. Except for bb%, once-interesting prospect's skill set is now stagnating everywhere. Contact skills, struggles vL are huge problems, GB% looks ingrained, running game has never developed. Just two years off big AAA numbers, still young enough for a career. But needs to show more before he's drafted anywhere.

Yr Tm	PA	R	HR	RBI	SB	BA	xHR	xSB	xBA	OBP	SLG	OPS+	vL+	vR+	bb%	ct%	Eye	G	L	F	h%	HctX	QBaB	Brl%	PX	xPX	HR/F	xHR/F	Spd	SBA%	SB%	RAR	BPX
17																																	
18 a/a	490	54	10	48	12	205		7		301	343	86			12	64	0.38				29				101				112	13%	79%		-10
19 MIA *	623	97	26	86	5	239	5	12	221	317	435	104	57	84	10	70	0.38	41	13	45	30	94	CAf	7%	110	106	9%	9%	100	8%	38%	-1.9	74
20 MIA	22	3	0	1	0	182	0	0	212	182	182	48	174	28	0	68	0.00	47	33	20	27	110	DCf		0	24	0%	0%	106	0%	0%	-2.7	-368
21 MIA *	389	38	8	29	1	195	6	2	210	285	313	82	60	88	11	68	0.40	46	19	35	26	89	CCf	4%	81	72	7%	10%	94	5%	23%	-24.9	-35
1st Half	171	12	4	16	0	182	3	1	213	288	312	83	50	82	13	66	0.43	45	23	32	24	81	CCf	4%	89	91	9%	14%	77	5%	0%	-10.0	-58
2nd Half	218	26	3	13	1	206	3	1	209	283	315	81	71	91	10	70	0.36	47	16	36	27	95	CCf	4%	75	59	6%	8%	113	5%	32%	-12.8	-15
22 Proj	**210**	**24**	**4**	**19**	**2**	**207**	**5**	**2**	**202**	**296**	**318**	**83**	**64**	**91**	**11**	**68**	**0.39**	**45**	**18**	**37**	**29**	**91**		**5%**	**77**	**80**	**8%**	**10%**	**104**	**6%**	**50%**	**-7.7**	**-83**

Díaz,Lewin

Age: 25	Pos: 1B	Health: A	LIMA Plan: D+
Bats: L	Ht: 6' 4" Wt: 217	PT/Exp: C	Rand Var: +2
		Consist: D	MM: 4211

8-13-.205 in 128 PA at MIA. Rookie flashed legit power (5 HR, .741 OPS over 93 PA) during first extended opportunity beginning in September. Won't hit for average, but challenged plate skills don't look hopeless. More patience, consistent exit velocity would work wonders. With any growth here, platoon role vR could yield... UP: 400 PA, 25 HR.

Yr Tm	PA	R	HR	RBI	SB	BA	xHR	xSB	xBA	OBP	SLG	OPS+	vL+	vR+	bb%	ct%	Eye	G	L	F	h%	HctX	QBaB	Brl%	PX	xPX	HR/F	xHR/F	Spd	SBA%	SB%	RAR	BPX
17																																	
18																																	
19 aa	262	30	14	43	0	240		2		301	506	112			8	77	0.37				26				145				88	2%	0%		252
20 MIA	41	2	0	3	0	154	1	0	152	195	205	53	0	76	5	69	0.17	41	11	48	22	73	DAd	11%	45	38	0%	8%	93	0%	0%	-6.0	-184
21 MIA *	427	57	23	53	2	204	7	1	228	255	422	93	66	109	6	74	0.26	31	15	54	22	112	CAf	10%	122	149	17%	15%	95	3%	100%	-30.5	142
1st Half	161	23	8	20	1	173	2	0	214	214	376	82	138	58	5	72	0.19	36	9	55	18	161	AAf	18%	121	182	33%	33%	92	3%	100%	-15.6	100
2nd Half	266	35	15	33	1	224	6	1	233	279	450	99	55	115	7	75	0.31	31	15	54	24	106	CAf	9%	123	145	14%	14%	103	3%	100%	-11.2	177
22 Proj	**245**	**32**	**12**	**33**	**1**	**233**	**20**	**1**	**230**	**284**	**446**	**99**	**53**	**120**	**7**	**75**	**0.28**	**31**	**15**	**54**	**26**	**95**		**8%**	**123**	**131**	**13%**	**22%**	**95**	**4%**	**78%**	**-1.6**	**127**

Díaz,Yandy

Age: 30	Pos: 1B 3B	Health: B	LIMA Plan: C+
Bats: R	Ht: 6' 2" Wt: 215	PT/Exp: A	Rand Var: 0
		Consist: B	MM: 1133

Plate skills, HctX look great, seemingly a small LD% bump away from a BA hike. 2nd half FB% spike, QBaB turnaround drove HR into double-digits again, teased as to what might be. But GB% and history reminds that little has changed in t profile and outlook. You're still buying an OBP/counting stat floor, hoping for PA, loft.

Yr Tm	PA	R	HR	RBI	SB	BA	xHR	xSB	xBA	OBP	SLG	OPS+	vL+	vR+	bb%	ct%	Eye	G	L	F	h%	HctX	QBaB	Brl%	PX	xPX	HR/F	xHR/F	Spd	SBA%	SB%	RAR	BPX
17 CLE *	536	69	4	39	3	293	2	10	264	385	379	104	98	87	13	80	0.74	59	22	19	36	106	AFa	3%	56	60	0%	9%	106	3%	54%	-2.0	73
18 CLE *	520	54	3	44	1	264	2	5	246	353	353	95	96	112	12	76	0.58	53	23	23	34	125	AFb	4%	65	84	5%	10%	106	3%	29%	-2.7	50
19 TAM	347	53	14	38	2	267	13	3	276	340	476	113	137	101	10	80	0.57	51	17	32	29	118	AFc	10%	108	115	18%	16%	102	5%	50%	5.7	222
20 TAM	138	16	2	11	0	307	1	2	261	428	386	108	100	111	17	85	1.35	66	23	11	35	96	CFf	2%	41	22	18%	9%	104	0%	0%	2.0	160
21 TAM	541	62	13	64	1	256	16	4	242	353	387	102	110	95	13	82	0.81	52	16	32	29	116	BDf	7%	73	79	11%	13%	112	1%	50%	-9.9	181
1st Half	303	32	3	26	0	239	5	3	206	366	307	94	97	91	16	80	1.00	57	14	29	29	105	CFf	4%	42	56	5%	9%	106	1%	0%	-14.3	85
2nd Half	238	30	10	38	1	276	11	1	275	336	481	111	128	99	9	83	0.56	46	18	36	29	128	BCd	10%	108	105	15%	17%	114	1%	50%	0.0	277
22 Proj	**385**	**47**	**9**	**42**	**1**	**273**	**9**	**3**	**256**	**365**	**407**	**105**	**111**	**100**	**13**	**82**	**0.79**	**54**	**19**	**27**	**31**	**114**		**6%**	**75**	**76**	**12%**	**12%**	**102**	**4%**	**46%**	**6.7**	**111**

Dickerson,Alex

Age: 32	Pos: LF	Health: F	LIMA Plan: D+
Bats: L	Ht: 6' 2" Wt: 226	PT/Exp: C	Rand Var: +3
		Consist: D	MM: 3223

13-38-.233 in 306 PA at SF. Short-season 2020 looks like an outlier, as more injuries (shoulder, back, hamstring, foot) cu into his playing time and skills across the board. Already typecast as a vR-only bat, production will rebound with more durability. But history, age say limited upside comes with plenty of risk.

Yr Tm	PA	R	HR	RBI	SB	BA	xHR	xSB	xBA	OBP	SLG	OPS+	vL+	vR+	bb%	ct%	Eye	G	L	F	h%	HctX	QBaB	Brl%	PX	xPX	HR/F	xHR/F	Spd	SBA%	SB%	RAR	BPX
17																																	
18																																	
19 2 NL *	316	43	9	43	1	270	9	5	252	329	450	108	78	117	8	77	0.38	35	23	41	32	108	BBc	9%	97	108	11%	16%	115	3%	50%	-0.5	137
20 SF	170	28	10	27	0	298	9	1	288	371	576	126	115	128	9	80	0.53	41	20	39	32	133	AAc	11%	144	113	21%	19%	88	0%	0%	9.9	332
21 SF *	353	42	14	40	1	230	14	1	239	288	412	96	119	98	7	73	0.30	36	23	42	27	95	CBd	10%	105	104	15%	16%	77	1%	100%	-12.7	62
1st Half	180	21	8	24	1	230	6	0	244	288	405	97	97	97	8	73	0.30	37	26	38	27	97	CBd	10%	97	100	16%	14%	84	1%	100%	-7.2	50
2nd Half	173	21	7	16	0	230	8	0	232	288	419	96	142	99	8	73	0.30	34	19	47	27	93	CAf	11%	113	109	14%	19%	79	1%	0%	-6.5	85
22 Proj	**315**	**42**	**14**	**40**	**1**	**243**	**16**	**2**	**251**	**316**	**453**	**104**	**107**	**104**	**8**	**75**	**0.36**	**37**	**22**	**42**	**28**	**105**		**10%**	**119**	**107**	**15%**	**17%**	**88**	**3%**	**76%**	**2.9**	**142**

Dickerson,Corey

Age: 33	Pos: LF	Health: D	LIMA Plan: C
Bats: L	Ht: 6' 1" Wt: 200	PT/Exp: B	Rand Var: 0
		Consist: B	MM: 2333

Lost 7 weeks to mid-season foot injury, showed a little better in 2nd half return. But stale exit velocity and inability to significantly reverse soaring GB% from 2020 made for meh fantasy value. BA/contact skills look healthy enough, but combination of age, sub-par power, recent struggles vL threaten his playing time. Glory days they pass you by.

Yr Tm	PA	R	HR	RBI	SB	BA	xHR	xSB	xBA	OBP	SLG	OPS+	vL+	vR+	bb%	ct%	Eye	G	L	F	h%	HctX	QBaB	Brl%	PX	xPX	HR/F	xHR/F	Spd	SBA%	SB%	RAR	BPX
17 TAM	628	84	27	62	4	282	25	8	265	325	490	111	111	109	6	74	0.23	42	22	36	34	101	CCb	7%	122	106	17%	16%	118	5%	57%	1.4	130
18 PIT	533	65	13	55	8	300	18	6	284	330	474	108	97	109	4	84	0.26	38	27	35	34	106	CBb	6%	100	101	9%	12%	129	9%	73%	14.3	217
19 2 NL *	314	36	12	62	1	286	11	3	287	327	520	117	111	129	6	78	0.28	36	25	39	33	105	CBd	8%	133	112	15%	14%	95	2%	100%	7.5	219
20 MIA	209	25	7	17	1	258	7	2	237	311	402	95	84	98	7	82	0.43	52	14	34	28	102	DCf	6%	70	71	13%	13%	109	4%	50%	-6.8	132
21 2 TM	365	43	6	29	6	271	9	4	254	326	408	101	87	103	7	80	0.37	49	19	32	32	112	CCf	3%	79	85	7%	10%	135	12%	55%	-10.2	146
1st Half	225	27	2	14	2	263	5	3	252	324	380	98	97	99	7	78	0.36	50	21	29	33	99	DDf	3%	73	73	4%	11%	123	12%	33%	-8.9	92
2nd Half	140	16	4	15	4	282	4	2	257	329	450	105	34	109	6	82	0.39	46	17	37	32	131	BCc	3%	88	103	10%	10%	139	12%	80%	-0.3	219
22 Proj	**315**	**38**	**9**	**34**	**4**	**276**	**10**	**6**	**259**	**322**	**441**	**104**	**90**	**106**	**6**	**80**	**0.34**	**46**	**20**	**35**	**32**	**111**		**5%**	**92**	**92**	**10%**	**12%**	**123**	**11%**	**64%**	**4.9**	**150**

Difo,Wilmer

Age: 30	Pos: 2B	Health: A	LIMA Plan: D
Bats: R	Ht: 5' 11" Wt: 200	PT/Exp: D	Rand Var: -5
		Consist: D	MM: 1311

4-24-.269 in 239 PA at PIT. Spd rebounded from small sample 2020 blip, obviously helped him out-hit xBA. But the good news ended there. Subterranean SBA% neutralized his only plus skill; average plate skills, soft contact / power lived up low expectations. Bench utility can't be rostered if he can't run, and the upside isn't worth it.

Yr Tm	PA	R	HR	RBI	SB	BA	xHR	xSB	xBA	OBP	SLG	OPS+	vL+	vR+	bb%	ct%	Eye	G	L	F	h%	HctX	QBaB	Brl%	PX	xPX	HR/F	xHR/F	Spd	SBA%	SB%	RAR	BPX
17 WAS *	409	51	5	22	10	258	5	6	256	310	351	90	115	85	7	78	0.35	51	24	25	32	73	DDc	2%	53	54	8%	8%	158	11%	91%	-7.1	58
18 WAS	456	55	7	42	10	230	6	10	246	298	350	87	60	93	9	80	0.48	42	24	34	27	62	FCd	2%	67	54	6%	5%	150	12%	77%	-4.2	123
19 WAS *	394	49	5	29	9	247	1	8	240	303	335	88	108	80	7	75	0.32	48	24	28	32	53	FCc	0%	51	33	7%	4%	112	16%	56%	-16.2	-30
20 WAS	18	1	0	1	0	71	0	0	219	222	71	39	22	48	17	71	0.75	27	36	36	10	53	CAc		0	-4	0%	0%	95	0%	0%	-2.0	-196
21 PIT *	284	29	4	25	1	256	4	3	216	315	358	93	75	107	8	74	0.34	44	19	37	33	77	FCf	4%	61	60	7%	7%	165	1%	100%	-4.6	54
1st Half	133	11	1	7	0	222	1	1	220	272	316	82	61	101	6	70	0.23	34	29	36	31	74	FCf	4%	61	73	5%	5%	131	1%	0%	-6.6	-65
2nd Half	151	18	3	18	1	287	3	2	217	351	397	101	80	111	9	79	0.48	49	13	38	35	80	FCf	5%	61	53	8%	8%	155	1%	100%	1.9	119
22 Proj	**245**	**28**	**4**	**21**	**2**	**253**	**3**	**3**	**232**	**310**	**361**	**91**	**80**	**95**	**8**	**76**	**0.36**	**45**	**22**	**33**	**31**	**69**		**3%**	**63**	**53**	**7%**	**6%**	**137**	**5%**	**65%**	**-1.7**	**1**

JOCK THOMPSON

Donaldson,Josh

Age: 36	Pos: 3B		Health	C	LIMA Plan	B
Bats: R	Ht: 6' 1"	Wt: 210	PT/Exp	A	Rand Var	+1
			Consist	A	MM	4125

Aging, durability-challenged slugger spent just 12 days on the IL (hamstring), reversed short-season GB% from 2020 and showed he has something left in the tank. Power-and-patience combo still check out, exit velocity, HctX, Brl% and HR/F all still offer plenty of verification. Health is always the big question, but he remains a viable injury portfolio pick.

Yr Tm	PA	R	HR	RBI	SB	BA	xHR	xSB	xBA	OBP	SLG	OPS+	vL+	vR+	bb%	ct%	Eye	G	L	F	h%	HctX	QBaB	Brl%	PX	xPX	HR/F	xHR/F	Spd	SBA%	SB%	RAR	BPX	R$
17 TOR	496	65	33	78	2	270	29	8	272	385	559	128	142	122	15	73	0.68	41	17	42	29	108	BCf	14%	164	132	26%	22%	66	3%	50%	30.2	233	$16
18 2 AL	219	30	8	23	2	246	9	2	252	352	449	107	119	100	14	71	0.57	48	17	35	30	108	BCd	10%	138	113	17%	19%	93	4%	100%	6.1	177	$4
19 ATL	659	96	37	94	4	259	36	5	270	379	521	125	117	126	15	72	0.65	42	21	36	29	118	ACd	16%	145	124	26%	25%	78	3%	67%	25.9	219	$21
20 MIN	102	14	6	11	0	222	4	1	226	373	469	112	82	118	18	70	0.75	55	10	34	24	98	ADf	7%	134	98	30%	20%	85	0%	0%	1.8	204	$4
21 MIN	543	73	26	72	0	247	36	2	253	352	475	114	128	107	14	75	0.65	43	17	40	27	123	ABd	17%	132	121	19%	26%	77	0%	0%	10.9	223	$14
1st Half	259	36	13	34	0	252	17	1	263	347	491	117	132	110	13	77	0.67	43	18	39	27	121	ACf	19%	135	124	19%	25%	89	0%	0%	5.3	269	$14
2nd Half	284	37	13	38	0	243	20	1	244	356	460	110	125	104	14	74	0.63	43	16	40	28	125	ABc	16%	129	117	18%	28%	68	0%	0%	2.5	188	$12
22 Proj	**560**	**78**	**29**	**73**	**1**	**245**	**32**	**1**	**251**	**359**	**480**	**114**	**118**	**112**	**15**	**73**	**0.64**	**46**	**16**	**38**	**27**	**115**		**14%**	**138**	**116**	**22%**	**24%**	**72**	**1%**	**75%**	**22.1**	**176**	**$15**

Dozier,Hunter

Age: 30	Pos: RF 3B		Health	B	LIMA Plan	C+
Bats: R	Ht: 6' 4"	Wt: 220	PT/Exp	A	Rand Var	+2
			Consist	C	MM	3305

2020 COVID victim struggled early before 2nd half rebound. April thumb injury, May concussion, 1st half h% all factors; all got better. BA skills look mediocre, and while has some plus HR power, recent FB%, HR/F, Brl% aren't convincing. Was 2019 exit velocity a fluke? Inconsistency here is obvious. Don't forget about him but don't chase him, either.

Yr Tm	PA	R	HR	RBI	SB	BA	xHR	xSB	xBA	OBP	SLG	OPS+	vL+	vR+	bb%	ct%	Eye	G	L	F	h%	HctX	QBaB	Brl%	PX	xPX	HR/F	xHR/F	Spd	SBA%	SB%	RAR	BPX	R$
17 a/a	110	12	3	9	1	200		1		272	369	87			9	49	0.20				37				160				108	11%	40%		-67	-$2
18 KC *	524	49	12	42	3	225	16	7	221	287	367	88	80	93	8	67	0.26	41	22	37	31	111	BCc	11%	102	132	12%	17%	107	6%	45%	-16.8	0	$5
19 KC	586	75	26	84	2	279	26	9	252	348	522	120	127	117	9	72	0.37	34	22	44	34	112	ABc	10%	132	144	16%	16%	156	3%	50%	19.6	222	$18
20 KC	186	29	6	12	4	228	6	3	221	344	392	98	98	98	15	70	0.56	36	24	40	29	87	DBd	8%	92	80	14%	14%	160	8%	100%	-1.6	124	$12
21 KC	543	55	16	54	5	216	20	7	226	285	394	93	87	96	8	68	0.28	38	19	42	28	102	BBc	9%	116	121	11%	14%	130	8%	56%	-21.6	88	$6
1st Half	250	23	7	25	1	170	9	2	217	236	341	80	74	83	8	68	0.26	35	19	46	22	99	BAd	10%	115	103	10%	13%	108	8%	50%	-19.8	46	-$2
2nd Half	293	32	9	29	4	256	11	5	233	328	442	104	97	107	9	69	0.30	40	20	39	34	105	BBc	8%	116	137	13%	15%	144	8%	57%	-2.8	119	$12
22 Proj	**455**	**54**	**15**	**44**	**5**	**231**	**17**	**7**	**226**	**311**	**414**	**98**	**94**	**99**	**10**	**68**	**0.34**	**37**	**21**	**41**	**30**	**102**		**9%**	**117**	**120**	**13%**	**15%**	**123**	**9%**	**66%**	**-2.9**	**72**	**$10**

Dubón,Mauricio

Age: 27	Pos: CF SS 2B		Health	A	LIMA Plan	D
Bats: R	Ht: 6' 0"	Wt: 173	PT/Exp	B	Rand Var	+1
			Consist	A	MM	2331

5-22-.240 with 2 SB in 184 PA at SF. Poor 1st half, team depth eventually squeezed him out in June; returned only briefly in September. Couldn't build on 2020 BA/OBP gains as HctX, power stagnated. Spd offers growth foundation, but SB% history, inconsistent bb% and QBaB make him difficult to bet on. Flyer at best; check his playing time in March.

Yr Tm	PA	R	HR	RBI	SB	BA	xHR	xSB	xBA	OBP	SLG	OPS+	vL+	vR+	bb%	ct%	Eye	G	L	F	h%	HctX	QBaB	Brl%	PX	xPX	HR/F	xHR/F	Spd	SBA%	SB%	RAR	BPX	R$
17 a/a	524	61	8	47	31	247		7		293	346	87			6	83	0.37				29				61				87	40%	65%		58	$17
18 aaa	109	12	3	12	4	283		4		292	460	101			1	79	0.06				34				109				107	40%	53%		130	$2
19 2 NL *	636	76	17	53	11	260	2	30	287	291	393	95	115	97	4	84	0.28	48	27	26	29	91	DCb	2%	68	74	18%	9%	119	15%	51%	-9.9	133	$15
20 SF	176	21	4	19	2	274	5	6	231	337	389	96	116	88	9	77	0.42	34	26	40	33	96	DBd	4%	61	108	8%	10%	166	10%	40%	-3.3	104	$12
21 SF *	453	47	10	42	8	248	6	7	240	294	368	91	99	84	6	79	0.31	40	22	38	29	90	DCd	4%	71	98	10%	12%	112	13%	62%	-18.6	77	$10
1st Half	185	21	5	23	2	256	6	3	234	294	388	95	97	86	5	76	0.23	40	21	39	31	85	DBc	5%	79	97	11%	13%	96	13%	67%	-5.2	38	$5
2nd Half	268	25	5	20	6	243	0	4	267	295	355	88	110	68	7	81	0.38	43	29	29	28	118	DDf	0%	66	103	0%	0%	131	13%	61%	-11.3	119	$7
22 Proj	**175**	**19**	**6**	**17**	**4**	**258**	**3**	**3**	**256**	**302**	**412**	**97**	**108**	**91**	**6**	**79**	**0.30**	**40**	**24**	**36**	**29**	**90**		**4%**	**86**	**95**	**12%**	**7%**	**126**	**12%**	**55%**	**0.4**	**81**	**$6**

Duffy,Matt

Age: 31	Pos: 3B 2B		Health	F	LIMA Plan	D
Bats: R	Ht: 6' 2"	Wt: 190	PT/Exp	D	Rand Var	-4
			Consist	B	MM	1331

Back strain shelved bench utility for a couple of months mid-season. Before and after, displayed plate/BA skills similar to career numbers (.283 BA, .341 OBP). Near-zero power, but all-fields approach, LD%, h% still intact. Versatility, competent running game are plusses. But IL time has long cut into his opportunities, keeping his production a WAG.

Yr Tm	PA	R	HR	RBI	SB	BA	xHR	xSB	xBA	OBP	SLG	OPS+	vL+	vR+	bb%	ct%	Eye	G	L	F	h%	HctX	QBaB	Brl%	PX	xPX	HR/F	xHR/F	Spd	SBA%	SB%	RAR	BPX	R$
17																																		
18 TAM	560	59	4	44	12	294	5	10	264	361	366	97	95	96	8	82	0.51	54	25	20	35	93	CFb	1%	48	44	5%	6%	112	10%	67%	-0.5	57	$16
19 TAM *	203	15	2	19	0	245	2	3	245	319	322	89	73	104	10	80	0.56	54	23	24	30	100	CFc	2%	48	52	4%	7%	87	2%	0%	-10.8	26	-$1
20																																		
21 CHC	322	45	5	30	8	287	6	5	256	357	381	101	92	105	8	78	0.40	48	26	25	35	85	CDa	4%	58	63	9%	11%	104	9%	89%	-4.0	31	$11
1st Half	106	16	1	12	3	278	2	2	265	377	356	102	88	111	11	80	0.61	48	29	23	34	76	CDa	4%	51	54	6%	12%	102	9%	100%	-1.0	58	$1
2nd Half	216	29	4	18	5	291	4	3	252	347	392	100	94	102	7	77	0.31	49	25	26	36	88	CDb	4%	62	67	10%	10%	109	9%	83%	-1.4	27	$10
22 Proj	**245**	**30**	**3**	**23**	**5**	**279**	**4**	**5**	**255**	**354**	**362**	**97**	**86**	**102**	**9**	**79**	**0.47**	**51**	**26**	**24**	**34**	**88**		**3%**	**53**	**56**	**7%**	**9%**	**100**	**8%**	**81%**	**1.0**	**0**	**$9**

Duggar,Steven

Age: 28	Pos: CF		Health	B	LIMA Plan	D
Bats: L	Ht: 6' 1"	Wt: 187	PT/Exp	C	Rand Var	-5
			Consist	D	MM	3403

8-35-.257 with 7 SB in 295 PA at SF. Another SF depth piece that performed well for a while (.323, 6 HR, 6 SB over May/June) before disappearing. Reported swing change, more aggressive approach fueled FB%, power bumps at the expense of ct%. Plus speed, CF defense keep him on the radar, but poor and fluctuating plate skills minimizes our interest.

Yr Tm	PA	R	HR	RBI	SB	BA	xHR	xSB	xBA	OBP	SLG	OPS+	vL+	vR+	bb%	ct%	Eye	G	L	F	h%	HctX	QBaB	Brl%	PX	xPX	HR/F	xHR/F	Spd	SBA%	SB%	RAR	BPX	R$
17 aaa	53	6	1	5	2	224		1		321	331	89			13	70	0.48				29				63				104	27%	52%		-30	-$1
18 SF *	495	56	4	32	13	232	3	16	214	290	352	86	112	83	8	64	0.23	43	23	34	35	70	DCb	4%	102	72	6%	9%	136	19%	69%	-12.4	-13	$7
19 SF *	378	44	6	38	3	246	5	10	232	306	365	93	67	94	8	70	0.29	50	21	29	33	80	DDb	4%	74	73	8%	10%	129	12%	25%	-8.4	-7	$4
20 SF	36	3	0	3	1	176	0	0	210	222	235	61	0	65	3	68	0.09	52	22	26	26	48	DDd		53	28	0%	0%	108	17%	100%	-3.7	-184	-$2
21 SF *	364	53	9	41	12	248	13	10	221	316	408	99	91	108	9	65	0.28	38	26	36	36	78	CBb	8%	107	112	13%	20%	141	14%	100%	-4.5	27	$12
1st Half	165	30	6	25	6	313	8	5	249	388	537	129	139	127	11	64	0.34	37	29	34	45	75	CCc	12%	158	119	19%	26%	134	14%	100%	12.5	177	$15
2nd Half	199	23	3	16	6	196	5	5	196	256	303	76	42	85	7	65	0.23	38	23	38	28	81	CBb	5%	67	103	6%	15%	145	14%	100%	-13.2	-92	$1
22 Proj	**280**	**37**	**6**	**28**	**7**	**243**	**9**	**6**	**221**	**309**	**391**	**95**	**84**	**98**	**8**	**66**	**0.26**	**41**	**24**	**34**	**35**	**77**		**6%**	**102**	**95**	**10%**	**15%**	**127**	**13%**	**80%**	**0.8**	**9**	**$9**

Duran,Jarren

Age: 25	Pos: CF		Health	A	LIMA Plan	C
Bats: L	Ht: 6' 2"	Wt: 200	PT/Exp	C	Rand Var	+3
			Consist	A	MM	2503

2-10-.215 BA with 2 SB in 135 PA at BOS. Plus-plus speed, running game have always been his carrying skills. 2020 alternate site swing change began to unlock power that bloomed at AAA early but never materialized in BOS. Rookie came with plenty of hype as a power/speed weapon, but batting eye, QBaB, GB% say he's a work-in-progress.

Yr Tm	PA	R	HR	RBI	SB	BA	xHR	xSB	xBA	OBP	SLG	OPS+	vL+	vR+	bb%	ct%	Eye	G	L	F	h%	HctX	QBaB	Brl%	PX	xPX	HR/F	xHR/F	Spd	SBA%	SB%	RAR	BPX	R$
17																																		
18																																		
19 aa	340	37	1	17	25	247		6		291	323	85			6	73	0.23				34				46				149	42%	75%		-48	$10
20																																		
21 BOS *	379	52	13	37	14	221	2	5	234	276	395	92	60	86	7	67	0.23	49	19	31	29	109	CDf	4%	110	105	10%	10%	131	25%	76%	-13.0	42	$10
1st Half	186	28	11	24	8	244		2	253	313	486	111	0	0	9	69	0.31	44	20	36	29	0		0%	145	-22	0%		110	25%	69%	0.1	165	$14
2nd Half	193	25	3	14	7	199	2	2	210	241	312	75	59	85	5	66	0.16	49	19	31	29	106	CDf	4%	76	105	10%	10%	142	25%	87%	-14.0	-85	$2
22 Proj	**350**	**46**	**8**	**30**	**17**	**230**	**7**	**11**	**221**	**277**	**365**	**87**	**59**	**96**	**6**	**68**	**0.22**	**47**	**20**	**32**	**31**	**95**		**4%**	**86**	**95**	**11%**	**10%**	**140**	**20%**	**77%**	**-5.9**	**-2**	**$13**

Duvall,Adam

Age: 33	Pos: RF LF CF		Health	A	LIMA Plan	B
Bats: R	Ht: 6' 1"	Wt: 215	PT/Exp	A	Rand Var	0
			Consist	A	MM	4315

So who else pegged him early as the NL RBI leader? Kidding aside, slugger still delivers plus power and production that plays in our game. BA and OBP are reliable but unhelpful, but not necessarily deal-breakers in this era. FB%, HR/F, launch angle look locked in and platoon splits aren't a problem. Even with 2018 outlier, R$ history looks instructive.

Yr Tm	PA	R	HR	RBI	SB	BA	xHR	xSB	xBA	OBP	SLG	OPS+	vL+	vR+	bb%	ct%	Eye	G	L	F	h%	HctX	QBaB	Brl%	PX	xPX	HR/F	xHR/F	Spd	SBA%	SB%	RAR	BPX	R$
17 CIN	647	78	31	99	5	249	27	7	247	301	480	106	125	98	6	71	0.23	33	18	49	30	91	CAc	9%	143	116	15%	13%	87	6%	63%	-7.5	118	$16
18 2 NL	427	48	15	61	2	195	21	3	224	274	365	86	84	84	9	70	0.32	30	22	48	24	94	CAc	10%	114	116	12%	16%	71	5%	50%	-16.7	33	$4
19 ATL *	534	72	33	89	1	223	12	4	221	284	479	106	157	104	8	70	0.29	27	12	60	25	109	AAf	16%	138	182	20%	24%	104	1%	100%	-13.6	148	$12
20 ATL	209	34	16	33	0	237	16	1	251	301	532	111	117	108	7	72	0.28	29	17	54	24	89	CAf	14%	162	136	22%	22%	93	0%	0%	0.0	240	$18
21 2 NL	555	67	38	113	5	228	41	1	231	281	491	106	83	114	6	66	0.20	30	17	53	26	97	BAd	16%	160	148	21%	23%	84	5%	100%	-9.8	123	$18
1st Half	273	35	18	56	5	221	20	1	223	271	474	104	90	109	6	66	0.20	31	15	55	25	105	AAd	16%	153	155	19%	22%	72	5%	100%	-5.9	92	$22
2nd Half	282	32	20	57	0	235	21	1	240	291	508	108	75	118	6	66	0.20	29	20	51	27	89	CAf	17%	167	142	23%	24%	95	5%	0%	-2.0	154	$18
22 Proj	**490**	**65**	**33**	**90**	**2**	**236**	**36**	**4**	**235**	**294**	**501**	**108**	**105**	**109**	**7**	**68**	**0.23**	**29**	**17**	**53**	**27**	**96**		**15%**	**158**	**146**	**20%**	**22%**	**89**	**5%**	**87%**	**5.9**	**138**	**$18**

JOCK THOMPSON

Eaton,Adam

Age: 33	Pos: RF	Health	C	LIMA Plan	D
Bats: L	Ht: 5' 9" Wt: 176	PT/Exp	B	Rand Var	+4
		Consist	B	MM	1421

Poor start quickly grew legs. Contact skills plummeted as balky hamstring became an issue in May, shelved him for 19 days in June. DFA'd in July and again in August. Seems a tad overdone, but trend vR looks freefall-ish, once-elite OBP, Sp now look anything but. Decline, problematic health and now age will dry up his opportunities. Not great, Bob.

Yr	Tm	PA	R	HR	RBI	SB	BA	xHR	xSB	xBA	OBP	SLG	OPS+	vL+	vR+	bb%	ct%	Eye	G	L	F	h%	HctX	QBaB	Brl%	PX	xPX	HR/F	xHR/F	Spd	SBA%	SB%	RAR	BPX
17	WAS	107	24	2	13	3	297	3	2	273	393	462	116	80	119	13	80	0.78	53	15	32	35	101	CDf	4%	99	87	9%	13%	142	13%	75%	3.7	215
18	WAS	370	55	5	33	9	301	6	11	267	394	411	108	73	112	10	80	0.59	47	26	26	36	96	CDb	3%	72	66	8%	9%	130	8%	90%	11.5	130
19	WAS	656	103	15	49	15	279	14	16	246	365	428	110	109	109	10	81	0.61	40	20	40	32	96	CBc	4%	74	95	8%	8%	158	10%	83%	3.3	196
20	WAS	176	22	4	17	3	226	5	2	276	285	384	89	48	102	7	80	0.38	49	24	28	26	101	DFf	5%	92	77	12%	15%	92	9%	100%	-6.7	144
21	2 AL	288	38	6	30	3	201	5	4	226	282	327	84	61	89	8	72	0.31	51	17	32	25	78	DDd	4%	78	78	10%	9%	109	5%	100%	-17.8	4
1st Half		207	31	5	27	2	202	4	3	236	300	348	90	50	98	10	71	0.37	54	17	29	25	87	DFc	6%	88	108	14%	11%	116	5%	100%	-10.6	46
2nd Half		81	7	1	3	1	197	1	1	199	235	276	69	79	66	4	74	0.15	44	16	40	25	58	FCf	2%	54	10	5%	5%	91	5%	100%	-7.2	-96
22	**Proj**	**175**	**24**	**4**	**15**	**3**	**232**	**4**	**2**	**239**	**302**	**363**	**90**	**72**	**95**	**8**	**77**	**0.36**	**47**	**19**	**34**	**28**	**84**		**4%**	**79**	**65**	**9%**	**9%**	**108**	**6%**	**92%**	**-4.0**	**65**

Edman,Tommy

Age: 27	Pos: 2B RF	Health	A	LIMA Plan	B
Bats: B	Ht: 5' 10" Wt: 180	PT/Exp	A	Rand Var	+2
		Consist	B	MM	1435

BA, contact skills rebounded into plus territory; xBA says he wasn't particularly fortunate. Running game again stood out, with SB%, SBA back at peak levels following 2020 short season. But it's Health, full season of top-of-the-order PA that fueled counting stats. Poor bb% keeps leadoff spot tentative, but ct%, SB, versatility make for a profitable floor.

Yr	Tm	PA	R	HR	RBI	SB	BA	xHR	xSB	xBA	OBP	SLG	OPS+	vL+	vR+	bb%	ct%	Eye	G	L	F	h%	HctX	QBaB	Brl%	PX	xPX	HR/F	xHR/F	Spd	SBA%	SB%	RAR	BPX
17	aa	233	18	2	23	4	232		3		278	323	82			6	84	0.40				27				55				103	12%	67%		76
18	a/a	550	65	5	32	23	263		11		306	342	87			6	81	0.34				31				50				121	21%	80%		53
19	STL *	557	89	16	59	22	288	10	17	273	323	470	110	134	111	5	81	0.28	41	25	35	33	116	CBb	5%	90	108	12%	11%	140	18%	96%	16.3	189
20	STL	227	29	5	26	2	250	4	6	248	317	368	91	111	85	7	76	0.33	51	23	26	30	92	DDd	4%	66	67	12%	10%	115	10%	33%	-9.0	36
21	STL	691	91	11	56	30	262	19	11	270	308	387	95	108	92	5	85	0.40	46	22	32	29	102	CDd	4%	73	79	6%	11%	116	22%	86%	-15.7	181
1st Half		361	44	4	23	15	264	8	6	275	308	377	95	129	87	5	88	0.45	47	23	31	29	98	DDf	3%	64	72	4%	9%	134	22%	83%	-7.6	208
2nd Half		330	47	7	33	15	260	10	5	265	307	398	95	90	97	6	83	0.36	45	21	34	30	106	CCc	5%	84	87	8%	12%	94	22%	88%	-4.5	150
22	**Proj**	**595**	**80**	**13**	**56**	**21**	**262**	**15**	**19**	**263**	**313**	**397**	**96**	**109**	**92**	**6**	**82**	**0.35**	**46**	**22**	**32**	**30**	**103**		**5%**	**77**	**83**	**9%**	**10%**	**113**	**17%**	**80%**	**2.6**	**154**

Engel,Adam

Age: 30	Pos: CF	Health	F	LIMA Plan	D+
Bats: R	Ht: 6' 2" Wt: 220	PT/Exp	D	Rand Var	+2
		Consist	C	MM	3413

7-18-.252 with 7 SB in 134 PA at CHW. 124 IL days (hamstring, shoulder); through it all he ran and hit for power when on the field. PRO: Retained most of 2020 HctX bump; swing change report validated by QBaB; SB%. CON: HR/F looks outlier-ish, xPX remains skeptical; ct%, BA still problems. Plus glove, recent effort vR have him on our radar.

Yr	Tm	PA	R	HR	RBI	SB	BA	xHR	xSB	xBA	OBP	SLG	OPS+	vL+	vR+	bb%	ct%	Eye	G	L	F	h%	HctX	QBaB	Brl%	PX	xPX	HR/F	xHR/F	Spd	SBA%	SB%	RAR	BPX
17	CHW *	516	49	12	35	11	172	6	5	191	228	316	74	87	62	7	62	0.19	41	14	45	25	64	FBf	4%	104	98	8%	8%	132	19%	71%	-39.0	-45
18	CHW	463	49	6	29	16	235	7	12	200	279	336	82	78	82	4	70	0.14	41	18	41	32	66	CBd	3%	69	64	5%	6%	145	24%	67%	-15.1	-37
19	CHW *	512	57	13	47	12	227	5	16	224	272	370	89	117	82	6	67	0.19	44	23	33	31	65	DCd	5%	87	73	13%	11%	143	18%	65%	-18.5	-22
20	CHW	93	11	3	12	1	295	2	3	251	333	477	108	100	111	3	78	0.16	44	18	38	35	106	DCf	6%	100	65	12%	8%	138	5%	100%	2.0	176
21	CHW *	196	25	8	21	10	223	5	1	251	276	422	96	87	129	7	70	0.25	42	23	35	27	90	CBd	9%	126	86	21%	15%	80	28%	91%	-4.0	85
1st Half		61	8	4	6	4	224	2	0	257	245	439	95	114	126	3	75	0.12	26	30	43	23	134	BAc	17%	114	141	30%	20%	88	28%	100%	-1.9	100
2nd Half		135	18	5	15	7	224	3	1	248	290	414	95	71	128	9	68	0.29	47	20	33	29	76	DCd	6%	132	68	17%	13%	82	28%	87%	-3.1	85
22	**Proj**	**315**	**39**	**13**	**29**	**14**	**233**	**9**	**11**	**234**	**300**	**417**	**97**	**90**	**101**	**6**	**69**	**0.20**	**41**	**22**	**37**	**29**	**90**		**8%**	**115**	**84**	**16%**	**12%**	**113**	**21%**	**82%**	**-0.6**	**60**

Escobar,Alcides

Age: 35	Pos: SS	Health	A	LIMA Plan	D+
Bats: R	Ht: 6' 1" Wt: 205	PT/Exp	B	Rand Var	-2
		Consist	B	MM	1223

4-28-.288 with 3 SB in 336 PA at WAS. Like he never left. Following 2-year MLB hiatus, one-trick pony rode plus ct%, LD% bump, inflated h% to 2nd-half fantasy relevance on a rebuilder with PA to spare. No sign of any power, can chip in a few SBs, glove is still passable. But even contact looks age-faded, and PA will soon again be in lockstep. Pass.

Yr	Tm	PA	R	HR	RBI	SB	BA	xHR	xSB	xBA	OBP	SLG	OPS+	vL+	vR+	bb%	ct%	Eye	G	L	F	h%	HctX	QBaB	Brl%	PX	xPX	HR/F	xHR/F	Spd	SBA%	SB%	RAR	BPX
17	KC	629	71	6	54	4	250	8	7	252	272	357	86	97	80	2	83	0.15	41	22	37	29	90	FCc	2%	65	90	3%	4%	116	9%	36%	-25.1	76
18	KC	531	54	4	34	8	231	7	7	250	279	313	79	84	76	5	85	0.39	46	22	32	27	95	DCc	2%	51	67	3%	5%	117	9%	80%	-13.8	93
19	aaa	389	36	7	49	4	216		4		261	333	82			6	77	0.26				26				70				76	10%	62%		0
20																																		
21	WAS *	477	67	7	38	4	265	5	6	262	298	381	93	101	103	4	79	0.23	44	27	30	32	67	FCd	3%	73	48	5%	6%	106	4%	100%	-6.8	69
1st Half		132	14	3	10	1	206		1	311	229	317	76	0	93	3	71	0.10	50	50	0	27	0		0%	74	-22	0%		88	4%	100%	-8.9	-96
2nd Half		345	53	4	28	3	289	5	5	273	341	406	101	101	102	5	83	0.31	44	26	30	34	70	FCd	3%	73	48	5%	6%	111	4%	100%	2.0	135
22	**Proj**	**315**	**38**	**3**	**28**	**3**	**242**	**4**	**2**	**245**	**286**	**337**	**85**	**89**	**83**	**5**	**80**	**0.23**	**44**	**24**	**32**	**29**	**83**		**3%**	**62**	**64**	**4%**	**6%**	**95**	**4%**	**74%**	**-9.8**	**14**

Escobar,Eduardo

Age: 33	Pos: 3B 2B	Health	B	LIMA Plan	B+
Bats: B	Ht: 5' 10" Wt: 210	PT/Exp	A	Rand Var	0
		Consist	D	MM	3235

As suspected, power rebounded with better conditioning following anomalous short season. Hamstring knocked him out of action in late August and it took a while to regain his groove. But it's often been in-season peaks-and-valleys with him. Launch angle, FB% look healthy, plate skills are holding steady, MI versatility is a new plus. Expect a repeat.

Yr	Tm	PA	R	HR	RBI	SB	BA	xHR	xSB	xBA	OBP	SLG	OPS+	vL+	vR+	bb%	ct%	Eye	G	L	F	h%	HctX	QBaB	Brl%	PX	xPX	HR/F	xHR/F	Spd	SBA%	SB%	RAR	BPX
17	MIN	499	62	21	73	5	254	22	6	250	309	449	103	99	103	7	79	0.34	34	21	45	28	100	CAc	8%	102	114	13%	13%	102	5%	83%	-8.4	127
18	2 TM	631	75	23	84	2	272	25	4	275	334	489	110	103	112	8	78	0.41	32	25	43	31	109	DAb	8%	136	133	12%	13%	62	4%	33%	14.7	190
19	ARI	699	94	35	118	5	269	30	6	268	320	511	115	123	111	7	80	0.38	33	23	45	29	114	CAa	7%	116	152	15%	13%	104	4%	83%	5.9	215
20	ARI	222	22	4	20	1	212	5	2	236	270	335	80	74	83	7	80	0.37	36	24	40	25	97	CAd	5%	64	80	6%	8%	108	2%	100%	-15.0	72
21	2 NL	599	77	28	90	1	253	30	4	254	314	472	108	119	104	8	77	0.39	32	21	47	28	110	CAd	9%	119	134	14%	15%	104	1%	100%	-4.0	208
1st Half		331	41	18	54	1	249	18	2	248	296	472	107	106	108	6	77	0.29	31	20	49	27	109	CAd	10%	119	134	16%	16%	94	1%	100%	-2.7	173
2nd Half		268	36	10	36	0	258	13	2	262	336	471	109	134	99	10	78	0.52	32	23	45	29	111	DAd	8%	119	134	12%	15%	108	1%	0%	2.2	242
22	**Proj**	**595**	**74**	**25**	**86**	**2**	**250**	**25**	**3**	**256**	**310**	**459**	**104**	**110**	**101**	**8**	**78**	**0.39**	**33**	**23**	**44**	**28**	**108**		**8%**	**114**	**125**	**13%**	**13%**	**96**	**3%**	**78%**	**8.7**	**181**

Espinal,Santiago

Age: 27	Pos: 3B	Health	A	LIMA Plan	D+
Bats: R	Ht: 5' 10" Wt: 181	PT/Exp	C	Rand Var	-5
		Consist	B	MM	1331

Rookie with plus plate skills and speed fared better in second MLB try. Combined these with HctX bump and lofty h% to generate modest fantasy value. Absent any power, seems unlikely to ever win regular AB for too long, and SB% needs confirmation. But on-base skills with potential SB-and-versatility combo is a worthy in-season waiver watch.

Yr	Tm	PA	R	HR	RBI	SB	BA	xHR	xSB	xBA	OBP	SLG	OPS+	vL+	vR+	bb%	ct%	Eye	G	L	F	h%	HctX	QBaB	Brl%	PX	xPX	HR/F	xHR/F	Spd	SBA%	SB%	RAR	BPX
17																																		
18	aa	159	14	1	17	2	261		2		315	360	91			7	83	0.48				31				64				106	8%	60%		110
19	a/a	507	49	6	62	10	262		6		314	361	93			7	82	0.44				31				57				87	20%	41%		67
20	TOR	66	10	0	6	1	267	1	2	253	308	333	85	96	69	6	73	0.25	30	40	30	36	77	FCc	2%	56	78	0%	8%	111	6%	100%	-1.9	-52
21	TOR	246	32	2	17	6	311	2	5	259	376	405	107	108	106	9	86	0.73	43	22	35	35	86	DCd	2%	58	56	3%	3%	134	9%	86%	5.1	204
1st Half		110	14	1	9	2	304	1	2	253	355	402	105	93	120	7	83	0.47	49	20	31	36	76	FDf	1%	58	65	4%	4%	142	9%	67%	0.2	150
2nd Half		136	18	1	8	4	317	1	3	264	393	408	108	133	98	10	89	1.08	39	23	37	35	95	DBc	2%	58	48	3%	3%	118	9%	100%	3.5	235
22	**Proj**	**245**	**29**	**1**	**21**	**5**	**291**	**2**	**5**	**261**	**349**	**380**	**99**	**103**	**95**	**8**	**85**	**0.60**	**40**	**26**	**34**	**34**	**85**		**2%**	**56**	**61**	**2%**	**3%**	**121**	**9%**	**70%**	**2.9**	**114**

Estrada,Thairo

Age: 26	Pos: SS	Health	A	LIMA Plan	D+
Bats: R	Ht: 5' 10" Wt: 185	PT/Exp	D	Rand Var	-4
		Consist	D	MM	3241

7-22-.273 in 130 PA at SF. Rookie shuttle piece performed when called upon. Improved ct%, power, Brl% all pleasantly surprised despite looking capped by lofty GB%. Young, healthy enough to swipe a few bases despite marginal SB% history. Versatility would be part of a more permanent bench role. Could be a useful 2022 stopgap.

Yr	Tm	PA	R	HR	RBI	SB	BA	xHR	xSB	xBA	OBP	SLG	OPS+	vL+	vR+	bb%	ct%	Eye	G	L	F	h%	HctX	QBaB	Brl%	PX	xPX	HR/F	xHR/F	Spd	SBA%	SB%	RAR	BPX
17	aa	528	70	7	47	8	294		9		339	385	98			6	88	0.55				32				48				117	13%	40%		118
18	aaa	33	1	0	3	0	135		0		135	161	40			0	73	0.00				18				23				101	0%	0%		-180
19	NYY *	322	43	10	38	6	239	2	1	269	274	408	94	58	111	5	77	0.21	53	20	27	28	74	CDb	4%	92	61	23%	15%	108	11%	85%	-8.8	89
20	NYY	52	8	1	3	1	167	1	1	189	231	229	61	93	36	2	60	0.05	59	21	21	25	67	FFf	3%	37	60	17%	17%	110	9%	100%	-4.9	-356
21	SF *	356	44	12	49	5	268	6	6	256	315	431	102	93	127	6	80	0.35	51	17	32	30	84	DDf	7%	90	108	23%	19%	109	12%	51%	0.0	158
1st Half		179	24	5	28	3	317	0	3	258	370	488	119	138	201	8	82	0.46	56	11	33	36	111	ACa	50%	99	145	33%	0%	102	12%	48%	7.9	208
2nd Half		177	20	7	22	2	221	6	2	246	259	377	86	90	114	5	79	0.25	51	17	32	24	80	DDf	6%	82	105	21%	21%	108	12%	59%	-7.4	100
22	**Proj**	**245**	**31**	**11**	**31**	**4**	**264**	**7**	**4**	**273**	**318**	**462**	**106**	**88**	**116**	**6**	**81**	**0.33**	**52**	**19**	**30**	**28**	**78**		**5%**	**105**	**87**	**20%**	**13%**	**111**	**10%**	**54%**	**3.3**	**162**

JOCK THOMPSON

Farmer,Kyle

Age: 31 Pos: SS	Health A	LIMA Plan D+	
Bats: R Ht: 6' 0" Wt: 205	PT/Exp A	Rand Var -1	
	Consist A	MM 2123	

Glove-first bench utility was handed SS job early out of expediency, stunned everyone with 2nd half offensive show. Surging h% helped, but HctX soared, power jumped as he began to pound RHP. Small sample invites skepticism, but recent contact skills, defense will likely keep him in PA for now. Maybe something, maybe nothing; but watchable.

Yr Tm	PA	R	HR	RBI	SB	BA	xHR	xSB	xBA	OBP	SLG	OPS+	vL+	vR+	bb%	ct%	Eye	G	L	F	h%	HctX	QBaB	Brl%	PX	xPX	HR/F	xHR/F	Spd	SBA%	SB%	RAR	BPX	R$
17 LA *	387	41	8	44	1	261	0	5	367	300	385	93	68	100	5	83	0.32	35	53	12	30	118	CDa	0%	73	106	0%	0%	75	7%	13%	-8.1	73	$6
18 LA *	376	27	5	34	1	227	0	3	265	261	343	81	83	85	4	78	0.21	43	28	28	28	112	CCc	0%	80	81	0%	0%	96	3%	36%	-9.8	50	$1
19 CIN	197	22	9	27	4	230	7	1	235	279	410	95	114	84	5	68	0.17	40	24	35	29	94	DAb	6%	103	80	20%	16%	73	13%	80%	-6.0	-41	$3
20 CIN	70	4	0	4	1	266	2	1	235	329	313	85	118	64	7	80	0.38	37	27	35	33	114	BAb	6%	36	101	0%	11%	88	5%	100%	-1.7	-36	$1
21 CIN	529	60	16	63	2	263	14	6	259	316	416	101	107	99	4	80	0.23	41	24	35	30	118	CBc	4%	85	109	12%	10%	108	4%	40%	-5.1	115	$13
1st Half	253	24	6	26	2	216	5	3	237	282	322	84	103	79	5	80	0.27	43	22	35	24	108	CBd	4%	57	96	9%	8%	91	4%	50%	-14.0	23	$4
2nd Half	276	36	10	37	0	305	9	3	277	348	500	115	109	117	4	80	0.19	40	25	35	35	128	CBb	4%	110	121	14%	12%	114	4%	0%	9.7	192	$17
22 Proj	**385**	**42**	**10**	**47**	**3**	**252**	**8**	**3**	**250**	**304**	**390**	**94**	**106**	**88**	**5**	**77**	**0.21**	**40**	**25**	**35**	**30**	**113**		**4%**	**82**	**100**	**10%**	**8%**	**86**	**4%**	**54%**	**-5.2**	**18**	**$7**

Fletcher,David

Age: 28 Pos: 2B SS	Health A	LIMA Plan B+	
Bats: R Ht: 5' 9" Wt: 185	PT/Exp A	Rand Var +2	
	Consist C	MM 0345	

H% regressed from lofty short-season levels. HctX, BA, OBP plunged as he became less selective, struggled uncharacteristically vR. But floor-setting elite ct% held firm, suggesting that this was overdone and will retrace some. And running game stepped forward, with SB% hinting at a repeat with opportunity. Buy for the BA, hope for the SBs.

Yr Tm	PA	R	HR	RBI	SB	BA	xHR	xSB	xBA	OBP	SLG	OPS+	vL+	vR+	bb%	ct%	Eye	G	L	F	h%	HctX	QBaB	Brl%	PX	xPX	HR/F	xHR/F	Spd	SBA%	SB%	RAR	BPX	R$
17 a/a	469	48	2	32	16	230		6		265	290	76			5	86	0.34				26				37				103	22%	71%		45	$6
18 LAA *	571	70	5	49	7	274	1	16	280	306	388	93	89	90	4	89	0.42	39	27	34	30	95	FCc	0%	69	49	1%	1%	111	7%	76%	1.3	183	$13
19 LAA	653	83	6	49	8	290	3	11	284	350	384	102	102	100	9	89	0.86	44	26	30	32	99	FCb	0%	49	56	4%	2%	123	6%	73%	1.0	193	$16
20 LAA	230	31	3	18	2	319	1	4	292	376	425	106	119	99	9	88	0.80	54	25	21	35	81	DFc	1%	61	25	8%	3%	114	4%	67%	7.6	216	$20
21 LAA	665	74	2	47	15	262	1	8	270	297	324	85	106	76	5	90	0.52	48	23	28	29	64	FDd	0%	37	10	1%	1%	128	11%	83%	-22.6	158	$16
1st Half	323	46	0	25	4	285	0	4	265	315	334	91	106	84	4	88	0.40	48	25	27	32	45	FDd	0%	33	1	0%	0%	130	11%	80%	-8.7	115	$15
2nd Half	342	28	2	22	11	241	1	4	275	281	315	81	105	68	5	92	0.68	49	22	29	26	82	FCd	0%	41	19	2%	1%	119	11%	85%	-17.5	192	$10
22 Proj	**630**	**74**	**5**	**47**	**12**	**275**	**2**	**12**	**277**	**319**	**358**	**92**	**105**	**85**	**6**	**90**	**0.61**	**48**	**25**	**28**	**30**	**79**		**0%**	**49**	**27**	**3%**	**1%**	**111**	**10%**	**79%**	**-0.2**	**150**	**$19**

Flores,Wilmer

Age: 30 Pos: 3B 1B 2B	Health C	LIMA Plan B	
Bats: R Ht: 6' 2" Wt: 213	PT/Exp A	Rand Var +1	
	Consist A	MM 2343	

Begins every season with job questions yet skills, decent production remain remarkably consistent. Contact skills at the core of his success look rock-solid; average power a tick better in his best seasons. Passable effort vR helps him avoid a short platoon; versatility is a valuable plus. Health, playing time questions will keep his draft price reasonable.

Yr Tm	PA	R	HR	RBI	SB	BA	xHR	xSB	xBA	OBP	SLG	OPS+	vL+	vR+	bb%	ct%	Eye	G	L	F	h%	HctX	QBaB	Brl%	PX	xPX	HR/F	xHR/F	Spd	SBA%	SB%	RAR	BPX	R$
17 NYM	362	42	18	52	1	271	13	4	271	307	488	108	116	102	5	84	0.31	36	18	46	28	120	CBc	6%	111	127	14%	10%	90	3%	50%	-7.0	191	$9
18 NYM	429	43	11	51	0	267	8	2	261	319	417	99	81	106	7	89	0.69	36	19	45	28	108	DBd	3%	85	109	7%	5%	76	0%	0%	-5.4	210	$9
19 ARI	285	31	9	37	0	317	7	1	290	361	487	117	137	104	5	88	0.48	37	25	38	33	114	CBc	5%	84	93	10%	8%	75	0%	0%	7.2	207	$7
20 SF	213	30	12	32	1	268	9	1	280	315	515	110	127	102	6	82	0.36	33	23	44	27	118	CAc	6%	125	130	17%	13%	92	2%	100%	-1.4	276	$20
21 SF	436	57	18	53	1	262	15	3	270	335	447	107	109	106	9	86	0.73	38	21	41	27	108	CAc	6%	92	107	13%	11%	99	1%	100%	-8.4	254	$12
1st Half	218	29	8	28	1	262	6	2	269	330	436	107	98	112	9	86	0.71	37	22	40	27	102	CBc	6%	87	110	12%	9%	110	1%	100%	-3.6	254	$10
2nd Half	218	28	10	25	0	263	10	2	268	339	459	108	122	101	10	86	0.75	38	20	42	26	115	BAc	6%	97	104	14%	14%	87	1%	0%	-1.9	262	$8
22 Proj	**385**	**49**	**16**	**50**	**1**	**272**	**14**	**2**	**272**	**332**	**466**	**108**	**115**	**104**	**8**	**86**	**0.58**	**36**	**22**	**42**	**28**	**112**		**6%**	**99**	**110**	**13%**	**11%**	**84**	**2%**	**94%**	**11.3**	**209**	**$14**

Fraley,Jake

Age: 27 Pos: LF	Health C	LIMA Plan D	
Bats: L Ht: 6' 0" Wt: 195	PT/Exp D	Rand Var -2	
	Consist D	MM 3301	

9-36-.217 with 10 SBs in 260 PA at SEA. Rookie IL'd early (hamstring), returned with .841 OPS in June before COVID, shoulder woes helped drag 2nd half. Soaring bb% held up throughout. Running game, power still hopeful. But abysmal ct%, struggles vL keep him marginal and platooning. Check in March; some health, consistency would help.

Yr Tm	PA	R	HR	RBI	SB	BA	xHR	xSB	xBA	OBP	SLG	OPS+	vL+	vR+	bb%	ct%	Eye	G	L	F	h%	HctX	QBaB	Brl%	PX	xPX	HR/F	xHR/F	Spd	SBA%	SB%	RAR	BPX	R$
17																																		
18																																		
19 SEA *	452	60	16	68	18	251	0	5	207	299	444	103	31	57	6	72	0.24	31	12	58	31	38	FAf	4%	111	2	0%	0%	109	29%	70%	-9.4	81	$17
20 SEA	29	3	0	0	2	154	0	1	182	241	269	68	19	83	7	58	0.18	27	33	40	27	47	FAc	7%	82	40	0%	0%	145	60%	67%	-3.4	-172	-$1
21 SEA *	311	33	11	41	12	218	8	29	224	352	379	100	72	112	17	64	0.58	39	26	34	29	79	DCc	6%	105	111	18%	16%	87	17%	79%	-8.0	12	$8
1st Half	149	21	8	23	8	266	3	17	242	430	512	131	102	152	22	63	0.78	35	27	38	34	62	FCf	7%	153	117	29%	13%	96	17%	89%	8.8	196	$12
2nd Half	163	12	3	17	4	178	5	12	209	280	271	75	40	86	12	65	0.41	43	26	32	25	93	DCc	5%	67	106	8%	19%	90	17%	63%	-14.0	-123	-$3
22 Proj	**245**	**27**	**8**	**33**	**9**	**222**	**6**	**6**	**225**	**331**	**376**	**96**	**69**	**108**	**14**	**66**	**0.46**	**40**	**26**	**34**	**30**	**81**		**6%**	**101**	**110**	**16%**	**12%**	**94**	**12%**	**76%**	**-1.6**	**-8**	**$9**

France,Ty

Age: 27 Pos: 1B DH 2B	Health A	LIMA Plan B	
Bats: R Ht: 5' 11" Wt: 217	PT/Exp A	Rand Var -2	
	Consist A	MM 2045	

Near-magical h%, LD% of the short season regressed some but both stayed healthy. And the retreat had little impact, as rebounding plus ct%, HctX helped average power play up. Enjoyed zero platoon splits, as Health, soaring PA fueled counting stats that made this season. Oh, and versatility. What good fantasy value looks like.

Yr Tm	PA	R	HR	RBI	SB	BA	xHR	xSB	xBA	OBP	SLG	OPS+	vL+	vR+	bb%	ct%	Eye	G	L	F	h%	HctX	QBaB	Brl%	PX	xPX	HR/F	xHR/F	Spd	SBA%	SB%	RAR	BPX	R$
17 aa	382	38	4	36	1	259		5		297	353	88			5	80	0.27				31				60				91	1%	100%		21	$4
18 a/a	543	63	16	72	2	223		2		272	372	86			6	80	0.33				25				88				89	7%	33%		100	$8
19 SD *	518	77	24	85	1	288	6	5	270	330	510	116	107	91	6	77	0.27	43	21	37	33	112	CBc	6%	118	96	14%	12%	99	3%	25%	6.9	167	$18
20 2 TM	155	19	4	23	0	305	6	1	265	368	468	111	82	130	7	74	0.30	38	31	32	39	95	DBc	9%	100	108	12%	18%	92	0%	0%	2.8	76	$13
21 SEA	650	85	18	73	0	291	24	3	268	368	445	112	119	108	7	81	0.43	46	23	31	33	112	CCc	7%	88	84	12%	16%	93	0%	0%	1.8	154	$21
1st Half	310	36	8	34	0	264	12	1	261	352	428	108	111	107	9	79	0.45	46	21	33	31	103	CCc	9%	101	86	11%	17%	81	0%	0%	-6.3	158	$13
2nd Half	340	49	10	39	0	315	12	2	274	382	460	114	124	108	7	83	0.42	45	25	30	35	119	CCb	5%	77	83	13%	16%	109	0%	0%	4.1	165	$22
22 Proj	**616**	**82**	**20**	**81**	**0**	**287**	**23**	**3**	**266**	**359**	**455**	**110**	**111**	**110**	**7**	**79**	**0.36**	**43**	**24**	**32**	**33**	**109**		**7%**	**97**	**91**	**14%**	**16%**	**88**	**2%**	**34%**	**16.0**	**102**	**$23**

Franco,Maikel

Age: 29 Pos: 3B	Health A	LIMA Plan D	
Bats: R Ht: 6' 1" Wt: 225	PT/Exp B	Rand Var +5	
	Consist C	MM 2221	

11-47-.210 in 403 PA at BAL. Sample size reminder to heed the skills, as 2020 success quickly turned into 2021 pumpkin. HctX, h% regressed back to mediocre as inconsistent power continued slow descent into sub-par. Only reliable plus has been ct%, but it's never looked more empty. An August DFA ended his season. Word.

Yr Tm	PA	R	HR	RBI	SB	BA	xHR	xSB	xBA	OBP	SLG	OPS+	vL+	vR+	bb%	ct%	Eye	G	L	F	h%	HctX	QBaB	Brl%	PX	xPX	HR/F	xHR/F	Spd	SBA%	SB%	RAR	BPX	R$
17 PHI	623	66	24	76	0	230	18	7	264	281	409	94	89	94	7	83	0.43	45	18	37	24	104	CCf	6%	95	86	13%	10%	60	0%	0%	-26.1	130	$7
18 PHI	465	48	22	68	1	270	16	1	272	314	467	105	85	109	6	86	0.47	49	17	34	27	87	CCf	6%	100	88	17%	13%	85	1%	100%	6.1	210	$14
19 PHI *	472	52	19	60	0	225	16	2	250	291	402	96	110	92	8	84	0.57	43	17	40	23	96	CBf	7%	84	78	13%	12%	79	0%	0%	-20.5	163	$6
20 KC	243	23	8	38	1	278	7	0	262	321	457	103	108	102	7	83	0.42	46	18	36	31	110	CDf	6%	99	94	12%	10%	51	2%	100%	0.0	164	$19
21 BAL *	437	34	11	47	0	204	11	1	242	247	339	80	77	87	5	82	0.32	49	18	33	22	95	CDf	5%	78	65	11%	11%	52	0%	0%	-33.3	69	$0
1st Half	309	27	9	42	0	221	9	0	260	265	376	89	96	87	6	83	0.34	49	20	32	24	95	CCf	6%	89	65	12%	12%	53	0%	0%	-16.3	119	$8
2nd Half	128	7	2	5	0	162	2	0	189	206	247	61	34	90	5	79	0.27	50	13	38	19	94	CDf	3%	51	62	7%	7%	77	0%	0%	-13.6	-27	-$10
22 Proj	**210**	**18**	**7**	**23**	**0**	**221**	**6**	**0**	**241**	**271**	**373**	**87**	**72**	**94**	**6**	**82**	**0.37**	**48**	**16**	**36**	**24**	**98**		**5%**	**84**	**75**	**11%**	**10%**	**66**	**1%**	**100%**	**-5.9**	**73**	**$3**

Franco,Wander

Age: 21 Pos: SS	Health A	LIMA Plan A	
Bats: B Ht: 5' 10" Wt: 189	PT/Exp D	Rand Var 0	
	Consist F	MM 3355	

7-39-.288 with 2 SB in 305 PA at TAM. Numbers alone don't wow until you realize precocious rookie did this at age 20 with just 180 high-minors PA under his belt. Power may be a few years away, but near-elite contact skills, Eye already make for plus hit tool. Monthly BAs from call-up through Sept: .194, .256, .313,. 340. He's arrived and will only get better.

Yr Tm	PA	R	HR	RBI	SB	BA	xHR	xSB	xBA	OBP	SLG	OPS+	vL+	vR+	bb%	ct%	Eye	G	L	F	h%	HctX	QBaB	Brl%	PX	xPX	HR/F	xHR/F	Spd	SBA%	SB%	RAR	BPX	R$
17																																		
18																																		
19																																		
20																																		
21 TAM *	484	81	13	71	7	293	8	8	291	347	496	116	139	96	8	86	0.61	45	20	34	32	102	CCf	5%	103	80	8%	10%	140	10%	56%	17.4	338	$21
1st Half	217	33	7	37	7	285	1	3	293	337	509	118	149	47	7	85	0.51	39	26	35	31	134	CCd	4%	111	139	9%	9%	145	10%	61%	7.1	335	$19
2nd Half	267	48	6	34	0	300	7	5	290	355	486	114	135	102	8	88	0.72	46	20	34	32	99	CCf	5%	96	72	8%	10%	132	10%	0%	10.8	331	$16
22 Proj	**595**	**93**	**17**	**83**	**8**	**301**	**17**	**12**	**292**	**356**	**509**	**117**	**163**	**92**	**8**	**87**	**0.62**	**43**	**22**	**35**	**32**	**113**		**6%**	**105**	**99**	**11%**	**10%**	**139**	**11%**	**57%**	**33.3**	**321**	**$29**

JOCK THOMPSON

Frazier,Adam

Frazier,Adam		Health	A	LIMA Plan	B+
Age: 30	Pos: 2B	PT/Exp	A	Rand Var	-2
Bats: L	Ht: 5' 10" Wt: 185	Consist	C	MM	1245

Bumped his already-plus contact skill to elite levels (seriously, 0.70 Eye might as well be the new 1.00 Eye), while doing nothing about poor quality of said contact. Barrels even converged to zero in second half. Sustaining a .300 BA out of tha isn't repeatable. Speed and OBP could be his best path to value, but age and poor SB% says that's unlikely.

Yr Tm	PA	R	HR	RBI	SB	BA	xHR	xSB	xBA	OBP	SLG	OPS+	vL+	vR+	bb%	ct%	Eye	G	L	F	h%	HctX	QBaB	Brl%	PX	xPX	HR/F	xHR/F	Spd	SBA%	SB%	RAR	BPX
17 PIT	454	55	6	53	9	276	6	7	288	344	399	101	91	101	8	86	0.63	48	25	27	31	96	DDa	2%	66	59	6%	6%	122	11%	64%	-4.7	155
18 PIT *	481	59	10	48	2	251	7	8	266	309	397	95	78	113	8	83	0.49	49	20	31	28	106	CCa	4%	87	79	12%	8%	106	8%	21%	-4.4	163
19 PIT	608	80	10	50	5	278	10	9	283	336	417	104	93	107	7	86	0.53	41	26	33	31	89	CCb	2%	70	69	6%	6%	127	7%	50%	2.3	204
20 PIT	230	22	7	23	1	230	6	2	250	297	364	88	70	92	7	83	0.49	44	21	35	25	85	DCd	4%	68	67	11%	10%	86	7%	25%	-11.2	120
21 2 NL	639	83	5	43	10	305	6	11	288	368	411	107	102	109	8	88	0.70	41	29	30	34	86	DCb	1%	62	53	3%	4%	127	8%	67%	5.0	219
1st Half	355	50	4	28	4	324	4	6	294	392	462	119	123	118	9	88	0.79	37	30	33	36	83	DBc	1%	79	52	4%	4%	134	8%	50%	13.9	288
2nd Half	284	33	1	15	6	282	2	5	281	338	347	93	80	98	6	88	0.58	46	29	25	32	89	DCb	0%	41	55	2%	3%	111	8%	86%	-5.1	127
22 Proj	**560**	**69**	**8**	**46**	**7**	**276**	**8**	**9**	**275**	**337**	**392**	**99**	**88**	**102**	**7**	**86**	**0.57**	**43**	**26**	**31**	**31**	**89**		**2%**	**65**	**62**	**6%**	**6%**	**110**	**8%**	**57%**	**5.5**	**150**

Frazier,Clint

Frazier,Clint		Health	F	LIMA Plan	D
Age: 27	Pos: LF RF	PT/Exp	C	Rand Var	+4
Bats: R	Ht: 5' 11" Wt: 212	Consist	F	MM	4311

Started off slowly in attempt to confirm his short-season explosion into relevance, then season ended in June due to bout of dizziness/blurred vision that were still unresolved by season's end. Assuming health cooperates at some point, patience and-power profile still worthy of a speculative buck, but long road from here to there.

Yr Tm	PA	R	HR	RBI	SB	BA	xHR	xSB	xBA	OBP	SLG	OPS+	vL+	vR+	bb%	ct%	Eye	G	L	F	h%	HctX	QBaB	Brl%	PX	xPX	HR/F	xHR/F	Spd	SBA%	SB%	RAR	BPX
17 NYY *	448	57	17	54	9	237	5	5	242	305	449	103	104	93	9	71	0.33	38	17	45	29	115	CCd	12%	132	158	10%	12%	106	13%	80%	-10.5	118
18 NYY *	250	40	10	18	3	274	1	5	276	345	487	112	152	70	10	67	0.33	52	29	19	37	106	CFd	5%	147	139	0%	25%	113	8%	59%	7.6	140
19 NYY *	511	60	20	59	3	240	11	5	240	287	430	99	101	114	6	72	0.23	39	20	42	29	86	CBc	11%	113	101	18%	17%	86	7%	38%	-16.0	63
20 NYY	160	24	8	26	3	267	6	3	253	394	511	120	115	121	16	66	0.57	41	25	34	34	86	BCc	13%	148	98	27%	20%	121	6%	100%	5.9	216
21 NYY	218	20	5	15	2	186	7	2	195	317	317	87	77	93	15	64	0.49	45	15	40	26	80	CCd	10%	95	105	11%	15%	79	4%	100%	-13.6	-38
1st Half	218	20	5	15	2	186	7	2	195	317	317	88	78	95	15	64	0.49	45	15	40	26	80	CCd	10%	95	105	11%	15%	79	4%	100%	-13.1	-42
2nd Half																								0%									
22 Proj	**210**	**27**	**8**	**22**	**3**	**235**	**9**	**2**	**231**	**331**	**430**	**103**	**94**	**107**	**12**	**67**	**0.41**	**41**	**19**	**40**	**30**	**90**		**11%**	**128**	**113**	**16%**	**18%**	**99**	**5%**	**78%**	**1.9**	**77**

Freeman,Freddie

Freeman,Freddie		Health	A	LIMA Plan	C
Age: 32	Pos: 1B	PT/Exp	A	Rand Var	0
Bats: L	Ht: 6' 5" Wt: 220	Consist	F	MM	4255

Trend line of full-season dollar values paints a picture of stability; dip in RBI just a function of circumstance (more time batting 2nd, loss of Acuña in front). Power trends are disparate: xPX eroding in the face of fewer FBs, but xHR/F sees still strong exit velocity, copious barrels and says he might yet hit us with... UP: 40 HR.

Yr Tm	PA	R	HR	RBI	SB	BA	xHR	xSB	xBA	OBP	SLG	OPS+	vL+	vR+	bb%	ct%	Eye	G	L	F	h%	HctX	QBaB	Brl%	PX	xPX	HR/F	xHR/F	Spd	SBA%	SB%	RAR	BPX
17 ATL	514	84	28	71	8	307	32	8	300	403	586	135	119	138	13	78	0.68	35	24	41	34	119	BBa	13%	157	156	20%	23%	102	9%	62%	29.5	294
18 ATL	707	94	23	98	10	309	36	11	290	388	505	120	122	116	11	79	0.58	36	32	31	36	121	CBa	9%	119	123	15%	23%	83	6%	77%	34.6	193
19 ATL	692	113	38	121	6	295	41	9	296	389	549	130	104	138	13	79	0.69	38	28	34	32	128	BBa	13%	128	133	24%	25%	90	5%	67%	36.0	267
20 ATL	262	51	13	53	2	341	17	3	326	462	640	146	93	163	17	83	1.22	32	31	37	37	146	ABa	15%	162	143	20%	26%	92	2%	100%	30.2	500
21 ATL	695	120	31	83	8	300	43	7	285	393	503	123	103	131	12	82	0.79	43	24	33	32	129	ACb	12%	104	115	19%	27%	103	5%	73%	19.2	265
1st Half	356	53	17	46	4	267	23	3	271	374	472	118	93	128	14	77	0.72	39	26	35	29	124	ACa	13%	110	139	21%	28%	87	5%	80%	4.1	204
2nd Half	339	67	14	37	4	333	21	4	301	413	535	128	114	134	11	87	0.92	47	23	30	35	134	BCc	10%	99	93	18%	27%	117	5%	67%	19.8	331
22 Proj	**665**	**118**	**34**	**104**	**7**	**304**	**42**	**8**	**301**	**401**	**552**	**129**	**105**	**138**	**13**	**82**	**0.83**	**39**	**27**	**34**	**32**	**131**		**12%**	**132**	**124**	**21%**	**26%**	**93**	**5%**	**74%**	**55.6**	**330**

Fuentes,Joshua

Fuentes,Joshua		Health	A	LIMA Plan	D
Age: 29	Pos: 3B 1B	PT/Exp	B	Rand Var	+4
Bats: R	Ht: 6' 2" Wt: 209	Consist	D	MM	2101

7-33-.225 in 285 PA at COL. Got a long look in COL in first half, where he replicated 2020's unremarkable skills, without the codpiece of 2020's 42% hit rate. COL decided they didn't like the 27% hit rate version at all, and sent him to minors for bulk of 2nd half. Skills are as stable as they are substandard, and he's getting kind of old for new tricks.

Yr Tm	PA	R	HR	RBI	SB	BA	xHR	xSB	xBA	OBP	SLG	OPS+	vL+	vR+	bb%	ct%	Eye	G	L	F	h%	HctX	QBaB	Brl%	PX	xPX	HR/F	xHR/F	Spd	SBA%	SB%	RAR	BPX
17 aa	433	39	13	58	6	299		6		330	498	113			4	78	0.21				36				115				114	11%	54%		145
18 aaa	564	58	10	59	2	281		9		298	432	98			2	80	0.12				34				91				119	7%	24%		110
19 COL *	474	49	15	47	2	213	1	4	222	241	364	84	42	119	4	67	0.11	46	20	34	29	59	DDc	3%	94	64	25%	8%	102	4%	58%	-36.5	-63
20 COL	103	14	2	17	1	306	1	1	243	320	439	101	102	100	2	70	0.07	49	24	27	42	84	FCc	1%	93	63	11%	5%	96	4%	100%	-1.7	-32
21 COL *	483	46	13	51	1	220	4	4	213	250	358	83	95	78	4	75	0.16	40	15	45	27	79	DAf	2%	83	79	7%	4%	118	6%	13%	-44.4	46
1st Half	238	26	7	31	0	233	4	2	221	265	383	90	106	83	4	74	0.17	39	17	44	29	86	DAd	3%	91	83	9%	5%	107	6%	0%	-15.4	42
2nd Half	245	20	6	20	1	207	0	2	183	234	334	77	40	59	3	76	0.15	42	5	53	25	41	FBf	0%	75	57	0%	0%	126	6%	13%	-25.1	42
22 Proj	**175**	**18**	**5**	**20**	**1**	**245**	**2**	**1**	**221**	**268**	**398**	**90**	**83**	**94**	**3**	**74**	**0.12**	**43**	**15**	**42**	**31**	**64**		**2%**	**95**	**66**	**9%**	**4%**	**105**	**6%**	**42%**	**-3.9**	**-2**

Gallo,Joey

Gallo,Joey		Health	B	LIMA Plan	B
Age: 28	Pos: RF LF	PT/Exp	A	Rand Var	+2
Bats: L	Ht: 6' 5" Wt: 250	Consist	D	MM	5205

Perfectly reasonable 1st half went off the rails after trade to NY. The 18% 2nd half h% looks like an obvious culprit, but there's more: as a Yankee, had an amazing 23/8/69 G/L/F split. He wasn't the first, nor will he the last, to get sucked in by that short porch in RF. First half shows the path to gobs of power without a poison-pill BA... if he could just stick to it.

Yr Tm	PA	R	HR	RBI	SB	BA	xHR	xSB	xBA	OBP	SLG	OPS+	vL+	vR+	bb%	ct%	Eye	G	L	F	h%	HctX	QBaB	Brl%	PX	xPX	HR/F	xHR/F	Spd	SBA%	SB%	RAR	BPX
17 TEX	532	85	41	80	7	209	43	7	237	333	537	118	114	117	14	56	0.38	28	18	54	25	106	AAc	22%	231	206	30%	32%	103	8%	78%	9.0	215
18 TEX	577	82	40	92	3	206	48	5	238	312	498	109	109	106	13	59	0.36	30	21	50	25	105	AAb	23%	213	180	28%	33%	75	6%	43%	4.6	183
19 TEX	297	54	22	49	4	253	28	3	240	389	598	136	163	124	18	53	0.46	27	26	47	37	95	AAc	26%	251	199	37%	47%	90	8%	67%	19.5	278
20 TEX	226	23	10	26	2	181	12	2	194	301	378	90	82	94	13	59	0.37	27	18	55	24	99	CAf	14%	137	173	17%	20%	89	4%	100%	-9.1	0
21 2 AL	616	90	38	77	6	199	42	5	212	351	458	111	104	115	18	57	0.52	33	17	51	25	88	BAf	19%	179	160	27%	30%	80	4%	100%	2.6	131
1st Half	325	47	20	46	6	236	22	3	224	394	492	123	131	118	20	61	0.63	34	20	47	30	95	BAf	18%	165	161	28%	31%	72	4%	100%	11.5	150
2nd Half	291	43	18	31	0	158	20	2	200	302	421	98	71	111	16	53	0.42	31	13	56	18	81	BAf	20%	195	159	26%	29%	95	4%	0%	-10.2	123
22 Proj	**595**	**87**	**39**	**84**	**5**	**214**	**45**	**4**	**218**	**346**	**491**	**114**	**109**	**116**	**16**	**57**	**0.44**	**30**	**18**	**52**	**28**	**93**		**19%**	**198**	**173**	**27%**	**31%**	**82**	**4%**	**82%**	**15.9**	**155**

Galvis,Freddy

Galvis,Freddy		Health	C	LIMA Plan	D+
Age: 32	Pos: SS	PT/Exp	A	Rand Var	0
Bats: B	Ht: 5' 10" Wt: 195	Consist	A	MM	2223

You know that beater car that you keep driving because it's paid off? It gets you around fine, and you convince yourself that the extras (like, say, power and speed) are worth the oil drips in the driveway. In reality, the moonroof doesn't open (SB are shot), and the engine HAS been making that foreboding noise for awhile (waning PA, xPX). Time for a new ride.

Yr Tm	PA	R	HR	RBI	SB	BA	xHR	xSB	xBA	OBP	SLG	OPS+	vL+	vR+	bb%	ct%	Eye	G	L	F	h%	HctX	QBaB	Brl%	PX	xPX	HR/F	xHR/F	Spd	SBA%	SB%	RAR	BPX
17 PHI	663	71	12	61	14	255	11	9	252	309	382	94	86	95	7	82	0.41	37	24	39	29	84	DBc	2%	71	85	6%	6%	121	12%	74%	-9.5	109
18 SD	656	62	13	67	8	248	15	11	239	299	380	91	103	84	7	76	0.31	41	22	37	31	112	CBc	4%	85	118	8%	9%	101	10%	57%	-0.9	53
19 2 TM	589	67	23	70	4	260	17	7	244	296	438	102	100	102	5	74	0.19	40	21	39	31	97	CBc	6%	98	100	14%	11%	89	5%	67%	-5.2	44
20 CIN	159	18	7	16	1	220	4	1	245	308	404	95	91	95	8	79	0.43	47	17	37	23	86	DCf	5%	95	109	18%	10%	80	5%	50%	-3.5	132
21 2 TM	393	53	14	40	1	242	12	3	244	302	407	97	104	95	7	78	0.35	39	20	41	27	93	DCf	5%	92	98	12%	10%	90	1%	100%	-4.8	115
1st Half	273	36	9	26	1	249	8	2	240	306	414	100	116	93	7	77	0.31	40	19	41	29	91	DCf	6%	95	105	12%	10%	87	1%	100%	-2.5	92
2nd Half	120	17	5	14	0	224	3	1	251	292	393	93	77	100	8	82	0.47	37	21	42	23	97	DBf	3%	84	84	13%	8%	97	1%	0%	-2.9	165
22 Proj	**350**	**44**	**12**	**38**	**2**	**238**	**9**	**2**	**241**	**300**	**395**	**94**	**93**	**95**	**7**	**78**	**0.36**	**40**	**20**	**40**	**27**	**94**		**4%**	**87**	**99**	**12%**	**9%**	**92**	**3%**	**63%**	**-3.7**	**71**

Gamel,Ben

Gamel,Ben		Health	A	LIMA Plan	C+
Age: 30	Pos: LF CF	PT/Exp	B	Rand Var	0
Bats: L	Ht: 5' 11" Wt: 177	Consist	A	MM	3125

Didn't stick in CLE after making Opening Day roster, eventually claimed by PIT in May and given a long look. Gradual uptick in barrels, FB%, and launch angle all show he's bought into the "revolution." xPX and xHR agree that there's more pop lurking. Clearly sees the strike zone well; a little more contact could yet unlock... UP: 20 HR.

Yr Tm	PA	R	HR	RBI	SB	BA	xHR	xSB	xBA	OBP	SLG	OPS+	vL+	vR+	bb%	ct%	Eye	G	L	F	h%	HctX	QBaB	Brl%	PX	xPX	HR/F	xHR/F	Spd	SBA%	SB%	RAR	BPX
17 SEA *	619	73	12	65	5	273	10	9	247	326	404	99	94	100	7	76	0.34	45	22	33	34	91	DCb	4%	79	80	8%	8%	128	5%	69%	-7.4	70
18 SEA *	384	51	2	31	10	276	4	6	256	349	387	99	88	98	10	78	0.51	47	25	28	35	75	CDb	3%	74	50	2%	7%	135	12%	77%	5.3	107
19 MIL	356	47	7	33	2	248	6	8	231	337	373	98	125	90	11	67	0.38	44	26	29	35	87	CCb	4%	85	89	11%	10%	113	4%	50%	-1.1	-22
20 MIL	127	13	3	10	0	237	3	1	261	315	404	95	87	97	10	66	0.33	37	39	24	33	78	CCc	7%	116	73	17%	17%	104	7%	0%	-3.8	40
21 2 TM	400	43	8	26	3	247	11	6	230	347	388	101	85	107	13	69	0.49	31	29	40	33	96	CBd	8%	94	128	9%	12%	129	8%	33%	-7.8	69
1st Half	152	15	4	8	0	222	3	2	240	291	393	95	56	108	9	70	0.34	30	28	43	29	100	CBc	9%	114	124	10%	8%	115	8%	0%	-5.1	96
2nd Half	248	28	4	18	3	263	8	4	224	381	385	104	99	106	15	69	0.58	32	29	39	36	94	CCf	7%	81	131	7%	15%	133	8%	38%	-1.3	46
22 Proj	**455**	**52**	**10**	**40**	**4**	**249**	**11**	**7**	**241**	**337**	**398**	**100**	**91**	**102**	**11**	**69**	**0.42**	**39**	**29**	**33**	**34**	**96**		**8%**	**100**	**101**	**11%**	**12%**	**118**	**8%**	**38%**	**0.1**	**15**

RAY MURPHY

García,Adolis

Age: 29	Pos: CF RF	Health	A	LIMA Plan	B
Bats: R	Ht: 6' 1" Wt: 205	PT/Exp	A	Rand Var	-5
		Consist	F	MM	4305

Initially, rode power surge and h% to cover ugly plate skills. Came crashing down in 2nd half as brutal Eye exposed the tiny margins of this profile type. Given age and how league adjusted, 1st half was likely his peak. Power and speed can deliver fantasy value, but plan for the BA/OBP drain, and know that any further drop-off will start costing him PT.

Yr	Tm	PA	R	HR	RBI	SB	BA	xHR	xSB	xBA	OBP	SLG	OPS+	vL+	vR+	bb%	ct%	Eye	G	L	F	h%	HctX	QBaB	Brl%	PX	xPX	HR/F	xHR/F	Spd	SBA%	SB%	RAR	BPX	R$
17	a/a	472	53	12	54	12	258		6		301	415	97			6	74	0.23				33				103				89	23%	55%		52	$12
18	STL *	433	49	16	54	7	209	0	7	228	227	384	82	0	60	2	72	0.09	50	10	40	25	53	DBf	0%	113	-2	0%	0%	100	18%	68%	-21.7	47	$7
19	aaa	507	71	23	71	10	205		8		230	396	87			3	62	0.09				28				118				116	31%	47%		-48	$10
20	TEX	7	0	0	0	0	0	0	0	0	143	0	19	0	67	14	33	0.25	50	0	50	0	0	FDf		0	-26	0%	0%	104	0%	0%	-1.1	-816	-$4
21	TEX	622	77	31	90	16	243	35	3	231	286	454	102	95	105	5	67	0.16	43	16	41	31	106	BBd	12%	134	127	20%	22%	112	18%	76%	-11.2	73	$23
1st Half		303	40	20	57	8	270	21	2	249	307	526	116	106	122	5	67	0.16	44	18	38	33	116	ACd	15%	152	140	27%	28%	129	18%	73%	3.9	162	$32
2nd Half		319	37	11	33	8	216	14	1	214	266	385	88	83	91	5	66	0.17	42	15	43	29	96	BBf	8%	118	113	13%	17%	100	18%	80%	-16.5	4	$14
22	Proj	525	65	23	70	12	227	24	10	225	265	424	93	87	96	4	67	0.13	43	16	41	29	104		11%	126	124	17%	17%	111	14%	65%	-7.1	36	$14

García,Avisail

Age: 31	Pos: RF	Health	B	LIMA Plan	B
Bats: R	Ht: 6' 4" Wt: 250	PT/Exp	A	Rand Var	-1
		Consist	D	MM	3135

Nagging injuries in 2020 sapped power, but it rebounded big time as the recovered Brl% was joined by 5-year highs in HctX, HR/F, and xPX for a career year. Only a September back injury kept him from 30 HR. Dwindling Spd and xSB says don't bet on SB repeat. xHR, xPX, and xHR/FB support the breakout and R$ points to a solid double-digit investment.

Yr	Tm	PA	R	HR	RBI	SB	BA	xHR	xSB	xBA	OBP	SLG	OPS+	vL+	vR+	bb%	ct%	Eye	G	L	F	h%	HctX	QBaB	Brl%	PX	xPX	HR/F	xHR/F	Spd	SBA%	SB%	RAR	BPX	R$
17	CHW	561	75	18	80	5	330	25	9	275	380	506	121	139	112	6	79	0.30	52	20	27	39	112	BDb	9%	98	89	16%	22%	131	5%	63%	25.3	139	$26
18	CHW *	412	51	22	56	3	240	21	4	247	282	455	99	107	91	5	70	0.20	48	17	34	28	99	BCc	12%	130	101	21%	24%	108	5%	75%	-1.0	100	$11
19	TAM	530	61	20	72	10	282	26	5	260	332	464	110	108	110	6	74	0.25	46	22	32	34	103	BCc	12%	100	90	17%	22%	98	11%	71%	-1.2	78	$18
20	MIL	207	20	2	15	1	238	5	3	232	333	326	88	114	75	10	73	0.41	48	24	27	32	80	CDc	4%	63	68	6%	14%	82	7%	25%	-10.8	-44	$6
21	MIL	515	68	29	86	8	262	31	4	265	330	490	113	127	108	7	74	0.31	47	21	32	30	113	BCc	12%	128	117	26%	28%	70	10%	67%	1.6	135	$21
1st Half		289	36	15	51	4	249	16	2	257	315	456	107	135	100	7	71	0.27	49	22	29	29	107	ADb	13%	120	98	28%	30%	68	10%	57%	-4.1	69	$22
2nd Half		226	32	14	35	4	280	15	2	277	350	535	120	119	120	8	77	0.39	45	19	36	30	120	BCd	12%	138	141	25%	26%	81	10%	80%	7.8	235	$17
22	Proj	560	73	26	81	7	264	28	8	258	331	464	108	119	103	7	74	0.31	47	21	32	31	104		10%	116	104	22%	23%	83	7%	59%	9.3	98	$22

García,Leury

Age: 31	Pos: 2B RF LF CF	Health	C	LIMA Plan	D+
Bats: B	Ht: 5' 8" Wt: 185	PT/Exp	A	Rand Var	0
		Consist	B	MM	1423

Better real life player with positional flexibility being his best asset. Spd was undercut by massive SBA% drop-off and age might hinder a full bounce back. Power was up from 2019's volume-based breakout and QBaB remains skeptical of any further growth. Super-deep league Swiss Army Knife with a tinge of SB upside.

Yr	Tm	PA	R	HR	RBI	SB	BA	xHR	xSB	xBA	OBP	SLG	OPS+	vL+	vR+	bb%	ct%	Eye	G	L	F	h%	HctX	QBaB	Brl%	PX	xPX	HR/F	xHR/F	Spd	SBA%	SB%	RAR	BPX	R$
17	CHW	326	41	9	33	8	270	7	4	271	316	423	101	93	101	4	77	0.19	55	21	24	32	83	DFb	4%	89	66	16%	13%	99	17%	62%	-3.2	58	$9
18	CHW	275	23	4	32	12	271	4	7	248	303	376	91	105	83	3	73	0.13	49	29	23	36	81	CDa	3%	63	63	10%	10%	135	19%	92%	0.0	-23	$8
19	CHW	618	93	8	40	15	279	10	20	252	310	378	95	109	88	3	76	0.15	55	22	24	36	75	CDb	4%	59	45	8%	10%	145	13%	75%	-11.7	11	$18
20	CHW	63	6	3	8	0	271	3	1	244	317	441	101	179	88	6	85	0.44	50	18	32	28	96	CDd	6%	77	78	19%	19%	88	0%	0%	0.4	168	$2
21	CHW	474	60	5	54	6	267	8	4	251	335	376	98	95	99	9	77	0.42	56	20	24	34	83	FFd	3%	69	59	6%	10%	123	6%	75%	-3.1	69	$12
1st Half		237	31	2	31	2	252	3	2	230	315	338	91	89	92	9	73	0.36	57	19	24	34	76	FFf	4%	55	52	5%	8%	125	6%	67%	-7.3	-23	$8
2nd Half		237	29	3	23	4	283	5	2	272	356	415	104	104	105	9	80	0.51	55	21	24	34	90	DFc	3%	82	66	8%	13%	117	6%	80%	2.1	158	$9
22	Proj	315	40	6	33	7	272	6	4	251	322	398	98	108	94	6	76	0.28	54	21	25	34	85		4%	76	62	10%	10%	117	7%	79%	3.4	42	$12

García,Luis

Age: 22	Pos: 2B	Health	A	LIMA Plan	B
Bats: L	Ht: 6' 2" Wt: 211	PT/Exp	B	Rand Var	+4
		Consist	A	MM	1145

6-22-.242 in 247 PA at WAS. NL's youngest player in 2021 has a building block in ability to put balls in play. Power also showed up in Triple-A (13 HR in 37 games) and xHR confirms MLB total even though Brl%, xPX signal there's still work to do. Speed won't be a factor, but the contact/pop combination at his age is worth tracking. A good start.

Yr	Tm	PA	R	HR	RBI	SB	BA	xHR	xSB	xBA	OBP	SLG	OPS+	vL+	vR+	bb%	ct%	Eye	G	L	F	h%	HctX	QBaB	Brl%	PX	xPX	HR/F	xHR/F	Spd	SBA%	SB%	RAR	BPX	R$
17																																			
18																																			
19	aa	542	68	4	31	11	268		8		292	350	89			3	84	0.20				31				46				128	13%	69%		67	$11
20	WAS	139	18	2	16	1	276	3	2	259	302	366	89	37	106	4	78	0.17	61	23	16	34	82	FFf	5%	55	41	12%	18%	88	6%	50%	-4.6	-24	$9
21	WAS *	401	50	17	42	1	257	7	3	288	300	458	104	105	90	6	81	0.32	56	20	24	28	105	CFd	5%	109	68	13%	15%	93	5%	21%	-5.0	208	$9
1st Half		158	20	9	18	1	277	0	2	272	334	503	117	138	83	8	78	0.39	79	7	14	30	137	FFf	0%	112	50	0%	0%	125	5%	42%	4.0	223	$7
2nd Half		243	29	8	24	0	245	6	2	293	278	430	96	102	90	4	83	0.27	55	21	25	26	105	CFd	6%	106	69	14%	14%	85	5%	0%	-6.7	208	$6
22	Proj	595	74	14	58	4	265	15	5	268	300	401	95	79	101	5	81	0.26	54	22	24	31	96		5%	77	58	13%	13%	90	5%	48%	0.1	74	$17

Gardner,Brett

Age: 38	Pos: CF LF	Health	A	LIMA Plan	D+
Bats: L	Ht: 5' 11" Wt: 195	PT/Exp	A	Rand Var	+1
		Consist	B	MM	2313

While a strong bb% is his core skill, it used to marry well with a good Eye and excellent Spd. But green light evaporated and at 38, the bags probably won't return. That leaves us with a part-time ground-ball hitter with eroding QBaB and BA/xBA, without the power to pick up the slack. May be in for a slight R$ rebound, but this is nearing the end.

Yr	Tm	PA	R	HR	RBI	SB	BA	xHR	xSB	xBA	OBP	SLG	OPS+	vL+	vR+	bb%	ct%	Eye	G	L	F	h%	HctX	QBaB	Brl%	PX	xPX	HR/F	xHR/F	Spd	SBA%	SB%	RAR	BPX	R$
17	NYY	682	96	21	63	23	264	13	11	266	350	428	106	80	112	11	79	0.59	44	22	33	30	92	DCc	4%	89	79	13%	8%	124	15%	82%	7.4	148	$23
18	NYY	609	95	12	45	16	236	9	17	247	322	368	93	83	94	11	80	0.61	49	18	33	27	81	CCd	3%	75	58	8%	6%	155	12%	89%	0.0	163	$15
19	NYY	550	86	28	74	10	251	11	10	275	325	503	115	91	122	9	78	0.48	44	18	38	27	92	CBd	4%	125	80	19%	8%	131	10%	83%	15.3	267	$18
20	NYY	158	20	5	15	3	223	4	3	233	354	392	99	59	107	16	73	0.74	37	23	41	27	99	CCc	5%	95	137	13%	11%	107	13%	50%	-1.7	140	$9
21	NYY	461	47	10	39	4	222	8	10	229	327	362	95	89	97	13	74	0.60	45	18	37	27	88	DCf	3%	83	82	9%	7%	117	3%	100%	-9.5	100	$4
1st Half		208	19	3	11	1	200	2	4	209	314	318	88	75	92	15	71	0.59	40	19	41	26	81	DBf	3%	75	59	6%	4%	119	3%	100%	-8.9	46	-$4
2nd Half		253	28	7	28	3	240	6	6	244	337	396	99	100	99	13	76	0.61	49	17	34	28	93	DDf	3%	89	99	12%	11%	108	3%	100%	-2.4	138	$7
22	Proj	280	35	7	27	4	231	6	3	233	334	378	97	83	101	13	75	0.62	44	19	37	28	90		4%	85	91	10%	8%	117	6%	75%	1.5	103	$7

Garlick,Kyle

Age: 30	Pos: OF	Health	F	LIMA Plan	D
Bats: R	Ht: 6' 1" Wt: 210	PT/Exp	F	Rand Var	0
		Consist	F	MM	4301

Hernia ended his season in early June. Relative playing time spike came more out of necessity than skills improvement. All-or-nothing power is the only draw as a weak Eye, modest HctX, and sharp PX/xPX split hold him back. Throw in a short-side platoon issue and this is an MLB 5th outfielder profile. Pass.

Yr	Tm	PA	R	HR	RBI	SB	BA	xHR	xSB	xBA	OBP	SLG	OPS+	vL+	vR+	bb%	ct%	Eye	G	L	F	h%	HctX	QBaB	Brl%	PX	xPX	HR/F	xHR/F	Spd	SBA%	SB%	RAR	BPX	R$
17	aa	290	36	14	34	1	205		3		265	392	89			8	66	0.24				25				117				90	2%	100%		3	$1
18	a/a	416	43	16	43	1	209		2		235	379	82			3	58	0.08				31				133				94	2%	100%		-77	$3
19	LA *	340	45	19	46	1	247	4	1	225	294	508	111	139	79	6	60	0.17	21	21	59	34	108	AAb	21%	178	213	18%	24%	93	4%	52%	-3.6	96	$7
20	PHI	23	0	0	3	0	136	0	0	162	174	182	47	53	55	0	68	0.00	47	20	33	20	110	CBa		41	7	0%	0%	95	0%	0%	-3.0	-252	-$4
21	MIN	107	17	5	10	1	232	8	0	253	280	465	102	119	76	6	68	0.19	37	22	41	29	81	CAb	13%	158	107	18%	29%	88	6%	100%	-1.7	142	$0
1st Half		107	17	5	10	1	232	8	0	253	280	465	104	121	77	6	68	0.19	37	22	41	29	81	CAb	13%	158	107	18%	29%	88	6%	100%	-2.2	142	-$1
2nd Half																									0%										
22	Proj	175	24	7	19	1	226	11	1	224	275	417	94	109	71	6	64	0.17	37	22	41	31	73		12%	136	96	16%	26%	89	6%	88%	-2.5	-10	$4

Garver,Mitch

Age: 31	Pos: CA	Health	D	LIMA Plan	C+
Bats: R	Ht: 6' 1" Wt: 220	PT/Exp	D	Rand Var	-1
		Consist	F	MM	4133

13-34-.256 in 243 PA at MIN. Toss out 2020 (like we all want to do) and let's compare 2021 to 2019. Drops in ct%, PX, and HR/F look like standard regression, fall vL highlights instability of platoon splits. Otherwise, this is a pure power profile with a flyball lean that is buoyed by HctX, QBaB, and xPX. While 2019 is likely the peak... Mash away, Mitch.

Yr	Tm	PA	R	HR	RBI	SB	BA	xHR	xSB	xBA	OBP	SLG	OPS+	vL+	vR+	bb%	ct%	Eye	G	L	F	h%	HctX	QBaB	Brl%	PX	xPX	HR/F	xHR/F	Spd	SBA%	SB%	RAR	BPX	R$
17	MIN *	416	55	15	44	2	255	1	6	254	344	471	111	103	71	12	70	0.46	45	16	39	32	92	CCd	3%	140	95	0%	8%	106	2%	100%	15.3	158	$8
18	MIN	335	38	7	45	0	268	9	3	246	335	414	100	83	106	9	76	0.40	40	23	38	33	114	CCd	6%	95	122	8%	10%	108	0%	0%	12.3	107	$7
19	MIN	359	70	31	67	0	273	26	1	278	365	630	138	163	124	11	72	0.47	39	14	47	28	118	ABd	16%	186	159	29%	24%	91	0%	0%	38.2	330	$15
20	MIN	81	8	2	5	0	167	2	0	150	247	264	68	107	49	9	49	0.19	39	22	39	30	82	AAf	8%	79	78	14%	14%	103	0%	0%	-5.1	-364	-$2
21	MIN *	271	32	13	35	1	247	17	0	242	341	479	113	100	136	12	65	0.41	31	23	46	32	122	AAc	17%	157	183	21%	27%	61	3%	50%	9.2	119	$6
1st Half		135	17	8	17	0	224	9	0	246	333	500	116	107	123	14	61	0.42	35	21	44	29	92	BAc	15%	196	151	26%	29%	69	3%	0%	4.9	200	$1
2nd Half		136	15	5	18	1	270	8	0	237	349	458	109	90	149	11	69	0.39	27	25	48	35	156	AAc	19%	123	217	16%	25%	69	3%	50%	4.6	73	$2
22	Proj	420	57	22	60	1	261	24	3	252	350	506	116	114	117	11	70	0.42	35	21	44	32	117		14%	153	155	19%	21%	82	3%	55%	26.3	164	$15

PAUL SPORER

Giménez,Andrés

Age: 23	Pos: SS 2B	Health	A	LIMA Plan	C
Bats: L	Ht: 5' 11" Wt: 161	PT/Exp	B	Rand Var	0
		Consist	B	MM	2513

5-16-.218 with 11 SB in 210 PA at CLE. Change of scenery didn't help, as 1st half ct% loss and h% regression tanked BA/OBP. But 2nd half was more promising. HctX, xPX gains show power potential and steady SBA% is sign of management's faith in his wheels. Still-young, steals are enough to drive value while we wait for further growth.

Yr	Tm	PA	R	HR	RBI	SB	BA	xHR	xSB	xBA	OBP	SLG	OPS+	vL+	vR+	bb%	ct%	Eye	G	L	F	h%	HctX	QBaB	Brl%	PX	xPX	HR/F	xHR/F	Spd	SBA%	SB%	RAR	BPX	R$
17																																			
18	aa	145	16	0	14	9	250		2		291	321	82			5	82	0.33				30				52				101	36%	73%		47	$
19	aa	456	54	9	37	28	235		19		276	363	88			5	74	0.21				30				74				124	47%	64%		11	$1
20	NYM	132	22	3	12	8	263	2	10	237	333	398	97	96	98	5	76	0.25	45	21	34	32	64	DCf	3%	70	35	10%	7%	177	25%	89%	-0.7	108	$1
21	CLE *	428	45	12	38	17	232	5	12	222	269	382	89	78	89	5	70	0.17	50	13	38	30	83	DDf	4%	99	86	10%	10%	112	26%	79%	-14.5	23	$1
1st Half		245	24	8	22	7	207	2	6	209	236	364	84	81	72	4	69	0.12	44	12	44	26	77	FDf	5%	103	79	9%	9%	105	26%	75%	-13.4	-4	$
2nd Half		183	21	4	17	10	269	3	7	229	314	408	98	74	100	6	73	0.24	53	13	34	35	89	DDf	2%	92	90	11%	11%	118	26%	81%	-0.1	54	$
22	**Proj**	**350**	**41**	**9**	**29**	**19**	**246**	**8**	**14**	**227**	**308**	**389**	**95**	**86**	**96**	**5**	**74**	**0.21**	**48**	**15**	**37**	**31**	**79**		**4%**	**88**	**73**	**10%**	**9%**	**141**	**21%**	**81%**	**-4.0**	**53**	**$1**

Goldschmidt,Paul

Age: 34	Pos: 1B	Health	A	LIMA Plan	D+
Bats: R	Ht: 6' 3" Wt: 220	PT/Exp	A	Rand Var	-1
		Consist	B	MM	4345

Has clearly established that sometimes h% will inflate BA to valuable heights, but xBA says safe bet is to target .265. And while he still has skill to exceed SB expectations, age and SBA% make return to single digits likely. On the other hand, xHR correctly called power rebound a year ago, so don't dismiss bullish 2021 mark lest you miss out on... UP: 40 HR

Yr	Tm	PA	R	HR	RBI	SB	BA	xHR	xSB	xBA	OBP	SLG	OPS+	vL+	vR+	bb%	ct%	Eye	G	L	F	h%	HctX	QBaB	Brl%	PX	xPX	HR/F	xHR/F	Spd	SBA%	SB%	RAR	BPX	R$
17	ARI	664	117	36	120	18	297	38	11	284	404	563	132	137	127	14	74	0.64	46	19	35	35	132	ACb	13%	154	160	25%	26%	108	12%	78%	34.7	242	$3
18	ARI	689	95	33	83	7	290	43	16	267	389	533	124	128	119	13	71	0.52	39	25	36	36	121	BBc	14%	153	139	22%	28%	120	6%	64%	35.7	233	$2
19	STL	680	97	34	97	3	260	39	8	251	346	476	114	134	108	11	72	0.47	38	22	39	30	119	BBb	11%	116	140	20%	23%	101	2%	75%	4.2	137	$2
20	STL	230	31	6	21	1	304	11	2	264	417	466	117	134	114	16	77	0.86	35	28	38	37	88	CCc	11%	97	114	11%	20%	99	1%	100%	6.5	204	$1
21	STL	679	102	31	99	12	294	49	5	269	365	514	121	145	115	10	77	0.49	36	24	40	33	131	ABc	14%	125	141	16%	26%	101	7%	100%	16.6	238	$3
1st Half		345	43	12	44	5	256	22	2	249	322	422	103	89	107	8	77	0.40	39	22	38	30	129	ABc	12%	95	130	13%	24%	104	7%	100%	-8.6	131	$2
2nd Half		334	59	19	55	7	334	27	3	291	410	614	139	202	122	12	78	0.59	33	25	42	38	133	ABb	15%	157	153	20%	28%	96	7%	100%	32.1	350	$4
22	**Proj**	**665**	**100**	**29**	**91**	**8**	**288**	**43**	**9**	**265**	**376**	**506**	**120**	**143**	**114**	**12**	**76**	**0.57**	**37**	**24**	**39**	**34**	**120**		**13%**	**127**	**138**	**17%**	**25%**	**97**	**6%**	**91%**	**39.2**	**221**	**$3**

Gomes,Yan

Age: 34	Pos: CA	Health	B	LIMA Plan	C+
Bats: R	Ht: 6' 2" Wt: 215	PT/Exp	B	Rand Var	+1
		Consist	B	MM	3333

Maintained 2020's ct% increase, proving that sometimes old dogs can learn new tricks. That has put recent xBA at best levels since 2013-14, and moved BA out of liability territory, and both would be helped further by return to plus power suggested by xPX. If he can find his way back to 425+ PA, not unreasonable to think 20 HR is once again in play.

Yr	Tm	PA	R	HR	RBI	SB	BA	xHR	xSB	xBA	OBP	SLG	OPS+	vL+	vR+	bb%	ct%	Eye	G	L	F	h%	HctX	QBaB	Brl%	PX	xPX	HR/F	xHR/F	Spd	SBA%	SB%	RAR	BPX	R$
17	CLE	383	43	14	56	0	232	11	5	223	309	399	96	115	86	8	71	0.31	41	17	42	29	84	DBd	6%	103	109	14%	11%	74	0%	0%	-2.2	21	$
18	CLE	435	52	16	48	0	266	20	2	251	313	449	102	111	97	5	70	0.18	32	27	41	34	112	CAb	8%	125	142	14%	17%	96	0%	0%	15.5	73	$1
19	WAS	358	36	12	43	2	223	13	1	230	316	389	97	122	89	11	73	0.45	39	19	42	27	83	CAc	7%	94	91	12%	13%	82	2%	100%	3.2	59	$
20	WAS	119	14	4	13	1	284	4	1	262	319	468	105	126	97	5	80	0.27	36	24	40	33	101	BAc	6%	99	93	11%	11%	118	4%	100%	3.9	184	$
21	2 TM	375	49	14	52	0	252	16	3	260	301	421	99	121	88	5	78	0.24	39	25	36	29	111	BCc	9%	95	118	14%	16%	88	0%	0%	0.4	96	$
1st Half		211	26	8	30	0	260	8	2	270	313	434	104	135	92	5	79	0.27	47	24	29	29	113	CCc	8%	94	96	18%	18%	94	0%	0%	2.1	123	$
2nd Half		164	23	6	22	0	242	8	1	248	287	405	94	109	81	5	76	0.22	27	27	45	28	109	AAb	10%	95	147	11%	15%	82	0%	0%	-1.3	62	$
22	**Proj**	**350**	**44**	**14**	**45**	**1**	**253**	**15**	**1**	**256**	**305**	**438**	**101**	**121**	**92**	**6**	**77**	**0.28**	**36**	**24**	**40**	**29**	**103**		**8%**	**105**	**115**	**14%**	**15%**	**91**	**2%**	**100%**	**8.9**	**99**	**$1**

Gonzalez,Erik

Age: 30	Pos: 3B	Health	D	LIMA Plan	F
Bats: R	Ht: 6' 3" Wt: 210	PT/Exp	D	Rand Var	+5
		Consist	A	MM	1111

2-21-.232 in 229 PA at PIT. New career highs in ct%, GB% suggest perhaps a bitter, all-consuming vendetta against worms? A love of watching acrobatic infield glovework in action? Hasn't led to success at the plate, because apart from mild value vL, he's unrosterable. When PIT removes you from their 40-man, it might be time to find a new career path.

Yr	Tm	PA	R	HR	RBI	SB	BA	xHR	xSB	xBA	OBP	SLG	OPS+	vL+	vR+	bb%	ct%	Eye	G	L	F	h%	HctX	QBaB	Brl%	PX	xPX	HR/F	xHR/F	Spd	SBA%	SB%	RAR	BPX	R$
17	CLE *	281	34	9	21	5	236	4	3	239	260	385	88	81	98	3	66	0.09	58	21	22	33	85	CFa	9%	97	94	25%	25%	136	15%	61%	-14.6	-30	$
18	CLE	143	17	1	16	3	265	2	3	257	301	375	91	75	100	3	75	0.15	55	22	23	35	108	BFc	3%	82	77	4%	9%	106	10%	100%	-1.3	20	$
19	PIT *	236	19	2	13	5	219	1	4	212	257	287	75	102	77	5	68	0.16	56	20	24	32	64	CFf	3%	44	31	4%	4%	147	14%	68%	-14.6	-141	-$
20	PIT	193	14	3	20	2	227	6	3	243	255	359	82	117	69	4	72	0.16	47	23	29	30	95	CFf	7%	91	97	8%	15%	109	16%	40%	-12.0	12	$
21	PIT *	275	21	2	23	2	211	4	5	246	241	278	71	103	65	4	80	0.20	62	19	19	26	72	CFc	3%	41	24	6%	12%	119	8%	50%	-23.8	0	-$
1st Half		229	17	2	21	2	232	4	5	249	258	300	78	104	65	4	82	0.20	62	19	19	28	74	CFc	3%	40	24	6%	12%	111	8%	50%	-15.6	8	$
2nd Half		46	4	0	2	0	103	0	0	199	153	165	43	0	0	6	71	0.21	44	20	36	14	0	FFf	0%	43	-22	0%	#DIV/0!	122	8%	0%	-6.2	-115	-$1
22	**Proj**	**105**	**9**	**1**	**9**	**1**	**235**	**2**	**1**	**239**	**267**	**335**	**82**	**93**	**76**	**4**	**74**	**0.16**	**56**	**21**	**23**	**31**	**84**		**4%**	**66**	**58**	**7%**	**12%**	**108**	**8%**	**39%**	**-4.3**	**-76**	**$**

Gonzalez,Marwin

Age: 33	Pos: 2B	Health	B	LIMA Plan	D
Bats: B	Ht: 6' 1" Wt: 205	PT/Exp	B	Rand Var	+4
		Consist	B	MM	2001

Precipitous slides in RAR, BPX, R$ highlight how little skill support there was in 2017, and now ct%, xPX have bottomed out with age. Sometimes big-picture view can give helpful perspective—career .250 xBA, 95 xPX, 12% HR/F aren't much better than what we've seen lately. Hard for him to sink much lower than 2020, but no case for big rebound either.

Yr	Tm	PA	R	HR	RBI	SB	BA	xHR	xSB	xBA	OBP	SLG	OPS+	vL+	vR+	bb%	ct%	Eye	G	L	F	h%	HctX	QBaB	Brl%	PX	xPX	HR/F	xHR/F	Spd	SBA%	SB%	RAR	BPX	R$
17	HOU	515	67	23	90	8	303	14	8	283	377	530	123	107	126	10	78	0.49	44	20	36	35	104	CCf	7%	132	94	18%	11%	83	8%	73%	31.5	194	$2
18	HOU	552	61	16	68	2	247	18	7	246	324	409	98	100	95	10	74	0.42	42	23	36	30	105	CCc	7%	101	123	13%	14%	91	4%	40%	4.1	87	$1
19	MIN	463	52	15	55	1	264	15	3	257	322	414	102	110	98	7	77	0.32	45	24	31	31	110	BCc	6%	81	99	15%	15%	83	1%	100%	-3.1	48	$
20	MIN	199	15	5	22	0	211	7	1	217	286	320	81	68	87	9	77	0.41	41	21	38	25	81	CCc	5%	58	105	10%	13%	83	0%	0%	-9.2	-8	$
21	2 AL	307	30	5	28	3	199	8	0	228	275	304	80	97	72	7	72	0.26	49	21	30	26	82	CDf	5%	73	67	9%	14%	63	8%	60%	-19.3	-77	$
1st Half		240	22	2	18	3	210	5	0	239	289	304	82	109	72	7	73	0.28	46	25	29	28	87	CDf	4%	71	76	4%	11%	62	8%	75%	-14.8	-58	$
2nd Half		67	8	3	10	0	161	3	0	191	224	306	72	70	73	6	66	0.19	61	7	32	18	66	DDf	6%	81	33	23%	23%	91	8%	0%	-6.3	-112	-$
22	**Proj**	**175**	**19**	**5**	**22**	**1**	**212**	**6**	**2**	**222**	**281**	**348**	**85**	**86**	**85**	**7**	**73**	**0.29**	**49**	**18**	**33**	**26**	**86**		**6%**	**81**	**78**	**14%**	**16%**	**84**	**6%**	**40%**	**-5.5**	**-54**	**$**

Goodrum,Niko

Age: 30	Pos: SS	Health	C	LIMA Plan	C+
Bats: B	Ht: 6' 3" Wt: 198	PT/Exp	B	Rand Var	0
		Consist	B	MM	3405

9-33-.214 with 14 SB in 325 PA at DET. Half-season ct% splits suggest free-swinging ways may have finally hit rock bottom, while xHR, xHR/F indicate he might have struck power gold while he was at it. Even if ct% rebound holds, 2018-19 xBA shows BA ceiling is quite low, but if you can live with that, could be in line for... UP: first 20 HR/20 SB season

Yr	Tm	PA	R	HR	RBI	SB	BA	xHR	xSB	xBA	OBP	SLG	OPS+	vL+	vR+	bb%	ct%	Eye	G	L	F	h%	HctX	QBaB	Brl%	PX	xPX	HR/F	xHR/F	Spd	SBA%	SB%	RAR	BPX	R$
17	MIN *	506	66	12	61	10	240	0	6	226	281	383	90	23	22	5	71	0.20	71	0	29	31	124	DCf	0%	90	81	0%	0%	126	17%	56%	-17.2	24	$1
18	DET	492	55	16	53	12	245	18	11	253	315	432	100	104	97	9	70	0.32	44	23	33	31	95	CCb	8%	127	103	16%	17%	114	15%	75%	5.5	120	$1
19	DET	472	61	12	45	12	248	12	11	245	322	421	103	129	94	10	67	0.33	41	28	31	34	93	BCb	6%	109	87	13%	13%	133	14%	80%	-6.4	67	$1
20	DET	179	15	5	20	7	184	6	3	181	263	335	79	140	63	10	56	0.26	36	18	46	29	92	CBd	10%	115	180	12%	14%	109	24%	88%	-8.6	-108	$
21	DET *	384	44	9	34	15	204	14	12	201	275	326	83	101	84	9	63	0.27	42	22	36	29	80	CCb	10%	83	107	13%	21%	115	23%	75%	-19.1	-96	$
1st Half		226	27	5	17	12	213	9	8	181	284	322	85	93	84	9	58	0.24	36	25	39	34	67	CBb	11%	80	105	11%	20%	117	23%	75%	-10.1	-188	$1
2nd Half		158	17	4	17	3	190	5	4	229	263	330	80	116	83	9	71	0.34	51	17	32	24	101	CDb	9%	87	109	18%	23%	111	23%	73%	-8.5	31	-$
22	**Proj**	**490**	**55**	**15**	**50**	**16**	**228**	**18**	**15**	**218**	**301**	**388**	**94**	**117**	**84**	**9**	**65**	**0.29**	**42**	**22**	**36**	**32**	**90**		**9%**	**108**	**117**	**14%**	**17%**	**116**	**18%**	**78%**	**-5.2**	**-2**	**$1**

Goodwin,Brian

Age: 31	Pos: RF CF	Health	C	LIMA Plan	D
Bats: L	Ht: 6' 0" Wt: 200	PT/Exp	B	Rand Var	+3
		Consist	B	MM	3211

8-29-.221 in 271 PA at CHW. Five teams in four seasons proves he's as replaceable as RAR suggests, with 2019 looking like a peak-age outlier. Doesn't make enough contact, and when bat does find ball, HctX and QBaB history say results are unremarkable. Being a lefty hitter who can play CF should keep him employed, but fantasy usefulness is waning.

Yr	Tm	PA	R	HR	RBI	SB	BA	xHR	xSB	xBA	OBP	SLG	OPS+	vL+	vR+	bb%	ct%	Eye	G	L	F	h%	HctX	QBaB	Brl%	PX	xPX	HR/F	xHR/F	Spd	SBA%	SB%	RAR	BPX	R$
17	WAS *	376	48	14	38	8	240	11	4	244	303	445	102	135	103	8	70	0.30	38	19	43	30	96	CBb	9%	135	133	16%	14%	101	12%	86%	-4.8	106	$
18	2 TM *	240	27	8	34	5	223	6	4	224	293	379	90	85	95	9	66	0.29	43	23	34	30	81	CCb	9%	110	83	17%	17%	93	13%	70%	-2.7	-3	$
19	LAA	458	65	17	47	7	262	16	8	242	326	470	110	113	108	8	69	0.29	33	24	43	34	90	CAc	6%	127	126	14%	13%	110	10%	70%	8.5	104	$1
20	2 TM	164	17	6	22	5	215	6	2	226	299	417	95	73	102	10	63	0.31	32	27	41	30	85	BAb	11%	139	96	16%	16%	111	15%	100%	-2.2	68	$1
21	CHW *	363	41	10	36	2	209	8	7	226	294	347	88	46	112	11	69	0.39	37	26	38	27	87	CBc	6%	89	79	12%	12%	86	6%	46%	-15.4	-12	$
1st Half		162	22	5	16	1	212	1	3	226	285	386	93	34	172	9	61	0.26	36	30	34	31	94	CBa	5%	131	92	20%	7%	98	6%	33%	-7.3	-12	$
2nd Half		201	19	5	20	1	206	7	4	229	303	314	84	51	93	12	76	0.57	37	25	39	24	88	CBc	6%	61	75	10%	13%	81	6%	100%	-10.0	12	$
22	**Proj**	**175**	**20**	**6**	**20**	**3**	**221**	**5**	**2**	**232**	**301**	**395**	**94**	**61**	**105**	**10**	**68**	**0.34**	**36**	**26**	**39**	**29**	**89**		**7%**	**114**	**94**	**15%**	**13%**	**97**	**6%**	**72%**	**-2.7**	**23**	**$**

BRANDON KRUSE

Gordon,Nick

Age: 26 Pos: CF
Bats: L Ht: 6' 0" Wt: 160

Health	A	LIMA Plan	C
PT/Exp	D	Rand Var	0
Consist	B	MM	1533

4-23-.240 with 10 SB in 216 PA at MIN. Spent Jun-Aug cementing future MLB role as speedy reserve who hits too many grounders, has negligible power. Then came Sept (.281, 3 HR, 5 SB in 70 PA). Can't forget all that came before, including mediocre contact rates, but speed, HctX are legit enough to place small bet on other pieces falling into place.

Yr	Tm	PA	R	HR	RBI	SB	BA	xHR	xSB	xBA	OBP	SLG	OPS+	vL+	vR+	bb%	ct%	Eye	G	L	F	h%	HctX	QBaB	Brl%	PX	xPX	HR/F	xHR/F	Spd	SBA%	SB%	RAR	BPX	R$
17	aa	567	74	8	61	12	262		8		325	394	98			8	74	0.35				34				83				125	14%	62%		55	$14
18	a/a	572	53	6	42	17	230		11		268	325	80			5	79	0.25				28				58				122	18%	76%		33	$9
19	aaa	307	41	3	33	12	271		6		307	417	100			5	76	0.21				35				94				104	26%	72%		74	$9
20																																			
21	MIN *	292	27	6	30	15	240	7	4	244	284	355	88	71	94	6	74	0.24	52	22	26	30	133	ACa	7%	68	88	11%	18%	133	26%	82%	-9.5	23	$9
1st Half		88	9	2	5	9	311	1	2	265	359	418	108	71	110	7	81	0.39	58	21	21	37	177	BCa	3%	56	71	11%	11%	135	26%	100%	3.9	92	$4
2nd Half		204	18	4	25	6	209	6	3	235	251	327	78	70	88	5	72	0.20	50	22	28	27	117	ACa	8%	74	95	10%	21%	132	26%	66%	-12.1	-8	$3
22	**Proj**	**420**	**44**	**8**	**40**	**19**	**249**	**13**	**16**	**254**	**299**	**378**	**92**	**70**	**98**	**6**	**76**	**0.25**	**53**	**22**	**25**	**31**	**141**		**6%**	**78**	**85**	**11%**	**17%**	**147**	**22%**	**82%**	**-1.8**	**65**	**$13**

Gorman,Nolan

Age: 22 Pos: 2B
Bats: L Ht: 6' 1" Wt: 210

Health	A	LIMA Plan	D
PT/Exp	B	Rand Var	
Consist	F	MM	2313

Prized STL prospect started year at AA and rose to AAA by end of June. Maintained power stroke (25 HR in 119 games), but more importantly, added nearly 10 points to ct% despite stiffer competition. Still doesn't like to take walks, but if move to 2B sticks, it adds to intrigue. MLB debut likely on tap in 2022, so now is the time to get in on ground floor.

Yr	Tm	PA	R	HR	RBI	SB	BA	xHR	xSB	xBA	OBP	SLG	OPS+	vL+	vR+	bb%	ct%	Eye	G	L	F	h%	HctX	QBaB	Brl%	PX	xPX	HR/F	xHR/F	Spd	SBA%	SB%	RAR	BPX	R$
17																																			
18																																			
19																																			
20																																			
21	a/a	505	48	16	51	5	230		5		269	368	87			5	74	0.20				28				81				88	6%	81%		-4	$8
1st Half		210	18	7	20	3	221		2		268	354	87			6	68	0.20				29				81				90	6%	100%		-81	$3
2nd Half		296	30	9	31	2	237		3	241	269	378	88			4	78	0.20	44	20	36	28	0			81	-22	0%		91	6%	65%	-14.6	50	$8
22	**Proj**	**280**	**31**	**10**	**32**	**3**	**231**	**9**	**2**	**233**	**268**	**383**	**88**	**88**	**88**	**5**	**74**	**0.19**	**44**	**20**	**36**	**28**	**97**		**14%**	**88**		**14%**	**13%**	**94**	**6%**	**83%**	**-6.8**	**-8**	**$7**

Gosselin,Phil

Age: 33 Pos: LF 3B 1B
Bats: R Ht: 6' 1" Wt: 188

Health	A	LIMA Plan	D
PT/Exp	B	Rand Var	-3
Consist	A	MM	1101

"Hey, Ohtani wasn't the only Angel to double previous HR career high! Why does he get all the press?" -Phil's mom (probably). Giving 32-year-old journeyman this many PA surely wasn't the plan coming into year, nor should it ever be again. Did whiff less with steadier PT in 2nd half, but not much happened on balls in play. Leave this "blah" bench bat be.

Yr	Tm	PA	R	HR	RBI	SB	BA	xHR	xSB	xBA	OBP	SLG	OPS+	vL+	vR+	bb%	ct%	Eye	G	L	F	h%	HctX	QBaB	Brl%	PX	xPX	HR/F	xHR/F	Spd	SBA%	SB%	RAR	BPX	R$
17	2 TM *	334	23	1	21	2	193	0	4	205	225	242	64	50	49	4	75	0.16	57	14	29	26	51	FCc	0%	34	-19	0%	0%	127	10%	36%	-39.1	-70	-$5
18	CIN *	339	33	5	30	0	192	0	4	239	247	292	72	254	13	7	72	0.26	50	25	25	25	50	DDc	6%	71	66	25%	0%	97	5%	0%	-24.4	-27	-$2
19	PHI *	396	42	6	40	2	244	2	4	234	311	364	93	92	76	9	72	0.35	41	24	35	32	118	CBb	6%	72	86	0%	12%	121	5%	45%	-15.6	11	$4
20	PHI	102	14	3	12	0	250	3	1	250	324	402	96	106	79	10	71	0.37	38	30	33	32	88	BBc	6%	97	98	14%	14%	92	0%	0%	-2.7	40	$4
21	LAA	373	40	7	47	4	261	9	2	218	314	362	93	95	91	6	77	0.30	45	18	37	32	89	CCd	3%	63	93	7%	9%	109	6%	67%	-16.2	15	$8
1st Half		103	9	3	16	0	319	4	1	214	379	468	118	150	92	8	71	0.30	44	17	39	42	65	CDc	6%	97	115	12%	15%	108	6%	0%	2.3	50	$1
2nd Half		270	31	4	31	4	239	5	2	218	289	323	83	72	90	6	78	0.30	45	18	37	29	97	DCd	2%	51	85	6%	7%	108	6%	80%	-16.9	4	$8
22	**Proj**	**140**	**15**	**3**	**16**	**1**	**251**	**3**	**2**	**223**	**311**	**362**	**91**	**100**	**83**	**8**	**74**	**0.31**	**43**	**21**	**36**	**32**	**91**		**5%**	**72**	**95**	**8%**	**10%**	**102**	**6%**	**49%**	**-2.3**	**-51**	**$3**

Grandal,Yasmani

Age: 33 Pos: CA
Bats: B Ht: 6' 2" Wt: 230

Health	C	LIMA Plan	B
PT/Exp	A	Rand Var	0
Consist	C	MM	4125

23-62-.240 in 375 PA at CHW. Even with seven-week IL stint for torn knee tendon, remained an OBP league deity. Early struggles largely h%-driven; HctX, PX, xPX all confirm he still packs a wallop, so some 1B/DH time should keep coming. Injury risk will always loom due to age, rigors of position, but spot in upper echelon of CA power bats pretty firm.

Yr	Tm	PA	R	HR	RBI	SB	BA	xHR	xSB	xBA	OBP	SLG	OPS+	vL+	vR+	bb%	ct%	Eye	G	L	F	h%	HctX	QBaB	Brl%	PX	xPX	HR/F	xHR/F	Spd	SBA%	SB%	RAR	BPX	R$
17	LA *	482	50	22	58	0	247	15	6	239	308	459	104	90	106	8	70	0.31	44	16	40	30	104	CCd	7%	134	125	18%	12%	68	1%	0%	8.1	85	$8
18	LA	518	65	24	68	2	241	26	1	248	349	466	109	96	111	14	72	0.58	41	17	42	28	108	CBd	12%	139	140	18%	20%	64	2%	67%	26.9	160	$13
19	MIL	632	79	28	77	5	246	28	4	259	380	468	117	129	112	17	73	0.78	39	23	38	28	115	BBc	11%	120	133	20%	20%	78	3%	83%	36.4	178	$15
20	CHW	194	27	8	27	0	230	7	1	222	351	422	103	118	99	15	64	0.52	36	23	41	31	109	BBc	8%	125	161	19%	16%	67	0%	0%	3.7	36	$11
21	CHW *	410	64	24	64	0	239	21	0	247	408	498	124	142	125	22	69	0.92	41	19	40	27	120	ACd	13%	150	153	28%	26%	59	0%	0%	24.9	227	$11
1st Half		243	42	14	38	0	190	13	0	229	388	441	116	149	105	25	65	0.95	43	16	41	19	110	ABd	15%	149	142	29%	27%	70	0%	0%	7.6	204	$11
2nd Half		167	22	10	26	0	305	7	0	276	433	574	136	130	163	18	74	0.87	38	23	39	35	133	ACf	11%	153	170	28%	22%	61	0%	0%	18.2	288	$9
22	**Proj**	**490**	**70**	**26**	**72**	**1**	**242**	**23**	**1**	**249**	**379**	**484**	**117**	**119**	**116**	**18**	**70**	**0.72**	**39**	**21**	**40**	**28**	**117**		**11%**	**145**	**152**	**24%**	**21%**	**61**	**1%**	**75%**	**31.3**	**167**	**$16**

Greene,Riley

Age: 21 Pos: OF
Bats: L Ht: 6' 3" Wt: 200

Health	A	LIMA Plan	C
PT/Exp	B	Rand Var	
Consist	F	MM	3503

At tender age of 20, elite DET prospect's first tour of high minors went well, with power developing as expected, and SB success hinting at tantalizing five-category potential. Walk rate encouraging, too, so it's just strikeouts that may delay launch into stardom. Even if there's short-term BA drag, contributions could come quick, only rise over time.

Yr	Tm	PA	R	HR	RBI	SB	BA	xHR	xSB	xBA	OBP	SLG	OPS+	vL+	vR+	bb%	ct%	Eye	G	L	F	h%	HctX	QBaB	Brl%	PX	xPX	HR/F	xHR/F	Spd	SBA%	SB%	RAR	BPX	R$
17																																			
18																																			
19																																			
20																																			
21	a/a	536	79	20	70	13	284		9		352	489	116			10	68	0.33				38				128				130	10%	93%		131	$24
1st Half		214	30	7	23	8	261		4		331	425	105			9	68	0.32				35				101				132	10%	88%		46	$14
2nd Half		321	48	12	46	5	296		5	250	361	525	120			9	68	0.32	44	20	36	40	0			144	-22	0%		138	10%	100%	15.5	185	$26
22	**Proj**	**385**	**56**	**10**	**50**	**9**	**268**	**10**	**8**	**226**	**334**	**436**	**105**	**104**	**105**	**9**	**68**	**0.31**	**44**	**20**	**36**	**37**	**98**		**6%**	**108**		**12%**	**12%**	**137**	**11%**	**93%**	**9.8**	**69**	**$16**

Gregorius,Didi

Age: 32 Pos: SS
Bats: L Ht: 6' 3" Wt: 205

Health	D	LIMA Plan	C+
PT/Exp	B	Rand Var	+4
Consist	D	MM	1223

Pain diagnosed as arthritic condition in surgically repaired elbow that arose in mid-April; injury—and meds to treat it—dogged him all year. Off-season surgery being mulled, but hadn't happened as of this writing. HctX, xPX were already trending in wrong direction, and now may accelerate. Too much risk, too little upside... DN: 250 PA, single-digit HR

Yr	Tm	PA	R	HR	RBI	SB	BA	xHR	xSB	xBA	OBP	SLG	OPS+	vL+	vR+	bb%	ct%	Eye	G	L	F	h%	HctX	QBaB	Brl%	PX	xPX	HR/F	xHR/F	Spd	SBA%	SB%	RAR	BPX	R$
17	NYY	569	73	25	87	3	287	10	7	274	318	478	108	88	113	4	87	0.36	36	20	44	29	81	DBc	4%	96	67	12%	5%	97	3%	75%	13.6	194	$20
18	NYY	569	89	27	86	10	268	14	5	282	335	494	111	101	113	8	86	0.70	39	20	42	26	114	CBc	5%	114	100	15%	8%	110	12%	63%	25.4	293	$23
19	NYY *	369	48	16	62	2	227	11	5	257	263	416	94	102	98	5	84	0.31	38	18	44	23	100	CAd	6%	88	99	13%	9%	97	5%	67%	-12.3	174	$7
20	PHI	237	34	10	40	3	284	5	3	273	339	488	110	93	117	6	87	0.54	36	21	43	29	102	FBd	4%	97	81	12%	6%	118	9%	60%	6.7	300	$25
21	PHI	408	35	13	54	3	209	8	4	240	270	370	88	76	92	6	82	0.37	37	18	45	22	81	DAf	2%	86	66	9%	6%	94	4%	100%	-15.8	146	$3
1st Half		136	11	5	23	1	232	2	1	226	272	392	92	81	96	5	78	0.21	36	17	47	26	70	DAf	2%	90	51	11%	4%	92	4%	100%	-4.0	81	$1
2nd Half		272	24	8	31	2	198	6	3	247	268	358	85	72	89	7	84	0.49	37	18	45	20	87	DBd	2%	84	73	9%	7%	97	4%	100%	-12.5	188	$3
22	**Proj**	**420**	**49**	**12**	**65**	**4**	**237**	**9**	**3**	**241**	**291**	**386**	**92**	**82**	**95**	**6**	**84**	**0.40**	**37**	**19**	**44**	**26**	**91**		**3%**	**79**	**77**	**8%**	**6%**	**98**	**5%**	**74%**	**-6.6**	**138**	**$11**

Grichuk,Randal

Age: 30 Pos: CF RF
Bats: R Ht: 6' 2" Wt: 216

Health	A	LIMA Plan	C+
PT/Exp	A	Rand Var	+1
Consist	B	MM	3123

In 1st half, looked like same ol' Randal: acceptable BA, power that might scare up 30 HR with enough PA. But slumped badly in July-Aug (.180 BA) as exit velocity, Brl%, xPX all plummeted; perhaps an unreported injury? Hit .273 in P/T play in September (only 55 AB) which gives hope he'll get back on track, but he may have a harder time finding full-time role.

Yr	Tm	PA	R	HR	RBI	SB	BA	xHR	xSB	xBA	OBP	SLG	OPS+	vL+	vR+	bb%	ct%	Eye	G	L	F	h%	HctX	QBaB	Brl%	PX	xPX	HR/F	xHR/F	Spd	SBA%	SB%	RAR	BPX	R$
17	STL *	511	63	27	69	6	236	25	5	249	279	478	103	89	105	6	67	0.18	36	21	43	29	109	CBc	16%	154	152	18%	21%	107	8%	86%	-10.3	109	$11
18	TOR	462	60	25	61	3	245	28	4	260	301	502	108	107	106	6	71	0.22	35	18	47	29	96	BAf	14%	167	136	18%	20%	90	6%	60%	4.4	197	$13
19	TOR	628	75	31	80	2	232	27	6	247	280	457	102	109	98	6	72	0.21	39	19	42	27	93	BBf	9%	122	93	17%	15%	119	3%	67%	-15.2	130	$12
20	TOR	231	38	12	35	1	273	11	1	262	312	481	105	124	97	6	77	0.27	41	22	37	30	109	CCf	11%	110	95	19%	18%	94	4%	50%	1.9	156	$23
21	TOR	545	59	22	81	0	241	23	3	239	281	423	97	100	96	5	78	0.24	40	17	43	27	107	BBf	8%	103	99	13%	13%	87	3%	0%	-16.5	119	$11
1st Half		323	35	14	54	0	262	15	2	252	291	456	104	120	99	4	77	0.17	40	20	40	30	111	ABd	11%	111	107	15%	16%	91	3%	0%	-6.3	123	$20
2nd Half		222	24	8	27	0	208	8	1	219	266	371	86	76	91	7	79	0.36	39	13	48	22	101	CAf	5%	91	86	10%	10%	84	3%	0%	-12.0	119	$2
22	**Proj**	**420**	**53**	**20**	**59**	**1**	**241**	**19**	**2**	**245**	**286**	**444**	**99**	**102**	**97**	**6**	**76**	**0.25**	**39**	**18**	**43**	**27**	**103**		**10%**	**116**	**101**	**15%**	**15%**	**90**	**4%**	**43%**	**2.4**	**99**	**$12**

KRIS OLSON

Grisham,Trent

Age: 25	Pos: CF	Health	B	LIMA Plan	B
Bats: L	Ht: 5' 11" Wt: 224	PT/Exp	A	Rand Var	+1
		Consist	B	MM	3225

Played well despite lower half injuries in first half, but pronounced second half swoon makes us wonder if the boo-boos finally got to him. Although lack of FB and contact rate cap HR and BA ceilings, 2020 metrics said there's a potentially valuable power/speed profile lurking. At 25, a full healthy season would help determine if that was aberration or floor.

Yr	Tm	PA	R	HR	RBI	SB	BA	xHR	xSB	xBA	OBP	SLG	OPS+	vL+	vR+	bb%	ct%	Eye	G	L	F	h%	HctX	QBaB	Brl%	PX	xPX	HR/F	xHR/F	Spd	SBA%	SB%	RAR	BPX	R$
17																																			
18	aa	394	42	7	29	10	225		7		341	330	90			15	72	0.62				29				67				116	11%	76%		27	$
19	MIL *	613	87	31	87	12	267	4	10	262	364	520	122	99	101	13	75	0.62	38	19	43	30	94	CBc	5%	129	90	13%	8%	86	11%	68%	33.8	219	$2
20	SD	251	42	10	26	10	251	13	5	247	352	456	107	98	110	12	70	0.48	41	25	34	31	95	DCf	11%	116	111	20%	26%	111	16%	91%	3.2	136	$2
21	SD	527	61	15	62	13	242	13	11	249	327	413	102	112	98	10	74	0.45	41	22	37	30	90	CCf	5%	106	95	12%	10%	72	14%	72%	-8.5	100	$1
1st Half		231	30	10	30	7	272	7	5	257	359	505	120	125	119	12	71	0.47	40	20	40	34	107	BCf	7%	143	118	18%	13%	88	14%	78%	8.3	200	$1
2nd Half		296	31	5	32	6	219	6	6	243	302	342	87	103	82	9	77	0.44	42	23	35	27	77	DCd	4%	79	79	7%	9%	65	14%	67%	-13.6	38	$
22	Proj	525	70	17	61	14	246	17	10	245	341	428	104	109	103	12	74	0.50	41	22	38	30	92		6%	108	97	14%	13%	81	10%	77%	12.3	152	$1

Groshans,Jordan

Age: 22	Pos: 3B SS	Health	A	LIMA Plan	D
Bats: R	Ht: 6' 3" Wt: 205	PT/Exp	D	Rand Var	0
		Consist	F	MM	3011

The 2018 first-rounder and TOR prospect spent all of 2021 at AA and hit well. Plate discipline and bat-to-ball skills stand out more than actual power for now. Bat plays at SS but may be better suited defensively at 3B, where he'll need to turn those doubles into homers to stick.

Yr	Tm	PA	R	HR	RBI	SB	BA	xHR	xSB	xBA	OBP	SLG	OPS+	vL+	vR+	bb%	ct%	Eye	G	L	F	h%	HctX	QBaB	Brl%	PX	xPX	HR/F	xHR/F	Spd	SBA%	SB%	RAR	BPX	R$
17																																			
18																																			
19																																			
20																																			
21	aa	303	35	6	30	0	255		3		317	390	97			8	76	0.37				32				92				85	0%	0%		77	$4
1st Half		154	19	4	17	0	219		1		275	352	87			7	74	0.29				27				84				99	0%	0%		35	-$
2nd Half		149	15	2	13	0	294		2	248	361	431	107			9	78	0.47	44	20	36	37	0			99	-22	0%		95	0%	0%	2.0	150	$0
22	Proj	175	19	4	17	0	252	4	1	236	313	401	97	96	97	8	73	0.33	42	20	38	32	91		5%	104		8%	8%	95	2%	0%	0.0	24	$4

Grossman,Robbie

Age: 32	Pos: LF RF	Health	A	LIMA Plan	B
Bats: B	Ht: 6' 0" Wt: 216	PT/Exp	A	Rand Var	-1
		Consist	B	MM	3325

Solidified 2020 gains (which pro-rated nicely to 2021) and unlocked post-peak power by maximizing fly ball rate, launch angle, and PT, resulting in full season breakout. Skills, expected stats backed increased output, but regression will most likely drag counting stats downward. We've seen his career year—at 32, don't overpay for the next step.

Yr	Tm	PA	R	HR	RBI	SB	BA	xHR	xSB	xBA	OBP	SLG	OPS+	vL+	vR+	bb%	ct%	Eye	G	L	F	h%	HctX	QBaB	Brl%	PX	xPX	HR/F	xHR/F	Spd	SBA%	SB%	RAR	BPX	R$
17	MIN	456	62	9	45	3	246	8	8	262	361	380	101	94	102	15	79	0.85	41	25	34	29	99	DCc	3%	81	83	9%	8%	90	3%	75%	-9.4	121	$6
18	MIN	465	50	5	48	0	273	7	5	247	367	384	101	117	91	13	79	0.72	39	24	37	33	92	CBb	2%	77	59	4%	6%	103	1%	0%	3.7	120	$8
19	OAK	482	57	6	38	9	240	8	3	250	334	348	94	76	96	12	80	0.69	41	25	34	29	95	CCc	2%	60	81	5%	7%	104	10%	69%	-15.6	89	$7
20	OAK	192	23	8	23	8	241	6	3	275	344	482	110	59	117	11	77	0.55	39	23	38	27	88	CBc	5%	134	98	16%	12%	95	20%	89%	0.0	272	$19
21	DET	671	88	23	67	20	239	24	23	229	357	415	106	117	101	15	72	0.63	29	24	46	29	81	CAb	8%	104	105	12%	13%	111	13%	80%	-8.1	138	$21
1st Half		351	40	10	36	10	224	13	12	219	343	383	101	120	94	15	71	0.60	30	23	47	28	82	CAb	8%	97	107	10%	13%	104	13%	77%	-9.3	88	$18
2nd Half		320	48	13	31	10	255	11	11	243	373	449	111	114	110	15	74	0.67	28	26	46	30	79	DAb	7%	112	103	14%	12%	112	13%	83%	3.0	192	$23
22	Proj	560	73	17	58	15	245	16	13	243	353	416	104	105	104	14	75	0.64	34	24	41	29	86		6%	101	94	11%	11%	103	11%	81%	8.9	163	$19

Guerrero Jr.,Vladimir

Age: 23	Pos: 1B DH	Health	A	LIMA Plan	C
Bats: R	Ht: 6' 2" Wt: 250	PT/Exp	A	Rand Var	-2
		Consist	C	MM	4155

Boy, that escalated quickly! Massive breakout supported across the board by rock-solid skills. Lack of loft suppressed prior expectations, but launch angle improved... and still has room for more. That's...terrifying. A touch of regression likely as he maximized PAs and outperformed xPX. But, UP: 55+ HR? Welcome to the first round, Vlad.

Yr	Tm	PA	R	HR	RBI	SB	BA	xHR	xSB	xBA	OBP	SLG	OPS+	vL+	vR+	bb%	ct%	Eye	G	L	F	h%	HctX	QBaB	Brl%	PX	xPX	HR/F	xHR/F	Spd	SBA%	SB%	RAR	BPX	R$
17																																			
18	a/a	378	59	19	71	3	383		6		438	634	144			9	89	0.89				39				133				86	5%	48%		360	$25
19	TOR *	548	58	18	76	1	277	18	5	259	343	448	109	89	113	9	81	0.53	50	17	33	31	98	BDd	8%	88	90	12%	15%	80	1%	48%	6.4	144	$13
20	TOR	243	34	9	33	1	262	9	1	283	329	462	105	116	101	8	83	0.53	55	17	28	28	130	AFc	9%	103	72	18%	18%	96	2%	100%	-1.1	244	$19
21	TOR	698	123	48	111	4	311	49	4	299	401	601	138	129	141	12	82	0.78	45	19	36	31	140	ACd	15%	146	128	27%	27%	84	2%	80%	56.5	369	$40
1st Half		350	66	27	69	2	337	23	2	317	440	673	155	125	164	15	80	0.85	46	21	33	35	138	ADc	16%	174	128	35%	29%	88	2%	67%	42.6	446	$48
2nd Half		348	57	21	42	2	287	26	2	280	362	532	121	129	118	10	84	0.70	44	17	39	28	141	ACd	15%	121	129	20%	25%	83	2%	100%	10.8	308	$29
22	Proj	665	102	37	101	3	300	37	4	288	376	546	125	119	127	10	83	0.67	48	18	34	31	129		12%	127	110	22%	22%	76	3%	74%	48.2	289	$34

Gurriel Jr.,Lourdes

Age: 28	Pos: LF	Health	B	LIMA Plan	B
Bats: R	Ht: 6' 4" Wt: 215	PT/Exp	A	Rand Var	0
		Consist	C	MM	4145

Played through early-season knee issues, achieving career highs in most counting stats. Combines above-average ct% with solid quality of contact to produce plenty of barrels despite ground ball tendencies. Robust xHR/F history, elite exit velocity in second half, decent speed, peak age hint at a high BA/HR extra gear, to the tune of... UP: 30 HR/.300 BA

Yr	Tm	PA	R	HR	RBI	SB	BA	xHR	xSB	xBA	OBP	SLG	OPS+	vL+	vR+	bb%	ct%	Eye	G	L	F	h%	HctX	QBaB	Brl%	PX	xPX	HR/F	xHR/F	Spd	SBA%	SB%	RAR	BPX	R$
17	aa	178	17	4	23	2	220		2		257	340	81			5	80	0.25				26				74				83	6%	100%		48	$0
18	TOR *	475	52	17	71	4	276	11	6	253	299	432	98	109	96	3	77	0.14	43	24	33	33	86	ACb	8%	92	92	17%	17%	108	8%	44%	-3.0	67	$15
19	TOR *	468	66	23	71	6	268	20	5	260	303	508	112	138	110	5	74	0.20	39	18	43	31	112	BBf	11%	133	145	20%	20%	117	14%	49%	-0.2	185	$16
20	TOR	224	28	11	33	3	308	10	4	282	348	534	117	108	120	6	77	0.29	41	26	33	36	94	ACd	12%	127	91	20%	19%	102	8%	75%	8.1	216	$26
21	TOR	541	62	21	84	1	276	26	7	267	319	466	108	101	111	6	80	0.31	45	21	34	31	106	BCc	10%	106	93	15%	19%	108	3%	25%	-4.6	188	$18
1st Half		289	30	9	33	1	259	11	3	248	278	416	97	90	100	3	78	0.14	47	18	35	30	91	CCd	7%	93	67	12%	14%	96	3%	33%	-11.8	96	$12
2nd Half		252	32	12	51	0	296	15	4	290	365	527	121	116	122	10	81	0.56	43	24	33	32	124	ACb	13%	121	124	20%	25%	123	3%	0%	9.2	304	$18
22	Proj	560	69	26	90	4	281	29	4	272	326	498	112	112	111	6	78	0.30	43	22	35	32	105		11%	122	107	18%	20%	102	5%	51%	19.3	159	$24

Gurriel,Yuli

Age: 38	Pos: 1B	Health	B	LIMA Plan	B
Bats: R	Ht: 6' 0" Wt: 215	PT/Exp	A	Rand Var	-5
		Consist	D	MM	1135

Huge BA bounceback, but was second half power outage due to neck injury or just Kronos catching up to him? Exit velocity, xPX, and even ct% all suffered while outperforming xBA by a wide margin. A worthy late source of BA, but hit rate regression, age say not to expect a full repeat.

Yr	Tm	PA	R	HR	RBI	SB	BA	xHR	xSB	xBA	OBP	SLG	OPS+	vL+	vR+	bb%	ct%	Eye	G	L	F	h%	HctX	QBaB	Brl%	PX	xPX	HR/F	xHR/F	Spd	SBA%	SB%	RAR	BPX	R$
17	HOU	564	69	18	75	3	299	12	7	293	332	486	111	94	116	4	88	0.35	46	19	35	31	125	BCd	3%	102	99	11%	7%	77	4%	60%	4.9	206	$19
18	HOU *	594	72	13	87	5	292	7	6	271	320	431	101	118	91	4	88	0.34	44	20	36	31	99	BCd	2%	80	87	8%	4%	106	4%	83%	8.8	190	$21
19	HOU	612	85	31	104	5	298	12	4	306	343	541	122	112	126	6	88	0.57	38	22	39	29	118	BBf	4%	113	79	16%	6%	80	6%	63%	26.5	304	$25
20	HOU	230	27	6	22	0	232	6	2	258	274	384	87	115	75	5	87	0.44	38	20	42	24	127	BCd	3%	78	123	8%	8%	96	2%	0%	-12.5	208	$9
21	HOU	605	83	15	81	1	319	13	3	263	383	462	116	126	111	10	87	0.87	41	20	39	34	120	BCf	3%	78	83	8%	7%	75	1%	50%	18.3	212	$25
1st Half		326	41	10	53	1	326	8	2	275	393	502	125	138	116	11	90	1.21	42	18	40	34	121	ACf	4%	92	83	10%	8%	70	1%	50%	14.1	296	$27
2nd Half		279	42	5	28	0	311	5	2	250	373	418	107	110	106	9	84	0.62	40	22	37	35	119	CCd	3%	62	82	6%	6%	85	1%	0%	0.6	123	$14
22	Proj	560	76	14	74	2	286	12	3	264	339	431	104	113	100	7	87	0.63	40	21	39	31	119		3%	79	91	8%	7%	82	2%	53%	10.5	172	$20

Gutierrez,Kelvin

Age: 27	Pos: 3B	Health	A	LIMA Plan	D
Bats: R	Ht: 6' 2" Wt: 220	PT/Exp	C	Rand Var	0
		Consist	D	MM	1303

3-20-.232 in 295 PA with KC/BAL. When you get DFA'd by the Royals, that's some real Mississippi Delta blues stuff. Has good speed and hits the ball reasonably hard, but more often than not it goes straight into the ground. There's always a chance he learns to lift; let him practice that skill on someone else's dime.

Yr	Tm	PA	R	HR	RBI	SB	BA	xHR	xSB	xBA	OBP	SLG	OPS+	vL+	vR+	bb%	ct%	Eye	G	L	F	h%	HctX	QBaB	Brl%	PX	xPX	HR/F	xHR/F	Spd	SBA%	SB%	RAR	BPX	R$
17																																			
18	aa	501	53	8	53	16	247		8		291	352	86			6	75	0.25				31				63				127	17%	78%		7	$13
19	KC *	391	35	7	43	10	247	1	11	239	308	350	91	134	71	8	71	0.30	68	16	16	33	79	BFa	4%	58	54	13%	13%	119	11%	90%	-13.4	-56	$7
20	KC	12	0	0	0	0	111	0	0	201	333	111	59	0	72	25	33	0.50	33	67	0	33	45	CDa		0	57	0%	#DIV/0!	103	0%	0%	-1.1	-732	-$4
21	2 AL *	425	31	6	32	1	223	4	4	218	266	322	81	96	79	5	73	0.21	61	15	24	29	91	BFd	4%	61	52	6%	9%	154	4%	17%	-26.3	0	$0
1st Half		179	10	1	11	0	222	2	2	223	254	308	78	72	78	4	77	0.19	63	13	24	28	109	AFd	4%	52	60	4%	8%	163	4%	0%	-14.3	35	-$6
2nd Half		246	21	5	21	1	225	2	2	219	275	333	82	114	79	7	69	0.23	58	18	24	30	74	CFd	3%	69	44	9%	9%	125	4%	37%	-14.8	-54	$1
22	Proj	280	23	4	25	4	233	4	3	225	288	325	83	106	74	6	73	0.24	62	16	22	31	86		4%	56	51	8%	10%	126	7%	67%	-10.0	-91	$5

ALAIN DE LEONARDIS

Guzmán,Ronald

Age: 27 Pos: 1B | Bats: L Ht: 6' 5" Wt: 235

Health	F	LIMA Plan	D
PT/Exp	F	Rand Var	+5
Consist	C	MM	4131

2021 wiped out by a right knee injury that required surgery in April. That xHR/F history says he's capable of hitting the ball hard, but more often than not he doesn't, as evidenced by poor average exit velocity, xPX, HctX. Low FB%, ct% stack the deck against him further. Several adjustments away from refining raw power.

Yr	Tm	PA	R	HR	RBI	SB	BA	xHR	xSB	xBA	OBP	SLG	OPS+	vL+	vR+	bb%	ct%	Eye	G	L	F	h%	HctX	QBaB	Brl%	PX	xPX	HR/F	xHR/F	Spd	SBA%	SB%	RAR	BPX	R$
17	aaa	507	60	9	48	3	264		7		318	376	94			7	80	0.40				31				64				110	3%	73%		67	$9
18	TEX	428	46	16	58	1	235	12	3	235	306	416	97	76	102	8	69	0.27	41	22	37	30	83	CBc	6%	119	81	16%	12%	88	1%	100%	-3.6	47	$8
19	TEX *	444	53	15	50	1	236	13	1	256	316	424	102	75	108	10	68	0.37	37	29	34	31	92	DBb	9%	120	92	17%	22%	69	3%	33%	-6.2	41	$6
20	TEX	86	10	4	9	1	244	4	1	247	314	436	100	71	108	8	69	0.29	50	24	26	30	93	DDf	7%	102	84	29%	29%	144	5%	100%	-1.8	80	$4
21	TEX	17	1	1	1	0	63	1	0	91	118	250	51	45	49	6	63	0.17	60	0	40	0	77	CCb	10%	111	128	25%	25%	96	0%	0%	-2.6	-69	-$3
1st Half		17	1	1	1	0	63	1	0	91	118	250	51	46	50	6	63	0.17	60	0	40	0	77	CCb	10%	111	128	25%	25%	96	0%	0%	-2.9	-73	-$10
2nd Half																									0%										
22	Proj	**210**	**25**	**9**	**25**	**1**	**242**	**8**	**1**	**261**	**316**	**452**	**104**	**75**	**113**	**9**	**71**	**0.34**	**44**	**25**	**31**	**29**	**90**		**8%**	**129**	**86**	**22%**	**18%**	**98**	**3%**	**55%**	**1.2**	**90**	**$3**

Haase,Eric

Age: 29 Pos: CA LF | Bats: R Ht: 5' 10" Wt: 210

Health	A	LIMA Plan	C
PT/Exp	C	Rand Var	-3
Consist	D	MM	4203

22-61-.231 in 381 PA with DET. Slugging catcher was a popular FA pickup in 2021—can he do it again? PRO: MiLB HR history; exit velocity, Brl%, xHR/F all confirm power; will retain C eligibility. CON: Outperformed xPX; problematic ct%. Catchers who mash and keep their BA above .200 usually play, but he could see more PA in the OF.

Yr	Tm	PA	R	HR	RBI	SB	BA	xHR	xSB	xBA	OBP	SLG	OPS+	vL+	vR+	bb%	ct%	Eye	G	L	F	h%	HctX	QBaB	Brl%	PX	xPX	HR/F	xHR/F	Spd	SBA%	SB%	RAR	BPX	R$
17	a/a	376	47	22	48	3	232		4		307	495	109			10	64	0.30				29				169				110	7%	58%		142	$7
18	CLE *	473	40	15	54	2	200	0	3	206	240	359	80	52	29	5	62	0.14	60	10	30	29	45	FCf	0%	121	73	0%	0%	84	4%	66%	-9.0	-63	$3
19	CLE *	400	52	23	49	1	185	1	3	178	254	413	92	81	0	8	52	0.19	50	0	50	27	67	CCb	13%	163	151	25%	25%	104	3%	39%	-4.2	-44	$3
20	DET	19	1	0	2	0	176	1	0	135	211	176	51	0	52	5	65	0.17	42	17	42	27	65	FAf	8%	0	36	0%	20%	97	0%	0%	-1.5	-396	-$3
21	DET *	408	50	23	65	3	234	23	1	233	290	460	103	123	91	7	65	0.23	38	20	41	29	96	ABd	14%	144	105	23%	24%	83	4%	100%	3.9	62	$10
1st Half		157	22	11	23	2	254	9	0	248	308	541	118	160	94	7	62	0.20	33	24	43	33	95	AAc	15%	188	117	31%	25%	103	4%	100%	7.0	181	$9
2nd Half		250	29	12	42	1	221	14	1	220	279	409	93	96	89	7	67	0.24	42	18	40	28	97	BBf	13%	118	99	18%	23%	70	4%	100%	-2.4	-4	$10
22	Proj	**420**	**50**	**21**	**59**	**2**	**224**	**19**	**2**	**218**	**281**	**434**	**97**	**116**	**87**	**7**	**62**	**0.20**	**38**	**20**	**42**	**30**	**96**		**14%**	**143**	**106**	**21%**	**19%**	**83**	**4%**	**80%**	**5.2**	**-6**	**$11**

Hampson,Garrett

Age: 27 Pos: CF 2B | Bats: R Ht: 5' 11" Wt: 196

Health	A	LIMA Plan	C+
PT/Exp	A	Rand Var	+1
Consist	A	MM	2515

Hot spring training led to...another disappointing year. It's hard to look at those Spd and xPX columns and not fantasize about a career season on the horizon. Still a mixed bag: ct% rebounded but not getting on base enough to maximize speed; weak exit velocity a drag on power. Grab for cheap, hope for more.

Yr	Tm	PA	R	HR	RBI	SB	BA	xHR	xSB	xBA	OBP	SLG	OPS+	vL+	vR+	bb%	ct%	Eye	G	L	F	h%	HctX	QBaB	Brl%	PX	xPX	HR/F	xHR/F	Spd	SBA%	SB%	RAR	BPX	R$
17																																			
18	COL *	528	60	8	32	27	281	1	10	249	341	411	101	136	97	8	81	0.48	44	20	36	33	85	DCd	4%	77	113	0%	11%	148	24%	83%	11.8	163	$20
19	COL *	439	50	9	33	19	243	6	15	224	290	378	92	100	92	6	72	0.24	43	19	37	32	75	DCd	4%	77	73	11%	8%	152	25%	79%	-6.8	33	$11
20	COL	184	25	5	11	6	234	7	7	204	287	383	89	71	100	7	64	0.22	36	25	39	33	68	FCd	8%	90	141	13%	18%	179	18%	86%	-6.4	-4	$13
21	COL	494	69	11	33	17	234	15	14	234	289	380	92	111	83	7	74	0.28	39	23	38	29	107	FCd	5%	87	140	9%	12%	174	23%	71%	-20.9	127	$13
1st Half		277	38	6	21	12	257	10	8	245	309	435	104	138	88	7	74	0.28	37	23	40	32	108	FCd	7%	109	152	8%	14%	165	23%	86%	-1.7	188	$18
2nd Half		217	31	5	12	5	205	5	6	221	264	310	78	80	76	7	74	0.28	43	22	35	25	106	FCf	3%	59	123	10%	10%	154	23%	50%	-16.2	12	$3
22	Proj	**490**	**65**	**13**	**32**	**18**	**243**	**15**	**16**	**228**	**297**	**392**	**93**	**99**	**90**	**7**	**72**	**0.27**	**40**	**22**	**38**	**31**	**93**		**5%**	**88**	**124**	**10%**	**12%**	**151**	**20%**	**74%**	**-1.5**	**57**	**$17**

Haniger,Mitch

Age: 31 Pos: RF DH | Bats: R Ht: 6' 2" Wt: 199

Health	C	LIMA Plan	B
PT/Exp	A	Rand Var	0
Consist	A	MM	4325

He may not have won the hardware, but 2021 was one heck of a comeback. Career-best xPX, xHR/F, full season of health combined to yield cornucopia of counting stats. Playing time regression could claw back a few PAs, but skills, prior success point to another season of power with acceptable BA and token SB.

Yr	Tm	PA	R	HR	RBI	SB	BA	xHR	xSB	xBA	OBP	SLG	OPS+	vL+	vR+	bb%	ct%	Eye	G	L	F	h%	HctX	QBaB	Brl%	PX	xPX	HR/F	xHR/F	Spd	SBA%	SB%	RAR	BPX	R$
17	SEA *	454	63	18	52	5	275	14	6	267	334	484	111	99	117	8	76	0.36	44	19	37	32	106	CCc	6%	124	120	16%	14%	109	8%	56%	7.1	158	$13
18	SEA	683	90	26	93	8	285	35	11	265	366	493	115	118	112	10	75	0.47	42	21	36	34	103	BCb	10%	128	110	16%	21%	114	5%	80%	30.9	200	$26
19	SEA	283	46	15	32	4	220	14	3	240	314	463	108	128	101	11	67	0.37	35	20	45	26	82	CAc	11%	143	116	20%	19%	107	7%	100%	-2.4	141	$5
20																																			
21	SEA	691	110	39	100	1	253	42	9	248	318	485	110	125	103	8	73	0.32	43	16	41	29	111	BBd	13%	131	133	21%	23%	120	1%	100%	4.9	188	$23
1st Half		341	52	18	47	0	255	20	4	256	305	484	110	107	111	7	74	0.27	47	16	37	29	105	BBd	12%	132	101	20%	23%	111	1%	0%	-0.3	196	$24
2nd Half		350	58	21	53	1	252	22	5	239	331	487	111	139	94	9	71	0.36	39	17	44	28	116	CBd	13%	130	166	21%	22%	130	1%	100%	2.8	188	$26
22	Proj	**630**	**99**	**32**	**87**	**5**	**255**	**35**	**4**	**248**	**330**	**480**	**110**	**122**	**104**	**9**	**72**	**0.36**	**41**	**18**	**41**	**30**	**103**		**11%**	**131**	**127**	**19%**	**21%**	**108**	**3%**	**83%**	**15.2**	**156**	**$24**

Happ,Ian

Age: 27 Pos: LF CF | Bats: B Ht: 6' 0" Wt: 205

Health	A	LIMA Plan	B
PT/Exp	A	Rand Var	+3
Consist	B	MM	4225

A tale of two half seasons, with the first as ugly as the second was promising. Plate skills, exit velocity, speed didn't change much; the differences were big positive swing in hit rate, better launch angle, stolen base success. Entering peak age, we could see a career year if he puts it all together. Go an extra buck.

Yr	Tm	PA	R	HR	RBI	SB	BA	xHR	xSB	xBA	OBP	SLG	OPS+	vL+	vR+	bb%	ct%	Eye	G	L	F	h%	HctX	QBaB	Brl%	PX	xPX	HR/F	xHR/F	Spd	SBA%	SB%	RAR	BPX	R$
17	CHC *	526	78	31	88	10	254	21	7	253	323	513	114	107	115	9	66	0.30	40	20	40	32	87	CCb	13%	163	122	25%	22%	101	13%	65%	3.7	133	$19
18	CHC	462	56	15	44	8	233	20	10	206	353	408	102	81	108	15	57	0.42	40	23	38	37	80	BCb	12%	141	126	18%	24%	105	9%	67%	1.0	13	$10
19	CHC *	569	77	23	72	9	225	10	8	222	319	420	102	107	128	12	66	0.41	43	16	42	29	79	BBd	14%	117	102	26%	24%	104	8%	80%	-11.7	59	$13
20	CHC	231	27	12	28	1	258	11	3	259	361	505	115	93	122	13	68	0.48	45	22	33	32	99	BDc	10%	150	121	27%	25%	95	7%	25%	3.5	196	$17
21	CHC	535	63	25	66	9	226	23	5	242	323	434	104	89	109	12	66	0.40	46	21	33	28	93	CCf	11%	133	115	24%	22%	89	9%	82%	-9.8	92	$13
1st Half		251	23	9	21	1	186	8	2	216	297	340	89	78	92	13	67	0.43	49	20	31	23	83	CDf	9%	96	83	20%	18%	92	9%	50%	-16.0	-8	$1
2nd Half		284	40	16	45	8	260	15	3	259	345	516	117	97	123	11	66	0.37	43	22	35	33	102	CCc	13%	164	142	28%	26%	91	9%	89%	6.0	185	$24
22	Proj	**560**	**70**	**28**	**71**	**9**	**247**	**27**	**8**	**242**	**343**	**474**	**111**	**94**	**116**	**12**	**66**	**0.41**	**44**	**21**	**35**	**32**	**91**		**12%**	**146**	**117**	**25%**	**23%**	**92**	**7%**	**70%**	**15.6**	**114**	**$20**

Harper,Bryce

Age: 29 Pos: RF | Bats: L Ht: 6' 3" Wt: 210

Health	B	LIMA Plan	C
PT/Exp	A	Rand Var	-4
Consist	C	MM	5355

Finally delivered a performance to rival his 2015 MVP season while playing through various injuries. Career-best exit velocity, Brl%, xHR/F supported even more homers. Fantasy managers expecting Bitcoin-level growth are missing those Brl%, R$ trends and the fact that he's been steady as IBM for many years. A true blue chipper.

Yr	Tm	PA	R	HR	RBI	SB	BA	xHR	xSB	xBA	OBP	SLG	OPS+	vL+	vR+	bb%	ct%	Eye	G	L	F	h%	HctX	QBaB	Brl%	PX	xPX	HR/F	xHR/F	Spd	SBA%	SB%	RAR	BPX	R$
17	WAS	492	95	29	87	4	319	25	8	293	413	595	137	108	145	14	76	0.69	40	22	38	36	106	ABb	12%	155	105	24%	21%	119	4%	67%	44.7	288	$26
18	WAS	695	103	34	100	13	249	37	7	262	393	496	119	114	119	19	69	0.77	40	22	38	30	108	ABb	12%	161	148	23%	25%	87	8%	81%	37.0	240	$26
19	PHI	682	98	35	114	15	260	40	9	261	372	510	122	132	116	15	69	0.56	38	24	38	32	115	ACc	15%	145	152	23%	27%	88	10%	83%	19.2	181	$27
20	PHI	244	41	13	33	8	268	20	6	266	420	542	128	126	128	20	77	1.14	36	18	46	28	125	BCc	17%	141	148	20%	30%	121	13%	80%	15.3	404	$31
21	PHI	599	101	35	84	13	309	45	14	293	429	615	143	109	159	17	73	0.75	41	22	37	36	129	ACc	18%	186	153	27%	34%	107	9%	81%	60.3	408	$35
1st Half		252	40	14	26	7	276	20	6	251	381	519	125	108	134	13	70	0.51	39	20	41	33	110	BBd	17%	147	138	23%	33%	107	9%	100%	12.0	219	$21
2nd Half		347	61	21	58	6	336	26	9	326	464	690	156	109	176	20	75	0.97	42	24	34	39	143	ACb	19%	215	163	30%	37%	106	9%	67%	51.3	554	$41
22	Proj	**630**	**106**	**40**	**104**	**15**	**282**	**48**	**11**	**287**	**408**	**595**	**136**	**116**	**144**	**17**	**73**	**0.78**	**39**	**21**	**40**	**31**	**123**		**17%**	**184**	**149**	**27%**	**31%**	**101**	**8%**	**80%**	**62.1**	**393**	**$36**

Harrison,Josh

Age: 34 Pos: 2B 3B OF | Bats: R Ht: 5' 8" Wt: 190

Health	D	LIMA Plan	B
PT/Exp	A	Rand Var	-3
Consist	B	MM	1235

Versatile utility man played mostly full-time and delivered surprising value. Ah, but--now say it with me--is it repeatable? PRO: Career-best exit velocity, xHR, xHR/F suggest more dingers are possible; superior ct% is bankable. CON: Sub-par Spd, SB%, age put SB at risk. Don't get greedy and enjoy a modest profit.

Yr	Tm	PA	R	HR	RBI	SB	BA	xHR	xSB	xBA	OBP	SLG	OPS+	vL+	vR+	bb%	ct%	Eye	G	L	F	h%	HctX	QBaB	Brl%	PX	xPX	HR/F	xHR/F	Spd	SBA%	SB%	RAR	BPX	R$
17	PIT	542	66	16	47	12	272	12	8	260	339	432	105	116	99	5	81	0.31	36	23	41	31	107	DBb	3%	89	120	10%	8%	102	12%	75%	0.7	121	$15
18	PIT	374	41	8	37	3	250	9	6	245	293	363	88	90	86	5	80	0.26	38	25	37	29	97	DBc	4%	67	114	8%	9%	97	3%	100%	-4.8	50	$6
19	DET *	174	11	1	10	4	170	4	1	212	220	250	65	70	66	6	80	0.33	36	18	45	21	77	DAc	5%	48	54	2%	8%	100	21%	67%	-16.3	11	-$4
20	WAS	91	11	3	14	1	278	3	3	264	352	418	102	105	98	7	85	0.50	41	25	35	30	80	FBa	4%	66	60	13%	13%	80	11%	33%	-0.4	124	$6
21	2 TM	557	58	8	60	9	279	15	9	264	341	400	102	105	101	6	85	0.41	39	24	37	32	98	CBb	4%	72	91	5%	9%	90	10%	64%	-2.4	146	$17
1st Half		271	25	4	24	4	278	8	5	249	354	378	102	101	102	7	83	0.43	37	25	38	32	89	CBa	4%	60	93	5%	11%	73	10%	67%	-3.4	62	$10
2nd Half		286	33	4	36	5	280	7	4	279	329	420	101	107	99	5	88	0.39	42	23	36	31	106	CCb	5%	82	89	5%	8%	100	10%	63%	-2.0	219	$15
22	Proj	**455**	**47**	**9**	**45**	**8**	**265**	**12**	**7**	**254**	**323**	**392**	**97**	**103**	**94**	**6**	**83**	**0.35**	**39**	**23**	**38**	**30**	**92**		**4%**	**74**	**83**	**7%**	**9%**	**89**	**8%**	**68%**	**0.6**	**104**	**$14**

ALAIN DE LEONARDIS

Hayes,Ke'Bryan

Age: 25 Pos: 3B | Bats: R Ht: 5' 10" Wt: 205
Health C | PT/Exp B | Consist F
LIMA Plan B+ | Rand Var +1 | MM 3345

6-38-.257 with 9 SB in 396 PA at PIT. April wrist injury lingered, costing him two months. Oct report revealed he played through a cyst in hand, explaining some of the downturn after a h%-puffed debut. Exhibited mature plate skills and some pop for a rookie, and the team says he'll be ready for spring. But this projection is largely health-dependent.

Yr	Tm	PA	R	HR	RBI	SB	BA	xHR	xSB	xBA	OBP	SLG	OPS+	vL+	vR+	bb%	ct%	Eye	G	L	F	h%	HctX	QBaB	Brl%	PX	xPX	HR/F	xHR/F	Spd	SBA%	SB%	RAR	BPX	R$
17																																			
18	aa	486	56	6	41	10	275		8		349	410	102			10	80	0.57				33				86				117	12%	66%		153	$
19	aaa	464	54	8	45	10	245		7		304	376	94			8	78	0.39				30				78				99	11%	90%		78	
20	PIT	95	17	5	11	1	376	4	2	305	442	682	149	175	140	9	76	0.45	48	22	31	45	138	ADd	9%	167	112	25%	20%	142	4%	100%	14.5	412	$
21	PIT *	421	53	7	40	9	254	10	4	251	312	378	95	101	92	8	75	0.34	57	18	25	32	110	BFd	5%	80	76	9%	14%	103	10%	90%	-13.4	54	$
1st Half		145	20	4	17	2	238	4	1	259	315	406	100	114	95	10	77	0.49	55	16	28	28	119	BFc	5%	97	90	13%	17%	118	10%	67%	-3.3	165	
2nd Half		276	33	3	23	7	262	6	3	244	312	363	91	95	90	7	75	0.28	57	19	24	34	106	BFd	5%	70	69	7%	13%	94	10%	100%	-7.6	-8	$
22	Proj	560	72	18	60	11	265	19	9	269	330	446	105	113	102	9	77	0.41	49	22	29	31	118		7%	107	86	16%	17%	98	8%	82%	12.5	162	$

Hays,Austin

Age: 26 Pos: LF RF | Bats: R Ht: 6' 0" Wt: 205
Health B | PT/Exp A | Consist A
LIMA Plan B+ | Rand Var 0 | MM 3235

Injuries to both hamstrings hampered 1st half, but does a late season surge (12 HR, .834 OPS in Aug-Sept) foretell next level? PRO: Above average vRHP in 2nd half; HctX, barrels on the rise. CON: Pedestrian QBaB; poor bb%; inconsistent HR/F. Age/experience hints that improvement is possible; but metrics say more baby steps than breakout.

Yr	Tm	PA	R	HR	RBI	SB	BA	xHR	xSB	xBA	OBP	SLG	OPS+	vL+	vR+	bb%	ct%	Eye	G	L	F	h%	HctX	QBaB	Brl%	PX	xPX	HR/F	xHR/F	Spd	SBA%	SB%	RAR	BPX	R$
17	BAL *	336	37	15	54	1	273	1	4	262	303	460	104	96	68	4	79	0.20	56	16	29	31	99	DDf	2%	100	79	8%	8%	90	3%	43%	0.8	97	
18	aa	282	25	10	32	4	209		1		234	363	80			3	77	0.14				24				89				99	16%	57%		53	
19	BAL *	384	55	15	45	10	242	2	6	260	282	438	100	48	177	5	75	0.22	41	22	37	28	80	ACa	6%	111	107	20%	10%	112	24%	63%	-5.5	126	$
20	BAL	134	20	4	9	2	279	3	5	236	328	393	96	95	96	6	80	0.32	49	19	32	32	62	DCf	4%	57	42	13%	10%	141	13%	40%	-2.1	80	$
21	BAL	529	73	22	71	4	256	25	9	261	308	461	106	122	94	5	78	0.26	43	18	38	29	98	CCf	9%	114	92	15%	17%	119	6%	57%	-2.0	200	$
1st Half		216	33	8	27	1	247	13	4	244	304	429	102	140	84	6	77	0.29	43	17	40	28	84	CCd	11%	99	99	13%	21%	133	6%	100%	-3.5	165	
2nd Half		313	40	14	44	3	262	12	5	271	311	483	107	113	102	5	79	0.24	43	19	38	29	108	CCf	8%	123	87	16%	14%	107	6%	50%	-0.9	219	$
22	Proj	560	77	23	67	4	260	20	7	255	305	448	102	98	104	5	78	0.25	45	19	36	29	88		7%	104	84	16%	14%	119	7%	48%	2.7	115	$

Hedges,Austin

Age: 29 Pos: CA | Bats: R Ht: 6' 1" Wt: 223
Health A | PT/Exp C | Consist A
LIMA Plan D | Rand Var +2 | MM 2201

Don't overthink this one. When the best you can do is "He touched 70% ct% for the first time in years," let's admit this will be a quick scan. The box does remind us that once upon a time, he had league-average punch and enough BA to get RAR into plus-territory. Tactical tip for auction leagues: Drop out when bidding hits $1.

Yr	Tm	PA	R	HR	RBI	SB	BA	xHR	xSB	xBA	OBP	SLG	OPS+	vL+	vR+	bb%	ct%	Eye	G	L	F	h%	HctX	QBaB	Brl%	PX	xPX	HR/F	xHR/F	Spd	SBA%	SB%	RAR	BPX	R$
17	SD	417	36	18	55	4	214	12	4	223	262	398	90	81	91	6	68	0.19	37	18	46	26	92	CAf	7%	116	114	15%	10%	61	7%	80%	-9.4	-3	$
18	SD *	355	34	16	44	3	239	11	3	235	288	445	98	90	96	6	69	0.23	38	18	44	30	94	DBf	7%	133	116	15%	12%	86	4%	100%	8.2	80	$
19	SD	347	28	11	36	1	176	10	1	200	252	311	78	67	80	8	65	0.25	32	22	46	23	71	CAd	8%	81	89	12%	11%	54	1%	100%	-12.7	-148	-$
20	2 TM	83	7	3	6	1	145	2	0	192	231	290	69	53	77	7	67	0.26	43	15	43	16	99	FCf	8%	83	143	15%	10%	85	14%	50%	-5.5	-96	-$
21	CLE	312	32	10	31	1	178	6	3	203	220	308	72	77	70	5	70	0.17	34	20	45	22	64	FBf	4%	78	77	11%	7%	69	2%	100%	-18.6	-100	-$
1st Half		142	11	4	13	0	155	2	2	178	209	256	65	51	69	6	63	0.17	34	22	44	21	51	FAf	3%	62	73	11%	6%	88	2%	0%	-10.8	-227	-$
2nd Half		170	21	6	18	1	197	5	2	224	229	350	78	92	71	4	75	0.18	34	19	46	22	74	DBf	5%	88	79	11%	9%	69	2%	100%	-7.4	8	-$
22	Proj	245	24	9	27	1	195	7	1	208	247	346	81	77	82	6	69	0.20	36	19	45	24	77		6%	94	98	13%	9%	67	2%	95%	-6.4	-81	$

Heim,Jonah

Age: 27 Pos: CA | Bats: B Ht: 6' 4" Wt: 220
Health A | PT/Exp C | Consist C
LIMA Plan D+ | Rand Var +4 | MM 2123

Shouldn't read too much into 1H/2H splits of this volume, but his first full MLB season gives some positive vibes: legit double-digit HR power; decent contact that ballparks his MLEs; and batted-ball quality that belies his sub-Mendoza BA. He's not young and hopefully he can close the vL/vR and xBA/BA gaps, but there are worse choices for a second catcher.

Yr	Tm	PA	R	HR	RBI	SB	BA	xHR	xSB	xBA	OBP	SLG	OPS+	vL+	vR+	bb%	ct%	Eye	G	L	F	h%	HctX	QBaB	Brl%	PX	xPX	HR/F	xHR/F	Spd	SBA%	SB%	RAR	BPX	R$
17																																			
18	aa	145	12	1	9	0	157		1		202	199	54			5	83	0.32				18				28				101	0%	0%		-10	-$
19	a/a	315	34	7	43	0	270		1		335	408	103			9	82	0.55				31				78				83	1%	0%		133	$
20	OAK	41	5	0	5	0	211	1	0	202	268	211	64	87	56	7	92	1.00	43	17	40	23	117	DBf	6%	0	66	0%	7%	117	0%	0%	-2.6	80	-$
21	TEX	285	22	10	32	3	196	10	0	239	239	358	82	99	75	5	78	0.26	40	18	42	21	117	CBf	6%	93	117	11%	11%	57	9%	75%	-11.9	62	$
1st Half		121	12	3	12	1	227	3	0	269	283	391	94	89	95	8	80	0.41	46	21	33	26	113	DCf	5%	102	88	10%	10%	68	9%	50%	-1.8	150	-$
2nd Half		164	10	7	20	2	174	7	0	216	207	335	73	103	59	4	77	0.17	36	16	49	18	119	CAf	7%	86	139	12%	12%	70	9%	100%	-9.7	23	-$
22	Proj	385	33	13	42	2	221	13	3	245	269	375	88	106	80	6	80	0.33	41	20	39	24	117		6%	88	119	11%	11%	62	6%	70%	-2.8	64	$

Hernandez,Cesar

Age: 32 Pos: 2B | Bats: B Ht: 5' 10" Wt: 195
Health A | PT/Exp A | Consist A
LIMA Plan B | Rand Var +2 | MM 2315

The age-old fantasy question of when to move on, personified. As he's aged and the game has changed, so has his approach, trading speed for power. In 2021, while it got him over the 20-HR barrier for the first time, the big-picture results question whether it was worth it (R$). That will be the quandary for us in the spring, too.

Yr	Tm	PA	R	HR	RBI	SB	BA	xHR	xSB	xBA	OBP	SLG	OPS+	vL+	vR+	bb%	ct%	Eye	G	L	F	h%	HctX	QBaB	Brl%	PX	xPX	HR/F	xHR/F	Spd	SBA%	SB%	RAR	BPX	R$
17	PHI	577	85	9	34	15	294	10	10	273	373	421	108	109	105	11	80	0.59	53	23	25	35	71	DFa	3%	74	61	9%	10%	167	11%	75%	13.9	155	$1
18	PHI	708	91	15	60	19	253	13	18	225	356	362	96	93	96	13	74	0.61	46	21	34	32	66	DCc	4%	65	63	10%	9%	128	11%	76%	6.1	57	$2
19	PHI	667	77	14	71	9	279	11	13	274	333	408	103	89	107	7	84	0.45	49	23	29	32	95	DCc	3%	67	55	10%	7%	105	6%	82%	0.2	130	$1
20	CLE	260	35	3	20	0	283	5	3	253	355	408	101	89	105	9	76	0.42	49	23	27	36	95	CFc	4%	88	93	6%	11%	95	0%	0%	2.9	88	$1
21	2 AL	637	84	21	62	1	232	20	3	239	308	386	95	104	91	9	76	0.44	47	18	35	27	88	DCc	7%	87	92	14%	13%	105	1%	50%	-13.0	104	$1
1st Half		342	48	13	33	0	220	13	2	247	301	400	98	111	90	10	75	0.44	45	19	35	25	103	CCc	9%	101	109	16%	16%	96	1%	0%	-8.9	127	$1
2nd Half		295	36	8	29	1	245	7	2	227	315	370	93	94	92	9	77	0.43	48	17	35	29	70	DCc	4%	71	72	11%	10%	106	1%	50%	-7.6	69	$
22	Proj	595	74	15	51	4	237	15	4	238	313	376	94	93	93	9	76	0.44	48	18	34	28	85		5%	83	80	11%	11%	112	4%	72%	-2.8	59	$1

Hernández,Kiké

Age: 30 Pos: CF 2B | Bats: R Ht: 5' 11" Wt: 190
Health B | PT/Exp A | Consist B
LIMA Plan A | Rand Var 0 | MM 3235

In hindsight, one can see seeds of his mad playoff run sowed in the 2nd half: best plate skills of his career watered with surging batted-ball and power metrics. An unlucky HR/F rate kept most of it underground until Oct (see xHR). And while we can't just double a half-season on a whim, his age, positional flexibility and growth curve could lead to ... UP: 30 HR

Yr	Tm	PA	R	HR	RBI	SB	BA	xHR	xSB	xBA	OBP	SLG	OPS+	vL+	vR+	bb%	ct%	Eye	G	L	F	h%	HctX	QBaB	Brl%	PX	xPX	HR/F	xHR/F	Spd	SBA%	SB%	RAR	BPX	R$
17	LA	342	46	11	37	3	215	10	4	259	308	421	99	128	67	12	73	0.51	42	19	40	26	116	CCd	7%	132	122	13%	11%	98	4%	100%	-4.0	161	$
18	LA	462	67	21	52	3	256	17	5	260	336	470	108	103	110	11	81	0.64	38	19	44	27	105	CBd	7%	115	105	15%	12%	110	3%	100%	17.2	237	$1
19	LA	460	57	17	64	4	237	15	3	242	304	411	99	105	94	8	77	0.37	36	21	43	27	107	CAc	6%	92	107	12%	11%	88	4%	100%	-4.3	89	$
20	LA	148	20	5	20	0	230	5	1	251	270	410	90	88	91	4	78	0.19	40	20	39	26	107	CBf	6%	101	104	12%	12%	121	4%	0%	-5.5	152	$
21	BOS	585	84	20	60	1	250	28	6	256	337	449	108	116	103	10	78	0.55	33	21	46	28	114	BAd	8%	116	123	11%	15%	122	1%	100%	4.5	254	$1
1st Half		284	40	10	28	1	241	11	2	243	313	435	104	115	97	8	75	0.37	35	18	47	28	99	BAd	7%	118	116	11%	12%	113	1%	100%	-3.3	188	$1
2nd Half		301	44	10	32	0	259	17	3	271	359	463	111	115	108	13	81	0.79	30	24	45	28	129	ABd	10%	115	130	10%	18%	125	1%	0%	5.5	315	$1
22	Proj	595	85	23	70	2	251	25	4	257	329	455	106	112	102	10	79	0.50	35	21	44	28	115		9%	115	116	13%	13%	108	4%	71%	16.4	201	$1

Hernández,Teoscar

Age: 29 Pos: RF LF | Bats: R Ht: 6' 2" Wt: 205
Health A | PT/Exp A | Consist C
LIMA Plan D+ | Rand Var -3 | MM 4335

And it keeps getting better. Replicated 2019-20's power (HR), benefitted from a more talented lineup (elite R/RBI), continued his stunning contract growth, and oh, yeah—doubled his SB. Seems unlikely to flirt with .300 again, but what if all those LDs stick and the h% is his new level? This is one impressive resume at his age, with no signs of slowing down.

Yr	Tm	PA	R	HR	RBI	SB	BA	xHR	xSB	xBA	OBP	SLG	OPS+	vL+	vR+	bb%	ct%	Eye	G	L	F	h%	HctX	QBaB	Brl%	PX	xPX	HR/F	xHR/F	Spd	SBA%	SB%	RAR	BPX	R$
17	2 AL *	538	78	25	81	15	253	7	6	246	322	495	111	87	135	9	69	0.33	28	23	49	32	79	CAc	17%	152	139	31%	27%	115	23%	60%	-4.2	161	$1
18	TOR	523	67	22	57	5	239	36	14	238	302	468	103	99	103	8	66	0.25	36	20	44	32	90	ABc	16%	157	149	16%	26%	148	10%	50%	-0.4	170	$1
19	TOR *	544	67	30	74	8	228	25	8	226	299	461	105	116	103	9	64	0.28	39	18	43	29	97	ABf	12%	138	144	23%	22%	119	10%	74%	-9.0	81	$1
20	TOR	206	33	16	34	6	289	17	3	262	340	579	122	122	121	7	67	0.22	36	26	38	35	133	ABb	18%	169	165	33%	35%	103	15%	86%	8.7	196	$3
21	TOR	595	92	32	116	12	296	37	13	268	346	524	119	157	108	6	73	0.24	38	25	36	35	109	ACc	14%	134	109	22%	25%	101	11%	75%	14.5	169	$3
1st Half		268	33	11	47	5	299	14	6	267	340	482	114	149	104	6	73	0.23	38	31	31	37	110	ACc	14%	112	104	19%	25%	108	11%	71%	3.9	100	$2
2nd Half		327	59	21	69	7	294	23	7	271	352	559	123	162	111	6	74	0.25	38	21	41	34	109	ABc	13%	152	113	24%	26%	94	11%	78%	12.0	227	$3
22	Proj	630	95	38	109	13	277	43	10	257	331	528	117	131	111	7	70	0.25	37	23	39	34	109		15%	152	131	24%	27%	102	9%	75%	27.5	163	$3

BRENT HERSHEY

Hernandez,Yadiel

Age: 34 Pos: LF
Bats: L Ht: 5' 9" Wt: 185

Health A | LIMA Plan D+
PT/Exp C | Rand Var 0
Consist C | MM 1223

9-32-.273 with 3 SB in 289 PA at WAS. Defected from Cuba at age 28, finally got an extended MLB shot and made the most of it. More of a bat-to-ball guy than pure slugger, proved he has enough exit velo/barrels to rack up some counting stats without killing your BA. The shelf life will be short, but a reasonable end-of-roster pickup even in a part-time role.

Yr	Tm	PA	R	HR	RBI	SB	BA	xHR	xSB	xBA	OBP	SLG	OPS+	vL+	vR+	bb%	ct%	Eye	G	L	F	h%	HctX	QBaB	Brl%	PX	xPX	HR/F	xHR/F	Spd	SBA%	SB%	RAR	BPX	R$
17	aa	438	41	8	43	4	228		6		300	335	86			9	79	0.48				27				64				85	7%	58%		36	$2
18	a/a	474	46	13	50	3	227		5		293	356	87			9	69	0.31				30				84				86	5%	54%		-33	$6
19	aaa	480	58	23	60	5	249		4		314	445	105			9	69	0.30				31				111				88	10%	42%		33	$12
20	WAS	28	3	1	6	0	192	1	0	231	214	423	85	81	85	4	54	0.08	53	20	27	31	87	CDa	7%	208	140	25%	25%	77	0%	0%	-1.8	56	-$1
21	WAS *	351	39	13	40	3	264	10	2	265	318	417	101	117	95	7	77	0.35	54	23	23	31	104	BFb	6%	83	94	19%	21%	98	5%	70%	-6.3	85	$9
1st Half		135	14	6	12	2	251	3	1	259	298	406	98	102	91	6	74	0.26	53	25	22	30	124	BFa	8%	85	106	18%	27%	91	5%	61%	-5.0	19	$1
2nd Half		216	25	7	28	1	273	7	1	269	330	424	102	119	96	8	80	0.42	55	22	23	31	98	CFc	5%	81	90	19%	19%	102	5%	100%	-2.3	123	$8
22	Proj	350	38	10	40	3	249	12	3	249	310	383	94	108	88	8	74	0.33	54	23	23	31	108		6%	79	96	19%	23%	97	5%	59%	-3.5	-22	$6

Hernandez,Yonny

Age: 24 Pos: 3B
Bats: B Ht: 5' 9" Wt: 140

Health A | LIMA Plan D
PT/Exp D | Rand Var +4
Consist D | MM 0521

0-6-.217 with 11 SB in 166 PA at TEX. Young legs are the attention-getter here, with 30+ SB in each three past full seasons. Will it translate? While his 10% MLB walk rate and MiLB OBPs of .370+ over that same span are in his favor, the stick badly needs some oomph, as his QBaB shows. Likely returns to minors for more seasoning and (hopefully) strength.

Yr	Tm	PA	R	HR	RBI	SB	BA	xHR	xSB	xBA	OBP	SLG	OPS+	vL+	vR+	bb%	ct%	Eye	G	L	F	h%	HctX	QBaB	Brl%	PX	xPX	HR/F	xHR/F	Spd	SBA%	SB%	RAR	BPX	R$
17	aa																																		
18	aa																																		
19	aa	199	26	0	15	15	283		5		389	343	101			15	85	1.18				33				31				142	27%	78%		148	$7
20																																			
21	TEX *	396	46	1	16	27	215	0	8	246	325	263	81	60	86	14	76	0.67	52	28	20	28	41	FFb	1%	34	9	0%	0%	137	34%	67%	-22.6	4	$11
1st Half		140	18	0	5	10	198		3	212	334	243	80	0	0	17	78	0.92	44	20	36	25	0		0%	36	-22	0%		132	34%	61%	-10.2	62	$1
2nd Half		256	28	1	10	16	224	0	5	242	321	273	80	59	84	12	75	0.56	52	28	20	30	40	FFb	1%	33	9	0%	0%	142	34%	71%	-14.9	-23	$10
22	Proj	175	17	0	8	12	231	0	11	250	352	273	85	66	92	14	78	0.75	52	28	20	30	36		1%	30	8	0%	0%	130	26%	69%	-5.5	-12	$6

Herrera,Odúbel

Age: 30 Pos: CF LF
Bats: L Ht: 5' 11" Wt: 205

Health A | LIMA Plan C+
PT/Exp B | Rand Var 0
Consist B | MM 2233

Seized the CF job after a domestic-violence suspension and put up best skills of his career, led by a ct% bump. But more of that contact went into the ground, his power, patience and OBP remained below average, and his running game is no longer a factor. Future value will depend on racking up the PAs, something that is by no means guaranteed.

Yr	Tm	PA	R	HR	RBI	SB	BA	xHR	xSB	xBA	OBP	SLG	OPS+	vL+	vR+	bb%	ct%	Eye	G	L	F	h%	HctX	QBaB	Brl%	PX	xPX	HR/F	xHR/F	Spd	SBA%	SB%	RAR	BPX	R$
17	PHI	563	67	14	56	8	281	13	7	265	325	452	106	107	103	6	76	0.25	44	21	35	35	90	CCc	6%	110	79	10%	9%	95	10%	62%	-0.2	103	$16
18	PHI	597	64	22	71	5	255	15	10	245	310	420	98	98	96	6	78	0.31	45	18	37	29	71	CCd	5%	93	64	14%	9%	111	5%	71%	1.5	113	$15
19	PHI	139	12	1	16	2	222	3	1	242	288	341	87	82	88	8	74	0.33	40	24	35	29	79	CCd	4%	80	62	3%	9%	91	14%	50%	-4.8	15	-$1
20																																			
21	PHI	491	59	13	51	6	260	12	6	273	310	416	100	93	103	6	83	0.38	48	21	31	29	102	CDf	5%	88	86	11%	10%	104	6%	86%	-8.6	181	$13
1st Half		238	32	5	22	4	245	3	3	257	298	389	96	102	91	6	80	0.33	48	19	34	29	89	CDf	3%	87	86	9%	5%	107	6%	100%	-6.2	138	$8
2nd Half		253	27	8	29	2	274	9	3	286	321	440	103	78	110	6	85	0.44	49	22	29	29	114	CDf	6%	89	86	14%	16%	99	6%	67%	-0.3	219	$10
22	Proj	420	47	11	47	5	255	11	4	258	307	408	97	92	99	6	80	0.34	46	21	33	30	91		5%	91	76	10%	10%	97	6%	68%	2.5	111	$12

Heyward,Jason

Age: 32 Pos: RF
Bats: L Ht: 6' 5" Wt: 240

Health C | LIMA Plan C+
PT/Exp A | Rand Var +5
Consist D | MM 2333

Turns out that 2019-2020's "rebound" was only fleeting. R$ dipped back into the single digits as GBs reappeared, lefties and righties gave him fits, power metrics faltered. Blame some of it on his three IL trips (hamstring, finger, concussion), but even his previously solid OBP fell to new depths. Yes, it's a low bar, but he's better than this.

Yr	Tm	PA	R	HR	RBI	SB	BA	xHR	xSB	xBA	OBP	SLG	OPS+	vL+	vR+	bb%	ct%	Eye	G	L	F	h%	HctX	QBaB	Brl%	PX	xPX	HR/F	xHR/F	Spd	SBA%	SB%	RAR	BPX	R$
17	CHC	480	59	11	59	4	259	10	7	262	326	389	97	89	98	9	84	0.61	47	20	33	29	87	CCd	4%	66	70	9%	8%	113	6%	50%	-12.2	133	$10
18	CHC	488	67	8	57	1	270	10	6	260	335	395	98	95	97	9	86	0.70	48	18	34	30	94	CCd	3%	71	69	6%	8%	108	2%	50%	2.4	180	$11
19	CHC	589	78	21	62	8	251	12	5	258	343	429	107	77	114	12	79	0.62	46	20	34	28	96	CCc	6%	88	82	15%	9%	110	7%	73%	-6.8	159	$14
20	CHC	181	20	6	22	2	265	5	3	271	392	456	113	74	125	17	75	0.81	46	28	27	32	119	CCa	4%	103	114	20%	17%	110	4%	100%	4.6	200	$13
21	CHC	353	35	8	30	5	214	10	3	245	280	347	86	84	87	8	79	0.40	51	17	33	25	99	CDf	5%	77	77	10%	12%	99	8%	83%	-20.7	92	$2
1st Half		210	23	5	15	3	193	6	2	239	281	332	85	80	87	11	75	0.48	52	16	32	23	87	CDf	6%	84	67	11%	13%	103	8%	100%	-12.3	88	$0
2nd Half		143	12	3	15	2	243	4	1	252	280	368	88	96	86	4	84	0.23	49	18	33	27	114	CDd	3%	68	90	8%	11%	92	8%	67%	-7.2	104	-$1
22	Proj	420	47	12	44	5	242	11	6	256	321	394	97	83	101	10	80	0.53	48	20	32	28	104		4%	84	86	12%	12%	101	7%	78%	-2.3	134	$11

Hicks,Aaron

Age: 32 Pos: CF
Bats: B Ht: 6' 1" Wt: 205

Health F | LIMA Plan C+
PT/Exp D | Rand Var +4
Consist B | MM 3213

This time, a torn tendon sheath in his wrist ended his season in mid-May. Prior, plate patience and batted ball metrics were on par; it was a h% dive and declining HR/F responsible for the tepid results. The owner of just one 400-PA season in his career; if you're looking for guaranteed volume, this is not the place.

Yr	Tm	PA	R	HR	RBI	SB	BA	xHR	xSB	xBA	OBP	SLG	OPS+	vL+	vR+	bb%	ct%	Eye	G	L	F	h%	HctX	QBaB	Brl%	PX	xPX	HR/F	xHR/F	Spd	SBA%	SB%	RAR	BPX	R$
17	NYY *	387	60	16	54	11	267	11	6	266	370	481	116	122	109	14	78	0.76	44	16	40	30	98	CCd	8%	122	119	16%	12%	90	15%	68%	12.7	203	$14
18	NYY	581	90	27	79	11	248	25	15	264	366	467	112	106	112	15	77	0.81	40	22	38	27	112	BCd	9%	122	131	19%	18%	111	8%	85%	26.1	237	$21
19	NYY	255	41	12	36	1	235	9	3	227	325	443	106	94	112	12	67	0.43	43	16	41	29	89	BCf	9%	122	98	19%	15%	92	5%	33%	1.6	78	$4
20	NYY	211	28	6	21	4	225	7	3	261	379	414	105	103	106	19	78	1.08	45	20	35	26	93	CCf	7%	105	75	13%	16%	115	8%	80%	2.2	276	$13
21	NYY	126	13	4	14	0	194	5	2	213	294	333	86	112	74	11	72	0.47	35	20	45	23	89	BAd	10%	81	109	11%	14%	87	0%	0%	-5.8	15	-$2
1st Half		126	13	4	14	0	194	5	2	213	294	333	87	114	76	11	72	0.47	35	20	45	23	89	BAd	10%	81	109	11%	14%	87	0%	0%	-6.4	19	-$4
2nd Half																									0%										
22	Proj	385	54	15	48	5	233	15	2	239	342	420	103	108	101	14	74	0.63	41	19	40	27	95		9%	108	105	15%	15%	98	3%	72%	7.8	128	$11

Hill,Derek

Age: 26 Pos: CF
Bats: R Ht: 6' 2" Wt: 190

Health B | LIMA Plan D
PT/Exp C | Rand Var -5
Consist F | MM 2501

3-14-.259 with 6 SB in 150 PA at DET. Collisions filled his year: outfield wall in June; teammate Akil Baddoo in Aug, and the ground by first base in Sept. All sent him to the IL; Oct knee surgery could affect 2022. Spd score hints that maybe he's just faster than he realizes. SB potential is the takeaway with caveat that ct%, batted ball quality need to improve.

Yr	Tm	PA	R	HR	RBI	SB	BA	xHR	xSB	xBA	OBP	SLG	OPS+	vL+	vR+	bb%	ct%	Eye	G	L	F	h%	HctX	QBaB	Brl%	PX	xPX	HR/F	xHR/F	Spd	SBA%	SB%	RAR	BPX	R$
17																																			
18																																			
19	aa	505	73	13	42	20	231		8		284	380	92			7	67	0.22				32				88				142	32%	58%		-7	$13
20	DET	12	3	0	0	0	91	0	0	130	167	91	34	0	41	8	45	0.17	60	20	20	20	110	ADb		0	-26	0%	0%	126	0%	0%	-1.6	-644	-$3
21	DET *	283	36	6	26	9	270	3	5	231	316	413	100	108	87	6	68	0.21	41	29	30	38	74	FFf	5%	85	89	11%	11%	222	18%	69%	-2.3	77	$9
1st Half		120	17	2	12	7	311	0	3	220	373	431	112	55	117	9	68	0.30	50	20	30	45	55	CBf	0%	78	78	0%	0%	178	18%	77%	3.2	27	$7
2nd Half		163	18	5	14	2	241	3	2	236	274	400	91	111	82	4	68	0.14	40	30	30	33	76	FFf	6%	90	91	13%	13%	219	18%	50%	-6.5	73	$1
22	Proj	245	32	6	22	8	237	4	7	216	289	385	92	106	79	6	68	0.20	48	18	34	33	68		5%	89	82	11%	8%	172	18%	66%	-3.1	-18	$8

Hilliard,Sam

Age: 28 Pos: CF
Bats: L Ht: 6' 5" Wt: 236

Health A | LIMA Plan C+
PT/Exp B | Rand Var +4
Consist A | MM 5413

14-34-.215 with 5 SB in 238 PA at COL. Power/speed prospect who's slow to make the leap. Ct% hole keeps getting deeper, OBP trend is ominous (and coincides with declining SB opps). HR promise is legit but BA cost is heavy. Profile that once seemed well-rounded now looks one-dimensional. Mostly bombs, a touch of SB, lots of Ks. Sound familiar?

Yr	Tm	PA	R	HR	RBI	SB	BA	xHR	xSB	xBA	OBP	SLG	OPS+	vL+	vR+	bb%	ct%	Eye	G	L	F	h%	HctX	QBaB	Brl%	PX	xPX	HR/F	xHR/F	Spd	SBA%	SB%	RAR	BPX	R$
17																																			
18	aa	468	45	8	31	18	247		7		300	364	89			7	64	0.21				37				89				112	30%	54%		-73	$11
19	COL *	622	83	32	77	16	233	5	18	241	287	478	106	155	133	7	65	0.22	43	19	39	30	83	ADc	13%	146	167	33%	24%	117	20%	74%	3.7	104	$19
20	COL	114	13	6	10	3	210	4	3	217	272	438	94	63	107	8	60	0.21	50	15	35	28	89	CCf	10%	141	98	27%	18%	138	14%	100%	-3.4	48	$6
21	COL *	439	50	23	55	8	205	14	7	228	271	436	97	115	101	8	61	0.23	44	18	38	27	82	BCf	15%	157	123	29%	29%	118	12%	87%	-15.3	88	$8
1st Half		232	23	10	23	3	178	2	3	229	233	387	86	113	55	7	60	0.18	39	28	33	24	82	DAc	17%	144	103	33%	33%	113	12%	70%	-15.0	19	$2
2nd Half		207	27	13	32	6	236	11	4	238	314	494	109	114	109	10	62	0.30	44	17	39	30	84	BCf	15%	171	126	29%	26%	109	12%	100%	2.4	154	$13
22	Proj	385	46	22	45	8	232	21	6	237	297	483	106	112	104	8	62	0.23	44	19	37	30	84		14%	165	123	27%	25%	122	11%	78%	7.9	118	$13

BRENT HERSHEY

Hiura,Keston

Age: 25 Pos: 1B | Bats: R Ht: 6' 0" Wt: 202

Health A | PT/Exp B | Consist D | LIMA Plan D | Rand Var +3 | MM 4201

4-19-.168 with 3 SB in 197 PA at MIL. A baffling fall for a prospect with a nearly can't-miss hit tool. But reasons to stay engaged: 1) The ct% trend frightens, but patience remains; 2) QBaB, Brl%, xPX all on the upswing; 3) elite, consistent xHR/F points to usable power. There's serious thump here and the shot to capitalize will come cheap.

Yr	Tm	PA	R	HR	RBI	SB	BA	xHR	xSB	xBA	OBP	SLG	OPS+	vL+	vR+	bb%	ct%	Eye	G	L	F	h%	HctX	QBaB	Brl%	PX	xPX	HR/F	xHR/F	Spd	SBA%	SB%	RAR	BPX	R$
17																																			
18	aa	300	34	6	19	10	264		4		315	408	97			7	78	0.34				32				92				112	22%	66%		120	$8
19	MIL *	579	85	35	85	14	298	20	16	262	351	577	128	94	140	7	66	0.24	38	24	38	39	101	ABb	14%	170	140	24%	25%	108	14%	73%	27.1	178	$28
20	MIL	246	30	13	32	3	212	14	5	211	297	410	94	89	95	7	61	0.19	43	20	37	28	72	CBc	13%	124	111	26%	28%	97	9%	60%	-16.7	-48	$1
21	MIL *	388	30	9	35	4	185	9	4	183	256	327	80	55	86	9	53	0.20	37	22	41	31	81	BBf	15%	125	133	10%	23%	87	7%	78%	-36.2	-158	-$
1st Half		246	25	8	26	3	223	7	3	205	295	396	96	52	91	9	57	0.24	37	23	40	35	87	BBf	15%	139	136	12%	21%	98	7%	73%	-12.0	-42	$7
2nd Half		142	5	2	8	1	127	1	1	138	196	219	56	65	54	8	47	0.16	38	15	46	25	74	CBf	14%	99	113	0%	17%	83	7%	100%	-19.6	-350	-$1
22	**Proj**	**245**	**24**	**11**	**25**	**4**	**234**	**13**	**3**	**218**	**309**	**442**	**102**	**82**	**112**	**8**	**61**	**0.21**	**39**	**20**	**41**	**33**	**85**		**14%**	**146**	**124**	**20%**	**22%**	**92**	**6%**	**72%**	**-1.2**	**-11**	**$4**

Hoerner,Nico

Age: 25 Pos: 2B | Bats: R Ht: 6' 1" Wt: 200

Health D | PT/Exp D | Consist C | LIMA Plan C | Rand Var -4 | MM 0223

0-16-.302 with 5 SB in 170 PA at CHC. Missed the season's final week due to "general soreness" attributed to forearm, hamstring, and oblique injuries. On the field, he's a solid ct% plus LD hitter, but QBaB, Brl%, xPX and FB% say don't hold your breath for his first MLB HR. Will steal a few bags, but SB% doesn't inspire confidence. Check back in a year.

Yr	Tm	PA	R	HR	RBI	SB	BA	xHR	xSB	xBA	OBP	SLG	OPS+	vL+	vR+	bb%	ct%	Eye	G	L	F	h%	HctX	QBaB	Brl%	PX	xPX	HR/F	xHR/F	Spd	SBA%	SB%	RAR	BPX	R$
17																																			
18																																			
19	CHC *	370	48	6	38	7	277	1	6	298	322	399	100	111	100	6	87	0.53	53	25	22	30	80	DFa	2%	60	48	20%	7%	135	12%	64%	-3.2	193	$9
20	CHC	125	19	0	13	3	222	1	3	230	312	259	76	81	73	10	78	0.50	55	21	24	29	92	CFf	1%	29	59	0%	5%	114	14%	60%	-6.7	-36	$6
21	CHC *	196	15	0	17	5	290	1	5	246	353	352	97	87	110	9	82	0.53	48	23	29	35	80	CDc	2%	48	41	0%	3%	110	13%	63%	-0.7	69	$4
1st Half		98	10	0	10	3,	322	1	3	270	385	402	109	103	122	9	81	0.54	52	26	23	40	84	CFc	3%	62	39	0%	7%	121	13%	75%	3.0	119	$0
2nd Half		98	5	0	8	2	258	0	3	219	321	303	84	74	99	8	82	0.52	45	19	35	31	76	FCd	0%	34	43	0%	0%	100	13%	50%	-3.7	23	-$5
22	**Proj**	**350**	**36**	**1**	**34**	**8**	**268**	**2**	**8**	**248**	**337**	**333**	**91**	**81**	**94**	**8**	**82**	**0.50**	**50**	**22**	**27**	**32**	**82**		**1%**	**46**	**46**	**1%**	**3%**	**102**	**11%**	**61%**	**-3.4**	**20**	**$11**

Hoskins,Rhys

Age: 29 Pos: 1B | Bats: R Ht: 6' 4" Wt: 245

Health C | PT/Exp A | Consist A | LIMA Plan B+ | Rand Var +1 | MM 5155

Had shaken off the ct% doldrums in July when a groin injury halted his whopping 2nd half and ended his season. Slugging returned to his highest level since his rookie year, supported by all the power metrics. Staying out of the trainer's room is key, and he's at the age for another step up. If better contact and gains vs. RHP stick, then ... UP: 45 HR.

Yr	Tm	PA	R	HR	RBI	SB	BA	xHR	xSB	xBA	OBP	SLG	OPS+	vL+	vR+	bb%	ct%	Eye	G	L	F	h%	HctX	QBaB	Brl%	PX	xPX	HR/F	xHR/F	Spd	SBA%	SB%	RAR	BPX	R$
17	PHI *	668	104	45	126	5	256	13	9	287	359	551	124	136	136	14	77	0.69	31	24	45	26	143	AAb	14%	158	178	32%	23%	77	4%	71%	14.0	258	$24
18	PHI	659	89	34	96	5	246	34	4	256	354	496	114	88	119	13	73	0.58	29	19	52	28	93	CAc	11%	157	146	16%	16%	66	5%	63%	10.9	220	$21
19	PHI	703	86	29	85	2	226	29	8	236	364	454	113	136	105	17	70	0.67	29	21	50	27	111	BAc	10%	131	143	14%	14%	106	2%	50%	-1.8	185	$12
20	PHI	185	35	10	26	1	245	11	1	247	384	503	118	162	100	16	72	0.67	29	19	52	28	94	BAc	15%	150	161	18%	20%	94	2%	100%	1.6	272	$16
21	PHI	443	64	27	71	3	247	36	2	267	334	530	119	127	115	11	72	0.44	29	20	51	27	101	AAc	17%	172	152	19%	25%	73	5%	60%	-1.1	277	$15
1st Half		336	42	18	46	2	225	22	1	245	301	460	106	123	97	9	71	0.34	33	20	48	26	90	AAd	13%	143	132	17%	21%	73	5%	100%	-10.4	154	$19
2nd Half		107	22	9	25	1	322	14	0	341	439	770	164	144	172	16	77	0.85	19	21	60	33	139	AAa	28%	262	217	22%	34%	80	5%	33%	14.4	677	$8
22	**Proj**	**504**	**85**	**34**	**87**	**3**	**255**	**38**	**4**	**281**	**370**	**576**	**128**	**136**	**125**	**14**	**73**	**0.62**	**29**	**20**	**51**	**27**	**112**		**17%**	**191**	**169**	**21%**	**23%**	**81**	**5%**	**49%**	**31.8**	**363**	**$23**

Hosmer,Eric

Age: 32 Pos: 1B | Bats: L Ht: 6' 4" Wt: 226

Health A | PT/Exp A | Consist C | LIMA Plan B | Rand Var 0 | MM 2135

Sigh. 2020 looked like the mini-breakthrough we'd been clamoring for (Get the ball in the air, Hos!) but was just small sample size variance. The gremlins all returned in 2021: 55%+ GB%; league-average HctX; "F" launch angle; poor Brl% and xPX; mid-teens R$. And now, the playing time is waning. Exhibit A of the perils of short-season analysis.

Yr	Tm	PA	R	HR	RBI	SB	BA	xHR	xSB	xBA	OBP	SLG	OPS+	vL+	vR+	bb%	ct%	Eye	G	L	F	h%	HctX	QBaB	Brl%	PX	xPX	HR/F	xHR/F	Spd	SBA%	SB%	RAR	BPX	R$
17	KC	671	98	25	94	6	318	21	12	298	385	498	120	103	125	10	83	0.63	56	22	22	35	99	BFb	7%	96	65	23%	19%	92	3%	86%	21.0	173	$30
18	SD	677	72	18	69	7	253	19	5	266	322	398	97	70	110	9	77	0.44	60	20	20	30	98	CFd	6%	90	68	19%	20%	86	7%	64%	-14.2	87	$15
19	SD	667	72	22	99	0	265	22	7	252	310	425	102	83	107	6	74	0.25	56	21	23	33	102	BFc	7%	89	77	21%	21%	86	2%	0%	-16.9	22	$15
20	SD	156	23	9	36	4	287	9	1	277	333	517	113	80	130	6	80	0.32	46	20	34	30	136	BDc	10%	116	159	23%	23%	70	11%	100%	1.4	196	$22
21	SD	565	53	12	65	5	269	16	9	255	337	395	101	92	104	8	81	0.48	55	19	26	31	107	BFf	6%	76	70	11%	15%	82	6%	56%	-20.8	104	$14
1st Half		300	25	6	36	4	252	8	5	252	311	350	92	97	91	7	83	0.46	58	19	23	28	117	AFd	5%	54	66	11%	15%	84	6%	67%	-16.5	65	$11
2nd Half		265	28	6	29	1	289	8	5	256	366	447	110	87	122	10	77	0.51	52	19	29	35	95	BFf	7%	103	76	11%	15%	85	6%	33%	0.1	154	$10
22	**Proj**	**525**	**60**	**17**	**71**	**5**	**275**	**19**	**5**	**261**	**336**	**435**	**105**	**85**	**113**	**8**	**79**	**0.40**	**54**	**20**	**27**	**32**	**109**		**7%**	**92**	**89**	**16%**	**18%**	**78**	**5%**	**63%**	**7.9**	**89**	**$19**

Ibáñez,Andy

Age: 29 Pos: 2B | Bats: R Ht: 5' 10" Wt: 170

Health A | PT/Exp C | Consist A | LIMA Plan D+ | Rand Var -1 | MM 2233

7-25-.277 in 272 PA at TEX. It's been a slow burn, but he's hit at every level, including a 1.051 OPS in 129 PA at Triple-A before his recall. That entire 2nd half is vs MLB pitching, where ct%, batted ball quality, and level platoon splits were very un-rookie-like. Late bloomer ingredients abound, meaning that if he happens upon full-time PA... UP: .280, 25 HR

Yr	Tm	PA	R	HR	RBI	SB	BA	xHR	xSB	xBA	OBP	SLG	OPS+	vL+	vR+	bb%	ct%	Eye	G	L	F	h%	HctX	QBaB	Brl%	PX	xPX	HR/F	xHR/F	Spd	SBA%	SB%	RAR	BPX	R$
17	aa	332	28	7	25	5	242		4		292	363	89			7	83	0.42				27				65				110	8%	82%		100	$3
18	aaa	494	45	9	40	1	244		6		291	346	85			6	82	0.37				28				61				93	7%	10%		63	$5
19	aaa	506	64	15	46	5	255		5		312	411	100			8	78	0.37				30				85				100	10%	41%		100	$10
20																																			
21	TEX *	394	45	12	43	1	274	9	5	262	317	448	105	122	93	6	84	0.40	37	20	43	30	106	CBd	7%	96	103	7%	9%	125	1%	100%	1.4	250	$10
1st Half		175	17	5	22	1	246	2	2	254	281	410	96	131	42	5	83	0.29	48	15	37	27	119	CCf	7%	93	94	5%	10%	89	1%	100%	-5.7	169	$3
2nd Half		219	29	7	21	0	296	7	3	267	345	480	112	119	110	7	85	0.51	33	21	45	32	103	CBc	7%	98	105	8%	9%	148	1%	0%	5.1	308	$9
22	**Proj**	**315**	**35**	**9**	**30**	**2**	**273**	**10**	**3**	**255**	**323**	**434**	**103**	**130**	**87**	**7**	**84**	**0.43**	**37**	**21**	**42**	**30**	**109**		**7%**	**88**	**101**	**9%**	**10%**	**128**	**5%**	**46%**	**6.1**	**147**	**$10**

Iglesias,José

Age: 32 Pos: SS | Bats: R Ht: 5' 11" Wt: 195

Health B | PT/Exp A | Consist F | LIMA Plan C+ | Rand Var 0 | MM 2253

Has rolled off impressive run of double-digit R$ seasons after being tagged with a lack of strength in his MiLB days. Contact/BA at the skills core, and there's no signs of that slipping just yet. But take close watch to his playing time, for all those 500-AB seasons support the Runs and RBI opportunities. More than some others, his 2022 team context matters.

Yr	Tm	PA	R	HR	RBI	SB	BA	xHR	xSB	xBA	OBP	SLG	OPS+	vL+	vR+	bb%	ct%	Eye	G	L	F	h%	HctX	QBaB	Brl%	PX	xPX	HR/F	xHR/F	Spd	SBA%	SB%	RAR	BPX	R$
17	DET	489	56	6	54	7	255	3	6	287	288	369	89	88	88	4	86	0.32	50	23	26	29	99	FDc	1%	71	46	6%	3%	78	11%	64%	-14.5	103	$9
18	DET	464	43	5	48	15	269	5	7	279	310	389	94	115	87	4	89	0.40	44	23	34	29	88	DCd	1%	73	45	4%	4%	106	20%	71%	-1.3	190	$13
19	CIN	530	62	11	59	6	288	8	16	284	318	407	100	96	101	4	86	0.29	52	24	24	32	91	DDc	3%	58	53	10%	8%	115	9%	50%	-10.3	130	$14
20	BAL	150	16	3	24	0	373	3	2	350	400	556	127	117	130	2	88	0.18	43	36	21	41	102	DDc	3%	109	53	11%	11%	72	0%	0%	14.4	268	$17
21	2 AL	511	65	9	48	5	271	8	3	263	309	391	96	107	92	4	84	0.28	42	23	34	31	85	DCd	3%	69	63	6%	6%	107	6%	71%	-7.1	138	$13
1st Half		268	33	7	26	2	272	5	1	265	302	397	97	101	96	3	84	0.19	46	23	31	30	86	DDc	4%	68	62	11%	8%	92	6%	67%	-3.8	96	$12
2nd Half		243	32	2	22	3	270	3	1	260	317	385	95	112	87	5	85	0.39	38	24	39	31	85	DCf	3%	70	65	3%	4%	115	6%	75%	-2.7	173	$7
22	**Proj**	**350**	**42**	**6**	**40**	**4**	**281**	**6**	**3**	**282**	**316**	**418**	**100**	**105**	**97**	**4**	**85**	**0.26**	**44**	**26**	**30**	**31**	**91**		**3%**	**81**	**57**	**7%**	**7%**	**90**	**6%**	**67%**	**2.8**	**143**	**$12**

India,Jonathan

Age: 25 Pos: 2B | Bats: R Ht: 6' 1" Wt: 200

Health A | PT/Exp A | Consist A | LIMA Plan B | Rand Var -1 | MM 3335

Alt-site wonderkid won job in March, skipped over Triple-A, and gained some serious momentum as year progressed despite a decidedly 'meh' 2019. Just about every measure improved after June, with G/L/F smoothing and power metrics popping. Even when Year 2 regression hits, the five-category baseline is appealing. He's just getting started.

Yr	Tm	PA	R	HR	RBI	SB	BA	xHR	xSB	xBA	OBP	SLG	OPS+	vL+	vR+	bb%	ct%	Eye	G	L	F	h%	HctX	QBaB	Brl%	PX	xPX	HR/F	xHR/F	Spd	SBA%	SB%	RAR	BPX	R$
17																																			
18																																			
19	aa	132	22	3	13	4	252		3		369	358	101			16	73	0.68				32				58				110	9%	100%		15	$1
20																																			
21	CIN	631	98	21	69	12	269	26	9	260	376	459	115	112	116	11	73	0.50	44	23	33	33	102	CCc	10%	118	97	16%	20%	104	8%	80%	10.5	169	$23
1st Half		285	39	6	31	7	264	9	5	235	380	400	109	116	107	13	74	0.58	50	18	32	34	95	CCd	9%	82	86	11%	16%	135	8%	70%	1.0	112	$17
2nd Half		346	59	15	38	5	273	17	5	279	373	505	119	109	123	11	73	0.44	39	26	35	33	108	CBb	10%	146	105	20%	22%	85	8%	100%	12.5	227	$26
22	**Proj**	**630**	**104**	**23**	**69**	**14**	**265**	**27**	**10**	**255**	**380**	**452**	**113**	**109**	**114**	**13**	**73**	**0.55**	**44**	**23**	**34**	**32**	**103**		**10%**	**114**	**97**	**17%**	**20%**	**91**	**7%**	**87%**	**26.5**	**159**	**$27**

BRENT HERSHEY

Isbel,Kyle

Age: 25 Pos: OF
Bats: L Ht: 5' 11" Wt: 183

Health	A	LIMA Plan	D+
PT/Exp	D	Rand Var	-1
Consist	F	MM	2403

1-7-.276 with 2 SB in 83 PA at KC. Season bookended by three-week MLB stints, the first a surprise, given no experience above High-A. In between, flashed power and speed in AAA, along with decent plate skills (0.49 Eye). Nothing screams "can't miss," but enough here that he should get better chance to make case for regular duty in 2022.

Yr	Tm	PA	R	HR	RBI	SB	BA	xHR	xSB	xBA	OBP	SLG	OPS+	vL+	vR+	bb%	ct%	Eye	G	L	F	h%	HctX	QBaB	Brl%	PX	xPX	HR/F	xHR/F	Spd	SBA%	SB%	RAR	BPX	R$
17																																			
18																																			
19																																			
20																																			
21	KC *	509	60	11	46	18	233	1	7	211	292	366	90	120	104	8	74	0.32	35	18	47	29	80	DAf	4%	81	52	4%	4%	136	21%	75%	-19.7	73	$14
1st Half		242	26	4	16	9	200	1	3	219	253	298	77	138	77	7	70	0.24	39	28	33	27	61	DFf	5%	58	48	0%	17%	158	21%	100%	-17.6	-35	$5
2nd Half		267	34	7	30	8	265	1	4	217	328	429	102	105	123	9	77	0.42	33	12	55	32	93	DAc	3%	100	54	6%	6%	109	21%	59%	-3.3	158	$16
22	Proj	**385**	**46**	**8**	**36**	**11**	**248**	**10**	**12**	**214**	**310**	**382**	**94**	**94**	**94**	**8**	**75**	**0.35**	**36**	**18**	**46**	**31**	**80**		**4%**	**82**	**52**	**6%**	**8%**	**123**	**17%**	**67%**	**-3.2**	**60**	**$9**

Jackson,Alex

Age: 26 Pos: CA
Bats: R Ht: 6' 2" Wt: 215

Health	D	LIMA Plan	D
PT/Exp	D	Rand Var	+3
Consist	B	MM	2403

3-12-.137 in 151 AB at ATL/MIA. Former first-round pick, converted OF continued power surge in AAA, but it came with 67% ct%. And in first extended MLB look, holes in bat grew even more massive. If everything breaks right, maybe he can still have Zunino-esque peak, but road to get there will be littered with BA land mines. Choose another path.

Yr	Tm	PA	R	HR	RBI	SB	BA	xHR	xSB	xBA	OBP	SLG	OPS+	vL+	vR+	bb%	ct%	Eye	G	L	F	h%	HctX	QBaB	Brl%	PX	xPX	HR/F	xHR/F	Spd	SBA%	SB%	RAR	BPX	R$
17	aa	120	12	5	20	0	232		2		298	379	92			9	67	0.29				30				90				93	0%	0%		-36	$0
18	a/a	359	36	7	35	0	185		1		243	325	76			7	61	0.20				28				116				99	0%	0%		-53	-$2
19	ATL *	338	44	22	55	1	193	0	1	212	235	428	92	23	15	5	58	0.13	25	25	50	24	0	FAf	0%	150	-36	0%	0%	82	2%	100%	-11.7	-41	$4
20	ATL	7	0	0	0	0	286	0	0	203	286	429	95	0	133	0	43	0.00	33	33	33	67	58	FCb		204	57	0%	0%	102	0%	0%	0.1	-128	-$3
21	2 NL *	267	29	11	40	1	185	3	1	192	252	382	87	39	78	8	52	0.19	34	19	47	29	77	BAd	7%	164	129	11%	11%	99	2%	100%	-7.8	-42	$0
1st Half		88	12	5	13	1	145	0	0	207	222	393	86	20	47	9	52	0.21	64	0	36	17	78	ACc	0%	184	114	0%	0%	124	2%	100%	-3.7	54	-$4
2nd Half		180	18	6	27	0	204	3	1	192	266	377	87	42	84	8	52	0.18	28	23	49	34	77	BAc	9%	154	132	13%	13%	89	2%	0%	-4.5	-88	$0
22	Proj	**280**	**32**	**5**	**41**	**1**	**195**	**4**	**2**	**166**	**308**	**305**	**83**	**45**	**96**	**8**	**57**	**0.19**	**42**	**14**	**44**	**32**	**77**		**5%**	**91**	**125**	**8%**	**6%**	**102**	**4%**	**100%**	**-8.7**	**-229**	**$3**

Jansen,Danny

Age: 27 Pos: CA
Bats: R Ht: 6' 2" Wt: 225

Health	C	LIMA Plan	B
PT/Exp	D	Rand Var	+3
Consist	A	MM	4143

11-28-.223 in 205 PA at TOR. Just as he was putting early HBP injury and super slow start behind him, hamstring took him out in June. Big 2nd half shows what can happen when health, h% cooperate. Yes, it's only 100 PA, but it's impressive across the board, especially the bountiful barrels. At minimum, he's CA with pop; if stars align... UP: .275, 25 HR

Yr	Tm	PA	R	HR	RBI	SB	BA	xHR	xSB	xBA	OBP	SLG	OPS+	vL+	vR+	bb%	ct%	Eye	G	L	F	h%	HctX	QBaB	Brl%	PX	xPX	HR/F	xHR/F	Spd	SBA%	SB%	RAR	BPX	R$
17	a/a	276	29	5	28	1	295		4		373	451	112			11	89	1.09				32				88				99	1%	100%		239	$6
18	TOR *	432	52	14	59	4	257	4	3	256	340	441	105	94	106	11	82	0.68	32	20	48	28	60	DAf	9%	111	69	10%	13%	104	4%	100%	20.4	233	$11
19	TOR	384	41	13	43	0	207	13	3	237	279	360	89	101	82	8	77	0.39	39	20	41	23	114	CBd	6%	78	97	12%	12%	87	1%	0%	-5.2	59	$1
20	TOR	147	18	6	20	0	183	6	1	243	313	358	89	55	105	14	74	0.68	36	25	39	19	65	FBf	9%	93	74	17%	17%	92	0%	0%	-2.7	116	$4
21	TOR *	229	36	12	31	0	221	10	0	272	292	459	103	79	119	9	77	0.43	31	24	45	23	105	BAf	9%	136	117	17%	16%	77	0%	0%	1.5	227	$3
1st Half		130	15	3	8	0	157	3	0	220	247	271	72	31	95	11	72	0.42	34	25	42	19	68	CAf	4%	72	69	9%	9%	95	0%	0%	-7.8	-12	-$7
2nd Half		100	22	9	23	0	303	7	0	340	350	695	141	150	153	7	83	0.44	27	24	49	28	157	AAf	14%	206	176	26%	23%	74	0%	0%	11.9	519	$6
22	Proj	**385**	**58**	**19**	**56**	**0**	**255**	**19**	**1**	**269**	**341**	**481**	**112**	**95**	**119**	**10**	**78**	**0.52**	**34**	**23**	**43**	**27**	**103**		**9%**	**126**	**108**	**16%**	**16%**	**76**	**1%**	**74%**	**11.7**	**196**	**$13**

Jeffers,Ryan

Age: 25 Pos: CA
Bats: R Ht: 6' 4" Wt: 235

Health	A	LIMA Plan	D
PT/Exp	D	Rand Var	+5
Consist	B	MM	4003

14-35-.199 in 293 PA at MIN. Demoted after 5-for-34 start, impressive power skills reemerged upon June return. xPX, Brl%, 111.2 max exit velo all confirm something's happening here, while bb%, small sample ct% history both suggest plate skills are not a lost cause. In meantime, HR will come with BA tax, but at least there should be plenty of them.

Yr	Tm	PA	R	HR	RBI	SB	BA	xHR	xSB	xBA	OBP	SLG	OPS+	vL+	vR+	bb%	ct%	Eye	G	L	F	h%	HctX	QBaB	Brl%	PX	xPX	HR/F	xHR/F	Spd	SBA%	SB%	RAR	BPX	R$
17																																			
18																																			
19	aa	95	12	4	8	0	279		1		343	467	112			9	77	0.42				32				101				102	0%	0%		148	-$1
20	MIN	62	5	3	7	0	273	4	0	182	355	436	105	93	110	8	65	0.26	53	17	31	36	110	ACf	14%	89	112	27%	36%	111	0%	0%	1.5	-60	$2
21	MIN *	389	38	18	47	0	196	17	1	217	269	394	91	99	88	9	61	0.25	42	21	37	26	98	BCc	14%	136	157	24%	29%	96	1%	0%	-9.0	4	$2
1st Half		212	21	9	27	0	191	6	1	218	286	379	93	152	59	12	64	0.37	50	17	33	24	95	BCc	15%	122	122	23%	27%	111	1%	0%	-4.1	50	$2
2nd Half		177	17	9	20	0	202	11	1	215	266	411	92	63	105	6	57	0.14	37	24	40	29	98	CBc	14%	155	182	24%	30%	84	1%	0%	-4.8	-35	$0
22	Proj	**350**	**34**	**17**	**42**	**0**	**214**	**20**	**1**	**215**	**293**	**416**	**96**	**100**	**94**	**8**	**60**	**0.23**	**45**	**20**	**36**	**30**	**100**		**14%**	**142**	**147**	**25%**	**29%**	**91**	**3%**	**0%**	**1.7**	**-64**	**$6**

Jiménez,Eloy

Age: 25 Pos: LF
Bats: R Ht: 6' 4" Wt: 235

Health	F	LIMA Plan	B
PT/Exp	C	Rand Var	+2
Consist	C	MM	4045

10-37-.249 in 231 AB at CHW. Missed about four months after ill-fated spring attempt to rob HR (torn pec). Late start may excuse stunted growth, but whatever cause, skills look much like 2019. But 2020 happened, too, and if that season's hard contact and xPX return with his health, his first full MLB campaign could be impactful.

Yr	Tm	PA	R	HR	RBI	SB	BA	xHR	xSB	xBA	OBP	SLG	OPS+	vL+	vR+	bb%	ct%	Eye	G	L	F	h%	HctX	QBaB	Brl%	PX	xPX	HR/F	xHR/F	Spd	SBA%	SB%	RAR	BPX	R$
17	aa	73	11	3	7	1	346		1		392	556	129			7	74	0.30				43				131				99	10%	48%		142	$2
18	a/a	446	58	21	68	0	315		6		361	544	121			7	81	0.39				35				128				95	1%	0%		240	$19
19	CHW *	526	71	32	80	0	268	30	3	255	310	509	113	109	116	6	71	0.21	48	18	34	31	94	ACc	13%	128	102	27%	26%	109	0%	0%	5.3	126	$16
20	CHW	226	26	14	41	0	296	15	1	268	332	559	118	112	120	5	74	0.21	52	20	28	34	132	AFd	16%	150	125	31%	33%	86	0%	0%	7.6	212	$24
21	CHW *	270	25	11	38	0	243	11	0	239	292	416	97	78	110	6	70	0.24	48	22	29	30	114	BDc	11%	108	104	22%	24%	67	0%	0%	-10.0	12	$4
1st Half																									0%										
2nd Half		270	25	11	38	0	243	11	0	239	292	416	97	78	110	6	70	0.24	48	22	29	30	114	BDc	11%	108	104	22%	24%	68	0%	0%	-9.4	15	$9
22	Proj	**595**	**68**	**32**	**93**	**0**	**263**	**34**	**1**	**265**	**308**	**494**	**109**	**94**	**113**	**6**	**74**	**0.24**	**49**	**20**	**30**	**30**	**114**		**13%**	**135**	**110**	**26%**	**27%**	**80**	**2%**	**0%**	**14.7**	**105**	**$21**

Joe,Connor

Age: 29 Pos: LF
Bats: R Ht: 6' 0" Wt: 205

Health	B	LIMA Plan	C+
PT/Exp	D	Rand Var	-3
Consist	D	MM	3135

8-35-.285 in 211 PA at COL. Cancer survivor and late bloomer was having 2nd half breakout before Sept hamstring injury ended year. Thin air helped (1.035 home OPS vs. .723 road), but HctX, xPX, Brl% all say he did his part. Walk rate shows good command of strike zone, too. Watch role, but in right situation, he could be a better-than-average Joe.

Yr	Tm	PA	R	HR	RBI	SB	BA	xHR	xSB	xBA	OBP	SLG	OPS+	vL+	vR+	bb%	ct%	Eye	G	L	F	h%	HctX	QBaB	Brl%	PX	xPX	HR/F	xHR/F	Spd	SBA%	SB%	RAR	BPX	R$
17	aa	333	29	4	32	2	187		5		282	277	76			12	76	0.56				23				50				133	10%	24%		30	-$3
18	a/a	405	50	12	40	2	243		6		320	415	99			10	70	0.38				31				116				101	4%	48%		90	$7
19	SF *	422	57	10	46	1	228	0	3	229	315	370	95	31	0	11	71	0.44	70	10	20	29	25	FFc	0%	87	-36	0%	0%	84	3%	22%	-16.4	19	$4
20																																			
21	COL *	311	34	14	49	1	273	9	4	272	355	477	114	128	112	11	75	0.51	33	28	38	32	120	CBc	10%	119	138	15%	17%	80	1%	100%	5.5	165	$9
1st Half		116	8	3	14	0	243	1	1	274	324	382	98	85	88	11	76	0.49	39	32	29	29	91	DCc	5%	85	64	0%	8%	87	1%	0%	-3.7	77	-$3
2nd Half		195	26	10	35	1	292	8	2	276	375	536	123	145	121	12	74	0.52	31	27	42	34	131	BBc	12%	141	168	19%	19%	83	1%	100%	8.9	235	$12
22	Proj	**455**	**55**	**15**	**64**	**2**	**258**	**12**	**3**	**253**	**346**	**424**	**104**	**113**	**101**	**11**	**73**	**0.48**	**34**	**29**	**37**	**32**	**115**		**9%**	**101**	**126**	**13%**	**11%**	**88**	**3%**	**49%**	**7.1**	**54**	**$14**

Jones,Jahmai

Age: 24 Pos: 2B
Bats: R Ht: 6' 0" Wt: 204

Health	A	LIMA Plan	D
PT/Exp	C	Rand Var	+5
Consist	F	MM	1403

0-3-.149 with 1 SB in 72 PA at BAL. Showed power and speed in minors, but by the time major league audition came, bat had cooled. MLB pitchers struck him out a lot and cut his AAA walk rate in half, drying up running opportunities. Still young enough to be get more chances to find groove, but he will have work to do before door opens again.

Yr	Tm	PA	R	HR	RBI	SB	BA	xHR	xSB	xBA	OBP	SLG	OPS+	vL+	vR+	bb%	ct%	Eye	G	L	F	h%	HctX	QBaB	Brl%	PX	xPX	HR/F	xHR/F	Spd	SBA%	SB%	RAR	BPX	R$
17																																			
18	aa	205	29	2	18	10	223		3		301	333	85			10	70	0.37				31				77				128	23%	90%		3	$4
19	aa	530	62	5	47	8	218		17		288	301	82			9	75	0.40				28				51				107	16%	42%		-19	$4
20	LAA	7	2	0	1	0	429	0	0	267	429	429	114	0	133	0	71	0.00	60	40	0	60	0	CFa		0	-26	0%		126	0%	0%	0.6	-292	-$1
21	BAL *	353	31	9	31	9	198	1	3	200	267	329	82	56	54	9	69	0.30	38	18	45	26	55	DAd	2%	82	66	0%	6%	136	16%	73%	-18.9	8	$3
1st Half		118	11	3	14	5	249		1	244	359	401	106	0	0	15	76	0.72	44	20	36	30	0		0%	90	-22	0%		126	16%	80%	0.5	177	$2
2nd Half		235	19	7	17	5	175	1	1	188	221	296	70	56	54	6	66	0.17	38	18	45	23	52	DAd	2%	77	66	0%	6%	128	16%	68%	-20.6	-92	-$1
22	Proj	**280**	**29**	**5**	**25**	**7**	**212**	**4**	**7**	**199**	**296**	**326**	**84**	**89**	**81**	**10**	**71**	**0.37**	**38**	**18**	**45**	**28**	**47**		**2%**	**73**	**59**	**6%**	**6%**	**129**	**14%**	**69%**	**-8.3**	**-25**	**$5**

KRIS OLSON

ones,Taylor

Age: 28	Pos: 1B		Health	A	LIMA Plan	F
Bats: R	Ht: 6' 7"	Wt: 230	PT/Exp	C	Rand Var	-3
			Consist	B	MM	2001

2-16-.245 in 108 PA at HOU. Again pounded AAA pitching (1.009 OPS), though not unexpected at his age. Struggled early but did better after August recall, only to be sent down after stay on COVID IL. For man his size, power has underwhelme in MLB, and plate skills are just so-so. Versatility (LF in HOU, 3B at AAA) may help him carve role, but clock is ticking.

Yr	Tm	PA	R	HR	RBI	SB	BA	xHR	xSB	xBA	OBP	SLG	OPS+	vL+	vR+	bb%	ct%	Eye	G	L	F	h%	HctX	QBaB	Brl%	PX	xPX	HR/F	xHR/F	Spd	SBA%	SB%	RAR	BPX	R$
17																																			
18	a/a	497	46	14	61	2	232		5		302	390	93			9	67	0.31				31				113				86	2%	100%		20	$
19	aaa	493	58	15	56	0	225		3		296	373	93			9	69	0.33				29				90				87	1%	0%		-19	$
20	HOU	22	3	1	3	0	190	1	0	203	227	381	81	0	100	5	67	0.14	50	7	43	23	96	ABb	14%	120	134	17%	17%	101	0%	0%	-1.7	16	-$
21	HOU *	305	34	9	44	0	246	3	1	229	304	413	98	124	79	8	69	0.27	49	16	35	32	76	BCc	7%	114	55	8%	12%	98	2%	0%	-10.1	62	$
1st Half		113	12	1	14	0	222	1	0	199	293	326	86	126	29	9	69	0.32	55	13	32	31	67	BCf	3%	81	18	0%	8%	81	2%	0%	-7.8	-62	-$
2nd Half		192	21	7	30	0	260	2	1	245	310	463	105	119	118	7	70	0.24	43	19	38	33	85	ACb	9%	132	93	14%	14%	120	2%	0%	-4.5	142	$
22	Proj	**210**	**23**	**4**	**28**	**0**	**238**	**6**	**1**	**213**	**296**	**367**	**90**	**112**	**81**	**8**	**69**	**0.29**	**48**	**17**	**35**	**33**	**78**		**7%**	**92**	**63**	**9%**	**12%**	**105**	**4%**	**27%**	**-4.5**	**-65**	**$**

udge,Aaron

Age: 30	Pos: RF CF DH		Health	C	LIMA Plan	D+
Bats: R	Ht: 6' 7"	Wt: 282	PT/Exp	A	Rand Var	0
			Consist	B	MM	5135

Dodged injury bug to produce best season yet in some respects (see ct%, HctX). No, he didn't match rookie HR total, but xHR suggests he should've come closer. GB% that doesn't stray far from 40% and QBaB confirm he's everything you want in a power anchor. Really, if not for history of strains and such, you could take 40 HR to the bank.

Yr	Tm	PA	R	HR	RBI	SB	BA	xHR	xSB	xBA	OBP	SLG	OPS+	vL+	vR+	bb%	ct%	Eye	G	L	F	h%	HctX	QBaB	Brl%	PX	xPX	HR/F	xHR/F	Spd	SBA%	SB%	RAR	BPX	R$
17	NYY	678	128	52	114	9	284	61	12	267	422	627	143	126	144	19	62	0.61	35	22	43	36	113	ABb	26%	223	175	36%	42%	94	6%	69%	67.0	282	$3
18	NYY	498	77	27	67	6	278	30	6	251	392	528	123	128	119	15	63	0.50	42	23	35	38	112	ACa	16%	175	126	29%	32%	77	6%	67%	31.8	160	$2
19	NYY	446	75	27	55	3	272	29	5	256	381	540	127	156	116	14	63	0.45	40	27	32	36	117	ACa	20%	163	150	35%	38%	88	4%	60%	22.1	141	$1
20	NYY	113	23	9	22	0	257	8	1	259	336	554	118	120	117	9	68	0.31	39	20	41	28	116	ABa	12%	166	111	32%	29%	72	4%	0%	3.0	192	$1
21	NYY	633	89	39	98	6	287	45	3	268	373	544	126	135	122	12	71	0.47	41	23	36	34	137	ACa	18%	149	141	28%	32%	53	4%	86%	36.2	177	$3
1st Half		323	45	19	43	0	284	22	1	263	381	529	127	137	122	13	69	0.51	39	26	35	34	139	ACa	20%	145	147	28%	32%	57	4%	0%	16.4	154	$2
2nd Half		310	44	20	55	6	290	23	1	275	365	559	125	132	122	11	73	0.44	43	21	36	33	134	ACb	16%	153	136	27%	32%	59	4%	86%	17.7	215	$3
22	Proj	**609**	**94**	**40**	**101**	**5**	**278**	**43**	**4**	**262**	**370**	**548**	**125**	**133**	**121**	**12**	**68**	**0.44**	**41**	**23**	**36**	**33**	**126**		**17%**	**162**	**136**	**30%**	**33%**	**63**	**3%**	**67%**	**40.2**	**177**	**$3**

ung,Josh

Age: 24	Pos: 3B		Health	A	LIMA Plan	C+
Bats: R	Ht: 6' 2"	Wt: 215	PT/Exp	D	Rand Var	
			Consist	F	MM	3015

By starting year with clear placeholders, TEX seemed to be putting 3B of future on fast track, but surgery on fractured foot scuttled those plans. Express lane is back open after .326/.398/.592 line with 19 HR and plate skills that were fine for a masher in AA/AAA. Last impediments to Opening Day nod may be slow spring or service time shenanigans.

Yr	Tm	PA	R	HR	RBI	SB	BA	xHR	xSB	xBA	OBP	SLG	OPS+	vL+	vR+	bb%	ct%	Eye	G	L	F	h%	HctX	QBaB	Brl%	PX	xPX	HR/F	xHR/F	Spd	SBA%	SB%	RAR	BPX	R$
17																																			
18																																			
19																																			
20																																			
21	a/a	329	43	15	48	2	288		3		341	506	116			7	72	0.29				36				136				86	5%	41%		150	$12
1st Half		65	8	3	13	0	271		1		327	453	109			8	74	0.32				31				96				101	5%	0%		81	-$3
2nd Half		264	35	12	36	2	294		3	263	347	524	118			8	71	0.28	44	20	36	37	0			147	-22	0%		91	5%	58%	9.5	185	$18
22	Proj	**490**	**60**	**16**	**67**	**2**	**266**	**16**	**4**	**236**	**325**	**433**	**103**	**102**	**103**	**8**	**72**	**0.31**	**44**	**20**	**36**	**34**	**98**		**10%**	**105**		**14%**	**14%**	**87**	**5%**	**35%**	**6.1**	**20**	**$16**

Kelenic,Jarred

Age: 22	Pos: CF		Health	A	LIMA Plan	B
Bats: L	Ht: 6' 1"	Wt: 190	PT/Exp	C	Rand Var	+2
			Consist	D	MM	3215

14-43-.181 with 6 SB in 377 PA at SEA. May never have had prayer of living up to hype, but outdid himself with 0-for-42 stretch. Still, 1.016 OPS in 30 AAA games speaks to talent, as does post-Sept 1 MLB work (.248, 7 HR, 3 SB in 118 PA), which came with 72% ct%, spikes in HctX, PX/xPX. 2022 may bring more growing pains, but ceiling may be worth risk.

Yr	Tm	PA	R	HR	RBI	SB	BA	xHR	xSB	xBA	OBP	SLG	OPS+	vL+	vR+	bb%	ct%	Eye	G	L	F	h%	HctX	QBaB	Brl%	PX	xPX	HR/F	xHR/F	Spd	SBA%	SB%	RAR	BPX	R$
17																																			
18																																			
19	aa	91	12	6	18	3	255		1		324	556	122			9	78	0.46				25				145				111	17%	100%		300	$1
20																																			
21	SEA *	514	63	21	64	11	206	18	4	230	280	393	92	67	96	9	71	0.36	43	16	42	24	86	CBd	10%	112	111	15%	19%	79	16%	67%	-18.6	73	$10
1st Half		220	28	9	26	8	189	3	2	223	259	362	86	32	62	9	75	0.37	40	14	46	21	75	CBc	7%	97	101	8%	12%	89	16%	87%	-12.0	85	$9
2nd Half		294	36	12	39	3	220	15	3	232	297	417	97	74	108	10	69	0.35	44	16	40	27	87	CCd	11%	125	115	17%	21%	83	16%	43%	-8.7	88	$12
22	Proj	**595**	**74**	**23**	**76**	**12**	**246**	**28**	**12**	**233**	**324**	**430**	**102**	**83**	**113**	**10**	**73**	**0.39**	**41**	**17**	**41**	**30**	**82**		**9%**	**110**	**109**	**14%**	**17%**	**84**	**11%**	**67%**	**9.4**	**101**	**$21**

Kelly,Carson

Age: 27	Pos: CA		Health	B	LIMA Plan	C+
Bats: R	Ht: 6' 2"	Wt: 210	PT/Exp	B	Rand Var	0
			Consist	C	MM	2025

Torrid April (.340, 6 HR) gave way to weaker rest of season, which was also interrupted by toe, wrist injuries. Profound platoon splits likely to keep him out of catching elite, though sustaining shift away from ground balls would keep 15 HR within reach. It all adds up to "he's fine," but there may be more exciting options.

Yr	Tm	PA	R	HR	RBI	SB	BA	xHR	xSB	xBA	OBP	SLG	OPS+	vL+	vR+	bb%	ct%	Eye	G	L	F	h%	HctX	QBaB	Brl%	PX	xPX	HR/F	xHR/F	Spd	SBA%	SB%	RAR	BPX	R$
17	STL *	346	35	8	40	0	236	1	5	244	307	360	91	38	65	9	83	0.59	56	16	28	26	110	FDc	0%	70	123	0%	6%	73	2%	0%	-4.5	91	$2
18	STL *	372	30	5	34	0	217	1	2	186	300	304	81	24	50	10	82	0.64	54	7	39	25	87	DCd	7%	53	98	0%	9%	88	0%	0%	-5.5	60	$0
19	ARI	365	46	18	47	0	245	15	1	263	348	478	114	157	97	13	75	0.61	37	22	41	27	126	CBc	9%	126	168	19%	15%	80	0%	0%	11.4	196	$7
20	ARI	129	11	5	19	0	221	4	0	232	264	385	86	61	101	5	76	0.21	42	19	39	25	109	DBc	4%	91	100	14%	11%	84	0%	0%	-2.9	56	$4
21	ARI	359	41	13	46	0	240	14	2	245	343	411	104	138	83	12	76	0.59	31	25	44	28	101	CAc	9%	96	115	13%	14%	93	0%	0%	5.2	131	$6
1st Half		187	22	8	26	0	260	10	1	257	385	460	118	168	96	16	75	0.74	29	26	45	30	124	CAc	11%	113	151	15%	19%	88	0%	0%	8.1	188	$6
2nd Half		172	19	5	20	0	221	4	1	234	297	364	89	117	67	9	77	0.44	34	24	43	26	79	CAc	6%	79	81	10%	8%	106	0%	0%	-2.8	85	-$1
22	Proj	**455**	**49**	**16**	**59**	**0**	**240**	**15**	**1**	**241**	**324**	**403**	**99**	**119**	**88**	**10**	**77**	**0.49**	**37**	**22**	**41**	**28**	**107**		**7%**	**92**	**120**	**13%**	**12%**	**78**	**1%**	**0%**	**9.1**	**57**	**$10**

Kemp,Tony

Age: 30	Pos: 2B LF		Health	A	LIMA Plan	D+
Bats: L	Ht: 5' 6"	Wt: 160	PT/Exp	B	Rand Var	-3
			Consist	B	MM	1323

Sustained supreme strike zone control, but what happens when bat leaves shoulder just isn't cutting it. When barrels are 1-in-100 proposition and exit velocity is stuck in lowest tier, PT tends to be tenuous. xHR says he was lucky to even get to 8 HR twice. SBA% seems to be fading with age. May be on verge of entering cling-to-bench-role phase of career.

Yr	Tm	PA	R	HR	RBI	SB	BA	xHR	xSB	xBA	OBP	SLG	OPS+	vL+	vR+	bb%	ct%	Eye	G	L	F	h%	HctX	QBaB	Brl%	PX	xPX	HR/F	xHR/F	Spd	SBA%	SB%	RAR	BPX	R$
17	HOU *	565	66	6	43	16	252	0	7	217	282	346	85	71	66	4	89	0.37	44	9	47	27	90	DAa	0%	48	75	0%	0%	156	20%	65%	-22.7	152	$11
18	HOU *	467	59	6	43	18	259	3	14	261	331	363	93	89	102	9	85	0.70	45	23	32	29	94	FCb	1%	61	80	9%	5%	112	19%	76%	1.0	143	$14
19	2 TM	279	31	8	29	4	212	3	7	241	291	380	93	103	90	8	81	0.49	41	16	43	23	99	DBc	2%	80	110	10%	4%	124	13%	50%	-11.5	159	$2
20	OAK	114	15	0	4	3	247	1	3	253	363	301	88	16	94	13	85	1.07	35	29	35	29	92	FAb	1%	39	97	0%	4%	99	11%	75%	-2.6	116	$4
21	OAK	397	54	8	37	8	279	5	10	254	382	418	110	100	113	13	85	1.02	35	23	42	31	90	DBc	1%	75	98	7%	4%	124	8%	80%	9.4	246	$13
1st Half		205	28	4	18	4	261	2	5	252	388	422	113	105	117	17	80	1.00	35	23	42	31	67	FBd	0%	94	69	7%	4%	111	8%	80%	4.1	242	$7
2nd Half		192	26	4	19	4	296	3	5	256	375	414	107	93	109	10	89	1.06	35	23	42	31	113	DBb	2%	59	124	6%	5%	130	8%	80%	3.4	254	$8
22	Proj	**280**	**38**	**4**	**24**	**7**	**253**	**3**	**5**	**248**	**346**	**368**	**97**	**88**	**99**	**11**	**85**	**0.84**	**37**	**23**	**40**	**28**	**95**		**1%**	**63**	**100**	**5%**	**4%**	**117**	**8%**	**73%**	**1.4**	**167**	**$9**

Kepler,Max

Age: 29	Pos: RF CF		Health	B	LIMA Plan	B+
Bats: L	Ht: 6' 4"	Wt: 225	PT/Exp	A	Rand Var	+3
			Consist	A	MM	3335

Growing evidence that sitting him vL is right call, but while your competitors fixate on ugly BA "trend," you see more barrels than ever, nothing wrong with exit velocity. If he keeps running—and SB% says he should—that helps, too. 2019 HR total is clear outlier, but at this point, everyone realizes it. As a result, there may be a bit of profit to be mined here.

Yr	Tm	PA	R	HR	RBI	SB	BA	xHR	xSB	xBA	OBP	SLG	OPS+	vL+	vR+	bb%	ct%	Eye	G	L	F	h%	HctX	QBaB	Brl%	PX	xPX	HR/F	xHR/F	Spd	SBA%	SB%	RAR	BPX	R$
17	MIN	568	67	19	69	6	243	11	7	256	312	425	100	61	111	8	78	0.41	43	18	40	28	104	CCd	4%	107	93	12%	7%	85	6%	86%	-7.8	121	$10
18	MIN	611	80	20	58	4	224	20	6	249	319	408	97	99	95	12	82	0.74	38	16	46	24	112	BBd	7%	104	120	10%	10%	97	6%	44%	-6.6	217	$10
19	MIN	596	98	36	90	1	252	22	4	275	336	519	118	122	116	10	81	0.61	36	17	47	25	119	BAd	9%	131	113	18%	11%	69	5%	17%	9.0	267	$18
20	MIN	196	27	9	23	3	228	7	1	257	321	439	101	49	120	11	79	0.61	32	22	46	24	103	CAd	5%	112	95	15%	11%	80	7%	100%	-1.2	216	$14
21	MIN	490	61	19	54	10	211	23	6	249	306	413	99	69	110	11	77	0.56	37	19	44	23	113	BBd	11%	112	134	13%	16%	109	9%	100%	-10.4	215	$9
1st Half		196	25	6	27	7	200	8	2	240	296	388	95	68	106	11	74	0.50	39	18	43	23	104	BAd	10%	113	90	11%	15%	108	9%	100%	-6.6	169	$7
2nd Half		294	36	13	27	3	219	15	4	255	313	430	101	69	111	11	80	0.62	36	19	45	23	119	CBd	11%	111	161	14%	16%	109	9%	100%	-5.6	246	$10
22	Proj	**560**	**76**	**24**	**67**	**8**	**230**	**23**	**8**	**252**	**319**	**438**	**103**	**76**	**112**	**11**	**79**	**0.57**	**36**	**19**	**45**	**25**	**111**		**9%**	**115**	**119**	**14%**	**13%**	**91**	**8%**	**87%**	**2.8**	**228**	**$17**

KRIS OLSON

Kieboom,Carter

Age: 24 Pos: 3B
Bats: R Ht: 6' 2" Wt: 210

Health	A	LIMA Plan	D+
PT/Exp	C	Rand Var	+4
Consist	C	MM	1115

6-20-.207 in 249 PA at WAS. Admit it, you're dying to pull trigger on tweet, "More like 'Kie-bust', amirite?" Holding fire looked wise as he rapped 6 HR in August, but atypical barrel barrage became mirage as he closed on 9-for-81 skid. We're obliged to cite age, 2019 AAA line and say, "Stand down for now." But keep that tweet in Drafts.

Yr	Tm	PA	R	HR	RBI	SB	BA	xHR	xSB	xBA	OBP	SLG	OPS+	vL+	vR+	bb%	ct%	Eye	G	L	F	h%	HctX	QBaB	Brl%	PX	xPX	HR/F	xHR/F	Spd	SBA%	SB%	RAR	BPX	R$
17																																			
18	aa	267	31	4	20	3	247		3		300	366	89			7	75	0.30				31				83				102	7%	70%		40	$3
19	WAS *	507	65	15	63	4	262	2	6	221	344	418	105	55	70	11	72	0.45	48	13	39	33	109	ACc	9%	90	137	22%	22%	97	4%	64%	-6.6	52	$12
20	WAS	122	15	0	9	0	202	0	2	196	344	212	74	103	58	14	67	0.52	41	30	29	30	56	DCc	0%	9	27	0%	0%	112	2%	0%	-10.0	-248	$0
21	WAS *	416	45	10	37	1	208	6	3	229	294	324	85	84	85	11	74	0.46	49	21	30	25	90	DDd	4%	71	69	13%	13%	97	2%	40%	-25.7	12	$1
1st Half		155	18	4	17	0	218		1	231	306	352	92	69	0	11	75	0.51	44	20	36	26	0		0%	82	-22	0%		94	2%	0%	-7.2	73	-$1
2nd Half		261	27	6	20	1	202	6	2	222	287	308	80	83	84	11	73	0.43	49	21	30	25	89	DDd	4%	63	69	13%	13%	105	2%	100%	-16.0	-15	$0
22	**Proj**	**490**	**58**	**13**	**46**	**2**	**233**	**11**	**4**	**235**	**336**	**357**	**94**	**109**	**86**	**11**	**72**	**0.45**	**46**	**25**	**29**	**29**	**76**		**2%**	**76**	**52**	**14%**	**12%**	**99**	**4%**	**47%**	**-7.0**	**-45**	**$6**

Kiermaier,Kevin

Age: 32 Pos: CF
Bats: L Ht: 6' 1" Wt: 210

Health	C	LIMA Plan	C+
PT/Exp	A	Rand Var	-3
Consist	A	MM	2523

Made customary three trips to IL (COVID/wrist/quad), but they were mercifully short. SB opps dried up some, but Spd, xSB say he could reach double digits again, while BA just needed some hit-rate love. Beyond that, there's little here. USDA would stamp "rejected" on QBaB, and GB% further buries HR potential. Roster for end-game speed only.

Yr	Tm	PA	R	HR	RBI	SB	BA	xHR	xSB	xBA	OBP	SLG	OPS+	vL+	vR+	bb%	ct%	Eye	G	L	F	h%	HctX	QBaB	Brl%	PX	xPX	HR/F	xHR/F	Spd	SBA%	SB%	RAR	BPX	R$
17	TAM	421	56	15	39	16	276	11	6	252	338	450	107	92	114	7	74	0.31	50	18	32	34	95	CDd	5%	99	70	17%	12%	134	21%	70%	3.9	97	$16
18	TAM	367	44	7	29	10	217	7	10	240	282	370	88	73	92	7	73	0.27	50	19	31	28	84	DDf	5%	91	70	10%	10%	152	20%	67%	-8.7	80	$5
19	TAM	480	60	14	55	19	228	14	12	261	278	398	94	109	87	5	77	0.25	54	17	29	27	88	CDd	6%	88	59	14%	14%	136	26%	79%	-12.5	115	$13
20	TAM	159	16	3	22	8	217	4	6	250	321	362	91	59	96	13	70	0.48	56	24	20	29	88	CFf	6%	85	75	16%	21%	130	23%	89%	-3.3	52	$13
21	TAM	390	54	4	37	9	259	6	15	243	328	388	98	92	101	8	72	0.33	57	18	25	35	82	DFf	4%	84	70	6%	10%	152	14%	64%	-5.5	69	$10
1st Half		195	22	1	13	5	227	2	7	219	282	304	82	77	84	6	67	0.20	59	19	22	33	72	CFf	3%	61	59	4%	7%	118	14%	83%	-11.6	-123	$1
2nd Half		195	32	3	24	4	293	4	8	267	374	479	115	110	118	11	76	0.53	56	17	27	37	93	DFf	4%	106	79	8%	11%	163	14%	50%	5.4	238	$10
22	**Proj**	**350**	**46**	**6**	**39**	**11**	**247**	**8**	**9**	**248**	**319**	**395**	**97**	**90**	**99**	**9**	**73**	**0.36**	**55**	**19**	**26**	**32**	**86**		**5%**	**90**	**70**	**10%**	**13%**	**144**	**14%**	**72%**	**1.7**	**83**	**$12**

Kim,Ha-Seong

Age: 26 Pos: SS 3B 2B
Bats: R Ht: 5' 9" Wt: 168

Health	A	LIMA Plan	C+
PT/Exp	A	Rand Var	+4
Consist	B	MM	2413

Honeymoon for heralded KBO arrival did not last long. Adjustment pains not unexpected, but depth of strikeout woes a surprise. Patient approach in 2nd half provides glimmer of hope, and SB skill at least made the trans-Pacific trip. Between age, four-year deal, he'll get more chances, though you may want to wait to see more ct% before you invest.

Yr	Tm	PA	R	HR	RBI	SB	BA	xHR	xSB	xBA	OBP	SLG	OPS+	vL+	vR+	bb%	ct%	Eye	G	L	F	h%	HctX	QBaB	Brl%	PX	xPX	HR/F	xHR/F	Spd	SBA%	SB%	RAR	BPX	R$
17	for	573	88	14	111	14	282		8		340	446	107			8	88	0.76				30	0			87				99	16%	62%	5.6	215	$24
18	for	554	93	12	82	7	268		13		325	415	99			8	85	0.57				30	0			82				116	7%	76%	7.9	193	$19
19	for	596	109	11	101	30	287		8		354	431	109			9	86	0.74				32	0			76				100	21%	87%	15.1	207	$31
20	for	528	98	16	97	1	283		18		356	434	105			10	88	0.98				29	0			73				98	1%	45%	8.5	256	$57
21	SD	298	27	8	34	6	202	6	2	224	270	352	85	91	83	7	73	0.31	41	17	41	24	87	DCf	4%	90	74	10%	7%	117	12%	86%	-16.8	65	$2
1st Half		189	17	5	21	5	208	4	1	225	265	353	86	105	79	6	74	0.24	39	20	41	25	81	DBf	4%	83	71	9%	8%	135	12%	83%	-10.2	65	$3
2nd Half		109	10	3	13	1	191	2	1	217	280	351	85	74	92	10	72	0.42	46	12	42	23	96	DCf	5%	105	80	10%	7%	97	12%	100%	-5.1	96	-$5
22	**Proj**	**385**	**45**	**10**	**49**	**9**	**240**	**8**	**7**	**226**	**312**	**389**	**95**	**93**	**96**	**9**	**76**	**0.40**	**43**	**15**	**42**	**29**	**90**		**5%**	**91**	**76**	**9%**	**7%**	**106**	**10%**	**87%**	**-2.0**	**93**	**$12**

Kiner-Falefa,Isiah

Age: 27 Pos: SS
Bats: R Ht: 5' 11" Wt: 190

Health	A	LIMA Plan	C+
PT/Exp	A	Rand Var	0
Consist	A	MM	0435

Early power (5 HR by May 2) predictably faded—there's zero skill here and tons of grounders to boot—but SB pace can be sustained, and contact skill should keep BA acceptable. Wild swings in monthly results almost entirely driven by h%. Hasn't caught since 2019, so no guarantee of eligibility bonus, but you're rostering him for his wheels.

Yr	Tm	PA	R	HR	RBI	SB	BA	xHR	xSB	xBA	OBP	SLG	OPS+	vL+	vR+	bb%	ct%	Eye	G	L	F	h%	HctX	QBaB	Brl%	PX	xPX	HR/F	xHR/F	Spd	SBA%	SB%	RAR	BPX	R$
17	aa	550	52	5	43	15	275		8		324	370	94			7	85	0.50				31				58				103	15%	70%		106	$14
18	TEX	396	43	4	34	7	261	2	10	271	325	357	91	106	82	7	83	0.45	51	25	24	31	89	DDc	1%	60	34	6%	3%	114	12%	58%	-3.5	97	$8
19	TEX *	324	31	3	31	5	230	2	5	235	283	327	84	75	91	7	78	0.33	50	17	33	29	98	CDc	1%	62	85	2%	4%	105	7%	100%	-17.7	33	$2
20	TEX	228	28	3	10	8	280	3	6	259	329	370	93	119	82	6	85	0.44	62	16	22	32	101	CFd	2%	42	33	8%	8%	199	20%	62%	-3.5	188	$20
21	TEX	677	74	8	53	20	271	7	21	263	312	357	92	79	98	4	86	0.31	54	20	26	31	95	DFc	2%	49	49	6%	5%	130	14%	80%	-14.9	123	$22
1st Half		356	44	6	28	15	269	5	10	271	304	376	95	74	104	4	83	0.22	58	20	22	31	99	DFc	2%	61	47	10%	8%	141	14%	88%	-5.4	119	$25
2nd Half		321	30	2	25	5	273	3	11	255	321	337	89	83	92	5	89	0.47	49	21	30	30	91	DDd	1%	37	51	2%	4%	112	14%	63%	-8.7	123	$10
22	**Proj**	**595**	**65**	**5**	**45**	**18**	**266**	**7**	**15**	**253**	**317**	**348**	**90**	**89**	**91**	**6**	**85**	**0.38**	**54**	**19**	**27**	**31**	**96**		**2%**	**48**	**52**	**4%**	**5%**	**120**	**12%**	**75%**	**-8.2**	**74**	**$20**

Kingery,Scott

Age: 28 Pos: OF
Bats: R Ht: 5' 10" Wt: 180

Health	D	LIMA Plan	D
PT/Exp	D	Rand Var	+1
Consist	C	MM	2401

0-0-.053 in 19 PA at PHI. July labrum surgery ended another lost year; maybe getting that cleaned up will give "Scotty Jetpacks" needed boost. In theory, still owns 2019 skills that earned "UP: 25 HR/25 SB" two years ago. No way you should bank on anything near that, but 28-year-olds with latent power/speed combos are what last roster spots were made for.

Yr	Tm	PA	R	HR	RBI	SB	BA	xHR	xSB	xBA	OBP	SLG	OPS+	vL+	vR+	bb%	ct%	Eye	G	L	F	h%	HctX	QBaB	Brl%	PX	xPX	HR/F	xHR/F	Spd	SBA%	SB%	RAR	BPX	R$
17	a/a	578	89	24	56	25	275		7		319	478	108			6	77	0.28				32				112				132	24%	82%		155	$25
18	PHI	484	55	8	35	10	226	12	14	220	267	338	81	78	81	5	72	0.19	35	24	41	30	71	DBb	5%	79	102	6%	9%	123	14%	77%	-18.1	3	$7
19	PHI	500	64	19	55	15	258	18	9	247	315	474	109	122	104	7	68	0.23	34	26	40	34	108	CAb	8%	134	123	15%	14%	125	19%	79%	6.5	119	$16
20	PHI	124	12	3	6	0	159	5	2	200	228	283	68	44	78	7	69	0.26	38	18	44	20	92	DBf	10%	80	156	9%	15%	117	0%	0%	-11.5	-28	-$3
21	PHI *	100	8	0	3	2	128	0	1	117	203	189	54	19	0	9	50	0.19	29	14	57	26	0	FAa	0%	59	-22	0%	0%	146	12%	100%	-11.8	-342	-$4
1st Half		100	8	0	3	2	128	0	1	117	203	189	55	20	0	9	50	0.19	29	14	57	26	0	FAa	0%	59	-22	0%	0%	146	12%	100%	-11.3	-346	-$10
2nd Half																									0%										
22	**Proj**	**210**	**23**	**6**	**14**	**4**	**226**	**5**	**4**	**215**	**286**	**374**	**90**	**80**	**93**	**7**	**68**	**0.24**	**36**	**22**	**42**	**30**	**92**		**8%**	**98**	**133**	**10%**	**8%**	**125**	**11%**	**84%**	**-4.3**	**-16**	**$4**

Kirilloff,Alex

Age: 24 Pos: 1B RF
Bats: L Ht: 6' 2" Wt: 195

Health	D	LIMA Plan	B
PT/Exp	D	Rand Var	+2
Consist	A	MM	3135

July wrist surgery hopefully put to rest injury dogging him since 2019, aggravated on head-first slide in May. xHR, exit velocity, Brl% speak to tantalizing power upside, and while it'll take some gumption to assume this risk, the reward might be well worth it. If injury fears soften former top prospect's market, buy and then backfill roster with surer things.

Yr	Tm	PA	R	HR	RBI	SB	BA	xHR	xSB	xBA	OBP	SLG	OPS+	vL+	vR+	bb%	ct%	Eye	G	L	F	h%	HctX	QBaB	Brl%	PX	xPX	HR/F	xHR/F	Spd	SBA%	SB%	RAR	BPX	R$
17																																			
18																																			
19	aa	402	44	8	40	7	276		6		324	402	101			7	79	0.34				33				69				105	13%	51%		67	$9
20																																			
21	MIN	231	23	8	34	1	251	15	2	260	299	423	99	106	96	6	76	0.27	49	22	29	30	108	ADb	13%	101	137	17%	31%	95	4%	50%	-7.7	104	$4
1st Half		185	17	6	28	1	264	12	2	270	303	437	103	107	101	5	76	0.24	49	25	26	32	107	AFb	14%	103	140	17%	34%	95	4%	50%	-4.2	104	$6
2nd Half		46	6	2	6	0	195	3	0	211	283	366	88	106	73	9	76	0.40	48	10	42	21	110	BCa	10%	92	123	15%	23%	112	4%	0%	-2.9	112	-$7
22	**Proj**	**490**	**53**	**22**	**68**	**4**	**268**	**37**	**4**	**255**	**319**	**474**	**108**	**122**	**98**	**6**	**77**	**0.26**	**49**	**16**	**36**	**31**	**109**		**11%**	**116**	**130**	**17%**	**29%**	**102**	**5%**	**47%**	**6.7**	**122**	**$18**

Kirk,Alejandro

Age: 23 Pos: CA
Bats: R Ht: 5' 8" Wt: 265

Health	C	LIMA Plan	C+
PT/Exp	F	Rand Var	0
Consist	F	MM	3043

8-24-.242 in 189 PA at TOR. Beefy backstop hit 60-day IL in early May, but healing, hit tool got him back to majors after 14 AAA games (.924 OPS). Things started to gel in Sept (4 HR, 1.29 Eye, 133 HctX), but 16% h% kept it on down low. Bat good enough to keep DH time coming, boosting counting stats. Window to roster at reasonable cost may close soon.

Yr	Tm	PA	R	HR	RBI	SB	BA	xHR	xSB	xBA	OBP	SLG	OPS+	vL+	vR+	bb%	ct%	Eye	G	L	F	h%	HctX	QBaB	Brl%	PX	xPX	HR/F	xHR/F	Spd	SBA%	SB%	RAR	BPX	R$
17																																			
18																																			
19																																			
20	TOR	25	4	1	3	0	375	1	0	291	400	583	131	37	168	4	83	0.25	55	20	25	42	135	ADb	5%	115	61	20%	20%	57	0%	0%	3.2	208	$1
21	TOR *	242	25	10	36	0	262	10	0	268	335	452	108	134	91	10	85	0.74	41	20	39	27	113	ABc	11%	98	97	14%	18%	22	0%	0%	6.7	181	$5
1st Half		63	11	4	11	0	259	2	0	289	362	521	123	95	123	14	85	1.05	38	21	41	24	81	BBf	9%	126	81	21%	14%	47	0%	0%	3.7	319	-$2
2nd Half		180	15	6	25	0	263	8	0	258	325	429	102	151	82	8	85	0.63	42	20	38	28	123	ABc	12%	89	102	12%	19%	25	0%	0%	3.4	150	$3
22	**Proj**	**315**	**39**	**15**	**50**	**0**	**262**	**16**	**0**	**271**	**347**	**468**	**111**	**129**	**101**	**10**	**85**	**0.77**	**41**	**20**	**39**	**26**	**106**		**11%**	**104**	**94**	**16%**	**17%**	**24**	**0%**	**0%**	**15.8**	**205**	**$11**

KRIS OLSON

Knizner,Andrew

Age: 27 Pos: CA | Bats: R Ht: 6' 1" Wt: 225
Health A | PT/Exp D | Consist B | LIMA Plan F | Rand Var +5 | MM 1101

Is there lonelier ballpark job than Yadier's understudy? Sardine vendor, maybe? Strong BA in minors is getting further in rear view, evidence of power growth has been scant, though playing time is too erratic to draw firm conclusions. Did show good patience, but he'll need to hit ball harder, higher to get our attention. Until real chance comes, safe to ignore.

Yr	Tm	PA	R	HR	RBI	SB	BA	xHR	xSB	xBA	OBP	SLG	OPS+	vL+	vR+	bb%	ct%	Eye	G	L	F	h%	HctX	QBaB	Brl%	PX	xPX	HR/F	xHR/F	Spd	SBA%	SB%	RAR	BPX	R$
17	aa	194	24	3	20	0	305		3		349	430	106			6	85	0.44				35				76				89	2%	0%		124	$4
18	a/a	355	32	5	35	0	273		2		315	366	91			6	84	0.39				31				58				86	0%	0%		73	$5
19	STL *	322	39	11	33	4	234	1	1	219	286	378	92	56	100	7	81	0.40	62	3	36	25	101	CDf	3%	71	85	14%	7%	83	6%	100%	-6.0	85	$4
20	STL	17	1	0	4	0	250	0	0	228	235	313	73	78	70	0	69	0.00	67	25	8	36	116	AFc	0%	56	57	0%	0%	82	0%	0%	-0.6	-208	-$2
21	STL	185	18	1	9	0	174	3	0	210	281	236	71	37	84	11	76	0.51	52	18	30	22	84	CDf	4%	45	58	3%	8%	75	0%	0%	-11.0	-54	-$4
1st Half		93	11	0	2	0	193	1	0	206	280	241	73	62	76	9	76	0.40	46	19	35	25	74	DBf	2%	40	26	0%	5%	95	0%	0%	-5.5	-62	-$8
2nd Half		92	7	1	7	0	154	2	0	209	283	231	69	20	93	13	76	0.63	58	17	25	19	94	CFf	7%	51	93	7%	13%	70	0%	0%	-5.8	-27	-$9
22	Proj	**245**	**25**	**4**	**19**	**1**	**217**	**5**	**0**	**218**	**301**	**311**	**83**	**40**	**98**	**9**	**79**	**0.47**	**55**	**14**	**31**	**26**	**90**		**4%**	**58**	**71**	**7%**	**9%**	**64**	**1%**	**83%**	**-4.4**	**-15**	**-$1**

La Stella,Tommy

Age: 33 Pos: 2B | Bats: L Ht: 5' 11" Wt: 180
Health F | PT/Exp C | Consist B | LIMA Plan D+ | Rand Var +3 | MM 1143

7-27-.250 in 240 PA at SF. Lost three months to hamstring, then was off to specialist (Achilles) as year ended. When healthy, platooned in way apropos of recent splits (only 25 PA vL), but even with protection, gave back gains in ct%, bb%, HctX. Between age, growing list of health woes, hard to see career arc bending back upward in any major way.

Yr	Tm	PA	R	HR	RBI	SB	BA	xHR	xSB	xBA	OBP	SLG	OPS+	vL+	vR+	bb%	ct%	Eye	G	L	F	h%	HctX	QBaB	Brl%	PX	xPX	HR/F	xHR/F	Spd	SBA%	SB%	RAR	BPX	R$
17	CHC *	266	28	6	26	0	231	3	4	249	311	345	89	135	113	10	81	0.59	43	23	34	27	105	CCb	3%	65	95	14%	8%	77	1%	0%	-13.0	58	$0
18	CHC	188	23	1	19	0	266	2	1	258	340	331	90	51	93	9	84	0.63	53	24	23	31	96	DDa	1%	45	56	3%	6%	85	2%	0%	-4.4	60	$1
19	LAA	315	49	16	44	0	295	11	2	291	346	486	115	99	121	6	90	0.71	45	21	33	28	135	CCb	5%	80	104	18%	13%	91	0%	0%	4.4	252	$10
20	2 AL	228	31	5	25	1	281	6	1	285	370	449	109	76	120	12	94	2.25	40	20	40	28	114	CBc	5%	82	77	7%	8%	108	2%	100%	3.2	396	$16
21	SF *	274	31	7	28	0	237	10	1	265	299	379	93	75	101	8	87	0.68	43	21	36	25	102	CCb	6%	75	84	10%	14%	80	0%	0%	-11.3	192	$2
1st Half		77	8	1	5	0	225	3	0	257	286	338	87	0	99	8	84	0.53	48	21	31	26	83	CCa	7%	61	77	6%	17%	114	0%	0%	-4.1	142	-$7
2nd Half		197	23	6	23	0	242	7	1	268	304	395	95	96	101	8	88	0.76	41	21	38	25	111	CBb	6%	80	87	12%	13%	66	0%	0%	-5.5	212	$3
22	Proj	**280**	**35**	**8**	**30**	**0**	**256**	**9**	**1**	**271**	**324**	**403**	**99**	**76**	**103**	**9**	**88**	**0.81**	**44**	**21**	**35**	**27**	**108**		**5%**	**76**	**83**	**10%**	**12%**	**91**	**2%**	**56%**	**2.7**	**191**	**$7**

Larnach,Trevor

Age: 25 Pos: LF RF | Bats: L Ht: 6' 4" Wt: 223
Health B | PT/Exp D | Consist D | LIMA Plan D | Rand Var +1 | MM 1303

7-28-.223 in 301 PA at MIN. For month or so, kept his head above water, but h% warned it wouldn't last. Sure enough, from June 15 to Aug 15, hit .193, as low Brl% zapped power, and then hand injury halted bid to find stroke at AAA. Minors track record suggests pop should get back on track, but he'll have to solve ct% issues if he's to become MLB mainstay.

Yr	Tm	PA	R	HR	RBI	SB	BA	xHR	xSB	xBA	OBP	SLG	OPS+	vL+	vR+	bb%	ct%	Eye	G	L	F	h%	HctX	QBaB	Brl%	PX	xPX	HR/F	xHR/F	Spd	SBA%	SB%	RAR	BPX	R$
17																																			
18																																			
19	aa	177	24	7	21	0	286		3		369	439	112			12	67	0.39				39				88				101	0%	0%		-26	$3
20																																			
21	MIN *	357	39	9	33	1	212	12	4	190	293	343	87	71	102	10	59	0.28	46	18	35	32	81	BCb	9%	101	84	13%	21%	82	1%	100%	-15.9	-135	$1
1st Half		193	25	8	18	0	250	9	2	214	330	441	107	87	121	11	61	0.31	43	18	38	36	94	BCb	13%	138	112	16%	24%	83	1%	0%	-0.6	15	$5
2nd Half		164	14	2	15	1	167	3	2	164	251	230	65	52	75	10	56	0.26	51	19	31	28	62	BCc	5%	54	38	6%	17%	96	1%	100%	-15.5	-308	-$7
22	Proj	**350**	**40**	**6**	**35**	**1**	**239**	**13**	**2**	**185**	**334**	**334**	**91**	**70**	**100**	**11**	**62**	**0.32**	**48**	**18**	**34**	**36**	**75**		**8%**	**72**	**68**	**10%**	**19%**	**95**	**3%**	**100%**	**-6.8**	**-216**	**$6**

Laureano,Ramón

Age: 27 Pos: CF | Bats: R Ht: 5' 11" Wt: 203
Health B | PT/Exp A | Consist C | LIMA Plan C+ | Rand Var +1 | MM 4223

PED penalty will cost him April. Silver lining? More time to heal from surgery on hernia, which reportedly dates to last winter and explains screeching halt of SB after 8 in first 9 games, 2nd half power outage. Still strikes out a bunch, so let xBA set expectations, but with clean bill of health, could be worth waiting for... UP: 2019 redux

Yr	Tm	PA	R	HR	RBI	SB	BA	xHR	xSB	xBA	OBP	SLG	OPS+	vL+	vR+	bb%	ct%	Eye	G	L	F	h%	HctX	QBaB	Brl%	PX	xPX	HR/F	xHR/F	Spd	SBA%	SB%	RAR	BPX	R$
17	aa	496	55	9	47	20	206		5		259	334	81			7	73	0.26				26				78				129	27%	79%		21	$6
18	OAK *	446	62	15	47	16	269	9	17	247	335	449	105	105	112	9	68	0.31	44	25	31	36	100	BCc	11%	124	86	15%	26%	112	17%	83%	8.5	83	$17
19	OAK	481	79	24	67	13	288	22	11	263	340	521	119	117	119	6	72	0.22	36	25	39	35	99	BBc	10%	134	108	19%	18%	101	14%	87%	13.4	137	$21
20	OAK	222	27	6	25	2	213	8	5	225	338	366	93	85	96	11	68	0.41	43	22	35	28	91	CCf	9%	96	100	13%	18%	86	5%	67%	-10.5	0	$10
21	OAK	378	43	14	39	12	246	20	3	253	317	443	104	117	98	7	71	0.28	43	22	35	31	94	CCc	11%	124	108	16%	24%	96	20%	71%	-10.5	112	$12
1st Half		276	37	13	30	8	237	17	2	251	319	457	108	117	103	8	71	0.31	42	20	38	28	96	CCd	13%	129	122	19%	25%	114	20%	73%	-6.3	162	$18
2nd Half		102	6	1	9	4	271	3	1	260	314	406	97	118	88	5	71	0.18	46	28	26	37	89	DCc	5%	109	74	6%	17%	77	20%	67%	-3.3	23	-$2
22	Proj	**420**	**49**	**15**	**47**	**10**	**252**	**19**	**10**	**248**	**322**	**440**	**103**	**109**	**101**	**7**	**70**	**0.27**	**43**	**22**	**35**	**32**	**94**		**9%**	**123**	**97**	**16%**	**20%**	**82**	**14%**	**69%**	**6.2**	**92**	**$15**

Lee,Khalil

Age: 24 Pos: RF | Bats: L Ht: 5' 10" Wt: 170
Health A | PT/Exp C | Consist B | LIMA Plan F | Rand Var -1 | MM 2301

0-1-.056 in 18 PA at NYM. After three-way trade, Mets let him play nearly full year at AAA. Beneath surface of .951 OPS were a ton of strikeouts (he whiffed in 13 of 18 MLB PA, too), though bb% history is a positive. And after huge SB total at AA in 2019, stumbled badly on basepaths, too. More time in minors to smooth out rough edges seems warranted.

Yr	Tm	PA	R	HR	RBI	SB	BA	xHR	xSB	xBA	OBP	SLG	OPS+	vL+	vR+	bb%	ct%	Eye	G	L	F	h%	HctX	QBaB	Brl%	PX	xPX	HR/F	xHR/F	Spd	SBA%	SB%	RAR	BPX	R$
17																																			
18	aa	111	13	2	9	2	234		1		299	332	85			8	72	0.33				31				72				99	15%	45%		-13	$0
19	aa	531	69	7	48	49	259		14		344	363	98			12	67	0.39				38				69				116	41%	80%		-67	$27
20																																			
21	NYM *	358	48	9	27	6	206	0	5	198	314	357	92	0	30	14	51	0.32	60	20	20	37	83	BFc	0%	136	28	0%	0%	117	21%	32%	-19.0	-88	$3
1st Half		141	16	1	9	2	185	0	2	190	284	278	78	0	30	12	54	0.30	60	20	20	33	89	BFc	0%	87	28	0%	0%	114	21%	26%	-11.9	-200	-$5
2nd Half		217	32	8	17	3	220		3	191	333	410	101	0	0	14	48	0.33	44	20	36	40	0		0%	173	-22	0%		120	21%	37%	-5.0	-4	$5
22	Proj	**210**	**27**	**3**	**16**	**9**	**222**	**3**	**6**	**188**	**315**	**330**	**88**	**87**	**88**	**12**	**58**	**0.32**	**46**	**20**	**34**	**36**	**84**		**4%**	**90**		**8%**	**8%**	**120**	**17%**	**61%**	**-6.9**	**-148**	**$6**

LeMahieu,DJ

Age: 33 Pos: 2B 1B 3B | Bats: R Ht: 6' 4" Wt: 220
Health A | PT/Exp A | Consist F | LIMA Plan B | Rand Var +3 | MM 1255

More so than for most, one column will dictate his 2022 fate: where did HctX go and is it coming back? Otherwise, cake is baked—too many grounders, not enough barrels. Age hints best days behind him, but mild rebound could happen, as xHR says he's owed a few. Still, if others are bidding on another batting title or 20+ HR, let them chase that pipe dream.

Yr	Tm	PA	R	HR	RBI	SB	BA	xHR	xSB	xBA	OBP	SLG	OPS+	vL+	vR+	bb%	ct%	Eye	G	L	F	h%	HctX	QBaB	Brl%	PX	xPX	HR/F	xHR/F	Spd	SBA%	SB%	RAR	BPX	R$
17	COL	682	95	8	64	6	310	6	12	289	374	409	107	130	97	9	85	0.66	56	25	20	35	105	BFa	2%	56	60	8%	6%	110	5%	55%	14.6	115	$23
18	COL	581	90	15	62	6	276	15	6	280	321	428	100	119	89	6	85	0.45	50	21	29	30	109	ADb	5%	88	97	11%	11%	102	8%	55%	10.1	180	$18
19	NYY	655	109	26	102	5	327	25	10	302	375	518	124	148	114	7	85	0.51	50	24	26	35	119	ADb	8%	92	90	19%	19%	108	4%	71%	40.9	230	$31
20	NYY	216	41	10	27	3	364	5	3	327	421	590	134	131	135	8	89	0.86	57	22	21	37	128	AFb	3%	104	76	27%	14%	134	4%	100%	26.2	396	$33
21	NYY	679	84	10	57	4	268	13	8	262	349	362	98	92	100	11	84	0.78	52	22	26	30	94	BFc	4%	53	62	8%	10%	100	3%	67%	-4.4	127	$15
1st Half		350	44	7	33	2	270	7	4	268	346	373	100	94	103	10	83	0.68	56	23	21	31	90	BFc	4%	57	61	13%	13%	92	3%	100%	-2.5	108	$17
2nd Half		329	40	3	24	2	266	6	4	256	353	350	95	90	97	11	86	0.90	48	22	30	30	99	ADd	4%	50	63	4%	8%	104	3%	50%	-5.4	150	$9
22	Proj	**630**	**94**	**14**	**67**	**5**	**278**	**15**	**6**	**280**	**345**	**409**	**102**	**103**	**102**	**9**	**86**	**0.70**	**52**	**22**	**25**	**30**	**107**		**4%**	**71**	**73**	**12%**	**12%**	**104**	**5%**	**70%**	**14.5**	**168**	**$22**

Lewis,Kyle

Age: 26 Pos: CF | Bats: R Ht: 6' 4" Wt: 205
Health F | PT/Exp C | Consist B | LIMA Plan C | Rand Var +1 | MM 4413

Opened year on IL after March run-in with wall and may never have fully healed, as same knee needed surgery by late May. Rehab hit snag and return never materialized, but what a tease those six weeks in between were: improved ct%, FB%, HctX, xPX. Sample is small, but if others lean "wait and see," maybe let them see his stats add up on your roster.

Yr	Tm	PA	R	HR	RBI	SB	BA	xHR	xSB	xBA	OBP	SLG	OPS+	vL+	vR+	bb%	ct%	Eye	G	L	F	h%	HctX	QBaB	Brl%	PX	xPX	HR/F	xHR/F	Spd	SBA%	SB%	RAR	BPX	R$
17																																			
18	aa	146	15	3	16	1	190		1		268	318	79			10	72	0.38				24				88				91	3%	100%		20	-$2
19	SEA *	587	70	17	74	3	248	6	6	202	323	404	101	72	140	10	61	0.28	51	14	35	37	69	BCa	23%	108	144	40%	40%	115	4%	57%	-1.5	-44	$11
20	SEA	242	37	11	28	5	262	10	3	215	364	437	106	105	106	14	66	0.48	43	20	36	35	87	CCd	11%	101	97	22%	20%	127	8%	83%	5.1	44	$24
21	SEA	147	15	5	11	2	246	8	3	224	333	392	100	88	103	11	72	0.43	33	24	43	31	101	BBd	14%	87	118	13%	20%	115	5%	100%	-1.0	54	$1
1st Half		147	15	5	11	2	246	8	3	224	333	392	101	90	105	11	72	0.43	33	24	43	31	101	BBd	14%	87	118	13%	20%	115	5%	100%	-1.7	54	$1
2nd Half																									0%										
22	Proj	**420**	**50**	**22**	**51**	**5**	**239**	**25**	**5**	**236**	**325**	**453**	**106**	**89**	**111**	**11**	**68**	**0.40**	**41**	**20**	**39**	**29**	**89**		**15%**	**130**	**118**	**22%**	**25%**	**108**	**6%**	**88%**	**11.3**	**74**	**$13**

KRIS OLSON

Lindor,Francisco

Age: 28 Pos: SS	Health B	LIMA Plan B+
Bats: B Ht: 5' 11" Wt: 190	PT/Exp A	Rand Var +2
	Consist B	MM 3335

Took time to adjust to new home, but 2nd half skills show that 2017-19 hitter is still there (note BPX), even with IL stint for oblique injury. And while his previous BA/SB level has diminished, 2nd half HR/xHR pace hints at possibility of a power rebound. One good half-season doesn't return him to the Top 15, but there's more value here than you might realize.

Yr	Tm	PA	R	HR	RBI	SB	BA	xHR	xSB	xBA	OBP	SLG	OPS+	vL+	vR+	bb%	ct%	Eye	G	L	F	h%	HctX	QBaB	Brl%	PX	xPX	HR/F	xHR/F	Spd	SBA%	SB%	RAR	BPX	R$
17	CLE	723	99	33	89	15	273	30	9	289	337	505	115	120	109	8	86	0.65	39	18	42	28	122	CBc	7%	120	122	14%	13%	101	11%	83%	27.1	267	$26
18	CLE	745	129	38	92	25	277	35	12	292	352	519	117	133	108	9	84	0.65	39	22	40	28	128	BBc	9%	131	135	17%	16%	93	20%	71%	45.5	297	$38
19	CLE	654	101	32	74	22	284	25	16	292	335	518	118	108	122	7	84	0.47	44	20	37	29	122	ACd	8%	115	104	17%	14%	106	19%	81%	24.7	274	$30
20	CLE	266	30	8	27	6	258	8	7	270	335	415	100	97	100	9	83	0.59	38	26	36	28	102	BCc	6%	85	82	11%	11%	97	12%	75%	1.0	192	$21
21	NYM	524	73	20	63	10	230	23	10	245	322	412	101	97	102	11	79	0.60	39	19	42	25	104	BCf	8%	96	114	13%	15%	108	11%	71%	-3.0	185	$14
1st Half		331	43	9	27	7	215	11	6	238	310	356	93	96	91	11	80	0.64	42	18	40	24	99	CCf	7%	77	95	10%	12%	103	11%	78%	-9.2	146	$13
2nd Half		193	30	11	36	3	256	12	4	258	344	506	115	98	125	12	76	0.55	35	20	45	27	113	BAd	10%	130	147	19%	21%	119	11%	60%	5.9	269	$13
22	Proj	**665**	**95**	**29**	**83**	**15**	**255**	**30**	**12**	**263**	**334**	**460**	**108**	**103**	**109**	**10**	**81**	**0.58**	**39**	**21**	**40**	**27**	**111**		**8%**	**108**	**115**	**15%**	**15%**	**104**	**9%**	**73%**	**16.5**	**230**	**$25**

Long Jr.,Shed

Age: 26 Pos: LF	Health F	LIMA Plan D
Bats: L Ht: 5' 8" Wt: 184	PT/Exp D	Rand Var +1
	Consist B	MM 2201

4-17-.198 with 1 SB in 121 PA at SEA. Second straight season that shin injuries have kept him out of action, and even when he's been able to take the field, subpar ct%, anemic power skills, and too-high GB% continue to plague his MLB performance. If leg issues are going to limit his running game, there's no reason left to invest.

Yr	Tm	PA	R	HR	RBI	SB	BA	xHR	xSB	xBA	OBP	SLG	OPS+	vL+	vR+	bb%	ct%	Eye	G	L	F	h%	HctX	QBaB	Brl%	PX	xPX	HR/F	xHR/F	Spd	SBA%	SB%	RAR	BPX	R$
17	aa	162	14	4	15	4	230		2		329	372	95			13	76	0.61				28				82				119	12%	80%		100	$1
18	aa	502	64	11	48	16	239		10		314	375	92			10	69	0.36				32				92				114	19%	71%		23	$13
19	SEA *	409	49	12	41	4	241	4	10	235	298	400	97	139	99	8	69	0.26	47	21	31	32	78	CCc	6%	94	64	14%	11%	114	11%	37%	-11.4	4	$6
20	SEA	128	10	3	9	4	171	4	1	208	242	291	71	27	87	9	68	0.30	64	10	26	22	76	CFf	6%	78	61	14%	19%	80	17%	100%	-8.7	-80	$2
21	SEA *	156	19	5	18	1	210	3	3	236	274	368	88	70	96	8	68	0.28	63	14	23	27	72	DFc	4%	102	73	25%	19%	102	3%	100%	-5.8	8	$0
1st Half		103	16	4	14	0	220	2	2	254	270	413	95	93	90	6	72	0.25	63	12	26	26	85	DFb	3%	118	94	27%	18%	111	3%	0%	-3.4	119	-$2
2nd Half		53	3	1	4	1	191	1	1	184	283	277	76	33	103	11	60	0.32	64	18	18	30	52	DFc	6%	62	41	20%	20%	93	3%	100%	-3.4	-231	-$8
22	Proj	**210**	**21**	**6**	**20**	**4**	**233**	**6**	**2**	**224**	**302**	**378**	**92**	**71**	**104**	**9**	**67**	**0.30**	**60**	**15**	**24**	**32**	**70**		**5%**	**94**	**63**	**20%**	**18%**	**91**	**4%**	**82%**	**-2.8**	**-53**	**$5**

Longoria,Evan

Age: 36 Pos: 3B	Health F	LIMA Plan C+
Bats: R Ht: 6' 1" Wt: 213	PT/Exp B	Rand Var -1
	Consist B	MM 4133

As exit velocity has spiked, power skills have rebounded. xHR, xHR/F both agree there's another 30-HR season in his bat if he can stay healthy enough to return to 500 PA. June shoulder injury clearly impacted 2nd half, and any worries over lowest ct% since rookie year should be mitigated by best bb% since 2011. Likely to be undervalued this spring.

Yr	Tm	PA	R	HR	RBI	SB	BA	xHR	xSB	xBA	OBP	SLG	OPS+	vL+	vR+	bb%	ct%	Eye	G	L	F	h%	HctX	QBaB	Brl%	PX	xPX	HR/F	xHR/F	Spd	SBA%	SB%	RAR	BPX	R$
17	TAM	677	71	20	86	6	261	19	9	266	313	424	100	92	101	7	82	0.42	43	20	37	29	114	CCd	5%	91	91	11%	10%	85	5%	86%	-12.5	130	$15
18	SF	512	51	16	54	3	244	20	4	250	281	413	93	99	88	4	79	0.22	42	18	39	28	120	CCc	8%	99	114	11%	13%	105	4%	75%	-11.7	123	$9
19	SF	508	59	20	69	3	254	24	6	250	325	437	105	118	99	8	75	0.38	41	22	37	30	115	BCa	8%	96	123	16%	19%	119	3%	75%	-8.9	119	$11
20	SF	209	26	7	28	0	254	13	1	258	297	425	96	112	89	5	80	0.28	50	18	32	29	125	ACb	11%	92	115	14%	26%	97	2%	0%	-6.4	136	$13
21	SF	291	45	13	46	1	261	17	1	255	351	482	114	148	102	12	73	0.51	41	19	40	31	130	ABb	13%	136	151	17%	23%	78	3%	50%	3.4	196	$8
1st Half		186	28	9	30	1	280	13	1	273	376	516	124	174	104	13	74	0.60	38	24	38	33	145	ABa	15%	142	171	20%	29%	82	3%	50%	7.7	242	$11
2nd Half		105	17	4	16	0	228	4	0	223	305	424	99	98	98	10	72	0.38	47	9	44	27	104	ABd	10%	125	114	13%	13%	79	3%	0%	-2.3	123	-$2
22	Proj	**420**	**61**	**19**	**65**	**1**	**258**	**22**	**2**	**253**	**325**	**468**	**108**	**124**	**101**	**9**	**76**	**0.39**	**44**	**17**	**39**	**30**	**120**		**11%**	**122**	**126**	**17%**	**20%**	**83**	**3%**	**54%**	**9.9**	**143**	**$15**

Lopez,Nicky

Age: 27 Pos: SS	Health A	LIMA Plan B+
Bats: L Ht: 5' 11" Wt: 175	PT/Exp A	Rand Var -5
	Consist D	MM 0435

Probably helped win some fantasy titles with surprising BA, SB output, but odds are against a repeat. High h% added 40 points to BA/OBP, which gave more opportunities to run, and even if SB% represents newly-learned skill, he's unlikely to be that elite again. Further SB growth will require higher SBA% that he has yet to own; be cautious with valuation.

Yr	Tm	PA	R	HR	RBI	SB	BA	xHR	xSB	xBA	OBP	SLG	OPS+	vL+	vR+	bb%	ct%	Eye	G	L	F	h%	HctX	QBaB	Brl%	PX	xPX	HR/F	xHR/F	Spd	SBA%	SB%	RAR	BPX	R$
17	aa	246	23	0	10	6	248		4		291	284	78			6	87	0.47				29				23				122	15%	60%		52	$2
18	a/a	553	61	7	43	12	281		17		345	376	97			9	89	0.87				31				48				140	12%	65%		187	$15
19	KC *	533	65	4	40	8	257	2	10	277	304	349	90	90	80	6	89	0.59	62	16	22	28	78	DFb	1%	50	5	3%	3%	125	10%	64%	-17.2	170	$8
20	KC	192	15	1	13	0	201	1	3	242	286	266	73	58	79	9	76	0.44	55	26	19	26	73	FFf	2%	47	51	4%	4%	89	11%	0%	-14.0	-44	-$1
21	KC	565	78	2	43	22	300	4	14	269	365	378	102	96	104	9	85	0.66	55	21	23	35	87	DFf	1%	46	48	2%	4%	154	13%	96%	8.8	165	$25
1st Half		243	33	0	12	8	266	1	6	258	353	329	95	97	95	12	85	0.88	56	20	23	31	84	FFf	0%	36	34	0%	3%	169	13%	100%	-3.2	165	$9
2nd Half		322	45	2	31	14	324	3	8	275	375	414	107	95	112	7	86	0.50	55	22	23	37	90	DFd	1%	52	58	4%	5%	137	13%	93%	9.5	154	$28
22	Proj	**595**	**72**	**3**	**45**	**15**	**270**	**4**	**16**	**263**	**335**	**345**	**92**	**87**	**94**	**8**	**84**	**0.59**	**57**	**21**	**22**	**32**	**83**		**1%**	**45**	**40**	**3%**	**4%**	**130**	**12%**	**73%**	**-3.4**	**91**	**$19**

Lowe,Brandon

Age: 27 Pos: 2B	Health B	LIMA Plan B+
Bats: L Ht: 5' 10" Wt: 185	PT/Exp A	Rand Var +3
	Consist B	MM 5335

He's been hitting dingers at a 40-HR clip since 2019, just needed the 600+ PA to prove it. Skills say he can do it again, though declining exit velocity could be something to monitor. The good news? Low h% kept him from full value, and 2nd half ct% jump hints at yet another level of potential value. UP: adding .285 BA, 110 R, 120 RBI to those 40 HR

Yr	Tm	PA	R	HR	RBI	SB	BA	xHR	xSB	xBA	OBP	SLG	OPS+	vL+	vR+	bb%	ct%	Eye	G	L	F	h%	HctX	QBaB	Brl%	PX	xPX	HR/F	xHR/F	Spd	SBA%	SB%	RAR	BPX	R$
17	aa	97	7	2	10	1	225		1		239	339	79			2	68	0.06				31				78				106	13%	44%		-76	-$1
18	TAM *	576	78	24	89	9	251	8	10	254	335	467	108	93	105	11	69	0.40	43	22	35	32	88	BBc	11%	146	100	19%	25%	97	10%	66%	17.8	147	$19
19	TAM	327	42	17	51	5	270	20	5	235	336	514	118	94	123	8	62	0.22	30	27	43	38	92	AAb	16%	156	130	22%	26%	119	7%	100%	10.2	93	$10
20	TAM	224	36	14	37	3	269	15	3	261	362	554	122	148	112	11	70	0.43	33	24	43	31	122	BAc	18%	161	154	24%	25%	122	5%	100%	12.8	280	$25
21	TAM	615	97	39	99	7	247	39	6	261	340	523	119	90	132	11	69	0.41	34	22	44	28	99	CBd	14%	171	137	24%	24%	90	6%	88%	20.3	242	$23
1st Half		314	41	16	39	4	204	19	3	224	312	422	102	60	122	12	63	0.36	40	18	42	25	84	CCd	14%	144	135	23%	27%	96	6%	80%	-6.7	88	$15
2nd Half		301	56	23	60	3	291	20	3	298	369	626	135	119	142	11	74	0.47	30	25	46	31	115	CAd	14%	194	139	25%	22%	88	6%	100%	26.0	392	$33
22	Proj	**595**	**93**	**36**	**100**	**8**	**261**	**38**	**7**	**256**	**347**	**529**	**119**	**106**	**124**	**11**	**68**	**0.37**	**34**	**23**	**43**	**32**	**103**		**15%**	**167**	**136**	**23%**	**25%**	**101**	**6%**	**91%**	**33.8**	**222**	**$28**

Lowe,Josh

Age: 24 Pos: OF	Health A	LIMA Plan D+
Bats: L Ht: 6' 4" Wt: 205	PT/Exp B	Rand Var 0
	Consist C	MM 3401

0-0-1.000 with 1 SB in 2 PA at TAM. His cup of coffee was more like a shot of espresso, as he crammed as much as he could into 2 PA. With a full season each at AA and AAA, plus a year spent at alternate training site, extended call-up could come at any time, and the potential for 20 SB/20 HR with it. There's little chance he's the next Moonlight Graham.

Yr	Tm	PA	R	HR	RBI	SB	BA	xHR	xSB	xBA	OBP	SLG	OPS+	vL+	vR+	bb%	ct%	Eye	G	L	F	h%	HctX	QBaB	Brl%	PX	xPX	HR/F	xHR/F	Spd	SBA%	SB%	RAR	BPX	R$
17																																			
18																																			
19	aa	507	68	17	61	29	241		8		329	419	104			12	67	0.40				32				107				117	31%	75%		52	$20
20																																			
21	TAM *	457	66	19	68	24	264	0	6	280	351	475	113	0	276	12	65	0.38	100	0	0	36	0	FF	0%	145	-22	0%	#DIV/0!	109	21%	100%	14.3	131	$25
1st Half		193	25	8	29	10	266		2	248	329	479	112	0	0	9	67	0.29	44	20	36	35	0		0%	144	-22	0%		103	21%	100%	3.8	131	$16
2nd Half		265	41	11	39	14	262	0	4	271	367	472	113	0	272	14	63	0.45	100	0	0	37	0	FF	0%	146	-22	0%	#DIV/0!	113	21%	100%	8.8	127	$25
22	Proj	**210**	**30**	**6**	**30**	**10**	**257**	**6**	**7**	**225**	**346**	**421**	**104**	**103**	**104**	**12**	**65**	**0.39**	**42**	**23**	**35**	**36**	**96**		**10%**	**114**		**14%**	**14%**	**109**	**16%**	**83%**	**4.9**	**45**	**$11**

Lowe,Nate

Age: 26 Pos: 1B	Health A	LIMA Plan B
Bats: L Ht: 6' 4" Wt: 220	PT/Exp A	Rand Var 0
	Consist A	MM 2325

Is there an award for hardest-hit grounders? Asking for a friend who owns frustrating combo of elite exit velocity, high GB%. 2nd half batted-ball output got so out of whack that it killed already-shaky power; it's probably time to set aside 2020 HR/F as small-sample outlier it was. Add in xBA downside, and he looks like wrong bat for bat-first position.

Yr	Tm	PA	R	HR	RBI	SB	BA	xHR	xSB	xBA	OBP	SLG	OPS+	vL+	vR+	bb%	ct%	Eye	G	L	F	h%	HctX	QBaB	Brl%	PX	xPX	HR/F	xHR/F	Spd	SBA%	SB%	RAR	BPX	R$
17																																			
18	a/a	325	47	14	50	1	278		5		360	483	113			11	77	0.55				32				121				93	2%	43%		187	$10
19	TAM *	558	76	20	71	1	252	7	3	244	350	432	108	136	101	13	69	0.49	40	24	36	32	99	ACc	11%	110	93	19%	19%	79	1%	100%	3.5	59	$12
20	TAM	76	10	4	11	1	224	3	0	229	316	433	99	48	114	12	58	0.32	46	28	26	31	60	CDa	15%	141	82	40%	30%	98	6%	100%	-1.5	4	$4
21	TEX	642	75	18	72	8	264	25	10	239	357	415	106	103	108	12	71	0.49	55	18	27	34	103	AFc	10%	94	88	17%	23%	114	4%	100%	-2.5	77	$19
1st Half		346	37	12	43	4	258	15	5	232	355	416	108	104	110	13	69	0.47	51	20	29	34	107	ADc	11%	96	101	20%	25%	114	4%	100%	-4.3	54	$20
2nd Half		296	38	6	29	4	270	10	4	247	358	413	104	102	105	12	73	0.52	59	16	26	35	99	BFc	9%	92	73	12%	20%	114	4%	100%	-2.6	108	$13
22	Proj	**595**	**76**	**16**	**73**	**5**	**265**	**23**	**7**	**244**	**356**	**416**	**105**	**98**	**107**	**12**	**72**	**0.50**	**50**	**21**	**28**	**34**	**93**		**11%**	**95**	**86**	**15%**	**21%**	**97**	**5%**	**93%**	**11.1**	**63**	**$19**

BRANDON KRUSE

Lowrie, Jed

Age: 38	Pos: 2B DH	Health: F	LIMA Plan: D+	
Bats: B	Ht: 6'0" Wt: 180	PT/Exp: B	Rand Var: -1	
		Consist: D	MM: 3033	

CON: He's old; only one season removed from catastrophic knee injury; troubling declines (setting aside 2019-20) in ct%, xBA. PRO: Just set new career bests in exit velocity and Brl%, and note PX/xPX gap. Look at xHR! Can't ignore risks, but he's hit 20+ HR before. VERDICT: Cons relegate him to later rounds, but he's a power sleeper there.

Yr	Tm	PA	R	HR	RBI	SB	BA	xHR	xSB	xBA	OBP	SLG	OPS+	vL+	vR+	bb%	ct%	Eye	G	L	F	h%	HctX	QBaB	Brl%	PX	xPX	HR/F	xHR/F	Spd	SBA%	SB%	RAR	BPX	R$
17	OAK	645	86	14	69	0	277	19	10	280	360	448	110	101	110	11	82	0.73	29	27	43	32	115	CAa	6%	103	115	7%	9%	101	1%	0%	16.3	203	$
18	OAK	680	78	23	99	0	267	21	3	260	353	448	107	95	111	11	79	0.61	33	23	43	31	117	CBc	5%	110	125	11%	10%	98	0%	0%	24.0	187	$
19	NYM *	55	5	1	2	0	160	0	0	208	221	258	66	0	20	7	60	0.19	33	33	33	23	0	FAf		61	-36	0%	0%	108	0%	0%	-4.6	-222	$
20																																			
21	OAK	512	55	14	69	0	245	26	5	244	318	398	98	93	101	10	76	0.45	36	22	41	29	115	BBb	9%	95	150	10%	18%	77	0%	0%	-4.6	100	$
1st Half		304	37	8	36	0	253	16	3	252	329	399	101	98	104	10	78	0.51	36	25	40	30	117	ABb	10%	90	150	10%	19%	87	0%	0%	-2.7	119	$
2nd Half		208	18	6	33	0	234	10	2	232	303	397	95	84	98	9	74	0.38	37	19	44	28	112	BBc	8%	104	150	10%	16%	73	0%	0%	-4.6	88	$
22	Proj	434	49	15	60	0	254	19	1	256	330	437	104	95	108	10	78	0.51	34	23	43	29	115		8%	110	138	11%	14%	84	2%	0%	9.9	122	$

Luplow, Jordan

Age: 28	Pos: CF	Health: D	LIMA Plan: D+	
Bats: R	Ht: 6'1" Wt: 195	PT/Exp: D	Rand Var: +3	
		Consist: B	MM: 4111	

11-28-.202 in 193 PA at CLE/TAM. If this was him swapping ct% for power, it was not a good trade. Double-digit HR almost entirely a product of FB%. That leaves no room for upside without more PA, which isn't likely. Why? Because BA/xBA have crashed so badly that even elite bb% isn't enough to salvage value. 2019's looking more like an outlier.

Yr	Tm	PA	R	HR	RBI	SB	BA	xHR	xSB	xBA	OBP	SLG	OPS+	vL+	vR+	bb%	ct%	Eye	G	L	F	h%	HctX	QBaB	Brl%	PX	xPX	HR/F	xHR/F	Spd	SBA%	SB%	RAR	BPX	R$
17	PIT *	541	71	22	60	4	263	2	8	242	326	453	106	90	88	8	78	0.42	38	16	46	30	88	DAf	5%	105	103	12%	8%	98	7%	44%	-1.7	133	$
18	PIT *	447	48	9	45	7	231	3	6	232	300	379	91	94	76	9	78	0.44	42	15	42	28	66	DBf	7%	91	75	10%	10%	122	11%	63%	-6.6	137	$
19	CLE *	314	51	17	43	5	275	12	6	265	370	533	125	164	79	13	71	0.53	40	21	39	33	100	BBc	12%	145	110	23%	19%	103	10%	59%	17.7	222	$
20	CLE	92	8	2	8	0	192	3	2	216	304	359	88	102	74	13	76	0.63	35	13	52	23	87	FAf	7%	99	90	6%	10%	131	5%	0%	-3.7	196	$
21	2AL *	246	29	13	35	1	197	10	2	224	315	435	103	94	123	15	66	0.51	31	14	54	23	87	DAf	10%	155	135	19%	18%	97	7%	24%	-4.2	192	$
1st Half		124	12	7	20	0	170	7	1	225	318	430	104	94	121	18	68	0.67	30	12	58	16	91	CAf	13%	161	152	18%	18%	90	7%	0%	-3.4	250	$
2nd Half		122	17	6	15	1	222	2	1	227	311	440	102	94	129	11	65	0.37	33	18	49	28	82	DAf	5%	150	106	21%	11%	113	7%	45%	-1.9	154	$
22	Proj	245	32	12	32	2	228	10	3	238	327	464	107	111	102	12	71	0.47	35	16	49	26	86		8%	144	109	16%	13%	107	7%	47%	5.2	165	$

Lux, Gavin

Age: 24	Pos: SS 2B	Health: B	LIMA Plan: B	
Bats: L	Ht: 6'2" Wt: 190	PT/Exp: B	Rand Var: 0	
		Consist: D	MM: 2425	

7-46-.242 with 4 SB in 381 PA at LA. Declining trends in HctX, PX/xPX, and SBA% capture frustration surrounding top prospect's MLB progress. Career PA total (532) is close to a full season, and suggests floor of 12-15 HR, 7-8 SB, though career .234 xBA remains area of weakness. Tiny September sample (.360 BA, 1.13 Eye over 60 PA) may be a spark.

Yr	Tm	PA	R	HR	RBI	SB	BA	xHR	xSB	xBA	OBP	SLG	OPS+	vL+	vR+	bb%	ct%	Eye	G	L	F	h%	HctX	QBaB	Brl%	PX	xPX	HR/F	xHR/F	Spd	SBA%	SB%	RAR	BPX	R$
17																																			
18	aa	115	17	3	7	2	287		2		352	424	104			9	79	0.47				34				79				120	13%	42%		113	$
19	LA *	588	94	24	72	10	304	2	14	268	369	513	122	58	104	9	74	0.40	39	27	33	37	135	CCa	6%	112	164	12%	12%	133	10%	63%	23.7	170	$2
20	LA	69	8	3	8	1	175	2	1	216	246	349	79	37	87	9	70	0.32	48	14	39	20	109	CCa	7%	101	110	18%	12%	103	8%	100%	-5.1	40	$
21	LA *	453	61	8	53	4	239	9	9	236	315	354	92	72	103	10	75	0.45	47	21	31	30	93	BCc	4%	69	80	9%	11%	143	4%	80%	-17.9	77	$
1st Half		272	35	6	33	3	228	8	5	232	309	357	93	59	105	10	74	0.44	47	20	33	28	92	BCc	6%	76	87	10%	13%	129	4%	75%	-12.6	69	$
2nd Half		181	26	2	20	1	255	1	4	245	326	351	91	110	101	9	77	0.45	49	24	27	32	93	CCc	0%	57	63	5%	5%	154	4%	100%	-6.6	77	$
22	Proj	490	71	12	52	8	252	11	7	244	327	395	98	79	103	9	76	0.42	46	22	32	31	104		5%	82	99	11%	10%	139	7%	71%	1.3	83	$

Machado, Manny

Age: 29	Pos: 3B	Health: A	LIMA Plan: D+	
Bats: R	Ht: 6'3" Wt: 218	PT/Exp: A	Rand Var: 0	
		Consist: D	MM: 3245	

Stat fluctuations have earned him D in Consistency, but 2019's odd ct% plunge aside, skills show more stability. xHR says he's usually good for 30+ HR, and career .280 BA/.268 xBA are nearly in agreement, leaving SB as one true wild card. (Let us never forget 2015's 20 SB followed up by 0 in 2016.) Pay for single-digit steals, rejoice if you get more.

Yr	Tm	PA	R	HR	RBI	SB	BA	xHR	xSB	xBA	OBP	SLG	OPS+	vL+	vR+	bb%	ct%	Eye	G	L	F	h%	HctX	QBaB	Brl%	PX	xPX	HR/F	xHR/F	Spd	SBA%	SB%	RAR	BPX	R$
17	BAL	690	81	33	95	9	259	33	8	266	310	471	106	112	102	7	82	0.43	42	16	42	27	131	ACd	11%	112	131	15%	15%	94	9%	69%	-5.2	185	$2
18	2 TM	709	84	37	107	14	297	36	11	281	367	538	121	122	119	10	84	0.67	40	18	42	31	119	ABc	11%	128	115	16%	16%	96	9%	88%	45.1	290	$3
19	SD	661	81	32	85	5	256	26	10	251	334	462	110	151	98	10	75	0.41	42	17	41	28	118	ACf	8%	101	121	17%	14%	100	5%	63%	-4.6	167	$1
20	SD	254	44	16	47	6	304	14	3	294	370	580	126	123	127	10	83	0.70	37	22	41	30	131	BBd	11%	134	108	21%	18%	107	14%	90%	15.4	384	$2
21	SD	640	92	28	106	12	278	36	13	271	347	489	115	109	117	10	82	0.62	39	20	41	30	137	ACf	13%	112	123	15%	19%	97	9%	80%	12.4	262	$2
1st Half		319	44	13	52	9	259	15	6	265	335	457	110	107	111	11	81	0.65	40	21	39	28	130	ACd	11%	104	115	15%	17%	114	9%	82%	2.8	246	$2
2nd Half		321	48	15	54	3	297	21	6	277	358	521	119	109	122	9	83	0.58	37	18	44	31	143	ABf	15%	120	130	15%	20%	85	9%	75%	13.5	285	$2
22	Proj	665	94	33	104	8	281	35	10	272	349	506	116	118	115	10	82	0.60	39	20	41	30	131		12%	118	120	16%	17%	93	8%	66%	33.3	254	$3

Madrigal, Nick

Age: 25	Pos: 2B	Health: D	LIMA Plan: B	
Bats: R	Ht: 5'8" Wt: 175	PT/Exp: D	Rand Var: 0	
		Consist: A	MM: 1353	

Once again season ended with surgery, this time to repair hamstring tear. Offers unicorn value as one of dwindling number of .300 hitters in MLB; what he'll add beyond that is an open question, as minor league SBA% has yet to materialize in majors. Mind the Health grade, but he racked up 532 PA in 2019—if that happens in 2022, he's a $20 player.

Yr	Tm	PA	R	HR	RBI	SB	BA	xHR	xSB	xBA	OBP	SLG	OPS+	vL+	vR+	bb%	ct%	Eye	G	L	F	h%	HctX	QBaB	Brl%	PX	xPX	HR/F	xHR/F	Spd	SBA%	SB%	RAR	BPX	R$
17																																			
18																																			
19	a/a	306	51	2	25	16	314		6		369	408	108			8	96	2.17				32				46				125	28%	63%		281	$
20	CHW	109	8	0	11	2	340	0	6	283	376	369	99	59	109	4	93	0.57	55	26	19	36	83	FFc	0%	19	10	0%	0%	119	8%	67%	0.3	132	$
21	2TM	215	30	2	21	1	305	1	5	302	349	425	106	135	94	5	92	0.65	60	20	20	33	81	DFc	1%	61	14	6%	3%	164	5%	33%	0.6	204	$
1st Half		215	30	2	21	1	305	1	5	302	349	425	108	136	96	5	92	0.65	60	20	20	33	81	DFc	1%	61	14	6%	3%	164	5%	33%	1.7	296	$
2nd Half																								0%											
22	Proj	420	54	4	40	9	318	3	7	302	364	416	106	116	102	5	93	0.82	58	23	19	33	82		1%	50	12	5%	5%	148	8%	58%	13.6	204	$2

Maldonado, Martin

Age: 35	Pos: CA	Health: A	LIMA Plan: D	
Bats: R	Ht: 6'0" Wt: 230	PT/Exp: A	Rand Var: +4	
		Consist: B	MM: 2003	

You're at the end of a long draft day, lost in a fog of computer-strained eyesight, running on the fumes of coffee and cheap donuts. You need a second catcher. A voice in your head whispers: *Maldonado*. His BA history makes you vomit in your mouth a little. (Stupid donuts!) But his xHR/F skill looks solid. "$1!" you cry, before passing out under the table.

Yr	Tm	PA	R	HR	RBI	SB	BA	xHR	xSB	xBA	OBP	SLG	OPS+	vL+	vR+	bb%	ct%	Eye	G	L	F	h%	HctX	QBaB	Brl%	PX	xPX	HR/F	xHR/F	Spd	SBA%	SB%	RAR	BPX	R$
17	LAA	471	43	14	38	0	221	15	5	221	276	368	88	85	87	3	72	0.13	49	15	37	27	78	DCd	9%	91	78	13%	14%	73	2%	0%	-16.0	-21	$
18	2 AL	404	39	9	44	0	225	9	1	227	276	351	84	86	82	4	74	0.16	41	21	38	28	86	DBc	5%	83	86	9%	9%	68	1%	0%	-4.9	-23	$
19	3 TM	374	46	12	27	0	213	13	1	237	293	378	93	96	91	9	74	0.37	48	17	35	25	103	CCc	8%	95	94	15%	15%	69	0%	0%	-1.4	48	$
20	HOU	165	19	6	24	1	215	5	0	217	350	378	97	113	88	16	62	0.53	35	28	37	29	64	DBd	7%	106	79	19%	16%	58	2%	100%	0.6	-52	$
21	HOU	426	40	12	36	0	172	12	2	200	272	300	79	91	73	11	66	0.37	37	21	42	22	75	CBd	6%	82	101	12%	12%	73	0%	0%	-20.5	-99	$
1st Half		223	21	5	21	0	181	5	1	207	269	296	79	106	64	9	65	0.29	36	26	38	25	82	CBc	5%	77	104	10%	10%	82	0%	0%	-11.1	-131	$
2nd Half		203	19	7	15	0	161	7	1	189	276	305	78	67	83	13	67	0.47	38	15	47	19	68	DAf	7%	88	98	13%	13%	65	0%	0%	-9.0	-46	$
22	Proj	385	41	12	38	0	202	10	0	211	297	348	87	96	84	11	68	0.38	39	21	40	26	78		6%	93	93	13%	11%	60	1%	0%	-3.9	39	$

Mancini, Trey

Age: 30	Pos: 1B DH	Health: A	LIMA Plan: B+	
Bats: R	Ht: 6'4" Wt: 230	PT/Exp: A	Rand Var: 0	
		Consist: D	MM: 3135	

A laudable comeback from cancer, and 2nd half power drop was likely caused by fatigue from missing all of 2020 and/or HR Derby hangover effect. If we operate under that assumption, 1st half xHR suggests that 30-HR power is still there, lying in wait. Forget about return to .290 BA—career xBA is .262—and your valuation should be right on target.

Yr	Tm	PA	R	HR	RBI	SB	BA	xHR	xSB	xBA	OBP	SLG	OPS+	vL+	vR+	bb%	ct%	Eye	G	L	F	h%	HctX	QBaB	Brl%	PX	xPX	HR/F	xHR/F	Spd	SBA%	SB%	RAR	BPX	R$
17	BAL	586	65	24	78	1	293	27	6	263	338	488	112	100	115	6	74	0.24	51	19	30	36	103	CDc	10%	112	113	20%	22%	121	1%	100%	7.5	112	$
18	BAL	636	69	24	58	0	242	28	3	249	299	416	96	86	98	7	74	0.29	55	19	26	29	91	BFb	12%	104	95	21%	24%	102	1%	0%	-5.5	80	$
19	BAL	679	106	35	97	1	291	30	4	283	364	535	124	127	123	9	76	0.44	46	22	32	33	98	BDc	11%	129	118	24%	20%	103	1%	100%	33.1	222	$2
20																																			
21	BAL	616	77	21	71	0	255	27	6	252	326	432	104	122	94	8	74	0.36	48	20	31	31	103	CCc	10%	108	94	16%	21%	82	0%	0%	-10.9	104	$
1st Half		339	45	15	53	0	257	17	4	254	330	457	110	130	100	9	74	0.38	49	19	32	30	102	CCc	12%	118	100	21%	24%	64	0%	0%	-5.1	119	$
2nd Half		277	32	6	18	0	254	10	3	247	321	401	98	115	86	8	74	0.34	48	21	31	32	105	BCc	8%	96	87	10%	17%	109	0%	0%	-10.2	81	$
22	Proj	630	80	26	71	0	263	28	3	261	329	461	107	114	103	8	75	0.34	47	21	31	31	100		10%	117	100	19%	21%	95	2%	60%	11.4	101	$

BRANDON KRUSE

Margot,Manuel

Age: 27	Pos: RF CF LF	Health	B	LIMA Plan	C+
Bats: R	Ht: 5' 11" Wt: 180	PT/Exp	A	Rand Var	0
		Consist	A	MM	1423

It's tempting to blame disappointing SB total on July 5 hamstring injury. While 2nd half SBA% didn't budge (and matched 2017-18 rates), his success rate plummeted. At this point, skill baseline is pretty well-established: he's a .250 hitter who can get you 10-12 HR and 15-20 SB. Target that value level, and hope he runs like it's 2019-20.

Yr Tm	PA	R	HR	RBI	SB	BA	xHR	xSB	xBA	OBP	SLG	OPS+	vL+	vR+	bb%	ct%	Eye	G	L	F	h%	HctX	QBaB	Brl%	PX	xPX	HR/F	xHR/F	Spd	SBA%	SB%	RAR	BPX	R$
17 SD	529	53	13	39	17	263	8	7	251	313	409	98	112	91	7	78	0.33	41	23	36	31	80	DCd	3%	79	75	9%	6%	167	19%	71%	-8.4	127	$14
18 SD	519	50	8	51	11	245	10	14	251	292	384	91	87	90	6	82	0.36	43	20	37	29	118	BCf	3%	81	106	6%	7%	150	19%	52%	-13.8	167	$10
19 SD	441	59	12	37	20	234	6	12	238	304	387	96	123	85	9	78	0.43	43	16	40	27	90	CBf	4%	81	82	10%	5%	153	24%	83%	-12.8	156	$12
20 TAM	159	19	1	11	12	269	3	6	251	327	352	90	83	92	8	83	0.52	45	23	32	32	97	DDf	4%	55	86	3%	8%	126	38%	75%	-3.7	124	$19
21 TAM	464	55	10	57	13	254	12	25	250	313	382	96	102	90	8	83	0.53	46	18	36	28	102	CCf	5%	69	81	8%	10%	136	18%	62%	-12.2	181	$15
1st Half	280	32	9	42	9	245	8	14	261	293	402	97	104	91	6	84	0.42	47	18	35	26	98	CCf	6%	81	80	12%	11%	128	18%	69%	-9.1	200	$19
2nd Half	184	23	1	15	4	269	4	12	233	344	350	94	101	87	11	83	0.70	46	18	36	32	107	CCc	3%	51	82	2%	8%	143	18%	50%	-5.2	150	$3
22 Proj	**420**	**51**	**9**	**43**	**14**	**256**	**9**	**12**	**249**	**318**	**390**	**96**	**103**	**92**	**8**	**82**	**0.51**	**45**	**19**	**36**	**29**	**100**		**4%**	**75**	**84**	**8%**	**8%**	**133**	**16%**	**71%**	**-0.1**	**146**	**$13**

Marsh,Brandon

Age: 24	Pos: CF	Health	A	LIMA Plan	C+
Bats: L	Ht: 6' 4" Wt: 215	PT/Exp	C	Rand Var	-1
		Consist	C	MM	2405

2-19-.254 with 6 SB in 260 PA at LAA. 41% MLB h% made him one of the luckiest hitters in baseball, and xBA might not even be true downside, as LD% will be tough to repeat. That said, moving toward 2019 SBA% could keep SB stable, and exit velocity, xPX, xHR are very intriguing. Low FB% is an obstacle, but next step forward might be double-digit HR.

Yr Tm	PA	R	HR	RBI	SB	BA	xHR	xSB	xBA	OBP	SLG	OPS+	vL+	vR+	bb%	ct%	Eye	G	L	F	h%	HctX	QBaB	Brl%	PX	xPX	HR/F	xHR/F	Spd	SBA%	SB%	RAR	BPX	R$
17																																		
18																																		
19 aa	405	45	7	40	17	281		6		361	404	106			11	72	0.44				37				77				100	19%	76%		11	$14
20																																		
21 LAA *	364	43	4	24	7	237	8	5	220	300	346	89	76	100	8	62	0.24	44	31	25	37	100	ADa	11%	84	122	6%	22%	129	9%	88%	-11.9	-104	$5
1st Half	68	9	1	1	1	135		1	186	241	218	64	0	0	12	63	0.37	44	20	36	20	0		0%	63	-22	0%		130	9%	100%	-6.7	-127	-$9
2nd Half	295	33	3	23	7	260	8	5	221	314	376	93	75	99	7	62	0.21	44	31	25	41	100	ADa	11%	88	122	6%	22%	126	9%	87%	-6.0	-112	$11
22 Proj	**560**	**66**	**9**	**36**	**14**	**241**	**12**	**10**	**214**	**317**	**355**	**91**	**72**	**100**	**10**	**65**	**0.30**	**47**	**23**	**30**	**35**	**90**		**10%**	**83**	**110**	**9%**	**12%**	**118**	**9%**	**85%**	**-2.3**	**-75**	**$14**

Marte,Ketel

Age: 28	Pos: CF 2B	Health	C	LIMA Plan	B+
Bats: B	Ht: 6' 1" Wt: 210	PT/Exp	A	Rand Var	-4
		Consist	F	MM	3355

Hamstrings gave equal opportunity IL stints—right in the 1st half, left in the 2nd. That might be reason not to give up on running game just yet, though Spd, SBA% trends are not good. Other 2021 skills compare favorably to 2019, suggesting that with return to health—and last year's grade was an A—he could bring upper-tier fantasy value once again.

Yr Tm	PA	R	HR	RBI	SB	BA	xHR	xSB	xBA	OBP	SLG	OPS+	vL+	vR+	bb%	ct%	Eye	G	L	F	h%	HctX	QBaB	Brl%	PX	xPX	HR/F	xHR/F	Spd	SBA%	SB%	RAR	BPX	R$
17 ARI *	582	70	9	45	8	276	5	8	273	332	416	102	97	100	8	86	0.59	45	21	34	31	98	CDc	3%	76	77	8%	8%	137	8%	69%	-3.3	188	$13
18 ARI	580	68	14	59	6	260	14	9	285	332	437	103	129	86	9	85	0.68	51	20	29	28	113	CDd	5%	93	84	11%	11%	128	5%	86%	11.3	243	$14
19 ARI	628	97	32	92	10	329	28	8	307	389	592	136	139	133	8	85	0.62	43	22	35	34	123	BCc	9%	122	107	19%	17%	117	7%	83%	66.6	337	$32
20 ARI	195	19	2	17	1	287	4	3	274	323	409	97	143	78	4	88	0.33	46	21	33	32	114	CDd	4%	71	80	4%	8%	108	2%	100%	-2.1	208	$11
21 ARI	374	52	14	50	2	318	15	3	295	377	532	125	159	109	8	82	0.52	46	22	32	35	134	ACd	9%	123	116	16%	17%	91	2%	100%	22.2	285	$17
1st Half	148	24	4	21	1	370	5	1	314	419	556	136	186	118	8	84	0.57	52	26	22	42	126	AFd	9%	111	85	16%	20%	92	2%	100%	15.5	281	$11
2nd Half	226	28	10	29	1	283	10	1	282	350	517	117	145	102	8	81	0.49	41	20	40	31	140	BCc	9%	131	138	15%	15%	90	2%	100%	8.4	288	$11
22 Proj	**595**	**79**	**23**	**73**	**5**	**300**	**21**	**4**	**295**	**355**	**515**	**118**	**149**	**104**	**7**	**84**	**0.50**	**46**	**22**	**33**	**32**	**125**		**7%**	**117**	**103**	**15%**	**14%**	**100**	**4%**	**90%**	**40.2**	**280**	**$27**

Marte,Starling

Age: 33	Pos: CF	Health	B	LIMA Plan	D+
Bats: R	Ht: 6' 1" Wt: 195	PT/Exp	A	Rand Var	-4
		Consist	B	MM	2545

PRO: Tied career high in SB cuz he's a crafty vet who's learned to pick his spots (see SB%), xHR says he could still pop 20, and while BA was fluky, xBA still above average. CON: Hit-rate-inflated OBP helped prop up SB total, and QBaB, declining xPX history don't suggest power rebound is imminent. But even mild overall pullback still yields elite value.

Yr Tm	PA	R	HR	RBI	SB	BA	xHR	xSB	xBA	OBP	SLG	OPS+	vL+	vR+	bb%	ct%	Eye	G	L	F	h%	HctX	QBaB	Brl%	PX	xPX	HR/F	xHR/F	Spd	SBA%	SB%	RAR	BPX	R$
17 PIT *	377	51	8	33	23	275	9	6	245	318	376	94	55	108	6	79	0.30	49	21	30	33	84	FCc	6%	54	77	10%	13%	138	25%	85%	-6.6	42	$16
18 PIT	606	81	20	72	33	277	27	22	272	327	460	106	96	107	6	81	0.32	51	17	32	31	99	CDc	8%	105	106	14%	19%	137	33%	70%	15.4	203	$31
19 PIT	586	97	23	82	25	295	25	27	297	342	503	117	108	119	4	83	0.27	50	21	28	32	108	CDc	8%	102	89	19%	20%	135	22%	81%	21.9	233	$30
20 2 NL	250	36	6	27	10	281	8	9	272	340	430	102	92	106	5	82	0.29	53	19	28	32	97	DFd	6%	83	74	12%	16%	123	19%	83%	1.0	172	$29
21 2 TM	526	89	12	55	47	308	18	20	276	381	456	115	104	120	8	79	0.43	55	21	24	37	106	CFd	8%	88	69	14%	20%	140	33%	90%	24.1	177	$42
1st Half	197	35	6	18	12	289	7	8	260	396	452	118	114	120	14	77	0.67	52	20	29	35	103	DFf	10%	92	81	17%	19%	132	33%	86%	7.5	185	$18
2nd Half	329	54	6	37	35	319	11	12	283	372	458	112	97	119	5	80	0.28	56	22	22	38	108	CFc	8%	85	63	12%	21%	137	33%	92%	14.4	162	$49
22 Proj	**560**	**89**	**14**	**61**	**37**	**290**	**21**	**31**	**271**	**353**	**442**	**108**	**97**	**112**	**7**	**80**	**0.36**	**53**	**20**	**27**	**34**	**103**		**8%**	**88**	**78**	**13%**	**19%**	**129**	**25%**	**86%**	**23.3**	**182**	**$37**

Martin,Austin

Age: 23	Pos: SS CF	Health	A	LIMA Plan	D
Bats: R	Ht: 6' 0" Wt: 185	PT/Exp	D	Rand Var	
		Consist	F	MM	1411

Top prospect led all of Double-A in OBP despite trade from TOR to MIN at trade deadline. While he was drafted as SS, played half the season in CF and might wind up a utility guy. Extremely smart hitter who can be too selective at times, power is still questionable; most observers see BA/OBP with double-digit steals as main drivers of early MLB value.

Yr Tm	PA	R	HR	RBI	SB	BA	xHR	xSB	xBA	OBP	SLG	OPS+	vL+	vR+	bb%	ct%	Eye	G	L	F	h%	HctX	QBaB	Brl%	PX	xPX	HR/F	xHR/F	Spd	SBA%	SB%	RAR	BPX	R$
17																																		
18																																		
19																																		
20																																		
21 aa	376	50	4	26	10	240		6		333	333	92			12	72	0.51				32				66				111	14%	70%		8	$7
1st Half	166	22	1	12	3	242		3		327	340	93			11	68	0.39				35				74				115	14%	58%		-38	$1
2nd Half	211	28	2	14	7	238		3	223	338	328	90			13	76	0.63	44	20	36	30	0			59	-22	0%		119	14%	77%	-4.4	58	$5
22 Proj	**140**	**19**	**2**	**10**	**4**	**255**	**2**	**4**	**232**	**346**	**355**	**95**	**94**	**95**	**12**	**73**	**0.51**	**45**	**25**	**30**	**34**	**0**		**4%**	**67**		**6%**	**6%**	**122**	**12%**	**72%**	**0.0**	**-1**	**$4**

Martin,Jason

Age: 26	Pos: LF	Health	A	LIMA Plan	F
Bats: L	Ht: 5' 9" Wt: 185	PT/Exp	D	Rand Var	-2
		Consist	D	MM	3211

6-17-.208 in 154 PA with 3 SB at TEX. Cleared outright waivers in Oct and elected free agency after mediocre season. Has flashed mildly promising power/speed combo at times, and has double-digit HR/SB potential if he ever gets platoon role vR. But weak BA history and subpar defense/arm holds him back, making reserve OF likeliest short-term outcome.

Yr Tm	PA	R	HR	RBI	SB	BA	xHR	xSB	xBA	OBP	SLG	OPS+	vL+	vR+	bb%	ct%	Eye	G	L	F	h%	HctX	QBaB	Brl%	PX	xPX	HR/F	xHR/F	Spd	SBA%	SB%	RAR	BPX	R$
17 aa	316	33	10	32	6	253		3		292	445	100			5	69	0.18				34				130				105	21%	49%		73	$6
18 a/a	505	57	10	45	10	246		15		301	375	91			7	74	0.30				31				78				132	19%	43%		50	$11
19 PIT *	434	43	6	42	9	233	2	9	253	282	359	89	111	83	6	76	0.29	52	20	28	29	91	AFa	8%	75	103	0%	29%	111	18%	58%	-24.5	48	$5
20 PIT	11	2	0	0	0	0	0	0	0	182	0	24	65	15	18	56	0.50	60	0	40	0	0	FAf		0	-26	0%	0%	111	0%	0%	-1.8	-420	-$4
21 TEX *	302	33	13	36	4	204	6	1	224	277	378	90	29	101	9	70	0.34	46	17	38	24	90	DCf	8%	100	119	16%	16%	92	14%	49%	-19.7	31	$3
1st Half	127	15	7	19	2	210	1	0	217	295	426	100	28	79	11	64	0.33	60	5	35	26	87	DDf	5%	136	91	14%	14%	101	14%	52%	-5.5	65	$2
2nd Half	176	18	6	17	2	200	5	1	227	264	346	83	30	107	8	75	0.35	42	20	38	23	95	DCf	8%	78	126	16%	16%	95	14%	46%	-13.3	31	-$1
22 Proj	**105**	**11**	**4**	**11**	**2**	**223**	**5**	**2**	**230**	**283**	**403**	**93**	**37**	**112**	**8**	**72**	**0.31**	**49**	**14**	**37**	**27**	**92**		**7%**	**104**	**112**	**15%**	**19%**	**105**	**12%**	**50%**	**-2.3**	**60**	**$3**

Martin,Richie

Age: 27	Pos: SS	Health	C	LIMA Plan	D
Bats: R	Ht: 5' 11" Wt: 190	PT/Exp	D	Rand Var	+2
		Consist	A	MM	1401

1-8-.235 in 105 PA at BAL. SB that were previously main source of value were M.I.A. in MLB, as he went 0-for-2 on basepaths while looking overmatched at the plate (.183 xBA). 2021 minor league SBA% shows he's still running, but even there, SB% was an issue. With subpar ct% and nonexistent power, paltry SB upside hardly seems worth ugly downside.

Yr Tm	PA	R	HR	RBI	SB	BA	xHR	xSB	xBA	OBP	SLG	OPS+	vL+	vR+	bb%	ct%	Eye	G	L	F	h%	HctX	QBaB	Brl%	PX	xPX	HR/F	xHR/F	Spd	SBA%	SB%	RAR	BPX	R$
17 aa	305	34	2	22	10	198		3		247	274	71			6	79	0.31				24				46				126	21%	74%		12	$0
18 aa	486	53	4	33	19	261		15		312	379	93			7	79	0.35				32				75				128	26%	63%		97	$13
19 BAL	309	29	6	23	10	208	4	10	224	260	322	80	89	70	5	71	0.17	49	20	31	27	61	FCd	2%	63	56	10%	7%	139	18%	91%	-21.9	-48	$2
20																																		
21 BAL *	227	20	2	13	5	201	1	3	201	254	277	73	81	73	7	71	0.25	51	16	33	27	61	FDf	0%	49	34	5%	5%	144	24%	41%	-18.0	-65	-$1
1st Half	53	2	0	1	3	136		1	166	228	163	54	0	0	11	66	0.35	44	20	36	21	0		0%	13	-22	0%		144	24%	70%	-5.6	-231	-$9
2nd Half	174	18	3	12	2	220	1	2	211	263	311	78	79	72	6	73	0.21	51	16	33	29	62	FDf	0%	59	34	5%	5%	129	24%	27%	-11.8	-42	-$2
22 Proj	**210**	**19**	**3**	**13**	**5**	**206**	**2**	**7**	**216**	**269**	**303**	**78**	**82**	**73**	**7**	**73**	**0.27**	**50**	**18**	**32**	**27**	**62**		**1%**	**59**	**43**	**6%**	**5%**	**136**	**20%**	**60%**	**-11.0**	**-52**	**$2**

BRANDON KRUSE

Martinez,J.D.

Age: 34 Pos: DH LF | Bats: R Ht: 6' 3" Wt: 230
Health A | PT/Exp A | Consist F
LIMA Plan B | Rand Var -1 | MM 4245

Projected bounceback occurred and alleviated concern over 2020's small-sample size disappointment. Despite stable ct% and high 1st half BA, xBA trend and gentle decline in HctX suggest full-season return to .300 isn't likely. But xPX indicates fairly steady power floor, and xHR, 160 PX vR (highest since 2018) point to potential climb back to 40 HR.

Yr	Tm	PA	R	HR	RBI	SB	BA	xHR	xSB	xBA	OBP	SLG	OPS+	vL+	vR+	bb%	ct%	Eye	G	L	F	h%	HctX	QBaB	Brl%	PX	xPX	HR/F	xHR/F	Spd	SBA%	SB%	RAR	BPX	R$
17	2 TM	489	85	45	104	4	303	45	6	305	376	690	145	183	132	11	70	0.41	38	19	43	33	140	ABb	19%	224	190	34%	34%	93	4%	100%	56.4	339	$27
18	BOS	649	111	43	130	6	330	48	7	298	402	629	138	128	139	11	74	0.47	43	23	34	38	123	ACa	16%	178	148	29%	33%	105	4%	86%	77.4	317	$41
19	BOS	656	98	36	105	2	304	37	6	280	383	557	130	192	109	11	76	0.52	43	22	35	35	121	ACa	12%	131	127	23%	24%	91	1%	100%	40.1	222	$27
20	BOS	237	22	7	27	1	213	11	0	238	291	389	90	89	91	9	72	0.37	35	21	44	26	104	BBc	11%	114	150	10%	16%	60	2%	100%	-7.9	72	$8
21	BOS	633	92	28	99	0	286	38	4	267	349	518	119	112	122	9	74	0.37	34	24	42	34	117	ABb	12%	142	140	16%	21%	91	0%	0%	25.2	212	$25
1st Half		336	58	17	56	0	303	20	2	270	369	557	129	122	132	10	75	0.42	36	21	43	36	117	ABc	12%	149	142	17%	20%	99	0%	0%	22.0	265	$33
2nd Half		297	34	11	43	0	267	19	2	265	327	474	108	103	111	8	73	0.31	33	27	40	33	117	ABa	13%	133	139	14%	24%	81	0%	0%	3.7	150	$14
22	Proj	630	87	31	102	1	279	40	2	266	348	519	118	121	116	10	73	0.40	36	23	41	33	117		13%	145	143	18%	23%	77	1%	88%	27.8	183	$23

Mateo,Jorge

Age: 27 Pos: OF | Bats: R Ht: 6' 0" Wt: 182
Health A | PT/Exp C | Consist D
LIMA Plan C | Rand Var -2 | MM 2503

After six years in minors, mid-season DFA from SD, former touted prospect appeared in danger of never reaching potential. However, 2nd half run with BAL brought performance gains that matched 2017 MLEs, though xBA, xPX cast doubt. Speed skills remain elite, so 2nd half bb%, ct% bumps could be key to finally unlocking valuable SB production.

Yr	Tm	PA	R	HR	RBI	SB	BA	xHR	xSB	xBA	OBP	SLG	OPS+	vL+	vR+	bb%	ct%	Eye	G	L	F	h%	HctX	QBaB	Brl%	PX	xPX	HR/F	xHR/F	Spd	SBA%	SB%	RAR	BPX	R$
17	aa	276	42	6	38	20	272		3		323	461	107			7	74	0.28				35				108				156	51%	64%		130	$14
18	aaa	493	40	2	36	20	209		27		245	320	76			5	68	0.15				30				70				162	35%	64%		-33	$6
19	aaa	554	72	13	60	18	249		21		279	418	96			4	69	0.13				34				98				145	30%	59%		26	$16
20	SD	28	4	0	2	1	154	0	0	207	185	269	60	67	44	4	58	0.09	13	47	40	27	102	CAd		122	107	0%	0%	109	50%	100%	-2.5	-116	-$2
21	2 TM	209	19	4	14	10	247	5	13	227	293	376	92	90	93	4	72	0.16	39	23	38	33	71	DCf	6%	86	61	8%	9%	119	29%	77%	-6.1	8	$5
1st Half		84	7	1	5	3	190	1	4	219	229	266	69	50	76	1	70	0.04	44	26	30	26	66	FDf	5%	55	52	6%	6%	104	29%	100%	-7.6	-162	-$6
2nd Half		125	12	3	9	7	287	4	9	235	336	452	107	107	106	7	73	0.26	35	21	44	37	74	DBc	6%	107	67	8%	11%	128	29%	70%	1.2	119	$3
22	Proj	350	37	7	30	16	243	8	13	224	291	386	92	96	89	5	71	0.17	39	23	38	33	71		6%	91	61	7%	9%	144	23%	69%	-7.5	24	$13

Mayfield,Jack

Age: 31 Pos: 3B | Bats: R Ht: 5' 11" Wt: 190
Health A | PT/Exp C | Consist C
LIMA Plan D | Rand Var 0 | MM 2201

10-39-.218 with 5 SB in 290 PA at SEA/LAA. Stuck with Angels in 2nd half after being DFA'd twice early on, and while he managed some power production, exit velocity and xPX say there's not much to see here. With subpar power, FB-heavy profile points toward abysmal BA/xBA combo. At his age, looking like a Quad-A player with no carrying skill.

Yr	Tm	PA	R	HR	RBI	SB	BA	xHR	xSB	xBA	OBP	SLG	OPS+	vL+	vR+	bb%	ct%	Eye	G	L	F	h%	HctX	QBaB	Brl%	PX	xPX	HR/F	xHR/F	Spd	SBA%	SB%	RAR	BPX	R$
17	a/a	442	46	14	46	7	221		4		254	380	86			4	74	0.16				27				97				92	12%	74%		30	$4
18	aaa	454	42	11	42	3	198		5		234	326	75			5	73	0.17				25				87				87	11%	38%		-3	$1
19	HOU *	468	57	19	54	4	200	2	4	231	241	381	86	97	51	5	73	0.20	35	19	46	23	84	DAf	4%	102	83	9%	9%	92	7%	77%	-29.4	52	$5
20	HOU	47	5	0	3	0	190	0	1	162	239	214	60	37	66	4	67	0.14	34	21	45	29	81	DAf	0%	22	51	0%	0%	102	0%	0%	-4.3	-292	-$3
21	2 AL *	369	39	13	46	6	222	9	2	228	264	389	90	95	88	5	76	0.25	39	15	46	25	85	FBf	6%	97	88	11%	10%	108	10%	80%	-15.5	112	$6
1st Half		117	11	3	10	1	211	1	1	202	236	327	78	54	47	3	78	0.15	50	8	42	25	77	FCf	4%	60	72	0%	10%	146	10%	29%	-9.7	50	-$4
2nd Half		252	28	10	36	5	227	8	1	239	285	419	95	108	90	7	76	0.29	38	16	46	26	86	FBf	7%	115	91	13%	10%	89	10%	100%	-7.9	138	$11
22	Proj	140	15	4	16	2	213	4	2	211	256	346	82	86	78	5	75	0.21	41	14	45	26	83		5%	82	83	8%	10%	99	9%	72%	-6.0	0	$2

McCann,James

Age: 32 Pos: CA | Bats: R Ht: 6' 3" Wt: 220
Health A | PT/Exp A | Consist C
LIMA Plan C | Rand Var 0 | MM 2115

Didn't deliver as hoped after big FA payday, as h% finally regressed and power was held down by second-lowest FB%, highest GB% of career. Underlying dips in HctX, QBaB, and Brl% also a factor, but history shows all of these swings are part of the package with him. 1st half xHR, xHR/F say plus power still there; just don't expect BA to return with it.

Yr	Tm	PA	R	HR	RBI	SB	BA	xHR	xSB	xBA	OBP	SLG	OPS+	vL+	vR+	bb%	ct%	Eye	G	L	F	h%	HctX	QBaB	Brl%	PX	xPX	HR/F	xHR/F	Spd	SBA%	SB%	RAR	BPX	R$
17	DET	391	39	13	49	1	253	15	5	260	318	415	100	125	87	7	75	0.29	38	28	34	30	116	CBc	8%	93	102	14%	16%	101	1%	100%	2.7	58	$6
18	DET	457	31	8	39	0	220	12	1	211	267	314	78	68	79	6	73	0.22	38	22	39	28	98	CBc	5%	63	90	7%	10%	69	3%	0%	-11.7	-77	$1
19	CHW	476	62	18	60	4	273	18	3	248	328	460	109	120	104	6	69	0.22	44	24	32	36	95	BCb	9%	113	89	19%	19%	85	5%	80%	10.3	22	$13
20	CHW	111	20	7	15	1	289	5	1	254	360	536	119	162	99	7	69	0.27	38	25	38	35	101	BBb	9%	139	125	27%	19%	98	7%	50%	6.4	132	$12
21	NYM	412	29	10	46	1	232	11	5	216	294	349	88	101	83	8	69	0.28	52	20	29	31	84	CDc	6%	74	79	13%	15%	99	3%	33%	-8.3	-58	$3
1st Half		236	16	7	29	0	247	9	3	199	309	381	96	118	89	8	67	0.25	53	19	28	34	85	CCb	8%	90	84	17%	22%	85	3%	0%	-1.1	-73	$5
2nd Half		176	13	3	17	1	213	3	2	222	273	306	78	87	73	8	73	0.33	50	21	29	27	83	DDd	4%	55	74	9%	9%	117	3%	33%	-7.5	-38	-$3
22	Proj	455	48	15	53	2	246	15	3	229	308	394	95	111	87	7	70	0.27	45	22	32	32	92		7%	90	91	16%	15%	89	4%	44%	4.8	-59	$11

McCarthy,Jake

Age: 24 Pos: OF | Bats: L Ht: 6' 3" Wt: 195
Health A | PT/Exp D | Consist F
LIMA Plan D | Rand Var 0 | MM 3501

2-4-.220 with 3 SB in 70 PA at ARI. Made brief MLB debut late in season, but sample is too small to draw conclusions. Reportedly bulked up and changed swing to add more power during scratched 2020 minor-league season. That provides potential for modest HR/SB value with extended run in 2022, and makes him an intriguing end game target.

Yr	Tm	PA	R	HR	RBI	SB	BA	xHR	xSB	xBA	OBP	SLG	OPS+	vL+	vR+	bb%	ct%	Eye	G	L	F	h%	HctX	QBaB	Brl%	PX	xPX	HR/F	xHR/F	Spd	SBA%	SB%	RAR	BPX	R$
17																																			
18																																			
19																																			
20																																			
21	ARI *	420	49	11	36	20	207	1	6	205	264	374	88	92	100	7	66	0.23	58	3	39	29	44	FFf	3%	104	82	14%	7%	173	35%	76%	-23.4	54	$10
1st Half		190	18	3	16	11	173		2	205	233	319	77	0	0	7	62	0.21	44	20	36	25	0		0%	99	-22	0%		153	35%	91%	-14.1	-38	$3
2nd Half		230	31	7	20	9	236	1	4	216	291	420	96	90	98	7	69	0.25	58	3	39	31	46	FFf	3%	108	82	14%	7%	173	35%	62%	-7.1	115	$11
22	Proj	210	25	6	18	10	221	4	10	210	295	402	95	94	94	7	66	0.22	58	3	39	30	41		2%	112	74	13%	7%	165	29%	75%	-4.0	49	$7

McCormick,Chas

Age: 27 Pos: LF CF RF | Bats: R Ht: 6' 0" Wt: 190
Health A | PT/Exp C | Consist B
LIMA Plan D+ | Rand Var -5 | MM 3313

Power was big surprise after minors profile built around ct% and speed, though skills all show HR outburst was legit. But it took massive trade-off in ct% to get there, leaving two questions: Is BA tenable when H% regresses (xBA says no), and will ct% return? For now, focus on pop; long-term, has potential to pair double-digit HR/SB with above-average BA.

Yr	Tm	PA	R	HR	RBI	SB	BA	xHR	xSB	xBA	OBP	SLG	OPS+	vL+	vR+	bb%	ct%	Eye	G	L	F	h%	HctX	QBaB	Brl%	PX	xPX	HR/F	xHR/F	Spd	SBA%	SB%	RAR	BPX	R$
17																																			
18	aa	271	30	2	25	11	253		4		312	318	84			8	86	0.59				29				40				101	21%	71%		77	$6
19	a/a	420	50	11	51	12	228		16		323	354	94			12	80	0.72				26				56				151	15%	73%		141	$9
20																																			
21	HOU	320	47	14	50	4	257	17	4	219	319	447	105	112	102	8	63	0.24	36	22	42	36	93	BAc	10%	128	144	18%	22%	97	8%	67%	0.5	12	$10
1st Half		150	27	9	29	2	233	8	2	240	300	481	109	99	115	9	66	0.30	35	21	44	28	89	BBd	11%	154	146	23%	20%	99	8%	100%	0.1	142	$8
2nd Half		170	20	5	21	2	277	8	2	203	335	419	102	136	94	7	61	0.20	36	23	41	42	97	AAa	10%	105	142	13%	21%	102	8%	50%	-1.0	-92	$5
22	Proj	315	43	13	44	7	234	17	4	231	303	416	98	108	94	9	71	0.33	36	22	42	28	94		10%	107	144	16%	20%	111	8%	69%	-1.9	57	$11

McCutchen,Andrew

Age: 35 Pos: LF | Bats: R Ht: 5' 11" Wt: 195
Health D | PT/Exp A | Consist A
LIMA Plan B | Rand Var +3 | MM 4235

Hit rate was to blame for lowest BA of his career and has been primary cause of subpar vR numbers last two seasons (24 h% for 2020-21). And while five-year ct% drop has lowered BA floor, Eye, xHR/F have remained largely stable. No longer the electric player of his prime, but can give you solid OBP and power production along with handful of steals.

Yr	Tm	PA	R	HR	RBI	SB	BA	xHR	xSB	xBA	OBP	SLG	OPS+	vL+	vR+	bb%	ct%	Eye	G	L	F	h%	HctX	QBaB	Brl%	PX	xPX	HR/F	xHR/F	Spd	SBA%	SB%	RAR	BPX	R$
17	PIT	650	94	28	88	11	279	24	10	276	363	486	116	153	103	11	80	0.63	41	22	37	31	114	CBc	8%	113	109	16%	14%	93	9%	69%	14.1	185	$24
18	2 TM	682	83	20	65	14	255	25	12	250	368	424	106	109	103	14	75	0.66	41	23	36	31	119	BCb	8%	105	125	13%	16%	102	12%	61%	8.3	143	$19
19	PHI	262	45	10	29	2	256	9	5	255	378	457	115	117	114	16	75	0.78	45	18	37	30	95	BCb	7%	109	101	17%	15%	100	4%	67%	4.4	193	$5
20	PHI	241	32	10	34	4	253	11	2	245	324	433	100	123	91	9	78	0.46	35	22	44	28	126	BAc	8%	96	151	14%	15%	93	7%	100%	-2.3	148	$21
21	PHI	574	78	27	80	6	222	26	6	252	334	444	107	140	90	14	73	0.61	40	19	40	25	108	CBd	9%	131	126	19%	18%	79	5%	86%	-5.3	188	$14
1st Half		310	42	13	41	6	229	14	4	244	352	427	108	132	92	16	72	0.69	46	18	36	26	102	CCc	10%	113	118	19%	21%	96	5%	86%	-2.3	165	$19
2nd Half		264	36	14	39	0	214	11	2	262	314	463	105	152	87	13	73	0.53	34	21	45	23	115	CAf	8%	150	134	18%	14%	70	5%	0%	-4.6	231	$10
22	Proj	490	69	23	65	6	243	20	4	253	346	458	109	135	98	13	75	0.61	39	20	40	27	112		8%	124	127	18%	16%	83	5%	79%	12.7	185	$17

DANIEL MARCUS

McGuire,Reese

Age: 27	Pos: CA	Health	A	LIMA Plan	D
Bats: L	Ht: 6' 0" Wt: 215	PT/Exp	D	Rand Var	-2
		Consist	F	MM	1221

Once-promising prospect has flatlined at big-league level. High ct%, LD% are most hopeful part of skill profile, but without any power to back it up, even BA can't get off the ground, making him a poor candidate for a post-hype breakout. Likely to stick around due to skills behind the plate, but fantasy upside is currently nonexistent.

Yr Tm	PA	R	HR	RBI	SB	BA	xHR	xSB	xBA	OBP	SLG	OPS+	vL+	vR+	bb%	ct%	Eye	G	L	F	h%	HctX	QBaB	Brl%	PX	xPX	HR/F	xHR/F	Spd	SBA%	SB%	RAR	BPX	R$
17 aa	129	17	6	17	2	266		2		345	470	111			11	82	0.68				28				105				109	9%	62%		209	$3
18 TOR *	384	32	8	37	4	224	1	5	233	287	338	84	83	133	8	74	0.34	36	27	36	28	99	FCa	9%	71	166	25%	13%	93	7%	63%	-2.3	0	$3
19 TOR *	368	39	9	35	3	246	2	4	273	303	387	96	95	127	8	80	0.41	40	28	32	28	88	DCc	4%	77	85	20%	8%	96	4%	100%	4.2	104	$4
20 TOR	45	2	1	1	0	73	0	0	191	73	146	29	0	50	0	73	0.00	66	10	24	7	35	FFf	3%	36	8	14%	0%	91	0%	0%	-5.6	-192	-$6
21 TOR	217	22	1	10	0	253	3	1	239	310	343	90	63	97	7	78	0.34	40	24	36	32	71	DCc	3%	69	59	2%	5%	91	0%	0%	-3.2	35	$0
1st Half	107	14	1	6	0	293	2	0	239	340	394	102	45	115	6	79	0.29	40	22	38	36	73	DCf	4%	71	69	3%	7%	93	0%	0%	1.7	50	-$2
2nd Half	110	8	0	4	0	212	1	0	241	282	293	78	78	78	8	77	0.39	40	25	35	28	69	CCb	1%	67	48	0%	4%	89	0%	0%	-4.5	23	-$9
22 Proj	**210**	**21**	**3**	**16**	**1**	**243**	**4**	**1**	**246**	**306**	**358**	**90**	**71**	**95**	**8**	**78**	**0.38**	**40**	**25**	**35**	**30**	**75**		**3%**	**75**	**64**	**6%**	**7%**	**91**	**2%**	**74%**	**0.6**	**16**	**$1**

McKinney,Billy

Age: 27	Pos: RF LF	Health	B	LIMA Plan	D
Bats: L	Ht: 6' 1" Wt: 205	PT/Exp	C	Rand Var	+5
		Consist	F	MM	3201

Has yet to earn true chance against LHP, and hasn't found his way into lineup regularly vs. RHP despite intriguing results (career 117 PX). PX, xPX have hinted at mild power upside during various points in career, while BA has been held down by stubbornly low h%. With playing time, HR production could come, but there's little hope for anything more.

Yr Tm	PA	R	HR	RBI	SB	BA	xHR	xSB	xBA	OBP	SLG	OPS+	vL+	vR+	bb%	ct%	Eye	G	L	F	h%	HctX	QBaB	Brl%	PX	xPX	HR/F	xHR/F	Spd	SBA%	SB%	RAR	BPX	R$
17 a/a	477	61	17	59	2	260		6		316	460	106			8	76	0.34				31				115				112	3%	63%		145	$10
18 2 AL *	453	47	19	47	2	217	6	3	253	283	433	96	73	110	8	72	0.33	37	24	39	25	88	CAc	8%	130	79	18%	18%	116	4%	62%	-5.4	150	$6
19 TOR *	423	51	15	44	1	225	8	4	248	294	426	100	86	98	9	73	0.36	39	21	41	27	95	CBd	7%	111	99	16%	11%	127	5%	21%	-16.4	148	$4
20 TOR	3	1	0	0	0	667	0	0	401	667	667	177	0	177	0	100	0.00	0	67	33	67	135	CAa		0	57	0%	0%	113	0%	0%	1.1	144	-$2
21 3 NL	300	32	9	27	2	192	10	1	221	280	358	88	97	85	11	70	0.41	37	20	43	24	92	CAd	6%	101	109	11%	12%	104	3%	100%	-16.6	62	$0
1st Half	194	23	8	19	2	216	8	1	250	284	426	99	82	104	9	71	0.33	37	24	39	26	101	CBd	8%	127	125	16%	16%	103	3%	100%	-5.7	138	$4
2nd Half	106	9	1	8	0	146	1	1	158	274	225	67	132	51	14	69	0.54	37	11	52	20	72	CAd	3%	49	75	3%	3%	109	3%	0%	-9.7	-88	-$9
22 Proj	**175**	**19**	**6**	**17**	**1**	**221**	**5**	**2**	**226**	**302**	**401**	**95**	**105**	**93**	**10**	**71**	**0.40**	**37**	**19**	**44**	**27**	**87**		**6%**	**107**	**93**	**12%**	**11%**	**109**	**5%**	**65%**	**-2.3**	**71**	**$3**

McKinstry,Zach

Age: 27	Pos: RF 2B	Health	B	LIMA Plan	D
Bats: L	Ht: 6' 0" Wt: 180	PT/Exp	C	Rand Var	+5
		Consist	A	MM	3111

7-29-.215 in 172 PA at LA. Gained additional buzz as prospect due to added weight while retooling grip and swing prior to 2019 season. Increased power didn't carry over in first substantial MLB sample, but xPX and HctX show above-average batted-ball skills. Enough potential thump here to keep him on your end-game radar, especially if he finds a role.

Yr Tm	PA	R	HR	RBI	SB	BA	xHR	xSB	xBA	OBP	SLG	OPS+	vL+	vR+	bb%	ct%	Eye	G	L	F	h%	HctX	QBaB	Brl%	PX	xPX	HR/F	xHR/F	Spd	SBA%	SB%	RAR	BPX	R$
17 aa	44	4	0	2	0	230		1		313	286	81			11	77	0.53				30				33				127	0%	0%		-6	-$2
18 aa	86	5	2	6	0	162		0		189	251	59			3	71	0.12				21				55				112	0%	0%		-90	-$4
19 a/a	462	55	15	62	6	259		2		311	432	103			7	75	0.30				31				94				107	15%	38%		85	$11
20 LA	7	1	0	0	0	286	0	0	275	286	429	95	0	95	0	57	0.00	50	50	0	50	173	DFf		153	99	0%		116	0%	0%	0.0	-44	-$2
21 LA *	331	42	12	43	4	213	7	1	239	267	388	90	88	93	7	73	0.27	43	18	39	25	111	CCa	8%	106	143	17%	17%	104	12%	51%	-17.0	92	$5
1st Half	142	19	5	26	2	257	4	1	253	315	441	105	93	114	8	72	0.31	44	22	34	32	100	CCa	6%	118	117	19%	15%	98	12%	62%	-0.5	119	$5
2nd Half	189	23	7	17	2	181	3	1	209	231	350	79	77	46	6	74	0.24	40	10	50	20	136	CBa	13%	97	211	13%	20%	115	12%	45%	-14.1	81	-$1
22 Proj	**175**	**22**	**7**	**23**	**2**	**223**	**8**	**2**	**236**	**277**	**414**	**94**	**104**	**89**	**7**	**72**	**0.26**	**44**	**17**	**40**	**27**	**122**		**10%**	**116**	**173**	**15%**	**18%**	**99**	**10%**	**50%**	**-3.4**	**75**	**$5**

McMahon,Ryan

Age: 27	Pos: 3B 2B	Health	A	LIMA Plan	B
Bats: L	Ht: 6' 2" Wt: 219	PT/Exp	A	Rand Var	+1
		Consist	B	MM	4225

Surge to begin season cooled in later months, and comparing 2021 to 2019 could make it tempting to think this is his ceiling. But there were several positive takeaways, including lower GB% along with big tick up in ct%. If he can bring PX closer to xPX while maintaining ct% growth as he hits peak age, there's potential for... UP: 30 HR

Yr Tm	PA	R	HR	RBI	SB	BA	xHR	xSB	xBA	OBP	SLG	OPS+	vL+	vR+	bb%	ct%	Eye	G	L	F	h%	HctX	QBaB	Brl%	PX	xPX	HR/F	xHR/F	Spd	SBA%	SB%	RAR	BPX	R$
17 COL *	526	59	17	69	8	333	0	8	291	380	534	124	27	85	7	80	0.38	86	0	14	39	70	FFa	0%	117	81	0%	0%	86	8%	72%	30.7	170	$25
18 COL *	436	42	13	49	3	243	4	4	242	292	410	94	128	82	6	68	0.21	46	24	30	33	85	BDc	5%	114	99	14%	11%	84	6%	56%	-8.5	10	$8
19 COL	539	70	24	83	5	250	20	5	246	329	450	108	109	106	10	67	0.35	51	21	28	32	102	ADb	9%	119	112	27%	22%	79	5%	83%	-5.4	30	$15
20 COL	193	23	9	26	0	215	9	2	214	295	419	95	97	93	9	62	0.27	50	15	35	29	100	BCc	11%	131	158	24%	24%	108	2%	0%	-7.8	16	$9
21 COL	596	80	23	86	6	254	24	3	254	331	449	107	90	114	10	72	0.40	39	24	38	31	114	BBc	7%	122	140	16%	17%	87	6%	75%	-4.2	131	$18
1st Half	314	47	16	45	4	251	17	1	255	312	481	110	93	117	9	70	0.32	36	24	39	30	123	ABb	9%	141	173	20%	22%	98	6%	80%	0.8	158	$23
2nd Half	282	33	7	41	2	257	8	2	251	351	412	103	88	110	12	75	0.52	41	23	36	32	103	CCc	5%	101	103	11%	12%	80	6%	67%	-1.8	112	$12
22 Proj	**595**	**78**	**25**	**88**	**5**	**253**	**23**	**6**	**247**	**329**	**453**	**106**	**101**	**108**	**10**	**70**	**0.36**	**42**	**23**	**35**	**32**	**104**		**8%**	**127**	**129**	**19%**	**17%**	**85**	**5%**	**67%**	**11.6**	**86**	**$20**

McNeil,Jeff

Age: 30	Pos: 2B LF	Health	B	LIMA Plan	B
Bats: L	Ht: 6' 1" Wt: 195	PT/Exp	A	Rand Var	+3
		Consist	C	MM	1245

Value enhanced by PA volume took several hits, as hamstring injury cost him 36 days in 1st half and BA/OBP tumbled after heightened h% proved unsustainable. Making matters worse, OPS+ and xPX fell to new lows as GB% continued to inch up. Output in 2021 likely set floor, but slide in production vs. LHP raises concern of more lost opportunity.

Yr Tm	PA	R	HR	RBI	SB	BA	xHR	xSB	xBA	OBP	SLG	OPS+	vL+	vR+	bb%	ct%	Eye	G	L	F	h%	HctX	QBaB	Brl%	PX	xPX	HR/F	xHR/F	Spd	SBA%	SB%	RAR	BPX	R$
17 aaa	73	8	1	4	1	196		1		221	281	68			3	82	0.18				23				55				101	9%	100%		33	-$2
18 NYM *	613	85	16	68	11	292	6	12	270	339	464	108	108	114	7	86	0.52	39	22	40	32	96	CBd	2%	92	103	4%	8%	141	8%	92%	23.4	253	$23
19 NYM	567	83	23	75	5	318	18	9	297	384	531	127	115	130	6	85	0.47	43	22	35	34	111	CCa	5%	107	94	15%	12%	107	7%	45%	32.9	270	$23
20 NYM	209	19	4	23	0	311	5	3	280	383	454	111	97	118	10	87	0.83	44	24	32	34	109	CCc	2%	81	81	8%	10%	111	3%	0%	5.5	268	$15
21 NYM	426	48	7	35	3	249	11	4	256	317	358	93	86	95	7	85	0.50	47	20	33	28	100	CCc	4%	62	70	6%	10%	112	3%	100%	-14.9	150	$6
1st Half	162	16	3	10	1	236	5	2	247	321	326	90	90	90	8	86	0.65	46	21	33	26	97	CCd	5%	47	69	7%	12%	111	3%	100%	-6.6	131	-$2
2nd Half	264	32	4	25	2	256	6	2	261	314	376	93	83	98	6	84	0.42	47	20	33	29	103	CCc	4%	71	70	6%	9%	110	3%	100%	-6.2	162	$7
22 Proj	**490**	**59**	**11**	**51**	**4**	**279**	**13**	**5**	**268**	**346**	**417**	**104**	**95**	**107**	**7**	**86**	**0.54**	**45**	**22**	**34**	**31**	**104**		**4%**	**78**	**80**	**8%**	**10%**	**112**	**5%**	**62%**	**10.2**	**153**	**$16**

Meadows,Austin

Age: 27	Pos: LF DH	Health	A	LIMA Plan	B
Bats: L	Ht: 6' 3" Wt: 225	PT/Exp	A	Rand Var	+3
		Consist	D	MM	4125

Shift to extreme FB% remained, but that isn't a good thing. BA has gone from notable positive to mediocre, with no xPX or xHR jump to make up for loss in value. Now Spd, SBA%, and SB% suggest mere handful of SB should be new baseline. Limitations vs. LHP are one more reason for alarm, despite entering what should be prime of career.

Yr Tm	PA	R	HR	RBI	SB	BA	xHR	xSB	xBA	OBP	SLG	OPS+	vL+	vR+	bb%	ct%	Eye	G	L	F	h%	HctX	QBaB	Brl%	PX	xPX	HR/F	xHR/F	Spd	SBA%	SB%	RAR	BPX	R$
17 aaa	306	43	3	33	10	236		4		291	336	85			7	82	0.43				28				66				89	19%	76%		70	$5
18 2 TM *	467	59	16	54	15	276	6	11	272	314	463	104	122	93	5	81	0.30	41	21	37	31	111	CCb	6%	111	139	12%	12%	117	18%	83%	7.3	200	$18
19 TAM	591	83	33	89	12	291	33	16	270	364	558	128	116	132	9	75	0.41	34	23	43	33	118	BBc	13%	137	139	19%	19%	108	13%	63%	27.2	233	$26
20 TAM	152	19	4	13	2	205	5	2	194	296	371	89	51	102	11	62	0.34	26	20	54	29	93	BAd	7%	119	122	9%	11%	97	9%	67%	-8.1	-8	$5
21 TAM	591	79	27	106	4	234	25	6	245	315	458	106	77	120	10	76	0.48	29	19	53	25	110	BAd	9%	127	130	13%	12%	74	6%	57%	-12.0	200	$16
1st Half	331	48	16	54	2	235	16	4	237	326	478	112	82	126	11	71	0.44	27	16	57	28	105	BAc	11%	151	152	14%	14%	79	6%	100%	-1.6	204	$22
2nd Half	260	31	11	52	2	231	10	3	255	300	432	99	71	113	9	83	0.58	30	21	49	23	116	CAd	7%	100	108	11%	10%	84	6%	40%	-8.9	223	$14
22 Proj	**525**	**70**	**23**	**80**	**7**	**245**	**22**	**4**	**243**	**318**	**458**	**105**	**84**	**115**	**9**	**75**	**0.42**	**31**	**20**	**49**	**28**	**109**		**9%**	**124**	**129**	**13%**	**13%**	**83**	**5%**	**64%**	**6.7**	**174**	**$19**

Mejia,Francisco

Age: 26	Pos: CA	Health	B	LIMA Plan	D+
Bats: B	Ht: 5' 8" Wt: 188	PT/Exp	D	Rand Var	-3
		Consist	F	MM	3233

Change of scenery allowed for yet another chance to get MLB career on track. Hints of growth in ct%, Eye would have been more impactful if there was similar jump in QBaB, xPX, or HctX. Promise and pedigree as a prospect continue to slowly fade into the past, but chance for double-digit HR and solid BA is enough to move the needle at CA position.

Yr Tm	PA	R	HR	RBI	SB	BA	xHR	xSB	xBA	OBP	SLG	OPS+	vL+	vR+	bb%	ct%	Eye	G	L	F	h%	HctX	QBaB	Brl%	PX	xPX	HR/F	xHR/F	Spd	SBA%	SB%	RAR	BPX	R$
17 CLE *	382	44	12	44	6	278	0	5	320	319	447	104	45	52	6	85	0.40	50	30	20	30	138	ADc	0%	91	49	0%	0%	83	9%	73%	8.9	155	$11
18 2 TM *	507	44	12	56	0	234	2	5	234	269	373	86	68	100	4	76	0.19	54	16	30	28	98	CDf	8%	90	74	27%	18%	78	0%	0%	-2.5	33	$5
19 SD *	311	37	11	30	1	273	7	2	248	312	467	108	97	106	5	77	0.24	36	20	44	32	95	CAd	5%	105	94	11%	9%	127	3%	50%	5.9	152	$6
20 SD	42	5	1	2	0	77	0	0	196	143	179	43	33	47	2	77	0.11	40	13	47	7	114	FAf		56	115	7%	0%	96	0%	0%	-5.0	-44	-$5
21 TAM	277	31	6	35	0	260	6	2	241	322	416	101	102	101	6	80	0.35	41	16	42	30	79	DBf	4%	90	72	7%	7%	114	0%	0%	1.9	162	$4
1st Half	143	11	3	14	0	256	3	1	227	317	388	98	104	94	6	81	0.33	48	15	37	29	75	DCf	5%	80	59	8%	8%	99	0%	0%	-0.5	127	-$2
2nd Half	134	20	3	21	0	264	4	1	240	328	446	105	99	109	7	79	0.36	34	18	48	31	84	DBf	4%	101	85	7%	9%	118	0%	0%	2.7	188	$1
22 Proj	**315**	**36**	**11**	**39**	**1**	**260**	**9**	**1**	**253**	**316**	**454**	**105**	**98**	**109**	**6**	**79**	**0.30**	**42**	**17**	**41**	**29**	**87**		**5%**	**109**	**78**	**12%**	**10%**	**101**	**3%**	**65%**	**10.2**	**153**	**$9**

DANIEL MARCUS

Melendez,MJ

Age: 23 Pos: CA
Bats: L Ht: 6' 1" Wt: 185

Health	A	LIMA Plan	D
PT/Exp	B	Rand Var	
Consist	F	MM	3111

After hitting .163 with 55% ct% at Single-A in 2019, KC prospect made massive leap in 2021. Dramatically cut down on the whiffs while leading minors in home runs. Some regression should probably be expected given the magnitude of this breakout, but a catcher with this level of power potential is worth gambling on.

Yr	Tm	PA	R	HR	RBI	SB	BA	xHR	xSB	xBA	OBP	SLG	OPS+	vL+	vR+	bb%	ct%	Eye	G	L	F	h%	HctX	QBaB	Brl%	PX	xPX	HR/F	xHR/F	Spd	SBA%	SB%	RAR	BPX	R$
17																																			
18																																			
19																																			
20																																			
21	a/a	505	73	29	79	2	251		6		336	500	115			11	73	0.47				28				143				98	8%	25%		227	$
1st Half		205	21	10	30	2	247		2		327	468	111			11	72	0.42				29				133				92	8%	26%		169	
2nd Half		302	53	19	50	1	257		4	276	347	532	119			12	73	0.52	44	20	36	28	0			153	-22	0%		125	8%	25%	16.0	308	$
22	**Proj**	**175**	**29**	**6**	**33**	**1**	**252**	**5**	**2**	**234**	**339**	**432**	**105**	**104**	**105**	**12**	**73**	**0.48**	**38**	**20**	**42**	**31**	**98**		**8%**	**107**		**13%**	**10%**	**114**	**8%**	**33%**	**5.7**	**104**	**$**

Mendick,Danny

Age: 28 Pos: 2B SS
Bats: R Ht: 5' 10" Wt: 195

Health	A	LIMA Plan	F
PT/Exp	C	Rand Var	+2
Consist	A	MM	1101

2-20-.220 in 186 PA at CHW. Minor league numbers said speed was most logical path to fantasy relevance, but 340 PA int[o] big league career, he's still searching for that elusive first SB. Awful OBP and complete lack of power don't really help his case for a regular role, either. There's no reason to have him on your radar.

Yr	Tm	PA	R	HR	RBI	SB	BA	xHR	xSB	xBA	OBP	SLG	OPS+	vL+	vR+	bb%	ct%	Eye	G	L	F	h%	HctX	QBaB	Brl%	PX	xPX	HR/F	xHR/F	Spd	SBA%	SB%	RAR	BPX	R$
17	aa	164	13	3	19	1	182		2		266	274	73			10	79	0.54				21				54				88	8%	29%		21	-$
18	aa	506	55	13	53	18	220		6		301	357	88			10	77	0.50				26				86				86	25%	61%		80	$1
19	CHW *	566	63	16	52	14	235	0	18	242	303	369	93	65	141	9	75	0.39	44	22	33	28	74	DCa	0%	74	75	22%	0%	111	18%	60%	-18.9	44	$1
20	CHW	114	11	3	6	0	243	2	3	248	281	383	88	81	91	5	77	0.24	49	22	29	29	67	DDf	2%	77	40	13%	8%	135	4%	0%	-3.5	84	$
21	CHW *	287	25	4	25	1	213	2	2	212	276	289	78	75	86	8	74	0.33	42	22	36	27	68	FCc	2%	49	57	5%	5%	88	4%	22%	-17.3	-77	-$
1st Half		127	12	2	17	0	213	1	1	213	317	296	86	71	96	12	72	0.50	32	26	42	28	70	FAb	1%	53	69	6%	3%	79	4%	0%	-6.6	-73	-$
2nd Half		160	13	2	8	1	213	0	1	210	251	283	72	82	65	5	75	0.20	59	16	25	27	63	FDd	2%	46	35	0%	0%	110	4%	34%	-12.3	-73	-$
22	**Proj**	**175**	**17**	**3**	**15**	**2**	**221**	**1**	**2**	**223**	**284**	**314**	**81**	**79**	**82**	**8**	**75**	**0.34**	**44**	**22**	**34**	**28**	**66**		**2%**	**58**	**46**	**7%**	**3%**	**104**	**5%**	**47%**	**-6.3**	**-74**	**$**

Mercado,Oscar

Age: 27 Pos: LF RF
Bats: R Ht: 6' 2" Wt: 197

Health	A	LIMA Plan	C+
PT/Exp	B	Rand Var	+4
Consist	D	MM	2413

6-19-.224 with 7 SB in 238 PA at CLE. PRO: Plus speed, recent efficiency on bases suggest SB are bankable when he's getting consistent AB; ct% bounced back to prior levels. CON: The 2019 HctX, xPX looking more and more like aberration. His h%/BA should bounce back some, but still looking like a speed-only play.

Yr	Tm	PA	R	HR	RBI	SB	BA	xHR	xSB	xBA	OBP	SLG	OPS+	vL+	vR+	bb%	ct%	Eye	G	L	F	h%	HctX	QBaB	Brl%	PX	xPX	HR/F	xHR/F	Spd	SBA%	SB%	RAR	BPX	R$
17	aa	504	66	11	40	33	265		7		305	386	94			5	75	0.23				33				72				122	45%	61%		24	$2
18	aaa	524	66	6	36	29	251		31		307	348	88			7	80	0.40				30				64				105	33%	68%		63	$1
19	CLE *	614	89	18	66	26	268	11	26	257	318	441	105	108	103	7	78	0.34	40	22	39	31	108	CBd	4%	94	105	11%	8%	122	24%	78%	-3.8	148	$2
20	CLE	93	6	1	6	3	128	1	2	161	174	174	46	46	46	5	69	0.19	43	13	43	17	68	CCf	2%	29	44	4%	4%	107	21%	100%	-13.0	-224	-$
21	CLE *	424	46	9	34	13	199	5	11	239	268	335	83	111	78	9	79	0.44	43	18	39	23	82	DBf	4%	82	59	9%	7%	120	18%	85%	-30.5	138	$
1st Half		203	20	3	15	6	170	0	4	173	235	295	74	55	86	8	76	0.35	40	0	60	21	124	CAa	0%	79	203	0%	0%	130	18%	83%	-19.5	88	-$
2nd Half		221	26	6	19	7	227	5	7	252	305	374	92	113	77	9	82	0.56	43	19	38	25	82	DBf	4%	84	50	10%	8%	105	18%	88%	-9.5	177	$
22	**Proj**	**350**	**43**	**8**	**30**	**15**	**242**	**7**	**9**	**237**	**303**	**383**	**93**	**107**	**84**	**8**	**79**	**0.39**	**43**	**18**	**40**	**28**	**84**		**4%**	**84**	**62**	**8%**	**7%**	**113**	**14%**	**75%**	**-4.6**	**117**	**$1**

Mercedes,Yermín

Age: 29 Pos: DH
Bats: R Ht: 5' 11" Wt: 235

Health	A	LIMA Plan	D
PT/Exp	B	Rand Var	-5
Consist	F	MM	1201

7-37-.271 in 262 PA at CHW. Took the league by storm with 5 HR, .415 BA in April. Season quickly took a turn for the worse and he even announced retirement in July before changing his mind a day later. With middling plate skills, little power, and no defensive position, path back to relevance will be tough to navigate. But he'll always have April.

Yr	Tm	PA	R	HR	RBI	SB	BA	xHR	xSB	xBA	OBP	SLG	OPS+	vL+	vR+	bb%	ct%	Eye	G	L	F	h%	HctX	QBaB	Brl%	PX	xPX	HR/F	xHR/F	Spd	SBA%	SB%	RAR	BPX	R$
17	aa	46	4	1	6	1	242		1		271	335	83			4	78	0.18				29				57				98	10%	100%		-6	-$
18																																			
19	a/a	368	45	20	67	2	274		4		341	504	117			9	76	0.42				31				119				80	2%	100%		156	$1
20	CHW	1	0	0	0	0	0	0	0	0	0	0	0	0	0	0	100	0.00	100	0	0	0	405	AF		0	-26	0%		85	7%	0%	-0.1	112	-$
21	CHW *	491	47	14	56	2	239	11	6	226	282	368	89	124	92	6	79	0.28	41	18	41	27	76	CBc	7%	70	74	9%	14%	108	3%	66%	-19.4	69	$
1st Half		270	26	7	37	0	268	11	4	228	323	400	101	125	93	7	79	0.39	41	18	41	31	77	CBc	7%	74	74	9%	14%	105	3%	0%	-3.2	96	$1
2nd Half		221	21	7	19	2	206		2	234	232	331	76	0	0	3	79	0.16	44	20	36	23	0		0%	65	-22	0%		89	3%	100%	-15.8	8	$
22	**Proj**	**140**	**14**	**3**	**18**	**1**	**241**	**6**	**1**	**218**	**286**	**356**	**87**	**107**	**79**	**6**	**78**	**0.28**	**41**	**18**	**41**	**29**	**69**		**6%**	**65**	**67**	**8%**	**14%**	**76**	**3%**	**82%**	**-4.9**	**-18**	**$**

Merrifield,Whit

Age: 33 Pos: 2B OF
Bats: R Ht: 6' 1" Wt: 195

Health	A	LIMA Plan	D+
PT/Exp	A	Rand Var	0
Consist	A	MM	1545

Once again among league leaders in PA, and successful on 33 of first 34 SB tries. Production did fall off in 2nd half, as ct% and power metrics slipped, and he had just 2 SB over final month. He'll likely fall short of full repeat, but speed, durability remain firmly intact, providing high floor and helping maintain status as an attractive early-round target.

Yr	Tm	PA	R	HR	RBI	SB	BA	xHR	xSB	xBA	OBP	SLG	OPS+	vL+	vR+	bb%	ct%	Eye	G	L	F	h%	HctX	QBaB	Brl%	PX	xPX	HR/F	xHR/F	Spd	SBA%	SB%	RAR	BPX	R$
17	KC *	665	84	21	85	35	291	20	9	274	323	469	108	108	104	4	85	0.32	38	22	40	31	105	CBb	5%	94	111	9%	10%	133	29%	79%	14.1	200	$3
18	KC	707	88	12	60	45	304	20	32	269	367	438	108	125	99	9	82	0.54	35	30	35	36	111	CBb	5%	85	100	7%	11%	110	27%	82%	33.9	160	$3
19	KC	735	105	16	74	20	302	17	33	276	348	463	112	113	111	6	81	0.36	38	29	33	35	108	CBa	4%	83	95	9%	9%	163	16%	67%	17.5	207	$2
20	KC	265	38	9	30	12	282	7	6	275	325	440	101	101	101	5	87	0.36	37	26	37	30	83	DBb	5%	79	78	11%	9%	94	23%	80%	2.3	196	$3
21	KC	720	97	10	74	40	277	16	24	263	317	395	98	98	98	6	84	0.39	41	24	35	32	90	DCb	3%	70	85	5%	8%	123	25%	91%	0.9	169	$3
1st Half		358	50	8	45	23	287	9	13	275	338	435	108	109	107	7	86	0.57	42	23	35	31	96	CCb	4%	81	90	8%	9%	116	25%	96%	7.6	238	$4
2nd Half		362	47	2	29	17	268	7	11	253	296	356	88	88	88	4	83	0.25	39	26	35	32	85	DBc	3%	60	80	2%	7%	125	25%	85%	-9.9	104	$2
22	**Proj**	**665**	**92**	**13**	**69**	**30**	**284**	**16**	**25**	**267**	**326**	**415**	**101**	**102**	**100**	**6**	**84**	**0.37**	**40**	**26**	**35**	**32**	**94**		**4%**	**76**	**87**	**7%**	**9%**	**119**	**20%**	**83%**	**14.7**	**177**	**$3**

Meyers,Jake

Age: 26 Pos: CF
Bats: R Ht: 6' 0" Wt: 200

Health	A	LIMA Plan	C
PT/Exp	D	Rand Var	-5
Consist	D	MM	2313

6-28-.260 with 3 SB in 163 PA at HOU. With plus defense in CF, improved power, and 95th percentile sprint speed, he has our attention, but still has work to do. BA was saved by high h% following August call-up, but low ct%, bb% may limit SB opportunities. Worth going an extra buck, though, as you don't have to squint too hard to see the upside.

Yr	Tm	PA	R	HR	RBI	SB	BA	xHR	xSB	xBA	OBP	SLG	OPS+	vL+	vR+	bb%	ct%	Eye	G	L	F	h%	HctX	QBaB	Brl%	PX	xPX	HR/F	xHR/F	Spd	SBA%	SB%	RAR	BPX	R$
17																																			
18																																			
19	aa	99	8	1	5	3	193		2		273	241	71			10	75	0.44				25				21				140	24%	45%		-70	-$3
20																																			
21	HOU *	451	57	17	62	10	270	7	5	248	313	451	105	122	93	6	71	0.22	43	24	33	34	96	CDb	10%	113	117	19%	22%	95	13%	73%	1.6	58	$17
1st Half		203	24	10	23	3	266		2	250	307	469	108	0	0	6	72	0.21	44	20	36	32	0		0%	121	-22	0%		89	13%	58%	-0.4	104	$1
2nd Half		247	33	7	39	6	272	7	3	239	319	435	102	120	92	6	69	0.22	43	24	33	36	94	CDb	10%	106	117	19%	22%	104	13%	84%	0.1	27	$16
22	**Proj**	**385**	**50**	**12**	**55**	**10**	**252**	**16**	**7**	**237**	**311**	**405**	**97**	**113**	**87**	**6**	**70**	**0.21**	**43**	**24**	**33**	**33**	**85**		**9%**	**99**	**105**	**14%**	**19%**	**90**	**10%**	**80%**	**1.7**	**11**	**$15**

Miller,Brad

Age: 32 Pos: 1B OF
Bats: L Ht: 6' 2" Wt: 195

Health	A	LIMA Plan	D+
PT/Exp	B	Rand Var	+1
Consist	A	MM	4313

Still playing all over and getting job done vR, which helped him reach 20 MLB HR for first time since 2016. Displayed improved ct% and elite Brl% in strong 2nd half that would have been even better if not for low h%. Struggles vL cap upside, but 91st percentile exit velocity says he's still a decent end game power source if you have solid BA foundation.

Yr	Tm	PA	R	HR	RBI	SB	BA	xHR	xSB	xBA	OBP	SLG	OPS+	vL+	vR+	bb%	ct%	Eye	G	L	F	h%	HctX	QBaB	Brl%	PX	xPX	HR/F	xHR/F	Spd	SBA%	SB%	RAR	BPX	R$
17	TAM	407	43	9	40	5	201	13	6	214	327	337	90	92	88	15	67	0.57	47	17	36	27	105	BCc	6%	88	94	11%	16%	129	7%	63%	-25.9	36	$1
18	2 TM *	283	23	8	30	1	236	11	4	210	300	391	93	87	97	8	64	0.25	40	20	40	34	98	ACc	11%	114	150	12%	18%	116	2%	100%	-9.0	0	$2
19	2 TM *	323	48	21	45	3	246	12	2	237	322	518	116	82	129	10	67	0.33	40	13	47	29	97	AAc	13%	154	110	26%	24%	116	10%	41%	-0.1	174	$9
20	STL	171	21	7	25	1	232	9	3	249	357	451	107	85	110	15	68	0.54	42	24	34	29	99	BCd	12%	136	120	21%	27%	110	2%	100%	-2.7	172	$10
21	PHI	377	53	20	49	3	227	20	4	236	321	453	106	73	116	12	66	0.40	45	18	37	28	116	ACd	12%	136	132	25%	25%	124	3%	100%	-10.8	138	$8
1st Half		161	22	6	20	3	239	5	2	220	329	408	103	98	105	12	61	0.35	48	23	29	35	101	ACc	8%	113	90	24%	20%	121	3%	100%	-4.3	-12	$5
2nd Half		216	31	14	29	0	217	15	2	248	315	487	109	41	122	12	70	0.46	44	15	42	23	128	ACd	15%	151	159	25%	27%	118	3%	0%	-4.1	238	$8
22	**Proj**	**280**	**37**	**14**	**37**	**2**	**230**	**15**	**3**	**235**	**326**	**454**	**106**	**76**	**112**	**12**	**66**	**0.41**	**43**	**19**	**38**	**29**	**108**		**12%**	**138**	**126**	**22%**	**24%**	**114**	**5%**	**77%**	**2.9**	**109**	**$8**

BRIAN RUDD

Miller,Owen

Age: 25 Pos: 2B | Bats: R Ht: 6' 0" Wt: 190
Health A | PT/Exp B | Consist B | LIMA Plan D | Rand Var 0 | MM 1213

4-18-.204 with 2 SB in 204 PA at CLE. Earned May call-up following hot start at AAA, but was sent back down after posting 50% ct% in first 48 PA. Contact rate improved in 2nd half, but he still couldn't sniff a .300 OBP. Since he lacks power and speed he'll need to contribute strong BA, which doesn't look too promising in the short-term.

Yr Tm	PA	R	HR	RBI	SB	BA	xHR	xSB	xBA	OBP	SLG	OPS+	vL+	vR+	bb%	ct%	Eye	G	L	F	h%	HctX	QBaB	Brl%	PX	xPX	HR/F	xHR/F	Spd	SBA%	SB%	RAR	BPX	R$
17																																		
18																																		
19 aa	547	65	10	58	4	261		7		315	380	96			7	81	0.42				30				65				98	7%	44%		89	$10
20																																		
21 CLE *	399	34	9	33	2	223	5	4	228	270	347	85	72	78	6	69	0.20	54	20	25	30	81	DDc	6%	85	80	11%	14%	96	3%	100%	-17.3	-50	$2
1st Half	183	16	3	11	0	218	0	2	207	275	321	83	27	50	7	64	0.21	65	17	17	32	45	FFd	0%	78	0	0%	0%	117	3%	0%	-10.2	-119	-$4
2nd Half	215	18	6	22	2	228	5	2	243	266	369	86	91	84	5	73	0.19	52	21	27	28	93	CDb	7%	90	96	13%	16%	87	3%	100%	-9.5	4	$2
22 Proj	**280**	**26**	**4**	**25**	**2**	**244**	**5**	**2**	**230**	**292**	**344**	**86**	**84**	**88**	**6**	**72**	**0.24**	**50**	**22**	**27**	**32**	**74**		**4%**	**69**	**58**	**8%**	**10%**	**97**	**4%**	**68%**	**-5.4**	**-94**	**$2**

Molina,Yadier

Age: 39 Pos: CA | Bats: R Ht: 5' 11" Wt: 225
Health C | PT/Exp A | Consist A | LIMA Plan D+ | Rand Var -1 | MM 1123

Got off to blazing start with .323 BA, 5 HR in late April when he landed on IL with foot injury. Made quick return but never got much going the rest of the way, though xHR and xPX say he deserved a few more HR. Still a useful 2nd catcher, but xBA and durability aren't what they once were, so upside is pretty limited heading into final year.

Yr Tm	PA	R	HR	RBI	SB	BA	xHR	xSB	xBA	OBP	SLG	OPS+	vL+	vR+	bb%	ct%	Eye	G	L	F	h%	HctX	QBaB	Brl%	PX	xPX	HR/F	xHR/F	Spd	SBA%	SB%	RAR	BPX	R$
17 STL	543	60	18	82	9	273	19	7	274	312	439	102	115	97	5	85	0.38	42	20	37	29	126	CBb	6%	88	118	11%	12%	66	11%	69%	9.9	133	$17
18 STL	503	55	20	74	4	261	17	6	279	314	436	101	106	97	6	86	0.44	39	24	37	27	140	CBb	6%	92	130	14%	12%	55	6%	57%	13.3	153	$15
19 STL	452	45	10	57	6	270	13	3	281	312	399	98	120	93	5	86	0.40	39	27	34	29	125	CCb	4%	67	108	8%	11%	56	6%	100%	0.2	100	$10
20 STL	156	12	4	16	0	262	4	1	231	303	359	88	99	85	4	86	0.29	42	21	37	28	88	DCd	2%	44	83	9%	9%	61	0%	0%	-1.8	20	$6
21 STL	472	45	11	66	3	252	16	0	238	297	370	92	116	87	5	82	0.30	42	19	39	29	110	CBc	5%	67	111	8%	11%	57	3%	100%	-4.4	42	$10
1st Half	244	26	8	38	2	258	9	0	262	307	427	102	136	96	7	81	0.38	40	21	39	29	110	BBc	6%	97	111	11%	13%	58	3%	100%	3.0	138	$12
2nd Half	228	19	3	28	1	247	7	0	211	285	312	81	95	78	4	83	0.22	44	17	39	29	110	CBc	4%	36	111	4%	10%	64	3%	100%	-7.6	-46	$3
22 Proj	**420**	**40**	**9**	**56**	**3**	**246**	**13**	**1**	**242**	**291**	**353**	**87**	**104**	**83**	**5**	**84**	**0.33**	**42**	**21**	**37**	**27**	**112**		**4%**	**59**	**107**	**7%**	**11%**	**55**	**2%**	**87%**	**-1.7**	**36**	**$10**

Moncada,Yoán

Age: 27 Pos: 3B | Bats: B Ht: 6' 2" Wt: 225
Health A | PT/Exp A | Consist D | LIMA Plan C+ | Rand Var 0 | MM 3225

It was easy to chalk up 2020 struggles to COVID and small sample, but what can explain 2021? Not all was bad, as ct% rebounded and xHR, HctX say he should have had more HR. But he stopped running for second straight year and power potential is capped by growing GB lean. Count on improvement, but it's tough not to see 2019 as an outlier.

Yr Tm	PA	R	HR	RBI	SB	BA	xHR	xSB	xBA	OBP	SLG	OPS+	vL+	vR+	bb%	ct%	Eye	G	L	F	h%	HctX	QBaB	Brl%	PX	xPX	HR/F	xHR/F	Spd	SBA%	SB%	RAR	BPX	R$
17 CHW *	583	78	18	52	17	246	7	9	213	339	405	101	87	107	12	63	0.38	46	19	35	36	91	CCb	10%	105	112	18%	16%	134	17%	61%	-6.0	3	$15
18 CHW	650	73	17	61	12	235	24	16	213	315	400	96	78	100	10	62	0.31	37	23	40	35	84	ABc	10%	123	113	12%	17%	120	12%	67%	-3.5	23	$14
19 CHW *	581	88	27	84	10	317	28	12	264	365	551	127	118	130	7	70	0.25	42	23	35	41	96	ACa	12%	135	103	20%	23%	126	9%	77%	35.2	159	$27
20 CHW	231	28	6	24	0	225	6	4	213	320	385	94	92	94	12	64	0.39	40	22	37	32	86	CCf	6%	103	101	13%	13%	145	0%	0%	-4.8	32	$8
21 CHW	616	74	14	61	3	263	20	3	247	375	412	108	95	113	14	70	0.54	44	27	30	35	116	BCc	8%	102	96	13%	19%	87	3%	60%	4.8	62	$14
1st Half	310	34	5	35	2	280	9	2	238	403	394	111	100	115	16	69	0.61	43	29	28	39	99	BCb	8%	83	79	10%	18%	86	3%	67%	3.0	4	$14
2nd Half	306	40	9	26	1	248	12	1	257	346	429	105	89	110	12	71	0.45	44	24	31	32	132	BCc	8%	120	112	15%	20%	92	3%	50%	-2.0	127	$10
22 Proj	**630**	**80**	**18**	**67**	**5**	**268**	**23**	**6**	**239**	**361**	**437**	**108**	**98**	**111**	**12**	**69**	**0.43**	**42**	**24**	**33**	**36**	**104**		**9%**	**112**	**102**	**14%**	**18%**	**110**	**5%**	**66%**	**17.5**	**58**	**$20**

Mondesi,Adalberto

Age: 26 Pos: 3B | Bats: B Ht: 6' 1" Wt: 200
Health F | PT/Exp D | Consist A | LIMA Plan C+ | Rand Var +3 | MM 3503

6-17-.230 with 15 SB in 136 PA at KC. This year's injury checklist: oblique, hamstring, and foot issues cost him most of the season. Massive ceiling was on display in limited sample, as constant green light and modest power somewhat offset major contact/BA issues. He's a speed monster when healthy, but can't count on anything close to a full season of PA.

Yr Tm	PA	R	HR	RBI	SB	BA	xHR	xSB	xBA	OBP	SLG	OPS+	vL+	vR+	bb%	ct%	Eye	G	L	F	h%	HctX	QBaB	Brl%	PX	xPX	HR/F	xHR/F	Spd	SBA%	SB%	RAR	BPX	R$
17 KC *	395	47	11	46	22	270	1	4	259	302	453	103	62	61	4	70	0.16	34	34	31	36	73	CCb	6%	114	120	11%	11%	138	35%	81%	1.8	70	$17
18 KC *	417	62	18	54	40	262	16	16	254	293	479	104	111	104	4	72	0.16	41	21	38	32	115	BBf	10%	132	130	20%	13%	130	61%	85%	10.3	150	$27
19 KC *	488	62	10	64	45	258	14	36	226	293	418	98	88	103	5	67	0.15	47	19	34	37	88	CCd	9%	95	82	9%	14%	153	55%	85%	-10.2	4	$27
20 KC	233	33	6	22	24	256	8	16	216	294	416	94	136	80	5	68	0.16	49	13	39	35	100	DCf	7%	101	102	11%	15%	161	67%	75%	-4.2	52	$40
21 KC *	201	25	8	21	19	209	9	12	218	241	392	87	113	93	4	67	0.13	43	14	43	27	105	CBf	13%	118	146	18%	26%	116	70%	89%	-8.0	31	$9
1st Half	67	8	5	11	2	279	5	3	267	298	589	124	159	174	3	67	0.08	33	17	50	35	148	BAb	23%	207	217	33%	42%	103	70%	71%	2.6	277	$0
2nd Half	134	17	3	9	16	173	4	8	195	213	292	68	90	64	5	67	0.16	47	13	40	23	87	DBf	8%	74	115	9%	18%	131	70%	93%	-9.5	-81	$6
22 Proj	**420**	**56**	**13**	**47**	**38**	**254**	**22**	**35**	**224**	**289**	**428**	**97**	**107**	**93**	**4**	**68**	**0.14**	**44**	**16**	**39**	**34**	**104**		**11%**	**113**	**130**	**13%**	**21%**	**131**	**55%**	**84%**	**0.5**	**85**	**$28**

Moore,Dylan

Age: 29 Pos: 2B LF | Bats: R Ht: 6' 0" Wt: 185
Health B | PT/Exp B | Consist D | LIMA Plan C | Rand Var +4 | MM 2403

Strikeouts continued to pile up, but this time without the plus power, which along with FB% spike resulted in h% and BA collapse. Did salvage some fantasy value with aggressiveness on bases, and light should remain green with SB% trending up. Just don't count on him as primary SB source, as limited real-life value puts playing time at risk.

Yr Tm	PA	R	HR	RBI	SB	BA	xHR	xSB	xBA	OBP	SLG	OPS+	vL+	vR+	bb%	ct%	Eye	G	L	F	h%	HctX	QBaB	Brl%	PX	xPX	HR/F	xHR/F	Spd	SBA%	SB%	RAR	BPX	R$
17 aa	465	45	6	39	9	175		6		253	238	67			9	72	0.38				23				39				91	17%	50%		-91	-$3
18 a/a	433	51	11	42	17	250		9		294	429	97			6	80	0.31				29				106				118	30%	67%		177	$13
19 SEA *	313	33	9	33	12	199	8	11	201	270	362	87	104	91	9	65	0.28	37	16	47	27	75	CAd	7%	104	100	13%	11%	125	33%	55%	-18.0	0	$5
20 SEA	159	26	8	17	12	255	7	7	254	358	496	113	99	120	9	69	0.33	35	25	40	31	100	BAc	14%	150	137	22%	19%	110	43%	71%	2.3	188	$24
21 SEA	377	42	12	43	21	181	12	19	194	276	334	84	93	77	11	67	0.36	32	18	50	23	65	DAf	9%	97	89	11%	11%	115	33%	81%	-18.9	8	$9
1st Half	207	22	7	26	13	186	7	9	210	275	361	89	88	89	10	63	0.29	33	23	44	25	64	DBf	11%	122	84	14%	14%	91	33%	87%	-9.8	-8	$10
2nd Half	170	20	5	17	8	174	6	9	173	276	302	78	96	56	12	71	0.47	30	13	58	21	66	DAf	6%	70	96	8%	10%	148	33%	73%	-11.3	42	$3
22 Proj	**350**	**44**	**10**	**38**	**20**	**220**	**13**	**16**	**206**	**311**	**372**	**93**	**98**	**89**	**10**	**69**	**0.35**	**35**	**18**	**47**	**29**	**74**		**9%**	**97**	**102**	**10%**	**13%**	**117**	**25%**	**70%**	**-5.7**	**34**	**$14**

Moran,Colin

Age: 29 Pos: 1B | Bats: L Ht: 6' 4" Wt: 200
Health C | PT/Exp B | Consist A | LIMA Plan C+ | Rand Var 0 | MM 2025

10-50-.258 in 359 PA at PIT. Small sample 2020 HR/F spike proved to be a fluke, which along with low FB% means he won't provide much of a power boost. Not looking like a BA asset anymore either after ct% failed to rebound. Consistent production vR shows he can still be a useful bat, but he's stretched as an everyday player and lacking in upside.

Yr Tm	PA	R	HR	RBI	SB	BA	xHR	xSB	xBA	OBP	SLG	OPS+	vL+	vR+	bb%	ct%	Eye	G	L	F	h%	HctX	QBaB	Brl%	PX	xPX	HR/F	xHR/F	Spd	SBA%	SB%	RAR	BPX	R$
17 HOU *	333	37	13	43	0	244	0	4	259	291	415	96	189	146	6	77	0.29	50	20	30	28	94	ACb	0%	93	74	33%	0%	115	6%	0%	-19.2	100	$4
18 PIT	465	49	11	58	0	277	13	5	265	340	407	100	67	104	8	80	0.48	45	26	29	32	97	CCa	5%	78	91	11%	13%	105	2%	0%	-3.8	113	$11
19 PIT	503	46	13	80	0	277	18	2	254	322	429	104	95	105	6	75	0.26	44	24	32	35	89	CCb	7%	90	80	12%	16%	83	1%	0%	-7.9	37	$11
20 PIT	200	28	10	23	0	247	11	1	246	325	472	106	85	114	10	71	0.37	56	15	29	29	115	ADc	13%	134	98	28%	31%	95	0%	0%	-4.1	160	$13
21 PIT *	386	32	11	57	1	250	11	1	239	325	387	98	75	108	10	72	0.40	50	23	27	32	91	CDc	8%	85	85	16%	18%	74	1%	100%	-16.2	0	$7
1st Half	183	12	5	27	1	279	4	0	257	335	421	105	73	115	8	71	0.29	45	30	25	37	85	CDc	7%	96	89	14%	14%	80	1%	100%	-2.9	8	$5
2nd Half	203	19	7	30	0	223	6	0	215	315	356	91	76	101	12	73	0.51	54	18	28	27	96	CFf	9%	75	82	18%	18%	83	1%	0%	-10.6	15	$2
22 Proj	**455**	**43**	**14**	**61**	**0**	**252**	**16**	**2**	**241**	**322**	**402**	**98**	**78**	**105**	**9**	**73**	**0.38**	**50**	**22**	**29**	**31**	**96**		**9%**	**92**	**87**	**16%**	**18%**	**81**	**2%**	**46%**	**-0.9**	**-11**	**$11**

Mountcastle,Ryan

Age: 25 Pos: 1B DH LF | Bats: R Ht: 6' 3" Wt: 210
Health A | PT/Exp A | Consist C | LIMA Plan B | Rand Var +1 | MM 4235

Started slow with .226 BA, 5 HR through end of May, then power took off and was well-supported by xHR and xPX. He bumped up xBA in 2nd half, and even without a full ct% rebound, he shouldn't be a total BA drag in current environment. This breakout looks pretty legit, and next step just might be... UP: 40 HR.

Yr Tm	PA	R	HR	RBI	SB	BA	xHR	xSB	xBA	OBP	SLG	OPS+	vL+	vR+	bb%	ct%	Eye	G	L	F	h%	HctX	QBaB	Brl%	PX	xPX	HR/F	xHR/F	Spd	SBA%	SB%	RAR	BPX	R$
17 aa	156	16	3	13	0	181		1		196	283	65			2	74	0.07				23				68				92	0%	0%		-42	-$3
18 aa	414	49	11	46	2	267		2		302	406	95			5	79	0.24				31				81				108	2%	100%		80	$9
19 aaa	540	66	22	68	2	281		3		307	466	107			4	73	0.14				35				105				89	3%	60%		48	$15
20 BAL	140	12	5	23	0	333	5	2	230	386	492	117	86	126	8	76	0.37	44	19	37	41	107	CCf	7%	88	91	14%	14%	124	2%	0%	5.4	120	$13
21 BAL	586	77	33	89	4	255	33	3	248	309	487	109	115	106	7	70	0.25	35	22	43	30	97	CBd	12%	139	126	20%	20%	99	6%	57%	-6.3	138	$20
1st Half	307	36	14	47	3	259	15	2	238	300	458	106	117	101	5	69	0.18	35	24	42	33	96	CBd	10%	124	126	17%	18%	105	6%	60%	-6.3	73	$21
2nd Half	279	41	19	42	1	250	18	2	259	319	520	114	112	114	9	71	0.35	36	21	44	27	98	CAd	14%	155	125	24%	23%	95	6%	50%	1.5	219	$19
22 Proj	**560**	**68**	**34**	**87**	**3**	**262**	**31**	**6**	**256**	**310**	**503**	**110**	**108**	**111**	**6**	**73**	**0.25**	**37**	**21**	**41**	**30**	**100**		**11%**	**138**	**117**	**21%**	**20%**	**108**	**6%**	**58%**	**12.9**	**128**	**$22**

BRIAN RUDD

Moustakas,Mike

Age: 33 Pos: 3B | Bats: L Ht: 6' 0" Wt: 225

Health D | PT/Exp C | Consist B | LIMA Plan C | Rand Var +3 | MM 4135

Started slow before illness and foot ailments wiped out most of his season. Brl% dropped and took power down with it, while ct% didn't rebound and well-established low h% combined for BA dip. Even though we already gave him a mulligan last year, strong track record in xPX, HctX, Eye warn against writing him off. Health is key.

Yr	Tm	PA	R	HR	RBI	SB	BA	xHR	xSB	xBA	OBP	SLG	OPS+	vL+	vR+	bb%	ct%	Eye	G	L	F	h%	HctX	QBaB	Brl%	PX	xPX	HR/F	xHR/F	Spd	SBA%	SB%	RAR	BPX	R$
17	KC	598	75	38	85	0	272	30	7	279	314	521	114	103	115	6	83	0.36	35	20	46	27	107	CAc	9%	124	120	18%	14%	68	0%	0%	6.6	197	$
18	2 TM	635	66	28	95	4	251	29	1	264	315	459	104	96	105	8	82	0.48	34	20	46	26	124	BAd	9%	116	130	13%	13%	71	4%	80%	3.1	200	$
19	MIL	584	80	35	87	3	254	31	3	277	329	516	117	122	114	9	81	0.54	36	19	45	25	117	BBf	10%	127	129	18%	16%	76	2%	100%	4.7	259	$
20	CIN	163	13	8	27	1	230	6	1	256	331	468	106	85	114	11	74	0.50	36	20	44	25	114	CBc	10%	137	123	17%	13%	61	3%	100%	-1.3	192	
21	CIN	206	21	6	22	0	208	6	1	232	282	372	90	45	101	9	75	0.39	36	19	46	24	83	CAf	6%	104	64	9%	9%	57	0%	0%	-11.1	73	-
1st Half		104	15	4	13	0	241	3	0	248	337	437	108	70	117	12	79	0.67	39	17	44	26	77	DBf	4%	110	48	13%	9%	75	0%	0%	-0.5	208	-
2nd Half		102	6	2	9	0	177	3	0	219	225	313	73	20	86	6	71	0.21	32	21	47	23	89	CAf	7%	98	81	6%	9%	51	0%	0%	-9.0	-35	-
22	**Proj**	**455**	**53**	**21**	**67**	**1**	**232**	**20**	**0**	**253**	**305**	**449**	**102**	**80**	**110**	**9**	**76**	**0.41**	**35**	**19**	**45**	**25**	**100**		**9%**	**127**	**97**	**15%**	**14%**	**52**	**0%**	**94%**	**2.6**	**142**	

Mullins,Cedric

Age: 27 Pos: CF | Bats: L Ht: 5' 8" Wt: 175

Health A | PT/Exp A | Consist D | LIMA Plan B+ | Rand Var -4 | MM 3525

How does a light-hitting speedster produce first-round value? Easy: 1) Give up switch-hitting, 2) Make harder contact (PX/xPX, Brl%), and 3) Come to bat nearly 700 times. But can he repeat? It's unwise to bet on this much volume again, but his skills generally support the results. His true talent looks much closer to 2021 than to previous years.

Yr	Tm	PA	R	HR	RBI	SB	BA	xHR	xSB	xBA	OBP	SLG	OPS+	vL+	vR+	bb%	ct%	Eye	G	L	F	h%	HctX	QBaB	Brl%	PX	xPX	HR/F	xHR/F	Spd	SBA%	SB%	RAR	BPX	R$
17	aa	333	44	11	31	7	220		4		277	365	87			7	78	0.35				25				80				105	22%	49%		70	$
18	BAL *	663	83	14	48	18	247	3	19	246	300	389	92	60	99	7	82	0.41	51	12	37	28	80	CCd	3%	84	66	9%	7%	136	15%	82%	-0.6	173	$1
19	BAL *	580	68	9	38	28	188	1	12	211	249	279	73	34	50	7	80	0.41	53	8	39	22	52	DBf	2%	47	18	0%	5%	122	31%	78%	-38.8	41	$
20	BAL	153	16	3	12	7	271	2	7	229	315	407	96	65	106	5	74	0.22	43	22	35	35	64	FCf	3%	73	44	9%	6%	154	24%	78%	-1.2	44	$1
21	BAL	674	91	30	59	30	291	28	25	270	360	518	121	107	128	9	79	0.47	39	20	41	32	108	CCd	8%	125	109	15%	14%	137	22%	79%	31.3	300	$3
1st Half		354	46	14	30	15	313	13	14	274	381	535	128	119	132	9	79	0.48	38	22	40	36	104	CCc	7%	126	115	14%	13%	137	22%	79%	22.2	296	$3
2nd Half		320	45	16	29	15	266	15	11	268	335	500	113	97	125	9	80	0.47	40	17	42	28	111	CCf	9%	125	102	17%	16%	127	22%	79%	6.7	292	$2
22	**Proj**	**630**	**78**	**24**	**52**	**25**	**269**	**20**	**22**	**249**	**335**	**460**	**108**	**95**	**114**	**8**	**79**	**0.39**	**41**	**18**	**41**	**31**	**85**		**5%**	**104**	**73**	**13%**	**11%**	**133**	**18%**	**76%**	**20.7**	**196**	**$3**

Muncy,Max

Age: 31 Pos: 1B 2B | Bats: L Ht: 6' 0" Wt: 215

Health B | PT/Exp A | Consist D | LIMA Plan B | Rand Var +3 | MM 4135

Mashed his way through another strong season, as June oblique injury barely slowed him down. Contact and exit velocity ("A" in QBaB) surpassed previous norms, while both xHR and xBA hint at what could've been with better luck. With plus skills across the board, no platoon split, and dual eligibility, he's poised for a four-category repeat.

Yr	Tm	PA	R	HR	RBI	SB	BA	xHR	xSB	xBA	OBP	SLG	OPS+	vL+	vR+	bb%	ct%	Eye	G	L	F	h%	HctX	QBaB	Brl%	PX	xPX	HR/F	xHR/F	Spd	SBA%	SB%	RAR	BPX	R$
17	aaa	357	46	9	33	2	251		5		328	394	98			10	67	0.35				34				99				94	10%	23%		0	$
18	LA *	517	80	36	82	3	262	32	7	267	382	571	128	118	132	16	68	0.60	34	21	45	30	118	BAa	17%	192	176	29%	27%	79	2%	100%	30.6	277	$2
19	LA	589	101	35	98	4	251	31	4	262	374	515	123	124	122	15	69	0.60	38	23	39	29	110	BBb	12%	146	150	27%	23%	83	3%	80%	14.9	193	$2
20	LA	248	36	12	27	1	192	14	2	217	331	389	96	104	91	16	70	0.65	44	14	42	21	118	CBd	12%	107	168	20%	23%	88	2%	100%	-12.3	108	$1
21	LA	592	95	36	94	2	249	45	2	279	368	527	123	131	120	14	76	0.69	38	21	41	26	122	ABc	16%	153	154	23%	29%	68	2%	67%	6.8	292	$2
1st Half		286	49	18	44	1	261	20	1	289	416	553	135	139	133	20	76	1.00	40	23	37	27	118	ABc	17%	157	135	29%	32%	70	2%	100%	14.0	346	$2
2nd Half		306	46	18	50	1	240	25	1	269	324	506	112	122	109	9	76	0.43	37	18	45	25	126	ABc	16%	149	170	19%	27%	73	2%	50%	-3.5	254	$2
22	**Proj**	**560**	**85**	**34**	**85**	**3**	**256**	**35**	**3**	**261**	**371**	**520**	**121**	**125**	**119**	**14**	**73**	**0.61**	**39**	**20**	**41**	**28**	**119**		**15%**	**150**	**159**	**24%**	**25%**	**77**	**3%**	**68%**	**27.6**	**228**	**$2**

Murphy,Sean

Age: 27 Pos: CA | Bats: R Ht: 6' 3" Wt: 228

Health A | PT/Exp B | Consist B | LIMA Plan B | Rand Var +5 | MM 4025

Delivered marginal second-catcher value until late slump pushed him to backup role. Regression of 2020's bb% and exit velocity spikes were expected; good news is he held onto HctX and xPX, solidifying power foundation. Though xBA says the BA will drag, he's a reasonable play behind the dish right now, and he's young enough to take another step.

Yr	Tm	PA	R	HR	RBI	SB	BA	xHR	xSB	xBA	OBP	SLG	OPS+	vL+	vR+	bb%	ct%	Eye	G	L	F	h%	HctX	QBaB	Brl%	PX	xPX	HR/F	xHR/F	Spd	SBA%	SB%	RAR	BPX	R$
17	aa	207	20	3	18	0	183		2		248	261	69			8	81	0.46				21				47				93	0%	0%		24	-$
18	a/a	285	42	6	34	2	248		1		301	416	96			7	79	0.36				29				110				99	4%	100%		170	$
19	OAK *	191	33	11	31	0	253	3	1	281	320	512	115	103	135	9	70	0.33	46	27	27	30	85	BDb	8%	147	99	40%	30%	90	3%	0%	9.4	159	$
20	OAK	140	21	7	14	0	233	7	1	233	364	457	109	99	113	17	68	0.65	43	18	39	28	94	ABc	13%	134	109	23%	23%	102	0%	0%	4.9	188	$
21	OAK	448	47	17	59	0	216	22	1	237	306	405	98	86	103	9	71	0.35	39	20	41	26	99	CBc	11%	120	115	15%	19%	64	0%	0%	-4.0	73	$
1st Half		262	28	10	40	0	221	14	0	235	321	420	103	76	120	10	71	0.36	41	17	42	27	102	BBd	13%	129	126	15%	21%	68	0%	0%	-0.2	108	$
2nd Half		186	19	7	19	0	210	8	0	239	285	383	90	107	85	9	71	0.33	38	23	39	25	95	CBc	9%	108	99	15%	17%	75	0%	0%	-3.4	50	-$
22	**Proj**	**455**	**59**	**21**	**56**	**0**	**241**	**23**	**1**	**251**	**331**	**455**	**107**	**98**	**110**	**11**	**72**	**0.42**	**41**	**21**	**37**	**28**	**95**		**11%**	**131**	**108**	**19%**	**21%**	**77**	**1%**	**47%**	**16.3**	**107**	**$1**

Murphy,Tom

Age: 31 Pos: CA | Bats: R Ht: 6' 1" Wt: 218

Health B | PT/Exp C | Consist D | LIMA Plan D | Rand Var +1 | MM 3103

Came back from lost 2020 (broken foot) to produce as expected in part-time role. PX, QBaB, HctX were middling, but contact woes killed BA and further limited power production. Intriguing 2nd half bb% spike, if repeated, would not only be a boon in OBP leagues but could also net continued playing time. But he's still a fringy CA option at best.

Yr	Tm	PA	R	HR	RBI	SB	BA	xHR	xSB	xBA	OBP	SLG	OPS+	vL+	vR+	bb%	ct%	Eye	G	L	F	h%	HctX	QBaB	Brl%	PX	xPX	HR/F	xHR/F	Spd	SBA%	SB%	RAR	BPX	R$
17	COL *	173	16	3	14	0	196	0	1	192	233	320	75	37	0	5	58	0.12	40	20	40	32	47	FBf	0%	104	40	0%	0%	86	0%	0%	-8.7	-139	-$
18	COL *	345	29	13	40	2	214	3	1	234	252	415	89	84	84	5	60	0.13	31	33	37	31	73	DAc	6%	154	85	11%	17%	103	10%	41%	-2.7	23	$
19	SEA	281	32	18	40	2	273	15	3	240	324	535	119	153	90	7	67	0.22	34	19	47	34	87	BAc	11%	150	133	22%	19%	91	3%	100%	18.4	107	$
20																																			
21	SEA	322	35	11	34	0	202	12	4	188	304	350	90	108	70	12	64	0.40	44	14	41	27	100	CBf	9%	97	116	15%	16%	86	0%	0%	-6.4	-46	$
1st Half		174	20	6	16	0	192	8	1	198	264	353	86	103	69	9	61	0.25	38	19	43	27	108	BAf	12%	117	138	14%	19%	97	0%	0%	-5.8	-54	-$
2nd Half		148	15	5	18	0	215	4	2	170	351	347	94	113	71	17	69	0.66	51	10	39	27	90	DCf	6%	74	91	15%	12%	85	0%	0%	-0.6	-19	-$
22	**Proj**	**280**	**29**	**10**	**33**	**1**	**232**	**10**	**1**	**206**	**308**	**400**	**96**	**114**	**79**	**10**	**64**	**0.30**	**40**	**18**	**41**	**32**	**91**		**8%**	**113**	**110**	**16%**	**14%**	**83**	**2%**	**60%**	**3.9**	**-71**	**$**

Myers,Wil

Age: 31 Pos: RF | Bats: R Ht: 6' 3" Wt: 207

Health B | PT/Exp A | Consist D | LIMA Plan C+ | Rand Var -1 | MM 4325

Returned to "normal" after 2020's outburst, which is now the clear outlier. Skills suggest a diminished profile as exit velocity, xPX, and ct% dropped, HctX tanked severely, and running game faltered. On the plus side, bb% and narrow platoon splits should keep him in the lineup, where his now middling bat should still produce modest all-around value.

Yr	Tm	PA	R	HR	RBI	SB	BA	xHR	xSB	xBA	OBP	SLG	OPS+	vL+	vR+	bb%	ct%	Eye	G	L	F	h%	HctX	QBaB	Brl%	PX	xPX	HR/F	xHR/F	Spd	SBA%	SB%	RAR	BPX	R$
17	SD	649	80	30	74	20	243	27	9	242	328	464	108	107	106	11	68	0.39	38	20	43	30	114	BBd	9%	138	144	18%	16%	126	17%	77%	-1.5	136	$1
18	SD	343	39	11	39	13	253	11	7	266	318	446	102	107	97	9	70	0.32	44	28	29	33	120	BCc	7%	137	121	17%	17%	94	19%	93%	5.8	123	$1
19	SD	490	58	18	53	16	239	20	14	220	321	418	102	122	97	10	61	0.30	43	22	35	35	100	BCf	11%	119	121	20%	22%	114	20%	70%	-13.2	-4	$14
20	SD	218	34	15	40	2	288	16	5	287	353	606	127	136	122	8	72	0.32	38	23	38	33	139	BCc	15%	182	175	28%	30%	118	7%	67%	12.6	348	$27
21	SD	500	56	17	63	8	256	18	7	230	334	434	106	113	103	11	68	0.38	45	18	37	34	83	CCf	8%	117	104	15%	16%	116	10%	62%	-3.7	92	$15
1st Half		261	23	9	29	5	244	10	3	222	314	406	100	85	105	10	70	0.35	49	15	36	31	86	DDf	8%	100	100	16%	17%	114	10%	50%	-7.1	54	$1
2nd Half		239	33	8	34	3	269	8	3	237	356	466	111	134	100	12	66	0.41	40	20	39	37	79	CCf	7%	138	110	15%	15%	117	10%	100%	5.2	142	$13
22	**Proj**	**525**	**67**	**21**	**71**	**10**	**260**	**23**	**9**	**242**	**336**	**465**	**109**	**120**	**104**	**10**	**68**	**0.35**	**42**	**21**	**37**	**34**	**101**		**10%**	**135**	**125**	**18%**	**20%**	**109**	**9%**	**72%**	**13.0**	**110**	**$21**

Naquin,Tyler

Age: 31 Pos: CF LF RF | Bats: L Ht: 6' 2" Wt: 195

Health D | PT/Exp B | Consist D | LIMA Plan B | Rand Var -1 | MM 3235

Feasted on righties to produce best season, which ended in Sept due to rib injury. Improved walk rate and normalized HR/F luck in new home park helped, but playing time was the real value driver as ct% and HctX were consistent with previous baselines. Weakness vL will continue to limit PA, but profile strongly supports 2021 as a baseline.

Yr	Tm	PA	R	HR	RBI	SB	BA	xHR	xSB	xBA	OBP	SLG	OPS+	vL+	vR+	bb%	ct%	Eye	G	L	F	h%	HctX	QBaB	Brl%	PX	xPX	HR/F	xHR/F	Spd	SBA%	SB%	RAR	BPX	R$
17	CLE *	359	37	8	41	4	257	0	5	261	311	392	96	68	70	7	75	0.31	59	21	21	32	94	FFa	0%	82	69	0%	0%	113	9%	46%	-10.2	48	$6
18	CLE	183	22	3	23	1	264	4	2	242	295	356	87	75	87	3	76	0.14	54	23	23	33	107	CDa	5%	61	63	10%	13%	90	5%	50%	-3.6	-37	$2
19	CLE *	317	37	12	39	4	286	12	3	263	318	486	111	116	107	4	76	0.19	44	21	36	34	106	BCd	9%	112	84	13%	16%	100	9%	67%	9.8	122	$9
20	CLE	141	15	4	20	0	218	7	1	240	248	383	84	6	98	4	70	0.13	43	23	34	28	107	ACc	9%	105	107	13%	22%	105	5%	0%	-8.5	16	$4
21	CIN	454	52	19	70	5	270	22	4	264	333	477	111	77	118	8	74	0.33	47	21	32	32	109	CDd	10%	123	105	19%	22%	96	8%	63%	3.6	162	$16
1st Half		252	26	13	47	4	248	14	2	249	313	469	109	84	113	8	73	0.31	44	17	39	28	124	BCd	11%	129	123	20%	22%	63	8%	67%	-0.8	123	$17
2nd Half		202	26	6	23	1	297	8	2	282	356	486	114	70	124	8	76	0.36	50	26	24	37	91	CDd	10%	115	83	18%	24%	129	8%	50%	6.3	196	$8
22	**Proj**	**455**	**53**	**16**	**63**	**4**	**265**	**21**	**6**	**258**	**313**	**451**	**104**	**73**	**110**	**6**	**74**	**0.25**	**47**	**22**	**31**	**32**	**105**		**9%**	**114**	**94**	**17%**	**21%**	**107**	**7%**	**54%**	**9.5**	**85**	**$16**

ARIK FLORIMONTE

Narváez,Omar

Age: 30 Pos: CA	Health A	LIMA Plan D+	
Bats: B Ht: 5' 11" Wt: 220	PT/Exp A	Rand Var -1	
	Consist D	MM 1025	

Quickly put 2020 in rearview with near-full BA rebound, as h% and ct% both snapped right back to normal. 2019 HR total a clear outlier given subpar Brl% and xHR/F, but bb% baseline locks in decent OBP and playing time floor. Not much of a ceiling, but modest four-category production like this from a catcher has deep-league value.

Yr	Tm	PA	R	HR	RBI	SB	BA	xHR	xSB	xBA	OBP	SLG	OPS+	vL+	vR+	bb%	ct%	Eye	G	L	F	h%	HctX	QBaB	Brl%	PX	xPX	HR/F	xHR/F	Spd	SBA%	SB%	RAR	BPX	R$
17	CHW	295	23	2	14	0	277	1	6	257	373	340	97	90	96	13	82	0.84	44	28	29	33	65	FCb	0%	41	27	3%	2%	76	0%	0%	2.8	36	$2
18	CHW	322	30	9	30	0	275	5	1	270	366	429	106	75	111	12	77	0.58	42	29	29	33	81	DCa	3%	94	84	15%	8%	77	2%	0%	14.4	103	$6
19	SEA	482	63	22	55	0	278	15	3	263	353	460	113	97	115	10	79	0.51	33	26	41	31	81	DAa	5%	88	94	16%	11%	82	0%	0%	16.1	115	$12
20	MIL	126	8	2	10	0	176	3	0	197	294	269	75	67	76	13	64	0.41	39	25	36	25	52	FAb	7%	67	64	8%	12%	65	0%	0%	-5.9	-172	-$3
21	MIL	445	54	11	49	0	266	13	1	251	342	402	102	59	111	9	79	0.49	33	26	41	31	82	DAc	5%	81	98	9%	10%	68	0%	0%	7.0	77	$10
1st Half		228	31	7	25	0	303	8	1	266	395	462	119	92	124	12	80	0.67	35	27	39	35	95	DBb	8%	90	121	11%	13%	77	0%	0%	12.7	158	$12
2nd Half		217	23	4	24	0	230	5	0	235	286	342	85	34	97	7	77	0.33	32	25	43	28	69	FAc	2%	71	75	6%	7%	67	0%	0%	-5.2	4	$1
22	**Proj**	**455**	**52**	**12**	**48**	**0**	**255**	**12**	**1**	**242**	**338**	**388**	**99**	**69**	**105**	**10**	**77**	**0.50**	**36**	**25**	**39**	**30**	**74**		**5%**	**79**	**83**	**10%**	**10%**	**64**	**1%**	**0%**	**10.2**	**9**	**$8**

Naylor,Josh

Age: 25 Pos: RF	Health D	LIMA Plan B	
Bats: L Ht: 5' 11" Wt: 250	PT/Exp C	Rand Var 0	
	Consist B	MM 2035	

Broke camp with starting RF gig; season ended abruptly with ankle surgery after late-June outfield collision. He gave back short-season ct% gains, putting xBA in lockstep with mediocre BA while PX/xPX and GB% stroke cap any HR upside. A former first rounder at pre-peak age, but if there's a step forward to be had, we're not seeing it in the skills.

Yr	Tm	PA	R	HR	RBI	SB	BA	xHR	xSB	xBA	OBP	SLG	OPS+	vL+	vR+	bb%	ct%	Eye	G	L	F	h%	HctX	QBaB	Brl%	PX	xPX	HR/F	xHR/F	Spd	SBA%	SB%	RAR	BPX	R$
17	aa	171	17	2	18	2	247		2		312	341	89			9	77	0.41				31				65				88	7%	65%		12	$1
18	aa	557	63	14	65	4	274		7		347	404	101			10	85	0.73				30				72				90	6%	45%		153	$15
19	SD *	522	65	15	62	2	257	6	3	261	321	420	103	94	100	9	80	0.46	53	17	30	30	114	BFf	6%	91	89	14%	11%	49	3%	63%	-10.8	93	$10
20	2 TM	103	13	1	6	1	247	1	1	269	291	330	82	156	76	5	88	0.42	53	22	25	27	100	CDd	4%	41	44	5%	5%	92	4%	100%	-4.8	92	$3
21	CLE	249	28	7	21	1	253	9	1	254	301	399	96	70	111	6	81	0.31	49	19	32	29	93	BDf	7%	85	85	12%	15%	60	2%	100%	-5.9	85	$3
1st Half		249	28	7	21	1	253	9	1	254	301	399	97	71	113	6	81	0.31	49	19	32	29	93	BDf	7%	85	85	12%	15%	60	2%	100%	-6.9	85	$7
2nd Half																									0%										
22	**Proj**	**490**	**57**	**13**	**50**	**3**	**257**	**12**	**1**	**261**	**316**	**401**	**97**	**88**	**100**	**7**	**82**	**0.45**	**51**	**19**	**29**	**29**	**100**		**6%**	**81**	**74**	**12%**	**11%**	**55**	**1%**	**70%**	**-1.7**	**105**	**$13**

Newman,Kevin

Age: 28 Pos: SS	Health A	LIMA Plan C+	
Bats: R Ht: 6' 0" Wt: 200	PT/Exp A	Rand Var +4	
	Consist C	MM 0335	

The type of PA total where counting stats should start to accumulate. Spoiler alert: They didn't. QBaB with a damning summary of the (lack of) contact quality here, while 2020's red light hung around all year. One of the better bat-on-ballers in the game, but xBA doubts that translates to a plus BA. Speculate on higher ceilings elsewhere in the end game.

Yr	Tm	PA	R	HR	RBI	SB	BA	xHR	xSB	xBA	OBP	SLG	OPS+	vL+	vR+	bb%	ct%	Eye	G	L	F	h%	HctX	QBaB	Brl%	PX	xPX	HR/F	xHR/F	Spd	SBA%	SB%	RAR	BPX	R$
17	a/a	535	57	3	36	10	245		7		281	331	83			5	87	0.39				28				52				113	11%	74%		106	$6
18	PIT *	558	64	3	33	22	250	1	9	263	288	326	82	115	53	5	85	0.35	55	20	25	29	59	FFa	1%	51	45	0%	6%	103	28%	61%	-13.0	80	$14
19	PIT *	565	65	12	65	16	302	7	27	281	342	435	108	101	113	6	87	0.46	49	22	28	33	80	DDb	2%	63	50	10%	6%	150	16%	64%	7.2	204	$21
20	PIT	172	12	1	10	0	224	1	4	236	281	276	74	100	67	7	87	0.57	49	21	30	25	96	DDf	1%	31	74	2%	2%	115	2%	0%	-9.8	84	$0
21	PIT	554	50	5	39	6	226	6	4	258	265	309	79	82	77	5	92	0.66	44	20	36	24	83	FDf	2%	45	50	3%	4%	118	6%	86%	-28.1	196	$4
1st Half		292	24	2	12	2	208	3	2	251	251	263	72	67	73	5	93	0.79	47	20	33	22	74	DDf	1%	29	40	2%	4%	113	6%	100%	-20.7	162	-$3
2nd Half		262	26	3	27	4	247	3	2	264	280	362	87	96	82	5	91	0.55	41	20	39	26	93	FCf	2%	64	62	3%	3%	126	6%	80%	-7.9	246	$6
22	**Proj**	**560**	**54**	**5**	**44**	**7**	**243**	**6**	**7**	**256**	**287**	**325**	**83**	**91**	**80**	**5**	**89**	**0.53**	**47**	**21**	**33**	**27**	**84**		**2%**	**46**	**56**	**3%**	**4%**	**121**	**7%**	**61%**	**-18.3**	**114**	**$10**

Nido,Tomás

Age: 28 Pos: CA	Health B	LIMA Plan D	
Bats: R Ht: 6' 0" Wt: 211	PT/Exp F	Rand Var +2	
	Consist F	MM 1411	

A decent May (.298 BA, 3 HR), but rest of season was littered with injuries (June wrist, Aug thumb) and ineffectiveness. We could maybe look to xPX as a sign of life, but PX baseline (ignore 2020's small sample) has us skeptical while brutal bb%/OBP could cost him PT. An easy pass when diving through the second-catcher clearance bin.

Yr	Tm	PA	R	HR	RBI	SB	BA	xHR	xSB	xBA	OBP	SLG	OPS+	vL+	vR+	bb%	ct%	Eye	G	L	F	h%	HctX	QBaB	Brl%	PX	xPX	HR/F	xHR/F	Spd	SBA%	SB%	RAR	BPX	R$
17	NYM *	409	40	8	62	0	217	0	5	286	279	336	84	0	104	8	80	0.43	25	38	38	25	81	BCa	0%	70	161	0%	0%	75	0%	0%	-11.7	52	$1
18	NYM *	329	28	4	31	0	204	1	1	252	230	312	73	83	52	3	77	0.15	51	24	25	25	91	DDc	2%	75	75	7%	7%	92	0%	0%	-11.9	13	-$1
19	NYM *	183	11	4	17	0	202	3	0	189	236	304	75	90	70	4	70	0.15	55	15	30	27	79	CDd	5%	62	66	14%	10%	69	0%	0%	-11.1	-148	-$3
20	NYM	26	4	2	6	0	292	1	0	266	346	583	123	203	81	8	75	0.33	67	11	22	31	101	CFb	11%	153	98	50%	25%	91	0%	0%	2.1	268	$1
21	NYM	161	16	3	13	1	222	5	1	230	261	327	81	73	83	3	71	0.11	41	28	31	29	110	CCb	6%	65	132	9%	15%	122	3%	100%	-6.4	-65	-$1
1st Half		91	12	3	11	0	238	3	1	246	297	393	96	89	99	5	71	0.17	48	25	27	30	102	CDa	8%	87	124	19%	19%	124	3%	0%	-1.3	15	-$3
2nd Half		70	4	0	2	1	203	2	0	215	214	246	62	50	66	1	71	0.05	33	31	37	29	119	BCb	4%	39	141	0%	11%	112	3%	100%	-5.1	-177	-$9
22	**Proj**	**245**	**21**	**5**	**21**	**1**	**212**	**6**	**2**	**232**	**245**	**318**	**77**	**79**	**75**	**4**	**73**	**0.14**	**45**	**25**	**30**	**27**	**101**		**5%**	**69**	**109**	**9%**	**10%**	**101**	**4%**	**100%**	**-7.7**	**-99**	**$2**

Nimmo,Brandon

Age: 29 Pos: CF	Health F	LIMA Plan B	
Bats: L Ht: 6' 3" Wt: 206	PT/Exp C	Rand Var -2	
	Consist B	MM 3335	

8-28-.292 with 5 SB in 386 PA at NYM. Injury woes continued; this time it was a finger in May, hamstring in Sept. Held 2020's ct% gains and OBP foundation is firm, but troubling signs elsewhere: dwindling PX kept xBA in neutral, xPX says he deserved it, and SB effectiveness is waning. A rebound candidate with health, but 2018 looks like his high-water mark.

Yr	Tm	PA	R	HR	RBI	SB	BA	xHR	xSB	xBA	OBP	SLG	OPS+	vL+	vR+	bb%	ct%	Eye	G	L	F	h%	HctX	QBaB	Brl%	PX	xPX	HR/F	xHR/F	Spd	SBA%	SB%	RAR	BPX	R$
17	NYM *	403	42	7	33	2	221	6	6	225	335	353	94	72	117	14	65	0.49	43	24	33	32	92	CCb	7%	99	106	13%	15%	101	2%	100%	-12.0	0	$1
18	NYM	535	77	17	47	9	263	15	8	254	404	483	119	98	125	15	68	0.57	45	22	33	35	93	BCd	7%	148	114	18%	15%	146	9%	60%	24.4	217	$16
19	NYM *	295	42	9	34	5	212	5	5	226	356	386	103	166	93	18	65	0.65	39	23	38	28	81	BCc	7%	110	103	16%	10%	96	6%	100%	2.2	59	$4
20	NYM	225	33	8	18	1	280	8	5	263	404	484	118	85	130	15	77	0.77	47	20	32	33	67	CDd	8%	107	70	17%	17%	154	4%	33%	7.3	284	$17
21	NYM *	418	54	8	28	5	278	7	7	251	378	413	109	112	117	14	77	0.69	47	22	30	34	106	CDd	4%	81	72	11%	9%	138	7%	56%	3.3	162	$11
1st Half		123	13	2	10	2	287	2	2	258	375	407	109	145	131	12	74	0.54	56	25	19	37	72	CFc	8%	82	46	20%	20%	120	7%	67%	1.5	88	$0
2nd Half		295	41	6	18	3	274	6	5	249	388	415	109	105	110	14	78	0.76	45	22	33	33	116	CCf	3%	80	79	9%	9%	140	7%	50%	3.4	185	$11
22	**Proj**	**490**	**67**	**14**	**41**	**6**	**264**	**13**	**9**	**253**	**382**	**439**	**111**	**106**	**113**	**14**	**73**	**0.63**	**47**	**22**	**31**	**33**	**89**		**6%**	**106**	**79**	**15%**	**14%**	**127**	**8%**	**61%**	**19.4**	**140**	**$16**

Nola,Austin

Age: 32 Pos: CA	Health D	LIMA Plan C+	
Bats: R Ht: 6' 0" Wt: 197	PT/Exp D	Rand Var +2	
	Consist B	MM 2033	

2-29-.272 in 194 PA at SD. A lost season that featured numerous ailments: broken finger in March, knee sprain in May, thumb surgery in Sept. Can't take much away from this—injuries likely fueled power collapse, ct% spike probably a small-sample anomaly—as successful offseason rehab could yield return to 2019-20 production.

Yr	Tm	PA	R	HR	RBI	SB	BA	xHR	xSB	xBA	OBP	SLG	OPS+	vL+	vR+	bb%	ct%	Eye	G	L	F	h%	HctX	QBaB	Brl%	PX	xPX	HR/F	xHR/F	Spd	SBA%	SB%	RAR	BPX	R$
17	a/a	286	23	2	25	2	189		4		271	252	71			10	79	0.54				23				41				83	6%	50%		-6	-$3
18	aaa	246	19	1	23	1	212		2		276	283	75			8	75	0.36				28				56				82	2%	100%		-33	-$2
19	SEA *	482	60	15	55	4	256	6	4	232	322	417	102	124	103	9	73	0.36	40	19	41	32	85	CBc	3%	93	90	14%	8%	114	4%	73%	3.1	70	$10
20	2 TM	184	24	7	28	0	273	7	2	267	353	472	110	79	124	10	79	0.53	40	23	37	31	119	BCc	8%	107	105	15%	15%	91	0%	0%	7.7	200	$14
21	SD *	230	17	3	31	0	261	3	1	260	317	362	93	112	89	7	86	0.59	40	24	36	29	111	BBf	1%	63	94	4%	5%	73	2%	0%	-1.0	131	$2
1st Half		59	4	1	11	0	217	1	0	249	373	326	97	153	67	15	93	2.67	45	18	36	21	96	ACf	2%	55	98	6%	6%	84	2%	0%	-0.8	288	-$6
2nd Half		171	13	2	20	0	274	2	0	264	312	373	93	97	97	5	84	0.35	38	26	36	32	117	CBf	0%	66	92	3%	5%	79	2%	0%	-0.6	96	$0
22	**Proj**	**420**	**40**	**13**	**59**	**1**	**265**	**11**	**2**	**261**	**347**	**427**	**105**	**113**	**100**	**9**	**82**	**0.56**	**41**	**22**	**37**	**29**	**106**		**3%**	**90**	**96**	**11%**	**9%**	**78**	**2%**	**46%**	**14.8**	**125**	**$12**

Nootbaar,Lars

Age: 24 Pos: RF	Health A	LIMA Plan D	
Bats: L Ht: 6' 3" Wt: 210	PT/Exp F	Rand Var 0	
	Consist A	MM 1201	

5-15-.239 in 124 PA at STL. Parlayed AAA success (.308/.404/.496 in 136 PA) into part-time audition late in season. Tough to expect 2nd half power "surge" to continue given 15 career HR in 750 MiLB PA, subpar small-sample xPX. Plate skills could lead to passable OBP, but without any SB upside, there isn't enough here to warrant an end game bid.

Yr	Tm	PA	R	HR	RBI	SB	BA	xHR	xSB	xBA	OBP	SLG	OPS+	vL+	vR+	bb%	ct%	Eye	G	L	F	h%	HctX	QBaB	Brl%	PX	xPX	HR/F	xHR/F	Spd	SBA%	SB%	RAR	BPX	R$
17																																			
18																																			
19	aa	106	10	0	3	1	245		2		339	281	86			12	75	0.56				33				22				134	6%	44%		-56	-$2
20																																			
21	STL *	252	29	9	28	3	244	4	3	221	317	396	98	118	98	10	75	0.43	46	15	39	29	89	CDf	5%	81	67	16%	13%	107	13%	37%	-8.4	69	$5
1st Half		122	14	3	15	1	229	0	2	230	305	355	92	17	79	10	76	0.46	52	17	30	27	108	CCf	0%	62	22	0%	0%	137	13%	23%	-5.9	65	-$1
2nd Half		130	16	6	13	2	257	4	2	222	328	434	103	156	101	10	74	0.40	43	14	43	30	80	DDf	7%	100	85	21%	17%	89	13%	48%	-1.5	88	$1
22	**Proj**	**175**	**20**	**5**	**16**	**2**	**246**	**4**	**4**	**215**	**321**	**374**	**94**	**96**	**94**	**11**	**75**	**0.47**	**47**	**16**	**38**	**30**	**91**		**4%**	**71**	**60**	**10%**	**10%**	**115**	**11%**	**45%**	**-2.2**	**9**	**$4**

RYAN BLOOMFIELD

Nuñez,Dom

Age: 27 Pos: CA	Health A	LIMA Plan D+	
Bats: L Ht: 6' 0" Wt: 175	PT/Exp D	Rand Var +1	
	Consist A	MM 4201	

Started slow in first extended MLB look, which came almost exclusively vR, before playing time dried up in 2nd half. Held 2019's PX gains and plate patience kept OBP on life support, but awful ct% and FB% stroke cemented brutal BA. Power skills make him mildly attractive when sifting through the second-catcher bin, but he's probably best left there.

Yr	Tm	PA	R	HR	RBI	SB	BA	xHR	xSB	xBA	OBP	SLG	OPS+	vL+	vR+	bb%	ct%	Eye	G	L	F	h%	HctX	QBaB	Brl%	PX	xPX	HR/F	xHR/F	Spd	SBA%	SB%	RAR	BPX	R$
17	aa	342	31	10	24	6	203		5		308	350	90			13	73	0.56				24				86				108	8%	85%		64	$
18	aa	361	27	8	34	6	212		4		294	321	82			10	77	0.50				25				67				85	14%	50%		33	$
19	COL *	279	32	14	31	1	209	1	4	215	283	448	101	0	93	9	64	0.29	30	13	57	26	115	CAb	9%	151	224	15%	8%	112	2%	100%	-1.8	115	$
20																																			
21	COL	263	31	10	33	0	189	9	3	209	293	399	95	73	100	13	60	0.37	32	18	50	26	93	DAd	9%	150	170	15%	13%	107	0%	0%	-2.6	77	$
1st Half		164	19	5	20	0	160	6	2	190	256	340	83	52	88	12	56	0.30	35	17	48	24	93	DAf	9%	139	172	13%	15%	112	0%	0%	-6.8	-19	-$
2nd Half		99	12	5	13	0	238	3	1	242	354	500	116	98	120	15	67	0.54	29	20	52	29	92	DAc	11%	167	166	17%	10%	111	0%	0%	4.6	254	-$
22	**Proj**	**245**	**26**	**12**	**28**	**1**	**208**	**8**	**1**	**224**	**304**	**440**	**101**	**84**	**104**	**12**	**65**	**0.40**	**30**	**19**	**51**	**26**	**92**		**10%**	**150**	**168**	**16%**	**11%**	**103**	**3%**	**62%**	**4.9**	**104**	**$**

O Hearn,Ryan

Age: 28 Pos: DH RF 1B	Health A	LIMA Plan D	
Bats: L Ht: 6' 3" Wt: 220	PT/Exp C	Rand Var 0	
	Consist B	MM 2301	

9-29-.225 in 254 PA at KC. Buoyed between AAA and MLB in 1st half, grip on platoon role weakened by Sept. We could previously cite plus power as the reason to stay in, but xHR/F continued its steady descent, bb% unraveled, and BA/xBA tanked in 2nd half. Uncertain whether he can hold an MLB roster spot at this point; he shouldn't have one for you.

Yr	Tm	PA	R	HR	RBI	SB	BA	xHR	xSB	xBA	OBP	SLG	OPS+	vL+	vR+	bb%	ct%	Eye	G	L	F	h%	HctX	QBaB	Brl%	PX	xPX	HR/F	xHR/F	Spd	SBA%	SB%	RAR	BPX	R$
17	a/a	523	45	16	53	1	227		6		292	393	93			8	68	0.29				30				110				91	1%	100%		24	$
18	KC *	557	59	20	70	2	219	9	2	230	295	408	94	62	146	10	70	0.36	35	19	46	27	108	AAc	13%	127	160	25%	19%	78	2%	100%	-7.2	83	$
19	KC *	512	47	20	58	0	209	15	2	234	289	397	95	71	93	10	71	0.38	46	18	36	25	104	BCc	9%	107	97	17%	18%	82	1%	0%	-17.7	52	$
20	KC	132	7	2	18	0	195	4	0	199	303	301	80	109	77	14	67	0.49	46	21	33	27	113	BCb	6%	77	131	8%	16%	75	0%	0%	-8.7	-68	$
21	KC *	332	38	16	46	2	240	9	2	237	284	432	98	54	93	6	71	0.21	43	20	38	28	98	BBc	8%	110	85	14%	14%	104	3%	100%	-11.2	65	$
1st Half		176	26	13	30	2	258	5	1	246	300	525	115	59	105	6	70	0.20	35	17	48	28	73	BAb	10%	150	89	20%	17%	84	3%	100%	-0.8	154	$1
2nd Half		156	12	3	16	0	218	4	1	218	269	324	80	49	85	6	72	0.23	48	21	31	28	115	ACd	7%	64	83	9%	12%	121	3%	0%	-12.4	-42	-$
22	**Proj**	**210**	**19**	**7**	**27**	**1**	**221**	**8**	**1**	**223**	**289**	**379**	**91**	**68**	**95**	**9**	**70**	**0.32**	**43**	**19**	**37**	**28**	**103**		**9%**	**98**	**104**	**14%**	**16%**	**93**	**4%**	**90%**	**-6.3**	**-27**	**$**

O Neill,Tyler

Age: 27 Pos: LF	Health B	LIMA Plan B	
Bats: R Ht: 5' 11" Wt: 200	PT/Exp A	Rand Var -5	
	Consist D	MM 4315	

Earned starting gig in camp and never looked back. PRO: Power skills look top-notch, xHR hints at room for even more; took full advantage of green light. CON: Ct%, xBA hint at swift BA correction; owns 162 MLB games of a .229 BA, 21 HR, 6 SB before 2021. Tough to buy in coming off (likely) career year, but still a reasonable bet to approach 35/15 again.

Yr	Tm	PA	R	HR	RBI	SB	BA	xHR	xSB	xBA	OBP	SLG	OPS+	vL+	vR+	bb%	ct%	Eye	G	L	F	h%	HctX	QBaB	Brl%	PX	xPX	HR/F	xHR/F	Spd	SBA%	SB%	RAR	BPX	R$
17	aaa	540	64	25	79	12	224		6		288	434	98			8	68	0.28				28				131				94	13%	84%		76	$1
18	STL *	402	77	28	73	4	265	10	8	240	319	539	115	106	106	7	64	0.22	29	23	48	33	107	AAb	23%	179	169	25%	28%	123	6%	79%	16.6	177	$1
19	STL *	337	42	15	38	3	236	5	3	213	283	413	96	91	101	6	62	0.17	38	23	40	33	100	CAd	7%	111	108	14%	14%	97	4%	100%	-13.5	-67	$
20	STL	157	20	7	19	3	173	7	1	221	261	360	82	60	88	10	69	0.35	43	15	41	19	92	CBf	8%	110	115	18%	18%	95	14%	75%	-10.8	56	$
21	STL	537	89	34	80	15	286	43	12	254	352	560	125	140	122	7	65	0.23	36	23	41	37	114	AAc	18%	176	153	26%	33%	121	15%	79%	21.2	208	$3
1st Half		240	37	15	36	6	279	21	4	267	333	562	125	99	130	6	66	0.18	31	27	42	35	112	AAc	19%	189	160	24%	34%	94	15%	67%	6.7	219	$2
2nd Half		297	52	19	44	9	293	22	7	244	367	559	125	170	116	9	64	0.27	40	20	40	39	115	ABd	17%	166	148	28%	32%	146	15%	90%	16.2	204	$3
22	**Proj**	**560**	**87**	**31**	**81**	**13**	**257**	**37**	**12**	**235**	**325**	**486**	**110**	**111**	**110**	**8**	**65**	**0.25**	**37**	**21**	**41**	**33**	**106**		**14%**	**147**	**138**	**22%**	**26%**	**105**	**12%**	**77%**	**14.8**	**103**	**$2**

Odor,Rougned

Age: 28 Pos: 2B 3B	Health B	LIMA Plan D	
Bats: L Ht: 5' 11" Wt: 200	PT/Exp A	Rand Var +1	
	Consist B	MM 4001	

Fell into semi-regular playing time after April DFA by TEX. Several reasons to steer clear: declining Brl%, xHR/F mean all those flyballs will be cans of corn; xBA, h% baseline give little hope for BA growth; hasn't attempted a steal since 2019. Young enough to recapture 2018-19 R$ if someone lets him play, which isn't all that likely.

Yr	Tm	PA	R	HR	RBI	SB	BA	xHR	xSB	xBA	OBP	SLG	OPS+	vL+	vR+	bb%	ct%	Eye	G	L	F	h%	HctX	QBaB	Brl%	PX	xPX	HR/F	xHR/F	Spd	SBA%	SB%	RAR	BPX	R$
17	TEX	651	79	30	75	15	204	23	6	239	252	397	88	61	96	5	73	0.20	42	16	42	23	109	CBf	6%	109	116	16%	12%	90	19%	71%	-30.2	58	$
18	TEX	535	76	18	63	12	253	18	14	238	326	424	101	94	102	8	73	0.34	41	20	39	31	122	BBd	7%	107	121	14%	14%	99	18%	50%	2.1	87	$1
19	TEX	581	77	30	93	11	205	32	10	230	283	439	100	113	93	9	66	0.29	35	17	48	25	104	AAd	14%	142	157	19%	20%	84	19%	55%	-17.8	81	$1
20	TEX	148	15	10	30	0	167	8	2	223	209	413	83	53	98	5	66	0.15	33	17	50	16	83	DAf	12%	145	112	22%	18%	65	6%	0%	-9.6	44	$
21	NYY	361	42	15	39	0	202	15	2	210	286	379	91	103	86	7	69	0.27	37	15	47	24	94	CAf	9%	109	111	15%	15%	73	1%	0%	-14.9	8	$
1st Half		168	18	8	18	0	211	8	1	230	286	414	97	119	90	7	72	0.28	38	17	45	24	102	CAf	9%	122	91	17%	17%	87	1%	0%	-5.8	104	$
2nd Half		193	24	7	21	0	194	8	1	191	286	347	86	92	82	8	66	0.26	37	14	49	25	86	DAf	9%	97	131	13%	15%	73	1%	0%	-11.1	-62	$
22	**Proj**	**245**	**30**	**12**	**34**	**2**	**209**	**12**	**1**	**219**	**280**	**411**	**94**	**92**	**94**	**7**	**68**	**0.24**	**37**	**16**	**47**	**25**	**96**		**10%**	**124**	**121**	**17%**	**16%**	**72**	**2%**	**44%**	**-4.7**	**11**	**$**

Ohtani,Shohei

Age: 27 Pos: DH	Health B	LIMA Plan D+	
Bats: L Ht: 6' 4" Wt: 210	PT/Exp A	Rand Var 0	
	Consist D	MM 5435	

Not too shabby, coverboy. Highest xHR total of any hitter since 2017, so yeah, the power's legit and FB% spike let it flourish. Ditto the bags given green light, elite wheels. But is he a top-five pick? League format caveats aside, 2nd half ct% plunge raises BA questions, PA looks like an outlier given history. A special talent; just know there's risk at his price.

Yr	Tm	PA	R	HR	RBI	SB	BA	xHR	xSB	xBA	OBP	SLG	OPS+	vL+	vR+	bb%	ct%	Eye	G	L	F	h%	HctX	QBaB	Brl%	PX	xPX	HR/F	xHR/F	Spd	SBA%	SB%	RAR	BPX	R$
17	for	209	22	5	30	0	312		3		371	482	116			8	70	0.31				42	0			116				96	2%	0%	0.0	67	$
18	LAA	366	59	22	61	10	285	24	3	279	361	564	124	87	138	10	69	0.36	44	24	33	35	109	ACb	16%	181	129	30%	32%	114	16%	71%	0.0	253	$1
19	LAA	423	51	18	62	12	286	19	11	276	343	505	117	110	119	8	71	0.30	50	26	24	36	123	ADa	12%	121	111	26%	28%	142	15%	80%	0.0	159	$1
20	LAA	175	23	7	24	7	190	8	3	228	291	366	87	82	89	13	67	0.44	50	17	33	23	93	CDd	11%	108	109	21%	24%	89	21%	88%	0.0	36	$1
21	LAA	639	103	46	100	26	257	59	22	270	372	592	133	133	132	15	65	0.51	38	21	41	30	120	ABc	22%	208	162	33%	42%	148	23%	72%	0.0	392	$3
1st Half		313	59	30	66	12	278	34	9	306	367	700	149	141	152	12	68	0.41	37	21	43	29	125	ABc	25%	250	182	38%	44%	129	23%	80%	0.0	527	$4
2nd Half		326	44	16	34	14	235	24	13	233	377	481	116	126	108	19	61	0.59	40	22	38	32	114	ABc	19%	160	140	26%	39%	161	23%	67%	0.0	235	$2
22	**Proj**	**595**	**86**	**35**	**87**	**21**	**251**	**43**	**20**	**258**	**352**	**525**	**119**	**116**	**120**	**13**	**67**	**0.46**	**41**	**22**	**37**	**31**	**113**		**17%**	**170**	**135**	**28%**	**34%**	**127**	**18%**	**75%**	**23.7**	**255**	**$3**

Olivares,Edward

Age: 26 Pos: RF	Health A	LIMA Plan C+	
Bats: R Ht: 6' 2" Wt: 188	PT/Exp B	Rand Var 0	
	Consist B	MM 2333	

5-12-.238 in 111 PA at KC. Logged serious mileage with EIGHT (8!) separate call-ups from AAA, where he hit .313 with 15/12 HR/SB in 292 PA. Held his own in majors too with plus contact (81%) despite 2nd half h% that torpedoed BA. Needs to turn primo wheels into more SB, but a fine five-category flyer if he can cash in those miles for a permanent stay.

Yr	Tm	PA	R	HR	RBI	SB	BA	xHR	xSB	xBA	OBP	SLG	OPS+	vL+	vR+	bb%	ct%	Eye	G	L	F	h%	HctX	QBaB	Brl%	PX	xPX	HR/F	xHR/F	Spd	SBA%	SB%	RAR	BPX	R$
17																																			
18																																			
19	aa	525	73	14	66	30	254		7		307	397	97			7	78	0.35				30				77				99	34%	73%		70	$2
20	2 TM	101	9	3	10	0	240	2	4	237	267	375	85	69	94	4	74	0.16	48	23	30	29	79	FDf	6%	71	65	14%	10%	140	10%	0%	-4.9	20	$
21	KC *	387	52	15	37	10	254	4	6	253	303	425	100	74	112	7	80	0.36	47	17	36	28	105	CDf	6%	90	117	17%	13%	143	19%	61%	-5.9	196	$1
1st Half		177	25	6	17	9	293	0	3	283	330	441	107	64	96	5	76	0.23	63	25	13	35	65	FFf	0%	80	51	33%	0%	138	19%	79%	1.7	88	$1
2nd Half		210	27	8	20	2	219	4	3	248	280	412	94	77	120	8	84	0.52	41	14	46	22	125	CCd	8%	97	143	15%	15%	137	19%	28%	-8.9	273	$
22	**Proj**	**350**	**45**	**13**	**36**	**11**	**256**	**7**	**10**	**258**	**314**	**430**	**101**	**80**	**116**	**6**	**79**	**0.31**	**49**	**19**	**32**	**29**	**96**		**5%**	**93**	**96**	**16%**	**9%**	**124**	**16%**	**63%**	**-1.5**	**130**	**$1**

Olson,Matt

Age: 28 Pos: 1B	Health A	LIMA Plan B+	
Bats: L Ht: 6' 5" Wt: 225	PT/Exp A	Rand Var 0	
	Consist D	MM 4245	

Didn't quite reach last year's "UP: 50 HR", but no complaints here. Breakout season featured the elite power we've come to expect; this time he paired it with biggest ct% jump from 2020 of any other hitter (min. 150 PA). Fair to expect some BA pullback given track record, but with ironclad QBaB and xHR/F in place, this is otherwise repeatable.

Yr	Tm	PA	R	HR	RBI	SB	BA	xHR	xSB	xBA	OBP	SLG	OPS+	vL+	vR+	bb%	ct%	Eye	G	L	F	h%	HctX	QBaB	Brl%	PX	xPX	HR/F	xHR/F	Spd	SBA%	SB%	RAR	BPX	R$
17	OAK *	545	78	41	93	2	245	16	7	257	325	536	117	102	144	11	69	0.38	38	16	46	27	113	ABd	16%	168	178	41%	28%	81	2%	100%	7.8	176	$
18	OAK	660	85	29	84	2	247	37	3	247	335	453	106	93	110	11	72	0.43	36	21	43	29	125	AAd	12%	132	140	16%	21%	84	2%	67%	10.1	140	$
19	OAK *	570	75	37	92	0	262	38	2	269	330	531	119	107	131	9	72	0.37	31	24	45	29	125	AAc	15%	145	161	24%	25%	77	0%	0%	16.7	174	$
20	OAK	245	28	14	42	1	195	13	1	220	310	424	97	91	99	14	63	0.44	35	21	44	23	110	AAd	13%	136	143	24%	22%	88	2%	100%	-8.0	72	$
21	OAK	673	101	39	111	4	271	41	3	279	371	540	125	131	121	13	80	0.78	40	16	44	28	119	ABf	13%	145	129	19%	20%	76	3%	80%	25.8	335	$
1st Half		335	51	20	53	3	282	22	2	281	370	554	129	128	129	12	81	0.69	38	17	45	29	121	ABf	14%	145	136	19%	21%	84	3%	75%	12.5	346	$
2nd Half		338	50	19	58	1	259	18	2	275	373	525	122	134	114	15	79	0.86	42	16	42	26	116	BBf	12%	145	121	20%	19%	75	3%	100%	8.9	335	$
22	**Proj**	**665**	**94**	**40**	**108**	**3**	**263**	**42**	**4**	**265**	**361**	**523**	**120**	**119**	**120**	**13**	**76**	**0.60**	**37**	**19**	**44**	**28**	**118**		**13%**	**143**	**139**	**21%**	**21%**	**71**	**3%**	**84%**	**33.6**	**239**	**$**

RYAN BLOOMFIELD

Ortega,Rafael

Age: 31 Pos: CF	Health A	LIMA Plan C+	11-33-.291 with 12 SB in 330 PA at CHC. Career journeyman fell into everyday role in July and took off, but this was likely just a well-timed heater. SB production has staying power, but 35% MLB h% and xBA cast major doubt on BA repeat while hard contact (Brl%, xHR/F) was few and far between. A fun story, but one where the sequel won't be as hot.
Bats: L Ht: 5' 11" Wt: 160	PT/Exp C	Rand Var -5	
	Consist B	MM 2523	

Yr Tm	PA	R	HR	RBI	SB	BA	xHR	xSB	xBA	OBP	SLG	OPS+	vL+	vR+	bb%	ct%	Eye	G	L	F	h%	HctX	QBaB	Brl%	PX	xPX	HR/F	xHR/F	Spd	SBA%	SB%	RAR	BPX	R$
17 aaa	448	44	4	34	17	250		6		298	355	89			6	86	0.49				28				62				111	26%	66%		127	$10
18 MIA *	457	49	1	28	14	225	1	20	245	300	302	81	94	69	10	85	0.72	46	22	32	26	88	DCc	0%	40	37	0%	3%	177	15%	81%	-14.8	157	$6
19 ATL *	572	71	17	55	14	229	2	12	245	300	398	97	23	88	9	74	0.39	41	21	38	28	81	CCd	5%	98	85	8%	8%	124	19%	62%	-7.4	115	$12
20																																		
21 CHC *	399	51	13	40	13	271	9	7	245	336	439	106	57	124	9	76	0.40	34	25	41	32	86	CBc	6%	96	86	12%	10%	145	19%	63%	-1.0	165	$16
1st Half	129	12	4	11	3	199	2	2	240	249	345	83	31	100	6	75	0.27	32	27	41	23	71	BBd	7%	84	70	12%	12%	119	19%	44%	-9.5	69	-$2
2nd Half	270	39	9	29	10	307	7	5	249	379	485	117	61	128	10	76	0.47	34	25	41	37	89	DBc	5%	102	90	12%	9%	149	19%	71%	11.4	208	$23
22 Proj	**385**	**46**	**9**	**34**	**12**	**248**	**9**	**12**	**243**	**317**	**389**	**96**	**56**	**103**	**9**	**78**	**0.43**	**37**	**24**	**39**	**29**	**83**		**5%**	**81**	**73**	**9%**	**8%**	**144**	**17%**	**66%**	**0.6**	**108**	**$10**

Ozuna,Marcell

Age: 31 Pos: LF	Health F	LIMA Plan C+	On the field: A two-month slump driven mostly by softer contact, paltry h%, and then missed time with two broken fingers. Off the field: Arrested on domestic violence charges May 29 and didn't play another game. 2022 outlook obviously in flux as legal process runs its course. A wild card at this point.
Bats: R Ht: 6' 1" Wt: 225	PT/Exp B	Rand Var +5	
	Consist F	MM 4233	

Yr Tm	PA	R	HR	RBI	SB	BA	xHR	xSB	xBA	OBP	SLG	OPS+	vL+	vR+	bb%	ct%	Eye	G	L	F	h%	HctX	QBaB	Brl%	PX	xPX	HR/F	xHR/F	Spd	SBA%	SB%	RAR	BPX	R$
17 MIA	679	93	37	124	1	312	32	11	275	376	548	126	109	128	9	77	0.44	47	19	34	36	121	BCc	9%	130	106	23%	20%	91	2%	25%	37.6	176	$31
18 STL	627	69	23	88	3	280	33	4	248	325	433	102	119	95	6	81	0.35	47	18	35	31	135	ACc	10%	81	112	14%	20%	96	2%	100%	6.5	107	$21
19 STL	549	80	29	89	12	243	30	3	275	330	474	111	105	112	11	76	0.54	41	23	35	26	127	ACc	12%	118	119	22%	23%	78	11%	86%	1.9	178	$19
20 ATL	267	38	18	56	0	338	20	5	283	431	636	142	173	133	14	74	0.63	37	23	40	39	138	ABd	15%	166	146	26%	29%	70	0%	0%	31.5	316	$38
21 ATL	208	21	7	26	0	213	9	0	233	288	356	89	82	91	9	76	0.41	37	23	41	24	87	BBd	10%	81	80	12%	16%	51	0%	0%	-11.3	8	$0
1st Half	208	21	7	26	0	213	9	0	233	288	356	90	83	92	9	76	0.41	37	23	41	24	87	BBd	10%	81	80	12%	16%	51	0%	0%	-12.0	12	$2
2nd Half																								0%										
22 Proj	**350**	**44**	**19**	**56**	**2**	**267**	**19**	**1**	**262**	**341**	**489**	**113**	**117**	**111**	**10**	**77**	**0.47**	**41**	**22**	**38**	**29**	**118**		**11%**	**121**	**110**	**20%**	**21%**	**75**	**1%**	**82%**	**13.4**	**146**	**$14**

Pache,Cristian

Age: 23 Pos: CF	Health B	LIMA Plan D	1-4-.111 in 68 PA at ATL. Pair of early IL stints didn't help, but was overmatched in limited MLB sample (60% ct%, .171 xBA) before AAA demotion in May. A step back in minors too, as more whiffs torpedoed BA, PX dropped, and he remained ineffective on basepaths. Prospect pedigree is still a reason to speculate; just don't expect immediate returns.
Bats: R Ht: 6' 2" Wt: 215	PT/Exp B	Rand Var +2	
	Consist C	MM 2201	

Yr Tm	PA	R	HR	RBI	SB	BA	xHR	xSB	xBA	OBP	SLG	OPS+	vL+	vR+	bb%	ct%	Eye	G	L	F	h%	HctX	QBaB	Brl%	PX	xPX	HR/F	xHR/F	Spd	SBA%	SB%	RAR	BPX	R$
17																																		
18 aa	108	9	1	7	0	256		2		287	329	83			4	72	0.16				35				49				116	8%	0%		-83	-$1
19 a/a	528	62	11	60	8	273		6		330	448	108			8	74	0.33				35				103				117	17%	41%		119	$13
20 ATL	4	0	0	0	0	250	0	0	0	250	250	66	261	0	0	50	0.00	100	0	0	50	0	FFa		0	-26	0%		118	0%	0%	-0.2	-648	-$3
21 ATL *	413	47	10	40	7	217	2	1	191	267	338	83	73	42	6	66	0.20	50	11	39	30	40	FFf	5%	85	82	7%	14%	74	18%	49%	-27.8	-119	$5
1st Half	154	16	3	12	1	156	2	0	178	198	270	65	74	42	5	58	0.13	50	11	39	24	36	FFf	5%	100	82	7%	14%	79	18%	100%	-15.5	-196	-$7
2nd Half	260	31	7	28	7	254		1	217	308	379	93	0	0	7	70	0.26	44	20	36	33	0		0%	78	-22	0%		91	18%	46%	-9.7	-46	$13
22 Proj	**210**	**23**	**5**	**20**	**3**	**234**	**6**	**5**	**205**	**290**	**375**	**90**	**134**	**76**	**6**	**68**	**0.21**	**50**	**11**	**39**	**31**	**32**		**5%**	**94**	**74**	**10%**	**12%**	**103**	**14%**	**50%**	**-5.7**	**-51**	**$5**

Paredes,Isaac

Age: 23 Pos: 2B	Health B	LIMA Plan D+	1-5-.208 in 85 PA at DET. Sporadic MLB playing time given frequent call-ups/send-downs and June hip injury. Plate skills held up fine (0.91 MLB Eye), though xBA questions how that translates to BA. Not much else jumps out—career-high 15 HR in a season, PX remained subpar, running game has gone dormant—so place your end game chips elsewhere.
Bats: R Ht: 5' 11" Wt: 213	PT/Exp B	Rand Var +2	
	Consist D	MM 1223	

Yr Tm	PA	R	HR	RBI	SB	BA	xHR	xSB	xBA	OBP	SLG	OPS+	vL+	vR+	bb%	ct%	Eye	G	L	F	h%	HctX	QBaB	Brl%	PX	xPX	HR/F	xHR/F	Spd	SBA%	SB%	RAR	BPX	R$
17																																		
18 aa	148	18	3	20	1	311		2		389	441	111			11	83	0.77				36				82				89	2%	100%		167	$3
19 aa	534	64	13	67	5	286		4		360	424	109			10	87	0.93				30				68				94	5%	62%		204	$15
20 DET	108	7	1	6	0	220	1	1	212	278	290	75	118	67	7	76	0.33	47	21	32	28	57	DDf	0%	46	36	4%	4%	91	0%	0%	-6.0	-56	-$1
21 DET *	385	41	10	41	0	240	1	4	245	353	394	103	96	79	15	82	0.96	37	21	43	26	106	DAf	2%	80	93	4%	4%	130	0%	0%	0.4	238	$5
1st Half	192	18	4	20	0	236	1	2	230	334	361	97	74	100	13	82	0.83	38	19	42	27	91	DCf	4%	61	94	9%	9%	170	0%	0%	-4.0	215	$0
2nd Half	193	22	7	21	0	245	0	2	260	373	429	109	111	64	17	81	1.10	35	22	43	26	117	DAf	0%	101	93	0%	0%	84	0%	0%	2.7	258	$3
22 Proj	**280**	**29**	**6**	**29**	**1**	**253**	**5**	**1**	**242**	**346**	**384**	**99**	**115**	**90**	**12**	**82**	**0.78**	**39**	**21**	**40**	**29**	**94**		**1%**	**74**	**79**	**8%**	**6%**	**90**	**2%**	**69%**	**3.5**	**107**	**$6**

Park,Hoy Jun

Age: 26 Pos: 2B	Health A	LIMA Plan D	3-14-.195 in 150 PA at NYY/PIT. Traded to PIT in July; struggled in near-everyday audition over final two months. Plus plate patience wasn't enough to nudge MLB OBP over .300, while excellent Spd was wasted with just two SB attempts in majors. Green light is a path to relevance, but with major BA concerns and limited power, that path is rocky at best.
Bats: L Ht: 6' 1" Wt: 175	PT/Exp C	Rand Var +1	
	Consist A	MM 1401	

Yr Tm	PA	R	HR	RBI	SB	BA	xHR	xSB	xBA	OBP	SLG	OPS+	vL+	vR+	bb%	ct%	Eye	G	L	F	h%	HctX	QBaB	Brl%	PX	xPX	HR/F	xHR/F	Spd	SBA%	SB%	RAR	BPX	R$
17																																		
18																																		
19 aa	469	54	3	37	18	252		9		336	339	93			11	76	0.52				33				51				128	22%	62%		26	$11
20																																		
21 2 TM *	416	51	10	39	9	223	4	7	219	337	365	96	135	76	15	71	0.60	44	18	38	28	85	DBc	7%	87	107	9%	11%	137	13%	62%	-6.2	100	$7
1st Half	190	29	6	20	6	258		4	241	374	422	111	0	0	16	73	0.70	44	20	36	32	0		0%	98	-22	0%		121	13%	61%	3.2	162	$10
2nd Half	226	22	4	19	4	194	4	4	207	306	317	84	133	75	14	69	0.52	44	18	38	26	83	DBc	7%	78	107	9%	11%	143	13%	64%	-9.5	42	$0
22 Proj	**140**	**17**	**2**	**13**	**4**	**227**	**3**	**4**	**222**	**336**	**339**	**92**	**76**	**95**	**14**	**72**	**0.58**	**48**	**20**	**32**	**30**	**75**		**6%**	**71**	**96**	**8%**	**11%**	**136**	**13%**	**63%**	**-1.5**	**13**	**$3**

Pederson,Joc

Age: 30 Pos: LF RF CF	Health A	LIMA Plan B	Mild rebound from 2020 featured July trade to ATL; still couldn't snag everyday role. Careful with recent gains vL (35% h%, 108 AB since 2020), as career .284 OBP and 79 PX say platoon likely sticks. xHR shows consistent power despite swings in HR, but he's still just a BA-challenged part-timer with pop (a.k.a. dime-a-dozen later in drafts).
Bats: L Ht: 6' 1" Wt: 220	PT/Exp A	Rand Var -1	
	Consist C	MM 4125	

Yr Tm	PA	R	HR	RBI	SB	BA	xHR	xSB	xBA	OBP	SLG	OPS+	vL+	vR+	bb%	ct%	Eye	G	L	F	h%	HctX	QBaB	Brl%	PX	xPX	HR/F	xHR/F	Spd	SBA%	SB%	RAR	BPX	R$
17 LA *	392	50	13	42	5	199	11	5	258	288	379	91	81	103	11	75	0.50	47	19	34	22	100	BCf	9%	110	101	15%	15%	72	9%	61%	-19.7	103	$2
18 LA	443	65	25	56	1	248	21	5	281	321	522	113	67	118	9	78	0.47	39	17	44	26	122	ABc	8%	156	134	18%	15%	90	7%	17%	8.6	287	$13
19 LA	514	83	36	74	1	249	26	6	271	339	538	121	70	126	10	75	0.45	42	17	41	25	118	ABd	10%	141	124	26%	19%	109	2%	50%	9.1	252	$16
20 LA	137	21	7	16	1	190	7	1	238	285	397	90	96	90	8	72	0.32	48	15	36	20	107	ACc	10%	114	126	23%	23%	89	4%	100%	-7.6	96	$6
21 2 NL	481	55	18	61	2	238	24	4	235	310	422	101	99	101	8	73	0.33	39	19	42	29	101	BCf	10%	108	118	14%	18%	101	5%	40%	-14.3	100	$9
1st Half	265	29	11	33	2	226	14	2	222	298	417	100	85	104	8	69	0.29	37	18	45	28	105	AAf	12%	114	118	15%	19%	108	5%	40%	-11.4	77	$10
2nd Half	216	26	7	28	0	253	10	2	251	324	428	102	114	98	8	77	0.40	42	20	38	30	96	CCf	8%	103	118	13%	18%	93	5%	0%	-4.2	138	$6
22 Proj	**455**	**63**	**22**	**59**	**2**	**241**	**24**	**4**	**248**	**318**	**458**	**105**	**90**	**108**	**9**	**74**	**0.36**	**41**	**18**	**41**	**27**	**106**		**10%**	**124**	**121**	**18%**	**19%**	**93**	**5%**	**50%**	**3.8**	**138**	**$14**

Peralta,David

Age: 34 Pos: LF	Health B	LIMA Plan B	Skills base remained largely intact, with ct% nudging up and xBA tempering BA drop. But his power - UGH - that was one big splat. Three years of spiraling xPX and HR/F make his power stroke look unrecoverable. BA floor may keep him marginally rosterable, but there's not much else here, especially at age where further skill erosion is more likely than not.
Bats: L Ht: 6' 1" Wt: 220	PT/Exp A	Rand Var +4	
	Consist A	MM 2335	

Yr Tm	PA	R	HR	RBI	SB	BA	xHR	xSB	xBA	OBP	SLG	OPS+	vL+	vR+	bb%	ct%	Eye	G	L	F	h%	HctX	QBaB	Brl%	PX	xPX	HR/F	xHR/F	Spd	SBA%	SB%	RAR	BPX	R$
17 ARI	577	82	14	57	8	293	14	9	278	352	444	108	96	110	7	82	0.46	55	18	26	34	106	CFd	4%	86	80	12%	12%	111	8%	67%	3.3	145	$19
18 ARI	614	75	30	87	4	293	26	9	280	352	516	116	92	125	8	78	0.39	51	20	29	33	140	ADc	8%	124	120	23%	20%	103	3%	100%	30.0	197	$25
19 ARI	423	48	12	57	0	275	10	3	274	343	461	111	98	116	8	77	0.40	51	21	28	33	116	BDd	5%	105	89	15%	12%	100	0%	0%	2.7	156	$9
20 ARI	218	19	5	34	1	300	4	1	251	339	433	103	82	109	6	78	0.29	49	22	29	37	106	CDf	5%	77	67	11%	9%	100	2%	100%	1.0	68	$18
21 ARI	538	57	8	63	2	259	10	4	269	325	402	100	100	100	9	81	0.50	55	19	26	30	107	BFd	5%	83	56	8%	10%	113	2%	67%	-11.3	169	$10
1st Half	302	29	4	38	1	252	6	2	272	311	399	99	89	101	8	82	0.49	55	18	27	29	99	BFf	6%	83	60	7%	10%	123	2%	50%	-9.5	196	$9
2nd Half	236	28	4	25	1	268	3	2	265	343	407	101	114	99	10	79	0.51	55	20	26	32	118	CDd	4%	84	50	9%	7%	93	2%	100%	-3.2	131	$6
22 Proj	**490**	**52**	**10**	**61**	**2**	**265**	**10**	**4**	**264**	**328**	**413**	**101**	**92**	**103**	**8**	**79**	**0.43**	**53**	**20**	**27**	**31**	**113**		**5%**	**87**	**70**	**10%**	**10%**	**102**	**4%**	**81%**	**4.4**	**117**	**$13**

RYAN BLOOMFIELD

Perdomo,Geraldo

Health	A	LIMA Plan	F
PT/Exp	F	Rand Var	-2
Consist	F	MM	1401

Age: 22 Pos: SS
Bats: B Ht: 6' 2" Wt: 184

0-5-.258 in 37 PA at ARI. Excellent speed, a 16% career bb% in minors, and strong defense up the middle are good starting points. However, SB%, ct% show there is still plenty of work to do, and he also hasn't tapped into much power yet. Pedigree points to bright future, but probably at least another year away from making much of an impact.

Yr	Tm	PA	R	HR	RBI	SB	BA	xHR	xSB	xBA	OBP	SLG	OPS+	vL+	vR+	bb%	ct%	Eye	G	L	F	h%	HctX	QBaB	Brl%	PX	xPX	HR/F	xHR/F	Spd	SBA%	SB%	RAR	BPX
17																																		
18																																		
19																																		
20																																		
21	ARI *	366	38	4	23	5	202	1	6	168	282	297	80	111	109	10	71	0.38	33	13	54	28	46	DBf	4%	58	51	0%	8%	153	13%	47%	-20.6	-8
1st Half		178	14	1	7	1	127	0	3	134	241	169	57	0	76	13	67	0.46	57	0	43	18	0	FFf	0%	28	-22	0%	0%	134	13%	39%	-18.5	-154
2nd Half		190	26	3	17	4	278	1	4	193	338	424	103	170	122	8	74	0.34	24	18	59	36	71	CAb	6%	84	81	0%	10%	158	13%	53%	1.1	108
22	Proj	**210**	**24**	**2**	**14**	**3**	**217**	**2**	**5**	**202**	**295**	**321**	**84**	**83**	**84**	**10**	**71**	**0.38**	**45**	**17**	**38**	**30**	**86**		**2%**	**63**		**4%**	**4%**	**161**	**14%**	**51%**	**-7.4**	**-38**

Perez,Salvador

Health	F	LIMA Plan	B
PT/Exp	A	Rand Var	0
Consist	D	MM	4045

Age: 32 Pos: CA DH
Bats: R Ht: 6' 3" Wt: 250

Showed that lofty 2020 HR/F wasn't a fluke, as he repeated the mark and tied for league lead in HR. Lowest ct% of caree but this is a trade-off worth making, as xBA confirms that even with more whiffs he can produce a positive BA. Can't ban on PA total again or a full power repeat, but still worthy of consideration as the first catcher off the board.

Yr	Tm	PA	R	HR	RBI	SB	BA	xHR	xSB	xBA	OBP	SLG	OPS+	vL+	vR+	bb%	ct%	Eye	G	L	F	h%	HctX	QBaB	Brl%	PX	xPX	HR/F	xHR/F	Spd	SBA%	SB%	RAR	BPX
17	KC	498	57	27	80	1	268	29	6	266	297	495	108	106	106	3	80	0.18	33	20	47	28	123	CAb	9%	121	142	15%	16%	49	1%	100%	12.4	121
18	KC *	568	55	28	84	1	238	29	0	258	262	444	95	93	95	3	79	0.15	35	20	45	25	134	AAb	11%	116	149	15%	16%	43	2%	50%	7.9	103
19																																		
20	KC	156	22	11	32	1	333	12	1	302	353	633	131	117	135	2	76	0.08	36	27	37	38	131	ABb	14%	168	175	26%	28%	66	3%	100%	16.9	256
21	KC	665	88	48	121	1	273	54	2	270	316	544	118	134	112	4	73	0.16	37	23	40	30	130	ABd	16%	152	153	26%	30%	57	1%	100%	29.4	150
1st Half		335	40	20	50	0	283	24	1	269	310	520	116	157	101	2	73	0.09	38	25	36	33	124	ABc	14%	138	134	24%	28%	69	1%	0%	13.3	108
2nd Half		330	48	28	71	1	261	29	1	271	321	569	120	112	124	6	73	0.24	36	20	44	26	136	ABd	19%	166	174	29%	30%	52	1%	100%	16.9	204
22	Proj	**595**	**78**	**38**	**106**	**1**	**267**	**42**	**0**	**272**	**304**	**517**	**111**	**113**	**110**	**4**	**75**	**0.15**	**38**	**23**	**39**	**29**	**131**		**14%**	**139**	**158**	**23%**	**25%**	**50**	**0%**	**76%**	**28.4**	**123**

Peters,DJ

Health	A	LIMA Plan	D
PT/Exp	B	Rand Var	+2
Consist	B	MM	3203

Age: 26 Pos: CF LF
Bats: R Ht: 6' 6" Wt: 225

13-38-.197 in 240 PA at LA/TEX. Power stroke was lacking for much of season (4 HR in 204 PA at AAA), but it was on ful display late with 12 HR after August recall. Abysmal plate skills ensure low BA/OBP, which will make it tough to hold dow regular job, and decent speed isn't translating to SB. That power you're hoping for comes at a cost everywhere else.

Yr	Tm	PA	R	HR	RBI	SB	BA	xHR	xSB	xBA	OBP	SLG	OPS+	vL+	vR+	bb%	ct%	Eye	G	L	F	h%	HctX	QBaB	Brl%	PX	xPX	HR/F	xHR/F	Spd	SBA%	SB%	RAR	BPX
17																																		
18	aa	523	59	22	45	1	201		5		250	383	85			6	55	0.15				31				146				105	3%	25%		-50
19	a/a	502	56	19	64	2	213		3		284	378	92			9	57	0.23				32				114				94	3%	58%		-111
20																																		
21	2 TM *	432	45	16	50	3	189	12	4	191	235	356	81	67	105	6	62	0.16	39	13	49	26	102	CBf	11%	115	176	19%	17%	112	6%	69%	-33.9	-46
1st Half		156	15	2	11	0	153	0	2	124	255	243	69	80	182	12	51	0.28	33	8	58	27	70	BAf	8%	80	103	14%	0%	113	6%	0%	-15.9	-273
2nd Half		276	29	13	39	3	208	12	2	219	223	414	86	62	99	2	68	0.06	39	13	48	25	114	CBf	11%	128	183	19%	19%	111	6%	69%	-20.0	50
22	Proj	**385**	**41**	**14**	**42**	**2**	**210**	**13**	**3**	**199**	**265**	**371**	**86**	**80**	**92**	**7**	**63**	**0.19**	**38**	**18**	**44**	**29**	**96**		**10%**	**111**	**151**	**14%**	**13%**	**99**	**6%**	**67%**	**-9.2**	**-99**

Peterson,Jace

Health	B	LIMA Plan	D
PT/Exp	C	Rand Var	0
Consist	A	MM	1313

Age: 32 Pos: 2B 1B OF
Bats: L Ht: 6' 0" Wt: 215

6-31-.247 with 10 SB in 302 PA at MIL. Accumulated most MLB PA since 2016 and high bb%, SB% helped him stay in lineup and provide some value. But rarely plays vL, ct% too low for a player with limited power, and age puts already suspect speed into question. Multi-position eligibility keeps him mildly interesting, but most signs point to a step back.

Yr	Tm	PA	R	HR	RBI	SB	BA	xHR	xSB	xBA	OBP	SLG	OPS+	vL+	vR+	bb%	ct%	Eye	G	L	F	h%	HctX	QBaB	Brl%	PX	xPX	HR/F	xHR/F	Spd	SBA%	SB%	RAR	BPX
17	ATL *	364	31	3	38	8	210	4	6	217	314	297	83	71	86	13	74	0.59	58	12	30	27	88	DFc	5%	55	80	5%	10%	101	9%	86%	-18.7	0
18	2 AL	246	21	3	28	13	200	5	3	232	310	324	85	52	90	13	72	0.53	48	19	34	26	74	CCd	3%	88	66	6%	10%	80	28%	81%	-6.7	37
19	BAL *	467	55	9	44	13	236	2	16	257	300	373	93	99	77	8	78	0.41	43	25	32	28	95	CCb	4%	74	97	8%	8%	95	17%	73%	-10.6	67
20	MIL	61	6	2	5	1	200	2	2	181	393	356	99	52	102	25	56	0.75	54	15	31	30	86	BDa	8%	110	117	25%	25%	104	5%	100%	-0.4	-24
21	MIL *	362	43	9	42	11	233	8	4	228	326	371	96	85	101	12	70	0.46	41	23	35	30	71	CCd	5%	88	77	9%	12%	91	13%	91%	-7.9	15
1st Half		168	25	6	29	5	231	2	2	231	338	433	108	118	119	14	66	0.48	38	20	42	31	77	CBc	6%	136	99	11%	7%	101	13%	100%	1.0	131
2nd Half		194	18	3	13	6	235	6	2	226	325	318	87	72	91	11	74	0.44	43	25	32	30	69	CCd	5%	52	66	8%	15%	83	13%	86%	-7.0	-62
22	Proj	**280**	**30**	**5**	**30**	**10**	**225**	**6**	**5**	**227**	**319**	**342**	**90**	**80**	**92**	**12**	**73**	**0.48**	**44**	**21**	**34**	**29**	**79**		**5%**	**76**	**80**	**8%**	**10%**	**86**	**9%**	**84%**	**-3.1**	**25**

Pham,Tommy

Health	A	LIMA Plan	B
PT/Exp	A	Rand Var	+3
Consist	C	MM	2325

Age: 34 Pos: LF
Bats: R Ht: 6' 1" Wt: 223

Power/speed combo was in full effect early on; xHR said he deserved even better. But season went off the rails in 2nd ha low h% was to blame for sub-.200 BA, with added fallout of one SB attempt after July 17. At his age, once speed starts t go it often doesn't come back, so don't expect a pre-2020 rebound.

Yr	Tm	PA	R	HR	RBI	SB	BA	xHR	xSB	xBA	OBP	SLG	OPS+	vL+	vR+	bb%	ct%	Eye	G	L	F	h%	HctX	QBaB	Brl%	PX	xPX	HR/F	xHR/F	Spd	SBA%	SB%	RAR	BPX
17	STL *	631	107	26	87	29	292	21	11	277	384	497	120	130	123	13	73	0.56	52	22	26	36	106	BDa	9%	121	104	27%	24%	101	21%	73%	23.0	145
18	2 TM	570	102	21	63	15	275	26	22	258	367	464	111	116	108	12	72	0.48	48	24	28	35	128	ADb	10%	113	123	21%	26%	144	13%	68%	16.9	153
19	TAM	654	77	21	68	25	273	23	15	281	369	450	113	131	105	12	78	0.66	53	22	25	32	118	AFc	8%	95	95	19%	21%	106	16%	86%	11.6	178
20	SD	125	13	3	12	6	211	5	3	223	312	312	83	126	66	12	75	0.56	62	13	24	25	145	AFd	7%	54	101	15%	25%	98	18%	100%	-6.2	0
21	SD	561	74	15	49	14	229	22	16	244	340	383	99	94	101	14	73	0.61	48	20	32	28	111	ADd	10%	95	116	14%	20%	103	13%	70%	-14.5	112
1st Half		305	42	9	29	12	258	14	10	243	377	417	111	103	113	15	74	0.70	46	21	33	32	105	ADc	12%	91	125	14%	22%	123	13%	80%	0.5	146
2nd Half		256	32	6	20	2	197	8	6	243	297	345	87	86	87	13	72	0.52	51	20	30	25	117	ADd	8%	100	106	13%	17%	81	13%	40%	-15.9	77
22	Proj	**525**	**69**	**16**	**51**	**11**	**236**	**22**	**11**	**247**	**339**	**396**	**100**	**109**	**96**	**13**	**74**	**0.57**	**50**	**20**	**30**	**28**	**121**		**9%**	**96**	**109**	**16%**	**21%**	**100**	**11%**	**71%**	**1.2**	**103**

Phillips,Brett

Health	A	LIMA Plan	D
PT/Exp	C	Rand Var	-2
Consist	A	MM	4501

Age: 28 Pos: CF RF
Bats: L Ht: 6' 0" Wt: 195

Excellent speed shows he can be a force on bases even with subpar OBP, and check out that 2nd half power! However, ct completely tanked, tying for worst in majors (min. 250 PA), and he continued to be helpless vL. These are skills of a 5th OF in a deep league; one that will only be useful in small stretches for those truly desperate for SB.

Yr	Tm	PA	R	HR	RBI	SB	BA	xHR	xSB	xBA	OBP	SLG	OPS+	vL+	vR+	bb%	ct%	Eye	G	L	F	h%	HctX	QBaB	Brl%	PX	xPX	HR/F	xHR/F	Spd	SBA%	SB%	RAR	BPX
17	MIL *	513	65	20	67	11	265	3	7	226	324	466	107	42	114	8	61	0.22	38	25	38	39	73	CBd	9%	139	101	20%	15%	142	10%	91%	3.6	48
18	2 TM *	428	42	6	27	8	192	2	7	190	257	314	77	51	83	8	56	0.20	49	21	31	32	76	DCc	4%	97	87	9%	9%	149	11%	89%	-20.2	-110
19	KC *	466	62	14	46	19	196	1	11	200	307	382	95	88	67	14	61	0.41	42	16	42	28	83	CCf	4%	108	132	11%	6%	178	19%	94%	-7.0	52
20	2 AL	59	10	2	5	6	196	1	2	242	305	392	93	121	88	14	71	0.53	40	29	31	24	87	FCc	8%	94	116	18%	9%	163	50%	86%	-1.0	144
21	TAM	292	50	13	44	14	202	13	18	202	297	415	98	51	117	11	55	0.29	36	21	43	30	79	CAb	11%	157	157	22%	22%	138	28%	82%	-6.2	50
1st Half		174	22	3	18	11	199	5	13	188	314	315	88	50	108	14	54	0.36	43	27	30	34	62	DCc	7%	98	83	13%	21%	120	28%	79%	-7.8	-150
2nd Half		118	28	10	26	3	206	9	5	228	271	551	111	53	127	8	57	0.20	26	15	59	24	102	AAa	16%	233	252	28%	25%	143	28%	100%	-0.1	288
22	Proj	**245**	**38**	**10**	**33**	**11**	**205**	**9**	**9**	**200**	**289**	**405**	**94**	**66**	**102**	**10**	**58**	**0.27**	**36**	**21**	**42**	**30**	**84**		**9%**	**140**	**149**	**18%**	**16%**	**139**	**22%**	**90%**	**-0.5**	**48**

Pillar,Kevin

Health	B	LIMA Plan	D+
PT/Exp	A	Rand Var	+1
Consist	C	MM	3331

Age: 33 Pos: CF LF RF
Bats: R Ht: 6' 0" Wt: 200

Big jump in fly balls and strikeouts suggests he sold out for more power, but even with HR spike, pop still graded out as just league average. Low BA had full "support" from xBA - no thank you. SB game cratered despite still-solid speed skills Appeal is limited without the bags, while awful OBP, declining CF defense make it tough to hold a regular role.

Yr	Tm	PA	R	HR	RBI	SB	BA	xHR	xSB	xBA	OBP	SLG	OPS+	vL+	vR+	bb%	ct%	Eye	G	L	F	h%	HctX	QBaB	Brl%	PX	xPX	HR/F	xHR/F	Spd	SBA%	SB%	RAR	BPX
17	TOR	632	72	16	42	15	256	13	8	269	300	404	96	127	84	5	84	0.35	43	20	36	28	93	DCc	3%	85	69	9%	7%	107	16%	71%	-17.8	145
18	TOR	542	65	15	59	14	252	15	9	273	282	426	95	91	95	3	81	0.18	36	27	38	29	101	CBc	6%	108	90	9%	9%	99	18%	82%	-2.7	160
19	2 TM	645	83	21	88	14	259	17	13	276	287	432	100	114	93	3	85	0.20	44	20	36	27	110	DBc	5%	86	71	11%	9%	106	15%	74%	-2.9	185
20	2 TM	223	34	6	26	5	288	7	6	266	336	462	106	126	93	6	80	0.32	41	24	35	34	119	CCc	5%	93	106	10%	12%	145	13%	71%	2.0	212
21	NYM	347	40	15	47	4	231	12	6	232	277	415	95	92	96	3	75	0.14	35	19	46	26	98	DAd	7%	102	100	13%	11%	128	10%	57%	-16.2	112
1st Half		189	23	8	22	2	218	8	3	233	259	402	92	80	96	4	75	0.18	30	22	49	25	98	CAc	9%	104	120	12%	12%	112	10%	50%	-9.7	104
2nd Half		158	17	7	25	2	247	5	3	231	297	432	99	99	97	2	75	0.08	41	15	43	28	97	DAf	6%	99	75	15%	10%	129	10%	67%	-5.0	96
22	Proj	**245**	**31**	**10**	**33**	**4**	**252**	**8**	**4**	**252**	**294**	**439**	**99**	**106**	**95**	**4**	**79**	**0.17**	**39**	**20**	**41**	**28**	**104**		**6%**	**103**	**91**	**13%**	**11%**	**113**	**9%**	**69%**	**0.9**	**131**

BRIAN RUDD

Pinder,Chad

Age: 30	Pos: RF	Health	D	LIMA Plan	D
Bats: R	Ht: 6' 2" Wt: 210	PT/Exp	D	Rand Var	0
		Consist	A	MM	3221

6-27-.243 in 233 PA at OAK. Injuries plagued him again, as knee and hamstring issues led to extended absences. Continued to struggle getting on base, but power metrics mirrored 2018 marks and Brl%, xHR show that he was deserving of several more HR. Hard to envision much upside, but could be cheap source of power in deeper leagues.

Yr	Tm	PA	R	HR	RBI	SB	BA	xHR	xSB	xBA	OBP	SLG	OPS+	vL+	vR+	bb%	ct%	Eye	G	L	F	h%	HctX	QBaB	Brl%	PX	xPX	HR/F	xHR/F	Spd	SBA%	SB%	RAR	BPX	R$
17	OAK *	377	38	16	44	4	235	17	4	231	282	430	97	100	101	6	66	0.19	41	19	40	31	89	BCb	11%	127	119	19%	22%	104	8%	62%	-9.8	33	$5
18	OAK	333	43	13	27	0	258	20	5	233	332	436	103	111	94	8	70	0.31	44	19	37	32	120	ACb	14%	112	136	17%	26%	115	2%	0%	1.3	80	$6
19	OAK	370	45	13	47	0	240	13	1	258	290	416	98	104	92	5	74	0.23	49	22	29	29	105	ADc	8%	101	91	17%	17%	75	1%	0%	-11.5	48	$5
20	OAK	61	8	2	8	0	232	3	0	229	295	393	91	77	101	8	77	0.38	49	14	37	27	116	ACc	9%	93	90	13%	19%	104	0%	0%	-1.7	124	$1
21	OAK *	262	34	7	33	1	239	14	1	248	289	408	96	120	76	7	70	0.24	48	21	31	31	109	ADc	16%	116	137	13%	30%	102	2%	100%	-6.8	73	$4
1st Half		148	18	4	14	0	218	8	1	228	259	368	87	110	68	5	70	0.18	53	16	31	29	114	AFd	17%	107	139	11%	30%	100	2%	0%	-8.2	27	-$2
2nd Half		115	16	4	19	1	265	6	1	265	327	460	106	133	89	8	71	0.31	42	27	30	34	101	ACc	15%	128	133	15%	30%	103	2%	100%	0.7	135	$1
22	**Proj**	**245**	**32**	**9**	**30**	**1**	**247**	**10**	**1**	**246**	**302**	**432**	**100**	**111**	**89**	**7**	**71**	**0.24**	**47**	**20**	**33**	**31**	**109**		**13%**	**120**	**119**	**16%**	**20%**	**95**	**4%**	**62%**	**-0.5**	**55**	**$4**

Piscotty,Stephen

Age: 31	Pos: RF	Health	D	LIMA Plan	D
Bats: R	Ht: 6' 4" Wt: 211	PT/Exp	D	Rand Var	+1
		Consist	A	MM	2313

Wrist issue sidelined him for a couple weeks in June, eventually led to season-ending surgery in August. Jump in FB% couldn't revive power stroke, and recent health, ct%, BA trends don't offer much reason for optimism. Maybe going under the knife can fix him, but probably safe to avoid until we see positive signs in spring.

Yr	Tm	PA	R	HR	RBI	SB	BA	xHR	xSB	xBA	OBP	SLG	OPS+	vL+	vR+	bb%	ct%	Eye	G	L	F	h%	HctX	QBaB	Brl%	PX	xPX	HR/F	xHR/F	Spd	SBA%	SB%	RAR	BPX	R$
17	STL *	446	46	12	45	3	235	12	7	240	336	384	98	98	94	13	75	0.60	49	18	33	28	99	DCb	7%	91	112	11%	14%	86	8%	33%	-12.7	76	$4
18	OAK	605	78	27	88	2	267	31	5	287	331	491	110	103	111	7	79	0.37	45	22	33	29	124	CCb	10%	134	113	19%	22%	76	2%	100%	15.2	207	$20
19	OAK *	417	49	14	46	2	248	15	2	246	304	406	98	142	86	7	77	0.34	44	20	36	29	105	CCa	8%	104	102	13%	15%	93	2%	100%	-9.0	67	$7
20	OAK	171	17	5	29	4	226	6	1	221	271	358	84	69	90	5	67	0.17	46	23	31	31	107	CCc	6%	85	95	15%	18%	94	11%	100%	-7.8	-96	$12
21	OAK	188	14	5	16	1	220	8	3	220	282	353	87	97	76	7	72	0.27	39	20	41	28	71	DBd	9%	85	84	10%	16%	83	3%	100%	-9.1	-4	-$1
1st Half		141	11	4	11	1	217	6	2	238	284	357	89	99	77	8	74	0.33	38	24	39	26	76	DBd	9%	86	101	11%	16%	80	3%	100%	-7.1	31	-$3
2nd Half		47	3	1	5	0	227	2	1	152	277	341	84	93	73	4	66	0.13	45	7	48	32	56	DAf	7%	82	30	7%	14%	105	3%	0%	-2.8	-108	-$8
22	**Proj**	**280**	**29**	**8**	**34**	**3**	**237**	**11**	**2**	**232**	**303**	**384**	**93**	**99**	**89**	**8**	**74**	**0.32**	**45**	**19**	**37**	**29**	**87**		**8%**	**91**	**80**	**12%**	**16%**	**95**	**4%**	**86%**	**-4.6**	**16**	**$7**

Polanco,Gregory

Age: 30	Pos: RF	Health	D	LIMA Plan	D
Bats: L	Ht: 6' 5" Wt: 235	PT/Exp	C	Rand Var	0
		Consist	D	MM	3301

11-36-.208 with 14 SB in 382 PA at PIT. Futility at the plate led to his release by PIT in late August. Still had value in our game, as plus power held firm and SB prowess returned. But xSB and Spd cast doubt on the steals holding up, xBA is still on life support, and not being good in real life tends to limit the playing time. Temper expectations.

Yr	Tm	PA	R	HR	RBI	SB	BA	xHR	xSB	xBA	OBP	SLG	OPS+	vL+	vR+	bb%	ct%	Eye	G	L	F	h%	HctX	QBaB	Brl%	PX	xPX	HR/F	xHR/F	Spd	SBA%	SB%	RAR	BPX	R$
17	PIT	410	39	11	35	8	251	9	5	262	305	391	95	79	97	7	84	0.45	42	20	38	27	88	DCd	4%	78	77	9%	8%	80	10%	89%	-9.6	115	$7
18	PIT	532	75	23	81	12	254	25	8	257	340	499	113	102	114	11	75	0.52	33	19	48	29	93	CAc	9%	150	123	14%	15%	107	12%	86%	18.5	250	$20
19	PIT *	218	27	7	25	4	236	6	3	214	302	405	98	96	101	9	66	0.28	37	19	44	33	87	BAd	10%	109	120	13%	13%	98	10%	82%	-7.4	-4	$3
20	PIT	173	12	7	22	3	153	8	1	194	214	325	72	64	73	8	59	0.20	33	21	46	20	112	AAc	13%	121	155	16%	18%	67	17%	75%	-14.7	-124	$3
21	PIT *	479	50	19	55	18	230	18	9	224	299	411	98	60	98	9	70	0.33	38	18	44	28	105	BBf	10%	111	116	10%	17%	88	18%	95%	-8.7	58	$15
1st Half		251	23	9	23	8	199	13	5	207	275	362	89	49	102	10	67	0.34	38	18	44	25	88	CCf	11%	102	116	13%	19%	98	18%	100%	-11.4	-4	$8
2nd Half		228	27	10	32	10	262	4	5	242	319	464	106	75	92	8	74	0.32	39	17	44	31	134	AAf	7%	119	116	5%	11%	83	18%	91%	1.4	127	$17
22	**Proj**	**210**	**22**	**7**	**26**	**6**	**223**	**7**	**5**	**214**	**290**	**382**	**91**	**77**	**96**	**9**	**69**	**0.30**	**37**	**19**	**45**	**29**	**107**		**9%**	**104**	**123**	**11%**	**13%**	**86**	**13%**	**89%**	**-3.9**	**19**	**$6**

Polanco,Jorge

Age: 28	Pos: 2B SS	Health	A	LIMA Plan	B+
Bats: B	Ht: 5' 11" Wt: 208	PT/Exp	A	Rand Var	0
		Consist	D	MM	3245

His 1st half xHR hinted at a power surge, but 2nd half explosion was quite the surprise. His Spd, SB% suggest he could lose a handful of steals, but offers rock solid BA floor, and FB%, PX, xHR spikes say most of the power gains could stick. He can't be expected to maintain 2nd half pace, but another 30-HR campaign is well within reach.

Yr	Tm	PA	R	HR	RBI	SB	BA	xHR	xSB	xBA	OBP	SLG	OPS+	vL+	vR+	bb%	ct%	Eye	G	L	F	h%	HctX	QBaB	Brl%	PX	xPX	HR/F	xHR/F	Spd	SBA%	SB%	RAR	BPX	R$
17	MIN	544	60	13	74	13	256	10	7	258	313	410	98	90	100	8	84	0.53	38	19	43	28	94	DBc	3%	86	89	7%	6%	93	15%	72%	-3.7	152	$14
18	MIN	333	38	6	42	7	288	5	8	255	345	427	104	83	112	8	79	0.40	36	26	38	35	94	DAc	4%	86	76	7%	6%	106	16%	50%	7.2	120	$10
19	MIN	704	107	22	79	4	295	25	18	267	356	485	116	101	122	9	82	0.52	29	26	44	33	112	CAb	7%	97	132	10%	11%	122	4%	57%	24.6	222	$23
20	MIN	226	22	4	19	4	258	4	2	243	304	354	87	105	81	6	83	0.37	36	25	39	29	82	DBc	3%	53	75	6%	6%	90	11%	67%	-6.1	64	$14
21	MIN	644	97	33	98	11	269	36	8	273	323	503	114	109	116	7	80	0.38	32	23	45	29	109	CAd	10%	128	117	16%	17%	78	12%	65%	14.8	235	$28
1st Half		313	45	9	32	6	250	14	4	258	319	414	102	104	101	9	83	0.56	35	22	43	27	118	CBc	9%	92	111	9%	14%	85	12%	67%	-3.8	192	$18
2nd Half		331	52	24	66	5	286	22	4	286	326	584	123	115	127	6	77	0.26	29	24	47	30	101	CAf	11%	162	123	22%	20%	78	12%	63%	15.5	288	$36
22	**Proj**	**630**	**91**	**29**	**90**	**8**	**273**	**32**	**10**	**268**	**327**	**485**	**110**	**106**	**112**	**7**	**81**	**0.40**	**33**	**24**	**43**	**30**	**101**		**7%**	**114**	**106**	**14%**	**15%**	**91**	**10%**	**62%**	**22.9**	**218**	**$27**

Pollock,A.J.

Age: 34	Pos: LF	Health	F	LIMA Plan	C+
Bats: R	Ht: 6' 1" Wt: 210	PT/Exp	A	Rand Var	-2
		Consist	B	MM	4243

Showed that healthy 2020 was the product of short season, as he was back on IL twice with hamstring injuries. But after so-so start, power and xBA returned to peak form in 2nd half, and he even got a little h% boost. Still a potent bat with durability issues (has seen 500 AB once in 10-yr career) and profile supports near-repeat both PA and production.

Yr	Tm	PA	R	HR	RBI	SB	BA	xHR	xSB	xBA	OBP	SLG	OPS+	vL+	vR+	bb%	ct%	Eye	G	L	F	h%	HctX	QBaB	Brl%	PX	xPX	HR/F	xHR/F	Spd	SBA%	SB%	RAR	BPX	R$
17	ARI	466	73	14	49	20	266	12	6	299	330	471	109	115	103	8	83	0.49	45	23	32	29	118	CDd	6%	113	111	12%	11%	117	26%	77%	-0.4	230	$18
18	ARI	460	61	21	65	13	257	23	15	265	316	484	107	98	110	7	76	0.31	42	19	38	29	124	CCc	10%	132	146	17%	19%	117	15%	87%	7.1	197	$18
19	LA	342	49	15	47	5	266	14	7	258	327	468	110	126	102	7	76	0.31	43	20	37	31	115	BCd	8%	106	94	17%	16%	98	7%	83%	0.0	122	$10
20	LA	210	30	16	34	2	276	12	2	281	314	566	117	155	101	6	77	0.27	40	20	40	28	130	BCc	10%	150	158	26%	20%	85	10%	50%	4.8	268	$24
21	LA	422	53	21	69	9	297	23	6	283	355	536	123	119	124	7	79	0.38	40	22	39	33	122	BCf	11%	135	127	18%	19%	94	10%	90%	17.0	265	$21
1st Half		189	22	8	29	2	257	7	2	254	312	451	106	111	103	7	77	0.32	41	19	40	29	105	BCf	8%	113	105	15%	13%	98	10%	100%	-2.6	162	$9
2nd Half		233	31	13	40	7	330	16	4	305	391	608	135	125	140	8	81	0.44	39	23	38	36	135	BCd	13%	152	144	20%	25%	86	10%	88%	19.6	346	$24
22	**Proj**	**420**	**58**	**22**	**66**	**9**	**284**	**22**	**6**	**276**	**341**	**525**	**118**	**124**	**114**	**7**	**78**	**0.35**	**41**	**21**	**38**	**31**	**123**		**10%**	**134**	**130**	**19%**	**19%**	**86**	**8%**	**81%**	**21.5**	**235**	**$22**

Posey,Buster

Age: 35	Pos: CA	Health	B	LIMA Plan	D+
Bats: R	Ht: 6' 1" Wt: 213	PT/Exp	A	Rand Var	-5
		Consist	D	MM	0003

After turning back the clock with peak power/BA levels, we already had him projected for an 11-47-.276, $13 season when the news came through about his retirement. Hall of Fame-worthy career joins an elite group of mononymous superstars who went out after a solid season - Brett, Chipper, Mariano, Papi - and now Buster.

Yr	Tm	PA	R	HR	RBI	SB	BA	xHR	xSB	xBA	OBP	SLG	OPS+	vL+	vR+	bb%	ct%	Eye	G	L	F	h%	HctX	QBaB	Brl%	PX	xPX	HR/F	xHR/F	Spd	SBA%	SB%	RAR	BPX	R$
17	SF	568	62	12	67	6	320	15	10	285	400	462	117	138	107	11	87	0.92	44	23	33	35	116	CCb	4%	81	113	8%	10%	81	4%	86%	37.2	179	$21
18	SF	448	47	5	41	3	284	11	4	264	359	382	99	110	92	10	87	0.85	47	22	31	32	116	CCb	5%	61	93	5%	10%	79	4%	60%	14.5	137	$10
19	SF	445	43	7	38	0	257	14	3	259	320	368	95	80	101	8	82	0.48	49	23	28	30	102	CDc	5%	63	87	7%	15%	78	0%	0%	-4.4	78	$4
20																																			
21	SF	454	68	18	56	0	304	19	6	279	390	499	122	143	114	12	78	0.64	46	25	28	35	98	CDc	8%	112	89	20%	22%	75	0%	0%	33.1	196	$18
1st Half		230	33	12	27	0	327	12	3	277	417	548	134	149	128	13	78	0.70	45	24	31	37	105	BCc	10%	118	95	24%	24%	79	0%	0%	23.7	231	$18
2nd Half		224	35	6	29	0	281	8	2	281	362	449	110	136	101	12	78	0.59	48	27	25	34	91	CDc	6%	106	82	15%	21%	77	0%	0%	9.4	165	$10
22	Proj																																		

Pratto,Nick

Age: 23	Pos: DH	Health	A	LIMA Plan	D+
Bats: L	Ht: 6' 1" Wt: 195	PT/Exp	B	Rand Var	
		Consist	F	MM	4313

Swing change paid dividends as power came on strong and BA took step forward from .191 mark at Single-A in 2019. But ct%, including 53% in 135 PA vL in 2021, shows there are still some holes in the swing. Headed in right direction and even brings some speed to the table, but be sure you have a BA cushion before you invest in this KC prospect.

Yr	Tm	PA	R	HR	RBI	SB	BA	xHR	xSB	xBA	OBP	SLG	OPS+	vL+	vR+	bb%	ct%	Eye	G	L	F	h%	HctX	QBaB	Brl%	PX	xPX	HR/F	xHR/F	Spd	SBA%	SB%	RAR	BPX	R$
17																																			
18																																			
19																																			
20																																			
21	a/a	508	74	25	74	9	232		6		328	487	112			12	63	0.38				31				173				113	14%	62%		192	$15
1st Half		212	27	10	30	5	246		3		353	492	118			14	65	0.47				32				163				111	14%	46%		204	$13
2nd Half		297	49	15	46	5	227		3	248	316	494	109			11	61	0.34	44	20	36	30	0			184	-22	0%		125	14%	100%	-3.3	212	$20
22	**Proj**	**280**	**43**	**12**	**43**	**6**	**216**	**12**	**5**	**227**	**298**	**444**	**101**	**100**	**101**	**10**	**63**	**0.31**	**34**	**22**	**44**	**29**	**89**		**7%**	**158**		**17%**	**17%**	**120**	**12%**	**63%**	**-3.8**	**146**	**$9**

BRIAN RUDD

Profar,Jurickson

Age: 29 Pos: LF RF 1B	Health A	LIMA Plan D+
Bats: B Ht: 6' 0" Wt: 184	PT/Exp A	Rand Var +2
	Consist C	MM 1333

Didn't sniff a 2020 repeat as BA tumbled, homers disappeared, and PA started to wane. Plate skills held strong, but that's the best we can come up with since xHR/F and HctX collapsed, h% settled back to "normal", and he wasn't as sharp on basepaths. Still a double-digit HR/SB threat and BA should improve, but now he has to prove he merits PT.

Yr	Tm	PA	R	HR	RBI	SB	BA	xHR	xSB	xBA	OBP	SLG	OPS+	vL+	vR+	bb%	ct%	Eye	G	L	F	h%	HctX	QBaB	Brl%	PX	xPX	HR/F	xHR/F	Spd	SBA%	SB%	RAR	BPX	R$
17	TEX *	430	46	5	39	5	236	1	6	274	311	338	88	99	64	10	87	0.83	41	25	34	26	92	DCd	2%	62	82	0%	7%	94	6%	83%	-19.7	142	$
18	TEX	594	82	20	77	10	254	16	7	288	335	458	106	105	105	9	83	0.61	44	22	34	27	114	CCc	5%	115	98	13%	11%	114	7%	100%	8.8	263	$1
19	OAK	518	65	20	67	9	218	17	5	277	301	410	98	116	92	9	84	0.64	41	22	37	22	109	CCd	7%	93	99	14%	12%	82	9%	90%	-17.2	200	$1
20	SD	202	28	7	25	7	278	5	3	276	343	428	102	100	103	7	84	0.54	44	25	31	30	99	CCf	3%	74	58	15%	11%	101	14%	88%	-0.4	176	$2
21	SD	411	47	4	33	10	227	5	10	239	329	320	89	65	96	12	82	0.75	42	21	37	27	78	DBf	3%	57	53	4%	5%	117	13%	67%	-20.7	127	$
1st Half		262	32	1	20	9	224	2	7	232	330	296	87	75	90	13	81	0.81	43	21	36	27	78	DBf	1%	48	44	2%	3%	119	13%	82%	-14.1	104	-$
2nd Half		149	15	3	13	1	231	3	4	250	329	362	93	55	110	10	82	0.65	41	22	38	26	79	DCd	5%	72	68	8%	8%	110	13%	25%	-7.9	165	-$
22	**Proj**	**315**	**39**	**8**	**33**	**7**	**240**	**7**	**7**	**261**	**326**	**385**	**96**	**87**	**100**	**10**	**83**	**0.65**	**42**	**23**	**35**	**26**	**91**		**4%**	**79**	**70**	**10%**	**8%**	**103**	**11%**	**70%**	**-1.7**	**169**	**$**

Pujols,Albert

Age: 42 Pos: 1B	Health B	LIMA Plan D
Bats: R Ht: 6' 3" Wt: 235	PT/Exp B	Rand Var 0
	Consist A	MM 2221

LAA finally cut the cord with May DFA; he then carved out short-side platoon gig in LA. Recent skills vL (85% ct%, 107 PX since 2019) suggest that's a niche he can fill, and while raw power upticks give him an outside shot at 700 career HR (he's 21 away), that hinges on a team giving him enough PA. They probably shouldn't (see RAR); nor should you.

Yr	Tm	PA	R	HR	RBI	SB	BA	xHR	xSB	xBA	OBP	SLG	OPS+	vL+	vR+	bb%	ct%	Eye	G	L	F	h%	HctX	QBaB	Brl%	PX	xPX	HR/F	xHR/F	Spd	SBA%	SB%	RAR	BPX	R$
17	LAA	636	53	23	101	3	241	22	8	251	286	386	91	82	92	6	84	0.40	43	18	38	25	120	CCc	5%	72	105	12%	11%	53	2%	100%	-38.3	73	$1
18	LAA	498	50	19	64	1	245	19	1	272	289	411	94	89	94	6	86	0.43	40	22	37	25	134	BCd	6%	88	122	13%	13%	58	1%	100%	-15.0	150	$1
19	LAA	545	55	23	93	3	244	19	1	261	305	430	102	115	94	8	86	0.63	46	15	39	24	116	CCd	6%	86	90	14%	11%	60	2%	100%	-13.7	181	$1
20	LAA	163	15	6	25	0	224	5	0	253	270	395	88	82	92	6	84	0.36	40	20	41	23	103	CBf	5%	89	94	12%	10%	56	0%	0%	-11.2	140	$
21	2 TM	296	29	17	50	2	236	15	0	252	284	433	98	128	69	5	84	0.31	46	16	38	23	130	BCf	9%	90	105	19%	17%	64	3%	100%	-15.7	142	$
1st Half		191	18	11	31	1	223	11	0	249	267	419	96	141	61	4	85	0.27	43	16	42	20	132	ACd	9%	88	108	17%	17%	69	3%	100%	-11.7	162	$
2nd Half		105	11	6	19	1	260	5	0	253	314	458	105	112	92	7	80	0.37	53	17	31	27	126	BDf	9%	94	100	25%	21%	69	3%	100%	-1.9	123	$
22	**Proj**	**140**	**14**	**7**	**23**	**1**	**241**	**6**	**1**	**252**	**291**	**420**	**97**	**109**	**86**	**6**	**84**	**0.39**	**45**	**17**	**37**	**24**	**122**		**7%**	**88**	**101**	**16%**	**15%**	**64**	**3%**	**100%**	**-1.5**	**111**	**$**

Quinn,Roman

Age: 29 Pos: CF	Health F	LIMA Plan D
Bats: B Ht: 5' 10" Wt: 175	PT/Exp F	Rand Var +5
	Consist B	MM 1501

Last year, we asked "Can this guy catch a break?" No, apparently, as he lacerated a finger and ruptured an Achilles in May; the latter required season-ending surgery and could bleed into 2022. Not much to take away here—elite Spd, green light continued despite 4-for-7 start on basepaths—but a one-trick pony with a bum limb is no place to speculate.

Yr	Tm	PA	R	HR	RBI	SB	BA	xHR	xSB	xBA	OBP	SLG	OPS+	vL+	vR+	bb%	ct%	Eye	G	L	F	h%	HctX	QBaB	Brl%	PX	xPX	HR/F	xHR/F	Spd	SBA%	SB%	RAR	BPX	R$
17	aaa	190	21	2	11	9	242		3		304	340	88			8	67	0.27				35				67				132	30%	66%		-58	$
18	PHI *	251	25	4	21	20	256	1	12	236	307	394	94	117	86	7	74	0.29	49	18	33	33	59	CDc	2%	81	79	7%	3%	180	42%	80%	-0.1	107	$
19	PHI *	150	23	4	13	9	216	3	9	205	288	354	89	90	92	9	65	0.29	48	16	36	30	72	CCd	5%	79	62	18%	14%	138	29%	88%	-3.1	-48	$
20	PHI	116	14	2	7	12	213	2	4	214	261	315	76	94	68	4	64	0.13	47	28	26	31	59	FFf	3%	67	30	13%	13%	135	50%	100%	-6.7	-156	$1
21	PHI	62	8	0	2	4	173	1	5	218	306	288	82	40	120	10	63	0.32	43	30	27	27	79	FDf	3%	77	53	0%	13%	149	47%	57%	-5.5	-69	-$
1st Half		62	8	0	2	4	173	1	5	218	306	288	83	41	122	10	63	0.32	43	30	27	27	79	FDf	3%	77	53	0%	13%	149	47%	57%	-5.3	-65	-$
2nd Half																									0%										
22	**Proj**	**210**	**27**	**3**	**13**	**15**	**214**	**4**	**14**	**220**	**298**	**340**	**87**	**75**	**94**	**8**	**67**	**0.25**	**46**	**24**	**30**	**30**	**69**		**3%**	**80**	**54**	**8%**	**11%**	**165**	**38%**	**68%**	**-6.9**	**-25**	**$**

Raleigh,Cal

Age: 25 Pos: CA	Health A	LIMA Plan D+
Bats: R Ht: 6' 3" Wt: 215	PT/Exp D	Rand Var +1
	Consist A	MM 4113

2-13-.180 in 148 PA at SEA. Example #724 of catcher prospect struggling early. He tore up AAA (.324/.377/.608) in 199 PA, but fell flat after July call-up and lost grip on regular gig by September. Didn't make much contact in majors (63% ct%) and xPX, xHR/F say it was of the softer variety. Worth a late 2nd-catcher stab; just be ready to move on quickly.

Yr	Tm	PA	R	HR	RBI	SB	BA	xHR	xSB	xBA	OBP	SLG	OPS+	vL+	vR+	bb%	ct%	Eye	G	L	F	h%	HctX	QBaB	Brl%	PX	xPX	HR/F	xHR/F	Spd	SBA%	SB%	RAR	BPX	R$
17																																			
18																																			
19	aa	159	16	7	16	0	217		2		287	403	95			9	63	0.26				29				115				96	0%	0%		-22	-$
20																																			
21	SEA *	334	31	8	39	2	224	4	2	239	265	399	91	79	72	5	73	0.21	36	18	45	28	65	CBf	7%	120	78	5%	10%	78	8%	47%	-7.3	96	$
1st Half		176	23	6	25	2	256		1	289	299	460	106	0	0	6	83	0.37	44	20	36	28	0		0%	121	-22	0%		94	8%	47%	1.9	273	$
2nd Half		158	7	3	14	0	190	4	1	198	226	330	75	77	71	4	63	0.13	36	18	45	28	55	CBf	7%	119	78	5%	10%	76	8%	0%	-8.3	-81	-$
22	**Proj**	**385**	**36**	**13**	**45**	**1**	**227**	**11**	**3**	**230**	**274**	**417**	**94**	**93**	**94**	**6**	**69**	**0.20**	**36**	**18**	**45**	**29**	**50**		**6%**	**132**	**70**	**12%**	**10%**	**74**	**6%**	**50%**	**1.6**	**36**	**$**

Ramirez,Harold

Age: 27 Pos: LF RF CF	Health A	LIMA Plan C
Bats: R Ht: 5' 10" Wt: 232	PT/Exp B	Rand Var 0
	Consist F	MM 1133

Recalled from alternate site in May and started hot, but missed three weeks in Aug (knee) and limped to finish in Sept. Perhaps the 2nd half power collapse was injury-related, but PX says he's never had plus pop in minors and GB% stroke caps HR ceiling anyway. Strong ct% should help buoy BA, but it's not enough to make him mixed-league relevant.

Yr	Tm	PA	R	HR	RBI	SB	BA	xHR	xSB	xBA	OBP	SLG	OPS+	vL+	vR+	bb%	ct%	Eye	G	L	F	h%	HctX	QBaB	Brl%	PX	xPX	HR/F	xHR/F	Spd	SBA%	SB%	RAR	BPX	R$
17	aa	471	39	5	45	4	247		6		291	335	85			6	84	0.38				28				51				96	6%	57%		58	$
18	aa	485	50	9	58	13	292		4		324	429	101			5	79	0.23				35				94				81	13%	86%		87	$1
19	MIA *	560	71	14	62	3	282	11	11	271	312	433	103	92	103	4	79	0.21	57	20	23	34	95	CFb	6%	82	63	14%	14%	102	4%	57%	-6.8	78	$1
20	MIA	11	2	0	1	0	200	0	0	176	273	200	63	65	60	9	80	0.50	50	13	38	25	81	FCf		0	161	0%	0%	90	33%	0%	-1.5	-128	-$
21	CLE	361	33	7	41	3	268	11	12	260	305	398	97	105	92	4	83	0.25	53	17	30	30	121	ADd	6%	77	92	8%	13%	73	5%	75%	-12.9	104	$
1st Half		177	22	6	22	2	274	8	6	295	322	463	109	118	103	5	86	0.35	54	18	27	29	119	AFd	9%	101	101	15%	21%	80	5%	100%	-1.2	231	$
2nd Half		184	11	1	19	1	263	3	6	220	288	337	85	90	82	3	81	0.18	52	16	32	32	122	BDd	4%	52	82	2%	7%	70	5%	50%	-10.5	-15	-$
22	**Proj**	**385**	**38**	**8**	**43**	**3**	**265**	**11**	**3**	**256**	**303**	**397**	**95**	**100**	**92**	**4**	**81**	**0.24**	**54**	**18**	**28**	**31**	**114**		**6%**	**79**	**83**	**9%**	**13%**	**77**	**4%**	**69%**	**-2.8**	**73**	**$**

Ramírez,José

Age: 29 Pos: 3B	Health A	LIMA Plan C
Bats: B Ht: 5' 9" Wt: 190	PT/Exp A	Rand Var +1
	Consist D	MM 4455

More stat-stuffing goodness from one of the greats. Plenty of reasons to take him early in the first round: power stroke is only getting stronger (see Brl%, xHR/F); elite SB% means light should stay green; xBA hints at room for BA rebound; fou $35+ seasons in one box. We could go on (oh, he's under 30!)... but just do it.

Yr	Tm	PA	R	HR	RBI	SB	BA	xHR	xSB	xBA	OBP	SLG	OPS+	vL+	vR+	bb%	ct%	Eye	G	L	F	h%	HctX	QBaB	Brl%	PX	xPX	HR/F	xHR/F	Spd	SBA%	SB%	RAR	BPX	R$
17	CLE	645	107	29	83	17	318	19	9	320	374	583	130	129	128	8	88	0.75	39	21	40	32	121	CBc	5%	138	102	14%	9%	104	15%	77%	51.2	342	$
18	CLE	698	110	39	105	34	270	28	15	299	387	552	126	107	131	15	86	1.33	33	21	46	25	115	CAc	8%	146	119	17%	12%	89	21%	85%	53.6	403	$4
19	CLE	542	68	23	83	24	255	20	14	273	327	479	112	110	112	10	85	0.70	33	21	46	26	118	CAc	6%	109	114	12%	10%	94	24%	86%	6.6	278	$2
20	CLE	254	45	17	46	10	292	14	9	285	386	607	132	184	113	12	80	0.72	30	19	51	30	108	CAc	10%	163	134	19%	16%	101	20%	77%	20.9	436	$4
21	CLE	636	111	36	103	27	266	35	18	287	355	538	123	120	124	11	84	0.83	36	19	45	26	137	BAf	11%	136	125	17%	17%	102	20%	87%	29.5	388	$3
1st Half		310	54	18	50	6	265	18	8	296	345	537	123	116	127	10	86	0.82	34	21	46	25	138	AAd	12%	137	130	17%	17%	83	20%	75%	9.5	388	$3
2nd Half		326	57	18	53	21	268	16	10	281	365	539	122	124	121	13	83	0.84	38	18	45	27	136	CAf	11%	136	119	17%	15%	121	20%	91%	16.4	396	$4
22	**Proj**	**630**	**106**	**38**	**104**	**28**	**273**	**31**	**18**	**288**	**362**	**557**	**125**	**130**	**122**	**12**	**84**	**0.82**	**34**	**19**	**46**	**27**	**125**		**10%**	**145**	**123**	**17%**	**14%**	**102**	**15%**	**85%**	**45.3**	**431**	**$4**

Ramos,Wilson

Age: 34 Pos: CA	Health D	LIMA Plan D
Bats: R Ht: 6' 1" Wt: 245	PT/Exp C	Rand Var +5
	Consist B	MM 2111

8-20-.205 in 163 PA at DET/CLE. Popped six HR in April, then it fell apart with back problems in May, DFA in June, knee surgery in Sept. Skills weren't too far off 2018-19 peak—h% did most of the BA damage while ct%, HctX, Brl% say contact quality was just fine. But we can't count on much volume from a mid-30s catcher with lingering injury issues.

Yr	Tm	PA	R	HR	RBI	SB	BA	xHR	xSB	xBA	OBP	SLG	OPS+	vL+	vR+	bb%	ct%	Eye	G	L	F	h%	HctX	QBaB	Brl%	PX	xPX	HR/F	xHR/F	Spd	SBA%	SB%	RAR	BPX	R$
17	TAM *	251	22	13	39	0	252	11	3	258	287	444	99	109	94	5	84	0.31	52	18	30	25	113	DDc	9%	94	106	21%	21%	48	0%	0%	1.4	115	$
18	2 TM	416	39	15	70	0	306	15	1	266	358	487	113	121	108	8	79	0.40	55	20	25	36	114	AFb	7%	107	90	20%	20%	64	0%	0%	31.9	127	$
19	NYM	524	52	14	73	1	288	13	0	269	351	416	106	132	98	8	85	0.64	62	18	19	31	94	BFc	5%	63	50	18%	17%	52	1%	100%	21.1	100	$
20	NYM	155	13	5	15	0	239	6	0	231	297	387	91	100	86	6	78	0.32	53	18	29	27	102	CDf	7%	81	80	15%	18%	42	0%	0%	-1.5	20	
21	2 AL *	222	19	10	26	0	214	8	0	245	248	389	88	69	96	4	79	0.22	54	18	28	22	117	BDf	11%	93	67	25%	25%	49	0%	0%	-6.4	62	
1st Half		126	12	6	13	0	200	5	0	253	238	392	88	44	101	5	76	0.21	53	20	27	21	116	BDf	10%	108	58	24%	20%	56	0%	0%	-4.2	69	-
2nd Half		96	7	4	13	0	232	3	0	207	262	386	88	120	78	4	83	0.24	60	12	28	24	109	CFf	16%	76	98	29%	43%	55	0%	0%	-2.0	81	-
22	**Proj**	**245**	**21**	**9**	**31**	**0**	**252**	**13**	**0**	**238**	**294**	**410**	**96**	**105**	**91**	**6**	**80**	**0.30**	**55**	**18**	**28**	**28**	**107**		**10%**	**85**	**79**	**18%**	**26%**	**47**	**0%**	**100%**	**3.9**	**21**	

RYAN BLOOMFIELD

Realmuto,J.T.

Age: 31 Pos: CA	Health A	LIMA Plan B	
Bats: R Ht: 6' 1" Wt: 212	PT/Exp A	Rand Var -1	
	Consist A	MM 3325	

While HR output was down slightly from his peak, this was still darn good, and with a steals bonus. Contact issues lingered for a second season, and related xBA trend is foreboding. But he's still just 31, has a solid, stable skills set, and there's nothing here to keep me from bidding $20.

Yr	Tm	PA	R	HR	RBI	SB	BA	xHR	xSB	xBA	OBP	SLG	OPS+	vL+	vR+	bb%	ct%	Eye	G	L	F	h%	HctX	QBaB	Brl%	PX	xPX	HR/F	xHR/F	Spd	SBA%	SB%	RAR	BPX	R$
17	MIA	579	68	17	65	8	278	17	8	267	332	451	107	113	103	6	80	0.34	48	18	34	32	108	CCc	6%	97	98	12%	12%	126	7%	80%	16.9	152	$17
18	MIA	529	74	21	74	3	277	24	7	272	340	484	111	86	116	7	78	0.37	40	23	37	32	111	CBc	9%	123	110	15%	17%	108	4%	60%	28.0	200	$18
19	PHI	592	92	25	83	9	275	22	5	272	328	493	114	118	111	7	77	0.33	39	23	38	32	122	BBb	9%	117	118	16%	14%	112	8%	90%	21.0	189	$21
20	PHI	195	33	11	32	4	266	13	3	244	349	491	112	142	100	8	72	0.33	48	14	38	31	110	BCd	14%	124	121	23%	28%	94	10%	80%	7.8	140	$23
21	PHI	537	64	17	73	13	263	20	11	249	343	439	107	99	111	9	73	0.37	46	20	33	33	107	BCc	9%	107	99	15%	17%	132	12%	81%	13.8	142	$19
1st Half		244	27	7	30	4	258	10	5	253	357	431	110	105	112	12	74	0.51	47	21	31	32	106	BCc	9%	104	105	14%	20%	131	12%	67%	5.9	165	$11
2nd Half		293	37	10	43	9	266	10	5	247	331	446	105	93	110	7	72	0.27	46	20	35	33	107	BCc	8%	110	94	15%	15%	124	12%	90%	7.2	115	$22
22	Proj	525	70	20	73	11	267	22	10	250	340	454	108	108	107	8	74	0.35	45	20	35	32	110		10%	110	107	15%	17%	108	10%	82%	23.1	131	$19

Rendon,Anthony

Age: 32 Pos: 3B	Health F	LIMA Plan B	
Bats: R Ht: 6' 1" Wt: 200	PT/Exp B	Rand Var +3	
	Consist D	MM 4245	

Knee, triceps, groin, and hammy problems got the headlines, but it was a right hip impingement that was the root of the latter two injuries, ultimately ending his season. Given all that, it's probably safe to give him a mulligan for 2021. Expected to be at full strength by spring, so a rebound seems a good bet—but no, probably not to 2019 levels.

Yr	Tm	PA	R	HR	RBI	SB	BA	xHR	xSB	xBA	OBP	SLG	OPS+	vL+	vR+	bb%	ct%	Eye	G	L	F	h%	HctX	QBaB	Brl%	PX	xPX	HR/F	xHR/F	Spd	SBA%	SB%	RAR	BPX	R$
17	WAS	605	81	25	100	7	301	21	10	282	403	533	127	153	118	14	84	1.02	34	19	47	32	116	BAc	7%	127	112	12%	10%	92	5%	78%	41.1	285	$25
18	WAS	597	88	24	92	2	308	30	6	292	374	535	122	123	119	9	84	0.67	33	24	44	33	118	BAc	10%	130	122	12%	15%	95	2%	67%	43.1	303	$26
19	WAS	646	117	34	126	5	319	36	5	296	412	598	140	146	137	12	84	0.93	33	21	46	33	130	BAb	12%	136	160	16%	17%	97	3%	83%	59.7	374	$33
20	LAA	232	29	9	31	0	286	8	3	270	418	497	122	131	117	16	84	1.23	35	21	44	30	146	BAb	6%	108	119	13%	12%	107	0%	0%	12.4	352	$18
21	LAA	249	24	6	34	0	240	7	1	245	329	382	98	87	103	12	81	0.71	31	22	47	27	99	CAb	6%	84	98	7%	8%	70	0%	0%	-4.0	146	$2
1st Half		246	23	5	33	0	237	6	0	242	325	367	97	87	101	12	81	0.68	32	22	46	27	98	BAc	5%	79	95	6%	7%	70	0%	0%	-7.0	127	$5
2nd Half		3	1	1	1	0	500	0	0	762	667	2000	361	134	340	33	100	0.00	0	0	100	0	204	DAa	14%	554	352	50%	0%	101	0%	0%	2.5	2085	-$9
22	Proj	525	71	23	82	2	284	21	2	277	378	510	121	122	120	13	83	0.85	33	22	45	30	120		8%	123	120	13%	12%	88	2%	78%	32.6	288	$22

Renfroe,Hunter

Age: 30 Pos: RF	Health A	LIMA Plan B	
Bats: R Ht: 6' 1" Wt: 230	PT/Exp A	Rand Var -2	
	Consist D	MM 4125	

It sounds simple: The more often you hit the ball, the more chances you have to get a hit. But it bears out, as even this modest contact improvement was the difference—that and an attractive barrels rebound-plus. And yes, xHR likes it even more. Even with some pullback to the mean, he's again a solid power option with some respectable upside.

Yr	Tm	PA	R	HR	RBI	SB	BA	xHR	xSB	xBA	OBP	SLG	OPS+	vL+	vR+	bb%	ct%	Eye	G	L	F	h%	HctX	QBaB	Brl%	PX	xPX	HR/F	xHR/F	Spd	SBA%	SB%	RAR	BPX	R$
17	SD *	538	63	29	70	4	253	22	6	251	296	493	107	145	85	6	70	0.21	38	17	45	30	99	CBf	11%	149	131	19%	16%	82	4%	100%	-2.3	115	$13
18	SD *	483	57	27	71	2	241	24	3	259	291	483	104	107	106	6	73	0.26	37	20	43	27	126	BAd	12%	148	137	20%	19%	78	3%	67%	3.8	160	$13
19	SD	494	64	33	64	5	216	28	2	236	289	489	108	126	101	9	65	0.30	36	16	48	25	106	BAd	12%	159	144	24%	20%	75	6%	100%	-4.8	111	$11
20	TAM	139	18	8	22	2	156	7	1	227	252	393	86	105	75	10	70	0.38	42	10	48	14	98	BBf	9%	137	124	20%	17%	71	9%	100%	-7.9	128	$5
21	BOS	572	89	31	96	1	259	37	6	260	315	501	112	120	107	8	75	0.34	39	18	43	29	111	BBf	14%	141	114	18%	22%	66	3%	33%	6.9	192	$20
1st Half		286	44	12	44	0	267	16	3	256	322	465	110	136	97	8	76	0.36	41	20	39	31	108	ABf	13%	116	107	15%	20%	77	3%	0%	0.2	150	$19
2nd Half		286	45	19	52	1	251	21	2	266	308	536	114	107	118	8	74	0.32	37	15	48	27	113	BBf	16%	167	122	20%	23%	58	3%	100%	4.6	246	$22
22	Proj	560	80	33	89	4	241	33	2	248	305	489	108	118	102	8	72	0.32	39	16	45	27	109		13%	148	125	20%	20%	62	2%	80%	11.1	165	$20

Rengifo,Luis

Age: 25 Pos: SS	Health A	LIMA Plan D	
Bats: R Ht: 5' 10" Wt: 195	PT/Exp C	Rand Var 0	
	Consist C	MM 1311	

6-18-.201 with 1 SB in 190 PA at LAA. PRO: Improved contact; occasional pop born from launch-angle step-up; BPX was not -124 again! CON: Exit velocity, barrels highlight that this remains a weak bat overall; MLB running game still nil; walk rate regressed badly. Seeds of value here, but only if his very best individual skills all arrive at once.

Yr	Tm	PA	R	HR	RBI	SB	BA	xHR	xSB	xBA	OBP	SLG	OPS+	vL+	vR+	bb%	ct%	Eye	G	L	F	h%	HctX	QBaB	Brl%	PX	xPX	HR/F	xHR/F	Spd	SBA%	SB%	RAR	BPX	R$
17																																			
18	a/a	376	55	4	36	14	246		6		317	364	91			9	82	0.59				29				68				135	25%	62%		153	$10
19	LAA *	523	54	11	42	4	234	9	18	241	304	362	92	85	99	9	74	0.39	48	22	30	29	83	CCc	6%	73	50	9%	11%	132	10%	32%	-24.4	56	$5
20	LAA	106	12	1	3	3	156	1	2	190	269	200	62	46	71	13	71	0.54	59	14	27	21	83	DFf	2%	26	55	6%	6%	115	15%	75%	-8.8	-124	-$1
21	LAA *	408	50	11	38	9	229	7	8	240	267	361	86	72	78	5	80	0.25	48	17	35	26	95	DCf	6%	72	78	13%	15%	114	18%	60%	-18.5	85	$8
1st Half		191	26	5	18	4	222	3	3	223	263	359	87	16	85	5	80	0.27	55	6	39	25	104	DCf	8%	74	90	11%	16%	128	18%	47%	-10.1	112	$4
2nd Half		217	24	6	20	5	235	4	4	250	271	362	86	97	74	5	80	0.24	44	23	33	27	89	DCf	5%	70	70	14%	14%	98	18%	80%	-7.8	58	$6
22	Proj	140	17	3	11	3	233	4	4	233	297	359	89	76	95	8	77	0.37	50	17	33	28	90		5%	71	68	10%	12%	113	15%	61%	-3.3	43	$3

Reyes,Franmil

Age: 26 Pos: DH	Health B	LIMA Plan B	
Bats: R Ht: 6' 5" Wt: 265	PT/Exp A	Rand Var 0	
	Consist A	MM 4125	

Crushes it when he hits it, as exit velocity and barrels show in spades. But bat path issues continue to deny him a massive power explosion, and we have enough data in (see G/F, launch angle) to know that's not changing without a swing overhaul. And even the power can't save BA if whiffs keep rising. This is a 50-HR bat mired in a 30-HR swing.

Yr	Tm	PA	R	HR	RBI	SB	BA	xHR	xSB	xBA	OBP	SLG	OPS+	vL+	vR+	bb%	ct%	Eye	G	L	F	h%	HctX	QBaB	Brl%	PX	xPX	HR/F	xHR/F	Spd	SBA%	SB%	RAR	BPX	R$
17	aa	550	73	22	95	4	246		7		306	433	101			8	72	0.31				30				114				82	7%	47%		70	$13
18	SD *	521	71	27	68	0	275	14	5	246	345	487	112	136	99	10	68	0.34	49	21	30	35	111	ADd	12%	135	115	30%	26%	81	0%	0%	18.7	90	$17
19	2 TM	548	69	37	81	0	249	37	0	255	310	512	114	123	110	9	68	0.30	44	21	34	29	112	ACd	15%	145	140	31%	31%	51	0%	0%	3.0	89	$15
20	CLE	241	27	9	34	0	275	12	1	214	344	450	105	86	111	10	67	0.35	50	16	33	37	100	ACb	11%	111	104	18%	24%	87	0%	0%	3.9	24	$18
21	CLE	466	57	30	85	4	254	34	2	250	324	522	116	119	115	9	64	0.29	46	18	36	32	115	ACd	17%	171	153	31%	35%	88	5%	80%	10.9	158	$17
1st Half		163	21	11	29	1	268	13	0	274	325	577	126	108	135	7	66	0.24	53	14	33	33	125	ADc	21%	193	163	33%	39%	116	5%	100%	7.1	277	$10
2nd Half		303	36	19	56	3	245	20	1	236	323	491	110	126	104	10	63	0.31	42	20	38	31	110	ACf	15%	157	147	29%	31%	60	5%	75%	3.8	73	$22
22	Proj	560	70	33	93	3	259	36	4	246	325	504	112	115	111	9	66	0.30	47	18	34	32	112		15%	153	137	28%	31%	72	4%	77%	14.8	100	$22

Reyes,Victor

Age: 27 Pos: RF CF	Health B	LIMA Plan C+	
Bats: B Ht: 6' 5" Wt: 194	PT/Exp C	Rand Var -4	
	Consist A	MM 2533	

5-22-.258 with 5 SB in 220 PA at DET. Struggled early, then spent a month on IL with a ribcage muscle strain. That and MiLB time set him back, but then looked better upon return; LD history is intriguing. But 2nd half h%, lagging plate skills say to pump the brakes a bit, at least until we get a 500-PA MLB season to evaluate.

Yr	Tm	PA	R	HR	RBI	SB	BA	xHR	xSB	xBA	OBP	SLG	OPS+	vL+	vR+	bb%	ct%	Eye	G	L	F	h%	HctX	QBaB	Brl%	PX	xPX	HR/F	xHR/F	Spd	SBA%	SB%	RAR	BPX	R$
17	aa	501	49	3	43	15	276		7		309	382	94			4	82	0.26				33				65				117	21%	61%		76	$13
18	DET	219	35	1	12	9	222	3	6	246	239	288	71	64	71	2	78	0.11	50	26	24	28	100	DDc	3%	39	63	3%	8%	154	23%	90%	-14.3	-7	$3
19	DET *	592	71	12	73	17	287	3	19	278	318	428	103	99	108	4	79	0.21	45	29	26	35	110	CCa	2%	78	70	5%	5%	121	20%	64%	-7.2	93	$21
20	DET	213	30	4	14	8	277	6	7	251	315	391	94	103	91	4	78	0.20	46	26	28	34	86	BCa	4%	62	77	9%	14%	158	19%	80%	-6.6	72	$21
21	DET *	306	36	6	30	9	278	7	9	258	315	436	103	117	87	5	74	0.21	49	23	28	36	91	CDc	8%	95	65	12%	17%	149	18%	72%	-5.4	112	$11
1st Half		137	15	2	9	4	219	2	3	250	267	334	84	47	70	6	73	0.24	46	27	27	29	78	CDc	3%	77	27	7%	13%	113	18%	100%	-9.1	15	-$1
2nd Half		168	22	4	21	5	326	5	5	266	356	519	118	162	97	4	75	0.18	51	21	28	42	99	CDb	11%	110	88	15%	19%	168	18%	61%	5.4	185	$10
22	Proj	350	45	6	33	11	277	9	10	258	308	414	98	111	93	4	76	0.19	48	25	27	35	95		5%	81	68	9%	13%	152	16%	74%	0.5	84	$15

Reynolds,Bryan

Age: 27 Pos: CF	Health A	LIMA Plan B+	
Bats: B Ht: 6' 3" Wt: 205	PT/Exp A	Rand Var -2	
	Consist F	MM 4345	

Proved 2020 was the outlier with this stellar campaign. But look closer... that second half was even better than the stats showed. If those contact, exit velocity, and launch angle gains stick, we could be talking about a guy who not only hits for average, but also... well, take a look at xHR. And wipe off that drool; it's embarrassing. UP: 35 HR

Yr	Tm	PA	R	HR	RBI	SB	BA	xHR	xSB	xBA	OBP	SLG	OPS+	vL+	vR+	bb%	ct%	Eye	G	L	F	h%	HctX	QBaB	Brl%	PX	xPX	HR/F	xHR/F	Spd	SBA%	SB%	RAR	BPX	R$
17																																			
18	aa	367	47	6	39	3	275		6		347	392	99			10	76	0.46				35				76				108	7%	43%		67	$8
19	PIT *	601	91	20	77	5	315	19	10	275	375	513	123	105	128	9	75	0.39	46	24	30	39	111	BCa	7%	111	108	14%	17%	130	5%	56%	26.8	178	$23
20	PIT	207	24	7	19	1	189	8	2	230	275	357	84	82	84	10	69	0.37	44	22	34	23	105	CCc	10%	97	116	16%	18%	129	5%	50%	-13.3	60	$5
21	PIT	646	93	24	90	5	302	35	10	281	390	522	125	125	126	12	79	0.63	39	26	36	35	111	BCc	10%	122	109	15%	22%	131	4%	71%	31.6	296	$28
1st Half		328	46	15	46	3	310	18	5	281	396	540	130	141	126	12	77	0.58	42	23	35	36	104	CCc	11%	135	114	19%	23%	103	4%	75%	18.9	277	$30
2nd Half		318	47	9	44	2	294	17	5	281	384	504	120	107	125	12	81	0.70	36	28	36	34	118	BBc	10%	109	105	11%	21%	152	4%	67%	11.3	312	$21
22	Proj	630	88	26	89	5	284	31	8	271	371	508	119	113	121	12	77	0.56	39	25	36	33	111		10%	125	110	17%	20%	124	6%	59%	40.6	233	$27

ROD TRUESDELL

Riley,Austin

Age: 25	Pos: 3B	Health	A	LIMA Plan	B
Bats: R	Ht: 6' 3" Wt: 240	PT/Exp	A	Rand Var	-5
		Consist	C	MM	4035

Improved approach against RHP and reversal of flyball fortune in 2nd half drove this breakout. Of course, that 2nd-half h rate is unsustainable so expect BA to drop some, although xBA says it won't crater to 2019-20 levels. But you'll buy for that hot-corner power, and he's got it. An easy, 30-HR baseline.

Yr	Tm	PA	R	HR	RBI	SB	BA	xHR	xSB	xBA	OBP	SLG	OPS+	vL+	vR+	bb%	ct%	Eye	G	L	F	h%	HctX	QBaB	Brl%	PX	xPX	HR/F	xHR/F	Spd	SBA%	SB%	RAR	BPX
17	aa	200	29	8	28	2	296		3		372	467	114			11	69	0.39				39				103				109	3%	100%		39
18	a/a	419	51	16	59	1	280		3		329	484	109			7	67	0.22				38				144				94	1%	100%		87
19	ATL *	488	75	30	85	0	244	17	1	248	296	505	111	137	93	7	67	0.22	26	25	49	29	97	BAd	14%	152	160	22%	21%	76	2%	0%	-6.4	96
20	ATL	206	24	8	27	0	239	10	1	247	301	415	95	103	92	8	74	0.33	42	24	35	28	101	ACd	10%	97	90	17%	21%	106	0%	0%	-6.4	92
21	ATL	662	91	33	107	0	303	37	3	264	367	531	123	102	130	8	72	0.31	38	25	37	38	103	BBd	13%	138	111	21%	23%	94	1%	0%	26.3	162
1st Half		322	40	14	39	0	274	16	2	247	354	466	114	104	117	10	70	0.36	43	24	33	34	104	BCf	12%	117	113	21%	24%	94	1%	0%	3.8	88
2nd Half		340	51	19	68	0	330	20	2	278	379	589	131	100	140	7	73	0.26	34	26	40	40	103	BBd	14%	155	109	21%	22%	93	1%	0%	26.9	227
22	Proj	**630**	**87**	**32**	**101**	**0**	**281**	**35**	**2**	**256**	**344**	**508**	**116**	**111**	**117**	**8**	**71**	**0.29**	**36**	**25**	**39**	**35**	**102**		**13%**	**138**	**116**	**20%**	**22%**	**87**	**2%**	**37%**	**29.2**	**101**

Ríos,Edwin

Age: 28	Pos: 1B	Health	F	LIMA Plan	D
Bats: L	Ht: 6' 3" Wt: 220	PT/Exp	F	Rand Var	+5
		Consist	F	MM	4001

Surgery to repair partially torn right shoulder labrum ended season in May. He later revealed he was playing through pair prior. The numbers confirm it—even the bb% spike suggests it hurt just to swing the bat! While he's expected to be ready by spring, he'll need time to rebuild things. But don't forget: With health, he still owns prodigious power.

Yr	Tm	PA	R	HR	RBI	SB	BA	xHR	xSB	xBA	OBP	SLG	OPS+	vL+	vR+	bb%	ct%	Eye	G	L	F	h%	HctX	QBaB	Brl%	PX	xPX	HR/F	xHR/F	Spd	SBA%	SB%	RAR	BPX
17	a/a	502	58	20	75	1	276		6		315	473	107			5	73	0.21				34				122				76	3%	27%		79
18	aaa	326	35	8	42	0	260		2		298	407	94			5	58	0.13				42				130				82	1%	0%		-83
19	LA *	474	61	26	72	1	226	4	2	227	281	464	103	112	143	7	54	0.17	46	27	27	35	107	AFa	27%	173	184	57%	57%	100	4%	37%	-16.4	0
20	LA	83	13	8	17	0	250	8	0	311	301	645	126	170	113	5	76	0.22	34	19	47	22	157	ABc	14%	211	236	29%	29%	76	0%	0%	2.2	436
21	LA	60	4	1	1	0	78	2	0	132	217	137	49	0	62	12	65	0.39	42	9	48	9	88	BCf	12%	34	152	6%	13%	100	0%	0%	-8.4	-223
1st Half		60	4	1	1	0	78	2	0	132	217	137	49	0	63	12	65	0.39	42	9	48	9	88	BCf	12%	34	152	6%	13%	100	0%	0%	-8.0	-223
2nd Half																									0%									
22	Proj	**210**	**21**	**12**	**33**	**0**	**253**	**18**	**0**	**205**	**332**	**476**	**110**	**94**	**114**	**8**	**62**	**0.23**	**39**	**13**	**48**	**34**	**116**		**13%**	**149**	**186**	**20%**	**31%**	**73**	**1%**	**27%**	**3.3**	**-24**

Rizzo,Anthony

Age: 32	Pos: 1B	Health	A	LIMA Plan	B+
Bats: L	Ht: 6' 3" Wt: 240	PT/Exp	A	Rand Var	+2
		Consist	C	MM	2145

Missed some time with COVID in August. Otherwise, a year fairly typical of his post-peak self. How's that, you say, with that drop in HR and another low BA? As xHR shows, power metrics have suggested a pullback for a while now. And while gradually dwindling, plate skills still support a slightly better BA. Overall? Expect similar numbers in 2022.

Yr	Tm	PA	R	HR	RBI	SB	BA	xHR	xSB	xBA	OBP	SLG	OPS+	vL+	vR+	bb%	ct%	Eye	G	L	F	h%	HctX	QBaB	Brl%	PX	xPX	HR/F	xHR/F	Spd	SBA%	SB%	RAR	BPX
17	CHC	691	99	32	109	10	273	30	12	291	392	507	122	119	121	13	84	1.01	41	20	39	28	117	CBc	9%	119	107	17%	16%	70	7%	71%	19.7	248
18	CHC	665	74	25	101	6	283	22	8	286	376	470	113	91	119	11	86	0.88	38	25	37	29	108	BBc	7%	100	93	14%	12%	77	5%	60%	24.6	233
19	CHC	613	89	27	94	5	293	21	6	300	405	520	128	112	132	12	83	0.83	43	25	32	31	107	CCb	7%	109	95	20%	15%	78	4%	71%	30.7	252
20	CHC	243	26	11	24	3	222	6	1	267	342	414	100	80	106	12	81	0.74	38	24	38	22	116	CBd	7%	94	99	18%	10%	65	6%	75%	-6.7	180
21	2 TM	576	73	22	61	6	248	22	6	264	344	440	108	123	101	9	82	0.60	41	19	40	26	108	BBd	8%	100	88	13%	13%	84	5%	75%	-9.2	212
1st Half		290	30	10	32	4	245	12	3	271	341	434	108	125	103	11	82	0.67	43	21	36	26	117	ABd	9%	101	100	13%	16%	84	5%	67%	-6.9	219
2nd Half		286	43	12	29	2	251	10	3	257	346	445	107	120	99	8	83	0.52	39	17	43	26	100	CBd	6%	99	75	13%	11%	84	5%	100%	-6.3	212
22	Proj	**560**	**75**	**23**	**70**	**6**	**260**	**20**	**5**	**268**	**361**	**451**	**110**	**110**	**110**	**10**	**83**	**0.67**	**40**	**22**	**38**	**27**	**109**		**7%**	**99**	**91**	**14%**	**13%**	**75**	**4%**	**74%**	**14.0**	**212**

Robert,Luis

Age: 24	Pos: CF	Health	D	LIMA Plan	C+
Bats: R	Ht: 6' 2" Wt: 210	PT/Exp	C	Rand Var	-5
		Consist	D	MM	4435

Out half the season with a hip flexor strain, but was dynamite after his return in early August. 2nd-half skills support the excellence, with gains across the board featuring elite power. Now, expect the running game to return with full health, to Was drafted too early in most leagues in 2021, but maybe this is the year... UP: 30 HR, 25 SB

Yr	Tm	PA	R	HR	RBI	SB	BA	xHR	xSB	xBA	OBP	SLG	OPS+	vL+	vR+	bb%	ct%	Eye	G	L	F	h%	HctX	QBaB	Brl%	PX	xPX	HR/F	xHR/F	Spd	SBA%	SB%	RAR	BPX
17																																		
18																																		
19	a/a	449	79	23	61	25	288		6		322	535	119			5	72	0.18				35				135				132	38%	75%		170
20	CHW	225	33	11	31	9	233	14	10	218	302	436	98	105	96	9	64	0.27	37	20	43	31	77	CBd	13%	129	120	20%	25%	110	22%	82%	-1.9	44
21	CHW *	329	45	14	45	7	327	18	11	277	364	544	125	168	119	5	76	0.25	37	26	37	39	111	ACc	13%	130	116	16%	23%	112	9%	88%	22.9	215
1st Half		103	11	1	8	4	316	4	3	259	359	463	114	139	109	7	71	0.25	35	34	31	44	68	CCc	10%	111	48	5%	19%	130	9%	80%	3.6	100
2nd Half		226	34	13	37	3	333	14	8	285	365	581	128	178	123	5	79	0.24	37	23	40	37	133	ABc	14%	138	147	20%	24%	97	9%	100%	18.2	262
22	Proj	**504**	**76**	**21**	**67**	**17**	**279**	**29**	**8**	**258**	**330**	**493**	**112**	**139**	**103**	**6**	**72**	**0.24**	**37**	**25**	**38**	**34**	**100**		**12%**	**132**	**111**	**16%**	**23%**	**116**	**9%**	**80%**	**22.8**	**165**

Robles,Victor

Age: 25	Pos: CF	Health	A	LIMA Plan	C
Bats: R	Ht: 6' 0" Wt: 205	PT/Exp	A	Rand Var	+3
		Consist	B	MM	2313

2-19-.203 with 8 SB in 369 PA at WAS. Well, yikes. Finally exiled to AAA in September and never returned. Portrait of a very bad QBaB/Brl% profile: It does no good to loft the ball if exit velocity and barrels are among the worst in baseball, and that paints 2019 stats as the clear outliers. Age and pedigree are about all he has on his side now.

Yr	Tm	PA	R	HR	RBI	SB	BA	xHR	xSB	xBA	OBP	SLG	OPS+	vL+	vR+	bb%	ct%	Eye	G	L	F	h%	HctX	QBaB	Brl%	PX	xPX	HR/F	xHR/F	Spd	SBA%	SB%	RAR	BPX
17	WAS *	177	23	3	16	10	298	0	2	264	341	455	108	0	111	6	82	0.36	53	12	35	35	105	CDb	5%	93	135	0%	0%	124	33%	70%	1.7	164
18	WAS *	240	30	5	19	16	271	2	11	237	332	411	100	129	106	8	82	0.51	27	24	49	31	107	DAc	6%	84	106	14%	9%	124	39%	65%	1.3	167
19	WAS	617	86	17	65	28	255	15	32	248	326	419	103	103	102	6	74	0.25	41	23	37	31	64	FBc	5%	95	57	12%	10%	125	25%	76%	-0.3	89
20	WAS	189	20	3	15	4	220	2	7	216	293	315	81	107	70	5	68	0.17	35	30	35	30	63	FAc	2%	60	62	8%	5%	117	11%	80%	-12.1	-124
21	WAS *	461	48	5	25	13	218	6	7	230	289	339	86	78	86	9	71	0.35	36	25	39	29	70	FBf	3%	89	80	2%	7%	102	19%	65%	-24.5	27
1st Half		237	24	1	10	8	218	5	4	229	314	314	87	90	89	12	74	0.54	35	26	39	29	76	FBd	4%	72	92	2%	9%	109	19%	61%	-11.3	50
2nd Half		224	24	4	15	5	218	2	3	230	263	363	85	61	80	6	69	0.19	37	24	39	30	61	FBf	1%	106	61	3%	6%	93	19%	72%	-11.6	8
22	Proj	**385**	**46**	**7**	**29**	**14**	**233**	**7**	**10**	**231**	**317**	**363**	**92**	**95**	**91**	**7**	**73**	**0.28**	**36**	**25**	**39**	**30**	**70**		**3%**	**87**	**71**	**7%**	**7%**	**105**	**14%**	**70%**	**-6.2**	**33**

Rodgers,Brendan

Age: 25	Pos: 2B SS	Health	D	LIMA Plan	B
Bats: R	Ht: 6' 0" Wt: 204	PT/Exp	C	Rand Var	-5
		Consist	F	MM	2135

PRO: Nice gains in hard contact skills; actually hit better away from Coors Field; still owns 1st-round-pick status. CON: Subpar Statcast metrics suggest a pull-back; couldn't maintain early bb% gains; again missed nearly two months to inju (hammy). Has promise, but still putting it together. Don't rule out more growing (and actual) pains.

Yr	Tm	PA	R	HR	RBI	SB	BA	xHR	xSB	xBA	OBP	SLG	OPS+	vL+	vR+	bb%	ct%	Eye	G	L	F	h%	HctX	QBaB	Brl%	PX	xPX	HR/F	xHR/F	Spd	SBA%	SB%	RAR	BPX
17	aa	157	17	6	15	0	263		2		295	412	96			4	77	0.20				31				83				96	6%	0%		42
18	a/a	449	39	14	49	9	250		3		289	416	94			5	78	0.25				29				102				92	14%	73%		113
19	COL *	234	31	7	21	0	284	1	5	254	325	436	105	66	74	6	75	0.24	49	22	29	35	79	CDf	4%	87	66	0%	7%	128	0%	0%	3.1	74
20	COL	21	1	0	2	0	95	0	0	165	95	143	32	43	22	0	71	0.00	73	0	27	13	39	FFf		41	23	0%	0%	96	0%	0%	-3.4	-200
21	COL	415	49	15	51	0	284	16	2	267	328	470	110	134	101	5	78	0.23	51	20	29	33	122	CDd	6%	105	97	17%	18%	97	0%	0%	3.3	142
1st Half		132	10	5	19	0	276	5	1	263	356	457	113	136	104	9	79	0.46	48	22	30	31	119	BDb	6%	95	99	18%	18%	111	0%	0%	2.1	177
2nd Half		283	39	10	32	0	288	11	1	269	314	476	107	131	99	3	78	0.13	52	19	29	34	123	CFf	6%	109	96	16%	18%	95	0%	0%	3.2	135
22	Proj	**455**	**51**	**16**	**52**	**2**	**274**	**15**	**2**	**260**	**324**	**449**	**105**	**122**	**98**	**5**	**78**	**0.26**	**50**	**20**	**30**	**32**	**111**		**6%**	**99**	**89**	**16%**	**15%**	**87**	**2%**	**61%**	**10.5**	**87**

Rodríguez,Julio

Age: 21	Pos: RF	Health	A	LIMA Plan	C+
Bats: R	Ht: 6' 3" Wt: 180	PT/Exp	F	Rand Var	
		Consist	F	MM	3323

Consensus Top-3 prospect destroyed MiLB pitching (1.001 OPS overall), hitting even better after promotion to Double-A. Oh yes, he also led the Dominican Republic to a bronze at the Tokyo Olympics. Not a bad summer for a 20-year-old! He'll likely spend some 2022 time in AAA, a la Jarred Kelenic, but this is a future Mariners star.

Yr	Tm	PA	R	HR	RBI	SB	BA	xHR	xSB	xBA	OBP	SLG	OPS+	vL+	vR+	bb%	ct%	Eye	G	L	F	h%	HctX	QBaB	Brl%	PX	xPX	HR/F	xHR/F	Spd	SBA%	SB%	RAR	BPX
17																																		
18																																		
19																																		
20																																		
21	aa	198	29	6	22	13	325		3		408	479	122			12	75	0.56				41				95				92	26%	75%		115
1st Half		25	2	1	3	1	298		0		415	455	121			17	50	0.40				56				138				123	26%	100%		-69
2nd Half		173	27	5	18	13	329		3	253	407	482	120			12	78	0.62	44	20	36	39	0			92	-22	0%		114	26%	74%	9.5	181
22	Proj	**350**	**46**	**12**	**38**	**14**	**265**	**11**	**13**	**246**	**341**	**433**	**105**	**104**	**105**	**10**	**75**	**0.46**	**44**	**20**	**36**	**32**	**102**		**8%**	**100**		**14%**	**13%**	**107**	**19%**	**72%**	**5.9**	**111**

ROD TRUESDELL

Rogers,Jake

Age: 27 Pos: CA	Health	B	LIMA Plan	D
Bats: R Ht: 6' 1" Wt: 205	PT/Exp	F	Rand Var	-5
	Consist	C	MM	4401

Went down in July with a right elbow that ultimately required Tommy John surgery. PRO: Power growth is enticing; good stuff vL; nice walk rate; while Spd is skewed by a few triples, he actually can run a little. CON: So, so many whiffs, which tend to emaciate BA and OBP. He'll miss a good chunk of 2022, but keep him on your "CA-with-pop" list.

Yr	Tm	PA	R	HR	RBI	SB	BA	xHR	xSB	xBA	OBP	SLG	OPS+	vL+	vR+	bb%	ct%	Eye	G	L	F	h%	HctX	QBaB	Brl%	PX	xPX	HR/F	xHR/F	Spd	SBA%	SB%	RAR	BPX	R$
17																																			
18	aa	385	47	14	46	6	197		4		266	362	84			9	66	0.28				25				111				97	10%	84%		10	$5
19	DET *	412	52	17	54	0	199	3	5	207	287	391	94	138	50	11	63	0.33	37	17	46	26	62	FAf	5%	119	99	15%	11%	98	0%	0%	-0.3	0	$3
20																																			
21	DET	127	17	6	17	1	239	6	2	226	306	496	110	124	102	9	59	0.24	20	32	48	34	80	CAd	11%	175	133	19%	19%	182	4%	100%	3.4	196	$1
1st Half		103	12	4	12	1	226	3	2	204	280	430	99	88	104	7	57	0.18	17	35	48	35	79	DAd	10%	143	127	16%	12%	168	4%	100%	-0.2	35	-$2
2nd Half		24	5	2	5	0	300	3	0	337	417	800	165	206	81	17	70	0.67	29	21	50	33	82	AAf	16%	294	157	29%	43%	147	4%	0%	4.4	746	-$7
22	**Proj**	**140**	**17**	**6**	**17**	**1**	**234**	**4**	**1**	**209**	**302**	**429**	**99**	**117**	**92**	**9**	**61**	**0.24**	**25**	**28**	**47**	**33**	**72**		**8%**	**132**	**116**	**16%**	**12%**	**114**	**6%**	**93%**	**3.0**	**-7**	**$1**

Rojas,Jose

Age: 29 Pos: RF	Health	A	LIMA Plan	D
Bats: L Ht: 6' 0" Wt: 200	PT/Exp	B	Rand Var	+5
	Consist	B	MM	3221

6-15-.208 in with 2 SB in 184 PA at LAA. Long-time marginal prospect finally got a look, and brought some of the slugging ability he'd been growing in the minors. He also brought a low BA, although xBA says it wasn't quite that bad. Can play around the infield as well as outfield, so he could carve out a couple of years as a "utility man with muscle."

Yr	Tm	PA	R	HR	RBI	SB	BA	xHR	xSB	xBA	OBP	SLG	OPS+	vL+	vR+	bb%	ct%	Eye	G	L	F	h%	HctX	QBaB	Brl%	PX	xPX	HR/F	xHR/F	Spd	SBA%	SB%	RAR	BPX	R$
17	aa	177	15	4	19	0	205		2		230	324	75			3	76	0.13				25				73				97	4%	0%		3	-$2
18	a/a	407	47	12	50	7	231		2		280	385	89			6	72	0.24				29				100				96	15%	60%		40	$8
19	aaa	551	60	21	64	2	219		8		269	406	94			6	68	0.22				28				114				100	7%	33%		30	$7
20																																			
21	LAA *	413	44	10	34	4	192	8	3	229	246	331	79	114	86	7	74	0.28	35	22	43	23	105	BAc		90	127	12%	16%	95	8%	65%	-35.5	46	$0
1st Half		217	23	5	16	3	173	5	1	231	220	324	76	123	71	6	73	0.23	37	19	44	21	94	CAf	7%	103	127	8%	14%	90	8%	67%	-21.2	62	-$2
2nd Half		195	21	5	18	2	214	3	2	236	276	340	83	83	120	8	75	0.34	31	28	41	26	134	AAa	13%	74	127	23%	23%	106	8%	62%	-13.1	31	$0
22	**Proj**	**175**	**19**	**7**	**18**	**2**	**226**	**8**	**2**	**243**	**279**	**412**	**94**	**93**	**94**	**6**	**73**	**0.25**	**33**	**25**	**42**	**27**	**118**		**10%**	**112**	**127**	**14%**	**16%**	**99**	**8%**	**58%**	**-3.7**	**56**	**$4**

Rojas,Josh

Age: 28 Pos: 2B SS RF	Health	A	LIMA Plan	B
Bats: L Ht: 6' 1" Wt: 200	PT/Exp	A	Rand Var	-5
	Consist	F	MM	2225

PRO: Walk rate sets OBP floor, and means SB upside; does a little in a lot of categories; carries position flexibility. CON: It took a lot of PA to get some mediocre counting stats; Statcast metrics point to little or no additional power to come; average contact keeps a lid on that OBP. Perhaps an unsexy pick, but provides reliable value at the right price.

Yr	Tm	PA	R	HR	RBI	SB	BA	xHR	xSB	xBA	OBP	SLG	OPS+	vL+	vR+	bb%	ct%	Eye	G	L	F	h%	HctX	QBaB	Brl%	PX	xPX	HR/F	xHR/F	Spd	SBA%	SB%	RAR	BPX	R$
17																																			
18	aa	436	56	6	40	23	222		6		304	339	86			11	78	0.53				27				75				111	38%	59%		93	$12
19	ARI *	616	82	18	76	28	265	5	30	270	338	450	109	108	79	10	78	0.50	44	23	33	31	111	CCc	6%	99	139	6%	16%	109	28%	67%	8.6	167	$25
20	ARI	70	9	0	2	1	180	1	3	185	257	180	58	65	52	10	74	0.44	50	20	30	24	89	DFf	0%	0	98	0%	7%	119	11%	50%	-7.1	-184	-$2
21	ARI	546	69	11	44	9	264	13	10	251	341	411	103	105	103	11	72	0.42	49	23	28	35	86	CDb	5%	99	90	11%	13%	117	9%	69%	-2.3	92	$15
1st Half		307	41	10	26	5	251	11	5	254	326	425	105	110	103	10	71	0.38	52	21	27	32	99	CDb	7%	113	106	19%	21%	113	9%	83%	-0.4	112	$16
2nd Half		239	28	1	18	4	282	2	5	246	361	392	102	99	103	11	73	0.48	46	25	29	38	69	CCa	2%	82	70	2%	4%	117	9%	57%	0.7	69	$7
22	**Proj**	**490**	**63**	**9**	**45**	**11**	**255**	**10**	**8**	**252**	**330**	**400**	**99**	**100**	**98**	**10**	**74**	**0.46**	**48**	**23**	**30**	**32**	**89**		**4%**	**94**	**98**	**10%**	**10%**	**113**	**9%**	**56%**	**3.8**	**88**	**$15**

Rojas,Miguel

Age: 33 Pos: SS	Health	B	LIMA Plan	B
Bats: R Ht: 6' 0" Wt: 188	PT/Exp	A	Rand Var	0
	Consist	D	MM	1345

Despite the occasional spike or dip in a category from year to year, this is a fairly stable skill set. Consistently solid contact rate sets BA floor at... well, pretty much what he hit in 2021, but there's still upside. Spike in speed skills look like new path to value, but at 33, last year's SB output could be his peak. Double-digit HR/SB remain his annual goal.

Yr	Tm	PA	R	HR	RBI	SB	BA	xHR	xSB	xBA	OBP	SLG	OPS+	vL+	vR+	bb%	ct%	Eye	G	L	F	h%	HctX	QBaB	Brl%	PX	xPX	HR/F	xHR/F	Spd	SBA%	SB%	RAR	BPX	R$
17	MIA	306	37	1	26	2	290	1	5	285	361	375	100	96	99	9	88	0.84	48	25	27	33	72	FCd	0%	52	32	2%	2%	121	3%	67%	1.8	155	$6
18	MIA	527	44	11	53	6	252	6	3	260	297	346	86	84	85	5	86	0.35	47	24	29	27	85	DCc	1%	51	45	9%	5%	78	7%	67%	-6.6	63	$10
19	MIA	526	52	5	46	9	284	6	7	275	331	379	98	105	95	6	87	0.52	47	24	30	32	107	CDb	3%	54	65	4%	5%	104	10%	64%	-5.6	137	$12
20	MIA	143	20	4	20	5	304	2	3	292	392	496	118	186	90	11	86	0.89	41	25	35	33	107	CCc	1%	103	91	11%	5%	105	15%	83%	8.7	324	$17
21	MIA	539	66	9	48	13	265	8	13	265	322	392	98	120	89	7	85	0.50	45	21	34	30	86	DCc	3%	73	60	6%	6%	122	12%	81%	-2.6	196	$16
1st Half		247	36	4	23	5	251	4	6	259	324	390	99	128	86	8	85	0.61	39	21	40	28	92	CCc	2%	80	73	5%	5%	128	12%	83%	-2.4	238	$10
2nd Half		292	30	5	25	8	276	4	7	270	320	393	96	113	90	6	85	0.41	50	21	29	31	82	DCc	3%	68	49	7%	6%	109	12%	80%	-1.0	158	$14
22	**Proj**	**525**	**63**	**9**	**54**	**11**	**276**	**7**	**11**	**271**	**336**	**405**	**101**	**127**	**90**	**7**	**86**	**0.56**	**45**	**23**	**32**	**31**	**93**		**2%**	**74**	**63**	**7%**	**5%**	**104**	**10%**	**77%**	**7.1**	**181**	**$19**

Rooker,Brent

Age: 27 Pos: LF	Health	A	LIMA Plan	D
Bats: R Ht: 6' 3" Wt: 225	PT/Exp	C	Rand Var	+5
	Consist	C	MM	4103

9-16-.201 in 213 PA at MIN. Intriguing power prospect continues to struggle to put bat on ball, with predictable results. Shows some oomph when he does make contact (see exit velocity, Brl%), but a troublesome launch angle is keeping the lid on HR output as well. Too many warts to see a breakout coming, but enough here to keep us watching.

Yr	Tm	PA	R	HR	RBI	SB	BA	xHR	xSB	xBA	OBP	SLG	OPS+	vL+	vR+	bb%	ct%	Eye	G	L	F	h%	HctX	QBaB	Brl%	PX	xPX	HR/F	xHR/F	Spd	SBA%	SB%	RAR	BPX	R$
17																																			
18	aa	546	56	18	62	5	224		6		285	398	92			8	67	0.26				30				121				97	6%	81%		43	$9
19	aaa	256	33	11	38	2	248		2		332	464	110			11	53	0.27				41				167				86	3%	100%		-11	$5
20	MIN	21	4	1	5	0	316	1	0	324	381	579	127	99	140	0	74	0.00	36	43	21	38	107	CFf	14%	164	134	33%	33%	96	0%	0%	0.7	228	$0
21	MIN *	462	54	23	52	1	201	12	1	225	278	418	96	95	94	9	59	0.26	36	25	39	27	90	ACc	13%	153	123	20%	26%	87	3%	23%	-23.5	27	$4
1st Half		215	21	12	25	1	189	1	1	196	284	415	97	0	79	12	56	0.30	38	13	50	26	43	DCf	13%	165	88	13%	13%	95	3%	23%	-11.3	35	$3
2nd Half		247	33	12	26	0	212	11	1	237	274	420	94	109	96	8	62	0.23	36	27	37	28	102	ACc	13%	144	129	21%	29%	88	3%	0%	-11.1	35	$6
22	**Proj**	**315**	**37**	**13**	**38**	**1**	**233**	**16**	**2**	**213**	**327**	**424**	**102**	**86**	**110**	**10**	**61**	**0.27**	**37**	**21**	**42**	**33**	**91**		**13%**	**137**	**113**	**18%**	**22%**	**88**	**4%**	**63%**	**-0.2**	**-30**	**$8**

Rosario,Amed

Age: 26 Pos: SS	Health	A	LIMA Plan	C+
Bats: R Ht: 6' 2" Wt: 190	PT/Exp	A	Rand Var	-2
	Consist	C	MM	1525

Reclaimed SS job after Andres Giménez faltered. After that, the now-familiar cry of "why doesn't he run more?" rang out from his fantasy managers across the land. And it's a fair question, as he still owns the 20-plus steal speed. And yet, he's still earning $20 without it. Imagine the possibilities a green light would bring... UP: 30+ SB, $30+ R$.

Yr	Tm	PA	R	HR	RBI	SB	BA	xHR	xSB	xBA	OBP	SLG	OPS+	vL+	vR+	bb%	ct%	Eye	G	L	F	h%	HctX	QBaB	Brl%	PX	xPX	HR/F	xHR/F	Spd	SBA%	SB%	RAR	BPX	R$
17	NYM *	582	65	10	53	21	267	2	8	246	294	381	92	112	82	4	77	0.17	51	20	29	33	75	DDb	3%	65	73	12%	6%	169	23%	68%	-11.9	58	$18
18	NYM	592	76	9	51	24	256	11	20	253	295	381	91	99	86	5	79	0.24	50	21	30	31	80	CDc	4%	75	71	7%	9%	163	27%	69%	-6.4	117	$19
19	NYM	655	75	15	72	19	287	13	26	266	323	432	104	123	98	5	80	0.25	48	22	29	34	92	BDb	4%	75	65	10%	9%	149	18%	66%	-5.8	133	$23
20	NYM	147	20	4	15	0	252	3	4	231	272	371	85	101	73	3	76	0.12	58	16	27	30	68	DFc	4%	62	40	14%	10%	152	3%	0%	-5.4	32	$7
21	CLE	588	77	11	57	13	282	11	7	255	321	409	100	114	94	5	78	0.26	51	21	28	34	92	CFd	3%	74	58	9%	9%	156	9%	100%	2.6	119	$22
1st Half		285	39	5	23	7	264	5	4	254	316	377	97	108	90	6	78	0.32	50	24	26	32	89	CFc	3%	60	56	9%	9%	183	9%	100%	-2.7	119	$15
2nd Half		303	38	6	34	6	298	6	4	255	327	439	104	121	96	4	78	0.21	53	17	30	37	94	CDd	3%	87	60	9%	9%	134	9%	100%	6.3	123	$19
22	**Proj**	**630**	**81**	**13**	**64**	**14**	**275**	**12**	**12**	**251**	**307**	**405**	**97**	**111**	**90**	**4**	**78**	**0.21**	**52**	**20**	**28**	**33**	**85**		**3%**	**74**	**58**	**10%**	**9%**	**143**	**10%**	**77%**	**2.4**	**66**	**$24**

Rosario,Eddie

Age: 30 Pos: LF	Health	C	LIMA Plan	B
Bats: L Ht: 6' 1" Wt: 180	PT/Exp	A	Rand Var	+3
	Consist	A	MM	3345

14-62-.259 with 11 SB in 412 PA at MIN/ATL. Hit for a cycle in Sept, but a see-saw fits season better. After poor start with MIN, ended mercifully by July ab strain, got traded to ATL and raked (.903 OPS in 106 PA). The 2019 HR total is unlikely to repeat, but fine contact skills and late-year reversion to form peg him as a decent rebound pick.

Yr	Tm	PA	R	HR	RBI	SB	BA	xHR	xSB	xBA	OBP	SLG	OPS+	vL+	vR+	bb%	ct%	Eye	G	L	F	h%	HctX	QBaB	Brl%	PX	xPX	HR/F	xHR/F	Spd	SBA%	SB%	RAR	BPX	R$
17	MIN	589	79	27	78	9	290	25	7	281	328	507	114	92	121	6	80	0.33	42	20	37	32	103	CCc	7%	119	121	16%	15%	107	13%	53%	8.2	191	$23
18	MIN	592	87	24	77	8	288	24	11	259	323	479	108	96	111	5	81	0.29	36	20	44	32	109	CAd	8%	108	126	12%	12%	106	7%	80%	15.1	187	$24
19	MIN	590	91	32	109	3	276	31	6	278	300	500	111	107	111	4	85	0.26	37	20	42	28	114	CBd	9%	104	120	16%	15%	87	3%	75%	2.1	215	$22
20	MIN	231	31	13	42	3	257	10	2	258	316	476	105	70	117	8	84	0.56	35	18	47	25	103	CBf	6%	103	135	16%	12%	101	8%	75%	-0.3	264	$24
21	2 TM *	464	47	17	73	11	246	17	5	268	291	425	98	89	107	6	84	0.40	37	23	40	26	108	CBf	6%	93	111	11%	13%	99	15%	79%	-13.8	208	$15
1st Half		301	28	6	45	9	255	9	4	255	298	381	95	92	96	6	83	0.36	39	23	38	29	101	CCf	4%	73	98	7%	10%	94	15%	82%	-11.5	127	$18
2nd Half		163	19	11	28	2	228	7	1	288	278	504	106	71	132	6	86	0.48	32	22	47	20	128	CAf	10%	128	143	20%	17%	113	15%	67%	-3.8	362	$6
22	**Proj**	**490**	**62**	**25**	**82**	**8**	**265**	**23**	**9**	**270**	**307**	**483**	**107**	**84**	**115**	**6**	**84**	**0.40**	**36**	**21**	**44**	**27**	**112**		**8%**	**110**	**126**	**15%**	**14%**	**100**	**12%**	**74%**	**11.0**	**244**	**$22**

ROD TRUESDELL

Ruf,Darin

Age: 35	Pos: 1B LF	Health	B	LIMA Plan	C+
Bats: R	Ht: 6' 2" Wt: 232	PT/Exp	B	Rand Var	-1
		Consist	A	MM	4253

Missed some time with hammy and oblique injuries, but otherwise, a nice follow-up in his first full year back from Korea. Sure, the ct% plunge is a bit troubling, but 2nd half was better. And even in mid-30s, his power seems sustainable given step up in metrics. He's not even lost vR, but probably too late for him to graduate from part-time slugger role.

Yr	Tm	PA	R	HR	RBI	SB	BA	xHR	xSB	xBA	OBP	SLG	OPS+	vL+	vR+	bb%	ct%	Eye	G	L	F	h%	HctX	QBaB	Brl%	PX	xPX	HR/F	xHR/F	Spd	SBA%	SB%	RAR	BPX
17	for	563	88	19	121	2	293		8		354	475	113			9	80	0.48				33	0			107				75	3%	45%	8.9	148
18	for	558	95	20	122	5	308		5		372	513	119			9	80	0.52				35	0			118				105	5%	57%	32.2	223
19	for	536	78	13	98	5	272		6		360	443	111			12	83	0.78				31	0			91				96	6%	62%	4.9	215
20	SF	100	11	5	18	1	276	4	1	283	370	517	118	116	113	13	74	0.57	39	28	33	32	88	BCd	9%	141	87	24%	19%	66	4%	100%	3.9	220
21	SF	312	41	16	43	2	271	18	3	263	385	519	124	137	114	15	67	0.53	43	26	31	35	110	ACc	14%	155	136	29%	33%	97	2%	100%	12.7	200
1st Half		122	19	6	15	1	240	6	1	249	369	470	117	135	101	17	63	0.54	50	23	27	32	113	ADb	14%	156	119	35%	35%	84	2%	100%	1.5	142
2nd Half		190	22	10	28	1	290	12	2	270	395	549	128	138	120	14	69	0.52	38	28	34	36	109	ACc	14%	155	146	26%	32%	101	2%	100%	10.6	235
22	Proj	315	43	17	49	2	277	16	2	281	377	535	124	133	114	13	72	0.56	42	27	31	32	105		12%	152	123	27%	26%	72	2%	84%	20.2	234

Ruiz,Keibert

Age: 23	Pos: CA	Health	A	LIMA Plan	C+
Bats: R	Ht: 6' 0" Wt: 225	PT/Exp	C	Rand Var	-1
		Consist	C	MM	2033

3-15-.273 in 96 PA at LA/WAS. This 22-year-old top catching prospect looked the part in first extended MLB stint. Impressively, he struck out just 9 times in those 96 MLB PA, flashing the outstanding plate skills he's shown through his ascent to the majors. Still a work-in-progress defensively, but the seeds are there for a real asset at the dish.

Yr	Tm	PA	R	HR	RBI	SB	BA	xHR	xSB	xBA	OBP	SLG	OPS+	vL+	vR+	bb%	ct%	Eye	G	L	F	h%	HctX	QBaB	Brl%	PX	xPX	HR/F	xHR/F	Spd	SBA%	SB%	RAR	BPX
17																																		
18	aa	397	35	10	37	0	240		4		278	351	84			5	90	0.55				24				58				87	1%	0%		153
19	a/a	338	32	5	28	0	236		2		289	312	83			7	92	0.97				24				35				95	0%	0%		156
20	LA	8	1	1	1	0	250	1	0	264	250	625	116	0	116	0	63	0.00	20	20	60	25	51	CAf	20%	214	123	33%	33%	100	0%	0%	0.3	212
21	2 NL *	403	48	20	60	0	280	2	1	274	332	513	116	103	102	7	88	0.64	42	15	43	27	105	DAc	3%	118	64	9%	6%	76	0%	0%	20.8	327
1st Half		152	23	10	22	0	258	1	0	251	326	551	122	0	117	9	82	0.56	50	0	50	25	336	ABa	50%	156	352	100%	100%	77	0%	0%	8.3	373
2nd Half		251	25	10	38	0	293	1	1	266	336	490	112	105	98	6	91	0.74	42	16	43	29	102	DAc	1%	98	56	6%	3%	77	0%	0%	12.0	312
22	Proj	420	46	15	53	0	263	16	1	264	327	430	103	98	105	7	89	0.66	41	19	41	26	92		6%	85	50	10%	11%	82	2%	0%	12.5	187

Ruiz,Rio

Age: 28	Pos: 2B	Health	A	LIMA Plan	D
Bats: L	Ht: 6' 1" Wt: 215	PT/Exp	C	Rand Var	+1
		Consist	A	MM	2111

3-10-.168 in 141 PA at BAL/COL. When you're released by the worst team in the American League, let's just say it's not a good sign for your long-term career outlook. Not that he fared any better in the senior circuit. Fortunately for him, lefty-hitting infielders do tend to get extra chances. It's just that we have to squint hard to see a "hitter" here.

Yr	Tm	PA	R	HR	RBI	SB	BA	xHR	xSB	xBA	OBP	SLG	OPS+	vL+	vR+	bb%	ct%	Eye	G	L	F	h%	HctX	QBaB	Brl%	PX	xPX	HR/F	xHR/F	Spd	SBA%	SB%	RAR	BPX
17	ATL *	599	64	17	68	2	199	5	7	214	277	335	83	193	69	10	68	0.33	56	13	30	26	91	CFc	6%	87	123	12%	15%	78	3%	45%	-40.6	-39
18	ATL *	543	58	7	57	2	234	0	3	233	280	332	82	0	46	6	79	0.31	57	14	29	28	125	BFf	0%	62	116	0%	0%	91	3%	59%	-24.4	27
19	BAL *	436	36	13	52	0	231	8	3	240	303	372	93	87	95	9	76	0.44	45	21	34	27	92	CCf	3%	73	91	13%	8%	95	1%	0%	-20.4	48
20	BAL	204	25	9	32	1	222	5	0	252	286	427	95	102	93	8	75	0.37	47	17	36	25	95	CCf	9%	118	89	18%	10%	74	8%	33%	-8.2	144
21	2 TM *	377	33	7	26	4	217	3	3	232	267	346	84	117	64	6	76	0.29	49	16	35	26	66	DDf	4%	83	63	10%	10%	83	7%	75%	-24.6	38
1st Half		223	20	5	12	3	212	3	2	237	269	360	88	115	71	7	74	0.30	44	18	38	26	54	DCf	5%	98	56	13%	13%	98	7%	72%	-12.6	77
2nd Half		154	13	3	14	1	225	1	1	216	265	327	80	121	49	5	79	0.26	61	11	29	27	93	CFd	4%	63	76	0%	13%	72	7%	100%	-9.7	4
22	Proj	140	14	3	15	1	221	3	1	231	272	352	85	122	78	7	76	0.32	51	16	33	26	85		5%	81	82	10%	10%	83	6%	63%	-3.6	12

Rutschman,Adley

Age: 24	Pos: CA	Health	A	LIMA Plan	D+
Bats: R	Ht: 6' 2" Wt: 216	PT/Exp	B	Rand Var	0
		Consist	F	MM	2123

A top-3 prospect on most lists, the former Oregon State star reached AAA in his first full MiLB season. Sporting an enticin combination of power and plate skills, he's almost certain to reach the majors in BAL at some point in 2022. Keep in mind the game can move fast for a rookie catcher. But long-term, this one's a keeper league gem.

Yr	Tm	PA	R	HR	RBI	SB	BA	xHR	xSB	xBA	OBP	SLG	OPS+	vL+	vR+	bb%	ct%	Eye	G	L	F	h%	HctX	QBaB	Brl%	PX	xPX	HR/F	xHR/F	Spd	SBA%	SB%	RAR	BPX
17																																		
18																																		
19																																		
20																																		
21	a/a	511	65	19	56	2	249		6		336	428	105			12	79	0.61				28				100				95	4%	40%		185
1st Half		221	28	9	25	1	238		3		337	414	104			13	80	0.74				26				94				91	4%	39%		188
2nd Half		289	36	10	30	2	255		3	256	330	433	103			10	78	0.50	44	20	36	29	0			102	-22	0%		109	4%	40%	5.1	181
22	Proj	315	40	10	34	2	259	10	3	248	342	417	103	102	103	11	78	0.59	42	21	37	30	85		8%	91		12%	12%	94	5%	50%	10.4	104

Sánchez,Gary

Age: 29	Pos: CA	Health	C	LIMA Plan	D+
Bats: R	Ht: 6' 2" Wt: 230	PT/Exp	A	Rand Var	+1
		Consist	D	MM	4003

PRO: Contact rate returned to nearly tolerable levels; great Brl%; strong 1st half. CON: Exit velocity cratered in 2nd half, and power, BA with it (.350 SLG?!?); career-worst HctX, xPX. Maybe his Aug bout with COVID affected the pop, but then July wasn't any better. Overall, this is what he is now, and a full-time job is no longer guaranteed. DN: 250 PA

Yr	Tm	PA	R	HR	RBI	SB	BA	xHR	xSB	xBA	OBP	SLG	OPS+	vL+	vR+	bb%	ct%	Eye	G	L	F	h%	HctX	QBaB	Brl%	PX	xPX	HR/F	xHR/F	Spd	SBA%	SB%	RAR	BPX
17	NYY	525	79	33	90	2	278	32	7	275	345	531	119	119	117	8	75	0.33	42	21	37	31	111	BCc	12%	140	114	25%	25%	84	2%	67%	28.2	161
18	NYY *	402	54	22	56	1	184	23	1	241	279	417	93	116	84	11	70	0.44	43	14	43	19	91	BBf	14%	147	116	18%	23%	50	1%	100%	3.0	123
19	NYY	446	62	34	77	0	232	36	2	252	316	525	116	106	119	9	68	0.32	32	20	48	24	100	AAd	19%	156	141	26%	28%	76	1%	0%	19.3	152
20	NYY	178	19	10	24	0	147	10	0	200	253	365	82	79	82	10	59	0.28	38	16	46	16	99	AAd	17%	143	147	24%	24%	62	0%	0%	-8.1	-32
21	NYY	440	54	23	54	0	204	24	1	228	307	423	100	114	95	12	68	0.43	36	18	46	23	86	BAc	14%	131	103	19%	20%	79	0%	0%	-1.0	108
1st Half		240	30	14	32	0	233	14	1	246	342	485	115	127	110	13	69	0.49	37	18	45	26	89	AAd	14%	153	106	22%	22%	66	0%	0%	7.9	185
2nd Half		200	24	9	22	0	169	10	0	205	265	350	83	97	77	11	67	0.36	35	17	48	19	83	CAc	14%	105	100	16%	18%	109	0%	0%	-7.7	35
22	Proj	385	49	22	53	0	203	23	1	225	299	430	99	107	96	11	67	0.36	37	17	46	23	92		15%	138	119	21%	22%	68	1%	51%	4.6	54

Sánchez,Jesús

Age: 24	Pos: RF LF	Health	B	LIMA Plan	B
Bats: L	Ht: 6' 3" Wt: 222	PT/Exp	C	Rand Var	-5
		Consist	F	MM	4235

14-36-.251 in 251 PA at MIA. The power that scouts had predicted finally started to show. Cranked a career-best 24 HR between AAA and the majors, cresting with an impressive 8 round-trippers in Sept for the Marlins. Still some holes in his plate skills, but it's exciting to see a toolsy hitter turn some of those tools into results. The arrow's trending up.

Yr	Tm	PA	R	HR	RBI	SB	BA	xHR	xSB	xBA	OBP	SLG	OPS+	vL+	vR+	bb%	ct%	Eye	G	L	F	h%	HctX	QBaB	Brl%	PX	xPX	HR/F	xHR/F	Spd	SBA%	SB%	RAR	BPX
17																																		
18	aa	108	12	1	10	1	191		1		263	290	74			9	76	0.40				24				76				95	10%	45%		40
19	a/a	454	49	12	63	5	245		7		310	369	94			9	74	0.36				31				67				103	8%	54%		0
20	MIA	29	1	0	2	0	40	0	0	138	172	80	34	0	45	14	56	0.36	57	14	29	7	97	ADf	7%	44	80	0%	0%	97	0%	0%	-4.4	-324
21	MIA *	402	46	22	61	1	271	15	3	255	326	510	115	109	112	7	70	0.27	45	21	34	33	108	BDc	13%	137	141	27%	29%	133	2%	45%	6.0	173
1st Half		200	19	9	30	1	288	2	2	249	329	490	114	111	91	6	73	0.23	55	15	30	35	97	AFf	8%	112	103	17%	17%	128	2%	100%	3.9	131
2nd Half		201	27	13	31	0	253	13	1	258	323	531	115	107	117	9	66	0.30	42	23	35	31	108	BCc	14%	166	155	31%	33%	129	2%	0%	3.5	215
22	Proj	525	61	26	73	3	260	30	4	255	328	486	110	112	109	8	71	0.31	47	20	33	31	104		12%	130	134	23%	26%	117	5%	49%	12.1	120

Sanó,Miguel

Age: 29	Pos: 1B	Health	C	LIMA Plan	B
Bats: R	Ht: 6' 4" Wt: 272	PT/Exp	A	Rand Var	+2
		Consist	B	MM	5015

Archetypical all-or-nothing slugger took a baby step forward. Statcast metrics still show his prodigious clout, but trimming the whiffs a smidgen in the 2nd half turned him into a real asset—without killing power. As we often say, regression is a mighty force, so let's see that ct% again to really believe it. But if it sticks? UP: .250 BA, 40 HR (still)

Yr	Tm	PA	R	HR	RBI	SB	BA	xHR	xSB	xBA	OBP	SLG	OPS+	vL+	vR+	bb%	ct%	Eye	G	L	F	h%	HctX	QBaB	Brl%	PX	xPX	HR/F	xHR/F	Spd	SBA%	SB%	RAR	BPX
17	MIN	483	75	28	77	0	264	28	7	229	352	507	117	134	109	11	59	0.31	39	21	40	38	107	ACc	16%	166	148	27%	27%	99	0%	0%	8.8	73
18	MIN *	334	34	15	45	0	204	14	1	201	290	404	93	85	91	11	58	0.29	44	15	41	29	91	BCd	11%	156	121	21%	22%	71	0%	0%	-6.0	7
19	MIN *	474	78	35	84	0	245	34	2	246	336	562	124	140	122	12	58	0.32	37	21	42	33	105	ABd	21%	210	175	37%	37%	90	1%	0%	17.1	193
20	MIN	205	31	13	25	0	204	15	0	224	278	478	100	72	109	9	52	0.20	36	24	40	30	100	AAb	23%	222	148	34%	39%	75	0%	0%	-6.7	104
21	MIN	532	68	30	75	2	223	31	0	229	312	466	107	96	112	11	61	0.32	39	18	43	29	114	AAf	18%	169	138	24%	25%	47	3%	67%	-9.3	69
1st Half		234	28	14	34	0	191	13	0	204	274	421	97	75	111	10	57	0.26	37	17	46	25	95	AAf	14%	161	123	25%	23%	57	3%	0%	-13.5	-12
2nd Half		298	40	16	41	2	249	18	0	247	342	502	114	120	112	12	64	0.38	40	20	40	32	128	ABc	20%	174	149	24%	27%	51	3%	67%	0.9	142
22	Proj	525	72	32	76	1	224	34	2	230	310	484	108	100	111	11	58	0.29	39	20	42	30	108		19%	189	145	28%	30%	63	2%	60%	6.1	87

ROD TRUESDELL

Santana,Carlos

Age: 36 Pos: 1B | Bats: B Ht: 5' 11" Wt: 210
Health A | PT/Exp A | Consist C | LIMA Plan C | Rand Var +2 | MM 2225

In terms of R$, this was his worst season since his rookie year. It was a tale of two halves; strong early results came in spite of underperforming HR/F, then bottom fell out of hit and HR/F rates late. Rand Var summarizes support for rebound, and multiplying his 1st half by two gets you to his prior baseline. With enough PT, there's still profit here.

Yr Tm	PA	R	HR	RBI	SB	BA	xHR	xSB	xBA	OBP	SLG	OPS+	vL+	vR+	bb%	ct%	Eye	G	L	F	h%	HctX	QBaB	Brl%	PX	xPX	HR/F	xHR/F	Spd	SBA%	SB%	RAR	BPX	R$
17 CLE	667	90	23	79	5	259	24	10	278	363	455	111	105	113	13	84	0.94	41	20	39	28	112	CCf	8%	106	102	12%	13%	87	3%	83%	4.2	221	$16
18 PHI	679	82	24	86	2	229	23	5	253	352	414	103	108	99	16	83	1.18	40	16	44	23	101	CBf	7%	101	112	12%	11%	82	2%	67%	7.3	243	$13
19 CLE	686	110	34	93	4	281	28	4	276	397	515	126	136	121	16	81	1.00	45	17	38	29	121	ACd	10%	114	112	19%	16%	77	2%	100%	37.9	267	$24
20 CLE	255	34	8	30	0	199	10	1	231	349	350	93	99	89	18	79	1.09	43	18	40	21	109	CCf	7%	79	106	12%	15%	72	0%	0%	-9.7	160	$9
21 KC	659	66	19	69	2	214	27	1	235	319	342	91	98	88	13	82	0.84	46	18	37	23	113	BCf	7%	66	98	11%	16%	61	1%	100%	-31.9	104	$6
1st Half	347	44	13	47	2	247	17	0	247	366	411	108	117	105	16	83	1.06	43	18	39	26	121	BCf	9%	82	113	14%	18%	70	1%	100%	-4.4	192	$20
2nd Half	312	22	6	22	0	180	9	0	214	266	270	73	80	69	11	81	0.63	48	18	34	20	105	BCf	5%	49	82	8%	12%	61	1%	0%	-30.5	23	-$5
22 Proj	525	62	17	59	1	235	20	2	241	349	386	100	107	96	15	81	0.94	44	18	38	25	111		7%	80	102	12%	14%	68	2%	92%	0.5	135	$8

Santander,Anthony

Age: 27 Pos: RF DH | Bats: B Ht: 6' 2" Wt: 225
Health C | PT/Exp A | Consist C | LIMA Plan B+ | Rand Var 0 | MM 3035

Just when we thought a breakout was in cards, he stumbles out of gate. Was 2020 a short-season anomaly, or is there still hope for more? PRO: QBaB, xPX spikes in 2nd half; surging pre-'21 xPX. CON: Mid-70s ct% seems like his true baseline; xBA three of last four years gives little hope for improvement there. Buy the homers, hope for more. UP: 30 HR

Yr Tm	PA	R	HR	RBI	SB	BA	xHR	xSB	xBA	OBP	SLG	OPS+	vL+	vR+	bb%	ct%	Eye	G	L	F	h%	HctX	QBaB	Brl%	PX	xPX	HR/F	xHR/F	Spd	SBA%	SB%	RAR	BPX	R$
17 BAL *	87	12	4	14	0	300	0	1	304	352	535	121	51	95	7	76	0.34	22	35	43	35	121	CAc	0%	139	115	0%	0%	80	0%	0%	4.3	173	$2
18 BAL *	370	31	7	29	4	209	3	1	236	242	327	76	75	71	4	81	0.23	39	20	41	24	94	CBf	5%	69	77	3%	9%	98	8%	78%	-21.5	67	$1
19 BAL *	608	69	24	80	3	246	17	6	245	282	431	99	113	103	5	78	0.23	39	18	43	28	102	BBd	8%	99	110	16%	13%	90	6%	43%	-17.7	104	$13
20 BAL	165	24	11	32	0	261	8	1	308	315	575	118	85	126	6	84	0.40	24	27	50	25	124	CAc	10%	159	129	17%	13%	75	4%	0%	4.4	396	$16
21 BAL	438	54	18	50	1	241	19	2	251	286	433	99	95	101	5	75	0.23	34	23	43	28	110	BAd		115	109	13%	14%	64	2%	50%	-10.3	92	$8
1st Half	212	19	5	21	0	236	6	1	254	280	385	92	98	90	5	74	0.22	37	26	36	29	100	CCd	8%	99	83	9%	11%	65	2%	0%	-9.4	35	$1
2nd Half	226	35	13	29	1	246	13	1	251	292	479	104	92	113	5	76	0.24	31	19	50	27	119	AAd	9%	130	133	16%	16%	75	2%	100%	-2.4	165	$11
22 Proj	560	71	25	75	2	244	25	2	258	287	453	100	93	103	5	78	0.24	33	22	45	27	110		8%	119	112	14%	13%	72	3%	47%	-2.6	138	$16

Schoop,Jonathan

Age: 30 Pos: 1B 2B | Bats: R Ht: 6' 1" Wt: 225
Health A | PT/Exp A | Consist A | LIMA Plan B | Rand Var -2 | MM 2225

One of the more consistent profiles around. Has proven that $20 threshold is fully dependent on batting average. xBA tells the true story there; he's a .250 hitter. Still, 20 homers from a middle-infielder is nothing to sneeze at, and xHR fully validates that level of power in spite of consistently marginal QBaB.

Yr Tm	PA	R	HR	RBI	SB	BA	xHR	xSB	xBA	OBP	SLG	OPS+	vL+	vR+	bb%	ct%	Eye	G	L	F	h%	HctX	QBaB	Brl%	PX	xPX	HR/F	xHR/F	Spd	SBA%	SB%	RAR	BPX	R$
17 BAL	675	92	32	105	1	293	22	9	270	338	503	114	129	107	5	77	0.25	42	21	37	33	113	CCd	7%	120	113	18%	12%	67	1%	100%	10.7	112	$25
18 2 TM	501	61	21	61	1	233	14	1	249	266	416	91	86	92	4	76	0.17	45	18	37	26	78	DCf	5%	110	79	16%	11%	72	2%	50%	-11.7	73	$10
19 MIN	464	61	23	59	1	256	18	2	256	304	473	108	128	100	4	73	0.17	43	20	37	30	98	CCd	9%	119	103	20%	15%	78	2%	50%	-3.2	81	$11
20 DET	176	26	8	23	0	278	6	2	255	324	475	106	96	108	5	76	0.21	51	18	30	32	74	CDf	6%	100	49	21%	16%	147	0%	0%	-0.6	156	$14
21 DET	674	85	22	84	2	278	24	2	253	320	435	104	126	95	5	79	0.28	48	19	33	32	98	CCf	7%	90	66	13%	15%	85	1%	100%	-8.3	96	$21
1st Half	333	42	16	49	1	283	15	1	261	330	490	114	128	109	6	78	0.31	48	18	34	32	103	CCf	9%	113	77	20%	18%	94	1%	100%	1.0	169	$25
2nd Half	341	43	6	35	1	273	9	1	245	311	382	94	124	80	5	80	0.25	48	21	32	33	94	CCf	5%	69	56	7%	11%	79	1%	100%	-13.7	35	$14
22 Proj	595	80	23	77	1	263	21	3	252	306	437	101	114	96	5	77	0.22	47	19	33	31	92		7%	98	71	16%	14%	88	3%	80%	4.2	72	$19

Schrock,Max

Age: 27 Pos: LF | Bats: L Ht: 5' 9" Wt: 185
Health B | PT/Exp D | Consist C | LIMA Plan D | Rand Var -4 | MM 1211

3-14-.288 in 134 PA at CIN. Shiny batting average in majors will draw attention, but it's not sticking. In fact, 25-point gap with xBA, mid-80s exit velocity, and tiny barrel rate all inhibit any value he can provide with his bat. Only path to value is with his legs, as backed by Spd trend. But xSB history makes us disinterested there too. Pass.

Yr Tm	PA	R	HR	RBI	SB	BA	xHR	xSB	xBA	OBP	SLG	OPS+	vL+	vR+	bb%	ct%	Eye	G	L	F	h%	HctX	QBaB	Brl%	PX	xPX	HR/F	xHR/F	Spd	SBA%	SB%	RAR	BPX	R$
17 aa	444	45	5	37	3	286		7		329	369	95			6	89	0.60				31				46				95	4%	59%		109	$9
18 aaa	435	31	3	32	8	212		3		245	278	70			4	90	0.45				23				42				85	16%	57%		103	$1
19 aaa	292	32	1	24	9	230		6		302	315	85			9	79	0.49				29				56				98	16%	80%		37	$3
20 STL	17	1	1	1	0	176	0	0	183	176	353	70	457	18	0	65	0.00	36	18	45	20	71	FAf	9%	97	19	20%	0%	104	0%	0%	-1.7	-116	-$3
21 CIN *	268	30	8	28	1	264	2	2	240	301	415	98	52	112	5	78	0.24	31	25	44	31	109	DAa	3%	84	93	7%	4%	130	3%	50%	-7.1	115	$5
1st Half	58	5	2	5	0	266	1	0	235	299	457	105	0	119	4	76	0.20	32	18	50	32	127	ABa	5%	109	183	9%	9%	138	3%	0%	-0.9	169	-$6
2nd Half	210	25	6	24	1	263	1	2	244	302	403	95	57	108	5	78	0.26	31	26	43	31	104	FAb	3%	78	69	6%	3%	111	3%	50%	-6.9	85	$6
22 Proj	245	24	4	22	3	251	5	2	233	291	368	89	41	93	6	82	0.32	31	23	45	29	113		3%	68	115	5%	5%	109	5%	67%	-4.8	57	$6

Schwarber,Kyle

Age: 29 Pos: LF | Bats: L Ht: 6' 0" Wt: 225
Health B | PT/Exp A | Consist D | LIMA Plan C+ | Rand Var -2 | MM 5135

Take away the 2020 sprint season and check out his BPX trend. Those soaring skills suggest he hasn't peaked yet, especially if his gains against southpaws stick. Elite barrel rate confirms his upper-tier production upside. Only nit here is likely hit rate erosion given its prior baseline. Don't let it prevent you from speculating on... UP: 40 HR

Yr Tm	PA	R	HR	RBI	SB	BA	xHR	xSB	xBA	OBP	SLG	OPS+	vL+	vR+	bb%	ct%	Eye	G	L	F	h%	HctX	QBaB	Brl%	PX	xPX	HR/F	xHR/F	Spd	SBA%	SB%	RAR	BPX	R$
17 CHC *	527	74	33	66	1	217	30	7	234	315	476	108	87	109	12	64	0.40	38	15	46	25	94	BAd	15%	163	125	24%	24%	76	2%	50%	-5.7	109	$8
18 CHC	510	64	26	61	4	238	26	4	243	356	467	110	87	113	15	67	0.56	44	19	37	29	100	ACc	13%	143	120	25%	25%	99	5%	57%	11.6	153	$13
19 CHC	610	82	38	92	2	250	40	4	263	339	531	120	105	123	11	71	0.45	38	20	42	28	102	ABc	15%	154	140	24%	25%	77	4%	40%	13.4	196	$18
20 CHC	224	30	11	24	1	188	11	1	220	308	393	93	78	99	13	65	0.45	51	15	35	22	108	ADd	11%	124	128	26%	26%	86	2%	100%	-10.5	64	$9
21 2 TM	471	76	32	71	1	266	36	2	263	374	554	127	107	137	14	68	0.50	38	21	41	31	109	ABc	18%	174	136	29%	32%	69	2%	50%	18.0	238	$18
1st Half	303	42	25	53	1	253	26	1	266	340	570	127	102	137	10	67	0.35	40	20	40	28	105	ABc	19%	189	144	35%	37%	63	2%	50%	7.9	231	$27
2nd Half	168	34	7	18	0	291	10	1	257	435	522	129	116	136	20	71	0.85	35	22	43	36	116	ABd	15%	148	120	17%	24%	90	2%	0%	10.2	269	$7
22 Proj	560	89	34	78	2	256	36	3	252	369	518	120	104	126	15	68	0.54	41	19	40	30	107		15%	161	130	26%	27%	79	2%	59%	29.6	188	$21

Schwindel,Frank

Age: 30 Pos: 1B | Bats: R Ht: 6' 1" Wt: 215
Health A | PT/Exp C | Consist D | LIMA Plan B+ | Rand Var -5 | MM 2135

14-43-.326 in 259 PA at OAK/CHC. Hitting for both average and power at AAA got him another MLB look, and boy did he take advantage of it. Triple-digit BPVs in Aug/Sep seem to back it up, but a deeper look reveals warts. Batted ball quality just wasn't there, and these circa age-30 breakouts rarely stick. Expect pullback.

Yr Tm	PA	R	HR	RBI	SB	BA	xHR	xSB	xBA	OBP	SLG	OPS+	vL+	vR+	bb%	ct%	Eye	G	L	F	h%	HctX	QBaB	Brl%	PX	xPX	HR/F	xHR/F	Spd	SBA%	SB%	RAR	BPX	R$
17 a/a	542	55	17	79	0	291		6		308	465	105			2	82	0.13				33				103				73	1%	0%		118	$16
18 aaa	536	49	16	71	2	243		1		279	413	93			5	84	0.31				26				100				81	4%	39%		173	$10
19 KC *	386	42	13	56	0	223	0	2	227	257	372	87	21	0	4	81	0.25	38	15	46	24	108	DAf	0%	76	60	0%	0%	90	1%	0%	-26.2	89	$4
20																																		
21 2 TM *	494	71	24	73	2	275	11	5	272	312	498	111	146	126	5	79	0.25	41	20	39	30	103	CCf	8%	125	106	18%	14%	98	3%	67%	-6.1	219	$18
1st Half	204	28	11	29	0	244	1	2	247	275	458	102	161	84	4	77	0.18	22	22	56	27	70	AA	100%	119	89	20%	20%	93	3%	0%	-8.1	154	$9
2nd Half	290	43	14	45	2	298	10	3	281	339	528	117	143	125	6	81	0.32	42	20	39	33	106	CCf	8%	129	107	18%	14%	98	3%	67%	6.0	265	$23
22 Proj	560	66	18	69	2	266	19	3	255	303	432	100	107	97	5	81	0.25	42	20	39	30	95		7%	96	96	11%	12%	92	4%	53%	0.3	101	$17

Seager,Corey

Age: 28 Pos: SS | Bats: L Ht: 6' 4" Wt: 215
Health F | PT/Exp A | Consist B | LIMA Plan B | Rand Var -3 | MM 3255

Short-season gave his brittle body a Band-Aid, acting as a tease for his elite bat potential. Indeed, maturing plate skills, huge 2nd half remind us he's a top 10 bat...when healthy. But that's the rub; alternating healthy seasons isn't a risk profile you want from your 1st round pick. Use a .300 BA and 20 HR as your baseline until he proves otherwise.

Yr Tm	PA	R	HR	RBI	SB	BA	xHR	xSB	xBA	OBP	SLG	OPS+	vL+	vR+	bb%	ct%	Eye	G	L	F	h%	HctX	QBaB	Brl%	PX	xPX	HR/F	xHR/F	Spd	SBA%	SB%	RAR	BPX	R$
17 LA	613	85	22	77	4	295	26	10	271	375	479	116	124	110	11	76	0.51	42	25	33	35	135	BCb	9%	111	136	16%	19%	80	3%	67%	28.5	118	$21
18 LA	115	13	2	13	0	267	4	1	280	348	396	100	88	104	10	83	0.65	45	28	27	30	108	ACa	8%	74	79	9%	17%	108	0%	0%	2.5	150	$0
19 LA	541	82	19	87	1	272	21	2	278	335	483	113	98	120	8	80	0.45	39	22	39	31	117	CCc	7%	117	130	12%	14%	87	1%	100%	12.1	215	$16
20 LA	232	38	15	41	1	307	18	1	297	358	585	125	108	133	7	83	0.46	38	23	39	31	174	ACb	16%	137	171	22%	26%	100	2%	100%	18.5	344	$30
21 LA	409	54	16	57	1	306	23	4	283	394	521	126	125	126	12	81	0.73	46	21	33	34	136	ACc	12%	117	125	16%	24%	109	2%	50%	27.7	296	$16
1st Half	169	20	4	22	1	265	7	2	271	361	422	109	114	106	11	80	0.66	49	23	28	31	128	ADc	8%	86	101	12%	21%	124	2%	100%	2.5	200	$4
2nd Half	240	34	12	35	0	335	16	2	292	417	592	137	134	137	12	82	0.78	44	19	37	36	142	BCc	15%	139	141	19%	25%	97	2%	0%	25.6	365	$18
22 Proj	525	75	21	79	1	297	29	4	281	371	509	120	112	123	10	81	0.59	43	22	35	33	138		12%	116	131	16%	22%	98	4%	64%	33.3	236	$23

STEPHEN NICKRAND

Seager,Kyle	Health	B	LIMA Plan	B+
Age: 34 Pos: 3B	PT/Exp	A	Rand Var	+2
Bats: L Ht: 6' 0" Wt: 216	Consist	A	MM	4125

Opening up swing meant best power of career, and xHR says it should've been even better. Sum of parts didn't move R$ needle as BA eroded to Mendoza territory, but xBA says it should have been better too. Any PA dip or regression would cu into totals, but as both barrels and flyballs have inched upward, a near repeat could be in the offing.

Yr	Tm	PA	R	HR	RBI	SB	BA	xHR	xSB	xBA	OBP	SLG	OPS+	vL+	vR+	bb%	ct%	Eye	G	L	F	h%	HctX	QBaB	Brl%	PX	xPX	HR/F	xHR/F	Spd	SBA%	SB%	RAR	BPX	R
17	SEA	650	72	27	88	2	249	28	9	251	323	450	105	103	104	9	81	0.53	31	17	52	27	117	CAb	9%	110	142	11%	12%	75	2%	67%	-0.3	164	$
18	SEA	630	62	22	78	2	221	22	1	247	273	400	90	93	87	6	76	0.28	34	21	45	25	104	BAb	6%	112	127	11%	11%	62	4%	50%	-15.3	93	
19	SEA *	484	58	23	68	2	234	21	2	261	308	446	104	131	98	9	78	0.48	33	23	44	25	102	BAb	8%	107	140	17%	16%	67	4%	50%	-6.7	141	
20	SEA	248	35	9	40	5	241	11	1	250	355	433	105	85	113	13	84	0.97	35	16	48	25	133	CAf	9%	100	156	11%	13%	62	7%	100%	1.9	244	$
21	SEA	670	73	35	101	3	212	40	5	239	285	438	99	95	101	9	73	0.37	32	17	51	23	110	CAf	12%	131	163	16%	18%	71	3%	75%	-16.0	150	$
1st Half		347	31	15	49	2	220	20	3	230	288	422	99	94	101	8	71	0.31	31	19	50	26	120	BAd	13%	123	177	13%	18%	82	3%	67%	-11.4	104	$
2nd Half		323	42	20	52	1	203	20	2	249	282	455	100	96	102	10	76	0.44	33	16	51	20	100	CAf	12%	139	149	18%	18%	63	3%	100%	-8.9	208	$
22	**Proj**	**595**	**72**	**29**	**91**	**5**	**232**	**31**	**2**	**246**	**311**	**448**	**103**	**100**	**104**	**10**	**77**	**0.46**	**33**	**18**	**49**	**25**	**112**		**10%**	**121**	**152**	**14%**	**16%**	**61**	**2%**	**83%**	**4.9**	**166**	**$**

Segura,Jean	Health	B	LIMA Plan	B
Age: 32 Pos: 2B	PT/Exp	A	Rand Var	-1
Bats: R Ht: 5' 10" Wt: 220	Consist	A	MM	1245

Maintaining modest multi-category returns in spite of poor batted ball quality is a skill in itself. Health, consistency grades tell us he can keep doing it. But his power foundation remains full of cracks and his green light on basepaths has dried up (and speed is a skill of the young) so further upside is limited. Still, a decent second-tier 2Bman.

Yr	Tm	PA	R	HR	RBI	SB	BA	xHR	xSB	xBA	OBP	SLG	OPS+	vL+	vR+	bb%	ct%	Eye	G	L	F	h%	HctX	QBaB	Brl%	PX	xPX	HR/F	xHR/F	Spd	SBA%	SB%	RAR	BPX	R
17	SEA	565	80	11	45	22	300	11	9	279	349	427	106	111	102	6	84	0.41	54	19	26	34	96	CDa	3%	73	66	9%	9%	113	19%	73%	11.0	130	$
18	SEA	632	91	10	63	20	304	13	20	272	341	415	101	106	97	5	88	0.46	51	19	29	33	84	CDc	4%	63	59	7%	9%	116	18%	65%	19.0	167	$
19	PHI	618	79	12	60	10	280	13	15	291	323	420	103	126	95	5	87	0.41	52	21	27	30	100	CDc	3%	72	61	9%	9%	106	8%	83%	-0.5	185	$
20	PHI	217	28	7	25	2	266	6	5	240	347	422	102	108	99	11	77	0.51	48	18	34	31	96	CCf	6%	80	64	14%	12%	148	7%	50%	2.1	152	$
21	PHI	567	76	14	58	9	290	15	8	275	348	436	108	120	102	7	85	0.50	52	19	29	32	100	CDd	6%	79	68	11%	12%	107	8%	75%	11.4	192	$
1st Half		220	26	3	21	6	327	5	3	276	377	455	116	116	116	6	82	0.39	57	20	23	39	87	CFc	6%	77	52	8%	13%	112	8%	100%	10.9	150	$
2nd Half		347	50	11	37	3	266	10	4	273	329	423	102	124	94	7	87	0.60	49	19	32	28	108	DDf	6%	80	78	13%	11%	95	8%	50%	0.0	215	$
22	**Proj**	**560**	**73**	**14**	**56**	**8**	**278**	**14**	**8**	**267**	**334**	**419**	**102**	**114**	**97**	**7**	**84**	**0.46**	**51**	**19**	**29**	**31**	**97**		**5%**	**77**	**65**	**11%**	**11%**	**106**	**8%**	**65%**	**10.9**	**153**	**$**

Semien,Marcus	Health	A	LIMA Plan	B+
Age: 31 Pos: 2B SS	PT/Exp	A	Rand Var	0
Bats: R Ht: 6' 0" Wt: 195	Consist	D	MM	4335

MLB record for homers by a second baseman made this a historic season. Even if xHR points to regression, QBaB gives him higher floor than before. xPX trend backed by steady gains in swing path creates sturdy foundation for elite power. Just don't bank on double-digit steals again given eroding Spd and tempering xSB.

Yr	Tm	PA	R	HR	RBI	SB	BA	xHR	xSB	xBA	OBP	SLG	OPS+	vL+	vR+	bb%	ct%	Eye	G	L	F	h%	HctX	QBaB	Brl%	PX	xPX	HR/F	xHR/F	Spd	SBA%	SB%	RAR	BPX	R
17	OAK	386	53	10	40	12	249	8	5	237	325	398	98	90	99	10	75	0.45	37	20	42	30	92	CBc	5%	92	110	9%	7%	108	14%	92%	-1.0	85	$
18	OAK	703	89	15	70	14	255	19	15	248	318	388	95	100	90	9	79	0.47	39	23	38	30	95	CBc	5%	83	90	8%	10%	108	12%	70%	2.5	117	$
19	OAK	747	123	33	92	10	285	32	17	290	369	522	123	129	120	12	84	0.85	41	20	39	30	123	CBc	9%	114	105	15%	15%	136	9%	56%	35.2	352	$
20	OAK	236	28	7	23	4	223	7	4	225	305	374	90	103	86	11	76	0.50	33	20	47	26	86	DAf	5%	85	111	9%	9%	125	7%	100%	-4.9	136	$
21	TOR	724	115	45	102	15	265	37	8	272	334	538	120	106	125	9	78	0.45	31	21	48	28	114	BAc	10%	150	145	18%	15%	98	10%	94%	31.9	308	$
1st Half		368	63	21	54	10	289	17	5	265	353	548	125	123	126	9	74	0.38	34	21	45	33	107	BAc	10%	152	141	19%	15%	105	10%	91%	20.9	262	$
2nd Half		356	52	24	48	5	241	20	4	282	315	528	114	89	123	9	82	0.56	28	21	51	22	121	BAc	10%	148	148	18%	15%	90	10%	100%	7.5	354	$
22	**Proj**	**665**	**98**	**33**	**82**	**9**	**255**	**29**	**10**	**258**	**328**	**484**	**110**	**106**	**111**	**10**	**79**	**0.51**	**32**	**21**	**47**	**27**	**107**		**8%**	**125**	**125**	**15%**	**13%**	**103**	**9%**	**82%**	**24.4**	**254**	**$**

Senzel,Nick	Health	F	LIMA Plan	D+
Age: 27 Pos: CF	PT/Exp	F	Rand Var	+2
Bats: R Ht: 6' 1" Wt: 205	Consist	B	MM	1223

1-8-.252 in 124 PA at CIN. Former 1st-round pick spent another year mostly on injured list. Three reasons to roll the dice, but only at the right price: 1) Pre-injury returns featured another bump in contact; 2) xPX, Spd flashes confirm his multi-category potential; 3) the chase of upside and investment in hope is what makes fantasy fun. Right?

Yr	Tm	PA	R	HR	RBI	SB	BA	xHR	xSB	xBA	OBP	SLG	OPS+	vL+	vR+	bb%	ct%	Eye	G	L	F	h%	HctX	QBaB	Brl%	PX	xPX	HR/F	xHR/F	Spd	SBA%	SB%	RAR	BPX	R
17	aa	237	42	12	36	5	345		4		423	588	138			12	78	0.61				40				137				98	12%	56%		227	$1
18	aaa	187	19	5	21	7	280		3		342	457	107			9	74	0.36				35				114				102	19%	75%		123	$
19	CIN *	447	61	13	44	14	254	14	13	243	309	419	101	126	94	7	72	0.28	48	19	33	32	100	CCc	8%	95	77	13%	16%	147	19%	74%	1.2	85	$1
20	CIN	77	8	2	8	2	186	2	1	252	247	357	80	46	101	8	79	0.40	38	20	43	21	119	CBc	4%	106	143	8%	8%	87	27%	67%	-5.2	172	$
21	CIN *	161	22	1	10	2	250	3	6	263	314	326	88	101	85	8	87	0.74	46	24	30	28	100	CCc	4%	45	59	3%	10%	125	17%	29%	-8.9	162	$
1st Half		124	18	1	8	2	252	3	5	252	323	315	89	102	86	10	86	0.75	46	24	30	29	98	CCc	4%	38	59	3%	10%	109	17%	29%	-6.7	104	-$
2nd Half		37	4	0	2	0	243		1	277	276	359	86	0	0	4	93	0.65	44	20	36	26	0		0%	65	-22	0%		128	17%	0%	-1.6	281	-$
22	**Proj**	**315**	**45**	**6**	**32**	**8**	**259**	**10**	**8**	**241**	**328**	**380**	**96**	**89**	**98**	**9**	**78**	**0.48**	**44**	**22**	**35**	**31**	**105**		**5%**	**74**	**89**	**7%**	**13%**	**103**	**13%**	**53%**	**0.6**	**75**	**$**

Severino,Pedro	Health	A	LIMA Plan	D+
Age: 28 Pos: CA	PT/Exp	A	Rand Var	-3
Bats: R Ht: 6' 1" Wt: 220	Consist	A	MM	2213

Your second catcher slot usually is a place to speculate on upside. But it can also be a risk reducer. Here, we might have a combination of both; he's a steady producer with a hint of untapped upside coming off power-fueled 2nd half. Consider 2021 as his floor and its 2nd half doubled as his upside. Actually, from there it's not far to... UP: 20 HR, .265

Yr	Tm	PA	R	HR	RBI	SB	BA	xHR	xSB	xBA	OBP	SLG	OPS+	vL+	vR+	bb%	ct%	Eye	G	L	F	h%	HctX	QBaB	Brl%	PX	xPX	HR/F	xHR/F	Spd	SBA%	SB%	RAR	BPX	R
17	WAS *	254	14	4	27	1	207	0	3	192	252	275	72	77	52	6	76	0.24	47	16	37	26	64	FCf	0%	40	66	0%	0%	80	4%	42%	-13.9	-82	-$
18	WAS *	347	26	7	26	1	197	3	2	230	248	309	75	74	63	6	77	0.30	40	21	38	23	63	FBf	2%	71	49	4%	6%	75	1%	100%	-10.7	10	-$
19	BAL	341	37	13	44	3	249	12	1	252	321	420	102	113	93	9	76	0.40	40	23	37	29	87	CCf	9%	90	91	15%	14%	67	5%	75%	7.8	56	$
20	BAL	178	17	5	21	1	250	6	2	239	322	388	94	82	98	9	75	0.40	42	24	34	30	85	CDf	7%	75	88	12%	15%	113	2%	100%	0.4	56	$
21	BAL	419	32	11	46	0	248	13	2	228	308	383	95	111	84	8	71	0.31	39	24	37	32	91	CBf	8%	87	90	11%	13%	75	0%	0%	-1.2	-15	$
1st Half		211	18	3	15	0	229	4	1	225	308	319	87	96	82	10	74	0.45	41	24	34	29	73	CBf	3%	60	59	6%	8%	83	0%	0%	-4.7	-31	-$
2nd Half		208	14	8	31	0	267	9	1	231	308	445	102	125	86	6	69	0.20	37	23	40	35	108	CCd	12%	116	123	15%	17%	80	0%	0%	3.9	19	$
22	**Proj**	**420**	**35**	**12**	**49**	**1**	**243**	**13**	**1**	**232**	**305**	**382**	**93**	**105**	**86**	**8**	**73**	**0.32**	**40**	**23**	**37**	**30**	**88**		**8%**	**85**	**89**	**12%**	**12%**	**77**	**1%**	**82%**	**4.0**	**-42**	**$**

Sheets,Gavin	Health	A	LIMA Plan	D+
Age: 26 Pos: DH	PT/Exp	B	Rand Var	0
Bats: L Ht: 6' 4" Wt: 230	Consist	A	MM	4011

11-34-.250 in 179 PA at CHW. September flash (.931 OPS) elevated him from so-so prospect to something more. Problem is, xHR thought power burst was overstated, as did xPX. You'll want more pop potential from a bat that you can only slot at DH to begin the season, especially one with contact issues. Cap bidding at $5 for profit.

Yr	Tm	PA	R	HR	RBI	SB	BA	xHR	xSB	xBA	OBP	SLG	OPS+	vL+	vR+	bb%	ct%	Eye	G	L	F	h%	HctX	QBaB	Brl%	PX	xPX	HR/F	xHR/F	Spd	SBA%	SB%	RAR	BPX	R
17																																			
18																																			
19	aa	517	55	17	82	3	256		7		332	404	102			10	76	0.48				30				78				90	3%	73%		59	$1
20																																			
21	CHW *	424	48	19	66	1	241	9	3	236	302	437	102	37	124	8	72	0.31	45	17	38	29	117	BCd	10%	118	110	24%	20%	52	2%	37%	-11.4	65	$
1st Half		193	19	7	31	1	243	1	1	254	293	404	97	0	221	7	75	0.28	47	24	29	29	162	AAb	14%	95	199	40%	20%	70	2%	100%	-8.7	46	$
2nd Half		231	29	12	35	0	240	8	2	239	310	465	105	49	113	9	70	0.34	45	15	39	29	107	BCd	10%	140	96	22%	20%	60	2%	0%	-5.8	115	$
22	**Proj**	**245**	**28**	**13**	**38**	**1**	**246**	**13**	**1**	**238**	**320**	**464**	**106**	**51**	**112**	**9**	**73**	**0.35**	**45**	**15**	**39**	**28**	**96**		**9%**	**127**	**86**	**20%**	**20%**	**60**	**2%**	**55%**	**1.3**	**84**	**$**

Sierra,Magneuris	Health	A	LIMA Plan	D
Age: 26 Pos: CF	PT/Exp	C	Rand Var	0
Bats: L Ht: 5' 11" Wt: 178	Consist	A	MM	0511

Slap hitters don't get more slap-happy than this one, as the last time he barreled a ball was in Little League. You'll buy him for speed, and he does have it in spades. But he'll never hit enough to get a full-time role, so the best you can hope for is 20 steals as a part-timer. That has value, but only as your fifth outfielder in a deep league.

Yr	Tm	PA	R	HR	RBI	SB	BA	xHR	xSB	xBA	OBP	SLG	OPS+	vL+	vR+	bb%	ct%	Eye	G	L	F	h%	HctX	QBaB	Brl%	PX	xPX	HR/F	xHR/F	Spd	SBA%	SB%	RAR	BPX	R
17	STL *	408	38	1	36	17	266	0	6	275	305	331	87	125	81	5	81	0.29	53	28	19	33	21	FFb	0%	44	-3	0%	0%	151	23%	70%	-19.6	48	$1
18	MIA *	513	51	2	21	15	219	0	16	240	245	272	69	99	50	3	76	0.14	57	23	19	29	55	FFf	0%	36	18	0%	0%	168	21%	67%	-34.8	-30	$
19	MIA *	587	80	6	28	35	262	0	21	255	299	361	91	278	102	5	81	0.28	62	14	24	31	76	CDd	0%	50	33	0%	0%	179	35%	70%	-29.6	107	$2
20	MIA	53	8	0	7	4	250	0	3	256	333	364	93	121	89	9	80	0.56	59	15	26	31	68	FFf		70	40	0%	0%	151	38%	80%	-1.2	160	$
21	MIA	225	27	0	5	11	230	0	13	221	281	268	75	67	78	7	76	0.30	50	22	28	30	47	FDf	0%	28	-4	0%	0%	154	20%	100%	-15.2	-42	$
1st Half		113	15	0	0	5	235	0	7	225	310	265	80	73	82	10	78	0.50	51	22	27	30	36	FDd	0%	24	-12	0%	0%	137	20%	100%	-6.3	-19	-$
2nd Half		112	12	0	5	6	224	0	6	216	252	271	71	63	74	4	74	0.14	50	22	28	30	57	FDf	0%	32	4	0%	0%	148	20%	100%	-8.3	-96	-$
22	**Proj**	**245**	**28**	**0**	**10**	**12**	**250**	**0**	**9**	**233**	**291**	**298**	**80**	**86**	**78**	**5**	**77**	**0.25**	**52**	**23**	**24**	**32**	**44**		**0%**	**32**	**1**	**0%**	**0%**	**160**	**18%**	**83%**	**-6.2**	**-61**	**$**

STEPHEN NICKRAND

Simmons,Andrelton

Age: 32 Pos: SS
Bats: R Ht: 6' 2" Wt: 195

Health	C	LIMA Plan	D+
PT/Exp	A	Rand Var	+2
Consist	B	MM	0215

We gave him a mulligan for his struggles in 2020, since they were injury related. Perhaps early COVID stint drove this disaster? Batted ball metrics went from bad to flunking. Power has been MIA for three seasons now, so double-digit homers ain't coming back. Neither is speed, given subpar Spd and constant red light. You can do better.

Yr Tm	PA	R	HR	RBI	SB	BA	xHR	xSB	xBA	OBP	SLG	OPS+	vL+	vR+	bb%	ct%	Eye	G	L	F	h%	HctX	QBaB	Brl%	PX	xPX	HR/F	xHR/F	Spd	SBA%	SB%	RAR	BPX	R$
17 LAA	647	77	14	69	19	278	10	9	286	331	421	102	93	103	7	89	0.70	50	19	31	30	105	DDd	3%	78	82	8%	6%	105	16%	76%	5.0	197	$22
18 LAA	600	68	11	75	10	292	11	17	281	337	417	101	100	100	6	92	0.80	50	19	31	30	122	CDf	4%	65	82	7%	7%	140	8%	83%	14.9	253	$21
19 LAA	424	47	7	40	10	264	5	5	261	309	364	93	116	85	6	91	0.65	54	14	32	28	108	CCf	2%	51	33	6%	4%	92	11%	83%	-14.1	167	$9
20 LAA	127	19	0	10	2	297	0	3	260	346	356	93	85	97	6	86	0.50	55	21	25	34	93	DDf	0%	42	32	0%	0%	110	5%	100%	-0.3	108	$9
21 MIN	451	37	3	31	1	223	2	4	230	283	274	77	86	71	7	85	0.52	54	18	28	26	65	FFf	1%	31	23	3%	2%	83	1%	100%	-26.3	23	$0
1st Half	234	26	3	17	0	245	1	2	246	313	330	90	109	79	8	82	0.50	55	21	24	29	61	FFf	1%	52	25	7%	2%	94	1%	0%	-7.2	62	$2
2nd Half	217	11	0	14	1	200	0	2	207	251	215	63	64	63	6	88	0.54	54	16	31	23	68	FDf	0%	11	22	0%	0%	82	1%	100%	-17.9	0	-$7
22 Proj	**490**	**43**	**4**	**36**	**3**	**245**	**2**	**3**	**238**	**297**	**312**	**83**	**86**	**81**	**6**	**85**	**0.47**	**54**	**18**	**28**	**28**	**85**		**1%**	**41**	**35**	**3%**	**2%**	**94**	**3%**	**77%**	**-15.2**	**17**	**$4**

Siri,Jose

Age: 26 Pos: OF
Bats: R Ht: 6' 2" Wt: 175

Health	A	LIMA Plan	D+
PT/Exp	B	Rand Var	-5
Consist	B	MM	4503

4-9-.304 with 3 SB in 49 PA at HOU. Hey Siri, how do I get called up? Power/speed package in minors gave him the pathway, and he showed it at MLB level, too. But the contact warts that have stymied his development were the same in the bigs (63% ct%, 0.06 Eye). Worth a gamble as your 4th or 5th outfielder; any bigger investment isn't worth the risk.

Yr Tm	PA	R	HR	RBI	SB	BA	xHR	xSB	xBA	OBP	SLG	OPS+	vL+	vR+	bb%	ct%	Eye	G	L	F	h%	HctX	QBaB	Brl%	PX	xPX	HR/F	xHR/F	Spd	SBA%	SB%	RAR	BPX	R$
17																																		
18 aa	274	36	11	29	12	211		4		271	426	93			8	59	0.20				30				147				155	35%	69%		63	$7
19 a/a	506	48	10	46	22	214		21		273	326	83			7	58	0.19				34				80				103	28%	71%		-200	$10
20																																		
21 HOU *	428	56	15	56	19	253	5	6	189	284	433	99	147	123	4	58	0.11	34	14	52	39	82	BBa	17%	137	150	27%	33%	138	29%	80%	-6.5	-15	$18
1st Half	190	22	6	27	9	252		3	202	285	404	96	0	0	4	59	0.11	44	20	36	39	0		0%	118	-22	0%		102	29%	79%	-5.2	-115	$12
2nd Half	237	34	9	29	10	253	5	3	197	283	456	100	145	121	4	58	0.10	34	14	52	39	82	BBa	17%	152	150	27%	33%	158	29%	81%	-3.2	46	$17
22 Proj	**280**	**35**	**11**	**33**	**10**	**236**	**12**	**11**	**204**	**303**	**428**	**99**	**120**	**87**	**5**	**59**	**0.14**	**39**	**19**	**42**	**36**	**74**		**16%**	**139**	**135**	**17%**	**18%**	**137**	**23%**	**74%**	**-2.7**	**-7**	**$11**

Slater,Austin

Age: 29 Pos: CF LF RF
Bats: R Ht: 6' 1" Wt: 204

Health	A	LIMA Plan	C
PT/Exp	C	Rand Var	+1
Consist	D	MM	3433

Continues to mash southpaws, giving him path to short-side platoon work. But the more he plays, the more he gets exposed. Tanking production against righties, erosion in QBaB eliminate hope for daily playing time. Still, he'll help you in multiple categories when he does play, and hit rate correction will send his BA north.

Yr Tm	PA	R	HR	RBI	SB	BA	xHR	xSB	xBA	OBP	SLG	OPS+	vL+	vR+	bb%	ct%	Eye	G	L	F	h%	HctX	QBaB	Brl%	PX	xPX	HR/F	xHR/F	Spd	SBA%	SB%	RAR	BPX	R$
17 SF *	323	37	6	38	3	277	3	5	235	322	391	97	110	95	6	75	0.27	61	14	25	35	73	CFc	3%	71	48	14%	14%	115	8%	48%	-6.6	18	$7
18 SF *	435	43	4	45	13	263	3	6	251	323	371	93	87	83	8	70	0.30	63	21	16	37	97	CFa	2%	83	31	5%	14%	102	14%	84%	0.0	-7	$11
19 SF *	467	55	13	55	5	245	8	10	246	337	410	103	117	92	12	65	0.40	52	25	23	34	102	CFb	10%	107	113	20%	32%	112	6%	69%	4.4	26	$9
20 SF	104	18	5	7	8	282	5	2	266	408	506	121	147	98	15	74	0.73	40	29	32	33	94	CCb	14%	114	120	25%	25%	153	26%	89%	6.0	264	$16
21 SF	306	39	12	32	15	241	14	11	255	320	423	102	122	69	9	69	0.33	51	24	26	30	82	DDb	9%	113	89	25%	29%	97	23%	88%	-3.7	65	$12
1st Half	183	20	8	20	7	201	6	6	232	284	372	91	103	78	10	63	0.30	58	22	21	26	85	CFb	8%	103	93	38%	29%	127	23%	78%	-8.1	-15	$6
2nd Half	123	19	4	12	8	300	7	5	288	374	500	118	140	41	8	78	0.42	42	27	31	35	78	DCc	11%	125	83	15%	26%	84	23%	100%	6.5	219	$7
22 Proj	**280**	**39**	**10**	**28**	**14**	**264**	**12**	**10**	**260**	**351**	**446**	**108**	**128**	**82**	**10**	**72**	**0.41**	**49**	**25**	**26**	**33**	**88**		**10%**	**113**	**90**	**21%**	**25%**	**102**	**17%**	**89%**	**11.0**	**130**	**$14**

Smith,Dominic

Age: 27 Pos: LF
Bats: L Ht: 6' 0" Wt: 239

Health	B	LIMA Plan	C+
PT/Exp	A	Rand Var	+2
Consist	D	MM	3035

Skills went south just as it looked like he was on the verge of a breakout. Often the best breakout targets are the failed ones from the prior year. Soaring OPS+ vR and barrel rate pre-2021 tell us we need to give him another shot. xHR, xPX both confirm that his power wasn't as bad as it seemed. UP: 20 HR

Yr Tm	PA	R	HR	RBI	SB	BA	xHR	xSB	xBA	OBP	SLG	OPS+	vL+	vR+	bb%	ct%	Eye	G	L	F	h%	HctX	QBaB	Brl%	PX	xPX	HR/F	xHR/F	Spd	SBA%	SB%	RAR	BPX	R$
17 NYM *	672	74	22	82	1	256	8	9	242	307	418	99	59	95	7	75	0.30	50	16	34	31	113	BCa	8%	98	112	23%	20%	51	1%	40%	-16.0	33	$12
18 NYM *	509	48	9	38	2	208	6	1	228	251	328	78	77	91	5	71	0.20	34	26	40	27	80	CBc	6%	86	106	13%	16%	74	2%	100%	-28.8	-33	$1
19 NYM	197	35	11	25	1	282	8	1	274	355	525	122	122	121	10	75	0.43	40	23	37	32	96	CBc	8%	129	89	22%	16%	79	6%	33%	5.7	181	$5
20 NYM	199	27	10	42	0	316	12	1	308	377	616	132	117	137	7	75	0.31	41	26	33	38	114	BCb	13%	183	142	22%	27%	53	0%	0%	15.0	308	$24
21 NYM	493	43	11	58	2	244	17	1	240	304	363	92	107	86	6	75	0.29	38	26	36	30	107	CBb	6%	74	107	9%	14%	61	3%	67%	-21.9	-27	$7
1st Half	283	27	8	34	2	260	10	0	252	329	394	101	124	93	7	74	0.31	42	28	30	32	99	CCb	7%	80	104	14%	17%	67	3%	67%	-8.3	-8	$12
2nd Half	210	16	3	24	0	224	7	0	227	271	323	80	89	76	6	76	0.26	34	24	42	28	118	BBb	6%	67	111	5%	11%	62	3%	0%	-14.6	-46	-$2
22 Proj	**455**	**52**	**17**	**68**	**1**	**258**	**20**	**1**	**258**	**317**	**444**	**103**	**105**	**102**	**7**	**75**	**0.29**	**39**	**25**	**37**	**31**	**106**		**8%**	**114**	**112**	**14%**	**17%**	**55**	**2%**	**53%**	**4.7**	**76**	**$14**

Smith,Pavin

Age: 26 Pos: 1B RF CF LF
Bats: L Ht: 6' 2" Wt: 210

Health	A	LIMA Plan	B
PT/Exp	A	Rand Var	-1
Consist	A	MM	2435

Former 7th overall pick at a crossroads after so-so first full season in majors. As a groundball hitter whose pop has never materialized at any professional level, where does he go from here? Absence of hope from QBaB gives him cloudy path at turning draft upside into results. Only dual infield/outfield eligibility keeps us mildly interested.

Yr Tm	PA	R	HR	RBI	SB	BA	xHR	xSB	xBA	OBP	SLG	OPS+	vL+	vR+	bb%	ct%	Eye	G	L	F	h%	HctX	QBaB	Brl%	PX	xPX	HR/F	xHR/F	Spd	SBA%	SB%	RAR	BPX	R$
17																																		
18																																		
19 aa	497	58	11	63	2	282		9		364	457	114			11	85	0.87				31				86				128	2%	63%		270	$12
20 ARI	44	7	1	4	1	270	1	1	269	341	405	99	112	96	11	78	0.63	45	32	23	32	92	CDf	6%	58	46	14%	14%	148	8%	100%	-0.6	116	$2
21 ARI	545	68	11	49	1	267	16	9	253	328	404	101	83	107	8	79	0.40	47	21	32	32	111	CDf	5%	81	94	9%	13%	126	1%	100%	-19.2	135	$12
1st Half	317	40	7	28	1	266	11	5	259	319	410	101	85	107	7	80	0.35	48	21	30	31	111	DDf	6%	82	103	10%	15%	123	1%	100%	-9.6	138	$13
2nd Half	228	28	4	21	0	268	6	4	246	342	395	100	80	108	9	78	0.46	45	21	33	33	112	CCc	4%	80	81	8%	11%	125	1%	0%	-6.0	123	$5
22 Proj	**455**	**56**	**10**	**46**	**1**	**271**	**14**	**5**	**260**	**341**	**422**	**104**	**84**	**111**	**9**	**80**	**0.50**	**47**	**21**	**32**	**32**	**112**		**5%**	**87**	**90**	**9%**	**13%**	**139**	**5%**	**79%**	**6.2**	**136**	**$13**

Smith,Will

Age: 27 Pos: CA
Bats: R Ht: 5' 10" Wt: 195

Health	A	LIMA Plan	B
PT/Exp	A	Rand Var	0
Consist	D	MM	4435

The mini-breakout we saw coming, and he's not done yet. Power output turned elite in 2nd half and was backed by a trifecta of ace batted ball skills. Mature plate approach and vR+ dominance make him a true frontliner. If durability (or NL DH?) nets him 600+ plate appearances, he'll be a gem among backstop group... UP: .300 BA, 35 HR

Yr Tm	PA	R	HR	RBI	SB	BA	xHR	xSB	xBA	OBP	SLG	OPS+	vL+	vR+	bb%	ct%	Eye	G	L	F	h%	HctX	QBaB	Brl%	PX	xPX	HR/F	xHR/F	Spd	SBA%	SB%	RAR	BPX	R$
17																																		
18 a/a	383	44	15	45	4	200		3		265	376	86			8	64	0.25				26				126				86	6%	100%		0	$4
19 LA *	447	65	30	81	3	236	10	4	248	315	515	115	95	140	10	72	0.41	29	17	54	25	112	BAb	11%	147	168	23%	15%	95	3%	100%	12.9	211	$13
20 LA	137	23	8	25	0	289	6	1	301	401	579	130	110	138	15	81	0.91	24	27	49	30	133	BAb	13%	153	161	17%	13%	88	0%	0%	13.2	412	$14
21 LA	501	71	25	76	3	258	27	3	258	365	495	118	100	126	12	76	0.57	31	22	46	28	115	BAc	11%	131	140	17%	18%	104	2%	100%	23.4	246	$17
1st Half	251	36	10	29	1	261	11	1	267	363	469	116	79	136	12	79	0.62	32	25	43	29	115	BAd	10%	116	119	14%	15%	93	2%	100%	9.5	235	$13
2nd Half	250	35	15	47	2	256	15	2	250	368	522	120	135	117	13	72	0.54	31	19	50	28	115	AAa	12%	147	163	19%	19%	119	2%	100%	13.4	273	$17
22 Proj	**504**	**79**	**30**	**89**	**3**	**261**	**26**	**4**	**258**	**363**	**518**	**120**	**101**	**127**	**12**	**74**	**0.54**	**29**	**22**	**49**	**29**	**118**		**11%**	**145**	**153**	**18%**	**16%**	**98**	**4%**	**100%**	**35.3**	**242**	**$22**

Solak,Nick

Age: 27 Pos: 2B
Bats: R Ht: 5' 11" Wt: 185

Health	A	LIMA Plan	C+
PT/Exp	A	Rand Var	0
Consist	B	MM	1325

11-49-.242 with 7 SB in 511 PA at TEX. Multi-category flashes in minors are carrying limiting factors in big leagues, such as poor batted ball skills (see second half QBaB) and ominous xPX and xBA. Consistently good Spd says path to value for now could be with legs, but recent SBA%/SB% is not cooperating. In need of a consolidation year.

Yr Tm	PA	R	HR	RBI	SB	BA	xHR	xSB	xBA	OBP	SLG	OPS+	vL+	vR+	bb%	ct%	Eye	G	L	F	h%	HctX	QBaB	Brl%	PX	xPX	HR/F	xHR/F	Spd	SBA%	SB%	RAR	BPX	R$
17 aa	129	15	2	9	1	275		2		330	416	101			8	78	0.37				34				89				108	6%	48%		100	$1
18 aa	536	77	16	65	18	250		7		331	389	97			11	73	0.44				31				85				110	17%	73%		50	$19
19 TEX *	588	77	26	71	6	264	5	16	261	326	461	109	150	103	8	73	0.34	53	20	28	31	73	CDd	9%	106	64	21%	21%	127	6%	71%	6.5	130	$17
20 TEX	233	27	2	23	7	268	6	4	224	326	344	89	92	87	8	80	0.43	49	17	34	33	113	BCd	5%	49	91	3%	10%	128	13%	88%	-3.5	60	$19
21 TEX *	601	68	12	53	7	249	12	13	236	300	364	91	99	90	6	77	0.31	53	17	30	31	92	DDf	6%	69	86	11%	12%	125	9%	53%	-16.8	54	$12
1st Half	336	42	9	33	3	231	10	7	233	301	366	93	110	84	6	73	0.22	49	20	31	29	95	CDd	8%	80	101	13%	14%	134	9%	50%	-14.8	31	$13
2nd Half	265	26	3	20	4	273	2	6	233	331	361	94	74	101	8	82	0.48	60	13	27	32	83	FFf	4%	57	60	6%	6%	115	9%	55%	-5.3	100	$7
22 Proj	**525**	**63**	**13**	**51**	**9**	**255**	**13**	**9**	**242**	**327**	**389**	**97**	**104**	**93**	**8**	**77**	**0.38**	**54**	**17**	**30**	**31**	**90**		**6%**	**79**	**77**	**12%**	**12%**	**128**	**9%**	**68%**	**1.1**	**51**	**$16**

STEPHEN NICKRAND

Solano,Donovan

Age: 34	Pos: 2B	Health	C	LIMA Plan	D+
Bats: R	Ht: 5' 8" Wt: 210	PT/Exp	B	Rand Var	0
		Consist	B	MM	1233

Late-season mauling of southpaws reminded us that he can be good in stretches. Indeed, if he were 10 years younger, that trend in barrel rate might catch our attention, especially after 2nd half xPX. But with pessimistic xBA and no speed, double-digit homers and a good average are the best we can hope for. Stash him in your MI slot in deep leagues.

Yr	Tm	PA	R	HR	RBI	SB	BA	xHR	xSB	xBA	OBP	SLG	OPS+	vL+	vR+	bb%	ct%	Eye	G	L	F	h%	HctX	QBaB	Brl%	PX	xPX	HR/F	xHR/F	Spd	SBA%	SB%	RAR	BPX
17	aaa	392	34	4	37	1	225		4		261	314	78			5	79	0.24				27				62				78	1%	100%		3
18	aaa	324	26	3	29	3	241		1		265	323	79			3	83	0.20				28				55				85	6%	68%		33
19	SF *	321	35	5	34	0	307	5	4	280	343	419	105	117	107	5	79	0.26	37	34	29	37	104	CBb	4%	64	77	8%	10%	103	1%	0%	5.5	41
20	SF	203	22	3	29	0	326	4	1	265	365	463	110	113	108	5	79	0.26	36	28	36	40	110	CBc	5%	86	90	5%	7%	97	0%	0%	6.5	112
21	SF	344	35	7	31	2	280	11	1	261	344	404	103	112	97	7	81	0.43	40	26	34	33	98	CCb	7%	74	98	8%	13%	70	2%	100%	-1.6	81
1st Half		196	21	3	18	1	278	5	0	261	332	386	100	95	102	7	80	0.40	41	28	32	33	86	CCc	6%	68	70	7%	11%	72	2%	100%	-1.3	50
2nd Half		148	14	4	13	1	282	7	0	261	361	427	107	134	91	8	82	0.48	40	23	37	32	114	CCa	9%	82	136	10%	18%	68	2%	100%	1.3	127
22	**Proj**	**350**	**36**	**7**	**37**	**1**	**287**	**11**	**2**	**264**	**340**	**415**	**102**	**112**	**96**	**6**	**81**	**0.34**	**39**	**27**	**34**	**34**	**104**		**7%**	**77**	**99**	**8%**	**12%**	**79**	**3%**	**85%**	**8.0**	**57**

Soler,Jorge

Age: 30	Pos: RF DH	Health	B	LIMA Plan	B+
Bats: R	Ht: 6' 4" Wt: 235	PT/Exp	A	Rand Var	+4
		Consist	B	MM	4125

That 1st half had us wondering if his 2019 would ever come back. His 2nd half confirmed it still exists, and the expected metrics say it could've been even better. Plus, late contact rate was the best we've seen from him over a prolonged perio He'll be undervalued now. A premium place to target profit—if you can surround him with BA padding.

Yr	Tm	PA	R	HR	RBI	SB	BA	xHR	xSB	xBA	OBP	SLG	OPS+	vL+	vR+	bb%	ct%	Eye	G	L	F	h%	HctX	QBaB	Brl%	PX	xPX	HR/F	xHR/F	Spd	SBA%	SB%	RAR	BPX
17	KC *	421	45	19	52	1	205	3	5	217	300	394	94	78	61	12	65	0.39	38	18	44	26	82	CAd	7%	122	88	7%	11%	60	1%	100%	-16.7	9
18	KC	257	27	9	28	3	265	13	1	251	354	466	110	141	98	11	69	0.41	47	19	34	34	109	BCb	10%	144	111	17%	25%	91	6%	75%	6.4	143
19	KC	676	95	48	117	3	265	51	6	270	354	569	128	121	129	11	70	0.41	39	20	41	30	113	ABc	17%	168	141	28%	30%	70	3%	75%	27.6	215
20	KC	172	17	8	24	0	228	10	1	222	326	443	102	94	103	11	60	0.32	38	23	39	32	102	ABd	19%	151	159	23%	29%	68	0%	0%	-2.8	16
21	2 TM	594	74	27	70	0	223	37	1	234	316	432	103	115	98	11	72	0.47	42	15	43	25	111	ABd	13%	126	122	17%	23%	74	0%	0%	-13.0	146
1st Half		292	24	6	28	0	185	14	1	189	281	311	82	83	82	11	67	0.36	42	14	44	25	85	ABc	12%	91	76	8%	18%	70	0%	0%	-22.1	-54
2nd Half		302	50	21	42	0	260	23	1	277	351	550	122	144	113	12	77	0.63	42	17	42	26	135	BBd	13%	155	162	25%	27%	84	0%	0%	9.8	331
22	**Proj**	**595**	**78**	**33**	**86**	**1**	**237**	**37**	**1**	**246**	**329**	**478**	**110**	**119**	**106**	**11**	**69**	**0.42**	**41**	**18**	**41**	**28**	**110**		**14%**	**149**	**132**	**22%**	**25%**	**71**	**1%**	**76%**	**12.1**	**126**

Sosa,Edmundo

Age: 26	Pos: SS 2B	Health	A	LIMA Plan	C
Bats: R	Ht: 5' 11" Wt: 170	PT/Exp	C	Rand Var	-4
		Consist	A	MM	1323

His slow start hid some nice gains late in the year. Huge August (1.071 OPS, 209 Spd) teases his upside, and 98th-percentile Statcast sprint speed validates potential value on basepaths, which has been held back by poor success rate. While he won't deliver power, and the BA foundation is shaky, there's untapped speed here. UP: 15 SB

Yr	Tm	PA	R	HR	RBI	SB	BA	xHR	xSB	xBA	OBP	SLG	OPS+	vL+	vR+	bb%	ct%	Eye	G	L	F	h%	HctX	QBaB	Brl%	PX	xPX	HR/F	xHR/F	Spd	SBA%	SB%	RAR	BPX
17	aa																																	
18	STL *	472	52	9	46	5	237	0	5	114	266	358	84	0	66	4	77	0.18	0	0	100	29	0	DA	0%	80	-27	0%	0%	106	10%	52%	-16.3	50
19	STL *	476	58	13	49	3	254	0	8	288	276	387	92	0	100	3	77	0.13	50	33	17	31	88	FFd	0%	69	5	0%	0%	139	6%	43%	-13.2	41
20																																		
21	STL	325	39	6	27	4	271	8	9	248	346	389	101	93	104	5	78	0.27	52	21	27	33	78	DFf	4%	63	66	10%	13%	200	9%	50%	-8.0	135
1st Half		151	17	1	7	3	246	3	4	231	331	313	90	67	97	5	80	0.26	58	16	26	30	64	DFf	4%	40	54	4%	11%	166	9%	43%	-8.7	50
2nd Half		174	22	5	20	1	292	5	5	260	358	455	110	111	110	6	77	0.28	47	25	28	35	91	CCc	4%	84	76	15%	15%	199	9%	100%	3.0	185
22	**Proj**	**350**	**43**	**7**	**33**	**4**	**262**	**6**	**8**	**248**	**331**	**384**	**97**	**88**	**100**	**5**	**78**	**0.22**	**51**	**21**	**28**	**32**	**80**		**4%**	**69**	**67**	**10%**	**8%**	**155**	**11%**	**52%**	**-3.9**	**23**

Soto,Juan

Age: 23	Pos: RF	Health	A	LIMA Plan	C
Bats: L	Ht: 6' 1" Wt: 220	PT/Exp	A	Rand Var	-1
		Consist	F	MM	4255

Took a while to round into form, but wow, was he electric in the 2nd half. Annual Eye gains continue to raise his floor. Batted ball profile only dinged by chronic groundball stroke. That low launch angle is the only thing between him and an MVP season, but his post-July results suggest he can get there in spite of it. UP: .330 BA, 40 HR

Yr	Tm	PA	R	HR	RBI	SB	BA	xHR	xSB	xBA	OBP	SLG	OPS+	vL+	vR+	bb%	ct%	Eye	G	L	F	h%	HctX	QBaB	Brl%	PX	xPX	HR/F	xHR/F	Spd	SBA%	SB%	RAR	BPX
17																																		
18	WAS *	528	80	24	79	6	293	24	8	277	404	519	124	112	125	16	76	0.78	54	17	29	34	98	BDc	10%	135	105	25%	27%	94	5%	75%	39.0	247
19	WAS	659	110	34	110	12	282	39	8	280	401	548	131	118	137	16	76	0.82	42	21	37	32	108	ACc	12%	138	139	22%	25%	102	7%	92%	39.0	289
20	WAS	196	39	13	37	6	351	15	3	335	490	695	157	158	155	21	82	1.46	52	20	29	36	139	AFd	18%	179	140	36%	42%	82	12%	75%	31.8	556
21	WAS	654	111	29	95	9	313	35	18	285	465	534	137	119	148	22	81	1.56	53	19	29	34	130	ADd	13%	113	99	24%	29%	99	6%	56%	52.8	354
1st Half		296	46	9	37	5	278	16	7	272	399	433	116	110	119	17	82	1.11	55	20	25	31	121	AFd	11%	81	82	18%	32%	98	6%	56%	6.1	219
2nd Half		358	65	20	58	4	346	19	11	296	520	630	156	125	176	27	81	1.98	51	17	32	37	139	ADf	15%	142	116	29%	28%	103	6%	57%	50.5	485
22	**Proj**	**665**	**118**	**34**	**108**	**12**	**315**	**40**	**11**	**293**	**455**	**574**	**140**	**125**	**147**	**21**	**80**	**1.28**	**50**	**19**	**31**	**34**	**125**		**14%**	**138**	**118**	**26%**	**31%**	**93**	**6%**	**69%**	**75.5**	**369**

Springer,George

Age: 32	Pos: CF DH	Health	F	LIMA Plan	B+
Bats: R	Ht: 6' 3" Wt: 221	PT/Exp	A	Rand Var	0
		Consist	B	MM	4345

Nearly 100 days on injured list derailed him in 1st half, but once healthy, $20+ baseline returned. Top barrel rate of care best power foundation since rookie season, and another uptick in flyballs all put HR explosion within reach. The wild card here is the health risk, but that shouldn't keep you from viewing him as an upper-tier bat. UP: 45 HR

Yr	Tm	PA	R	HR	RBI	SB	BA	xHR	xSB	xBA	OBP	SLG	OPS+	vL+	vR+	bb%	ct%	Eye	G	L	F	h%	HctX	QBaB	Brl%	PX	xPX	HR/F	xHR/F	Spd	SBA%	SB%	RAR	BPX
17	HOU	627	112	34	85	5	283	30	10	285	367	522	121	131	115	10	80	0.58	48	18	34	30	119	BCc	9%	128	113	23%	20%	96	7%	42%	25.5	221
18	HOU	616	102	22	71	6	265	30	9	249	346	434	105	111	100	10	78	0.52	49	16	35	31	96	CCc	9%	101	100	15%	20%	110	6%	60%	16.3	157
19	HOU	556	96	39	96	6	292	37	8	289	383	591	135	126	137	12	76	0.59	45	20	36	31	119	BCd	14%	146	127	30%	28%	114	5%	75%	47.5	307
20	HOU	220	37	14	32	1	265	14	4	276	359	540	119	106	124	11	80	0.63	36	21	43	26	118	CAd	12%	132	112	21%	21%	150	5%	33%	8.4	376
21	TOR	341	59	22	50	4	264	22	3	273	352	555	125	128	123	11	74	0.47	33	21	47	29	103	BAc	15%	168	138	21%	21%	100	6%	80%	16.4	319
1st Half		60	10	5	10	1	245	3	1	268	383	571	133	99	155	18	73	0.85	33	17	50	23	92	BBb	17%	171	138	28%	17%	93	6%	100%	3.8	373
2nd Half		281	49	17	40	3	268	19	2	275	345	552	121	136	117	9	74	0.39	32	22	46	30	106	BAd	15%	168	138	20%	22%	102	6%	75%	11.2	308
22	**Proj**	**560**	**98**	**37**	**86**	**6**	**267**	**35**	**7**	**271**	**360**	**544**	**123**	**115**	**125**	**12**	**76**	**0.56**	**38**	**19**	**43**	**28**	**107**		**14%**	**150**	**126**	**23%**	**22%**	**107**	**7%**	**70%**	**38.2**	**293**

Stallings,Jacob

Age: 32	Pos: CA	Health	A	LIMA Plan	D+
Bats: R	Ht: 6' 5" Wt: 220	PT/Exp	B	Rand Var	0
		Consist	A	MM	1015

PRO: Eye on steady upswing; hit RHers for first time in career; xHR supports double-digit homers. CON: Shoddy barrel rate cratered in 2nd half; swing path not conducive to power; skills tanked late. SIS Fielding Bible Award winner as best defensive catcher, but all that buys you is the promise of PT. In sum, still carries value as your second catcher.

Yr	Tm	PA	R	HR	RBI	SB	BA	xHR	xSB	xBA	OBP	SLG	OPS+	vL+	vR+	bb%	ct%	Eye	G	L	F	h%	HctX	QBaB	Brl%	PX	xPX	HR/F	xHR/F	Spd	SBA%	SB%	RAR	BPX
17	PIT *	246	31	3	33	1	258	0	3	301	305	365	91	108	135	6	84	0.42	42	33	25	30	57	FDa	0%	68	57	0%	0%	92	5%	25%	-2.6	97
18	PIT *	308	28	2	33	1	222	0	2	245	256	307	75	37	74	4	75	0.19	52	24	24	29	96	BCa	0%	65	33	0%	0%	94	7%	22%	-9.3	-20
19	PIT *	264	34	7	18	0	252	7	3	244	306	395	97	134	86	7	79	0.37	48	19	34	29	95	CCb	6%	77	74	12%	14%	105	0%	0%	-1.5	93
20	PIT	143	13	3	18	0	248	3	1	210	326	376	93	126	80	10	68	0.38	40	21	40	34	84	CCb	5%	88	110	9%	9%	100	0%	0%	0.5	-16
21	PIT	427	38	8	53	0	246	10	2	245	335	369	97	81	105	11	77	0.58	44	23	33	30	106	CCc	4%	77	100	8%	11%	90	0%	0%	1.1	88
1st Half		233	18	5	32	0	222	7	1	249	309	372	95	81	101	10	78	0.52	45	20	35	26	103	CCc	7%	93	106	9%	13%	80	0%	0%	-2.6	123
2nd Half		194	20	3	21	0	275	3	1	240	366	365	99	82	111	13	77	0.64	43	26	30	34	111	CCb	2%	56	93	8%	8%	107	0%	0%	3.1	42
22	**Proj**	**455**	**46**	**10**	**52**	**0**	**249**	**9**	**2**	**237**	**324**	**374**	**95**	**95**	**94**	**10**	**76**	**0.45**	**44**	**22**	**34**	**31**	**100**		**4%**	**79**	**96**	**9%**	**9%**	**102**	**3%**	**28%**	**6.6**	**-5**

Stanton,Giancarlo

Age: 32	Pos: DH OF	Health	F	LIMA Plan	C+
Bats: R	Ht: 6' 6" Wt: 245	PT/Exp	A	Rand Var	0
		Consist	A	MM	4135

Top exit velocity since rookie season sparked resurgent BA and HR. While xBA points to pullback, power was backed by xHR and continued elite rate of barrels. The rub here continues to be spotty health, especially as he approaches his mid-30s. So if we build in the likelihood of some time missed to injury, 30 HR is the right baseline to use.

Yr	Tm	PA	R	HR	RBI	SB	BA	xHR	xSB	xBA	OBP	SLG	OPS+	vL+	vR+	bb%	ct%	Eye	G	L	F	h%	HctX	QBaB	Brl%	PX	xPX	HR/F	xHR/F	Spd	SBA%	SB%	RAR	BPX
17	MIA	692	123	59	132	2	281	53	10	296	376	631	137	164	127	12	73	0.52	45	16	39	29	114	ACf	17%	197	131	34%	31%	60	2%	50%	56.8	282
18	NYY	705	102	38	100	5	266	41	5	250	343	509	114	137	105	10	66	0.33	45	19	37	34	103	ACd	15%	164	113	25%	27%	106	3%	100%	27.8	160
19	NYY	72	8	3	13	0	288	4	1	218	403	492	124	147	116	17	59	0.50	44	22	33	44	86	ADf	25%	138	116	25%	33%	76	0%	0%	3.2	22
20	NYY	93	12	4	11	1	250	5	0	268	387	500	118	97	124	16	64	0.56	47	27	27	33	122	ADc	18%	175	86	31%	38%	69	8%	50%	2.9	212
21	NYY	579	64	35	97	0	273	35	6	241	354	516	119	121	119	11	69	0.40	45	19	37	33	118	ACf	16%	144	113	27%	27%	66	0%	0%	21.9	138
1st Half		258	27	14	39	0	269	15	3	223	364	489	119	102	126	13	67	0.47	49	17	34	34	117	ADd	16%	133	92	27%	29%	84	0%	0%	8.7	112
2nd Half		321	37	21	58	0	275	20	3	253	346	537	119	135	113	9	71	0.35	41	20	39	32	119	ACf	15%	152	128	26%	25%	59	0%	0%	12.9	165
22	**Proj**	**525**	**70**	**31**	**89**	**1**	**262**	**31**	**0**	**252**	**346**	**504**	**115**	**119**	**114**	**11**	**69**	**0.40**	**45**	**21**	**34**	**31**	**112**		**18%**	**145**	**109**	**27%**	**28%**	**58**	**0%**	**77%**	**17.7**	**104**

STEPHEN NICKRAND

Stassi,Max

Age: 31	Pos: CA		Health	C	LIMA Plan	D+
Bats: R	Ht: 5' 10"	Wt: 200	PT/Exp	C	Rand Var	-4
			Consist	F	MM	3003

Perpetual backup backstop showing signs of something more? Back-to-back double-digit barrel rates are encouraging and hint at untapped upside. Problem is, that huge 2020 ct% jump looks like a sample-size mirage, and his 1st half BA spike is due to a h% bump. Any power burst will come with a hurtful BA but if you can stomach it... UP: 20 HR

Yr Tm	PA	R	HR	RBI	SB	BA	xHR	xSB	xBA	OBP	SLG	OPS+	vL+	vR+	bb%	ct%	Eye	G	L	F	h%	HctX	QBaB	Brl%	PX	xPX	HR/F	xHR/F	Spd	SBA%	SB%	RAR	BPX	R$
17 HOU *	309	46	12	30	1	212	3	4	199	300	391	94	99	108	11	66	0.37	38	10	52	27	89	CAf	14%	118	105	18%	27%	79	3%	37%	-3.4	24	$1
18 HOU	250	28	8	27	0	226	10	1	224	316	394	95	90	96	9	67	0.31	52	18	31	30	88	BDf	9%	121	112	18%	22%	83	0%	0%	3.4	27	$2
19 2 AL	147	7	1	5	0	136	2	0	164	211	167	52	27	61	8	63	0.24	46	21	33	21	100	BCd	4%	19	55	4%	7%	87	0%	0%	-11.5	-326	-$6
20 LAA	105	12	7	20	0	278	7	0	265	352	533	118	134	100	10	77	0.52	40	22	38	29	103	ABd	11%	126	98	26%	26%	72	0%	0%	6.6	208	$9
21 LAA	319	45	13	35	0	241	14	2	229	326	426	103	87	108	9	64	0.28	44	23	33	33	79	BCf	11%	121	107	22%	23%	100	0%	0%	2.4	12	$5
1st Half	115	22	5	14	0	294	5	1	259	374	480	119	121	118	9	67	0.29	47	31	22	40	80	AFc	10%	119	81	33%	33%	102	0%	0%	5.9	46	$3
2nd Half	204	23	8	21	0	211	9	1	212	299	394	94	59	103	9	63	0.27	42	18	39	29	79	CBf	12%	123	123	18%	20%	96	0%	0%	-2.8	-8	$1
22 Proj	**350**	**44**	**14**	**41**	**0**	**231**	**16**	**1**	**226**	**312**	**404**	**97**	**95**	**98**	**9**	**67**	**0.31**	**43**	**22**	**34**	**30**	**89**		**9%**	**108**	**95**	**20%**	**23%**	**74**	**1%**	**50%**	**4.9**	**-43**	**$5**

Stephenson,Tyler

Age: 25	Pos: CA 1B		Health	A	LIMA Plan	C+
Bats: R	Ht: 6' 4"	Wt: 225	PT/Exp	B	Rand Var	+1
			Consist	D	MM	2043

11th overall pick in 2015 draft finally showed signs of becoming a full timer and now he gets an unobstructed chance. That pedigree, plus soaring contact rate, lack of lefty/righty splits, and dual C/IF eligibility color us intrigued. Groundball stroke, shaky power foundation warn of some caution, but this is a growth stock worthy of investment.

Yr Tm	PA	R	HR	RBI	SB	BA	xHR	xSB	xBA	OBP	SLG	OPS+	vL+	vR+	bb%	ct%	Eye	G	L	F	h%	HctX	QBaB	Brl%	PX	xPX	HR/F	xHR/F	Spd	SBA%	SB%	RAR	BPX	R$
17																																		
18																																		
19 aa	347	42	6	40	0	266		5		339	387	100			10	78	0.50				33				71				97	0%	0%		67	$5
20 CIN	20	4	2	6	0	294	1	0	225	400	647	139	84	196	10	47	0.22	38	25	38	50	71	BBa	13%	268	161	67%	33%	113	0%	0%	2.1	236	$1
21 CIN	402	56	10	45	0	286	10	2	271	366	431	109	111	109	10	79	0.55	50	25	25	34	96	CDc	5%	89	67	14%	14%	96	0%	0%	14.6	142	$11
1st Half	205	31	5	22	0	273	6	1	273	376	426	112	115	109	12	79	0.65	54	23	23	32	100	BDa	7%	94	59	16%	19%	97	0%	0%	6.4	177	$7
2nd Half	197	25	5	23	0	299	5	1	269	355	437	107	106	108	9	78	0.45	45	28	27	36	93	CDf	4%	83	74	13%	13%	99	0%	0%	7.8	112	$7
22 Proj	**406**	**55**	**12**	**47**	**0**	**277**	**11**	**2**	**273**	**354**	**433**	**107**	**107**	**106**	**10**	**78**	**0.52**	**49**	**26**	**25**	**33**	**96**		**5%**	**93**	**68**	**16%**	**15%**	**100**	**3%**	**0%**	**18.8**	**92**	**$13**

Stevenson,Andrew

Age: 28	Pos: CF LF		Health	B	LIMA Plan	F
Bats: L	Ht: 6' 0"	Wt: 192	PT/Exp	D	Rand Var	-2
			Consist	F	MM	1201

5-23-.229 in 213 PA at WAS. Groundball hitters with big holes in their swing just aren't good speculations. Powered up in 2nd half as barrel rate doubled, but those flashes haven't stuck for him in the past. 96th percentile Statcast sprint speed makes us interested in his legs, but he'll keep being just a tease with that mediocre contact rate.

Yr Tm	PA	R	HR	RBI	SB	BA	xHR	xSB	xBA	OBP	SLG	OPS+	vL+	vR+	bb%	ct%	Eye	G	L	F	h%	HctX	QBaB	Brl%	PX	xPX	HR/F	xHR/F	Spd	SBA%	SB%	RAR	BPX	R$
17 WAS *	480	48	2	33	10	233	0	7	247	285	288	78	18	72	7	73	0.27	62	24	14	32	61	DFb	0%	37	-6	0%	0%	126	12%	70%	-31.7	-76	$4
18 WAS *	405	43	6	37	11	220	1	7	232	283	304	79	80	82	8	71	0.30	46	28	26	29	66	CDb	4%	57	103	8%	8%	102	20%	59%	-17.8	-67	$6
19 WAS *	445	55	6	40	11	287	1	15	235	332	410	103	278	126	6	70	0.22	50	22	28	40	51	DCc	11%	74	88	0%	20%	160	15%	65%	5.6	4	$13
20 WAS	47	11	2	12	2	366	1	1	332	447	732	156	65	159	11	73	0.45	34	34	31	46	128	BDc	7%	235	111	22%	11%	110	18%	100%	8.4	548	$8
21 WAS *	270	30	7	29	2	260	6	7	221	303	378	94	90	85	6	70	0.20	49	20	30	35	94	CDf	6%	77	78	13%	15%	98	4%	71%	-8.0	-58	$5
1st Half	111	14	2	10	0	228	2	3	206	272	308	81	99	79	6	68	0.19	55	20	25	32	70	DFf	4%	51	41	13%	13%	118	4%	0%	-6.9	-146	-$4
2nd Half	159	16	5	19	2	282	3	4	229	324	426	101	78	91	6	71	0.22	44	20	36	37	119	BDf	8%	93	115	13%	13%	85	4%	100%	0.4	-8	$4
22 Proj	**140**	**16**	**2**	**14**	**2**	**255**	**3**	**2**	**225**	**312**	**355**	**91**	**73**	**93**	**6**	**70**	**0.24**	**51**	**23**	**27**	**35**	**85**		**4%**	**66**	**70**	**9%**	**12%**	**104**	**6%**	**63%**	**-1.4**	**-107**	**$4**

Stewart,D.J.

Age: 28	Pos: LF RF		Health	B	LIMA Plan	D+
Bats: L	Ht: 6' 0"	Wt: 230	PT/Exp	C	Rand Var	+1
			Consist	A	MM	4103

PRO: Swing plane now conducive to power; late xPX surge backed by elite rate of barrels; added 10 points of contact (though faint praise). CON: OPS +vL makes him a platoon guy; xBA confirms ugly BA is here to stay; should be showing more growth by this age. If he taps back into elite Brl% from 2020 and contact returns to pre-'20 levels... UP: 25 HR

Yr Tm	PA	R	HR	RBI	SB	BA	xHR	xSB	xBA	OBP	SLG	OPS+	vL+	vR+	bb%	ct%	Eye	G	L	F	h%	HctX	QBaB	Brl%	PX	xPX	HR/F	xHR/F	Spd	SBA%	SB%	RAR	BPX	R$
17 aa	514	65	17	64	16	229		7		314	379	94			11	77	0.55				26				82				99	16%	78%		85	$12
18 BAL *	512	56	14	55	11	209	1	9	204	284	354	86	44	121	9	73	0.38	34	14	52	26	74	DBf	7%	95	119	20%	7%	82	16%	66%	-20.3	40	$8
19 BAL *	418	53	15	58	5	244	4	8	248	330	434	106	104	93	11	76	0.55	48	14	37	28	92	CCf	7%	103	87	11%	11%	72	12%	43%	-6.1	130	$9
20 BAL	112	13	7	15	0	193	5	2	208	355	455	107	70	115	18	57	0.53	41	16	43	23	88	CCf	19%	174	121	33%	24%	86	0%	0%	-1.4	120	$4
21 BAL	318	39	12	33	0	204	14	1	201	324	374	96	73	100	14	67	0.49	35	16	49	25	85	CAf	9%	108	112	14%	16%	69	0%	0%	-14.0	19	$1
1st Half	199	23	7	21	0	209	7	0	200	317	360	94	78	98	13	67	0.45	37	17	45	27	83	CBf	7%	94	104	13%	13%	73	0%	0%	-9.4	-23	$1
2nd Half	119	16	5	12	0	194	7	0	205	336	398	99	60	104	16	66	0.58	31	13	56	23	88	CAf	14%	134	127	14%	19%	75	0%	0%	-3.9	112	-$4
22 Proj	**350**	**44**	**15**	**41**	**2**	**207**	**16**	**1**	**212**	**329**	**403**	**99**	**82**	**103**	**14**	**67**	**0.50**	**38**	**15**	**47**	**25**	**88**		**12%**	**123**	**112**	**16%**	**16%**	**70**	**1%**	**57%**	**-2.1**	**42**	**$7**

Story,Trevor

Age: 29	Pos: SS		Health	A	LIMA Plan	D+
Bats: R	Ht: 6' 2"	Wt: 213	PT/Exp	A	Rand Var	+2
			Consist	B	MM	4525

Some might be fearful of further erosion after this apparent pullback, but it was really more of the same. Power, speed skills back that assertion. Culprit for 40-point loss from batting average baseline lays squarely on sharp reduction in hit rate, which history says should correct. But if he moves to sea level, 2021 repeat makes a very nice baseline expectation

Yr Tm	PA	R	HR	RBI	SB	BA	xHR	xSB	xBA	OBP	SLG	OPS+	vL+	vR+	bb%	ct%	Eye	G	L	F	h%	HctX	QBaB	Brl%	PX	xPX	HR/F	xHR/F	Spd	SBA%	SB%	RAR	BPX	R$
17 COL	555	68	24	82	7	239	21	6	224	308	457	104	140	89	9	62	0.26	34	18	48	33	101	BAc	11%	156	166	16%	14%	119	8%	78%	2.5	85	$12
18 COL	656	88	37	108	27	291	38	9	271	348	567	123	142	112	7	72	0.28	34	23	43	35	118	ABc	13%	172	155	20%	20%	120	23%	82%	53.5	257	$38
19 COL	656	111	35	85	23	294	26	23	259	363	554	127	130	125	9	70	0.33	33	24	42	36	108	ABb	9%	147	132	20%	15%	139	19%	74%	37.9	226	$34
20 COL	259	41	11	28	15	289	11	9	242	355	519	116	136	107	9	73	0.38	30	23	48	35	121	BAc	9%	129	146	13%	13%	170	28%	83%	14.6	268	$40
21 COL	595	88	24	75	20	251	29	22	250	329	471	110	133	101	9	74	0.38	37	19	44	30	115	BBd	10%	132	136	14%	17%	131	20%	77%	9.2	227	$24
1st Half	296	39	10	39	15	255	13	12	249	328	445	108	113	105	9	75	0.42	36	22	42	30	115	BBd	9%	113	132	12%	15%	112	20%	79%	3.0	177	$26
2nd Half	299	49	14	36	5	247	17	11	252	331	498	112	156	98	9	72	0.35	38	15	47	29	115	AAd	11%	152	139	16%	19%	143	20%	71%	5.3	277	$20
22 Proj	**595**	**92**	**27**	**77**	**22**	**275**	**29**	**17**	**249**	**346**	**512**	**117**	**138**	**108**	**9**	**72**	**0.35**	**35**	**20**	**45**	**34**	**115**		**10%**	**143**	**141**	**16%**	**16%**	**131**	**16%**	**79%**	**29.6**	**237**	**$33**

Straw,Myles

Age: 27	Pos: CF		Health	A	LIMA Plan	C+
Bats: R	Ht: 5' 10"	Wt: 178	PT/Exp	A	Rand Var	-3
			Consist	D	MM	0515

Steals have been declining each season since 2016, making one-trick ponies like this more attractive than they used to be. Speedy wheels validated by 96th percentile sprint speed. That combined with good SB success rate and patience at plate give him more upside there. Just heed BA downside and know he won't help you anywhere else. UP: 50 SB

Yr Tm	PA	R	HR	RBI	SB	BA	xHR	xSB	xBA	OBP	SLG	OPS+	vL+	vR+	bb%	ct%	Eye	G	L	F	h%	HctX	QBaB	Brl%	PX	xPX	HR/F	xHR/F	Spd	SBA%	SB%	RAR	BPX	R$
17 aa	52	8	0	3	2	214		1		303	214	70			11	77	0.56				28				0				117	13%	100%		-91	-$1
18 HOU *	581	78	2	25	57	246	0	18	181	318	298	83	0	141	10	77	0.47	44	11	44	31	95	DCa	11%	34	139	25%	0%	170	41%	84%	-7.9	30	$27
19 HOU *	427	59	1	30	21	259	1	31	234	330	317	90	109	95	10	78	0.48	48	23	29	33	86	DDa	1%	34	60	0%	4%	169	22%	78%	-8.9	37	$12
20 HOU	86	8	0	8	6	207	1	2	195	244	256	66	9	99	5	73	0.18	36	22	42	28	79	CBb	2%	41	83	0%	4%	115	47%	75%	-7.0	-112	$5
21 2 AL	638	86	4	48	30	271	5	52	239	349	348	96	81	103	11	79	0.55	41	26	34	34	70	DCa	1%	53	52	3%	3%	139	19%	83%	-5.5	81	$26
1st Half	313	36	2	27	13	268	2	26	237	349	338	96	80	104	11	79	0.59	46	24	31	33	68	DDa	2%	46	34	3%	3%	151	19%	72%	-6.2	81	$19
2nd Half	325	50	2	21	17	274	3	25	240	348	356	95	81	101	10	78	0.52	36	28	36	34	73	CBa	1%	59	69	2%	4%	123	19%	94%	-1.9	77	$23
22 Proj	**560**	**77**	**2**	**38**	**33**	**264**	**4**	**20**	**227**	**338**	**330**	**91**	**70**	**100**	**10**	**78**	**0.51**	**41**	**25**	**35**	**33**	**76**		**1%**	**45**	**61**	**2%**	**3%**	**138**	**16%**	**84%**	**1.6**	**28**	**$25**

Suárez,Eugenio

Age: 30	Pos: 3B SS		Health	A	LIMA Plan	B
Bats: R	Ht: 5' 11"	Wt: 213	PT/Exp	A	Rand Var	+5
			Consist	C	MM	4125

One of just five bats that can claim 30+ homers in each of the last three full seasons. The downside is his batting average, which has hovered around Mendoza levels for consecutive years. QBaB deserves partial blame, but steady pre-2020 hit rate suggests it can come back. And latest xHR gives power an even higher ceiling. There's careful profit here.

Yr Tm	PA	R	HR	RBI	SB	BA	xHR	xSB	xBA	OBP	SLG	OPS+	vL+	vR+	bb%	ct%	Eye	G	L	F	h%	HctX	QBaB	Brl%	PX	xPX	HR/F	xHR/F	Spd	SBA%	SB%	RAR	BPX	R$
17 CIN	632	87	26	82	4	260	19	10	258	367	461	113	121	108	13	72	0.57	39	24	37	31	99	DBb	7%	118	116	18%	13%	82	5%	44%	4.3	115	$16
18 CIN	606	79	34	104	1	283	34	6	269	366	526	120	135	111	11	73	0.45	38	25	37	33	131	ABa	10%	143	150	23%	23%	94	1%	50%	30.1	193	$25
19 CIN	662	87	49	103	3	271	39	4	260	358	572	129	138	125	11	67	0.37	36	22	42	32	108	BAb	14%	166	145	30%	23%	96	3%	60%	25.2	196	$25
20 CIN	231	29	15	38	2	202	14	1	238	312	470	104	98	105	13	66	0.45	35	18	47	22	93	CAc	14%	160	147	24%	23%	61	4%	100%	-3.9	156	$16
21 CIN	574	71	31	79	0	198	37	2	228	286	428	98	84	103	10	66	0.33	36	17	47	23	94	CAc	15%	146	132	20%	23%	55	1%	0%	-24.8	73	$7
1st Half	326	38	16	45	0	176	19	1	208	258	369	87	66	94	9	65	0.28	40	16	45	20	93	CBd	14%	121	128	19%	22%	64	1%	0%	-21.6	-15	$9
2nd Half	248	33	15	34	0	228	18	1	255	323	507	112	100	118	12	67	0.40	32	19	49	26	96	BAb	17%	180	138	21%	25%	58	1%	0%	1.4	215	$10
22 Proj	**525**	**69**	**32**	**80**	**2**	**226**	**32**	**1**	**243**	**320**	**480**	**109**	**103**	**110**	**11**	**67**	**0.39**	**36**	**19**	**45**	**26**	**100**		**14%**	**157**	**139**	**22%**	**23%**	**63**	**1%**	**64%**	**9.4**	**126**	**$15**

STEPHEN NICKRAND

Swanson,Dansby

Age: 28 Pos: SS	Health A	LIMA Plan B	
Bats: R Ht: 6' 1" Wt: 190	PT/Exp A	Rand Var 0	
	Consist B	MM 4325	

2021 Forecaster tagged him with "UP: 30-HR" based on multi-year growth in power metrics and he took a good run at it. Better yet, both xHR and xPX re-confirm this is his true power level. While his ct% and xBA agree that pop will continue to come with a .250 BA, the smattering of SB are a nice topper on a valuable overall package.

Yr	Tm	PA	R	HR	RBI	SB	BA	xHR	xSB	xBA	OBP	SLG	OPS+	vL+	vR+	bb%	ct%	Eye	G	L	F	h%	HctX	QBaB	Brl%	PX	xPX	HR/F	xHR/F	Spd	SBA%	SB%	RAR	BPX	R$
17	ATL *	594	63	7	55	4	229	7	9	239	314	321	86	100	82	11	75	0.49	47	23	29	29	89	CDc	3%	60	73	6%	6%	108	5%	56%	-19.6	15	$
18	ATL	533	51	14	59	10	238	13	6	240	304	395	94	85	94	8	74	0.36	42	20	38	29	98	CCd	4%	99	89	10%	10%	122	12%	71%	2.2	107	$1
19	ATL	545	77	17	65	10	251	22	11	252	325	422	103	112	101	9	74	0.41	37	26	37	30	109	BBb	10%	96	106	13%	16%	120	11%	67%	-2.9	115	$1
20	ATL	264	49	10	35	5	274	12	5	243	345	464	107	67	116	8	70	0.31	37	24	39	35	110	CBc	11%	120	134	16%	19%	98	8%	100%	7.4	96	$2
21	ATL	653	78	27	88	9	248	33	8	245	311	449	104	104	105	8	72	0.31	40	20	40	30	98	CCc	11%	124	123	16%	19%	109	9%	75%	3.1	138	$2
1st Half		330	33	13	34	5	226	18	4	236	283	419	98	109	95	7	69	0.24	40	20	40	28	96	BBc	12%	121	137	15%	21%	127	9%	63%	-7.7	104	$1
2nd Half		323	45	14	54	4	272	15	5	254	341	481	111	99	115	9	74	0.41	40	19	41	32	101	CCc	11%	126	109	16%	17%	94	9%	100%	10.3	181	$2
22	**Proj**	**665**	**87**	**28**	**89**	**10**	**254**	**30**	**9**	**248**	**321**	**458**	**106**	**98**	**108**	**9**	**72**	**0.34**	**39**	**22**	**40**	**31**	**102**		**10%**	**124**	**115**	**16%**	**17%**	**99**	**8%**	**77%**	**13.7**	**128**	**$2**

Tapia,Raimel

Age: 28 Pos: LF	Health B	LIMA Plan C+	
Bats: L Ht: 6' 3" Wt: 175	PT/Exp A	Rand Var +2	
	Consist B	MM 1545	

Carried over short-season value, but the journey was wrought with drastic 1st half/2nd half, home/away splits (.292 BA/6 HR in 284 home PA), and toe injury cost him most of August. PRO: Contact % gains, bb% and SBA% support the SB output. CON: Terrible quality of contact and amazing GB% block other value paths, locking him as an empty SB source.

Yr	Tm	PA	R	HR	RBI	SB	BA	xHR	xSB	xBA	OBP	SLG	OPS+	vL+	vR+	bb%	ct%	Eye	G	L	F	h%	HctX	QBaB	Brl%	PX	xPX	HR/F	xHR/F	Spd	SBA%	SB%	RAR	BPX	R$
17	COL *	443	59	4	37	14	325	2	6	284	352	468	112	86	107	4	81	0.22	42	28	29	39	71	FCb	2%	85	69	6%	6%	159	16%	76%	10.5	155	$2
18	COL *	482	57	9	45	13	261	1	10	229	296	424	96	52	115	5	79	0.23	24	24	53	32	64	DAa	6%	100	120	11%	11%	136	17%	80%	-3.6	157	$1
19	COL	447	54	9	44	9	275	9	12	263	309	415	100	97	101	5	77	0.21	52	22	26	34	80	CDb	4%	78	64	11%	11%	141	12%	75%	-8.4	81	$1
20	COL	204	26	1	17	8	321	2	6	257	369	402	102	113	98	7	79	0.37	56	23	21	40	103	DFd	2%	49	57	3%	6%	166	16%	80%	1.9	88	$2
21	COL	533	69	6	50	20	273	6	14	282	327	372	96	91	98	8	86	0.57	67	16	16	31	86	DFd	2%	58	38	9%	9%	126	19%	77%	-13.3	169	$2
1st Half		334	49	5	38	11	289	4	9	287	338	399	103	99	104	7	85	0.53	67	17	16	33	97	CFd	2%	67	42	12%	10%	109	19%	79%	-3.9	169	$2
2nd Half		199	20	1	12	9	246	2	5	271	308	324	86	78	88	8	86	0.64	68	15	17	28	67	FFf	2%	44	33	4%	7%	153	19%	75%	-10.6	169	$
22	**Proj**	**490**	**60**	**5**	**43**	**19**	**279**	**7**	**16**	**271**	**327**	**386**	**97**	**94**	**98**	**7**	**82**	**0.39**	**60**	**20**	**21**	**33**	**83**		**2%**	**63**	**49**	**7%**	**8%**	**149**	**17%**	**78%**	**2.3**	**114**	**$2**

Tatis Jr.,Fernando

Age: 23 Pos: SS RF	Health C	LIMA Plan D+	
Bats: R Ht: 6' 3" Wt: 217	PT/Exp A	Rand Var +1	
	Consist B	MM 5445	

Troublesome left shoulder landed him on IL twice; he opted against offseason surgery. When active, he again showcased an elite collection of skills. Elite Brl%, HctX, and xPX allows him to post a strong BA/xBA despite ct% slip. xSB casts doubts a SB repeat, but that's nitpicking. A clear top pick, but the shoulder casts a shadow.

Yr	Tm	PA	R	HR	RBI	SB	BA	xHR	xSB	xBA	OBP	SLG	OPS+	vL+	vR+	bb%	ct%	Eye	G	L	F	h%	HctX	QBaB	Brl%	PX	xPX	HR/F	xHR/F	Spd	SBA%	SB%	RAR	BPX	R$
17	aa	57	6	1	6	3	268		1		294	341	86			3	71	0.12				36				45				104	20%	100%		-124	$
18	aa	383	70	14	39	14	274		11		331	472	108			8	67	0.26				37				136				122	21%	74%		107	$1
19	SD	372	61	22	53	16	317	20	15	265	379	590	134	176	122	8	67	0.27	47	22	31	42	97	BDd	13%	150	126	32%	29%	177	22%	73%	29.8	219	$2
20	SD	257	50	17	45	11	277	20	8	279	366	571	124	105	132	11	73	0.44	48	16	35	31	162	ADb	19%	161	176	29%	34%	115	22%	79%	16.7	308	$4
21	SD	546	99	42	97	25	282	48	16	281	364	611	134	132	135	11	68	0.41	40	20	40	33	134	ACd	21%	203	172	32%	37%	114	23%	86%	47.8	358	$3
1st Half		278	63	26	57	17	301	25	8	307	385	695	150	124	158	13	68	0.45	44	20	36	34	142	ACf	22%	240	169	43%	42%	113	23%	89%	36.9	481	$5
2nd Half		268	36	16	40	8	264	23	8	256	343	527	118	137	110	10	68	0.36	37	20	44	32	125	ABd	21%	167	176	23%	32%	110	23%	80%	11.2	238	$2
22	**Proj**	**525**	**94**	**38**	**85**	**19**	**286**	**42**	**17**	**274**	**361**	**594**	**130**	**132**	**128**	**10**	**69**	**0.36**	**43**	**20**	**38**	**34**	**131**		**19%**	**186**	**164**	**31%**	**34%**	**118**	**18%**	**81%**	**44.3**	**313**	**$3**

Taveras,Leody

Age: 23 Pos: CF	Health A	LIMA Plan C+	
Bats: B Ht: 6' 2" Wt: 195	PT/Exp B	Rand Var +5	
	Consist B	MM 2505	

3-9-.161 with 10 SB in 185 PA. Was sent to AAA after terrible 50 PA in April and didn't return until late Aug, when his power/speed combo flashed. There is much more work to be done, but Sept/Oct's 73% ct% is a good start toward unlocking SB in majors (8 SB in MLB Aug/Sept). Still flawed, but a worthy entry on your "late speed" target list.

Yr	Tm	PA	R	HR	RBI	SB	BA	xHR	xSB	xBA	OBP	SLG	OPS+	vL+	vR+	bb%	ct%	Eye	G	L	F	h%	HctX	QBaB	Brl%	PX	xPX	HR/F	xHR/F	Spd	SBA%	SB%	RAR	BPX	R$
17																																			
18																																			
19	aa	286	30	3	29	10	273		5		330	391	100			8	77	0.38				34				64				134	24%	56%		70	$
20	TEX	134	20	4	6	8	227	4	5	227	308	395	93	106	86	10	64	0.33	38	29	33	32	91	DCf	6%	113	110	17%	17%	152	27%	100%	-1.2	56	$1
21	TEX *	543	56	16	50	20	192	4	15	223	260	346	83	68	64	8	66	0.27	52	16	32	25	92	DFf	6%	102	95	9%	11%	111	27%	75%	-30.6	0	$
1st Half		256	26	7	23	7	186	1	8	204	257	318	80	66	20	9	60	0.24	62	14	24	27	75	FFf	4%	98	74	0%	20%	99	27%	68%	-18.1	-119	$
2nd Half		287	31	8	27	12	198	3	8	241	263	370	86	68	79	8	72	0.31	50	16	34	24	102	DDf	7%	105	100	10%	10%	120	27%	79%	-15.0	100	$1
22	**Proj**	**455**	**52**	**8**	**38**	**18**	**235**	**13**	**17**	**224**	**305**	**357**	**90**	**105**	**82**	**9**	**70**	**0.31**	**50**	**19**	**31**	**32**	**91**		**6%**	**81**	**95**	**9%**	**15%**	**130**	**21%**	**77%**	**-4.5**	**2**	**$1**

Taylor,Chris

Age: 31 Pos: CF 2B LF SS	Health A	LIMA Plan B	
Bats: R Ht: 6' 1" Wt: 196	PT/Exp A	Rand Var -1	
	Consist A	MM 4425	

Neck pain likely contributed to Sept crash (60% ct%, .114 BA, 1 HR in 67 PA). Despite that finish, new HR and SB career highs attributed to more playing time, fly balls, and SB success. However, power metrics are mixed, all the fly balls drag down xBA, and he's at an age where speed begins to fade. Despite post-season heroics, reset expectations to 2018-19.

Yr	Tm	PA	R	HR	RBI	SB	BA	xHR	xSB	xBA	OBP	SLG	OPS+	vL+	vR+	bb%	ct%	Eye	G	L	F	h%	HctX	QBaB	Brl%	PX	xPX	HR/F	xHR/F	Spd	SBA%	SB%	RAR	BPX	R$
17	LA *	614	91	22	76	18	280	18	8	263	343	483	112	113	114	9	73	0.36	42	23	36	35	96	CCb	8%	123	103	16%	14%	143	16%	73%	11.8	164	$2
18	LA	604	85	17	63	9	254	22	16	238	331	444	104	100	104	9	67	0.31	34	28	39	35	95	CBa	8%	134	117	12%	16%	153	11%	60%	8.6	137	$1
19	LA	414	52	12	52	8	262	11	7	254	333	462	110	120	103	9	69	0.32	38	27	35	35	90	DCa	6%	126	106	14%	13%	118	9%	100%	11.9	111	$1
20	LA	214	30	8	32	3	270	10	4	263	366	476	112	90	119	12	70	0.47	46	27	28	34	104	DDb	11%	122	142	23%	29%	136	9%	60%	4.3	184	$2
21	LA	582	92	20	73	13	254	26	11	226	344	438	107	122	101	11	67	0.38	36	22	42	34	86	CBc	10%	119	111	14%	18%	141	9%	93%	1.6	112	$21
1st Half		309	59	10	42	7	269	14	7	239	382	454	116	137	107	14	69	0.51	41	23	36	36	88	CCc	10%	115	97	16%	22%	155	9%	88%	7.8	165	$2
2nd Half		273	33	10	31	6	239	12	4	214	301	421	98	106	95	8	65	0.26	31	21	48	32	85	DAd	10%	124	127	13%	16%	113	9%	100%	-3.9	46	$1
22	**Proj**	**490**	**72**	**18**	**63**	**10**	**258**	**21**	**9**	**239**	**340**	**456**	**108**	**111**	**106**	**10**	**68**	**0.36**	**38**	**24**	**38**	**34**	**92**		**9%**	**128**	**119**	**16%**	**19%**	**122**	**9%**	**83%**	**17.0**	**122**	**$1**

Taylor,Michael A.

Age: 31 Pos: CF	Health A	LIMA Plan C+	
Bats: R Ht: 6' 4" Wt: 215	PT/Exp A	Rand Var -3	
	Consist A	MM 2205	

Roller-coaster career was on another upswing in 2021, but underlying metrics paint a different picture. While xHR backs HR output, xBA and xSB illustrate potential downside. History says he might be lucky to find 525 PA again, but if he does, something near a 2021 repeat is probably the best-case scenario. Buy only with accompanying BA salve in hand.

Yr	Tm	PA	R	HR	RBI	SB	BA	xHR	xSB	xBA	OBP	SLG	OPS+	vL+	vR+	bb%	ct%	Eye	G	L	F	h%	HctX	QBaB	Brl%	PX	xPX	HR/F	xHR/F	Spd	SBA%	SB%	RAR	BPX	R$
17	WAS *	460	57	20	56	19	262	16	5	243	311	473	107	115	106	7	66	0.21	43	20	37	35	90	CCc	10%	141	109	20%	17%	130	27%	73%	-0.8	88	$17
18	WAS	385	46	6	28	24	227	10	13	227	287	357	86	82	87	8	67	0.25	51	18	31	32	80	CDc	6%	99	83	9%	14%	126	38%	80%	-6.5	10	$1
19	WAS *	336	41	9	33	15	226	3	14	224	292	393	95	108	81	8	62	0.24	46	21	33	33	103	ADf	7%	119	141	6%	18%	103	33%	67%	-6.2	-22	$8
20	WAS	99	11	5	16	0	196	7	2	244	253	424	90	91	89	6	71	0.22	43	17	40	22	75	CCf	15%	139	100	20%	28%	77	0%	0%	-4.1	124	$3
21	KC	528	58	12	54	14	244	17	3	218	297	356	90	105	84	6	70	0.23	44	22	34	32	94	CCc	7%	71	89	10%	15%	116	17%	67%	-19.0	-46	$14
1st Half		269	31	7	30	5	241	8	2	202	294	357	91	83	94	6	65	0.20	46	20	34	34	75	CCc	7%	75	90	13%	15%	140	17%	63%	-11.4	-88	$11
2nd Half		259	27	5	24	9	248	8	2	235	300	355	88	125	73	6	76	0.28	43	23	34	31	113	CCc	6%	67	88	8%	13%	90	17%	69%	-10.0	-8	$11
22	**Proj**	**455**	**53**	**12**	**45**	**12**	**232**	**15**	**9**	**222**	**288**	**373**	**90**	**101**	**84**	**7**	**68**	**0.23**	**45**	**21**	**35**	**31**	**92**		**9%**	**95**	**99**	**12%**	**15%**	**96**	**12%**	**63%**	**-7.5**	**-33**	**$13**

Taylor,Tyrone

Age: 28 Pos: LF RF	Health B	LIMA Plan C	
Bats: R Ht: 6' 0" Wt: 194	PT/Exp D	Rand Var -3	
	Consist A	MM 4423	

12-43-.247 with 6 SB in 271 PA. Injuries (shoulder, oblique) prompted two IL stints. While not finding everyday role, did manage to blend roughly average ct%, xBA, bb%, HctX, Brl%, and xPX along with good Spd, for a package that bears watching in deeper leagues. Looks capable of being a productive fill-in type when short-term opportunities find him.

Yr	Tm	PA	R	HR	RBI	SB	BA	xHR	xSB	xBA	OBP	SLG	OPS+	vL+	vR+	bb%	ct%	Eye	G	L	F	h%	HctX	QBaB	Brl%	PX	xPX	HR/F	xHR/F	Spd	SBA%	SB%	RAR	BPX	R$
17	aa	93	15	1	6	2	241		1		305	372	92			9	77	0.40				30				85				120	15%	65%		91	$0
18	aaa	464	48	14	52	8	228		8		257	394	87			4	80	0.20				25				92				117	16%	65%		133	$
19	MIL *	367	33	11	44	4	232	0	7	264	277	387	92	0	166	6	70	0.21	89	11	0	30	54	FFa	0%	95	-36	0%	#DIV/0!	100	6%	100%	-6.7	0	$
20	MIL	41	6	2	6	0	237	2	0	266	293	500	105	92	113	5	79	0.25	43	10	47	25	138	CBf	13%	153	165	14%	14%	94	0%	0%	-0.4	312	$0
21	MIL *	302	40	14	50	6	263	10	3	251	321	486	111	114	103	8	76	0.36	41	16	43	30	106	CBd	8%	122	90	15%	13%	144	10%	86%	3.0	242	$11
1st Half		155	20	8	26	4	257	6	1	250	321	495	114	128	94	9	74	0.37	42	15	43	29	90	CBf	11%	132	81	16%	16%	131	10%	80%	2.2	235	$
2nd Half		148	20	6	23	2	268	4	1	252	321	477	108	98	111	7	78	0.36	40	16	43	30	122	BBc	5%	113	99	14%	10%	140	10%	100%	2.0	238	$
22	**Proj**	**280**	**34**	**13**	**41**	**5**	**250**	**8**	**4**	**247**	**314**	**466**	**106**	**111**	**103**	**7**	**76**	**0.30**	**41**	**16**	**43**	**28**	**109**		**7%**	**120**	**92**	**15%**	**9%**	**115**	**9%**	**82%**	**3.5**	**173**	**$11**

GREG PYRON

Tellez,Rowdy

Age: 27 Pos: 1B · Bats: L Ht: 6' 4" Wt: 255

Health B · PT/Exp C · Consist C · LIMA Plan B · Rand Var +3 · MM 4045

11-26-.242 in 325 PA with TOR/MIL. Plagued by inconsistency in 2021, but 2020's power+contact combo flashed again in small 2nd half sample, before strained right patella shelved him for most of Sept. HctX and exit velocity show hard contact; restored FB% bodes well for HR. Small investment could pay nicely if those small samples show over 500 PA.

Yr	Tm	PA	R	HR	RBI	SB	BA	xHR	xSB	xBA	OBP	SLG	OPS+	vL+	vR+	bb%	ct%	Eye	G	L	F	h%	HctX	QBaB	Brl%	PX	xPX	HR/F	xHR/F	Spd	SBA%	SB%	RAR	BPX	R$
17	aaa	491	44	6	55	6	223		6		296	339	86			9	78	0.46				27				78				84	7%	85%		58	$3
18	TOR *	501	48	15	58	6	263	4	4	268	318	431	100	43	158	7	78	0.37	38	26	36	31	115	CCd	12%	106	138	22%	22%	70	9%	59%	-6.5	117	$13
19	TOR *	514	66	27	72	1	249	20	4	257	310	484	110	116	96	8	69	0.28	39	24	38	30	99	BCc	13%	138	114	22%	21%	55	2%	50%	-4.8	74	$12
20	TOR	127	20	8	23	0	283	7	1	288	346	540	118	106	121	9	82	0.55	46	20	34	28	123	BCc	8%	125	97	25%	22%	84	3%	0%	1.7	296	$13
21	2 TM *	383	40	14	45	0	242	16	2	252	298	425	99	99	99	7	77	0.35	41	21	38	27	112	ACf	12%	104	111	12%	18%	86	0%	0%	-17.1	131	$6
1st Half		203	19	8	17	0	223	7	1	251	277	397	94	106	81	7	75	0.31	40	24	37	26	90	ACf	13%	99	87	10%	18%	88	0%	0%	-11.5	88	$1
2nd Half		181	23	8	30	0	272	9	1	265	334	485	111	94	115	9	80	0.46	43	18	39	30	133	ABd	10%	118	132	14%	18%	86	0%	0%	0.2	223	$7
22	**Proj**	**490**	**61**	**23**	**70**	**1**	**258**	**25**	**1**	**266**	**324**	**472**	**108**	**98**	**111**	**8**	**78**	**0.40**	**41**	**21**	**37**	**29**	**114**		**11%**	**120**	**113**	**18%**	**20%**	**76**	**1%**	**43%**	**8.7**	**150**	**$13**

Thomas,Alek

Age: 22 Pos: CF · Bats: L Ht: 5' 11" Wt: 175

Health A · PT/Exp C · Consist F · LIMA Plan D · Rand Var · MM 2311

2nd round pick for ARI in the 2018 draft began 2021 at AA and ended it with 166 PA at AAA. Possesses a well-rounded skill set, though none are elite. Speed projects as his best fantasy asset, but lousy SB% has kept him from tapping into it so far. Remaining skills are average. Prospect with a decent floor, but don't expect an immediate contribution.

Yr	Tm	PA	R	HR	RBI	SB	BA	xHR	xSB	xBA	OBP	SLG	OPS+	vL+	vR+	bb%	ct%	Eye	G	L	F	h%	HctX	QBaB	Brl%	PX	xPX	HR/F	xHR/F	Spd	SBA%	SB%	RAR	BPX	R$
17																																			
18																																			
19																																			
20																																			
21	a/a	468	55	11	38	8	266		7		318	448	105			7	75	0.30				33				106				145	19%	40%		165	$13
1st Half		191	22	3	16	3	248		3		318	421	103			9	74	0.39				32				102				154	19%	30%		165	$3
2nd Half		279	36	8	23	6	286		4	258	331	485	110			6	76	0.27	44	20	36	35	0			114	-22	0%		153	19%	51%	3.4	208	$16
22	**Proj**	**210**	**26**	**3**	**17**	**4**	**256**	**2**	**6**	**228**	**309**	**407**	**97**	**96**	**97**	**7**	**70**	**0.26**	**45**	**20**	**36**	**35**	**93**		**4%**	**97**		**6%**	**5%**	**151**	**17%**	**41%**	**-0.5**	**23**	**$6**

Thomas,Lane

Age: 26 Pos: CF · Bats: R Ht: 6' 0" Wt: 185

Health A · PT/Exp C · Consist D · LIMA Plan C+ · Rand Var 0 · MM 3305

7-28-.235 with 6 SB in 264 PA with STL/WAS. COVID shaded his 2020. Lots of 'buts' here: plus bb% but only passable ct%, good speed but poor SB%, makes hard contact but launch angle is a struggle. Excelled in everyday role in Sept (.277, 7 HR, 3 SB, 73% ct, 12% bb%, 168 xPX) with most of damage coming vR. Worth a flyer in deeper leagues.

Yr	Tm	PA	R	HR	RBI	SB	BA	xHR	xSB	xBA	OBP	SLG	OPS+	vL+	vR+	bb%	ct%	Eye	G	L	F	h%	HctX	QBaB	Brl%	PX	xPX	HR/F	xHR/F	Spd	SBA%	SB%	RAR	BPX	R$
17																																			
18	a/a	553	65	20	68	13	228		7		280	398	91			7	71	0.26				28				105				110	22%	54%		60	$14
19	STL *	333	39	11	46	10	239	2	10	251	303	415	99	164	145	8	68	0.29	47	27	27	31	102	ADc	13%	105	114	50%	25%	136	24%	55%	-3.3	56	$8
20	STL	40	5	1	2	0	111	0	1	187	200	250	60	33	67	10	64	0.31	39	13	48	14	67	ABf	4%	100	93	9%	0%	103	0%	0%	-4.4	-44	-$4
21	2 NL *	399	49	11	45	8	235	8	3	232	323	404	100	150	84	11	70	0.43	42	19	39	31	122	ACd	7%	110	124	11%	13%	131	14%	60%	-9.0	123	$9
1st Half		112	6	1	5	3	172	0	1	184	273	260	74	104	29	12	64	0.38	47	17	37	26	84	CDf	3%	64	37	0%	0%	137	14%	56%	-9.2	-104	-$7
2nd Half		287	44	10	39	5	259	8	2	249	342	460	109	163	97	11	72	0.45	41	20	39	32	133	ACd	8%	125	144	13%	15%	127	14%	63%	2.8	196	$18
22	**Proj**	**455**	**55**	**12**	**51**	**11**	**242**	**14**	**10**	**222**	**316**	**397**	**97**	**149**	**75**	**10**	**69**	**0.35**	**43**	**18**	**38**	**32**	**113**		**6%**	**101**	**101**	**11%**	**13%**	**122**	**12%**	**58%**	**1.1**	**27**	**$14**

Torkelson,Spencer

Age: 22 Pos: 1B · Bats: R Ht: 6' 1" Wt: 220

Health A · PT/Exp D · Consist F · LIMA Plan C+ · Rand Var · MM 2223

1st overall pick in the 2020 amateur draft rose from Single-A to AAA in his first professional season. Immense power and disciplined approach continued to be on full display, as he hit 30 HR with a 15% bb% and 0.68 Eye in 530 PA combined. Likely to debut with DET in 2022 and is capable of providing HR/RBI/OBP value from the get-go.

Yr	Tm	PA	R	HR	RBI	SB	BA	xHR	xSB	xBA	OBP	SLG	OPS+	vL+	vR+	bb%	ct%	Eye	G	L	F	h%	HctX	QBaB	Brl%	PX	xPX	HR/F	xHR/F	Spd	SBA%	SB%	RAR	BPX	R$
17																																			
18																																			
19																																			
20																																			
21	a/a	364	56	21	52	2	230		4		320	479	110			12	73	0.48				25				145				94	4%	60%		231	$9
1st Half		68	8	4	10	1	240		1		334	467	112			12	78	0.63				24				119				100	4%	100%		238	-$3
2nd Half		296	48	16	42	1	227		3	266	315	479	107			11	71	0.45	44	20	36	25	0			151	-22	0%		103	4%	43%	-5.9	238	$16
22	**Proj**	**350**	**51**	**12**	**50**	**3**	**245**	**12**	**3**	**240**	**331**	**409**	**100**	**99**	**100**	**11**	**74**	**0.50**	**44**	**20**	**36**	**29**	**102**		**6%**	**98**		**14%**	**14%**	**87**	**4%**	**80%**	**1.1**	**84**	**$11**

Toro,Abraham

Age: 25 Pos: 2B 3B · Bats: B Ht: 6' 0" Wt: 206

Health A · PT/Exp B · Consist F · LIMA Plan B · Rand Var 0 · MM 2225

11-46-6-.239 in 375 PA with HOU/SEA. Substantial jump in ct% obscured by low LD%. 2nd half FB% spike also lifted xHR, but BA/xBA offset was substantial. Don't expect more than a handful of SB given ordinary Spd/history of poor SB%. 2nd half Brl%/xPX hints at another modest step forward, if sustained and paired with ct% gains.

Yr	Tm	PA	R	HR	RBI	SB	BA	xHR	xSB	xBA	OBP	SLG	OPS+	vL+	vR+	bb%	ct%	Eye	G	L	F	h%	HctX	QBaB	Brl%	PX	xPX	HR/F	xHR/F	Spd	SBA%	SB%	RAR	BPX	R$
17																																			
18	aa	193	15	2	20	3	211		2		273	337	82			8	72	0.30				28				96				97	17%	46%		37	$0
19	HOU *	577	78	16	73	4	271	2	14	259	341	437	108	39	118	10	78	0.49	50	18	32	32	90	CDc	5%	89	64	11%	11%	109	5%	56%	5.4	141	$15
20	HOU	97	13	3	9	1	149	2	1	233	237	276	68	81	63	3	74	0.13	50	20	30	16	84	DDf	3%	69	52	16%	11%	90	11%	50%	-9.4	-56	-$1
21	2 AL *	436	52	12	53	7	245	15	7	234	312	384	96	86	98	9	84	0.60	42	15	43	26	103	CCf	7%	74	99	9%	12%	98	10%	64%	-7.6	162	$10
1st Half		130	17	4	22	2	264	1	2	255	347	425	108	120	96	11	83	0.72	47	18	35	29	106	CBf	5%	82	52	17%	6%	105	10%	51%	0.1	200	$4
2nd Half		306	35	8	31	5	236	14	5	228	310	367	92	80	98	8	84	0.55	41	14	45	26	102	CCf	8%	71	110	8%	13%	96	10%	71%	-9.9	154	$11
22	**Proj**	**525**	**61**	**17**	**66**	**7**	**245**	**14**	**8**	**252**	**330**	**416**	**101**	**91**	**105**	**9**	**80**	**0.50**	**46**	**17**	**37**	**27**	**97**		**6%**	**95**	**75**	**12%**	**10%**	**96**	**8%**	**58%**	**3.4**	**155**	**$16**

Torrens,Luis

Age: 26 Pos: DH CA · Bats: R Ht: 6' 0" Wt: 208

Health A · PT/Exp C · Consist A · LIMA Plan D+ · Rand Var 0 · MM 3123

15-47-.243 in 378 PA with SEA. Demoted to AAA after posting .519 OPS through 96 PA; returned in June and put up .803 OPS with 13 HR in 282 PA. Above-average pop is backed by xPX, Brl%, and robust 333 ft average flyball distance, but GB%/bad launch angle stifles HR upside. Lack of production vR raises platoon risk, but viable 2nd CA material.

Yr	Tm	PA	R	HR	RBI	SB	BA	xHR	xSB	xBA	OBP	SLG	OPS+	vL+	vR+	bb%	ct%	Eye	G	L	F	h%	HctX	QBaB	Brl%	PX	xPX	HR/F	xHR/F	Spd	SBA%	SB%	RAR	BPX	R$
17	SD	139	7	0	7	0	163	1	2	206	243	203	61	78	52	9	76	0.40	59	16	25	22	67	DFc	1%	27	49	0%	4%	102	0%	0%	-10.7	-76	-$5
18																																			
19	SD *	403	45	12	53	1	268	0	5	319	338	433	107	46	106	10	78	0.49	50	38	13	31	169	CFf	13%	91	151	0%	0%	92	2%	44%	7.4	126	$8
20	2 TM	78	5	1	6	0	257	1	0	244	325	371	92	86	96	9	79	0.47	42	24	35	31	165	ACc	2%	75	123	5%	5%	89	0%	0%	0.0	84	$0
21	SEA *	458	47	19	60	0	231	17	1	240	290	423	98	116	89	8	70	0.28	51	18	31	28	102	BDd	10%	118	115	20%	22%	87	0%	0%	-0.9	65	$7
1st Half		223	24	12	29	0	193	8	1	240	252	415	93	110	89	7	69	0.25	53	17	30	21	93	BDf	13%	135	116	28%	28%	60	0%	0%	-5.2	73	$4
2nd Half		235	23	7	31	0	266	10	1	236	323	430	102	118	88	8	71	0.30	50	19	31	35	107	ADc	9%	102	114	15%	21%	115	0%	0%	4.8	65	$7
22	**Proj**	**350**	**33**	**13**	**44**	**0**	**235**	**13**	**1**	**242**	**298**	**409**	**96**	**112**	**85**	**8**	**73**	**0.33**	**51**	**19**	**30**	**28**	**107**		**7%**	**104**	**103**	**18%**	**18%**	**87**	**2%**	**50%**	**-5.9**	**26**	**$7**

Torres,Gleyber

Age: 25 Pos: SS · Bats: R Ht: 6' 1" Wt: 205

Health B · PT/Exp A · Consist B · LIMA Plan B · Rand Var -1 · MM 2225

Spent a month on IL (sprained thumb) in 2nd half. Just as he wasn't as good as he looked in 2019, he wasn't as bad as he looked in 2021; in particular note xHR's view on those two years. 2nd half (fueled by late move back to 2B?) gives reason to hope for a rebound. How much? Look toward 2018 (with a little less BA) as season closest to his baseline.

Yr	Tm	PA	R	HR	RBI	SB	BA	xHR	xSB	xBA	OBP	SLG	OPS+	vL+	vR+	bb%	ct%	Eye	G	L	F	h%	HctX	QBaB	Brl%	PX	xPX	HR/F	xHR/F	Spd	SBA%	SB%	RAR	BPX	R$
17	a/a	230	29	8	32	7	280		4		372	476	115			13	75	0.59				34				117				100	21%	51%		158	$8
18	NYY *	537	59	25	87	7	276	24	16	247	340	479	110	121	104	9	72	0.35	33	25	43	33	102	CAb	9%	122	115	18%	18%	104	7%	69%	21.6	123	$21
19	NYY	604	96	38	90	5	278	31	6	270	337	535	121	125	118	8	76	0.37	37	21	42	30	105	CAb	10%	130	116	21%	18%	87	5%	71%	18.4	200	$24
20	NYY	160	17	3	16	1	243	4	2	235	356	368	96	96	96	14	79	0.79	42	19	39	29	98	CBb	4%	75	64	7%	10%	89	2%	100%	-1.0	136	$6
21	NYY	516	50	9	51	14	259	18	3	235	331	366	96	109	90	10	77	0.48	42	22	36	32	81	CBd	8%	67	81	7%	14%	86	14%	70%	-6.5	38	$15
1st Half		294	24	3	26	5	240	8	2	219	328	310	89	85	91	12	77	0.58	45	21	35	30	69	DCd	6%	45	60	4%	12%	93	14%	71%	-8.9	-8	$7
2nd Half		222	26	6	25	9	284	10	1	254	335	438	105	138	89	7	78	0.36	38	24	38	34	97	CBc	10%	95	107	10%	16%	86	14%	69%	3.0	112	$14
22	**Proj**	**595**	**69**	**20**	**71**	**11**	**265**	**23**	**12**	**247**	**339**	**430**	**104**	**117**	**99**	**10**	**77**	**0.48**	**39**	**22**	**39**	**31**	**94**		**8%**	**97**	**92**	**12%**	**14%**	**83**	**10%**	**66%**	**11.6**	**99**	**$22**

GREG PYRON

Torreyes,Ronald

Age: 29	Pos: 3B SS		Health	B	LIMA Plan	D
Bats: R	Ht: 5' 8"	Wt: 155	PT/Exp	D	Rand Var	-2
			Consist	C	MM	0321

7-41-.242 with 2 SB in 344 PA with PHI. Landed on COVID list in mid-April, returned a month later, and found much more playing time than expected. Puts bat on the ball at a near-elite rate, but nothing good ever comes of it. Pick a metric: Hct is bleak, xPX is rock-bottom, Brl% doesn't even register. Oh, and he's fast but doesn't steal bases.

Yr	Tm	PA	R	HR	RBI	SB	BA	xHR	xSB	xBA	OBP	SLG	OPS+	vL+	vR+	bb%	ct%	Eye	G	L	F	h%	HctX	QBaB	Brl%	PX	xPX	HR/F	xHR/F	Spd	SBA%	SB%	RAR	BPX	R$
17	NYY	336	35	3	36	2	292	1	5	251	314	375	94	100	90	3	86	0.26	52	17	30	33	61	FDc	1%	49	37	4%	1%	133	2%	100%	-6.2	100	
18	NYY *	205	16	0	13	0	244	1	2	253	272	302	77	92	86	4	85	0.26	45	25	30	29	82	FCf	1%	41	29	0%	4%	135	0%	0%	-8.7	77	-$
19	MIN *	334	40	9	34	3	216	0	2	228	237	330	79	0	83	3	87	0.22	38	15	46	22	23	FAf	0%	53	-36	0%	0%	132	7%	68%	-20.0	141	$
20	PHI	7	1	0	0	0	143	0	0	326	143	286	57	0	100	0	100	0.00	57	14	29	14	173	ADa		87	223	0%	0%	110	7%	0%	-0.8	420	-$
21	PHI *	377	32	7	44	2	240	3	5	252	287	343	86	103	77	6	86	0.47	46	20	33	26	61	FCf	0%	56	50	8%	3%	124	3%	67%	-17.9	154	$
1st Half		150	11	2	19	0	251	1	2	240	291	357	90	106	79	5	82	0.32	44	20	35	29	50	FBf	0%	68	38	6%	3%	117	3%	0%	-5.3	119	-$
2nd Half		227	21	5	25	2	232	2	3	256	283	333	83	100	76	7	88	0.63	47	20	32	24	67	FCf	1%	48	57	8%	3%	140	3%	67%	-10.7	192	$
22	**Proj**	**245**	**23**	**3**	**25**	**1**	**241**	**2**	**2**	**249**	**277**	**330**	**82**	**93**	**77**	**5**	**86**	**0.36**	**47**	**21**	**32**	**27**	**65**		**1%**	**50**	**43**	**5%**	**3%**	**122**	**6%**	**72%**	**-8.4**	**56**	**$**

Trammell,Taylor

Age: 24	Pos: CF		Health	A	LIMA Plan	D
Bats: L	Ht: 6' 2"	Wt: 215	PT/Exp	B	Rand Var	+1
			Consist	A	MM	3201

8-18-2-.160 in 178 PA with SEA. 2016 first round pick flashed his as-advertised above-average raw power in first MLB stint, but 52% contact rate undermined any optimism. Optioned to AAA in July, struggled mightily there in 2nd half and didn't get called up again. Still young, but clearly needs more polish.

Yr	Tm	PA	R	HR	RBI	SB	BA	xHR	xSB	xBA	OBP	SLG	OPS+	vL+	vR+	bb%	ct%	Eye	G	L	F	h%	HctX	QBaB	Brl%	PX	xPX	HR/F	xHR/F	Spd	SBA%	SB%	RAR	BPX	R$
17																																			
18																																			
19	aa	495	53	8	37	17	214		9		308	310	86			12	70	0.45				29				55				131	20%	67%		-37	$
20																																			
21	SEA *	481	54	17	54	8	194	5	4	200	273	356	86	55	99	10	61	0.28	42	16	42	27	82	DCf	7%	116	111	24%	15%	87	14%	60%	-24.2	-50	$
1st Half		250	31	12	32	4	214	5	2	216	275	434	99	56	103	8	58	0.20	41	16	43	30	78	DCf	8%	165	113	24%	15%	85	14%	59%	-8.3	31	$1
2nd Half		231	23	4	22	4	174	0	2	213	270	273	73	0	0	12	65	0.38	100	0	0	24	0	FAf	0%	68	-22	0%	#DIV/0!	99	14%	61%	-17.9	-115	-$
22	**Proj**	**175**	**19**	**6**	**18**	**4**	**213**	**5**	**3**	**205**	**309**	**383**	**94**	**61**	**110**	**11**	**64**	**0.34**	**41**	**16**	**43**	**29**	**70**		**7%**	**111**	**102**	**15%**	**11%**	**102**	**11%**	**64%**	**-1.7**	**-27**	**$**

Trevino,Jose

Age: 29	Pos: CA		Health	B	LIMA Plan	D+
Bats: R	Ht: 5' 11"	Wt: 210	PT/Exp	D	Rand Var	0
			Consist	B	MM	1133

5-30-.239 in 302 PA with TEX. Missed most of July due to forearm contusion. Free swinger makes lots of contact with a line drive stroke, but not a whole lot happens when bat meets ball, per Brl% and xPX. While defense/pitch framing keeps earning him opportunities, this looks locked in with this backup CA profile.

Yr	Tm	PA	R	HR	RBI	SB	BA	xHR	xSB	xBA	OBP	SLG	OPS+	vL+	vR+	bb%	ct%	Eye	G	L	F	h%	HctX	QBaB	Brl%	PX	xPX	HR/F	xHR/F	Spd	SBA%	SB%	RAR	BPX	R$
17	aa	418	33	6	35	1	215		5		245	285	72			4	88	0.33				23				37				85	3%	27%		48	-$
18	TEX *	202	14	2	15	0	203	0	1	167	243	280	70	66	66	5	84	0.32	57	0	43	23	44	FCf	0%	45	-27	0%	0%	94	3%	0%	-7.5	33	-$
19	TEX *	278	28	3	28	1	219	2	1	250	243	323	78	122	75	3	78	0.15	46	23	31	27	104	CDd	2%	66	77	7%	7%	91	2%	100%	-8.2	0	-$
20	TEX	83	10	2	9	0	250	4	0	280	280	434	95	104	89	4	80	0.20	41	24	35	29	122	CCf	13%	115	128	9%	18%	83	0%	0%	0.0	188	$
21	TEX *	324	27	6	33	1	238	9	0	253	270	345	84	65	92	4	80	0.22	44	25	31	28	98	CDf	4%	67	77	7%	13%	64	3%	50%	-9.6	8	$
1st Half		174	14	3	17	0	230	6	0	239	244	309	77	68	81	2	79	0.11	42	26	32	28	93	CDd	5%	45	84	7%	14%	76	3%	0%	-8.2	-73	-$
2nd Half		150	13	3	16	1	246	3	0	268	294	387	92	62	108	6	81	0.35	47	22	31	29	105	CCf	3%	91	68	7%	10%	68	3%	100%	-0.9	119	-$
22	**Proj**	**315**	**27**	**6**	**30**	**1**	**226**	**6**	**1**	**253**	**257**	**337**	**81**	**77**	**82**	**4**	**81**	**0.23**	**44**	**24**	**32**	**26**	**105**		**5%**	**67**	**86**	**7%**	**8%**	**75**	**3%**	**53%**	**-6.4**	**5**	**$**

Trout,Mike

Age: 30	Pos: CF		Health	F	LIMA Plan	D+
Bats: R	Ht: 6' 2"	Wt: 235	PT/Exp	C	Rand Var	-5
			Consist	D	MM	5355

Right calf strain suffered on May 17 eventually ended his season. Reportedly fully healed and expected to have a normal off-season. Health grade and slow ct% decline bears watching; but remind yourself he's not yet played a season in which his age started with a "3". Don't let this quality-of-contact slip too far; still a premium bat even if SB dip into single digits.

Yr	Tm	PA	R	HR	RBI	SB	BA	xHR	xSB	xBA	OBP	SLG	OPS+	vL+	vR+	bb%	ct%	Eye	G	L	F	h%	HctX	QBaB	Brl%	PX	xPX	HR/F	xHR/F	Spd	SBA%	SB%	RAR	BPX	R$
17	LAA	507	92	33	72	22	306	32	9	296	442	629	146	122	149	19	78	1.04	37	18	45	32	120	CBc	13%	173	133	23%	23%	116	16%	85%	61.1	373	$3
18	LAA	607	101	39	79	24	312	40	22	281	460	628	146	132	148	20	74	0.98	31	23	45	35	121	AAa	17%	182	156	25%	25%	120	12%	92%	87.6	397	$3
19	LAA	600	110	45	104	11	291	48	14	290	438	645	150	138	154	18	74	0.92	24	27	49	30	113	AAa	19%	180	172	26%	28%	89	7%	85%	71.6	396	$3
20	LAA	241	41	17	46	1	281	18	4	269	390	603	132	102	142	15	72	0.63	25	24	50	31	123	AAb	14%	174	157	23%	24%	129	3%	50%	19.5	384	$2
21	LAA	146	23	8	18	2	333	9	2	270	466	624	150	104	169	18	65	0.66	42	24	34	46	101	ACb	18%	191	123	31%	35%	116	4%	100%	19.4	335	$
1st Half		146	23	8	18	2	333	9	2	270	466	624	152	105	171	19	65	0.66	42	24	34	46	101	ACb	18%	191	123	31%	35%	116	4%	100%	19.0	335	$1
2nd Half																									0%										
22	**Proj**	**560**	**98**	**37**	**91**	**10**	**286**	**40**	**7**	**278**	**422**	**604**	**139**	**112**	**149**	**18**	**71**	**0.77**	**32**	**24**	**44**	**32**	**114**		**17%**	**185**	**147**	**26%**	**28%**	**102**	**5%**	**86%**	**65.3**	**389**	**$3**

Tsutsugo,Yoshitomo

Age: 30	Pos: 1B RF		Health	B	LIMA Plan	D
Bats: L	Ht: 6' 1"	Wt: 225	PT/Exp	B	Rand Var	+1
			Consist	B	MM	3003

8-32-.217 in 262 PA at TAM/LA/PIT. Struggled in limited MLB action during first half, but found regular playing time with PIT in Aug/Sept and surged to a .268/.347/.535 line with 8 HR in 144 MLB PA. Corresponding 2nd half jumps in ct%, HctX, QBaB, Brl% and xPX will need confirmation, but finally hint at the useful player that his foreign MLEs projected.

Yr	Tm	PA	R	HR	RBI	SB	BA	xHR	xSB	xBA	OBP	SLG	OPS+	vL+	vR+	bb%	ct%	Eye	G	L	F	h%	HctX	QBaB	Brl%	PX	xPX	HR/F	xHR/F	Spd	SBA%	SB%	RAR	BPX	R$
17	for	578	83	17	92	1	265		9		360	426	107			13	78	0.69				31	0			96				79	1%	100%	-0.1	127	$1
18	for	559	75	23	87	0	275		3		358	486	113			12	80	0.64				31	0			124				88	0%	0%	21.5	230	$1
19	for	535	72	18	77	0	253		2		352	417	106			13	71	0.53				32	0			96				85	0%	0%	-1.8	59	$1
20	TAM	185	27	8	24	0	197	8	1	214	314	395	94	102	91	14	68	0.52	40	15	45	23	87	BBf	9%	114	119	16%	16%	93	0%	0%	-6.6	88	$
21	3 TM *	425	44	14	51	0	205	9	1	210	287	368	90	97	94	10	70	0.38	41	14	45	25	105	BBd	7%	103	101	11%	13%	84	1%	0%	-22.5	35	$
1st Half		176	9	2	11	0	138	1	0	148	226	203	60	51	65	10	60	0.29	47	14	39	21	84	BCd	2%	53	56	0%	4%	87	1%	0%	-21.2	-262	-$1
2nd Half		249	35	12	40	0	253	8	1	249	331	487	111	113	123	10	77	0.50	37	15	48	28	122	BAc	11%	131	131	17%	17%	83	1%	0%	0.3	227	$1
22	**Proj**	**315**	**39**	**12**	**42**	**0**	**240**	**12**	**1**	**220**	**330**	**426**	**103**	**106**	**101**	**12**	**71**	**0.46**	**41**	**15**	**45**	**29**	**102**		**8%**	**113**	**106**	**14%**	**13%**	**77**	**2%**	**7%**	**1.7**	**58**	**$**

Tucker,Cole

Age: 25	Pos: SS		Health	A	LIMA Plan	D
Bats: B	Ht: 6' 3"	Wt: 205	PT/Exp	C	Rand Var	+3
			Consist	A	MM	1401

2-12-.222 with 2 SB in 131 PA at PIT. First round pick in 2014 MLB draft has mustered just a .217/.272/.330 slash line in 406 lifetime MLB PA. Held back in extended spring training to work on his swing, but no evidence of gains here, either in ct% or in Brl%/xPX. BB% growth is helpful, but shaky SB% muzzles decent Spd. Still safe to ignore at draft.

Yr	Tm	PA	R	HR	RBI	SB	BA	xHR	xSB	xBA	OBP	SLG	OPS+	vL+	vR+	bb%	ct%	Eye	G	L	F	h%	HctX	QBaB	Brl%	PX	xPX	HR/F	xHR/F	Spd	SBA%	SB%	RAR	BPX	R$
17	aa	186	23	2	17	10	251		3		330	364	94			10	81	0.62				30				55				170	26%	76%		130	$
18	aa	564	66	4	38	30	240		22		304	326	84			8	79	0.43				30				53				132	30%	70%		53	$1
19	PIT *	501	58	8	36	9	228	3	19	253	293	363	91	80	89	8	74	0.35	49	24	27	29	83	CDc	5%	77	58	7%	10%	120	11%	73%	-10.7	48	$6
20	PIT	116	17	1	8	1	220	1	2	192	252	275	70	91	61	4	72	0.16	49	16	34	30	58	FCf	3%	37	34	4%	4%	121	4%	100%	-9.0	-144	$2
21	PIT *	380	38	6	26	8	196	2	4	221	285	308	82	58	99	11	71	0.43	52	18	31	26	82	CDc	2%	72	58	8%	8%	127	15%	60%	-25.4	12	$
1st Half		141	12	1	8	3	170	0	1	237	252	270	73	0	73	10	76	0.45	55	18	27	21	84	CFa	0%	64	46	0%	0%	130	15%	60%	-12.2	54	-$
2nd Half		239	26	5	18	5	211	2	3	215	305	331	86	66	101	12	68	0.42	51	18	31	29	79	CCc	3%	78	59	9%	9%	122	15%	60%	-11.4	-12	$
22	**Proj**	**210**	**24**	**3**	**15**	**5**	**212**	**2**	**5**	**222**	**283**	**314**	**81**	**76**	**83**	**9**	**73**	**0.37**	**50**	**19**	**31**	**28**	**74**		**3%**	**64**	**51**	**7%**	**6%**	**126**	**13%**	**68%**	**-8.1**	**-23**	**$**

Tucker,Kyle

Age: 25	Pos: RF		Health	A	LIMA Plan	C
Bats: L	Ht: 6' 4"	Wt: 199	PT/Exp	A	Rand Var	-2
			Consist	C	MM	4445

Showcased five-category skill set with nary a wart in his first full season. Terrific QBaB, Brl%, xPX and xHR fully confirm the power, while xSB and SB/SB% history raise the ceiling on running game. Uptick in Eye paired with elite HctX pushed xBA up in tandem with BA. And nearly everything improved in 2nd half, opening door to... UP: .300/40 HR/20 SB.

Yr	Tm	PA	R	HR	RBI	SB	BA	xHR	xSB	xBA	OBP	SLG	OPS+	vL+	vR+	bb%	ct%	Eye	G	L	F	h%	HctX	QBaB	Brl%	PX	xPX	HR/F	xHR/F	Spd	SBA%	SB%	RAR	BPX	R$
17	aa	306	35	15	42	7	251		3		299	481	106			6	75	0.28				29				136				88	20%	63%		158	$8
18	HOU *	514	73	19	73	16	264	2	14	256	323	447	103	131	41	8	77	0.38	49	16	35	31	95	BBf	4%	109	76	0%	11%	110	17%	74%	6.2	153	$21
19	HOU *	578	81	29	81	27	229	4	11	238	292	452	103	117	119	8	71	0.31	34	19	47	26	116	ABa	13%	124	176	18%	18%	95	30%	83%	-9.9	115	$23
20	HOU	228	33	9	42	8	268	9	9	266	325	512	111	91	120	8	78	0.39	38	20	42	31	119	BBd	9%	127	125	13%	13%	150	19%	89%	6.1	304	$29
21	HOU	565	83	30	92	14	294	38	15	289	359	557	126	124	127	9	82	0.59	34	22	44	31	132	ABb	12%	141	139	16%	20%	107	12%	88%	34.2	365	$31
1st Half		303	44	13	47	5	264	19	8	276	323	476	111	94	122	8	82	0.52	36	22	42	28	138	ABc	11%	115	124	14%	20%	108	12%	83%	2.7	281	$24
2nd Half		262	39	17	45	9	330	19	7	304	401	652	142	164	131	11	82	0.67	31	21	48	34	124	BAa	12%	171	157	19%	21%	107	12%	90%	31.4	462	$31
22	**Proj**	**630**	**91**	**33**	**102**	**18**	**279**	**35**	**12**	**275**	**345**	**538**	**120**	**125**	**117**	**9**	**79**	**0.46**	**36**	**20**	**44**	**30**	**121**		**11%**	**142**	**140**	**17%**	**18%**	**114**	**11%**	**83%**	**35.3**	**321**	**$35**

GREG PYRON

Turner,Justin

Age: 37 Pos: 3B	Health B	LIMA Plan B+
Bats: R Ht: 5' 11" Wt: 202	PT/Exp A	Rand Var 0
	Consist A	MM 3335

Unlikely season of full health drove this late-30s R$ spike, but there's plenty to like in this skill set: ct% as solid as ever; gentle decline isn't that significant in the face of league-wide K% trend. QBaB and HctX remain pristine, xHR validates the power. Don't pay for a return to .300 or another 600+ PA, but a return to high-teens R$ is very attainable.

Yr Tm	PA	R	HR	RBI	SB	BA	xHR	xSB	xBA	OBP	SLG	OPS+	vL+	vR+	bb%	ct%	Eye	G	L	F	h%	HctX	QBaB	Brl%	PX	xPX	HR/F	xHR/F	Spd	SBA%	SB%	RAR	BPX	R$
17 LA	543	72	21	71	7	322	25	10	282	415	530	129	159	112	11	88	1.05	31	21	48	33	138	BAa	9%	108	154	11%	13%	71	5%	88%	32.9	252	$24
18 LA	426	62	14	52	2	312	17	4	290	406	518	124	136	115	11	85	0.87	29	26	44	34	141	CAa	8%	120	154	10%	12%	81	2%	67%	27.7	283	$16
19 LA	549	80	27	67	2	290	25	4	283	372	509	122	131	117	9	82	0.58	34	26	40	31	142	BAa	8%	107	151	17%	16%	91	1%	100%	15.5	222	$18
20 LA	175	26	4	23	1	307	9	2	251	400	460	114	97	122	10	83	0.69	34	22	44	35	163	BBa	11%	84	191	7%	16%	117	2%	100%	4.8	224	$16
21 LA	612	87	27	87	3	278	29	4	260	361	471	114	111	115	10	82	0.62	35	21	44	30	135	AAb	8%	101	143	14%	15%	86	2%	100%	8.7	212	$23
1st Half	326	48	13	41	0	295	13	2	265	387	484	121	125	120	12	80	0.68	36	23	40	33	130	AAb	8%	104	133	14%	14%	77	2%	0%	12.4	200	$24
2nd Half	286	39	14	46	3	258	15	2	254	332	456	107	95	111	8	84	0.54	33	19	47	26	142	BAb	8%	97	154	14%	15%	97	2%	100%	-0.3	231	$19
22 Proj	**560**	**83**	**22**	**80**	**3**	**273**	**47**	**4**	**260**	**359**	**459**	**111**	**110**	**111**	**10**	**82**	**0.60**	**35**	**22**	**43**	**30**	**144**		**19%**	**100**	**157**	**13%**	**27%**	**97**	**4%**	**95%**	**18.9**	**192**	**$19**

Turner,Trea

Age: 29 Pos: SS 2B	Health A	LIMA Plan D+
Bats: R Ht: 6' 2" Wt: 185	PT/Exp A	Rand Var -5
	Consist C	MM 3555

Should he be No. 1 overall pick in 2022? PRO: 2020-21 R$ say he's already there. Speed, PA track records set the requisite high floor. xHR validates his five-category resume, and new team context suited him just fine in 2nd half. CON: Mediocre QBaB; elevated h% trend both point to BA regression. Even still - VERDICT: A very defensible No. 1 overall.

Yr Tm	PA	R	HR	RBI	SB	BA	xHR	xSB	xBA	OBP	SLG	OPS+	vL+	vR+	bb%	ct%	Eye	G	L	F	h%	HctX	QBaB	Brl%	PX	xPX	HR/F	xHR/F	Spd	SBA%	SB%	RAR	BPX	R$
17 WAS	447	75	11	45	46	284	11	6	268	338	451	107	85	112	7	81	0.38	52	15	34	33	87	CDc	5%	94	85	10%	10%	183	49%	85%	6.8	206	$30
18 WAS	740	103	19	73	43	271	18	60	253	344	416	102	105	99	9	80	0.52	49	18	33	31	93	CCc	6%	82	79	11%	10%	160	26%	83%	15.5	183	$36
19 WAS	569	96	19	57	35	298	19	23	276	353	497	118	113	118	8	78	0.38	47	20	33	35	102	BCc	7%	108	87	14%	14%	158	29%	88%	29.2	237	$32
20 WAS	259	46	12	41	12	335	12	13	300	394	588	130	155	122	8	85	0.61	45	21	35	36	126	BCd	10%	124	115	17%	17%	169	23%	75%	22.8	428	$47
21 2 NL	646	107	28	77	32	328	27	25	283	375	536	125	156	114	6	82	0.37	45	21	34	37	117	BCc	7%	112	91	17%	16%	146	21%	86%	42.5	285	$47
1st Half	341	50	14	38	18	318	14	13	275	367	513	122	141	116	7	79	0.33	45	23	32	37	109	CCc	7%	106	95	18%	18%	146	21%	86%	19.5	231	$42
2nd Half	305	57	14	39	14	338	13	12	292	384	562	128	173	112	6	84	0.43	46	19	36	36	126	BCc	8%	119	86	16%	15%	141	21%	88%	26.3	342	$39
22 Proj	**595**	**102**	**24**	**74**	**32**	**303**	**25**	**21**	**280**	**358**	**512**	**118**	**139**	**111**	**7**	**82**	**0.43**	**46**	**20**	**34**	**34**	**114**		**7%**	**112**	**93**	**16%**	**16%**	**147**	**18%**	**84%**	**38.7**	**283**	**$42**

Upton,Justin

Age: 34 Pos: LF	Health F	LIMA Plan D
Bats: R Ht: 6' 1" Wt: 215	PT/Exp B	Rand Var +1
	Consist B	MM 3103

A continuation of his limited late-career value proposition: Lots of strikeouts and fly balls. When health cooperates for a stretch, as it did in 1st half, those FBs still clear the fence with some regularity. But as 2nd half (multiple IL stints with back problems) shows, those stretches of health—and value—are now measured in weeks, maybe months.

Yr Tm	PA	R	HR	RBI	SB	BA	xHR	xSB	xBA	OBP	SLG	OPS+	vL+	vR+	bb%	ct%	Eye	G	L	F	h%	HctX	QBaB	Brl%	PX	xPX	HR/F	xHR/F	Spd	SBA%	SB%	RAR	BPX	R$
17 2 AL	635	100	35	109	14	273	34	9	263	361	540	123	156	111	12	68	0.41	37	20	44	34	112	CBb	13%	176	151	21%	21%	68	13%	74%	20.5	173	$27
18 LAA	613	80	30	85	8	257	30	12	239	344	463	108	79	115	10	67	0.36	42	22	36	33	108	BCc	14%	132	137	23%	23%	96	6%	80%	12.2	83	$21
19 LAA	256	34	12	40	1	215	11	2	211	309	416	100	75	110	13	64	0.41	38	16	46	27	92	CAc	12%	120	114	18%	16%	72	3%	50%	-6.2	7	$3
20 LAA	166	20	9	22	0	204	7	1	223	289	422	94	104	86	7	71	0.26	42	13	45	22	120	AAd	9%	122	118	19%	15%	66	6%	0%	-10.0	64	$7
21 LAA	361	47	17	41	4	211	19	3	217	296	409	97	114	90	11	66	0.36	43	14	43	26	98	BBf	12%	125	114	18%	20%	83	6%	80%	-14.9	54	$5
1st Half	256	40	14	32	3	247	16	2	233	336	480	114	137	105	12	67	0.41	40	16	44	30	107	ABf	13%	147	124	21%	24%	82	6%	75%	0.6	135	$17
2nd Half	105	7	3	9	1	126	3	1	172	200	242	60	67	57	9	65	0.27	49	10	41	15	76	DCf	8%	74	89	12%	12%	87	6%	100%	-12.7	-131	-$9
22 Proj	**315**	**38**	**14**	**40**	**3**	**224**	**14**	**3**	**210**	**306**	**410**	**97**	**101**	**95**	**10**	**67**	**0.33**	**43**	**14**	**43**	**28**	**98**		**11%**	**116**	**113**	**18%**	**17%**	**77**	**5%**	**64%**	**-2.6**	**-11**	**$8**

Urías,Luis

Age: 25 Pos: 3B SS 2B	Health A	LIMA Plan B+
Bats: R Ht: 5' 9" Wt: 186	PT/Exp A	Rand Var +1
	Consist C	MM 3235

A box full of skill consolidation: Rediscovered his plate discipline from minors, stopped pounding balls into the ground, and much goodness followed. xHR endorses the power, 2nd half ct%/xBA says there's room for more BA, and xSB/prior Spd levels hint at some bags. RandVar confirms he wasn't out over his skis. Now with multi-position eligibility!

Yr Tm	PA	R	HR	RBI	SB	BA	xHR	xSB	xBA	OBP	SLG	OPS+	vL+	vR+	bb%	ct%	Eye	G	L	F	h%	HctX	QBaB	Brl%	PX	xPX	HR/F	xHR/F	Spd	SBA%	SB%	RAR	BPX	R$
17 aa	505	74	3	36	7	294		10		382	373	103			13	85	0.96				34				48				123	7%	56%		130	$14
18 SD *	551	65	8	37	2	248	1	8	243	318	366	92	163	53	9	73	0.38	63	16	21	33	83	CFf	3%	81	78	25%	13%	120	2%	69%	-10.5	47	$7
19 SD *	570	71	17	60	5	248	5	6	254	317	408	100	124	78	9	75	0.41	49	20	31	30	95	CCb	4%	87	89	8%	10%	131	6%	60%	-16.7	115	$11
20 MIL	120	11	0	11	2	239	1	2	218	308	294	80	92	74	8	71	0.31	63	18	18	34	71	CFf	1%	40	23	0%	7%	127	13%	50%	-8.1	-112	$3
21 MIL	567	77	23	75	5	249	24	10	257	345	445	108	109	108	11	76	0.54	41	21	38	28	109	CCf	9%	112	125	16%	17%	93	4%	83%	-3.3	181	$16
1st Half	295	38	10	39	3	236	13	5	241	325	415	103	112	101	10	72	0.42	43	19	38	29	102	CCf	10%	111	127	14%	18%	97	4%	100%	-5.0	112	$14
2nd Half	272	39	13	36	2	263	11	5	276	365	478	114	106	117	12	81	0.75	40	22	38	27	117	CCf	9%	114	122	18%	15%	92	4%	67%	5.0	269	$16
22 Proj	**560**	**72**	**22**	**68**	**6**	**260**	**17**	**6**	**255**	**348**	**448**	**108**	**118**	**104**	**10**	**76**	**0.47**	**44**	**21**	**35**	**30**	**100**		**7%**	**107**	**97**	**17%**	**13%**	**105**	**5%**	**63%**	**12.5**	**128**	**$19**

Urías,Ramón

Age: 28 Pos: SS 2B	Health A	LIMA Plan C
Bats: R Ht: 5' 11" Wt: 180	PT/Exp C	Rand Var -1
	Consist F	MM 2233

7-38-.279 in 296 PA at BAL. There are some profiles where you can't even find a foundational skill to build on. He's got one: He hits the ball pretty hard, per QBaB and HctX. But it's the search for the second skill that comes up empty: not enough contact, or fly balls, or speed to conjur a path to value from those hard hits. And time is getting short.

Yr Tm	PA	R	HR	RBI	SB	BA	xHR	xSB	xBA	OBP	SLG	OPS+	vL+	vR+	bb%	ct%	Eye	G	L	F	h%	HctX	QBaB	Brl%	PX	xPX	HR/F	xHR/F	Spd	SBA%	SB%	RAR	BPX	R$
17																																		
18 a/a	329	36	9	33	1	254		3		294	421	96			5	79	0.27				29				108				86	5%	25%		137	$5
19 a/a	357	41	7	41	3	223		3		295	348	89			9	74	0.40				28				78				86	5%	73%		22	$3
20 BAL	27	3	1	3	0	360	1	0	298	407	560	128	140	123	7	76	0.33	47	32	21	44	178	ADa	5%	121	144	25%	25%	109	0%	0%	2.8	200	$1
21 BAL *	391	43	10	47	2	261	10	2	244	327	405	101	97	113	9	70	0.33	50	24	26	35	102	BFf	10%	96	89	15%	21%	110	5%	35%	-2.0	38	$9
1st Half	184	21	6	21	1	236	4	1	250	296	405	98	68	140	8	71	0.29	47	24	29	30	98	CDf	13%	107	112	18%	24%	98	5%	24%	-5.2	62	$3
2nd Half	207	22	4	26	1	284	6	2	236	367	404	104	108	101	10	69	0.36	51	24	24	39	103	BFd	8%	85	79	13%	19%	117	5%	50%	1.1	8	$6
22 Proj	**385**	**43**	**11**	**45**	**2**	**268**	**14**	**5**	**253**	**344**	**422**	**104**	**91**	**114**	**8**	**73**	**0.34**	**49**	**24**	**26**	**34**	**101**		**10%**	**100**	**92**	**16%**	**21%**	**120**	**7%**	**46%**	**5.6**	**16**	**$12**

Urshela,Gio

Age: 30 Pos: 3B SS	Health B	LIMA Plan B
Bats: R Ht: 6' 0" Wt: 215	PT/Exp A	Rand Var -2
	Consist B	MM 2335

First half was outwardly fairly representative of prior levels, albeit with some ominous losses of contact and line drives. Caught COVID in July, pulled hamstring shortly after that. After he returned, contact was there but virtually nothing else. 1st-half-times-two seems like an attainable rebound target, and newfound SS eligibility could make that more playable.

Yr Tm	PA	R	HR	RBI	SB	BA	xHR	xSB	xBA	OBP	SLG	OPS+	vL+	vR+	bb%	ct%	Eye	G	L	F	h%	HctX	QBaB	Brl%	PX	xPX	HR/F	xHR/F	Spd	SBA%	SB%	RAR	BPX	R$
17 CLE *	478	40	6	41	0	231	2	6	254	269	313	79	72	75	5	85	0.35	46	23	31	26	84	CCb	2%	48	60	2%	5%	85	0%	0%	-28.2	45	$0
18 TOR *	280	28	3	22	0	234	1	2	195	267	320	79	136	67	4	82	0.25	45	9	45	28	64	DAf	6%	55	41	7%	7%	121	0%	0%	-11.9	63	$0
19 NYY	476	73	21	74	1	314	20	1	293	355	534	123	122	123	5	80	0.29	41	25	33	35	122	BCb	7%	117	122	18%	17%	78	2%	50%	22.6	189	$19
20 NYY	174	24	6	30	1	298	6	1	294	368	490	114	89	120	10	83	0.72	41	27	32	33	107	ACb	7%	104	64	14%	14%	76	2%	100%	7.6	252	$17
21 NYY	442	42	14	49	1	267	17	4	248	301	419	99	106	95	5	74	0.18	48	22	30	33	85	CDc	8%	91	82	15%	18%	114	1%	100%	-5.6	54	$10
1st Half	283	27	10	34	1	272	14	2	248	314	442	105	110	103	6	72	0.22	47	22	31	34	86	BDd	10%	104	94	17%	23%	106	1%	100%	-1.7	69	$14
2nd Half	159	15	4	15	0	258	3	1	245	277	381	89	101	84	3	77	0.11	50	23	28	31	84	CCa	5%	69	64	12%	9%	119	1%	0%	-6.6	19	-$1
22 Proj	**455**	**52**	**16**	**57**	**1**	**273**	**10**	**2**	**263**	**315**	**441**	**103**	**101**	**103**	**6**	**79**	**0.28**	**45**	**23**	**32**	**32**	**97**		**6%**	**96**	**81**	**15%**	**10%**	**89**	**3%**	**88%**	**7.4**	**84**	**$15**

VanMeter,Josh

Age: 27 Pos: 2B 3B	Health A	LIMA Plan D
Bats: L Ht: 5' 11" Wt: 190	PT/Exp C	Rand Var -1
	Consist F	MM 3213

6-36-.212 in 310 PA at ARI. Journeyman got a decent-sized look on a bad team and... confirmed what we already knew: he draws walks, but strikes out too much. Has some pop, but (per QBaB) it mostly comes from selling out for FBs, which cements the low BA. Double-digit SBs from minors haven't translated. He's already wringing max value from these skills.

Yr Tm	PA	R	HR	RBI	SB	BA	xHR	xSB	xBA	OBP	SLG	OPS+	vL+	vR+	bb%	ct%	Eye	G	L	F	h%	HctX	QBaB	Brl%	PX	xPX	HR/F	xHR/F	Spd	SBA%	SB%	RAR	BPX	R$
17 aa	533	48	6	58	16	257		8		337	359	95			11	77	0.53				32				70				83	13%	83%		39	$12
18 a/a	472	45	11	50	8	235		8		306	408	96			9	76	0.42				29				114				101	14%	60%		147	$8
19 CIN *	462	69	21	59	16	273	7	9	263	352	499	118	64	105	11	76	0.50	36	23	41	31	124	BBb	4%	122	132	11%	10%	91	19%	71%	17.9	189	$19
20 2 NL	79	9	2	6	1	129	3	1	201	228	257	64	82	60	9	66	0.29	43	17	39	16	87	CBf	7%	87	109	11%	17%	94	8%	100%	-8.1	-16	-$2
21 ARI *	390	39	11	47	4	226	8	5	220	317	395	98	119	84	12	68	0.41	35	20	45	30	99	CAd	5%	116	120	7%	9%	93	7%	64%	-9.6	65	$5
1st Half	194	24	6	21	1	216	3	3	204	338	393	102	90	78	15	62	0.48	40	15	45	31	94	CBf	7%	128	115	4%	11%	98	7%	100%	-2.4	54	$2
2nd Half	196	15	5	26	3	235	5	2	233	296	397	94	132	87	8	73	0.33	32	22	45	30	104	BAc	4%	106	122	8%	8%	94	7%	60%	-5.4	85	$3
22 Proj	**280**	**30**	**7**	**34**	**5**	**241**	**7**	**3**	**226**	**325**	**396**	**98**	**116**	**95**	**11**	**72**	**0.42**	**37**	**19**	**43**	**31**	**102**		**5%**	**102**	**120**	**8%**	**10%**	**90**	**6%**	**69%**	**1.2**	**67**	**$8**

RAY MURPHY

Varsho, Daulton

Health: A	LIMA Plan: B	
Age: 25	Pos: CA CF	PT/Exp: B	Rand Var: 0
Bats: L	Ht: 5'10"	Wt: 205	Consist: D	MM: 3425

11-38-.246 with 6 SB in 315 PA at ARI. A profile full of intrigue, and surprising balance: power comes more via launch angle than exit velocity (per QBaB), but xHR backs it up. He's not trashing his BA/xBA to get there; for a CA that 2nd half BA is near-elite. And those sweet, sweet SBs. Top-5 backstop in the making (if he sticks there), but beware the hype train.

Yr	Tm	PA	R	HR	RBI	SB	BA	xHR	xSB	xBA	OBP	SLG	OPS+	vL+	vR+	bb%	ct%	Eye	G	L	F	h%	HctX	QBaB	Brl%	PX	xPX	HR/F	xHR/F	Spd	SBA%	SB%	RAR	BPX
17																																		
18																																		
19	aa	437	80	16	55	20	289		7		355	502	119			9	83	0.60				31				103				131	23%	78%		274
20	ARI	115	16	3	9	3	188	4	3	218	287	366	87	44	108	10	67	0.36	39	19	42	25	76	FBf	4%	110	87	11%	15%	137	17%	75%	-2.9	84
21	ARI *	399	51	16	52	7	243	14	8	254	307	447	104	111	101	8	76	0.39	36	22	43	28	106	DBf	7%	118	119	12%	16%	97	9%	100%	7.3	181
1st Half		159	18	5	17	2	194	2	3	237	254	351	84	57	62	7	74	0.31	32	26	43	23	100	CAd	7%	96	90	0%	0%	94	9%	100%	-5.7	65
2nd Half		240	33	11	35	5	276	12	5	269	343	512	116	123	112	9	78	0.46	37	20	43	31	109	DBf	7%	132	128	16%	17%	99	9%	100%	13.8	258
22	Proj	455	65	15	54	15	252	19	7	243	321	437	103	95	106	9	76	0.40	36	22	42	30	98		7%	108	106	11%	14%	116	9%	89%	16.1	183

Vaughn, Andrew

Health: A	LIMA Plan: B	
Age: 24	Pos: LF	PT/Exp: C	Rand Var: 0
Bats: R	Ht: 6'0"	Wt: 215	Consist: F	MM: 2025

With four blank lines, it's no surprise to see a bunch of pros and cons here. You can see the future value proposition: top-shelf exit velocity, with both xPX and xHR pointing to more power on the way. 2nd half contact gains are also encouraging. But GBs, launch angle, and significant struggles vR all highlight the work still ahead. Still.... UP: 25 HR.

Yr	Tm	PA	R	HR	RBI	SB	BA	xHR	xSB	xBA	OBP	SLG	OPS+	vL+	vR+	bb%	ct%	Eye	G	L	F	h%	HctX	QBaB	Brl%	PX	xPX	HR/F	xHR/F	Spd	SBA%	SB%	RAR	BPX
17																																		
18																																		
19																																		
20																																		
21	CHW	469	56	15	48	1	235	22	5	244	309	396	97	128	84	9	76	0.41	44	20	36	28	110	ACd	11%	97	118	13%	19%	88	2%	50%	-18.4	104
1st Half		244	34	8	22	1	247	11	2	258	316	433	104	147	82	9	71	0.32	42	25	33	31	105	ADc	12%	124	114	15%	21%	97	2%	100%	-5.0	123
2nd Half		225	22	7	26	0	223	11	3	222	302	356	89	101	86	9	81	0.54	45	15	39	24	115	BCd	10%	71	121	11%	17%	88	2%	0%	-12.2	104
22	Proj	560	65	20	60	1	242	27	3	241	323	406	99	127	87	10	77	0.47	44	19	37	28	111		11%	95	118	14%	19%	83	3%	39%	-0.5	62

Vázquez, Christian

Health: A	LIMA Plan: C+	
Age: 31	Pos: CA	PT/Exp: A	Rand Var: 0
Bats: R	Ht: 5'9"	Wt: 205	Consist: B	MM: 1125

PRO: A catcher in his peak years makes near peak contact, but every metric that measures the quality of that contact tanks? That suggests "hidden injury." CON: 2019 HR spike was just a juiced ball product, 2020 BA spike was a short-season fluke, and 2021 is who he really is. VERDICT: Modest rebound potential, just don't chase it too hard.

Yr	Tm	PA	R	HR	RBI	SB	BA	xHR	xSB	xBA	OBP	SLG	OPS+	vL+	vR+	bb%	ct%	Eye	G	L	F	h%	HctX	QBaB	Brl%	PX	xPX	HR/F	xHR/F	Spd	SBA%	SB%	RAR	BPX
17	BOS	345	43	5	32	7	290	6	5	268	330	404	100	101	98	5	80	0.27	47	25	28	35	86	DDb	3%	70	58	7%	8%	86	10%	78%	5.4	45
18	BOS	269	24	3	16	4	207	4	3	237	257	283	72	80	68	5	84	0.32	42	21	36	24	85	CCb	2%	48	51	4%	5%	74	9%	80%	-8.6	23
19	BOS	521	66	23	72	4	276	18	6	270	320	477	110	124	103	6	79	0.33	39	23	38	31	92	CBf	5%	103	100	16%	13%	82	5%	70%	24.3	141
20	BOS	189	22	7	23	4	283	5	2	242	344	457	106	102	108	8	75	0.37	42	20	38	34	94	CBf	5%	100	96	14%	16%	90	14%	57%	6.0	108
21	BOS	498	51	6	49	8	258	9	9	238	308	352	91	75	98	7	82	0.39	41	22	38	30	76	DCd	3%	58	67	4%	6%	75	10%	67%	-6.2	42
1st Half		274	29	4	32	8	261	6	5	230	307	356	92	66	104	6	79	0.30	39	22	39	32	78	CBf	3%	60	76	5%	8%	62	10%	89%	-1.8	-12
2nd Half		224	22	2	17	0	254	3	4	247	309	346	89	85	91	8	85	0.55	43	21	36	29	73	DCd	2%	56	57	3%	5%	94	10%	0%	-4.0	115
22	Proj	490	53	11	50	7	262	12	7	245	314	387	95	91	97	7	81	0.39	41	22	37	30	83		4%	74	75	8%	9%	80	7%	60%	-2.4	65

Verdugo, Alex

Health: B	LIMA Plan: B	
Age: 26	Pos: LF CF RF	PT/Exp: A	Rand Var: 0
Bats: L	Ht: 6'0"	Wt: 192	Consist: B	MM: 2445

Predictably gave back short-season h% spike, but a bunch of skill upticks smoothed that over: a little more ct%, fewer GBs, another pinch of progress vR, a few more barrels. Minor pickups all, but positive impact over 600+ PA. Don't get too excited about xHR; Fenway is tough on LH power. But this is a broad base of skills and may not have peaked yet.

Yr	Tm	PA	R	HR	RBI	SB	BA	xHR	xSB	xBA	OBP	SLG	OPS+	vL+	vR+	bb%	ct%	Eye	G	L	F	h%	HctX	QBaB	Brl%	PX	xPX	HR/F	xHR/F	Spd	SBA%	SB%	RAR	BPX
17	LA *	498	57	6	53	8	279	0	8	328	340	387	99	54	78	8	87	0.70	58	32	11	31	74	FFa	5%	62	40	50%	0%	98	9%	64%	-8.7	136
18	LA *	455	47	9	40	6	287	2	7	265	341	409	100	74	99	7	84	0.52	62	16	22	32	121	CFb	5%	73	68	7%	14%	104	7%	74%	4.4	147
19	LA *	377	43	12	44	4	294	10	4	297	342	475	113	117	111	7	86	0.53	49	23	29	32	130	BDc	6%	90	91	14%	12%	96	5%	80%	7.6	219
20	BOS	221	36	6	15	4	308	6	3	271	367	478	112	103	117	8	78	0.38	52	20	27	33	102	CDd	6%	104	82	14%	16%	128	5%	100%	5.9	196
21	BOS	604	88	13	63	6	289	20	9	271	351	426	107	75	123	8	82	0.53	50	22	29	33	104	BDc	7%	80	71	10%	16%	110	5%	75%	-1.6	173
1st Half		330	52	9	33	4	273	11	5	282	339	421	106	68	126	9	85	0.62	52	21	27	30	101	BDc	5%	80	66	13%	16%	101	5%	80%	-3.3	204
2nd Half		274	36	4	30	2	308	10	4	258	365	433	108	84	121	7	79	0.45	47	22	31	38	106	BCc	9%	81	78	7%	16%	125	5%	67%	3.1	150
22	Proj	595	85	15	61	7	295	18	8	273	354	451	109	91	118	8	82	0.50	50	21	29	34	111		7%	91	78	12%	14%	117	6%	80%	22.3	167

Villar, Jonathan

Health: B	LIMA Plan: C	
Age: 31	Pos: 3B SS	PT/Exp: A	Rand Var: 0
Bats: B	Ht: 6'0"	Wt: 233	Consist: C	MM: 2313

Former speedster making the transition to a more balanced profile in his 30s: legs no longer burn, and ongoing decline in SB% makes us question how much longer the light stays green. But his most impressive skill is continually finding playing time. That gets tougher from here, though he'll remain a category-filler when he plays.

Yr	Tm	PA	R	HR	RBI	SB	BA	xHR	xSB	xBA	OBP	SLG	OPS+	vL+	vR+	bb%	ct%	Eye	G	L	F	h%	HctX	QBaB	Brl%	PX	xPX	HR/F	xHR/F	Spd	SBA%	SB%	RAR	BPX
17	MIL	436	49	11	40	23	241	9	6	240	293	372	90	82	93	7	67	0.23	57	21	22	33	90	CFd	5%	94	83	19%	16%	94	32%	74%	-20.6	-45
18	2TM	515	54	14	46	35	260	15	24	235	325	384	95	97	93	8	70	0.30	56	20	24	34	80	CFd	5%	79	71	18%	19%	101	29%	88%	-2.6	-20
19	BAL	713	111	24	73	40	274	23	30	253	339	453	110	103	112	9	73	0.35	49	20	31	34	73	CDd	7%	100	70	17%	16%	111	27%	82%	0.4	85
20	2TM	207	13	2	15	16	232	2	8	215	301	292	79	77	79	9	71	0.35	60	19	21	32	75	DFf	1%	40	23	7%	7%	88	38%	76%	-13.0	-148
21	NYM	505	63	18	42	14	249	17	26	243	322	416	101	98	103	9	71	0.35	49	21	31	31	84	CDf	7%	101	84	18%	17%	103	17%	67%	-12.6	15
1st Half		212	30	7	16	8	246	8	11	253	332	422	105	86	112	11	73	0.43	47	21	31	30	98	CCf	8%	108	98	17%	19%	102	17%	67%	-3.4	119
2nd Half		293	33	11	26	6	251	9	15	234	315	412	98	104	95	8	70	0.30	50	20	30	32	75	CFf	7%	96	74	20%	16%	99	17%	67%	-6.2	15
22	Proj	350	40	10	30	17	250	10	18	235	319	390	96	93	97	9	71	0.33	52	20	28	32	81		6%	68	68	16%	15%	98	13%	75%	-0.8	-2

Vogelbach, Daniel

Health: C	LIMA Plan: D	
Age: 29	Pos: 1B	PT/Exp: C	Rand Var: 0
Bats: L	Ht: 6'0"	Wt: 270	Consist: A	MM: 3001

9-24-.219 in 258 PA at MIL. Continues to carve out a living by hitting the ball hard (when he hits it). Still, he's practically an automatic out vL, and when he hits the ball on the ground. Luckily for him, most MLB pitchers are right-handed, so he should be able to keep doing this for a while longer. But his weaknesses are debilitating and preclude larger opportunities.

Yr	Tm	PA	R	HR	RBI	SB	BA	xHR	xSB	xBA	OBP	SLG	OPS+	vL+	vR+	bb%	ct%	Eye	G	L	F	h%	HctX	QBaB	Brl%	PX	xPX	HR/F	xHR/F	Spd	SBA%	SB%	RAR	BPX
17	SEA *	550	51	14	69	2	242	0	8	273	328	372	95	68	73	11	74	0.49	32	37	32	30	141	CCa	5%	81	145	0%	0%	46	2%	67%	-26.1	-3
18	SEA *	457	49	19	58	0	229	5	1	246	349	416	102	36	108	15	74	0.71	44	21	34	26	143	ACb	12%	112	161	19%	24%	48	1%	0%	-4.3	107
19	SEA	558	73	30	76	0	208	25	0	240	341	439	108	84	116	16	68	0.62	33	22	45	23	90	CBc	11%	130	123	21%	18%	33	0%	0%	-8.7	74
20	3TM	136	16	6	16	0	209	5	0	233	331	391	96	46	102	15	71	0.61	46	21	33	24	92	BCc	9%	101	77	22%	19%	44	0%	0%	-6.3	44
21	MIL	316	35	11	29	0	220	8	0	224	351	375	100	50	108	17	72	0.71	44	20	35	27	98	ACc	8%	91	98	16%	14%	50	0%	0%	-12.8	38
1st Half		198	23	7	16	0	216	6	0	242	323	386	99	63	105	14	75	0.64	43	20	36	25	98	BCd	7%	99	91	15%	13%	52	0%	0%	-8.3	100
2nd Half		118	12	4	13	0	228	2	0	193	397	355	102	0	113	23	66	0.84	49	21	31	31	109	ADa	14%	73	133	22%	22%	66	0%	0%	-2.8	-69
22	Proj	210	24	9	24	0	220	8	0	226	354	397	102	48	112	17	70	0.68	43	21	36	26	103		11%	104	114	20%	18%	47	0%	36%	0.6	14

Voit, Luke

Health: F	LIMA Plan: B	
Age: 31	Pos: 1B	PT/Exp: C	Rand Var: 0
Bats: R	Ht: 6'3"	Wt: 255	Consist: C	MM: 4025

11-35-.239 in 241 PA at NYY. Lost season of injuries (knee, oblique) for 2020's short-season HR champ. But before you write him an injury-related pass on 2021, it's concerning that he didn't hold 2020's contact gains, which now look like an anomaly. If that ct% stays below 70%, he's just another in the bottomless pool of sub-.250 BA power sources.

Yr	Tm	PA	R	HR	RBI	SB	BA	xHR	xSB	xBA	OBP	SLG	OPS+	vL+	vR+	bb%	ct%	Eye	G	L	F	h%	HctX	QBaB	Brl%	PX	xPX	HR/F	xHR/F	Spd	SBA%	SB%	RAR	BPX
17	STL *	415	51	14	57	1	268	5	5	261	320	455	105	100	95	7	76	0.32	48	18	34	32	126	ACa	10%	116	142	14%	18%	60	2%	39%	-9.9	94
18	2TM *	458	60	25	68	0	276	16	3	274	347	512	115	155	134	10	73	0.40	35	28	37	32	126	ABa	20%	141	158	41%	43%	99	1%	0%	20.7	183
19	NYY	510	72	21	62	0	263	25	2	245	378	464	117	110	118	14	67	0.50	40	26	35	35	90	BCb	13%	120	118	21%	25%	82	0%	0%	12.3	67
20	NYY	234	41	22	52	0	277	19	0	283	308	610	126	118	128	7	75	0.31	41	20	39	27	125	CBd	13%	167	134	35%	30%	67	0%	0%	10.5	276
21	NYY *	292	34	15	46	0	249	15	1	233	312	472	108	103	106	8	65	0.26	40	20	40	32	99	BBb	16%	142	144	20%	27%	74	0%	0%	-2.9	54
1st Half		134	17	7	16	0	227	6	0	226	285	441	101	64	94	8	64	0.23	48	16	36	29	84	CCc	13%	135	125	15%	30%	93	0%	0%	-5.6	35
2nd Half		158	17	9	29	0	268	10	0	240	335	500	113	125	114	9	66	0.29	35	23	42	35	110	AAb	18%	147	156	23%	29%	64	0%	0%	0.8	77
22	Proj	490	66	29	82	0	253	34	1	248	336	492	112	109	114	9	68	0.32	40	22	38	30	107		15%	144	139	25%	30%	69	1%	26%	12.2	85

RAY MURPHY

Votto,Joey

Health C | LIMA Plan A | Age: 38 | Pos: 1B | PT/Exp A | Rand Var 0 | Bats: L | Ht: 6' 2" | Wt: 220 | Consist B | MM 4245

36-99-.266 in 533 PA at CIN. Missed most of May with broken thumb. We typically say that "selling out for power" is bad, but we've never seen it done like this. We'll trade -6% in ct% for +8% in Brl% anytime. Emergence of "aces" QBaB, with more LD and FB, is where the magic happened. Didn't even sacrifice his hallmark patience. He can do this again.

Yr Tm	PA	R	HR	RBI	SB	BA	xHR	xSB	xBA	OBP	SLG	OPS+	vL+	vR+	bb%	ct%	Eye	G	L	F	h%	HctX	QBaB	Brl%	PX	xPX	HR/F	xHR/F	Spd	SBA%	SB%	RAR	BPX	R$
17 CIN	707	106	36	100	5	320	33	14	309	454	578	140	133	140	19	85	1.61	39	23	38	33	125	CBa	9%	130	141	20%	18%	85	2%	83%	58.4	333	$32
18 CIN	623	67	12	67	2	284	21	5	276	417	419	112	101	116	17	80	1.07	38	31	31	34	121	CCa	7%	83	129	10%	17%	82	1%	100%	15.0	157	$16
19 CIN	608	79	15	47	5	261	20	3	253	357	411	106	91	112	13	77	0.62	37	25	38	32	110	CBa	7%	86	116	10%	13%	88	3%	100%	-4.7	107	$12
20 CIN	223	32	11	22	0	226	11	2	262	354	446	106	88	112	17	77	0.86	38	22	39	23	113	CBa	9%	117	144	20%	20%	84	0%	0%	-3.9	248	$12
21 CIN *	555	74	36	100	1	260	42	2	278	366	549	126	96	145	14	71	0.58	32	26	42	29	131	AAb	17%	167	173	26%	31%	78	1%	100%	13.9	281	$21
1st Half	235	25	11	38	1	247	14	1	265	317	456	108	79	131	9	74	0.40	42	25	34	28	130	ACa	13%	120	149	23%	29%	78	1%	100%	-4.4	142	$11
2nd Half	320	49	25	62	0	271	28	1	292	400	624	139	107	153	18	69	0.71	24	28	48	29	132	AAb	20%	208	191	28%	32%	80	1%	0%	23.0	404	$29
22 Proj	**595**	**81**	**31**	**85**	**2**	**259**	**36**	**2**	**270**	**373**	**499**	**118**	**95**	**128**	**15**	**75**	**0.70**	**34**	**26**	**40**	**29**	**123**		**13%**	**137**	**153**	**20%**	**24%**	**78**	**2%**	**97%**	**28.6**	**221**	**$18**

Wade Jr.,LaMonte

Health C | LIMA Plan B | Age: 28 | Pos: RF LF 1B | PT/Exp C | Rand Var -2 | Bats: L | Ht: 6' 1" | Wt: 205 | Consist C | MM 3333

18-56-.253 with 6 SB in 381 PA at SF. Earned "Late Night LaMonte" nickname on the back of some serious QBaB gains, which were also endorsed by xPX, Brl%, and HctX. This was the power breakout scouts have been waiting for throughout his pro career. Reduction in GB, healthy bb%, and success vR all point to a sustainable run at this level.

Yr Tm	PA	R	HR	RBI	SB	BA	xHR	xSB	xBA	OBP	SLG	OPS+	vL+	vR+	bb%	ct%	Eye	G	L	F	h%	HctX	QBaB	Brl%	PX	xPX	HR/F	xHR/F	Spd	SBA%	SB%	RAR	BPX	R$
17 aa	491	68	6	61	8	278		9		377	386	104			14	83	0.92				32				63				105	6%	79%		127	$14
18 a/a	476	45	9	40	8	234		7		318	340	88			11	81	0.65				27				57				122	9%	71%		103	$7
19 MIN *	404	52	6	28	6	217	2	7	249	335	330	92	42	108	15	81	0.92	45	21	34	25	107	CCd	6%	61	97	13%	13%	113	8%	64%	-19.2	141	$3
20 MIN	44	3	0	1	1	231	0	1	203	318	308	83	0	92	9	77	0.44	37	17	47	30	104	DBf	0%	61	107	0%	0%	91	18%	50%	-2.7	16	-$1
21 SF *	435	60	20	61	6	244	20	10	248	319	464	108	53	119	10	72	0.40	33	23	44	29	111	CAd	11%	128	138	16%	18%	109	8%	73%	-2.4	177	$13
1st Half	177	25	9	22	2	242	4	4	259	326	462	110	18	135	11	75	0.50	38	23	39	27	105	BAd	6%	120	99	21%	12%	116	8%	62%	-0.4	212	$7
2nd Half	258	35	11	39	4	246	17	6	242	318	465	106	71	110	9	71	0.34	30	23	47	30	113	CAd	13%	135	159	14%	22%	101	8%	80%	-0.7	158	$15
22 Proj	**385**	**50**	**17**	**44**	**6**	**240**	**18**	**6**	**256**	**338**	**449**	**107**	**47**	**115**	**11**	**77**	**0.56**	**36**	**23**	**41**	**26**	**109**		**9%**	**115**	**126**	**16%**	**17%**	**107**	**8%**	**73%**	**5.2**	**192**	**$12**

Wade,Tyler

Health A | LIMA Plan D+ | Age: 27 | Pos: SS 3B OF | PT/Exp D | Rand Var -5 | Bats: L | Ht: 6' 1" | Wt: 188 | Consist B | MM 1501

May have won some AL-only leagues with that SB outburst in 2nd half. Other than those wheels, there's precious little to get excited about in this box, as perhaps best captured by QBaB. We've got to ask, though: What are pitchers so afraid of, that they're walking this noodle bat 11% of the time? Throw strikes already! And get off my lawn!

Yr Tm	PA	R	HR	RBI	SB	BA	xHR	xSB	xBA	OBP	SLG	OPS+	vL+	vR+	bb%	ct%	Eye	G	L	F	h%	HctX	QBaB	Brl%	PX	xPX	HR/F	xHR/F	Spd	SBA%	SB%	RAR	BPX	R$
17 NYY *	436	68	7	30	24	268	1	6	239	333	397	99	35	66	9	74	0.38	51	15	33	35	54	DDd	0%	85	70	0%	8%	131	28%	79%	0.5	70	$17
18 NYY *	465	46	5	27	10	214	1	16	218	273	305	77	22	73	7	73	0.30	60	13	28	28	50	DFb	2%	64	42	9%	9%	116	19%	53%	-20.8	-17	$3
19 NYY *	427	56	6	40	17	250	2	11	210	302	358	91	98	94	7	70	0.25	52	13	35	34	64	CCd	6%	67	64	9%	9%	121	23%	75%	-12.9	-44	$11
20 NYY	105	19	3	10	4	170	1	3	243	288	307	79	33	94	11	75	0.55	37	29	35	19	71	FCf	1%	77	77	14%	5%	107	21%	80%	-5.7	76	$5
21 NYY	144	31	0	5	17	268	1	7	220	354	323	93	100	90	11	71	0.43	59	18	23	38	48	FFf	1%	42	27	0%	5%	172	51%	74%	-2.4	-23	$9
1st Half	53	14	0	2	4	224	0	2	211	283	265	76	109	39	8	71	0.29	72	9	19	31	8	FFf	0%	18	2	0%	0%	180	51%	67%	-3.8	-112	-$3
2nd Half	91	17	0	3	13	295	1	5	228	396	359	102	83	106	13	71	0.52	50	24	26	42	73	FDf	2%	58	43	0%	8%	135	51%	76%	0.9	-8	$6
22 Proj	**210**	**39**	**2**	**13**	**16**	**240**	**2**	**17**	**221**	**323**	**324**	**88**	**81**	**90**	**10**	**72**	**0.40**	**53**	**19**	**28**	**32**	**55**		**2%**	**57**	**46**	**5%**	**6%**	**143**	**40%**	**74%**	**-4.8**	**5**	**$11**

Walker,Christian

Health B | LIMA Plan C | Age: 31 | Pos: 1B | PT/Exp A | Rand Var 0 | Bats: R | Ht: 6' 0" | Wt: 210 | Consist B | MM 3223

Failed to replicate 2019's power outburst, which now looks more fluke than breakout. Oddly, that failure came amid trends in ct% (up) and GBs (down) that should be helpful for power. The problem showed up in QBaB and Brl%: he didn't find the sweet spot like he did in 2019. PX, HR/F trends are damning which doesn't bode well for much of a rebound.

Yr Tm	PA	R	HR	RBI	SB	BA	xHR	xSB	xBA	OBP	SLG	OPS+	vL+	vR+	bb%	ct%	Eye	G	L	F	h%	HctX	QBaB	Brl%	PX	xPX	HR/F	xHR/F	Spd	SBA%	SB%	RAR	BPX	R$
17 ARI *	566	66	23	73	3	250	2	6	229	301	464	104	204	53	7	75	0.29	29	14	57	29	174	ABc	43%	122	330	50%	50%	116	4%	56%	-18.8	148	$12
18 ARI *	392	46	13	47	2	211	4	2	198	248	383	85	91	61	5	65	0.14	37	11	52	29	53	DAc	15%	123	112	21%	29%	104	3%	100%	-23.2	3	$4
19 ARI	603	86	29	73	8	259	34	5	248	348	476	114	110	115	11	71	0.43	42	20	38	31	113	ABc	13%	122	127	20%	24%	91	6%	89%	4.0	119	$18
20 ARI	243	35	7	34	1	271	9	2	270	333	459	105	99	107	8	77	0.38	43	23	34	32	140	BCf	6%	114	117	12%	16%	94	4%	50%	-4.3	180	$19
21 ARI	445	55	10	46	0	244	12	4	234	315	382	96	90	98	9	74	0.36	39	22	39	31	107	CBd	6%	89	103	9%	10%	97	0%	0%	-22.7	54	$6
1st Half	190	24	4	19	0	222	4	1	239	274	341	86	90	84	6	77	0.29	45	22	33	27	106	CCd	5%	70	87	9%	9%	118	0%	0%	-14.1	50	$0
2nd Half	255	31	6	27	0	262	9	2	232	345	413	103	89	109	10	71	0.40	34	22	43	34	108	BBc	8%	105	116	9%	13%	82	0%	0%	-5.3	62	$7
22 Proj	**420**	**55**	**13**	**50**	**2**	**250**	**20**	**2**	**239**	**317**	**421**	**100**	**93**	**103**	**8**	**73**	**0.33**	**39**	**21**	**40**	**31**	**115**		**8%**	**108**	**111**	**12%**	**18%**	**89**	**2%**	**74%**	**0.0**	**64**	**$11**

Walls,Taylor

Health A | LIMA Plan D | Age: 25 | Pos: SS | PT/Exp D | Rand Var 0 | Bats: B | Ht: 5' 10" | Wt: 180 | Consist B | MM 1301

1-15-.211 with 4 SB in 176 PA at TAM. Glove-first rookie got his call following Adames trade, then got Wally Pipp'd by Wander Franco. Defense is supposedly good enough to give him a career on its own; healthy bb% and double-digit SB could be the start of a useful offensive profile. Next step is to stabilize ct%, but he'll get some chances to do that.

Yr Tm	PA	R	HR	RBI	SB	BA	xHR	xSB	xBA	OBP	SLG	OPS+	vL+	vR+	bb%	ct%	Eye	G	L	F	h%	HctX	QBaB	Brl%	PX	xPX	HR/F	xHR/F	Spd	SBA%	SB%	RAR	BPX	R$
17																																		
18																																		
19 aa	236	40	5	19	14	252		4		332	445	108			11	72	0.43				32				111				147	44%	59%		167	$8
20																																		
21 TAM *	387	48	8	39	12	212	3	5	211	326	339	91	83	84	15	64	0.47	47	20	33	31	91	CCb	3%	95	118	3%	9%	93	20%	61%	-12.2	-31	$7
1st Half	156	17	3	15	5	243	3	2	197	364	363	101	93	92	16	64	0.52	33	22	45	36	102	CBa	5%	94	178	4%	12%	87	20%	52%	-1.7	-42	$3
2nd Half	231	31	5	24	8	191	0	3	230	301	323	85	69	77	14	64	0.44	64	17	19	27	77	DFc	0%	95	48	0%	0%	105	20%	69%	-9.9	-19	$6
22 Proj	**245**	**33**	**2**	**23**	**10**	**222**	**2**	**8**	**208**	**329**	**318**	**88**	**86**	**89**	**14**	**66**	**0.47**	**49**	**20**	**32**	**33**	**87**		**2%**	**76**	**100**	**4%**	**5%**	**113**	**16%**	**62%**	**-6.0**	**-52**	**$7**

Walsh,Jared

Health B | LIMA Plan B | Age: 28 | Pos: 1B | PT/Exp A | Rand Var -3 | Bats: L | Ht: 6' 0" | Wt: 210 | Consist D | MM 4135

Confirmed short-season emergence as a masher vR (19 HR, .994 OPS in 348 PA), overall numbers actually tamped down because he flailed in a long look vL (.565 OPS in 182 PA). 2nd half shift toward ct% and LDs over power may have related to a July intercostal strain. Could be a case where stricter platoon causes dip in counting stats but better rates.

Yr Tm	PA	R	HR	RBI	SB	BA	xHR	xSB	xBA	OBP	SLG	OPS+	vL+	vR+	bb%	ct%	Eye	G	L	F	h%	HctX	QBaB	Brl%	PX	xPX	HR/F	xHR/F	Spd	SBA%	SB%	RAR	BPX	R$
17 aa	72	7	3	8	1	210		1		240	367	83			4	51	0.08				36				133				95	9%	100%		-152	-$1
18 a/a	352	41	11	44	1	221		4		277	388	89			7	62	0.20				32				131				83	2%	100%		-23	$4
19 LAA *	505	60	25	57	0	239	3	2	241	303	466	106	104	81	8	61	0.23	39	27	34	33	115	ACc	14%	150	134	7%	20%	75	0%	0%	-2.5	19	$9
20 LAA	108	19	9	26	0	293	7	1	317	324	646	129	101	143	5	85	0.33	48	15	37	27	146	CCc	13%	159	111	28%	22%	142	0%	0%	6.2	484	$14
21 LAA	585	70	29	98	2	277	25	1	269	340	509	117	77	137	8	71	0.32	48	22	30	34	105	BDf	11%	144	97	25%	22%	76	2%	67%	10.0	162	$22
1st Half	325	43	20	60	2	284	15	1	277	345	564	127	77	150	8	69	0.27	49	20	31	35	111	BDf	14%	178	103	32%	24%	78	2%	100%	10.1	223	$31
2nd Half	260	27	9	38	0	269	10	1	257	335	440	105	76	121	9	75	0.39	47	24	29	33	97	BDf	8%	104	90	18%	20%	79	2%	0%	-4.0	100	$11
22 Proj	**560**	**75**	**26**	**95**	**1**	**266**	**25**	**4**	**260**	**326**	**484**	**110**	**84**	**120**	**8**	**71**	**0.29**	**46**	**22**	**32**	**32**	**114**		**12%**	**133**	**106**	**22%**	**21%**	**98**	**4%**	**56%**	**14.0**	**111**	**$21**

Ward,Taylor

Health A | LIMA Plan D+ | Age: 28 | Pos: RF | PT/Exp C | Rand Var 0 | Bats: R | Ht: 6' 1" | Wt: 200 | Consist A | MM 3321

8-33-.250 in 237 PA at LAA. Nothing but small samples to work with, at least at the MLB level. There are multiple hints of a productive bat here: LDs beget healthy hit rates, QBaB shows flashes of promise. Even holds his own vR. A touch more ct% could be the key to unlocking a new level, but getting to an age where more chances aren't guaranteed.

Yr Tm	PA	R	HR	RBI	SB	BA	xHR	xSB	xBA	OBP	SLG	OPS+	vL+	vR+	bb%	ct%	Eye	G	L	F	h%	HctX	QBaB	Brl%	PX	xPX	HR/F	xHR/F	Spd	SBA%	SB%	RAR	BPX	R$
17 aa	139	13	3	18	0	260		3		367	351	98			14	83	1.02				29				47				93	0%	0%		91	$1
18 LAA *	567	62	16	58	15	255	5	2	213	326	396	97	101	65	10	69	0.34	35	21	44	34	76	CBc	8%	97	99	15%	13%	81	13%	80%	-0.6	-7	$17
19 LAA *	518	66	19	45	7	226	1	9	243	309	412	100	63	95	11	68	0.37	37	26	37	29	98	ACc	11%	116	121	14%	14%	95	12%	52%	-14.0	52	$8
20 LAA	102	16	0	5	2	277	3	2	238	333	383	95	83	103	8	70	0.29	44	29	27	39	95	ACb	5%	74	98	0%	17%	158	8%	100%	-0.7	20	$5
21 LAA *	291	42	10	39	2	262	10	4	264	328	466	109	116	101	9	72	0.35	36	26	38	33	98	CBa	10%	135	113	14%	18%	109	5%	68%	2.3	188	$7
1st Half	197	26	7	28	1	244	9	3	259	332	436	107	107	107	9	74	0.40	35	25	40	29	105	CBa	12%	121	127	14%	18%	102	5%	50%	-2.5	169	$7
2nd Half	94	16	3	11	1	297	1	1	282	353	526	119	168	81	8	69	0.27	42	29	29	40	73	FCc	3%	167	41	14%	14%	115	5%	100%	4.1	235	$0
22 Proj	**245**	**36**	**6**	**26**	**3**	**265**	**8**	**3**	**249**	**344**	**435**	**106**	**127**	**95**	**9**	**70**	**0.34**	**39**	**26**	**34**	**35**	**86**		**7%**	**117**	**86**	**12%**	**15%**	**116**	**6%**	**78%**	**3.9**	**85**	**$8**

RAY MURPHY

Welker,Colton

Age: 24 Pos: 3B | Bats: R Ht: 6' 2" Wt: 195 | Health A | PT/Exp F | Consist C | LIMA Plan D | Rand Var +1 | MM 2221

0-2-.189 in 37 AB at COL. Corner infield prospect with good bat-to-ball skills and line-drive stroke made MLB debut as Sept callup after 80-game PED suspension. Lengthy Double-A stint in 2019, alt-site time in 2020 and short Triple-A stint in 2021 mean he's about as ready as he's going to be. Pedestrian profile, but a good one to take advantage of Coors Field.

Yr	Tm	PA	R	HR	RBI	SB	BA	xHR	xSB	xBA	OBP	SLG	OPS+	vL+	vR+	bb%	ct%	Eye	G	L	F	h%	HctX	QBaB	Brl%	PX	xPX	HR/F	xHR/F	Spd	SBA%	SB%	RAR	BPX	R$
17																																			
18																																			
19	aa	386	37	11	53	2	272		5		333	448	108			8	81	0.49				31				96				89	3%	66%		174	$
20																																			
21	COL *	131	15	2	13	0	229	1	2	244	291	340	87	40	76	8	73	0.32	19	38	42	30	115	CAd	0%	71	132	0%	9%	122	0%	0%	-7.4	12	-$
1st Half																									0%										
2nd Half		131	15	2	13	0	229	1	2	244	291	340	0	40	76	8	73	0.32	19	38	42	30	115	CAd	0%	71	132	0%	9%	123	0%	0%	-6.6	15	-$
22	Proj	210	25	4	27	0	248	5	1	248	309	382	94	65	108	8	76	0.37	34	28	37	30	104		4%	83	119	8%	9%	101	3%	67%	-1.5	41	$

Wendle,Joe

Age: 32 Pos: 3B SS | Bats: L Ht: 6' 1" Wt: 195 | Health C | PT/Exp A | Consist B | LIMA Plan B | Rand Var -1 | MM 2335

If you can find the guy who makes decent contact and is going to get 500 PA, he's a good bet for double-digit value even if he lacks any plus skills. In the end, all value starts and ends with playing time. That all said, the odds of another 500+ PA here seem poor. But his floor is reasonably high enough to prevent any real damage.

Yr	Tm	PA	R	HR	RBI	SB	BA	xHR	xSB	xBA	OBP	SLG	OPS+	vL+	vR+	bb%	ct%	Eye	G	L	F	h%	HctX	QBaB	Brl%	PX	xPX	HR/F	xHR/F	Spd	SBA%	SB%	RAR	BPX	R$
17	OAK *	506	52	6	45	10	234	0	5	257	256	350	83	0	130	3	80	0.15	50	20	30	28	129	ACc	10%	69	124	33%	0%	121	16%	66%	-28.8	58	$
18	TAM	545	62	7	61	16	300	10	14	261	354	435	106	107	104	7	80	0.39	46	22	32	36	109	CCc	3%	86	77	5%	8%	104	14%	80%	16.7	123	$2
19	TAM	263	32	3	19	8	231	2	5	254	293	340	88	49	98	5	80	0.30	44	23	32	28	89	CCc	2%	62	56	5%	3%	122	19%	73%	-14.2	74	$
20	TAM	184	24	4	17	8	286	4	5	268	342	435	103	90	106	5	79	0.29	49	24	28	34	98	CFf	4%	83	91	11%	11%	123	21%	80%	1.1	132	$2
21	TAM	501	73	11	54	8	265	10	14	259	319	422	102	82	109	6	75	0.25	49	21	30	33	97	CDd	5%	99	79	11%	10%	124	12%	57%	-6.9	119	$1
1st Half		266	42	7	33	5	275	6	8	272	338	454	110	65	126	7	76	0.30	48	22	30	34	93	CDc	6%	115	82	13%	11%	113	12%	50%	-1.8	177	$1
2nd Half		235	31	4	21	3	255	4	7	244	298	386	93	100	90	5	75	0.20	51	20	29	33	102	CFf	3%	81	75	8%	8%	132	12%	75%	-8.1	54	$
22	Proj	455	62	9	45	12	265	8	9	256	319	406	98	81	103	6	78	0.26	48	22	30	32	98		3%	86	76	9%	8%	119	11%	71%	-0.2	105	$1

White,Eli

Age: 28 Pos: LF CF | Bats: R Ht: 6' 3" Wt: 195 | Health C | PT/Exp C | Consist B | LIMA Plan D | Rand Var +1 | MM 2301

6-15-.177 in 220 PA at TEX. Joined the launch angle revolution, unlocking some power while shoving his already sub-Mendoza BA even lower. That was bad news for his running game, which had previously looked like his best path to fantasy relevance. Worst news of all was torn UCL in August, which likely impacts his readiness for Opening Day. Pass.

Yr	Tm	PA	R	HR	RBI	SB	BA	xHR	xSB	xBA	OBP	SLG	OPS+	vL+	vR+	bb%	ct%	Eye	G	L	F	h%	HctX	QBaB	Brl%	PX	xPX	HR/F	xHR/F	Spd	SBA%	SB%	RAR	BPX	R$
17																																			
18	aa	551	63	6	43	14	266		9		328	386	96			9	74	0.36				35				80				125	17%	58%		60	$1
19	aaa	470	45	11	31	10	221		10		274	355	87			7	65	0.21				31				83				130	17%	63%		-63	$
20	TEX	52	5	0	3	1	188	1	1	220	231	229	61	18	94	6	67	0.19	42	33	24	28	82	CBa	3%	38	49	0%	13%	122	20%	50%	-4.9	-208	-$
21	TEX *	295	39	8	23	6	201	6	9	193	273	334	83	62	88	9	66	0.29	40	16	44	27	53	FBf	7%	85	82	11%	11%	159	15%	59%	-16.4	-4	$
1st Half		221	32	6	20	5	233	4	7	207	301	369	93	67	101	9	66	0.29	44	18	38	32	48	DCf	7%	86	67	12%	12%	171	15%	61%	-8.2	19	$
2nd Half		74	7	2	3	1	106	2	1	165	203	227	58	53	61	10	64	0.29	32	12	56	13	62	FAf	6%	83	112	9%	9%	109	15%	50%	-8.8	-96	-$1
22	Proj	210	24	6	14	4	208	6	4	193	290	359	88	71	98	9	67	0.29	36	15	49	28	56		6%	97	94	10%	10%	118	13%	58%	-7.2	-32	$

White,Evan

Age: 26 Pos: 1B | Bats: R Ht: 6' 3" Wt: 220 | Health F | PT/Exp D | Consist D | LIMA Plan D | Rand Var +5 | MM 2103

Spent first six weeks of season showing precious little progress from 2020's rough rookie campaign, then a hip injury ended his season. If you squint, small-sample ct% gains might have been the first step in figuring things out, but a lengthy journey still lies ahead. Little reason to speculate until he shows next step.

Yr	Tm	PA	R	HR	RBI	SB	BA	xHR	xSB	xBA	OBP	SLG	OPS+	vL+	vR+	bb%	ct%	Eye	G	L	F	h%	HctX	QBaB	Brl%	PX	xPX	HR/F	xHR/F	Spd	SBA%	SB%	RAR	BPX	R$
17																																			
18																																			
19	aa	394	61	18	55	2	281		6		334	474	112			7	71	0.28				35				103				111	2%	100%		67	$1
20	SEA	202	19	8	26	1	176	11	1	179	252	346	79	60	88	9	54	0.21	43	15	42	27	75	ACc	13%	131	147	20%	27%	84	8%	33%	-16.7	-136	$
21	SEA	104	8	2	9	0	144	2	1	184	202	237	60	47	67	6	68	0.19	42	17	41	19	76	DAc	5%	62	58	7%	7%	74	0%	0%	-12.9	-158	-$
1st Half		104	8	2	9	0	144	2	1	184	202	237	61	47	68	6	68	0.19	42	17	41	19	76	DAc	5%	62	58	7%	7%	74	0%	0%	-13.9	-162	-$
2nd Half																									0%										
22	Proj	315	32	10	36	1	219	12	1	198	281	358	87	64	96	7	67	0.24	43	16	41	29	76		8%	89	94	12%	15%	88	2%	48%	-11.4	-118	$

Williams,Luke

Age: 25 Pos: OF | Bats: R Ht: 6' 1" Wt: 180 | Health A | PT/Exp D | Consist A | LIMA Plan F | Rand Var -2 | MM 1401

1-6-.245 with 2 SB in 108 PA at PHI. Swiss Army-type (played 7 positions in 58 MLB games) showed some plate patience in first cup-of-coffee, but little else. Speed is the carrying skill from minors profile; versatility plus willingness to take a walk give it at least a chance to flourish. But there's likely a lot of nose-holding if you chase these bags.

Yr	Tm	PA	R	HR	RBI	SB	BA	xHR	xSB	xBA	OBP	SLG	OPS+	vL+	vR+	bb%	ct%	Eye	G	L	F	h%	HctX	QBaB	Brl%	PX	xPX	HR/F	xHR/F	Spd	SBA%	SB%	RAR	BPX	R$
17																																			
18																																			
19	aa	485	69	11	46	27	219		6		290	368	91			9	70	0.34				29				93				111	37%	73%		33	$1
20																																			
21	PHI *	242	22	1	16	7	240	1	4	220	297	301	82	101	64	8	74	0.32	55	19	26	32	69	FFf	0%	42	40	6%	6%	142	19%	56%	-16.9	-35	$
1st Half		129	14	1	10	3	300	0	2	245	349	408	105	132	57	7	73	0.28	58	19	22	40	68	FFf	0%	74	55	13%	0%	137	19%	41%	-1.7	38	$
2nd Half		113	8	0	7	4	171	0	2	189	240	179	57	71	69	8	75	0.36	52	18	30	23	70	FDf	0%	6	24	0%	0%	131	19%	79%	-12.6	-142	-$
22	Proj	210	21	2	16	8	223	0	6	220	285	298	79	91	60	8	73	0.32	54	19	27	29	69		0%	51	36	5%	0%	133	16%	67%	-9.1	-79	$

Winker,Jesse

Age: 28 Pos: LF | Bats: L Ht: 6' 3" Wt: 215 | Health D | PT/Exp A | Consist B | LIMA Plan B | Rand Var 0 | MM 4155

Just a monster first half, but cooled in July and then intercostal strain shelved him for most of Aug/Sept. It takes some cherry-picking, but if you glue together the skills he has displayed on multiple occasions over past few years: contact, peak exit velocity, potent HctX, recent Brl% gains, you can pretty clearly justify... UP: 35 HR, .300 BA.

Yr	Tm	PA	R	HR	RBI	SB	BA	xHR	xSB	xBA	OBP	SLG	OPS+	vL+	vR+	bb%	ct%	Eye	G	L	F	h%	HctX	QBaB	Brl%	PX	xPX	HR/F	xHR/F	Spd	SBA%	SB%	RAR	BPX	R$
17	CIN *	468	48	9	49	3	283	4	8	247	355	409	104	48	139	10	81	0.60	53	16	31	33	118	CDb	7%	77	100	23%	13%	80	7%	32%	-3.6	100	$1
18	CIN	334	38	7	43	0	299	10	4	265	405	431	112	92	115	15	84	1.07	42	24	34	34	135	ACb	6%	79	107	9%	13%	68	0%	0%	13.2	167	$
19	CIN	384	51	16	38	0	269	10	2	301	357	473	115	62	122	10	82	0.63	49	26	25	29	117	CDb	4%	99	88	23%	14%	102	2%	0%	3.4	226	$
20	CIN	183	27	12	23	1	255	10	1	275	388	544	124	116	126	15	69	0.61	48	23	29	29	137	ACb	13%	166	137	40%	33%	78	2%	100%	7.5	260	$1
21	CIN	485	77	24	71	1	305	25	3	306	394	556	130	78	148	11	82	0.71	42	25	33	32	124	BCc	11%	136	113	21%	22%	88	1%	100%	29.4	338	$2
1st Half		328	56	19	48	1	314	20	2	297	393	572	135	75	155	10	81	0.60	42	23	34	33	128	ACc	13%	135	128	23%	25%	96	1%	100%	22.1	319	$3
2nd Half		157	21	5	23	0	286	5	1	326	395	519	124	86	134	13	85	1.00	42	27	31	31	114	CCf	8%	139	80	14%	14%	83	1%	0%	6.2	400	$
22	Proj	504	72	25	78	1	288	22	2	299	389	536	126	89	135	12	80	0.72	44	25	32	31	124		9%	138	106	23%	20%	74	2%	60%	35.7	272	$2

Wisdom,Patrick

Age: 30 Pos: 3B | Bats: R Ht: 6' 2" Wt: 220 | Health A | PT/Exp C | Consist F | LIMA Plan C+ | Rand Var -5 | MM 4205

28-61-.231 in 375 PA at CHC. Embodiment of the extremes in today's game? Brl% is in elite territory behind optimized QBaB. But ct% is appalling. His bb% and (slightly) better MLE ct% give hope for some improvement; it wouldn't take much to make the power legitimately exciting. But at his age, this was more likely the peak than a growth step.

Yr	Tm	PA	R	HR	RBI	SB	BA	xHR	xSB	xBA	OBP	SLG	OPS+	vL+	vR+	bb%	ct%	Eye	G	L	F	h%	HctX	QBaB	Brl%	PX	xPX	HR/F	xHR/F	Spd	SBA%	SB%	RAR	BPX	R$
17	aaa	485	52	23	68	2	203		4		251	404	89			6	63	0.17				26				137				82	5%	39%		0	$
18	STL *	459	58	14	54	10	234	3	4	217	295	387	91	107	123	8	64	0.24	35	26	39	33	106	BBf	13%	113	134	33%	25%	94	13%	74%	-11.2	-27	$1
19	TEX *	461	46	22	50	5	191	0	6	239	258	380	88	48	53	8	62	0.23	9	45	45	25	107	AAa	0%	117	123	0%	0%	81	8%	68%	-31.8	-63	$
20	CHC	2	0	0	0	0	0	0	0	0	0	0	0	0	0	0	100	0.00	0	0	100	0	0	CAa		0	-26	0%	0%	97	7%	0%	-0.3	124	-$
21	CHC *	403	58	30	68	5	223	25	3	220	292	507	110	113	113	9	54	0.21	31	19	49	31	100	AAc	16%	214	181	31%	27%	79	8%	82%	-4.9	112	$1
1st Half		132	22	13	26	3	242	9	1	232	310	595	126	140	138	9	51	0.20	25	20	55	33	111	AAa	24%	271	208	39%	32%	91	8%	72%	3.7	262	$1
2nd Half		271	36	17	42	2	213	15	2	213	292	463	102	99	103	9	55	0.22	34	19	47	30	96	BAd	13%	188	170	27%	24%	77	8%	100%	-5.9	50	$1
22	Proj	490	58	25	62	5	218	24	5	207	296	427	98	97	98	8	58	0.22	34	21	45	31	103		16%	150	172	21%	21%	81	6%	70%	-4.8	-40	$1

RAY MURPHY

Witt Jr.,Bobby

Age: 22 Pos: SS	Health A	LIMA Plan B	
Bats: R Ht: 6' 1" Wt: 190	PT/Exp B	Rand Var	
	Consist F	MM 4423	

Royals briefly flirted with having him start year in majors; instead he spent the season lighting up the high minors. Power emergence rates as biggest news here, given 2019 debut featured only 1 HR in 180 rookie-ball PA. While we might wish for a bit more contact, power/speed confirms elite prospect status, and he's arriving soon.

Yr	Tm	PA	R	HR	RBI	SB	BA	xHR	xSB	xBA	OBP	SLG	OPS+	vL+	vR+	bb%	ct%	Eye	G	L	F	h%	HctX	QBaB	Brl%	PX	xPX	HR/F	xHR/F	Spd	SBA%	SB%	RAR	BPX	R$
17																																			
18																																			
19																																			
20																																			
21	a/a	537	78	24	76	23	263		5		318	488	111			7	73	0.30				32				138				97	31%	68%		185	$27
1st Half		224	31	10	34	11	278		3		334	490	115			8	72	0.30				34				123				147	31%	59%		181	$22
2nd Half		314	48	14	44	13	256		3	277	312	497	109			8	74	0.31	44	20	36	30	0			152	-22	0%		102	31%	79%	6.2	246	$28
22	**Proj**	**420**	**62**	**17**	**61**	**19**	**263**	**17**	**15**	**250**	**322**	**483**	**109**	**108**	**109**	**8**	**73**	**0.32**	**35**	**21**	**44**	**32**	**0**		**6%**	**135**		**14%**	**14%**	**109**	**23%**	**69%**	**11.1**	**207**	**$20**

Wong,Kolten

Age: 31 Pos: 2B	Health C	LIMA Plan B	
Bats: L Ht: 5' 7" Wt: 185	PT/Exp A	Rand Var 0	
	Consist B	MM 2335	

In between three IL stints (oblique x2, calf), more hard contact and barrels lifted power skills to, depending on your perspective, "career-high levels" or "barely above average." Unfortunately, Spd fell below the waterline, as so often happens in one's 30s. Nets out to a profile good for a bit of everything, but not much of anything.

Yr	Tm	PA	R	HR	RBI	SB	BA	xHR	xSB	xBA	OBP	SLG	OPS+	vL+	vR+	bb%	ct%	Eye	G	L	F	h%	HctX	QBaB	Brl%	PX	xPX	HR/F	xHR/F	Spd	SBA%	SB%	RAR	BPX	R$
17	STL	411	55	4	42	8	285	4	7	270	376	412	107	95	108	10	83	0.68	48	20	32	33	95	DCc	3%	79	72	4%	4%	107	8%	80%	3.1	148	$11
18	STL	407	41	9	38	6	249	7	6	263	332	388	96	81	99	8	83	0.52	49	20	31	28	86	CDd	3%	80	59	10%	8%	91	11%	55%	-3.5	137	$7
19	STL	549	61	11	59	24	285	8	10	258	361	423	108	103	109	9	83	0.57	44	20	36	33	97	DCd	2%	71	83	8%	6%	101	18%	86%	11.8	137	$21
20	STL	208	26	1	16	5	265	2	8	240	350	326	90	86	90	10	83	0.67	50	21	29	31	83	DDf	1%	31	44	2%	5%	139	11%	71%	-6.2	84	$14
21	MIL	492	70	14	50	12	272	13	7	273	335	447	107	107	107	6	81	0.37	42	22	35	31	113	CCc	5%	102	107	11%	10%	90	15%	71%	-1.2	188	$18
1st Half		214	30	7	20	6	291	6	3	286	346	485	116	123	113	6	83	0.36	42	23	35	32	129	CCd	7%	110	131	13%	11%	90	15%	60%	3.7	235	$14
2nd Half		278	40	7	30	6	257	6	4	263	327	418	101	96	103	7	80	0.38	43	22	36	30	101	CCb	4%	96	89	10%	8%	91	15%	86%	-2.4	154	$15
22	**Proj**	**525**	**71**	**11**	**53**	**11**	**270**	**10**	**12**	**260**	**342**	**410**	**102**	**99**	**103**	**8**	**82**	**0.47**	**45**	**21**	**34**	**31**	**101**		**4%**	**80**	**84**	**8%**	**8%**	**101**	**11%**	**69%**	**7.9**	**156**	**$19**

Yastrzemski,Mike

Age: 31 Pos: RF CF	Health A	LIMA Plan B	
Bats: L Ht: 5' 10" Wt: 178	PT/Exp A	Rand Var +4	
	Consist D	MM 4225	

Over the course of 1000+ PA spanning parts of three seasons, plate skills and power metrics have all lived in a very narrow range. Launch angle also remains in locked position, even though LD/FB mix wiggles around a bit. The one metric that bounces around a lot is h%, and xBA shows you that's where the profit opportunity lies here.

Yr	Tm	PA	R	HR	RBI	SB	BA	xHR	xSB	xBA	OBP	SLG	OPS+	vL+	vR+	bb%	ct%	Eye	G	L	F	h%	HctX	QBaB	Brl%	PX	xPX	HR/F	xHR/F	Spd	SBA%	SB%	RAR	BPX	R$
17	a/a	388	48	12	47	2	213		5		282	361	88			9	67	0.29				28				92				115	5%	49%		-9	$2
18	a/a	467	44	8	43	6	198		4		265	321	78			8	71	0.31				26				85				105	13%	48%		3	$2
19	SF *	563	91	28	73	3	264	22	10	253	328	508	116	131	113	9	70	0.32	34	23	43	32	103	BAc	11%	139	142	18%	19%	113	8%	34%	18.3	163	$17
20	SF	225	39	10	35	2	297	12	4	263	400	568	128	130	127	13	71	0.55	39	19	42	37	108	CAf	11%	159	152	17%	21%	148	5%	67%	15.7	344	$25
21	SF	532	75	25	71	4	224	27	4	247	311	457	105	70	117	10	72	0.39	34	19	47	26	89	CAd	10%	140	134	16%	17%	89	4%	100%	-6.9	185	$12
1st Half		268	40	12	31	1	228	13	2	260	332	483	114	70	129	11	74	0.49	36	17	48	26	97	BBf	11%	155	149	15%	16%	96	4%	100%	1.2	277	$12
2nd Half		264	35	13	40	3	220	15	2	235	289	432	98	69	106	8	70	0.30	32	22	46	25	81	CAc	9%	125	118	17%	19%	88	4%	100%	-6.0	100	$13
22	**Proj**	**525**	**77**	**25**	**72**	**4**	**252**	**29**	**5**	**247**	**333**	**491**	**112**	**97**	**117**	**10**	**71**	**0.38**	**34**	**20**	**45**	**30**	**95**		**11%**	**144**	**137**	**17%**	**19%**	**112**	**5%**	**66%**	**13.9**	**191**	**$19**

Yelich,Christian

Age: 30 Pos: LF	Health C	LIMA Plan C+	
Bats: L Ht: 6' 3" Wt: 195	PT/Exp A	Rand Var +3	
	Consist F	MM 3435	

Landed on IL twice in 1st half (back problems), then again with COVID in July. 2nd half ct% recovery was the only good news here. Look at the bell curve among post-contact metrics: 2019 is the peak, with 2017 and 2021 forming the mirror image endpoints. Still owns those peak skills and too young to write off, but trends are breaking the wrong way here.

Yr	Tm	PA	R	HR	RBI	SB	BA	xHR	xSB	xBA	OBP	SLG	OPS+	vL+	vR+	bb%	ct%	Eye	G	L	F	h%	HctX	QBaB	Brl%	PX	xPX	HR/F	xHR/F	Spd	SBA%	SB%	RAR	BPX	R$
17	MIA	694	100	18	81	16	282	21	11	272	369	439	110	97	112	12	77	0.58	55	19	25	34	110	BFb	7%	94	77	15%	18%	110	9%	89%	9.7	127	$25
18	MIL	651	118	36	110	22	326	38	14	310	402	598	134	130	133	10	76	0.50	52	25	24	37	134	AFb	13%	156	128	35%	37%	135	14%	85%	68.2	313	$44
19	MIL	580	100	44	97	30	329	41	16	306	429	671	152	130	164	14	76	0.68	43	21	36	36	133	ACc	16%	172	146	33%	31%	114	18%	94%	77.5	389	$42
20	MIL	247	39	12	22	4	205	12	8	234	356	430	104	139	89	19	62	0.61	51	19	30	26	103	ADb	12%	143	112	32%	32%	117	9%	67%	-2.6	148	$16
21	MIL	475	70	9	51	9	248	12	9	245	362	373	101	83	108	15	72	0.62	54	22	24	32	102	BFf	8%	81	84	13%	18%	119	8%	75%	-7.9	73	$12
1st Half		210	39	5	23	6	252	7	5	234	414	399	113	94	119	22	64	0.78	52	25	24	36	107	AFd	9%	101	122	20%	28%	126	8%	86%	2.1	85	$12
2nd Half		265	31	4	28	3	246	5	4	250	321	356	92	77	98	10	77	0.45	56	20	24	31	99	BFf	7%	70	61	9%	12%	112	8%	60%	-11.2	65	$7
22	**Proj**	**560**	**89**	**20**	**67**	**12**	**261**	**18**	**11**	**257**	**374**	**450**	**112**	**108**	**113**	**15**	**71**	**0.60**	**52**	**21**	**27**	**33**	**111**		**10%**	**115**	**104**	**22%**	**20%**	**116**	**9%**	**78%**	**20.3**	**151**	**$23**

Zimmer,Bradley

Age: 29 Pos: CF RF	Health D	LIMA Plan D	
Bats: L Ht: 6' 5" Wt: 220	PT/Exp D	Rand Var -5	
	Consist C	MM 2403	

8-35-.227 with 15 SB in 348 PA at CLE. Bookending an awful lot of missed time across 2018-20, 2021 stats and skills look a lot like they did back in 2017. Back then, he was a 24-year old prospect with a promising power/speed blend. Now, he's an oft-injured 29-year old with disqualifying ct% problems baked in. Life comes at you fast.

Yr	Tm	PA	R	HR	RBI	SB	BA	xHR	xSB	xBA	OBP	SLG	OPS+	vL+	vR+	bb%	ct%	Eye	G	L	F	h%	HctX	QBaB	Brl%	PX	xPX	HR/F	xHR/F	Spd	SBA%	SB%	RAR	BPX	R$
17	CLE *	469	58	12	50	25	248	12	6	237	309	410	98	84	95	8	66	0.26	48	20	32	35	90	CDd	9%	112	83	13%	20%	121	28%	85%	-3.9	27	$16
18	CLE *	146	16	3	10	6	208	4	5	195	259	306	76	102	72	6	58	0.16	48	24	28	33	93	CDb	8%	82	124	13%	25%	102	23%	86%	-5.8	-183	$0
19	CLE *	51	7	2	4	2	218	0	1	231	270	407	94	0	17	7	61	0.18	80	0	20	32	35	FFa	0%	127	113	0%	0%	124	29%	100%	-1.0	-7	-$2
20	CLE	50	3	1	3	2	162	1	3	145	360	243	80	43	86	14	62	0.50	48	9	43	23	52	FBf	4%	47	49	10%	10%	118	18%	67%	-3.1	-188	-$1
21	CLE *	414	50	9	40	18	223	13	12	188	294	332	86	76	97	9	57	0.23	48	22	30	37	79	CDd	9%	85	100	16%	25%	120	22%	76%	-16.8	-188	$11
1st Half		164	17	1	13	7	215	2	5	154	307	267	80	64	99	12	50	0.27	41	27	32	42	70	CCa	12%	49	88	0%	15%	142	22%	65%	-10.1	-350	$1
2nd Half		250	33	8	27	11	227	10	6	211	304	373	92	80	95	8	60	0.21	50	21	29	34	85	CDf	9%	105	103	21%	26%	100	22%	85%	-8.7	-104	$14
22	**Proj**	**280**	**34**	**7**	**27**	**13**	**224**	**10**	**9**	**198**	**314**	**345**	**89**	**81**	**92**	**9**	**59**	**0.23**	**47**	**23**	**30**	**35**	**84**		**9%**	**92**	**99**	**14%**	**22%**	**110**	**17%**	**79%**	**-4.8**	**-159**	**$10**

Zimmerman,Ryan

Age: 37 Pos: 1B	Health D	LIMA Plan D+	
Bats: R Ht: 6' 3" Wt: 215	PT/Exp D	Rand Var -1	
	Consist A	MM 4131	

Came back from 2020 opt-out to post a credible bad-side platoon season. If he wants to, he can do it again, but late-season indications seemed to point toward retirement. If this is the end of the line, he finishes with a career .277 BA, 284 HR, 1061 RBI, and of course that 2019 World Series ring. Well done, "Mr. National."

Yr	Tm	PA	R	HR	RBI	SB	BA	xHR	xSB	xBA	OBP	SLG	OPS+	vL+	vR+	bb%	ct%	Eye	G	L	F	h%	HctX	QBaB	Brl%	PX	xPX	HR/F	xHR/F	Spd	SBA%	SB%	RAR	BPX	R$
17	WAS	576	90	36	108	1	303	31	8	289	358	573	127	140	120	8	76	0.35	46	20	34	34	124	ADc	12%	152	138	26%	23%	89	1%	100%	22.8	209	$26
18	WAS	323	33	13	51	1	264	18	2	282	337	486	110	152	95	9	81	0.55	49	17	34	29	118	ADd	14%	129	128	16%	23%	96	3%	50%	3.7	253	$8
19	WAS	190	20	6	27	0	257	7	1	246	321	415	102	134	88	9	77	0.44	47	20	33	30	110	ACd	8%	86	118	14%	16%	87	0%	0%	-3.8	89	$1
20																																			
21	WAS	273	27	14	46	0	243	13	2	239	286	471	104	123	89	6	70	0.21	51	16	33	29	111	ADf	11%	144	117	23%	22%	82	0%	0%	-10.1	127	$5
1st Half		154	16	9	24	0	250	8	1	253	279	480	106	118	96	4	73	0.15	47	19	33	28	124	BDf	12%	133	122	25%	22%	86	0%	0%	-4.7	131	$5
2nd Half		119	11	5	22	0	234	6	1	222	294	458	102	129	80	9	65	0.27	56	11	33	31	93	ADf	9%	160	110	21%	25%	82	0%	0%	-3.5	127	-$1
22	**Proj**	**245**	**26**	**11**	**41**	**0**	**246**	**12**	**1**	**252**	**304**	**461**	**104**	**127**	**91**	**8**	**73**	**0.32**	**50**	**17**	**33**	**29**	**111**		**10%**	**132**	**120**	**20%**	**22%**	**84**	**2%**	**56%**	**2.0**	**105**	**$7**

Zunino,Mike

Age: 31 Pos: CA	Health B	LIMA Plan C+	
Bats: R Ht: 6' 2" Wt: 235	PT/Exp B	Rand Var 0	
	Consist C	MM 5203	

Impressive rebound of exit velocity breathed life into this skill set. Behold the combo of ct% and HctX: despite that abysmal ct%, he hit so many balls hard that his HctX still reached league average. Consistent launch angle means HR will keep coming, but ridiculous success vL (16 HR in 129 PA) has to regress, so don't chase a repeat.

Yr	Tm	PA	R	HR	RBI	SB	BA	xHR	xSB	xBA	OBP	SLG	OPS+	vL+	vR+	bb%	ct%	Eye	G	L	F	h%	HctX	QBaB	Brl%	PX	xPX	HR/F	xHR/F	Spd	SBA%	SB%	RAR	BPX	R$
17	SEA *	479	57	29	72	1	250	24	6	245	317	515	113	119	110	9	61	0.25	32	22	46	34	96	BAc	15%	186	141	24%	23%	76	1%	100%	18.0	109	$11
18	SEA	405	37	20	44	0	201	23	1	212	259	410	90	76	94	6	60	0.16	37	19	44	27	87	BAd	14%	156	132	20%	23%	68	0%	0%	-1.2	-3	$3
19	TAM	289	30	9	32	0	165	13	0	187	232	312	75	65	80	7	63	0.20	40	14	46	22	85	CAf	11%	93	96	12%	17%	68	0%	0%	-12.8	-133	-$3
20	TAM	84	8	4	10	0	147	5	0	184	238	360	79	45	94	7	51	0.16	21	18	61	21	76	CAf	16%	177	197	17%	22%	67	0%	0%	-4.6	-72	-$1
21	TAM	375	64	33	62	0	216	34	1	246	301	559	118	175	88	9	60	0.26	30	16	54	23	100	BAf	24%	223	179	30%	31%	96	0%	0%	11.3	265	$11
1st Half		193	30	18	36	0	205	19	1	240	290	550	117	172	85	10	56	0.24	27	18	56	22	92	AAd	28%	241	176	33%	35%	58	0%	0%	4.5	215	$12
2nd Half		182	34	15	26	0	228	15	1	254	313	568	119	179	90	9	65	0.28	33	14	52	24	109	BAf	21%	206	180	27%	27%	127	0%	0%	7.3	315	$9
22	**Proj**	**385**	**54**	**25**	**55**	**0**	**222**	**27**	**1**	**226**	**300**	**484**	**106**	**128**	**95**	**8**	**61**	**0.23**	**32**	**19**	**50**	**28**	**93**		**19%**	**174**	**163**	**23%**	**26%**	**73**	**1%**	**100%**	**10.5**	**87**	**$11**

RAY MURPHY

THE NEXT TIER

The preceding section provided player boxes and analysis for 441 batters. As we know, far more than 441 batters will play in the major leagues in 2022. Many of those additional hitters are covered in the minor league section, but that still leaves a gap: established major leaguers who don't play enough, or well enough, to merit a player box.

This section looks to fill that gap. Here, you will find "The Next Tier" of batters who are mostly past their growth years, but who are likely to see some playing time in 2022. We are including their 2020-21 statline here for reference for you to do your own analysis. (Years that include MLEs are marked by an asterisk.) This way, if you're dredging through the catcher pool in July and Kevin Plawecki has come upon some MLB playing time, this is a good reminder that in both of his past two seasons, he had an OPS+ in the triple digits. Or you can use Daniel Johnson's sub-60% contact rate the past two seasons to steer you away from picking him up as a reserve OFer.

Batter	Yr	B	Age	Pos	PA	R	HR	RBI	SB	BA	xBA	OPS+	vL+	vR+	bb%	ct%	Eye	GLF	HctX	PX	xPX	Spd	SBA%	SB%	BPX
Adrianza, Ehire	20	B	30	o	101	10	0	3	1	191	225	74	70	76	11	74	0.48	37/25/38	82	65	89	99	5	100	8
	21	B	31		209	32	5	28	0	247	252	100	93	103	10	77	0.50	41/24/35	90	89	80	106	0	0	127
Almora, Albert	20	R	26	8	34	4	0	1	0	167	165	62	70	57	9	70	0.33	57/10/33	54	29	9	122	0	0	-160
	21*	R	27		214	18	4	11	1	175	221	66	55	36	5	80	0.25	54/14/31	122	53	85	97	20	17	12
Arcia, Orlando	20	R	25	7	189	22	5	20	2	260	269	97	83	103	7	82	0.44	46/23/31	121	86	110	88	5	100	152
	21*	R	26		399	50	14	42	5	225	258	92	107	67	8	82	0.47	51/16/33	70	88	50	84	11	57	165
Barnes, Austin	20	R	30	2	104	14	1	9	3	244	196	89	95	87	13	72	0.54	44/17/38	99	47	88	115	9	100	-48
	21	R	31		225	28	6	23	1	215	213	88	87	89	9	72	0.36	43/17/40	91	81	95	103	2	100	15
Cabrera, Asdrúbal	20	B	34	5	213	23	8	31	0	242	258	100	131	88	9	79	0.48	44/18/38	118	106	127	118	0	0	224
	21	B	35		352	34	7	42	1	230	236	93	99	90	10	74	0.45	41/21/38	99	92	106	70	1	100	50
Camargo, Johan	20	B	26	345	127	16	4	9	0	200	228	81	82	81	5	71	0.17	49/15/35	71	108	44	96	0	0	40
	21*	B	27		438	53	14	50	0	255	237	101	0	20	8	77	0.39	60/10/30	94	97	128	96	1	0	119
Casali, Curtis	20	R	31	2	93	10	6	8	2	224	235	115	131	103	15	62	0.48	26/23/51	112	176	202	84	8	100	180
	21	R	32		231	20	5	26	0	210	208	91	57	102	11	67	0.39	32/21/47	99	98	136	105	0	0	8
Castro, Jason	20	L	33	2	92	8	2	9	0	188	208	89	71	94	13	59	0.36	32/17/51	121	163	212	79	0	0	68
	21	L	34		179	22	8	21	0	235	242	110	76	126	14	64	0.46	37/27/36	97	140	152	92	0	0	96
Castro, Starlin	20	R	30	5	63	9	2	4	0	267	248	100	167	74	5	78	0.23	36/21/43	74	98	80	130	0	0	168
	21	R	31		345	25	3	38	0	283	244	97	109	93	8	80	0.42	49/23/28	101	63	78	95	1	0	65
Cave, Jake	20	L	27	78	123	17	4	15	0	221	223	89	71	96	4	61	0.11	50/25/25	86	106	95	126	8	0	-88
	21*	L	28		212	18	4	17	1	205	220	78	33	88	6	61	0.18	50/30/20	59	76	60	102	7	31	-181
Chirinos, Robinson	20	R	36	2	82	4	1	7	0	162	193	63	107	36	7	72	0.29	48/19/33	59	55	52	67	0	0	-128
	21*	R	37		154	17	7	19	0	223	197	103	107	107	10	57	0.27	34/13/52	79	160	122	104	0	0	38
Culberson, Charlie	20	R	31	5	7	2	0	1	0	143	178	57	0	133	0	43	0.00	33/33/33	116	204	306	94	-	0	-136
	21	R	32		271	23	5	22	7	243	244	93	127	53	6	74	0.27	47/21/32	79	89	63	118	14	88	65
Davis, Khristopher	20	R	32	0	99	9	2	10	0	200	222	84	105	68	10	69	0.38	32/25/43	80	88	107	79	0	0	-20
	21*	R	33		183	20	9	25	0	214	238	97	88	85	7	70	0.24	47/14/40	98	133	119	118	0	0	142
Drury, Brandon	20	R	27	o	49	3	0	1	0	152	216	47	74	21	4	80	0.22	34/26/39	69	17	72	94	0	0	-100
	21*	R	28		313	24	9	33	0	204	210	80	120	98	5	70	0.16	52/16/32	97	93	95	65	0	0	-54
Dyson, Jarrod	20	L	35	789	66	9	0	5	6	180	222	55	86	50	6	82	0.36	50/23/27	72	0	67	105	40	100	-100
	21	L	36		149	17	0	10	10	207	257	75	67	78	7	76	0.30	57/24/19	50	56	25	132	52	67	8
Fowler, Dexter	20	B	34	9	101	14	4	15	1	233	216	94	37	107	10	69	0.36	44/19/37	76	89	82	105	8	50	0
	21	B	35		21	3	0	1	1	250	136	74	109	62	5	70	0.17	36/14/50	61	0	50	116	17	100	-281
Greiner, Grayson	20	R	27	2	55	8	3	8	0	118	203	68	92	61	5	61	0.15	32/16/52	103	143	183	86	0	0	-12
	21*	R	28		210	14	2	14	0	189	169	72	71	99	9	53	0.21	41/24/34	68	74	82	86	0	0	-312
Guillorme, Luis	20	L	25	5	68	6	0	9	2	333	263	115	55	125	15	70	0.59	49/32/20	111	92	89	94	9	100	56
	21*	L	26		181	16	1	6	0	259	220	91	80	99	14	83	0.97	52/20/28	87	23	64	116	3	0	62
Hamilton, Billy	20	B	29	8	36	10	1	2	6	125	171	52	69	42	6	78	0.29	19/27/54	35	43	41	131	160	75	0
	21	B	30		135	23	2	11	9	220	210	85	103	74	3	63	0.09	36/24/40	58	115	69	174	47	100	15
Heredia, Guillermo	20	R	29	78	36	6	2	5	1	212	230	89	85	89	8	73	0.33	17/33/50	74	89	119	94	13	100	36
	21	R	30		347	46	5	26	0	220	244	91	103	87	9	73	0.40	42/23/35	91	98	90	95	0	0	81
Higashioka, Kyle	20	R	30	2	48	7	4	10	0	250	232	102	33	137	0	77	0.00	39/8/53	110	132	140	97	0	0	180
	21	R	31		211	20	10	29	0	181	233	87	108	77	8	69	0.29	28/21/51	107	130	187	62	0	0	69
Holt, Brock	20	L	32	5	106	12	0	5	1	211	232	74	121	66	8	75	0.38	46/25/29	80	52	53	92	4	100	-48
	21	L	33		260	21	2	23	5	209	246	79	49	86	9	79	0.47	48/22/30	76	60	53	81	11	83	31
Inciarte, Ender	20	L	29	8	131	17	1	10	4	190	215	68	82	64	9	78	0.48	45/20/34	44	32	38	132	17	80	0
	21*	L	30		174	17	2	16	1	209	206	76	92	79	7	72	0.27	47/19/33	59	53	57	82	5	44	-112

THE NEXT TIER

Batters

Batter	Yr	B	Age	Pos	PA	R	HR	RBI	SB	BA	xBA	OPS+	vL+	vR+	bb%	ct%	Eye	GLF	HctX	PX	xPX	Spd	SBA%	SB%	BPX
Johnson Jr., Daniel	20	L	24	o	13	0	0	0	0	83	91	31	0	32	8	58	0.20	43/14/43	67	0	80	104	0	0	-468
	21*	L	25		384	33	13	31	6	186	178	81	136	83	7	56	0.18	28/20/52	69	119	113	100	10	83	-123
Jones, JaCoby	20	R	28	8	108	19	5	14	1	268	259	113	139	105	6	65	0.21	45/22/33	78	172	75	101	9	50	172
	21*	R	29		394	32	7	28	3	181	187	70	49	73	6	55	0.15	47/26/28	51	80	26	95	10	38	-269
Knapp, Andrew	20	B	28	2	89	9	2	15	0	278	263	113	90	118	17	74	0.79	40/30/30	88	98	82	114	0	0	172
	21	B	29		159	13	2	11	0	152	157	59	42	67	6	58	0.16	42/19/39	72	49	117	96	0	0	-327
Lagares, Juan	20	R	31	789	0	0	0	0	0	0	0	0	0	0	0	0	0.00	0/0/0	0	0	0	0	-	0	0
	21	R	32		327	39	6	38	1	236	247	88	100	80	4	75	0.16	45/22/33	117	88	119	93	5	33	35
Lamb, Jake	20	L	29	o	99	7	3	10	0	193	249	84	93	82	8	72	0.32	33/29/38	129	100	144	76	5	0	28
	21*	L	30		236	29	9	24	0	189	207	88	71	97	11	65	0.38	39/18/43	96	109	114	95	0	0	8
Locastro, Tim	20	R	27	8	82	15	2	7	4	290	269	114	88	170	10	80	0.57	35/30/35	86	95	75	153	16	100	248
	21	R	28		156	15	2	7	5	180	200	71	91	59	4	76	0.21	43/16/41	70	45	36	131	23	63	-31
Marisnick, Jake	20	R	29	78	34	4	2	5	0	333	286	127	143	110	3	70	0.10	52/26/22	98	173	71	110	0	0	232
	21	R	30		198	21	5	24	4	216	210	91	101	81	6	63	0.17	37/24/39	85	107	96	147	12	80	-15
Marmolejos, José	20	L	27	3	115	12	6	18	0	206	230	89	72	94	6	70	0.22	44/17/39	106	118	110	69	5	0	40
	21*	L	28		452	56	21	63	0	231	226	104	52	82	11	67	0.39	29/22/49	72	128	85	70	0	0	58
Maybin, Cameron	20	R	33	o	101	8	1	7	3	247	250	92	96	91	7	73	0.28	56/18/26	100	97	69	108	14	100	72
	21*	R	34		121	8	1	5	2	80	139	35	19	33	7	55	0.16	67/7/27	42	30	-5	92	13	100	-431
Mazara, Nomar	20	L	25	9	149	13	1	15	0	228	207	78	105	72	7	68	0.23	52/23/25	89	52	63	92	3	0	-176
	21	L	26		181	12	3	19	0	212	219	82	37	89	8	73	0.33	48/20/32	88	65	67	124	0	0	0
Mercer, Jordy	20	R	33	4	22	2	0	0	0	200	189	63	99	46	9	90	1.00	61/11/28	61	0	-13	92	0	0	32
	21	R	34		127	13	2	9	0	254	237	92	99	88	7	71	0.26	39/27/33	104	79	91	92	0	0	-27
Moreland, Mitch	20	L	34	0	152	22	10	29	0	265	265	119	91	125	10	76	0.47	45/14/42	104	156	121	65	0	0	288
	21	L	35		252	28	10	30	0	227	244	96	76	101	7	75	0.31	45/18/37	100	109	105	77	0	0	96
Núñez, Renato	20	R	26	3	216	29	12	31	0	256	244	108	85	114	8	67	0.27	32/23/45	70	145	91	94	0	0	124
	21*	R	27		410	48	18	50	1	201	207	87	79	99	6	65	0.18	49/11/41	86	120	93	84	1	100	-19
Panik, Joe	20	L	29	45	141	18	1	7	0	225	232	85	101	78	14	78	0.74	48/23/29	101	51	66	91	0	0	32
	21	L	30		257	17	3	18	2	208	248	75	50	82	7	86	0.50	45/22/33	79	45	51	74	4	100	62
Perez, Michael	20	L	27	2	93	7	1	13	0	167	205	63	148	52	8	68	0.26	33/28/40	90	51	107	69	0	0	-196
	21	L	28		231	19	7	21	0	143	204	70	74	69	8	68	0.28	46/14/40	78	95	125	85	3	0	-35
Piña, Manny	20	R	33	2	45	4	2	5	0	231	268	99	76	119	7	72	0.27	18/36/46	125	98	143	78	0	0	16
	21	R	34		208	27	13	33	0	189	250	101	116	88	11	79	0.58	38/14/48	99	128	130	44	0	0	208
Plawecki, Kevin	20	R	29	2	89	8	1	17	1	341	265	114	117	110	6	83	0.36	43/25/32	104	70	73	128	4	100	156
	21	R	30		173	15	3	15	0	287	231	101	108	95	7	83	0.46	40/20/40	90	59	89	98	0	0	100
Reddick, Josh	20	L	33	9	209	22	4	23	1	245	240	92	98	88	10	78	0.48	36/23/41	88	80	63	107	2	100	112
	21*	L	34		242	23	4	28	0	229	226	82	61	104	5	74	0.19	37/23/40	106	72	106	77	0	0	-35
Refsnyder, Rob	20	R	29	78	34	4	0	1	0	200	170	66	82	41	6	63	0.18	45/20/35	103	32	98	102	0	0	-304
	21*	R	30		232	30	5	22	1	246	235	97	107	80	11	72	0.45	42/23/35	101	88	126	78	2	100	27
Romine, Austin	20	R	31	2	135	12	2	17	0	238	197	77	105	72	3	64	0.09	45/24/31	77	63	72	95	0	0	-228
	21	R	32		62	5	1	5	0	217	167	74	173	24	3	63	0.09	53/13/34	68	62	77	96	0	0	-227
Sandoval, Pablo	20	B	33	0	94	5	1	6	0	214	194	73	104	67	9	77	0.42	50/20/30	133	26	110	59	0	0	-128
	21	B	34		86	11	4	11	0	178	203	89	74	90	13	66	0.44	35/21/44	84	92	114	52	0	0	-73
Santana, Danny	20	B	29	o	63	6	1	7	2	145	186	68	54	74	11	56	0.29	47/16/38	114	114	137	79	20	100	-136
	21*	B	30		189	24	8	21	7	207	219	92	82	82	8	73	0.33	43/9/48	66	109	77	117	24	77	127
Shaw, Travis	20	L	30	35	180	17	6	17	0	239	226	95	96	95	9	69	0.32	31/22/47	81	111	100	68	0	0	24

The following section contains player boxes for every pitcher who had significant playing time in 2021 and/or is expected to get fantasy roster-worthy innings in 2022. You will find some prospects here, specifically the most impactful names who we project to play in 2022. For more complete prospect coverage, see our Prospects section.

Snapshot Section

The top band of each player box contains the following information:

Age as of Opening Day 2022.

Throws right (R) or left (L).

Role: Starters (SP) are those projected to face 20+ batters per game; the rest are relievers (RP).

Ht/Wt: Each batter's height and weight.

Type evaluates the extent to which a pitcher allows the ball to be put into play and his ground ball or fly ball tendency. CON (contact) represents pitchers who allow the ball to be put into play a great deal. PWR (power) represents those with high strikeout and/or walk totals who keep the ball out of play. GB are those who have a ground ball rate more than 50%; xGB are those who have a GB rate more than 55%. FB are those who have a fly ball rate more than 40%; xFB are those who have a FB rate more than 45%.

Reliability Grades analyze each pitcher's forecast risk, on an A-F scale. High grades go to those who have accumulated few disabled list days (Health), have a history of substantial and regular major league playing time (PT/Exp) and have displayed consistent performance over the past three years, using xERA (Consist).

LIMA Plan Grade evaluates how well that pitcher would be a good fit for a team using the LIMA Plan draft strategy. Best grades go to pitchers who have excellent base skills and had a 2021 dollar value less than $20. Lowest grades will go to poor skills and values more than $20.

Random Variance Score (Rand Var) measures the impact random variance had on the pitcher's 2021 stats and the probability that his 2022 performance will exceed or fall short of 2021. The variables tracked are those prone to regression—H%, S%, HR/F and xERA to ERA variance. Players are rated on a scale of −5 to +5 with positive scores indicating rebounds and negative scores indicating corrections. Note that this score is computer-generated and the projections will override it on occasion.

Mayberry Method (MM) acknowledges the imprecision of the forecasting process by projecting player performance in broad strokes. The four digits of MM each represent a fantasy-relevant skill—ERA, strikeout rate, saves potential and playing time (IP)—and are all on a scale of 0 to 5.

Commentaries for each pitcher provide a brief analysis of his skills and the potential impact on performance in 2022. MLB statistics are listed first for those who played only a portion of 2021 at the major league level. Note that these commentaries generally look at performance related issues only. Role and playing time expectations may impact these analyses, so you will have to adjust accordingly. Upside (UP) and downside (DN) statistical potential appears for some players; these are less grounded in hard data and more speculative of skills potential.

Player Stat Section

The past five years' statistics represent the total accumulated in the majors as well as in Triple-A, Double-A ball and various foreign leagues during each year. All non-major league stats have been converted to a major league equivalent (MLE) performance level. Minor league levels below Double-A are not included.

Nearly all baseball publications separate a player's statistical experiences in the major leagues from the minor leagues and outside leagues. While this may be appropriate for official record-keeping purposes, it is not an easy-to-analyze snapshot of a player's complete performance for a given year.

Bill James has proven that minor league statistics (converted to MLEs), at Double-A level or above, provide as accurate a record of a player's performance as major league statistics. Other researchers have also devised conversion factors for foreign leagues. Since these are adequate barometers, we include them in the pool of historical data for each year.

Team designations: An asterisk (*) appearing with a team name means that Triple-A and/or Double-A numbers are included in that year's stat line. Any stints of less than 10 IP are not included (to screen out most rehab appearances). A designation of "a/a" means the stats were accumulated at both AA and AAA levels that year. "for" represents a foreign or independent league. The designation "2TM" appears whenever a player was on more than one major league team, crossing leagues, in a season. "2AL" and "2NL" represent more than one team in the same league. Players who were cut during the season and finished 2021 as a free agent are designated as FAA (Free agent, AL) and FAN (Free agent, NL).

Stats: Descriptions of all the categories appear in the Encyclopedia.

- The leading decimal point has been suppressed on some categories to conserve space.
- Data for platoons (vL+, vR+), SwK, balls-in-play (G/L/F), HR/F and xHR/F, consistency (GS, APC, DOM, DIS), xWHIP and velocity (Vel) are for major league performance only.
- Formulas that use BIP data, like xERA and BPV, are used for years in which G/L/F data is available. Where feasible, older versions of these formulas are used otherwise.

Earned run average and WHIP are presented first next to each other, then skills-based xERA and xWHIP for comparison. Next is opponents' OPS splits vs. left-handed and right-handed batters (indexed to league average). Batters faced per game (BF/G) provide a quick view of a pitcher's role—starters will generally have levels over 20.

Basic pitching skills are measured by percentage of batters faced: BB% or walk rate, K% or strikeout rate, and K-BB%. xBB% and Swinging strike rate (SwK) are also presented with these basic skills; compare xBB% to BB% and our research shows that SwK serves as a skills-based indicator of K%. Vel is the pitcher's average fastball velocity.

Once the ball leaves the bat, it will either be a (G)round ball, (L)ine drive or (F)ly ball.

Random variance indicators include hit rate (H%)—often referred to as batting average on balls-in-play (BABIP)—which tends to regress to 30%. Normal strand rates (S%) fall within the tolerances of 65% to 80%. The ratio of home runs to fly balls (HR/F) is another sanity check; levels far from the league average of 14% are prone to regression, as is HR/F vs. xHR/F disparity.

In looking at consistency for starting pitchers, we track games started (GS), average pitch counts (APC) for all outings (for starters and relievers), the percentage of DOMinating starts (PQS 4 or 5) and DISaster starts (PQS 0 or 1). The larger the variance between DOM and DIS, the greater the consistency of good or bad performance.

For relievers, we look at their saves success rate (Sv%) and Leverage Index (LI). A Doug Dennis study showed little correlation between saves success and future opportunity. However, you can increase your odds by prospecting for pitchers who have *both* a high saves percentage (80% or better) *and* high skills. Relievers with LI levels over 1.0 are being used more often by managers to win ballgames.

The final section includes several overall performance measures: runs above replacement (RAR), Base performance index (BPX, which is BPV indexed to each year's league average) and the Rotisserie value (R$).

2022 Projections

Forecasts are computed from a player's trends over the past five years. Adjustments were made for leading indicators and variances between skill and statistical output. After reviewing the leading indicators, you might opt to make further adjustments.

Although each year's numbers include all playing time at the Double-A level or above, the 2022 forecast only represents potential playing time at the major league level, and again is highly preliminary.

Note that the projected Rotisserie values in this book will not necessarily align with each player's historical actuals. Since we currently have no idea who is going to close games for the Phillies, or whether Grayson Rodriguez is going to break camp with the Orioles, it is impossible to create a finite pool of playing time, something which is required for valuation. So the projections are roughly based on a 12-team AL/NL league, and include an inflated number of innings, league-wide. This serves to flatten the spread of values and depress individual player dollar projections. In truth, a $25 player in this book might actually be worth $21, or $28. This level of precision is irrelevant in a process that is driven by market forces anyway. So, don't obsess over it.

Be aware of other sources that publish perfectly calibrated Rotisserie values over the winter. They are likely making arbitrary decisions as to where free agents are going to sign and who is going to land jobs in the spring. We do not make those leaps of faith here.

Bottom line… It is far too early to be making definitive projections for 2022, especially on playing time. Focus on the skill levels and trends, then consult BaseballHQ.com for playing time revisions as players change teams and roles become more defined. A free projections update will be available online in March.

Do-it-yourself analysis

Here are some data points you can look at in doing your own player analysis:

- Variance between vL+ and vR+ (opposition OPS)
- Variance in 2021 HR/F rate from 13-14%
- Variance in HR/F and xHR/F each year
- Variance in 2021 hit rate (H%) from 30%
- Variance in 2021 strand rate (S%) to tolerances (65% - 80%)
- Variance between ERA and xERA each year
- Growth or decline in base performance index (BPX)
- Spikes in innings pitched
- Trends in average pitch counts (APC)
- Trends in DOM/DIS splits
- Trends in saves success rate (Sv%)
- Variance between K% changes and corresponding SwK levels
- Variance between BB% changes and corresponding xBB% levels
- Improvement or decline in velocity

Abreu,Bryan

Age: 25	Th: R	Role: RP	Health: C	LIMA Plan: D+	
Ht: 6' 1"	Wt: 225	Type: Pwr	PT/Exp: D	Rand Var: 0	
			Consist: F	MM: 2300	

3-3, 5.75 ERA in 36 IP at HOU. Opened year in MLB bullpen, spent June on IL (calf), and 2nd half LI shows how he fell out of favor on his way to AAA. GB% is a nice starting skill, paired with healthy SwK% that hints at even more K%. However, horrid BB% (confirmed by xBB%) is disqualifying. Late-inning ceiling, but not close to emerging.

Yr	Tm	W	Sv	IP	K	ERA	WHIP	xERA	xWHIP	vL+	vR+	BF/G	BB%	K%	K-BB%	xBB%	SwK	Vel	G	L	F	H%	S%	HR/F	xHR/F	GS	APC	DOM%	DIS%	Sv%	LI	RAR	BPX	R$
17																																		
18																																		
19	HOU *	6	2	87	102	6.39	1.53	4.23	1.50	19	80	14.0	15%	27%	12%	9%	19.2%	95.1	50	25	25	33%	57%	0%	1%	0	21			67	0.44	-20.2	92	-$7
20	HOU	0	0	3	3	2.70	2.40	14.18		41	160	5.0	35%	15%	-20%		5.3%	92.9	38	25	38	14%	88%	0%	0%	0	19			0	0.49	0.7	-394	-$8
21	HOU *	3	1	52	56	4.49	1.47	4.07	1.46	107	99	4.9	13%	25%	12%	12%	13.5%	95.7	48	20	32	32%	70%	12%	16%	0	22			17	1.32	-1.4	92	-$4
1st Half		2	1	31	28	3.80	1.17	2.97	1.42	89	98	4.9	11%	23%	11%	12%	13.4%	95.3	51	17	31	25%	70%	14%	19%	0	22			25	1.52	1.8	88	-$1
2nd Half		1	0	21	28	5.48	1.90	5.65	1.52	125	106	4.8	16%	28%	12%	12%	13.6%	96.5	41	26	32	42%	70%	9%	10%	0	24			0	0.89	-3.2	102	-$14
Proj		**3**	**0**	**44**	**50**	**4.39**	**1.44**	**4.14**	**1.49**	**103**	**99**	**5.6**	**15%**	**27%**	**12%**	**12%**	**13.4%**	**95.3**	**51**	**17**	**31**	**31%**	**70%**	**11%**	**17%**	**0**						**0.4**	**72**	**-$4**

Akin,Keegan

Age: 27	Th: L	Role: RP	Health: B	LIMA Plan: D+	
Ht: 6' 0"	Wt: 225	Type: Pwr/FB	PT/Exp: C	Rand Var: +5	
			Consist: C	MM: 0103	

Missed a couple weeks in 2nd half (COVID), then late-September left adductor strain eventually required abdominal surgery. Career-high K% from 2020's truncated season didn't stick as SwK, K% regressed to below-average. Showed much better skills as RP (20% K-BB% in 18 IP), but still not enough here for fantasy relevance.

Yr	Tm	W	Sv	IP	K	ERA	WHIP	xERA	xWHIP	vL+	vR+	BF/G	BB%	K%	K-BB%	xBB%	SwK	Vel	G	L	F	H%	S%	HR/F	xHR/F	GS	APC	DOM%	DIS%	Sv%	LI	RAR	BPX	R$
17																																		
18	aa	14	0	139	117	3.68	1.32	4.15				23.1	10%	20%	10%							28%	77%									8.1	68	$8
19	aaa	6	0	113	105	5.66	1.68	5.35				20.3	12%	21%	8%							35%	67%									-16.1	61	-$10
20	BAL	1	0	26	35	4.56	1.44	4.09	1.18	80	108	14.5	9%	30%	22%	8%	13.6%	91.9	35	25	41	39%	71%	11%	13%	6	63	33%	33%	0	0.85	-0.3	157	-$4
21	BAL	2	0	95	82	6.63	1.58	5.33	1.41	119	112	17.8	9%	19%	10%	7%	10.2%	92.1	36	21	43	33%	60%	13%	17%	17	74	12%	65%	0	0.68	-27.7	57	-$17
1st Half		0	0	41	38	7.46	1.68	5.10	1.35	126	118	16.9	9%	20%	12%	6%	11.0%	91.7	36	23	41	36%	58%	17%	17%	7	71	0%	86%	0	0.60	-16.2	77	-$18
2nd Half		2	0	54	44	6.00	1.50	5.50	1.46	99	112	18.5	10%	18%	8%	7%	9.5%	92.4	36	19	45	31%	62%	11%	17%	10	76	20%	50%	0	0.75	-11.6	42	-$13
Proj		**6**	**0**	**131**	**114**	**5.28**	**1.55**	**5.25**	**1.45**	**112**	**108**	**18.9**	**10%**	**20%**	**10%**	**6%**	**10.1%**	**92.1**	**36**	**20**	**43**	**33%**	**69%**	**12%**	**17%**	**27**						**-13.3**	**53**	**-$10**

Alcala,Jorge

Age: 26	Th: R	Role: RP	Health: B	LIMA Plan: A	
Ht: 6' 3"	Wt: 205	Type: Pwr	PT/Exp: D	Rand Var: 0	
			Consist: C	MM: 4310	

Converted minors SP emerging as a bullpen weapon? Confirmed his dominance vR; 2nd half pitch mix adjustments (more sliders and change-ups) brought better results vL, also helped spike GB%. Gaudy second-half BPX highlights closer-worthiness. With opportunity... UP: 25 Sv

Yr	Tm	W	Sv	IP	K	ERA	WHIP	xERA	xWHIP	vL+	vR+	BF/G	BB%	K%	K-BB%	xBB%	SwK	Vel	G	L	F	H%	S%	HR/F	xHR/F	GS	APC	DOM%	DIS%	Sv%	LI	RAR	BPX	R$
17																																		
18	aa	2	1	62	48	5.14	1.60	5.04				19.6	11%	17%	6%							33%	68%									-7.6	56	-$8
19	MIN *	6	0	115	95	7.23	1.66	6.03		263	22	15.6	9%	18%	10%		17.2%	94.1	0	40	60	37%	56%	0%	0%	0	15			0	0.05	-38.7	52	-$16
20	MIN	2	0	24	27	2.63	1.21	3.84	1.21	148	57	5.9	9%	29%	20%	10%	13.9%	97.0	38	22	40	31%	85%	13%	11%	0	25			0	0.56	5.4	132	$3
21	MIN	3	1	60	61	3.92	0.97	3.47	1.11	102	77	3.9	6%	27%	21%	5%	15.0%	97.4	44	19	37	25%	67%	18%	19%	0	15			20	0.97	2.5	148	$3
1st Half		1	0	32	26	4.83	0.98	4.19	1.25	115	81	3.7	7%	21%	15%	5%	15.0%	97.2	41	16	43	19%	61%	22%	20%	0	14			0	0.74	-2.2	99	-$4
2nd Half		2	1	28	35	2.89	0.96	2.68	0.97	79	76	4.2	5%	33%	28%	5%	15.0%	97.6	48	23	29	31%	72%	11%	17%	0	16			50	1.27	4.7	204	$2
Proj		**3**	**8**	**58**	**66**	**3.30**	**1.10**	**3.34**	**1.09**	**103**	**84**	**5.7**	**6%**	**29%**	**23%**	**5%**	**15.0%**	**97.5**	**45**	**20**	**34**	**30%**	**76%**	**15%**	**18%**	**0**						**8.2**	**171**	**$6**

Alcantara,Sandy

Age: 26	Th: R	Role: SP	Health: A	LIMA Plan: D+	
Ht: 6' 5"	Wt: 200	Type: /GB	PT/Exp: A	Rand Var: 0	
			Consist: B	MM: 3205	

One of only four pitchers to crack 200 IP mark in 2021, he got there with a skills flourish. Pitch mix changes (improved slider, more change-ups/fewer curves) took 2020 skills pop to a new level: K-BB%, GB%, velocity all jumped. Even got a handle on lefty hitters. DOM/DIS% shows how far he has come; 2nd half BPX suggests... UP: Cy Young

Yr	Tm	W	Sv	IP	K	ERA	WHIP	xERA	xWHIP	vL+	vR+	BF/G	BB%	K%	K-BB%	xBB%	SwK	Vel	G	L	F	H%	S%	HR/F	xHR/F	GS	APC	DOM%	DIS%	Sv%	LI	RAR	BPX	R$
17	STL *	7	0	134	98	5.36	1.61	5.38	1.54	108	126	17.9	10%	17%	6%		17.4%	98.3	26	43	30	33%	68%	29%	14%	0	19			0	0.08	-16.5	45	-$9
18	MIA *	8	0	151	106	4.13	1.36	3.93	1.47	86	112	25.3	10%	17%	7%	10%	10.6%	95.5	48	16	36	29%	70%	9%	8%	6	95	33%	33%			0.4	65	$1
19	MIA	6	0	197	151	3.88	1.32	5.11	1.49	100	90	26.2	10%	18%	8%	7%	11.4%	95.6	45	19	36	28%	74%	11%	14%	32	97	25%	28%			15.3	51	$7
20	MIA	3	0	42	39	3.00	1.19	4.08	1.32	119	63	24.6	9%	23%	14%	8%	11.3%	96.5	49	22	29	28%	78%	12%	13%	7	95	29%	29%			7.5	102	$8
21	MIA	9	0	206	201	3.19	1.07	3.44	1.17	96	78	25.4	6%	24%	18%	5%	13.9%	97.9	53	19	28	28%	74%	13%	16%	33	94	48%	18%			27.2	143	$23
1st Half		5	0	113	97	2.96	1.09	3.75	1.27	88	79	25.3	7%	21%	14%	6%	13.0%	97.7	54	18	28	27%	76%	11%	14%	18	92	50%	22%			18.2	110	$21
2nd Half		4	0	93	104	3.48	1.05	3.10	1.05	93	81	25.5	4%	28%	23%	5%	14.9%	98.1	52	20	28	31%	71%	16%	20%	15	96	47%	13%			9.0	184	$20
Proj		**14**	**0**	**196**	**187**	**3.27**	**1.14**	**3.69**	**1.23**	**99**	**80**	**23.7**	**7%**	**24%**	**17%**	**6%**	**12.7%**	**96.9**	**50**	**19**	**31**	**28%**	**75%**	**13%**	**15%**	**33**						**28.6**	**128**	**$22**

Alexander,Tyler

Age: 27	Th: L	Role: RP	Health: A	LIMA Plan: B+	
Ht: 6' 2"	Wt: 200	Type: Con/FB	PT/Exp: C	Rand Var: -2	
			Consist: D	MM: 1101	

xERA shows this wasn't really a step forward. Good control and effectiveness vL are assets, but frightening DOM/DIS% and paltry SwK/K% are all results of getting exposed vR in the SP role. Lifetime K-BB% (13% SP, 17% RP) confirm he's best suited to 'pen work, though same platoon split will preclude high leverage opps.

Yr	Tm	W	Sv	IP	K	ERA	WHIP	xERA	xWHIP	vL+	vR+	BF/G	BB%	K%	K-BB%	xBB%	SwK	Vel	G	L	F	H%	S%	HR/F	xHR/F	GS	APC	DOM%	DIS%	Sv%	LI	RAR	BPX	R$
17	aa	8	0	138	99	6.32	1.68	6.85				23.0	4%	16%	12%							39%	64%									-33.4	80	-$15
18	a/a	6	0	140	76	5.94	1.78	7.36				24.8	4%	12%	8%							39%	68%									-30.8	48	-$22
19	DET *	6	0	153	131	6.25	1.57	6.68	1.26	89	117	20.3	5%	20%	15%	5%	8.8%	90.7	36	26	38	37%	64%	13%	16%	8	71	0%	50%	0	0.59	-32.8	73	-$14
20	DET	2	0	36	34	3.96	1.32	4.20	1.21	72	130	10.9	6%	22%	16%	8%	9.3%	90.6	45	18	37	31%	80%	21%	17%	2	43	0%	50%	0	0.81	2.2	129	$1
21	DET	2	0	106	87	3.81	1.26	4.82	1.27	77	104	11.0	6%	19%	13%	6%	9.0%	90.4	38	18	44	30%	75%	11%	14%	15	40	13%	67%	0	0.56	6.0	93	$0
1st Half		0	0	35	32	4.67	1.38	4.61	1.15	82	118	6.7	4%	21%	17%	4%	10.4%	91.0	41	17	43	35%	73%	14%	15%	2	24	0%	100%	0	0.37	-1.7	139	-$8
2nd Half		2	0	72	55	3.39	1.20	4.92	1.34	61	101	16.4	7%	19%	11%	7%	8.3%	90.1	36	19	45	27%	77%	9%	13%	13	61	15%	62%	0	0.81	7.7	70	$5
Proj		**4**	**0**	**116**	**95**	**4.59**	**1.40**	**4.67**	**1.26**	**84**	**119**	**12.2**	**6%**	**19%**	**14%**	**6%**	**9.2%**	**90.5**	**39**	**19**	**42**	**33%**	**73%**	**13%**	**15%**	**5**						**-1.9**	**106**	**-$4**

Allard,Kolby

Age: 24	Th: L	Role: RP	Health: A	LIMA Plan: D+	
Ht: 6' 1"	Wt: 195	Type: Con/FB	PT/Exp: C	Rand Var: +3	
			Consist: B	MM: 0101	

Began and ended 2021 in bullpen with three months as SP in between. PRO: BB% improvement pulled K-BB% to MLB average. CON: K%/SwK remained subpar; throwing more strikes led to more hard contact/HR issues (xHR/F, 11% Brl%). VERDICT: K% spiked as RP (25% vs. 17% as SP), suggesting that might be his best path forward.

Yr	Tm	W	Sv	IP	K	ERA	WHIP	xERA	xWHIP	vL+	vR+	BF/G	BB%	K%	K-BB%	xBB%	SwK	Vel	G	L	F	H%	S%	HR/F	xHR/F	GS	APC	DOM%	DIS%	Sv%	LI	RAR	BPX	R$
17	aa	8	0	150	120	4.34	1.49	4.77				24.0	8%	19%	11%							35%	72%									0.4	82	$0
18	ATL *	7	0	121	80	3.77	1.39	4.39	1.38	203	158	23.2	7%	16%	9%	12%	4.3%	89.4	32	29	39	32%	74%	20%	27%	1	54	0%	100%	0	0.56	5.7	70	$0
19	TEX *	11	0	160	121	4.71	1.54	5.36	1.44	100	98	23.3	8%	17%	9%	8%	8.2%	92.5	45	26	29	34%	72%	7%	8%	9	93	11%	44%			-4.0	52	-$3
20	TEX	0	0	34	32	7.75	1.51	5.89	1.57	125	89	13.8	13%	21%	8%	8%	10.0%	91.6	33	19	48	30%	47%	9%	12%	8	60	13%	50%	0	0.60	-13.7	23	-$15
21	TEX	3	0	125	104	5.41	1.28	4.70	1.25	111	103	16.7	6%	19%	14%	7%	9.2%	91.6	39	20	41	29%	65%	18%	18%	17	64	12%	41%	0	0.78	-17.7	101	-$6
1st Half		2	0	52	49	3.46	1.08	4.13	1.16	67	93	13.2	5%	23%	18%	6%	10.6%	91.7	37	22	41	28%	73%	11%	14%	6	54	17%	17%	0	0.86	5.2	128	$3
2nd Half		1	0	73	55	6.81	1.42	5.13	1.32	129	112	20.2	6%	17%	11%	7%	8.1%	91.5	39	19	42	29%	59%	22%	21%	11	75	9%	55%	0	0.69	-22.8	80	-$18
Proj		**3**	**0**	**102**	**84**	**4.70**	**1.39**	**4.82**	**1.36**	**112**	**100**	**10.6**	**8%**	**20%**	**11%**	**7%**	**9.2%**	**91.8**	**39**	**21**	**40**	**30%**	**71%**	**14%**	**15%**	**-7**						**-3.1**	**76**	**-$5**

Allen,Logan

Age: 25	Th: L	Role: RP	Health: A	LIMA Plan: D+	
Ht: 6' 3"	Wt: 220	Type:	PT/Exp: D	Rand Var: +5	
			Consist: B	MM: 0100	

2-7, 6.26 ERA in 50 IP with CLE. Continued to be overmatched at MLB level (career: 5.89 ERA, 1.61 WHIP, 5.05 xERA) and was even worse at AAA. Improved BB%/xBB% in 2nd half, but SwK%/K% and K-BB% all remain far below our minimum thresholds. Plus, xHR/F column shows far too much hard contact. Stay far away.

Yr	Tm	W	Sv	IP	K	ERA	WHIP	xERA	xWHIP	vL+	vR+	BF/G	BB%	K%	K-BB%	xBB%	SwK	Vel	G	L	F	H%	S%	HR/F	xHR/F	GS	APC	DOM%	DIS%	Sv%	LI	RAR	BPX	R$
17																																		
18	a/a	14	0	150	134	2.62	1.09	2.58				23.5	8%	23%	15%							27%	78%									28.3	118	$21
19	2 TM *	7	0	108	87	7.08	1.78	6.97	1.48	147	121	18.4	10%	18%	8%	8%	10.2%	92.7	49	29	22	36%	63%	20%	27%	4	50	25%	50%	0	0.60	-34.2	22	-$17
20	CLE	0	0	11	7	3.38	1.78	6.19	1.76	43	132	16.3	14%	14%	0%	12%	8.6%	94.1	47	21	32	32%	83%	9%	12%	0	62			0	0.29	1.4	-32	-$7
21	CLE *	4	0	101	81	7.33	1.70	6.86	1.46	125	115	17.5	10%	18%	8%	10%	8.4%	92.7	45	22	33	34%	59%	22%	24%	11	62	9%	64%	0	0.70	-38.0	20	-$22
1st Half		1	0	39	26	10.06	1.88	8.07	1.61	142	135	16.5	12%	14%	3%	12%	7.8%	92.5	45	19	36	34%	47%	35%	32%	6	66	0%	83%			-27.6	-18	-$25
2nd Half		3	0	62	55	5.64	1.58	6.11	1.36	107	106	18.2	9%	20%	11%	8%	8.8%	92.9	45	24	31	34%	68%	13%	19%	5	60	20%	40%	0	0.67	-10.5	47	-$12
Proj		**3**	**0**	**58**	**48**	**5.51**	**1.60**	**4.94**	**1.44**	**121**	**113**	**18.5**	**10%**	**19%**	**9%**	**9%**	**8.3%**	**92.7**	**45**	**22**	**33**	**33%**	**70%**	**17%**	**24%**	**12**						**-7.5**	**60**	**-$8**

GREG PYRON

Alvarado,José

Age: 27 Th: L Role RP	Health D	LIMA Plan D+	
Ht: 6' 2" Wt: 245 Type Pwr/xGB	PT/Exp D	Rand Var +1	
	Consist B	MM 2410	

Luster of terrific 2018 has dulled, but he's spent about 150 day on the IL since then, including a recurrence of 2020 shoulder inflammation. Obscene BB%, career-worst 42% hard-hit rate allowed, and recent history vR are major concerns. We can hope for prior skills, but it will all come down to health. At 27, there's still time, and hope.

Yr Tm	W	Sv	IP	K	ERA	WHIP	xERA	xWHIP	vL+	vR+	BF/G	BB%	K%	K-BB%	xBB%	SwK	Vel	G	L	F	H%	S%	HR/F	xHR/F	GS	APC	DOM%	DIS%	Sv%	LI	RAR	BPX	R$
17 TAM *	2	1	59	65	3.92	1.17	2.41	1.36	97	61	3.9	12%	27%	16%		11.4%	98.2	54	16	30	27%	66%	4%	12%	0	13			33	1.15	3.2	131	$2
18 TAM	1	8	64	80	2.39	1.11	3.13	1.26	79	69	3.8	11%	31%	20%	9%	13.2%	97.4	55	17	28	29%	77%	2%	9%	0	15			67	1.48	13.9	144	$8
19 TAM	1	7	30	39	4.80	1.87	5.29	1.71	71	113	4.2	19%	27%	8%	12%	12.8%	98.2	48	22	30	37%	74%	9%	10%	1	17	0%	100%	78	1.17	-1.1	19	-$3
20 TAM	0	0	9	13	6.00	1.67	4.41	1.40	35	140	5.0	13%	29%	16%	11%	10.8%	96.9	42	25	33	36%	69%	25%	29%	0	22			0	0.42	-1.7	104	-$8
21 PHI	7	5	56	68	4.20	1.60	4.21	1.67	65	113	3.9	19%	27%	8%	12%	12.8%	99.4	57	21	22	29%	75%	18%	16%	0	16			63	1.29	0.4	30	$0
1st Half	5	3	31	42	4.06	1.55	4.08	1.63	76	96	4.3	19%	30%	11%	12%	11.8%	99.3	56	19	25	28%	76%	18%	17%	0	18			60	1.44	0.8	46	$1
2nd Half	2	2	25	26	4.38	1.66	4.37	1.72	48	145	3.5	18%	24%	5%	12%	14.2%	99.4	59	23	18	30%	74%	18%	15%	0	14			67	1.13	-0.3	12	-$7
Proj	5	2	65	79	3.96	1.52	4.15	1.57	65	106	3.8	17%	28%	11%	12%	13.1%	98.7	55	21	24	31%	74%	11%	13%	0						4.0	57	-$1

Alvarez,Jose

Age: 33 Th: L Role RP	Health C	LIMA Plan B	
Ht: 5' 11" Wt: 195 Type Con	PT/Exp D	Rand Var -5	
	Consist A	MM 1000	

Shiny ERA/WHIP masked an underwhelming skill set. Big changes to pitch mix around mid-season, including elimination of four-seam fastball and heavy reliance on sinker and change-up, sparked 2nd half SwK/K% decline and GB% surge. Could notch some Holds, but not enough for fantasy relevance.

Yr Tm	W	Sv	IP	K	ERA	WHIP	xERA	xWHIP	vL+	vR+	BF/G	BB%	K%	K-BB%	xBB%	SwK	Vel	G	L	F	H%	S%	HR/F	xHR/F	GS	APC	DOM%	DIS%	Sv%	LI	RAR	BPX	R$
17 LAA	0	1	49	45	3.88	1.27	4.18	1.23	95	101	3.2	6%	22%	16%	6%	11.1%	91.1	39	24	37	32%	75%	13%	13%	0	12			33	1.02	2.8	128	-$2
18 LAA	6	1	63	59	2.71	1.16	3.97	1.30	82	87	3.4	8%	23%	14%	6%	11.1%	91.6	45	20	35	29%	77%	5%	14%	0	13			25	1.24	11.2	103	$5
19 PHI	3	1	59	51	3.36	1.42	4.36	1.33	87	115	3.8	7%	20%	13%	6%	11.5%	91.5	49	24	27	33%	82%	16%	14%	1	15	0%	0%	33	1.17	8.4	101	$0
20 PHI	0	0	6	6	1.42	1.58	4.05		146	75	3.4	11%	22%	11%	9%	12.4%	91.7	50	33	17	37%	90%	0%	4%	0	16			0	0.68	2.4	75	-$6
21 SF	5	0	65	42	2.37	1.11	4.46	1.37	71	78	4.0	7%	16%	9%	6%	9.3%	91.3	51	20	29	27%	79%	3%	7%	1	14	0%	100%	0	1.00	15.2	68	$5
1st Half	2	0	30	20	2.73	1.15	4.81	1.38	75	82	4.4	7%	16%	9%	6%	11.0%	91.0	46	17	37	27%	78%	6%	8%	0	17			0	0.69	5.6	65	-$1
2nd Half	3	0	35	22	2.06	1.09	4.16	1.37	61	78	3.6	7%	15%	8%	6%	7.7%	91.6	55	23	23	27%	79%	0%	5%	1	13	0%	100%	0	1.21	9.5	71	$3
Proj	4	0	58	45	3.85	1.27	4.28	1.33	84	94	3.6	7%	19%	12%	6%	10.2%	91.4	48	22	30	31%	70%	7%	10%	0						4.3	89	-$1

Alzolay,Adbert

Age: 27 Th: R Role SP	Health C	LIMA Plan B+	
Ht: 6' 1" Wt: 208 Type	PT/Exp C	Rand Var +4	
	Consist B	MM 2203	

Two IL trips (finger, hamstring) marred his first full MLB season. PRO: Dominant vR; exciting BB%/xBB% gains; and slight GB% uptick while maintaining plus-SwK/K%. CON: Toxic xHR/F and serious difficulties vL. Spent September in bullpen to manage workload, but figures to get another shot in rotation in 2021.

Yr Tm	W	Sv	IP	K	ERA	WHIP	xERA	xWHIP	vL+	vR+	BF/G	BB%	K%	K-BB%	xBB%	SwK	Vel	G	L	F	H%	S%	HR/F	xHR/F	GS	APC	DOM%	DIS%	Sv%	LI	RAR	BPX	R$
17 aa	0	0	33	26	3.92	1.37	3.23				19.5	10%	19%	10%							33%	68%									1.8	109	-$4
18 aaa	2	0	41	23	5.06	1.47	4.91				22.1	7%	13%	6%							32%	66%									-4.6	43	-$6
19 CHC *	3	0	78	88	5.84	1.52	5.34	1.47	133	109	17.9	13%	26%	13%	10%	11.1%	94.4	32	24	43	32%	66%	25%	18%	2	56	0%	100%	0	0.54	-12.9	60	-$7
20 CHC	1	0	21	29	2.95	1.17	3.59	1.37	90	66	14.5	15%	33%	18%	9%	11.4%	94.7	43	27	30	26%	75%	8%	12%	4	65	25%	0%	0	0.72	3.9	105	$1
21 CHC	5	1	126	128	4.58	1.16	3.74	1.18	128	74	17.9	7%	25%	18%	6%	12.4%	93.9	45	21	34	28%	68%	22%	23%	21	67	29%	38%	100	0.84	-4.9	134	$3
1st Half	4	0	72	76	4.48	1.08	3.69	1.18	122	72	21.0	7%	26%	19%	6%	11.9%	93.7	44	21	35	24%	68%	24%	23%	14	81	36%	29%			-1.9	134	$6
2nd Half	1	1	53	52	4.73	1.28	3.79	1.18	120	81	15.0	6%	24%	18%	6%	13.2%	94.3	47	21	32	32%	68%	19%	24%	7	55	14%	57%	100	0.89	-3.0	136	-$4
Proj	5	0	145	133	4.25	1.31	4.19	1.31	125	78	20.9	8%	22%	14%	6%	12.7%	94.0	46	21	33	30%	73%	17%	24%	29						3.6	101	$1

Anderson,Brett

Age: 34 Th: L Role SP	Health F	LIMA Plan D+	
Ht: 6' 4" Wt: 230 Type Con/xGB	PT/Exp B	Rand Var 0	
	Consist A	MM 1001	

Spent nearly two months on the IL (shoulder, knee, hamstring) and has now had IL stints in 10 of the past 12 seasons. Aside from GB%, the rest of these skills are dreadful, including SwK/K%, DOM/DIS%, xHR/F, and xBB%. Plunging APC also zaps chances for any Wins-aided fantasy value. All risk, no reward.

Yr Tm	W	Sv	IP	K	ERA	WHIP	xERA	xWHIP	vL+	vR+	BF/G	BB%	K%	K-BB%	xBB%	SwK	Vel	G	L	F	H%	S%	HR/F	xHR/F	GS	APC	DOM%	DIS%	Sv%	LI	RAR	BPX	R$
17 2 TM *	7	0	92	52	6.14	1.75	6.04	1.51	143	112	20.1	8%	12%	4%	8%	8.9%	90.5	49	29	22	36%	64%	12%	12%	13	69	0%	46%			-20.3	33	-$12
18 OAK *	6	0	113	73	4.25	1.34	4.51	1.26	99	109	19.6	4%	15%	11%	8%	7.8%	90.3	56	20	25	33%	69%	15%	17%	17	71	12%	47%			-1.3	98	-$1
19 OAK	13	0	176	90	3.89	1.31	4.93	1.46	77	103	24.0	7%	12%	6%	8%	8.0%	90.8	54	20	25	28%	73%	13%	20%	31	86	0%	42%			13.4	51	$9
20 MIL	4	0	47	32	4.21	1.28	4.32	1.29	103	103	20.2	5%	16%	11%	9%	8.5%	89.8	58	16	26	30%	70%	15%	17%	10	75	10%	60%			1.4	107	$4
21 MIL	4	0	96	58	4.22	1.35	4.29	1.38	105	102	17.0	7%	14%	7%	12%	6.8%	89.1	58	22	21	30%	71%	17%	27%	24	63	8%	58%			0.6	69	-$3
1st Half	2	0	48	31	4.69	1.46	4.51	1.39	112	108	17.8	7%	15%	8%	12%	5.8%	89.4	55	23	22	32%	71%	19%	31%	12	68	17%	58%			-2.5	68	-$7
2nd Half	2	0	48	27	3.75	1.25	4.06	1.38	88	99	16.3	7%	14%	7%	11%	8.0%	88.7	60	21	19	28%	71%	14%	21%	12	58	0%	58%			3.1	70	-$3
Proj	5	0	87	52	4.43	1.39	4.46	1.42	101	104	20.7	7%	14%	7%	10%	7.7%	89.6	57	20	23	30%	70%	15%	21%	18						0.3	65	-$3

Anderson,Ian

Age: 24 Th: R Role SP	Health D	LIMA Plan C+	
Ht: 6' 3" Wt: 170 Type Pwr	PT/Exp C	Rand Var 0	
	Consist B	MM 2303	

9-5, 3.58 ERA in 128 IP at ATL. Missed several weeks in 2nd half (shoulder inflammation), which contributed to 2nd half fade. Pre-injury skills looked a lot like 2020 except for drop in K%, which was actually regression foretold by 2020 SwK. BB% remains his main flaw, so best to pay for a full-season repeat rather than a step forward.

Yr Tm	W	Sv	IP	K	ERA	WHIP	xERA	xWHIP	vL+	vR+	BF/G	BB%	K%	K-BB%	xBB%	SwK	Vel	G	L	F	H%	S%	HR/F	xHR/F	GS	APC	DOM%	DIS%	Sv%	LI	RAR	BPX	R$
17																																	
18 aa	2	0	20	21	2.87	1.24	2.47				20.4	11%	26%	15%							31%	74%									3.2	136	-$2
19 a/a	8	0	137	147	4.77	1.45	4.37				22.5	12%	25%	13%							32%	69%									-4.4	83	$0
20 ATL	3	0	32	41	1.95	1.08	3.45	1.24	55	80	23.0	10%	30%	20%	10%	12.3%	94.1	53	20	28	28%	82%	5%	3%	6	95	17%	0%			10.0	148	$11
21 ATL *	9	0	145	141	3.64	1.25	3.61	1.36	89	92	21.0	11%	24%	13%	10%	12.4%	94.6	49	20	31	28%	74%	15%	20%	24	91	17%	21%			11.2	88	$9
1st Half	5	0	89	90	3.35	1.14	3.64	1.26	76	88	22.7	9%	25%	16%	9%	12.5%	94.9	50	22	28	28%	73%	12%	18%	16	94	19%	6%			10.0	118	$14
2nd Half	4	0	56	51	4.10	1.43	4.53	1.52	99	112	19.8	13%	21%	8%	11%	12.2%	94.0	47	16	37	28%	76%	20%	24%	8	85	13%	50%			1.1	57	-$1
Proj	11	0	167	174	3.59	1.29	4.04	1.38	84	95	21.1	11%	25%	14%	10%	12.3%	94.3	49	19	32	29%	75%	12%	17%	33						17.7	93	$11

Anderson,Nick

Age: 31 Th: R Role RP	Health F	LIMA Plan C	
Ht: 6' 4" Wt: 205 Type Pwr	PT/Exp D	Rand Var -5	
	Consist F	MM 2310	

Diagnosed with partially torn UCL (elbow) in late March that ultimately required October UCL brace surgery. Not expected back until sometime after 2022 All-Star break. Prior to injury, he had become an elite RP backed by a tremendous K-BB% and BPX. Given severity of surgery, it's best not to expect much in 2022.

Yr Tm	W	Sv	IP	K	ERA	WHIP	xERA	xWHIP	vL+	vR+	BF/G	BB%	K%	K-BB%	xBB%	SwK	Vel	G	L	F	H%	S%	HR/F	xHR/F	GS	APC	DOM%	DIS%	Sv%	LI	RAR	BPX	R$
17 aa	2	9	34	27	1.66	1.01	1.77				4.4	6%	21%	15%							28%	82%									11.2	152	$6
18 aaa	8	4	60	65	5.26	1.52	5.86				6.7	9%	25%	16%							35%	71%									-8.3	71	-$2
19 2 TM	5	1	65	110	3.32	1.08	2.80	0.94	102	72	3.9	7%	42%	35%	5%	20.3%	96.1	29	30	42	38%	74%	15%	16%	0	16			20	1.19	9.5	233	$7
20 TAM	2	6	16	26	0.55	0.49	3.05	0.82	63	27	3.1	5%	45%	40%	4%	21.9%	95.2	21	7	72	17%	100%	5%	14%	0	12			100	1.55	7.9	240	$17
21 TAM	0	1	6	1	4.50	1.00	7.55		114	90	4.0	8%	4%	-4%	8%	8.8%	93.0	15	15	70	11%	75%	14%	26%	0	17			100	0.45	-0.2	-67	-$5
1st Half																																	
2nd Half	0	1	6	1	4.50	1.00	7.55		108	92	4.0	8%	4%	-4%	8%	8.8%	93.0	15	15	70	11%	75%	14%	26%	0	17			100	0.45	-0.2	-67	-$11
Proj	3	2	29	32	3.47	1.20	3.85	1.18	124	85	4.6	7%	28%	20%	5%	20.3%	96.1	29	30	42	31%	75%	12%	15%	0						3.5	130	-$1

Anderson,Tyler

Age: 32 Th: L Role SP	Health F	LIMA Plan B+	
Ht: 6' 2" Wt: 213 Type Con/FB	PT/Exp B	Rand Var 0	
	Consist B	MM 1103	

Enjoyed spurts of success, including three months of sub-3.50 ERA, but only one month with an xERA better than 4.65. Improved control was backed by xBB% and SwK hints at some K% upside. However, FB% and meh velocity make him susceptible to HR issues. Best treated as a matchups-based streaming option.

Yr Tm	W	Sv	IP	K	ERA	WHIP	xERA	xWHIP	vL+	vR+	BF/G	BB%	K%	K-BB%	xBB%	SwK	Vel	G	L	F	H%	S%	HR/F	xHR/F	GS	APC	DOM%	DIS%	Sv%	LI	RAR	BPX	R$
17 COL	6	0	86	81	4.81	1.33	4.07	1.27	98	115	21.3	7%	23%	15%	6%	12.2%	92.0	44	23	33	31%	69%	20%	16%	15	83	13%	33%	0	0.78	-4.8	121	$0
18 COL	7	0	176	164	4.55	1.27	4.30	1.29	113	103	23.0	8%	22%	14%	6%	12.3%	91.8	37	24	39	29%	70%	15%	11%	32	89	25%	34%			-8.7	97	$2
19 COL	0	0	21	23	11.76	2.13	5.45	1.44	154	155	21.2	11%	22%	12%	7%	11.4%	91.3	41	26	33	41%	47%	35%	32%	5	86	0%	40%			-18.5	76	-$12
20 SF	4	0	60	41	4.37	1.39	5.89	1.52	119	92	20.0	10%	16%	6%	7%	10.9%	90.2	28	27	44	29%	69%	6%	9%	11	73	9%	36%	0	0.95	0.6	18	$2
21 2 TM	7	0	167	134	4.53	1.25	4.75	1.25	96	103	22.7	5%	19%	14%	5%	12.0%	90.2	35	22	43	30%	69%	12%	13%	31	84	19%	39%			-5.4	96	$2
1st Half	3	0	85	72	4.75	1.23	4.51	1.25	55	117	23.9	6%	20%	14%	5%	11.8%	89.9	39	22	39	29%	67%	15%	16%	15	90	20%	27%			-5.1	100	$0
2nd Half	4	0	82	62	4.30	1.26	4.98	1.24	131	93	21.6	5%	18%	13%	4%	12.1%	90.6	32	22	47	31%	70%	10%	10%	16	79	19%	50%			-0.3	93	$4
Proj	8	0	160	130	4.67	1.29	4.72	1.32	109	100	21.2	7%	20%	13%	6%	11.9%	90.8	35	23	42	30%	68%	12%	12%	31						-4.3	84	$1

GREG PYRON

Antone,Tejay

Age: 28	Th: R	Role: RP	Health: F	LIMA Plan: B+
Ht: 6' 4"	Wt: 230	Type: Pwr	PT/Exp: D	Rand Var: -5
			Consist: D	MM: 3300

Landed on IL in mid-June with right forearm inflammation and ultimately required Tommy John surgery in late August. Timing was terrible, as electric SwK/K%, GB% tilt, and xBB% were gelling into an impressive package. This is 2nd career TJS, so not only will he likely miss all of 2022, the path beyond that is rarely-traveled.

Yr	Tm	W	Sv	IP	K	ERA	WHIP	xERA	xWHIP	vL+	vR+	BF/G	BB%	K%	K-BB%	xBB%	SwK	Vel	G	L	F	H%	S%	HR/F	xHR/F	GS	APC	DOM%	DIS%	Sv%	LI	RAR	BPX	R$
17																																		
18																																		
19	a/a	11	0	149	112	5.47	1.74	6.10				25.2	9%	16%	7%							37%	69%									-17.7	45	-$11
20	CIN	0	0	35	45	2.80	1.02	3.62	1.25	98	59	10.8	11%	32%	21%	9%	13.2%	95.7	49	10	41	23%	78%	13%	13%	4	46	0%	25%	0	0.77	7.2	139	$5
21	CIN	2	3	34	42	2.14	0.89	2.98	1.17	77	59	5.6	10%	33%	23%	6%	13.6%	96.8	47	21	31	21%	81%	14%	21%	0	23			43	1.54	8.8	146	$4
1st Half		2	3	34	42	1.87	0.86	2.90	1.14	73	60	5.8	9%	33%	24%	6%	13.7%	96.9	47	21	31	21%	85%	14%	21%	0	24			43	1.60	9.9	154	$8
2nd Half		0	0	0	0	0.00	0.00	0.00		0	0	1.0						94.0				0%	0%	0%		0	5			0	0.22	0.0	-24	-$13
Proj		**0**	**0**	**7**	**8**	**3.05**	**1.13**	**3.65**	**1.26**	**103**	**72**	**8.8**	**10%**	**29%**	**19%**	**8%**	**13.5%**	**96.4**	**48**	**17**	**35**	**27%**	**77%**	**12%**	**18%**	**0**						**1.3**	**127**	**-$5**

Archer,Chris

Age: 33	Th: R	Role: RP	Health: F	LIMA Plan: C
Ht: 6' 2"	Wt: 195	Type: Pwr/FB	PT/Exp: D	Rand Var: -1
			Consist: A	MM: 1301

Briefly returned from missed 2020 season (thoracic outlet surgery) before forearm/hip injuries shelved him for nearly all of 2021. Tough to draw much from 2021 sample, but velocity drop, FB% spike, and decision to stop throwing sinker are notable. Best case from here is some strikeout upside, in between continued blowups (DIS%) and more missed time.

Yr	Tm	W	Sv	IP	K	ERA	WHIP	xERA	xWHIP	vL+	vR+	BF/G	BB%	K%	K-BB%	xBB%	SwK	Vel	G	L	F	H%	S%	HR/F	xHR/F	GS	APC	DOM%	DIS%	Sv%	LI	RAR	BPX	R$
17	TAM	10	0	201	249	4.07	1.26	3.54	1.14	101	90	25.1	7%	29%	22%	8%	13.8%	95.5	42	22	36	34%	72%	14%	12%	34	100	35%	12%			7.0	178	$14
18	2 TM	6	0	148	162	4.31	1.38	3.71	1.22	110	103	23.6	8%	25%	18%	7%	13.4%	94.7	45	23	32	35%	72%	14%	16%	27	93	26%	33%			-2.9	138	$0
19	PIT	3	0	120	143	5.19	1.41	4.47	1.34	105	106	22.9	11%	28%	17%	8%	13.3%	94.1	36	24	39	31%	69%	20%	18%	23	91	17%	39%			-10.1	104	-$4
20																																		
21	TAM	1	0	19	21	4.66	1.34	4.83	1.31	73	111	13.8	10%	25%	16%	8%	12.8%	92.0	31	17	52	31%	70%	11%	20%	5	55	0%	20%	0	0.82	-0.9	93	-$5
1st Half		0	0	4	6	6.23	1.85	3.95		52	132	10.5	5%	29%	24%	7%	13.8%	91.6	29	36	36	53%	63%	0%	8%	1	47	0%	0%	0	0.85	-1.1	192	-$9
2nd Half		1	0	15	15	4.20	1.20	5.10	1.40	73	106	15.5	11%	24%	13%	9%	12.5%	92.2	33	10	58	23%	73%	13%	22%	4	58	0%	25%			0.1	65	-$8
Proj		**4**	**0**	**87**	**97**	**4.75**	**1.33**	**4.28**	**1.29**	**100**	**103**	**19.6**	**10%**	**27%**	**17%**	**8%**	**13.1%**	**93.8**	**38**	**19**	**44**	**31%**	**70%**	**15%**	**18%**	**18**						**-3.2**	**112**	**-$2**

Arihara,Kohei

Age: 29	Th: R	Role: SP	Health: F	LIMA Plan: D+
Ht: 6' 2"	Wt: 211	Type: Con	PT/Exp: A	Rand Var: +5
			Consist: C	MM: 1001

Japanese import's first four MLB starts included two PQS-4 outings, but struggled with reduced velocity in next three outings before landing on IL (finger). It was then discovered he needed surgery to repair a shoulder aneurysm and artery damage. Cleared waivers and was outrighted to AAA in September. Deep-league flyer at best.

Yr	Tm	W	Sv	IP	K	ERA	WHIP	xERA	xWHIP	vL+	vR+	BF/G	BB%	K%	K-BB%	xBB%	SwK	Vel	G	L	F	H%	S%	HR/F	xHR/F	GS	APC	DOM%	DIS%	Sv%	LI	RAR	BPX	R$
17	for	10	0	169	83	5.89	1.52	6.09				29.3	7%	11%	5%							31%	66%									-31.9	2	-$11
18	for	8	0	111	83	5.64	1.37	6.12				23.2	4%	18%	14%							31%	66%									-20.4	69	-$6
19	for	15	0	164	153	3.07	1.03	2.94				26.3	8%	24%	16%							24%	78%									29.1	99	$24
20	for	8	0	133	101	4.29	1.29	4.48				27.3	7%	18%	12%							30%	71%									2.7	71	$18
21	TEX	2	0	41	24	6.64	1.43	5.36	1.43	119	135	17.8	7%	13%	6%	10%	7.6%	90.9	41	21	39	27%	60%	21%	26%	10	70	20%	60%			-11.9	41	-$9
1st Half		2	0	29	17	6.59	1.53	5.66	1.53	93	152	18.1	9%	13%	4%	11%	6.7%	91.0	40	21	38	28%	62%	19%	27%	7	72	29%	71%			-8.2	14	-$11
2nd Half		0	0	12	7	6.75	1.17	4.71	1.20	149	95	17.0	2%	14%	12%	8%	10.1%	90.5	41	20	39	25%	50%	25%	25%	3	63	0%	33%			-3.7	103	-$13
Proj		**5**	**0**	**102**	**73**	**4.91**	**1.35**	**4.77**	**1.38**	**96**	**149**	**22.7**	**7%**	**17%**	**10%**	**11%**	**6.7%**	**91.0**	**40**	**21**	**38**	**29%**	**70%**	**18%**	**24%**	**19**						**-5.7**	**68**	**-$4**

Arrieta,Jake

Age: 36	Th: R	Role: RP	Health: F	LIMA Plan: D+
Ht: 6' 4"	Wt: 230	Type:	PT/Exp: B	Rand Var: +5
			Consist: A	MM: 0100

Began 2021 with CHC, released in August only to be signed by SD, but two IL stints cost him most of remainder of 2021 (hamstring, right adductor strain). Skill set has been deteriorating since 2017, and at this point what's most remarkable is how consistently his BPX has declined, like bringing a car to a gentle stop. Time to put it in park.

Yr	Tm	W	Sv	IP	K	ERA	WHIP	xERA	xWHIP	vL+	vR+	BF/G	BB%	K%	K-BB%	xBB%	SwK	Vel	G	L	F	H%	S%	HR/F	xHR/F	GS	APC	DOM%	DIS%	Sv%	LI	RAR	BPX	R$
17	CHC	14	0	168	163	3.53	1.22	4.04	1.29	112	83	23.6	8%	23%	15%	8%	9.0%	92.1	45	21	34	29%	76%	14%	12%	30	91	20%	27%			17.2	121	$16
18	PHI	10	0	173	138	3.96	1.29	4.03	1.34	111	92	23.4	8%	19%	11%	8%	8.4%	93.0	52	20	29	29%	73%	14%	15%	31	89	23%	39%			4.0	91	$6
19	PHI	8	0	136	110	4.64	1.47	4.58	1.42	123	91	24.8	9%	19%	10%	8%	7.6%	92.5	51	23	26	32%	73%	19%	20%	24	91	8%	33%			-2.3	75	-$2
20	PHI	4	0	44	32	5.08	1.51	4.60	1.42	121	101	21.1	8%	17%	8%	10%	7.5%	92.1	52	24	24	33%	69%	18%	21%	9	81	11%	56%			-3.4	67	-$3
21	2 NL	5	0	99	83	7.39	1.77	5.15	1.44	131	127	19.5	9%	18%	8%	9%	7.5%	91.4	43	26	31	35%	62%	23%	24%	24	73	4%	71%			-38.0	54	-$22
1st Half		5	0	73	62	5.57	1.57	5.14	1.45	115	111	20.8	10%	19%	8%	9%	8.2%	91.2	42	24	34	31%	70%	20%	23%	16	80	6%	63%			-11.7	49	-$8
2nd Half		0	0	26	21	12.46	2.35	5.18	1.39	152	169	17.0	8%	16%	8%	9%	5.7%	91.9	47	30	23	45%	47%	35%	27%	8	59	0%	88%			-26.3	68	-$33
Proj		**1**	**0**	**15**	**12**	**5.90**	**1.73**	**4.80**	**1.40**	**133**	**122**	**19.8**	**9%**	**18%**	**9%**	**9%**	**7.3%**	**92.0**	**48**	**25**	**27**	**36%**	**71%**	**23%**	**22%**	**3**						**-2.6**	**71**	**-$7**

Ashby,Aaron

Age: 24	Th: L	Role: RP	Health: A	LIMA Plan: A
Ht: 6' 2"	Wt: 181	Type: Pwr/GB	PT/Exp: F	Rand Var: +5
			Consist: F	MM: 5501

3-2, 4.55 ERA in 32 IP with MIL. Failed to complete one inning (4 ER) in June MLB debut and was immediately returned to AAA. Returned in August, finished strong with 9 of 12 appearances as a RP. 2nd half blend of elite SwK/K%, good BB%, extreme GB%, and vR makes him an intriguing end-gamer for 2022, assuming another rotation shot awaits.

Yr	Tm	W	Sv	IP	K	ERA	WHIP	xERA	xWHIP	vL+	vR+	BF/G	BB%	K%	K-BB%	xBB%	SwK	Vel	G	L	F	H%	S%	HR/F	xHR/F	GS	APC	DOM%	DIS%	Sv%	LI	RAR	BPX	R$
17																																		
18																																		
19																																		
20																																		
21	MIL *	8	1	96	127	4.42	1.30	3.55	1.20	121	76	11.6	11%	32%	22%	6%	13.3%	96.6	61	14	25	34%	66%	20%	21%	4	41	0%	50%	33	0.75	-1.8	134	$3
1st Half		4	0	41	50	6.17	1.67	4.94		262	153	13.1	14%	27%	14%		5.1%	96.4	67	33	0	38%	61%	0%		1	39	0%	100%			-9.6	99	-$8
2nd Half		4	1	57	77	2.99	0.98	2.29	1.02	102	72	10.9	7%	35%	28%	6%	14.0%	96.6	61	12	27	29%	73%	20%	21%	3	41	0%	33%	50	0.75	9.0	179	$16
Proj		**5**	**0**	**73**	**94**	**3.76**	**1.20**	**2.92**	**1.20**	**135**	**82**	**11.6**	**10%**	**32%**	**22%**	**6%**	**14.0%**	**96.6**	**61**	**12**	**27**	**32%**	**70%**	**15%**	**19%**	**4**						**6.2**	**169**	**$3**

Bard,Daniel

Age: 37	Th: R	Role: RP	Health: A	LIMA Plan: B+
Ht: 6' 4"	Wt: 197	Type: Pwr	PT/Exp: C	Rand Var: +4
			Consist: A	MM: 2410

First full season since 2013 was a mixed bag. PRO: Strong 1st half skills, including a stellar K-BB% and GB% lean. CON: Some of those early Ks turned to BBs, GBs to FBs, and by late August he lost the closer gig. RandVar and xERA say he deserved better, but severe issues vL cap our optimism, and age removes patience from the equation.

Yr	Tm	W	Sv	IP	K	ERA	WHIP	xERA	xWHIP	vL+	vR+	BF/G	BB%	K%	K-BB%	xBB%	SwK	Vel	G	L	F	H%	S%	HR/F	xHR/F	GS	APC	DOM%	DIS%	Sv%	LI	RAR	BPX	R$
17																																		
18																																		
19																																		
20	COL	4	6	25	27	3.65	1.30	4.08	1.30	109	72	4.6	9%	25%	16%	6%	12.9%	97.1	48	17	35	32%	73%	9%	13%	0	18			100	1.42	2.4	118	$12
21	COL	7	20	66	80	5.21	1.60	4.22	1.37	139	77	4.5	12%	26%	15%	8%	13.4%	97.5	42	26	31	37%	69%	14%	13%	0	18			71	1.07	-7.6	92	$3
1st Half		4	12	35	47	4.08	1.56	3.62	1.23	134	82	4.8	10%	29%	19%	7%	14.2%	97.7	46	26	29	40%	76%	15%	16%	0	20			71	1.20	0.8	142	$6
2nd Half		3	8	30	33	6.53	1.65	4.98	1.54	128	76	4.3	14%	23%	9%	10%	12.5%	97.2	39	27	34	33%	61%	14%	9%	0	17			73	0.93	-8.5	36	-$4
Proj		**4**	**8**	**58**	**69**	**4.62**	**1.42**	**4.00**	**1.34**	**128**	**70**	**4.1**	**12%**	**28%**	**16%**	**8%**	**13.2%**	**97.4**	**42**	**26**	**32**	**33%**	**70%**	**15%**	**12%**	**0**						**-1.2**	**105**	**$0**

Barlow,Joe

Age: 26	Th: R	Role: RP	Health: A	LIMA Plan: B
Ht: 6' 3"	Wt: 195	Type: Pwr/FB	PT/Exp: F	Rand Var: -5
			Consist: D	MM: 1220

0-2, 1.55 ERA with 11 Sv in 29 IP at TEX. Made MLB debut on June 24 and worked his way into closer role by mid-August. However, his BPV deteriorated with each passing month (105, 71, 9), masked by fortuitous H%/S% and HR/F. Though xBB% hints at potential for better BB%, the 2nd half K-BB%, FB%, and BPX aren't nearly closer-worthy... DN: 4.50 ERA.

Yr	Tm	W	Sv	IP	K	ERA	WHIP	xERA	xWHIP	vL+	vR+	BF/G	BB%	K%	K-BB%	xBB%	SwK	Vel	G	L	F	H%	S%	HR/F	xHR/F	GS	APC	DOM%	DIS%	Sv%	LI	RAR	BPX	R$
17																																		
18																																		
19	a/a	2	0	34	39	6.74	1.93	5.55				5.1	19%	24%	6%							37%	64%									-9.4	75	-$9
20																																		
21	TEX *	0	18	50	50	2.16	0.83	3.93	1.32	51	64	3.8	11%	27%	16%	7%	12.3%	94.5	38	17	46	17%	77%	6%	11%	0	15			95	0.84	13.0	130	$13
1st Half		0	7	23	26	3.12	0.85	0.90		26	136	4.4	11%	31%	20%		16.2%	94.8	25	50	25	19%	63%	0%	0%	0	19			100	0.15	3.2	149	$2
2nd Half		0	11	27	24	1.33	0.81	4.47	1.39	50	62	3.6	11%	23%	13%	7%	12.0%	94.5	38	15	47	15%	90%	6%	12%	0	14			92	0.89	9.8	67	$12
Proj		**2**	**10**	**58**	**59**	**3.87**	**1.41**	**4.78**	**1.45**	**112**	**112**	**4.4**	**12%**	**24%**	**12%**	**7%**	**12.0%**	**94.5**	**38**	**15**	**47**	**30%**	**76%**	**11%**	**10%**	**0**						**4.1**	**63**	**$2**

GREG PYRON

Barlow,Scott

Age: 29	Th: R	Role RP	Health A	LIMA Plan C+
Ht: 6' 3"	Wt: 215	Type Pwr	PT/Exp C	Rand Var -5
			Consist B	MM 2421

Repeated 2020 skill gains in 1st half, which propelled him to closer role by mid-season. Everything turned in 2nd half: K% fell sharply though SwK% says not to worry. More troublesome was GB/FB flip, which would have dragged ERA toward xERA if HR/F had normalized. RandVar and xERA make it tough to fully endorse, even if he opens season as closer.

Yr Tm	W	Sv	IP	K	ERA	WHIP	xERA	xWHIP	vL+	vR+	BF/G	BB%	K%	K-BB%	xBB%	SwK	Vel	G	L	F	H%	S%	HR/F	xHR/F	GS	APC	DOM%	DIS%	Sv%	LI	RAR	BPX	R$
17 a/a	7	0	140	132	3.92	1.22	3.42				21.7	10%	23%	13%							27%	71%									7.6	94	$
18 KC *	2	1	66	57	6.59	1.70	6.65	1.38	84	101	15.0	9%	19%	10%	5%	11.4%	90.6	38	26	36	37%	64%	12%	19%	0	40			50	1.33	-19.9	42	-$1
19 KC	3	1	70	92	4.22	1.44	4.19	1.35	112	88	5.1	12%	30%	18%	8%	14.8%	94.1	40	23	37	35%	72%	9%	11%	0	21			33	1.13	2.5	111	-$
20 KC	2	2	30	39	4.20	1.20	3.31	1.10	103	85	3.9	7%	31%	24%	8%	17.2%	94.9	47	19	34	34%	69%	16%	21%	0	16			100	0.95	0.9	184	$
21 KC	5	16	74	91	2.42	1.20	3.68	1.20	93	78	4.3	9%	30%	21%	8%	16.2%	95.4	39	23	38	32%	81%	6%	14%	0	17			73	1.26	16.9	136	$1
1st Half	2	4	41	59	1.99	1.20	2.94	1.14	83	75	4.4	10%	34%	24%	8%	16.6%	95.8	49	23	28	36%	83%	4%	19%	0	18			80	1.15	11.4	176	$
2nd Half	3	12	34	32	2.94	1.19	4.53	1.27	97	85	4.2	8%	24%	16%	9%	15.7%	94.8	29	23	48	29%	78%	7%	12%	0	17			71	1.40	5.5	89	$1
Proj	**4**	**20**	**73**	**84**	**3.60**	**1.28**	**3.88**	**1.24**	**106**	**86**	**4.8**	**9%**	**28%**	**19%**	**8%**	**16.0%**	**94.9**	**40**	**22**	**38**	**33%**	**74%**	**10%**	**15%**	**0**						**7.6**	**130**	**$1**

Barnes,Matt

Age: 32	Th: R	Role RP	Health C	LIMA Plan B
Ht: 6' 4"	Wt: 208	Type Pwr	PT/Exp B	Rand Var +1
			Consist B	MM 4520

Tremendous 1st half, then "poof." Late-season bout with COVID didn't help, but collapse in late June was due to sudden/dramatic loss of K-BB%, corresponding dip in spin rates. It all points to a sticky stuff issue. Getting left off ALCS roster was a strong statement about org's lack of confidence. 2022 value could depend on rules/what ball is used.

Yr Tm	W	Sv	IP	K	ERA	WHIP	xERA	xWHIP	vL+	vR+	BF/G	BB%	K%	K-BB%	xBB%	SwK	Vel	G	L	F	H%	S%	HR/F	xHR/F	GS	APC	DOM%	DIS%	Sv%	LI	RAR	BPX	R$
17 BOS	7	1	70	83	3.88	1.22	3.38	1.25	105	78	4.1	10%	29%	19%	10%	12.9%	95.2	49	23	28	31%	71%	14%	11%	0	17			33	0.95	4.1	147	$
18 BOS	6	0	62	96	3.65	1.26	2.88	1.18	88	85	4.3	12%	36%	25%	11%	14.9%	96.6	53	14	33	35%	73%	11%	16%	0	18			0	1.08	3.8	185	$
19 BOS	5	4	64	110	3.78	1.38	3.10	1.22	84	91	4.1	13%	39%	25%	10%	15.4%	96.7	47	22	31	38%	77%	20%	14%	0	19			33	1.42	5.8	173	$
20 BOS	1	9	23	31	4.30	1.39	3.96	1.38	68	115	4.3	14%	30%	17%	9%	11.6%	95.6	45	23	32	29%	75%	24%	27%	0	19			69	1.32	0.4	106	$
21 BOS	6	24	55	84	3.79	1.12	3.08	1.05	80	89	3.7	9%	38%	29%	6%	15.1%	95.9	42	12	46	32%	72%	15%	16%	0	15			80	1.30	3.2	197	$1
1st Half	4	18	36	61	2.75	0.83	2.31	0.84	69	67	3.7	7%	46%	39%	5%	17.1%	96.2	41	13	46	30%	73%	14%	11%	0	15			82	1.63	6.7	256	$2
2nd Half	2	6	19	23	5.79	1.66	4.85	1.41	85	130	3.7	13%	26%	14%	10%	12.2%	95.4	42	12	46	35%	70%	17%	22%	0	15			75	0.80	-3.5	84	-$
Proj	**6**	**16**	**58**	**86**	**4.16**	**1.32**	**3.33**	**1.19**	**88**	**96**	**3.7**	**12%**	**36%**	**24%**	**9%**	**14.3%**	**96.1**	**46**	**16**	**39**	**34%**	**72%**	**16%**	**16%**	**0**						**2.1**	**166**	**$**

Barria,Jaime

Age: 25	Th: R	Role RP	Health A	LIMA Plan D+
Ht: 6' 1"	Wt: 210	Type Con/FB	PT/Exp C	Rand Var -2
			Consist C	MM 0001

2-4, 4.61 ERA in 57 IP with LAA. Began year at AAA, then made 11 MLB starts in 2nd half. Altered pitch mix, throwing more sinkers and four-seamers at the expense of slider and change-up. That change was net-negative: GB% jumped accordingly, but SwK/K%, xERA, BPX, and DOM/DIS% were awful. Time to go back to the lab, try something else.

Yr Tm	W	Sv	IP	K	ERA	WHIP	xERA	xWHIP	vL+	vR+	BF/G	BB%	K%	K-BB%	xBB%	SwK	Vel	G	L	F	H%	S%	HR/F	xHR/F	GS	APC	DOM%	DIS%	Sv%	LI	RAR	BPX	R$
17 a/a	3	0	76	54	3.38	1.26	3.99				20.7	5%	17%	12%							31%	76%									9.2	97	$
18 LAA *	10	0	147	115	3.37	1.27	4.02	1.37	84	115	19.5	8%	19%	11%	9%	10.8%	91.2	37	20	43	28%	78%	10%	12%	26	84	15%	42%			14.2	70	$
19 LAA *	7	0	132	113	7.17	1.52	6.90	1.32	96	142	19.7	6%	20%	13%	10%	9.6%	91.7	34	19	46	33%	59%	20%	16%	13	79	0%	62%	0	0.81	-43.3	30	-$1
20 LAA	1	0	32	27	3.62	1.11	4.84	1.30	117	64	18.9	7%	20%	14%	6%	10.8%	92.1	34	21	45	27%	70%	7%	5%	5	73	20%	40%	0	0.73	3.3	90	$
21 LAA *	5	0	106	63	4.32	1.43	5.48	1.35	116	111	19.5	6%	14%	8%	9%	8.4%	93.1	44	23	33	32%	74%	13%	14%	11	71	9%	55%	0	0.80	-0.7	42	-$
1st Half	2	0	40	20	4.42	1.43	4.99		96	125	18.9	6%	12%	6%	12%	9.6%	93.1	36	23	41	32%	71%	0%	7%	0	58			0	0.96	-0.8	41	-$
2nd Half	3	0	66	43	4.25	1.43	5.79	1.32	111	112	19.9	6%	15%	10%	8%	8.2%	93.0	44	23	32	32%	77%	15%	15%	11	73	9%	55%			0.1	43	-$
Proj	**5**	**0**	**116**	**82**	**4.71**	**1.36**	**4.93**	**1.34**	**107**	**109**	**19.3**	**6%**	**17%**	**11%**	**8%**	**9.7%**	**92.2**	**38**	**21**	**40**	**31%**	**69%**	**12%**	**12%**	**23**						**-3.7**	**75**	**-$**

Bass,Anthony

Age: 34	Th: R	Role RP	Health B	LIMA Plan C
Ht: 6' 2"	Wt: 200	Type	PT/Exp C	Rand Var 0
			Consist B	MM 1111

Again relied heavily upon sinker/slider combo, but this time flipped usage rates to favor the slider, throwing it 50% of the time (sinker 42%). It had a negative impact: GB% plunged, K% didn't budge, he allowed more hard contact, and vL issues reemerged. Regardless of pitch mix, history of BPX tells the tale: he nets out as a tick below average.

Yr Tm	W	Sv	IP	K	ERA	WHIP	xERA	xWHIP	vL+	vR+	BF/G	BB%	K%	K-BB%	xBB%	SwK	Vel	G	L	F	H%	S%	HR/F	xHR/F	GS	APC	DOM%	DIS%	Sv%	LI	RAR	BPX	R$
17 TEX *	3	0	81	63	6.38	1.87	6.89	1.45	168	135	19.0	9%	17%	8%		8.1%	92.3	43	27	30	40%	67%	11%	1%	0	56			0	0.39	-20.2	42	-$1
18 CHC *	0	3	47	32	3.86	1.50	5.36	1.28	112	93	4.8	5%	16%	11%	10%	8.2%	94.1	53	27	20	36%	76%	11%	5%	0	15			60	0.69	1.7	83	-$
19 SEA *	3	14	69	58	3.44	1.05	2.48	1.37	69	79	4.2	9%	22%	13%	9%	11.4%	95.4	52	21	28	23%	70%	14%	16%	0	17			64	1.28	9.1	93	$1
20 TOR	2	7	26	21	3.51	1.01	4.04	1.36	58	85	3.8	9%	21%	12%	10%	11.9%	94.7	62	4	33	23%	67%	9%	8%	0	15			78	1.45	3.0	99	$1
21 MIA	3	0	61	58	3.82	1.29	4.31	1.34	139	72	3.7	9%	22%	13%	7%	12.2%	95.4	44	22	34	28%	78%	18%	18%	1	14	0%	100%	0	1.09	3.4	88	-$
1st Half	1	0	31	28	4.70	1.21	4.50	1.35	150	54	3.6	9%	22%	12%	8%	12.0%	95.4	41	19	40	25%	68%	18%	16%	0	13			0	1.12	-1.6	79	-$
2nd Half	2	0	31	30	2.93	1.37	4.13	1.32	112	89	3.9	9%	23%	14%	6%	12.4%	95.4	46	25	29	31%	86%	19%	22%	1	15	0%	100%	0	1.05	5.0	96	-$
Proj	**3**	**2**	**73**	**62**	**4.01**	**1.35**	**4.36**	**1.35**	**126**	**84**	**4.4**	**8%**	**21%**	**12%**	**8%**	**12.0%**	**95.4**	**46**	**22**	**32**	**31%**	**74%**	**14%**	**19%**	**0**						**3.9**	**89**	**-$**

Bassitt,Chris

Age: 33	Th: R	Role SP	Health D	LIMA Plan D+
Ht: 6' 5"	Wt: 217	Type	PT/Exp A	Rand Var -2
			Consist A	MM 2203

Missed just over a month after taking a line drive to the head in mid-August. Failed to duplicate 2020 career "year," but he didn't give it all back, either, thanks to K-BB% uptick to career-best levels. He now owns a track record of beating his xERA across multiple years running, but next step in ERA is still more likely toward 4.00 rather than 3.00.

Yr Tm	W	Sv	IP	K	ERA	WHIP	xERA	xWHIP	vL+	vR+	BF/G	BB%	K%	K-BB%	xBB%	SwK	Vel	G	L	F	H%	S%	HR/F	xHR/F	GS	APC	DOM%	DIS%	Sv%	LI	RAR	BPX	R$
17 aaa	4	0	38	23	7.95	1.82	6.15				10.3	10%	13%	3%							37%	54%									-16.7	33	-$1
18 OAK *	7	0	131	101	4.68	1.51	4.89	1.39	79	93	19.6	8%	18%	10%	8%	7.2%	92.0	45	22	34	34%	69%	9%	14%	7	73	14%	43%	0	0.69	-8.6	71	-$
19 OAK	10	0	144	141	3.81	1.19	4.42	1.30	92	93	21.9	8%	23%	15%	7%	9.3%	93.5	41	21	38	28%	74%	14%	13%	25	87	24%	36%	0	0.71	12.3	107	$1
20 OAK	5	0	63	55	2.29	1.16	4.46	1.27	104	78	23.7	7%	21%	15%	7%	10.4%	92.9	44	18	38	29%	85%	9%	11%	11	86	27%	18%			16.8	111	$2
21 OAK	12	0	157	159	3.15	1.06	3.81	1.16	85	85	23.6	6%	25%	19%	6%	10.8%	93.0	42	20	38	28%	74%	9%	12%	27	88	44%	15%			21.7	135	$2
1st Half	9	0	107	109	3.04	1.03	3.71	1.16	75	89	25.5	6%	25%	19%	6%	10.9%	93.2	44	20	37	28%	73%	9%	10%	17	94	41%	12%			16.2	138	$2
2nd Half	3	0	51	50	3.38	1.11	4.02	1.16	91	83	20.4	6%	25%	19%	6%	10.6%	92.5	38	20	42	29%	74%	10%	14%	10	78	50%	20%			5.6	130	$
Proj	**10**	**0**	**145**	**135**	**3.63**	**1.19**	**4.13**	**1.25**	**95**	**89**	**21.5**	**7%**	**23%**	**16%**	**7%**	**10.0%**	**92.9**	**42**	**20**	**38**	**30%**	**73%**	**10%**	**12%**	**27**						**14.6**	**115**	**$1**

Bauer,Trevor

Age: 31	Th: R	Role SP	Health B	LIMA Plan C+
Ht: 6' 1"	Wt: 205	Type Pwr/FB	PT/Exp A	Rand Var -5
			Consist B	MM 3400

Spent 2nd half on administrative leave while MLB investigated sexual assault claims against him. 1st half skills weren't as electric as truncated 2020 sample, with K-BB% receding. FB% spike stuck and became problematic as he allowed much more hard contact. xERA/xWHIP capture these trends and reflect the downside, if he plays at all in 2022.

Yr Tm	W	Sv	IP	K	ERA	WHIP	xERA	xWHIP	vL+	vR+	BF/G	BB%	K%	K-BB%	xBB%	SwK	Vel	G	L	F	H%	S%	HR/F	xHR/F	GS	APC	DOM%	DIS%	Sv%	LI	RAR	BPX	R$
17 CLE	17	0	176	196	4.19	1.37	3.72	1.23	111	97	23.4	8%	26%	18%	10%	9.5%	94.0	46	22	32	34%	74%	16%	14%	31	98	19%	23%	0	0.77	3.8	146	$1
18 CLE	12	1	175	221	2.21	1.09	3.16	1.13	78	83	25.6	8%	31%	23%	8%	13.7%	94.5	45	21	34	31%	81%	6%	10%	27	102	59%	11%	100	0.80	42.0	171	$2
19 2 TM	11	0	213	253	4.48	1.25	4.18	1.26	108	91	26.8	9%	28%	19%	8%	12.6%	94.6	38	22	40	30%	69%	15%	15%	34	108	47%	15%			0.7	125	$1
20 CIN	5	0	73	100	1.73	0.79	3.22	0.99	84	56	25.3	6%	36%	30%	8%	13.5%	93.5	34	18	48	23%	90%	12%	10%	11	106	64%	0%			24.6	200	$4
21 LA	8	0	108	137	2.59	1.00	3.70	1.14	106	67	25.4	9%	32%	23%	8%	13.2%	94.0	33	19	47	24%	87%	16%	17%	17	105	53%	6%			22.2	147	$1
1st Half	8	0	108	137	2.59	1.00	3.70	1.14	100	69	25.4	9%	32%	23%	8%	13.2%	94.0	33	19	47	24%	87%	16%	17%	17	105	53%	6%			22.2	147	$3
2nd Half																																	
Proj	**2**	**0**	**29**	**36**	**3.50**	**1.17**	**3.63**	**1.17**	**104**	**82**	**25.0**	**9%**	**32%**	**22%**	**8%**	**12.8%**	**94.1**	**38**	**20**	**42**	**30%**	**75%**	**13%**	**14%**	**5**						**3.4**	**150**	**-$**

Baz,Shane

Age: 23	Th: R	Role RP	Health A	LIMA Plan C+
Ht: 6' 3"	Wt: 190	Type Pwr/FB	PT/Exp F	Rand Var -1
			Consist F	MM 5403

2-0, 2.03 ERA in 13 IP with TAM. Opened 2021 in AA, pitched in the Olympics, and made three September MLB starts. Mechanical adjustments, improved command, better pitch sequencing, and upgraded secondary pitches paid huge dividends. Further development of change-up could unlock frontline starter upside, but that might take time.

Yr Tm	W	Sv	IP	K	ERA	WHIP	xERA	xWHIP	vL+	vR+	BF/G	BB%	K%	K-BB%	xBB%	SwK	Vel	G	L	F	H%	S%	HR/F	xHR/F	GS	APC	DOM%	DIS%	Sv%	LI	RAR	BPX	R$
17																																	
18																																	
19																																	
20																																	
21 TAM *	7	0	94	119	2.24	0.82	2.11	0.94	115	48	17.0	5%	35%	30%	6%	16.7%	97.0	43	11	46	25%	83%	23%	19%	3	66	33%	33%			23.4	234	$1
1st Half	3	0	53	69	2.28	0.83	1.74				17.7	4%	35%	31%							29%	76%	0%		0	0					13.0	279	$1
2nd Half	4	0	40	50	2.18	0.81	2.59	0.98	109	49	16.3	5%	34%	29%	6%	16.7%	97.0	43	11	46	21%	93%	23%	19%	3	66	33%	33%			10.4	185	$1
Proj	**10**	**0**	**145**	**183**	**3.53**	**1.01**	**3.20**	**1.00**			**17.7**	**5%**	**33%**	**28%**				**37**	**21**	**42**	**30%**	**72%**	**15%**	**0%**	**24**						**16.6**	**196**	**$1**

GREG PYRON

Bednar,David

Age: 27	Th: R	Role: RP	Health: B	LIMA Plan: B+
Ht: 6' 1"	Wt: 249	Type: Pwr/FB	PT/Exp: D	Rand Var: -4
			Consist: F	MM: 4420

Former 35th round pick blossomed after coming over from SD in the Musgrove trade. Mechanical tweaks seemed to help velocity, K-BB% gains. Both splitter and curve had SwK spikes, so multiple pitches improving suggests K% gains are sustainable, while xBB% hints at potential for even better BB%. Closer-worthy skills with ... UP: 30 Sv.

Yr Tm	W	Sv	IP	K	ERA	WHIP	xERA	xWHIP	vL+	vR+	BF/G	BB%	K%	K-BB%	xBB%	SwK	Vel	G	L	F	H%	S%	HR/F	xHR/F	GS	APC	DOM%	DIS%	Sv%	LI	RAR	BPX	R$
17																																	
18																																	
19 SD *	2	14	69	83	4.30	1.37	4.31	1.25	107	129	5.1	9%	29%	20%	8%	14.8%	95.3	30	22	48	36%	71%	23%	16%	0	15			93	0.62	1.8	118	$5
20 SD	0	0	6	5	7.11	2.05	6.20	1.37	135	129	8.0	6%	16%	9%	6%	13.6%	95.8	36	24	40	44%	67%	10%	20%	0	30			0	0.25	-2.1	74	-$10
21 PIT	3	3	61	77	2.23	0.97	3.26	1.10	73	81	3.9	8%	32%	24%	5%	17.0%	96.8	41	20	39	27%	81%	9%	11%	0	15			60	0.82	15.3	163	$9
1st Half	1	0	31	39	3.48	1.13	3.31	1.15	95	90	3.6	9%	31%	22%	6%	16.1%	96.8	45	21	33	28%	77%	20%	17%	0	15			0	0.67	3.0	155	-$1
2nd Half	2	3	30	38	0.91	0.81	3.20	1.05	46	74	4.3	7%	34%	27%	4%	18.2%	96.7	37	18	45	26%	88%	0%	5%	0	16			75	1.03	12.3	172	$10
Proj	**3**	**15**	**65**	**82**	**3.08**	**1.11**	**3.44**	**1.13**	**81**	**95**	**4.2**	**8%**	**32%**	**24%**	**5%**	**17.3%**	**96.7**	**40**	**20**	**40**	**31%**	**75%**	**9%**	**10%**	**0**						**11.0**	**164**	**$11**

Beede,Tyler

Age: 29	Th: R	Role: RP	Health: F	LIMA Plan: D
Ht: 6' 2"	Wt: 216	Type: Pwr	PT/Exp: D	Rand Var: 0
			Consist: D	MM: 0101

0-0, 27.00 ERA in 1 IP with SF. 2014 first round pick seemed poised to take a step forward in 2020, but underwent Tommy John surgery in March. Walks were a huge issue in his 2021 return, but on brightside, velocity was up a tick before a lower back injury ended season. Worth monitoring this spring for those in NL-only leagues.

Yr Tm	W	Sv	IP	K	ERA	WHIP	xERA	xWHIP	vL+	vR+	BF/G	BB%	K%	K-BB%	xBB%	SwK	Vel	G	L	F	H%	S%	HR/F	xHR/F	GS	APC	DOM%	DIS%	Sv%	LI	RAR	BPX	R$
17 aaa	6	0	109	70	5.74	1.66	5.82				25.7	8%	14%	6%							35%	66%									-18.6	38	-$11
18 SF *	4	0	82	70	7.53	1.97	6.37	1.74	111	131	11.2	16%	18%	2%	12%	11.4%	92.3	45	27	27	36%	61%	0%	1%	2	83	0%	0%			-34.0	44	-$21
19 SF *	7	0	153	151	4.56	1.42	4.93	1.37	109	105	21.0	9%	23%	14%	9%	11.7%	94.3	44	22	34	32%	73%	18%	19%	22	85	14%	41%	0	0.74	-1.0	69	$0
20																																	
21 SF *	0	0	51	40	7.37	2.05	6.74		277	153	14.7	18%	16%	-2%		14.3%	95.8	33	33	33	34%	64%	0%	6%	0	28			0	0.08	-19.6	28	-$19
1st Half	0	0	37	30	6.80	1.98	6.40				14.9	18%	17%	-1%							33%	66%	0%		0	0					-11.7	34	-$18
2nd Half	0	0	14	10	8.89	2.23	7.65		262	156	14.1	18%	14%	-4%		14.3%	95.8	33	33	33	35%	59%	0%	6%	0	28			0	0.08	-8.0	13	-$20
Proj	**3**	**0**	**87**	**72**	**5.14**	**1.54**	**5.12**	**1.59**	**113**	**102**	**15.3**	**13%**	**19%**	**6%**	**9%**	**11.7%**	**94.3**	**44**	**22**	**34**	**30%**	**68%**	**14%**	**17%**	**13**						**-7.3**	**21**	**-$8**

Beeks,Jalen

Age: 28	Th: L	Role: RP	Health: F	LIMA Plan: C
Ht: 5' 11"	Wt: 215	Type: Pwr	PT/Exp: D	Rand Var: 0
			Consist: D	MM: 2200

Didn't pitch in 2021 (Sept 2020 Tommy John surgery). Emerged in 2020 as effective multi-inning reliever and worked his way into higher leverage spots. Ditched curve and focused on four-seam/change-up/cutter mix, producing stellar K-BB% backed by elite SwK/xBB% and a knack for avoiding barrels in tiny sample. Expected ready for spring; watch role.

Yr Tm	W	Sv	IP	K	ERA	WHIP	xERA	xWHIP	vL+	vR+	BF/G	BB%	K%	K-BB%	xBB%	SwK	Vel	G	L	F	H%	S%	HR/F	xHR/F	GS	APC	DOM%	DIS%	Sv%	LI	RAR	BPX	R$
17 a/a	11	0	145	125	4.69	1.48	4.67				24.0	10%	20%	10%							33%	70%									-5.9	71	$0
18 2 AL *	10	0	139	134	4.73	1.41	4.75	1.31	80	120	19.6	9%	23%	14%	10%	11.9%	91.8	47	21	32	33%	69%	13%	12%	1	63	0%	100%	0	0.88	-9.9	81	-$2
19 TAM	6	1	104	89	4.31	1.49	4.79	1.41	114	102	14.1	9%	19%	11%	8%	10.2%	92.2	46	24	31	33%	73%	12%	14%	3	55	0%	67%	100	0.77	2.5	75	-$1
20 TAM	1	1	19	26	3.26	1.29	3.11	1.01	89	95	6.8	5%	32%	27%	4%	17.6%	93.1	43	27	31	41%	75%	7%	3%	0	27			100	1.16	2.8	213	$0
21																																	
1st Half																																	
2nd Half																																	
Proj	**4**	**0**	**58**	**57**	**4.07**	**1.36**	**4.11**	**1.32**	**99**	**101**	**16.6**	**9%**	**23%**	**14%**	**9%**	**10.9%**	**92.0**	**46**	**23**	**31**	**32%**	**73%**	**14%**	**13%**	**10**						**2.7**	**104**	**-$2**

Bender,Anthony

Age: 27	Th: R	Role: RP	Health: A	LIMA Plan: B+
Ht: 6' 4"	Wt: 205	Type: Pwr/GB	PT/Exp: D	Rand Var: -1
			Consist: F	MM: 4310

Signed minor league deal with MIA after playing independent ball in 2019-20. Power sinker/slider combo generated GB% tilt and plus K%, but unremarkable SwK% suggests 2nd-half K% is closer to his true level; normalized H%/S% actually say everything about second half is the better baseline. That's not world-beating, but potentially still useful... UP: 20 Sv

Yr Tm	W	Sv	IP	K	ERA	WHIP	xERA	xWHIP	vL+	vR+	BF/G	BB%	K%	K-BB%	xBB%	SwK	Vel	G	L	F	H%	S%	HR/F	xHR/F	GS	APC	DOM%	DIS%	Sv%	LI	RAR	BPX	R$
17																																	
18																																	
19																																	
20																																	
21 MIA	3	3	61	71	2.79	1.06	3.15	1.16	100	77	4.1	8%	29%	21%	8%	11.7%	96.9	50	23	28	28%	77%	12%	11%	1	16	0%	0%	60	1.02	11.2	150	$6
1st Half	0	0	24	31	0.74	0.74	2.51	1.05	64	46	3.9	8%	35%	27%	7%	12.5%	96.9	53	18	29	23%	89%	0%	1%	0	16			0	0.76	10.6	184	$3
2nd Half	3	3	37	40	4.14	1.27	3.59	1.23	109	100	4.3	8%	25%	17%	8%	11.2%	96.9	48	25	27	31%	71%	19%	16%	1	16	0%	0%	75	1.19	0.6	127	$1
Proj	**3**	**5**	**65**	**76**	**3.47**	**1.13**	**3.24**	**1.17**	**106**	**82**	**4.0**	**8%**	**29%**	**21%**	**8%**	**11.7%**	**96.9**	**50**	**22**	**28**	**30%**	**71%**	**12%**	**10%**	**0**						**7.9**	**155**	**$5**

Berríos,José

Age: 28	Th: R	Role: SP	Health: A	LIMA Plan: D+
Ht: 6' 0"	Wt: 205	Type:	PT/Exp: A	Rand Var: 0
			Consist: A	MM: 2205

Tagged with "UP: sub-3.50 ERA" in last year's book and he pretty much nailed it. PRO: regained superb BB%, sported career-best DOM/DIS% and dominated vR. CON: SwK points to a touch of negative K% regression, surrendered more hard contact, and xHR/F indicates some HR/F luck. Unlikely to match 2021, but shouldn't fall far.

Yr Tm	W	Sv	IP	K	ERA	WHIP	xERA	xWHIP	vL+	vR+	BF/G	BB%	K%	K-BB%	xBB%	SwK	Vel	G	L	F	H%	S%	HR/F	xHR/F	GS	APC	DOM%	DIS%	Sv%	LI	RAR	BPX	R$
17 MIN *	17	0	185	170	3.43	1.18	3.28	1.29	104	83	23.2	8%	23%	15%	8%	10.0%	93.5	39	21	40	29%	74%	9%	10%	25	92	32%	32%	0	0.78	21.3	114	$21
18 MIN	12	0	192	202	3.84	1.14	3.79	1.22	93	91	24.9	8%	25%	18%	8%	11.7%	93.2	42	20	38	28%	71%	13%	12%	32	96	38%	25%			7.4	130	$16
19 MIN	14	0	200	195	3.68	1.22	4.30	1.23	93	95	26.3	6%	23%	17%	6%	11.2%	92.8	42	21	37	31%	74%	12%	14%	32	98	25%	25%			20.3	126	$17
20 MIN	5	0	63	68	4.00	1.32	4.34	1.32	98	92	22.6	10%	25%	15%	8%	12.3%	94.3	40	24	36	31%	73%	13%	14%	12	92	17%	42%			3.5	105	$10
21 2 AL	12	0	192	204	3.52	1.06	3.54	1.12	109	72	24.4	6%	26%	20%	6%	10.2%	94.0	43	23	34	29%	71%	13%	18%	32	95	44%	16%			17.8	149	$22
1st Half	7	0	95	96	3.52	1.14	3.64	1.17	120	67	24.3	6%	25%	19%	6%	10.4%	94.1	43	26	31	30%	73%	14%	18%	16	94	31%	19%			8.7	136	$16
2nd Half	5	0	97	108	3.51	0.99	3.46	1.08	88	80	24.6	5%	27%	22%	6%	10.1%	93.9	43	20	37	28%	68%	12%	18%	16	96	56%	13%			9.0	163	$25
Proj	**14**	**0**	**203**	**200**	**3.71**	**1.18**	**3.92**	**1.22**	**103**	**85**	**23.5**	**7%**	**25%**	**18%**	**6%**	**10.9%**	**93.7**	**42**	**22**	**36**	**30%**	**72%**	**12%**	**15%**	**35**						**18.6**	**126**	**$18**

Bickford,Phil

Age: 26	Th: R	Role: RP	Health: A	LIMA Plan: A
Ht: 6' 4"	Wt: 200	Type: Pwr	PT/Exp: F	Rand Var: -4
			Consist: A	MM: 3310

2015 1st round pick was claimed off waivers in May and found a home in bullpen, earning higher leverage opportunities in 2nd half. Velocity spike helped four-seamer and the slider, his second pitch, garnered a 17% SwK. Elite xBB% represents BB% upside. GB% tilt helps limit HR. Nice end game target for Holds leagues.

Yr Tm	W	Sv	IP	K	ERA	WHIP	xERA	xWHIP	vL+	vR+	BF/G	BB%	K%	K-BB%	xBB%	SwK	Vel	G	L	F	H%	S%	HR/F	xHR/F	GS	APC	DOM%	DIS%	Sv%	LI	RAR	BPX	R$
17																																	
18																																	
19																																	
20 MIL	0	0	1	2	36.00	4.00	3.75		173	195	9.0	0%	22%	22%		15.2%	89.4	0	80	20	83%	0%	0%	1%	0	33			0	0.10	-3.9	341	-$10
21 2 NL	4	1	51	59	2.81	1.07	3.54	1.22	102	77	3.6	9%	29%	19%	6%	13.9%	93.9	47	18	35	25%	81%	16%	17%	0	14			33	0.72	9.2	133	$4
1st Half	4	1	18	23	2.50	1.11	2.88	1.12	146	54	4.1	8%	32%	23%	6%	14.8%	93.5	51	22	27	32%	79%	9%	16%	0	16			100	0.48	3.9	171	-$3
2nd Half	0	0	33	36	2.97	1.05	3.90	1.27	67	92	3.4	10%	27%	17%	5%	13.4%	94.2	45	16	40	22%	83%	18%	17%	0	12			0	0.84	5.3	113	$4
Proj	**4**	**2**	**58**	**67**	**3.56**	**1.25**	**3.65**	**1.22**	**119**	**87**	**3.7**	**9%**	**29%**	**19%**	**6%**	**14.0%**	**93.9**	**47**	**18**	**35**	**31%**	**76%**	**15%**	**17%**	**0**						**6.4**	**141**	**$2**

Bieber,Shane

Age: 27	Th: R	Role: SP	Health: F	LIMA Plan: B+
Ht: 6' 3"	Wt: 200	Type: Pwr	PT/Exp: A	Rand Var: +1
			Consist: B	MM: 5403

Landed on IL in mid-June (shoulder strain) and didn't return until late Sept. Even before injury, skills were "good, just not 2020-good". Velocity history suggests he just aired it out in 2020 sprint, while similarity of 2018/2019/2021 metrics demonstrates his full-season baseline with remarkable clarity. Assuming shoulder is sound, that's what to bid for.

Yr Tm	W	Sv	IP	K	ERA	WHIP	xERA	xWHIP	vL+	vR+	BF/G	BB%	K%	K-BB%	xBB%	SwK	Vel	G	L	F	H%	S%	HR/F	xHR/F	GS	APC	DOM%	DIS%	Sv%	LI	RAR	BPX	R$
17 aa	2	0	54	38	2.99	1.31	4.13				25.0	2%	17%	15%							36%	77%									9.2	205	$0
18 CLE *	17	0	196	183	3.45	1.16	3.64	1.11	124	91	23.6	4%	23%	19%	6%	11.8%	93.1	47	22	31	33%	73%	12%	17%	19	90	42%	21%	0	0.79	16.9	178	$19
19 CLE	15	0	214	259	3.28	1.05	3.34	1.05	90	86	25.3	5%	30%	25%	6%	14.3%	93.1	44	21	35	31%	76%	16%	17%	33	98	48%	9%	0	0.76	32.5	188	$30
20 CLE	8	0	77	122	1.63	0.87	2.34	0.93	58	75	24.8	7%	41%	34%	8%	18.0%	94.2	48	22	30	29%	88%	15%	21%	12	103	67%	0%			26.9	244	$48
21 CLE	7	0	97	134	3.17	1.21	3.11	1.09	105	78	25.3	8%	33%	25%	7%	16.6%	92.8	44	24	32	34%	78%	15%	20%	16	97	38%	6%			13.1	179	$9
1st Half	7	0	91	130	3.28	1.25	3.07	1.10	100	84	27.4	9%	34%	25%	7%	17.0%	92.9	44	24	32	35%	78%	16%	21%	14	105	43%	0%			11.1	183	$17
2nd Half	0	0	6	4	1.50	0.67	3.67		92	23	11.0	0%	18%	18%	8%	9.5%	91.2	39	28	33	24%	75%	0%	17%	2	42	0%	50%			2.0	137	-$9
Proj	**13**	**0**	**174**	**216**	**3.26**	**1.12**	**3.08**	**1.05**	**96**	**82**	**24.7**	**6%**	**32%**	**25%**	**7%**	**15.7%**	**93.3**	**46**	**22**	**32**	**33%**	**75%**	**13%**	**19%**	**28**						**25.6**	**189**	**$22**

GREG PYRON

Bielak,Brandon

Age: 26	Th: R	Role	RP	Health	A	LIMA Plan	D+
Ht: 6' 2"	Wt: 208	Type		PT/Exp	D	Rand Var	-1
				Consist	D	MM	1100

3-4, 1 Sv in 50 IP at HOU. Last year we called him a "flyball pitcher with control problems," so I guess he gets points for addressing one of those bugaboos outright and showing some minor improvement on the other. Punching up the K% is nice too, although it came without SwK support. Steps forward, but they just move him from "avoid" to "unremarkable."

Yr Tm	W	Sv	IP	K	ERA	WHIP	xERA	xWHIP	vL+	vR+	BF/G	BB%	K%	K-BB%	xBB%	SwK	Vel	G	L	F	H%	S%	HR/F	xHR/F	GS	APC	DOM%	DIS%	Sv%	LI	RAR	BPX	R$
17																																	
18 aa	2	0	62	50	2.88	1.32	3.82				23.4	9%	19%	11%							31%	80%									9.8	86	$C
19 a/a	11	0	123	103	5.22	1.35	4.19				22.3	10%	20%	10%							29%	63%									-10.8	64	$1
20 HOU	3	0	32	26	6.75	1.75	5.98	1.56	92	179	12.3	12%	18%	6%	10%	11.1%	93.3	36	23	41	32%	68%	21%	18%	6	50	0%	67%	0	0.62	-9.1	19	-$10
21 HOU *	5	1	68	64	3.84	1.32	3.84	1.31	85	106	8.3	9%	23%	14%	8%	11.1%	93.8	44	23	33	32%	72%	10%	12%	2	30	0%	50%	50	0.60	3.6	99	$C
1st Half	3	0	34	28	5.80	1.38	4.67	1.33	82	116	6.8	8%	20%	12%	8%	9.4%	93.4	40	23	37	32%	58%	11%	13%	0	27			0	0.67	-6.5	72	-$6
2nd Half	2	1	36	37	1.75	1.18	2.62	1.29	80	88	11.2	10%	25%	16%	9%	13.9%	94.4	51	24	24	30%	86%	8%	9%	2	36	0%	50%	100	0.44	11.2	125	$4
Proj	**4**	**0**	**58**	**51**	**4.36**	**1.38**	**4.50**	**1.39**	**84**	**117**	**11.7**	**10%**	**21%**	**11%**	**9%**	**11.8%**	**93.8**	**44**	**23**	**32**	**31%**	**71%**	**13%**	**12%**	**3**						**0.7**	**75**	**-$3**

Boxberger,Brad

Age: 34	Th: R	Role	RP	Health	B	LIMA Plan	B+
Ht: 5' 10"	Wt: 211	Type	Pwr/FB	PT/Exp	D	Rand Var	-1
				Consist	C	MM	3410

Sign of the times: 34-year old dials up career-best velocity, spikes his SwK and K% accordingly, and xERA falls into the happy zone. Bet on a repeat? Let's put it this way: his seasons with sub-3.50 xERAs are 2014, 2017, 2021. If you play "guess the next number in the series," we're looking at 2026. Spend a buck to see if he can beat that, no more.

Yr Tm	W	Sv	IP	K	ERA	WHIP	xERA	xWHIP	vL+	vR+	BF/G	BB%	K%	K-BB%	xBB%	SwK	Vel	G	L	F	H%	S%	HR/F	xHR/F	GS	APC	DOM%	DIS%	Sv%	LI	RAR	BPX	R$
17 TAM	4	0	29	40	3.38	1.16	3.39	1.15	77	102	4.0	9%	33%	24%		12.6%	92.3	42	16	42	31%	77%	14%	12%	0	17			0	1.14	3.6	180	$C
18 ARI	3	32	53	71	4.39	1.43	3.89	1.37	115	92	3.9	14%	30%	17%	8%	11.2%	91.4	46	16	38	31%	75%	18%	16%	0	16			80	1.31	-1.6	108	$10
19 KC *	2	2	43	42	5.88	1.73	5.73	1.61	87	114	4.7	14%	21%	8%	9%	12.1%	90.2	39	21	39	34%	68%	10%	9%	0	17			40	0.75	-7.3	50	-$7
20 MIA	1	0	18	18	3.00	1.39	4.59	1.38	86	110	3.4	10%	23%	13%	11%	10.4%	92.5	51	12	37	30%	86%	16%	18%	0	16			0	1.05	3.2	94	-$2
21 MIL	5	4	65	83	3.34	1.07	3.59	1.17	61	103	3.7	10%	32%	22%	8%	13.7%	93.6	37	20	43	27%	74%	13%	13%	0	15			44	1.22	7.4	142	$7
1st Half	3	3	34	37	3.21	1.07	3.90	1.29	60	105	3.9	10%	27%	17%	9%	13.7%	93.5	39	23	39	24%	75%	13%	12%	0	16			75	1.32	4.4	103	$4
2nd Half	2	1	31	46	3.48	1.06	3.28	1.06	56	106	3.6	9%	37%	28%	6%	13.7%	93.7	36	16	48	30%	72%	13%	15%	0	14			20	1.11	3.0	185	$2
Proj	**4**	**2**	**65**	**82**	**3.80**	**1.19**	**3.73**	**1.21**	**76**	**105**	**3.7**	**10%**	**31%**	**21%**	**8%**	**13.0%**	**93.1**	**39**	**18**	**43**	**30%**	**73%**	**14%**	**14%**	**0**						**5.3**	**141**	**$3**

Boyd,Matthew

Age: 31	Th: L	Role	SP	Health	F	LIMA Plan	C
Ht: 6' 3"	Wt: 234	Type	/FB	PT/Exp	A	Rand Var	-2
				Consist	B	MM	1201

Hung his best half-season performance in years, though xERA and BPX columns say it was same-old cromulent skill set. Elbow injury ended his season in July, led to September surgery to repair torn flexor tendon, which puts 2022 readiness in doubt. Unless surgery makes that tendon like the "Rookie of the Year" kid's, little reason to be interested here.

Yr Tm	W	Sv	IP	K	ERA	WHIP	xERA	xWHIP	vL+	vR+	BF/G	BB%	K%	K-BB%	xBB%	SwK	Vel	G	L	F	H%	S%	HR/F	xHR/F	GS	APC	DOM%	DIS%	Sv%	LI	RAR	BPX	R$
17 DET *	9	0	186	151	4.97	1.46	5.03	1.41	94	115	23.4	9%	19%	10%	8%	10.4%	92.0	38	22	40	32%	69%	11%	12%	25	91	12%	48%	0	0.74	-14.0	60	-$3
18 DET	9	0	170	159	4.39	1.16	4.55	1.26	89	100	22.9	7%	22%	15%	8%	10.7%	90.4	29	21	50	27%	67%	11%	10%	31	92	16%	26%			-5.0	98	$8
19 DET	9	0	185	238	4.56	1.23	3.90	1.12	94	104	24.6	6%	30%	24%	6%	14.8%	92.0	36	20	45	33%	71%	18%	16%	32	97	34%	13%			-1.4	170	$10
20 DET	3	0	60	60	6.71	1.48	4.92	1.32	58	131	22.6	8%	22%	14%	9%	13.2%	91.7	37	21	42	32%	59%	20%	17%	12	91	8%	50%			-16.8	99	-$11
21 DET	3	0	79	67	3.89	1.27	4.64	1.29	98	95	22.5	7%	20%	13%	5%	11.1%	92.0	38	21	41	31%	73%	9%	13%	15	85	27%	33%			3.6	91	-$1
1st Half	3	0	71	56	3.44	1.20	4.67	1.29	95	89	22.9	6%	19%	12%	5%	11.1%	91.9	39	20	41	30%	73%	7%	12%	13	86	31%	31%			7.2	88	$5
2nd Half	0	0	8	11	7.88	1.88	4.35	1.27	66	152	19.5	10%	28%	18%	8%	11.0%	92.4	35	26	39	41%	67%	33%	27%	2	77	0%	50%			-3.6	125	-$14
Proj	**4**	**0**	**87**	**84**	**4.66**	**1.28**	**4.41**	**1.26**	**90**	**105**	**22.3**	**7%**	**23%**	**16%**	**7%**	**12.1%**	**91.6**	**36**	**21**	**44**	**30%**	**68%**	**13%**	**13%**	**16**						**-2.2**	**109**	**-$1**

Bradley,Archie

Age: 29	Th: R	Role	RP	Health	D	LIMA Plan	B+
Ht: 6' 4"	Wt: 215	Type	Pwr/GB	PT/Exp	C	Rand Var	-2
				Consist	B	MM	2210

Velocity isn't everything, but when you throw your fastball ~70% of the time, long-term mph decline is a big deal. He's compensated by throwing more sinkers/change-ups instead of fastballs/curves. GB% likes that change, but BB% and K% both suffered dramatic losses. Sometimes the problem isn't the recipe, it's the ingredients.

Yr Tm	W	Sv	IP	K	ERA	WHIP	xERA	xWHIP	vL+	vR+	BF/G	BB%	K%	K-BB%	xBB%	SwK	Vel	G	L	F	H%	S%	HR/F	xHR/F	GS	APC	DOM%	DIS%	Sv%	LI	RAR	BPX	R$
17 ARI	3	1	73	79	1.73	1.04	3.31	1.18	77	75	4.6	7%	27%	20%	6%	10.5%	96.4	48	23	29	29%	86%	7%	12%	0	18			14	1.29	23.7	158	$10
18 ARI	4	3	72	75	3.64	1.14	3.51	1.18	67	111	3.9	7%	25%	19%	5%	9.3%	95.6	49	17	33	29%	73%	14%	16%	0	16			27	1.37	4.5	148	$4
19 ARI	4	18	72	87	3.52	1.44	4.09	1.36	104	88	4.8	11%	28%	16%	8%	10.6%	95.5	45	25	30	35%	77%	9%	12%	1	19	0%	100%	86	1.11	8.7	106	$9
20 2 NL	2	6	18	18	2.95	1.09	3.71	1.10	58	115	4.6	4%	25%	21%	6%	9.4%	94.2	39	27	33	32%	74%	6%	16%	0	17			86	1.55	3.4	154	$9
21 PHI	7	2	51	40	3.71	1.43	4.52	1.45	99	102	4.2	10%	18%	8%	8%	7.5%	94.0	56	17	27	31%	76%	12%	15%	0	17			40	0.92	3.5	62	$C
1st Half	3	1	19	13	4.26	1.63	5.32	1.70	128	103	3.9	14%	15%	1%	9%	6.7%	93.5	53	23	23	28%	79%	21%	30%	0	16			50	0.58	0.0	-12	-$5
2nd Half	4	1	32	27	3.38	1.31	4.10	1.30	73	105	4.5	7%	20%	12%	8%	8.0%	94.3	57	13	30	32%	75%	7%	8%	0	19			33	1.16	3.5	105	$C
Proj	**6**	**2**	**65**	**62**	**4.02**	**1.34**	**4.08**	**1.36**	**93**	**98**	**4.1**	**10%**	**23%**	**13%**	**8%**	**8.7%**	**94.9**	**51**	**19**	**29**	**31%**	**72%**	**12%**	**15%**	**0**						**3.5**	**97**	**$1**

Brash,Matt

Age: 24	Th: R	Role	SP	Health	A	LIMA Plan	B+
Ht: 6' 1"	Wt: 170	Type	Pwr	PT/Exp	F	Rand Var	0
				Consist	F	MM	2400

Skinny SEA flamethrower has a fastball that touches triple digits, plus a devastating slider. Work-in-progress change-up will likely make or break him as a starter, but fastball/slider combo screams "just make him a closer" if starting doesn't work out. Multiple paths to fantasy value make him a nice stash.

Yr Tm	W	Sv	IP	K	ERA	WHIP	xERA	xWHIP	vL+	vR+	BF/G	BB%	K%	K-BB%	xBB%	SwK	Vel	G	L	F	H%	S%	HR/F	xHR/F	GS	APC	DOM%	DIS%	Sv%	LI	RAR	BPX	R$
17																																	
18																																	
19																																	
20																																	
21 aa	3	0	55	72	2.39	1.06	2.06				21.3	11%	34%	23%							28%	79%									12.7	154	$5
1st Half																																	
2nd Half	3	0	55	72	2.39	1.06	2.06		0	0	21.3	11%	34%	23%							28%	79%	0%		0	0					12.7	154	$12
Proj	**2**	**0**	**51**	**60**	**3.98**	**1.26**	**3.91**	**1.29**			**24.9**	**11%**	**29%**	**18%**				**43**	**18**	**39**	**30%**	**72%**	**13%**	**0%**	**8**						**3.0**	**121**	**-$1**

Brentz,Jake

Age: 27	Th: L	Role	RP	Health	A	LIMA Plan	B+
Ht: 6' 1"	Wt: 195	Type	Pwr	PT/Exp	D	Rand Var	-2
				Consist	D	MM	3410

High-velocity southpaw hung a nice—but thoroughly undeserved—first half ERA, then quietly fixed his BB% issues amid ERA correction. That sample is sketchy, but 2nd-half skill set is very playable if he confirms it, keeps more balls in the park, and improves his control. From there it's likely only one more step forward to... UP: 20 Saves. Admittedly, maybe 2-3 steps.

Yr Tm	W	Sv	IP	K	ERA	WHIP	xERA	xWHIP	vL+	vR+	BF/G	BB%	K%	K-BB%	xBB%	SwK	Vel	G	L	F	H%	S%	HR/F	xHR/F	GS	APC	DOM%	DIS%	Sv%	LI	RAR	BPX	R$
17																																	
18																																	
19 a/a	1	8	54	46	5.47	1.79	5.91				6.1	12%	18%	6%							36%	70%									-6.5	50	-$5
20																																	
21 KC	5	2	64	76	3.66	1.28	4.04	1.41	68	98	3.9	13%	28%	14%	10%	13.0%	97.0	49	16	35	27%	75%	13%	17%	0	15			29	1.00	4.8	87	$2
1st Half	2	0	38	43	2.82	1.25	4.89	1.55	61	90	4.1	16%	27%	10%	11%	13.1%	96.8	49	17	34	23%	80%	10%	18%	0	16			0	0.87	6.8	48	$1
2nd Half	3	2	26	33	4.91	1.32	3.59	1.22	74	111	3.6	10%	29%	19%	10%	12.9%	97.2	49	15	35	33%	67%	17%	16%	0	14			40	1.15	-2.0	144	-$3
Proj	**5**	**2**	**65**	**78**	**3.73**	**1.28**	**3.79**	**1.31**	**69**	**104**	**3.9**	**12%**	**29%**	**17%**	**10%**	**13.0%**	**97.0**	**49**	**16**	**35**	**30%**	**74%**	**14%**	**17%**	**0**						**5.8**	**119**	**$2**

Brogdon,Connor

Age: 27	Th: R	Role	RP	Health	C	LIMA Plan	B+
Ht: 6' 6"	Wt: 205	Type		PT/Exp	D	Rand Var	-3
				Consist	B	MM	2210

Elite SwK carried over from 2020 micro-sample, but didn't translate to K%. Accompanying GB spike (more cutters) was a nice consolation prize. COVID bug, elbow tendinitis both bit him in 2nd half, likely explain that SwK dip. Another strong Sept (7 IP, 1 BB / 7 K, with the cutter shelved) leave us right where we were a year ago: intrigued by a tiny sample.

Yr Tm	W	Sv	IP	K	ERA	WHIP	xERA	xWHIP	vL+	vR+	BF/G	BB%	K%	K-BB%	xBB%	SwK	Vel	G	L	F	H%	S%	HR/F	xHR/F	GS	APC	DOM%	DIS%	Sv%	LI	RAR	BPX	R$
17																																	
18																																	
19 a/a	4	4	58	73	3.49	1.05	3.23				5.5	9%	32%	23%							25%	76%									7.3	122	$
20 PHI	1	0	11	17	3.97	0.88	3.27	1.14	72	89	4.9	11%	39%	27%	7%	16.8%	95.3	36	18	45	12%	71%	30%	14%	0	20			0	0.73	0.7	169	-$
21 PHI	5	1	58	50	3.43	1.13	4.30	1.29	86	89	4.2	8%	21%	14%	8%	13.8%	96.0	44	18	38	27%	73%	10%	10%	1	16	0%	100%	20	0.97	5.9	95	$
1st Half	4	1	31	28	4.40	1.27	4.18	1.35	86	101	3.9	9%	22%	13%	8%	15.6%	96.2	54	13	33	28%	69%	14%	12%	0	15			25	1.00	-0.5	93	-$
2nd Half	1	0	27	22	2.33	0.96	4.38	1.23	74	80	4.6	6%	21%	15%	6%	11.5%	95.8	33	24	42	25%	79%	6%	8%	1	18	0%	100%	0	0.93	6.4	98	-$
Proj	**4**	**1**	**58**	**55**	**3.88**	**1.22**	**4.15**	**1.26**	**94**	**98**	**4.6**	**8%**	**24%**	**16%**	**7%**	**14.4%**	**95.9**	**42**	**20**	**39**	**30%**	**71%**	**11%**	**10%**	**0**						**4.1**	**114**	**$**

RAY MURPHY

Brubaker,Jonathan

Age: 28	Th: R	Role: SP	Health: C	LIMA Plan: C	
Ht: 6' 3"	Wt: 185	Type:	PT/Exp: C	Rand Var: +5	
			Consist: A	MM: 2203	

Spent first half flirting with our "UP: sub-4.00 ERA" from last year's box. Then came a barrage of walks, line drives, and HRs. He may not have been healthy, as thumb and shoulder injuries popped up; latter ended his year early. BPX shows those half-season splits weren't as massive as ERA indicates. If arm is sound, first half redux is in play... but not assured.

Yr Tm	W	Sv	IP	K	ERA	WHIP	xERA	xWHIP	vL+	vR+	BF/G	BB%	K%	K-BB%	xBB%	SwK	Vel	G	L	F	H%	S%	HR/F	xHR/F	GS	APC	DOM%	DIS%	Sv%	LI	RAR	BPX	R$
17 aa	7	0	130	87	6.08	1.81	6.30				23.1	8%	14%	6%							39%	66%									-27.5	47	-$17
18 a/a	10	0	154	103	3.51	1.47	4.58				23.6	7%	16%	9%							34%	76%									12.2	74	$2
19 aaa	2	0	21	15	3.42	1.34	4.57				21.8	5%	17%	13%							33%	78%									2.8	89	-$3
20 PIT	1	0	47	48	4.94	1.37	4.18	1.29	113	91	18.6	8%	23%	15%	8%	11.7%	93.7	47	22	31	33%	66%	14%	18%	9	73	11%	44%	0	0.77	-2.9	115	-$4
21 PIT	5	0	124	129	5.36	1.29	4.03	1.21	115	102	22.4	7%	24%	17%	8%	12.4%	93.2	43	22	35	30%	65%	22%	19%	24	81	17%	25%			-16.7	126	-$4
1st Half	4	0	84	81	4.09	1.14	3.76	1.15	87	107	23.3	5%	23%	18%	6%	12.8%	93.1	48	18	34	28%	72%	20%	16%	15	82	27%	20%			1.8	143	$8
2nd Half	1	0	41	48	7.97	1.62	4.58	1.34	140	97	20.9	11%	26%	15%	10%	11.9%	93.2	33	29	38	34%	56%	27%	24%	9	79	0%	33%			-18.6	91	-$19
Proj	**8**	**0**	**152**	**145**	**4.33**	**1.30**	**4.20**	**1.28**	**113**	**89**	**20.1**	**8%**	**23%**	**15%**	**8%**	**12.1%**	**93.3**	**41**	**24**	**35**	**30%**	**73%**	**17%**	**20%**	**31**						**2.4**	**106**	**$3**

Bubic,Kris

Age: 24	Th: L	Role: RP	Health: A	LIMA Plan: D+	
Ht: 6' 3"	Wt: 220	Type: Pwr	PT/Exp: C	Rand Var: +1	
			Consist: A	MM: 1103	

Jumped from Single-A to majors in 2020 and lived to tell the tale. But as you scan across this box and look for sophomore year growth, there is none to be found. Even mild second-half improvement, which peaked with a 2.05 ERA over final five starts, featured a 3.89 xERA. Just a flat profile with no short-term upside as presently configured.

Yr Tm	W	Sv	IP	K	ERA	WHIP	xERA	xWHIP	vL+	vR+	BF/G	BB%	K%	K-BB%	xBB%	SwK	Vel	G	L	F	H%	S%	HR/F	xHR/F	GS	APC	DOM%	DIS%	Sv%	LI	RAR	BPX	R$
17																																	
18																																	
19																																	
20 KC	1	0	50	49	4.32	1.48	4.61	1.38	123	101	22.2	10%	22%	12%	10%	10.5%	91.5	47	21	32	32%	76%	17%	18%	10	93	10%	30%			0.8	87	-$4
21 KC	6	0	130	114	4.43	1.38	4.52	1.43	117	102	19.2	11%	21%	10%	9%	10.0%	90.9	47	21	32	28%	73%	18%	22%	20	76	15%	45%	0	0.79	-2.7	62	-$2
1st Half	2	0	52	44	4.99	1.51	4.97	1.51	112	115	16.4	12%	19%	7%	10%	9.3%	90.4	47	18	35	28%	75%	22%	21%	7	65	0%	57%	0	0.83	-4.7	39	-$8
2nd Half	4	0	78	70	4.06	1.30	4.23	1.38	111	96	21.8	10%	21%	12%	8%	10.5%	91.3	47	23	30	28%	73%	15%	23%	13	86	23%	38%	0	0.75	2.0	78	$4
Proj	**6**	**0**	**131**	**118**	**4.54**	**1.42**	**4.53**	**1.43**	**119**	**103**	**19.5**	**11%**	**21%**	**11%**	**9%**	**10.1%**	**91.1**	**47**	**21**	**32**	**30%**	**73%**	**18%**	**21%**	**27**						**-1.4**	**70**	**-$3**

Buehler,Walker

Age: 27	Th: R	Role: SP	Health: B	LIMA Plan: D+	
Ht: 6' 2"	Wt: 185	Type: Pwr	PT/Exp: A	Rand Var: -5	
			Consist: A	MM: 4305	

LA finally took the restrictor plates off him; thanks to SF for creating a pennant race and to seemingly every other LA SP for getting hurt. Despite big R$ season, yellow flags abound: concurrent decay of Vel, SwK, K%; ERA/xERA gap growing to unsustainable level. GBs, volume, team context all say he's still a top-tier SP, just expect a 3.00+ ERA.

Yr Tm	W	Sv	IP	K	ERA	WHIP	xERA	xWHIP	vL+	vR+	BF/G	BB%	K%	K-BB%	xBB%	SwK	Vel	G	L	F	H%	S%	HR/F	xHR/F	GS	APC	DOM%	DIS%	Sv%	LI	RAR	BPX	R$
17 LA *	4	1	82	97	4.79	1.33	3.90	1.22	67	172	10.9	9%	29%	19%		10.4%	98.1	67	17	17	34%	65%	50%	29%	0	24			100	0.33	-4.4	126	$0
18 LA	8	0	137	151	2.62	0.96	3.14	1.14	78	76	22.5	7%	28%	21%	6%	11.8%	96.2	50	18	32	26%	77%	11%	10%	23	91	39%	9%	0	0.79	25.9	162	$21
19 LA	14	0	182	215	3.26	1.04	3.45	1.08	81	88	24.6	5%	29%	24%	5%	12.8%	96.6	43	23	35	31%	73%	12%	11%	30	95	43%	13%			28.1	177	$26
20 LA	1	0	37	42	3.44	0.95	3.92	1.17	76	88	18.4	7%	29%	21%	8%	12.8%	96.9	35	23	42	22%	75%	18%	15%	8	75	38%	25%			4.6	142	$6
21 LA	16	0	208	212	2.47	0.97	3.56	1.15	82	76	24.7	6%	26%	20%	6%	12.3%	95.4	45	20	35	26%	79%	10%	12%	33	96	45%	12%			46.0	140	$39
1st Half	8	0	103	101	2.35	0.90	3.67	1.13	79	75	24.8	6%	26%	20%	5%	12.3%	95.4	41	18	40	23%	83%	12%	15%	16	98	38%	13%			24.4	138	$33
2nd Half	8	0	104	111	2.59	1.04	3.45	1.17	77	81	24.6	7%	27%	20%	6%	12.3%	95.3	48	21	31	28%	76%	7%	8%	17	93	53%	12%			21.6	141	$36
Proj	**14**	**0**	**196**	**213**	**3.20**	**1.02**	**3.46**	**1.14**	**83**	**83**	**20.8**	**7%**	**28%**	**21%**	**6%**	**12.4%**	**96.0**	**43**	**21**	**36**	**27%**	**73%**	**12%**	**12%**	**36**						**30.3**	**152**	**$28**

Bukauskas,J.B.

Age: 25	Th: R	Role: SP	Health: D	LIMA Plan: D	
Ht: 6' 0"	Wt: 196	Type: Pwr	PT/Exp: F	Rand Var: +5	
			Consist: C	MM: 0110	

Former SP prospect converted to relief, club hoped he would slide into high-lev role in this (ahem) unsettled pen. Control problems were expected, but underwhelming K% was more of a surprise. Of course, the frequent HRs were sub-optimal, too. He'll get more chances, and there's more stuff than showed here... but he's more than one adjustment away.

Yr Tm	W	Sv	IP	K	ERA	WHIP	xERA	xWHIP	vL+	vR+	BF/G	BB%	K%	K-BB%	xBB%	SwK	Vel	G	L	F	H%	S%	HR/F	xHR/F	GS	APC	DOM%	DIS%	Sv%	LI	RAR	BPX	R$
17																																	
18																																	
19 aa	2	1	94	91	7.74	1.93	6.32				20.3	15%	20%	5%							37%	59%									-37.6	50	-$21
20																																	
21 ARI	2	0	17	14	7.79	1.79	4.97	1.41	162	110	3.9	9%	18%	9%	8%	12.2%	94.5	47	24	29	36%	59%	24%	27%	0	14			0	0.97	-7.5	63	-$8
1st Half	1	0	10	8	7.45	2.07	5.42	1.50	144	122	4.0	10%	17%	6%	8%	12.4%	94.4	46	29	26	40%	67%	22%	17%	0	14			0	0.80	-3.8	35	-$11
2nd Half	1	0	8	6	8.22	1.43	4.43	1.28	161	98	3.7	6%	19%	13%	8%	12.0%	94.6	50	17	33	31%	44%	25%	38%	0	13			0	1.21	-3.7	100	-$12
Proj	**1**	**2**	**51**	**44**	**5.01**	**1.64**	**5.40**	**1.64**			**21.2**	**14%**	**19%**	**5%**				**45**	**21**	**34**	**30%**	**73%**	**15%**	**0%**	**11**						**-3.5**	**9**	**-$7**

Bumgarner,Madison

Age: 32	Th: L	Role: SP	Health: F	LIMA Plan: B+	
Ht: 6' 4"	Wt: 255	Type: Con/FB	PT/Exp: A	Rand Var: 0	
			Consist: C	MM: 1103	

Shoulder inflammation cost him six weeks in June/July; 2nd half ERA/WHIP would have you believe he spent that IL stint finding what he left in San Francisco. All he found was a little bit of H%/S% regression, when what we were looking for was his former Vel/SwK/K%. Alas, those are still lost in the Bay Area.

Yr Tm	W	Sv	IP	K	ERA	WHIP	xERA	xWHIP	vL+	vR+	BF/G	BB%	K%	K-BB%	xBB%	SwK	Vel	G	L	F	H%	S%	HR/F	xHR/F	GS	APC	DOM%	DIS%	Sv%	LI	RAR	BPX	R$
17 SF	4	0	111	101	3.32	1.09	4.05	1.17	70	100	26.5	4%	23%	18%	6%	10.6%	91.0	41	18	41	28%	77%	13%	13%	17	98	53%	12%			14.2	147	$10
18 SF	6	0	130	109	3.26	1.24	4.35	1.33	87	99	26.2	8%	20%	12%	8%	9.4%	90.9	43	22	35	29%	78%	10%	16%	21	98	29%	14%			14.2	88	$7
19 SF	9	0	208	203	3.90	1.13	4.22	1.18	73	102	24.8	5%	24%	19%	6%	12.0%	91.4	36	23	42	30%	71%	13%	16%	34	95	35%	18%			15.5	133	$17
20 ARI	1	0	42	30	6.48	1.44	5.66	1.39	106	131	21.1	7%	16%	9%	6%	8.0%	88.4	32	26	42	28%	64%	22%	25%	9	79	11%	56%			-10.4	57	-$11
21 ARI	7	0	146	124	4.67	1.18	4.70	1.26	92	101	23.6	6%	20%	14%	6%	10.1%	90.4	33	22	45	28%	65%	12%	14%	26	88	23%	42%			-7.4	92	$3
1st Half	4	0	60	62	5.73	1.26	4.52	1.22	94	108	21.5	7%	24%	17%	6%	11.0%	91.1	32	20	48	31%	57%	12%	15%	12	86	25%	50%			-10.8	115	-$3
2nd Half	3	0	87	62	3.95	1.13	4.82	1.30	84	100	25.4	6%	18%	12%	5%	9.4%	89.8	34	23	43	26%	71%	12%	13%	14	90	21%	36%			3.4	76	$8
Proj	**7**	**0**	**160**	**134**	**4.70**	**1.23**	**4.55**	**1.28**	**91**	**107**	**22.4**	**7%**	**21%**	**14%**	**6%**	**9.9%**	**90.2**	**35**	**23**	**43**	**28%**	**68%**	**15%**	**16%**	**29**						**-4.9**	**95**	**$2**

Bummer,Aaron

Age: 28	Th: L	Role: RP	Health: D	LIMA Plan: A	
Ht: 6' 3"	Wt: 215	Type: Pwr/xGB	PT/Exp: D	Rand Var: +2	
			Consist: A	MM: 5300	

Let's get the bad news out of the way first: yes, he allows too many walks. But he made some progress on that in 2nd half, xBB% says there's reason to hope that continues. The good news is, if he doesn't walk you, you're very likely either striking out or hitting a groundball. Would like to see a bit more success vR, but still... UP: 25 Sv.

Yr Tm	W	Sv	IP	K	ERA	WHIP	xERA	xWHIP	vL+	vR+	BF/G	BB%	K%	K-BB%	xBB%	SwK	Vel	G	L	F	H%	S%	HR/F	xHR/F	GS	APC	DOM%	DIS%	Sv%	LI	RAR	BPX	R$
17 CHW *	2	3	60	51	4.00	1.47	4.22	1.59	82	105	5.2	13%	20%	7%		11.5%	93.2	54	14	32	29%	75%	22%	15%	0	12			75	1.55	2.7	65	-$1
18 CHW *	2	0	64	60	3.72	1.48	4.16	1.29	82	114	4.0	8%	22%	14%	11%	10.5%	93.1	61	22	16	37%	73%	6%	16%	0	16			0	0.92	3.4	117	-$3
19 CHW	0	1	68	60	2.13	0.99	3.15	1.34	60	75	4.5	9%	23%	14%	8%	11.0%	95.6	72	11	17	23%	81%	14%	9%	0	18			33	1.23	19.8	117	$7
20 CHW	1	0	9	14	0.96	1.07	2.42	1.22	64	51	4.2	13%	37%	24%	8%	12.9%	95.7	68	16	16	29%	90%	0%	32%	0	17			0	0.77	4.0	179	$0
21 CHW	5	2	56	75	3.51	1.26	2.47	1.27	45	90	3.9	12%	31%	19%	9%	13.2%	95.4	76	11	13	32%	72%	18%	20%	0	16			25	1.05	5.2	159	$3
1st Half	1	2	30	43	3.26	1.42	2.56	1.28	49	100	4.2	13%	32%	19%	10%	15.0%	95.9	74	12	14	36%	78%	20%	24%	0	16			29	1.14	3.7	160	-$2
2nd Half	4	0	26	32	3.81	1.08	2.37	1.26	35	82	3.6	11%	30%	19%	8%	11.1%	94.8	79	10	11	27%	63%	14%	14%	0	15			0	0.96	1.5	158	$1
Proj	**4**	**0**	**65**	**72**	**2.94**	**1.23**	**2.86**	**1.30**	**56**	**90**	**4.0**	**11%**	**27%**	**17%**	**9%**	**11.9%**	**94.9**	**73**	**13**	**14**	**30%**	**77%**	**14%**	**16%**	**0**						**12.1**	**141**	**$3**

Bundy,Dylan

Age: 29	Th: R	Role: RP	Health: D	LIMA Plan: C	
Ht: 6' 1"	Wt: 225	Type: Pwr	PT/Exp: A	Rand Var: +5	
			Consist: B	MM: 1201	

xERA and RandVar agree that he didn't deserve all of this 6+ ERA, but that's cold comfort. Once we cast off 2020 as a short-season mirage, what emerges across his full-season xERA history is a quite-stable (and unexciting) skill set. Can't rule out future glimpses of 2020 form, but regression always wins in the long run.

Yr Tm	W	Sv	IP	K	ERA	WHIP	xERA	xWHIP	vL+	vR+	BF/G	BB%	K%	K-BB%	xBB%	SwK	Vel	G	L	F	H%	S%	HR/F	xHR/F	GS	APC	DOM%	DIS%	Sv%	LI	RAR	BPX	R$
17 BAL	13	0	170	152	4.24	1.20	4.62	1.30	102	91	24.9	7%	22%	14%	7%	11.8%	92.2	33	20	47	28%	69%	11%	12%	28	101	25%	29%			2.4	100	$12
18 BAL	8	0	172	184	5.45	1.41	4.37	1.22	128	108	24.2	7%	25%	17%	6%	13.2%	91.6	34	20	46	33%	69%	18%	15%	31	92	35%	32%			-27.6	126	-$7
19 BAL	7	0	162	162	4.79	1.35	4.60	1.33	103	105	23.3	8%	23%	15%	7%	13.3%	91.2	41	21	38	31%	70%	16%	13%	30	93	17%	37%			-5.6	103	$1
20 LAA	6	0	66	72	3.29	1.04	3.72	1.15	95	69	24.3	6%	27%	21%	6%	13.2%	90.2	41	24	36	29%	70%	8%	9%	11	93	45%	27%			9.4	151	$23
21 LAA	2	0	91	84	6.06	1.36	4.64	1.33	104	115	17.3	9%	21%	13%	7%	10.1%	90.8	41	21	39	29%	60%	19%	19%	19	66	16%	42%	0	0.69	-20.0	86	-$10
1st Half	1	0	67	63	6.58	1.39	4.44	1.27	110	117	19.5	7%	22%	14%	6%	11.4%	91.2	42	20	38	31%	56%	20%	19%	14	75	14%	43%	0	0.73	-19.1	106	-$13
2nd Half	1	0	24	21	4.56	1.27	5.25	1.53	58	117	13.0	13%	20%	8%	10%	6.5%	89.7	37	22	41	21%	72%	18%	20%	5	50	20%	40%	0	0.62	-0.9	27	-$8
Proj	**6**	**0**	**116**	**113**	**4.66**	**1.32**	**4.42**	**1.33**	**101**	**108**	**17.7**	**9%**	**24%**	**14%**	**7%**	**10.7%**	**90.7**	**39**	**22**	**40**	**29%**	**70%**	**16%**	**16%**	**21**						**-3.0**	**94**	**-$1**

RAY MURPHY

Burnes,Corbin

Age: 27	Th: R	Role SP	Health B	LIMA Plan D+
Ht: 6' 3"	Wt: 225	Type Pwr	PT/Exp A	Rand Var -2
			Consist F	MM 5503

After successfully rebooting his arsenal (eliminating 4-seamer in favor of sinker) in 2020, he introduced 3.0 version in 2021 (now throwing >50% cutters) to rave reviews. Of course, four plus pitches make it hard to go wrong. Pre-2021 IP totals raise workload concern, but Health grade says those are largely theoretical. Maybe not a horse, but definitely an ace.

Yr Tm	W	Sv	IP	K	ERA	WHIP	xERA	xWHIP	vL+	vR+	BF/G	BB%	K%	K-BB%	xBB%	SwK	Vel	G	L	F	H%	S%	HR/F	xHR/F	GS	APC	DOM%	DIS%	Sv%	LI	RAR	BPX	R$
17 aa	3	0	86	73	3.22	1.26	3.35				21.9	7%	21%	14%							33%	74%									12.1	126	$3
18 MIL *	10	1	118	103	4.33	1.32	3.99	1.32	70	89	10.0	8%	21%	13%	6%	15.9%	95.3	49	21	30	31%	68%	13%	14%	0	19			33	0.96	-2.6	92	$2
19 MIL *	1	1	72	91	9.06	1.84	8.03	1.26	167	111	8.4	9%	27%	18%	8%	17.7%	95.2	45	24	31	43%	53%	39%	29%	4	28	0%	75%	100	1.05	-40.5	53	-$19
20 MIL	4	0	60	88	2.11	1.02	2.99	1.11	80	57	20.0	10%	37%	27%	10%	15.0%	96.0	46	19	34	30%	80%	5%	16%	9	84	56%	11%	0	0.84	17.2	187	$25
21 MIL	11	0	167	234	2.43	0.94	2.55	0.94	78	63	23.5	5%	36%	30%	6%	17.5%	96.9	49	21	30	33%	75%	6%	8%	28	93	50%	4%			37.9	224	$32
1st Half	4	0	82	120	2.41	0.90	2.40	0.89	77	62	23.0	5%	37%	33%	6%	17.4%	96.7	50	18	31	33%	73%	5%	6%	14	91	50%	0%			18.7	243	$24
2nd Half	7	0	85	114	2.44	0.98	2.70	0.99	71	67	23.9	6%	34%	28%	6%	17.7%	97.1	47	23	29	32%	76%	7%	10%	14	94	50%	7%			19.2	207	$32
Proj	**12**	**0**	**174**	**233**	**2.93**	**1.04**	**2.81**	**1.02**	**86**	**70**	**23.2**	**7%**	**35%**	**28%**	**7%**	**16.9%**	**96.3**	**47**	**21**	**31**	**32%**	**74%**	**11%**	**15%**	**25**						**32.8**	**203**	**$27**

Cabrera,Edward

Age: 24	Th: R	Role RP	Health A	LIMA Plan B+
Ht: 6' 4"	Wt: 175	Type Pwr	PT/Exp F	Rand Var +4
			Consist A	MM 2311

0-3, 5.81 ERA in 26 IP at MIA. Tall, big-armed prospect spent final six weeks in Marlins rotation, flashing skills consistent with scouting reports. Generated promising levels of GB%, SwK%, but struggled with command: both in terms of BB% and in missing spots (LD%, HR/F). Projects as mid-rotation type, but needs more high-minors finishing school.

Yr Tm	W	Sv	IP	K	ERA	WHIP	xERA	xWHIP	vL+	vR+	BF/G	BB%	K%	K-BB%	xBB%	SwK	Vel	G	L	F	H%	S%	HR/F	xHR/F	GS	APC	DOM%	DIS%	Sv%	LI	RAR	BPX	R$
17																																	
18																																	
19 aa	4	0	40	38	3.78	1.26	4.37				20.5	9%	23%	14%							27%	78%									3.6	67	$0
20																																	
21 MIA *	3	0	82	97	4.50	1.41	4.56	1.39	131	110	19.4	13%	28%	15%	12%	12.7%	96.7	42	25	33	30%	73%	27%	32%	7	69	0%	43%			-2.4	81	-$4
1st Half	1	0	16	16	1.37	0.83	1.98				19.6	7%	27%	20%							20%	97%	0%		0	0					5.7	135	-$1
2nd Half	2	0	69	81	5.09	1.49	4.92	1.42	124	113	19.7	14%	27%	14%	12%	12.7%	96.7	42	25	33	31%	70%	27%	32%	7	69	0%	43%			-7.0	75	-$7
Proj	**5**	**2**	**87**	**93**	**4.00**	**1.23**	**3.89**	**1.33**	**116**	**101**	**19.9**	**11%**	**26%**	**16%**	**12%**	**12.7%**	**96.7**	**42**	**25**	**33**	**27%**	**73%**	**21%**	**29%**	**17**						**4.9**	**100**	**$3**

Cabréra,Genesis

Age: 25	Th: L	Role RP	Health A	LIMA Plan B
Ht: 6' 2"	Wt: 180	Type Pwr	PT/Exp C	Rand Var -3
			Consist C	MM 1211

Starting to curtail BB% was a good sign, in a "first step is admitting you have a problem" way. Unfortunately, K% tracked downward concurrently, leaving K-BB% worse off. Velocity is here in spades, SwK and GB ticked up in 2nd half. Raw stuff alone makes him worth watching, but we won't get excited until he at least sniffs 20% K-BB%.

Yr Tm	W	Sv	IP	K	ERA	WHIP	xERA	xWHIP	vL+	vR+	BF/G	BB%	K%	K-BB%	xBB%	SwK	Vel	G	L	F	H%	S%	HR/F	xHR/F	GS	APC	DOM%	DIS%	Sv%	LI	RAR	BPX	R$
17 aa	5	0	65	46	4.36	1.74	5.94				24.6	9%	16%	6%							37%	76%									-0.1	47	-$5
18 a/a	8	0	141	125	4.41	1.33	3.68				21.7	11%	21%	10%							29%	68%									-4.5	83	$1
19 STL *	5	1	119	107	6.49	1.61	6.11	1.42	157	83	16.0	9%	20%	11%	8%	7.8%	96.3	36	26	38	35%	62%	8%	12%	2	29	0%	100%	50	0.57	-29.2	44	-$13
20 STL	4	1	22	32	2.42	1.16	4.11	1.46	44	100	5.1	17%	33%	17%	12%	14.9%	96.2	34	25	41	18%	87%	17%	18%	0	21			100	0.92	5.6	79	$9
21 STL	4	0	70	77	3.73	1.26	4.24	1.39	105	73	4.2	12%	26%	14%	9%	11.8%	97.7	42	20	38	29%	69%	5%	11%	0	17			0	1.08	4.6	80	$1
1st Half	1	0	39	45	3.23	1.31	4.28	1.39	104	75	4.3	13%	27%	14%	10%	11.1%	97.4	41	19	40	30%	76%	5%	12%	0	17			0	1.16	5.0	83	-$1
2nd Half	3	0	31	32	4.35	1.19	4.18	1.39	91	74	4.0	12%	25%	13%	8%	12.7%	98.0	43	22	35	27%	61%	4%	9%	0	16			0	0.98	-0.3	78	-$3
Proj	**4**	**5**	**73**	**70**	**3.94**	**1.38**	**4.57**	**1.42**	**124**	**88**	**6.8**	**11%**	**23%**	**12%**	**8%**	**12.0%**	**97.8**	**42**	**20**	**37**	**31%**	**73%**	**8%**	**10%**	**0**						**4.6**	**72**	**$1**

Canning,Griffin

Age: 26	Th: R	Role SP	Health C	LIMA Plan C
Ht: 6' 2"	Wt: 180	Type Pwr/FB	PT/Exp C	Rand Var +2
			Consist B	MM 1201

Spent a half-season getting knocked around; was sent down in July and immediately shut down with season-ending back injury (stress fracture). Reports of UCL damage post-2019 still seem relevant here: he's avoided Tommy John surgery, but K-BB% trend suggests that's been a pyrrhic victory. These are not the directional arrows you want in a 26-year-old.

Yr Tm	W	Sv	IP	K	ERA	WHIP	xERA	xWHIP	vL+	vR+	BF/G	BB%	K%	K-BB%	xBB%	SwK	Vel	G	L	F	H%	S%	HR/F	xHR/F	GS	APC	DOM%	DIS%	Sv%	LI	RAR	BPX	R$
17																																	
18 a/a	4	0	106	100	4.02	1.29	3.61				19.0	8%	23%	14%							32%	69%									1.7	107	$1
19 LAA *	6	0	106	111	3.97	1.17	3.61	1.24	92	104	20.2	8%	26%	19%	9%	14.0%	93.9	38	18	44	29%	70%	13%	13%	17	86	35%	29%	0	0.86	7.0	111	$6
20 LAA	2	0	56	56	3.99	1.37	4.81	1.36	100	107	21.6	10%	24%	14%	10%	11.8%	92.8	36	20	43	31%	75%	12%	15%	11	88	9%	36%			3.2	86	$2
21 LAA	5	0	63	62	5.60	1.48	4.88	1.38	108	118	19.8	10%	22%	12%	9%	14.1%	93.6	35	24	41	31%	68%	18%	16%	13	77	15%	62%	0	0.79	-10.3	71	-$7
1st Half	5	0	63	62	5.60	1.48	4.88	1.38	102	120	19.8	10%	22%	12%	9%	14.1%	93.6	35	24	41	31%	68%	18%	14%	13	77	15%	62%	0	0.79	-10.3	71	-$5
2nd Half																																	
Proj	**6**	**0**	**109**	**108**	**4.55**	**1.35**	**4.56**	**1.33**	**98**	**108**	**21.8**	**9%**	**24%**	**14%**	**9%**	**13.4%**	**93.4**	**36**	**21**	**43**	**31%**	**71%**	**13%**	**14%**	**21**						**-1.3**	**91**	**-$1**

Carrasco,Carlos

Age: 35	Th: R	Role SP	Health F	LIMA Plan C+
Ht: 6' 4"	Wt: 224	Type Pwr	PT/Exp B	Rand Var +5
			Consist A	MM 3303

Torn hamstring in spring kept him out until late July. Came back with intact Vel, but SwK and K% were both down significantly. Between hamstring injury, shortened 2020, and 2019 leukemia bout, that's a lot of choppy half-seasons, and he's reached an age where it's unwise to give mulligans. Some rebound potential, but best to lower expectations.

Yr Tm	W	Sv	IP	K	ERA	WHIP	xERA	xWHIP	vL+	vR+	BF/G	BB%	K%	K-BB%	xBB%	SwK	Vel	G	L	F	H%	S%	HR/F	xHR/F	GS	APC	DOM%	DIS%	Sv%	LI	RAR	BPX	R$
17 CLE	18	0	200	226	3.29	1.10	3.26	1.11	96	85	24.9	6%	28%	23%	6%	13.9%	94.3	45	22	33	31%	74%	12%	14%	32	96	50%	13%			26.5	180	$28
18 CLE	17	0	192	231	3.38	1.13	3.07	1.06	96	89	24.5	5%	29%	24%	6%	15.7%	93.5	47	21	32	33%	74%	13%	15%	30	93	47%	17%	0	0.80	18.3	191	$23
19 CLE	6	1	80	96	5.29	1.35	3.73	1.09	111	118	14.8	5%	28%	23%	6%	15.3%	93.5	41	23	36	36%	68%	22%	21%	12	55	42%	25%	50	0.70	-7.7	180	-$1
20 CLE	3	0	68	82	2.91	1.21	3.70	1.23	97	83	23.3	10%	29%	20%	8%	15.4%	93.6	44	22	34	30%	81%	14%	15%	12	92	33%	8%			12.9	137	$16
21 NYM	1	0	54	50	6.04	1.43	4.59	1.29	96	126	19.8	8%	21%	14%	6%	12.9%	93.3	42	21	36	32%	63%	20%	20%	12	74	8%	33%			-11.7	98	-$9
1st Half																																	
2nd Half	1	0	54	50	6.04	1.43	4.59	1.29	91	128	19.8	8%	21%	14%	6%	12.9%	93.3	42	21	36	32%	63%	20%	20%	12	74	8%	33%			-11.7	99	-$13
Proj	**7**	**0**	**131**	**145**	**4.25**	**1.24**	**3.65**	**1.16**	**98**	**102**	**22.7**	**7%**	**27%**	**20%**	**6%**	**14.5%**	**93.5**	**44**	**22**	**35**	**31%**	**72%**	**18%**	**18%**	**23**						**3.3**	**150**	**$5**

Castillo,Diego

Age: 28	Th: R	Role RP	Health C	LIMA Plan B
Ht: 6' 3"	Wt: 250	Type Pwr/GB	PT/Exp C	Rand Var -2
			Consist B	MM 5420

Seemed to tame the most fickle of roles—Rays closer—for four months, before getting flipped to Seattle. Spent a couple of weeks on IL (sore shoulder) soon after arrival, which knocked him out of closer committee. Strong final month (2.13 ERA, 4% BB, 33% K%) says he finished up healthy, and BPX history is clearly worthy of more Save opps.

Yr Tm	W	Sv	IP	K	ERA	WHIP	xERA	xWHIP	vL+	vR+	BF/G	BB%	K%	K-BB%	xBB%	SwK	Vel	G	L	F	H%	S%	HR/F	xHR/F	GS	APC	DOM%	DIS%	Sv%	LI	RAR	BPX	R$
17 a/a	4	15	72	79	3.55	1.26	3.29				5.7	7%	27%	20%							35%	71%									7.1	155	$10
18 TAM *	4	4	84	93	2.55	0.94	1.99	1.15	70	81	5.1	8%	29%	22%	8%	13.7%	97.7	45	18	37	25%	77%	12%	14%	11	21	0%	36%	57	1.20	16.5	152	$12
19 TAM	5	8	69	81	3.41	1.24	3.53	1.25	101	85	4.5	9%	28%	19%	8%	14.0%	98.3	57	13	30	31%	77%	15%	15%	6	17	0%	83%	80	1.16	9.3	146	$7
20 TAM	3	4	22	23	1.66	1.06	3.81	1.41	70	81	4.0	12%	26%	13%	9%	15.6%	96.2	60	11	28	19%	95%	20%	11%	0	15			80	1.39	7.5	98	$12
21 2AL	5	16	58	75	2.78	0.98	3.02	1.07	113	69	3.8	7%	32%	25%	7%	15.6%	94.7	49	15	36	26%	81%	19%	13%	0	15			73	1.34	10.7	180	$14
1st Half	2	12	30	42	3.30	1.10	3.04	1.04	98	88	4.0	7%	35%	27%	6%	18.0%	95.0	45	15	39	31%	79%	19%	14%	0	16			86	1.58	3.6	195	$8
2nd Half	3	4	28	33	2.22	0.85	2.99	1.11	116	52	3.6	7%	29%	22%	7%	13.1%	94.5	53	15	32	20%	85%	19%	11%	0	15			50	1.10	7.1	166	$9
Proj	**4**	**14**	**58**	**69**	**3.03**	**1.04**	**3.20**	**1.13**	**101**	**73**	**4.1**	**8%**	**31%**	**23%**	**7%**	**14.6%**	**96.0**	**50**	**15**	**34**	**27%**	**76%**	**15%**	**13%**	**0**						**10.2**	**167**	**$11**

Castillo,Luis

Age: 29	Th: R	Role SP	Health A	LIMA Plan A
Ht: 6' 2"	Wt: 190	Type Pwr/xGB	PT/Exp A	Rand Var 0
			Consist B	MM 4305

7.22 ERA through May, then 2.73 from June onward. xERA smooths that out, as monthly levels were all between 3.22 and 4.96. The case against him as an ace has long hinged on his weaker WHIP/xWHIP. Higher WHIP=more runners, thus more chances for S% to burn him, as in April/May. Bottom line: he is what his full-season xERA history says he is.

Yr Tm	W	Sv	IP	K	ERA	WHIP	xERA	xWHIP	vL+	vR+	BF/G	BB%	K%	K-BB%	xBB%	SwK	Vel	G	L	F	H%	S%	HR/F	xHR/F	GS	APC	DOM%	DIS%	Sv%	LI	RAR	BPX	R$
17 CIN *	7	0	170	166	3.70	1.22	3.70	1.23	83	87	23.6	7%	24%	17%	8%	13.2%	97.5	59	12	29	31%	73%	17%	11%	15	99	40%	20%			13.8	120	$12
18 CIN	10	0	170	165	4.30	1.22	3.77	1.23	120	82	22.8	7%	23%	16%	7%	13.9%	95.8	46	22	32	29%	70%	18%	19%	31	90	26%	32%			-3.1	128	$7
19 CIN	15	0	191	226	3.40	1.14	3.43	1.27	89	78	24.4	10%	29%	19%	10%	16.4%	96.5	55	18	27	27%	74%	18%	15%	32	99	28%	16%			26.0	135	$23
20 CIN	4	0	70	89	3.21	1.23	3.01	1.15	106	74	24.3	8%	30%	22%	7%	16.0%	97.5	58	19	22	34%	75%	13%	13%	12	96	25%	0%			10.7	179	$17
21 CIN	8	0	188	192	3.98	1.36	3.67	1.30	101	98	24.3	9%	24%	15%	8%	13.5%	97.3	57	19	25	32%	73%	15%	15%	33	96	30%	24%			6.6	114	$4
1st Half	3	0	90	86	5.08	1.46	4.13	1.36	99	100	23.5	10%	22%	12%	8%	12.7%	97.0	52	23	26	33%	66%	13%	14%	17	92	24%	35%			-9.1	90	-$6
2nd Half	5	0	97	106	2.96	1.27	3.25	1.25	92	99	25.2	9%	26%	17%	8%	14.3%	97.5	62	15	24	31%	81%	17%	17%	16	100	38%	13%			15.7	136	$18
Proj	**11**	**0**	**189**	**206**	**3.67**	**1.27**	**3.43**	**1.25**	**102**	**89**	**23.6**	**9%**	**27%**	**18%**	**8%**	**14.5%**	**97.1**	**56**	**18**	**25**	**32%**	**74%**	**16%**	**15%**	**33**						**18.2**	**138**	**$13**

RAY MURPHY

Castro,Miguel

Age: 27 | Th: R | Role: RP | Ht: 6' 7" | Wt: 205 | Type: Pwr/GB
Health: A | PT/Exp: C | Consist: C
LIMA Plan: B | Rand Var: -3 | MM: 1200

Bunches of strikeouts and grounders are great, but last year we said we were waiting for BB% to fall into single digits, and we're still waiting. Plus, actual BB% underperformed xBB% by ~3% every year. Sub-1.00 LI history shows how managers run from those BBs in big spots. In danger of establishing permanent residency on the "one skill away" list.

Yr Tm	W	Sv	IP	K	ERA	WHIP	xERA	xWHIP	vL+	vR+	BF/G	BB%	K%	K-BB%	xBB%	SwK	Vel	G	L	F	H%	S%	HR/F	xHR/F	GS	APC	DOM%	DIS%	Sv%	LI	RAR	BPX	R$
17 BAL *	6	0	91	48	4.05	1.26	3.59	1.56	112	77	8.2	9%	13%	4%	9%	10.2%	95.6	49	17	34	25%	70%	12%	13%	1	26	0%	100%	0	0.90	3.4	45	$2
18 BAL	2	0	86	57	3.96	1.45	5.25	1.68	106	94	6.0	13%	15%	2%	10%	10.1%	95.5	49	19	32	26%	75%	11%	16%	1	23	0%	100%	0	0.99	2.0	-8	-$4
19 BAL	1	2	73	71	4.66	1.42	4.93	1.54	102	91	4.9	13%	22%	9%	11%	12.1%	97.4	49	17	34	28%	70%	14%	13%	0	19			40	0.87	-1.4	52	-$3
20 2 TM	2	1	25	38	4.01	1.66	3.50	1.23	138	97	4.4	11%	33%	22%	9%	14.1%	98.1	51	19	30	43%	81%	21%	15%	0	18			33	1.29	1.3	170	-$1
21 NYM	3	0	70	77	3.45	1.29	4.20	1.49	81	87	4.4	14%	25%	11%	11%	12.8%	98.1	52	16	32	25%	76%	13%	16%	2	18	0%	50%	0	0.84	7.0	64	$1
1st Half	2	0	35	39	3.38	1.38	4.32	1.56	85	94	4.6	16%	26%	10%	12%	13.7%	98.3	52	19	29	24%	81%	20%	26%	2	19	0%	50%	0	1.08	3.8	48	-$2
2nd Half	1	0	36	38	3.53	1.21	4.10	1.42	68	84	4.2	13%	25%	13%	10%	11.8%	97.9	53	13	34	26%	71%	6%	8%	0	17			0	0.63	3.2	81	-$3
Proj	2	0	65	60	4.00	1.34	4.59	1.54	92	87	4.8	14%	22%	9%	11%	11.8%	97.2	51	17	33	26%	72%	12%	15%	0						3.6	47	-$2

Cavalli,Cade

Age: 23 | Th: R | Role: SP | Ht: 0' 0" | Wt: 0 | Type: Pwr
Health: A | PT/Exp: F | Consist: F
LIMA Plan: D+ | Rand Var: +2 | MM: 1300

Nats' 2020 first-rounder sailed through three levels in first pro season, topping out at Triple-A. Demonstrated strikeout prowess at every level, but BB% and K-BB% eroded as he reached the upper levels. Could be just a quick Triple-A refresher away from his big-league debut, though could be a bumpy transition until he stabilizes that K-BB%.

Yr Tm	W	Sv	IP	K	ERA	WHIP	xERA	xWHIP	vL+	vR+	BF/G	BB%	K%	K-BB%	xBB%	SwK	Vel	G	L	F	H%	S%	HR/F	xHR/F	GS	APC	DOM%	DIS%	Sv%	LI	RAR	BPX	R$
17																																	
18																																	
19																																	
20																																	
21 a/a	4	0	84	87	4.86	1.55	4.35				21.7	13%	24%	11%							34%	68%									-6.2	90	-$7
1st Half	0	0	18	22	4.12	1.42	3.59				25.8	14%	28%	14%							32%	71%									0.3	109	-$7
2nd Half	4	0	68	65	4.89	1.53	4.29				21.3	12%	22%	9%							34%	67%									-5.2	85	-$6
Proj	2	0	58	61	4.97	1.49	4.64	1.48			22.8	13%	24%	11%				44	20	36	31%	68%	12%	12%	11						-3.7	63	-$6

Cease,Dylan

Age: 26 | Th: R | Role: SP | Ht: 6' 2" | Wt: 200 | Type: Pwr/FB
Health: A | PT/Exp: B | Consist: C
LIMA Plan: C+ | Rand Var: 0 | MM: 2403

Proof that rebooting a pitcher can take many forms: this skills transformation came without introduction of a new pitch; instead he changed his arm slot, which added some spin and made his entire existing arsenal more effective. Velocity was never a problem, now SwK% is commensurate. Has become a strikeout asset with much less ratio risk. UP: 3.25 ERA

Yr Tm	W	Sv	IP	K	ERA	WHIP	xERA	xWHIP	vL+	vR+	BF/G	BB%	K%	K-BB%	xBB%	SwK	Vel	G	L	F	H%	S%	HR/F	xHR/F	GS	APC	DOM%	DIS%	Sv%	LI	RAR	BPX	R$
17																																	
18 aa	3	0	53	68	2.33	1.16	2.60				21.1	12%	32%	20%							29%	83%									11.9	141	$4
19 CHW *	9	0	142	143	5.56	1.63	5.65	1.43	120	102	21.8	11%	23%	12%	11%	11.1%	96.5	46	21	34	36%	68%	21%	16%	14	97	14%	36%			-18.4	64	-$8
20 CHW	5	0	58	44	4.01	1.44	5.74	1.66	121	101	21.3	13%	17%	4%	12%	9.9%	97.5	40	22	39	24%	81%	18%	18%	12	90	0%	42%			3.2	-2	$5
21 CHW	13	0	166	226	3.91	1.25	3.78	1.18	94	88	22.1	10%	32%	22%	9%	15.5%	96.7	33	23	44	33%	72%	11%	15%	32	92	22%	16%			7.2	145	$13
1st Half	7	0	82	103	3.75	1.29	3.98	1.24	75	103	22.0	10%	29%	19%	9%	15.6%	96.2	36	23	41	32%	74%	11%	15%	16	92	19%	19%			5.2	125	$11
2nd Half	6	0	84	123	4.07	1.21	3.60	1.12	104	79	22.3	9%	35%	25%	8%	15.4%	97.3	31	22	48	34%	70%	12%	15%	16	93	25%	13%			2.0	165	$16
Proj	13	0	174	208	3.61	1.26	3.99	1.27	100	87	20.7	10%	29%	19%	10%	13.4%	96.9	37	22	41	30%	77%	14%	16%	34						18.2	119	$15

Cessa,Luis

Age: 30 | Th: R | Role: RP | Ht: 6' 0" | Wt: 208 | Type: Con
Health: C | PT/Exp: C | Consist: B
LIMA Plan: B | Rand Var: -5 | MM: 2110

Started out as another bland season of slightly below-average middle relief. Something interesting happened in 2nd half upon arrival in Cincinnati: skills growth was driven by a retooled change-up. Parsing half-season sample sizes for relievers is dicey, and 2nd half xERA rather than ERA is your baseline, but he may have moved to the good side of average.

Yr Tm	W	Sv	IP	K	ERA	WHIP	xERA	xWHIP	vL+	vR+	BF/G	BB%	K%	K-BB%	xBB%	SwK	Vel	G	L	F	H%	S%	HR/F	xHR/F	GS	APC	DOM%	DIS%	Sv%	LI	RAR	BPX	R$
17 NYY *	4	0	114	85	4.80	1.55	5.46	1.47	73	139	20.8	9%	17%	8%	9%	10.6%	95.6	45	18	36	32%	73%	18%	18%	5	62	0%	60%	0	0.60	-6.3	42	-$6
18 NYY *	4	2	82	69	4.54	1.24	3.76	1.22	99	110	13.8	6%	21%	15%	7%	12.4%	94.8	47	23	30	32%	63%	12%	13%	5	44	0%	60%	67	0.39	-4.0	120	$0
19 NYY	2	1	81	75	4.11	1.31	4.46	1.38	102	99	8.0	9%	22%	13%	8%	13.2%	94.5	49	18	33	28%	75%	18%	12%	0	31			100	0.67	3.9	92	$0
20 NYY	0	1	22	17	3.32	1.25	5.10	1.37	94	94	5.8	8%	18%	11%	8%	12.5%	93.7	40	21	40	29%	76%	7%	10%	0	23			100	0.59	3.0	75	-$2
21 2 TM	5	0	65	54	2.51	1.14	3.92	1.28	90	82	4.9	7%	21%	13%	7%	12.0%	93.6	51	20	28	28%	81%	9%	13%	0	18			0	0.76	14.0	102	$5
1st Half	1	0	33	29	3.31	1.38	4.38	1.43	76	96	5.5	11%	20%	10%	8%	11.4%	93.2	54	18	28	31%	77%	7%	15%	0	20			0	0.41	3.9	71	-$4
2nd Half	4	0	32	25	1.69	0.91	3.46	1.12	93	67	4.4	3%	21%	18%	5%	12.7%	94.0	48	23	29	25%	88%	12%	11%	0	16			0	1.10	10.2	134	$7
Proj	4	1	65	55	3.37	1.21	4.05	1.29	91	92	6.7	7%	21%	14%	7%	12.3%	94.3	49	21	30	29%	76%	12%	13%	0						8.7	104	$2

Chafin,Andrew

Age: 32 | Th: L | Role: RP | Ht: 6' 2" | Wt: 235 | Type: Pwr
Health: C | PT/Exp: D | Consist: B
LIMA Plan: B | Rand Var: -5 | MM: 3310

Mid-season trade from CHC to OAK vaulted him into Saves mix with his new team. That's partially a statement about how the entire OAK pen was imploding, but also reflective of how the H%/S%/HR/F trio had his back. Stable xERA history shows his true skill level, which isn't closer-worthy unless the rest of your pen is completely on fire (hi, Oakland).

Yr Tm	W	Sv	IP	K	ERA	WHIP	xERA	xWHIP	vL+	vR+	BF/G	BB%	K%	K-BB%	xBB%	SwK	Vel	G	L	F	H%	S%	HR/F	xHR/F	GS	APC	DOM%	DIS%	Sv%	LI	RAR	BPX	R$
17 ARI	1	0	51	61	3.51	1.34	3.26	1.26	75	107	3.1	10%	28%	18%	10%	11.7%	93.7	56	21	22	34%	77%	17%	17%	0	12			0	1.02	5.4	153	-$1
18 ARI	1	0	49	53	3.10	1.34	3.71	1.39	91	80	2.7	12%	25%	13%	10%	14.6%	93.5	50	26	24	32%	74%	0%	10%	0	11			0	1.20	6.4	91	-$1
19 ARI	2	0	53	68	3.76	1.33	3.49	1.17	89	95	2.9	8%	30%	22%	7%	15.8%	93.8	43	28	29	36%	75%	15%	17%	0	12			0	1.23	4.8	160	-$1
20 2 NL	1	1	10	13	6.52	1.66	4.26	1.30	109	125	3.0	11%	29%	18%	10%	10.3%	93.6	41	26	33	39%	64%	22%	19%	0	12			33	1.38	-2.5	126	-$5
21 2 TM	2	5	69	64	1.83	0.93	3.84	1.22	65	73	3.7	7%	24%	17%	6%	12.1%	92.0	45	16	39	24%	83%	6%	13%	0	13			63	1.14	20.6	117	$11
1st Half	0	0	35	31	1.54	0.80	3.56	1.24	58	61	3.5	8%	24%	16%	6%	11.6%	92.7	53	13	34	20%	81%	3%	9%	0	13			0	1.17	11.8	115	$4
2nd Half	2	5	34	33	2.14	1.07	4.12	1.20	67	85	4.0	7%	24%	18%	6%	12.7%	91.4	37	20	43	28%	85%	8%	16%	0	14			71	1.12	8.8	120	$7
Proj	2	4	58	62	3.60	1.11	3.58	1.21	82	86	3.1	8%	27%	19%	8%	13.5%	92.8	46	21	33	29%	70%	12%	14%	0						6.1	136	$3

Chapman,Aroldis

Age: 34 | Th: L | Role: RP | Ht: 6' 4" | Wt: 218 | Type: Pwr
Health: C | PT/Exp: B | Consist: B
LIMA Plan: C+ | Rand Var: +1 | MM: 5530

Elbow inflammation cost him a couple of weeks in August. SwK remains top-notch, and leveling of the slow velocity decline is nice to see. Long-standing BB% issues got worse, joined by a new gotcha in the form of gopheritis that carried over from 2020 micro-sample. That combo speaks to increased volatility, but there's still plenty left in this tank.

Yr Tm	W	Sv	IP	K	ERA	WHIP	xERA	xWHIP	vL+	vR+	BF/G	BB%	K%	K-BB%	xBB%	SwK	Vel	G	L	F	H%	S%	HR/F	xHR/F	GS	APC	DOM%	DIS%	Sv%	LI	RAR	BPX	R$
17 NYY	4	22	50	69	3.22	1.13	3.17	1.17	76	80	4.0	10%	33%	23%	5%	14.2%	100.1	49	16	35	32%	72%	7%	9%	0	17			85	1.14	7.1	183	$13
18 NYY	3	32	51	93	2.45	1.05	2.48	1.13	64	70	3.9	14%	44%	30%	8%	16.2%	98.9	44	19	37	30%	77%	6%	8%	0	17			94	1.10	10.7	200	$19
19 NYY	3	37	57	85	2.21	1.11	3.08	1.16	61	75	3.9	11%	36%	26%	7%	14.7%	98.4	42	28	30	32%	82%	8%	8%	0	16			88	1.05	16.1	169	$22
20 NYY	1	3	12	22	3.09	0.86	2.50	0.87	38	104	3.5	9%	49%	40%	5%	20.1%	98.1	22	22	56	27%	75%	20%	17%	0	15			60	1.29	2.0	251	$4
21 NYY	6	30	56	97	3.36	1.31	3.14	1.27	66	98	4.0	16%	40%	24%	10%	17.0%	98.5	43	19	38	30%	82%	23%	28%	0	16			88	1.39	6.3	149	$16
1st Half	5	16	29	49	3.77	1.36	2.89	1.26	74	99	3.9	16%	40%	25%	8%	17.0%	99.0	46	25	29	33%	77%	27%	33%	0	15			84	1.58	1.8	154	$12
2nd Half	1	14	28	48	2.93	1.27	3.39	1.27	53	100	4.0	16%	40%	24%	12%	17.1%	98.0	39	14	47	27%	87%	21%	25%	0	18			93	1.19	4.6	144	$12
Proj	5	30	65	108	3.16	1.20	2.96	1.20	66	86	3.8	15%	41%	27%	8%	16.1%	98.7	43	20	37	30%	78%	16%	18%	0						10.4	169	$18

Cimber,Adam

Age: 31 | Th: R | Role: RP | Ht: 6' 3" | Wt: 195 | Type: Con/xGB
Health: A | PT/Exp: D | Consist: C
LIMA Plan: B | Rand Var: -5 | MM: 2000

Continues to defy league-wide velocity fetish, instead featuring a sinker/slider arsenal that keeps the ball on the ground, with enough K-BB% to survive. But what's unsustainable about these results was the HR/F; once that falls back in line, ERA will converge to xERA. That doesn't make him unplayable, but lack of K's makes him a tough fit in our lineups.

Yr Tm	W	Sv	IP	K	ERA	WHIP	xERA	xWHIP	vL+	vR+	BF/G	BB%	K%	K-BB%	xBB%	SwK	Vel	G	L	F	H%	S%	HR/F	xHR/F	GS	APC	DOM%	DIS%	Sv%	LI	RAR	BPX	R$
17 a/a	5	5	81	50	3.67	1.09	3.78				6.4	3%	16%	13%							27%	73%									6.8	116	$7
18 2 TM	3	0	68	58	3.42	1.24	3.39	1.24	145	85	4.1	6%	20%	14%	4%	10.4%	86.5	57	21	21	32%	74%	12%	7%	0	14			0	0.88	6.1	129	$1
19 CLE	6	1	57	41	4.45	1.32	4.45	1.41	124	86	3.6	8%	17%	9%	5%	10.2%	85.2	56	20	24	30%	68%	14%	13%	0	12			33	1.32	0.4	76	$0
20 CLE	0	0	11	5	3.97	1.32	5.48	1.37	57	120	3.5	4%	10%	6%	4%	10.7%	85.9	52	12	36	31%	71%	7%	12%	0	13			0	0.75	0.7	66	-$6
21 2 TM	3	1	72	51	2.26	1.07	3.89	1.27	79	82	4.0	6%	18%	12%	6%	10.2%	87.1	54	17	29	28%	79%	3%	9%	0	14			100	0.79	17.7	102	$7
1st Half	2	0	37	22	2.70	1.17	4.39	1.40	83	87	4.3	7%	15%	7%	7%	8.8%	86.9	50	21	29	28%	74%	0%	6%	0	15			0	0.74	7.1	58	$0
2nd Half	1	1	35	29	1.80	0.97	3.41	1.13	65	81	3.7	4%	21%	18%	4%	11.7%	87.2	57	14	29	28%	84%	7%	13%	0	13			100	0.83	10.6	148	$4
Proj	3	0	58	43	3.95	1.23	4.01	1.31	109	90	4.0	7%	18%	12%	5%	10.4%	86.6	55	18	26	30%	69%	11%	10%	0						3.6	101	-$1

RAY MURPHY

Cisnero,José

Age: 33	Th: R	Role RP	Health B	LIMA Plan B
Ht: 6' 3"	Wt: 245	Type Pwr	PT/Exp C	Rand Var -1
			Consist B	MM 1210

Validated 2020's K-BB% growth in first half, then turned into a pumpkin. Problem appears to be reduced slider usage in favor of a sinker as year went on. GB% spiked as a result, but everything else went awry. Slider was also less effective later, so perhaps change was injury-related? There was something decent here, unclear if he can get it back.

Yr Tm	W	Sv	IP	K	ERA	WHIP	xERA	xWHIP	vL+	vR+	BF/G	BB%	K%	K-BB%	xBB%	SwK	Vel	G	L	F	H%	S%	HR/F	xHR/F	GS	APC	DOM%	DIS%	Sv%	LI	RAR	BPX	R$
17																																	
18																																	
19 DET *	1	7	75	75	4.21	1.71	5.62	1.56	123	95	5.1	13%	22%	9%	6%	13.0%	96.4	37	21	41	35%	78%	12%	9%	0	18			58	0.88	2.7	59	-$3
20 DET	3	0	30	34	3.03	1.11	4.01	1.21	72	82	4.2	8%	28%	20%	9%	15.2%	96.3	37	22	41	31%	72%	3%	13%	0	18			0	1.00	5.2	134	$7
21 DET	4	4	62	62	3.65	1.33	4.35	1.42	105	83	4.0	12%	24%	12%	9%	9.9%	96.6	46	21	34	29%	75%	11%	15%	0	16			50	1.29	4.7	71	$1
1st Half	1	3	36	44	2.75	1.17	3.70	1.18	71	90	3.9	9%	30%	21%	7%	10.4%	96.9	36	26	38	31%	79%	9%	18%	0	16			75	1.25	6.7	136	$3
2nd Half	3	1	26	18	4.91	1.56	5.43	1.78	143	76	4.0	16%	16%	0%	12%	9.3%	96.3	57	15	28	26%	70%	14%	11%	0	16			25	1.34	-2.0	-24	-$8
Proj	**4**	**2**	**65**	**61**	**4.08**	**1.34**	**4.51**	**1.45**	**117**	**81**	**4.0**	**11%**	**22%**	**11%**	**8%**	**10.6%**	**96.5**	**46**	**20**	**34**	**29%**	**72%**	**11%**	**13%**	**0**						**3.0**	**67**	**$0**

Civale,Aaron

Age: 27	Th: R	Role SP	Health D	LIMA Plan C+
Ht: 6' 2"	Wt: 215	Type Con	PT/Exp B	Rand Var -1
			Consist A	MM 1103

Very nice (albeit not skills-supported) 1st half ended with a late June finger injury. Returned in Sept. to absorb overdue ERA regression, with HR/F leading the charge. Substandard velocity and SwK leave him on the edge of the knife; absent another trick (pinpoint control, GB spike, etc) he's a 4.00 ERA guy, plus or minus the error bars of H%, S% and HR/F.

Yr Tm	W	Sv	IP	K	ERA	WHIP	xERA	xWHIP	vL+	vR+	BF/G	BB%	K%	K-BB%	xBB%	SwK	Vel	G	L	F	H%	S%	HR/F	xHR/F	GS	APC	DOM%	DIS%	Sv%	LI	RAR	BPX	R$
17																																	
18 aa	5	0	107	66	5.27	1.53	5.91				22.2	5%	14%	9%							35%	68%									-14.8	54	-$10
19 CLE *	10	0	132	104	2.83	1.19	3.59	1.31	91	81	23.0	6%	20%	13%	9%	9.0%	92.6	40	22	37	29%	80%	7%	6%	10	86	40%	40%			27.2	95	$14
20 CLE	4	0	74	69	4.74	1.32	4.07	1.19	91	125	26.0	5%	22%	17%	7%	10.6%	91.8	44	25	31	34%	68%	16%	16%	12	100	17%	42%			-2.6	136	$4
21 CLE	12	0	124	99	3.84	1.12	4.23	1.26	91	107	23.7	6%	20%	14%	8%	9.6%	91.6	45	18	37	25%	74%	17%	18%	21	91	29%	29%			6.6	100	$11
1st Half	10	0	98	76	3.32	1.06	4.10	1.25	93	93	25.6	6%	20%	14%	8%	9.9%	91.7	45	19	36	25%	76%	14%	15%	15	97	33%	27%			11.4	101	$22
2nd Half	2	0	27	23	5.74	1.31	4.69	1.29	61	156	19.0	7%	20%	13%	8%	8.9%	91.1	44	13	43	26%	69%	26%	26%	6	75	17%	33%			-4.8	97	-$9
Proj	**9**	**0**	**160**	**131**	**4.14**	**1.26**	**4.36**	**1.27**	**87**	**125**	**22.1**	**6%**	**20%**	**14%**	**8%**	**9.5%**	**91.7**	**44**	**19**	**38**	**29%**	**75%**	**17%**	**17%**	**30**						**6.2**	**106**	**$5**

Clase,Emmanuel

Age: 24	Th: R	Role RP	Health A	LIMA Plan C
Ht: 6' 2"	Wt: 206	Type /xGB	PT/Exp D	Rand Var -5
			Consist B	MM 5230

Turns out, throwing 100 with a heavy GB tilt plays pretty well at this level. Was approaching Vintage Eck Territory in 2nd half, where that 2% walk rate represents 3 BB in 36 IP. Add in a healthy dose of HR suppression, and that doesn't leave a lot of ways to beat him. In a desert of reliable closers, he's an emerging oasis. UP: 40 Sv.

Yr Tm	W	Sv	IP	K	ERA	WHIP	xERA	xWHIP	vL+	vR+	BF/G	BB%	K%	K-BB%	xBB%	SwK	Vel	G	L	F	H%	S%	HR/F	xHR/F	GS	APC	DOM%	DIS%	Sv%	LI	RAR	BPX	R$
17																																	
18																																	
19 TEX *	3	12	63	54	3.78	1.24	3.46	1.24	90	90	4.7	6%	21%	15%	6%	11.3%	99.3	61	20	20	32%	69%	15%	16%	1	16	0%	100%	86	1.00	5.6	119	$6
20																																	
21 CLE	4	24	70	74	1.29	0.96	2.71	1.11	61	69	3.9	6%	27%	21%	5%	17.6%	100.3	68	14	18	29%	88%	6%	9%	0	15			83	1.11	25.6	178	$22
1st Half	3	11	34	37	1.07	1.22	2.94	1.25	58	82	4.1	9%	26%	17%	6%	16.5%	100.1	72	12	16	33%	90%	0%	8%	0	15			92	1.10	13.3	147	$12
2nd Half	1	13	36	37	1.50	0.72	2.48	0.97	57	58	3.8	2%	27%	25%	5%	18.7%	100.5	64	17	20	25%	83%	11%	9%	0	15			76	1.12	12.3	206	$21
Proj	**4**	**32**	**65**	**66**	**2.21**	**1.00**	**2.72**	**1.12**	**66**	**73**	**3.9**	**6%**	**26%**	**21%**	**5%**	**17.8%**	**100.3**	**67**	**15**	**18**	**29%**	**78%**	**8%**	**9%**	**0**						**18.1**	**178**	**$22**

Clevinger,Mike

Age: 31	Th: R	Role SP	Health F	LIMA Plan C+
Ht: 6' 4"	Wt: 215	Type Pwr	PT/Exp C	Rand Var 0
			Consist B	MM 2303

Underwent Tommy John surgery in November 2020, was reportedly throwing from flat ground by September. Still has hurdles to clear, but it's possible that he'll be ready for Opening Day. Even in that scenario, best to not expect a full-SP workload. But if pre-injury skills are near-intact, he'll be very good on a per-IP basis.

Yr Tm	W	Sv	IP	K	ERA	WHIP	xERA	xWHIP	vL+	vR+	BF/G	BB%	K%	K-BB%	xBB%	SwK	Vel	G	L	F	H%	S%	HR/F	xHR/F	GS	APC	DOM%	DIS%	Sv%	LI	RAR	BPX	R$
17 CLE *	15	0	156	164	3.27	1.32	3.64	1.42	108	77	19.0	12%	25%	13%	11%	12.8%	92.5	39	24	36	29%	79%	12%	13%	21	78	33%	24%	0	0.71	20.8	98	$15
18 CLE	13	0	200	207	3.02	1.16	3.85	1.24	99	82	25.3	8%	26%	17%	8%	12.4%	93.6	40	20	39	29%	78%	10%	11%	32	102	31%	13%			28.0	120	$22
19 CLE	13	0	126	169	2.71	1.06	3.22	1.09	85	74	23.8	7%	34%	26%	8%	15.7%	95.5	41	24	36	32%	77%	10%	12%	21	100	57%	10%			27.8	180	$21
20 2 TM	3	0	42	40	3.02	1.15	4.19	1.29	102	91	20.3	9%	25%	16%	9%	13.3%	95.2	34	27	39	27%	81%	15%	14%	8	81	25%	25%			7.3	97	$9
21																																	
1st Half																																	
2nd Half																																	
Proj	**11**	**0**	**131**	**142**	**3.62**	**1.20**	**3.93**	**1.25**	**104**	**84**	**21.8**	**9%**	**27%**	**18%**	**9%**	**13.6%**	**94.4**	**38**	**24**	**38**	**30%**	**73%**	**12%**	**13%**	**24**						**13.4**	**120**	**$11**

Clippard,Tyler

Age: 37	Th: R	Role RP	Health F	LIMA Plan C
Ht: 6' 3"	Wt: 200	Type Pwr/xFB	PT/Exp D	Rand Var -5
			Consist B	MM 0210

And you thought nothing went right in Arizona this year? Shoulder sprain cost him first half; upon return he rode his sub-90mph FB, appalling K-BB%, helplessness vL, and flammable FB tilt all the way to the de-facto closer role. He's been sneering at our xERA formula for years now, but this was just silly. Avoid, regardless of March role.

Yr Tm	W	Sv	IP	K	ERA	WHIP	xERA	xWHIP	vL+	vR+	BF/G	BB%	K%	K-BB%	xBB%	SwK	Vel	G	L	F	H%	S%	HR/F	xHR/F	GS	APC	DOM%	DIS%	Sv%	LI	RAR	BPX	R$
17 3 AL	2	5	60	72	4.77	1.29	4.66	1.38	90	99	3.9	12%	28%	16%	8%	14.4%	91.1	32	17	51	27%	68%	13%	9%	0	17			45	1.11	-3.1	94	$1
18 TOR	4	7	69	85	3.67	1.17	4.25	1.16	82	115	3.9	8%	30%	22%	7%	15.1%	90.9	19	20	60	29%	78%	13%	11%	1	16	0%	100%	54	1.02	4.1	134	$6
19 CLE	1	0	62	64	2.90	0.85	4.30	1.18	61	100	4.5	6%	27%	21%	6%	14.1%	90.0	32	13	56	21%	73%	9%	10%	3	18	0%	67%	0	0.82	12.3	129	$6
20 MIN	2	0	26	26	2.77	0.88	4.07	1.09	66	81	3.8	4%	27%	22%	8%	12.5%	89.2	29	21	50	26%	71%	6%	12%	2	16	0%	50%	0	1.04	5.4	149	$7
21 ARI	1	6	25	21	3.20	1.30	5.61	1.45	129	74	4.3	10%	19%	9%	11%	11.0%	88.9	26	20	54	27%	80%	8%	16%	0	16			67	1.04	3.3	36	-$1
1st Half																																	
2nd Half	1	6	25	21	3.20	1.30	5.61	1.45	123	76	4.3	10%	19%	9%	11%	11.0%	88.9	26	20	54	27%	80%	8%	16%	0	16			67	1.04	3.3	36	$0
Proj	**2**	**4**	**65**	**67**	**4.22**	**1.31**	**4.83**	**1.31**	**110**	**106**	**4.1**	**9%**	**25%**	**16%**	**8%**	**13.3%**	**90.0**	**27**	**18**	**55**	**30%**	**74%**	**12%**	**12%**	**0**						**1.9**	**91**	**$0**

Cobb,Alex

Age: 34	Th: R	Role SP	Health F	LIMA Plan B+
Ht: 6' 3"	Wt: 205	Type /GB	PT/Exp C	Rand Var -1
			Consist B	MM 2103

Mid-30s return to relevance built on (stop us if you've heard this before) a revamped pitch mix. In his case, it's a sinker/splitter mix that he now leans on ~80% of the time. The splitter feeds the SwK%/K% spike while the sinker yields GBs, and both offerings work vL and vR. Half-season S% silliness aside, he's relevant again, but heed the Health grade.

Yr Tm	W	Sv	IP	K	ERA	WHIP	xERA	xWHIP	vL+	vR+	BF/G	BB%	K%	K-BB%	xBB%	SwK	Vel	G	L	F	H%	S%	HR/F	xHR/F	GS	APC	DOM%	DIS%	Sv%	LI	RAR	BPX	R$
17 TAM	12	0	179	128	3.66	1.22	4.27	1.32	90	99	25.6	6%	17%	11%	8%	7.1%	91.7	48	22	30	29%	74%	13%	13%	29	98	38%	17%			15.4	98	$14
18 BAL	5	0	152	102	4.90	1.41	4.57	1.36	105	120	23.6	7%	15%	9%	8%	7.6%	92.0	50	19	31	31%	69%	15%	16%	28	87	21%	36%			-14.2	78	-$7
19 BAL	0	0	12	8	10.95	1.86	5.49	1.31	130	203	20.0	3%	15%	10%	7%	10.5%	92.3	46	24	30	31%	57%	60%	55%	3	76	0%	67%			-9.8	98	-$9
20 BAL	2	0	52	38	4.30	1.34	4.42	1.39	109	92	22.6	8%	17%	9%	8%	9.8%	92.5	54	24	22	29%	73%	22%	27%	10	81	0%	40%			1.0	75	$0
21 LAA	8	0	93	98	3.76	1.26	3.50	1.25	84	90	21.8	8%	25%	17%	8%	11.3%	92.8	53	23	24	33%	70%	8%	11%	18	88	33%	22%			5.8	126	$4
1st Half	6	0	61	69	4.60	1.22	2.91	1.15	67	107	21.1	7%	27%	20%	8%	12.1%	92.5	58	24	18	34%	61%	10%	13%	12	86	42%	25%			-2.5	163	$5
2nd Half	2	0	33	29	2.20	1.35	4.66	1.43	107	70	23.3	11%	21%	10%	8%	9.8%	93.2	45	22	33	30%	86%	6%	10%	6	91	17%	17%			8.3	60	-$1
Proj	**9**	**0**	**131**	**110**	**3.65**	**1.32**	**4.14**	**1.35**	**99**	**92**	**22.3**	**8%**	**20%**	**12%**	**8%**	**9.6%**	**92.5**	**51**	**22**	**27**	**31%**	**75%**	**13%**	**15%**	**24**						**12.9**	**92**	**$6**

Cole,Gerrit

Age: 31	Th: R	Role SP	Health B	LIMA Plan C
Ht: 6' 4"	Wt: 220	Type Pwr/FB	PT/Exp A	Rand Var 0
			Consist B	MM 5505

Wrong question: Was second-half fade a lost spider-tack issue, or just residue from hamstring issue? Better question: What second-half fade? BB% slippage qualifies as noise, only thing out of range in 2nd half line is H% (thanks, Gleyber). Health and Consistency grades, robust R$ history all say this is still your first SP off the board.

Yr Tm	W	Sv	IP	K	ERA	WHIP	xERA	xWHIP	vL+	vR+	BF/G	BB%	K%	K-BB%	xBB%	SwK	Vel	G	L	F	H%	S%	HR/F	xHR/F	GS	APC	DOM%	DIS%	Sv%	LI	RAR	BPX	R$
17 PIT	12	0	203	196	4.26	1.25	3.92	1.23	105	93	25.7	7%	23%	17%	7%	9.9%	96.0	46	21	34	31%	71%	16%	14%	33	100	24%	18%			2.6	138	$12
18 HOU	15	0	200	276	2.88	1.03	3.13	1.07	71	94	25.0	8%	35%	27%	6%	14.7%	96.6	36	21	43	30%	76%	10%	12%	32	102	50%	0%			31.5	184	$31
19 HOU	20	0	212	326	2.50	0.89	2.71	0.93	77	76	24.8	6%	40%	34%	6%	17.6%	97.2	40	20	39	29%	81%	17%	13%	33	102	42%	12%			52.5	231	$46
20 NYY	7	0	73	94	2.84	0.96	3.43	1.04	106	77	24.0	6%	33%	27%	6%	16.0%	96.7	37	20	43	26%	84%	19%	17%	12	100	50%	8%			14.6	189	$33
21 NYY	16	0	181	243	3.23	1.06	3.14	1.00	92	82	24.2	6%	33%	28%	6%	14.9%	97.7	43	16	41	32%	76%	13%	17%	30	99	37%	7%			23.2	201	$28
1st Half	8	0	102	129	2.66	0.90	3.01	0.96	86	73	24.3	4%	33%	29%	6%	14.9%	97.5	44	15	41	28%	79%	14%	16%	16	99	44%	0%			20.2	205	$33
2nd Half	8	0	80	114	3.95	1.26	3.29	1.05	89	97	24.1	7%	34%	27%	7%	14.8%	98.0	42	18	40	37%	72%	13%	18%	14	100	29%	14%			3.1	196	$17
Proj	**17**	**0**	**189**	**256**	**3.06**	**1.05**	**3.07**	**1.01**	**91**	**84**	**24.3**	**6%**	**35%**	**29%**	**6%**	**15.2%**	**97.3**	**41**	**19**	**41**	**31%**	**78%**	**15%**	**16%**	**30**						**32.3**	**202**	**$31**

RAY MURPHY

Colomé,Alex

Age: 33	Th: R	Role: RP	Health: A	LIMA Plan: B+	
Ht: 6' 1"	Wt: 225	Type: /GB	PT/Exp: B	Rand Var: 0	
			Consist: A	MM: 2220	

Longtime closer got overdue comeuppance early, lost 9th-inning role with horrific April (8.31 ERA). Gradually reduced HR, walks; regained job again in August. GB%, SwK still headline otherwise mediocre peripherals, but "experienced closer's" 2nd-half keeps him relevant. Will find save opps again, but more in-season volatility seems inevitable.

Yr Tm	W	Sv	IP	K	ERA	WHIP	xERA	xWHIP	vL+	vR+	BF/G	BB%	K%	K-BB%	xBB%	SwK	Vel	G	L	F	H%	S%	HR/F	xHR/F	GS	APC	DOM%	DIS%	Sv%	LI	RAR	BPX	R$
17 TAM	2	47	67	58	3.24	1.20	4.25	1.35	90	81	4.3	8%	21%	12%	7%	12.0%	95.1	49	18	34	29%	74%	6%	9%	0	15			89	1.41	9.2	101	$23
18 2 AL	7	12	68	72	3.04	1.18	3.49	1.20	67	106	4.0	7%	26%	18%	6%	14.2%	95.1	46	24	30	30%	78%	13%	16%	0	16			71	1.37	9.3	139	$10
19 CHW	4	30	61	55	2.80	1.07	4.53	1.39	77	86	4.0	9%	22%	13%	8%	13.5%	94.4	45	18	37	23%	79%	11%	18%	0	16			91	1.18	12.8	84	$18
20 CHW	2	12	22	16	0.81	0.94	4.21	1.42	46	79	4.3	9%	18%	9%	8%	15.3%	94.4	52	24	24	22%	90%	0%	5%	0	17			92	1.40	10.0	67	$22
21 MIN	4	17	65	58	4.15	1.40	4.25	1.32	124	83	4.3	8%	20%	12%	8%	13.0%	93.8	54	18	29	32%	73%	14%	23%	0	16			71	1.04	0.9	99	$5
1st Half	2	2	30	28	4.85	1.55	4.47	1.38	132	84	4.3	9%	20%	11%	8%	13.8%	93.8	52	20	28	33%	73%	19%	26%	0	17			40	0.91	-2.2	84	-$6
2nd Half	2	15	35	30	3.57	1.27	4.06	1.27	104	86	4.3	7%	20%	13%	6%	12.1%	93.9	55	16	29	31%	74%	9%	21%	0	16			79	1.15	3.0	112	$12
Proj	**4**	**15**	**65**	**60**	**4.09**	**1.29**	**4.05**	**1.31**	**106**	**92**	**4.0**	**8%**	**22%**	**14%**	**7%**	**13.2%**	**94.3**	**50**	**19**	**31**	**30%**	**73%**	**16%**	**19%**	**0**						**3.0**	**107**	**$6**

Contreras,Roansy

Age: 22	Th: R	Role: SP	Health: B	LIMA Plan: C+	
Ht: 6' 0"	Wt: 175	Type: Pwr	PT/Exp: F	Rand Var: -3	
			Consist: F	MM: 3400	

0-0, 0.00 ERA in 3 IP at PIT. Undersized talent with stuff and pitchability showed an uptick in both at AA before forearm strain shelved him in July and August. Emerged in September unscathed, and impressive in AAA and MLB cameos. Age, just 58 high-minors IP say he needs time, and health risk is now in play. But legit prospect is coming quickly.

Yr Tm	W	Sv	IP	K	ERA	WHIP	xERA	xWHIP	vL+	vR+	BF/G	BB%	K%	K-BB%	xBB%	SwK	Vel	G	L	F	H%	S%	HR/F	xHR/F	GS	APC	DOM%	DIS%	Sv%	LI	RAR	BPX	R$
17																																	
18																																	
19																																	
20																																	
21 PIT *	3	0	63	73	2.48	0.94	2.12		90	95	17.0	5%	31%	25%		13.0%	96.4	57	0	43	28%	76%	0%	18%	1	46	0%	0%			13.9	188	$7
1st Half	3	0	46	54	2.42	0.94	1.95				19.2	6%	31%	25%							29%	76%	0%		0	0					10.5	190	$9
2nd Half	0	0	17	18	2.67	0.95	2.58		85	97	13.1	5%	27%	23%		13.0%	96.4	57	0	43	28%	77%	0%	18%	1	46	0%	0%			3.4	190	-$6
Proj	**3**	**0**	**44**	**54**	**4.15**	**1.28**	**3.57**	**1.16**			**22.5**	**8%**	**30%**	**22%**				**45**	**18**	**37**	**35%**	**69%**	**10%**	**0%**	**8**						**1.6**	**162**	**-$2**

Coonrod,Sam

Age: 29	Th: R	Role: RP	Health: D	LIMA Plan: C	
Ht: 6' 1"	Wt: 225	Type: Pwr	PT/Exp: D	Rand Var: +2	
			Consist: C	MM: 3300	

Hard-thrower earned late-inning chances before late-May meltdowns, June IL stint (forearm tendinitis) knocked him out for a couple of months. Plus GB%, 2nd-half SwK intrigue; both K%, BB% are trending in the right direction and BPX, xWHIP, xERA say he deserved better. Historical H% and Consistency are red flags, but he's on our radar.

Yr Tm	W	Sv	IP	K	ERA	WHIP	xERA	xWHIP	vL+	vR+	BF/G	BB%	K%	K-BB%	xBB%	SwK	Vel	G	L	F	H%	S%	HR/F	xHR/F	GS	APC	DOM%	DIS%	Sv%	LI	RAR	BPX	R$
17 aa	4	0	104	77	6.47	1.62	4.99				19.2	10%	17%	7%							35%	58%									-27.0	62	-$13
18																																	
19 SF *	7	3	61	53	6.52	1.74	5.73	1.60	101	80	4.2	13%	19%	6%	11%	10.1%	96.5	50	15	35	35%	62%	12%	11%	0	14			38	0.67	-15.1	48	-$7
20 SF	0	3	15	15	9.82	1.64	5.10	1.41	159	93	3.9	10%	21%	11%	10%	11.1%	98.0	43	20	37	36%	36%	12%	10%	0	17			60	0.72	-9.7	80	-$10
21 PHI	2	2	42	48	4.04	1.32	3.48	1.22	97	91	4.4	8%	26%	18%	7%	11.5%	98.0	57	16	27	34%	73%	16%	18%	2	17	0%	0%	33	0.91	1.2	145	-$2
1st Half	1	2	28	30	4.18	1.29	3.77	1.25	96	93	4.5	8%	25%	17%	6%	10.5%	98.0	54	16	30	30%	74%	21%	20%	0	16			40	1.13	0.3	130	-$3
2nd Half	1	0	14	18	3.77	1.40	2.91	1.16	86	95	4.3	8%	28%	20%	7%	13.2%	98.1	64	15	21	40%	70%	0%	13%	2	18	0%	0%	0	0.51	0.9	177	-$9
Proj	**3**	**0**	**58**	**62**	**3.91**	**1.33**	**3.66**	**1.27**	**108**	**97**	**5.1**	**9%**	**26%**	**17%**	**6%**	**11.0%**	**98.0**	**54**	**16**	**30**	**32%**	**75%**	**18%**	**18%**	**0**						**3.9**	**128**	**-$1**

Corbin,Patrick

Age: 32	Th: L	Role: SP	Health: A	LIMA Plan: C	
Ht: 6' 3"	Wt: 210	Type:	PT/Exp: A	Rand Var: +5	
			Consist: A	MM: 2203	

Disaster followed 2020 disappointment, as thrashing from RHB continued unchecked. One-time frontliner led NL pitchers in HR allowed, BA against. K-BB% is trending poorly, S% didn't help. All overdone, and ERA should rebound with regression. GB%, 2nd-half velocity bump, Aug/Sept K% turnaround are all positives. But a lot here needs fixing.

Yr Tm	W	Sv	IP	K	ERA	WHIP	xERA	xWHIP	vL+	vR+	BF/G	BB%	K%	K-BB%	xBB%	SwK	Vel	G	L	F	H%	S%	HR/F	xHR/F	GS	APC	DOM%	DIS%	Sv%	LI	RAR	BPX	R$
17 ARI	14	0	190	178	4.03	1.42	4.06	1.29	86	112	25.0	7%	22%	14%	8%	11.5%	92.4	50	20	30	34%	76%	15%	14%	32	93	31%	28%	0	0.76	7.6	122	$8
18 ARI	11	0	200	246	3.15	1.05	2.81	1.06	95	81	24.2	6%	31%	25%	8%	16.2%	90.8	48	24	27	32%	72%	11%	16%	33	95	39%	0%			24.7	192	$25
19 WAS	14	0	202	238	3.25	1.18	3.65	1.22	67	94	25.3	8%	29%	20%	9%	14.7%	91.9	50	18	33	30%	77%	14%	19%	33	100	30%	27%			31.2	147	$24
20 WAS	2	0	66	60	4.66	1.57	4.56	1.26	101	116	26.8	6%	20%	14%	7%	11.1%	90.2	44	26	31	37%	74%	15%	17%	11	97	18%	45%			-1.7	117	-$6
21 WAS	9	0	172	143	5.82	1.47	4.51	1.35	85	122	24.2	8%	19%	11%	8%	11.6%	92.5	47	22	31	31%	66%	23%	23%	31	89	19%	48%			-32.9	82	-$13
1st Half	5	0	87	70	5.56	1.40	4.48	1.34	81	117	23.5	8%	19%	11%	8%	11.3%	91.7	47	23	31	30%	65%	20%	19%	16	86	19%	50%			-14.0	81	-$5
2nd Half	4	0	84	73	6.08	1.54	4.53	1.35	81	133	25.0	8%	20%	11%	8%	11.9%	93.3	47	21	31	32%	66%	25%	27%	15	92	20%	47%			-18.9	84	-$13
Proj	**9**	**0**	**167**	**158**	**4.60**	**1.41**	**4.11**	**1.28**	**87**	**113**	**24.4**	**8%**	**22%**	**15%**	**8%**	**12.4%**	**91.8**	**47**	**22**	**31**	**33%**	**73%**	**19%**	**21%**	**29**						**-3.1**	**114**	**-$1**

Cortes,Nestor

Age: 27	Th: L	Role: RP	Health: D	LIMA Plan: B+	
Ht: 5' 11"	Wt: 210	Type: Pwr/xFB	PT/Exp: D	Rand Var: -3	
			Consist: F	MM: 1203	

2-3, 2.90 ERA in 93 IP at NYY. Deceptive soft-tossing swingman delivered season no one expected, the final two months from the rotation. Had everything in his favor: H%, S%, HR/F, sudden command vR and a K-BB% for which history gave no warning. Obviously regression is coming, and GLF looks scary. But now at least a worthy end-gamer.

Yr Tm	W	Sv	IP	K	ERA	WHIP	xERA	xWHIP	vL+	vR+	BF/G	BB%	K%	K-BB%	xBB%	SwK	Vel	G	L	F	H%	S%	HR/F	xHR/F	GS	APC	DOM%	DIS%	Sv%	LI	RAR	BPX	R$
17 a/a	7	0	100	88	2.86	1.26	3.18				14.1	8%	22%	13%							31%	77%									18.5	115	$8
18 BAL *	6	0	122	87	4.91	1.43	5.18		196	183	18.5	9%	17%	8%	8%	10.2%	88.0	47	16	37	30%	70%	29%	19%	0	27			0	0.97	-11.5	39	-$6
19 NYY *	7	0	108	103	5.27	1.39	5.02	1.37	131	103	11.3	9%	23%	14%	8%	10.9%	89.6	34	22	44	31%	67%	18%	13%	1	39	0%	100%	0	0.72	-10.2	64	-$2
20 SEA	0	0	8	8	15.26	2.35	7.09	1.67	208	176	8.8	14%	19%	5%	12%	7.9%	88.1	37	19	44	31%	42%	50%	25%	1	33	0%	100%	0	0.51	-10.2	-7	-$15
21 NYY *	3	1	108	117	2.71	1.03	3.16	1.12	94	87	15.4	6%	28%	22%	7%	11.0%	90.7	27	21	51	27%	82%	11%	11%	14	69	21%	14%	100	0.64	20.7	139	$12
1st Half	0	0	18	25	1.02	1.08	3.24	1.18	72	65	10.0	11%	36%	24%	6%	13.5%	90.5	38	24	38	31%	89%	0%	7%	0	41			0	0.45	7.1	148	-$2
2nd Half	2	0	75	78	3.35	1.08	4.37	1.14	93	94	20.3	6%	26%	20%	8%	10.5%	90.8	25	21	54	27%	79%	13%	12%	14	82	21%	14%	0	0.73	8.6	128	$12
Proj	**5**	**0**	**131**	**132**	**4.02**	**1.27**	**4.46**	**1.27**	**114**	**94**	**14.2**	**8%**	**25%**	**17%**	**8%**	**11.4%**	**90.4**	**31**	**22**	**47**	**30%**	**75%**	**13%**	**11%**	**16**						**7.0**	**104**	**$4**

Cousins,Jake

Age: 27	Th: R	Role: RP	Health: B	LIMA Plan: B+	
Ht: 6' 4"	Wt: 185	Type: Pwr	PT/Exp: F	Rand Var: -2	
			Consist: F	MM: 4510	

2-4, 2.67 ERA in 50 IP at MIL. Just 19 dominant IP (30/5 K/BB) between AA, AAA fueled June MLB promotion—and he stuck. Sinking FB, nasty swing-and-miss slider combo earned high-leverage innings work despite 2nd-half control woes. Minor league track record says these are fixable. If that happens, SwK, K% say closer-in-waiting.

Yr Tm	W	Sv	IP	K	ERA	WHIP	xERA	xWHIP	vL+	vR+	BF/G	BB%	K%	K-BB%	xBB%	SwK	Vel	G	L	F	H%	S%	HR/F	xHR/F	GS	APC	DOM%	DIS%	Sv%	LI	RAR	BPX	R$
17																																	
18																																	
19																																	
20																																	
21 MIL *	2	4	50	68	2.67	1.09	2.45	1.22	77	78	4.2	12%	35%	22%	8%	17.6%	95.5	47	16	37	25%	80%	14%	17%	0	18			80	0.87	9.9	136	$5
1st Half	1	4	25	35	2.16	0.92	1.81		26	41	4.6	9%	38%	29%	8%	24.2%	96.6	75	0	25	26%	82%	0%	0%	0	23			80	0.37	6.4	180	$4
2nd Half	1	0	26	33	3.16	1.25	3.05	1.42	84	85	3.9	15%	31%	16%	8%	16.3%	95.3	45	17	38	25%	79%	15%	18%	0	17			0	0.95	3.5	110	-$4
Proj	**2**	**4**	**58**	**78**	**3.24**	**1.16**	**3.40**	**1.27**	**90**	**87**	**4.2**	**13%**	**34%**	**21%**	**8%**	**16.3%**	**95.3**	**45**	**17**	**38**	**27%**	**76%**	**14%**	**16%**	**0**						**8.7**	**134**	**$4**

Crismatt,Nabil

Age: 27	Th: R	Role: RP	Health: A	LIMA Plan: C	
Ht: 6' 1"	Wt: 220	Type: /GB	PT/Exp: D	Rand Var: -1	
			Consist: C	MM: 2101	

Rookie quickly became bullpen workhorse as injuries mounted. Logged 29 multi-IP appearances over 45 games despite ping-ponging between SD and AAA for most of the year. Historically strong GB%, BB% improved as season progressed. But unimpressive K%, velocity say role is unlikely to change. He's more valuable in the real game than in ours.

Yr Tm	W	Sv	IP	K	ERA	WHIP	xERA	xWHIP	vL+	vR+	BF/G	BB%	K%	K-BB%	xBB%	SwK	Vel	G	L	F	H%	S%	HR/F	xHR/F	GS	APC	DOM%	DIS%	Sv%	LI	RAR	BPX	R$
17																																	
18 a/a	11	0	146	120	5.01	1.51	4.99				23.5	9%	19%	10%							34%	68%									-15.6	70	-$7
19 a/a	4	0	133	134	5.67	1.39	5.37				20.8	6%	24%	18%							34%	63%									-19.2	90	-$6
20 STL	0	0	8	8	3.24	0.84	3.28	1.05	135	58	5.2	3%	26%	23%	5%	14.0%	89.5	50	18	32	21%	80%	29%	21%	0	19			0	0.19	1.2	174	-$4
21 SD	3	0	81	71	3.76	1.36	4.16	1.27	106	101	7.8	7%	20%	13%	8%	12.0%	89.9	51	17	33	33%	76%	13%	14%	0	30			0	0.51	5.0	108	-$2
1st Half	2	0	40	38	3.86	1.44	4.11	1.29	101	108	8.2	8%	22%	14%	9%	12.8%	89.4	47	21	32	35%	75%	11%	11%	0	29			0	0.49	2.0	104	-$4
2nd Half	1	0	42	33	3.67	1.30	4.22	1.26	100	98	7.4	6%	19%	13%	8%	11.5%	90.3	53	14	33	31%	77%	14%	17%	0	30			0	0.53	3.1	111	-$4
Proj	**3**	**0**	**73**	**64**	**4.02**	**1.37**	**4.17**	**1.28**	**106**	**102**	**10.2**	**7%**	**21%**	**14%**	**8%**	**11.9%**	**89.9**	**51**	**16**	**33**	**33%**	**75%**	**14%**	**14%**	**1**						**3.9**	**113**	**-$2**

JOCK THOMPSON

Crochet,Garrett

Age: 23	Th: L	Role RP	Health B	LIMA Plan B+	
Ht: 6' 6"	Wt: 218	Type Pwr	PT/Exp D	Rand Var -5	
			Consist D	MM 2400	

2020 1st-round pick developing out of MLB pen. 2nd half control gains came as early H% woes subsided; stuff, luck checked HR all season. Just 12 IL days (back) following 2020 flexor strain was more good news. Average SwK points to change-up, SP repertoire in-progress; delivery may keep him in the pen. Either way he seems likely to build on this.

Yr	Tm	W	Sv	IP	K	ERA	WHIP	xERA	xWHIP	vL+	vR+	BF/G	BB%	K%	K-BB%	xBB%	SwK	Vel	G	L	F	H%	S%	HR/F	xHR/F	GS	APC	DOM%	DIS%	Sv%	LI	RAR	BPX	R$
17																																		
18																																		
19																																		
20	CHW	0	0	6	8	0.00	0.50	2.24		40	46	4.4	0%	36%	36%		16.5%	100.2	62	0	38	25%	100%	0%	9%	0	17			0	0.57	3.3	289	-$
21	CHW	3	0	54	65	2.82	1.27	4.03	1.33	69	87	4.3	12%	29%	17%	10%	12.7%	96.7	40	22	38	31%	78%	4%	8%	0	17			0	1.00	9.7	100	$
1st Half		2	0	25	31	2.92	1.50	4.41	1.45	69	95	4.7	15%	28%	14%	12%	13.3%	96.8	39	26	34	34%	81%	5%	6%	0	19			0	1.20	4.1	70	-$
2nd Half		1	0	30	34	2.73	1.08	3.73	1.22	62	82	3.9	9%	29%	20%	8%	12.1%	96.6	41	18	41	29%	74%	3%	10%	0	16			0	0.84	5.6	126	-$
Proj		4	0	65	78	3.50	1.25	3.97	1.33	68	94	4.1	12%	29%	17%	10%	12.6%	96.7	40	21	38	30%	74%	9%	8%	0						7.7	107	$

Crowe,Wil

Age: 27	Th: R	Role SP	Health A	LIMA Plan D+	
Ht: 6' 2"	Wt: 228	Type Pwr	PT/Exp C	Rand Var +2	
			Consist F	MM 0103	

Soft-tossing rookie added some clicks to his fastball and SwK while eating some innings for a rebuilder; none of it was enough. Poor control continues to be a problem, glaringly so when paired with marginal K%. Modest GB% made no difference as HR were an issue and hitters from both sides banged him around at will. Just nothing to see here.

Yr	Tm	W	Sv	IP	K	ERA	WHIP	xERA	xWHIP	vL+	vR+	BF/G	BB%	K%	K-BB%	xBB%	SwK	Vel	G	L	F	H%	S%	HR/F	xHR/F	GS	APC	DOM%	DIS%	Sv%	LI	RAR	BPX	R$
17																																		
18	aa	0	0	27	12	7.53	1.97	7.44				26.0	12%	9%	-3%							33%	63%									-11.3	-18	-$1
19	a/a	7	0	150	106	6.33	1.60	5.74				25.5	8%	16%	8%							35%	61%									-33.8	44	-$1
20	WAS	0	0	8	8	11.88	2.64	8.30	1.88	238	149	15.3	17%	17%	0%	12%	6.2%	91.4	28	24	48	37%	65%	36%	35%	3	65	0%	100%			-7.6	-81	-$1
21	PIT	4	0	117	111	5.48	1.57	4.92	1.43	110	122	20.2	11%	21%	10%	11%	10.8%	93.6	43	19	38	32%	71%	19%	19%	25	84	16%	56%	0	0.76	-17.4	62	-$1
1st Half		1	0	50	46	6.26	1.61	4.95	1.46	98	129	19.2	11%	20%	9%	11%	9.2%	94.0	45	21	34	32%	66%	21%	21%	11	80	18%	64%	0	0.73	-12.4	55	-$1
2nd Half		3	0	66	65	4.88	1.54	4.90	1.42	108	121	21.0	11%	22%	11%	11%	12.1%	93.2	41	17	42	31%	75%	18%	18%	14	86	14%	50%			-5.1	67	-$
Proj		5	0	131	116	5.32	1.57	5.01	1.44	109	123	20.9	10%	20%	10%	11%	10.9%	93.5	43	19	39	33%	71%	16%	19%	27						-13.9	63	-$1

Cueto,Johnny

Age: 36	Th: R	Role SP	Health F	LIMA Plan B+	
Ht: 5' 11"	Wt: 229	Type	PT/Exp B	Rand Var 0	
			Consist A	MM 1101	

Not the same since 2017 arm woes segued into 2018 Tommy John surgery. Held his own early until barking elbow IL'd him twice for almost 7 weeks in Aug/Sept. BB% looked vintage, but K% and trend vR are stagnant, DOM%/DIS% mediocre. Still has his bag of tricks and off-season rest might help. But ongoing injuries, age suggest otherwise.

Yr	Tm	W	Sv	IP	K	ERA	WHIP	xERA	xWHIP	vL+	vR+	BF/G	BB%	K%	K-BB%	xBB%	SwK	Vel	G	L	F	H%	S%	HR/F	xHR/F	GS	APC	DOM%	DIS%	Sv%	LI	RAR	BPX	R$
17	SF	8	0	147	136	4.52	1.45	4.53	1.35	110	107	25.9	8%	21%	13%	8%	11.1%	91.3	39	25	36	33%	73%	14%	15%	25	101	20%	40%			-2.9	95	$
18	SF	3	0	53	38	3.23	1.11	4.21	1.29	96	98	23.8	6%	18%	12%	9%	9.6%	89.4	44	19	37	25%	78%	14%	18%	9	88	33%	56%			6.0	90	$
19	SF	1	0	16	13	5.06	1.25	4.92	1.63	149	60	16.8	14%	20%	6%	11%	7.9%	91.3	53	16	30	20%	65%	23%	26%	4	66	0%	25%			-1.1	28	-$
20	SF	2	0	63	56	5.40	1.37	4.88	1.40	110	93	23.1	9%	20%	11%	9%	8.6%	91.3	41	25	34	30%	63%	14%	14%	12	95	17%	50%			-7.4	71	-$
21	SF	7	0	115	98	4.08	1.37	4.45	1.25	112	105	22.3	6%	20%	14%	7%	10.5%	91.8	38	26	36	33%	74%	12%	16%	21	85	14%	33%	0	0.77	2.6	100	$
1st Half		6	0	72	58	4.00	1.31	4.32	1.21	115	99	23.4	5%	19%	15%	8%	10.4%	91.9	39	26	35	33%	74%	13%	15%	13	89	23%	38%			2.4	110	$
2nd Half		1	0	43	40	4.22	1.48	4.67	1.33	93	122	20.7	9%	22%	13%	6%	10.6%	91.6	36	26	38	34%	74%	10%	17%	8	80	0%	25%	0	0.76	0.2	82	-$
Proj		5	0	102	87	4.24	1.35	4.52	1.32	106	103	22.1	8%	21%	13%	8%	10.0%	91.1	39	24	36	31%	72%	13%	16%	19						2.6	89	-$

Darvish,Yu

Age: 35	Th: R	Role SP	Health F	LIMA Plan B	
Ht: 6' 5"	Wt: 220	Type Pwr	PT/Exp A	Rand Var 0	
			Consist B	MM 4403	

Began 2021 (and 2nd half) in ace territory, ended it as a question mark. Clearly hip/back issues that shelved him in July/Aug contributed to velocity and near across-the-board 2nd half peripheral sags. HR, S% crushed him after June too, though xERA, BPX say this was overdone. Health is still firmly an issue and he's not getting any younger.

Yr	Tm	W	Sv	IP	K	ERA	WHIP	xERA	xWHIP	vL+	vR+	BF/G	BB%	K%	K-BB%	xBB%	SwK	Vel	G	L	F	H%	S%	HR/F	xHR/F	GS	APC	DOM%	DIS%	Sv%	LI	RAR	BPX	R$
17	2 TM	10	0	187	209	3.86	1.16	3.70	1.20	103	81	24.7	8%	27%	20%	7%	12.6%	94.2	41	22	37	29%	72%	15%	11%	31	99	35%	26%			11.5	150	$1
18	CHC	1	0	40	49	4.95	1.43	4.15	1.35	115	97	22.5	12%	27%	16%	10%	11.2%	93.9	38	23	40	31%	70%	18%	18%	8	93	13%	50%			-3.9	100	-$
19	CHC	6	0	179	229	3.98	1.10	3.36	1.14	101	83	23.6	8%	31%	24%	6%	14.0%	94.2	45	21	34	28%	72%	23%	19%	31	92	32%	16%			11.6	168	$1
20	CHC	8	0	76	93	2.01	0.96	3.02	1.01	84	70	24.8	5%	31%	27%	5%	15.0%	95.5	43	26	31	31%	82%	9%	11%	12	96	58%	0%			22.9	197	$4
21	SD	8	0	166	199	4.22	1.09	3.74	1.10	99	93	22.7	6%	29%	23%	6%	12.4%	94.5	37	18	45	29%	68%	15%	14%	30	92	33%	20%			0.9	159	$1
1st Half		7	0	102	123	2.65	0.95	3.59	1.06	78	88	23.6	6%	31%	25%	6%	13.0%	94.9	34	18	49	27%	79%	10%	9%	17	94	41%	6%			20.4	165	$3
2nd Half		1	0	64	76	6.72	1.32	3.98	1.16	119	103	21.5	7%	27%	20%	7%	11.5%	94.1	41	18	41	32%	54%	22%	22%	13	90	23%	38%			-19.4	148	-$1
Proj		9	0	160	193	3.95	1.10	3.42	1.10	99	86	21.8	7%	31%	24%	6%	12.8%	94.5	40	21	39	30%	70%	16%	16%	29						9.9	168	$1

Davies,Zachary

Age: 29	Th: R	Role SP	Health C	LIMA Plan D+	
Ht: 6' 0"	Wt: 180	Type	PT/Exp A	Rand Var +1	
			Consist C	MM 0003	

Almost predictably, short-season magic dissipated along with K% spike and fortunate H%/S%. Soaring BB% didn't help, but mostly deserved, per xBB%. Mediocre skills occasionally tempered by H% were laid bare in 2nd half, as GB% tilt vanished and HR began to fly. Health, R$ history are more reminders that you're always rolling the dice here.

Yr	Tm	W	Sv	IP	K	ERA	WHIP	xERA	xWHIP	vL+	vR+	BF/G	BB%	K%	K-BB%	xBB%	SwK	Vel	G	L	F	H%	S%	HR/F	xHR/F	GS	APC	DOM%	DIS%	Sv%	LI	RAR	BPX	R$
17	MIL	17	0	191	124	3.90	1.35	4.48	1.39	104	98	24.8	7%	15%	9%	9%	7.8%	89.7	50	23	27	31%	74%	12%	11%	33	94	12%	48%			10.7	76	$1
18	MIL *	3	0	94	70	5.35	1.43	4.46	1.45	107	105	20.0	10%	18%	8%	9%	8.5%	89.9	48	22	30	31%	63%	13%	13%	13	86	8%	38%			-13.9	62	-$
19	MIL	10	0	160	102	3.55	1.29	5.30	1.46	99	95	21.7	8%	15%	8%	10%	7.4%	88.5	40	24	36	28%	77%	11%	13%	31	86	6%	32%			18.8	48	$
20	SD	7	0	69	63	2.73	1.07	4.20	1.25	70	99	23.0	7%	23%	16%	10%	10.4%	88.6	41	22	37	26%	82%	13%	19%	12	88	42%	17%			14.8	113	$2
21	CHC	6	0	148	114	5.78	1.60	5.26	1.53	114	116	20.9	11%	17%	6%	11%	9.2%	88.0	42	25	32	31%	67%	17%	19%	32	81	3%	56%			-27.6	24	-$1
1st Half		5	0	83	55	4.32	1.43	5.30	1.62	90	99	21.4	12%	15%	3%	10%	9.2%	87.8	46	23	31	28%	70%	8%	16%	17	80	6%	53%			-0.6	3	-$
2nd Half		1	0	65	59	7.65	1.82	5.21	1.44	127	143	20.3	10%	20%	9%	11%	9.2%	88.3	38	27	34	36%	64%	27%	23%	15	81	0%	60%			-27.0	52	-$2
Proj		8	0	160	126	4.80	1.45	4.87	1.44	105	112	20.9	10%	18%	9%	10%	9.0%	88.5	42	24	34	30%	71%	16%	18%	33						-6.8	56	-$

De Geus,Brett

Age: 24	Th: R	Role RP	Health A	LIMA Plan D	
Ht: 6' 1"	Wt: 190	Type /GB	PT/Exp F	Rand Var +5	
			Consist F	MM 0000	

Rule 5 pick with zero high-minors IP waived by TEX in June, didn't do any better in ARI afterward. GB tilt followed him from the minors and he maintained average velocity. But unsurprisingly plus command (36/7 K/BB over 31 A+ IP in 2019) lagged behind, as MLB hitters had their way. Needs more minor league experience, seems likely to get it in 2022.

Yr	Tm	W	Sv	IP	K	ERA	WHIP	xERA	xWHIP	vL+	vR+	BF/G	BB%	K%	K-BB%	xBB%	SwK	Vel	G	L	F	H%	S%	HR/F	xHR/F	GS	APC	DOM%	DIS%	Sv%	LI	RAR	BPX	R$
17																																		
18																																		
19																																		
20																																		
21	2 TM	3	0	50	41	7.56	1.74	4.81	1.49	153	98	5.1	11%	17%	7%	10%	7.2%	93.8	52	24	24	36%	56%	15%	18%	0	19			0	0.73	-20.3	45	-$1
1st Half		0	0	30	28	8.01	1.58	3.99	1.38	125	107	6.1	9%	20%	11%	10%	8.0%	93.9	55	25	20	35%	48%	22%	18%	0	23			0	0.51	-14.0	87	-$1
2nd Half		3	0	20	13	6.86	1.98	6.15	1.66	170	89	4.1	12%	13%	1%	11%	6.2%	93.7	48	23	30	37%	65%	10%	17%	0	16			0	0.93	-6.3	-17	-$1
Proj		3	0	29	22	5.46	1.65	5.07	1.58	147	87	4.3	12%	17%	5%	11%	6.9%	93.8	51	24	26	33%	68%	14%	17%	0						-3.6	25	-$

deGrom,Jacob

Age: 34	Th: R	Role SP	Health F	LIMA Plan C+	
Ht: 6' 4"	Wt: 180	Type Pwr	PT/Exp A	Rand Var -5	
			Consist B	MM 5503	

Imagine! $28 earnings for half season of work. Physical woes began in May as lat inflammation shelved him for 14 days. Balky forearm limited starts in June. Tossed final game in early July, landing on 60 day IL. Through it all, skills, velocity remained pristine. Prudence says to wait on off-season news; suddenly he's the ultimate risk/reward proposition.

Yr	Tm	W	Sv	IP	K	ERA	WHIP	xERA	xWHIP	vL+	vR+	BF/G	BB%	K%	K-BB%	xBB%	SwK	Vel	G	L	F	H%	S%	HR/F	xHR/F	GS	APC	DOM%	DIS%	Sv%	LI	RAR	BPX	R$
17	NYM	15	0	201	239	3.53	1.19	3.40	1.15	92	91	26.7	7%	29%	22%	6%	14.0%	95.2	45	21	34	32%	76%	16%	12%	31	102	48%	23%			20.5	173	$2
18	NYM	10	0	217	269	1.70	0.91	2.75	1.01	79	64	26.1	6%	32%	27%	5%	15.9%	96.0	46	22	32	29%	84%	6%	9%	32	100	75%	0%			65.6	200	$4
19	NYM	11	0	204	255	2.43	0.97	3.18	1.05	82	74	25.1	6%	32%	26%	6%	16.1%	96.9	44	21	35	30%	80%	11%	10%	32	103	66%	13%			52.3	187	$3
20	NYM	4	0	68	104	2.38	0.96	2.77	0.96	85	68	22.3	7%	39%	32%	6%	22.0%	98.6	42	21	37	31%	81%	13%	16%	12	95	50%	8%			17.4	230	$3
21	NYM	7	0	92	146	1.08	0.55	2.00	0.74	61	49	21.6	3%	45%	42%	4%	22.4%	99.3	44	17	39	23%	89%	9%	13%	15	82	80%	0%			36.2	274	$2
1st Half		7	0	85	136	0.95	0.55	2.02	0.75	58	46	21.4	4%	45%	42%	4%	22.6%	99.3	43	18	39	24%	88%	7%	10%	14	82	79%	0%			34.7	273	$4
2nd Half		0	0	7	10	2.57	0.57	1.73		60	94	24.0	0%	42%	42%	4%	20.0%	98.9	57	14	29	17%	100%	50%	49%	1	85	100%	0%			1.5	293	-$
Proj		10	0	145	198	2.87	0.99	2.82	0.99	88	73	23.7	6%	36%	30%	5%	18.9%	97.6	44	20	36	31%	74%	11%	11%	23						28.3	210	$2

JOCK THOMPSON

DeSclafani,Anthony

Age:	32	Th:	R	Role	SP	Health	F	LIMA Plan	D+
Ht:	6' 1"	Wt:	200	Type		PT/Exp	A	Rand Var	-2
						Consist	D	MM	1103

Built fast 1st-half start on improved health, fortunate H% with all of his metrics near career bests. Spent most of August on the IL (shoulder, ankle), but finished strong with uptick in walk-and-HR evasion. Peaked with career year as free agent-to-be; we should all be so lucky. Health, Consistency, x-stats say he won't be again; regression will bite.

Yr	Tm	W	Sv	IP	K	ERA	WHIP	xERA	xWHIP	vL+	vR+	BF/G	BB%	K%	K-BB%	xBB%	SwK	Vel	G	L	F	H%	S%	HR/F	xHR/F	GS	APC	DOM%	DIS%	Sv%	LI	RAR	BPX	R$
17																																		
18	CIN *	7	0	135	125	5.15	1.32	5.42	1.21	125	94	22.4	6%	22%	16%	7%	10.2%	93.6	41	22	36	31%	69%	20%	15%	21	85	14%	24%			-16.6	76	-$3
19	CIN	9	0	167	167	3.89	1.20	4.30	1.26	105	85	22.5	7%	24%	17%	8%	10.4%	94.7	43	19	38	29%	75%	16%	13%	31	86	23%	26%			12.7	122	$12
20	CIN	1	0	34	25	7.22	1.69	5.81	1.53	136	106	17.6	10%	16%	6%	12%	9.8%	94.9	39	27	35	33%	60%	18%	20%	7	67	14%	43%	0	0.71	-11.5	25	-$15
21	SF	13	0	168	152	3.17	1.09	4.00	1.21	96	77	21.8	6%	22%	16%	7%	11.5%	94.1	44	19	36	28%	76%	11%	16%	31	83	26%	23%			22.7	118	$21
1st Half		8	0	93	86	2.91	1.03	3.96	1.23	93	65	23.0	7%	23%	16%	8%	11.7%	94.1	46	17	37	25%	77%	12%	15%	16	86	31%	25%			15.5	116	$23
2nd Half		5	0	75	66	3.48	1.17	4.06	1.19	88	95	20.5	5%	21%	16%	6%	11.3%	94.1	43	22	35	31%	74%	10%	18%	15	78	20%	20%			7.3	122	$12
Proj		**9**	**0**	**160**	**142**	**4.08**	**1.27**	**4.26**	**1.28**	**111**	**88**	**20.1**	**7%**	**22%**	**14%**	**8%**	**10.8%**	**94.3**	**42**	**21**	**36**	**30%**	**73%**	**15%**	**16%**	**32**						**7.4**	**105**	**$7**

Detmers,Reid

Age:	22	Th:	L	Role	RP	Health	C	LIMA Plan	A
Ht:	6' 2"	Wt:	210	Type	Pwr/FB	PT/Exp	F	Rand Var	+2
						Consist	F	MM	3503

1-3, 7.40 ERA in 21 IP at LAA. 2020 1st-round pick and command-first arm with stuff uptick at AA/AAA (108/19 K/BB, 3.19 ERA over 62 IP). Success didn't follow on to August MLB debut, where hitters were tougher. COVID bout essentially ended his season. Limiting HR damage will be critical, but killer breaking stuff, age give him time. He's close.

Yr	Tm	W	Sv	IP	K	ERA	WHIP	xERA	xWHIP	vL+	vR+	BF/G	BB%	K%	K-BB%	xBB%	SwK	Vel	G	L	F	H%	S%	HR/F	xHR/F	GS	APC	DOM%	DIS%	Sv%	LI	RAR	BPX	R$
17																																		
18																																		
19																																		
20																																		
21	LAA *	4	0	83	114	4.14	1.29	4.50	1.09	134	120	17.9	8%	34%	25%	8%	11.6%	92.9	34	21	46	35%	74%	16%	17%	5	76	0%	80%			1.3	132	$1
1st Half		2	0	46	74	4.27	1.30	4.89				18.9	8%	39%	31%							38%	76%	0%		0	0					0.0	143	$0
2nd Half		2	0	37	40	4.64	1.39	4.80	1.24	127	123	17.2	8%	26%	17%	8%	11.6%	92.9	34	21	46	34%	70%	16%	17%	5	76	0%	80%			-1.7	98	-$6
Proj		**7**	**0**	**131**	**169**	**4.52**	**1.35**	**3.76**	**1.16**	**119**	**107**	**19.7**	**8%**	**31%**	**23%**	**8%**	**11.6%**	**92.9**	**34**	**21**	**46**	**34%**	**74%**	**19%**	**15%**	**27**						**-1.1**	**155**	**$1**

Diaz,Edwin

Age:	28	Th:	R	Role	RP	Health	A	LIMA Plan	C+
Ht:	6' 3"	Wt:	223	Type	Pwr/FB	PT/Exp	B	Rand Var	-2
						Consist	B	MM	5530

Top-shelf skills still minimize the ratio inconsistencies. SwK, K% took dives, still finished firmly in elite territory as short-season BB% concerns moderated. Gyrating H% landed in his favor as unfortunate S% took a chunk out of 2nd-half ERA. Owned hitters from both sides again, per usual. Buy Ks, saves, and you're unlikely to be disappointed.

Yr	Tm	W	Sv	IP	K	ERA	WHIP	xERA	xWHIP	vL+	vR+	BF/G	BB%	K%	K-BB%	xBB%	SwK	Vel	G	L	F	H%	S%	HR/F	xHR/F	GS	APC	DOM%	DIS%	Sv%	LI	RAR	BPX	R$
17	SEA	4	34	66	89	3.27	1.15	3.83	1.27	87	80	4.2	12%	32%	21%	8%	16.8%	97.3	39	15	46	26%	79%	14%	8%	0	17			87	1.64	8.8	141	$20
18	SEA	0	57	73	124	1.96	0.79	2.01	0.83	61	68	3.8	6%	44%	38%	6%	19.7%	97.3	44	20	35	30%	79%	11%	9%	0	16			93	1.40	19.8	276	$36
19	NYM	2	26	58	99	5.59	1.38	3.19	1.04	91	124	3.8	9%	39%	30%	6%	18.5%	97.5	37	20	44	40%	68%	27%	14%	0	16			79	1.18	-7.7	217	$8
20	NYM	2	6	26	50	1.75	1.25	2.45	1.06	85	75	4.2	13%	45%	33%	9%	21.5%	97.8	43	23	34	42%	90%	13%	9%	0	19			67	1.22	8.5	230	$15
21	NYM	5	32	63	89	3.45	1.05	3.24	1.09	76	81	4.1	9%	35%	26%	7%	16.7%	98.8	34	23	43	31%	67%	5%	7%	0	16			84	1.35	6.3	168	$19
1st Half		2	17	32	41	2.84	1.01	3.19	1.09	68	74	3.9	8%	33%	25%	6%	16.1%	99.2	35	26	39	31%	69%	0%	9%	0	16			94	1.31	5.6	160	$13
2nd Half		3	15	31	48	4.06	1.10	3.28	1.10	76	92	4.3	10%	36%	26%	8%	17.4%	98.5	33	19	48	31%	65%	10%	6%	0	16			75	1.39	0.8	176	$16
Proj		**4**	**30**	**65**	**94**	**3.35**	**1.08**	**3.15**	**1.07**	**78**	**89**	**3.8**	**9%**	**37%**	**28%**	**7%**	**17.8%**	**98.1**	**37**	**20**	**43**	**31%**	**73%**	**12%**	**9%**	**0**						**8.9**	**184**	**$18**

Diekman,Jake

Age:	35	Th:	L	Role	RP	Health	B	LIMA Plan	B+
Ht:	6' 4"	Wt:	195	Type	Pwr	PT/Exp	C	Rand Var	0
						Consist	C	MM	2510

Extreme 2020 dominance vR vanished with H%, S% regression. Ability to handle hitters from both sides, elite K% remain foundational skills keeping him in late-inning work, but entrenched control woes keep ratios in flux. And now missing GB% has made HR an issue. FA has marginal saves potential if opportunity returns, but only in the right pen.

Yr	Tm	W	Sv	IP	K	ERA	WHIP	xERA	xWHIP	vL+	vR+	BF/G	BB%	K%	K-BB%	xBB%	SwK	Vel	G	L	F	H%	S%	HR/F	xHR/F	GS	APC	DOM%	DIS%	Sv%	LI	RAR	BPX	R$
17	TEX	0	1	11	13	2.53	1.31	4.36	1.82	62	76	4.1	22%	29%	7%		12.2%	94.7	59	14	27	15%	85%	17%	17%	0	17			100	1.10	2.4	8	-$3
18	2 TM	1	2	53	66	4.73	1.50	3.94	1.39	120	87	3.4	13%	27%	14%	11%	11.8%	95.0	48	20	32	35%	68%	9%	12%	0	14			67	1.07	-3.8	98	-$5
19	2 AL	1	0	61	81	4.72	1.44	3.98	1.44	88	91	3.7	14%	29%	15%	8%	15.7%	95.8	47	27	26	34%	66%	8%	9%	0	16			0	1.16	-1.6	92	-$4
20	OAK	2	0	21	31	0.42	0.94	2.99	1.27	90	34	4.0	14%	37%	23%	7%	17.8%	95.1	62	3	36	19%	100%	7%	14%	0	17			0	1.25	10.6	157	$9
21	OAK	3	7	61	83	3.86	1.34	4.03	1.32	99	95	3.9	13%	32%	19%	10%	14.1%	95.4	35	21	44	30%	77%	16%	18%	0	17			50	1.03	3.1	108	$2
1st Half		2	6	34	45	3.21	1.28	4.09	1.28	106	88	4.0	12%	31%	19%	9%	14.5%	95.2	33	20	47	29%	84%	16%	17%	0	17			60	1.19	4.4	115	$4
2nd Half		1	1	27	38	4.67	1.41	3.95	1.37	78	107	3.8	15%	32%	18%	11%	13.5%	95.7	37	22	41	31%	71%	17%	21%	0	16			25	0.85	-1.3	99	-$7
Proj		**2**	**7**	**58**	**78**	**4.01**	**1.37**	**3.93**	**1.37**	**96**	**91**	**3.5**	**14%**	**32%**	**18%**	**10%**	**13.8%**	**95.4**	**40**	**22**	**38**	**31%**	**74%**	**14%**	**16%**	**0**						**3.1**	**104**	**$1**

Dobnak,Randy

Age:	27	Th:	R	Role	RP	Health	F	LIMA Plan	D+
Ht:	6' 1"	Wt:	230	Type	Con/xGB	PT/Exp	C	Rand Var	+5
						Consist	C	MM	1001

1-7, 7.64 ERA in 51 IP at MIN. Spring training flash (19/0 K/BB in 15 IP) vanished as xGBer struggled in long relief early, then as SP. Strained finger sent him to IL in June and again in September following lone 2nd-half start. Abysmal K%, marginal BB% are trending poorly, and suddenly he's coughing up HR. Not this awful, but can be safely ignored for now.

Yr	Tm	W	Sv	IP	K	ERA	WHIP	xERA	xWHIP	vL+	vR+	BF/G	BB%	K%	K-BB%	xBB%	SwK	Vel	G	L	F	H%	S%	HR/F	xHR/F	GS	APC	DOM%	DIS%	Sv%	LI	RAR	BPX	R$
17																																		
18																																		
19	MIN *	11	1	143	100	2.93	1.16	3.17	1.30	54	105	19.6	5%	18%	12%	5%	13.8%	92.7	53	25	22	29%	76%	5%	11%	5	47	20%	40%	100	0.50	27.7	103	$16
20	MIN	6	0	47	27	4.05	1.35	4.34	1.39	108	85	20.0	7%	14%	7%	8%	9.4%	91.6	62	17	21	31%	70%	9%	12%	10	75	0%	20%			2.3	75	$7
21	MIN *	1	1	69	37	6.65	1.57	6.06	1.46	132	114	16.7	8%	12%	5%	8%	7.8%	91.7	55	23	22	32%	59%	27%	31%	6	55	0%	50%	100	0.87	-20.2	16	-$14
1st Half		1	1	58	34	6.92	1.57	6.40	1.43	134	122	15.9	7%	13%	6%	8%	8.3%	91.7	54	23	23	32%	58%	30%	33%	5	52	0%	60%	100	0.86	-18.9	13	-$17
2nd Half		0	0	13	4	4.28	1.26	2.96		90	45	27.0	7%	7%	0%	11%	4.6%	91.4	65	19	15	26%	62%	0%	20%	1	88	0%	0%			0.0	41	-$11
Proj		**5**	**0**	**102**	**62**	**4.85**	**1.40**	**4.38**	**1.39**	**111**	**95**	**17.6**	**7%**	**15%**	**8%**	**8%**	**8.7%**	**91.7**	**57**	**21**	**22**	**31%**	**67%**	**16%**	**24%**	**19**						**-4.9**	**74**	**-$5**

Doval,Camilo

Age:	24	Th:	R	Role	RP	Health	A	LIMA Plan	C+
Ht:	6' 2"	Wt:	180	Type	Pwr	PT/Exp	F	Rand Var	+2
						Consist	F	MM	4521

5-1, 3.00 ERA with 3 Sv in 27 IP at SF. Inexperienced flamethrower hit turbulence in both his MLB and high minors debuts in the 1st half. Things began clicking in August, MLB promotion yielded 16 scoreless IP, 24/3 K/BB and closer work in late September. Control still a work in progress, but K%, GB% say he has all of the ninth inning necessities. UP: 25 Sv

Yr	Tm	W	Sv	IP	K	ERA	WHIP	xERA	xWHIP	vL+	vR+	BF/G	BB%	K%	K-BB%	xBB%	SwK	Vel	G	L	F	H%	S%	HR/F	xHR/F	GS	APC	DOM%	DIS%	Sv%	LI	RAR	BPX	R$
17																																		
18																																		
19																																		
20																																		
21	SF *	8	4	59	73	3.93	1.35	3.79	1.33	104	65	4.3	13%	30%	17%	7%	14.4%	98.7	48	19	32	31%	73%	20%	18%	0	16			50	1.02	2.4	107	$3
1st Half		2	0	23	26	7.12	1.72	6.64	1.51	152	101	4.0	14%	25%	11%	12%	10.6%	98.3	50	13	37	32%	63%	36%	25%	0	17			0	1.06	-8.0	37	-$11
2nd Half		6	4	37	47	1.95	1.12	2.02	1.22	56	40	4.6	11%	33%	22%	4%	17.9%	99.1	47	25	28	30%	82%	0%	10%	0	15			100	0.98	10.4	156	$14
Proj		**6**	**18**	**73**	**93**	**3.79**	**1.26**	**3.37**	**1.27**	**115**	**83**	**4.2**	**12%**	**31%**	**20%**	**4%**	**17.9%**	**99.1**	**48**	**22**	**30**	**32%**	**71%**	**13%**	**9%**	**0**						**5.9**	**136**	**$11**

Duffey,Tyler

Age:	31	Th:	R	Role	RP	Health	A	LIMA Plan	B+
Ht:	6' 3"	Wt:	220	Type	Pwr	PT/Exp	D	Rand Var	-3
						Consist	B	MM	3310

Seemingly established back-of-the-pen arm and speculative saves candidate took a step backward. Lost GB% tilt from short-season; H%, S% normalization also factored in. But ballooning BB% / plummeting SwK combo was front and center as LHB began to solve him again—and now future HR regression looms. Use 2nd half xERA as your baseline.

Yr	Tm	W	Sv	IP	K	ERA	WHIP	xERA	xWHIP	vL+	vR+	BF/G	BB%	K%	K-BB%	xBB%	SwK	Vel	G	L	F	H%	S%	HR/F	xHR/F	GS	APC	DOM%	DIS%	Sv%	LI	RAR	BPX	R$
17	MIN	2	1	71	67	4.94	1.37	4.02	1.23	99	96	5.5	6%	22%	16%	6%	11.4%	92.1	50	19	31	34%	66%	13%	19%	0	20			33	1.00	-5.1	143	-$3
18	MIN *	6	3	84	65	5.39	1.44	5.25	1.36	126	101	7.2	8%	18%	10%	7%	10.5%	93.0	34	28	38	32%	66%	19%	25%	1	22	0%	100%	38	0.99	-12.9	54	-$5
19	MIN *	5	1	73	98	2.34	1.03	2.69	1.06	77	80	4.3	7%	35%	28%	6%	16.0%	94.0	38	25	37	30%	84%	16%	15%	0	17			33	0.97	19.5	173	$10
20	MIN	1	0	24	31	1.88	0.79	2.53	1.03	65	67	4.2	7%	34%	27%	6%	16.8%	92.6	56	22	22	23%	82%	17%	14%	0	17			0	1.28	7.6	206	$7
21	MIN	3	3	62	61	3.18	1.22	4.11	1.38	109	71	4.0	11%	24%	13%	9%	9.7%	92.5	46	21	34	28%	75%	7%	13%	0	16			60	1.06	8.4	81	$3
1st Half		0	2	31	28	3.45	1.31	4.50	1.52	98	73	3.9	13%	22%	8%	11%	9.1%	92.4	46	24	30	27%	74%	8%	11%	0	16			67	1.10	3.2	40	-$4
2nd Half		3	1	31	33	2.90	1.13	3.76	1.24	109	71	4.0	9%	27%	18%	8%	10.2%	92.7	46	17	37	29%	76%	7%	15%	0	17			50	1.02	5.2	121	$2
Proj		**4**	**8**	**65**	**71**	**3.60**	**1.17**	**3.72**	**1.24**	**99**	**76**	**4.5**	**9%**	**27%**	**18%**	**8%**	**11.3%**	**92.7**	**45**	**21**	**34**	**29%**	**72%**	**11%**	**15%**	**0**						**6.9**	**128**	**$6**

JOCK THOMPSON

Duffy,Danny

Duffy,Danny			Health	F	LIMA Plan	B+
Age: 33	Th: L	Role SP	PT/Exp	B	Rand Var	-5
Ht: 6' 3"	Wt: 185	Type Pwr/FB	Consist	A	MM	1200

Thrived with velocity uptick, improved change-up until flexor strain sent him to the IL in mid-May, then again for good in late July. SwK, K% at the top of his range helped him outpitch his xERA, as did S%, HR avoidance. But history of arm injuries say this is as good as it gets. More elbow surgery may be on the table.

Yr Tm	W	Sv	IP	K	ERA	WHIP	xERA	xWHIP	vL+	vR+	BF/G	BB%	K%	K-BB%	xBB%	SwK	Vel	G	L	F	H%	S%	HR/F	xHR/F	GS	APC	DOM%	DIS%	Sv%	LI	RAR	BPX	R
17 KC	9	0	146	130	3.81	1.26	4.38	1.28	60	104	25.4	7%	22%	15%	6%	12.1%	92.8	39	20	41	32%	71%	8%	10%	24	95	38%	25%			9.8	111	$
18 KC	8	0	155	141	4.88	1.49	5.01	1.42	90	110	24.7	10%	20%	10%	9%	10.1%	93.1	35	22	43	32%	71%	11%	14%	28	99	11%	39%			-13.9	58	-$
19 KC	7	0	131	115	4.34	1.31	4.99	1.38	104	101	24.1	8%	21%	12%	8%	10.7%	92.4	36	22	42	29%	72%	13%	15%	23	94	13%	30%			2.7	77	$
20 KC	4	0	56	57	4.95	1.33	4.93	1.33	80	105	20.2	9%	24%	15%	8%	11.0%	92.2	32	23	46	30%	68%	14%	14%	11	79	9%	27%	0	0.78	-3.5	89	$
21 KC	4	0	61	65	2.51	1.21	4.33	1.26	94	85	19.4	9%	26%	17%	8%	13.9%	93.7	33	22	44	30%	84%	8%	12%	12	78	17%	17%	0	0.74	13.2	105	$
1st Half	4	0	52	57	2.60	1.23	4.29	1.23	59	96	19.7	8%	26%	18%	8%	14.5%	93.9	32	23	44	31%	83%	8%	13%	10	80	20%	20%	0	0.74	10.7	114	$
2nd Half	0	0	9	8	2.00	1.11	4.53	1.43	361	34	17.5	11%	23%	11%	8%	9.9%	92.6	39	17	43	22%	89%	10%	9%	2	66	0%	0%			2.5	58	-$
Proj	**4**	**0**	**58**	**57**	**3.99**	**1.32**	**4.56**	**1.32**	**81**	**101**	**21.4**	**9%**	**24%**	**15%**	**8%**	**11.9%**	**93.0**	**34**	**22**	**43**	**31%**	**74%**	**11%**	**13%**	**11**						**3.3**	**92**	**-$**

Dunn,Justin

Dunn,Justin			Health	F	LIMA Plan	D+
Age: 26	Th: R	Role SP	PT/Exp	C	Rand Var	-5
Ht: 6' 2"	Wt: 185	Type Pwr/xFB	Consist	B	MM	0200

Stuff-first project seemed to be figuring some things out in May (25 IP, 2.52 ERA, 28% K). But June shoulder strain intervened and (stop us if you've heard this) ended his season early. SwK, velocity jumped; BB% still a problem though xBB% is hopeful. Ominous FB% tilt offset a tad by dominance vR. Health is mandatory before we're interested again.

Yr Tm	W	Sv	IP	K	ERA	WHIP	xERA	xWHIP	vL+	vR+	BF/G	BB%	K%	K-BB%	xBB%	SwK	Vel	G	L	F	H%	S%	HR/F	xHR/F	GS	APC	DOM%	DIS%	Sv%	LI	RAR	BPX	R
17																																	
18 aa	6	0	91	92	4.67	1.45	4.33				26.0	10%	24%	14%							35%	68%									-5.8	99	-$
19 SEA *	9	0	140	143	5.22	1.50	5.12	1.35	88	40	20.9	9%	24%	15%	12%	6.6%	92.5	44	6	50	35%	67%	0%	3%	4	34	0%	0%			-12.3	80	-$
20 SEA	4	0	46	38	4.34	1.36	6.17	1.73	113	85	19.8	16%	19%	4%	11%	8.6%	91.2	32	20	47	19%	77%	17%	15%	10	80	10%	60%			0.7	-23	$
21 SEA	1	0	50	49	3.75	1.31	5.32	1.52	102	74	19.8	13%	22%	9%	8%	10.2%	93.7	34	15	51	25%	75%	9%	14%	11	79	9%	18%			3.2	33	-$
1st Half	1	0	50	49	3.75	1.31	5.32	1.52	97	76	19.8	13%	22%	9%	8%	10.2%	93.7	34	15	51	25%	75%	9%	14%	11	79	9%	18%			3.2	32	-$
2nd Half																																	
Proj	**3**	**0**	**58**	**55**	**4.37**	**1.39**	**5.21**	**1.50**	**110**	**86**	**20.5**	**13%**	**23%**	**10%**	**9%**	**9.6%**	**92.7**	**33**	**17**	**49**	**28%**	**72%**	**10%**	**15%**	**12**						**0.6**	**42**	**-$**

Dunning,Dane

Dunning,Dane			Health	B	LIMA Plan	C
Age: 27	Th: R	Role RP	PT/Exp	C	Rand Var	+2
Ht: 6' 4"	Wt: 225	Type Pwr/GB	Consist	A	MM	2203

1st half H%, 2nd half HR woes hurt; x-stats say he deserved better. Lost 4 weeks late (ankle, then COVID). Still owns plus GB% but velocity, SwK drooped throughout; K%, BB% look average at best. "Stagnancy" might be the word if not for 2019 Tommy John surgery, ongoing IP management, age. Has time to develop, but upside looks limited.

Yr Tm	W	Sv	IP	K	ERA	WHIP	xERA	xWHIP	vL+	vR+	BF/G	BB%	K%	K-BB%	xBB%	SwK	Vel	G	L	F	H%	S%	HR/F	xHR/F	GS	APC	DOM%	DIS%	Sv%	LI	RAR	BPX	R
17																																	
18 aa	5	0	62	59	3.87	1.58	4.32				24.8	10%	22%	12%							38%	73%									2.2	110	-$
19																																	
20 CHW	2	0	34	35	3.97	1.12	4.11	1.30	103	60	20.3	9%	25%	15%	10%	11.6%	91.9	45	22	33	26%	68%	13%	12%	7	82	29%	29%			2.0	109	$
21 TEX	5	0	118	114	4.51	1.44	3.89	1.30	108	102	18.9	8%	22%	14%	7%	10.3%	90.4	54	20	26	34%	71%	14%	20%	25	71	12%	36%	0	0.72	-3.6	110	-$
1st Half	3	0	74	79	4.38	1.51	3.74	1.25	100	104	20.3	8%	24%	16%	7%	11.2%	90.5	54	20	27	38%	72%	11%	18%	16	75	19%	38%			-1.0	128	-$
2nd Half	2	0	44	35	4.74	1.31	4.16	1.37	106	103	16.9	9%	19%	10%	8%	8.8%	90.1	54	20	26	28%	68%	21%	22%	9	64	0%	33%	0	0.64	-2.6	80	-$
Proj	**8**	**0**	**145**	**137**	**4.15**	**1.36**	**4.03**	**1.33**	**107**	**92**	**19.1**	**9%**	**23%**	**13%**	**8%**	**10.2%**	**90.7**	**52**	**20**	**28**	**32%**	**71%**	**13%**	**19%**	**29**						**5.5**	**103**	**$**

Eflin,Zach

Eflin,Zach			Health	F	LIMA Plan	B+
Age: 28	Th: R	Role SP	PT/Exp	A	Rand Var	+2
Ht: 6' 6"	Wt: 220	Type Con	Consist	B	MM	2201

Right patella (knee) tendinitis shelved him in mid-July. Rehab setbacks and eventually a late-August COVID bout kept him from returning. Before this, put up 1st-half numbers commensurate with established median skills; exquisite control partially offset predictable K% fade from short season. History of knee issues limits gap between ceiling and floor.

Yr Tm	W	Sv	IP	K	ERA	WHIP	xERA	xWHIP	vL+	vR+	BF/G	BB%	K%	K-BB%	xBB%	SwK	Vel	G	L	F	H%	S%	HR/F	xHR/F	GS	APC	DOM%	DIS%	Sv%	LI	RAR	BPX	R
17 PHI *	2	0	108	68	6.02	1.52	5.96	1.38	123	116	24.6	6%	15%	9%	6%	7.5%	92.7	44	18	38	33%	64%	19%	17%	11	93	0%	36%			-22.0	36	-$1
18 PHI *	13	0	148	136	4.46	1.32	4.29	1.25	115	93	21.9	7%	22%	15%	6%	11.1%	94.3	41	21	38	33%	68%	11%	12%	24	85	29%	29%			-5.7	103	$
19 PHI	10	0	163	129	4.13	1.35	4.83	1.36	113	95	22.0	7%	18%	12%	6%	9.4%	93.6	45	21	35	30%	76%	16%	13%	28	80	21%	43%	0	0.74	7.5	87	$
20 PHI	4	0	59	70	3.97	1.27	3.45	1.11	125	84	22.3	6%	29%	23%	6%	10.7%	93.9	47	21	31	35%	73%	16%	16%	10	83	30%	10%	0	0.74	3.5	176	$
21 PHI	4	0	106	99	4.17	1.25	3.83	1.11	102	106	24.6	4%	22%	19%	5%	10.9%	92.6	43	24	33	34%	71%	14%	16%	18	90	28%	22%			1.2	149	$
1st Half	3	0	96	89	4.13	1.23	3.85	1.10	104	100	24.9	3%	22%	19%	5%	10.9%	92.7	43	23	34	33%	71%	14%	15%	16	90	25%	19%			1.7	152	$
2nd Half	1	0	10	10	4.66	1.45	3.60	1.22	39	197	21.5	7%	23%	16%	7%	10.9%	92.3	48	31	21	37%	69%	17%	20%	2	88	50%	50%			-0.5	130	-$1
Proj	**7**	**0**	**123**	**113**	**3.98**	**1.31**	**4.07**	**1.20**	**116**	**94**	**22.7**	**6%**	**22%**	**17%**	**6%**	**10.3%**	**93.4**	**44**	**21**	**35**	**33%**	**74%**	**14%**	**14%**	**22**						**7.2**	**130**	**$**

Eovaldi,Nathan

Eovaldi,Nathan			Health	D	LIMA Plan	B
Age: 32	Th: R	Role RP	PT/Exp	B	Rand Var	0
Ht: 6' 2"	Wt: 217	Type	Consist	B	MM	3303

Injury magnet finally avoided serious downtime to post career year. Carried over plus K/BB metrics from 2020 to post another elite K-BB%; elevated DOM%/DIS% points to season-long consistency. HR/F and H% fortunes will regress, but with similar durability he should be profitable again.

Yr Tm	W	Sv	IP	K	ERA	WHIP	xERA	xWHIP	vL+	vR+	BF/G	BB%	K%	K-BB%	xBB%	SwK	Vel	G	L	F	H%	S%	HR/F	xHR/F	GS	APC	DOM%	DIS%	Sv%	LI	RAR	BPX	R
17																																	
18 2AL	6	0	111	101	3.81	1.13	3.75	1.15	101	88	20.7	4%	22%	18%	5%	11.3%	97.2	46	19	35	30%	70%	12%	12%	21	82	24%	19%	0	0.75	4.6	147	$
19 BOS	2	0	68	70	5.99	1.58	4.89	1.46	126	107	13.1	12%	23%	12%	9%	10.9%	97.5	45	19	36	32%	68%	23%	18%	12	55	8%	58%	0	0.88	-12.3	71	-$
20 BOS	4	0	48	52	3.72	1.20	3.35	1.05	86	128	22.1	4%	26%	23%	5%	13.8%	97.4	49	21	30	34%	76%	20%	19%	9	83	22%	33%			4.3	188	$
21 BOS	11	0	182	195	3.75	1.19	3.67	1.09	91	97	23.9	5%	26%	21%	5%	12.9%	96.9	42	23	35	34%	70%	8%	12%	32	91	41%	13%			11.6	161	$1
1st Half	9	0	98	90	3.41	1.20	3.79	1.15	76	101	23.9	5%	22%	17%	5%	12.3%	97.1	45	25	30	34%	71%	5%	10%	17	91	35%	12%			10.3	137	$1
2nd Half	2	0	85	105	4.15	1.18	3.56	1.02	97	97	23.8	4%	29%	25%	5%	13.6%	96.6	38	21	41	35%	69%	12%	14%	15	92	47%	13%			1.3	188	$
Proj	**9**	**0**	**174**	**186**	**3.83**	**1.17**	**3.59**	**1.13**	**93**	**96**	**18.7**	**6%**	**27%**	**21%**	**5%**	**12.6%**	**97.1**	**44**	**21**	**35**	**32%**	**71%**	**13%**	**15%**	**32**						**13.3**	**157**	**$1**

Espino,Paolo

Espino,Paolo			Health	A	LIMA Plan	B+
Age: 35	Th: R	Role RP	PT/Exp	D	Rand Var	0
Ht: 5' 10"	Wt: 215	Type Con/FB	Consist	D	MM	0001

Well-traveled swing-man flourished out of the pen in 1st half, courtesy of plus control, H%, S% and HR luck; wasn't as fortunate afterward as a SP. Apart from BB%, poor SwK and soft-tosser velocity, nothing stands out good or bad. Health, deception may be his next-best skills. Can be ignored on draft day.

Yr Tm	W	Sv	IP	K	ERA	WHIP	xERA	xWHIP	vL+	vR+	BF/G	BB%	K%	K-BB%	xBB%	SwK	Vel	G	L	F	H%	S%	HR/F	xHR/F	GS	APC	DOM%	DIS%	Sv%	LI	RAR	BPX	R
17 2TM *	5	0	103	75	6.14	1.62	6.73	1.36	131	104	15.7	6%	16%	10%		8.0%	88.6	38	19	42	35%	67%	23%	24%	2	37	0%	50%	0	0.53	-22.5	33	-$1
18 aaa	4	0	60	43	6.73	1.91	7.52				12.9	10%	15%	6%							38%	67%									-19.1	15	-$1
19 aaa	8	0	93	68	7.41	1.64	6.73				24.4	7%	16%	10%							36%	57%									-33.4	32	-$1
20 WAS	0	0	6	7	4.50	1.67	3.95		117	113	13.5	7%	26%	19%	11%	10.9%	90.3	44	28	28	41%	78%	20%	37%	1	55	0%	100%	0	0.43	0.0	147	-$
21 WAS	5	1	110	92	4.27	1.21	4.56	1.23	106	99	13.0	6%	20%	15%	7%	8.9%	89.0	36	21	43	29%	71%	14%	16%	19	50	11%	37%	100	0.59	0.0	104	$
1st Half	2	1	40	28	2.48	0.93	4.55	1.23	78	74	8.3	5%	18%	14%	6%	7.3%	89.4	38	18	44	23%	79%	8%	13%	4	30	0%	25%	100	0.39	8.8	95	$
2nd Half	3	0	70	64	5.30	1.38	4.56	1.23	114	114	18.6	6%	22%	16%	7%	9.6%	88.8	35	23	42	32%	68%	17%	18%	15	73	13%	40%	0	0.82	-8.9	109	-$
Proj	**5**	**0**	**102**	**79**	**4.83**	**1.43**	**4.99**	**1.33**	**119**	**112**	**14.1**	**7%**	**18%**	**12%**	**6%**	**8.8%**	**89.0**	**36**	**21**	**43**	**32%**	**71%**	**13%**	**16%**	**12**						**-4.7**	**80**	**-$**

Estevez,Carlos

Estevez,Carlos			Health	D	LIMA Plan	C
Age: 29	Th: R	Role RP	PT/Exp	C	Rand Var	+1
Ht: 6' 6"	Wt: 277	Type Pwr	Consist	B	MM	1210

14 consecutive scoreless IP beginning in late July earned him the 9th inning role in late August - all fueled by GB and S% spikes. History says neither will last. Consistent top-shelf velocity, average peripherals almost across the board will keep him in late-inning work, health permitting. But this is not his first rodeo, and closer skills still look tenuous.

Yr Tm	W	Sv	IP	K	ERA	WHIP	xERA	xWHIP	vL+	vR+	BF/G	BB%	K%	K-BB%	xBB%	SwK	Vel	G	L	F	H%	S%	HR/F	xHR/F	GS	APC	DOM%	DIS%	Sv%	LI	RAR	BPX	R
17 COL *	6	4	66	56	3.66	1.41	4.21	1.39	105	104	4.1	9%	20%	11%	9%	11.3%	97.1	45	28	26	32%	76%	11%	8%	0	16			57	0.62	5.7	86	$
18 aaa	0	1	29	26	7.52	1.92	8.38				4.9	9%	19%	10%							40%	65%									-12.1	15	-$1
19 COL	2	0	72	81	3.75	1.29	4.38	1.24	112	91	4.3	7%	26%	19%	6%	14.4%	97.9	38	20	42	32%	78%	14%	14%	0	17			0	0.93	6.7	131	$
20 COL	1	1	24	27	7.50	1.75	5.00	1.28	140	132	4.5	8%	23%	16%	6%	11.7%	96.9	31	29	40	40%	61%	19%	17%	0	17			25	1.16	-9.0	113	-$1
21 COL	3	11	62	60	4.38	1.49	4.35	1.28	109	109	4.2	8%	22%	14%	8%	11.7%	97.1	44	21	36	36%	74%	12%	14%	0	16			65	1.32	-0.9	106	$
1st Half	2	2	26	25	5.47	1.44	4.73	1.33	102	110	4.1	9%	22%	13%	8%	12.4%	96.6	38	21	42	34%	63%	9%	13%	0	16			50	1.35	-3.9	85	-$
2nd Half	1	9	35	35	3.57	1.53	4.06	1.24	105	111	4.3	7%	23%	16%	7%	11.2%	97.6	48	21	31	37%	82%	15%	16%	0	15			69	1.30	3.0	122	$
Proj	**3**	**10**	**65**	**64**	**4.10**	**1.44**	**4.30**	**1.29**	**107**	**102**	**4.1**	**8%**	**23%**	**15%**	**8%**	**12.2%**	**97.3**	**43**	**22**	**35**	**34%**	**75%**	**13%**	**13%**	**0**						**2.8**	**109**	**$**

JOCK THOMPSON

Fairbanks,Peter

Age: 28 | Th: R | Role: RP | Ht: 6' 6" | Wt: 225 | Type: Pwr
Health: D | PT/Exp: D | Consist: C
LIMA Plan: C+ | Rand Var: 0 | MM: 4510

April rotator cuff strain sidelined him early for a month, shoulder inflammation did likewise in late July. These and two elbow surgeries in his past keep his Health sketchy. Control is an ongoing issue; ditto a chronically elevated H%. Premium K%, velocity and HR avoidance keep him relevant. A late-inning arm still too inconsistent to rely upon.

Yr	Tm	W	Sv	IP	K	ERA	WHIP	xERA	xWHIP	vL+	vR+	BF/G	BB%	K%	K-BB%	xBB%	SwK	Vel	G	L	F	H%	S%	HR/F	xHR/F	GS	APC	DOM%	DIS%	Sv%	LI	RAR	BPX	R$
17																																		
18																																		
19	2 AL *	4	2	53	74	6.87	1.47	5.46	1.14	65	167	4.6	8%	32%	24%	8%	14.0%	97.4	43	27	30	39%	55%	28%	19%	0	18			40	0.80	-15.5	115	-$6
20	TAM	6	0	27	39	2.70	1.39	3.55	1.25	84	89	4.3	12%	33%	21%	9%	16.9%	97.5	47	19	34	37%	83%	10%	9%	2	18	0%	50%	0	1.02	5.8	152	$10
21	TAM	3	5	43	56	3.59	1.43	3.94	1.28	128	62	4.0	11%	30%	19%	8%	13.7%	97.2	43	20	37	37%	75%	5%	10%	0	16			71	1.23	3.6	125	$0
1st Half		1	3	23	26	3.91	1.61	4.79	1.47	112	85	4.2	13%	25%	11%	9%	14.2%	96.9	44	19	38	36%	75%	4%	10%	0	17			75	1.31	1.0	63	-$5
2nd Half		2	2	20	30	3.20	1.22	3.08	1.06	132	36	3.8	8%	36%	27%	6%	13.1%	97.4	41	22	37	39%	74%	6%	11%	0	16			67	1.13	2.6	198	-$2
Proj		4	7	51	70	3.64	1.20	3.36	1.19	128	49	3.8	11%	34%	23%	8%	13.5%	97.2	42	21	37	32%	73%	12%	11%	0						5.1	157	$4

Falter,Bailey

Age: 25 | Th: L | Role: RP | Ht: 6' 4" | Wt: 175 | Type: /FB
Health: C | PT/Exp: F | Consist: D
LIMA Plan: B+ | Rand Var: 0 | MM: 2201

2-1, 5.61 ERA in 31 IP at PHI. Minor league starter's results ticked up early at AAA (1.76 ERA, 44/8 K/BB over 31 IP), found the going tougher, less fortunate as MLB long reliever. Lost momentum and a month to COVID in 2nd half as K%, GB%, S% plunged, H% soared. Has two promising pitches and some projection, but watchable from afar for now.

Yr	Tm	W	Sv	IP	K	ERA	WHIP	xERA	xWHIP	vL+	vR+	BF/G	BB%	K%	K-BB%	xBB%	SwK	Vel	G	L	F	H%	S%	HR/F	xHR/F	GS	APC	DOM%	DIS%	Sv%	LI	RAR	BPX	R$
17																																		
18																																		
19	aa	6	0	78	57	4.94	1.44	5.53				23.8	5%	17%	12%							34%	69%									-4.2	74	-$3
20																																		
21	PHI *	4	0	66	72	3.79	1.12	3.64	1.09	97	98	8.7	5%	28%	22%	6%	10.3%	91.8	36	23	41	31%	70%	13%	11%	1	25	0%	100%	0	0.66	3.8	152	$2
1st Half		2	0	45	52	2.14	0.99	2.88	1.04	82	73	13.2	5%	30%	25%	5%	11.0%	92.2	41	26	32	29%	86%	18%	16%	0	35			0	0.48	11.8	180	$7
2nd Half		2	0	21	20	7.40	1.41	5.29	1.19	100	115	5.1	6%	23%	17%	8%	9.9%	91.7	33	21	46	35%	46%	10%	9%	1	21	0%	100%	0	0.73	-8.0	101	-$12
Proj		6	0	80	77	4.32	1.27	4.25	1.20	102	112	8.2	6%	24%	18%	8%	9.9%	91.7	33	21	46	32%	70%	11%	8%	0						1.3	123	$1

Familia,Jeurys

Age: 32 | Th: R | Role: RP | Ht: 6' 3" | Wt: 240 | Type: Pwr
Health: C | PT/Exp: C | Consist: B
LIMA Plan: B+ | Rand Var: +3 | MM: 2400

Horrendous 2nd-half HR luck undid his early ERA work. But he held it under 4 again, and xERA says it was deserved this time. Near-elite K%, velocity, GB% still keep him in innings, but poor control keeps runners on the basepaths. BB%, WHIP histories are instructive; forget ninth inning work unless they improve (Narrator: They won't).

Yr	Tm	W	Sv	IP	K	ERA	WHIP	xERA	xWHIP	vL+	vR+	BF/G	BB%	K%	K-BB%	xBB%	SwK	Vel	G	L	F	H%	S%	HR/F	xHR/F	GS	APC	DOM%	DIS%	Sv%	LI	RAR	BPX	R$
17	NYM	2	6	25	25	4.38	1.46	4.05	1.53	101	73	4.3	14%	23%	9%		10.5%	95.9	60	21	19	31%	69%	8%	6%	0	16			86	1.08	-0.1	65	-$1
18	2 TM	8	18	72	83	3.13	1.22	3.58	1.24	99	69	4.3	9%	27%	18%	7%	14.7%	96.2	46	21	33	32%	74%	5%	9%	0	17			75	1.28	9.1	134	$13
19	NYM	4	0	60	63	5.70	1.73	5.05	1.63	117	106	4.2	15%	23%	8%	10%	11.3%	96.0	51	19	30	34%	68%	14%	14%	0	16			0	0.81	-8.8	32	-$8
20	NYM	2	0	27	23	3.71	1.46	5.07	1.72	129	72	4.8	16%	19%	3%	11%	11.4%	96.6	60	15	25	26%	76%	11%	14%	0	18			0	0.82	2.4	5	-$1
21	NYM	9	1	59	72	3.94	1.42	3.64	1.28	118	93	4.0	10%	28%	17%	8%	13.0%	96.7	51	22	27	33%	78%	23%	17%	0	16			14	1.06	2.4	126	$2
1st Half		3	1	25	29	3.28	1.58	3.85	1.44	97	91	4.3	13%	26%	12%	8%	11.8%	96.7	57	24	19	36%	79%	8%	11%	0	17			33	1.01	3.0	85	-$2
2nd Half		6	0	35	43	4.41	1.30	3.51	1.16	124	97	3.8	8%	29%	21%	8%	13.9%	96.6	47	20	33	30%	78%	30%	20%	0	15			0	1.10	-0.6	155	$2
Proj		6	0	51	59	4.13	1.44	3.86	1.34	114	91	4.0	12%	27%	16%	8%	13.0%	96.4	50	21	29	33%	75%	18%	14%	0						2.0	111	-$1

Fedde,Erick

Age: 29 | Th: R | Role: SP | Ht: 6' 4" | Wt: 200 | Type: /GB
Health: D | PT/Exp: B | Consist: B
LIMA Plan: D+ | Rand Var: +4 | MM: 1103

Consistent GB% remains big carrying skill. Anemic SwK finally spiked, pushing K% up at least to healthy levels. And xERA offers more hope than previously despite atrocious 2nd-half H%, S% luck. But consistently mediocre control, abominable HR history are both more ingrained, predictable. Risk-takers will need a strong stomach and reserve list.

Yr	Tm	W	Sv	IP	K	ERA	WHIP	xERA	xWHIP	vL+	vR+	BF/G	BB%	K%	K-BB%	xBB%	SwK	Vel	G	L	F	H%	S%	HR/F	xHR/F	GS	APC	DOM%	DIS%	Sv%	LI	RAR	BPX	R$
17	WAS *	4	0	106	80	5.38	1.47	5.04	1.35	111	196	14.2	7%	18%	11%		5.7%	92.9	62	17	21	34%	65%	50%	32%	3	99	0%	100%			-13.3	69	-$6
18	WAS *	5	0	122	105	5.58	1.63	5.61	1.34	120	115	21.8	8%	19%	11%	12%	9.1%	93.7	53	22	24	38%	66%	22%	28%	11	86	9%	64%			-21.6	75	-$13
19	WAS *	7	0	114	70	5.36	1.50	5.55	1.52	121	91	17.6	9%	14%	5%	11%	7.3%	92.3	51	22	27	30%	68%	16%	18%	12	61	0%	67%	0	0.60	-12.1	20	-$6
20	WAS	2	0	50	28	4.29	1.37	5.32	1.57	82	118	20.2	10%	13%	3%	12%	6.1%	93.5	54	20	26	25%	76%	23%	21%	8	77	25%	50%	0	0.64	1.0	18	-$2
21	WAS	7	0	133	128	5.47	1.44	4.22	1.30	116	102	20.3	8%	22%	14%	10%	9.5%	93.9	50	19	31	33%	66%	19%	23%	27	83	11%	41%	0	0.76	-19.8	105	-$8
1st Half		4	0	55	50	3.90	1.23	4.28	1.42	96	81	21.0	11%	22%	11%	10%	8.9%	93.8	51	16	32	25%	72%	15%	20%	11	83	18%	36%			2.5	72	$3
2nd Half		3	0	78	78	6.58	1.59	4.18	1.23	119	117	19.9	6%	22%	15%	10%	9.8%	93.9	49	21	31	37%	62%	21%	24%	16	83	6%	44%	0	0.75	-22.2	129	-$17
Proj		8	0	160	129	4.96	1.46	4.47	1.39	114	107	20.1	9%	19%	10%	11%	8.4%	93.5	51	20	29	31%	70%	19%	22%	34						-10.0	79	-$6

Feyereisen,J.P.

Age: 29 | Th: R | Role: RP | Ht: 6' 2" | Wt: 215 | Type: Pwr/xFB
Health: C | PT/Exp: D | Consist: C
LIMA Plan: B | Rand Var: -5 | MM: 0200

Shelved for a month with shoulder discomfort and biceps tendinitis in late July. Before this he'd earned a high-leverage bullpen role with big swing-and-miss secondaries and fortunate H%, S%. Not so fortunate afterward, as luck regressed and 1st-half GB tilt disappeared. Walks are a serious problem, along with HR spike potential. The x-stats are a red flag.

Yr	Tm	W	Sv	IP	K	ERA	WHIP	xERA	xWHIP	vL+	vR+	BF/G	BB%	K%	K-BB%	xBB%	SwK	Vel	G	L	F	H%	S%	HR/F	xHR/F	GS	APC	DOM%	DIS%	Sv%	LI	RAR	BPX	R$
17	a/a	2	4	63	51	4.63	1.46	4.50				7.3	11%	19%	7%							30%	71%									-2.1	59	-$3
18	aaa	6	1	60	49	4.60	1.61	5.44				7.2	10%	18%	8%							34%	74%									-3.3	54	-$5
19	aaa	10	7	62	75	3.14	1.28	3.45				6.4	13%	29%	16%							27%	81%									10.5	99	$9
20	MIL	0	0	9	7	5.79	0.96	5.76	1.64	107	84	6.2	14%	19%	5%	12%	16.7%	93.4	33	8	58	5%	50%	21%	13%	0	25			0	0.16	-1.5	3	-$6
21	2 TM	4	3	56	53	2.73	1.23	5.13	1.55	106	68	4.3	14%	23%	9%	10%	15.6%	93.1	37	16	47	23%	81%	7%	12%	0	18			50	1.17	10.6	28	$4
1st Half		4	3	37	35	1.95	1.03	4.45	1.53	71	65	3.9	14%	24%	10%	11%	16.3%	93.4	45	14	41	17%	86%	9%	10%	0	16			50	1.34	10.6	42	$9
2nd Half		0	0	19	18	4.26	1.63	6.40	1.59	147	77	4.9	13%	20%	7%	9%	14.6%	92.7	25	19	56	32%	76%	6%	15%	0	22			0	0.83	0.0	4	-$12
Proj		4	0	58	56	4.33	1.45	5.34	1.52	139	77	5.4	13%	22%	10%	10%	15.2%	93.0	33	17	50	30%	72%	8%	13%	0						0.9	37	-$3

Finnegan,Kyle

Age: 30 | Th: R | Role: RP | Ht: 6' 2" | Wt: 200 | Type: Pwr
Health: B | PT/Exp: D | Consist: A
LIMA Plan: B | Rand Var: -3 | MM: 1210

Inherited closer role in late July, was effective early on, courtesy of sinker/slider combo with velocity and big GB%. And August luck (23% H%, 100% S% in 10 IP) was as good as it gets. But minus good fortune, chronic control and middling SwK were obvious (10 runs over 14 IP) the rest of the way. Profile bets he won't lock down 9th inning role for too long.

Yr	Tm	W	Sv	IP	K	ERA	WHIP	xERA	xWHIP	vL+	vR+	BF/G	BB%	K%	K-BB%	xBB%	SwK	Vel	G	L	F	H%	S%	HR/F	xHR/F	GS	APC	DOM%	DIS%	Sv%	LI	RAR	BPX	R$
17	a/a	2	12	60	43	4.77	1.64	5.72				5.9	10%	16%	6%							34%	74%									-3.0	40	-$1
18	a/a	1	14	44	34	5.13	1.54	4.54				5.7	10%	18%	8%							34%	65%									-5.4	75	-$1
19	a/a	3	14	52	55	2.98	1.36	3.72				5.2	10%	25%	16%							33%	79%									9.8	107	$7
20	WAS	1	0	25	27	2.92	1.38	4.17	1.41	82	90	4.3	12%	25%	13%	8%	12.2%	95.1	51	22	28	31%	81%	11%	15%	0	17			0	1.13	4.7	88	-$1
21	WAS	5	11	66	68	3.55	1.48	4.54	1.42	98	104	4.3	12%	23%	12%	8%	11.2%	95.6	48	17	35	32%	81%	14%	14%	0	18			79	1.18	5.9	74	$4
1st Half		3	0	30	36	3.86	1.62	4.62	1.44	101	101	4.2	12%	26%	14%	8%	12.1%	95.5	42	20	38	36%	80%	13%	13%	0	18			0	1.05	1.5	84	-$4
2nd Half		2	11	36	32	3.28	1.37	4.46	1.44	86	111	4.4	11%	21%	10%	7%	10.4%	95.8	52	15	33	28%	82%	15%	16%	0	18			79	1.30	4.3	65	$7
Proj		4	10	65	61	4.11	1.48	4.59	1.42	93	106	4.8	11%	22%	11%	7%	11.1%	95.7	48	17	35	33%	74%	10%	14%	0						2.8	75	$1

Flaherty,Jack

Age: 26 | Th: R | Role: SP | Ht: 6' 4" | Wt: 225 | Type: Pwr
Health: F | PT/Exp: B | Consist: A
LIMA Plan: B | Rand Var: -2 | MM: 3303

Was sailing along through 1st half until oblique injury shelved him for 10+ weeks. Shoulder strain and HR barrage sent him back to the IL three games into his return; finished the season with three games in short relief. Only wobbly BB%, SwK% and suspect durability mar otherwise attractive skill set. If he's healthy this spring, buy the projection.

Yr	Tm	W	Sv	IP	K	ERA	WHIP	xERA	xWHIP	vL+	vR+	BF/G	BB%	K%	K-BB%	xBB%	SwK	Vel	G	L	F	H%	S%	HR/F	xHR/F	GS	APC	DOM%	DIS%	Sv%	LI	RAR	BPX	R$
17	STL *	14	0	170	142	3.12	1.21	3.58	1.28	145	79	22.1	7%	21%	14%		14.2%	93.2	48	22	30	30%	78%	21%	16%	5	60	0%	80%	0	0.65	25.9	108	$18
18	STL *	12	0	184	216	3.17	1.07	2.83	1.19	83	92	21.7	9%	30%	21%	8%	14.1%	92.7	42	21	37	27%	76%	15%	11%	28	92	21%	18%			22.3	132	$23
19	STL	11	0	196	231	2.75	0.97	3.59	1.15	81	76	23.4	7%	30%	23%	8%	14.2%	93.9	40	22	38	25%	79%	14%	13%	33	96	42%	12%			42.5	153	$32
20	STL	4	0	40	49	4.91	1.21	3.53	1.23	106	76	18.9	9%	29%	19%	8%	14.7%	93.6	43	32	26	29%	63%	23%	22%	9	80	22%	22%			-2.3	137	$5
21	STL	9	0	78	85	3.22	1.06	3.86	1.21	82	93	18.9	8%	26%	18%	10%	12.3%	93.3	39	23	38	25%	77%	16%	22%	15	80	33%	27%	0	0.72	10.1	123	$9
1st Half		8	0	62	67	2.90	1.03	3.84	1.21	86	77	23.2	8%	26%	18%	9%	12.8%	93.6	36	26	38	26%	77%	12%	20%	11	98	36%	18%			10.4	122	$16
2nd Half		1	0	16	18	4.41	1.16	3.89	1.24	50	171	11.2	9%	27%	18%	11%	10.3%	92.3	49	12	40	22%	79%	29%	29%	4	46	25%	50%	0	0.67	-0.3	128	-$8
Proj		12	0	160	179	3.77	1.11	3.63	1.21	80	104	21.9	9%	29%	20%	9%	12.8%	93.2	43	22	36	26%	74%	20%	21%	29						13.4	135	$16

JOCK THOMPSON

Fleming,Josh

Age: 26	Th: L	Role	RP	Health	A	LIMA Plan	C
Ht: 6' 2"	Wt: 220	Type	Con/xGB	PT/Exp	C	Rand Var	+2
				Consist	C	MM	1001

A finesse groundballer who needs everything working to succeed. Workload dipped in 2nd half due to role change into 1-2 inning guy—he was tagged with 1.045 OPS the third time through the lineup—but his already-flimsy skills cratered further. Lack of K% upside and a HR problem despite low FB% taint his potential. Nah.

Yr Tm	W	Sv	IP	K	ERA	WHIP	xERA	xWHIP	vL+	vR+	BF/G	BB%	K%	K-BB%	xBB%	SwK	Vel	G	L	F	H%	S%	HR/F	xHR/F	GS	APC	DOM%	DIS%	Sv%	LI	RAR	BPX	R$
17																																	
18																																	
19 a/a	12	0	150	96	4.53	1.38	4.89				25.3	5%	15%	11%							33%	69%									-0.4	77	$2
20 TAM	5	0	32	25	2.78	1.08	3.63	1.24	100	86	18.6	5%	19%	14%	9%	10.0%	90.6	64	14	23	26%	83%	23%	18%	5	67	40%	60%	0	0.94	6.7	130	$11
21 TAM	10	1	104	65	5.09	1.35	4.48	1.38	107	95	17.2	7%	15%	8%	7%	9.1%	91.2	56	19	25	30%	63%	13%	19%	11	63	9%	45%	100	0.94	-10.6	69	-$2
1st Half	6	0	66	40	3.39	1.06	3.97	1.33	95	78	20.5	6%	15%	9%	6%	10.0%	91.2	59	18	23	24%	71%	15%	18%	6	75	17%	33%	0	0.80	7.1	84	$10
2nd Half	4	1	38	25	8.05	1.87	5.37	1.46	112	125	14.0	8%	14%	5%	8%	7.7%	91.2	50	22	28	39%	55%	10%	20%	5	50	0%	60%	100	1.08	-17.8	43	-$19
Proj	6	0	87	58	4.62	1.41	4.37	1.36	107	102	17.2	7%	16%	9%	8%	8.9%	91.0	56	18	25	32%	69%	14%	19%	15						-1.7	84	-$3

Flexen,Chris

Age: 28	Th: R	Role	SP	Health	A	LIMA Plan	C+
Ht: 6' 3"	Wt: 250	Type	Con	PT/Exp	A	Rand Var	-2
				Consist	F	MM	1103

Honed skills in KBO during 2020 and returned with immaculate control fueled by a new cutter. Improvement vR was a major key while off-speed heavy arsenal (just 40% fastball usage) fueled success vL. Low K% and a weak SwK to match caps value and widens the range of outcomes given his dependence on defense. Don't pay the tax on a career year.

Yr Tm	W	Sv	IP	K	ERA	WHIP	xERA	xWHIP	vL+	vR+	BF/G	BB%	K%	K-BB%	xBB%	SwK	Vel	G	L	F	H%	S%	HR/F	xHR/F	GS	APC	DOM%	DIS%	Sv%	LI	RAR	BPX	R$
17 NYM *	9	0	97	81	5.15	1.46	5.03	1.48	120	142	19.7	11%	20%	9%	10%	8.6%	92.4	41	21	38	30%	69%	19%	11%	9	65	0%	89%	0	0.61	-9.4	48	-$2
18 NYM *	6	0	98	70	4.59	1.62	5.73	1.41	171	180	19.8	8%	16%	8%	12%	4.0%	92.6	40	23	37	35%	74%	18%	20%	1	38	0%	100%	0	0.77	-5.4	50	-$7
19 NYM *	5	0	94	88	5.53	1.72	6.37	1.39	91	120	12.2	8%	21%	12%	12%	8.0%	94.3	32	21	47	39%	70%	5%	9%	1	30	0%	100%	0	1.09	-11.9	62	-$9
20 for	8	0	117	125	3.73	1.21	3.44				22.4	8%	27%	19%							32%	71%									10.5	127	$29
21 SEA	14	0	180	125	3.61	1.25	4.60	1.28	90	104	23.9	5%	17%	11%	7%	9.1%	92.8	42	21	37	30%	74%	9%	14%	31	91	32%	45%			14.6	86	$12
1st Half	6	0	79	52	3.97	1.30	4.49	1.29	91	110	23.3	5%	16%	11%	6%	9.7%	92.7	49	18	34	31%	72%	9%	18%	14	89	36%	50%			2.9	89	$5
2nd Half	8	0	100	73	3.32	1.22	4.68	1.28	81	104	24.4	6%	18%	12%	8%	8.6%	92.8	37	24	39	30%	77%	9%	11%	17	92	29%	41%			11.7	85	$20
Proj	12	0	174	142	4.08	1.36	4.56	1.31	93	108	20.9	7%	20%	13%	8%	8.9%	92.7	42	21	37	32%	73%	10%	13%	35						8.1	93	$5

Floro,Dylan

Age: 31	Th: R	Role	RP	Health	B	LIMA Plan	C+
Ht: 6' 2"	Wt: 203	Type	/GB	PT/Exp	C	Rand Var	-4
				Consist	B	MM	2220

New team, same Floro... until the 2nd half. Season K-BB% masks massive 2nd half skills burst as SwK soared and led to elite K%. BB% was also back in line and season xBB% is even more encouraging. GB lean mitigates xHR/F a bit. Dominance vR is a foundation for success in leveraged spots and if K% jump holds, he can continue closing.

Yr Tm	W	Sv	IP	K	ERA	WHIP	xERA	xWHIP	vL+	vR+	BF/G	BB%	K%	K-BB%	xBB%	SwK	Vel	G	L	F	H%	S%	HR/F	xHR/F	GS	APC	DOM%	DIS%	Sv%	LI	RAR	BPX	R$
17 CHC *	3	2	70	36	5.31	1.65	6.79	1.36	135	129	8.6	4%	12%	7%		9.0%	91.3	50	19	31	36%	72%	18%	12%	0	44			67	0.15	-8.2	32	-$7
18 2 NL	6	0	64	58	2.25	1.25	3.79	1.32	103	78	5.0	8%	21%	13%	7%	11.6%	93.3	55	18	26	31%	83%	6%	8%	0	18			0	1.06	15.0	106	$5
19 LA	5	0	47	42	4.24	1.29	4.21	1.30	123	75	4.0	7%	21%	14%	6%	13.1%	93.9	51	20	28	32%	68%	10%	11%	0	15			0	1.14	1.5	111	$0
20 LA	3	0	24	19	2.59	1.11	3.58	1.19	63	95	3.9	4%	19%	15%	6%	10.2%	93.4	56	24	20	31%	77%	7%	9%	0	15			0	0.79	5.6	136	$5
21 MIA	6	15	64	62	2.81	1.22	4.09	1.32	89	69	4.0	9%	23%	14%	7%	10.5%	93.7	49	20	31	30%	76%	4%	14%	0	16			71	1.20	11.5	98	$11
1st Half	2	2	34	28	3.18	1.41	4.83	1.47	83	74	4.0	10%	18%	8%	7%	8.5%	93.5	50	21	28	32%	75%	0%	10%	0	16			33	1.21	4.6	52	-$1
2nd Half	4	13	30	34	2.40	1.00	3.34	1.15	88	66	3.9	8%	29%	21%	6%	13.0%	94.1	47	19	34	27%	79%	8%	18%	0	16			87	1.18	6.9	149	$18
Proj	6	20	65	60	3.18	1.25	3.96	1.30	104	76	4.3	8%	23%	14%	6%	11.5%	93.7	50	20	30	31%	76%	8%	13%	0						10.2	109	$12

Foltynewicz,Mike

Age: 30	Th: R	Role	SP	Health	D	LIMA Plan	C
Ht: 6' 4"	Wt: 195	Type	Con/FB	PT/Exp	C	Rand Var	+1
				Consist	F	MM	1101

Now 3 years removed from dream 2018 with many of the skills that drove it having faded or outright disappeared: K%, SwK, Velocity, S%, HR/F and work vL. MLB-worst 2.1 HR/9 since 2019 (min. 250 IP) and xHR/F doesn't offer much hope for improvement. Best avenue for a rebirth might be shift to RP in hopes of velocity and K% recovery; as SP, an easy pass.

Yr Tm	W	Sv	IP	K	ERA	WHIP	xERA	xWHIP	vL+	vR+	BF/G	BB%	K%	K-BB%	xBB%	SwK	Vel	G	L	F	H%	S%	HR/F	xHR/F	GS	APC	DOM%	DIS%	Sv%	LI	RAR	BPX	R$
17 ATL	10	0	154	143	4.79	1.48	4.68	1.37	116	97	23.9	9%	21%	12%	9%	9.9%	95.3	39	24	36	34%	70%	12%	12%	28	96	11%	36%	0	0.76	-8.2	89	-$1
18 ATL	13	0	183	202	2.85	1.08	3.70	1.24	84	81	24.0	9%	27%	18%	8%	10.8%	96.4	43	19	38	26%	77%	10%	11%	31	98	39%	23%			29.3	126	$25
19 ATL *	13	0	169	139	4.84	1.36	4.66	1.39	97	105	22.8	8%	20%	12%	7%	10.8%	94.9	37	23	40	31%	68%	17%	15%	21	90	24%	29%			-7.0	64	$3
20 ATL	0	0	3	3	16.20	2.40	8.39		125	334	16.0	25%	19%	-6%		5.7%	90.5	44	0	56	14%	40%	60%	36%	1	70	0%	100%			-4.8	-140	-$11
21 TEX	2	0	139	97	5.44	1.26	4.94	1.32	126	105	20.9	6%	17%	10%	7%	8.2%	93.6	38	21	41	26%	65%	19%	18%	24	80	21%	33%	0	0.70	-20.1	73	-$8
1st Half	2	0	87	62	5.17	1.34	4.87	1.29	128	102	23.3	5%	17%	11%	7%	8.0%	93.9	38	23	39	30%	68%	17%	18%	16	89	13%	38%			-9.7	83	-$7
2nd Half	0	0	52	35	5.88	1.12	5.07	1.39	105	117	17.8	7%	16%	9%	8%	8.7%	92.8	37	18	45	19%	57%	23%	18%	8	67	38%	25%	0	0.62	-10.4	54	-$9
Proj	4	0	102	83	4.82	1.24	4.61	1.34	109	101	20.8	8%	20%	12%	8%	9.5%	94.4	39	21	41	27%	67%	16%	15%	20						-4.6	83	-$2

Foster,Matt

Age: 27	Th: R	Role	RP	Health	A	LIMA Plan	C
Ht: 6' 0"	Wt: 210	Type	/FB	PT/Exp	D	Rand Var	+3
				Consist	B	MM	1200

2-1, 6.00 ERA in 39 IP at CHW. Ominous xHR/F highlighted in 2021 Forecaster came to fruition. Was better in 2nd half thanks to jump vL, but xHR/F was looming and platoons were rough overall. FB lean means he needs above average K%, H%, and S% to succeed, and if he can't trim the longball problem, he will struggle to find a late-inning role.

Yr Tm	W	Sv	IP	K	ERA	WHIP	xERA	xWHIP	vL+	vR+	BF/G	BB%	K%	K-BB%	xBB%	SwK	Vel	G	L	F	H%	S%	HR/F	xHR/F	GS	APC	DOM%	DIS%	Sv%	LI	RAR	BPX	R$
17																																	
18 aa	0	1	32	26	5.79	1.76	6.33				6.1	10%	18%	8%							37%	68%									-6.5	45	-$9
19 a/a	4	5	66	63	4.19	1.24	4.28				6.3	8%	23%	15%							28%	73%									2.6	76	$3
20 CHW	6	0	29	31	2.20	0.87	3.83	1.20	72	65	4.7	8%	28%	20%	6%	13.8%	93.8	36	22	42	22%	78%	7%	18%	2	19	0%	0%	0	1.04	8.0	128	$17
21 CHW *	2	1	55	59	5.52	1.34	5.31	1.17	107	112	4.5	7%	26%	19%	8%	10.7%	93.6	29	21	50	33%	64%	15%	18%	0	20			33	0.76	-8.5	94	-$6
1st Half	2	0	25	32	6.57	1.58	4.45	1.18	121	116	4.8	8%	28%	20%	8%	12.7%	93.9	27	24	49	38%	66%	21%	14%	0	20			0	0.83	-7.0	139	-$9
2nd Half	0	1	31	27	4.67	1.15	3.87	1.17	61	109	4.5	5%	22%	17%	8%	6.7%	93.2	31	17	52	30%	62%	8%	22%	0	18			50	0.62	-1.5	121	-$7
Proj	1	0	29	29	4.69	1.40	4.62	1.28	118	105	5.1	8%	23%	16%	8%	12.7%	93.9	27	24	49	33%	72%	14%	13%	0						-0.9	99	-$5

Freeland,Kyle

Age: 29	Th: L	Role	SP	Health	D	LIMA Plan	D+
Ht: 6' 4"	Wt: 204	Type	Con	PT/Exp	B	Rand Var	0
				Consist	C	MM	1003

Shoulder injury sidelined him until late-May and influenced slow start (first 5 starts: 9.58 ERA, 2.32 WHIP). Delivered a solid 3.24 ERA/1.24 WHIP rest of way as skills looked similar to 2018 breakout. Has found some relative ERA success in Coors (career 4.44), but the high WHIP (1.41) and mediocre or worse K% (<=21%) keeps fantasy value down.

Yr Tm	W	Sv	IP	K	ERA	WHIP	xERA	xWHIP	vL+	vR+	BF/G	BB%	K%	K-BB%	xBB%	SwK	Vel	G	L	F	H%	S%	HR/F	xHR/F	GS	APC	DOM%	DIS%	Sv%	LI	RAR	BPX	R$
17 COL	11	0	156	107	4.10	1.49	4.72	1.49	100	109	20.8	9%	16%	6%	10%	8.0%	92.0	54	19	28	31%	75%	13%	10%	28	78	14%	68%	0	0.69	5.0	54	$2
18 COL	17	0	202	173	2.85	1.25	4.19	1.34	71	98	25.6	8%	20%	12%	8%	9.6%	91.6	46	19	35	29%	80%	8%	11%	33	98	33%	21%			32.5	90	$21
19 COL *	3	0	136	100	7.40	1.68	6.80	1.49	103	126	21.8	9%	16%	7%	8%	9.9%	91.9	47	21	33	34%	59%	22%	18%	22	81	9%	59%			-48.4	13	-$22
20 COL	2	0	71	46	4.33	1.42	4.72	1.42	113	101	23.4	8%	15%	8%	8%	9.4%	91.9	52	23	25	31%	73%	16%	17%	13	86	0%	46%			1.1	64	-$2
21 COL	7	0	121	105	4.33	1.42	4.35	1.30	109	109	22.4	7%	20%	13%	8%	9.2%	91.4	45	21	34	32%	75%	16%	17%	23	82	22%	35%			-0.9	96	-$2
1st Half	1	0	38	29	5.50	1.67	4.92	1.45	135	125	21.4	9%	17%	8%	9%	8.0%	91.4	50	18	32	33%	74%	24%	22%	8	82	25%	50%			-5.7	54	-$12
2nd Half	6	0	83	76	3.80	1.30	4.11	1.23	90	105	22.9	6%	22%	16%	6%	9.8%	91.3	43	23	35	32%	75%	13%	14%	15	82	20%	27%			4.8	115	$10
Proj	7	0	145	114	4.39	1.46	4.61	1.37	108	110	22.4	8%	18%	10%	8%	9.3%	91.6	47	21	32	32%	75%	16%	16%	28						1.2	79	-$3

Fried,Max

Age: 28	Th: L	Role	SP	Health	D	LIMA Plan	D+
Ht: 6' 4"	Wt: 190	Type	/GB	PT/Exp	A	Rand Var	-1
				Consist	A	MM	3205

Hit the Goldilocks "just right" level this past season after bad fortune of 2019 swung to good in 2020. Hamstring and finger injuries prevented new IP high, but the career high BF/G is promising. Career bests in velocity and BB% along with a full year of 2020's vR dominance suggests there could be another level here. UP: 200 Ks and Cy Young consideration.

Yr Tm	W	Sv	IP	K	ERA	WHIP	xERA	xWHIP	vL+	vR+	BF/G	BB%	K%	K-BB%	xBB%	SwK	Vel	G	L	F	H%	S%	HR/F	xHR/F	GS	APC	DOM%	DIS%	Sv%	LI	RAR	BPX	R$
17 ATL *	3	0	119	103	6.63	1.69	5.41	1.51	91	118	17.8	12%	19%	8%		9.0%	92.4	65	18	17	35%	60%	21%	23%	4	47	0%	75%	0	0.38	-33.2	61	-$16
18 ATL *	4	0	113	115	4.40	1.46	4.12	1.39	114	88	16.7	11%	24%	13%	10%	14.4%	93.0	51	28	20	34%	70%	20%	14%	5	41	20%	20%	0	0.64	-3.4	98	-$4
19 ATL	17	0	166	173	4.02	1.33	3.54	1.21	86	103	21.3	7%	25%	18%	7%	11.9%	93.8	54	24	22	34%	74%	20%	16%	30	81	17%	23%	0	0.80	9.9	144	$12
20 ATL	7	0	56	50	2.25	1.09	3.85	1.31	94	81	20.4	8%	22%	14%	8%	11.8%	93.0	53	19	28	27%	80%	5%	10%	11	82	36%	18%			15.2	105	$24
21 ATL	14	0	166	158	3.04	1.09	3.47	1.18	98	81	23.8	6%	24%	18%	6%	11.7%	93.9	52	21	28	29%	75%	12%	16%	28	91	36%	18%			25.0	136	$22
1st Half	5	0	63	62	4.16	1.31	3.97	1.28	81	103	22.3	8%	23%	15%	6%	12.1%	93.7	45	24	31	32%	71%	13%	18%	12	85	17%	25%			0.8	108	$3
2nd Half	9	0	103	96	2.36	0.95	3.16	1.12	98	69	25.0	5%	24%	19%	6%	11.4%	94.0	56	19	26	27%	79%	11%	15%	16	96	50%	13%			24.2	154	$40
Proj	16	0	181	174	3.36	1.17	3.54	1.22	98	88	20.7	7%	24%	17%	7%	12.0%	93.6	52	22	26	30%	73%	12%	14%	35						24.4	133	$20

PAUL SPORER

Fulmer,Michael

Age: 29	Th: R	Role: RP	Health: F	LIMA Plan: B	
Ht: 6' 3"	Wt: 246	Type:	PT/Exp: D	Rand Var: -2	
			Consist: F	MM: 2221	

Shift to RP was a success (2.53 ERA, 21% K-BB in 57 IP) as velocity returned to pre-injury levels and SwK soared. Health continued to elude him (shoulder, spine IL stints), but career-high 40% slider usage fueled domination vL and aided new high in K%. Gaudy S% and HR/F drove 2nd half ERA, but xERA and core skills are good enough for high leverage role.

Yr	Tm	W	Sv	IP	K	ERA	WHIP	xERA	xWHIP	vL+	vR+	BF/G	BB%	K%	K-BB%	xBB%	SwK	Vel	G	L	F	H%	S%	HR/F	xHR/F	GS	APC	DOM%	DIS%	Sv%	LI	RAR	BPX	R$
17	DET	10	0	165	114	3.83	1.15	4.19	1.32	90	83	27.0	6%	17%	11%	8%	9.8%	95.8	49	22	29	28%	68%	9%	11%	25	99	36%	32%			10.8	96	$12
18	DET	3	0	132	110	4.69	1.31	4.29	1.35	108	100	23.3	8%	20%	11%	7%	11.1%	95.8	44	22	34	29%	68%	15%	15%	24	90	25%	33%			-8.9	83	-$3
19																																		
20	DET	0	0	28	20	8.78	2.06	6.21	1.50	98	194	13.6	9%	15%	6%	12%	7.8%	93.1	36	28	36	39%	61%	22%	18%	10	53	0%	80%			-14.8	29	-$22
21	DET	5	14	70	73	2.97	1.28	3.87	1.19	77	108	5.7	7%	25%	18%	8%	13.6%	95.7	45	21	34	33%	80%	10%	15%	4	23	0%	50%	78	1.31	11.1	135	$9
1st Half		4	6	40	42	4.05	1.30	3.87	1.18	78	108	7.0	6%	24%	18%	8%	13.2%	95.7	45	23	32	33%	74%	16%	17%	4	27	0%	50%	75	1.26	1.1	139	$4
2nd Half		1	8	30	31	1.52	1.25	3.86	1.20	64	112	4.6	7%	25%	18%	8%	14.1%	95.6	46	17	37	34%	89%	3%	11%	0	19			80	1.37	10.1	131	$7
Proj		4	18	73	68	3.25	1.26	4.02	1.25	85	101	7.5	7%	23%	16%	8%	12.5%	95.7	46	21	34	32%	77%	10%	14%	0						10.8	118	$10

Funkhouser,Kyle

Age: 28	Th: R	Role: RP	Health: A	LIMA Plan: B	
Ht: 6' 3"	Wt: 225	Type: Pwr/GB	PT/Exp: D	Rand Var: -3	
			Consist: C	MM: 0100	

Successful 1st half came from a tremendous GB rate that severely stifled hits and low FB rate mitigated HR/F impact. 2nd half regression only hurt the WHIP as a low HR/F artificially protected his ERA, but xERA doesn't buy it. Without that excellent GB rate, his below average K-BB% is exposed and casts him in a middle man role at best.

Yr	Tm	W	Sv	IP	K	ERA	WHIP	xERA	xWHIP	vL+	vR+	BF/G	BB%	K%	K-BB%	xBB%	SwK	Vel	G	L	F	H%	S%	HR/F	xHR/F	GS	APC	DOM%	DIS%	Sv%	LI	RAR	BPX	R$
17																																		
18	a/a	4	0	99	76	5.22	1.71	5.85				23.7	12%	17%	5%							34%	71%									-13.1	40	-$12
19	a/a	6	0	89	73	9.53	2.07	6.84				19.9	14%	17%	2%							39%	51%									-55.3	41	-$27
20	DET	1	0	17	12	7.27	1.90	6.00	1.70	127	124	6.2	14%	15%	1%	11%	10.0%	95.3	47	28	26	34%	63%	20%	15%	0	25			0	0.30	-6.0	-19	-$12
21	DET	7	1	68	63	3.42	1.40	4.53	1.51	97	87	5.2	13%	21%	8%	11%	11.1%	95.6	53	17	29	29%	78%	11%	12%	2	21	0%	0%	20	1.14	7.1	50	$2
1st Half		2	0	28	21	2.93	1.19	3.57	1.46	88	71	5.4	11%	19%	8%	8%	9.5%	95.6	73	12	16	25%	77%	17%	17%	1	21	0%	0%	0	1.03	4.6	75	-$1
2nd Half		5	1	41	42	3.76	1.55	5.13	1.55	94	100	5.1	14%	23%	9%	12%	12.0%	95.6	40	21	39	31%	78%	9%	10%	1	21	0%	0%	20	1.21	2.5	33	$0
Proj		5	0	65	57	4.46	1.52	4.84	1.58	104	95	7.4	13%	20%	7%	12%	11.1%	95.6	53	17	30	30%	72%	11%	13%	0						-0.1	35	-$4

Gallegos,Giovanny

Age: 30	Th: R	Role: RP	Health: A	LIMA Plan: C+	
Ht: 6' 2"	Wt: 215	Type: Pwr/xFB	PT/Exp: C	Rand Var: -4	
			Consist: B	MM: 3420	

Finally got an extended shot at closing even as skills came down some after 2020 outlier. But BB% and K%/SwK along with level platoon splits remained consistently elite, LI grew and the saves followed. Won't be able to outrun xHR/F forever, but xERA and xWHIP are palatable even when regression hits. We'll say it for the third straight year ... UP: 35 Sv

Yr	Tm	W	Sv	IP	K	ERA	WHIP	xERA	xWHIP	vL+	vR+	BF/G	BB%	K%	K-BB%	xBB%	SwK	Vel	G	L	F	H%	S%	HR/F	xHR/F	GS	APC	DOM%	DIS%	Sv%	LI	RAR	BPX	R$
17	NYY *	4	5	64	78	3.58	1.17	3.72	1.11	108	94	5.8	7%	31%	24%		14.3%	94.1	36	22	42	32%	75%	12%	15%	0	23			63	0.43	6.1	153	$6
18	2 TM *	2	4	56	55	3.29	1.09	2.69	1.16	138	81	6.1	6%	25%	19%	5%	9.3%	94.4	34	24	41	30%	70%	17%	15%	0	30			80	0.16	6.0	155	$3
19	STL	3	1	74	93	2.31	0.81	3.44	1.04	68	76	4.2	6%	33%	28%	5%	16.7%	93.7	34	19	47	23%	80%	11%	12%	0	17			25	0.94	20.0	178	$12
20	STL	2	4	15	21	3.60	0.87	2.91	1.00	55	69	3.6	7%	37%	30%	4%	21.0%	93.7	42	19	39	27%	58%	8%	15%	0	14			100	1.17	1.6	206	$7
21	STL	6	14	80	95	3.02	0.88	3.51	1.07	75	75	4.2	6%	31%	24%	6%	16.6%	94.5	33	20	47	25%	68%	7%	12%	0	17			64	1.37	12.3	156	$18
1st Half		5	1	43	49	2.53	0.70	3.23	1.06	64	54	4.5	6%	31%	25%	6%	15.5%	94.2	36	20	45	19%	67%	7%	10%	0	18			20	1.30	9.1	157	$13
2nd Half		1	13	38	46	3.58	1.09	3.81	1.09	77	100	4.1	7%	30%	24%	6%	17.7%	94.7	30	20	49	32%	68%	7%	13%	0	16			76	1.44	3.2	155	$12
Proj		3	25	65	76	3.07	0.96	3.59	1.09	79	84	4.5	6%	31%	24%	6%	16.8%	94.3	33	20	47	28%	71%	8%	12%	0						11.2	160	$17

Gallen,Zac

Age: 26	Th: R	Role: SP	Health: D	LIMA Plan: B+	
Ht: 6' 2"	Wt: 198	Type: Pwr	PT/Exp: B	Rand Var: +1	
			Consist: B	MM: 2303	

April injury (forearm) was a 1st half harbinger as two more followed (elbow, hamstring) and bred volatility. SwK dip didn't hurt K% much. Rally down the stretch (3.19 ERA, 1.13 WHIP in 48 IP) salvaged his season. Still a bright future thanks to a deep arsenal, neutral platoon, and a GB lean that lays a steady foundation. With health... UP: 200 Ks

Yr	Tm	W	Sv	IP	K	ERA	WHIP	xERA	xWHIP	vL+	vR+	BF/G	BB%	K%	K-BB%	xBB%	SwK	Vel	G	L	F	H%	S%	HR/F	xHR/F	GS	APC	DOM%	DIS%	Sv%	LI	RAR	BPX	R$
17	a/a	5	0	92	54	4.54	1.44	4.96				23.1	6%	14%	7%							32%	71%									-2.1	51	-$3
18	aaa	8	0	134	117	4.08	1.59	5.41				23.6	8%	20%	12%							37%	76%									1.1	77	-$4
19	2 NL *	12	0	172	190	2.54	1.01	2.51	1.21	88	87	22.7	8%	29%	21%	7%	13.2%	92.9	39	24	37	26%	81%	11%	11%	15	92	27%	7%			41.8	130	$28
20	ARI	3	0	72	82	2.75	1.11	3.64	1.21	86	82	24.3	9%	28%	20%	8%	12.3%	93.3	46	22	33	28%	82%	15%	15%	12	93	33%	8%			15.1	140	$20
21	ARI	4	0	121	139	4.30	1.29	4.01	1.26	97	100	22.7	9%	27%	17%	9%	9.9%	93.4	44	19	37	30%	72%	16%	16%	23	91	17%	30%			-0.5	120	$1
1st Half		1	0	41	49	4.17	1.39	4.18	1.35	117	72	20.3	11%	27%	15%	10%	11.0%	93.7	44	19	36	32%	73%	13%	11%	9	81	11%	33%			0.5	101	-$4
2nd Half		3	0	80	90	4.37	1.24	3.93	1.22	79	119	24.3	8%	27%	18%	8%	9.4%	93.2	43	19	37	30%	71%	17%	18%	14	98	21%	29%			-1.0	130	$5
Proj		7	0	167	181	3.71	1.26	3.93	1.26	97	93	22.3	9%	27%	17%	8%	11.1%	93.3	43	21	36	30%	75%	14%	14%	30						15.4	121	$10

Gant,John

Age: 29	Th: R	Role: RP	Health: B	LIMA Plan: D+	
Ht: 6' 4"	Wt: 200	Type: Pwr	PT/Exp: C	Rand Var: -2	
			Consist: D	MM: 0101	

Fantasy managers played chicken with wild early season run as many refused to roster the tiny ERA because of a comical 2% K-BB in first 10 starts (1.60 ERA, 1.52 WHIP!). Wheels predictably fell off with a 6.22 ERA rest of the way. Sharp velocity plunge played role in SwK and K% drops. Career 1.46 WHIP as SP says he is RP-only even if the skills rebound.

Yr	Tm	W	Sv	IP	K	ERA	WHIP	xERA	xWHIP	vL+	vR+	BF/G	BB%	K%	K-BB%	xBB%	SwK	Vel	G	L	F	H%	S%	HR/F	xHR/F	GS	APC	DOM%	DIS%	Sv%	LI	RAR	BPX	R$
17	STL *	6	0	121	88	4.81	1.53	5.38	1.37	131	109	21.0	7%	17%	10%		10.0%	93.0	54	13	33	35%	71%	22%	8%	2	41	0%	100%	0	0.38	-6.7	62	-$4
18	STL *	12	0	163	128	3.01	1.33	3.70	1.48	90	88	19.9	11%	19%	8%	8%	12.0%	93.3	45	21	34	28%	80%	8%	9%	19	72	16%	26%	0	0.79	22.8	73	$11
19	STL	11	3	66	60	3.66	1.28	4.47	1.52	102	76	4.2	13%	22%	10%	8%	12.6%	95.9	46	27	27	27%	72%	9%	7%	0	17			50	1.17	6.9	50	$6
20	STL	0	0	15	18	2.40	1.07	3.12	1.29	66	58	3.6	11%	30%	18%	6%	13.3%	93.9	63	17	20	27%	75%	0%	12%	0	14			0	1.00	3.8	138	-$2
21	2 TM	5	0	110	92	4.09	1.51	5.17	1.65	103	93	12.6	15%	19%	4%	12%	10.0%	91.8	47	24	29	28%	74%	11%	14%	21	51	0%	52%	0	0.87	2.4	4	-$4
1st Half		4	0	69	52	3.54	1.60	5.64	1.76	98	97	17.2	16%	17%	1%	12%	9.6%	91.2	45	28	28	28%	80%	11%	16%	14	70	0%	57%	0	0.72	6.2	-31	-$2
2nd Half		1	0	41	40	5.01	1.35	4.45	1.47	98	91	8.6	12%	22%	10%	11%	10.7%	92.8	51	17	31	28%	63%	11%	12%	7	34	0%	43%	0	1.00	-3.8	62	-$8
Proj		8	0	116	99	4.49	1.45	4.83	1.55	106	94	9.3	13%	20%	7%	10%	11.0%	93.1	47	23	30	30%	70%	10%	11%	0						-0.6	36	-$2

Garcia,Deivi

Age: 23	Th: R	Role: RP	Health: A	LIMA Plan: D+	
Ht: 5' 9"	Wt: 163	Type: Pwr/FB	PT/Exp: D	Rand Var: 0	
			Consist: D	MM: 0200	

0-2, 6.48 ERA in 8 IP at NYY. Couldn't build on a promising debut as HRs remained and were made worse by massive control problems. In AAA, lefties crushed him with 1.084 OPS, 0.5% K-BB, and 13 HR. Young enough to rebound, but size and durability questions are now joined by command and platoon issues, which make an RP future more likely.

Yr	Tm	W	Sv	IP	K	ERA	WHIP	xERA	xWHIP	vL+	vR+	BF/G	BB%	K%	K-BB%	xBB%	SwK	Vel	G	L	F	H%	S%	HR/F	xHR/F	GS	APC	DOM%	DIS%	Sv%	LI	RAR	BPX	R$
17																																		
18																																		
19	a/a	5	0	95	119	5.37	1.46	4.61				18.5	12%	29%	18%							35%	65%									-10.2	96	-$4
20	NYY	3	0	34	33	4.98	1.19	4.66	1.15	80	109	24.3	4%	23%	19%	6%	11.5%	92.0	33	20	47	31%	63%	12%	13%	6	89	67%	17%			-2.2	140	$1
21	NYY *	3	0	101	92	7.60	1.92	7.57	1.68	153	81	18.3	15%	19%	4%	11%	11.8%	92.3	23	19	58	34%	64%	7%	19%	2	77	0%	50%			-41.3	8	-$27
1st Half		1	0	44	43	8.80	1.84	6.93	1.60	145	83	16.9	14%	21%	7%	11%	11.8%	92.3	23	19	58	35%	52%	7%	19%	2	77	0%	50%			-24.4	30	-$22
2nd Half		2	0	57	49	6.68	1.98	8.06		0	0	19.5	16%	18%	2%							33%	72%	0%		0	0					-17.0	-8	-$25
Proj		3	0	58	57	5.53	1.58	5.30	1.55	100	129	18.6	14%	22%	9%	6%	11.5%	92.0	33	20	47	30%	70%	17%	12%	12						-7.7	30	-$8

Garcia,Jarlin

Age: 29	Th: L	Role: RP	Health: B	LIMA Plan: B	
Ht: 6' 3"	Wt: 215	Type: Con	PT/Exp: D	Rand Var: -5	
			Consist: A	MM: 2110	

Parlayed shiny 2020 into an expanded role even though xERA and xWHIP were very leery. It paid off as a big SwK boost delivered a career-best K%. 2nd half K% fade in line with career norms, but did come with excellent control. Can give some extra length (20 of 58 appearances were >1 IP), but HRs curb late-inning appeal. Deep league filler.

Yr	Tm	W	Sv	IP	K	ERA	WHIP	xERA	xWHIP	vL+	vR+	BF/G	BB%	K%	K-BB%	xBB%	SwK	Vel	G	L	F	H%	S%	HR/F	xHR/F	GS	APC	DOM%	DIS%	Sv%	LI	RAR	BPX	R$
17	MIA	1	0	53	42	4.73	1.20	4.74	1.37	80	106	3.3	8%	19%	11%	8%	12.0%	94.2	39	20	41	27%	62%	9%	9%	0	13			0	0.96	-2.4	81	-$2
18	MIA *	5	0	116	67	5.15	1.44	5.36	1.49	109	110	12.7	9%	14%	5%	9%	8.3%	92.1	43	20	37	29%	69%	21%	22%	7	36	0%	29%	0	0.86	-14.4	18	-$8
19	MIA	4	0	51	39	3.02	1.11	4.60	1.38	79	81	3.9	8%	19%	11%	7%	9.1%	93.3	47	18	35	26%	75%	8%	13%	0	14			0	0.90	9.3	79	$3
20	SF	2	0	18	14	0.49	0.98	4.57	1.43	63	71	3.8	9%	19%	9%	8%	6.3%	93.8	46	18	36	23%	94%	0%	7%	0	15			0	0.80	9.0	62	$6
21	SF	6	1	69	68	2.62	0.96	3.74	1.18	71	97	4.6	7%	26%	19%	6%	9.9%	93.2	40	22	37	24%	81%	14%	13%	0	17			33	1.10	13.9	126	$9
1st Half		0	1	29	35	3.45	0.98	3.50	1.23	65	93	4.5	11%	31%	20%	7%	10.5%	93.2	42	22	37	21%	71%	17%	15%	0	18			50	0.81	2.9	127	-$1
2nd Half		6	0	40	33	2.03	0.95	3.91	1.14	68	102	4.7	4%	22%	18%	4%	9.4%	93.2	40	23	37	25%	88%	12%	11%	0	17			0	1.32	11.1	126	$12
Proj		5	2	65	55	3.69	1.16	4.22	1.27	86	102	4.8	7%	21%	14%	6%	9.6%	93.1	42	21	37	28%	73%	12%	14%	0						6.2	104	$3

PAUL SPORER

Garcia,Luis

Age: 25 Th: R Role SP	Health A	LIMA Plan C	
Ht: 6' 1" Wt: 244 Type Pwr	PT/Exp C	Rand Var -1	
	Consist B	MM 2303	

Won a rotation spot in the spring and made 28 starts in eye-opening rookie campaign. Good command of five pitches highlighted by cutter, with room for K% improvement per excellent SwK%. Favorable strand rate held down ERA a bit, but strong overall skills paint encouraging picture for a repeat.

Yr Tm	W	Sv	IP	K	ERA	WHIP	xERA	xWHIP	vL+	vR+	BF/G	BB%	K%	K-BB%	xBB%	SwK	Vel	G	L	F	H%	S%	HR/F	xHR/F	GS	APC	DOM%	DIS%	Sv%	LI	RAR	BPX	R$
17																																	
18																																	
19																																	
20 HOU	0	0	12	9	2.92	0.97	4.87	1.48	142	28	9.8	10%	18%	8%	12%	11.3%	94.0	41	21	38	19%	73%	8%	13%	1	41	0%	0%	0	0.67	2.3	44	-$3
21 HOU	11	0	155	167	3.30	1.17	3.97	1.21	113	73	21.1	8%	26%	18%	8%	13.8%	93.3	38	21	41	29%	77%	11%	14%	28	83	25%	14%	0	0.74	18.4	123	$16
1st Half	6	0	80	90	3.14	1.12	4.05	1.20	104	73	20.5	8%	27%	19%	8%	13.5%	93.3	36	18	45	28%	77%	10%	13%	14	84	29%	14%	0	0.71	11.2	125	$16
2nd Half	5	0	75	77	3.48	1.23	3.89	1.21	109	76	21.8	8%	25%	18%	8%	14.2%	93.3	41	23	36	30%	77%	14%	16%	14	83	21%	14%			7.3	121	$11
Proj	11	0	174	185	3.70	1.21	3.97	1.22	114	75	21.0	8%	26%	19%	8%	13.9%	93.3	39	21	40	30%	73%	12%	15%	33						16.1	127	$14

Garrett,Amir

Age: 30 Th: L Role RP	Health B	LIMA Plan C	
Ht: 6' 5" Wt: 239 Type Pwr	PT/Exp D	Rand Var +5	
	Consist C	MM 2410	

Horrible season not quite as bad as it looked. Both H% and S% were unfriendly, as xERA was nearly two full runs below ERA; xBB% suggests ballooning walk rate was overstated. Still, he's proven walk and homer prone, placing pressure on K% to be otherworldly. A risky bet for saves without improved control and command.

Yr Tm	W	Sv	IP	K	ERA	WHIP	xERA	xWHIP	vL+	vR+	BF/G	BB%	K%	K-BB%	xBB%	SwK	Vel	G	L	F	H%	S%	HR/F	xHR/F	GS	APC	DOM%	DIS%	Sv%	LI	RAR	BPX	R$
17 CIN *	5	0	138	115	7.42	1.71	6.79	1.50	126	126	20.9	11%	18%	8%	9%	9.1%	91.7	43	18	38	33%	60%	28%	17%	14	77	14%	50%	0	0.77	-52.3	15	-$22
18 CIN	1	0	63	71	4.29	1.29	3.83	1.26	99	103	4.0	9%	27%	17%	10%	14.3%	95.1	38	25	37	31%	70%	13%	11%	0	15			0	0.97	-1.1	118	-$2
19 CIN	5	0	56	78	3.21	1.41	3.66	1.39	84	99	3.6	14%	32%	17%	10%	16.6%	95.3	54	18	28	32%	82%	19%	10%	0	14			0	1.47	8.9	115	$2
20 CIN	1	1	18	26	2.45	0.93	2.86	1.10	36	107	3.3	10%	38%	28%	11%	18.1%	94.7	44	22	33	19%	92%	33%	27%	0	14			50	1.22	4.5	180	$4
21 CIN	0	7	48	61	6.04	1.57	4.15	1.40	97	117	3.4	13%	28%	15%	8%	14.7%	94.8	51	15	35	34%	65%	21%	19%	0	13			64	1.09	-10.4	97	-$7
1st Half	0	5	25	32	7.20	1.56	4.52	1.44	97	141	3.4	14%	29%	14%	9%	14.6%	94.8	42	15	44	28%	61%	30%	21%	0	12			71	1.28	-9.0	79	-$9
2nd Half	0	2	23	29	4.76	1.59	3.72	1.36	85	99	3.5	13%	28%	15%	8%	14.9%	94.8	60	15	26	39%	69%	6%	16%	0	14			50	0.88	-1.4	116	-$10
Proj	3	2	58	71	4.34	1.41	3.95	1.38	91	104	3.7	13%	29%	16%	9%	14.5%	94.7	49	18	33	31%	74%	18%	15%	0						0.8	104	-$2

Gausman,Kevin

Age: 31 Th: R Role SP	Health D	LIMA Plan D+	
Ht: 6' 2" Wt: 190 Type Pwr	PT/Exp A	Rand Var -2	
	Consist A	MM 4305	

After an amuse-bouche in 2020, we got the pièce de résistance in 2021. Can we get a second helping? PRO: Command metrics whipped to stiff peaks; SwK aging like fine wine; delectable splitter. CON: Regression looming after overachieving ERA, WHIP. Don't be a glutton and you won't be disappointed.

Yr Tm	W	Sv	IP	K	ERA	WHIP	xERA	xWHIP	vL+	vR+	BF/G	BB%	K%	K-BB%	xBB%	SwK	Vel	G	L	F	H%	S%	HR/F	xHR/F	GS	APC	DOM%	DIS%	Sv%	LI	RAR	BPX	R$
17 BAL	11	0	187	179	4.68	1.49	4.44	1.35	107	109	24.0	9%	22%	13%	8%	11.3%	95.0	43	22	35	34%	73%	15%	15%	34	99	29%	35%			-7.3	101	$0
18 2 TM	10	0	184	148	3.92	1.30	4.21	1.29	98	110	25.0	6%	19%	13%	7%	11.6%	93.6	46	21	33	31%	75%	14%	16%	31	97	26%	42%			5.2	102	$6
19 2 NL	3	0	102	114	5.72	1.42	4.24	1.24	105	106	14.5	7%	25%	18%	6%	15.5%	94.0	38	27	35	36%	62%	15%	16%	17	54	29%	41%	0	0.79	-15.3	131	-$6
20 SF	3	0	60	79	3.62	1.11	3.34	1.06	94	85	20.4	7%	32%	26%	6%	16.0%	95.1	42	22	36	32%	72%	15%	15%	10	81	20%	0%	0	0.71	6.1	191	$14
21 SF	14	0	192	227	2.81	1.04	3.42	1.10	83	82	23.5	6%	29%	23%	5%	15.8%	94.6	42	22	36	29%	78%	11%	16%	33	91	48%	18%			34.4	163	$31
1st Half	8	0	102	116	1.68	0.81	3.33	1.09	70	57	24.3	6%	30%	23%	6%	16.1%	94.5	44	16	40	22%	85%	8%	14%	16	93	63%	13%			32.4	162	$40
2nd Half	6	0	90	111	4.08	1.31	3.51	1.11	88	109	22.8	6%	29%	22%	5%	15.4%	94.8	40	28	33	36%	73%	15%	18%	17	89	35%	24%			2.0	164	$12
Proj	12	0	181	210	3.52	1.11	3.44	1.12	88	89	22.9	7%	29%	23%	6%	15.1%	94.6	41	23	35	30%	73%	14%	16%	31						20.9	161	$20

Germán,Domingo

Age: 29 Th: R Role SP	Health D	LIMA Plan A	
Ht: 6' 2" Wt: 181 Type Pwr/FB	PT/Exp C	Rand Var -2	
	Consist A	MM 2301	

Rollercoaster year after domestic violence suspension included two-week April demotion and right shoulder injury that shelved him almost two months. Skills peaked over small-sample second half thanks to a few solid relief appearances and one dominant start. Has the tools to succeed, but carries baggage with it.

Yr Tm	W	Sv	IP	K	ERA	WHIP	xERA	xWHIP	vL+	vR+	BF/G	BB%	K%	K-BB%	xBB%	SwK	Vel	G	L	F	H%	S%	HR/F	xHR/F	GS	APC	DOM%	DIS%	Sv%	LI	RAR	BPX	R$
17 NYY *	8	0	124	117	4.05	1.40	4.50	1.32	82	94	19.3	9%	22%	14%		11.5%	96.4	55	21	24	33%	74%	13%	8%	0	36			0	0.35	4.7	89	$3
18 NYY	2	0	86	102	5.57	1.33	3.98	1.23	114	100	17.9	9%	27%	18%	7%	15.2%	94.7	37	22	40	32%	62%	16%	11%	14	70	14%	36%	0	0.68	-15.0	132	-$6
19 NYY	18	0	143	153	4.03	1.15	4.20	1.21	103	87	22.0	7%	26%	19%	6%	13.4%	93.6	38	21	41	28%	75%	19%	15%	24	83	25%	13%	0	0.90	8.4	134	$16
20																																	
21 NYY	4	0	98	98	4.58	1.18	4.26	1.20	87	104	18.6	7%	24%	17%	6%	14.8%	93.5	42	14	44	29%	67%	14%	16%	18	72	28%	22%	0	0.75	-3.8	126	$1
1st Half	4	0	76	68	4.50	1.24	4.52	1.23	94	106	21.5	6%	21%	15%	6%	13.3%	93.4	43	14	43	29%	71%	15%	16%	15	81	27%	27%			-2.2	115	$2
2nd Half	0	0	22	30	4.84	0.99	3.42	1.12	43	108	12.6	9%	34%	25%	7%	19.8%	94.0	40	14	46	27%	50%	9%	13%	3	51	33%	0%	0	0.75	-1.6	163	-$7
Proj	6	0	123	139	4.09	1.20	3.92	1.20	90	104	20.8	8%	28%	20%	7%	16.0%	93.9	40	17	43	30%	71%	14%	14%	24						5.5	138	$5

Gibson,Kyle

Age: 34 Th: R Role SP	Health B	LIMA Plan C+	
Ht: 6' 6" Wt: 215 Type /GB	PT/Exp A	Rand Var -1	
	Consist A	MM 2103	

According to ERA, a tale of two halves: first he pitched like a Cy Young candidate, then, well... not. But skills weren't as stark. Earlier work was heavily indebted to very friendly H%, S% and good HR suppression. The latter was marred by a reversal in luck and eroding command. Fulsome innings, inconsistent results. Consult xERA for future insight.

Yr Tm	W	Sv	IP	K	ERA	WHIP	xERA	xWHIP	vL+	vR+	BF/G	BB%	K%	K-BB%	xBB%	SwK	Vel	G	L	F	H%	S%	HR/F	xHR/F	GS	APC	DOM%	DIS%	Sv%	LI	RAR	BPX	R$
17 MIN *	13	0	175	137	4.93	1.53	5.34	1.42	110	111	23.8	9%	18%	9%	9%	10.4%	92.0	51	23	26	33%	71%	18%	18%	29	90	17%	45%			-12.3	52	-$3
18 MIN	10	0	197	179	3.62	1.30	3.95	1.36	100	94	25.8	10%	22%	12%	11%	11.7%	93.0	50	22	28	29%	76%	15%	15%	32	101	22%	28%			13.0	90	$10
19 MIN	13	0	160	160	4.84	1.44	4.02	1.30	107	100	20.8	8%	23%	15%	9%	13.4%	93.3	51	25	24	34%	70%	20%	20%	29	81	21%	31%	0	0.88	-6.6	115	$2
20 TEX	2	0	67	58	5.35	1.53	4.47	1.43	118	106	25.1	10%	19%	9%	11%	9.6%	92.3	51	27	22	32%	69%	27%	24%	12	95	17%	58%			-7.4	68	-$9
21 2 TM	10	0	182	155	3.71	1.22	4.07	1.34	102	79	24.3	8%	21%	12%	9%	10.8%	92.5	52	19	29	28%	72%	11%	13%	30	93	23%	17%	0	0.78	12.5	91	$11
1st Half	6	0	96	81	1.98	1.03	3.84	1.29	76	75	23.7	8%	21%	14%	9%	11.7%	92.7	51	19	30	25%	85%	9%	9%	16	92	25%	13%			27.0	102	$26
2nd Half	4	0	86	74	5.63	1.42	4.33	1.39	114	87	25.0	9%	20%	10%	11%	9.9%	92.2	53	19	29	32%	61%	14%	16%	14	94	21%	21%	0	0.81	-14.5	78	-$8
Proj	9	0	174	153	4.23	1.36	4.15	1.37	109	92	23.4	9%	21%	12%	10%	10.9%	92.6	51	22	27	31%	72%	16%	17%	31						4.8	90	$3

Gil,Luis

Age: 24 Th: R Role RP	Health A	LIMA Plan B+	
Ht: 6' 3" Wt: 176 Type Pwr/xFB	PT/Exp F	Rand Var 0	
	Consist F	MM 1401	

1-1, 3.07 ERA in 29 IP at NYY. Top SP prospect hurdled two MiLB levels, got off to a hot MLB start, was displaced by Luis Severino's return, then finished with three less successful outings. Big, high-spin fastball is nice but has work to do throwing strikes. You know the drill with high-risk, high-reward arms.

Yr Tm	W	Sv	IP	K	ERA	WHIP	xERA	xWHIP	vL+	vR+	BF/G	BB%	K%	K-BB%	xBB%	SwK	Vel	G	L	F	H%	S%	HR/F	xHR/F	GS	APC	DOM%	DIS%	Sv%	LI	RAR	BPX	R$
17																																	
18																																	
19																																	
20																																	
21 NYY *	6	1	112	139	4.11	1.36	3.87	1.40	74	88	18.0	14%	30%	16%	10%	14.1%	96.1	32	15	52	29%	73%	11%	12%	6	89	33%	0%			2.1	99	$2
1st Half	2	0	46	56	3.89	1.39	4.43				19.5	12%	29%	17%							32%	77%	0%		0	0					2.2	92	-$2
2nd Half	4	1	66	83	4.27	1.33	3.47	1.43	71	90	17.0	15%	31%	15%	10%	14.1%	96.1	32	15	52	28%	70%	11%	12%	6	89	33%	0%			-0.1	104	$5
Proj	6	0	116	147	4.34	1.40	4.46	1.40	89	107	19.6	14%	30%	16%	10%	14.1%	96.1	32	15	52	30%	73%	13%	11%	24						1.6	85	$0

Gilbert,Logan

Age: 25 Th: R Role SP	Health A	LIMA Plan B+	
Ht: 6' 6" Wt: 225 Type Pwr/xFB	PT/Exp D	Rand Var +1	
	Consist C	MM 2303	

Much heralded prospect made his MLB debut and mostly held his own as SEA carefully managed workload. Broad skills foundation, with K-BB%, SwK, velocity all comfortably above average. Extreme fly ball tendencies can be nerve-racking, but he does many things well enough. Solid growth potential.

Yr Tm	W	Sv	IP	K	ERA	WHIP	xERA	xWHIP	vL+	vR+	BF/G	BB%	K%	K-BB%	xBB%	SwK	Vel	G	L	F	H%	S%	HR/F	xHR/F	GS	APC	DOM%	DIS%	Sv%	LI	RAR	BPX	R$
17																																	
18																																	
19 aa	4	0	50	51	4.20	1.19	2.92				22.3	8%	25%	17%							31%	63%									1.9	123	$0
20																																	
21 SEA	6	0	119	128	4.68	1.17	4.21	1.14	92	101	21.0	6%	25%	20%	8%	12.8%	95.3	32	21	46	31%	63%	11%	14%	24	89	25%	17%			-6.0	139	$3
1st Half	2	0	42	45	4.10	1.10	3.96	1.13	82	101	19.1	6%	26%	20%	8%	12.9%	94.9	34	22	44	30%	66%	10%	15%	9	81	33%	11%			0.8	142	$0
2nd Half	4	0	78	83	4.98	1.21	4.34	1.14	91	104	22.1	5%	25%	20%	8%	12.8%	95.5	31	21	47	32%	62%	11%	14%	15	93	20%	20%			-6.9	139	$3
Proj	8	0	145	154	4.20	1.18	4.09	1.17	89	98	20.3	7%	27%	20%	8%	12.9%	95.3	33	21	46	31%	67%	10%	14%	29						4.6	135	$8

ALAIN DE LEONARDIS

Gilbert,Tyler

Age: 28 Th: L Role SP | Ht: 6' 3" Wt: 190 Type Con
Health B | PT/Exp F | Consist B
LIMA Plan C+ | Rand Var -3 | MM 1001

2-2, 3.15 ERA in 40 IP at ARI. MiLB Rule 5 draft pick threw a no-hitter in first MLB start, then shut down in September with left elbow inflammation. Relied heavily on location, defense, helpful H% with cutter-first approach as velocity, SwK among lowest for any SP. Volatile profile, health picture murky; let's see him do it again.

Yr Tm	W	Sv	IP	K	ERA	WHIP	xERA	xWHIP	vL+	vR+	BF/G	BB%	K%	K-BB%	xBB%	SwK	Vel	G	L	F	H%	S%	HR/F	xHR/F	GS	APC	DOM%	DIS%	Sv%	LI	RAR	BPX	R$
17																																	
18 a/a	7	5	72	59	3.82	1.10	3.40				5.9	6%	21%	15%							28%	69%									3.0	112	$6
19 aaa	2	2	49	39	3.36	1.25	3.78				5.6	7%	19%	12%							29%	76%									7.0	82	$1
20																																	
21 ARI *	7	0	93	63	3.08	1.14	3.02	1.40	47	103	18.5	8%	17%	9%	6%	8.7%	89.7	39	19	42	26%	75%	8%	13%	6	67	17%	50%	0	0.93	13.6	76	$7
1st Half	4	0	30	20	3.74	1.24	3.30				17.5	8%	16%	8%							28%	69%	0%		0	0					1.9	76	-$1
2nd Half	3	0	63	43	2.77	1.10	2.89	1.39	45	105	19.0	8%	17%	9%	6%	8.7%	89.7	39	19	42	24%	78%	8%	13%	6	67	17%	50%	0	0.93	11.6	77	$9
Proj	8	0	102	74	3.97	1.16	4.62	1.37	58	128	20.7	8%	18%	11%	6%	8.7%	89.7	39	19	42	27%	68%	8%	12%	20						6.1	70	$5

Giles,Ken

Age: 31 Th: R Role RP | Ht: 6' 3" Wt: 210 Type Pwr
Health F | PT/Exp D | Consist F
LIMA Plan B+ | Rand Var 0 | MM 4520

Missed all of 2021 recovering from Tommy John surgery. Pre-injury skill levels were definitely closer-worthy, as K-BB%, SwK, velocity all truly elite. Risky for sure, but if he recovers dominant stuff, he should be in the saves mix by midseason, if not earlier.

Yr Tm	W	Sv	IP	K	ERA	WHIP	xERA	xWHIP	vL+	vR+	BF/G	BB%	K%	K-BB%	xBB%	SwK	Vel	G	L	F	H%	S%	HR/F	xHR/F	GS	APC	DOM%	DIS%	Sv%	LI	RAR	BPX	R$
17 HOU	1	34	63	83	2.30	1.04	3.14	1.12	77	74	3.9	9%	34%	25%	6%	16.6%	98.1	44	18	38	30%	80%	7%	7%	0	15			89	1.11	15.9	186	$21
18 2 AL	0	26	50	53	4.65	1.21	3.54	1.06	89	110	3.9	3%	25%	22%	4%	16.4%	97.3	44	20	36	35%	64%	11%	14%	0	14			100	0.99	-3.1	183	$7
19 TOR	2	23	53	83	1.87	1.00	2.93	1.01	75	77	3.9	8%	40%	32%	6%	19.3%	97.0	39	19	42	32%	88%	11%	12%	0	15			96	1.10	17.2	210	$17
20 TOR	0	1	4	6	9.82	2.18	5.85		74	216	4.8	21%	32%	11%		24.6%	94.4	33	22	44	32%	67%	50%	40%	0	17			100	0.62	-2.4	12	-$8
21																																	
1st Half																																	
2nd Half																																	
Proj	1	18	51	69	3.52	1.19	3.33	1.12	87	90	3.9	9%	34%	25%	5%	17.7%	97.4	42	19	39	34%	73%	10%	12%	0						5.9	175	$8

Giolito,Lucas

Age: 27 Th: R Role SP | Ht: 6' 6" Wt: 245 Type Pwr/FB
Health C | PT/Exp A | Consist A
LIMA Plan C+ | Rand Var 0 | MM 3305

Third straight season of excellence, cementing him as one of the top SP options out there. If not for his 1 inning, 7 ER blowup on Patriot's Day, his ERA would have been 3.19. Strikeout rate, SwK both slipped but compensated with superior walk rate in line with xBB%. History of suppressing H%, xHR/F puts a bow on the whole package. Bid with confidence.

Yr Tm	W	Sv	IP	K	ERA	WHIP	xERA	xWHIP	vL+	vR+	BF/G	BB%	K%	K-BB%	xBB%	SwK	Vel	G	L	F	H%	S%	HR/F	xHR/F	GS	APC	DOM%	DIS%	Sv%	LI	RAR	BPX	R$
17 CHW *	9	0	174	152	4.49	1.40	4.63	1.44	84	88	23.7	10%	21%	10%	8%	10.7%	92.1	45	20	35	30%	72%	18%	11%	7	101	29%	14%			-2.8	62	$2
18 CHW	10	0	173	125	6.13	1.48	5.29	1.58	114	105	24.2	12%	16%	5%	11%	8.6%	92.4	44	18	37	28%	60%	13%	14%	32	94	16%	41%			-42.3	15	-$14
19 CHW	14	0	177	228	3.41	1.06	3.66	1.15	74	96	24.3	8%	32%	24%	6%	15.5%	94.3	36	21	43	28%	74%	14%	12%	29	97	38%	10%			23.8	158	$24
20 CHW	4	0	72	97	3.48	1.04	3.38	1.16	82	73	24.0	10%	34%	24%	7%	17.9%	94.0	41	21	38	27%	70%	13%	12%	12	101	33%	17%			8.6	161	$22
21 CHW	11	0	179	201	3.53	1.10	3.87	1.16	89	92	23.2	7%	28%	21%	7%	15.6%	93.9	33	25	42	28%	75%	14%	12%	31	96	32%	16%			16.3	134	$19
1st Half	6	0	94	111	3.84	1.10	3.81	1.16	74	113	23.6	8%	29%	21%	6%	15.6%	93.8	33	23	44	26%	74%	18%	14%	16	98	25%	13%			4.9	138	$15
2nd Half	5	0	85	90	3.18	1.11	3.93	1.16	99	75	22.9	6%	26%	20%	8%	15.7%	94.0	33	26	41	30%	75%	10%	10%	15	93	40%	20%			11.4	131	$19
Proj	11	0	181	205	3.62	1.11	3.73	1.18	90	89	22.8	8%	29%	21%	8%	15.5%	93.7	37	23	40	28%	73%	14%	12%	31						18.7	139	$19

Givens,Mychal

Age: 32 Th: R Role RP | Ht: 6' 0" Wt: 230 Type Pwr
Health B | PT/Exp C | Consist A
LIMA Plan B+ | Rand Var -3 | MM 2310

Missed three weeks with a back strain before deadline deal from COL to CIN, where he closed by default. Control and dominance metrics headed south as BPX sunk to five-year low; fortunate S% saved his bacon. Unless he rediscovers SwK magic, these skills should be kept far away from the ninth inning.

Yr Tm	W	Sv	IP	K	ERA	WHIP	xERA	xWHIP	vL+	vR+	BF/G	BB%	K%	K-BB%	xBB%	SwK	Vel	G	L	F	H%	S%	HR/F	xHR/F	GS	APC	DOM%	DIS%	Sv%	LI	RAR	BPX	R$
17 BAL	8	0	79	88	2.75	1.04	3.66	1.20	82	83	4.6	8%	28%	20%	8%	12.5%	95.6	43	17	40	26%	81%	13%	12%	0	19			0	1.13	15.6	150	$11
18 BAL	0	9	77	79	3.99	1.19	4.08	1.30	94	81	4.6	9%	25%	15%	6%	12.1%	95.1	36	24	39	29%	66%	5%	7%	0	18			69	1.34	1.5	99	$3
19 BAL	2	11	63	86	4.57	1.19	3.65	1.20	122	79	4.5	10%	33%	23%	7%	16.7%	95.3	38	23	39	28%	69%	23%	18%	0	19			58	1.45	-0.5	149	$5
20 2 TM	1	1	22	25	3.63	1.16	4.98	1.35	103	100	4.2	11%	27%	16%	8%	13.3%	94.7	23	18	59	22%	81%	15%	12%	0	19			33	1.02	2.3	83	$1
21 2 NL	4	8	51	54	3.35	1.37	4.48	1.43	98	103	4.0	13%	25%	13%	10%	11.8%	94.8	36	27	37	29%	81%	14%	15%	0	16			73	1.30	5.7	62	$3
1st Half	2	0	23	25	2.78	1.28	4.28	1.37	86	115	3.9	12%	27%	15%	11%	11.2%	94.3	27	33	40	26%	88%	18%	17%	0	16			0	1.35	4.2	73	-$2
2nd Half	2	8	28	29	3.81	1.45	4.63	1.48	98	99	4.1	13%	24%	11%	10%	12.3%	95.2	43	22	35	30%	76%	11%	14%	0	16			80	1.27	1.6	54	$2
Proj	2	5	65	73	3.96	1.27	4.15	1.34	102	90	4.2	11%	27%	16%	8%	12.9%	95.1	37	24	38	29%	73%	14%	14%	0						4.0	97	$1

Glasnow,Tyler

Age: 28 Th: R Role SP | Ht: 6' 8" Wt: 225 Type Pwr
Health F | PT/Exp B | Consist A
LIMA Plan B | Rand Var -2 | MM 5500

Was on a tear before season-ending UCL injury and Tommy John surgery; will be lucky to see any action in 2022. SwK spiked to career high, as did BF/G--wait, did heavier workload contribute to injury? Maybe, but brittle even in years past when IP were carefully managed. Lamborghini on legs.

Yr Tm	W	Sv	IP	K	ERA	WHIP	xERA	xWHIP	vL+	vR+	BF/G	BB%	K%	K-BB%	xBB%	SwK	Vel	G	L	F	H%	S%	HR/F	xHR/F	GS	APC	DOM%	DIS%	Sv%	LI	RAR	BPX	R$
17 PIT *	11	0	155	167	4.64	1.48	4.59	1.42	139	128	22.3	12%	25%	13%	12%	8.4%	94.6	43	21	36	33%	71%	18%	16%	13	81	8%	54%	0	0.81	-5.4	86	$1
18 2 TM	2	0	112	136	4.27	1.27	3.44	1.30	93	97	10.4	11%	29%	18%	10%	12.2%	96.6	50	20	30	29%	70%	18%	21%	11	41	27%	9%	0	0.56	-1.7	127	$1
19 TAM	6	0	61	76	1.78	0.89	2.98	1.05	55	78	19.2	6%	33%	27%	7%	12.1%	97.0	50	16	34	27%	84%	9%	11%	12	75	58%	8%			20.4	190	$11
20 TAM	5	0	57	91	4.08	1.13	3.08	1.06	84	98	21.6	9%	38%	29%	8%	14.5%	97.0	39	23	38	31%	72%	23%	20%	11	88	27%	9%			2.6	204	$16
21 TAM	5	0	88	123	2.66	0.93	2.87	1.04	65	84	24.3	8%	36%	28%	6%	17.5%	97.0	45	18	37	26%	78%	14%	17%	14	96	64%	7%			17.4	192	$13
1st Half	5	0	88	123	2.66	0.93	2.87	1.04	62	85	24.3	8%	36%	28%	6%	17.5%	97.0	45	18	37	26%	78%	14%	17%	14	96	64%	7%			17.4	192	$25
2nd Half																																	
Proj	1	0	15	19	3.29	1.09	3.12	1.10	80	88	22.9	10%	37%	27%	8%	13.7%	96.7	46	19	35	29%	75%	16%	17%	2						2.1	174	-$3

Gomber,Austin

Age: 28 Th: L Role SP | Ht: 6' 5" Wt: 220 Type
Health D | PT/Exp C | Consist C
LIMA Plan B+ | Rand Var +1 | MM 1201

Potential breakout campaign bookended by awful April and August was cut short by season-ending stress fracture in his lower spine. First half surge was built on solid BB%, GB%, with some help from H% and HR/F. Skills faded after return from month-long elbow injury. Spring's in doubt; jury's still out.

Yr Tm	W	Sv	IP	K	ERA	WHIP	xERA	xWHIP	vL+	vR+	BF/G	BB%	K%	K-BB%	xBB%	SwK	Vel	G	L	F	H%	S%	HR/F	xHR/F	GS	APC	DOM%	DIS%	Sv%	LI	RAR	BPX	R$
17 aa	10	0	143	111	4.38	1.36	4.40				23.0	9%	19%	10%							29%	71%									-0.3	63	$3
18 STL *	13	0	144	127	4.18	1.44	4.73	1.34	102	112	15.0	8%	21%	12%	8%	9.5%	92.5	38	27	35	33%	73%	9%	17%	11	42	18%	27%	0	0.95	-0.5	80	$2
19 a/a	4	0	50	42	3.41	1.40	4.49				19.2	9%	20%	11%							32%	79%									6.8	73	$0
20 STL	1	0	29	27	1.86	1.17	4.50	1.49	98	68	8.5	13%	23%	10%	10%	10.1%	92.5	49	18	34	25%	85%	4%	5%	4	38	0%	0%	0	1.01	9.3	59	$4
21 COL	9	0	115	113	4.53	1.24	4.23	1.29	91	99	21.2	8%	23%	15%	7%	11.7%	91.6	44	19	37	28%	69%	17%	17%	23	80	30%	26%			-3.7	103	$3
1st Half	6	0	78	76	3.68	1.07	3.77	1.22	71	89	21.1	7%	24%	17%	6%	11.4%	91.8	48	20	32	26%	69%	13%	17%	15	81	40%	13%			5.7	123	$13
2nd Half	3	0	37	37	6.32	1.59	5.22	1.41	127	121	21.4	11%	22%	11%	8%	12.4%	91.4	38	18	45	31%	69%	22%	17%	8	79	13%	50%			-9.4	65	-$12
Proj	9	0	109	100	4.26	1.31	4.44	1.32	99	102	20.3	8%	22%	14%	8%	11.4%	91.8	41	21	38	30%	73%	15%	17%	22						2.6	93	$2

Gonsolin,Tony

Age: 28 Th: R Role RP | Ht: 6' 3" Wt: 205 Type Pwr/FB
Health F | PT/Exp C | Consist B
LIMA Plan B+ | Rand Var -5 | MM 1301

Pitched around two lengthy stints on the IL due to right shoulder inflammation and posted passable results despite skills erosion. Injuries may well have caused BB% to balloon and velocity to drop; generous H% and S% bailed him out. If healthy he's intriguing, but shoulder issues can linger. Caveat emptor.

Yr Tm	W	Sv	IP	K	ERA	WHIP	xERA	xWHIP	vL+	vR+	BF/G	BB%	K%	K-BB%	xBB%	SwK	Vel	G	L	F	H%	S%	HR/F	xHR/F	GS	APC	DOM%	DIS%	Sv%	LI	RAR	BPX	R$
17																																	
18 aa	6	0	45	41	2.58	1.10	2.64				19.7	8%	23%	15%							27%	79%									8.8	119	$4
19 LA *	6	1	82	78	3.83	1.30	3.67	1.42	75	79	14.1	10%	23%	13%	10%	12.3%	93.7	42	15	44	29%	73%	9%	9%	6	63	17%	50%	100	0.65	6.8	87	$3
20 LA	2	0	47	46	2.31	0.84	3.75	1.08	74	67	19.6	4%	26%	22%	6%	14.6%	95.1	34	24	42	26%	73%	4%	9%	8	78	25%	0%	0	0.81	12.3	153	$17
21 LA	4	0	56	65	3.23	1.35	4.69	1.46	90	98	15.9	14%	27%	13%	11%	13.0%	93.8	37	18	45	26%	82%	13%	11%	13	66	15%	23%	0	0.73	7.1	60	$0
1st Half	1	0	16	22	2.81	1.56	5.08	1.57	76	102	14.4	18%	31%	13%	12%	13.1%	93.6	30	19	51	32%	83%	5%	5%	4	63	0%	25%	0	0.71	2.9	36	-$5
2nd Half	3	0	40	43	3.40	1.26	4.55	1.42	89	99	16.7	13%	26%	13%	10%	13.0%	93.9	39	18	43	24%	81%	16%	13%	9	68	22%	22%	0	0.74	4.2	70	$1
Proj	6	0	94	102	3.84	1.31	4.51	1.37	92	95	16.2	11%	26%	15%	9%	13.2%	94.0	36	19	45	30%	73%	9%	9%	15						7.2	85	$2

ALAIN DE LEONARDIS

Gonzales,Marco

Age: 30	Th: L	Role: SP	Health: C	LIMA Plan: B
Ht: 6' 1"	Wt: 197	Type: Con/FB	PT/Exp: A	Rand Var: -3
			Consist: C	MM: 1103

Rough 1st half included month-long IL stint due to left forearm strain, while 2nd half was more prosperous. However, overall skills were nearly identical each half... and not all that good. K% took a dive and FB lean - which led to HR - got extreme. Survives on control, exit velocity suppression, defense, and a bit of luck. Crafty leftying ain't easy.

Yr Tm	W	Sv	IP	K	ERA	WHIP	xERA	xWHIP	vL+	vR+	BF/G	BB%	K%	K-BB%	xBB%	SwK	Vel	G	L	F	H%	S%	HR/F	xHR/F	GS	APC	DOM%	DIS%	Sv%	LI	RAR	BPX	R$
17 2 TM *	9	0	120	88	4.52	1.37	4.60	1.34	110	129	21.0	7%	17%	11%	8%	9.7%	91.5	45	23	32	32%	70%	18%	14%	8	64	0%	75%	0	0.59	-2.3	73	$1
18 SEA	13	0	167	145	4.00	1.22	3.71	1.18	95	101	23.7	5%	21%	16%	5%	9.7%	90.1	45	25	30	32%	70%	11%	13%	29	88	28%	14%			3.2	135	$9
19 SEA	16	0	203	147	3.99	1.31	5.12	1.38	108	95	25.5	6%	17%	11%	6%	8.3%	88.9	41	21	38	31%	72%	9%	9%	34	95	26%	32%			12.9	75	$12
20 SEA	7	0	70	64	3.10	0.95	4.02	1.08	97	77	25.2	3%	23%	21%	5%	8.7%	88.2	38	21	41	28%	72%	10%	14%	11	96	55%	18%			11.6	159	$28
21 SEA	10	0	143	108	3.96	1.17	5.00	1.33	83	108	23.4	7%	18%	11%	7%	9.4%	88.4	32	20	48	24%	75%	14%	17%	25	93	16%	36%			5.5	67	$9
1st Half	1	0	51	46	6.00	1.47	5.06	1.37	67	147	22.3	9%	21%	12%	8%	9.9%	88.3	30	26	43	30%	66%	19%	25%	10	86	20%	40%			-10.9	65	-$11
2nd Half	9	0	92	62	2.83	1.00	4.97	1.31	88	90	24.1	6%	17%	11%	6%	9.1%	88.5	33	16	51	21%	83%	12%	13%	15	98	13%	33%			16.4	68	$29
Proj	12	0	174	139	4.10	1.26	4.65	1.29	96	105	23.7	6%	20%	13%	6%	9.2%	88.8	36	21	42	29%	73%	12%	15%	30						7.7	91	$8

González,Chi Chi

Age: 30	Th: R	Role: RP	Health: F	LIMA Plan: D+
Ht: 6' 3"	Wt: 210	Type: Con	PT/Exp: C	Rand Var: +5
			Consist: B	MM: 0001

A renowned screenwriter once told me that when giving notes, you should always say three nice things first, then you can say whatever you want. So, here goes: didn't walk many in 2021; was one of only 141 SP to throw 80+ IP; his grandfather gave him the nickname Chi Chi. Eh, let's just leave it at that.

Yr Tm	W	Sv	IP	K	ERA	WHIP	xERA	xWHIP	vL+	vR+	BF/G	BB%	K%	K-BB%	xBB%	SwK	Vel	G	L	F	H%	S%	HR/F	xHR/F	GS	APC	DOM%	DIS%	Sv%	LI	RAR	BPX	R$
17																																	
18																																	
19 COL *	6	0	150	102	6.40	1.70	6.48	1.59	113	97	22.6	10%	15%	5%	11%	8.5%	92.2	43	25	32	33%	66%	18%	16%	12	82	0%	75%	0	0.76	-35.0	11	-$18
20 COL	0	0	20	16	6.86	1.63	5.59	1.54	129	114	15.2	11%	18%	7%	12%	7.5%	92.2	33	32	35	33%	59%	14%	11%	4	58	0%	75%	0	0.61	-5.8	22	-$12
21 COL	3	0	102	56	6.46	1.52	5.27	1.40	113	133	18.7	6%	13%	6%	7%	7.3%	91.8	39	28	33	32%	60%	16%	20%	18	68	0%	67%	0	0.72	-27.5	43	-$16
1st Half	2	0	77	42	5.52	1.41	5.02	1.39	110	116	20.3	6%	13%	7%	6%	7.2%	91.9	41	26	33	30%	64%	16%	18%	12	75	0%	58%	0	0.77	-11.8	49	-$10
2nd Half	1	0	25	14	9.36	1.88	6.01	1.44	98	188	15.4	7%	11%	5%	9%	7.7%	91.6	36	31	34	38%	50%	15%	26%	6	55	0%	83%	0	0.61	-15.7	29	-$22
Proj	3	0	87	51	5.92	1.58	5.41	1.47	107	140	17.1	8%	13%	6%	8%	7.8%	91.8	39	28	33	32%	66%	17%	21%	16						-15.7	33	-$12

Graterol,Brusdar

Age: 23	Th: R	Role: RP	Health: D	LIMA Plan: B+
Ht: 6' 1"	Wt: 265	Type: /GB	PT/Exp: D	Rand Var: +5
			Consist: B	MM: 3110

3-0, 4.59 ERA in 33 IP at LA. Got off to slow start in camp and missed two months with forearm tightness. Owner of one of the fastest and heaviest sinkers in baseball, with nice xBB% to boot, but MLB SwK/K% stuck in first gear. If he can approach his 13% SwK from AA--and iron out those vL/R splits--we may have something here.

Yr Tm	W	Sv	IP	K	ERA	WHIP	xERA	xWHIP	vL+	vR+	BF/G	BB%	K%	K-BB%	xBB%	SwK	Vel	G	L	F	H%	S%	HR/F	xHR/F	GS	APC	DOM%	DIS%	Sv%	LI	RAR	BPX	R$
17																																	
18																																	
19 MIN *	8	1	70	59	2.84	1.12	2.60	1.39	100	91	10.6	9%	21%	12%	4%	9.0%	99.0	48	30	22	26%	76%	17%	13%	0	14			100	1.49	14.4	96	$8
20 LA	1	0	23	13	3.09	0.90	3.57	1.24	125	54	3.8	3%	15%	11%	4%	6.5%	99.3	62	16	22	24%	65%	7%	11%	2	13	0%	0%	0	0.84	3.9	112	$2
21 LA *	5	1	52	44	4.99	1.23	3.30	1.30	134	79	4.1	8%	21%	13%	5%	9.0%	100.0	58	23	18	30%	58%	11%	12%	1	15	0%	100%	20	0.93	-4.6	100	-$2
1st Half	3	0	15	12	5.82	1.11	2.22		170	59	3.7	8%	20%	12%		4.6%	99.6	62	23	15	29%	42%	0%	0%	0	13			0	0.83	-2.9	123	-$5
2nd Half	2	1	36	32	4.65	1.28	3.74	1.32	122	84	4.3	9%	21%	13%	4%	9.7%	100.1	58	23	19	31%	64%	12%	13%	1	16	0%	100%	25	0.95	-1.7	91	-$5
Proj	7	2	65	55	3.92	1.28	3.68	1.34	126	84	4.9	9%	21%	12%	4%	9.6%	100.1	58	23	19	31%	69%	11%	12%	0						4.3	99	$3

Graveman,Kendall

Age: 31	Th: R	Role: RP	Health: F	LIMA Plan: C+
Ht: 6' 2"	Wt: 200	Type: /GB	PT/Exp: D	Rand Var: -5
			Consist: D	MM: 3210

Flourished in first full season working out of pen despite missing almost three weeks on COVID IL. Does he have stuff to close? PRO: Elite GB%; velocity up almost two ticks; LI shows he's had managers' trust. CON: K% downside due to meh SwK; had plenty of help from H%, S%. Solid but regression may hit hard.

Yr Tm	W	Sv	IP	K	ERA	WHIP	xERA	xWHIP	vL+	vR+	BF/G	BB%	K%	K-BB%	xBB%	SwK	Vel	G	L	F	H%	S%	HR/F	xHR/F	GS	APC	DOM%	DIS%	Sv%	LI	RAR	BPX	R$
17 OAK	6	0	105	70	4.19	1.39	4.52	1.40	91	116	23.4	7%	16%	9%	9%	7.0%	93.4	51	19	30	31%	72%	12%	16%	19	88	16%	47%			2.2	75	$0
18 OAK *	3	0	58	39	6.89	1.87	7.92	1.43	125	126	24.9	8%	14%	7%	11%	7.8%	93.7	55	16	28	38%	66%	27%	28%	7	90	0%	71%			-19.7	5	-$15
19																																	
20 SEA	1	0	19	15	5.79	1.23	4.82	1.46	44	127	7.0	10%	19%	9%	12%	7.3%	94.8	48	17	35	26%	52%	11%	10%	2	30	0%	50%	0	1.15	-3.1	59	-$5
21 2 AL	5	10	56	61	1.77	0.98	3.06	1.22	103	46	4.2	9%	27%	18%	8%	11.3%	96.6	55	22	23	25%	85%	10%	14%	0	16			67	1.38	17.3	135	$13
1st Half	2	7	25	23	1.07	0.67	2.96	1.12	100	28	4.1	5%	25%	20%	8%	11.4%	96.6	52	21	26	17%	93%	13%	20%	0	17			78	1.55	10.0	142	$9
2nd Half	3	3	31	38	2.35	1.24	3.11	1.29	97	63	4.2	11%	29%	18%	9%	11.1%	96.6	57	22	21	31%	81%	7%	8%	0	16			50	1.25	7.3	128	$5
Proj	5	5	65	61	3.31	1.25	3.78	1.31	108	80	6.3	9%	23%	14%	9%	9.6%	95.4	54	20	25	30%	76%	13%	17%	0						9.2	110	$4

Gray,Jonathan

Age: 30	Th: R	Role: SP	Health: F	LIMA Plan: B+
Ht: 6' 4"	Wt: 225	Type: Pwr	PT/Exp: B	Rand Var: +1
			Consist: D	MM: 2203

Besides losing three weeks in 1st half to right elbow flexor strain, posted fairly typical ho-hum results overall. Second half skills surged with velocity, Swk, K% all ticking up, but results marred by unhelpful H%, S%. Might get a boost with change of scenery as BPX, xERA history confirm mid-rotation starter status.

Yr Tm	W	Sv	IP	K	ERA	WHIP	xERA	xWHIP	vL+	vR+	BF/G	BB%	K%	K-BB%	xBB%	SwK	Vel	G	L	F	H%	S%	HR/F	xHR/F	GS	APC	DOM%	DIS%	Sv%	LI	RAR	BPX	R$
17 COL	10	0	110	112	3.67	1.30	3.62	1.21	92	101	23.1	7%	24%	18%	7%	9.4%	96.0	49	23	29	34%	74%	11%	10%	20	92	35%	20%			9.4	151	$8
18 COL	12	0	172	183	5.12	1.35	3.63	1.20	113	100	24.0	7%	25%	18%	8%	12.9%	94.8	47	22	30	34%	65%	18%	15%	31	90	29%	29%			-20.6	142	-$1
19 COL	11	0	150	150	3.84	1.35	4.02	1.33	108	96	24.5	9%	24%	15%	8%	12.3%	96.1	50	23	26	32%	76%	17%	17%	25	91	28%	32%	0	1.01	12.3	108	$8
20 COL	2	0	39	22	6.69	1.44	5.82	1.43	119	99	21.8	6%	13%	6%	8%	9.9%	94.0	37	25	38	31%	54%	11%	13%	8	82	13%	50%			-10.8	43	-$10
21 COL	8	0	149	157	4.59	1.33	4.03	1.29	101	100	22.2	9%	24%	15%	8%	11.5%	94.9	48	18	33	31%	69%	15%	15%	29	87	14%	28%			-6.0	112	$1
1st Half	5	0	74	65	3.89	1.24	4.28	1.39	95	86	22.5	10%	21%	11%	9%	11.1%	94.4	52	17	30	27%	72%	14%	13%	14	87	21%	36%			3.4	78	$6
2nd Half	3	0	75	92	5.28	1.41	3.80	1.19	97	117	21.9	8%	28%	20%	8%	12.0%	95.4	44	19	37	36%	66%	16%	16%	15	88	7%	20%			-9.4	147	-$4
Proj	9	0	160	154	4.41	1.31	4.10	1.30	104	97	21.5	8%	23%	15%	8%	11.4%	95.0	46	21	33	31%	70%	15%	14%	31						0.9	108	$4

Gray,Josiah

Age: 24	Th: R	Role: SP	Health: B	LIMA Plan: B+
Ht: 6' 1"	Wt: 190	Type: Pwr/xFB	PT/Exp: F	Rand Var: 0
			Consist: D	MM: 1203

2-2, 5.48 ERA in 70 IP at LA/WAS. Top SP prospect sidelined two months with early-season shoulder injury, then debuted with two promising breaking pitches (each over 20% SwK). Shape and command of fastball need work to reach full potential. Expect bumps but seeds are there to grow into useful rotation piece.

Yr Tm	W	Sv	IP	K	ERA	WHIP	xERA	xWHIP	vL+	vR+	BF/G	BB%	K%	K-BB%	xBB%	SwK	Vel	G	L	F	H%	S%	HR/F	xHR/F	GS	APC	DOM%	DIS%	Sv%	LI	RAR	BPX	R$
17																																	
18																																	
19 aa	3	0	40	36	3.45	1.23	2.90				18.1	7%	22%	15%							33%	69%									5.2	134	$0
20																																	
21 2 NL *	3	0	88	94	4.91	1.21	4.67	1.29	112	113	19.7	10%	27%	17%	8%	14.7%	94.6	31	16	54	24%	69%	19%	18%	13	87	0%	31%	0	0.74	-7.0	64	-$2
1st Half	0	0	7	9	2.54	0.70	1.27				12.3	8%	37%	28%							17%	74%	0%		0	0					1.5	191	-$6
2nd Half	3	0	81	85	5.11	1.25	4.97	1.31	106	115	20.6	10%	26%	16%	8%	14.7%	94.6	31	16	54	25%	69%	19%	18%	13	87	0%	31%	0	0.74	-8.5	55	$0
Proj	8	0	145	143	4.29	1.25	4.59	1.30	106	111	20.9	9%	24%	16%	8%	14.7%	94.6	31	16	54	28%	71%	13%	16%	28						2.9	94	$5

Gray,Sonny

Age: 32	Th: R	Role: SP	Health: D	LIMA Plan: B
Ht: 5' 10"	Wt: 195	Type: Pwr	PT/Exp: A	Rand Var: +1
			Consist: A	MM: 3303

Back, groin, rib issues cost a chunk of season and may have contributed to 2nd half swoon as skills sagged. 2019 looks like an outlier but behold the consistency of those xERA and xWHIP columns. Low SwK/high K% not ideal and health is shaky, but GB%, command history offer a nice floor.

Yr Tm	W	Sv	IP	K	ERA	WHIP	xERA	xWHIP	vL+	vR+	BF/G	BB%	K%	K-BB%	xBB%	SwK	Vel	G	L	F	H%	S%	HR/F	xHR/F	GS	APC	DOM%	DIS%	Sv%	LI	RAR	BPX	R$
17 2 AL	10	0	162	153	3.55	1.21	3.82	1.31	85	93	25.1	8%	23%	14%	9%	12.2%	93.0	53	20	28	28%	75%	15%	16%	27	99	37%	30%			16.2	118	$14
18 NYY	11	0	130	123	4.90	1.50	4.14	1.39	99	113	19.4	10%	21%	11%	10%	10.4%	93.3	50	23	27	34%	69%	13%	13%	23	75	22%	43%	0	0.72	-12.1	86	-$4
19 CIN	11	0	175	205	2.87	1.08	3.55	1.26	81	80	22.8	10%	29%	19%	10%	11.8%	93.3	51	18	31	27%	77%	13%	15%	31	94	39%	13%			35.3	135	$24
20 CIN	5	0	56	72	3.70	1.21	3.32	1.26	86	78	21.4	11%	31%	20%	10%	11.6%	93.0	51	26	23	31%	70%	13%	15%	11	88	18%	18%			5.2	141	$14
21 CIN	7	0	135	155	4.19	1.22	3.67	1.22	94	93	22.1	9%	27%	18%	8%	11.0%	92.4	47	21	32	30%	70%	17%	11%	26	86	31%	15%			1.3	132	$6
1st Half	1	0	55	73	3.27	1.29	3.31	1.16	78	111	21.5	9%	31%	22%	8%	11.7%	92.9	46	24	29	34%	81%	20%	13%	11	85	27%	18%			6.7	161	$2
2nd Half	6	0	80	82	4.82	1.17	3.92	1.27	98	84	22.5	9%	24%	16%	8%	10.5%	92.1	48	18	34	27%	68%	15%	10%	15	86	33%	13%			-5.5	114	$8
Proj	10	0	160	183	3.71	1.22	3.54	1.25	90	90	20.9	10%	28%	19%	9%	11.2%	92.8	49	22	29	30%	73%	16%	13%	31						14.6	132	$12

ALAIN DE LEONARDIS

Green,Chad

Age: 31 Th: R Role RP	Health A	LIMA Plan C+	
Ht: 6' 3" Wt: 215 Type Pwr/xFB	PT/Exp C	Rand Var -3	
	Consist A	MM 4410	

Typically excellent skills rewarded by Wins windfall and handful of Saves, boosting roto value to impressive heights. K% fully supported by robust SwK; xBB% history a real beaut. He'll give up a few homers due to extreme fly ball lean that may hinder saves chances, but this is one of the most reliable middle relief profiles out there.

Yr Tm	W	Sv	IP	K	ERA	WHIP	xERA	xWHIP	vL+	vR+	BF/G	BB%	K%	K-BB%	xBB%	SwK	Vel	G	L	F	H%	S%	HR/F	xHR/F	GS	APC	DOM%	DIS%	Sv%	LI	RAR	BPX	R$
17 NYY *	7	0	96	130	3.20	1.10	2.48	1.08	54	64	8.3	8%	35%	27%	8%	15.9%	95.8	26	27	47	33%	71%	7%	10%	1	29	0%	0%	0	0.95	13.7	194	$11
18 NYY	8	0	76	94	2.50	1.04	3.36	1.01	88	89	4.7	5%	32%	27%	5%	13.6%	96.2	31	23	46	32%	83%	10%	15%	0	20			0	1.12	15.4	187	$10
19 NYY	4	2	69	98	4.17	1.23	3.55	1.06	96	100	5.5	6%	33%	27%	6%	14.1%	96.5	35	22	42	37%	71%	14%	14%	15	24	7%	40%	100	0.95	2.8	192	$3
20 NYY	3	1	26	32	3.51	0.82	3.66	1.13	57	84	4.5	8%	32%	24%	5%	15.8%	95.5	42	10	47	17%	69%	18%	13%	0	19			33	1.00	3.0	165	$9
21 NYY	10	6	84	99	3.12	0.88	3.64	1.03	87	82	4.7	5%	31%	26%	6%	15.9%	95.7	27	20	53	24%	75%	13%	15%	0	20			50	1.47	11.8	162	$17
1st Half	2	2	40	40	2.48	0.80	3.93	1.10	70	72	4.6	5%	27%	22%	6%	14.3%	95.4	32	12	56	21%	78%	9%	14%	0	19			67	1.49	8.8	136	$8
2nd Half	8	4	44	59	3.71	0.96	3.37	0.97	93	94	4.8	5%	35%	30%	5%	17.2%	96.0	23	27	51	27%	73%	18%	15%	0	20			44	1.46	3.0	186	$18
Proj	**7**	**8**	**65**	**83**	**3.26**	**1.01**	**3.46**	**1.03**	**91**	**88**	**5.0**	**6%**	**33%**	**27%**	**6%**	**15.1%**	**96.0**	**29**	**22**	**49**	**29%**	**75%**	**13%**	**14%**	**0**						**9.6**	**180**	**$11**

Greene,Hunter

Age: 22 Th: R Role SP	Health A	LIMA Plan B+	
Ht: 6' 4" Wt: 215 Type Pwr	PT/Exp F	Rand Var 0	
	Consist F	MM 1301	

Elite CIN prospect with overwhelming fastball and four-pitch mix made mincemeat of AA hitters (28% K-BB%) before slowing down a bit in AAA (20% K-BB%). Control ahead of command for now but has the size and tools to make an impact at the MLB level, whether out of the bullpen or in the rotation. Patience.

Yr Tm	W	Sv	IP	K	ERA	WHIP	xERA	xWHIP	vL+	vR+	BF/G	BB%	K%	K-BB%	xBB%	SwK	Vel	G	L	F	H%	S%	HR/F	xHR/F	GS	APC	DOM%	DIS%	Sv%	LI	RAR	BPX	R$
17																																	
18																																	
19																																	
20																																	
21 a/a	10	0	107	127	4.00	1.30	4.30				21.0	9%	29%	19%							32%	74%									3.5	105	$5
1st Half	6	0	59	76	3.90	1.26	3.72				21.9	10%	32%	21%							32%	73%									2.7	120	$7
2nd Half	4	0	48	51	4.12	1.35	5.01				20.0	8%	26%	18%							33%	76%									0.9	89	$0
Proj	**7**	**0**	**73**	**78**	**4.43**	**1.35**	**4.27**	**1.31**			**20.9**	**10%**	**26%**	**16%**				**42**	**18**	**40**	**31%**	**71%**	**14%**	**0%**	**14**						**0.2**	**106**	**$0**

Greinke,Zack

Age: 38 Th: R Role SP	Health C	LIMA Plan B	
Ht: 6' 2" Wt: 200 Type Con	PT/Exp A	Rand Var 0	
	Consist A	MM 2103	

Fantastic late-30s run encumbered as minor ailments, age may finally be catching up with him. K% plummeted alongside SwK while H% papered over skills losses. More DISaster than DOMinating starts for only the second time in 14 years. Ever the sphinx, but even the mighty statue of Ozymandias succumbed to the sands of time.

Yr Tm	W	Sv	IP	K	ERA	WHIP	xERA	xWHIP	vL+	vR+	BF/G	BB%	K%	K-BB%	xBB%	SwK	Vel	G	L	F	H%	S%	HR/F	xHR/F	GS	APC	DOM%	DIS%	Sv%	LI	RAR	BPX	R$
17 ARI	17	0	202	215	3.20	1.07	3.44	1.13	87	90	25.0	6%	27%	21%	8%	12.9%	91.0	47	18	35	29%	76%	13%	14%	32	99	50%	22%			28.8	172	$29
18 ARI	15	0	208	199	3.21	1.08	3.53	1.15	88	96	25.4	5%	24%	19%	7%	11.3%	89.6	45	23	32	28%	77%	15%	16%	33	97	45%	15%			24.1	147	$25
19 2 TM	18	0	209	187	2.93	0.98	3.74	1.14	80	86	24.5	4%	23%	19%	7%	10.7%	90.0	45	22	33	28%	74%	11%	12%	33	94	45%	18%			40.5	145	$33
20 HOU	3	0	67	67	4.03	1.13	3.75	1.08	73	112	22.8	3%	25%	21%	9%	10.8%	87.1	41	25	34	33%	66%	9%	17%	12	88	25%	17%			3.5	168	$11
21 HOU	11	0	171	120	4.16	1.17	4.33	1.27	78	110	23.2	5%	17%	12%	8%	9.5%	88.9	44	23	32	27%	71%	17%	16%	29	86	24%	48%	0	0.78	2.3	93	$9
1st Half	8	0	104	74	3.65	1.15	4.32	1.25	70	104	24.4	5%	18%	13%	8%	9.4%	88.9	40	25	34	28%	73%	12%	14%	17	91	29%	41%			7.9	93	$16
2nd Half	3	0	67	46	4.95	1.20	4.33	1.29	79	127	21.8	5%	16%	11%	9%	9.6%	88.9	50	21	29	25%	69%	27%	18%	12	79	17%	58%	0	0.78	-5.6	93	-$2
Proj	**10**	**0**	**160**	**133**	**4.17**	**1.16**	**3.91**	**1.19**	**82**	**110**	**22.9**	**5%**	**21%**	**16%**	**8%**	**10.3%**	**88.9**	**45**	**23**	**32**	**29%**	**69%**	**16%**	**16%**	**28**						**5.7**	**127**	**$9**

Guerra,Deolis

Age: 33 Th: R Role RP	Health A	LIMA Plan B+	
Ht: 6' 5" Wt: 245 Type /xFB	PT/Exp D	Rand Var -2	
	Consist B	MM 1200	

Journeyman reliever posted serviceable season while skills registered exactly league-average. Splits reveal big 2nd half SwK bump without expected jump in K%, a curious multi-year trend. Uses five-pitch mix to effectively suppress hard contact; if he can build on those whiffs, a $1 bid could return a modest profit.

Yr Tm	W	Sv	IP	K	ERA	WHIP	xERA	xWHIP	vL+	vR+	BF/G	BB%	K%	K-BB%	xBB%	SwK	Vel	G	L	F	H%	S%	HR/F	xHR/F	GS	APC	DOM%	DIS%	Sv%	LI	RAR	BPX	R$
17 LAA *	6	2	66	54	3.10	1.06	2.74	1.34	95	100	5.1	8%	21%	13%		15.1%	91.7	37	10	53	25%	75%	11%	15%	0	22			40	0.73	10.2	104	$7
18 aaa	2	2	60	51	5.26	1.36	4.80				6.3	8%	20%	12%							31%	64%									-8.3	70	-$5
19 MIL *	4	0	69	67	2.89	1.12	3.22		395	112	5.9	7%	25%	18%		17.6%	91.8	0	67	33	29%	79%	50%	18%	0	17			0	0.25	13.7	119	$5
20 PHI	1	0	7	8	8.59	1.64	4.23	1.19	41	199	4.0	6%	22%	17%	6%	16.2%	91.8	54	13	33	36%	56%	38%	23%	0	14			0	0.68	-3.7	161	-$8
21 OAK	4	0	66	62	4.11	1.11	4.56	1.25	88	87	5.1	7%	23%	16%	8%	12.8%	90.8	34	16	50	27%	66%	9%	10%	0	20			0	0.54	1.2	100	$1
1st Half	1	0	30	25	3.94	0.94	4.77	1.34	41	97	5.5	9%	22%	13%	8%	10.7%	90.9	29	17	54	20%	60%	7%	9%	0	23			0	0.35	1.2	68	-$2
2nd Half	3	0	36	37	4.25	1.25	4.38	1.20	112	82	4.8	6%	24%	18%	8%	14.5%	90.6	38	16	47	32%	70%	10%	11%	0	19			0	0.67	0.1	126	-$2
Proj	**4**	**0**	**65**	**60**	**4.00**	**1.24**	**4.64**	**1.28**	**99**	**94**	**5.4**	**7%**	**23%**	**15%**	**8%**	**13.0%**	**90.7**	**35**	**16**	**50**	**30%**	**71%**	**9%**	**10%**	**0**						**3.7**	**101**	**$0**

Gutierrez,Vladimir

Age: 26 Th: R Role SP	Health A	LIMA Plan D+	
Ht: 6' 0" Wt: 190 Type /FB	PT/Exp D	Rand Var 0	
	Consist F	MM 0101	

9-6, 4.74 ERA in 114 IP at CIN. Made MLB debut in May after 80-game suspension in 2020 for PEDs. Soft skill set lowlighted by subpar SwK, K% calls attention to lackluster fastball quality and velocity. Improved 2nd half BB%, GB% encouraging but we'd need to see progress on other fronts before recommending.

Yr Tm	W	Sv	IP	K	ERA	WHIP	xERA	xWHIP	vL+	vR+	BF/G	BB%	K%	K-BB%	xBB%	SwK	Vel	G	L	F	H%	S%	HR/F	xHR/F	GS	APC	DOM%	DIS%	Sv%	LI	RAR	BPX	R$
17																																	
18 aa	9	0	147	126	5.78	1.41	5.25				23.1	7%	20%	14%							33%	61%									-29.6	76	-$9
19 aaa	6	0	137	103	7.90	1.66	7.01				22.7	9%	17%	8%							33%	55%									-57.3	7	-$23
20																																	
21 CIN *	11	0	131	106	4.59	1.38	4.99	1.43	118	101	22.0	10%	19%	9%	8%	10.3%	93.3	43	16	40	28%	73%	14%	13%	22	83	18%	45%			-5.2	43	$0
1st Half	5	0	55	48	4.52	1.33	4.80	1.48	86	123	22.9	12%	21%	9%	9%	10.4%	93.0	38	18	44	24%	74%	15%	17%	7	89	14%	57%			-1.7	38	$0
2nd Half	6	0	76	58	4.64	1.41	4.84	1.39	124	93	21.7	8%	18%	10%	8%	10.2%	93.4	46	16	38	30%	72%	14%	11%	15	80	20%	40%			-3.5	68	$0
Proj	**6**	**0**	**116**	**94**	**4.87**	**1.44**	**4.96**	**1.41**	**119**	**108**	**22.3**	**9%**	**19%**	**10%**	**8%**	**10.3%**	**93.3**	**43**	**17**	**41**	**30%**	**72%**	**15%**	**14%**	**22**						**-5.9**	**67**	**-$5**

Hader,Josh

Age: 28 Th: L Role RP	Health A	LIMA Plan C+	
Ht: 6' 3" Wt: 180 Type Pwr/xFB	PT/Exp A	Rand Var -5	
	Consist B	MM 5530	

Ohhh-weee! Snapped right back to über-dominant form after (slightly) down 2020, posting the lowest ERA of any reliever with at least 2 saves. Threw harder than ever, adding two ticks--which no doubt helped goose his SwK and K%--while throwing fewer IP in a more traditional closer role. Stud, full stop.

Yr Tm	W	Sv	IP	K	ERA	WHIP	xERA	xWHIP	vL+	vR+	BF/G	BB%	K%	K-BB%	xBB%	SwK	Vel	G	L	F	H%	S%	HR/F	xHR/F	GS	APC	DOM%	DIS%	Sv%	LI	RAR	BPX	R$
17 MIL *	5	0	100	112	3.90	1.29	4.12	1.41	60	82	8.7	12%	27%	15%	7%	17.6%	94.3	34	14	51	26%	78%	9%	8%	0	22			0	1.14	5.6	80	$4
18 MIL	6	12	81	143	2.43	0.81	2.37	0.93	48	77	5.6	10%	47%	37%	6%	19.8%	94.5	29	23	48	24%	77%	15%	14%	0	24			71	1.31	17.2	233	$21
19 MIL	3	37	76	138	2.62	0.81	2.57	0.84	82	78	4.7	7%	48%	41%	5%	24.0%	95.6	22	23	55	26%	85%	21%	15%	0	19			84	1.71	17.6	252	$29
20 MIL	1	13	19	31	3.79	0.95	3.54	1.17	96	70	3.7	13%	40%	27%	9%	16.7%	94.6	26	15	59	18%	67%	15%	11%	0	18			87	1.63	1.6	159	$17
21 MIL	4	34	59	102	1.23	0.84	2.54	0.98	52	58	3.7	11%	46%	35%	6%	21.9%	96.4	31	23	46	26%	89%	7%	8%	0	16			97	1.37	22.0	210	$28
1st Half	3	20	33	55	0.55	0.73	2.48	0.96	46	45	3.7	10%	45%	36%	6%	21.2%	96.2	32	23	45	24%	92%	0%	2%	0	16			100	1.57	15.0	213	$24
2nd Half	1	14	26	47	2.08	0.96	2.62	1.01	55	73	3.8	12%	46%	34%	8%	22.7%	96.7	29	24	48	28%	86%	15%	15%	0	16			93	1.14	7.0	206	$16
Proj	**3**	**35**	**58**	**99**	**2.13**	**0.89**	**2.64**	**0.97**	**62**	**73**	**4.3**	**11%**	**46%**	**36%**	**6%**	**21.6%**	**95.7**	**29**	**22**	**49**	**26%**	**84%**	**15%**	**12%**	**0**						**16.6**	**214**	**$24**

Hancock,Emerson

Age: 23 Th: R Role SP	Health C	LIMA Plan D+	
Ht: 6' 4" Wt: 213 Type Con	PT/Exp F	Rand Var +2	
	Consist F	MM 1000	

2020 No. 6 overall draft pick made it to AA in first year of professional ball while battling recurring shoulder woes that cost him some time. Four-pitch mix fronted by mid-90s heat and strong secondaries. Combination of stuff and polish could allow him to advance quickly to SEA, but shoulder concerns may slow things down.

Yr Tm	W	Sv	IP	K	ERA	WHIP	xERA	xWHIP	vL+	vR+	BF/G	BB%	K%	K-BB%	xBB%	SwK	Vel	G	L	F	H%	S%	HR/F	xHR/F	GS	APC	DOM%	DIS%	Sv%	LI	RAR	BPX	R$
17																																	
18																																	
19																																	
20																																	
21 aa	1	0	15	12	3.25	0.97	1.58				19.2	7%	21%	14%							26%	63%									1.9	134	-$4
1st Half																																	
2nd Half	1	0	15	12	3.25	0.97	1.58				19.2	7%	21%	14%							26%	63%									1.9	134	-$7
Proj	**3**	**0**	**44**	**31**	**4.23**	**1.28**	**4.73**	**1.35**			**23.1**	**7%**	**17%**	**10%**				**42**	**20**	**38**	**29%**	**71%**	**12%**	**0%**	**8**						**1.2**	**75**	**-$3**

ALAIN DE LEONARDIS

Hand,Brad

Age: 32	Th: L	Role: RP	Health: A	LIMA Plan: C+	
Ht: 6' 3"	Wt: 215	Type: Pwr	PT/Exp: B	Rand Var: -1	
			Consist: B	MM: 1210	

Velocity bounced back, which had been the concern of the past two off-seasons. Curiously, though, SwK/K% didn't get the memo and took deep plunges anyway. The first half looked like rebound, but once H%/S% corrected, the carousel started. He'll still end up in someone's pen, but we likely have seen his final double-digit saves season.

Yr Tm	W	Sv	IP	K	ERA	WHIP	xERA	xWHIP	vL+	vR+	BF/G	BB%	K%	K-BB%	xBB%	SwK	Vel	G	L	F	H%	S%	HR/F	xHR/F	GS	APC	DOM%	DIS%	Sv%	LI	RAR	BPX	R$
17 SD	3	21	79	104	2.16	0.93	2.81	1.04	78	78	4.3	6%	34%	27%	8%	13.7%	93.5	46	20	34	27%	85%	15%	11%	0	17			81	1.35	21.6	210	$21
18 2 TM	2	32	72	106	2.75	1.11	2.83	1.09	73	102	4.4	9%	35%	26%	8%	13.7%	93.6	45	21	34	31%	81%	15%	15%	0	18			82	1.36	12.4	192	$19
19 CLE	6	34	57	84	3.30	1.24	3.52	1.08	66	102	4.0	7%	35%	27%	5%	14.0%	92.7	27	31	42	38%	77%	11%	11%	0	16			87	1.31	8.6	181	$19
20 CLE	2	16	22	29	2.05	0.77	3.53	0.96	48	67	3.7	5%	35%	30%	8%	10.7%	91.4	27	16	57	28%	71%	0%	8%	0	16			100	1.10	6.5	197	$27
21 3 TM	6	21	65	61	3.90	1.27	4.58	1.35	92	100	4.1	9%	22%	13%	8%	8.2%	93.0	40	20	40	28%	74%	12%	17%	0	16			72	1.15	2.9	80	$10
1st Half	4	18	35	33	2.60	1.07	4.05	1.28	80	86	4.3	9%	23%	15%	8%	8.3%	93.1	42	22	36	24%	82%	12%	18%	0	16			90	1.13	7.1	99	$16
2nd Half	2	3	30	28	5.40	1.50	5.20	1.42	92	124	3.9	10%	21%	10%	8%	8.1%	93.0	37	18	45	31%	68%	13%	16%	0	15			33	1.17	-4.2	58	-$7
Proj	**3**	**2**	**44**	**43**	**4.18**	**1.23**	**4.28**	**1.32**	**83**	**101**	**3.9**	**9%**	**24%**	**15%**	**8%**	**10.9%**	**93.1**	**39**	**22**	**39**	**28%**	**69%**	**12%**	**15%**	**0**						**1.4**	**96**	**-$1**

Happ,J.A.

Age: 39	Th: L	Role: SP	Health: B	LIMA Plan: C	
Ht: 6' 5"	Wt: 205	Type: Con/FB	PT/Exp: A	Rand Var: +1	
			Consist: B	MM: 1101	

Keeps chugging along as a 30-start machine, but a lot of trends (velocity, K%, xERA, BPX) remind us that he's pushing 40 years old. Right handed batters can now pretty much dig in; the fly-ball increase is leading to more HR. An underrated player a few years ago, now there's very little to grab onto in hopes of a turnaround.

Yr Tm	W	Sv	IP	K	ERA	WHIP	xERA	xWHIP	vL+	vR+	BF/G	BB%	K%	K-BB%	xBB%	SwK	Vel	G	L	F	H%	S%	HR/F	xHR/F	GS	APC	DOM%	DIS%	Sv%	LI	RAR	BPX	R$
17 TOR	10	0	145	142	3.53	1.31	4.13	1.28	73	99	25.0	7%	23%	15%	8%	10.1%	91.8	47	19	34	32%	77%	12%	10%	25	99	24%	28%			14.9	128	$10
18 2 AL	17	0	178	193	3.65	1.13	3.81	1.17	67	101	23.6	7%	26%	19%	8%	10.8%	92.0	40	17	42	29%	74%	13%	15%	31	98	26%	23%			11.0	143	$19
19 NYY	12	0	161	140	4.91	1.30	4.74	1.33	86	111	21.9	7%	21%	13%	8%	10.7%	91.3	40	21	39	29%	69%	18%	15%	30	87	7%	43%	0	0.76	-8.0	92	$4
20 NYY	2	0	49	42	3.47	1.05	4.26	1.30	80	91	21.8	8%	22%	14%	8%	10.7%	90.9	44	20	36	23%	75%	17%	9%	9	87	33%	56%			6.0	97	$9
21 2 TM	10	0	152	122	5.79	1.48	5.23	1.34	93	120	22.4	7%	18%	11%	8%	8.6%	90.6	35	21	45	32%	65%	14%	17%	30	89	0%	40%			-28.6	73	-$11
1st Half	4	0	75	59	6.09	1.50	5.42	1.35	86	128	22.3	7%	18%	10%	8%	8.4%	90.6	34	19	47	32%	64%	14%	16%	15	93	0%	40%			-17.0	68	-$11
2nd Half	6	0	77	63	5.49	1.45	5.04	1.32	89	116	22.4	7%	19%	12%	8%	8.8%	90.6	36	22	42	32%	66%	14%	19%	15	85	0%	40%			-11.7	78	-$5
Proj	**8**	**0**	**116**	**100**	**4.84**	**1.32**	**4.60**	**1.31**	**86**	**110**	**21.8**	**7%**	**21%**	**13%**	**8%**	**9.6%**	**90.9**	**39**	**20**	**41**	**30%**	**69%**	**15%**	**15%**	**22**						**-5.5**	**92**	**-$1**

Harvey,Hunter

Age: 27	Th: R	Role: RP	Health: F	LIMA Plan: C	
Ht: 6' 3"	Wt: 210	Type:	PT/Exp: D	Rand Var: -1	
			Consist: B	MM: 1100	

There are worse late dart-throws, but it's really a blindfolded exercise by now. Long past the "Can he start?" question, his high-90s fastball and killer curve have the makings of a late-inning arsenal. But when your target can't stay on the field (oblique/lat/triceps the 2021 culprits), well, might as well cross both pinkies while holding a rabbit's foot before you toss.

Yr Tm	W	Sv	IP	K	ERA	WHIP	xERA	xWHIP	vL+	vR+	BF/G	BB%	K%	K-BB%	xBB%	SwK	Vel	G	L	F	H%	S%	HR/F	xHR/F	GS	APC	DOM%	DIS%	Sv%	LI	RAR	BPX	R$
17																																	
18 aa	1	0	33	24	6.31	1.51	5.32				15.9	6%	17%	10%							35%	58%									-8.8	71	-$8
19 BAL *	4	1	84	76	6.11	1.55	6.44		90	88	11.1	9%	21%	12%	7%	12.4%	98.4	45	27	27	32%	67%	33%	11%	0	20			50	1.49	-16.6	29	-$8
20 BAL	0	0	9	6	4.15	1.15	4.89	1.31	60	115	3.7	5%	16%	11%	6%	11.0%	97.4	39	25	36	25%	75%	20%	16%	0	15			0	1.38	0.3	83	-$6
21 BAL	0	0	9	6	4.15	1.27	4.59	1.41	85	113	4.0	8%	17%	8%	6%	5.8%	97.1	48	22	30	28%	70%	13%	10%	0	15			0	1.14	0.1	59	-$6
1st Half	0	0	9	6	4.15	1.27	4.59	1.41	81	115	4.0	8%	17%	8%	6%	5.8%	97.1	48	22	30	28%	70%	13%	10%	0	15			0	1.14	0.1	60	-$8
2nd Half																																	
Proj	**2**	**1**	**51**	**42**	**4.77**	**1.37**	**4.33**	**1.34**			**12.1**	**8%**	**20%**	**12%**	**6%**	**9.0%**	**97.0**	**48**	**22**	**30**	**30%**	**71%**	**21%**	**14%**	**4**						**-2.0**	**90**	**-$5**

Harvey,Matt

Age: 33	Th: R	Role: SP	Health: F	LIMA Plan: D+	
Ht: 6' 4"	Wt: 220	Type: Con	PT/Exp: C	Rand Var: +5	
			Consist: B	MM: 0001	

While some say we're in the Golden Era of pitching ... this skill set received 28 starts until a Sept knee injury (mercifully) ended his season. Strand rate has be a chronic problem, consistently pushing ERA above xERA. Falling strikeouts and tons of hard contact have led to a string of negative RARs and R$. There's seemingly no escape. The future is dark, Knight.

Yr Tm	W	Sv	IP	K	ERA	WHIP	xERA	xWHIP	vL+	vR+	BF/G	BB%	K%	K-BB%	xBB%	SwK	Vel	G	L	F	H%	S%	HR/F	xHR/F	GS	APC	DOM%	DIS%	Sv%	LI	RAR	BPX	R$
17 NYM	5	0	93	67	6.70	1.69	5.53	1.58	136	105	22.7	11%	16%	5%	8%	7.9%	93.8	43	23	34	31%	65%	21%	16%	18	89	0%	61%	0	0.79	-26.8	18	-$13
18 2 NL	7	0	155	131	4.94	1.30	4.28	1.24	110	106	20.7	6%	20%	14%	6%	9.9%	94.0	42	20	38	31%	67%	15%	16%	28	79	25%	25%	0	0.74	-15.0	114	-$2
19 LAA *	4	0	83	62	7.52	1.62	6.17	1.54	127	109	19.3	10%	17%	7%	10%	9.6%	93.2	43	27	30	32%	55%	22%	20%	12	83	8%	58%			-30.7	20	-$14
20 KC	0	0	12	10	11.57	2.74	6.42	1.43	185	169	9.3	8%	15%	8%	10%	7.3%	94.1	42	26	32	48%	65%	38%	32%	4	35	0%	100%	0	0.44	-10.2	62	-$19
21 BAL	6	0	128	95	6.27	1.54	5.05	1.33	106	117	20.8	6%	16%	10%	8%	8.5%	93.2	43	22	35	35%	61%	12%	16%	28	80	4%	39%			-31.6	78	-$16
1st Half	3	0	72	58	7.34	1.71	5.24	1.36	102	130	20.4	7%	17%	10%	8%	9.1%	93.4	42	24	34	37%	58%	14%	19%	17	80	0%	41%			-27.4	72	-$21
2nd Half	3	0	55	37	4.88	1.32	4.79	1.29	99	103	21.5	5%	16%	11%	6%	7.7%	92.8	44	19	38	31%	65%	10%	12%	11	79	9%	36%			-4.2	85	-$5
Proj	**5**	**0**	**102**	**76**	**5.65**	**1.49**	**4.87**	**1.38**	**116**	**110**	**20.1**	**8%**	**17%**	**10%**	**8%**	**8.8%**	**93.4**	**43**	**22**	**35**	**33%**	**65%**	**15%**	**16%**	**22**						**-15.0**	**73**	**-$9**

Heaney,Andrew

Age: 31	Th: L	Role: RP	Health: D	LIMA Plan: C+	
Ht: 6' 2"	Wt: 200	Type: Pwr/FB	PT/Exp: B	Rand Var: +5	
			Consist: A	MM: 2301	

BB, K skills would indicate above-average ERA/WHIP, but LD and FB are hit into the gaps or over the fence. Five years of declining strand rates may indicate a vulnerability to pitch with men on base. xERA indicates some upside, but we've been saying that for 4 years. Health cooperated in 2021, but that excellent K% is going to waste.

Yr Tm	W	Sv	IP	K	ERA	WHIP	xERA	xWHIP	vL+	vR+	BF/G	BB%	K%	K-BB%	xBB%	SwK	Vel	G	L	F	H%	S%	HR/F	xHR/F	GS	APC	DOM%	DIS%	Sv%	LI	RAR	BPX	R$
17 LAA *	2	0	39	39	5.36	1.50	7.11	1.30	103	160	21.1	8%	23%	15%		13.7%	91.9	30	22	48	31%	79%	40%	27%	5	83	0%	60%			-4.8	21	-$5
18 LAA	9	0	180	180	4.15	1.20	3.75	1.18	74	107	25.0	6%	24%	18%	6%	12.1%	92.0	41	24	35	31%	70%	15%	16%	30	92	37%	13%			0.0	138	$9
19 LAA	4	0	95	118	4.91	1.29	4.11	1.18	121	98	22.7	7%	29%	22%	7%	14.5%	92.5	34	23	44	33%	69%	18%	16%	18	94	17%	28%			-4.7	148	$0
20 LAA	4	0	67	70	4.46	1.23	4.21	1.20	95	97	23.3	7%	25%	18%	6%	13.0%	91.5	39	22	39	31%	67%	12%	17%	12	90	25%	17%			0.0	133	$8
21 2 AL	8	0	130	150	5.83	1.32	4.19	1.18	107	108	18.6	7%	27%	20%	7%	13.0%	92.0	33	22	45	32%	61%	18%	16%	23	78	30%	30%	0	0.69	-25.0	133	-$5
1st Half	4	0	72	89	5.40	1.34	4.02	1.16	100	102	21.9	8%	29%	21%	7%	13.9%	92.2	31	25	44	34%	65%	17%	19%	14	93	36%	29%			-10.0	142	-$2
2nd Half	4	0	58	61	6.36	1.29	4.40	1.20	102	121	15.7	7%	24%	18%	8%	11.9%	91.8	35	19	46	30%	57%	20%	13%	9	64	22%	33%	0	0.62	-15.0	124	-$6
Proj	**7**	**0**	**116**	**129**	**4.29**	**1.29**	**4.05**	**1.19**	**105**	**107**	**19.3**	**7%**	**27%**	**20%**	**7%**	**13.1%**	**92.0**	**35**	**22**	**43**	**31%**	**75%**	**18%**	**16%**	**23**						**2.4**	**136**	**$3**

Hearn,Taylor

Age: 27	Th: L	Role: SP	Health: F	LIMA Plan: D+	
Ht: 6' 6"	Wt: 230	Type: /FB	PT/Exp: D	Rand Var: 0	
			Consist: A	MM: 1103	

Stayed healthy all year, and roughly split the season in relief and then as starter. Showed second-half glimmers that intrigue, including much better BB% (though K% dropped also) at a slightly lower velocity. It's still mid-90s from the left side, though, which is why the team will give him every chance to start. Let's see what another year can do.

Yr Tm	W	Sv	IP	K	ERA	WHIP	xERA	xWHIP	vL+	vR+	BF/G	BB%	K%	K-BB%	xBB%	SwK	Vel	G	L	F	H%	S%	HR/F	xHR/F	GS	APC	DOM%	DIS%	Sv%	LI	RAR	BPX	R$
17																																	
18 aa	4	0	129	113	4.67	1.40	4.35				22.7	10%	21%	11%							31%	68%									-8.3	76	-$4
19 TEX *	1	0	20	20	6.66	1.69	5.60		66	312	18.4	16%	22%	5%		2.6%	91.6	50	25	25	30%	63%	0%	3%	1	39	0%	100%			-5.4	42	-$7
20 TEX	0	0	17	23	3.63	1.38	4.91	1.44	123	67	5.4	14%	30%	16%	9%	9.9%	95.0	27	20	54	30%	77%	9%	8%	0	25			0	0.51	1.8	74	-$4
21 TEX	6	0	104	92	4.66	1.32	4.77	1.38	87	106	10.5	10%	21%	11%	8%	10.0%	94.8	39	19	42	28%	69%	14%	14%	11	41	9%	45%	0	0.78	-5.1	68	-$2
1st Half	2	0	38	43	5.40	1.64	4.71	1.44	70	136	7.0	13%	25%	12%	8%	10.8%	95.5	42	22	37	33%	74%	23%	22%	1	29	0%	100%	0	0.87	-5.4	68	-$9
2nd Half	4	0	66	49	4.23	1.14	4.78	1.35	93	91	15.6	8%	18%	11%	7%	9.4%	94.2	38	17	45	26%	66%	9%	11%	10	58	10%	40%	0	0.64	0.3	69	$5
Proj	**8**	**0**	**152**	**135**	**4.45**	**1.36**	**4.78**	**1.40**	**85**	**107**	**21.5**	**10%**	**21%**	**11%**	**8%**	**10.0%**	**94.7**	**40**	**19**	**41**	**29%**	**72%**	**13%**	**15%**	**24**						**0.0**	**70**	**$1**

Helsley,Ryan

Age: 27	Th: R	Role: RP	Health: D	LIMA Plan: D+	
Ht: 6' 2"	Wt: 230	Type: Pwr	PT/Exp: D	Rand Var: -1	
			Consist: D	MM: 0100	

Throws hard, but does he know where it's going? All the double-digit walk rates say "Not really," though xBB% indicates he deserved better. For now, he tamed his fly ball fetish and took care of both LHH and RHH. Elbow and knee injuries cut his season short, but the teeny 14-inning second half sample is promising and what a best-case scenario would look like.

Yr Tm	W	Sv	IP	K	ERA	WHIP	xERA	xWHIP	vL+	vR+	BF/G	BB%	K%	K-BB%	xBB%	SwK	Vel	G	L	F	H%	S%	HR/F	xHR/F	GS	APC	DOM%	DIS%	Sv%	LI	RAR	BPX	R$
17 a/a	3	0	39	37	3.48	1.44	4.35				23.5	11%	22%	12%							32%	79%									4.2	82	-$2
18 a/a	5	0	69	63	4.47	1.17	3.08				23.0	10%	23%	13%							26%	63%									-2.7	96	$0
19 STL *	4	1	75	65	4.20	1.34	3.96	1.47	100	95	7.6	10%	21%	11%	6%	10.7%	97.8	34	21	46	29%	71%	10%	9%	0	24			50	0.65	2.8	72	$0
20 STL	1	1	12	10	5.25	1.33	6.20	1.72	108	101	4.3	15%	19%	4%	10%	14.4%	96.9	33	15	52	17%	69%	18%	13%	0	16			33	0.97	-1.2	-18	-$4
21 STL	6	1	47	47	4.56	1.42	4.69	1.50	88	91	4.0	13%	23%	10%	10%	11.8%	97.5	42	26	32	29%	68%	10%	16%	0	16			33	1.03	-1.7	46	-$2
1st Half	4	1	34	30	5.08	1.51	5.08	1.63	92	95	4.1	15%	20%	5%	11%	10.4%	97.3	47	24	29	29%	67%	11%	18%	0	16			100	0.89	-3.4	12	-$4
2nd Half	2	0	14	17	3.29	1.17	3.84	1.18	68	85	4.0	9%	30%	21%	10%	16.2%	98.0	26	32	41	32%	73%	7%	13%	0	14			0	1.40	1.6	129	-$6
Proj	**4**	**0**	**44**	**39**	**4.21**	**1.43**	**4.85**	**1.49**	**104**	**98**	**7.2**	**12%**	**21%**	**9%**	**8%**	**10.5%**	**97.5**	**42**	**22**	**36**	**29%**	**74%**	**12%**	**14%**	**0**						**1.3**	**48**	**-$3**

BRENT HERSHEY

Hendricks,Kyle

Age: 32 **Th:** R **Role** SP **Health** B **LIMA Plan** B+
Ht: 6' 3" **Wt:** 190 **Type** Con **PT/Exp** A **Rand Var** 0
Consist B **MM** 2005

Pre-2021, out-pitching his x-indicators, luck was his M.O. Cue up a career-worst skills season, where of course results matched xERA/xWHIP. We're tempted to call "track record," as BB%/K% drops are within standard variance. But if his change-up stops neutralizing lefties, all bets are off. Not old, but a unique set of skills. This could go either way.

Yr	Tm	W	Sv	IP	K	ERA	WHIP	xERA	xWHIP	vL+	vR+	BF/G	BB%	K%	K-BB%	xBB%	SwK	Vel	G	L	F	H%	S%	HR/F	xHR/F	GS	APC	DOM%	DIS%	Sv%	LI	RAR	BPX	R$
17	CHC	7	0	140	123	3.03	1.19	3.83	1.28	93	86	23.8	7%	22%	15%	8%	8.7%	85.8	50	21	29	29%	80%	15%	12%	24	95	21%	17%			22.9	121	$13
18	CHC	14	0	199	161	3.44	1.15	3.85	1.23	91	98	24.6	5%	20%	15%	6%	9.6%	86.9	47	21	32	29%	74%	12%	13%	33	92	24%	30%			17.5	118	$18
19	CHC	11	0	177	150	3.46	1.13	4.26	1.21	88	94	24.3	4%	21%	16%	5%	10.5%	86.9	41	24	35	30%	73%	10%	10%	30	90	30%	27%			22.9	122	$17
20	CHC	6	0	81	64	2.88	1.00	3.82	1.12	78	93	26.3	3%	20%	18%	5%	12.0%	87.4	47	21	32	28%	77%	13%	13%	12	97	42%	17%			15.8	145	$28
21	CHC	14	0	181	131	4.77	1.35	4.64	1.29	123	99	24.5	6%	17%	11%	6%	9.2%	87.3	43	23	34	31%	69%	16%	17%	32	88	25%	41%			-11.3	87	$1
1st Half		10	0	93	74	3.98	1.27	4.42	1.22	121	94	24.6	5%	19%	14%	5%	10.0%	87.1	41	24	35	30%	79%	19%	19%	16	86	31%	38%			3.2	108	$12
2nd Half		4	0	88	57	5.60	1.43	4.89	1.37	113	109	24.4	6%	15%	8%	7%	8.4%	87.6	45	22	32	32%	62%	12%	14%	16	90	19%	44%			-14.6	65	-$9
Proj		10	0	189	144	4.07	1.23	4.21	1.25	104	97	23.9	5%	19%	14%	6%	9.9%	87.2	45	22	33	30%	71%	14%	14%	32						9.0	108	$9

Hendriks,Liam

Age: 33 **Th:** R **Role** RP **Health** B **LIMA Plan** C
Ht: 6' 0" **Wt:** 230 **Type** Pwr/xFB **PT/Exp** A **Rand Var** 0
Consist A **MM** 5530

Let's play everyone's favorite game - Pick a Headline: 1) When your 2.54 ERA/0.73 WHIP is rock-solid legit. 2) When your SwK outpaces many hurlers' K%. 3) When your 51% FB% doesn't matter. 4) How to add velocity in your early 30s. And of course, 5) How to win over new teammates. Remember that regression is undefeated, but he's Closer King right now.

Yr	Tm	W	Sv	IP	K	ERA	WHIP	xERA	xWHIP	vL+	vR+	BF/G	BB%	K%	K-BB%	xBB%	SwK	Vel	G	L	F	H%	S%	HR/F	xHR/F	GS	APC	DOM%	DIS%	Sv%	LI	RAR	BPX	R$
17	OAK	4	1	64	78	4.22	1.25	3.84	1.21	84	92	3.9	8%	29%	20%	8%	12.9%	94.7	42	19	39	33%	68%	10%	14%	0	17			25	1.03	1.1	156	$2
18	OAK *	4	6	50	53	3.90	1.33	4.07	1.18	89	117	4.3	7%	25%	19%	9%	11.4%	94.4	40	21	39	35%	72%	11%	6%	8	18	0%	63%	86	0.64	1.6	131	$1
19	OAK	4	25	85	124	1.80	0.96	3.27	0.99	93	57	4.4	6%	38%	31%	6%	17.7%	96.5	31	19	49	33%	84%	6%	7%	2	18	0%	100%	78	1.37	28.4	202	$25
20	OAK	3	14	25	37	1.78	0.67	2.48	0.82	77	40	3.8	3%	41%	37%	5%	20.0%	96.1	32	30	38	27%	75%	5%	11%	0	15			93	1.36	8.4	246	$30
21	CHW	8	38	71	113	2.54	0.73	2.55	0.76	60	80	3.9	3%	42%	40%	6%	20.1%	97.7	33	17	51	28%	78%	15%	15%	0	16			86	1.54	15.2	269	$32
1st Half		3	21	35	53	2.57	0.80	2.90	0.82	82	67	3.7	3%	39%	36%	5%	19.0%	97.4	30	18	52	28%	82%	15%	16%	0	16			88	1.69	7.3	248	$21
2nd Half		5	17	36	60	2.50	0.67	2.22	0.69	26	95	4.1	2%	46%	44%	6%	21.2%	98.1	36	15	49	28%	74%	15%	12%	0	17			85	1.37	7.8	290	$31
Proj		5	35	65	93	2.84	0.94	2.96	0.92	72	83	3.9	5%	38%	33%	6%	18.1%	96.9	35	17	48	31%	76%	11%	13%	0						13.0	225	$24

Hentges,Sam

Age: 25 **Th:** L **Role** RP **Health** A **LIMA Plan** C
Ht: 6' 8" **Wt:** 245 **Type** Pwr **PT/Exp** D **Rand Var** +5
Consist F **MM** 1201

Hit/Strand rate duo laid waste to this hard-throwing rookie's 1st half results, which never fully recovered. But some promising seeds emerged after June, including domination of LHH, BB% improvement, and a significant GB lean. Groomed as a starter, pitched well out of the pen in 2021; short-term role is still TBD. Could take a sneaky next step up.

Yr	Tm	W	Sv	IP	K	ERA	WHIP	xERA	xWHIP	vL+	vR+	BF/G	BB%	K%	K-BB%	xBB%	SwK	Vel	G	L	F	H%	S%	HR/F	xHR/F	GS	APC	DOM%	DIS%	Sv%	LI	RAR	BPX	R$
17																																		
18																																		
19	aa	2	0	130	107	7.32	1.99	7.13				24.1	11%	17%	6%							40%	63%									-45.2	35	-$28
20																																		
21	CLE	1	0	69	68	6.68	1.78	4.84	1.39	90	125	10.6	10%	21%	11%	11%	10.4%	94.4	46	19	35	39%	63%	13%	21%	12	42	0%	67%	0	0.49	-20.5	78	-$16
1st Half		1	0	38	41	8.22	2.06	5.31	1.46	107	140	13.4	12%	22%	10%	12%	10.7%	94.6	43	19	38	43%	61%	15%	25%	7	53	0%	57%	0	0.61	-18.7	60	-$21
2nd Half		0	0	30	27	4.75	1.42	4.25	1.30	58	112	8.1	8%	21%	13%	8%	10.0%	94.0	49	19	31	34%	68%	10%	15%	5	32	0%	80%	0	0.39	-1.8	101	-$11
Proj		1	0	73	67	4.45	1.28	4.28	1.37	61	95	10.3	10%	23%	13%	10%	10.3%	94.3	47	19	34	29%	68%	12%	19%	1						0.1	87	-$3

Hernández,Carlos

Age: 25 **Th:** R **Role** SP **Health** A **LIMA Plan** B
Ht: 6' 4" **Wt:** 250 **Type** /FB **PT/Exp** D **Rand Var** -1
Consist C **MM** 0103

6-2, 3.68 ERA in 86 IP at KC. High-octane arm who seemed to arrive in the 2nd half, making 11 starts with eye-catching ERA/WHIP. But good fortune in H% and HR/F masked very similar BPX scores to 1st half. Nearly doubled his MLB K% as a RP vs. SP (31% vs. 16%), but walks went up also. Young and watchable ... but still searching for that sweet spot.

Yr	Tm	W	Sv	IP	K	ERA	WHIP	xERA	xWHIP	vL+	vR+	BF/G	BB%	K%	K-BB%	xBB%	SwK	Vel	G	L	F	H%	S%	HR/F	xHR/F	GS	APC	DOM%	DIS%	Sv%	LI	RAR	BPX	R$
17																																		
18																																		
19																																		
20	KC	0	0	15	13	4.91	1.70	5.21	1.40	151	106	13.4	9%	19%	10%	10%	11.4%	96.2	38	26	36	35%	81%	24%	21%	3	51	0%	67%	0	0.66	-0.8	68	-$9
21	KC *	8	0	113	94	3.93	1.30	3.93	1.42	79	96	15.5	10%	20%	10%	10%	11.4%	97.2	40	20	40	28%	73%	7%	13%	11	60	27%	27%	0	0.65	4.6	71	$3
1st Half		3	0	44	43	5.16	1.59	5.82	1.41	122	107	12.1	11%	22%	11%	11%	13.7%	97.9	42	16	42	34%	71%	11%	15%	0	34			0	0.54	-4.9	55	-$7
2nd Half		5	0	69	51	3.15	1.12	4.76	1.43	63	94	19.6	9%	19%	9%	10%	10.6%	97.0	39	21	40	24%	74%	6%	12%	11	78	27%	27%	0	0.72	9.5	50	$12
Proj		9	0	145	121	4.05	1.31	4.84	1.44	90	99	20.8	10%	20%	10%	10%	12.0%	97.4	40	19	41	28%	71%	9%	13%	22						7.2	59	$5

Hernandez,Elieser

Age: 27 **Th:** R **Role** SP **Health** F **LIMA Plan** B+
Ht: 6' 0" **Wt:** 214 **Type** /xFB **PT/Exp** D **Rand Var** +1
Consist B **MM** 1203

1-3, 4.18 ERA in 52 IP at MIA. Missed two, two-month stretches with biceps and quad injuries but contributed more solid numbers down the stretch. Walks trendline stands out, and makes his FB-heavy profile less toxic. Expanded change-up usage and it scored well (plus movement, 14% SwK) but LHH still feasted. With health, only a few tweaks away.

Yr	Tm	W	Sv	IP	K	ERA	WHIP	xERA	xWHIP	vL+	vR+	BF/G	BB%	K%	K-BB%	xBB%	SwK	Vel	G	L	F	H%	S%	HR/F	xHR/F	GS	APC	DOM%	DIS%	Sv%	LI	RAR	BPX	R$
17																																		
18	MIA	2	0	66	45	5.21	1.45	5.69	1.49	121	102	8.9	10%	16%	6%	10%	8.8%	90.7	28	21	51	29%	68%	10%	12%	6	35	0%	67%	0	0.69	-8.6	20	-$7
19	MIA *	6	0	130	143	3.72	1.22	4.02	1.24	120	99	17.6	8%	27%	19%	6%	11.7%	90.6	34	17	49	30%	76%	18%	12%	15	69	13%	20%	0	0.67	12.7	106	$8
20	MIA	1	0	26	34	3.16	1.01	3.54	1.00	100	84	17.7	5%	32%	27%	5%	13.9%	91.4	34	22	45	29%	81%	17%	13%	6	76	33%	17%			4.1	202	$3
21	MIA *	1	0	78	81	3.81	1.10	4.24	1.12	140	87	18.0	6%	26%	21%	4%	11.7%	90.9	38	19	43	27%	76%	20%	18%	11	74	0%	18%			4.4	116	$2
1st Half		0	0	25	27	4.12	0.94	3.48	1.03	97	88	16.0	4%	28%	24%	5%	12.4%	91.0	38	19	44	24%	66%	21%	7%	3	62	0%	33%			0.5	159	-$4
2nd Half		1	0	53	54	3.65	1.18	4.60	1.15	145	89	19.1	6%	26%	20%	4%	11.5%	90.8	39	18	43	29%	80%	20%	21%	8	79	0%	13%			4.0	101	$1
Proj		3	0	131	128	3.97	1.18	4.30	1.22	119	82	21.8	7%	25%	18%	6%	11.7%	90.7	35	19	47	28%	74%	14%	16%	22						7.8	120	$5

Hernández,Jonathan

Age: 25 **Th:** R **Role** RP **Health** F **LIMA Plan** B+
Ht: 6' 3" **Wt:** 190 **Type** **PT/Exp** D **Rand Var** 0
Consist F **MM** 2210

An off-season closer favorite heading into 2021 before a late spring UCL injury led to TJ surgery in April; now likely out through June with no setbacks. Might be worth stashing to see if his stopper-level fastball/slider combo and control come all the way back, but it's a stretch to count on him for 2022 saves. Better to check back in a year.

Yr	Tm	W	Sv	IP	K	ERA	WHIP	xERA	xWHIP	vL+	vR+	BF/G	BB%	K%	K-BB%	xBB%	SwK	Vel	G	L	F	H%	S%	HR/F	xHR/F	GS	APC	DOM%	DIS%	Sv%	LI	RAR	BPX	R$
17																																		
18	aa	4	0	64	48	6.33	1.68	5.35				24.0	14%	17%	3%							32%	62%									-17.2	41	-$11
19	TEX *	7	0	113	96	7.20	1.77	6.56	1.53	113	81	16.7	11%	19%	8%	12%	13.0%	96.9	52	17	30	36%	61%	21%	17%	2	37	0%	50%	0	0.49	-37.5	32	-$17
20	TEX	5	0	31	31	2.90	1.03	3.94	1.18	102	71	4.6	6%	25%	19%	9%	14.5%	97.8	46	14	41	28%	73%	6%	7%	0	18			0	0.89	5.9	139	$12
21																																		
1st Half																																		
2nd Half																																		
Proj		5	2	44	43	3.80	1.14	3.85	1.22	124	90	7.6	7%	25%	18%	9%	14.5%	97.8	46	14	41	29%	69%	11%	6%	0						3.5	130	$2

Heuer,Codi

Age: 25 **Th:** R **Role** RP **Health** A **LIMA Plan** B
Ht: 6' 5" **Wt:** 190 **Type** Con **PT/Exp** D **Rand Var** -1
Consist B **MM** 1010

The Jekyll & Hyde flip of ERA and WHIP compared to x-stats over the first and second halves is ... freaky. But it's actually a good reminder of how half-season splits for relievers are often noisy. By contrast, the yearly consistency of xBB%, SwK, velocity and G/L/F paints a cautiously favorable impression—one that could provide modest profit in the end game.

Yr	Tm	W	Sv	IP	K	ERA	WHIP	xERA	xWHIP	vL+	vR+	BF/G	BB%	K%	K-BB%	xBB%	SwK	Vel	G	L	F	H%	S%	HR/F	xHR/F	GS	APC	DOM%	DIS%	Sv%	LI	RAR	BPX	R$
17																																		
18																																		
19	aa	2	9	30	19	2.67	1.32	3.40				5.7	6%	15%	9%							33%	78%									6.8	94	$2
20	CHW	3	1	24	25	1.52	0.89	3.61	1.28	56	62	4.4	10%	27%	17%	8%	15.0%	97.6	50	21	29	21%	85%	6%	9%	0	18			100	1.02	8.6	121	$11
21	2 TM	7	2	67	56	4.28	1.31	4.44	1.34	125	80	4.3	8%	20%	12%	7%	14.0%	95.9	44	22	35	30%	69%	10%	12%	0	16			40	1.26	-0.1	81	$1
1st Half		4	0	31	33	5.46	1.47	3.70	1.10	143	93	4.2	5%	25%	20%	6%	15.6%	96.7	43	26	31	39%	64%	14%	17%	0	16			0	1.15	-4.6	159	-$5
2nd Half		3	2	36	23	3.25	1.17	5.16	1.59	97	69	4.4	12%	16%	4%	8%	12.5%	95.2	44	18	38	22%	74%	8%	8%	0	16			40	1.36	4.5	12	$2
Proj		6	9	65	50	3.77	1.30	4.64	1.38	119	79	4.6	8%	18%	10%	7%	13.8%	95.8	44	21	35	30%	72%	7%	11%	0						5.5	72	$5

BRENT HERSHEY

Hicks,Jordan

Age: 25	Th: R	Role RP	Health F	LIMA Plan D+
Ht: 6' 2"	Wt: 220	Type Pwr/GB	PT/Exp D	Rand Var -3
			Consist D	MM 3210

Late-fall chatter has him pegged for 2022 rotation. Reasons to be dubious: 1) History of high walk rates; 2) Tommy John surgery (2019), opt-out (2020), more elbow woes (2021) have severely limited innings; 3) Just two starts in the AFL before departure. Triple-digit fastball? Yes. Elite GB rate? Yes. Track record to start? No. A red-light risk in any role.

Yr Tm	W	Sv	IP	K	ERA	WHIP	xERA	xWHIP	vL+	vR+	BF/G	BB%	K%	K-BB%	xBB%	SwK	Vel	G	L	F	H%	S%	HR/F	xHR/F	GS	APC	DOM%	DIS%	Sv%	LI	RAR	BPX	R$
17																																	
18 STL	3	6	78	70	3.59	1.34	3.95	1.55	98	64	4.6	13%	21%	7%	10%	10.0%	100.5	61	21	19	28%	72%	5%	7%	0	17			46	1.25	5.3	51	$2
19 STL	2	14	29	31	3.14	0.94	2.86	1.27	106	44	3.8	10%	28%	18%	11%	12.1%	101.2	67	16	16	22%	68%	18%	16%	0	16			93	0.94	4.8	138	$6
20																																	
21 STL	0	0	10	10	5.40	1.50	4.77	1.97	72	79	4.4	23%	23%	0%	12%	8.7%	99.3	71	13	17	22%	60%	0%	1%	0	21			0	0.47	-1.4	-35	-$6
1st Half	0	0	10	10	5.40	1.50	4.77	1.97	69	80	4.4	23%	23%	0%	12%	8.7%	99.3	71	13	17	22%	60%	0%	1%	0	21			0	0.47	-1.4	-35	-$
2nd Half																																	
Proj	2	5	44	43	3.85	1.34	3.80	1.50	108	67	4.9	14%	24%	10%	10%	10.0%	100.5	61	21	19	29%	69%	5%	6%	0						3.2	71	-$1

Hill,Rich

Age: 42	Th: L	Role SP	Health F	LIMA Plan B
Ht: 6' 5"	Wt: 221	Type /FB	PT/Exp B	Rand Var -1
			Consist B	MM 1201

Rays magic: Squeezing out the most IP and games started SINCE 2007. Outpitched estimators again, and though skills rebounded from 2020, the trends are in decline just about everywhere—as you'd expect at his age. Volume, then, becomes even more important, and that's not exactly his strong suit. This time, know the hat could end up rabbit-less.

Yr Tm	W	Sv	IP	K	ERA	WHIP	xERA	xWHIP	vL+	vR+	BF/G	BB%	K%	K-BB%	xBB%	SwK	Vel	G	L	F	H%	S%	HR/F	xHR/F	GS	APC	DOM%	DIS%	Sv%	LI	RAR	BPX	R$
17 LA	12	0	136	166	3.32	1.09	3.72	1.20	112	79	22.1	9%	30%	21%	6%	11.8%	89.0	37	17	46	27%	75%	13%	12%	25	89	28%	24%			17.4	151	$18
18 LA	11	0	133	150	3.66	1.12	3.66	1.17	95	96	21.9	8%	28%	20%	5%	11.1%	89.3	39	21	40	28%	74%	15%	16%	24	84	29%	17%	0	0.81	8.0	144	$12
19 LA	4	0	59	72	2.45	1.13	3.36	1.15	70	99	18.6	8%	30%	23%	5%	11.4%	90.3	50	18	32	29%	89%	22%	12%	13	74	15%	23%			14.8	166	$5
20 MIN	2	0	39	31	3.03	1.16	4.86	1.48	71	82	19.5	11%	20%	9%	8%	6.6%	87.7	41	23	37	24%	76%	8%	18%	8	77	13%	13%			6.8	47	$5
21 2 TM	7	0	159	150	3.86	1.21	4.45	1.30	78	102	20.7	8%	23%	14%	6%	10.3%	88.0	35	22	43	28%	73%	11%	14%	31	78	13%	42%	0	0.77	8.0	90	$8
1st Half	6	0	83	80	3.70	1.11	4.13	1.30	76	97	20.8	9%	24%	15%	6%	10.5%	88.2	40	19	40	24%	73%	15%	17%	16	78	13%	31%			5.7	96	$13
2nd Half	1	0	76	70	4.03	1.32	4.78	1.29	72	111	20.6	8%	21%	14%	6%	10.1%	87.7	30	24	46	32%	72%	8%	11%	15	78	13%	53%	0	0.76	2.2	85	$0
Proj	6	0	123	116	4.26	1.27	4.42	1.32	84	102	20.8	9%	23%	14%	6%	9.9%	88.4	38	21	40	30%	70%	11%	14%	24						3.0	94	$3

Hill,Tim

Age: 32	Th: L	Role RP	Health A	LIMA Plan B+
Ht: 6' 4"	Wt: 200	Type /xGB	PT/Exp D	Rand Var +1
			Consist A	MM 2100

Lefty sidewinder pairs elite GB% with a nasty HR/F habit. SwK and xBB% point in the way of better command, but RHH have no problems and the velocity is only average. First-half S% coincided with manager confidence, but still just resulted in a single save. Could have some holds value, which makes him worth checking up on in March.

Yr Tm	W	Sv	IP	K	ERA	WHIP	xERA	xWHIP	vL+	vR+	BF/G	BB%	K%	K-BB%	xBB%	SwK	Vel	G	L	F	H%	S%	HR/F	xHR/F	GS	APC	DOM%	DIS%	Sv%	LI	RAR	BPX	R$
17 aa	1	4	69	57	6.29	1.80	5.98				8.9	7%	18%	11%							42%	62%									-16.5	90	-$11
18 KC	1	2	46	42	4.53	1.31	3.38	1.26	78	108	2.8	7%	21%	14%	6%	9.0%	91.0	62	19	19	33%	66%	15%	15%	0	11			50	1.16	-2.2	132	-$3
19 KC *	3	4	71	61	3.21	1.19	3.39	1.29	61	101	3.9	7%	21%	14%	7%	9.6%	90.2	57	17	26	30%	76%	15%	12%	0	14			67	1.39	11.3	101	$5
20 SD	3	0	18	20	4.50	1.28	3.71	1.22	91	112	3.4	8%	25%	18%	7%	10.3%	90.7	53	20	27	31%	70%	21%	13%	0	15			0	0.96	-0.1	147	$1
21 SD	6	1	60	56	3.62	1.24	3.78	1.33	86	106	3.3	9%	22%	13%	6%	11.0%	91.7	61	12	27	27%	77%	20%	21%	0	12			20	1.23	4.7	107	$2
1st Half	5	1	33	36	2.45	1.21	3.30	1.24	98	77	3.6	8%	25%	17%	6%	12.4%	91.9	64	12	23	30%	86%	19%	22%	0	14			50	1.49	7.4	144	$5
2nd Half	1	0	27	20	5.06	1.28	4.38	1.45	62	153	2.9	10%	18%	8%	7%	9.3%	91.4	56	12	32	25%	66%	21%	20%	0	11			0	0.95	-2.6	61	-$9
Proj	4	0	58	51	3.87	1.31	3.86	1.32	81	114	3.3	8%	21%	13%	6%	10.1%	91.2	60	14	26	30%	74%	16%	18%	0						4.2	109	-$1

Hoffman,Jeff

Age: 29	Th: R	Role RP	Health D	LIMA Plan C
Ht: 6' 5"	Wt: 215	Type Pwr/FB	PT/Exp D	Rand Var -1
			Consist C	MM 1300

3-5, 4.56 ERA in 73 IP at CIN. A $9 gain couldn't even make him draftable. New org coaxed out more Ks and better fortune, but walks also spiked, the LD laser show continued, and LHBs thrived. Was better in relief (32% K% and 20% K-BB%), which should be his role. If we somehow got $9 more this season, THEN we'd have something.

Yr Tm	W	Sv	IP	K	ERA	WHIP	xERA	xWHIP	vL+	vR+	BF/G	BB%	K%	K-BB%	xBB%	SwK	Vel	G	L	F	H%	S%	HR/F	xHR/F	GS	APC	DOM%	DIS%	Sv%	LI	RAR	BPX	R$
17 COL *	9	0	149	118	6.03	1.48	4.87	1.45	94	129	19.4	9%	18%	9%	8%	8.5%	94.4	41	18	41	32%	60%	12%	12%	16	70	31%	44%	0	0.59	-30.7	59	-$8
18 COL *	6	0	116	83	6.06	1.67	5.48	1.53	177	92	19.3	11%	16%	5%	10%	8.3%	92.8	52	35	13	34%	63%	0%	1%	1	30	0%	100%	0	0.48	-27.3	47	-$16
19 COL *	8	0	156	142	7.80	1.69	7.30	1.44	103	152	22.0	9%	20%	11%	8%	9.8%	93.7	35	21	43	34%	58%	24%	20%	15	84	0%	53%			-63.4	15	-$24
20 COL	2	1	21	20	9.28	1.92	5.57	1.40	133	134	6.5	9%	19%	11%	9%	9.3%	94.5	36	25	39	42%	50%	11%	14%	0	25			100	1.07	-12.7	72	-$13
21 CIN *	3	0	89	95	4.17	1.51	5.11	1.46	125	92	11.0	13%	25%	12%	11%	12.4%	94.3	38	24	39	31%	78%	15%	14%	11	44	9%	64%	0	0.44	1.1	63	-$4
1st Half	3	0	51	49	3.71	1.47	4.05	1.56	98	101	16.8	14%	22%	8%	11%	11.6%	93.6	36	29	36	30%	76%	10%	15%	10	77	10%	60%			3.5	80	-$2
2nd Half	0	0	38	46	4.78	1.55	6.54	1.33	146	85	7.6	11%	28%	16%	11%	13.5%	95.2	41	16	43	32%	80%	22%	13%	1	28	0%	100%	0	0.28	-2.4	43	-$11
Proj	2	0	58	64	4.75	1.50	4.60	1.39	117	107	12.9	11%	25%	14%	10%	12.4%	94.3	38	21	41	32%	74%	17%	15%	6						-2.1	85	-$5

Holland,Greg

Age: 36	Th: R	Role RP	Health D	LIMA Plan D+
Ht: 5' 10"	Wt: 205	Type Pwr	PT/Exp C	Rand Var 0
			Consist C	MM 1210

Welp, the 2018-19 guy we mused about last year DID resurface, right down to the 4.50-plus ERA, double-digit walk rate and a BPX below average. The saves came early (just one in Aug-Sep) and not often, so there was no overriding the negative R$. At 36, he'll still notch a K per IP, but there are younger, more skilled choices available for just as cheap.

Yr Tm	W	Sv	IP	K	ERA	WHIP	xERA	xWHIP	vL+	vR+	BF/G	BB%	K%	K-BB%	xBB%	SwK	Vel	G	L	F	H%	S%	HR/F	xHR/F	GS	APC	DOM%	DIS%	Sv%	LI	RAR	BPX	R$
17 COL	3	41	57	70	3.61	1.15	3.94	1.30	71	98	3.9	11%	30%	19%	8%	15.6%	93.5	42	13	45	26%	73%	11%	9%	0	14			91	1.33	5.3	129	$20
18 2 NL	2	3	46	47	4.66	1.62	5.06	1.61	90	102	3.8	15%	22%	7%	10%	13.8%	93.0	40	25	35	33%	70%	4%	9%	0	15			50	0.84	-2.9	17	-$5
19 ARI	1	17	36	41	4.54	1.37	4.77	1.57	82	100	3.8	16%	27%	11%	10%	12.5%	91.6	45	16	38	25%	70%	15%	15%	0	15			77	1.20	-0.2	50	$4
20 KC	3	6	28	31	1.91	0.95	3.25	1.12	63	98	4.0	6%	28%	22%	7%	13.2%	93.0	51	19	30	28%	81%	5%	13%	0	16			100	1.00	8.9	165	$18
21 KC	3	8	56	53	4.85	1.35	4.76	1.41	107	91	4.3	11%	22%	11%	9%	12.8%	92.8	42	21	38	28%	68%	15%	24%	0	17			67	0.89	-4.0	67	-$1
1st Half	2	5	33	34	4.05	1.38	4.74	1.42	99	99	4.2	12%	23%	12%	9%	13.2%	92.9	40	21	38	27%	79%	19%	19%	0	18			56	1.03	0.9	66	$0
2nd Half	1	3	22	19	6.04	1.30	4.79	1.39	106	84	4.4	9%	20%	10%	9%	12.2%	92.7	43	19	37	29%	52%	8%	32%	0	17			100	0.65	-4.9	67	-$8
Proj	3	2	58	59	4.36	1.38	4.63	1.47	96	93	3.9	13%	24%	11%	9%	13.1%	92.7	42	20	38	29%	71%	12%	19%	0						0.7	60	-$2

Holloway,Jordan

Age: 26	Th: R	Role RP	Health C	LIMA Plan D
Ht: 6' 6"	Wt: 230	Type Pwr	PT/Exp F	Rand Var 0
			Consist F	MM 0100

2-3, 4.00 ERA in 36 IP at MIA. Was called up/sent down six times, in addition to a month-long IL stint (groin), in the season's first four months. With such starts and stops, the MLB line looks passable (1.36 WHIP), but all of 2021 tells a different story. Walks galore, not enough Ks and a second-half HR problem. Big arm, but needs more time to marinate.

Yr Tm	W	Sv	IP	K	ERA	WHIP	xERA	xWHIP	vL+	vR+	BF/G	BB%	K%	K-BB%	xBB%	SwK	Vel	G	L	F	H%	S%	HR/F	xHR/F	GS	APC	DOM%	DIS%	Sv%	LI	RAR	BPX	R$
17																																	
18																																	
19																																	
20 MIA	0	0	0	0	0.00	9.00	44.28		138	266	4.0	25%	0%	-25%		0.0%	97.1	67	0	33	68%	100%	0%	45%	0	16			0	0.57	0.2	-773	-$8
21 MIA *	2	0	68	60	4.92	1.45	4.30	1.59	86	83	13.8	14%	21%	7%	11%	10.4%	95.6	41	20	40	27%	68%	8%	14%	4	51	0%	75%	0	0.57	-5.5	59	-$7
1st Half	1	0	37	31	4.90	1.46	3.97	1.52	101	80	12.1	12%	20%	8%	12%	10.3%	95.2	40	19	40	31%	65%	4%	11%	3	43	0%	67%	0	0.42	-2.9	77	-$8
2nd Half	1	0	31	28	4.93	1.44	4.68	1.70	49	91	16.7	16%	21%	4%	10%	10.5%	96.1	41	20	38	22%	72%	13%	19%	1	69	0%	100%	0	0.90	-2.6	39	-$10
Proj	1	0	44	38	4.88	1.46	5.35	1.64	93	104	14.5	15%	20%	6%	11%	10.4%	95.7	41	20	39	26%	69%	13%	16%	6						-2.3	9	-$6

Holmes,Clay

Age: 29	Th: R	Role RP	Health C	LIMA Plan B+
Ht: 6' 5"	Wt: 230	Type Pwr/xGB	PT/Exp D	Rand Var +1
			Consist C	MM 5311

The 1st half/2nd half splits don't do this transformation justice. July trade was the turning point (PIT: 4.93 ERA/1.43 WHIP/10% K-BB%; NYY: 1.61 ERA/0.79 WHIP/29% K-BB%). More sinkers; fewer curves seemed to do the trick. Still need to see it again, but by adding command to rising velocity and GB rate, there's suddenly a potential impact reliever here.

Yr Tm	W	Sv	IP	K	ERA	WHIP	xERA	xWHIP	vL+	vR+	BF/G	BB%	K%	K-BB%	xBB%	SwK	Vel	G	L	F	H%	S%	HR/F	xHR/F	GS	APC	DOM%	DIS%	Sv%	LI	RAR	BPX	R$
17 aaa	10	0	113	79	4.54	1.62	4.44				20.0	13%	16%	3%							32%	71%									-2.5	64	-$3
18 PIT *	9	0	122	100	4.69	1.68	5.03	1.52	105	122	16.7	12%	18%	7%	12%	7.6%	94.3	57	21	22	35%	71%	11%	10%	4	45	25%	75%	0	0.44	-8.2	69	-$8
19 PIT *	4	1	71	68	6.45	1.80	5.28	1.73	107	93	7.0	16%	21%	4%	12%	9.7%	94.3	60	18	22	34%	63%	17%	19%	0	26			20	0.57	-17.1	61	-$11
20 PIT	0	0	1	1	0.00	1.50	3.77		92	89	6.0	0%	17%	17%		18.2%	92.4	60	20	20	42%	100%	0%	0%	0	22			0	1.12	0.7	180	-$6
21 2 TM	8	0	70	78	3.60	1.17	2.96	1.27	112	63	4.2	10%	27%	17%	8%	11.6%	96.1	69	13	18	29%	70%	16%	18%	0	16			0	1.06	5.7	139	$5
1st Half	2	0	35	35	4.33	1.42	3.64	1.51	112	69	4.4	13%	22%	9%	9%	11.8%	95.6	71	14	14	29%	69%	14%	19%	0	17			0	0.95	-0.3	72	-$5
2nd Half	6	0	35	43	2.86	0.92	2.38	1.02	96	58	4.0	6%	32%	26%	6%	11.4%	96.5	66	12	22	28%	72%	17%	18%	0	15			0	1.17	6.0	207	$10
Proj	7	4	73	78	3.29	1.11	2.93	1.21	104	65	5.6	9%	27%	19%	8%	11.0%	95.7	66	14	20	29%	72%	14%	18%	0						10.4	156	$8

BRENT HERSHEY

Houck,Tanner

Age: 26	Th: R	Role: RP	Health	A	LIMA Plan	B
Ht: 6' 5"	Wt: 230	Type: Pwr	PT/Exp	D	Rand Var	+2
			Consist	C	MM	4403

1-5, 3.52 ERA in 69 IP at BOS. Team moved him on/off the roster at seemingly every turn; he responded by pitching well both as a starter and in relief. A skills jump like this—velocity, K% and BB%—along with solid GB% and ability to get both-handed hitters out bodes well for an extended rotation look. And if inflated ERA/WHIP depresses the price, all the better.

Yr Tm	W	Sv	IP	K	ERA	WHIP	xERA	xWHIP	vL+	vR+	BF/G	BB%	K%	K-BB%	xBB%	SwK	Vel	G	L	F	H%	S%	HR/F	xHR/F	GS	APC	DOM%	DIS%	Sv%	LI	RAR	BPX	R$
17																																	
18																																	
19 a/a	8	1	109	88	5.50	1.63	5.21				14.7	10%	18%	8%							36%	66%									-13.3	61	-$7
20 BOS	3	0	17	21	0.53	0.88	3.38	1.35	61	59	21.0	14%	33%	19%	12%	12.1%	92.1	47	19	34	16%	100%	9%	16%	3	88	0%	0%			8.2	109	$8
21 BOS *	1	1	90	108	4.22	1.20	3.14	1.13	88	77	15.1	8%	30%	22%	8%	13.7%	94.1	48	20	32	34%	64%	7%	14%	13	64	46%	31%	100	1.11	0.5	150	$0
1st Half	0	0	30	31	4.60	1.27	4.12	1.04	64	148	15.1	3%	26%	22%	5%	13.9%	94.5	53	20	27	37%	63%	13%	23%	2	53	0%	50%	0	1.99	-1.2	210	-$6
2nd Half	1	1	63	77	3.88	1.13	2.46	1.19	88	65	15.5	10%	31%	21%	8%	13.6%	94.1	47	20	33	30%	65%	7%	13%	11	66	55%	27%	100	0.93	3.0	148	$5
Proj	4	0	160	192	3.59	1.14	3.27	1.16	112	77	14.6	8%	30%	22%	8%	13.6%	94.1	47	20	33	31%	70%	11%	12%	20						17.0	158	$12

Houser,Adrian

Age: 29	Th: R	Role: RP	Health	B	LIMA Plan	C+
Ht: 6' 3"	Wt: 222	Type: /xGB	PT/Exp	B	Rand Var	-3
			Consist	A	MM	2003

Surface stats look like he reclaimed 2019 success, but 5 reasons not to fall in that trap: 1) Walks rising; 2) SwK plunging; 3) xERA/xWHIP in lockstep with 2020, not 2019; 4) That's not a DOM/DIS of a sub-3.25 ERA pitcher; 5) H%/S% worked overtime to paper over 2nd-half collapse. Elite GB% provides a foundation, but there are no walls on this House-r.

Yr Tm	W	Sv	IP	K	ERA	WHIP	xERA	xWHIP	vL+	vR+	BF/G	BB%	K%	K-BB%	xBB%	SwK	Vel	G	L	F	H%	S%	HR/F	xHR/F	GS	APC	DOM%	DIS%	Sv%	LI	RAR	BPX	R$
17																																	
18 MIL *	2	0	94	63	5.65	1.70	6.23	1.43	63	131	15.2	8%	15%	7%	9%	10.6%	94.3	40	21	40	37%	68%	0%	5%	0	32			0	0.24	-17.4	41	-$15
19 MIL *	8	0	133	136	3.34	1.18	3.55	1.24	109	83	13.7	8%	25%	18%	8%	10.4%	94.4	53	21	26	29%	76%	18%	13%	18	52	11%	39%	0	1.00	19.1	108	$12
20 MIL	1	0	56	44	5.30	1.50	4.20	1.39	137	78	20.5	9%	18%	9%	8%	10.3%	93.4	59	23	19	33%	67%	24%	20%	11	77	18%	55%	0	0.69	-5.9	83	-$10
21 MIL	10	0	142	105	3.22	1.28	4.19	1.49	105	78	21.4	11%	18%	7%	10%	8.0%	93.7	59	20	21	26%	77%	14%	16%	26	84	8%	46%	0	0.80	18.3	52	$10
1st Half	5	0	82	65	3.94	1.35	3.97	1.42	104	92	21.8	10%	19%	9%	11%	8.3%	93.7	60	20	20	28%	75%	23%	22%	15	86	7%	60%	0	0.78	3.4	72	$4
2nd Half	5	0	60	40	2.25	1.18	4.49	1.59	93	63	20.9	12%	16%	4%	10%	7.7%	93.8	57	20	23	24%	80%	3%	9%	11	81	9%	27%	0	0.82	14.9	24	$12
Proj	8	0	145	114	3.95	1.33	4.13	1.43	117	79	18.0	10%	19%	9%	9%	8.9%	93.8	57	21	22	29%	72%	15%	15%	27						9.0	73	$4

Howard,Spencer

Age: 25	Th: R	Role: RP	Health	B	LIMA Plan	C
Ht: 6' 3"	Wt: 210	Type: Pwr/FB	PT/Exp	D	Rand Var	+3
			Consist	D	MM	1201

0-5, 7.43 ERA in 50 IP at PHI/TEX. Rough ride so far, though PHI's always-shifting plans were no way to treat a top rookie. Strong K% and promising control are among the highlights, though the LD% is troublesome and stamina/durability has been a surprising challenge. Change of scenery is probably a good thing, but there's likely growing pains ahead.

Yr Tm	W	Sv	IP	K	ERA	WHIP	xERA	xWHIP	vL+	vR+	BF/G	BB%	K%	K-BB%	xBB%	SwK	Vel	G	L	F	H%	S%	HR/F	xHR/F	GS	APC	DOM%	DIS%	Sv%	LI	RAR	BPX	R$
17																																	
18																																	
19 aa	1	0	32	34	2.96	1.05	2.54				20.8	8%	27%	19%							27%	74%									6.1	134	$0
20 PHI	1	0	24	23	5.92	1.64	5.26	1.38	148	93	18.8	9%	20%	12%	7%	10.7%	94.1	38	24	38	34%	71%	20%	13%	6	73	0%	50%			-4.4	78	-$9
21 2 TM *	1	0	75	77	5.47	1.43	4.41	1.39	100	118	12.2	11%	24%	13%	8%	10.6%	94.2	36	23	40	32%	62%	12%	13%	15	49	0%	47%	0	0.75	-11.2	84	-$9
1st Half	1	0	36	42	3.82	1.28	2.89	1.50	79	116	11.2	16%	29%	13%	8%	12.1%	94.5	34	20	46	25%	72%	8%	10%	5	49	0%	20%	0	0.71	2.0	106	-$3
2nd Half	0	0	39	36	6.98	1.57	5.78	1.30	107	124	13.3	8%	21%	13%	9%	9.2%	93.9	38	26	37	37%	55%	15%	15%	10	50	0%	60%			-13.1	72	-$18
Proj	2	0	116	119	4.77	1.36	4.47	1.34	86	103	16.0	10%	25%	15%	9%	10.5%	94.1	36	23	41	32%	66%	10%	13%	18						-4.5	90	-$4

Hudson,Dakota

Age: 27	Th: R	Role: SP	Health	F	LIMA Plan	B
Ht: 6' 5"	Wt: 215	Type: /xGB	PT/Exp	C	Rand Var	-5
			Consist	D	MM	1103

1-0, 2.08 ERA in 9 IP at STL. Spent the season defying expectations after Sept 2020 TJ surgery. Played catch, faced hitters, rehabbed in minors, activated by STL, started MLB game—everything was ahead of schedule. GB, control returned in the short sample, maybe velocity, Ks are next? Still more floor than ceiling, but potential 2022 profit center in end game.

Yr Tm	W	Sv	IP	K	ERA	WHIP	xERA	xWHIP	vL+	vR+	BF/G	BB%	K%	K-BB%	xBB%	SwK	Vel	G	L	F	H%	S%	HR/F	xHR/F	GS	APC	DOM%	DIS%	Sv%	LI	RAR	BPX	R$
17 a/a	10	0	153	78	3.75	1.45	4.31				26.1	8%	12%	4%							32%	74%									11.5	54	$3
18 STL *	17	0	141	90	2.75	1.38	3.45	1.48	104	57	13.1	9%	15%	6%	11%	9.9%	96.0	61	20	19	31%	78%	0%	5%	0	17			0	1.35	24.3	81	$12
19 STL	16	1	175	136	3.35	1.41	4.61	1.55	108	90	22.9	11%	18%	7%	11%	10.2%	93.7	57	22	21	28%	81%	20%	20%	32	86	16%	41%	100	0.95	24.9	45	$13
20 STL	3	0	39	31	2.77	1.00	4.13	1.41	66	95	18.9	10%	21%	11%	9%	10.0%	92.9	57	13	31	19%	79%	16%	14%	8	74	25%	38%			8.1	79	$11
21 STL *	2	0	27	13	1.33	0.98	1.50	1.46	82	68	17.0	8%	13%	5%	8%	7.6%	92.1	65	8	27	22%	85%	0%	1%	1	66	0%	0%	0	1.05	9.7	82	$0
1st Half																																	
2nd Half	2	0	27	13	1.33	0.98	1.50	1.46	78	70	17.0	8%	13%	5%	8%	7.6%	92.1	65	8	27	22%	85%	0%	1%	1	66	0%	0%	0	1.05	9.7	82	$1
Proj	9	0	131	107	3.93	1.38	4.27	1.42	90	104	21.5	10%	20%	10%	10%	10.1%	93.2	57	16	27	31%	71%	7%	17%	25						8.4	79	$3

Iglesias,Raisel

Age: 32	Th: R	Role: RP	Health	A	LIMA Plan	C
Ht: 6' 2"	Wt: 190	Type: Pwr	PT/Exp	B	Rand Var	-1
			Consist	B	MM	5530

Under-the-radar gem. Skills growth since 2018 is almost without fail; pick just about any column and work your way down. Faves include K%/SwK, which resulted in triple-digit strikeouts; BB%, which morphed from league average to elite; and a sub-1.00 WHIP repeat over 70 IP. Yes, closers are fickle, but there's no reason he can't repeat.

Yr Tm	W	Sv	IP	K	ERA	WHIP	xERA	xWHIP	vL+	vR+	BF/G	BB%	K%	K-BB%	xBB%	SwK	Vel	G	L	F	H%	S%	HR/F	xHR/F	GS	APC	DOM%	DIS%	Sv%	LI	RAR	BPX	R$
17 CIN	3	28	76	92	2.49	1.11	3.38	1.20	94	61	4.9	9%	30%	21%	6%	14.7%	96.4	42	25	32	30%	80%	8%	9%	0	20			93	0.99	17.5	156	$20
18 CIN	2	30	72	80	2.38	1.07	3.59	1.22	91	87	4.4	9%	28%	19%	7%	15.7%	95.2	38	26	35	25%	89%	19%	18%	0	17			88	1.02	15.8	129	$19
19 CIN	3	34	67	89	4.16	1.22	3.83	1.14	105	94	4.1	8%	32%	24%	7%	16.0%	95.5	30	26	44	33%	73%	17%	12%	0	17			85	1.54	2.8	160	$16
20 CIN	4	8	23	31	2.74	0.91	3.02	0.99	74	65	4.1	6%	34%	29%	5%	19.7%	96.2	42	23	36	31%	70%	5%	11%	0	16			80	1.79	4.9	210	$20
21 LAA	7	34	70	103	2.57	0.93	2.67	0.88	89	78	4.2	4%	38%	33%	4%	21.1%	96.4	39	22	39	31%	83%	18%	16%	0	16			87	1.43	14.6	234	$27
1st Half	5	16	37	58	3.38	0.88	2.40	0.86	80	83	4.4	5%	41%	36%	4%	22.6%	96.3	45	17	38	29%	73%	24%	18%	0	18			84	1.50	4.1	252	$19
2nd Half	2	18	33	45	1.65	0.98	2.97	0.92	89	76	4.0	4%	35%	31%	4%	19.2%	96.6	33	27	40	33%	93%	13%	14%	0	15			90	1.35	10.5	217	$23
Proj	4	35	65	87	2.73	1.04	3.09	1.02	95	80	4.1	7%	35%	28%	5%	18.0%	96.0	37	25	39	30%	83%	17%	15%	0						13.9	193	$22

Irvin,Cole

Age: 28	Th: L	Role: SP	Health	A	LIMA Plan	B
Ht: 6' 4"	Wt: 217	Type: Con	PT/Exp	C	Rand Var	-1
			Consist	B	MM	0003

Command/control soft tosser kept opponents off balance—for a half-season, anyway. Then the swings and misses went down, the walks went up, the hits got harder, and HR propensity returned. Hasn't really handled LHH or RHH all that well over his career, and the xERA string confirms that the first three months is probably as good as it will get.

Yr Tm	W	Sv	IP	K	ERA	WHIP	xERA	xWHIP	vL+	vR+	BF/G	BB%	K%	K-BB%	xBB%	SwK	Vel	G	L	F	H%	S%	HR/F	xHR/F	GS	APC	DOM%	DIS%	Sv%	LI	RAR	BPX	R$
17 aa	5	0	84	58	4.92	1.27	4.48				26.6	7%	17%	10%							28%	66%									-5.8	54	-$1
18 aaa	14	0	162	114	3.21	1.22	3.71				25.2	6%	17%	12%							30%	76%									18.7	95	$14
19 PHI *	8	1	137	87	5.00	1.50	5.95	1.34	123	98	17.9	5%	15%	10%	6%	10.0%	89.8	34	31	34	34%	71%	16%	16%	3	40	33%	67%	100	0.57	-8.4	52	-$4
20 PHI	0	0	4	4	17.18	3.27	5.77		254	158	7.3	5%	18%	14%		7.3%	92.4	41	29	29	61%	45%	20%	23%	0	27			0	0.46	-5.8	146	-$13
21 OAK	10	0	178	125	4.24	1.33	4.90	1.30	106	98	24.0	6%	16%	11%	5%	9.6%	90.7	38	24	38	31%	71%	10%	12%	32	84	19%	44%			0.6	79	$2
1st Half	6	0	101	73	3.56	1.21	4.64	1.24	101	90	24.9	5%	17%	13%	5%	10.4%	90.7	37	24	39	31%	73%	8%	11%	17	85	18%	35%			8.7	95	$12
2nd Half	4	0	77	52	5.12	1.49	5.24	1.37	100	113	23.0	7%	15%	8%	6%	8.8%	90.7	38	25	37	32%	70%	13%	14%	15	82	20%	53%			-8.2	58	-$8
Proj	10	0	160	109	4.38	1.36	4.83	1.33	111	100	22.3	6%	16%	11%	5%	9.5%	90.5	37	26	37	31%	71%	12%	14%	30						1.4	76	$1

Jackson,Luke

Age: 30	Th: R	Role: RP	Health	A	LIMA Plan	B+
Ht: 6' 2"	Wt: 210	Type: Pwr/GB	PT/Exp	C	Rand Var	-5
			Consist	D	MM	3300

The H%/S% duo is responsible for 2021's pretty stage face, but in this case there's valid screenwriting underneath. A big K%, burgeoning velocity, and an elite GB% undergird the show, and though he walks too many, xBB says subsequent seasons should fix that criticism. Is the second half a teaser of things to come? If so, UP: 20 Sv

Yr Tm	W	Sv	IP	K	ERA	WHIP	xERA	xWHIP	vL+	vR+	BF/G	BB%	K%	K-BB%	xBB%	SwK	Vel	G	L	F	H%	S%	HR/F	xHR/F	GS	APC	DOM%	DIS%	Sv%	LI	RAR	BPX	R$
17 ATL *	2	1	75	52	5.85	1.67	5.23	1.59	80	118	6.5	11%	15%	4%	8%	10.7%	94.7	45	19	36	34%	64%	7%	12%	0	19			100	0.54	-13.8	49	-$10
18 ATL *	3	1	63	72	3.62	1.37	3.41	1.35	88	111	5.8	12%	27%	16%	9%	11.7%	94.3	48	23	29	33%	73%	9%	11%	0	20			50	0.89	4.1	121	$0
19 ATL	9	18	73	106	3.84	1.40	2.74	1.11	72	113	4.5	8%	34%	25%	8%	17.0%	96.1	60	18	22	40%	77%	26%	25%	0	18			72	1.28	6.0	204	$12
20 ATL	2	0	26	20	6.84	1.97	5.08	1.51	124	109	6.9	10%	15%	5%	9%	10.7%	94.4	62	20	19	41%	64%	11%	9%	0	26			0	0.65	-7.7	49	-$13
21 ATL	2	0	64	70	1.98	1.16	3.67	1.33	80	84	3.7	11%	27%	16%	9%	13.4%	95.9	53	17	30	26%	88%	13%	19%	0	15			0	1.07	18.0	108	$5
1st Half	1	0	29	29	1.86	1.28	4.18	1.40	81	93	3.6	12%	24%	12%	9%	11.1%	95.8	51	17	32	26%	94%	16%	21%	0	14			0	1.03	8.6	81	-$1
2nd Half	1	0	35	41	2.08	1.07	3.27	1.26	71	79	3.8	11%	29%	19%	9%	15.3%	95.9	54	18	29	26%	83%	9%	17%	0	15			0	1.11	9.4	130	$2
Proj	3	0	65	75	3.07	1.30	3.64	1.30	79	96	4.3	11%	28%	17%	9%	13.6%	95.5	53	19	29	31%	79%	12%	18%	0						11.2	122	$2

BRENT HERSHEY

ames,Josh

Age: 29	Th: R	Role RP	Health F	LIMA Plan C	
Ht: 6' 3"	Wt: 234	Type Pwr/FB	PT/Exp D	Rand Var +5	
			Consist F	MM 2400	

0-0, 5.40 ERA in 5 IP at HOU. Off-season hip surgery cascaded into a hamstring issue that led to just 5 Sept MLB appearances. A hard thrower gets whiffs, but any type of post-hype worthiness will need to come from some combination of getting ahold of his walk, fly ball and home run rates. All while staying healthy. It's a tall task.

Yr	Tm	W	Sv	IP	K	ERA	WHIP	xERA	xWHIP	vL+	vR+	BF/G	BB%	K%	K-BB%	xBB%	SwK	Vel	G	L	F	H%	S%	HR/F	xHR/F	GS	APC	DOM%	DIS%	Sv%	LI	RAR	BPX	R$
17	aa	4	3	76	63	5.51	1.66	4.81				16.2	10%	18%	9%							38%	64%									-10.8	90	-$7
18	HOU *	8	1	140	169	3.37	1.14	2.85	1.22	94	73	19.2	10%	30%	20%	6%	14.6%	97.1	42	15	43	29%	73%	13%	13%	3	58	33%	0%	50	0.75	13.4	136	$1
19	HOU	5	1	61	100	4.70	1.32	3.70	1.24	93	92	5.4	13%	38%	24%	10%	16.6%	97.2	35	19	46	33%	69%	17%	9%	1	23	0%	0%	33	0.80	-1.4	151	$1
20	HOU	1	0	17	21	7.27	1.85	6.37	1.84	126	117	6.4	20%	25%	5%	12%	10.3%	96.3	33	19	49	28%	64%	19%	20%	2	26	0%	100%	0	0.98	-6.0	-35	-$10
21	HOU *	1	1	25	29	3.79	1.33	3.49		63	153	4.2	10%	28%	18%		13.0%	94.8	55	9	36	35%	71%	25%	27%	0	14			100	0.12	1.5	128	-$4
1st Half																																		
2nd Half		1	1	24	27	3.94	1.30	3.39		60	156	4.2	9%	27%	18%		13.0%	94.8	55	9	36	34%	68%	25%	27%	0	14			100	0.12	1.0	131	-$6
Proj		**2**	**0**	**44**	**52**	**4.37**	**1.34**	**4.12**	**1.28**	**107**	**106**	**6.5**	**11%**	**29%**	**18%**	**10%**	**13.6%**	**97.2**	**35**	**19**	**46**	**33%**	**70%**	**12%**	**8%**	**0**						**0.4**	**115**	**-$3**

ansen,Kenley

Age: 34	Th: R	Role RP	Health A	LIMA Plan C	
Ht: 6' 5"	Wt: 265	Type Pwr/FB	PT/Exp A	Rand Var -5	
			Consist A	MM 3430	

If you knew nothing of his context and just looked at this box, there would be far less hand-wringing about his future. A first-half crazy (and unsubstantiated) BB% and H%/S% combo pulled a few indicators down; after June, order was mostly restored. That's not to say completely ignore his age (or his landing spot), but any cracks at this point are just hairlines.

Yr	Tm	W	Sv	IP	K	ERA	WHIP	xERA	xWHIP	vL+	vR+	BF/G	BB%	K%	K-BB%	xBB%	SwK	Vel	G	L	F	H%	S%	HR/F	xHR/F	GS	APC	DOM%	DIS%	Sv%	LI	RAR	BPX	R$
17	LA	5	41	68	109	1.32	0.75	2.26	0.77	85	43	4.0	3%	42%	40%	4%	18.6%	93.3	38	21	41	32%	89%	9%	8%	0	16			98	1.30	25.6	300	$34
18	LA	1	38	72	82	3.01	0.99	3.62	1.10	78	97	4.2	6%	28%	22%	5%	13.9%	92.3	35	21	44	25%	81%	16%	13%	0	17			90	1.15	10.0	162	$21
19	LA	5	33	63	80	3.71	1.06	3.79	1.11	83	91	4.2	6%	30%	24%	5%	16.3%	92.0	32	24	43	30%	71%	13%	11%	0	17			80	1.24	6.1	168	$19
20	LA	3	11	24	33	3.33	1.15	3.93	1.15	72	94	3.8	9%	32%	24%	6%	15.7%	92.4	25	25	50	32%	73%	7%	7%	0	17			85	1.39	3.4	150	$19
21	LA	4	38	69	86	2.22	1.04	3.93	1.33	76	61	4.0	13%	31%	18%	6%	15.8%	93.9	37	19	44	23%	81%	6%	9%	0	16			88	1.53	17.4	99	$25
1st Half		0	21	34	39	1.34	0.98	4.17	1.49	54	56	4.0	16%	30%	14%	7%	14.6%	93.8	39	16	45	16%	88%	3%	7%	0	16			91	1.78	12.2	58	$17
2nd Half		4	17	35	47	3.06	1.10	3.72	1.20	87	67	4.1	10%	32%	22%	5%	16.9%	94.1	35	21	44	29%	75%	8%	10%	0	15			85	1.30	5.3	138	$22
Proj		**4**	**32**	**58**	**74**	**3.59**	**1.12**	**3.60**	**1.16**	**89**	**79**	**4.0**	**9%**	**32%**	**23%**	**5%**	**15.9%**	**93.2**	**36**	**21**	**44**	**30%**	**71%**	**10%**	**10%**	**0**						**6.2**	**151**	**$17**

avier,Cristian

Age: 25	Th: R	Role RP	Health A	LIMA Plan B	
Ht: 6' 1"	Wt: 213	Type Pwr/xFB	PT/Exp C	Rand Var -3	
			Consist D	MM 2401	

Surprising move to the bullpen in late May, but team relished the flexibility. Was more effective as a SP (3.14/1.027) than RP (3.93/1.329) at run/baserunner prevention, and K% remained stable (31% as RP vs. 30% as a SP). All of which may not matter much if the fly balls, homers and walks continue at this rate. Young enough for a step up, but work ahead.

Yr	Tm	W	Sv	IP	K	ERA	WHIP	xERA	xWHIP	vL+	vR+	BF/G	BB%	K%	K-BB%	xBB%	SwK	Vel	G	L	F	H%	S%	HR/F	xHR/F	GS	APC	DOM%	DIS%	Sv%	LI	RAR	BPX	R$
17																																		
18																																		
19	a/a	6	3	85	115	2.47	1.00	1.64				17.1	13%	35%	22%							22%	79%									21.3	144	$14
20	HOU	5	0	54	54	3.48	0.99	4.58	1.28	109	61	17.8	8%	25%	17%	10%	8.9%	92.3	29	19	52	20%	77%	15%	10%	10	74	0%	30%	0	0.70	6.5	99	$17
21	HOU	4	2	101	130	3.55	1.18	4.21	1.32	103	78	11.8	13%	31%	18%	11%	13.6%	93.6	28	24	49	25%	77%	14%	17%	9	50	44%	11%	50	1.01	8.9	95	$7
1st Half		3	1	68	83	2.91	1.03	4.17	1.31	82	75	16.0	12%	31%	18%	11%	13.2%	93.4	27	22	51	20%	79%	12%	17%	9	69	44%	11%	100	0.85	11.4	93	$13
2nd Half		1	1	33	47	4.86	1.50	4.27	1.34	129	88	8.0	13%	31%	18%	12%	14.5%	94.0	29	27	44	33%	74%	20%	16%	0	33			33	1.15	-2.4	99	-$8
Proj		**6**	**0**	**116**	**147**	**3.92**	**1.22**	**4.15**	**1.31**	**110**	**75**	**11.5**	**12%**	**31%**	**19%**	**11%**	**12.8%**	**93.4**	**28**	**23**	**48**	**27%**	**74%**	**15%**	**15%**	**6**						**7.6**	**103**	**$6**

ax,Griffin

Age: 27	Th: R	Role SP	Health A	LIMA Plan D+	
Ht: 6' 2"	Wt: 195	Type Con/xFB	PT/Exp D	Rand Var +3	
			Consist B	MM 0001	

4-5, 6.37 ERA in 82 IP at MIN. By nature, having a "Con/xFB" type designation is rough; being a rookie without plus control just adds to the anxiety. In this case, things worked out how one might expect: a 6+ ERA that somehow lasted enough for 14 starts. Maybe there's a bit of K% upside if you squint; but he shouldn't be working through these issues in MLB.

Yr	Tm	W	Sv	IP	K	ERA	WHIP	xERA	xWHIP	vL+	vR+	BF/G	BB%	K%	K-BB%	xBB%	SwK	Vel	G	L	F	H%	S%	HR/F	xHR/F	GS	APC	DOM%	DIS%	Sv%	LI	RAR	BPX	R$
17																																		
18																																		
19	a/a	5	0	128	75	4.06	1.40	4.49				23.5	6%	14%	8%							33%	71%									7.0	67	$0
20																																		
21	MIN *	8	0	124	93	5.82	1.41	5.48	1.43	117	115	20.2	9%	18%	9%	8%	9.9%	92.7	32	16	52	29%	63%	17%	19%	14	77	0%	57%	0	0.65	-23.9	31	-$9
1st Half		4	0	49	38	6.28	1.71	5.98	1.55	87	163	20.1	11%	17%	6%	7%	7.6%	92.1	27	19	54	34%	64%	19%	13%	1	66	0%	100%	0	0.27	-12.1	40	-$11
2nd Half		4	0	75	55	5.53	1.22	5.15	1.34	118	105	20.3	7%	18%	11%	8%	10.6%	92.9	33	15	52	24%	63%	16%	21%	13	82	0%	54%			-11.7	30	-$2
Proj		**6**	**0**	**116**	**82**	**5.14**	**1.41**	**5.62**	**1.43**	**101**	**111**	**20.9**	**8%**	**17%**	**9%**	**8%**	**9.3%**	**92.6**	**31**	**16**	**53**	**30%**	**68%**	**10%**	**18%**	**23**						**-9.8**	**46**	**-$6**

ohnson,Pierce

Age: 31	Th: R	Role RP	Health C	LIMA Plan B+	
Ht: 6' 2"	Wt: 202	Type Pwr/FB	PT/Exp D	Rand Var -2	
			Consist A	MM 2411	

Was a down-ballot closing candidate prior to 2021, and one can see hints of it here. Finally tamed RHH, elite-level Ks for two seasons, a xBB that points to strong BB% upside, and emerging managerial confidence. At the very least, a Holds source, and with opportunity, one that could see .... UP: 20 Sv.

Yr	Tm	W	Sv	IP	K	ERA	WHIP	xERA	xWHIP	vL+	vR+	BF/G	BB%	K%	K-BB%	xBB%	SwK	Vel	G	L	F	H%	S%	HR/F	xHR/F	GS	APC	DOM%	DIS%	Sv%	LI	RAR	BPX	R$
17	CHC *	3	9	55	62	4.94	1.67	4.88		88	113	5.6	12%	25%	13%		13.8%	92.2	50	25	25	39%	69%	0%	0%	0	29			82	0.91	-4.0	104	-$1
18	SF *	3	4	68	59	4.90	1.29	3.38	1.46	93	109	5.2	11%	21%	10%	10%	10.5%	93.7	38	20	43	27%	62%	9%	11%	0	22			100	0.49	-6.3	84	-$2
19																																		
20	SD	3	0	20	27	2.70	1.20	3.73	1.22	49	105	3.3	11%	34%	23%	8%	16.8%	96.4	30	30	41	31%	82%	11%	12%	0	13			0	0.83	4.3	133	$4
21	SD	3	0	59	77	3.22	1.26	3.87	1.24	97	87	3.9	11%	32%	20%	8%	13.3%	95.5	34	22	43	32%	78%	10%	13%	2	17	0%	100%	0	0.80	7.6	124	$1
1st Half		2	0	26	37	3.16	1.25	3.48	1.19	95	71	3.5	11%	35%	24%	8%	12.6%	95.7	35	25	40	32%	79%	13%	16%	0	15			0	0.61	3.5	146	-$1
2nd Half		1	0	33	40	3.27	1.27	4.18	1.28	88	100	4.2	11%	29%	18%	8%	13.8%	95.4	33	21	46	31%	77%	8%	11%	2	18	0%	100%	0	0.98	4.0	107	-$3
Proj		**4**	**2**	**73**	**92**	**3.89**	**1.35**	**4.08**	**1.29**	**97**	**95**	**4.3**	**11%**	**30%**	**19%**	**8%**	**12.6%**	**95.1**	**35**	**22**	**43**	**33%**	**73%**	**9%**	**13%**	**0**						**5.0**	**116**	**$1**

unis,Jakob

Age: 29	Th: R	Role RP	Health D	LIMA Plan C	
Ht: 6' 3"	Wt: 220	Type	PT/Exp C	Rand Var +1	
			Consist B	MM 1200	

2-4, 5.26 ERA in 39 IP at KC. Sent to minors in early June, pitched one more MLB game in August, ended the year on IL with shoulder impingement. With velocity down, batters of both hands teeing off, and a serious HR problem (1.6 HR/9 for season and career), it seems time for a bullpen tryout. xERA, BPX histories say "Good luck" in stereo.

Yr	Tm	W	Sv	IP	K	ERA	WHIP	xERA	xWHIP	vL+	vR+	BF/G	BB%	K%	K-BB%	xBB%	SwK	Vel	G	L	F	H%	S%	HR/F	xHR/F	GS	APC	DOM%	DIS%	Sv%	LI	RAR	BPX	R$
17	KC *	12	0	169	148	4.09	1.28	4.24	1.25	104	100	21.7	6%	21%	15%	8%	9.4%	91.2	40	20	40	32%	72%	12%	16%	16	76	19%	31%	0	0.88	5.6	108	$10
18	KC	9	0	177	164	4.37	1.27	4.06	1.20	107	106	25.3	6%	22%	16%	7%	10.0%	91.1	42	21	37	31%	72%	16%	17%	30	95	23%	30%			-4.9	128	$4
19	KC	9	0	175	164	5.24	1.43	4.65	1.33	110	104	24.9	8%	21%	14%	8%	10.0%	91.5	42	23	35	33%	68%	17%	18%	31	94	23%	29%			-15.8	99	-$3
20	KC	0	0	25	19	6.39	1.62	4.88	1.29	141	114	14.3	5%	17%	11%	6%	9.4%	91.0	45	23	32	35%	68%	25%	22%	6	49	0%	83%	0	0.79	-6.1	98	-$12
21	KC *	2	0	59	54	5.61	1.55	6.16	1.32	117	95	11.6	8%	21%	13%	7%	11.0%	90.9	42	22	37	35%	68%	17%	23%	6	39	33%	33%	0	0.60	-9.7	53	-$9
1st Half		2	0	46	43	6.59	1.73	7.35	1.31	122	87	11.0	8%	21%	13%	8%	11.3%	91.1	42	22	36	38%	66%	16%	25%	5	37	40%	40%	0	0.59	-13.1	41	-$14
2nd Half		0	0	13	10	2.11	0.94	1.88		0	157	16.0	8%	21%	13%		9.0%	89.9	42	17	42	21%	82%	20%	6%	1	78	0%	0%			3.4	101	-$7
Proj		**3**	**0**	**58**	**54**	**5.12**	**1.47**	**4.46**	**1.28**	**125**	**103**	**9.9**	**7%**	**22%**	**14%**	**8%**	**10.3%**	**91.2**	**42**	**22**	**37**	**34%**	**70%**	**16%**	**20%**	**0**						**-4.7**	**109**	**-$6**

Kahnle,Tommy

Age: 32	Th: R	Role RP	Health F	LIMA Plan A	
Ht: 6' 1"	Wt: 230	Type Pwr	PT/Exp D	Rand Var 0	
			Consist F	MM 5500	

Pre-Tommy John surgery (Aug 2020), had shown some impressive, impactful reliever skills in short stints. High velocity and K% the main attributes; xBB% says BB% should be better. Inconsistency and of course injury recovery make up the "risk" part of the equation, so best left to a mid-season watchlist. But the type of arm who could return late-inning value.

Yr	Tm	W	Sv	IP	K	ERA	WHIP	xERA	xWHIP	vL+	vR+	BF/G	BB%	K%	K-BB%	xBB%	SwK	Vel	G	L	F	H%	S%	HR/F	xHR/F	GS	APC	DOM%	DIS%	Sv%	LI	RAR	BPX	R$
17	2AL	2	0	63	96	2.59	1.12	2.79	0.98	97	71	3.7	7%	38%	31%	6%	17.5%	97.9	41	21	38	38%	79%	8%	10%	0	15			0	1.06	13.7	242	$6
18	NYY *	4	2	50	58	6.00	1.66	5.41	1.41	90	133	4.5	13%	26%	14%	9%	10.0%	95.1	35	24	40	37%	65%	12%	15%	0	20			67	0.79	-11.3	84	-$7
19	NYY	3	0	61	88	3.67	1.06	2.83	1.07	89	79	3.4	8%	35%	27%	7%	18.2%	96.5	50	21	28	30%	71%	23%	18%	0	14			0	1.03	6.3	197	$4
20	NYY	0	0	1	3	0.00	2.00	0.00		207	33	6.0	17%	50%	33%		30.0%	97.6	100	0	0	122%	100%	0%		0	20			0	1.86	0.5	363	-$6
21																																		
1st Half																																		
2nd Half																																		
Proj		**2**	**0**	**44**	**60**	**3.68**	**1.14**	**3.04**	**1.13**	**96**	**76**	**3.6**	**10%**	**35%**	**25%**	**6%**	**17.9%**	**97.0**	**47**	**21**	**32**	**31%**	**71%**	**17%**	**15%**	**0**						**4.1**	**176**	**$0**

BRENT HERSHEY

Kaprielian,James

Age: 28 | Th: R | Role: SP | Ht: 6' 3" | Wt: 225 | Type: Pwr/xFB
Health: C | PT/Exp: D | Consist: F
LIMA Plan: B | Rand Var: -1 | MM: 1203

After May debut, proved capable of handling starter's workload through July, but final two months included IL stint (shoulder), ineffectiveness (5.36 ERA), and ended with bullpen work. High FB% and struggles against LHB are two areas of concern, along with his minor-league injury history. Whether 2021 is a stepping stone or a reality check is the question.

Yr	Tm	W	Sv	IP	K	ERA	WHIP	xERA	xWHIP	vL+	vR+	BF/G	BB%	K%	K-BB%	xBB%	SwK	Vel	G	L	F	H%	S%	HR/F	xHR/F	GS	APC	DOM%	DIS%	Sv%	LI	RAR	BPX	R$
17																																		
18																																		
19	a/a	2	0	33	26	2.03	1.11	2.86				16.3	6%	20%	14%							28%	85%									10.2	108	$1
20	OAK	0	0	4	4	7.36	1.64	6.11		207	63	8.5	12%	24%	12%		15.5%	95.0	36	0	64	24%	75%	29%	33%	0	36			0	0.44	-1.3	66	-$8
21	OAK	8	0	119	123	4.07	1.22	4.48	1.26	119	80	20.9	8%	25%	16%	8%	11.6%	93.0	35	18	47	29%	72%	12%	16%	21	84	14%	33%	0	0.72	2.8	106	$5
1st Half		4	0	50	52	3.06	1.10	4.31	1.28	118	64	22.6	9%	26%	16%	8%	11.8%	92.8	38	15	47	24%	81%	13%	15%	9	91	0%	22%			7.4	102	$7
2nd Half		4	0	69	71	4.80	1.31	4.61	1.24	110	96	19.9	7%	24%	16%	8%	11.5%	93.1	33	20	47	32%	68%	12%	16%	12	80	25%	42%	0	0.69	-4.6	109	$0
Proj		8	0	131	126	4.17	1.31	4.71	1.35	120	83	21.0	10%	23%	14%	8%	11.6%	93.0	35	18	47	29%	73%	11%	16%	26						4.5	84	$4

Karinchak,James

Age: 26 | Th: R | Role: RP | Ht: 6' 3" | Wt: 215 | Type: Pwr
Health: A | PT/Exp: D | Consist: B
LIMA Plan: B | Rand Var: 0 | MM: 3510

Possible that injury or unknown factor altered trajectory of this season, but after a fantastic start, his results greatly suffered after foreign substance ban. From that point forward, strikeouts vanished, homers spiked (1.9 HR/9), and he was so ineffective he was briefly sent to AAA. In a way, the specific culprit is irrelevant; he still needs fixing.

Yr	Tm	W	Sv	IP	K	ERA	WHIP	xERA	xWHIP	vL+	vR+	BF/G	BB%	K%	K-BB%	xBB%	SwK	Vel	G	L	F	H%	S%	HR/F	xHR/F	GS	APC	DOM%	DIS%	Sv%	LI	RAR	BPX	R$
17																																		
18																																		
19	CLE *	1	8	33	63	3.64	1.22	2.69		23	85	4.2	13%	47%	33%		16.0%	97.1	38	31	31	39%	71%	0%	9%	0	19			100	0.09	3.6	185	$3
20	CLE	1	1	27	53	2.67	1.11	2.70	1.09	81	59	4.0	15%	49%	34%	9%	17.9%	95.5	23	31	46	36%	76%	6%	7%	0	17			25	1.01	6.0	198	$7
21	CLE	7	11	55	78	4.07	1.21	3.76	1.31	79	98	3.9	14%	33%	20%	11%	13.5%	95.9	39	20	40	25%	72%	18%	16%	0	17			69	1.43	1.4	115	$7
1st Half		4	9	36	62	2.48	1.02	3.02	1.20	62	76	3.9	15%	42%	27%	9%	15.8%	96.1	35	24	41	21%	82%	15%	16%	0	17			90	1.47	8.0	156	$14
2nd Half		3	2	19	16	7.11	1.58	5.40	1.52	100	136	4.0	11%	18%	7%	12%	9.4%	95.6	44	17	39	29%	60%	22%	16%	0	17			33	1.36	-6.7	34	-$9
Proj		7	9	65	89	3.92	1.32	3.82	1.32	83	104	3.9	13%	33%	20%	11%	11.8%	95.8	40	20	40	30%	75%	16%	16%	0						4.3	119	$6

Keller,Brad

Age: 26 | Th: R | Role: SP | Ht: 6' 5" | Wt: 250 | Type:
Health: C | PT/Exp: A | Consist: B
LIMA Plan: D+ | Rand Var: +3 | MM: 1103

Experienced pullback that was projected by short-season xERA and xWHIP, and once batted ball luck faded, lack of K% upside and BB% inconsistency were exposed. Both H% and xERA make the case that regression went too far, but his lack of foundational skills leaves little room for optimism. Filler.

Yr	Tm	W	Sv	IP	K	ERA	WHIP	xERA	xWHIP	vL+	vR+	BF/G	BB%	K%	K-BB%	xBB%	SwK	Vel	G	L	F	H%	S%	HR/F	xHR/F	GS	APC	DOM%	DIS%	Sv%	LI	RAR	BPX	R$
17	aa	10	0	131	96	6.27	1.76	5.70				23.0	10%	16%	6%							37%	63%									-30.8	56	-$15
18	KC	9	0	140	96	3.08	1.30	4.24	1.42	100	82	14.2	9%	16%	8%	9%	9.3%	93.9	54	19	27	30%	77%	6%	10%	20	54	30%	25%	0	0.97	18.5	65	$8
19	KC	7	0	165	122	4.19	1.35	4.92	1.51	95	94	25.3	10%	17%	7%	9%	8.6%	93.4	50	21	29	29%	70%	10%	13%	28	97	21%	36%			6.4	49	$3
20	KC	5	0	55	35	2.47	1.02	4.26	1.41	79	56	23.9	8%	16%	8%	8%	8.6%	92.8	53	23	25	24%	76%	5%	12%	9	95	44%	22%			13.4	67	$19
21	KC	8	0	134	120	5.39	1.66	4.74	1.44	115	110	23.6	10%	20%	9%	10%	9.5%	93.9	48	23	29	35%	70%	15%	26%	26	90	23%	54%			-18.5	60	-$13
1st Half		6	0	81	67	6.67	1.88	5.14	1.50	115	129	22.9	11%	17%	6%	10%	8.7%	93.9	49	26	26	38%	66%	17%	27%	17	89	12%	65%			-24.0	38	-$19
2nd Half		2	0	53	53	3.42	1.33	4.18	1.34	97	87	24.8	10%	24%	14%	10%	11.0%	93.9	47	19	35	31%	78%	12%	23%	9	92	44%	33%			5.5	95	$0
Proj		8	0	131	106	4.38	1.40	4.51	1.43	103	94	22.1	10%	19%	9%	9%	9.4%	93.6	50	21	29	30%	71%	12%	19%	25						1.2	67	-$1

Keller,Mitch

Age: 26 | Th: R | Role: SP | Ht: 6' 2" | Wt: 205 | Type: Pwr
Health: C | PT/Exp: D | Consist: B
LIMA Plan: C | Rand Var: +1 | MM: 1203

5-11, 6.17 ERA in 101 IP at PIT. Your written-in-ink confirmation of the havoc that a 10% H%, 87% S% can cause on a player's stats over 22 IP. He tried again in 2021, and the walks were still bad, the strikeouts sub-par, and (sadly) the xERA fit in perfectly with his MLB history. Poke us when he gets traded. (Sorry, Pirates fans.)

Yr	Tm	W	Sv	IP	K	ERA	WHIP	xERA	xWHIP	vL+	vR+	BF/G	BB%	K%	K-BB%	xBB%	SwK	Vel	G	L	F	H%	S%	HR/F	xHR/F	GS	APC	DOM%	DIS%	Sv%	LI	RAR	BPX	R$
17	aa	2	0	35	38	4.05	1.18	2.94				23.1	8%	27%	19%							31%	65%									1.3	143	-$1
18	a/a	12	0	139	111	4.10	1.38	4.02				24.3	9%	19%	10%							31%	71%									0.8	81	$3
19	PIT *	8	0	153	166	5.24	1.53	5.13	1.27	130	121	22.2	8%	25%	17%	6%	12.4%	95.4	39	29	32	38%	66%	13%	9%	11	85	9%	27%			-13.8	102	-$5
20	PIT	1	0	22	16	2.91	1.25	6.24	2.02	112	61	17.4	21%	18%	-2%	12%	7.8%	94.0	44	8	48	10%	87%	16%	20%	5	77	20%	40%			4.1	-68	-$1
21	PIT *	6	0	129	123	5.59	1.74	5.92	1.42	124	114	18.9	11%	21%	10%	9%	8.9%	93.9	40	26	34	38%	68%	9%	14%	23	81	4%	48%			-21.0	68	-$17
1st Half		3	0	59	60	6.19	1.69	5.70	1.48	120	116	16.5	13%	23%	10%	9%	9.4%	94.4	35	26	38	36%	64%	13%	14%	12	77	8%	50%			-13.9	66	-$13
2nd Half		3	0	72	62	4.92	1.71	5.82	1.39	115	117	21.9	9%	19%	10%	8%	8.4%	93.3	45	25	31	39%	71%	6%	14%	11	85	0%	45%			-5.9	71	-$13
Proj		8	0	138	131	5.00	1.55	4.60	1.37	109	101	21.0	9%	22%	12%	8%	9.8%	94.2	40	26	33	36%	68%	9%	13%	29						-9.2	83	-$7

Kelly,Merrill

Age: 33 | Th: R | Role: SP | Ht: 6' 2" | Wt: 210 | Type: Con
Health: D | PT/Exp: A | Consist: B
LIMA Plan: B+ | Rand Var: 0 | MM: 2103

Returned from thoracic outlet surgery with no visible impact on skills, as 2021 xERA was spot-on match for career 4.35 MLB xERA. Doesn't look likely to improve further due to lack of strikeouts and stagnant SwK. So what you've seen is what you'll get: a contact-reliant pitcher who can maintain mediocre results based on his ability to spot pitches.

Yr	Tm	W	Sv	IP	K	ERA	WHIP	xERA	xWHIP	vL+	vR+	BF/G	BB%	K%	K-BB%	xBB%	SwK	Vel	G	L	F	H%	S%	HR/F	xHR/F	GS	APC	DOM%	DIS%	Sv%	LI	RAR	BPX	R$
17	for	16	0	190	179	4.47	1.45	5.08				27.0	7%	22%	15%							35%	73%									-2.6	93	$5
18	for	12	0	158	161	4.10	1.26	3.95				23.0	7%	25%	18%							32%	70%									0.9	116	$8
19	ARI	13	0	183	158	4.42	1.31	4.69	1.34	101	101	24.3	7%	20%	13%	8%	10.1%	91.9	42	22	36	30%	71%	15%	19%	32	93	22%	41%			2.0	92	$7
20	ARI	3	0	31	29	2.59	0.99	3.91	1.13	73	99	25.0	4%	23%	19%	7%	10.1%	92.1	46	18	37	26%	85%	15%	17%	5	95	40%	40%			7.2	153	$9
21	ARI	7	0	158	130	4.44	1.29	4.36	1.26	90	111	24.7	6%	19%	13%	6%	9.5%	91.8	44	22	34	31%	69%	13%	15%	27	90	22%	26%			-3.5	101	$1
1st Half		5	0	98	89	4.67	1.27	4.05	1.22	88	111	24.4	6%	21%	15%	6%	10.1%	91.8	45	23	32	31%	67%	15%	15%	17	90	24%	24%			-4.9	119	$4
2nd Half		2	0	60	41	4.07	1.32	4.89	1.34	82	117	25.2	6%	16%	10%	6%	8.4%	91.6	42	19	39	31%	72%	9%	15%	10	89	20%	30%			1.4	73	-$3
Proj		10	0	167	142	4.13	1.24	4.23	1.25	89	107	24.1	6%	21%	15%	6%	9.5%	91.8	43	21	36	30%	71%	13%	16%	28						6.7	111	$7

Kennedy,Ian

Age: 37 | Th: R | Role: RP | Ht: 6' 0" | Wt: 210 | Type: Pwr/xFB
Health: D | PT/Exp: C | Consist: C
LIMA Plan: C+ | Rand Var: -5 | MM: 1320

Ended up as a decent late-round closer stab, but gap between ERA, xERA indicates those 26 saves were more luck than skill. Primary concern is high FB%, which led to HR problems that became particularly bad in PHI (2.6 HR/9). Maybe the K% bump and decent WHIP lead him to some save chances again, but you shouldn't invest heavily in that outcome.

Yr	Tm	W	Sv	IP	K	ERA	WHIP	xERA	xWHIP	vL+	vR+	BF/G	BB%	K%	K-BB%	xBB%	SwK	Vel	G	L	F	H%	S%	HR/F	xHR/F	GS	APC	DOM%	DIS%	Sv%	LI	RAR	BPX	R$
17	KC	5	0	154	131	5.38	1.32	5.10	1.42	108	107	21.8	9%	20%	11%	8%	9.7%	91.9	36	16	48	26%	66%	16%	15%	30	88	13%	57%			-19.3	67	-$3
18	KC	3	0	120	105	4.66	1.38	4.82	1.32	103	113	23.5	8%	20%	13%	7%	8.7%	91.9	30	26	44	31%	71%	13%	16%	22	94	14%	45%			-7.6	79	-$4
19	KC	3	30	63	73	3.41	1.28	3.88	1.17	85	95	4.2	6%	27%	21%	6%	11.0%	94.5	44	18	37	35%	76%	9%	13%	0	17			88	0.88	8.6	156	$15
20	KC	0	0	14	15	9.00	1.79	5.44	1.29	146	145	4.6	7%	22%	14%	5%	10.7%	93.6	38	15	47	35%	61%	32%	24%	1	17	0%	0%	0	0.86	-7.9	116	-$13
21	2 TM	3	26	56	62	3.20	1.10	4.36	1.18	106	86	4.1	7%	27%	20%	5%	13.8%	94.1	23	23	54	25%	84%	15%	14%	0	16			87	1.38	7.4	116	$14
1st Half		0	14	27	31	2.96	1.13	3.88	1.12	81	102	4.0	6%	28%	22%	4%	14.9%	94.4	30	25	45	29%	85%	16%	14%	0	14			93	1.15	4.4	142	$6
2nd Half		3	12	29	31	3.41	1.07	4.81	1.25	119	73	4.3	8%	26%	18%	6%	12.9%	94.0	17	20	63	22%	83%	15%	15%	0	18			80	1.60	3.0	93	$12
Proj		3	14	65	68	4.05	1.26	4.43	1.24	106	96	5.5	8%	25%	18%	6%	11.7%	93.5	30	22	49	30%	75%	14%	15%	0						3.3	113	$6

Kershaw,Clayton

Age: 34 | Th: L | Role: SP | Ht: 6' 4" | Wt: 225 | Type:
Health: F | PT/Exp: A | Consist: A
LIMA Plan: B | Rand Var: +1 | MM: 5303

Maintained elite control while logging career-best SwK, so relatively little concern when on the mound. That's the catch though—he's now spent at least 10 days on IL in six straight seasons, and was sidelined for much of 2nd half with forearm injury. Excellent on per-inning basis, but expecting more than 150 IP is ambitious.

Yr	Tm	W	Sv	IP	K	ERA	WHIP	xERA	xWHIP	vL+	vR+	BF/G	BB%	K%	K-BB%	xBB%	SwK	Vel	G	L	F	H%	S%	HR/F	xHR/F	GS	APC	DOM%	DIS%	Sv%	LI	RAR	BPX	R$
17	LA	18	0	175	202	2.31	0.95	3.02	1.03	97	77	25.1	4%	30%	25%	5%	14.6%	92.7	48	19	33	28%	85%	16%	14%	27	93	56%	7%			44.1	206	$36
18	LA	9	0	161	155	2.73	1.04	3.36	1.12	93	86	25.0	4%	24%	19%	5%	11.5%	90.9	48	23	30	29%	79%	13%	12%	26	91	35%	8%			28.2	159	$21
19	LA	16	0	178	189	3.03	1.04	3.55	1.15	84	90	24.3	6%	27%	21%	6%	13.7%	90.4	48	19	33	27%	80%	19%	16%	28	92	50%	14%	0	0.77	32.5	154	$27
20	LA	6	0	58	62	2.16	0.84	3.07	1.02	87	77	22.1	4%	28%	24%	5%	13.0%	91.6	53	16	31	24%	85%	17%	19%	10	89	60%	10%			16.5	192	$30
21	LA	10	0	122	144	3.55	1.02	3.06	1.01	61	95	22.2	4%	30%	25%	6%	17.1%	90.7	49	18	33	31%	70%	15%	18%	22	82	50%	23%			10.7	194	$15
1st Half		9	0	106	127	3.39	0.98	3.05	1.01	51	95	23.4	5%	30%	26%	6%	16.8%	90.8	48	17	34	29%	70%	14%	16%	18	87	50%	17%			11.5	194	$28
2nd Half		1	0	15	17	4.70	1.30	3.16	1.03	100	104	16.5	3%	26%	23%	6%	19.3%	90.1	51	24	24	38%	67%	18%	34%	4	60	50%	50%			-0.8	194	-$9
Proj		11	0	131	143	3.36	1.06	3.09	1.04	87	91	21.7	4%	28%	24%	5%	15.7%	90.8	50	20	30	31%	74%	17%	22%	23						17.6	189	$16

DANIEL MARCUS

Keuchel,Dallas

Age: 34	Th: L	Role SP	Health C	LIMA Plan D+
Ht: 6' 2"	Wt: 220	Type Con/xGB	PT/Exp A	Rand Var +1
			Consist A	MM 1003

SwK dipped back into single-digits, leading to career-worst K% and K-BB%, and worsening steady decline of xERA, xWHIP, and BPX. And even elite GB% hasn't been able to prevent the occasional HR/F spike. Can luck his way into success from time to time, but heed those xERA levels as his baseline.

Yr Tm	W	Sv	IP	K	ERA	WHIP	xERA	xWHIP	vL+	vR+	BF/G	BB%	K%	K-BB%	xBB%	SwK	Vel	G	L	F	H%	S%	HR/F	xHR/F	GS	APC	DOM%	DIS%	Sv%	LI	RAR	BPX	R$
17 HOU	14	0	146	125	2.90	1.12	3.23	1.31	58	90	25.4	8%	21%	13%	9%	11.3%	88.7	67	15	18	26%	78%	21%	16%	23	95	30%	22%			26.1	127	$19
18 HOU	12	0	205	153	3.74	1.31	4.02	1.32	97	98	25.7	7%	18%	11%	9%	8.6%	89.3	54	22	24	31%	73%	11%	11%	34	97	21%	29%			10.4	97	$8
19 ATL	8	0	113	91	3.75	1.37	4.04	1.38	82	106	25.6	8%	19%	11%	9%	9.4%	88.4	60	20	20	30%	78%	24%	22%	19	98	16%	47%			10.4	92	$4
20 CHW	6	0	63	42	1.99	1.09	4.21	1.35	57	78	23.4	7%	16%	10%	9%	10.1%	87.3	53	25	22	27%	82%	5%	12%	11	87	18%	27%			19.2	83	$24
21 CHW	9	0	162	95	5.28	1.53	4.89	1.47	114	110	22.5	8%	13%	5%	10%	8.9%	87.9	55	20	25	31%	69%	18%	23%	30	85	3%	63%	0	0.77	-20.2	43	-$12
1st Half	6	0	90	55	4.48	1.39	4.52	1.42	100	102	22.9	8%	14%	6%	9%	9.4%	87.6	56	21	23	30%	71%	17%	23%	16	87	6%	56%	0	0.78	-2.4	57	$0
2nd Half	3	0	72	40	6.28	1.70	5.35	1.52	120	124	22.1	9%	12%	3%	11%	8.3%	88.1	54	19	28	33%	66%	18%	22%	14	83	0%	71%	0	0.75	-17.8	26	-$21
Proj	**12**	**0**	**174**	**115**	**4.52**	**1.43**	**4.48**	**1.42**	**99**	**105**	**23.0**	**8%**	**16%**	**8%**	**10%**	**9.2%**	**88.0**	**56**	**21**	**24**	**31%**	**71%**	**16%**	**19%**	**32**						**-1.4**	**66**	**-$1**

Kikuchi,Yusei

Age: 31	Th: L	Role SP	Health A	LIMA Plan B+
Ht: 6' 0"	Wt: 200	Type Pwr	PT/Exp A	Rand Var +3
			Consist B	MM 2203

Breakout appeared inevitable after 1st half saw him sustain 2020's growth in SwK, velocity, and GB%. However, gave back gains in 2nd half and saw rise in hard contact (xHR/F), which coincided with foreign substance crackdown (Correlation? Causation?). Gap between xERA, ERA makes him interesting, but uncertainty about his 2022 landing spot raises risk.

Yr Tm	W	Sv	IP	K	ERA	WHIP	xERA	xWHIP	vL+	vR+	BF/G	BB%	K%	K-BB%	xBB%	SwK	Vel	G	L	F	H%	S%	HR/F	xHR/F	GS	APC	DOM%	DIS%	Sv%	LI	RAR	BPX	R$
17																																	
18																																	
19 SEA	6	0	162	116	5.46	1.52	5.30	1.41	108	121	22.5	7%	16%	9%	8%	8.9%	92.5	44	21	35	32%	70%	19%	15%	32	85	16%	50%			-18.9	69	-$9
20 SEA	2	0	47	47	5.17	1.30	3.93	1.35	91	92	21.6	10%	24%	14%	9%	12.8%	95.0	52	23	25	31%	59%	9%	9%	9	88	11%	22%			-4.2	100	-$2
21 SEA	7	0	157	163	4.41	1.32	3.92	1.30	66	110	23.0	9%	25%	15%	7%	12.7%	95.2	48	21	30	30%	72%	21%	25%	29	88	24%	28%			-2.9	108	$2
1st Half	6	0	93	93	3.18	1.03	3.42	1.24	55	91	24.4	8%	25%	17%	6%	13.8%	95.7	54	19	27	23%	78%	23%	21%	15	93	47%	13%			12.5	124	$19
2nd Half	1	0	64	70	6.22	1.74	4.65	1.36	71	141	21.4	10%	23%	13%	8%	11.4%	94.7	42	24	34	38%	68%	18%	29%	14	83	0%	43%			-15.3	87	-$20
Proj	**6**	**0**	**145**	**147**	**4.48**	**1.35**	**4.02**	**1.31**	**78**	**110**	**21.4**	**9%**	**24%**	**15%**	**8%**	**11.7%**	**94.6**	**47**	**22**	**31**	**31%**	**72%**	**19%**	**20%**	**28**						**-0.4**	**108**	**$0**

Kim,Kwang-Hyun

Age: 33	Th: L	Role RP	Health D	LIMA Plan B
Ht: 6' 2"	Wt: 195	Type Con	PT/Exp B	Rand Var -2
			Consist A	MM 1001

Back injury delayed start to season, and he ended up in bullpen after failing to complete 5 IP in 10 of 21 starts. After two seasons in MLB, SwK, K%, and velocity offer little hope for upside, and xERA, xWHIP don't scream success in any role. Surface numbers aren't bad, but at some point regression is likely to make fantasy usefulness vanish.

Yr Tm	W	Sv	IP	K	ERA	WHIP	xERA	xWHIP	vL+	vR+	BF/G	BB%	K%	K-BB%	xBB%	SwK	Vel	G	L	F	H%	S%	HR/F	xHR/F	GS	APC	DOM%	DIS%	Sv%	LI	RAR	BPX	R$
17																																	
18 for	11	0	136	123	3.70	1.26	4.74				22.2	7%	22%	15%							29%	80%									7.6	80	$8
19 for	17	0	190	171	3.12	1.37	4.63				26.5	6%	21%	16%							34%	81%									32.5	100	$17
20 STL	3	1	39	24	1.62	1.03	4.56	1.42	84	77	19.3	8%	16%	8%	8%	7.7%	89.9	50	22	28	23%	89%	9%	10%	7	77	14%	43%	100	0.67	13.7	60	$14
21 STL	7	1	107	80	3.46	1.28	4.68	1.40	63	100	16.7	9%	18%	9%	9%	9.2%	89.1	47	19	34	28%	77%	11%	15%	21	66	14%	29%	100	0.70	10.6	63	$5
1st Half	2	0	59	50	3.79	1.35	4.59	1.36	64	106	19.9	9%	19%	11%	10%	8.9%	89.0	45	22	33	31%	74%	10%	14%	13	78	8%	23%			3.5	77	-$1
2nd Half	5	1	47	30	3.04	1.20	4.79	1.45	50	98	13.8	9%	16%	7%	9%	9.6%	89.4	50	15	35	25%	80%	12%	16%	8	55	25%	38%	100	0.63	7.1	48	$6
Proj	**7**	**0**	**87**	**65**	**4.23**	**1.36**	**4.62**	**1.40**	**73**	**107**	**18.7**	**8%**	**18%**	**10%**	**9%**	**8.9%**	**89.4**	**49**	**19**	**33**	**30%**	**72%**	**12%**	**14%**	**17**						**2.4**	**71**	**$0**

Kimbrel,Craig

Age: 34	Th: R	Role RP	Health B	LIMA Plan C+
Ht: 6' 0"	Wt: 215	Type Pwr/xFB	PT/Exp C	Rand Var -4
			Consist B	MM 5520

Control was key in return to near-peak performance in 1st half, as 65% first-pitch strike rate was highest mark since 2017; fortunes (and SwK) seem to rise and fall with xBB%. Second half slump as setup man in CHW warns success isn't a given moving forward, but he's shown he still has skills to be an effective closer... sometimes.

Yr Tm	W	Sv	IP	K	ERA	WHIP	xERA	xWHIP	vL+	vR+	BF/G	BB%	K%	K-BB%	xBB%	SwK	Vel	G	L	F	H%	S%	HR/F	xHR/F	GS	APC	DOM%	DIS%	Sv%	LI	RAR	BPX	R$
17 BOS	5	35	69	126	1.43	0.68	1.90	0.75	76	45	3.8	6%	50%	44%	5%	20.2%	98.3	37	19	44	28%	88%	13%	19%	0	17			90	1.34	24.9	314	$32
18 BOS	5	42	62	96	2.74	0.99	3.16	1.16	86	71	3.9	13%	39%	26%	9%	17.6%	97.1	28	25	47	23%	78%	13%	11%	0	18			89	1.39	10.8	155	$25
19 CHC	0	13	21	30	6.53	1.60	4.62	1.35	114	159	4.2	13%	31%	19%	10%	14.8%	96.2	30	20	50	30%	75%	36%	25%	0	17			81	1.29	-5.2	111	-$1
20 CHC	0	2	15	28	5.28	1.43	3.60	1.34	121	65	3.8	17%	41%	23%	11%	13.3%	96.9	33	22	44	34%	65%	17%	23%	0	17			67	0.65	-1.6	132	-$3
21 2 TM	4	24	60	100	2.26	0.91	2.80	0.99	70	69	3.7	10%	43%	33%	8%	19.0%	96.5	30	22	48	27%	81%	12%	10%	0	16			83	1.53	14.7	204	$20
1st Half	1	20	31	53	0.59	0.65	2.23	0.89	48	37	3.5	9%	47%	38%	6%	19.4%	97.0	34	26	40	21%	95%	5%	7%	0	15			91	1.82	13.9	234	$22
2nd Half	3	4	29	47	4.03	1.17	3.42	1.10	90	95	3.9	11%	39%	28%	11%	18.7%	96.1	27	19	54	32%	72%	16%	13%	0	17			57	1.23	0.8	174	$4
Proj	**4**	**20**	**65**	**103**	**3.08**	**0.99**	**2.94**	**1.03**	**83**	**73**	**3.7**	**10%**	**42%**	**32%**	**8%**	**18.9%**	**97.0**	**31**	**22**	**47**	**29%**	**73%**	**12%**	**12%**	**0**						**11.0**	**197**	**$16**

King,John

Age: 27	Th: L	Role RP	Health F	LIMA Plan B+
Ht: 6' 2"	Wt: 215	Type Con/GB	PT/Exp D	Rand Var 0
			Consist C	MM 4000

Emerged as valuable multi-inning reliever, but chance to earn starts later in season was derailed by season-ending surgery to correct thoracic outlet syndrome. Profile remained consistent, with heavy reliance on sinker to induce GB% and limit HR (career 0.8 HR/9). That formula has proven effective, but also limits him to back-end SP or low-leverage RP role.

Yr Tm	W	Sv	IP	K	ERA	WHIP	xERA	xWHIP	vL+	vR+	BF/G	BB%	K%	K-BB%	xBB%	SwK	Vel	G	L	F	H%	S%	HR/F	xHR/F	GS	APC	DOM%	DIS%	Sv%	LI	RAR	BPX	R$
17																																	
18																																	
19																																	
20 TEX	1	0	10	9	6.10	1.65	4.75	1.37	108	115	8.5	8%	18%	10%	8%	8.6%	93.1	56	19	25	35%	67%	22%	16%	0	31			0	0.66	-2.1	92	-$7
21 TEX	7	0	46	40	3.52	1.15	3.45	1.23	56	98	7.1	6%	21%	15%	6%	12.4%	92.3	57	24	19	30%	70%	12%	15%	0	26			0	1.02	4.2	123	$2
1st Half	6	0	44	37	2.86	1.09	3.38	1.23	55	87	7.0	6%	20%	14%	5%	12.1%	92.3	58	24	18	29%	72%	4%	9%	0	25			0	1.05	7.6	122	$8
2nd Half	1	0	2	3	18.00	2.50	4.88		0	279	11.0	9%	27%	18%		16.3%	92.0	43	14	43	43%	33%	67%	59%	0	49			0	0.26	-3.4	156	-$13
Proj	**5**	**0**	**58**	**44**	**3.51**	**1.15**	**3.47**	**1.25**	**66**	**107**	**7.5**	**6%**	**19%**	**13%**	**5%**	**12.1%**	**92.3**	**58**	**24**	**18**	**30%**	**70%**	**11%**	**8%**	**0**						**6.8**	**118**	**$2**

King,Michael

Age: 27	Th: R	Role RP	Health D	LIMA Plan C
Ht: 6' 3"	Wt: 210	Type Pwr	PT/Exp D	Rand Var -1
			Consist B	MM 2300

Added slider to pitch mix in effort to induce whiffs that were previously lacking due to sinker-heavy approach. Experiment was interrupted for 68 days by July finger injury, but returned in final month to show promise as low-leverage reliever. Given struggles as SP (career 6.52 ERA, 8% K-BB%), that's likely to be his role moving forward.

Yr Tm	W	Sv	IP	K	ERA	WHIP	xERA	xWHIP	vL+	vR+	BF/G	BB%	K%	K-BB%	xBB%	SwK	Vel	G	L	F	H%	S%	HR/F	xHR/F	GS	APC	DOM%	DIS%	Sv%	LI	RAR	BPX	R$
17																																	
18 a/a	10	0	121	92	2.33	1.01	2.70				25.7	4%	20%	16%							27%	81%									27.2	144	$18
19 NYY *	3	0	41	31	7.04	1.42	5.21		66	54	22.0	5%	18%	13%		2.4%	91.5	38	13	50	34%	50%	0%	0%	0	41			0	0.00	-13.0	82	-$7
20 NYY	1	0	27	26	7.76	1.54	5.05	1.37	125	106	13.4	9%	21%	12%	8%	9.4%	93.1	40	20	40	34%	50%	15%	14%	4	52	0%	25%	0	0.70	-10.9	86	-$12
21 NYY	2	0	63	62	3.55	1.28	4.12	1.31	113	80	12.5	9%	23%	14%	7%	10.8%	94.1	45	24	31	30%	75%	11%	17%	6	46	0%	67%	0	0.69	5.6	98	-$1
1st Half	0	0	48	47	3.72	1.39	4.27	1.37	106	90	15.3	10%	22%	12%	8%	9.7%	93.9	48	22	30	31%	76%	12%	18%	6	56	0%	67%	0	0.61	3.2	85	-$4
2nd Half	2	0	15	15	3.00	0.93	3.64	1.12	111	56	7.6	5%	25%	20%	6%	14.5%	94.7	37	29	34	27%	69%	7%	14%	0	28			0	0.85	2.3	141	-$4
Proj	**2**	**0**	**29**	**31**	**4.14**	**1.33**	**4.08**	**1.33**	**135**	**78**	**12.7**	**10%**	**26%**	**15%**	**7%**	**12.5%**	**94.4**	**41**	**26**	**32**	**31%**	**72%**	**14%**	**16%**	**3**						**1.1**	**100**	**-$3**

Kinley,Tyler

Age: 31	Th: R	Role RP	Health A	LIMA Plan D+
Ht: 6' 4"	Wt: 220	Type Pwr/FB	PT/Exp D	Rand Var 0
			Consist B	MM 1200

Finally brought his BB% into single-digits, though xERA and BPX indicate that wasn't enough to change overall skill level. K% is hardly notable for a reliever, particularly given above-average SwK, and high FB% remains an ongoing concern. Like many, would benefit from move out of Coors (3.43 ERA, 17.1 K-BB% on the road), but for now he's safe to ignore.

Yr Tm	W	Sv	IP	K	ERA	WHIP	xERA	xWHIP	vL+	vR+	BF/G	BB%	K%	K-BB%	xBB%	SwK	Vel	G	L	F	H%	S%	HR/F	xHR/F	GS	APC	DOM%	DIS%	Sv%	LI	RAR	BPX	R$
17 aa	1	8	26	28	6.95	2.10	7.00				4.7	14%	22%	8%							43%	66%									-8.3	64	-$6
18 2 TM *	2	8	51	57	5.46	1.68	4.99	1.49	98	167	4.3	14%	25%	11%	8%	13.0%	96.6	54	11	34	37%	67%	17%	17%	0	18			80	0.33	-8.3	89	-$5
19 MIA *	3	3	67	61	3.28	1.39	3.44	1.70	101	93	4.2	16%	22%	6%	9%	13.5%	95.0	38	23	40	25%	79%	9%	8%	0	17			60	0.84	10.0	73	$2
20 COL	0	0	24	26	5.32	1.06	4.10	1.40	55	103	4.0	13%	27%	15%	8%	17.0%	95.9	46	15	39	21%	48%	10%	10%	0	15			0	0.68	-2.5	89	-$4
21 COL	3	0	70	68	4.73	1.21	4.49	1.31	96	99	4.2	9%	23%	14%	7%	13.9%	96.0	39	19	42	27%	66%	14%	13%	0	16			0	0.92	-4.1	92	-$2
1st Half	1	0	35	32	4.58	1.25	4.82	1.45	106	94	4.4	11%	21%	10%	9%	12.4%	95.5	41	18	41	24%	68%	15%	14%	0	17			0	0.88	-1.4	53	-$5
2nd Half	2	0	35	36	4.89	1.17	4.19	1.17	75	108	4.0	6%	25%	19%	6%	15.4%	96.5	37	20	43	29%	63%	14%	12%	0	16			0	0.96	-2.7	131	-$4
Proj	**3**	**0**	**58**	**58**	**4.60**	**1.34**	**4.63**	**1.41**	**94**	**98**	**4.1**	**11%**	**24%**	**13%**	**8%**	**14.0%**	**95.8**	**38**	**20**	**42**	**29%**	**69%**	**12%**	**12%**	**0**						**-1.0**	**72**	**-$3**

DANIEL MARCUS

Kirby,George

Age: 24 | Th: R | Role: SP | Ht: 6' 4" | Wt: 201 | Type: Con
Health: A | PT/Exp: F | Consist: F
LIMA Plan: C | Rand Var: +2 | MM: 2100

Regarded as high-floor draft prospect thanks to above-average fastball and control, though development of complementary pitches was slowed by cancellation of 2020 minor-league season. Passed initial test at AA to close out 2021 after cruising against High-A competition (26.8 K-BB%, 2.38 ERA in 41.2 IP). Could be in line for SEA debut in late 2022.

Yr	Tm	W	Sv	IP	K	ERA	WHIP	xERA	xWHIP	vL+	vR+	BF/G	BB%	K%	K-BB%	xBB%	SwK	Vel	G	L	F	H%	S%	HR/F	xHR/F	GS	APC	DOM%	DIS%	Sv%	LI	RAR	BPX	R$
17																																		
18																																		
19																																		
20																																		
21	aa	1	0	26	25	3.11	1.33	3.52				18.0	6%	23%	17%							37%	74%									3.7	141	-$4
1st Half																																		
2nd Half		1	0	26	25	3.11	1.33	3.52		0	0	18.0	6%	23%	17%							37%	74%	0%		0	0					3.7	142	-$6
Proj		**2**	**0**	**44**	**38**	**3.63**	**1.21**	**4.13**	**1.24**			**21.8**	**6%**	**21%**	**15%**				**44**	**20**	**36**	**30%**	**74%**	**11%**	**0%**	**8**						**4.4**	**117**	**-$2**

Kittredge,Andrew

Age: 32 | Th: R | Role: RP | Ht: 6' 1" | Wt: 230 | Type: Pwr/GB
Health: D | PT/Exp: D | Consist: C
LIMA Plan: C+ | Rand Var: -5 | MM: 5320

Showed elite skills nearly across the board, highlighted by K-BB%, all backed by SwK, xBB%, and consistently strong GB%. All those metrics reinforced 2019 success, though key step forward was gaining team's trust, as indicated by LI. Likely to be some ERA pullback, but has proven to be reliable high-leverage reliever who could be an option for saves in 2022.

Yr	Tm	W	Sv	IP	K	ERA	WHIP	xERA	xWHIP	vL+	vR+	BF/G	BB%	K%	K-BB%	xBB%	SwK	Vel	G	L	F	H%	S%	HR/F	xHR/F	GS	APC	DOM%	DIS%	Sv%	LI	RAR	BPX	R$
17	TAM *	6	2	84	77	2.04	1.22	3.19	1.28	97	85	6.0	7%	23%	15%		12.7%	94.5	47	19	35	31%	85%	13%	11%	0	16			50	0.61	23.9	127	$10
18	TAM *	9	2	84	76	5.57	1.63	5.88	1.34	101	150	7.0	8%	20%	12%	8%	10.3%	93.1	50	24	25	37%	67%	21%	22%	3	19	0%	100%	67	0.77	-14.7	69	-$7
19	TAM *	3	6	88	101	3.47	1.15	3.63	1.09	120	83	5.5	5%	29%	24%	5%	16.4%	95.0	50	22	28	33%	74%	18%	16%	7	22	0%	43%	86	0.56	11.2	159	$8
20	TAM	0	1	8	3	2.25	1.25	4.56	1.47	69	97	3.9	6%	10%	3%	4%	7.8%	94.0	54	27	19	29%	80%	0%	8%	1	14	0%	100%	100	1.23	2.2	36	-$4
21	TAM	9	8	72	77	1.88	0.98	3.07	1.08	90	75	4.9	5%	27%	22%	4%	16.4%	95.3	54	18	28	28%	87%	13%	17%	4	17	0%	50%	89	1.30	21.1	170	$17
1st Half		5	2	39	38	1.62	0.90	3.22	1.17	111	66	5.0	7%	25%	19%	5%	14.9%	95.1	53	20	27	23%	90%	15%	21%	4	17	0%	50%	100	1.17	12.7	138	$12
2nd Half		4	6	33	39	2.20	1.07	2.90	0.99	65	91	4.9	4%	30%	26%	4%	18.1%	95.5	55	16	29	34%	84%	12%	12%	0	17			86	1.45	8.3	207	$12
Proj		**6**	**14**	**58**	**65**	**3.00**	**1.18**	**3.18**	**1.11**	**93**	**89**	**5.4**	**6%**	**28%**	**22%**	**5%**	**15.3%**	**94.8**	**52**	**20**	**28**	**33%**	**79%**	**15%**	**17%**	**0**						**10.4**	**174**	**$10**

Kluber,Corey

Age: 36 | Th: R | Role: SP | Ht: 6' 4" | Wt: 215 | Type: Pwr
Health: F | PT/Exp: D | Consist: B
LIMA Plan: B+ | Rand Var: -1 | MM: 2301

Recurring shoulder, forearm injuries have limited one-time workhorse, both in innings and ability to work deep into individual starts (see BF/G). Skills have similarly fallen off, starting with velocity and trickling down to BB%, K%. Still limits HR effectively, and 1st half shows he can have brief stints of fantasy usefulness, but best days are well behind him.

Yr	Tm	W	Sv	IP	K	ERA	WHIP	xERA	xWHIP	vL+	vR+	BF/G	BB%	K%	K-BB%	xBB%	SwK	Vel	G	L	F	H%	S%	HR/F	xHR/F	GS	APC	DOM%	DIS%	Sv%	LI	RAR	BPX	R$
17	CLE	18	0	204	265	2.25	0.87	2.70	0.97	76	73	26.8	5%	34%	30%	5%	15.9%	92.6	45	22	33	28%	81%	13%	11%	29	102	66%	14%			52.9	229	$45
18	CLE	20	0	215	222	2.89	0.99	3.22	1.06	92	80	25.5	4%	26%	22%	6%	12.4%	92.0	44	22	33	29%	77%	13%	14%	33	96	58%	9%			33.4	174	$35
19	CLE	2	0	36	38	5.80	1.65	4.95	1.36	119	102	24.0	9%	23%	14%	8%	13.3%	91.6	40	23	37	39%	65%	10%	17%	7	87	29%	29%			-5.7	96	-$6
20	TEX	0	0	1	1	0.00	1.00	5.41		0	133	3.0	33%	33%	0%		5.6%	91.7	0	0	100	0%	0%	0%	0%	1	18	0%	0%			0.5	-116	-$6
21	NYY	5	0	80	82	3.83	1.34	4.29	1.32	74	108	21.3	10%	24%	14%	8%	12.9%	90.6	42	20	38	31%	74%	10%	12%	16	84	19%	31%			4.3	94	$0
1st Half		4	0	53	55	3.04	1.20	4.08	1.34	64	98	22.0	10%	25%	15%	8%	13.6%	90.8	46	17	37	27%	78%	10%	12%	10	85	30%	30%			8.1	95	$6
2nd Half		1	0	27	27	5.40	1.61	4.70	1.30	83	131	20.2	8%	23%	14%	8%	11.8%	90.3	36	25	40	38%	68%	9%	11%	6	82	0%	33%			-3.7	95	-$12
Proj		**8**	**0**	**116**	**123**	**4.19**	**1.34**	**4.05**	**1.24**	**92**	**104**	**22.0**	**8%**	**25%**	**17%**	**7%**	**12.9%**	**91.2**	**41**	**22**	**37**	**34%**	**71%**	**11%**	**13%**	**22**						**3.8**	**125**	**$2**

Knebel,Corey

Age: 30 | Th: R | Role: RP | Ht: 6' 3" | Wt: 224 | Type: Pwr
Health: F | PT/Exp: D | Consist: F
LIMA Plan: A | Rand Var: -5 | MM: 5510

Looked like he might be getting back to 2018 form out of the gates, only to have lat injury cost him three months. While 2nd half return saw significant dips in SwK% and K%, bounceback in velocity, strong postseason run (11:1 K:BB in 5.2 IP) suggest there's plenty of strong innings left. Any bid has to factor in sizable injury risk, but... UP: 30 saves, again

Yr	Tm	W	Sv	IP	K	ERA	WHIP	xERA	xWHIP	vL+	vR+	BF/G	BB%	K%	K-BB%	xBB%	SwK	Vel	G	L	F	H%	S%	HR/F	xHR/F	GS	APC	DOM%	DIS%	Sv%	LI	RAR	BPX	R$
17	MIL	1	39	76	126	1.78	1.16	3.03	1.16	67	85	4.1	13%	41%	28%	8%	14.7%	97.4	38	17	45	32%	89%	10%	9%	0	18			87	1.49	24.2	188	$27
18	MIL	4	16	55	88	3.58	1.08	2.44	1.05	84	99	3.9	10%	39%	30%	8%	13.8%	96.9	48	21	31	31%	72%	21%	21%	0	17			84	1.21	3.9	215	$10
19																																		
20	MIL	0	0	13	15	6.08	1.73	5.86	1.49	132	118	4.1	13%	24%	11%	11%	7.6%	94.4	31	15	54	33%	74%	19%	14%	0	18			0	0.56	-2.7	51	-$9
21	LA	4	3	26	30	2.45	0.97	3.33	1.18	66	75	3.7	9%	30%	21%	6%	13.0%	96.4	46	21	33	25%	78%	10%	12%	4	15	0%	75%	60	1.16	5.7	141	$2
1st Half		1	2	6	9	4.50	1.00	2.08		72	50	3.0	13%	38%	25%	7%	16.9%	96.4	67	25	8	27%	50%	0%	17%	0	11			67	1.28	-0.2	183	-$5
2nd Half		3	1	20	21	1.83	0.97	3.67	1.19	60	86	4.1	8%	27%	19%	6%	11.9%	96.4	41	20	39	24%	88%	11%	12%	4	16	0%	75%	50	1.11	5.9	129	$1
Proj		**4**	**2**	**44**	**60**	**2.34**	**1.05**	**3.16**	**1.13**	**71**	**88**	**3.9**	**10%**	**35%**	**25%**	**7%**	**13.2%**	**96.8**	**42**	**20**	**38**	**28%**	**83%**	**13%**	**14%**	**0**						**11.3**	**168**	**$5**

Kopech,Michael

Age: 26 | Th: R | Role: SP | Ht: 6' 3" | Wt: 225 | Type: Pwr/FB
Health: F | PT/Exp: D | Consist: F
LIMA Plan: A | Rand Var: 0 | MM: 3503

After two lost seasons, spikes in velocity, K%, and SwK—aided by RP work—were very encouraging. And while transition to rotation was stalled by mid-season hamstring injury, SP role is likely still long-term plan. Minor-league BB% rates, 1.4 career HR/9 suggest short-term caution is appropriate, but ingredients are there for former top prospect to break out.

Yr	Tm	W	Sv	IP	K	ERA	WHIP	xERA	xWHIP	vL+	vR+	BF/G	BB%	K%	K-BB%	xBB%	SwK	Vel	G	L	F	H%	S%	HR/F	xHR/F	GS	APC	DOM%	DIS%	Sv%	LI	RAR	BPX	R$
17	a/a	9	0	134	156	3.57	1.31	2.99				22.2	13%	28%	16%							31%	73%									13.1	128	$10
18	CHW *	8	0	141	166	4.45	1.40	4.18	1.30	102	177	21.3	11%	28%	17%	5%	10.5%	95.4	28	26	46	34%	70%	19%	22%	4	64	0%	0%			-5.3	109	$0
19																																		
20																																		
21	CHW	4	0	69	103	3.50	1.13	3.21	1.06	82	92	6.5	8%	36%	28%	7%	14.7%	97.4	38	19	44	33%	74%	13%	14%	4	26	0%	0%	0	0.95	6.5	189	$4
1st Half		3	0	32	45	1.67	0.99	3.33	1.11	68	75	8.5	9%	35%	26%	8%	13.9%	96.5	36	19	45	27%	90%	10%	11%	3	36	0%	0%	0	0.90	10.4	164	$6
2nd Half		1	0	37	58	5.11	1.24	3.10	1.01	89	106	5.4	8%	37%	29%	6%	15.5%	98.1	39	19	42	38%	63%	17%	18%	1	21	0%	0%	0	0.98	-3.8	211	-$5
Proj		**9**	**0**	**131**	**170**	**3.81**	**1.23**	**3.70**	**1.20**	**82**	**96**	**20.3**	**10%**	**32%**	**22%**	**6%**	**14.8%**	**97.5**	**38**	**19**	**43**	**32%**	**72%**	**11%**	**15%**	**26**						**10.4**	**147**	**$10**

Kowar,Jackson

Age: 25 | Th: R | Role: RP | Ht: 6' 5" | Wt: 180 | Type: Pwr
Health: A | PT/Exp: D | Consist: A
LIMA Plan: D+ | Rand Var: +5 | MM: 1201

0-6, 11.27 ERA in 30 IP at KC. Didn't skip a beat despite lack of 2020 game action, posting dominant stint at AAA (0.85 ERA, 34 K%) to earn big-league call-up. S%, H% indicate some bad luck played part in ugly numbers, but real issues were high BB%, HR/F, both confirmed by xBB, xHR/F. Long-term project, but price should be lower after initial failure.

Yr	Tm	W	Sv	IP	K	ERA	WHIP	xERA	xWHIP	vL+	vR+	BF/G	BB%	K%	K-BB%	xBB%	SwK	Vel	G	L	F	H%	S%	HR/F	xHR/F	GS	APC	DOM%	DIS%	Sv%	LI	RAR	BPX	R$
17																																		
18																																		
19	aa	2	0	75	64	4.83	1.51	5.31				25.0	7%	20%	13%							35%	70%									-3.0	73	-$5
20																																		
21	KC *	9	0	113	118	5.82	1.53	5.03	1.38	149	128	18.8	11%	24%	13%	12%	10.3%	95.7	35	25	40	34%	63%	17%	19%	8	70	0%	63%	0	0.73	-21.6	78	-$9
1st Half		5	0	46	46	4.14	1.34	3.69	1.33	148	171	17.4	10%	24%	14%	12%	5.8%	96.0	43	26	30	32%	69%	14%	17%	2	46	0%	100%	0	0.61	0.7	103	$1
2nd Half		4	0	66	72	6.99	1.66	5.96	1.42	138	120	19.8	12%	24%	12%	11%	11.6%	95.6	33	25	43	36%	59%	18%	19%	6	82	0%	50%			-22.3	62	-$17
Proj		**5**	**0**	**73**	**72**	**4.36**	**1.36**	**4.55**	**1.38**	**112**	**96**	**19.3**	**10%**	**24%**	**13%**	**11%**	**11.6%**	**95.6**	**33**	**25**	**43**	**30%**	**71%**	**12%**	**17%**	**15**						**0.9**	**75**	**-$2**

Kremer,Dean

Age: 26 | Th: R | Role: SP | Ht: 6' 3" | Wt: 185 | Type: /FB
Health: A | PT/Exp: D | Consist: B
LIMA Plan: D+ | Rand Var: +4 | MM: 0101

0-7, 6.99 ERA in 54 IP at BAL. Extreme FB% coupled with high HR/F ruined any chance of success. Displayed solid control in upper levels of minors, but that has yet to translate to time in MLB (11.3 BB% in 72 IP), and 2020 K% proved to be a mirage in larger sample, with SwK indicating little chance of improvement. Not much reason to draft him in 2022.

Yr	Tm	W	Sv	IP	K	ERA	WHIP	xERA	xWHIP	vL+	vR+	BF/G	BB%	K%	K-BB%	xBB%	SwK	Vel	G	L	F	H%	S%	HR/F	xHR/F	GS	APC	DOM%	DIS%	Sv%	LI	RAR	BPX	R$
17																																		
18	aa	5	0	53	54	2.46	1.21	3.05				23.8	9%	25%	16%							30%	82%									11.1	121	$4
19	a/a	9	0	106	89	5.06	1.49	5.22				24.1	8%	19%	12%							34%	68%									-7.3	67	-$3
20	BAL	1	0	19	22	4.82	1.45	5.28	1.51	77	113	20.8	14%	27%	12%	12%	10.4%	93.0	31	22	47	33%	63%	0%	14%	4	87	0%	25%			-0.8	49	-$5
21	BAL *	1	0	117	101	6.68	1.55	6.49	1.39	120	134	17.0	9%	20%	11%	10%	8.8%	92.6	30	19	51	32%	62%	20%	20%	13	76	0%	77%			-34.8	28	-$20
1st Half		0	0	65	63	6.92	1.53	6.07	1.42	112	129	18.8	11%	22%	11%	10%	8.7%	92.6	32	20	48	31%	59%	19%	19%	12	77	0%	75%			-21.2	35	-$18
2nd Half		1	0	52	38	6.38	1.57	7.01		153	195	15.2	6%	17%	11%		10.6%	93.2	18	6	76	33%	65%	23%	25%	1	66	0%	100%			-13.6	22	-$17
Proj		**3**	**0**	**80**	**69**	**5.47**	**1.47**	**5.00**	**1.36**	**113**	**125**	**21.1**	**8%**	**20%**	**12%**	**10%**	**8.7%**	**92.6**	**32**	**20**	**48**	**32%**	**67%**	**14%**	**17%**	**16**						**-10.0**	**74**	**-$8**

DANIEL MARCUS

Kuhl,Chad

						Health	F	LIMA Plan	D+
Age:	29	Th:	R	Role	SP	PT/Exp	C	Rand Var	+1
Ht:	6' 3"	Wt:	215	Type	Pwr	Consist	A	MM	1203

All you need to see is big goose egg in DOM% column, which screams "mediocre innings eater." COVID-IL stay prompted move to bullpen, where K%, SwK went up slightly, but results weren't good (10 ER, 4 HR in 12.1 IP). That sound you heard may have been window to establish himself as rotation factor closing for good.

Yr	Tm	W	Sv	IP	K	ERA	WHIP	xERA	xWHIP	vL+	vR+	BF/G	BB%	K%	K-BB%	xBB%	SwK	Vel	G	L	F	H%	S%	HR/F	xHR/F	GS	APC	DOM%	DIS%	Sv%	LI	RAR	BPX	R$
17	PIT	8	0	157	142	4.35	1.47	4.65	1.45	118	94	21.9	11%	21%	10%	9%	10.0%	95.5	42	23	35	32%	72%	11%	10%	31	87	16%	23%			0.2	66	$1
18	PIT	5	0	85	81	4.55	1.44	4.45	1.34	118	104	23.3	9%	22%	13%	10%	10.1%	95.4	36	26	37	32%	73%	15%	21%	16	90	6%	38%			-4.2	85	-$3
19																																		
20	PIT	2	0	46	44	4.27	1.36	4.95	1.58	97	101	17.9	14%	22%	8%	12%	10.3%	93.9	43	22	35	24%	75%	19%	24%	9	72	11%	44%	0	0.79	1.0	32	$0
21	PIT	5	0	80	75	4.82	1.43	4.66	1.48	119	100	12.5	12%	21%	9%	12%	11.1%	94.2	44	21	35	28%	71%	17%	16%	14	51	0%	29%	0	0.81	-5.5	51	-$5
1st Half		2	0	45	35	5.16	1.46	5.29	1.66	107	97	20.2	14%	17%	3%	12%	10.3%	94.2	47	21	33	26%	67%	14%	11%	10	83	0%	40%			-5.0	0	-$8
2nd Half		3	0	35	40	4.37	1.40	3.94	1.26	120	108	8.2	10%	27%	18%	11%	12.1%	94.2	40	21	38	32%	76%	21%	22%	4	34	0%	0%	0	0.81	-0.5	117	-$4
Proj		**8**	**0**	**131**	**126**	**4.54**	**1.42**	**4.64**	**1.44**	**115**	**101**	**20.8**	**12%**	**23%**	**11%**	**12%**	**10.8%**	**94.5**	**41**	**22**	**36**	**29%**	**73%**	**16%**	**19%**	**25**						**-1.4**	**66**	**-$1**

Lamet,Dinelson

						Health	F	LIMA Plan	C
Age:	29	Th:	R	Role	RP	PT/Exp	C	Rand Var	+1
Ht:	6' 3"	Wt:	228	Type	Pwr/FB	Consist	B	MM	2400

Decision to rehab elbow injury "worked" only in sense he pitched at all. By late June, he was back on IL (forearm), then returned in September as wild reliever (12.2 IP, 9 ER, 19/11 K/BB). Still uncorked plenty of elusive sliders, but velocity was down, and batters who made contact did more damage. Extreme durability concerns now cloud role, once-bright future.

Yr	Tm	W	Sv	IP	K	ERA	WHIP	xERA	xWHIP	vL+	vR+	BF/G	BB%	K%	K-BB%	xBB%	SwK	Vel	G	L	F	H%	S%	HR/F	xHR/F	GS	APC	DOM%	DIS%	Sv%	LI	RAR	BPX	R$
17	SD *	10	0	153	179	4.26	1.28	3.60	1.35	115	73	21.7	12%	29%	17%	9%	12.5%	95.0	37	20	43	29%	70%	15%	16%	21	92	24%	19%			1.9	109	$9
18																																		
19	SD *	4	0	88	120	4.26	1.22	3.91	1.17	98	93	20.9	10%	34%	24%	8%	14.4%	96.1	36	27	36	31%	71%	20%	17%	14	88	14%	7%			2.7	121	$3
20	SD	3	0	69	93	2.09	0.86	3.23	1.05	60	76	22.3	7%	35%	27%	6%	14.8%	97.1	37	21	42	25%	80%	8%	12%	12	87	42%	8%			20.1	184	$31
21	SD	2	0	47	57	4.40	1.49	4.28	1.30	117	90	9.5	11%	27%	17%	7%	15.7%	95.5	39	21	40	36%	73%	12%	14%	9	38	11%	44%	0	0.60	-0.8	109	-$5
1st Half		2	0	34	38	3.67	1.40	4.13	1.20	100	101	13.5	7%	26%	18%	6%	15.4%	95.5	39	22	39	36%	77%	11%	15%	9	53	11%	44%	0	0.71	2.5	130	-$3
2nd Half		0	0	13	19	6.39	1.74	4.77	1.56	153	75	5.5	18%	32%	13%	9%	16.5%	95.5	38	17	45	35%	65%	15%	10%	0	23			0	0.50	-3.3	53	-$14
Proj		**3**	**0**	**58**	**71**	**4.14**	**1.31**	**3.92**	**1.25**	**100**	**91**	**17.8**	**10%**	**30%**	**20%**	**7%**	**14.5%**	**95.9**	**37**	**22**	**40**	**32%**	**71%**	**12%**	**15%**	**10**						**2.2**	**126**	**-$1**

Lauer,Eric

						Health	B	LIMA Plan	C+
Age:	27	Th:	L	Role	SP	PT/Exp	C	Rand Var	-4
Ht:	6' 3"	Wt:	228	Type		Consist	F	MM	1203

On surface, 2nd half looks like breakout, but he's not quite a budding ace, as static xERA attests. The good: sustained SwK gain, fastball up a tick. The worrisome: Hit, strand rate luck could turn, and only low HR/F kept late fly ball spike from costing him. Performance may have bought him some rotation rope, but you should be less quick to commit.

Yr	Tm	W	Sv	IP	K	ERA	WHIP	xERA	xWHIP	vL+	vR+	BF/G	BB%	K%	K-BB%	xBB%	SwK	Vel	G	L	F	H%	S%	HR/F	xHR/F	GS	APC	DOM%	DIS%	Sv%	LI	RAR	BPX	R$
17	aa	4	0	55	41	5.36	1.46	5.04				23.6	8%	17%	10%							33%	65%									-6.8	61	-$5
18	SD *	8	0	134	119	4.01	1.45	4.73	1.38	115	110	21.2	9%	21%	11%	8%	9.0%	91.2	38	28	35	32%	75%	13%	12%	23	88	13%	43%			2.2	73	$0
19	SD	8	0	150	138	4.45	1.40	4.83	1.35	120	95	21.7	8%	21%	13%	7%	9.2%	91.9	40	22	38	33%	71%	12%	11%	29	84	10%	34%	0	0.82	1.0	92	$2
20	MIL	0	0	11	12	13.09	2.36	7.29	1.69	117	145	15.3	15%	20%	5%	12%	11.1%	91.6	21	34	45	44%	42%	12%	16%	2	61	0%	100%	0	0.59	-11.7	-26	-$17
21	MIL	7	0	119	117	3.19	1.14	4.32	1.28	88	85	20.4	8%	24%	16%	8%	11.1%	92.6	36	23	41	26%	78%	12%	14%	20	82	35%	20%	0	0.76	15.8	98	$11
1st Half		3	0	50	51	4.11	1.31	4.34	1.32	76	104	19.6	9%	24%	14%	8%	11.1%	92.3	39	26	35	28%	77%	20%	16%	8	76	25%	25%	0	0.78	0.9	93	$0
2nd Half		4	0	68	66	2.50	1.01	4.30	1.24	89	73	21.0	8%	24%	16%	7%	11.2%	92.8	33	21	46	25%	79%	7%	13%	12	86	42%	17%	0	0.75	14.9	102	$17
Proj		**9**	**0**	**145**	**135**	**4.06**	**1.28**	**4.46**	**1.32**	**102**	**92**	**20.6**	**9%**	**23%**	**14%**	**8%**	**10.3%**	**92.2**	**37**	**23**	**40**	**30%**	**72%**	**12%**	**13%**	**29**						**7.1**	**90**	**$5**

Leclerc,José

						Health	F	LIMA Plan	B+
Age:	28	Th:	R	Role	RP	PT/Exp	D	Rand Var	0
Ht:	6' 0"	Wt:	195	Type	Pwr/xFB	Consist	D	MM	2510

Dodged operating table for shoulder injury that cost him most of 2020. Wasn't as lucky with elbow in 2021, succumbing to Tommy John surgery in late March that may claim first two-plus months of 2022. When last healthy, racked up strikeouts but had trouble finding strike zone, which long layoff will hardly help. He's an extreme wild card, literally.

Yr	Tm	W	Sv	IP	K	ERA	WHIP	xERA	xWHIP	vL+	vR+	BF/G	BB%	K%	K-BB%	xBB%	SwK	Vel	G	L	F	H%	S%	HR/F	xHR/F	GS	APC	DOM%	DIS%	Sv%	LI	RAR	BPX	R$
17	TEX	2	2	46	60	3.94	1.38	4.94	1.70	91	69	4.3	20%	30%	10%	12%	16.1%	95.8	40	10	50	22%	73%	8%	6%	0	18			67	0.90	2.3	22	-$1
18	TEX	2	12	58	85	1.56	0.85	3.04	1.12	61	59	3.8	11%	38%	27%	9%	18.1%	95.3	32	21	47	23%	81%	2%	4%	0	16			75	1.30	18.4	165	$14
19	TEX	2	14	69	100	4.33	1.33	4.05	1.32	112	77	4.3	13%	33%	20%	10%	14.1%	96.8	35	20	45	32%	69%	10%	9%	3	18	0%	67%	78	0.90	1.5	121	$6
20	TEX	0	1	2	3	4.50	2.00	5.92		121		5.0	20%	30%	10%		12.8%	94.5	0	60	40	43%	75%	0%	1%	0	24			100	0.97	0.0	-25	-$6
21																																		
1st Half																																		
2nd Half																																		
Proj		**1**	**6**	**44**	**62**	**4.02**	**1.33**	**3.99**	**1.34**	**110**	**76**	**4.1**	**15%**	**34%**	**20%**	**11%**	**15.7%**	**96.1**	**35**	**18**	**47**	**32%**	**70%**	**7%**	**7%**	**0**						**2.3**	**111**	**$0**

Lester,Jon

						Health	D	LIMA Plan	D+
Age:	38	Th:	L	Role	SP	PT/Exp	A	Rand Var	0
Ht:	6' 4"	Wt:	240	Type	Con	Consist	A	MM	0003

Held on to finish 16th season and even managed not to disrupt STL's 17-game winning streak, but he's been on back nine for a while. K%, K-BB%, fastball velocity, and BPX all hit new full-season lows. HR allowed have been part of the package for a while, too. 5-year xERA trend is damning. Order a drink to toast him in the clubhouse—he'll be up soon.

Yr	Tm	W	Sv	IP	K	ERA	WHIP	xERA	xWHIP	vL+	vR+	BF/G	BB%	K%	K-BB%	xBB%	SwK	Vel	G	L	F	H%	S%	HR/F	xHR/F	GS	APC	DOM%	DIS%	Sv%	LI	RAR	BPX	R$
17	CHC	13	0	181	180	4.33	1.32	3.95	1.28	73	109	23.8	8%	24%	16%	9%	11.2%	91.1	46	21	32	32%	71%	16%	13%	32	98	25%	34%			0.5	126	$9
18	CHC	18	0	182	149	3.32	1.31	4.47	1.36	120	97	23.8	8%	20%	11%	9%	8.8%	91.0	38	26	36	29%	80%	12%	15%	32	98	22%	31%			18.6	73	$14
19	CHC	13	0	172	165	4.46	1.50	4.57	1.29	110	108	24.6	7%	22%	15%	8%	9.2%	90.3	43	23	33	36%	74%	15%	16%	31	98	19%	35%			1.0	112	$2
20	CHC	3	0	61	42	5.16	1.33	5.08	1.36	88	106	22.1	6%	16%	9%	9%	7.4%	89.2	47	17	36	29%	66%	15%	20%	12	84	8%	42%			-5.3	78	-$2
21	2 NL	7	0	141	91	4.71	1.51	5.31	1.47	91	116	22.4	9%	15%	6%	10%	8.9%	88.4	44	23	34	30%	74%	16%	17%	28	85	4%	71%			-7.8	35	-$8
1st Half		2	0	57	39	5.34	1.55	5.39	1.45	63	131	21.3	9%	15%	7%	9%	9.8%	88.8	41	22	36	31%	71%	16%	15%	12	84	0%	75%			-7.6	40	-$10
2nd Half		5	0	84	52	4.29	1.49	5.25	1.49	106	110	23.3	9%	14%	5%	11%	8.3%	88.1	45	23	32	30%	77%	16%	18%	16	86	6%	69%			-0.2	31	-$2
Proj		**8**	**0**	**131**	**96**	**4.95**	**1.44**	**4.87**	**1.41**	**97**	**111**	**22.2**	**8%**	**17%**	**9%**	**9%**	**8.8%**	**89.2**	**44**	**22**	**34**	**31%**	**70%**	**15%**	**17%**	**25**						**-7.9**	**64**	**-$5**

Liberatore,Matthew

						Health	A	LIMA Plan	B
Age:	22	Th:	L	Role	SP	PT/Exp	F	Rand Var	0
Ht:	6' 5"	Wt:	200	Type		Consist	F	MM	2200

STL was content to have 21-year-old prize from Arozarena deal pitch full season at AAA, where he worked to refine arsenal, including adding four-seam FB. Numbers don't jump off page, but he did close well (2.55 ERA, 1.15 WHIP with 53/14 K/BB in last 53 IP). He may not have more than mid-rotation upside, but should take first step to getting there in 2022.

Yr	Tm	W	Sv	IP	K	ERA	WHIP	xERA	xWHIP	vL+	vR+	BF/G	BB%	K%	K-BB%	xBB%	SwK	Vel	G	L	F	H%	S%	HR/F	xHR/F	GS	APC	DOM%	DIS%	Sv%	LI	RAR	BPX	R$
17																																		
18																																		
19																																		
20																																		
21	aaa	9	0	126	104	3.75	1.20	4.02				23.1	6%	20%	15%							30%	73%									8.0	102	$7
1st Half		3	0	45	36	4.13	1.12	3.60				22.2	6%	20%	15%							28%	66%									0.7	100	$1
2nd Half		6	0	81	68	3.54	1.25	4.25				23.6	5%	21%	15%							31%	76%									7.3	103	$11
Proj		**3**	**0**	**44**	**40**	**4.43**	**1.29**	**4.20**	**1.24**			**23.5**	**7%**	**22%**	**16%**				**43**	**20**	**37**	**31%**	**70%**	**14%**	**0%**	**8**						**0.1**	**118**	**-$3**

Littell,Zack

						Health	B	LIMA Plan	B+
Age:	26	Th:	R	Role	RP	PT/Exp	D	Rand Var	-4
Ht:	6' 4"	Wt:	220	Type	Pwr	Consist	F	MM	2300

Took big step showing he belongs in MLB, but would need to sustain 2nd half strikeout binge to get ball regularly in ninth. Yielded lots of hard contact, but H%, S%, HR/F luck minimized pain. Quest for third pitch to get LHB out continues, as split-finger didn't get job done. Still relatively young, so keep tabs on him, but there may be better spec save targets.

Yr	Tm	W	Sv	IP	K	ERA	WHIP	xERA	xWHIP	vL+	vR+	BF/G	BB%	K%	K-BB%	xBB%	SwK	Vel	G	L	F	H%	S%	HR/F	xHR/F	GS	APC	DOM%	DIS%	Sv%	LI	RAR	BPX	R$
17	aa	10	0	86	70	3.38	1.32	3.68				25.3	8%	20%	12%							32%	75%									10.4	102	$6
18	MIN *	6	0	149	121	5.38	1.60	5.27	1.41	141	115	20.6	9%	18%	9%	8%	8.0%	91.9	44	24	32	36%	66%	13%	13%	2	53	0%	50%	0	0.74	-22.7	67	-$13
19	MIN *	9	1	100	87	4.08	1.37	4.87	1.39	92	96	8.5	9%	21%	12%	6%	13.6%	93.9	38	28	34	30%	77%	11%	16%	0	19			50	0.81	5.2	59	$4
20	MIN	0	0	6	3	9.95	2.37	7.45	1.67	129	256	5.2	10%	10%	0%	8%	5.1%	94.0	29	25	46	32%	80%	45%	33%	0	20			0	0.29	-4.3	-35	-$12
21	SF	4	2	62	63	2.92	1.14	4.01	1.30	108	79	4.0	10%	25%	15%	7%	13.9%	95.0	47	16	38	26%	79%	12%	17%	2	16	0%	50%	33	1.07	10.2	105	$5
1st Half		0	0	26	19	3.16	1.25	4.29	1.47	118	84	3.5	10%	18%	8%	7%	12.7%	95.1	61	11	28	25%	79%	14%	27%	2	13	0%	50%	0	0.74	3.5	60	-$5
2nd Half		4	2	36	44	2.75	1.06	3.81	1.18	91	78	4.4	9%	30%	21%	7%	14.6%	94.9	35	20	45	27%	79%	10%	12%	0	19			33	1.37	6.7	135	$8
Proj		**4**	**0**	**58**	**62**	**3.83**	**1.24**	**3.98**	**1.28**	**111**	**89**	**6.1**	**9%**	**26%**	**17%**	**7%**	**13.9%**	**94.7**	**44**	**19**	**37**	**30%**	**72%**	**12%**	**17%**	**0**						**4.5**	**117**	**$0**

KRIS OLSON

Loaisiga,Jonathan

Age: 27	Th: R	Role RP	Health F	LIMA Plan B
Ht: 5' 11"	Wt: 165	Type Pwr/GB	PT/Exp D	Rand Var -4
			Consist B	MM 4320

Everything you'd want in high-leverage reliever... except health. Strikeouts don't jump off page, but Statcast data—needle pinned on soft contact, chase rate—does. Spent most of year throwing harder than ever, inducing career-high GB%, but Sept rotator cuff strain reminds us we may never be able to relax. If health cooperates... UP: 30 Sv. But it probably won't.

Yr Tm	W	Sv	IP	K	ERA	WHIP	xERA	xWHIP	vL+	vR+	BF/G	BB%	K%	K-BB%	xBB%	SwK	Vel	G	L	F	H%	S%	HR/F	xHR/F	GS	APC	DOM%	DIS%	Sv%	LI	RAR	BPX	R$
17																																	
18 NYY *	5	0	60	67	5.18	1.51	5.96	1.19	108	110	14.4	7%	26%	19%	8%	13.8%	96.0	49	27	24	37%	71%	20%	21%	4	55	25%	50%	0	0.44	-7.6	91	-$5
19 NYY *	2	0	51	55	5.41	1.40	5.05	1.36	110	108	10.2	10%	26%	15%	9%	14.4%	96.9	40	24	36	31%	66%	19%	13%	4	39	0%	75%	0	0.67	-5.7	67	-$5
20 NYY	3	0	23	22	3.52	1.22	3.84	1.25	96	103	8.3	7%	22%	15%	6%	10.2%	96.7	51	23	26	30%	76%	18%	19%	3	33	0%	0%	0	1.00	2.6	124	$3
21 NYY	9	5	71	69	2.17	1.02	3.10	1.15	86	66	5.0	6%	24%	19%	5%	13.8%	98.4	61	16	23	29%	80%	7%	8%	0	19			56	1.61	18.3	156	$14
1st Half	7	2	43	39	2.32	0.98	3.04	1.15	89	64	5.1	5%	23%	18%	6%	12.7%	97.9	64	13	23	28%	78%	8%	9%	0	19			50	1.64	10.2	153	$13
2nd Half	2	3	28	30	1.93	1.07	3.20	1.14	72	72	4.8	6%	26%	20%	5%	15.4%	99.1	56	19	25	31%	83%	5%	6%	0	19			60	1.57	8.1	161	$4
Proj	6	11	65	68	3.38	1.20	3.41	1.19	98	85	6.3	7%	26%	19%	6%	14.4%	98.2	54	19	27	31%	75%	14%	9%	0						8.7	149	$8

López,Jorge

Age: 29	Th: R	Role RP	Health B	LIMA Plan D+
Ht: 6' 2"	Wt: 205	Type	PT/Exp B	Rand Var +5
			Consist A	MM 1100

To steal line from Regina George in Mean Girls: "Stop trying to make Jorge happen." He looks the part—even more now with amped fastball—but hitters have no problem teeing off. H%/S% look less like bad luck, more like just who he is, and long ball issues have been hard earned. It doesn't take "ESPN" to see he's not long for anyone's rotation... or roster.

Yr Tm	W	Sv	IP	K	ERA	WHIP	xERA	xWHIP	vL+	vR+	BF/G	BB%	K%	K-BB%	xBB%	SwK	Vel	G	L	F	H%	S%	HR/F	xHR/F	GS	APC	DOM%	DIS%	Sv%	LI	RAR	BPX	R$
17 MIL *	8	7	106	89	6.60	1.62	5.37		146	135	11.7	10%	19%	9%		5.7%	94.8	44	33	22	35%	59%	0%	1%	0	35			78	0.04	-29.3	64	-$8
18 2 TM *	6	5	93	65	5.64	1.51	5.21	1.43	99	114	9.4	8%	16%	8%	8%	9.0%	93.7	45	23	32	33%	64%	11%	13%	7	52	29%	71%	71	0.57	-17.1	49	-$7
19 KC	4	1	124	109	6.33	1.47	4.75	1.36	129	100	14.1	8%	20%	12%	9%	9.2%	94.2	46	20	34	32%	61%	21%	23%	18	53	11%	39%	50	0.78	-27.9	92	-$10
20 2 AL	2	0	39	28	6.69	1.49	4.93	1.37	121	101	17.4	7%	16%	9%	11%	8.8%	93.8	49	20	31	32%	57%	18%	21%	6	64	0%	17%	0	0.76	-10.8	77	-$10
21 BAL	3	0	122	112	6.07	1.63	4.51	1.41	129	107	16.8	10%	20%	10%	9%	8.7%	95.2	50	22	28	34%	66%	20%	21%	25	66	12%	56%	0	0.88	-27.0	72	-$18
1st Half	2	0	81	77	6.02	1.60	4.42	1.40	109	116	21.4	10%	21%	11%	9%	9.1%	95.2	48	24	28	34%	65%	21%	19%	17	82	18%	59%			-17.5	76	-$15
2nd Half	1	0	41	35	6.15	1.68	4.71	1.44	146	95	11.9	10%	18%	8%	10%	8.0%	95.4	54	18	28	35%	66%	19%	24%	8	48	0%	50%	0	0.99	-9.5	64	-$16
Proj	2	0	44	36	5.40	1.48	4.56	1.41	123	97	13.3	9%	19%	10%	10%	8.7%	94.6	49	20	30	31%	67%	19%	21%	5						-5.1	74	-$7

López,Pablo

Age: 26	Th: R	Role SP	Health F	LIMA Plan B
Ht: 6' 4"	Wt: 225	Type	PT/Exp B	Rand Var 0
			Consist B	MM 3203

All was going fine as success with change-up-heavy approach continued, but then rotator cuff strain struck in mid-July, bringing seven-week stretch of elite command to sudden halt. This was third serious shoulder issue in four years, so injury specter will stay part of otherwise appealing package. If you can work around missed time, he'll help while he's able.

Yr Tm	W	Sv	IP	K	ERA	WHIP	xERA	xWHIP	vL+	vR+	BF/G	BB%	K%	K-BB%	xBB%	SwK	Vel	G	L	F	H%	S%	HR/F	xHR/F	GS	APC	DOM%	DIS%	Sv%	LI	RAR	BPX	R$
17																																	
18 MIA *	4	0	124	104	2.77	1.10	3.24	1.23	93	113	22.1	6%	21%	15%	7%	11.3%	92.4	50	21	29	27%	80%	16%	19%	10	95	10%	40%			21.1	112	$11
19 MIA *	5	0	126	109	5.89	1.38	4.92	1.30	116	84	20.4	7%	21%	14%	8%	10.6%	93.6	48	21	31	33%	59%	15%	16%	21	86	33%	29%			-21.7	78	-$7
20 MIA	6	0	57	59	3.61	1.19	3.78	1.23	99	73	21.8	8%	25%	17%	7%	12.6%	93.7	52	19	29	31%	70%	9%	12%	11	82	45%	27%			6.0	136	$15
21 MIA	5	0	103	115	3.07	1.12	3.32	1.12	92	92	20.9	6%	28%	21%	6%	12.6%	94.0	47	22	31	31%	77%	13%	16%	20	83	35%	20%			15.2	159	$9
1st Half	4	0	91	94	2.97	1.08	3.39	1.14	83	94	21.5	6%	26%	20%	6%	12.1%	94.0	49	21	30	29%	76%	12%	17%	17	85	41%	18%			14.6	148	$17
2nd Half	1	0	12	21	3.86	1.46	2.81	0.96	130	91	17.7	8%	40%	32%	4%	16.2%	94.0	33	30	37	48%	80%	20%	13%	3	72	0%	33%			0.6	241	-$9
Proj	7	0	131	125	3.40	1.16	3.64	1.21	96	88	20.9	7%	24%	17%	7%	11.8%	93.5	50	21	30	30%	74%	13%	16%	25						17.0	134	$11

López,Reynaldo

Age: 28	Th: R	Role RP	Health B	LIMA Plan D+
Ht: 6' 1"	Wt: 220	Type /FB	PT/Exp C	Rand Var +3
			Consist B	MM 0201

4-4, 3.43 ERA in 58 IP at CHW. Called to plug rotation hole, he surprised with early success despite AAA struggles, but no start was above PQS-2. Instead, bullpen looks like better fit—he's down to two pitches, and while it was just 20 IP, he thrived there (2.21 ERA, 26% K-BB%, 14.4% SwK). Time to cut ties with prospect past and move him already.

Yr Tm	W	Sv	IP	K	ERA	WHIP	xERA	xWHIP	vL+	vR+	BF/G	BB%	K%	K-BB%	xBB%	SwK	Vel	G	L	F	H%	S%	HR/F	xHR/F	GS	APC	DOM%	DIS%	Sv%	LI	RAR	BPX	R$
17 CHW *	9	0	169	145	4.51	1.36	4.45	1.42	107	91	23.5	9%	21%	11%	8%	9.1%	94.5	30	22	48	30%	71%	9%	9%	8	96	0%	50%			-3.3	68	$3
18 CHW	7	0	189	151	3.91	1.27	5.05	1.42	96	101	25.0	9%	19%	10%	8%	9.6%	95.5	33	20	47	27%	73%	9%	12%	32	96	31%	28%			5.5	51	$6
19 CHW	10	0	184	169	5.38	1.46	5.21	1.37	114	107	24.5	8%	21%	13%	8%	11.7%	95.5	35	21	44	32%	68%	14%	14%	33	96	24%	55%			-19.9	83	-$4
20 CHW	1	0	26	24	6.49	1.63	6.15	1.56	102	154	15.1	12%	20%	7%	9%	9.3%	94.2	35	13	53	27%	71%	22%	17%	8	63	0%	63%			-6.6	25	-$10
21 CHW *	5	0	97	95	5.57	1.44	5.30	1.30	96	85	13.7	9%	23%	15%	8%	11.9%	95.8	39	22	39	33%	64%	17%	16%	9	47	0%	33%	0	0.66	-15.5	72	-$8
1st Half	0	0	33	34	10.00	2.40	9.98				19.2	12%	20%	8%							47%	58%	0%		0	0					-23.3	18	-$27
2nd Half	5	0	64	61	3.27	0.94	2.87	1.15	91	87	11.4	6%	25%	20%	8%	11.9%	95.8	39	22	39	23%	73%	17%	16%	9	47	0%	33%	0	0.66	7.8	128	$16
Proj	3	0	73	67	5.31	1.45	4.88	1.36	118	106	17.7	9%	22%	13%	8%	10.9%	95.4	35	21	44	32%	67%	13%	13%	13						-7.6	79	-$6

Lorenzen,Michael

Age: 30	Th: R	Role RP	Health F	LIMA Plan D+
Ht: 6' 3"	Wt: 220	Type	PT/Exp C	Rand Var +2
			Consist A	MM 1110

Spring shoulder injury, initially played off as no big deal, cost him 3 1/2 months, and hamstring issue stole two more weeks. Velocity was still there, but SwK and K% waned, and he crashed and burned in brief turn as part of closer mix. Now on wrong side of 30, he's even less interesting. Place speculative bids elsewhere.

Yr Tm	W	Sv	IP	K	ERA	WHIP	xERA	xWHIP	vL+	vR+	BF/G	BB%	K%	K-BB%	xBB%	SwK	Vel	G	L	F	H%	S%	HR/F	xHR/F	GS	APC	DOM%	DIS%	Sv%	LI	RAR	BPX	R$
17 CIN	8	2	83	80	4.45	1.35	3.91	1.36	102	86	5.2	9%	22%	13%	9%	11.1%	96.4	55	20	25	31%	69%	15%	13%	0	20			29	1.00	-0.9	108	$2
18 CIN	4	1	81	54	3.11	1.38	4.50	1.50	109	89	7.6	10%	16%	6%	8%	7.3%	95.1	50	25	25	29%	79%	10%	12%	3	29	0%	33%	50	0.84	10.4	39	$1
19 CIN	1	7	83	85	2.92	1.15	4.04	1.28	83	88	4.7	8%	25%	17%	8%	14.6%	96.9	44	23	32	28%	79%	13%	10%	0	18			64	1.20	16.3	115	$8
20 CIN	3	0	34	35	4.28	1.40	4.57	1.42	82	106	8.2	12%	24%	12%	11%	15.0%	96.7	48	17	34	31%	70%	9%	10%	2	34	100%	0%	0	1.14	0.7	81	$1
21 CIN	1	4	29	21	5.59	1.38	5.02	1.54	95	87	4.6	11%	17%	6%	8%	12.7%	96.5	45	24	31	28%	58%	7%	5%	0	18			100	1.31	-4.7	25	-$5
1st Half																																	
2nd Half	1	4	29	21	5.59	1.38	5.02	1.54	91	88	4.6	11%	17%	6%	8%	12.7%	96.5	45	24	31	28%	58%	7%	5%	0	18			100	1.31	-4.7	25	-$7
Proj	3	2	65	56	4.46	1.38	4.50	1.44	97	93	5.6	10%	20%	10%	9%	12.4%	96.3	48	22	30	30%	68%	10%	9%	0						0.0	66	-$3

Loup,Aaron

Age: 34	Th: L	Role RP	Health F	LIMA Plan C+
Ht: 5' 11"	Wt: 210	Type Pwr/GB	PT/Exp D	Rand Var -5
			Consist B	MM 3300

A "loupe" is a small magnifying glass used by jewelers, but by now you hardly need one to see who he is: a nifty "LOOGY-plus" who can go on nice runs when healthy and when hit and strand rates smile on him. Ground ball rates further establish him as safe roster finisher, if not league winner. No need to tarry further; save loupe for more iffy assessments.

Yr Tm	W	Sv	IP	K	ERA	WHIP	xERA	xWHIP	vL+	vR+	BF/G	BB%	K%	K-BB%	xBB%	SwK	Vel	G	L	F	H%	S%	HR/F	xHR/F	GS	APC	DOM%	DIS%	Sv%	LI	RAR	BPX	R$
17 TOR	2	0	58	64	3.75	1.53	3.98	1.39	95	98	3.8	11%	24%	13%	8%	10.4%	91.9	53	20	26	36%	76%	10%	8%	0	14			0	1.01	4.4	106	-$2
18 2 TM	0	0	40	44	4.54	1.56	3.78	1.24	93	131	3.1	8%	24%	16%	6%	11.6%	92.0	49	23	28	39%	72%	12%	11%	0	12			0	0.51	-1.9	139	-$6
19 SD	0	0	3	5	0.00	0.90	2.11		165	17	3.5	7%	36%	29%		15.1%	91.7	57	29	14	31%	100%	0%	0%	0	13			0	0.88	1.9	223	-$4
20 TAM	3	0	25	22	2.52	0.84	3.54	1.13	80	89	4.0	4%	23%	19%	5%	8.5%	92.1	40	29	32	22%	78%	15%	17%	0	14			0	0.78	6.0	137	$9
21 NYM	6	0	57	57	0.95	0.94	3.20	1.18	61	73	3.4	7%	26%	19%	6%	12.1%	92.4	50	23	27	26%	90%	3%	6%	2	13	0%	50%	0	1.53	23.2	134	$11
1st Half	2	0	24	29	1.52	0.97	2.50	0.95	51	88	3.5	3%	31%	28%	5%	14.2%	92.9	49	31	20	35%	83%	0%	7%	0	14			0	1.64	8.0	214	$2
2nd Half	4	0	33	28	0.55	0.91	3.76	1.38	62	61	3.3	10%	23%	12%	7%	10.5%	92.1	51	18	31	20%	97%	4%	6%	2	12	0%	50%	0	1.45	15.1	78	$10
Proj	5	0	65	68	3.19	1.18	3.52	1.24	79	93	3.3	9%	26%	18%	6%	11.6%	92.2	51	22	27	30%	75%	11%	8%	0						10.1	131	$3

Luetge,Lucas

Age: 35	Th: L	Role RP	Health A	LIMA Plan B+
Ht: 6' 4"	Wt: 205	Type	PT/Exp D	Rand Var -4
			Consist B	MM 2200

Since last pitching in MLB in 2015, underwent Tommy John surgery in 2017, then reinvented himself as cutter master, though curve was most devastating offering in 2021 (19.1% SwK). He's past age to hold any dynasty allure, but can he parlay new pitch mix, pinpoint control into year or two of ratio help? Sure, why not? Never give up on your dreams, kids.

Yr Tm	W	Sv	IP	K	ERA	WHIP	xERA	xWHIP	vL+	vR+	BF/G	BB%	K%	K-BB%	xBB%	SwK	Vel	G	L	F	H%	S%	HR/F	xHR/F	GS	APC	DOM%	DIS%	Sv%	LI	RAR	BPX	R$
17 aaa	2	0	32	25	6.97	2.13	8.82				6.5	10%	16%	6%							41%	71%									-10.2	-2	-$11
18																																	
19 a/a	9	1	68	54	3.08	1.43	4.29				5.3	8%	19%	10%							33%	80%									11.9	77	$4
20																																	
21 NYY	4	1	72	78	2.74	1.13	3.74	1.10	72	93	5.3	5%	26%	21%	9%	13.6%		42	20	38	33%	79%	8%	9%	1	22	0%	100%	33	0.79	13.6	158	$6
1st Half	2	0	41	43	3.10	1.08	3.76	1.07	75	99	5.5	4%	26%	21%	9%	14.2%		40	20	40	31%	77%	11%	10%	0	21			0	0.77	5.9	162	$3
2nd Half	2	1	32	35	2.27	1.20	3.72	1.13	58	90	5.1	6%	27%	20%	8%	12.9%		45	19	36	35%	81%	3%	8%	1	23	0%	100%	50	0.82	7.8	154	$2
Proj	3	0	44	42	3.60	1.18	3.86	1.16	73	98	5.0	5%	24%	19%	8%	13.4%		43	19	38	32%	72%	10%	9%	0						4.6	144	$0

KRIS OLSON

Lugo,Seth

Lugo,Seth					
Age: 32	Th: R	Role: RP	Health: F	LIMA Plan: A	
Ht: 6' 4"	Wt: 225	Type: Pwr	PT/Exp: C	Rand Var: 0	
			Consist: A	MM: 3311	

Season start delayed 'til June due to Feb surgery to remove loose bodies from elbow, but once back, resumed role as high-leverage weapon. On surface, control looks a bit wonky; xBB% says not to fret, though issue was vs. LHB (16% BB%), which may keep save opps at bay. Injuries are ongoing concern. But for ratio and strikeout help, he's a solid bet.

Yr	Tm	W	Sv	IP	K	ERA	WHIP	xERA	xWHIP	vL+	vR+	BF/G	BB%	K%	K-BB%	xBB%	SwK	Vel	G	L	F	H%	S%	HR/F	xHR/F	GS	APC	DOM%	DIS%	Sv%	LI	RAR	BPX	R$
17	NYM	7	0	101	85	4.71	1.37	4.37	1.27	102	104	22.9	6%	20%	14%	7%	9.2%	91.1	42	24	34	33%	68%	12%	14%	18	86	17%	33%	0	0.79	-4.4	115	$0
18	NYM	3	3	101	103	2.66	1.08	3.54	1.19	75	88	7.6	7%	25%	18%	6%	10.5%	93.9	46	20	33	28%	79%	10%	12%	5	30	20%	40%	75	0.93	18.6	140	$1
19	NYM	7	6	80	104	2.70	0.90	3.17	1.01	71	77	5.1	5%	33%	28%	6%	11.8%	94.4	43	18	39	28%	75%	11%	11%	0	21			55	1.34	17.8	199	$15
20	NYM	3	3	37	47	5.15	1.36	3.30	1.09	114	110	10.0	6%	29%	23%	7%	14.3%	93.4	49	25	27	36%	69%	30%	25%	7	38	29%	29%	60	1.08	-3.2	190	$4
21	NYM	4	1	46	55	3.50	1.29	3.77	1.25	106	88	4.2	10%	28%	18%	6%	13.8%	93.8	42	25	34	32%	78%	15%	16%	0	16			25	1.25	4.4	124	$0
1st Half		1	1	13	18	2.77	1.31	3.11	1.20	102	67	4.2	11%	33%	22%	7%	15.0%	93.5	41	34	24	35%	81%	14%	17%	0	16			100	1.54	2.4	144	-$4
2nd Half		3	0	33	37	3.78	1.29	4.03	1.26	100	99	4.3	9%	26%	17%	6%	13.4%	94.0	42	21	37	30%	76%	15%	16%	0	16			0	1.14	2.0	115	-$2
Proj		**5**	**2**	**73**	**82**	**3.46**	**1.19**	**3.54**	**1.16**	**94**	**92**	**6.1**	**7%**	**28%**	**21%**	**6%**	**12.2%**	**93.6**	**44**	**21**	**34**	**32%**	**76%**	**14%**	**16%**	**0**						**8.9**	**154**	**$5**

Luzardo,Jesús

Luzardo,Jesús					
Age: 24	Th: L	Role: RP	Health: B	LIMA Plan: B+	
Ht: 6' 0"	Wt: 218	Type: Pwr	PT/Exp: C	Rand Var: +5	
			Consist: D	MM: 1201	

6-9, 6.69 ERA in 95.1 IP at OAK/MIA. Development often takes unexpected paths, but pinky broken playing video games is new twist. Post-injury work was super shaky, both in MLB bullpen and AAA rotation. MIA let him take lumps after trade, which led to some flashes, like 11-K finale. Here's hoping he can hit reset button and start over at level 2020.

Yr	Tm	W	Sv	IP	K	ERA	WHIP	xERA	xWHIP	vL+	vR+	BF/G	BB%	K%	K-BB%	xBB%	SwK	Vel	G	L	F	H%	S%	HR/F	xHR/F	GS	APC	DOM%	DIS%	Sv%	LI	RAR	BPX	R$
17																																		
18	a/a	8	0	96	89	3.47	1.19	3.34				19.3	6%	23%	17%							32%	72%									8.1	133	$6
19	OAK *	1	2	43	45	2.96	1.10	2.98	1.19	27	73	13.0	7%	27%	20%	10%	15.2%	96.4	42	15	42	30%	76%	9%	13%	0	29			100	0.85	8.2	144	$2
20	OAK	3	0	59	59	4.12	1.27	3.96	1.22	97	101	20.7	7%	24%	17%	8%	13.0%	95.5	45	24	31	31%	73%	18%	16%	9	78	33%	11%	0	0.70	2.4	130	$6
21	2 TM *	8	0	124	120	6.52	1.62	6.07	1.44	105	123	16.7	11%	22%	10%	10%	13.5%	95.5	38	21	40	34%	62%	18%	19%	18	69	11%	50%	0	0.69	-34.6	46	-$17
1st Half		2	0	48	48	7.20	1.72	7.32	1.37	114	126	12.9	10%	22%	12%	10%	12.5%	95.6	40	16	44	36%	62%	22%	21%	6	51	17%	33%	0	0.63	-17.4	30	-$16
2nd Half		6	0	78	71	5.91	1.51	5.04	1.48	87	126	21.3	12%	21%	9%	10%	14.2%	95.4	38	25	38	31%	62%	14%	18%	12	89	8%	58%			-15.9	57	-$8
Proj		**7**	**0**	**116**	**113**	**4.54**	**1.34**	**4.38**	**1.32**	**92**	**104**	**16.4**	**9%**	**23%**	**14%**	**10%**	**13.4%**	**95.5**	**40**	**22**	**38**	**31%**	**70%**	**14%**	**18%**	**19**						**-1.2**	**97**	**$0**

Lyles,Jordan

Lyles,Jordan					
Age: 31	Th: R	Role: RP	Health: C	LIMA Plan: D+	
Ht: 6' 5"	Wt: 230	Type: Con	PT/Exp: A	Rand Var: +1	
			Consist: C	MM: 0101	

Easy to dismiss journeyman innings eater out of hand, but SwK did rebound, and half of last 12 starts were PQS-DOM, albeit against mostly weak competition. That may keep him employed, but do you want him on YOUR roster? Heck no. He's still an equal opportunity hard-contact machine with long-standing HR issues. Okay, NOW you can dismiss him.

Yr	Tm	W	Sv	IP	K	ERA	WHIP	xERA	xWHIP	vL+	vR+	BF/G	BB%	K%	K-BB%	xBB%	SwK	Vel	G	L	F	H%	S%	HR/F	xHR/F	GS	APC	DOM%	DIS%	Sv%	LI	RAR	BPX	R$
17	2 NL *	2	0	90	70	7.11	1.66	6.52	1.38	136	119	9.3	7%	17%	10%	9%	9.5%	93.8	49	19	32	36%	59%	21%	16%	5	33	0%	40%	0	0.44	-30.5	38	-$15
18	2 NL	3	0	88	84	4.11	1.27	4.07	1.26	78	117	10.6	8%	23%	15%	7%	10.6%	93.6	46	17	37	30%	72%	13%	15%	8	40	38%	50%	0	0.65	0.5	117	$0
19	2 NL	12	0	141	146	4.15	1.32	4.63	1.34	121	88	21.4	9%	24%	15%	8%	10.7%	92.6	40	18	41	30%	75%	16%	15%	28	88	11%	29%			6.2	99	$8
20	TEX	1	0	58	36	7.02	1.56	6.13	1.51	112	116	22.2	9%	14%	5%	9%	6.9%	92.2	40	21	39	30%	58%	15%	14%	9	83	0%	67%	0	0.69	-18.3	25	-$19
21	TEX	10	0	180	146	5.15	1.39	4.79	1.32	112	113	24.0	7%	19%	12%	8%	10.6%	92.8	38	23	40	30%	69%	17%	17%	30	93	20%	40%	0	0.76	-19.6	79	-$5
1st Half		4	0	90	73	4.98	1.45	5.03	1.34	94	122	23.2	7%	19%	11%	8%	10.6%	92.8	35	23	42	32%	71%	14%	15%	16	87	0%	44%	0	0.74	-8.0	72	-$5
2nd Half		6	0	90	73	5.32	1.33	4.54	1.31	120	108	25.0	7%	20%	12%	8%	10.6%	92.9	40	22	38	28%	67%	21%	21%	14	99	43%	36%	0	0.77	-11.7	85	$0
Proj		**6**	**0**	**116**	**95**	**4.77**	**1.41**	**4.80**	**1.36**	**113**	**109**	**18.9**	**8%**	**19%**	**11%**	**8%**	**10.3%**	**92.8**	**40**	**21**	**39**	**30%**	**73%**	**17%**	**17%**	**23**						**-4.5**	**77**	**-$4**

Lynch,Daniel

Lynch,Daniel					
Age: 25	Th: L	Role: RP	Health: A	LIMA Plan: D+	
Ht: 6' 6"	Wt: 190	Type:	PT/Exp: F	Rand Var: +1	
			Consist: F	MM: 0101	

4-6, 5.69 ERA in 68 IP at KC. Despite next-to-no high minors experience, made MLB debut in May but lasted just 3 GS. After rest of mediocre 57 IP at AAA, got another try and fared better at first, though skill support was lacking, and minor injuries helped results head south. Third time's a charm? Maybe, but seeing some AAA dominance first would be nice.

Yr	Tm	W	Sv	IP	K	ERA	WHIP	xERA	xWHIP	vL+	vR+	BF/G	BB%	K%	K-BB%	xBB%	SwK	Vel	G	L	F	H%	S%	HR/F	xHR/F	GS	APC	DOM%	DIS%	Sv%	LI	RAR	BPX	R$
17																																		
18																																		
19																																		
20																																		
21	KC *	8	0	125	103	6.09	1.70	6.50	1.40	58	118	20.9	9%	18%	10%	10%	11.6%	93.7	39	24	37	37%	66%	11%	18%	15	84	13%	47%			-28.1	45	-$18
1st Half		4	0	55	44	7.04	1.88	7.45	1.38	120	178	21.6	8%	17%	9%	6%	12.1%	94.9	33	36	30	41%	63%	10%	33%	3	58	0%	33%			-18.9	42	-$18
2nd Half		4	0	72	59	5.16	1.51	5.46	1.41	48	111	20.8	9%	19%	10%	11%	11.5%	93.5	40	22	39	32%	69%	11%	16%	12	90	17%	50%			-8.0	49	-$7
Proj		**7**	**0**	**116**	**94**	**4.63**	**1.40**	**4.79**	**1.41**	**54**	**120**	**19.9**	**9%**	**19%**	**10%**	**11%**	**11.5%**	**93.5**	**40**	**22**	**39**	**30%**	**71%**	**14%**	**14%**	**24**						**-2.5**	**63**	**-$2**

Lynn,Lance

Lynn,Lance					
Age: 35	Th: R	Role: SP	Health: C	LIMA Plan: D+	
Ht: 6' 5"	Wt: 250	Type: Pwr/FB	PT/Exp: A	Rand Var: -4	
			Consist: A	MM: 3305	

A reliable starter to be sure—two IL stints (back, knee) were short—but skills say 2nd half was more accurate representation than 1st. Still, control has been locked in for three years, and K% rates like this don't grow on trees. FB% inching up could pose HR issues, and H%, S% luck won't last, so if others see "ace," bow out. Otherwise, a safe buy.

Yr	Tm	W	Sv	IP	K	ERA	WHIP	xERA	xWHIP	vL+	vR+	BF/G	BB%	K%	K-BB%	xBB%	SwK	Vel	G	L	F	H%	S%	HR/F	xHR/F	GS	APC	DOM%	DIS%	Sv%	LI	RAR	BPX	R$
17	STL	11	0	186	153	3.43	1.23	4.59	1.45	108	81	23.5	10%	20%	10%	11%	9.4%	91.8	44	20	36	25%	78%	14%	12%	33	95	15%	42%			21.3	64	$16
18	2 AL	10	0	157	161	4.77	1.53	4.08	1.39	115	94	22.6	11%	23%	12%	11%	10.7%	93.2	50	23	27	35%	69%	11%	13%	29	95	17%	34%	0	0.79	-12.0	88	-$5
19	TEX	16	0	208	246	3.67	1.22	3.90	1.17	94	88	26.5	7%	28%	21%	8%	12.9%	94.2	40	21	38	34%	73%	10%	12%	33	108	45%	12%			21.4	153	$2
20	TEX	6	0	84	89	3.32	1.06	4.18	1.21	76	103	26.5	7%	26%	19%	7%	11.6%	93.5	36	22	42	26%	76%	14%	11%	13	108	31%	8%			11.7	128	$2
21	CHW	11	0	157	176	2.69	1.07	3.89	1.15	94	71	22.9	7%	28%	21%	8%	12.5%	93.5	38	19	43	28%	81%	10%	10%	28	93	25%	14%			30.4	140	$23
1st Half		8	0	85	99	2.02	1.03	3.88	1.17	83	66	22.9	8%	29%	21%	8%	13.1%	93.6	35	20	45	27%	86%	8%	11%	15	93	27%	20%			23.5	134	$27
2nd Half		3	0	72	77	3.48	1.12	3.90	1.13	96	80	22.9	6%	26%	20%	6%	11.8%	93.3	41	18	41	30%	75%	12%	8%	13	93	23%	8%			7.0	148	$1
Proj		**13**	**0**	**189**	**205**	**3.41**	**1.15**	**3.84**	**1.20**	**94**	**84**	**23.0**	**8%**	**27%**	**20%**	**8%**	**11.9%**	**93.4**	**40**	**20**	**40**	**29%**	**75%**	**12%**	**10%**	**33**						**24.3**	**135**	**$2**

Maeda,Kenta

Maeda,Kenta					
Age: 34	Th: R	Role: RP	Health: F	LIMA Plan: C+	
Ht: 6' 1"	Wt: 185	Type: Pwr	PT/Exp: A	Rand Var: +1	
			Consist: C	MM: 3301	

Injury-ravaged season ended with Tommy John surgery, though use of internal brace could see him return by June. Earlier groin, arm injuries preserve shred of hope 2020 wasn't total outlier, as he got on roll in July, maybe his only healthy month. Still, smart money is to bid to 2019 value, discounted for missed time, and take anything more as a bonus.

Yr	Tm	W	Sv	IP	K	ERA	WHIP	xERA	xWHIP	vL+	vR+	BF/G	BB%	K%	K-BB%	xBB%	SwK	Vel	G	L	F	H%	S%	HR/F	xHR/F	GS	APC	DOM%	DIS%	Sv%	LI	RAR	BPX	R$
17	LA	13	1	134	140	4.22	1.15	3.94	1.18	103	88	19.2	6%	25%	19%	6%	12.9%	91.5	38	22	40	29%	69%	15%	10%	25	75	24%	36%	100	0.73	2.3	148	$1
18	LA	8	2	125	153	3.81	1.26	3.52	1.17	112	85	13.6	8%	29%	21%	6%	14.8%	91.9	40	24	35	34%	72%	11%	12%	20	53	35%	45%	100	1.04	5.3	152	$7
19	LA	10	3	154	169	4.04	1.07	4.01	1.24	99	72	16.9	8%	27%	19%	6%	15.1%	92.1	41	21	38	26%	67%	15%	10%	26	66	27%	19%	100	0.91	8.8	127	$16
20	MIN	6	0	67	80	2.70	0.75	2.80	0.97	73	64	22.5	4%	32%	28%	5%	18.1%	91.4	49	20	31	22%	73%	19%	19%	11	90	36%	0%			14.4	209	$34
21	MIN	6	0	106	113	4.66	1.30	4.02	1.20	107	97	21.6	7%	25%	18%	8%	14.3%	90.5	38	24	37	33%	68%	14%	14%	21	85	24%	24%			-5.1	126	$0
1st Half		3	0	57	54	5.56	1.55	4.56	1.30	113	115	21.4	8%	21%	13%	7%	13.7%	90.7	40	26	34	35%	69%	18%	18%	12	81	8%	42%			-9.0	95	-$9
2nd Half		3	0	50	59	3.62	1.01	3.45	1.07	86	80	21.8	6%	30%	24%	8%	14.9%	90.3	36	22	43	29%	67%	10%	9%	9	89	44%	0%			3.9	162	$7
Proj		**5**	**0**	**73**	**82**	**4.06**	**1.15**	**3.59**	**1.14**	**100**	**86**	**19.1**	**7%**	**28%**	**22%**	**7%**	**15.2%**	**91.1**	**41**	**22**	**37**	**30%**	**69%**	**14%**	**13%**	**14**						**3.5**	**154**	**$3**

Mahle,Tyler

Mahle,Tyler					
Age: 27	Th: R	Role: SP	Health: B	LIMA Plan: C+	
Ht: 6' 3"	Wt: 210	Type: Pwr	PT/Exp: A	Rand Var: 0	
			Consist: A	MM: 2303	

Despite giving back some SwK gains, was still a successful year, as few others can boast 33 starts, 200+ Ks. 2020 FB% spike was confirmed as small-sample fluke. Had sizable fastball spin rate decline after sticky stuff ban, but slider was off more, hurting him vR, yet he still brought ERA in under 4. xERA suggests he can white-knuckle that landing again.

Yr	Tm	W	Sv	IP	K	ERA	WHIP	xERA	xWHIP	vL+	vR+	BF/G	BB%	K%	K-BB%	xBB%	SwK	Vel	G	L	F	H%	S%	HR/F	xHR/F	GS	APC	DOM%	DIS%	Sv%	LI	RAR	BPX	R$
17	CIN *	11	0	164	135	2.88	1.21	3.41	1.29	118	81	23.7	7%	20%	14%		7.3%	92.9	52	15	33	30%	79%	0%	4%	4	92	0%	25%			30.0	111	$17
18	CIN *	9	0	143	127	4.62	1.51	5.53	1.43	135	98	22.1	10%	20%	10%	7%	10.5%	92.4	39	25	36	31%	75%	18%	14%	23	90	9%	39%			-8.3	44	-$5
19	CIN	3	0	130	129	5.14	1.31	4.08	1.23	115	92	22.2	6%	23%	17%	6%	10.0%	93.3	47	22	31	32%	66%	21%	17%	25	88	24%	32%			-10.1	133	-$2
20	CIN	2	0	48	60	3.59	1.15	4.36	1.27	88	92	20.1	10%	30%	19%	8%	14.7%	93.9	29	21	50	27%	73%	10%	12%	9	85	44%	33%	0	0.79	5.1	117	$8
21	CIN	13	0	180	210	3.75	1.23	3.76	1.20	79	111	23.0	9%	28%	19%	8%	12.0%	94.1	42	21	37	31%	74%	14%	14%	33	97	30%	24%			11.4	134	$15
1st Half		7	0	89	112	3.63	1.18	3.50	1.15	73	109	22.0	8%	30%	22%	8%	12.6%	94.4	43	20	36	31%	74%	15%	13%	17	94	29%	18%			7.0	154	$16
2nd Half		6	0	91	98	3.87	1.29	4.03	1.25	77	117	24.1	9%	26%	17%	8%	11.3%	93.8	41	22	37	31%	74%	13%	14%	16	100	31%	31%			4.4	116	$12
Proj		**10**	**0**	**174**	**192**	**3.83**	**1.24**	**3.92**	**1.24**	**92**	**100**	**21.4**	**9%**	**27%**	**19%**	**8%**	**11.9%**	**93.7**	**40**	**22**	**38**	**30%**	**74%**	**14%**	**14%**	**33**						**13.4**	**127**	**$11**

KRIS OLSON

Manaea,Sean

Age: 30	Th: L	Role SP	Health F	LIMA Plan B	
Ht: 6' 5"	Wt: 245	Type	PT/Exp B	Rand Var +1	
			Consist B	MM 3203	

Atypical perfect health may have added tick to fastball, boosted SwK, though seemed gassed in August (9.90 ERA) and off down stretch (4.15 xERA over last 11 GS). Between lack of overpowering stuff, low spin rates, and how much he's around plate, may never be true ace. But there's enough to keep netting sub-4 ERA, decent WHIP, and double-digit value.

Yr Tm	W	Sv	IP	K	ERA	WHIP	xERA	xWHIP	vL+	vR+	BF/G	BB%	K%	K-BB%	xBB%	SwK	Vel	G	L	F	H%	S%	HR/F	xHR/F	GS	APC	DOM%	DIS%	Sv%	LI	RAR	BPX	R$
17 OAK	12	0	159	140	4.37	1.40	4.49	1.35	79	109	23.9	8%	20%	12%	7%	11.7%	91.6	44	21	35	33%	71%	11%	12%	29	93	17%	38%			-0.2	97	$4
18 OAK	12	0	161	108	3.59	1.08	4.24	1.27	86	94	24.2	5%	17%	12%	5%	10.2%	90.5	44	21	35	26%	72%	12%	16%	27	88	26%	41%			11.2	95	$14
19 OAK *	7	0	58	63	2.54	0.84	2.14	1.11	74	64	21.1	6%	30%	24%	7%	12.2%	89.8	41	18	41	22%	80%	11%	12%	5	89	60%	20%			14.0	153	$9
20 OAK	4	0	54	45	4.50	1.20	3.93	1.16	106	94	20.2	4%	20%	17%	6%	10.2%	90.4	50	20	29	32%	66%	14%	13%	11	74	27%	27%			-0.3	143	$6
21 OAK	11	0	179	194	3.91	1.23	3.74	1.12	82	101	23.6	5%	26%	20%	5%	13.2%	92.2	42	22	36	32%	73%	14%	17%	32	93	41%	22%			7.8	153	$12
1st Half	6	0	98	102	3.13	1.24	3.88	1.16	75	97	23.9	6%	25%	19%	6%	13.2%	91.8	40	24	36	33%	78%	10%	12%	17	93	41%	18%			13.6	137	$16
2nd Half	5	0	82	92	4.85	1.21	3.57	1.07	80	110	23.1	5%	27%	22%	5%	13.2%	92.6	44	20	36	33%	65%	18%	22%	15	93	40%	27%			-5.9	173	$7
Proj	**13**	**0**	**174**	**172**	**3.83**	**1.18**	**3.71**	**1.14**	**86**	**98**	**21.9**	**5%**	**25%**	**19%**	**6%**	**11.9%**	**91.5**	**45**	**21**	**34**	**31%**	**73%**	**15%**	**16%**	**32**						**13.4**	**149**	**$14**

Manning,Matt

Age: 24	Th: R	Role SP	Health A	LIMA Plan D+	
Ht: 6' 6"	Wt: 195	Type Con	PT/Exp D	Rand Var +3	
			Consist F	MM 1001	

4-7, 5.80 ERA in 85 IP at DET. Amid wave of young pitching, he's wiped out hardest thus far. While strikeout rates had been fine in rise through minors, he missed few bats in first MLB tour. High average exit velocity confirms he's been no mystery, and xHR/F says it could've been even worse. For now, let him try to sort things out away from your roster.

Yr Tm	W	Sv	IP	K	ERA	WHIP	xERA	xWHIP	vL+	vR+	BF/G	BB%	K%	K-BB%	xBB%	SwK	Vel	G	L	F	H%	S%	HR/F	xHR/F	GS	APC	DOM%	DIS%	Sv%	LI	RAR	BPX	R$
17																																	
18																																	
19 aa	11	0	135	124	3.63	1.15	2.96				22.4	7%	23%	16%							29%	69%									14.6	114	$13
20																																	
21 DET *	5	0	118	86	7.09	1.58	6.36	1.41	105	108	20.9	8%	16%	8%	7%	7.5%	93.7	44	22	34	33%	57%	10%	16%	18	79	6%	50%			-41.3	25	-$20
1st Half	2	0	47	35	9.73	1.70	8.45	1.34	119	125	21.4	7%	16%	10%	8%	5.6%	93.4	40	25	35	34%	45%	16%	15%	3	77	0%	67%			-32.0	-13	-$23
2nd Half	3	0	71	51	5.32	1.51	5.18	1.46	95	108	21.3	9%	16%	7%	7%	7.8%	93.7	46	21	34	32%	65%	9%	16%	15	79	7%	47%			-9.3	45	-$10
Proj	**6**	**0**	**116**	**90**	**5.28**	**1.44**	**4.62**	**1.39**	**114**	**119**	**21.0**	**8%**	**18%**	**10%**	**7%**	**7.8%**	**93.7**	**46**	**21**	**34**	**32%**	**66%**	**15%**	**14%**	**24**						**-11.9**	**74**	**-$7**

Manoah,Alek

Age: 24	Th: R	Role SP	Health B	LIMA Plan B	
Ht: 6' 6"	Wt: 260	Type Pwr/FB	PT/Exp F	Rand Var -1	
			Consist F	MM 3303	

9-2, 3.22 ERA in 112 IP at TOR. Rocketed to majors after only 38 IP in minors. But after early success, workload may have taken toll, as 2nd half skills slipped and he danced around LHB (13% BB%). While some may see "future ace," long-term role might hinge on change-up development. 3.79 MLB xERA suggests he's less of finished product than it appears.

Yr Tm	W	Sv	IP	K	ERA	WHIP	xERA	xWHIP	vL+	vR+	BF/G	BB%	K%	K-BB%	xBB%	SwK	Vel	G	L	F	H%	S%	HR/F	xHR/F	GS	APC	DOM%	DIS%	Sv%	LI	RAR	BPX	R$
17																																	
18																																	
19																																	
20																																	
21 TOR *	12	0	130	150	2.87	0.99	2.37	1.16	98	66	21.5	9%	30%	22%	8%	13.4%	93.4	39	21	41	25%	76%	11%	12%	20	92	50%	20%			22.3	137	$21
1st Half	5	0	55	66	2.03	0.89	2.40	1.08	101	69	20.3	7%	33%	25%	6%	14.2%	93.8	40	13	47	22%	90%	16%	15%	7	89	57%	14%			15.0	148	$16
2nd Half	7	0	75	84	3.48	1.07	3.76	1.23	89	66	23.9	9%	27%	18%	8%	13.0%	93.2	38	24	37	27%	68%	7%	10%	13	94	46%	23%			7.3	118	$19
Proj	**12**	**0**	**152**	**176**	**3.76**	**1.16**	**3.78**	**1.19**	**106**	**72**	**22.4**	**8%**	**29%**	**21%**	**8%**	**13.5%**	**93.4**	**39**	**20**	**41**	**30%**	**70%**	**10%**	**12%**	**27**						**12.9**	**140**	**$14**

Márquez,Germán

Age: 27	Th: R	Role SP	Health B	LIMA Plan B	
Ht: 6' 1"	Wt: 230	Type	PT/Exp A	Rand Var +1	
			Consist A	MM 3205	

"What if he escaped Coors?" poster boy flipped script (3.67 home ERA), and if anyone can thrive in thin air, it's him, given GB tilt. Posted steady value through July, then, like many others, seemed to hit post-COVID-year wall (7.48 ERA, 9.5% SwK in last 9 GS). Yo-yoing above/below 4 ERA may be his fate, but if fork ever takes him off Rocky Road, go an extra buck.

Yr Tm	W	Sv	IP	K	ERA	WHIP	xERA	xWHIP	vL+	vR+	BF/G	BB%	K%	K-BB%	xBB%	SwK	Vel	G	L	F	H%	S%	HR/F	xHR/F	GS	APC	DOM%	DIS%	Sv%	LI	RAR	BPX	R$
17 COL	11	0	162	147	4.39	1.38	4.23	1.29	100	115	24.2	7%	21%	14%	6%	9.6%	95.0	45	22	33	32%	73%	15%	14%	29	92	10%	34%			-0.6	116	$5
18 COL	14	0	196	230	3.77	1.20	3.22	1.14	109	83	24.8	7%	28%	21%	6%	13.0%	95.2	47	23	30	32%	73%	16%	14%	33	95	36%	18%			9.3	166	$16
19 COL	12	0	174	175	4.76	1.20	3.69	1.16	104	93	25.8	5%	24%	19%	6%	13.0%	95.5	49	22	29	31%	65%	20%	19%	28	93	29%	18%			-5.4	154	$9
20 COL	4	0	82	73	3.75	1.26	4.09	1.28	95	87	26.5	7%	21%	14%	6%	12.6%	95.7	51	23	26	31%	71%	9%	13%	13	94	38%	23%			7.1	112	$12
21 COL	12	0	180	176	4.40	1.27	3.76	1.28	103	86	23.6	8%	23%	15%	8%	12.3%	94.8	52	22	26	30%	68%	16%	17%	32	87	25%	31%			-3.0	112	$7
1st Half	7	0	99	94	3.62	1.19	3.74	1.34	86	78	24.0	10%	23%	13%	8%	13.4%	94.8	54	21	25	28%	70%	11%	14%	17	87	35%	29%			7.9	96	$15
2nd Half	5	0	81	82	5.36	1.38	3.79	1.21	112	97	23.2	7%	24%	17%	8%	11.2%	94.7	49	24	28	33%	65%	21%	19%	15	87	13%	33%			-10.8	131	-$2
Proj	**12**	**0**	**189**	**186**	**3.96**	**1.27**	**3.71**	**1.24**	**104**	**90**	**23.8**	**7%**	**24%**	**17%**	**7%**	**12.3%**	**95.1**	**50**	**23**	**28**	**31%**	**73%**	**16%**	**16%**	**32**						**11.5**	**129**	**$11**

Martin,Brett

Age: 27	Th: L	Role RP	Health B	LIMA Plan B+	
Ht: 6' 4"	Wt: 200	Type Con/xGB	PT/Exp D	Rand Var -3	
			Consist F	MM 2010	

Even in unsettled bullpen, couldn't scavenge a single save, and LI shows he's not really viewed as back-ender. On plus side, did show that small-sample wildness in 2020 was aberration, while steady GB% sets decent ERA floor. Mediocrity vR, though, suggests role may never expand significantly. You can easily find more interesting ways to invest draft capital.

Yr Tm	W	Sv	IP	K	ERA	WHIP	xERA	xWHIP	vL+	vR+	BF/G	BB%	K%	K-BB%	xBB%	SwK	Vel	G	L	F	H%	S%	HR/F	xHR/F	GS	APC	DOM%	DIS%	Sv%	LI	RAR	BPX	R$
17																																	
18 aa	2	0	89	79	9.55	2.22	8.79				15.5	7%	18%	10%							48%	55%									-59.3	56	-$35
19 TEX	2	0	62	62	4.76	1.44	3.97	1.25	92	104	5.5	6%	22%	16%	6%	13.7%	93.9	54	23	23	36%	69%	15%	19%	2	20	0%	100%	0	0.65	-2.0	134	-$4
20 TEX	1	0	15	8	1.84	1.16	6.26	1.81	99	74	4.1	15%	13%	-2%	10%	8.1%	94.0	51	5	44	15%	93%	11%	4%	0	15			0	1.04	4.7	-36	-$1
21 TEX	4	0	62	42	3.18	1.30	4.13	1.29	82	99	4.0	5%	16%	11%	5%	11.4%	93.4	57	18	25	32%	78%	10%	11%	0	14			0	0.87	8.4	98	$0
1st Half	2	0	32	26	2.51	1.39	4.32	1.35	64	107	4.3	8%	18%	11%	6%	11.1%	93.4	53	21	26	33%	84%	7%	11%	0	16			0	0.92	7.0	86	-$1
2nd Half	2	0	30	16	3.90	1.20	3.92	1.23	93	93	3.7	2%	13%	11%	4%	11.9%	93.3	62	16	23	30%	70%	13%	11%	0	12			0	0.82	1.4	112	-$5
Proj	**3**	**2**	**65**	**50**	**4.16**	**1.27**	**3.87**	**1.28**	**84**	**95**	**4.7**	**6%**	**19%**	**13%**	**5%**	**12.1%**	**93.5**	**57**	**19**	**24**	**31%**	**69%**	**13%**	**13%**	**0**						**2.4**	**112**	**-$1**

Martin,Christopher

Age: 36	Th: R	Role RP	Health F	LIMA Plan C+	
Ht: 6' 8"	Wt: 225	Type Con	PT/Exp D	Rand Var 0	
			Consist B	MM 3110	

Everyone's favorite preseason saves vulture, but that play went cold due to early injuries. Upon return, most skills recovered, but SwK never did, leaving him exposed to bad H% luck before elbow sent him to IL again. Amid sky full of stars, his closer worthiness now looks like meteor that's burning out, given age, injury history. Seek out a higher power.

Yr Tm	W	Sv	IP	K	ERA	WHIP	xERA	xWHIP	vL+	vR+	BF/G	BB%	K%	K-BB%	xBB%	SwK	Vel	G	L	F	H%	S%	HR/F	xHR/F	GS	APC	DOM%	DIS%	Sv%	LI	RAR	BPX	R$
17 for	0	0	38	32	1.48	0.80	1.51				3.4	5%	23%	18%							21%	89%									13.4	160	$4
18 TEX	1	0	42	37	4.54	1.22	3.77	1.11	108	96	3.8	3%	21%	18%	6%	10.0%	95.2	40	27	32	34%	65%	12%	15%	0	15			0	0.90	-2.0	153	-$3
19 2TM	1	4	56	65	3.40	1.02	2.96	0.97	77	102	3.7	2%	30%	28%	4%	13.2%	95.7	50	20	30	32%	75%	20%	20%	0	15			67	0.95	7.6	213	$4
20 ATL	1	1	18	20	1.00	0.61	3.14	1.02	47	54	3.5	5%	30%	26%	6%	12.1%	94.1	39	24	37	19%	90%	7%	21%	0	15			100	0.98	7.7	177	$7
21 ATL	2	1	43	33	3.95	1.27	3.99	1.17	108	90	3.9	3%	18%	15%	4%	10.1%	94.8	49	20	31	34%	71%	10%	14%	0	14			20	0.94	1.7	128	-$3
1st Half	0	0	19	11	3.86	1.13	4.44	1.32	75	87	3.8	5%	14%	9%	4%	11.1%	94.7	48	19	33	28%	65%	5%	17%	0	14			0	1.06	0.9	77	-$7
2nd Half	2	1	25	22	4.01	1.38	3.67	1.07	117	95	4.0	2%	21%	19%	4%	9.4%	94.9	49	22	29	38%	74%	13%	12%	0	15			25	0.85	0.8	167	-$6
Proj	**2**	**2**	**65**	**58**	**3.71**	**1.17**	**3.64**	**1.11**	**99**	**90**	**3.7**	**3%**	**22%**	**19%**	**5%**	**10.7%**	**95.1**	**47**	**22**	**31**	**32%**	**72%**	**12%**	**15%**	**0**						**6.0**	**156**	**$1**

Martínez,Carlos

Age: 30	Th: R	Role RP	Health F	LIMA Plan C	
Ht: 6' 0"	Wt: 200	Type Pwr/GB	PT/Exp C	Rand Var +5	
			Consist D	MM 2201	

July thumb bruise suffered while batting turned out to be season-ending ligament tear, and season also featured IL stint for ankle. Beyond sustaining GB%, showed little sign of reviving career, as velocity was still down, SwK was still AWOL. Given 2019 success as harder-throwing reliever, it seems clear what to do here. But health will have to cooperate, too.

Yr Tm	W	Sv	IP	K	ERA	WHIP	xERA	xWHIP	vL+	vR+	BF/G	BB%	K%	K-BB%	xBB%	SwK	Vel	G	L	F	H%	S%	HR/F	xHR/F	GS	APC	DOM%	DIS%	Sv%	LI	RAR	BPX	R$
17 STL	12	0	205	217	3.64	1.22	3.63	1.26	104	82	26.8	8%	25%	17%	7%	11.0%	95.6	51	19	30	30%	75%	16%	11%	32	98	41%	19%			18.1	140	$18
18 STL	8	5	119	117	3.11	1.35	4.22	1.44	94	83	15.8	12%	22%	11%	8%	11.4%	93.6	49	19	32	30%	77%	5%	10%	18	60	33%	28%	100	0.97	15.2	74	$9
19 STL	4	24	48	53	3.17	1.18	3.60	1.27	86	73	4.2	9%	27%	18%	7%	13.2%	95.8	56	15	28	31%	73%	6%	13%	0	16			89	1.28	8.0	132	$13
20 STL	0	0	20	17	9.90	2.10	5.84	1.49	126	155	20.8	10%	17%	7%	8%	8.2%	92.9	51	18	30	40%	56%	26%	21%	5	80	0%	60%			-13.4	51	-$20
21 STL	4	0	82	57	6.23	1.37	4.85	1.50	101	98	22.7	10%	16%	6%	8%	8.6%	92.7	50	21	29	28%	53%	11%	21%	16	80	19%	50%			-20.0	37	-$10
1st Half	4	0	79	55	6.38	1.41	4.92	1.50	97	99	23.4	10%	16%	6%	8%	8.7%	92.8	50	21	29	29%	53%	10%	21%	15	82	20%	47%			-20.6	36	-$11
2nd Half	0	0	3	2	2.70	0.60	3.25		52	97	12.0	8%	17%	8%		6.8%	89.4	71	0	29	0%	0%	50%	40%	1	44	0%	100%			0.6	81	-$11
Proj	**6**	**0**	**87**	**81**	**4.27**	**1.30**	**4.13**	**1.38**	**100**	**85**	**10.3**	**10%**	**22%**	**12%**	**8%**	**10.9%**	**94.3**	**52**	**19**	**30**	**30%**	**68%**	**11%**	**15%**	**1**						**2.0**	**89**	**$0**

KRIS OLSON

Maton,Phil

Age: 29	Th: R	Role RP	Health B	LIMA Plan C+
Ht: 6' 2"	Wt: 206	Type Pwr	PT/Exp D	Rand Var +1
			Consist C	MM 2400

Thanks to K% and SwK growth, his 2020 and 1st half 2021 xERA, xWHIP, and BPX marks stand out amid sea of otherwise average-to-slightly-subpar skills. But even as he masters one area of game, problems seem to pop up elsewhere—too many walks here, too many fly balls there. If a team can help him find consistency, save opps could come quickly.

Yr Tm	W	Sv	IP	K	ERA	WHIP	xERA	xWHIP	vL+	vR+	BF/G	BB%	K%	K-BB%	xBB%	SwK	Vel	G	L	F	H%	S%	HR/F	xHR/F	GS	APC	DOM%	DIS%	Sv%	LI	RAR	BPX	R$
17 SD *	4	14	68	71	3.71	1.26	4.20	1.23	121	92	4.0	8%	25%	18%	7%	13.6%	93.0	45	22	32	31%	77%	26%	18%	0	16			100	0.99	5.5	106	$8
18 SD	0	0	47	55	4.37	1.54	4.42	1.34	99	109	4.8	11%	26%	15%	10%	14.7%	91.1	36	23	41	37%	71%	6%	6%	0	19			0	0.85	-1.3	97	-$6
19 2 TM *	2	5	67	70	5.04	1.34	4.61	1.28	104	109	5.3	8%	25%	17%	6%	11.8%	91.0	45	25	31	32%	66%	20%	13%	0	20			83	0.43	-4.4	87	-$1
20 CLE	3	0	22	32	4.57	1.34	2.97	1.02	96	98	4.2	6%	33%	27%	6%	17.9%	93.6	44	26	30	43%	64%	6%	4%	0	16			0	1.11	-0.3	219	$1
21 2 AL	6	0	67	85	4.73	1.44	4.10	1.28	100	106	4.6	11%	29%	18%	7%	16.5%	91.7	39	21	40	36%	68%	9%	12%	1	18	0%	0%	0	0.82	-3.8	117	-$3
1st Half	2	0	32	47	5.29	1.36	3.25	1.15	110	106	4.8	10%	34%	24%	6%	17.5%	91.9	41	24	35	37%	63%	15%	19%	1	20	0%	0%	0	0.72	-4.1	163	-$5
2nd Half	4	0	34	38	4.19	1.51	4.94	1.40	84	110	4.4	11%	24%	13%	8%	15.6%	91.4	38	18	44	35%	72%	5%	7%	0	17			0	0.91	0.3	74	-$4
Proj	3	0	58	71	4.25	1.38	3.87	1.22	100	102	4.5	9%	29%	20%	8%	16.0%	91.5	40	22	38	36%	71%	11%	12%	0						1.5	138	-$2

Matz,Steven

Age: 31	Th: L	Role SP	Health D	LIMA Plan B
Ht: 6' 2"	Wt: 201	Type	PT/Exp B	Rand Var 0
			Consist A	MM 2203

Seems clear now that 2020 disaster was due to shoulder impingement, as GB% disappeared and batters tattooed him. When healthy, mix of control and grounders is enough to make him viable mid-rotation SP. As he heads to free agency, maybe another change of scenery will finally unlock further upside, but skills say modest value is as good as it'll get.

Yr Tm	W	Sv	IP	K	ERA	WHIP	xERA	xWHIP	vL+	vR+	BF/G	BB%	K%	K-BB%	xBB%	SwK	Vel	G	L	F	H%	S%	HR/F	xHR/F	GS	APC	DOM%	DIS%	Sv%	LI	RAR	BPX	R$
17 NYM	2	0	67	48	6.08	1.53	4.73	1.36	101	120	22.9	6%	16%	10%	8%	7.4%	93.1	47	22	31	34%	63%	17%	16%	13	90	8%	38%			-14.1	87	-$8
18 NYM	5	0	154	152	3.97	1.25	3.98	1.31	92	104	21.8	9%	23%	15%	8%	9.7%	93.4	49	15	36	28%	74%	17%	13%	30	90	30%	27%			3.3	110	$5
19 NYM	11	0	160	153	4.21	1.34	4.37	1.31	106	103	21.6	8%	22%	15%	8%	10.1%	93.4	47	20	33	31%	74%	17%	18%	30	84	10%	33%	0	0.80	5.8	110	$7
20 NYM	0	0	31	36	9.68	1.70	4.61	1.21	132	146	15.8	7%	26%	18%	8%	10.7%	94.5	33	28	39	36%	50%	38%	25%	6	70	0%	67%	0	0.67	-19.8	138	-$20
21 TOR	14	0	151	144	3.82	1.33	4.08	1.23	100	97	22.3	7%	22%	16%	7%	9.9%	94.5	45	22	32	33%	75%	12%	14%	29	88	17%	31%			8.2	119	$8
1st Half	7	0	72	78	4.60	1.37	3.78	1.18	92	106	22.5	7%	25%	18%	7%	10.6%	94.9	46	23	31	35%	70%	15%	14%	14	88	29%	43%			-3.0	141	$4
2nd Half	7	0	78	66	3.10	1.30	4.35	1.28	97	92	22.1	7%	20%	13%	7%	9.2%	94.2	45	21	33	32%	80%	10%	13%	15	88	7%	20%			11.2	100	$13
Proj	11	0	160	156	3.99	1.30	4.01	1.24	100	103	21.8	7%	24%	17%	8%	9.9%	94.2	44	22	34	30%	78%	21%	17%	30						9.1	123	$7

Matzek,Tyler

Age: 31	Th: L	Role RP	Health A	LIMA Plan B+
Ht: 6' 3"	Wt: 230	Type Pwr	PT/Exp D	Rand Var -5
			Consist F	MM 2410

With surface stats and skills heading in opposite directions, would be wise to pump the brakes on notion that rising LI might lead to speculative profit. The parts are certainly here to make an assembly line closer—combine 2020's BB%, K% with 2021's 1st half GB%, and voila—but probably best to wait and see if he actually makes it to the showroom floor.

Yr Tm	W	Sv	IP	K	ERA	WHIP	xERA	xWHIP	vL+	vR+	BF/G	BB%	K%	K-BB%	xBB%	SwK	Vel	G	L	F	H%	S%	HR/F	xHR/F	GS	APC	DOM%	DIS%	Sv%	LI	RAR	BPX	R$
17																																	
18																																	
19 a/a	0	0	15	15	12.05	1.99	6.18				8.0	17%	21%	4%							37%	34%									-14.0	56	-$10
20 ATL	4	0	29	43	2.79	1.14	3.08	1.07	71	81	5.8	8%	36%	27%	5%	13.5%	94.4	43	22	35	36%	75%	4%	8%	0	23			0	0.76	5.9	200	$10
21 ATL	0	0	63	77	2.57	1.22	4.03	1.41	92	70	3.8	14%	30%	15%	10%	13.4%	96.1	40	24	36	27%	80%	6%	7%	0	15			0	1.14	13.2	80	$2
1st Half	0	0	31	40	3.23	1.37	3.73	1.43	68	93	4.0	16%	31%	16%	12%	12.9%	95.9	50	21	29	30%	78%	11%	12%	0	16			0	0.98	3.9	89	-$4
2nd Half	0	0	32	37	1.95	1.08	4.27	1.39	102	47	3.7	13%	28%	15%	8%	13.9%	96.2	32	26	42	24%	82%	3%	5%	0	15			0	1.29	9.2	74	$0
Proj	2	1	65	79	3.29	1.27	4.02	1.37	106	71	3.7	13%	30%	17%	9%	13.5%	96.1	39	24	37	30%	74%	5%	8%	0						9.4	95	$1

May,Dustin

Age: 24	Th: R	Role SP	Health F	LIMA Plan C+
Ht: 6' 6"	Wt: 180	Type Pwr/GB	PT/Exp C	Rand Var +5
			Consist C	MM 5400

Mid-May Tommy John surgery means we won't see him 'til mid-season 2022 at earliest, and given only 79 IP last two years, workload will likely be limited. It's a shame, too, because 2021 skills had breakout potential, with massive jump in K% aided by nasty cutter (25.8% SwK) adding final piece to complement elite BB%, GB%. Be patient, keep eye on 2023.

Yr Tm	W	Sv	IP	K	ERA	WHIP	xERA	xWHIP	vL+	vR+	BF/G	BB%	K%	K-BB%	xBB%	SwK	Vel	G	L	F	H%	S%	HR/F	xHR/F	GS	APC	DOM%	DIS%	Sv%	LI	RAR	BPX	R$
17																																	
18 aa	2	0	35	25	3.67	1.10	2.14				22.9	7%	18%	11%							28%	63%									2.1	114	-$1
19 LA *	8	0	143	129	3.76	1.17	3.12	1.22	116	64	16.8	6%	23%	17%	6%	9.2%	96.0	44	28	27	32%	67%	7%	13%	4	40	25%	0%	0	0.94	13.1	136	$10
20 LA	3	0	56	44	2.57	1.09	3.98	1.31	108	69	18.7	7%	20%	13%	6%	9.0%	98.1	55	19	26	24%	87%	21%	20%	10	72	0%	40%	0	0.86	13.0	103	$15
21 LA	1	0	23	35	2.74	0.96	2.13	0.95	79	81	18.6	7%	38%	32%	6%	14.7%	98.0	56	24	20	29%	83%	40%	35%	5	74	20%	0%			4.3	238	-$1
1st Half	1	0	23	35	2.74	0.96	2.13	0.95	75	82	18.6	7%	38%	32%	6%	14.7%	98.0	56	24	20	29%	83%	40%	35%	5	74	20%	0%			4.3	239	$0
2nd Half																																	
Proj	1	0	29	35	3.08	1.06	2.86	1.09	94	71	21.9	7%	31%	24%	6%	13.6%	97.5	53	24	24	29%	76%	19%	25%	5						4.9	181	-$1

May,Trevor

Age: 32	Th: R	Role RP	Health D	LIMA Plan B+
Ht: 6' 5"	Wt: 240	Type Pwr/xFB	PT/Exp C	Rand Var -1
			Consist B	MM 2411

Newfound 1st half control was backed by xBB%, and G/L/F stabilized to briefly put all the skill elements in place. But BB%, FB% fell apart in 2nd half, with xERA showing damage could have been much worse. Those flaws have been enough to keep LI, saves mostly at bay, despite all the Ks. Doesn't mean he'll never close, but does keep status as flyer-only.

Yr Tm	W	Sv	IP	K	ERA	WHIP	xERA	xWHIP	vL+	vR+	BF/G	BB%	K%	K-BB%	xBB%	SwK	Vel	G	L	F	H%	S%	HR/F	xHR/F	GS	APC	DOM%	DIS%	Sv%	LI	RAR	BPX	R$
17																																	
18 MIN *	4	5	52	54	4.92	1.53	5.09	1.39	84	94	6.2	11%	24%	13%	8%	15.6%	94.1	41	22	37	34%	70%	18%	16%	1	19	0%	100%	100	1.05	-5.0	76	-$3
19 MIN	5	2	64	79	2.94	1.07	4.09	1.26	75	80	4.1	10%	30%	20%	9%	13.5%	95.6	34	24	42	25%	79%	12%	14%	0	18			50	0.94	12.4	123	$7
20 MIN	1	2	23	38	3.86	1.16	3.15	0.98	95	89	4.0	7%	40%	32%	10%	19.2%	96.4	25	29	45	35%	77%	22%	20%	0	17			100	1.06	1.7	219	$3
21 NYM	7	4	63	83	3.59	1.26	3.95	1.17	108	84	3.9	9%	31%	22%	7%	16.0%	96.6	36	15	48	32%	78%	13%	14%	0	16			57	0.89	5.2	149	$5
1st Half	2	1	30	40	3.34	1.25	3.34	1.05	111	86	3.9	6%	32%	26%	6%	17.8%	96.3	41	20	39	35%	81%	17%	19%	0	16			33	0.91	3.4	188	$0
2nd Half	5	3	33	43	3.82	1.27	4.53	1.28	95	87	3.9	11%	30%	19%	8%	14.5%	96.8	33	11	57	30%	76%	11%	11%	0	17			75	0.88	1.8	114	$5
Proj	7	5	73	90	3.76	1.28	4.06	1.24	102	87	4.1	10%	30%	20%	8%	15.2%	96.3	35	17	48	31%	76%	13%	14%	0						6.2	130	$5

Mayers,Mike

Age: 30	Th: R	Role RP	Health D	LIMA Plan B+
Ht: 6' 2"	Wt: 220	Type Pwr/FB	PT/Exp C	Rand Var +1
			Consist D	MM 2310

While groovy, shagadelic 2020 performance had many shouting "Yeah, baby!", xERA made it clear declarations to "party on" were a bit premature. Even with slight pullback, elite K%, K-BB% still "Schwing!", but high FB% continues to say "Shyeah, right!" about aspirations for high-leverage role. So don't go bidding "One million dollars!" just yet.

Yr Tm	W	Sv	IP	K	ERA	WHIP	xERA	xWHIP	vL+	vR+	BF/G	BB%	K%	K-BB%	xBB%	SwK	Vel	G	L	F	H%	S%	HR/F	xHR/F	GS	APC	DOM%	DIS%	Sv%	LI	RAR	BPX	R$
17 STL *	5	0	114	77	4.53	1.66	6.09		233	143	15.1	7%	15%	8%		8.9%	94.2	28	22	50	36%	76%	22%	29%	0	34			0	0.12	-2.4	40	-$7
18 STL	2	1	52	49	4.70	1.43	4.17	1.24	99	127	4.5	7%	22%	15%	8%	10.7%	96.1	42	23	35	35%	70%	13%	13%	0	18			100	0.61	-3.5	119	-$4
19 STL *	0	6	39	34	5.31	1.69	6.41	1.52	148	99	4.9	10%	19%	9%	12%	12.0%	94.8	22	32	47	34%	73%	11%	13%	0	22			86	0.52	-3.9	31	-$5
20 LAA	2	2	30	43	2.10	0.90	3.45	1.04	43	90	4.2	7%	36%	28%	9%	15.6%	94.2	33	19	48	28%	80%	6%	10%	0	18			50	1.13	8.7	192	$13
21 LAA	5	2	75	90	3.84	1.29	3.88	1.18	105	98	4.4	8%	29%	20%	8%	13.5%	94.6	37	21	42	33%	76%	14%	16%	2	17	0%	100%	40	0.93	3.9	137	$2
1st Half	2	2	39	55	4.38	1.46	3.79	1.16	108	109	4.4	9%	32%	23%	8%	15.0%	94.8	36	20	44	38%	78%	19%	18%	0	18			40	1.07	-0.6	157	-$2
2nd Half	3	0	36	35	3.25	1.11	3.96	1.21	84	93	4.3	7%	25%	18%	6%	11.6%	94.3	38	21	40	29%	73%	8%	14%	2	16	0%	100%	0	0.76	4.5	117	$2
Proj	3	2	58	65	3.77	1.28	4.04	1.22	91	105	4.5	8%	27%	19%	8%	13.1%	94.8	37	21	42	32%	75%	11%	14%	0						4.9	130	$1

Mayza,Tim

Age: 30	Th: L	Role RP	Health B	LIMA Plan A
Ht: 6' 3"	Wt: 220	Type Pwr/GB	PT/Exp D	Rand Var +1
			Consist C	MM 4311

Return from 2019 Tommy John surgery went well, with velocity stable and strikeouts coming back in 2nd half. BB% appears to have been a bit over his skill level, but as xERA, BPX indicate, with elite GB% in the mix, he's got some under-the-radar upside. 18% K-BB% vs. RHB should help him overcome lefty bias. All in all, a solid speculative option.

Yr Tm	W	Sv	IP	K	ERA	WHIP	xERA	xWHIP	vL+	vR+	BF/G	BB%	K%	K-BB%	xBB%	SwK	Vel	G	L	F	H%	S%	HR/F	xHR/F	GS	APC	DOM%	DIS%	Sv%	LI	RAR	BPX	R$
17 TOR *	3	4	70	75	5.28	1.65	5.86	1.33	67	160	5.3	9%	24%	15%		17.1%	93.9	42	29	29	38%	71%	21%	14%	0	18			57	0.42	-7.9	81	-$5
18 TOR *	8	1	63	68	4.50	1.48	4.56	1.30	79	110	4.7	10%	25%	16%	8%	14.1%	93.9	45	16	39	36%	70%	8%	10%	0	16			25	0.81	-2.7	103	-$1
19 TOR	1	0	51	55	4.91	1.40	4.25	1.44	95	102	3.3	12%	24%	12%	11%	14.4%	94.2	53	21	26	29%	69%	22%	22%	0	14			0	1.04	-2.6	84	-$4
20																																	
21 TOR	5	1	53	57	3.40	0.98	2.87	1.10	62	87	3.4	6%	27%	21%	8%	11.4%	94.1	59	18	23	27%	68%	16%	11%	0	14			25	1.00	5.7	171	$4
1st Half	2	0	26	26	4.50	1.23	3.05	1.15	69	108	3.2	6%	24%	19%	8%	9.3%	94.0	64	15	21	34%	63%	13%	11%	0	13			0	1.06	-0.8	163	-$4
2nd Half	3	1	27	31	2.33	0.74	2.70	1.05	43	70	3.8	6%	30%	25%	8%	13.8%	94.1	52	22	25	20%	76%	19%	11%	0	15			50	0.92	6.4	178	$6
Proj	6	2	73	78	3.63	1.21	3.42	1.22	77	95	3.7	8%	27%	18%	8%	12.8%	94.1	54	19	27	31%	72%	12%	13%	0						7.4	141	$4

BRANDON KRUSE

McClanahan,Shane

Age: 25	Th: L	Role SP	Health A	LIMA Plan B+	
Ht: 6' 1"	Wt: 200	Type Pwr	PT/Exp D	Rand Var +1	
			Consist F	MM 4303	

A strong rookie debut. 2nd half fades in SwK, velocity were understandable given lost 2020 season and new high IP total as a pro. Looking ahead, H% regression should give WHIP a slight boost, and with elite K-BB% already in place, he's primed to maintain this ERA level while taking next step forward in workload. A promising long-term investment.

Yr	Tm	W	Sv	IP	K	ERA	WHIP	xERA	xWHIP	vL+	vR+	BF/G	BB%	K%	K-BB%	xBB%	SwK	Vel	G	L	F	H%	S%	HR/F	xHR/F	GS	APC	DOM%	DIS%	Sv%	LI	RAR	BPX	R$
17																																		
18																																		
19	aa	1	0	19	19	10.87	2.24	9.63				24.2	6%	20%	13%							48%	50%									-15.0	44	-$11
20																																		
21	TAM	10	0	123	141	3.43	1.27	3.49	1.16	98	92	20.7	7%	27%	20%	6%	15.1%	96.5	45	25	30	34%	77%	14%	21%	25	78	16%	16%			12.7	148	$9
1st Half		3	0	56	66	4.18	1.23	3.41	1.16	98	96	19.4	8%	28%	21%	6%	16.9%	97.4	49	21	30	31%	72%	20%	17%	12	75	17%	17%			0.6	153	$2
2nd Half		7	0	67	75	2.81	1.31	3.56	1.15	91	91	21.8	7%	27%	20%	6%	13.6%	95.8	43	28	29	36%	81%	9%	25%	13	81	15%	15%			12.1	146	$7
Proj		12	0	160	182	3.47	1.20	3.41	1.16	91	88	21.3	7%	28%	21%	6%	14.9%	96.4	45	25	29	32%	75%	14%	21%	30						19.4	154	$15

McCullers,Lance

Age: 28	Th: R	Role SP	Health F	LIMA Plan C	
Ht: 6' 1"	Wt: 202	Type Pwr/xGB	PT/Exp B	Rand Var -1	
			Consist A	MM 4303	

That F to your left, combined with forearm strain that ended post-season, casts an uneasy pall of risk over 2022. Skill-wise, his combo of high GB%, steady K% has kept xERA fairly stable, with walks looking like wart that's not going away anytime soon. He can repeat this performance; only question is whether he can repeat the innings.

Yr	Tm	W	Sv	IP	K	ERA	WHIP	xERA	xWHIP	vL+	vR+	BF/G	BB%	K%	K-BB%	xBB%	SwK	Vel	G	L	F	H%	S%	HR/F	xHR/F	GS	APC	DOM%	DIS%	Sv%	LI	RAR	BPX	R$
17	HOU	7	0	119	132	4.25	1.30	3.09	1.22	80	103	23.3	8%	26%	18%	8%	12.3%	94.2	61	19	20	34%	67%	13%	15%	22	92	32%	18%			1.6	165	$5
18	HOU	10	0	128	142	3.86	1.17	3.28	1.26	78	102	21.1	10%	27%	17%	8%	13.9%	94.3	55	18	27	29%	69%	13%	16%	22	84	36%	27%	0	0.91	4.6	135	$9
19																																		
20	HOU	3	0	55	56	3.93	1.16	3.46	1.27	91	102	20.6	9%	25%	16%	10%	11.8%	93.8	60	17	23	28%	68%	15%	25%	11	80	36%	36%			3.6	129	$9
21	HOU	13	0	162	185	3.16	1.22	3.53	1.32	95	76	24.4	11%	27%	16%	10%	11.9%	94.0	56	17	27	29%	76%	12%	14%	28	100	21%	21%			22.1	115	$18
1st Half		6	0	73	81	2.97	1.22	3.83	1.40	86	78	23.5	13%	26%	14%	11%	12.1%	93.6	54	17	29	26%	78%	11%	13%	13	97	23%	31%			11.6	90	$13
2nd Half		7	0	90	104	3.31	1.22	3.30	1.25	96	75	25.2	10%	28%	18%	8%	11.7%	94.3	59	16	25	30%	75%	12%	14%	15	102	20%	13%			10.5	137	$16
Proj		10	0	145	161	3.57	1.21	3.41	1.28	90	88	21.9	10%	27%	17%	9%	12.3%	94.1	57	17	25	29%	72%	13%	17%	27						15.8	129	$12

McGee,Jake

Age: 35	Th: L	Role RP	Health D	LIMA Plan C	
Ht: 6' 4"	Wt: 229	Type Con/FB	PT/Exp C	Rand Var -5	
			Consist F	MM 2120	

Couldn't maintain fluky K%, SwK gains from small-sample 2020, but got closer role and surprise $20 season anyway thanks to low H%, HR/F, and high S%. All those saves and that gap between surface stats and skills is going to cause someone to badly overpay this spring, especially since ERA/WHIP match 2020. What luck giveth, regression taketh away.

Yr	Tm	W	Sv	IP	K	ERA	WHIP	xERA	xWHIP	vL+	vR+	BF/G	BB%	K%	K-BB%	xBB%	SwK	Vel	G	L	F	H%	S%	HR/F	xHR/F	GS	APC	DOM%	DIS%	Sv%	LI	RAR	BPX	R$
17	COL	0	3	57	58	3.61	1.10	3.91	1.22	91	79	3.7	7%	25%	18%	6%	10.1%	94.9	41	19	41	29%	68%	6%	7%	0	15			50	1.09	5.3	138	$2
18	COL	2	1	51	47	6.49	1.46	4.51	1.28	129	118	3.7	7%	21%	14%	7%	10.6%	93.8	40	21	39	33%	58%	16%	15%	0	14			33	0.80	-14.8	104	-$8
19	COL	0	0	41	35	4.35	1.40	5.18	1.32	91	141	4.0	6%	19%	13%	8%	9.1%	93.5	36	19	46	31%	81%	19%	15%	0	14			0	0.59	0.8	94	-$4
20	LA	3	0	20	33	2.66	0.84	2.55	0.81	118	58	3.3	4%	42%	38%	4%	19.6%	95.0	40	17	43	33%	73%	11%	17%	0	14			0	0.76	4.5	277	$8
21	SF	3	31	60	58	2.72	0.91	4.03	1.10	69	79	3.9	4%	24%	20%	4%	10.6%	94.9	36	19	45	25%	77%	9%	12%	0	14			86	1.36	11.4	143	$20
1st Half		3	16	33	38	2.97	0.84	3.79	1.04	48	86	3.7	5%	29%	24%	4%	10.6%	94.8	30	19	51	23%	74%	12%	13%	0	13			89	1.46	5.3	163	$15
2nd Half		0	15	26	20	2.39	0.99	4.35	1.18	93	73	4.0	4%	19%	15%	4%	10.6%	95.1	42	19	39	27%	79%	6%	11%	0	15			83	1.22	6.1	117	$18
Proj		1	15	58	53	3.84	1.15	4.19	1.20	95	96	3.7	6%	23%	17%	5%	10.2%	94.4	38	19	43	29%	72%	13%	13%	0						4.4	123	$6

McHugh,Collin

Age: 35	Th: R	Role RP	Health F	LIMA Plan B	
Ht: 6' 2"	Wt: 191	Type Pwr	PT/Exp D	Rand Var -5	
			Consist C	MM 3310	

This was 2018 all over again, right down to artificially low ERA and matching BPX, R$, suggesting that bullpen/opener role is where he belongs. Return of GB% (best since 2015) was a nice addition, as was career-best 30% K-BB% vs. LHB. Leverage Index doesn't indicate saves are imminent, but skills are strong enough for him to get a shot.

Yr	Tm	W	Sv	IP	K	ERA	WHIP	xERA	xWHIP	vL+	vR+	BF/G	BB%	K%	K-BB%	xBB%	SwK	Vel	G	L	F	H%	S%	HR/F	xHR/F	GS	APC	DOM%	DIS%	Sv%	LI	RAR	BPX	R$
17	HOU *	5	0	79	71	4.07	1.43	4.61	1.32	107	94	19.8	7%	21%	14%	8%	12.6%	90.2	33	22	45	34%	74%	9%	9%	12	90	25%	33%			2.8	94	$0
18	HOU	6	0	72	94	1.99	0.91	3.18	1.06	95	58	4.9	7%	33%	26%	7%	13.8%	92.1	35	22	44	26%	83%	8%	12%	0	21			0	0.87	19.3	176	$12
19	HOU	4	0	75	82	4.70	1.23	4.35	1.32	85	108	9.1	9%	26%	16%	8%	11.9%	90.8	38	25	38	28%	66%	16%	15%	8	37	13%	38%	0	0.55	-1.8	105	$0
20																																		
21	TAM	6	1	64	74	1.55	0.94	3.13	1.02	61	79	6.7	5%	30%	25%	5%	14.4%	90.6	44	20	36	30%	86%	5%	6%	7	26	14%	43%	33	0.90	21.5	180	$12
1st Half		2	0	31	44	2.05	1.04	2.71	0.95	65	85	6.7	6%	37%	31%	5%	15.0%	90.8	43	21	36	36%	81%	4%	7%	3	27	33%	33%	0	0.85	8.4	218	$3
2nd Half		4	1	33	30	1.08	0.84	3.52	1.10	54	74	6.6	4%	24%	20%	5%	13.8%	90.2	45	19	36	25%	92%	6%	6%	4	25	0%	50%	33	0.95	13.1	145	$10
Proj		5	2	65	73	2.90	1.03	3.50	1.12	81	82	6.8	7%	29%	22%	6%	13.5%	90.8	40	21	39	29%	75%	9%	9%	0						12.5	156	$8

McKay,Brendan

Age: 26	Th: L	Role SP	Health F	LIMA Plan C	
Ht: 6' 2"	Wt: 220	Type Pwr	PT/Exp F	Rand Var 0	
			Consist F	MM 2300	

Shoulder problems scuttled all of 2020 and most of 2021, then August elbow injury finished the job. Former first-rounder has a lot to overcome and not much of a recent track record. But looking back to 2019, elite K% was at odds with average SwK, and high FB% had MLB xERA at 4.58. Probably best to wait and see.

Yr	Tm	W	Sv	IP	K	ERA	WHIP	xERA	xWHIP	vL+	vR+	BF/G	BB%	K%	K-BB%	xBB%	SwK	Vel	G	L	F	H%	S%	HR/F	xHR/F	GS	APC	DOM%	DIS%	Sv%	LI	RAR	BPX	R$
17																																		
18																																		
19	TAM *	8	0	124	145	2.88	1.12	3.02	1.16	75	117	17.5	7%	30%	22%	6%	10.9%	93.7	35	22	43	31%	78%	13%	13%	11	68	18%	27%	0	0.78	24.9	145	$15
20																																		
21																																		
1st Half																																		
2nd Half																																		
Proj		3	0	44	48	3.85	1.19	3.86	1.19	73	107	22.3	7%	27%	20%	6%	10.9%	93.7	35	22	43	31%	72%	12%	12%	8						3.2	134	-$1

McKenzie,Triston

Age: 24	Th: R	Role SP	Health B	LIMA Plan C+	
Ht: 6' 5"	Wt: 165	Type Pwr/xFB	PT/Exp D	Rand Var 0	
			Consist A	MM 2303	

5-9, 4.95 ERA in 120 IP at CLE. Uncharacteristic 1st half wildness was quickly tamed, and xBB% says he should be good for at least league average control. But with FB% still stubbornly high, it'll take more Ks to push MLB xERA consistently below 4.00. Slider (20.1% SwK), curve (18.8%) might be potent enough to eventually get him there. For now, baby steps.

Yr	Tm	W	Sv	IP	K	ERA	WHIP	xERA	xWHIP	vL+	vR+	BF/G	BB%	K%	K-BB%	xBB%	SwK	Vel	G	L	F	H%	S%	HR/F	xHR/F	GS	APC	DOM%	DIS%	Sv%	LI	RAR	BPX	R$
17																																		
18	aa	7	0	92	76	3.49	1.13	3.17				22.8	8%	21%	13%							26%	73%									7.5	92	$6
19																																		
20	CLE	2	0	33	42	3.24	0.90	3.45	1.07	100	68	15.9	7%	33%	26%	8%	13.1%	92.8	40	13	47	22%	75%	17%	20%	6	69	17%	33%	0	0.71	5.0	177	$9
21	CLE *	6	0	142	155	4.66	1.22	3.90	1.38	94	89	19.1	12%	27%	15%	8%	13.1%	92.1	30	22	48	24%	68%	15%	14%	24	79	29%	38%	0	0.74	-7.0	77	$2
1st Half		2	0	64	78	5.26	1.53	4.90	1.64	106	90	17.5	18%	28%	10%	12%	13.2%	91.4	23	19	58	25%	71%	15%	15%	10	74	10%	40%	0	0.72	-7.9	63	-$8
2nd Half		4	0	78	77	4.17	0.97	4.02	1.17	80	89	21.9	6%	25%	19%	5%	13.0%	92.7	33	23	44	23%	63%	14%	14%	14	83	43%	36%			0.9	123	$0
Proj		8	0	160	170	4.02	1.09	4.22	1.27	97	84	20.7	9%	27%	18%	8%	13.1%	92.3	32	19	49	24%	70%	14%	16%	30						8.4	107	$13

Means,John

Age: 29	Th: L	Role SP	Health D	LIMA Plan C+	
Ht: 6' 3"	Wt: 230	Type Con/xFB	PT/Exp B	Rand Var -2	
			Consist B	MM 2203	

Mid-season shoulder strain impacted 2nd half skills, but swings in half-season ERA/WHIP were also exaggerated by H%, S%. Biggest takeaway from pre-injury 1st half compared to 2019: this was skill-supported improvement. Not sub-3.00 ERA-level improvement, but he has enough helium that it will be difficult to buy low, and health risk is sizable.

Yr	Tm	W	Sv	IP	K	ERA	WHIP	xERA	xWHIP	vL+	vR+	BF/G	BB%	K%	K-BB%	xBB%	SwK	Vel	G	L	F	H%	S%	HR/F	xHR/F	GS	APC	DOM%	DIS%	Sv%	LI	RAR	BPX	R$
17	aa	9	0	142	107	5.17	1.60	5.87				24.2	6%	17%	11%							37%	70%									-14.3	63	-$7
18	BAL *	7	0	161	106	4.88	1.49	5.53		137	171	24.0	5%	15%	10%		12.1%	90.1	25	42	33	35%	69%	25%	23%	0	66			0	0.52	-14.6	70	-$9
19	BAL	12	0	155	121	3.60	1.14	5.23	1.33	73	100	20.5	6%	19%	13%	8%	10.2%	91.8	31	19	50	27%	75%	10%	10%	27	86	30%	44%	0	0.88	17.3	83	$15
20	BAL	2	0	44	42	4.53	0.98	4.09	1.11	106	93	17.6	4%	24%	20%	6%	12.8%	93.8	44	11	45	23%	68%	22%	16%	10	75	0%	50%			-0.4	157	$5
21	BAL	6	0	147	134	3.62	1.03	4.32	1.14	87	94	22.7	4%	23%	18%	7%	12.4%	92.8	33	20	47	25%	76%	15%	15%	26	90	31%	31%			11.7	127	$13
1st Half		4	0	71	69	2.28	0.83	3.92	1.11	75	77	22.3	5%	26%	21%	6%	14.6%	92.9	30	22	48	20%	89%	15%	16%	12	88	50%	33%			17.4	133	$19
2nd Half		2	0	76	65	4.88	1.22	4.70	1.17	92	109	23.0	4%	20%	16%	8%	10.6%	92.8	35	18	47	29%	68%	15%	14%	14	91	14%	29%			-5.7	121	$15
Proj		8	0	174	160	3.91	1.13	4.24	1.16	93	100	20.5	5%	23%	18%	7%	12.8%	92.8	35	18	47	28%	75%	15%	14%	33						11.7	131	$12

BRANDON KRUSE

Megill,Tylor

Age: 26 | Th: R | Role: SP | Ht: 6' 7" | Wt: 230 | Type: Pwr | Health: A | PT/Exp: F | Consist: F | LIMA Plan: B+ | Rand Var: +1 | MM: 3303

4-6, 4.52 ERA in 90 IP at NYM. Reasons to be cautious: 6.13 ERA, 1.40 WHIP over last 11 GS; severe platoon splits, even down to fly ball tendencies (53% FB%, 3.0 HR/9 vL; 30%, 1.1 vR). Reasons to take a chance anyway: 4.00 MLB xERA, elite K-BB%; late-season swoon mostly due to 64% S%, 24% HR/F. If he figures out lefties, could blossom quickly.

Yr	Tm	W	Sv	IP	K	ERA	WHIP	xERA	xWHIP	vL+	vR+	BF/G	BB%	K%	K-BB%	xBB%	SwK	Vel	G	L	F	H%	S%	HR/F	xHR/F	GS	APC	DOM%	DIS%	Sv%	LI	RAR	BPX	R$
17																																		
18																																		
19																																		
20																																		
21	NYM *	6	0	131	148	4.11	1.23	4.32	1.15	138	77	20.4	7%	28%	21%	7%	12.6%	94.7	42	16	41	31%	73%	19%	18%	18	86	22%	28%			2.5	113	$
1st Half		2	0	50	61	3.52	1.14	3.15	1.12	129	58	20.0	8%	31%	23%	8%	11.3%	94.9	50	13	38	32%	71%	22%	10%	2	89	0%	50%			4.7	148	$
2nd Half		4	0	80	87	4.48	1.28	4.03	1.18	131	81	21.2	7%	26%	19%	7%	12.8%	94.6	42	17	42	31%	73%	18%	19%	16	86	25%	25%			-2.1	138	$
Proj		**8**	**0**	**145**	**164**	**4.24**	**1.22**	**3.70**	**1.16**	**137**	**80**	**20.3**	**7%**	**28%**	**21%**	**7%**	**12.8%**	**94.6**	**42**	**17**	**42**	**31%**	**71%**	**17%**	**17%**	**27**						**3.8**	**151**	**$**

Mejía,Jean Carlos

Age: 25 | Th: R | Role: RP | Ht: 6' 4" | Wt: 240 | Type: | Health: A | PT/Exp: F | Consist: F | LIMA Plan: D+ | Rand Var: +5 | MM: 1100

1-7, 8.25 ERA in 52 IP at CLE. Entire season was torpedoed by subterranean S% and atmospheric HR/F, though extra walks and balls-in-play didn't help either. Still, there are positives: high GB%; xBB% suggests control will improve; MLB xERA was 4.78. That's not enough to justify a flyer this spring, but it's at least worth keeping an eye on his development.

Yr	Tm	W	Sv	IP	K	ERA	WHIP	xERA	xWHIP	vL+	vR+	BF/G	BB%	K%	K-BB%	xBB%	SwK	Vel	G	L	F	H%	S%	HR/F	xHR/F	GS	APC	DOM%	DIS%	Sv%	LI	RAR	BPX	R$
17																																		
18																																		
19																																		
20																																		
21	CLE *	2	0	78	69	7.94	1.62	6.80	1.48	146	93	12.9	11%	20%	8%	9%	9.1%	92.7	48	20	33	30%	55%	25%	21%	11	58	9%	55%	0	0.63	-35.5	11	-$1
1st Half		1	0	37	33	5.21	1.27	4.35	1.35	115	76	13.6	9%	22%	13%	8%	9.4%	93.0	46	23	31	28%	63%	17%	11%	6	53	17%	50%	0	0.66	-4.3	68	-$
2nd Half		1	0	42	36	10.33	1.92	8.96	1.60	159	114	12.4	13%	18%	5%	10%	8.8%	92.4	49	16	34	32%	50%	31%	30%	5	63	0%	60%	0	0.61	-31.2	-33	-$3
Proj		**1**	**0**	**58**	**51**	**5.01**	**1.44**	**4.56**	**1.41**	**120**	**81**	**12.2**	**10%**	**21%**	**11%**	**9%**	**9.0%**	**92.7**	**48**	**19**	**33**	**31%**	**69%**	**17%**	**22%**	**4**						**-4.0**	**74**	**-$**

Melancon,Mark

Age: 37 | Th: R | Role: RP | Ht: 6' 1" | Wt: 215 | Type: /xGB | Health: D | PT/Exp: B | Consist: B | LIMA Plan: D+ | Rand Var: -5 | MM: 3220

In 3 of these 5 years, high strand rate (essentially, his job) helped him outperform xERA, but at 37, with his SwK trend, that hold becomes tenuous. On the other hand, extreme GB% and history of good control have ensured that downside rarely strays past 4.00 ERA mark. Still, likely to be an overpriced talent in an overvalued role, so don't go overboard.

Yr	Tm	W	Sv	IP	K	ERA	WHIP	xERA	xWHIP	vL+	vR+	BF/G	BB%	K%	K-BB%	xBB%	SwK	Vel	G	L	F	H%	S%	HR/F	xHR/F	GS	APC	DOM%	DIS%	Sv%	LI	RAR	BPX	R$
17	SF	1	11	30	29	4.50	1.43	3.59	1.17	95	119	4.1	5%	22%	18%	8%	10.2%	92.2	53	22	26	38%	70%	13%	11%	0	16			69	1.12	-0.5	167	$
18	SF	1	3	39	31	3.23	1.59	4.17	1.37	105	108	4.2	8%	18%	10%	8%	10.4%	91.5	52	26	22	37%	80%	7%	20%	0	16			43	1.24	4.4	82	-$
19	2 NL	5	12	67	68	3.61	1.32	3.25	1.21	89	91	4.3	6%	24%	18%	8%	10.9%	92.2	62	21	17	35%	73%	12%	12%	0	16			100	0.86	7.4	151	$7
20	ATL	2	11	23	14	2.78	1.28	4.31	1.41	104	74	4.1	7%	15%	7%	7%	9.3%	91.7	59	19	22	30%	79%	7%	9%	0	14			85	1.21	4.7	70	$14
21	SD	4	39	65	59	2.23	1.22	3.56	1.34	57	102	4.1	9%	22%	13%	8%	9.2%	92.2	56	25	18	29%	84%	12%	18%	0	16			87	1.30	16.3	96	$22
1st Half		1	25	36	30	2.27	1.21	3.74	1.41	41	115	4.1	10%	21%	10%	8%	9.1%	92.0	58	24	18	25%	87%	22%	17%	0	16			86	1.44	8.8	77	$1
2nd Half		3	14	29	29	2.17	1.24	3.36	1.26	67	91	4.1	8%	24%	16%	6%	9.3%	92.2	54	27	19	33%	81%	0%	19%	0	17			88	1.14	7.5	122	$15
Proj		**4**	**23**	**65**	**60**	**3.20**	**1.34**	**3.63**	**1.29**	**80**	**100**	**4.1**	**8%**	**22%**	**14%**	**8%**	**9.9%**	**92.0**	**56**	**24**	**20**	**33%**	**77%**	**10%**	**17%**	**0**						**10.1**	**117**	**$1**

Merryweather,Julian

Age: 30 | Th: R | Role: RP | Ht: 6' 4" | Wt: 215 | Type: Con | Health: F | PT/Exp: F | Consist: B | LIMA Plan: C | Rand Var: +2 | MM: 1110

Contrary to last name, career has been plagued by unshakeable black cloud: Finally made it back from Tommy John surgery, looked like he might assume closer role, then oblique injury shut him down for 4+ months. Skills were ugly in small sample return, leaving us reduced visibility regarding future. If you take a flyer, do your storm prep first.

Yr	Tm	W	Sv	IP	K	ERA	WHIP	xERA	xWHIP	vL+	vR+	BF/G	BB%	K%	K-BB%	xBB%	SwK	Vel	G	L	F	H%	S%	HR/F	xHR/F	GS	APC	DOM%	DIS%	Sv%	LI	RAR	BPX	R$
17	a/a	7	0	129	92	7.52	1.74	6.80				23.5	7%	16%	9%							37%	57%									-50.2	35	-$2
18																																		
19																																		
20	TOR	0	0	13	15	4.15	1.31	3.70	1.32	43	101	6.9	11%	27%	16%	7%	12.0%	96.7	45	33	21	34%	65%	0%	3%	3	29	0%	33%	0	1.23	0.5	110	-$
21	TOR	0	2	13	12	4.85	1.31	4.47	1.27	165	86	4.2	7%	22%	15%	5%	10.6%	97.5	41	16	43	27%	77%	25%	24%	1	17	0%	100%	100	0.96	-0.9	103	-$
1st Half		0	2	4	7	0.00	0.46	2.11		85		3.5	7%	50%	43%		14.6%	98.2	17	33	50	16%	100%	0%	0%	0	14			100	1.70	2.3	220	-$
2nd Half		0	0	9	5	7.27	1.73	5.94	1.46	178	120	4.6	7%	12%	5%	6%	9.3%	97.2	45	13	42	29%	73%	31%	29%	1	18	0%	100%	0	0.63	-3.2	36	-$1
Proj		**3**	**5**	**58**	**47**	**4.63**	**1.33**	**4.61**	**1.31**			**4.8**	**7%**	**20%**	**13%**				**42**	**18**	**40**	**31%**	**69%**	**12%**	**0%**	**0**						**-1.2**	**94**	**-$**

Meyer,Max

Age: 23 | Th: R | Role: SP | Ht: 6' 0" | Wt: 196 | Type: Pwr | Health: A | PT/Exp: F | Consist: F | LIMA Plan: B | Rand Var: -3 | MM: 2301

Third overall pick from 2020 draft has SP1 upside thanks to fastball that touches 100 mph and slider with sick two-plane movement. Size is a slight concern, and MLEs show that control is still a work-in-progress, but posted 53% GB% at Double-A. If he can maintain that while turning those plus pitches into strikeouts, he'll be dominating in MIA soon enough.

Yr	Tm	W	Sv	IP	K	ERA	WHIP	xERA	xWHIP	vL+	vR+	BF/G	BB%	K%	K-BB%	xBB%	SwK	Vel	G	L	F	H%	S%	HR/F	xHR/F	GS	APC	DOM%	DIS%	Sv%	LI	RAR	BPX	R$
17																																		
18																																		
19																																		
20																																		
21	a/a	6	0	111	113	2.70	1.30	3.65				20.8	9%	25%	16%							32%	82%									21.5	107	$
1st Half		4	0	54	47	2.01	1.29	3.11				20.2	12%	21%	9%							27%	87%									15.0	87	$
2nd Half		2	0	57	66	3.38	1.32	4.21				21.4	6%	28%	22%							37%	77%									6.2	145	$
Proj		**4**	**0**	**87**	**91**	**3.51**	**1.39**	**4.16**	**1.33**			**21.4**	**10%**	**25%**	**15%**				**46**	**20**	**34**	**34%**	**76%**	**8%**	**11%**	**17**						**10.1**	**105**	**$1**

Mikolas,Miles

Age: 33 | Th: R | Role: SP | Ht: 6' 4" | Wt: 230 | Type: Con | Health: F | PT/Exp: C | Consist: A | LIMA Plan: B+ | Rand Var: 0 | MM: 2001

2-3, 4.23 ERA in 45 IP at STL. Flexor tendon injury and subsequent surgery that cost him all of 2020 was followed by spring shoulder issue and May recurrence of forearm pain that was treated with stem cell injection. If that's not enough to scare you off, just look at xERA, BPX trends. That $27 pitcher was both a mirage and a career peak; he's not coming back.

Yr	Tm	W	Sv	IP	K	ERA	WHIP	xERA	xWHIP	vL+	vR+	BF/G	BB%	K%	K-BB%	xBB%	SwK	Vel	G	L	F	H%	S%	HR/F	xHR/F	GS	APC	DOM%	DIS%	Sv%	LI	RAR	BPX	R$
17	for	14	0	188	177	2.79	1.08	3.09				27.1	4%	24%	20%							31%	77%									36.3	196	$27
18	STL	18	0	201	146	2.83	1.07	3.71	1.19	99	70	25.3	4%	18%	14%	5%	10.1%	93.9	49	22	28	29%	76%	9%	13%	32	94	38%	22%			32.8	126	$27
19	STL	9	0	184	144	4.16	1.22	4.18	1.23	103	99	23.9	4%	19%	15%	6%	10.2%	93.6	47	23	30	31%	71%	16%	16%	32	90	19%	44%			7.9	119	$
20																																		
21	STL *	4	0	76	45	4.11	1.28	4.59	1.33	102	90	19.4	5%	14%	9%	5%	7.9%	93.1	49	21	29	29%	72%	15%	18%	9	79	0%	33%			1.5	57	-$
1st Half		1	0	17	11	3.43	1.32	4.71		70	64	17.7	4%	16%	11%		5.1%	90.2	50	17	33	32%	78%	0%	0%	1	59	0%	0%			1.8	86	-$
2nd Half		3	0	59	34	4.35	1.27	4.61	1.35	98	96	20.0	6%	14%	8%	6%	8.2%	93.3	49	22	29	28%	70%	16%	19%	8	81	0%	38%			-0.6	50	-$
Proj		**7**	**0**	**116**	**81**	**4.24**	**1.25**	**4.17**	**1.25**	**108**	**94**	**21.5**	**5%**	**17%**	**13%**	**6%**	**9.2%**	**93.6**	**49**	**22**	**29**	**31%**	**69%**	**13%**	**17%**	**22**						**3.1**	**108**	**$**

Miley,Wade

Age: 35 | Th: L | Role: SP | Ht: 6' 2" | Wt: 220 | Type: Con | Health: F | PT/Exp: B | Consist: B | LIMA Plan: C+ | Rand Var: -2 | MM: 1003

Control improvement was nice, but main driver of best season since 2012 was S%. 2nd half shows how little room for error there is, as it only took small drops in K%, GB% to push xERA, xWHIP to alarming levels. Velocity trend, older pitcher, IL time in each of the last five years... that's a lot of risk for a guy who's a two-category contributor at best.

Yr	Tm	W	Sv	IP	K	ERA	WHIP	xERA	xWHIP	vL+	vR+	BF/G	BB%	K%	K-BB%	xBB%	SwK	Vel	G	L	F	H%	S%	HR/F	xHR/F	GS	APC	DOM%	DIS%	Sv%	LI	RAR	BPX	R$
17	BAL	8	0	157	142	5.61	1.73	4.90	1.57	88	118	22.8	13%	20%	7%	12%	8.4%	91.0	50	23	27	34%	70%	19%	17%	32	95	16%	63%			-24.2	37	-$13
18	MIL *	6	0	107	71	3.33	1.33	4.02	1.37	83	90	19.3	7%	16%	9%	10%	9.4%	90.8	53	24	24	31%	76%	5%	9%	16	81	19%	44%			10.8	73	$
19	HOU	14	0	167	140	3.98	1.34	4.60	1.40	86	100	21.8	8%	19%	11%	10%	9.6%	90.5	50	21	30	30%	75%	15%	11%	33	90	12%	48%			10.8	82	$
20	CIN	0	0	14	12	5.65	1.67	5.05	1.62	34	133	11.2	13%	18%	4%	12%	11.6%	90.2	50	32	18	33%	65%	13%	13%	4	48	0%	75%	0	0.56	-2.1	12	-$
21	CIN	12	0	163	125	3.37	1.33	4.26	1.33	80	102	24.6	7%	18%	11%	8%	10.5%	89.8	49	23	27	31%	78%	13%	16%	28	93	32%	29%			18.0	84	$1
1st Half		6	0	82	69	3.09	1.11	3.79	1.25	54	89	24.1	7%	20%	14%	8%	10.5%	89.7	53	21	25	28%	74%	10%	18%	14	93	36%	14%			11.9	113	$1
2nd Half		6	0	81	56	3.65	1.54	4.75	1.41	97	119	25.2	8%	16%	8%	8%	10.6%	90.0	46	26	29	33%	81%	15%	15%	14	92	29%	43%			6.2	57	$
Proj		**10**	**0**	**160**	**122**	**3.97**	**1.39**	**4.41**	**1.39**	**88**	**105**	**23.1**	**8%**	**18%**	**10%**	**9%**	**9.9%**	**90.3**	**50**	**23**	**27**	**31%**	**74%**	**14%**	**14%**	**29**						**9.5**	**76**	**$**

BRANDON KRUSE

Mills,Alec

Mills,Alec				Health	B	LIMA Plan	C
Age: 30	Th: R	Role	SP	PT/Exp	B	Rand Var	+1
Ht: 6' 4"	Wt: 205	Type	Con/GB	Consist	C	MM	1003

PRO: ERA/WHIP were hurt by H%, S%—skills were almost exactly the same as 2020's career-best season; BB%, GB% have been impressively stable. CON: Lack of K% limits upside; platoon splits are obstacle to sticking at SP; 2020's success aided by H% that kept WHIP artificially low. VERDICT: A little too run-of-the-Mills, even for an end-gamer.

Yr Tm	W	Sv	IP	K	ERA	WHIP	xERA	xWHIP	vL+	vR+	BF/G	BB%	K%	K-BB%	xBB%	SwK	Vel	G	L	F	H%	S%	HR/F	xHR/F	GS	APC	DOM%	DIS%	Sv%	LI	RAR	BPX	R$
17																																	
18 CHC *	5	0	144	107	5.53	1.44	4.52	1.40	73	78	20.5	8%	17%	9%	8%	12.0%	90.6	51	12	37	32%	61%	7%	13%	2	42	50%	50%	0	0.38	-24.5	70	-$11
19 CHC *	7	1	140	115	6.00	1.64	6.49	1.38	127	71	22.3	8%	18%	11%	8%	12.7%	89.7	49	20	32	36%	67%	17%	22%	4	61	25%	0%	100	0.54	-25.7	41	-$12
20 CHC	5	0	62	46	4.48	1.16	4.53	1.36	123	69	22.9	8%	18%	11%	8%	7.7%	90.0	47	20	33	24%	69%	21%	19%	11	86	9%	45%			-0.2	80	$9
21 CHC	6	1	119	87	5.07	1.44	4.40	1.33	132	88	16.2	7%	17%	10%	8%	8.2%	89.0	51	21	28	33%	67%	15%	15%	20	61	5%	50%	100	0.79	-11.8	86	-$7
1st Half	3	1	43	35	4.85	1.45	4.00	1.35	112	96	11.1	8%	19%	11%	9%	7.3%	89.6	58	20	22	34%	67%	14%	14%	5	41	20%	40%	100	0.81	-3.1	91	-$5
2nd Half	3	0	76	52	5.19	1.43	4.61	1.32	132	86	21.9	6%	16%	10%	6%	8.7%	88.7	48	21	31	32%	67%	15%	16%	15	82	0%	53%			-8.7	83	-$8
Proj	7	0	145	109	4.55	1.32	4.34	1.35	126	81	20.7	7%	18%	11%	8%	8.9%	89.4	50	20	29	30%	69%	15%	17%	19						-1.8	86	$0

Minor,Mike

Minor,Mike				Health	C	LIMA Plan	B+
Age: 34	Th: L	Role	SP	PT/Exp	A	Rand Var	+2
Ht: 6' 4"	Wt: 210	Type	/FB	Consist	A	MM	2203

While fluctuations in S% have had him running gamut from near-ace to utterly replaceable, xERA and BPX say he's essentially been same pitcher for last four years. 2020-21 bottoming out should provide nice opportunity to acquire him cheaply, which is key given history of shoulder problems, including impingement syndrome that ended season in Sept.

Yr Tm	W	Sv	IP	K	ERA	WHIP	xERA	xWHIP	vL+	vR+	BF/G	BB%	K%	K-BB%	xBB%	SwK	Vel	G	L	F	H%	S%	HR/F	xHR/F	GS	APC	DOM%	DIS%	Sv%	LI	RAR	BPX	R$
17 KC	6	6	78	88	2.55	1.02	3.58	1.16	56	90	4.7	7%	29%	22%	6%	12.7%	94.4	42	16	41	28%	77%	6%	7%	0	18			67	1.20	17.3	162	$13
18 TEX	12	0	157	132	4.18	1.12	4.39	1.24	109	100	22.9	6%	21%	15%	7%	10.1%	92.8	34	21	45	27%	68%	12%	15%	28	91	14%	43%			-0.7	103	$10
19 TEX	14	0	208	200	3.59	1.24	4.51	1.31	92	94	27.0	8%	23%	15%	7%	11.9%	92.6	40	20	40	29%	77%	13%	13%	32	105	28%	25%			23.6	103	$18
20 2AL	1	0	57	62	5.56	1.24	4.50	1.26	81	101	19.9	8%	26%	18%	7%	12.2%	90.6	36	19	45	29%	59%	16%	15%	11	82	27%	9%	0	0.75	-7.7	119	-$3
21 KC	8	0	159	149	5.05	1.24	4.37	1.21	98	101	23.9	6%	22%	16%	7%	11.1%	91.0	38	20	41	30%	63%	13%	18%	28	94	25%	29%			-15.3	116	$0
1st Half	6	0	96	95	5.33	1.29	4.40	1.24	103	101	24.1	7%	23%	16%	8%	11.1%	90.8	38	20	42	31%	61%	13%	17%	17	95	24%	29%			-12.6	113	$1
2nd Half	2	0	62	54	4.62	1.17	4.33	1.18	75	106	23.6	5%	21%	16%	6%	11.1%	91.2	39	20	41	29%	66%	14%	19%	11	91	27%	27%			-2.7	121	$0
Proj	7	0	145	139	4.65	1.20	4.21	1.23	88	100	22.5	7%	24%	17%	7%	11.4%	91.5	38	20	42	29%	66%	14%	16%	26						-3.4	119	$3

Mize,Casey

Mize,Casey				Health	A	LIMA Plan	B
Age: 25	Th: R	Role	RP	PT/Exp	C	Rand Var	-1
Ht: 6' 3"	Wt: 220	Type	Con	Consist	C	MM	1003

Highly-touted young arm seemingly had breakthrough season, but xERA, xWHIP show there was plenty of good fortune at work. And while BB%, GB% skills featured encouraging gains, unless he's able to find a path to more Ks—and there's no sign of that in SwK—he'll have a hard time keeping ERA below 4.00. More likely to plateau than grow in 2022.

Yr Tm	W	Sv	IP	K	ERA	WHIP	xERA	xWHIP	vL+	vR+	BF/G	BB%	K%	K-BB%	xBB%	SwK	Vel	G	L	F	H%	S%	HR/F	xHR/F	GS	APC	DOM%	DIS%	Sv%	LI	RAR	BPX	R$
17																																	
18																																	
19 aa	6	0	80	63	4.56	1.31	4.14				22.1	6%	19%	13%							33%	66%									-0.5	97	$0
20 DET	0	0	28	26	6.99	1.48	5.20	1.44	145	78	19.0	10%	20%	10%	10%	10.1%	93.7	39	26	35	29%	57%	23%	23%	7	78	0%	71%			-8.9	61	-$12
21 DET	7	0	150	118	3.71	1.14	4.17	1.29	117	80	20.4	7%	19%	13%	8%	9.8%	93.6	48	18	34	26%	74%	16%	22%	30	79	10%	33%			10.3	95	$10
1st Half	5	0	91	75	3.55	1.15	3.92	1.29	107	81	23.3	7%	20%	13%	8%	10.3%	93.9	51	20	29	26%	75%	17%	23%	16	90	19%	25%			8.1	99	$12
2nd Half	2	0	59	43	3.97	1.12	4.55	1.28	116	83	17.1	6%	18%	12%	8%	9.0%	93.2	44	16	40	25%	73%	15%	20%	14	65	0%	43%			2.2	91	$2
Proj	9	0	174	134	4.15	1.24	4.41	1.31	122	86	19.7	7%	19%	12%	8%	9.5%	93.5	47	17	36	29%	71%	14%	21%	35						6.4	93	$6

Montas,Frankie

Montas,Frankie				Health	A	LIMA Plan	C+
Age: 29	Th: R	Role	SP	PT/Exp	A	Rand Var	-1
Ht: 6' 2"	Wt: 255	Type	Pwr	Consist	B	MM	3305

Career year helped put 2020 into perspective (mix of sample size, bad luck, and late-season back tightness), and 2nd half skill improvement suggests he still hasn't peaked. K% increase came from throwing elite splitter (26.7% SwK) more than ever (27.7% usage in 2nd half). If he can maintain consistency over a full season, could be a $25+ pitcher.

Yr Tm	W	Sv	IP	K	ERA	WHIP	xERA	xWHIP	vL+	vR+	BF/G	BB%	K%	K-BB%	xBB%	SwK	Vel	G	L	F	H%	S%	HR/F	xHR/F	GS	APC	DOM%	DIS%	Sv%	LI	RAR	BPX	R$
17 OAK *	1	0	61	65	6.59	1.54	5.92	1.37	168	102	8.4	10%	24%	14%	8%	12.1%	97.7	35	24	41	33%	62%	26%	21%	0	27			0	0.43	-16.9	56	-$9
18 OAK *	9	0	138	92	4.77	1.47	4.76	1.42	121	99	21.2	8%	16%	8%	8%	9.2%	95.8	44	25	31	32%	68%	7%	15%	11	77	27%	36%	0	0.64	-10.5	58	-$5
19 OAK	9	0	96	103	2.63	1.11	3.54	1.16	85	87	24.6	6%	26%	20%	7%	11.7%	96.6	49	22	29	31%	80%	11%	10%	16	93	31%	13%			22.3	155	$13
20 OAK	3	0	53	60	5.60	1.51	4.60	1.32	147	76	21.5	10%	25%	16%	6%	12.1%	95.8	37	26	38	34%	67%	18%	17%	11	83	27%	55%			-7.5	105	-$5
21 OAK	13	0	187	207	3.37	1.18	3.73	1.18	92	89	24.3	7%	27%	19%	6%	14.3%	96.3	43	22	35	31%	75%	11%	17%	32	95	31%	16%			20.7	139	$19
1st Half	7	0	93	95	4.63	1.34	4.28	1.21	92	107	24.1	7%	23%	17%	6%	12.2%	96.2	41	21	38	33%	69%	13%	19%	17	93	18%	24%			-4.2	124	$5
2nd Half	6	0	94	112	2.11	1.02	3.19	1.14	82	70	24.6	8%	31%	22%	7%	16.6%	96.5	45	23	31	28%	82%	9%	15%	15	97	47%	7%			24.9	153	$33
Proj	14	0	181	204	3.48	1.18	3.58	1.17	102	80	24.4	7%	28%	21%	7%	14.3%	96.3	43	23	34	31%	74%	13%	16%	30						21.7	148	$19

Montero,Rafael

Montero,Rafael				Health	F	LIMA Plan	D+
Age: 31	Th: R	Role	RP	PT/Exp	C	Rand Var	+5
Ht: 6' 0"	Wt: 190	Type	Pwr	Consist	B	MM	1100

Awful luck on H%, S% helped turn five relief wins, seven saves into negative fantasy value. Even if you set that aside, declining K%, BPX, and rising xWHIP don't exactly scream great rebound candidate. Neither does 417 days of IL time since 2015. Nor a career 4.66 xERA. MLB managers look at velocity, GB%, and think "closer"; skills say otherwise.

Yr Tm	W	Sv	IP	K	ERA	WHIP	xERA	xWHIP	vL+	vR+	BF/G	BB%	K%	K-BB%	xBB%	SwK	Vel	G	L	F	H%	S%	HR/F	xHR/F	GS	APC	DOM%	DIS%	Sv%	LI	RAR	BPX	R$
17 NYM *	5	0	148	144	4.99	1.64	5.10	1.50	107	116	16.9	12%	22%	10%	9%	10.8%	93.7	48	19	32	35%	71%	11%	9%	18	65	17%	28%	0	0.71	-11.5	74	-$8
18																																	
19 TEX	2	0	29	34	2.48	0.97	3.34	1.04	48	131	5.1	4%	30%	26%	8%	13.1%	95.8	40	22	38	27%	87%	19%	23%	0	21			0	0.88	7.2	181	$1
20 TEX	0	8	18	19	4.08	1.02	4.57	1.25	73	103	4.2	9%	27%	19%	6%	11.1%	95.5	25	20	55	24%	63%	8%	16%	0	17			100	0.77	0.8	107	$7
21 2AL	5	7	49	42	6.39	1.54	4.36	1.33	117	99	5.1	8%	19%	11%	7%	11.1%	95.5	55	16	28	36%	57%	9%	11%	0	20			54	1.03	-12.9	96	-$5
1st Half	5	7	37	32	6.27	1.42	4.09	1.30	108	92	4.7	7%	19%	12%	8%	11.2%	95.5	59	14	27	34%	54%	9%	10%	0	18			54	1.16	-9.2	107	-$1
2nd Half	0	0	12	10	6.75	1.92	5.18	1.41	124	124	7.1	9%	18%	9%	7%	10.8%	95.7	44	23	33	42%	64%	8%	12%	0	29			0	0.44	-3.7	61	-$15
Proj	4	0	44	39	4.51	1.34	4.48	1.39	102	88	6.1	10%	22%	12%	8%	11.0%	94.7	45	20	35	30%	68%	11%	10%	0						-0.3	79	-$3

Montgomery,Jordan

Montgomery,Jordan				Health	F	LIMA Plan	B
Age: 29	Th: L	Role	SP	PT/Exp	C	Rand Var	0
Ht: 6' 6"	Wt: 228	Type	Pwr	Consist	A	MM	2203

After three seasons basically lost to Tommy John surgery, finally clawed way back to where he left off, with one notable exception: career-best SwK. That's the result of change-up (23.3% SwK) and curveball (21.2%) that are better weapons than they were four years ago. Health still a risk, but a repeat of this level is entirely plausible.

Yr Tm	W	Sv	IP	K	ERA	WHIP	xERA	xWHIP	vL+	vR+	BF/G	BB%	K%	K-BB%	xBB%	SwK	Vel	G	L	F	H%	S%	HR/F	xHR/F	GS	APC	DOM%	DIS%	Sv%	LI	RAR	BPX	R$
17 NYY	9	0	155	144	3.88	1.23	4.46	1.31	88	93	22.4	8%	22%	14%	8%	12.4%	92.0	41	18	42	29%	73%	11%	11%	29	87	17%	28%			9.1	107	$10
18 NYY	2	0	27	23	3.62	1.35	4.67	1.44	0	105	19.3	10%	20%	9%	8%	10.4%	90.3	46	16	38	29%	76%	10%	9%	6	76	0%	17%			1.8	62	-$3
19 NYY	0	0	4	5	6.75	1.75	4.05		66	195	9.5	0%	26%	26%		12.2%	91.7	29	36	36	49%	67%	20%	22%	1	41	0%	0%	0	0.75	-1.1	228	-$6
20 NYY	2	0	44	47	5.11	1.30	3.91	1.13	85	106	19.3	5%	24%	20%	6%	13.5%	92.5	43	26	32	35%	64%	17%	15%	10	75	10%	30%			-3.6	163	-$1
21 NYY	6	0	157	162	3.83	1.28	4.06	1.23	83	95	22.0	8%	25%	17%	7%	14.1%	92.5	43	21	36	32%	74%	12%	15%	30	86	23%	30%			8.4	120	$6
1st Half	3	0	86	86	4.17	1.25	4.15	1.23	64	100	22.6	7%	24%	17%	7%	13.2%	92.7	42	20	38	32%	69%	10%	15%	16	85	19%	31%			1.0	119	$4
2nd Half	3	0	71	76	3.42	1.31	3.95	1.24	95	93	21.4	8%	25%	17%	7%	15.1%	92.4	44	22	34	32%	80%	15%	13%	14	86	29%	29%			7.4	120	$6
Proj	7	0	160	163	3.93	1.28	3.98	1.23	86	96	20.7	7%	25%	18%	7%	13.8%	92.4	42	21	36	32%	74%	13%	14%	32						10.4	127	$7

Moore,Matt

Moore,Matt				Health	F	LIMA Plan	D+
Age: 33	Th: L	Role	RP	PT/Exp	C	Rand Var	0
Ht: 6' 3"	Wt: 210	Type	Pwr/FB	Consist	D	MM	0100

2-4, 6.29 ERA in 73 IP at PHI. What worked briefly in Japan in 2020 disappeared for his return stateside, as skills were worse than ever. Reality is, he's had two positive value seasons (2013, 2016), and the rest has been a nightmare of injuries and poor performance. If this was a boxing match, the crowd would be begging the ref to stop the fight.

Yr Tm	W	Sv	IP	K	ERA	WHIP	xERA	xWHIP	vL+	vR+	BF/G	BB%	K%	K-BB%	xBB%	SwK	Vel	G	L	F	H%	S%	HR/F	xHR/F	GS	APC	DOM%	DIS%	Sv%	LI	RAR	BPX	R$
17 SF	6	0	174	148	5.52	1.53	5.19	1.41	139	104	24.7	9%	19%	10%	7%	9.3%	92.0	38	20	42	33%	67%	12%	15%	31	90	16%	42%	0	0.75	-25.1	72	-$9
18 TEX	3	0	102	86	6.79	1.66	5.18	1.40	119	129	12.1	9%	18%	10%	7%	9.9%	92.4	38	21	41	35%	61%	14%	15%	12	46	8%	67%	0	0.68	-33.3	63	-$18
19 DET	0	0	10	9	0.00	0.40	2.79	1.04	0	30	16.5	3%	27%	24%	5%	15.4%	93.0	59	9	32	14%	100%	0%	10%	2	59	50%	0%			5.6	173	-$2
20 for	6	0	85	93	3.29	1.25	3.96				23.1	9%	27%	18%							30%	79%									12.2	102	$21
21 PHI *	2	0	93	80	6.16	1.65	6.55	1.53	106	122	14.4	12%	19%	7%	8%	9.5%	92.5	39	21	41	31%	68%	17%	16%	13	52	8%	69%	0	0.86	-21.8	17	-$16
1st Half	0	0	43	36	5.74	1.77	7.42	1.55	91	137	13.3	12%	18%	6%	7%	8.3%	91.9	39	19	42	32%	75%	16%	21%	4	42	0%	50%	0	0.96	-7.9	-1	-$15
2nd Half	2	0	50	44	6.52	1.55	5.33	1.50	106	119	16.1	12%	20%	8%	9%	10.1%	92.8	39	22	40	30%	61%	17%	14%	9	60	11%	78%	0	0.78	-13.8	36	-$15
Proj	2	0	65	59	5.68	1.55	5.09	1.45	110	117	15.4	11%	21%	10%	8%	9.4%	92.3	38	21	41	32%	68%	16%	16%	10						-9.9	58	-$9

BRANDON KRUSE

Morgan,Elijah

Age: 26	Th: R	Role	SP	Health	A	LIMA Plan	C
Ht: 5' 10"	Wt: 190	Type	/xFB	PT/Exp	D	Rand Var	+1
				Consist	B	MM	0101

5-7, 5.34 ERA in 89 IP at CLE. Not a top prospect, but there's modest value in these skills, especially in 2nd half. Offers potentially elite control on one end of talent spectrum, extreme FB% on the other, and mediocre K% lies somewhere in middle, with clear lack of put-away pitch vs. LHB (17% K%). More likely one for the watchlist than speculative bid.

Yr Tm	W	Sv	IP	K	ERA	WHIP	xERA	xWHIP	vL+	vR+	BF/G	BB%	K%	K-BB%	xBB%	SwK	Vel	G	L	F	H%	S%	HR/F	xHR/F	GS	APC	DOM%	DIS%	Sv%	LI	RAR	BPX	R$
17																																	
18																																	
19 a/a	6	0	107	90	5.28	1.56	5.63				23.4	8%	19%	11%							35%	69%									-10.3	55	-$6
20																																	
21 CLE *	5	0	112	98	5.13	1.29	4.90	1.28	114	106	20.1	7%	21%	14%	6%	11.1%	90.4	29	20	51	30%	65%	15%	18%	18	79	17%	39%			-12.0	68	-$4
1st Half	1	0	39	34	6.85	1.50	6.37	1.31	95	164	18.9	7%	20%	13%	6%	11.2%	90.0	21	24	55	33%	58%	22%	14%	5	72	0%	60%			-12.6	46	-$13
2nd Half	4	0	73	64	4.21	1.18	4.11	1.27	112	89	20.9	7%	22%	15%	6%	11.1%	90.6	32	19	50	27%	70%	12%	19%	13	81	23%	31%			0.5	81	$6
Proj	**4**	**0**	**87**	**75**	**4.95**	**1.31**	**4.86**	**1.32**	**100**	**108**	**20.5**	**7%**	**21%**	**13%**	**6%**	**11.1%**	**90.3**	**33**	**20**	**48**	**30%**	**67%**	**13%**	**17%**	**18**						**-5.4**	**85**	**-$3**

Morton,Charlie

Age: 38	Th: R	Role	SP	Health	C	LIMA Plan	C
Ht: 6' 5"	Wt: 215	Type	Pwr	PT/Exp	A	Rand Var	0
				Consist	B	MM	4403

Normally, if a 38-year-old suffered a fractured tibia that had to be surgically repaired, you'd probably think, "Well, that's the end of him." But this is Charlie Bleepin' Morton we're talking about. He threw 16 pitches on that broken leg. Dude had hip AND Tommy John surgery in 2011-12, and came back to post a 3.26 ERA in 2013. Underestimate him at your peril.

Yr Tm	W	Sv	IP	K	ERA	WHIP	xERA	xWHIP	vL+	vR+	BF/G	BB%	K%	K-BB%	xBB%	SwK	Vel	G	L	F	H%	S%	HR/F	xHR/F	GS	APC	DOM%	DIS%	Sv%	LI	RAR	BPX	R$
17 HOU	14	0	147	163	3.62	1.19	3.44	1.23	74	109	24.7	8%	27%	18%	8%	11.3%	95.0	52	19	29	31%	72%	13%	11%	25	95	40%	16%			13.3	153	$15
18 HOU	15	0	167	201	3.13	1.16	3.26	1.21	95	88	23.2	9%	29%	20%	8%	12.2%	95.7	47	22	30	29%	77%	15%	13%	30	90	27%	17%			21.1	146	$20
19 TAM	16	0	195	240	3.05	1.08	3.26	1.13	90	75	23.9	7%	30%	23%	6%	13.4%	94.4	48	22	30	31%	74%	10%	11%	33	95	48%	15%			34.9	168	$29
20 TAM	2	0	38	42	4.74	1.39	4.07	1.17	109	100	18.9	6%	25%	19%	6%	12.4%	93.3	42	25	34	37%	67%	11%	13%	9	73	0%	33%			-1.3	153	-$2
21 ATL	14	0	186	216	3.34	1.04	3.22	1.15	79	81	22.9	8%	29%	21%	7%	13.0%	95.3	48	23	29	28%	70%	12%	14%	33	91	33%	18%			21.1	152	$26
1st Half	7	0	87	100	3.74	1.13	3.30	1.18	87	79	22.8	8%	28%	20%	7%	13.5%	95.1	48	25	27	30%	69%	14%	15%	16	90	31%	25%			5.6	144	$15
2nd Half	7	0	99	116	3.00	0.97	3.15	1.12	66	88	23.1	7%	30%	22%	7%	12.5%	95.5	48	21	31	27%	72%	11%	13%	17	91	35%	12%			15.5	159	$33
Proj	**12**	**0**	**160**	**186**	**3.66**	**1.13**	**3.31**	**1.15**	**87**	**87**	**21.1**	**8%**	**29%**	**22%**	**7%**	**12.7%**	**94.8**	**47**	**23**	**30**	**31%**	**70%**	**12%**	**13%**	**30**						**15.6**	**158**	**$16**

Musgrove,Joe

Age: 29	Th: R	Role	SP	Health	D	LIMA Plan	C
Ht: 6' 5"	Wt: 235	Type	Pwr	PT/Exp	A	Rand Var	0
				Consist	B	MM	4305

A breakout season, but the league adjusted after a stellar April/May (34% K%, 15.0% SwK, 2.59 xERA), and fatigue set in down the stretch (4.88 ERA, 4.7 BB/9 over last 5 GS). Given that those peak K skills matched 2020, sure looks like that's his upside. With more experience, endurance under his belt, we could see... UP: sub-3.00 ERA, 250 K

Yr Tm	W	Sv	IP	K	ERA	WHIP	xERA	xWHIP	vL+	vR+	BF/G	BB%	K%	K-BB%	xBB%	SwK	Vel	G	L	F	H%	S%	HR/F	xHR/F	GS	APC	DOM%	DIS%	Sv%	LI	RAR	BPX	R$
17 HOU	7	2	109	98	4.77	1.33	4.10	1.25	101	112	12.2	6%	21%	15%	5%	12.4%	92.9	45	21	34	32%	69%	16%	14%	15	46	13%	53%	50	0.89	-5.6	127	$2
18 PIT *	7	0	132	112	4.17	1.16	3.61	1.17	106	86	23.8	5%	21%	17%	4%	12.2%	93.0	46	20	34	31%	66%	10%	11%	19	86	26%	11%			-0.3	133	$5
19 PIT	11	0	170	157	4.44	1.22	4.27	1.23	106	91	22.4	5%	22%	16%	5%	12.2%	92.4	44	20	35	31%	66%	12%	14%	31	83	35%	26%	0	0.80	1.4	126	$9
20 PIT	1	0	40	55	3.86	1.24	3.24	1.16	92	103	20.8	10%	33%	23%	6%	15.0%	92.5	48	20	31	33%	73%	17%	14%	8	84	25%	13%			2.9	172	$3
21 SD	11	0	181	203	3.18	1.08	3.53	1.16	100	76	23.4	7%	27%	20%	6%	13.5%	93.3	44	23	33	28%	76%	14%	16%	31	92	29%	29%	0	0.74	24.4	143	$23
1st Half	5	0	89	106	2.63	0.88	3.14	1.07	85	64	22.1	6%	30%	24%	6%	14.4%	93.2	45	21	35	24%	78%	15%	17%	15	88	40%	13%	0	0.71	18.0	171	$25
2nd Half	6	0	92	97	3.70	1.28	3.92	1.24	105	89	24.7	8%	25%	17%	6%	12.7%	93.4	42	25	33	31%	75%	13%	15%	16	96	19%	44%			6.4	117	$14
Proj	**12**	**0**	**189**	**215**	**3.49**	**1.12**	**3.39**	**1.13**	**99**	**85**	**20.7**	**7%**	**29%**	**22%**	**6%**	**14.1%**	**93.0**	**45**	**22**	**33**	**30%**	**73%**	**15%**	**15%**	**36**						**22.4**	**160**	**$21**

Neris,Héctor

Age: 33	Th: R	Role	RP	Health	A	LIMA Plan	B+
Ht: 6' 2"	Wt: 227	Type	Pwr/FB	PT/Exp	B	Rand Var	+1
				Consist	C	MM	4521

xBB% suggests that control flare-ups of last two seasons may be correctable, which could push ERA, WHIP targets closer to 2019. Whether it's too late to recover from damage those walks did to Sv%, LI remains to be seen, but he's lost and regained managerial trust before. If stock has dropped enough to acquire him in later rounds, he's worth a shot.

Yr Tm	W	Sv	IP	K	ERA	WHIP	xERA	xWHIP	vL+	vR+	BF/G	BB%	K%	K-BB%	xBB%	SwK	Vel	G	L	F	H%	S%	HR/F	xHR/F	GS	APC	DOM%	DIS%	Sv%	LI	RAR	BPX	R$
17 PHI	4	26	75	86	3.01	1.26	4.13	1.23	95	89	4.3	8%	27%	19%	6%	16.6%	94.7	33	23	44	32%	81%	10%	14%	0	17			90	1.10	12.4	136	$16
18 PHI *	3	12	68	100	4.14	1.21	3.90	1.06	122	100	3.8	9%	37%	28%	7%	19.7%	94.6	31	24	45	34%	72%	23%	21%	0	15			75	0.81	0.1	151	$6
19 PHI	3	28	68	89	2.93	1.02	3.35	1.16	78	84	4.0	9%	32%	24%	8%	18.0%	94.6	45	19	36	26%	80%	18%	13%	0	17			82	1.54	13.2	163	$19
20 PHI	2	5	22	27	4.57	1.71	4.61	1.42	99	82	4.3	13%	26%	14%	9%	17.8%	94.0	42	29	29	41%	70%	0%	9%	0	17			63	1.19	-0.3	86	$2
21 PHI	4	12	74	98	3.63	1.17	3.53	1.20	109	77	4.2	10%	32%	21%	7%	16.7%	94.4	47	13	40	28%	76%	17%	14%	0	17			63	1.11	5.8	147	$9
1st Half	1	11	31	37	3.52	1.27	3.88	1.28	124	71	4.1	11%	28%	17%	8%	16.0%	93.7	47	15	37	29%	79%	17%	16%	0	17			65	1.31	2.8	121	$4
2nd Half	3	1	44	61	3.71	1.10	3.31	1.15	88	85	4.3	10%	35%	24%	6%	17.2%	94.9	47	10	43	27%	73%	17%	12%	0	17			50	0.95	3.0	166	$5
Proj	**4**	**11**	**73**	**97**	**3.40**	**1.10**	**3.29**	**1.11**	**100**	**80**	**3.9**	**9%**	**34%**	**25%**	**7%**	**17.6%**	**94.5**	**42**	**17**	**41**	**29%**	**76%**	**17%**	**15%**	**0**						**9.4**	**175**	**$10**

Nola,Aaron

Age: 29	Th: R	Role	SP	Health	B	LIMA Plan	B+
Ht: 6' 2"	Wt: 200	Type	Pwr	PT/Exp	A	Rand Var	+3
				Consist	B	MM	5405

Yes, ERA/WHIP have been frustratingly inconsistent, but he maintained career-best K-BB% from 2020, and sudden shifts in GB%, FB% were very out of character. And just like 2018 was far enough outside skill parameters to leave him overvalued, 2021 has done the same at other end of spectrum. Career 3.45 xERA makes this a terrific buy-low opportunity.

Yr Tm	W	Sv	IP	K	ERA	WHIP	xERA	xWHIP	vL+	vR+	BF/G	BB%	K%	K-BB%	xBB%	SwK	Vel	G	L	F	H%	S%	HR/F	xHR/F	GS	APC	DOM%	DIS%	Sv%	LI	RAR	BPX	R$
17 PHI	12	0	168	184	3.54	1.21	3.50	1.19	98	84	25.7	7%	27%	20%	6%	11.5%	92.0	50	19	31	32%	74%	13%	13%	27	99	44%	15%			17.0	162	$16
18 PHI	17	0	212	224	2.37	0.97	3.17	1.16	76	81	25.2	7%	27%	20%	6%	12.9%	92.4	51	19	30	26%	79%	11%	12%	33	97	52%	15%			46.5	154	$38
19 PHI	12	0	202	229	3.87	1.27	3.79	1.29	96	93	25.1	9%	27%	18%	7%	11.5%	92.9	50	21	30	30%	74%	17%	17%	34	98	32%	26%			15.9	126	$15
20 PHI	5	0	71	96	3.28	1.08	2.97	1.09	92	79	24.1	8%	33%	25%	6%	14.1%	92.4	50	23	28	30%	75%	20%	17%	12	96	42%	8%			10.3	189	$23
21 PHI	9	0	181	223	4.63	1.13	3.48	1.04	93	94	23.4	5%	30%	25%	5%	13.3%	92.7	41	19	41	33%	62%	14%	14%	32	93	34%	22%			-8.2	183	$10
1st Half	5	0	95	118	4.44	1.22	3.46	1.06	107	89	23.6	6%	30%	24%	5%	13.4%	92.4	41	22	37	35%	68%	15%	17%	17	93	29%	18%			-2.0	179	$9
2nd Half	4	0	85	105	4.85	1.03	3.50	1.02	70	106	23.1	5%	30%	25%	6%	13.1%	93.0	40	15	44	30%	55%	12%	11%	15	93	40%	27%			-6.2	186	$12
Proj	**13**	**0**	**181**	**220**	**3.50**	**1.07**	**3.19**	**1.07**	**88**	**88**	**22.8**	**6%**	**31%**	**25%**	**6%**	**13.0%**	**92.6**	**45**	**20**	**35**	**30%**	**73%**	**15%**	**15%**	**31**						**21.4**	**183**	**$22**

Norris,Daniel

Age: 29	Th: L	Role	RP	Health	D	LIMA Plan	D+
Ht: 6' 2"	Wt: 185	Type	Pwr	PT/Exp	C	Rand Var	+5
				Consist	B	MM	1200

Well, so much for theory that he just needed to become full-time RP. Strand rate made things look worse, but regardless, these skills are not going to cut it in a modern pen. If LOOGYs were still a thing, he might be able to carve out a career on the fringes; instead, maybe some team will find way to germinate 2020's seeds and tap into once-promising talent.

Yr Tm	W	Sv	IP	K	ERA	WHIP	xERA	xWHIP	vL+	vR+	BF/G	BB%	K%	K-BB%	xBB%	SwK	Vel	G	L	F	H%	S%	HR/F	xHR/F	GS	APC	DOM%	DIS%	Sv%	LI	RAR	BPX	R$
17 DET	5	0	102	86	5.31	1.61	5.19	1.46	123	110	20.9	10%	19%	9%	11%	9.5%	93.2	39	22	39	35%	68%	10%	14%	18	83	6%	44%	0	0.65	-12.0	59	-$8
18 DET	0	0	44	51	5.68	1.47	4.40	1.29	119	107	18.2	10%	26%	16%	9%	10.8%	90.2	30	29	41	34%	65%	15%	17%	8	74	0%	25%	0	0.72	-8.4	104	-$7
19 DET	3	0	144	125	4.49	1.33	4.59	1.29	106	106	19.1	6%	21%	14%	7%	10.6%	90.8	43	21	36	31%	72%	16%	17%	29	74	14%	38%	0	0.76	0.3	106	$0
20 DET	3	0	28	28	3.25	1.16	3.59	1.18	72	90	8.3	6%	24%	18%	8%	12.0%	92.7	56	18	27	31%	73%	10%	24%	1	35	0%	100%	0	0.85	4.1	154	$5
21 2 TM	2	1	57	58	6.16	1.49	4.37	1.44	89	115	4.4	12%	23%	11%	11%	11.8%	92.8	46	24	30	31%	61%	19%	18%	0	18			25	0.69	-13.3	67	-$9
1st Half	0	0	29	31	6.44	1.64	3.96	1.33	92	131	4.5	10%	24%	14%	10%	12.6%	92.7	46	30	24	37%	61%	20%	24%	0	17			0	0.70	-7.9	96	-$13
2nd Half	2	1	28	27	5.86	1.34	4.83	1.56	74	104	4.4	15%	23%	9%	12%	11.1%	92.8	45	18	37	23%	59%	19%	13%	0	18			50	0.68	-5.4	35	-$8
Proj	**1**	**0**	**44**	**43**	**4.58**	**1.45**	**4.53**	**1.39**	**98**	**109**	**7.0**	**11%**	**23%**	**13%**	**10%**	**11.1%**	**91.9**	**41**	**23**	**35**	**31%**	**73%**	**16%**	**17%**	**0**						**-0.7**	**79**	**-$5**

Ober,Bailey

Age: 26	Th: R	Role	RP	Health	A	LIMA Plan	B+
Ht: 6' 9"	Wt: 260	Type	/xFB	PT/Exp	F	Rand Var	0
				Consist	F	MM	2303

3-3, 4.19 ERA in 92 IP at MIN. Surprise season from guy who was not considered a huge prospect. Control bona fides look legit, turned slider into plus pitch in 2nd half (14.4% SwK), and flashed serious K upside on change-up (23.8%) and curve (25.8%) in four September GS. High FB% holds him back from full sleeper potential, but definitely worth a flyer.

Yr Tm	W	Sv	IP	K	ERA	WHIP	xERA	xWHIP	vL+	vR+	BF/G	BB%	K%	K-BB%	xBB%	SwK	Vel	G	L	F	H%	S%	HR/F	xHR/F	GS	APC	DOM%	DIS%	Sv%	LI	RAR	BPX	R$
17																																	
18																																	
19 aa	3	0	24	28	1.08	0.62	0.59				20.7	2%	34%	31%							22%	89%									10.1	360	$3
20																																	
21 MIN *	4	0	108	113	4.11	1.22	4.66	1.14	116	98	18.3	6%	26%	20%	6%	11.8%	92.4	33	21	46	31%	74%	17%	18%	20	74	10%	35%			2.1	116	$2
1st Half	1	0	41	43	4.96	1.37	5.17	1.20	158	81	17.0	7%	25%	18%	6%	8.2%	92.0	27	27	46	34%	68%	21%	17%	6	71	17%	50%			-3.5	96	-$6
2nd Half	3	0	68	70	3.59	1.14	4.03	1.10	90	107	19.5	5%	26%	21%	6%	13.3%	92.5	35	19	46	30%	78%	15%	19%	14	75	7%	29%			5.6	148	$8
Proj	**8**	**0**	**145**	**151**	**3.98**	**1.18**	**4.08**	**1.15**	**115**	**87**	**18.0**	**6%**	**26%**	**20%**	**6%**	**12.3%**	**92.3**	**32**	**22**	**46**	**30%**	**74%**	**15%**	**18%**	**26**						**8.5**	**139**	**$9**

BRANDON KRUSE

Odorizzi,Jake

Age: 32	Th: R	Role	SP	PT/Exp	B	Rand Var	-1
Ht: 6' 2"	Wt: 190	Type	/xFB	Consist	A	MM	1203
				Health	F	LIMA Plan	B+

Well, that career year a couple seasons back seems like a distant memory. He hasn't fooled many hitters since, as that K-BB% sticks out like a sore thumb now. Burgeoning xERA speaks the truth: as a flyball pitcher with shaky skills coming off an ugly 2nd half, his risk/reward proposition is siding firmly on the former. DN: 5.00 ERA

Yr Tm	W	Sv	IP	K	ERA	WHIP	xERA	xWHIP	vL+	vR+	BF/G	BB%	K%	K-BB%	xBB%	SwK	Vel	G	L	F	H%	S%	HR/F	xHR/F	GS	APC	DOM%	DIS%	Sv%	LI	RAR	BPX	R$
17 TAM	10	0	143	127	4.14	1.24	5.06	1.44	91	105	21.6	10%	21%	11%	10%	11.5%	91.6	31	22	47	24%	76%	16%	12%	28	94	11%	50%			3.8	59	$8
18 MIN	7	0	164	162	4.49	1.34	4.81	1.36	104	101	22.2	10%	23%	13%	10%	10.8%	91.1	28	23	49	30%	69%	9%	12%	32	96	28%	31%			-6.9	72	$0
19 MIN	15	0	159	178	3.51	1.21	4.30	1.25	100	78	21.9	8%	27%	19%	8%	13.1%	92.9	35	21	44	31%	74%	9%	12%	30	93	33%	23%			19.5	123	$17
20 MIN	0	0	14	12	6.59	1.39	4.70	1.23	62	157	15.0	5%	20%	15%	8%	8.8%	93.0	36	24	40	31%	60%	24%	26%	4	71	0%	50%			-3.6	116	-$9
21 HOU	6	0	105	91	4.21	1.25	4.80	1.31	108	93	18.4	8%	21%	13%	8%	10.3%	92.2	35	20	45	28%	71%	12%	15%	23	77	13%	30%	0	0.76	0.7	82	$2
1st Half	3	0	41	40	3.70	0.97	4.13	1.22	94	69	16.2	8%	25%	18%	8%	11.8%	92.5	34	22	44	23%	66%	11%	14%	9	72	11%	22%	0	0.74	2.9	108	$3
2nd Half	3	0	63	51	4.55	1.44	5.26	1.37	110	107	19.9	8%	18%	10%	8%	9.3%	92.0	36	19	45	31%	74%	12%	15%	14	80	14%	36%			-2.2	66	$2
Proj	**8**	**0**	**131**	**123**	**4.60**	**1.34**	**4.71**	**1.32**	**110**	**97**	**22.1**	**9%**	**23%**	**14%**	**8%**	**11.1%**	**92.1**	**33**	**21**	**46**	**31%**	**69%**	**11%**	**13%**	**25**						**-2.4**	**88**	**$1**

Ohtani,Shohei

Age: 27	Th: R	Role	SP	PT/Exp	D	Rand Var	0
Ht: 6' 4"	Wt: 210	Type	Pwr	Consist	F	MM	4403
				Health	C	LIMA Plan	C+

Totally dominant once the calendar turned to July (see DOM/DIS%). Was driven by pinpoint control, and even if his 2nd-half walk rate was favorable given ball/strike mix, command gains were legit. Addition of groundball tilt is the cherry on top. Normally, we'd project further upside with this profile (UP: 180 IP, 220 K), but these are truly uncharted waters.

Yr Tm	W	Sv	IP	K	ERA	WHIP	xERA	xWHIP	vL+	vR+	BF/G	BB%	K%	K-BB%	xBB%	SwK	Vel	G	L	F	H%	S%	HR/F	xHR/F	GS	APC	DOM%	DIS%	Sv%	LI	RAR	BPX	R$
17 for	2	0	16	18	6.17	1.79	5.34				18.8	23%	24%	1%							23%	70%									-3.6	49	-$6
18 LAA	4	0	52	63	3.31	1.16	3.58	1.25	73	95	21.1	10%	30%	19%	9%	15.5%	96.7	39	24	37	28%	76%	13%	12%	10	85	30%	40%			5.4	128	$2
19																																	
20 LAA	0	0	2	3	37.80	6.60	65.84		180	129	8.0	50%	19%	-31%		6.3%	93.8	50	25	25	64%	36%	0%	14%	2	40	0%	50%			-6.9	-957	-$14
21 LAA	9	0	130	156	3.18	1.09	3.45	1.16	101	71	23.2	8%	29%	21%	8%	13.4%	95.7	45	20	36	28%	76%	13%	15%	23	88	35%	13%			17.5	148	$16
1st Half	3	0	60	83	3.60	1.27	3.42	1.32	93	74	21.4	14%	33%	19%	12%	14.5%	95.5	47	23	30	29%	74%	16%	17%	12	81	8%	17%			4.9	118	$5
2nd Half	6	0	70	73	2.82	0.94	3.46	1.03	102	70	25.1	3%	26%	23%	5%	12.4%	95.9	44	17	39	28%	77%	12%	13%	11	96	64%	9%			12.6	174	$13
Proj	**11**	**0**	**145**	**172**	**3.30**	**1.11**	**3.47**	**1.17**	**96**	**78**	**22.0**	**9%**	**30%**	**22%**	**8%**	**13.9%**	**96.0**	**44**	**21**	**36**	**28%**	**75%**	**14%**	**14%**	**26**						**20.7**	**149**	**$17**

Ottavino,Adam

Age: 36	Th: R	Role	RP	PT/Exp	C	Rand Var	-2
Ht: 6' 5"	Wt: 246	Type	Pwr/FB	Consist	A	MM	2410
				Health	B	LIMA Plan	B+

Sometimes it's better to be lucky than good. Highest leverage rate of career netted him save opps... that he absolutely didn't deserve. Yo-yo BPX confirms skills come and go, though last three years xERA had narrower range of mediocrity. Pedestrian whiff rate for a RP explains K-BB% loss. MLB managers won't trust him much longer; you shouldn't either.

Yr Tm	W	Sv	IP	K	ERA	WHIP	xERA	xWHIP	vL+	vR+	BF/G	BB%	K%	K-BB%	xBB%	SwK	Vel	G	L	F	H%	S%	HR/F	xHR/F	GS	APC	DOM%	DIS%	Sv%	LI	RAR	BPX	R$
17 COL	2	0	53	63	5.06	1.63	5.00	1.60	119	98	3.9	16%	26%	10%	12%	9.6%	94.4	37	22	41	31%	72%	14%	12%	0	17			0	0.89	-4.6	34	-$6
18 COL	6	6	78	112	2.43	0.99	2.95	1.17	77	65	4.1	12%	36%	25%	8%	12.7%	93.9	43	19	38	25%	78%	9%	9%	0	17			55	1.21	16.4	163	$14
19 NYY	6	2	66	88	1.90	1.31	4.26	1.41	99	75	3.9	14%	31%	17%	10%	11.4%	93.9	40	19	41	30%	89%	8%	8%	0	16			22	1.13	21.3	94	$8
20 NYY	2	0	18	25	5.89	1.58	3.93	1.27	112	100	3.5	11%	29%	19%	8%	9.7%	93.5	48	20	32	40%	63%	13%	16%	0	14			0	0.66	-3.3	144	-$5
21 BOS	7	11	62	71	4.21	1.45	4.50	1.42	106	94	4.0	13%	26%	13%	9%	10.8%	95.0	40	21	39	33%	72%	8%	9%	0	17			65	1.39	0.4	73	$4
1st Half	2	6	35	40	2.57	1.29	4.00	1.40	108	60	3.9	13%	27%	14%	9%	10.6%	94.7	48	20	33	31%	78%	0%	4%	0	16			67	1.43	7.3	87	$5
2nd Half	5	5	27	31	6.33	1.67	5.13	1.45	95	139	4.1	13%	24%	12%	11%	11.1%	95.3	31	22	47	35%	65%	14%	14%	0	17			63	1.35	-6.9	56	$4
Proj	**6**	**2**	**58**	**72**	**4.10**	**1.38**	**4.24**	**1.40**	**99**	**92**	**3.8**	**14%**	**30%**	**16%**	**10%**	**11.2%**	**94.5**	**39**	**20**	**41**	**31%**	**72%**	**10%**	**9%**	**0**						**2.6**	**90**	**$1**

Otto Jr.,Glenn

Age: 26	Th: R	Role	SP	PT/Exp	F	Rand Var	+5
Ht: 6' 5"	Wt: 240	Type	Pwr	Consist	F	MM	3201
				Health	C	LIMA Plan	B

0-3, 9.26 ERA in 23 IP at TEX. Late-blooming SP prospect quietly showed elite command in minors after adding slider to his repertoire. While results didn't follow suit after call-up, he did put up triple-digit skills over six starts. That makes him worthy of a dart throw in deep leagues, as long as you acknowledge his long pre-2021 injury history.

Yr Tm	W	Sv	IP	K	ERA	WHIP	xERA	xWHIP	vL+	vR+	BF/G	BB%	K%	K-BB%	xBB%	SwK	Vel	G	L	F	H%	S%	HR/F	xHR/F	GS	APC	DOM%	DIS%	Sv%	LI	RAR	BPX	R$
17																																	
18																																	
19																																	
20																																	
21 TEX *	9	0	121	137	4.87	1.25	3.67	1.13	158	100	21.3	7%	28%	21%	5%	9.6%	92.7	44	29	26	35%	60%	11%	22%	6	75	17%	33%			-8.9	146	$2
1st Half																																	
2nd Half	9	0	121	137	4.87	1.25	3.67	1.13	158	100	21.3	6%	49%	43%	5%	9.6%	92.7	44	29	26	35%	60%	11%	22%	6	75	17%	33%			-8.9	146	$2
Proj	**7**	**0**	**102**	**104**	**3.99**	**1.18**	**3.55**	**1.24**	**121**	**82**	**41.2**	**8%**	**26%**	**17%**	**5%**	**9.6%**	**92.7**	**44**	**29**	**26**	**30%**	**68%**	**15%**	**20%**	**10**						**5.8**	**122**	**$5**

Oviedo,Johan

Age: 24	Th: R	Role	SP	PT/Exp	D	Rand Var	0
Ht: 6' 5"	Wt: 245	Type	Pwr	Consist	A	MM	0100
				Health	A	LIMA Plan	D+

0-5, 4.91 ERA in 62 IP at STL. Transition from Cuba continues to be stuck somewhere in the Gulf of Mexico. Even after adding change-up as third strikeout pitch, a ball rate of nearly 40% just doesn't allow for the command you need from a starter. Ugly DOM/DIS%, 5-ish xERA confirm he's neither a growth stock nor a value play.

Yr Tm	W	Sv	IP	K	ERA	WHIP	xERA	xWHIP	vL+	vR+	BF/G	BB%	K%	K-BB%	xBB%	SwK	Vel	G	L	F	H%	S%	HR/F	xHR/F	GS	APC	DOM%	DIS%	Sv%	LI	RAR	BPX	R$
17																																	
18																																	
19 aa	7	0	113	109	6.73	1.74	5.53				22.4	12%	21%	9%							38%	60%									-30.9	69	-$14
20 STL	0	0	25	16	5.47	1.38	5.53	1.51	89	124	22.4	9%	14%	5%	10%	9.2%	94.9	40	27	33	28%	61%	11%	19%	5	89	0%	40%			-3.1	28	-$8
21 STL *	1	0	117	100	5.32	1.53	4.90	1.52	115	94	19.7	12%	20%	7%	10%	11.4%	94.9	48	22	30	31%	66%	14%	19%	13	78	15%	54%	0	0.81	-15.3	56	-$13
1st Half	0	0	57	42	5.63	1.54	5.29	1.54	111	97	19.1	11%	17%	6%	9%	11.4%	95.1	46	22	31	31%	65%	14%	14%	10	76	10%	60%	0	0.79	-9.6	38	-$14
2nd Half	1	0	60	58	5.03	1.52	4.54	1.52	104	92	20.2	13%	22%	9%	12%	11.5%	94.4	57	20	23	31%	68%	13%	52%	3	84	33%	33%			-5.7	72	-$13
Proj	**1**	**0**	**51**	**45**	**5.66**	**1.58**	**4.84**	**1.53**	**126**	**101**	**20.4**	**12%**	**20%**	**8%**	**9%**	**11.4%**	**95.1**	**46**	**22**	**31**	**33%**	**65%**	**13%**	**13%**	**11**						**-7.5**	**42**	**-$9**

Paddack,Chris

Age: 26	Th: R	Role	SP	PT/Exp	B	Rand Var	+3
Ht: 6' 5"	Wt: 217	Type	Con	Consist	A	MM	2103
				Health	D	LIMA Plan	C+

Oblique, elbow injuries torpedoed 2nd half after he had a better start to the season than it appeared. Before ailments, added curveball diversified arsenal and fueled highest swinging strike rate of career. Those gains were hidden by low strand rate. Monitor closely in the spring; if healthy, a $5 bid could net $10 of profit. UP: 200 K

Yr Tm	W	Sv	IP	K	ERA	WHIP	xERA	xWHIP	vL+	vR+	BF/G	BB%	K%	K-BB%	xBB%	SwK	Vel	G	L	F	H%	S%	HR/F	xHR/F	GS	APC	DOM%	DIS%	Sv%	LI	RAR	BPX	R$
17																																	
18 aa	3	0	39	33	2.16	0.76	1.09				20.1	3%	23%	21%							24%	71%									9.6	263	$4
19 SD	9	0	141	153	3.33	0.98	3.94	1.14	88	81	21.8	5%	27%	22%	4%	12.3%	93.9	40	18	42	26%	75%	15%	13%	26	88	42%	19%			20.4	153	$18
20 SD	4	0	59	58	4.73	1.22	3.87	1.15	117	105	20.4	5%	24%	19%	7%	11.7%	94.2	47	20	33	30%	71%	25%	22%	12	80	8%	17%			-2.0	152	$6
21 SD	7	0	108	99	5.07	1.26	4.12	1.17	83	120	20.0	5%	22%	17%	6%	11.7%	94.9	43	22	35	33%	62%	13%	18%	22	81	14%	36%	0	0.79	-10.7	131	-$2
1st Half	4	0	73	75	4.56	1.23	3.84	1.15	83	114	20.5	6%	25%	19%	7%	13.2%	95.0	43	22	34	32%	66%	14%	17%	15	84	13%	33%			-2.7	144	$3
2nd Half	3	0	35	24	6.11	1.33	4.70	1.22	68	131	19.0	3%	16%	13%	6%	8.8%	94.9	42	21	37	33%	55%	11%	19%	7	77	14%	43%	0	0.80	-8.1	105	$0
Proj	**11**	**0**	**160**	**145**	**4.56**	**1.16**	**3.90**	**1.16**	**85**	**109**	**22.2**	**5%**	**23%**	**18%**	**6%**	**11.1%**	**94.6**	**43**	**20**	**37**	**30%**	**65%**	**14%**	**18%**	**29**						**-2.2**	**140**	**$8**

Pagan,Emilio

Age: 31	Th: R	Role	RP	PT/Exp	C	Rand Var	0
Ht: 6' 2"	Wt: 208	Type	Pwr/xFB	Consist	B	MM	1300
				Health	A	LIMA Plan	C+

Epitome of the risk of an extreme flyball reliever. The barrel rate against him has surged for two straight seasons, and his most recent mark was in the bottom first percentile. That blowup risk won't make him trusted again as a late-game option; decreasing leverage confirms it. Consecutive xERAs pushing 5.00 should prevent you from trusting him, too.

Yr Tm	W	Sv	IP	K	ERA	WHIP	xERA	xWHIP	vL+	vR+	BF/G	BB%	K%	K-BB%	xBB%	SwK	Vel	G	L	F	H%	S%	HR/F	xHR/F	GS	APC	DOM%	DIS%	Sv%	LI	RAR	BPX	R$
17 SEA *	4	5	82	86	3.18	0.95	2.28	1.12	109	68	5.4	5%	28%	23%	5%	14.4%	93.6	22	21	57	27%	69%	9%	7%	0	21			83	1.09	11.9	188	$11
18 OAK	3	0	62	63	4.35	1.19	4.63	1.23	141	88	4.8	7%	24%	17%	7%	14.5%	93.8	27	18	55	27%	72%	14%	14%	0	19			0	0.56	-1.6	110	-$1
19 TAM	4	20	70	96	2.31	0.83	3.20	0.97	94	70	4.0	5%	36%	31%	4%	18.5%	95.5	34	19	47	25%	87%	16%	9%	0	16			71	1.47	18.9	206	$20
20 SD	0	2	22	23	4.50	1.05	4.70	1.33	98	76	4.0	10%	26%	16%	8%	12.3%	94.5	29	18	53	20%	63%	14%	16%	0	17			29	1.02	-0.1	87	$0
21 SD	4	0	63	69	4.83	1.17	4.74	1.18	107	109	3.9	7%	26%	19%	7%	14.6%	95.0	22	17	61	27%	69%	15%	18%	0	16			0	0.89	-4.4	118	-$1
1st Half	4	0	33	41	3.51	1.08	4.10	1.12	74	108	3.8	7%	30%	23%	6%	15.4%	94.9	26	19	55	28%	74%	11%	18%	0	16			0	0.86	3.1	143	$3
2nd Half	0	0	30	28	6.30	1.27	5.46	1.24	143	112	4.1	6%	22%	16%	7%	13.7%	95.1	19	14	67	25%	63%	18%	18%	0	16			0	0.93	-7.5	91	$0
Proj	**3**	**0**	**58**	**64**	**4.55**	**1.15**	**4.29**	**1.15**	**120**	**95**	**4.1**	**7%**	**28%**	**21%**	**6%**	**15.2%**	**94.7**	**25**	**18**	**57**	**28%**	**70%**	**15%**	**14%**	**0**						**-0.7**	**137**	**-$1**

STEPHEN NICKRAND

Patiño,Luis

Age: 22	Th: R	Role	RP	Health	A	LIMA Plan	B
Ht: 6' 0"	Wt: 192	Type	Pwr/xFB	PT/Exp	D	Rand Var	0
				Consist	F	MM	1303

5-3, 4.31 ERA in 77 IP at TAM. Top SP prospect was handled with kid gloves, going no more than 6 innings in any start. Flashed some filthy stuff with two pitches, highlighting both his upside and need for more development. For now, you'll have to put up with some volatility, especially given the high launch angle he allows. For 2022... UP: 3.75 ERA, 180 K

Yr Tm	W	Sv	IP	K	ERA	WHIP	xERA	xWHIP	vL+	vR+	BF/G	BB%	K%	K-BB%	xBB%	SwK	Vel	G	L	F	H%	S%	HR/F	xHR/F	GS	APC	DOM%	DIS%	Sv%	LI	RAR	BPX	R$
17																																	
18																																	
19																																	
20 SD	1	0	17	21	5.19	1.85	6.12	1.64	84	124	7.7	16%	25%	8%	11%	10.9%	96.8	35	16	49	35%	76%	13%	12%	1	32	0%	100%	0	0.64	-1.6	15	-$8
21 TAM *	8	0	107	111	4.12	1.26	3.99	1.28	115	79	16.9	9%	25%	16%	8%	12.2%	95.7	31	20	49	30%	71%	11%	14%	15	72	7%	40%	0	0.75	2.0	94	$4
1st Half	4	0	41	50	3.71	1.11	3.25	1.06	121	79	14.8	6%	31%	25%	8%	12.0%	95.1	32	20	48	32%	69%	11%	9%	4	64	0%	0%	0	0.82	2.8	166	$4
2nd Half	4	0	66	61	4.37	1.35	4.45	1.42	106	81	18.4	11%	22%	11%	7%	12.2%	95.9	30	20	49	28%	72%	11%	15%	11	76	9%	55%	0	0.72	-0.9	63	$0
Proj	10	0	131	135	4.09	1.25	4.51	1.29	112	76	16.8	9%	25%	16%	8%	12.1%	95.6	31	20	49	30%	71%	10%	13%	22						5.8	99	$7

Patton,Spencer

Age: 34	Th: R	Role	RP	Health	A	LIMA Plan	C
Ht: 6' 1"	Wt: 200	Type	Pwr	PT/Exp	C	Rand Var	-1
				Consist	C	MM	1310

Career minor leaguer went to Japan, then got first sniff of majors since 2016. It went pretty well, especially early on. His bugaboo throughout career has been shoddy control, and that wart reared its head as the season went along. Given his age, we can't expect big changes there, which gives him an underwhelming profile.

Yr Tm	W	Sv	IP	K	ERA	WHIP	xERA	xWHIP	vL+	vR+	BF/G	BB%	K%	K-BB%	xBB%	SwK	Vel	G	L	F	H%	S%	HR/F	xHR/F	GS	APC	DOM%	DIS%	Sv%	LI	RAR	BPX	R$
17 for	4	7	60	63	3.35	1.29	3.73				4.0	10%	26%	16%							31%	78%									7.4	107	$5
18 for	5	0	56	64	3.19	1.37	4.16				4.0	9%	27%	19%							35%	79%									6.6	123	$1
19 for	0	0	37	43	6.34	1.84	6.36				4.1	16%	25%	9%							36%	68%									-8.4	50	-$9
20 for	3	0	53	62	6.12	1.69	6.07				4.2	14%	26%	12%							34%	67%									-10.9	58	-$11
21 TEX	2	2	42	48	3.83	1.20	3.82	1.21	113	69	4.1	9%	28%	19%	8%	11.8%	93.4	41	20	39	31%	70%	10%	10%	0	17			40	0.77	2.3	128	-$1
1st Half	0	0	10	11	0.93	0.93	3.26	0.96	145	12	3.1	3%	30%	27%	6%	9.9%	93.5	36	24	40	33%	89%	0%	4%	0	13			0	0.71	4.0	190	-$5
2nd Half	2	2	33	37	4.68	1.29	3.99	1.29	97	89	4.5	10%	27%	17%	8%	12.3%	93.4	43	19	38	30%	66%	13%	12%	0	18			50	0.80	-1.7	110	-$3
Proj	3	2	58	66	4.87	1.62	4.43	1.39	135	119	4.3	12%	26%	14%	8%	12.3%	93.4	43	19	38	36%	73%	15%	11%	0						-2.9	92	-$5

Paxton,James

Age: 33	Th: L	Role	SP	Health	F	LIMA Plan	C+
Ht: 6' 4"	Wt: 227	Type	Pwr	PT/Exp	C	Rand Var	+5
				Consist	F	MM	3400

Underwent Tommy John surgery in late April and a late 2022 return might be best case scenario given his body's brittle nature. Consistently elite pre-injury skills put him in a good position to reclaim SP2 rosterability once healthy. If you're playing for 2023 already, there's injury profit here. Just don't forget that even when healthy, 160 IP is his ceiling.

Yr Tm	W	Sv	IP	K	ERA	WHIP	xERA	xWHIP	vL+	vR+	BF/G	BB%	K%	K-BB%	xBB%	SwK	Vel	G	L	F	H%	S%	HR/F	xHR/F	GS	APC	DOM%	DIS%	Sv%	LI	RAR	BPX	R$
17 SEA	12	0	136	156	2.98	1.10	3.38	1.15	61	85	23.0	7%	28%	22%	7%	12.8%	95.4	45	22	33	31%	74%	8%	6%	24	95	54%	21%			23.2	171	$19
18 SEA	11	0	160	208	3.76	1.10	3.22	1.05	119	86	23.0	7%	32%	26%	5%	14.8%	95.4	40	19	41	31%	71%	14%	15%	28	93	32%	18%			7.7	189	$16
19 NYY	15	0	151	186	3.82	1.28	4.08	1.22	88	101	21.8	9%	29%	21%	8%	14.7%	95.5	38	19	43	32%	76%	14%	13%	29	92	34%	31%			12.7	139	$14
20 NYY	1	0	20	26	6.64	1.48	4.46	1.18	116	118	18.0	8%	29%	21%	6%	14.3%	92.1	32	18	50	38%	58%	14%	16%	5	71	20%	60%			-5.5	151	-$7
21 SEA	0	0	1	2	6.75	0.75	0.00			33	5.0	20%	40%	20%		12.5%	94.1	50	50	0	0%	0%	0%		1	24	0%	0%			-0.4	97	-$6
1st Half	0	0	1	2	6.75	0.75	0.00			34	5.0	20%	40%	20%		12.5%	94.1	50	50	0	0%	0%	0%		1	24	0%	0%			-0.4	97	-$9
2nd Half																																	
Proj	5	0	58	71	4.06	1.18	3.54	1.14	93	91	21.9	8%	31%	23%	7%	14.3%	95.4	40	20	40	32%	69%	13%	12%	11						2.8	162	$1

Payamps,Joel

Age: 28	Th: R	Role	RP	Health	A	LIMA Plan	C
Ht: 6' 2"	Wt: 225	Type	Con/FB	PT/Exp	D	Rand Var	-4
				Consist	F	MM	1000

Career minor leaguers on three MLB clubs in two years aren't good investments. This one's conversion from starter to reliever hasn't yielded much of substance. Still doesn't miss enough bats to keep hitters off balance, and both hit and strand rates made results look superficially good. xERA tells the true tale. Pass.

Yr Tm	W	Sv	IP	K	ERA	WHIP	xERA	xWHIP	vL+	vR+	BF/G	BB%	K%	K-BB%	xBB%	SwK	Vel	G	L	F	H%	S%	HR/F	xHR/F	GS	APC	DOM%	DIS%	Sv%	LI	RAR	BPX	R$
17 a/a	8	0	104	56	5.39	1.50	5.60				23.7	5%	12%	7%							33%	66%									-13.3	40	-$6
18 a/a	9	0	117	101	3.99	1.19	3.45				15.1	6%	22%	16%							31%	67%									2.3	130	$6
19 ARI *	5	0	84	58	4.47	1.42	4.78		99	94	21.0	6%	16%	10%		7.6%	92.9	10	40	50	33%	70%	0%	22%	0	33			0	0.09	0.4	70	-$2
20 ARI	0	0	3	2	3.00	1.67	7.27		28	133	6.5	23%	15%	-8%		5.1%	94.2	13	63	25	24%	80%	0%	32%	0	30			0	0.09	0.5	-163	-$7
21 2 AL	1	0	50	38	3.40	1.15	4.62	1.31	75	98	5.5	7%	19%	12%	8%	10.4%	94.7	44	15	41	27%	75%	10%	9%	1	22	0%	100%	0	0.73	5.4	84	-$1
1st Half	0	0	30	22	2.70	1.07	4.70	1.42	47	94	5.4	9%	18%	9%	10%	12.0%	94.6	47	11	42	22%	79%	8%	9%	0	22			0	0.46	5.8	60	-$2
2nd Half	1	0	20	16	4.43	1.28	4.51	1.18	95	109	5.7	3%	19%	15%	5%	8.1%	94.9	41	20	39	33%	70%	12%	9%	1	23	0%	100%	0	1.14	-0.4	121	-$9
Proj	3	0	58	43	4.41	1.27	4.61	1.29	86	105	8.5	6%	18%	12%	7%	9.6%	94.8	43	16	41	31%	67%	9%	9%	0						0.3	96	-$3

Peacock,Matt

Age: 28	Th: R	Role	RP	Health	A	LIMA Plan	D+
Ht: 6' 1"	Wt: 180	Type	Con/xGB	PT/Exp	D	Rand Var	+1
				Consist	A	MM	1010

Extreme sinkerballer couldn't use that skill to establish high-floor profile, as nearly half of the contact he allowed was of the hard variety. That's why his elevated hit rate may not regress. Adding to reasons for pessimism are lack of missed bats and a low volume of strikes, which explain total lack of command. Let him strut his feathers elsewhere.

Yr Tm	W	Sv	IP	K	ERA	WHIP	xERA	xWHIP	vL+	vR+	BF/G	BB%	K%	K-BB%	xBB%	SwK	Vel	G	L	F	H%	S%	HR/F	xHR/F	GS	APC	DOM%	DIS%	Sv%	LI	RAR	BPX	R$
17																																	
18																																	
19 aa	8	0	116	65	4.44	1.53	4.51				24.0	10%	13%	3%							31%	70%									0.9	45	-$2
20																																	
21 ARI	5	0	86	50	4.90	1.56	4.71	1.43	132	101	11.0	7%	13%	6%	8%	8.3%	93.4	59	18	23	33%	72%	19%	18%	8	38	0%	75%	0	0.64	-6.8	57	-$8
1st Half	2	0	53	34	5.74	1.63	4.72	1.40	141	97	12.9	7%	14%	7%	8%	7.9%	93.2	58	18	23	35%	67%	18%	20%	7	46	0%	71%	0	0.65	-9.7	68	-$13
2nd Half	3	0	33	16	3.55	1.45	4.71	1.48	98	114	8.8	8%	11%	4%	9%	9.0%	93.8	61	17	22	29%	81%	20%	12%	1	28	0%	100%	0	0.64	2.9	40	-$5
Proj	5	2	65	36	4.42	1.53	4.79	1.49	117	102	11.7	8%	13%	4%	9%	8.5%	93.6	60	17	23	31%	74%	16%	16%	4						0.3	46	-$4

Pearson,Nate

Age: 25	Th: R	Role	SP	Health	D	LIMA Plan	C
Ht: 6' 6"	Wt: 250	Type	Pwr	PT/Exp	D	Rand Var	+1
				Consist	F	MM	2301

1-1, 3.72 ERA in 15 IP at TOR. Groin injury lingered for most of season, turning him from top prospect to post-hype play. Upside was evident in tiny 12 IP stint out of TOR bullpen in September (38% K%, 16.2% SwK%). Scouts still question whether he has durability to stick as a starter, since injury concerns continue to mount. A high-risk/reward play.

Yr Tm	W	Sv	IP	K	ERA	WHIP	xERA	xWHIP	vL+	vR+	BF/G	BB%	K%	K-BB%	xBB%	SwK	Vel	G	L	F	H%	S%	HR/F	xHR/F	GS	APC	DOM%	DIS%	Sv%	LI	RAR	BPX	R$
17																																	
18																																	
19 a/a	2	0	82	71	3.65	1.11	2.92				17.0	8%	22%	14%							26%	69%									8.7	99	$3
20 TOR	1	0	18	16	6.00	1.50	6.22	1.73	160	58	16.2	16%	20%	4%	10%	11.1%	96.4	38	17	44	21%	68%	22%	12%	4	65	0%	50%	0	0.62	-3.4	-18	-$7
21 TOR *	2	0	47	56	5.38	1.42	4.56	1.39	116	94	8.3	13%	28%	15%	12%	13.0%	97.9	41	13	46	30%	65%	11%	10%	1	25	0%	100%	0	0.31	-6.5	81	-$6
1st Half	1	0	29	29	6.75	1.54	4.99		279	53	17.8	14%	23%	10%		1.6%	95.7	36	9	55	31%	57%	0%	1%	1	64	0%	100%			-8.8	63	-$11
2nd Half	1	0	19	26	3.29	1.23	3.90	1.22	62	105	4.5	12%	34%	22%	10%	16.0%	98.5	43	14	43	29%	82%	17%	15%	0	22			0	0.27	2.2	112	-$6
Proj	4	0	94	108	4.41	1.30	4.08	1.34			21.6	12%	28%	16%				42	20	38	29%	70%	15%	0%	18						0.5	103	$0

Peralta,Freddy

Age: 26	Th: R	Role	SP	Health	B	LIMA Plan	D+
Ht: 5' 11"	Wt: 199	Type	Pwr/xFB	PT/Exp	B	Rand Var	-4
				Consist	B	MM	2403

2020 gave us a taste of what he could do, and he turned that momentum into a breakout. Sure, friendly hit and strand rates are what really kept ERA below 3.00. But elite command is cemented in his profile now thanks to whiff-inducing arsenal, giving him a legit mid-3's ERA baseline. With another uptick in durability... UP: 240 K

Yr Tm	W	Sv	IP	K	ERA	WHIP	xERA	xWHIP	vL+	vR+	BF/G	BB%	K%	K-BB%	xBB%	SwK	Vel	G	L	F	H%	S%	HR/F	xHR/F	GS	APC	DOM%	DIS%	Sv%	LI	RAR	BPX	R$
17 aa	2	1	64	81	3.36	1.29	2.80				20.1	13%	31%	18%							31%	74%									7.9	142	$2
18 MIL *	12	0	139	173	3.72	1.18	2.61	1.28	118	55	19.2	12%	31%	19%	9%	11.5%	90.8	31	18	52	29%	69%	9%	12%	14	86	29%	14%	0	0.75	7.4	138	$12
19 MIL	7	1	85	115	5.29	1.46	4.34	1.25	90	114	9.8	10%	30%	20%	7%	13.9%	93.6	32	24	44	37%	68%	15%	15%	8	41	25%	38%	50	0.88	-8.3	134	-$1
20 MIL	3	0	29	47	3.99	1.16	3.22	1.08	77	93	8.3	10%	38%	28%	10%	16.6%	93.0	35	22	43	36%	66%	8%	15%	1	37	0%	100%	0	1.02	1.7	196	$6
21 MIL	10	0	144	195	2.81	0.97	3.52	1.14	75	78	20.7	10%	34%	24%	9%	15.1%	93.4	33	20	47	25%	75%	10%	10%	27	84	30%	15%	0	0.76	26.0	149	$24
1st Half	7	0	87	122	2.17	0.87	3.41	1.15	72	59	21.1	11%	36%	25%	10%	14.9%	93.4	32	18	50	20%	81%	9%	11%	15	89	33%	7%	0	0.77	22.5	147	$31
2nd Half	3	0	57	73	3.77	1.12	3.69	1.13	69	109	20.3	8%	30%	22%	7%	15.4%	93.5	35	22	43	31%	69%	10%	8%	12	77	25%	25%			3.5	152	$7
Proj	11	0	160	204	3.43	1.17	3.85	1.22	86	89	23.2	10%	32%	22%	8%	14.1%	93.0	33	21	47	29%	74%	10%	11%	27						20.1	132	$17

STEPHEN NICKRAND

Peralta,Wandy

Age: 30 Th: L Role RP	Health C	LIMA Plan B	
Ht: 6' 0" Wt: 217 Type /GB	PT/Exp D	Rand Var -1	
	Consist A	MM 1100	

In this era of deep and much-used bullpens, a lefty specialist can extend career in absence of plus skills. And hey, he even got in saves mix. But his margin for error is razor thin. High SwK rate has never pushed K-BB% needle; most recent was four points below the average reliever. A fringe $1 LIMA reliever in deep leagues.

Yr Tm	W	Sv	IP	K	ERA	WHIP	xERA	xWHIP	vL+	vR+	BF/G	BB%	K%	K-BB%	xBB%	SwK	Vel	G	L	F	H%	S%	HR/F	xHR/F	GS	APC	DOM%	DIS%	Sv%	LI	RAR	BPX	R$
17 CIN	3	0	65	57	3.76	1.19	3.93	1.36	85	96	3.8	9%	22%	13%	8%	15.5%	96.5	54	16	30	26%	72%	15%	9%	0	15			0	0.81	4.8	102	$2
18 CIN *	3	0	60	39	5.04	1.88	5.84	1.73	110	107	3.9	14%	14%	0%	9%	10.1%	95.6	48	25	27	35%	72%	5%	8%	0	15			0	0.75	-6.6	40	-$11
19 2 NL	1	0	40	32	5.67	1.41	4.74	1.45	103	125	3.7	9%	19%	9%	10%	15.2%	95.3	51	19	30	27%	69%	31%	23%	0	14			0	0.79	-5.7	67	-$6
20 SF	1	0	27	25	3.29	1.21	4.23	1.37	78	96	4.6	10%	22%	12%	11%	13.1%	94.8	46	26	28	27%	77%	14%	14%	0	20			0	0.54	3.9	84	$0
21 2 TM	5	5	51	43	3.35	1.37	4.08	1.40	94	96	3.9	10%	20%	10%	8%	15.7%	95.2	58	19	23	30%	80%	17%	18%	1	14	0%	100%	83	1.25	5.7	80	$2
1st Half	3	2	24	17	5.32	1.39	4.64	1.43	134	85	3.4	9%	17%	8%	7%	15.3%	95.6	52	20	28	29%	66%	19%	16%	0	13			67	1.00	-3.1	59	-$4
2nd Half	2	3	27	26	1.65	1.35	3.58	1.37	52	110	4.5	10%	22%	12%	8%	16.1%	94.9	64	18	18	31%	91%	14%	23%	1	16	0%	100%	100	1.53	8.8	98	$1
Proj	4	0	58	47	4.08	1.46	4.48	1.47	98	103	3.8	11%	19%	8%	8%	14.3%	95.4	55	20	25	30%	76%	17%	17%	0						2.7	60	-$3

Peralta,Wily

Age: 33 Th: R Role RP	Health B	LIMA Plan D	
Ht: 6' 1" Wt: 255 Type	PT/Exp D	Rand Var -3	
	Consist C	MM 0001	

4-5, 3.07 ERA in 94 IP at DET. 4 reasons he'll be overvalued... 1) Four straight seasons of shoddy command; 2) Skills were disastrous in 6 out of 10 starts; 3) Those hit and strand rates aren't repeating; 4) The only good Peralta is Freddy. Few pitchers will feel the power of regression more than this one.

Yr Tm	W	Sv	IP	K	ERA	WHIP	xERA	xWHIP	vL+	vR+	BF/G	BB%	K%	K-BB%	xBB%	SwK	Vel	G	L	F	H%	S%	HR/F	xHR/F	GS	APC	DOM%	DIS%	Sv%	LI	RAR	BPX	R$
17 MIL *	6	1	73	60	6.99	1.79	6.08	1.60	136	118	10.6	12%	18%	5%	10%	9.1%	96.0	45	22	34	35%	61%	16%	16%	8	59	25%	50%	50	0.74	-23.8	38	-$12
18 KC *	1	15	69	63	4.91	1.77	5.59	1.64	94	111	5.8	15%	20%	5%	12%	10.1%	96.2	46	19	35	34%	74%	13%	18%	0	16			100	0.82	-6.5	55	-$5
19 KC	2	2	40	24	5.80	1.59	5.79	1.64	134	98	4.2	11%	14%	3%	11%	8.8%	94.4	45	21	34	30%	67%	16%	21%	0	16			40	0.91	-6.4	5	-$6
20																																	
21 DET *	5	0	115	73	3.22	1.35	4.38	1.50	85	114	19.2	10%	15%	5%	11%	8.8%	93.9	51	19	31	27%	81%	13%	15%	18	82	11%	61%	0	0.82	14.8	40	$3
1st Half	2	0	35	23	3.61	1.29	4.09	1.48	144	55	14.5	10%	16%	6%	12%	9.1%	93.6	52	18	30	25%	77%	15%	18%	3	60	33%	33%	0	1.05	2.8	43	-$3
2nd Half	3	0	80	50	3.05	1.38	5.02	1.51	72	130	22.9	10%	15%	5%	11%	8.7%	94.0	50	19	31	28%	83%	13%	15%	15	88	7%	67%			11.9	32	$4
Proj	4	0	102	71	4.39	1.52	5.27	1.57	106	112	8.3	11%	16%	5%	11%	9.1%	94.9	47	20	33	30%	75%	13%	17%	0						0.8	22	-$6

Pérez,Martin

Age: 31 Th: L Role SP	Health D	LIMA Plan D+	
Ht: 6' 0" Wt: 200 Type Con	PT/Exp A	Rand Var +2	
	Consist A	MM 1101	

Man, does it seem long ago that he was a 3x Top-50 prospect. Now just a swingman, he can get lefties out in a pinch, but chronic struggles against righties mean less is more as usage goes. Five straight seasons with a 4.50+ xERA seal his fate on your league's FA wire. Final data point to convince you: his lifetime MLB Roto earnings (in 10 years) are MINUS $62.

Yr Tm	W	Sv	IP	K	ERA	WHIP	xERA	xWHIP	vL+	vR+	BF/G	BB%	K%	K-BB%	xBB%	SwK	Vel	G	L	F	H%	S%	HR/F	xHR/F	GS	APC	DOM%	DIS%	Sv%	LI	RAR	BPX	R$
17 TEX	13	0	185	115	4.82	1.54	4.89	1.46	88	115	25.3	8%	14%	6%	9%	7.5%	93.1	47	25	28	33%	71%	13%	14%	32	97	9%	66%			-10.5	52	-$4
18 TEX	2	0	85	52	6.22	1.78	5.25	1.52	102	135	18.0	9%	13%	4%	9%	7.5%	92.7	51	20	29	35%	68%	18%	16%	15	64	0%	73%	0	0.83	-21.8	29	-$17
19 MIN	10	0	165	135	5.12	1.52	4.94	1.45	77	112	23.0	9%	18%	9%	7%	10.3%	94.1	48	23	29	33%	69%	15%	12%	29	87	21%	55%	0	0.73	-12.5	65	-$5
20 BOS	3	0	62	46	4.50	1.34	5.23	1.52	107	98	21.8	11%	18%	7%	11%	8.7%	92.1	38	26	35	27%	69%	13%	14%	12	86	25%	42%			-0.4	30	$1
21 BOS	7	0	114	97	4.74	1.51	4.56	1.31	92	117	14.1	7%	19%	12%	8%	8.5%	93.0	44	24	33	34%	73%	16%	20%	22	52	9%	45%	0	0.54	-6.6	91	-$6
1st Half	6	0	76	62	4.04	1.43	4.57	1.35	93	105	20.8	8%	19%	11%	8%	7.7%	92.7	44	24	32	33%	75%	12%	17%	16	77	13%	44%			2.1	78	$3
2nd Half	1	0	38	35	6.10	1.67	4.54	1.24	81	149	8.9	6%	20%	14%	6%	10.2%	93.5	44	23	34	38%	70%	23%	25%	6	32	0%	50%	0	0.35	-8.7	117	-$16
Proj	5	0	102	81	5.17	1.54	4.76	1.38	92	120	20.5	8%	18%	10%	8%	9.0%	93.0	44	24	32	33%	71%	17%	18%	22						-9.0	74	-$8

Peterson,David

Age: 26 Th: L Role SP	Health F	LIMA Plan C	
Ht: 6' 6" Wt: 240 Type Pwr	PT/Exp C	Rand Var +5	
	Consist B	MM 1201	

Former 20th overall pick in 2017 draft with some sneaky gains in spite of ugly stats. Surge in command backed by SwK% and xBB% combo, so there's more of that on the horizon. Most won't see this growth, especially since broken foot wiped away his 2nd half. You'll bid a buck and net some nice profit... UP: 3.75 ERA, 180 K

Yr Tm	W	Sv	IP	K	ERA	WHIP	xERA	xWHIP	vL+	vR+	BF/G	BB%	K%	K-BB%	xBB%	SwK	Vel	G	L	F	H%	S%	HR/F	xHR/F	GS	APC	DOM%	DIS%	Sv%	LI	RAR	BPX	R$
17																																	
18																																	
19 aa	3	0	116	106	5.96	1.65	5.72				21.6	8%	20%	13%							39%	64%									-20.8	75	-$12
20 NYM	6	0	50	40	3.44	1.21	4.93	1.52	70	90	20.5	12%	20%	8%	12%	10.8%	92.1	44	19	36	24%	75%	10%	13%	9	81	11%	56%	0	0.79	6.2	40	$13
21 NYM	2	0	67	69	5.54	1.40	3.90	1.34	106	108	19.1	10%	24%	14%	8%	11.5%	92.6	49	23	27	31%	63%	22%	26%	15	75	7%	47%			-10.4	98	-$7
1st Half	2	0	67	69	5.54	1.40	3.90	1.34	101	110	19.1	10%	24%	14%	8%	11.5%	92.6	49	23	27	31%	63%	22%	26%	15	75	7%	47%			-10.4	98	-$7
2nd Half																																	
Proj	6	0	102	95	4.13	1.35	4.29	1.39	97	103	20.5	10%	22%	12%	10%	11.2%	92.4	47	22	31	30%	73%	15%	20%	21						4.1	83	$0

Petit,Yusmeiro

Age: 37 Th: R Role RP	Health A	LIMA Plan B	
Ht: 6' 1" Wt: 252 Type Con/FB	PT/Exp C	Rand Var -5	
	Consist A	MM 1011	

After getting a 30%+ whiff rate with three separate pitches the last two seasons, only one reached that threshold in 2021. He'll always have a high floor given ability to avoid hard contact, but BPX/xERA trends, erosion of stuff, and age all warn that his 3.00 ERA baseline isn't likely coming back.

Yr Tm	W	Sv	IP	K	ERA	WHIP	xERA	xWHIP	vL+	vR+	BF/G	BB%	K%	K-BB%	xBB%	SwK	Vel	G	L	F	H%	S%	HR/F	xHR/F	GS	APC	DOM%	DIS%	Sv%	LI	RAR	BPX	R$
17 LAA	5	4	91	101	2.76	0.95	3.74	1.09	85	70	5.9	5%	29%	24%	6%	11.2%	89.6	33	18	49	28%	76%	8%	8%	1	22	100%	0%	80	0.92	18.0	171	$14
18 OAK	7	0	93	76	3.00	1.01	4.22	1.20	83	95	5.0	5%	21%	16%	5%	9.4%	89.3	36	20	44	25%	78%	11%	14%	0	18			0	1.06	13.2	114	$10
19 OAK	5	0	83	71	2.71	0.81	4.26	1.14	89	68	3.9	3%	23%	20%	6%	12.1%	89.2	30	21	49	22%	75%	10%	11%	0	14			0	1.36	18.4	128	$12
20 OAK	2	0	22	17	1.66	1.11	5.01	1.28	30	111	3.4	6%	19%	14%	5%	13.3%	88.2	33	17	49	27%	95%	10%	19%	0	12			0	0.99	7.5	93	$4
21 OAK	8	2	78	37	3.92	1.04	5.20	1.32	96	85	4.0	4%	12%	8%	6%	10.4%	87.7	37	19	44	24%	68%	11%	13%	0	14			25	1.23	3.3	60	$6
1st Half	7	2	43	23	3.16	1.05	5.16	1.28	85	86	4.3	4%	14%	10%	6%	10.6%	87.4	33	19	48	26%	73%	6%	9%	0	15			40	1.38	5.8	71	$9
2nd Half	1	0	35	14	4.84	1.02	5.24	1.37	98	87	3.7	4%	10%	6%	6%	10.3%	88.0	41	20	39	20%	61%	17%	18%	0	13			0	1.07	-2.5	46	-$6
Proj	5	2	73	49	4.00	1.18	4.75	1.25	109	98	4.3	4%	17%	13%	6%	10.6%	88.5	35	20	45	28%	73%	12%	13%	0						4.1	94	$2

Pineda,Michael

Age: 33 Th: R Role SP	Health F	LIMA Plan B	
Ht: 6' 7" Wt: 280 Type Con	PT/Exp B	Rand Var -1	
	Consist A	MM 2103	

Thigh, oblique issues were his injury culprits this go-round. He's a conundrum: has posted a 100+ BPX in every season, but hasn't thrown more than 150 innings since 2016. To put that into perspective, he's spent the equivalent of four full MLB seasons on the injured list in his career. So draft him for his hot stretches, but don't rely on him.

Yr Tm	W	Sv	IP	K	ERA	WHIP	xERA	xWHIP	vL+	vR+	BF/G	BB%	K%	K-BB%	xBB%	SwK	Vel	G	L	F	H%	S%	HR/F	xHR/F	GS	APC	DOM%	DIS%	Sv%	LI	RAR	BPX	R$
17 NYY	8	0	96	92	4.39	1.29	3.77	1.19	101	105	24.1	5%	22%	17%	6%	12.7%	93.9	51	19	31	32%	74%	22%	16%	17	91	35%	29%			-0.4	157	$3
18																																	
19 MIN	11	0	146	140	4.01	1.16	4.30	1.18	88	102	23.1	5%	23%	19%	5%	12.9%	92.6	36	23	41	30%	71%	13%	13%	26	88	27%	19%			9.0	134	$12
20 MIN	2	0	27	25	3.38	1.20	4.45	1.23	103	60	22.2	6%	23%	16%	7%	14.9%	92.1	38	21	41	33%	69%	0%	8%	5	91	20%	20%			3.5	118	$2
21 MIN	9	0	109	88	3.62	1.23	4.43	1.21	113	94	20.8	5%	19%	15%	5%	10.8%	90.7	40	22	38	31%	77%	13%	16%	21	78	5%	33%	0	0.77	8.7	112	$6
1st Half	3	0	56	51	3.70	1.14	4.41	1.23	98	87	21.0	7%	22%	16%	5%	10.8%	91.0	39	19	43	27%	76%	14%	18%	11	80	9%	18%			3.9	109	$4
2nd Half	6	0	53	37	3.54	1.33	4.46	1.18	119	103	20.6	3%	16%	14%	4%	10.8%	90.4	41	26	34	34%	78%	11%	14%	10	75	0%	50%	0	0.77	4.7	114	$4
Proj	9	0	131	111	3.84	1.24	4.15	1.19	107	99	21.1	5%	21%	16%	5%	11.6%	91.7	41	22	37	31%	76%	15%	15%	25						9.8	127	$7

Pivetta,Nick

Age: 29 Th: R Role SP	Health A	LIMA Plan B+	
Ht: 6' 5" Wt: 214 Type Pwr	PT/Exp C	Rand Var 0	
	Consist B	MM 2303	

Best season of career generated only a few bucks, and it's hard to see a path to something more. Hard-hit contact warts haven't gone away; max exit velocity was in the game's bottom five percent. That means the elevated hit rates that have haunted him in the past are headed back. The best you can hope for is a repeat.

Yr Tm	W	Sv	IP	K	ERA	WHIP	xERA	xWHIP	vL+	vR+	BF/G	BB%	K%	K-BB%	xBB%	SwK	Vel	G	L	F	H%	S%	HR/F	xHR/F	GS	APC	DOM%	DIS%	Sv%	LI	RAR	BPX	R$
17 PHI *	13	0	165	172	5.21	1.41	4.90	1.28	93	133	22.5	8%	25%	16%	8%	9.3%	94.4	44	20	36	34%	67%	18%	14%	26	94	12%	31%			-17.3	90	$1
18 PHI	7	0	164	188	4.77	1.30	3.53	1.17	107	99	21.0	7%	27%	20%	6%	12.5%	94.8	47	19	35	34%	67%	16%	15%	32	86	31%	38%	0	0.80	-12.6	156	$1
19 PHI *	9	1	135	138	4.89	1.43	4.85	1.41	114	116	14.7	11%	24%	13%	8%	10.7%	94.6	43	25	32	31%	70%	22%	20%	13	54	15%	46%	100	0.78	-6.3	66	$0
20 2 TM	2	0	16	17	6.89	1.53	5.16	1.30	148	109	14.2	8%	24%	15%	8%	10.0%	92.8	28	23	49	34%	60%	17%	18%	2	58	0%	0%	0	0.52	-4.7	100	-$6
21 BOS	9	1	155	175	4.53	1.30	4.29	1.29	102	97	21.3	10%	27%	17%	7%	11.1%	94.8	38	19	43	30%	70%	14%	14%	30	89	20%	43%	100	0.82	-5.0	106	$4
1st Half	6	0	85	99	4.43	1.32	4.39	1.32	99	102	22.8	11%	27%	16%	8%	11.5%	94.8	35	20	45	30%	71%	13%	16%	16	96	13%	38%			-1.7	96	$6
2nd Half	3	1	70	76	4.65	1.28	4.16	1.24	93	96	19.8	8%	26%	17%	6%	10.6%	94.8	42	17	41	31%	68%	14%	13%	14	81	29%	50%	100	0.89	-3.3	121	$2
Proj	7	0	131	143	4.59	1.34	4.09	1.28	102	100	21.2	9%	26%	17%	7%	11.0%	94.7	42	20	38	31%	70%	15%	15%	26						-2.2	117	$1

STEPHEN NICKRAND

Plesac,Zach

Age: 27 Th: R Role SP | Ht: 6' 3" Wt: 220 Type Con

Health D | PT/Exp B | Consist B | LIMA Plan B+ | Rand Var 0 | MM 1003

Well, we knew those short-season hit and strand rates weren't repeating. That didn't help, but erosion in K-BB% was the true culprit. There's a path to recover some of it; threw slider 2x as much as curveball, but lost 10 points in SwK with slider and gained nearly the same SwK with curve. Upside is low, but with pitch mix tweak, he can get ERA below 4.00.

Yr Tm	W	Sv	IP	K	ERA	WHIP	xERA	xWHIP	vL+	vR+	BF/G	BB%	K%	K-BB%	xBB%	SwK	Vel	G	L	F	H%	S%	HR/F	xHR/F	GS	APC	DOM%	DIS%	Sv%	LI	RAR	BPX	R$
17																																	
18 aa	3	0	22	18	3.35	1.26	3.74				22.4	4%	20%	16%							33%	74%									2.2	131	-$2
19 CLE *	12	0	181	142	3.27	1.13	3.37	1.34	90	105	23.1	7%	20%	13%	7%	9.9%	94.0	39	22	39	27%	76%	15%	14%	21	90	19%	29%			27.6	85	$19
20 CLE	4	0	55	57	2.28	0.80	3.46	1.01	85	70	25.8	3%	28%	25%	5%	14.7%	92.8	39	20	41	23%	83%	14%	16%	8	97	75%	0%			14.9	178	$25
21 CLE	10	0	143	100	4.67	1.20	4.67	1.30	95	103	23.9	6%	17%	11%	6%	11.5%	92.9	45	17	38	27%	66%	13%	17%	25	88	16%	44%			-7.1	86	$3
1st Half	4	0	59	38	4.14	1.02	4.29	1.28	83	88	23.5	5%	16%	11%	5%	11.8%	93.4	53	13	34	23%	65%	15%	18%	10	88	20%	40%			0.9	94	$4
2nd Half	6	0	84	62	5.04	1.32	4.93	1.31	94	117	24.2	6%	17%	11%	7%	11.3%	92.5	40	19	41	30%	66%	13%	16%	15	88	13%	47%			-8.0	81	$1
Proj	12	0	174	136	4.07	1.18	4.34	1.25	97	104	23.8	5%	20%	14%	6%	11.8%	93.1	43	18	39	28%	72%	14%	16%	29						8.3	107	$11

Poche,Colin

Age: 28 Th: L Role RP | Ht: 6' 3" Wt: 225 Type Pwr/xFB

Health F | PT/Exp F | Consist F | LIMA Plan A | Rand Var 0 | MM 3500

Went under knife for Tommy John surgery in July 2020 and wasn't rushed back. Showed filthy stuff in MLB debut before injury, including crazy 34% SwK with a four-seam fastball that he threw 90% of time. Jury's out if that approach will work long-term, and as xFB pitcher, he comes with risk. But hidden skills make him a potential LIMA reliever gem.

Yr Tm	W	Sv	IP	K	ERA	WHIP	xERA	xWHIP	vL+	vR+	BF/G	BB%	K%	K-BB%	xBB%	SwK	Vel	G	L	F	H%	S%	HR/F	xHR/F	GS	APC	DOM%	DIS%	Sv%	LI	RAR	BPX	R$
17																																	
18 a/a	6	2	66	96	1.02	0.89	1.23				6.1	8%	39%	31%							29%	91%									25.5	221	$15
19 TAM *	7	2	80	113	5.71	1.25	4.14	1.15	82	89	4.6	9%	35%	26%	6%	17.6%	93.0	18	19	62	34%	57%	13%	11%	0	17			29	1.63	-11.8	132	$1
20																																	
21																																	
1st Half																																	
2nd Half																																	
Proj	4	0	58	83	3.83	1.11	3.64	1.08	95	99	5.1	9%	36%	28%	6%	17.6%	93.0	18	19	62	32%	68%	9%	9%	0						4.4	166	$3

Pomeranz,Drew

Age: 33 Th: L Role RP | Ht: 6' 5" Wt: 246 Type Pwr

Health F | PT/Exp C | Consist A | LIMA Plan C | Rand Var -5 | MM 2300

Torn flexor tendon led to August surgery, which reminds us he's no longer durable enough to take the ball every 5th day. But skills out of 'pen the last two years prove he can be good in short stints. Note for holds leagues: Had holds in almost half his appearances in 2021, which really is his path to value at this point given likely role, brittle arm.

Yr Tm	W	Sv	IP	K	ERA	WHIP	xERA	xWHIP	vL+	vR+	BF/G	BB%	K%	K-BB%	xBB%	SwK	Vel	G	L	F	H%	S%	HR/F	xHR/F	GS	APC	DOM%	DIS%	Sv%	LI	RAR	BPX	R$
17 BOS	17	0	174	174	3.32	1.35	4.22	1.34	103	94	23.1	9%	24%	14%	9%	10.3%	91.3	43	22	35	32%	79%	11%	13%	32	96	19%	22%			22.3	104	$16
18 BOS *	3	0	101	77	6.35	1.76	6.70	1.66	96	132	14.5	14%	17%	3%	10%	7.5%	89.3	37	24	39	31%	69%	13%	16%	11	56	0%	64%	0	0.63	-27.5	5	-$18
19 2 NL	2	2	104	137	4.85	1.43	3.99	1.25	88	115	9.9	10%	30%	21%	8%	11.6%	92.7	39	23	38	35%	73%	21%	18%	18	43	11%	39%	100	0.99	-4.4	139	-$2
20 SD	1	4	19	29	1.45	1.02	3.23	1.20	54	63	3.7	14%	40%	26%	8%	15.2%	94.7	47	6	47	25%	89%	6%	7%	0	16			80	1.58	6.9	165	$9
21 SD	1	0	26	30	1.75	1.13	3.29	1.22	57	97	3.8	10%	29%	20%	7%	11.4%	94.0	45	29	26	29%	89%	13%	17%	0	16			0	0.91	8.0	129	-$1
1st Half	0	0	16	21	1.72	1.21	3.37	1.27	31	123	4.0	13%	33%	20%	9%	13.6%	94.1	34	40	26	30%	89%	11%	17%	0	17			0	0.87	4.9	116	-$4
2nd Half	1	0	10	9	1.80	1.00	3.18	1.15	117	70	3.5	5%	24%	18%	4%	7.6%	93.6	59	15	26	27%	89%	14%	17%	0	14			0	0.98	3.0	148	-$7
Proj	1	0	44	50	3.76	1.36	4.09	1.35	66	112	7.4	12%	28%	16%	9%	11.1%	92.2	38	29	33	30%	77%	17%	16%	0						3.7	95	-$3

Pop,Zach

Age: 25 Th: R Role RP | Ht: 6' 4" Wt: 220 Type Pwr/xGB

Health B | PT/Exp F | Consist F | LIMA Plan C | Rand Var 0 | MM 2100

Knowing who to target often involves identifying unique skills combos. As an extreme GBer who misses bats and prevents hard contact (96th-percentile exit velocity), he's got one. But he was playing with fire, as he threw first-pitch strikes only half the time and BB% hasn't seen single digits. If he attacks hitters more, this is a profitable $1 dart throw.

Yr Tm	W	Sv	IP	K	ERA	WHIP	xERA	xWHIP	vL+	vR+	BF/G	BB%	K%	K-BB%	xBB%	SwK	Vel	G	L	F	H%	S%	HR/F	xHR/F	GS	APC	DOM%	DIS%	Sv%	LI	RAR	BPX	R$
17																																	
18 aa	1	1	22	14	2.72	0.95	1.47				6.0	7%	17%	10%							24%	68%									3.9	118	-$1
19																																	
20																																	
21 MIA	1	0	55	51	4.12	1.43	4.05	1.38	100	94	4.9	10%	21%	11%	9%	11.5%	95.4	58	18	25	33%	71%	8%	14%	0	19			0	0.59	1.0	88	-$5
1st Half	1	0	29	30	5.28	1.28	3.67	1.31	87	93	5.3	10%	24%	14%	10%	12.6%	95.4	59	15	26	30%	59%	14%	21%	0	21			0	0.28	-3.6	114	-$7
2nd Half	0	0	26	21	2.81	1.60	4.50	1.46	103	98	4.6	10%	18%	8%	9%	10.3%	95.6	56	21	23	36%	80%	0%	7%	0	17			0	0.88	4.6	59	-$10
Proj	1	0	36	33	4.04	1.36	4.04	1.42	100	89	4.5	11%	22%	11%	9%	11.2%	95.5	57	18	24	31%	71%	10%	12%	0						1.8	84	-$4

Pressly,Ryan

Age: 33 Th: R Role RP | Ht: 6' 2" Wt: 206 Type Pwr/GB

Health C | PT/Exp B | Consist B | LIMA Plan C | Rand Var -3 | MM 5430

A power/groundballer has become a top-tier closer that keeps getting more reliable (see Sv% trend). Top-shelf K-BB% propped up by fantastic command sub-indicators, he's filthy against LH and RH bats, and GB rate limits blow-up risk. In sum, there are no dents in the armor here. A top closer target.

Yr Tm	W	Sv	IP	K	ERA	WHIP	xERA	xWHIP	vL+	vR+	BF/G	BB%	K%	K-BB%	xBB%	SwK	Vel	G	L	F	H%	S%	HR/F	xHR/F	GS	APC	DOM%	DIS%	Sv%	LI	RAR	BPX	R$
17 MIN	2	0	61	61	4.70	1.16	3.71	1.25	108	84	4.4	8%	24%	17%	6%	12.9%	95.8	51	17	33	27%	64%	19%	14%	0	16			0	0.94	-2.6	138	-$1
18 2 AL	2	2	71	101	2.54	1.11	2.71	1.04	70	92	3.8	8%	35%	27%	6%	18.0%	95.8	52	17	32	34%	81%	12%	12%	0	14			25	1.16	14.1	213	$7
19 HOU	2	3	54	72	2.32	0.90	2.56	1.01	48	96	3.8	6%	34%	29%	5%	18.0%	95.6	51	28	21	28%	81%	22%	20%	0	15			38	1.25	14.7	207	$8
20 HOU	1	12	21	29	3.43	1.33	3.25	1.11	97	101	4.0	8%	32%	24%	4%	17.8%	94.7	48	22	30	39%	77%	13%	6%	0	15			75	1.61	2.7	191	$14
21 HOU	5	26	64	81	2.25	0.97	2.66	1.00	72	76	3.9	5%	33%	27%	5%	15.2%	95.5	55	17	28	31%	79%	9%	17%	0	15			93	1.40	15.9	207	$21
1st Half	4	14	35	45	1.54	0.83	2.49	0.92	62	61	4.0	4%	34%	31%	4%	14.4%	95.6	52	19	30	30%	82%	4%	16%	0	16			93	1.42	11.8	223	$19
2nd Half	1	12	29	36	3.10	1.14	2.87	1.09	74	97	3.8	7%	31%	24%	5%	16.1%	95.2	59	15	26	32%	77%	16%	19%	0	14			92	1.38	4.2	188	$10
Proj	4	30	58	74	2.68	1.03	2.72	1.04	71	86	3.8	6%	33%	27%	5%	16.3%	95.6	54	19	27	31%	78%	14%	17%	0						12.7	203	$19

Price,David

Age: 36 Th: L Role RP | Ht: 6' 5" Wt: 215 Type

Health D | PT/Exp C | Consist B | LIMA Plan C | Rand Var -1 | MM 2201

Averaged 220 innings per season from 2010 to 2016. It's clear that mileage has caught up to him, and he spent most of the year dealing with elbow soreness. That likely explains huge plunge in whiffs and worst skills since rookie season. If he's going to resurrect his career at 36, it's probably going to happen in a bullpen. Bid accordingly.

Yr Tm	W	Sv	IP	K	ERA	WHIP	xERA	xWHIP	vL+	vR+	BF/G	BB%	K%	K-BB%	xBB%	SwK	Vel	G	L	F	H%	S%	HR/F	xHR/F	GS	APC	DOM%	DIS%	Sv%	LI	RAR	BPX	R$
17 BOS	6	0	75	76	3.38	1.19	4.17	1.26	65	94	19.8	8%	24%	16%	7%	12.8%	94.3	40	22	39	30%	75%	10%	13%	11	78	27%	36%	0	0.85	9.1	126	$5
18 BOS	16	0	176	177	3.58	1.14	3.86	1.20	92	97	24.1	7%	25%	18%	7%	10.2%	92.7	40	21	39	28%	74%	13%	15%	30	91	43%	27%			12.4	129	$18
19 BOS	7	0	107	128	4.28	1.31	3.89	1.18	88	104	20.8	7%	28%	21%	6%	11.8%	92.0	41	24	35	35%	71%	14%	16%	22	85	23%	23%			3.0	152	$4
20																																	
21 LA	5	1	74	58	4.03	1.43	4.56	1.37	107	101	8.4	8%	18%	10%	6%	9.5%	92.9	50	20	30	32%	74%	11%	12%	11	30	9%	18%	100	0.59	2.1	77	-$2
1st Half	3	1	26	25	3.86	1.68	3.81	1.22	129	100	5.5	6%	21%	15%	5%	10.0%	93.2	55	24	21	41%	80%	17%	14%	3	20	33%	33%	100	0.68	1.3	136	-$4
2nd Half	2	0	48	33	4.13	1.29	4.97	1.46	79	105	12.1	9%	16%	7%	6%	9.2%	92.8	48	17	35	27%	70%	10%	11%	8	44	0%	13%	0	0.46	0.8	45	-$4
Proj	7	0	87	82	3.92	1.33	4.14	1.28	102	99	11.1	8%	23%	15%	6%	10.5%	92.8	46	21	34	32%	74%	13%	14%	4						5.8	111	$1

Puk,A.J.

Age: 27 Th: L Role RP | Ht: 6' 7" Wt: 248 Type Pwr

Health F | PT/Exp F | Consist F | LIMA Plan C | Rand Var 0 | MM 2300

0-3, 6.08 ERA in 13 IP at OAK. One-time sixth overall pick continues to battle health demons, including multiple bouts with elbow and shoulder ailments—he's thrown just 100 innings total since the start of 2018. We know the healthy version has tantalizing stuff, but you can't invest more than a buck or two given his risk profile.

Yr Tm	W	Sv	IP	K	ERA	WHIP	xERA	xWHIP	vL+	vR+	BF/G	BB%	K%	K-BB%	xBB%	SwK	Vel	G	L	F	H%	S%	HR/F	xHR/F	GS	APC	DOM%	DIS%	Sv%	LI	RAR	BPX	R$
17 aa	2	0	64	71	4.95	1.48	4.08				21.2	9%	26%	17%							39%	64%									-4.7	137	-$4
18																																	
19 OAK *	6	0	31	37	4.64	1.27	4.50	1.23	117	73	5.1	9%	29%	20%	8%	14.4%	97.1	48	10	41	30%	70%	8%	2%	0	20			0	1.00	-0.5	95	-$1
20																																	
21 OAK *	2	1	64	62	5.94	1.70	6.84	1.31	95	105	7.0	8%	22%	13%	9%	10.3%	95.7	52	26	21	38%	69%	11%	10%	0	20			33	0.57	-13.1	53	-$12
1st Half	2	0	26	28	7.82	1.90	8.61		33	68	7.3	10%	23%	12%		9.2%	93.9	57	14	29	38%	65%	0%	1%	0	65			0	0.94	-11.6	8	-$14
2nd Half	0	1	37	34	4.60	1.56	5.58	1.25	148	109	6.8	7%	21%	14%	7%	10.7%	96.3	51	29	20	38%	72%	14%	13%	0	16			33	0.53	-1.6	92	-$11
Proj	4	0	58	60	4.23	1.31	4.03	1.28			7.0	9%	25%	16%				45	20	35	32%	71%	13%	0%	0						1.6	115	-$2

STEPHEN NICKRAND

Quantrill,Cal

Age: 27 Th: R Role RP	Health A	LIMA Plan C+	
Ht: 6' 3" Wt: 195 Type Con	PT/Exp C	Rand Var -4	
	Consist A	MM 1103	

Carried forward 2020 mini-breakout into a bigger one...or did he? Turns out hit and strand rates were the true drivers. Slide in skills explained by corresponding drop in whiffs, along with alignment of walks with xBB%. He'll be overvalued because of his 2nd-half surge, which xERA confirms really wasn't much of a surge at all. View as a 4.00 ERA pitcher.

Yr Tm	W	Sv	IP	K	ERA	WHIP	xERA	xWHIP	vL+	vR+	BF/G	BB%	K%	K-BB%	xBB%	SwK	Vel	G	L	F	H%	S%	HR/F	xHR/F	GS	APC	DOM%	DIS%	Sv%	LI	RAR	BPX	R$
17 aa	1	0	42	29	5.51	1.88	7.11				24.9	8%	15%	7%							39%	73%									-6.0	26	-$9
18 a/a	9	0	148	106	5.16	1.55	5.50				23.1	6%	16%	10%							36%	68%									-18.4	67	-$10
19 SD *	10	0	140	116	4.95	1.33	4.44	1.32	112	78	19.4	7%	20%	13%	8%	10.4%	94.5	44	21	35	32%	65%	14%	14%	18	77	11%	44%	0	0.83	-7.7	80	$2
20 2 TM	2	1	32	31	2.25	1.22	4.11	1.20	70	114	7.5	6%	23%	17%	8%	10.1%	94.9	44	19	37	31%	89%	12%	15%	3	28	0%	33%	50	1.39	8.7	134	$7
21 CLE	8	0	150	121	2.89	1.18	4.34	1.32	90	93	15.4	8%	20%	12%	8%	9.8%	94.3	43	22	35	27%	80%	11%	13%	22	59	14%	27%	0	0.60	25.5	83	$14
1st Half	0	0	50	39	4.11	1.41	4.66	1.36	103	97	9.2	8%	18%	10%	8%	9.7%	94.9	41	28	31	33%	72%	8%	15%	6	34	0%	50%	0	0.50	0.9	68	-$6
2nd Half	8	0	99	82	2.27	1.06	4.18	1.30	76	93	24.7	8%	21%	13%	8%	9.8%	94.0	45	19	37	24%	86%	12%	12%	16	96	19%	19%			24.5	91	$33
Proj	9	0	160	132	3.94	1.29	4.38	1.31	98	101	13.0	7%	20%	13%	8%	10.0%	94.5	43	22	35	30%	73%	12%	14%	15						10.2	95	$6

Rainey,Tanner

Age: 29 Th: R Role RP	Health D	LIMA Plan C	
Ht: 6' 2" Wt: 235 Type Pwr/xFB	PT/Exp D	Rand Var +5	
	Consist F	MM 2510	

Injury-marred season (COVID, broken leg) made it a dud. Pre-2021 skills showed some real reasons for optimism, including a surge backed by a SwK turned filthy in 2020 (2nd highest in game among relievers). You'll be able to get him for nothing now, and often the best speculations are last year's failed ones. UP: 20 Sv

Yr Tm	W	Sv	IP	K	ERA	WHIP	xERA	xWHIP	vL+	vR+	BF/G	BB%	K%	K-BB%	xBB%	SwK	Vel	G	L	F	H%	S%	HR/F	xHR/F	GS	APC	DOM%	DIS%	Sv%	LI	RAR	BPX	R$
17 aa	1	4	17	23	2.68	1.47	4.27				5.2	19%	32%	12%							24%	92%									3.5	85	-$1
18 CIN *	7	3	58	60	6.06	1.65	4.42	1.82	215	183	5.0	20%	23%	3%	12%	12.2%	97.8	31	23	46	27%	64%	33%	21%	0	24			50	0.41	-13.7	72	-$6
19 WAS *	4	2	66	99	4.20	1.54	4.06	1.49	124	70	4.3	18%	34%	17%	11%	17.7%	97.8	53	18	29	33%	75%	21%	22%	0	17			22	0.71	2.5	113	-$1
20 WAS	1	0	20	32	2.66	0.74	2.74	0.99	59	82	3.8	9%	43%	33%	8%	21.7%	96.6	31	23	46	14%	82%	25%	19%	0	15			0	1.34	4.5	204	$5
21 WAS	1	3	32	42	7.39	1.71	5.72	1.57	116	111	4.0	17%	28%	11%	10%	15.9%	96.4	25	15	60	33%	58%	12%	16%	0	18			50	1.09	-12.2	29	-$9
1st Half	1	1	25	31	6.93	1.66	6.04	1.63	116	107	3.9	17%	26%	9%	10%	16.7%	96.3	19	17	63	29%	61%	13%	17%	0	17			33	1.03	-8.1	4	-$11
2nd Half	0	2	7	11	9.00	1.86	4.54	1.38	91	137	4.3	15%	32%	18%	8%	13.1%	96.6	44	6	50	44%	50%	11%	10%	0	18			67	1.31	-4.1	114	-$13
Proj	4	9	65	93	3.83	1.32	4.04	1.33	115	83	3.8	14%	34%	20%	10%	17.1%	96.9	32	18	50	29%	77%	14%	19%	0						5.1	113	$5

Rasmussen,Drew

Age: 26 Th: R Role RP	Health A	LIMA Plan B	
Ht: 6' 1" Wt: 211 Type Pwr	PT/Exp D	Rand Var -4	
	Consist B	MM 2301	

Filled opener role with good results. Possibility for expansion into rotation tempered by two-pitch arsenal and unproven durability. And the more batters saw him, the less trouble they had making contact against him. Also, remember that pitchers with two Tommy John surgeries under their belt aren't growth stocks to target. He'll be overvalued.

Yr Tm	W	Sv	IP	K	ERA	WHIP	xERA	xWHIP	vL+	vR+	BF/G	BB%	K%	K-BB%	xBB%	SwK	Vel	G	L	F	H%	S%	HR/F	xHR/F	GS	APC	DOM%	DIS%	Sv%	LI	RAR	BPX	R$
17																																	
18																																	
19 aa	1	0	61	66	5.87	1.67	5.27				12.5	13%	24%	11%							36%	65%									-10.3	74	-$9
20 MIL	1	0	15	21	5.87	1.70	3.72	1.34	156	68	5.9	13%	30%	17%	8%	13.2%	97.7	54	24	22	39%	70%	33%	14%	0	25			0	0.52	-2.7	126	-$7
21 2 TM	4	1	76	73	2.84	1.08	3.80	1.26	76	78	8.8	8%	24%	16%	7%	11.2%	97.1	47	23	30	27%	75%	8%	11%	10	34	10%	20%	100	0.83	13.3	110	$7
1st Half	0	1	23	34	3.97	1.37	3.68	1.35	62	95	5.2	15%	34%	19%	10%	12.1%	97.4	38	30	32	32%	72%	13%	8%	1	23	0%	100%	100	0.84	0.8	108	-$5
2nd Half	4	0	53	39	2.36	0.96	3.85	1.22	75	73	13.0	5%	19%	14%	5%	10.8%	97.0	50	20	29	25%	77%	7%	13%	9	48	11%	11%	0	0.81	12.5	111	$12
Proj	4	0	116	122	3.73	1.26	3.92	1.33	82	90	8.6	10%	26%	15%	7%	11.4%	97.1	45	24	30	30%	71%	10%	11%	0						10.4	102	$4

Ray,Robbie

Age: 30 Th: L Role SP	Health D	LIMA Plan D+	
Ht: 6' 2" Wt: 215 Type Pwr/FB	PT/Exp A	Rand Var -2	
	Consist F	MM 3505	

Best season yet; can he do it again? Threw half of pitches in zone, which fueled the improved control that turned him elite. But... 1) Same rate of pitches in zone in 2016, which didn't stick; 2) Friendly hit and strand rates won't repeat; 3) Had a very similar season in 2017, which turned out to be a mirage. Expect an ERA closer to 4.00 than 3.00.

Yr Tm	W	Sv	IP	K	ERA	WHIP	xERA	xWHIP	vL+	vR+	BF/G	BB%	K%	K-BB%	xBB%	SwK	Vel	G	L	F	H%	S%	HR/F	xHR/F	GS	APC	DOM%	DIS%	Sv%	LI	RAR	BPX	R$
17 ARI	15	0	162	218	2.89	1.15	3.49	1.22	82	88	23.8	11%	33%	22%	8%	14.7%	94.3	40	19	40	28%	82%	16%	14%	28	97	43%	25%			29.4	156	$24
18 ARI	6	0	124	165	3.93	1.35	3.75	1.34	62	109	21.9	13%	31%	18%	9%	13.2%	93.7	39	22	39	30%	76%	17%	14%	24	95	17%	25%			3.3	110	$3
19 ARI	12	0	174	235	4.34	1.34	3.90	1.28	85	108	22.6	11%	32%	21%	8%	14.1%	92.4	37	26	37	32%	74%	20%	19%	33	93	18%	12%			3.6	127	$9
20 2 TM	2	0	52	68	6.62	1.90	6.14	1.67	91	135	20.9	18%	27%	9%	12%	13.0%	93.7	24	24	51	34%	71%	19%	18%	11	89	0%	55%	0	0.76	-13.8	4	-$17
21 TOR	13	0	193	248	2.84	1.04	3.46	1.06	82	91	24.2	7%	32%	25%	6%	16.3%	94.8	37	19	44	28%	83%	16%	17%	32	98	38%	22%			34.0	173	$31
1st Half	6	0	87	113	3.43	1.12	3.30	1.04	72	104	23.7	6%	32%	26%	6%	16.1%	95.3	43	18	39	30%	82%	22%	22%	15	96	20%	20%			9.0	190	$17
2nd Half	7	0	107	135	2.36	0.98	3.58	1.09	84	84	24.5	7%	32%	25%	6%	16.4%	94.4	32	19	49	27%	85%	12%	14%	17	100	53%	24%			25.0	159	$41
Proj	12	0	189	246	3.67	1.19	3.67	1.17	78	97	21.6	9%	33%	23%	8%	14.8%	94.1	35	21	44	30%	76%	15%	17%	35						18.3	150	$18

Reyes,Alex

Age: 27 Th: R Role RP	Health D	LIMA Plan D+	
Ht: 6' 4" Wt: 220 Type Pwr/FB	PT/Exp C	Rand Var -5	
	Consist C	MM 1411	

Finally, talented flamethrower produced value like we all thought he could. Problem is, the underlying support just wasn't there. Filthy arsenal offset by continued wildness, and xBB% doesn't offer much reason for hope there. It all started to unravel in 2nd half once hit and strand rates regressed. He's an ideal sell-high target.

Yr Tm	W	Sv	IP	K	ERA	WHIP	xERA	xWHIP	vL+	vR+	BF/G	BB%	K%	K-BB%	xBB%	SwK	Vel	G	L	F	H%	S%	HR/F	xHR/F	GS	APC	DOM%	DIS%	Sv%	LI	RAR	BPX	R$
17																																	
18 STL *	2	0	20	23	0.00	0.55	-0.83		86	92	22.7	9%	34%	25%		4.1%	94.8	40	20	40	13%	100%	0%	1%	1	73	0%	0%			10.4	211	$3
19 STL *	1	0	31	31	9.49	2.05	7.08		38	192	10.8	20%	21%	1%		5.6%	96.8	30	20	50	33%	54%	20%	12%	0	18			0	1.00	-19.1	23	-$13
20 STL	2	1	20	27	3.20	1.42	4.63	1.48	80	84	5.7	16%	32%	15%	12%	14.9%	97.6	37	16	47	31%	78%	5%	11%	1	25	0%	0%	100	1.09	3.0	73	$1
21 STL	10	29	72	95	3.24	1.35	4.57	1.50	84	81	4.6	16%	30%	14%	12%	14.8%	96.7	37	19	44	25%	81%	12%	11%	0	18			85	1.22	9.2	58	$18
1st Half	5	20	40	52	0.91	1.24	4.43	1.58	64	67	4.6	19%	31%	13%	12%	13.5%	96.8	40	17	43	21%	96%	6%	11%	0	19			100	1.21	16.4	45	$23
2nd Half	5	9	33	43	6.06	1.50	4.73	1.42	95	102	4.6	14%	28%	15%	9%	16.5%	96.6	34	20	46	30%	64%	18%	10%	0	17			64	1.24	-7.2	76	$3
Proj	3	10	73	90	4.03	1.40	4.52	1.46	92	92	5.0	15%	29%	14%	11%	15.3%	96.6	36	19	45	28%	77%	15%	10%	0						3.8	70	$3

Richards,Garrett

Age: 34 Th: R Role RP	Health F	LIMA Plan C	
Ht: 6' 2" Wt: 210 Type Pwr	PT/Exp C	Rand Var +1	
	Consist A	MM 1201	

Finally, the durability we've been waiting for! Most innings since 2015—but that wasn't a good thing. His stuff has gone from electric to mediocre given all the injuries. Skills surge in 2nd half gives us a twinge of hope again, but they were still below par. Needs to move into a full-time relief role; command was 2x better out of pen than as a starter.

Yr Tm	W	Sv	IP	K	ERA	WHIP	xERA	xWHIP	vL+	vR+	BF/G	BB%	K%	K-BB%	xBB%	SwK	Vel	G	L	F	H%	S%	HR/F	xHR/F	GS	APC	DOM%	DIS%	Sv%	LI	RAR	BPX	R$
17 LAA	0	0	28	27	2.28	0.90	3.34	1.19	68	64	18.0	7%	25%	19%		12.6%	95.8	54	17	29	25%	75%	5%	11%	6	71	17%	17%			7.1	154	$0
18 LAA	5	0	76	87	3.66	1.28	3.68	1.30	89	101	20.3	11%	27%	16%	10%	11.9%	95.9	49	19	31	29%	77%	17%	18%	16	82	13%	44%			4.7	119	$2
19 SD	0	0	9	11	8.31	1.85	4.79	1.52	92	226	13.7	15%	28%	13%	10%	10.2%	95.1	43	26	30	37%	57%	29%	35%	3	52	0%	67%			-4.1	64	-$7
20 SD	2	0	51	46	4.03	1.25	4.48	1.32	118	78	15.2	8%	22%	14%	8%	11.5%	95.2	40	24	35	29%	72%	13%	18%	10	56	0%	40%	0	0.63	2.7	93	$3
21 BOS	7	3	137	115	4.87	1.60	4.87	1.43	102	118	15.4	10%	19%	9%	8%	10.3%	94.4	47	21	32	34%	72%	14%	18%	22	58	5%	50%	100	0.89	-10.2	60	-$8
1st Half	4	0	87	69	4.88	1.68	5.09	1.49	109	118	23.4	11%	17%	7%	8%	9.4%	94.1	47	22	30	35%	73%	13%	17%	17	89	6%	47%			-6.6	40	-$10
2nd Half	3	3	50	46	4.86	1.44	4.52	1.32	66	124	9.5	8%	21%	13%	6%	11.8%	95.0	46	19	35	33%	70%	15%	19%	5	36	0%	60%	100	0.98	-3.7	94	-$3
Proj	5	1	102	94	4.46	1.43	4.43	1.37	97	110	13.0	9%	22%	12%	8%	11.1%	95.0	46	21	33	32%	73%	15%	18%	10						-0.1	87	-$2

Richards,Trevor

Age: 29 Th: R Role RP	Health A	LIMA Plan B	
Ht: 6' 2" Wt: 195 Type Pwr/xFB	PT/Exp C	Rand Var -2	
	Consist C	MM 1311	

Anatomy of a future closer? 1) SwK turned elite in 2nd half; 2) Handcuffs both lefty and righty bats; 3) Gained over 2 mph with fastball. But Statcast isn't as optimistic, as barrel rate has jumped in three straight seasons; latest was in bottom 6% of league. As an xFB pitcher prone to hard contact, he's speculation material only. UP: 20 Sv

Yr Tm	W	Sv	IP	K	ERA	WHIP	xERA	xWHIP	vL+	vR+	BF/G	BB%	K%	K-BB%	xBB%	SwK	Vel	G	L	F	H%	S%	HR/F	xHR/F	GS	APC	DOM%	DIS%	Sv%	LI	RAR	BPX	R$
17 aa	5	0	75	66	3.94	1.37	4.09				22.5	6%	21%	15%							35%	71%									3.9	119	$1
18 MIA *	7	0	166	161	3.92	1.29	3.99	1.29	91	116	22.1	8%	24%	15%	9%	11.2%	90.8	36	25	39	31%	73%	11%	13%	25	89	32%	32%			4.6	97	$5
19 2 TM	6	0	135	127	4.06	1.35	5.05	1.42	100	99	19.3	10%	22%	12%	8%	12.3%	90.9	35	22	43	30%	74%	12%	12%	23	76	22%	30%	0	0.78	7.5	70	$4
20 TAM	0	0	32	27	5.91	1.72	5.75	1.37	108	126	16.7	7%	18%	11%	7%	12.3%	90.5	32	25	43	38%	69%	13%	10%	4	64	0%	75%	0	0.71	-5.7	71	-$13
21 3 TM	7	1	64	78	3.50	0.96	3.84	1.16	82	83	4.7	9%	31%	22%	9%	14.7%	92.8	28	22	50	21%	74%	16%	17%	0	20			17	0.87	6.1	131	$8
1st Half	3	1	32	41	3.69	1.14	3.91	1.17	65	111	6.1	9%	32%	23%	9%	13.3%	92.5	23	29	48	28%	74%	14%	12%	0	25			33	0.63	2.2	130	$1
2nd Half	4	0	33	37	3.31	0.80	3.76	1.15	95	61	3.8	8%	30%	22%	10%	16.1%	93.0	33	15	52	14%	74%	18%	21%	0	16			0	1.02	3.9	132	$6
Proj	5	2	73	76	3.99	1.25	4.37	1.26	96	100	7.5	9%	26%	17%	8%	13.5%	91.8	31	22	46	29%	75%	14%	15%	0						4.2	108	$2

STEPHEN NICKRAND

Robertson,David

Health	F	LIMA Plan	C+
PT/Exp	F	Rand Var	+5
Consist	F	MM	4410

Age: 37 Th: R Role: RP
Ht: 5' 11" Wt: 195 Type: Pwr

Returned after slow road back from Tommy John surgery. So did pre-injury skills in tiny sample size. We know his stuff was eroding before surgery, and latest SwK doesn't offer hope that it's back. But it's too early to write him off as a late-game option given prior steady skills. Consider him a good buy-low target, especially in holds leagues.

Yr Tm	W	Sv	IP	K	ERA	WHIP	xERA	xWHIP	vL+	vR+	BF/G	BB%	K%	K-BB%	xBB%	SwK	Vel	G	L	F	H%	S%	HR/F	xHR/F	GS	APC	DOM%	DIS%	Sv%	LI	RAR	BPX	R$
17 2AL	9	14	68	98	1.84	0.85	2.74	1.06	58	71	4.3	9%	37%	28%	7%	17.3%	91.6	47	16	37	23%	85%	12%	11%	0	17			88	1.19	21.2	211	$2
18 NYY	8	5	70	91	3.23	1.03	3.22	1.15	85	80	4.1	9%	32%	23%	9%	13.9%	92.3	45	17	37	27%	72%	12%	16%	0	17			56	1.20	7.9	166	$1
19 PHI	0	0	7	6	5.40	2.10	7.45	1.92	75	174	4.7	18%	18%	0%	12%	11.0%	91.7	33	24	43	35%	77%	11%	11%	0	19			0	1.24	-0.7	-67	-$
20																																	
21 TAM	0	0	12	16	4.50	1.25	3.31	1.11	81	108	4.2	8%	32%	24%	8%	9.6%	92.0	40	27	33	34%	69%	20%	16%	1	17	0%	0%	0	0.87	-0.3	168	-$
1st Half																																	
2nd Half	0	0	12	16	4.50	1.25	3.31	1.11	77	110	4.2	8%	32%	24%	8%	9.6%	92.0	40	27	33	34%	69%	20%	16%	1	17	0%	0%	0	0.87	-0.3	168	-$1
Proj	**4**	**4**	**58**	**71**	**3.45**	**1.13**	**3.46**	**1.18**	**91**	**88**	**4.2**	**9%**	**31%**	**22%**	**8%**	**15.2%**	**92.1**	**46**	**17**	**37**	**29%**	**73%**	**13%**	**14%**	**0**						**7.2**	**153**	**$**

Robles,Hansel

Health	B	LIMA Plan	B
PT/Exp	C	Rand Var	0
Consist	C	MM	1310

Age: 31 Th: R Role: RP
Ht: 6' 0" Wt: 220 Type: Pwr/FB

As children, the story of Hansel and Gretel taught us not to trust strangers. Here, let's try to convince you not to trust Hansel. 1) Those saves were the product of opportunity, not skill; 2) Take away 2019 and his control has been bad for five straight seasons; 3) Exit velocity, barrel rates were in bottom 7% of league. See? That wasn't hard.

Yr Tm	W	Sv	IP	K	ERA	WHIP	xERA	xWHIP	vL+	vR+	BF/G	BB%	K%	K-BB%	xBB%	SwK	Vel	G	L	F	H%	S%	HR/F	xHR/F	GS	APC	DOM%	DIS%	Sv%	LI	RAR	BPX	R$
17 NYM *	7	4	80	78	5.39	1.54	5.31	1.54	94	104	5.4	13%	22%	9%	10%	9.4%	94.9	34	22	44	30%	70%	15%	15%	0	21			50	1.11	-10.2	49	-$
18 2TM	2	2	56	59	3.70	1.39	4.41	1.35	118	98	4.6	10%	24%	14%	9%	11.4%	96.0	35	24	41	31%	80%	14%	13%	0	18			67	0.99	3.1	87	-$
19 LAA	5	23	73	75	2.48	1.02	3.89	1.16	77	81	4.0	6%	27%	21%	6%	12.5%	97.1	39	21	40	29%	79%	8%	9%	1	16	0%	0%	85	1.12	18.2	142	$1
20 LAA	0	1	17	20	10.26	1.74	5.35	1.45	175	94	4.4	13%	25%	13%	9%	13.9%	95.5	33	23	44	36%	40%	19%	20%	0	18			33	0.58	-11.9	67	-$1
21 2AL	3	14	69	76	4.43	1.38	4.39	1.41	110	92	4.1	12%	26%	13%	8%	11.1%	96.8	43	18	39	30%	70%	12%	19%	0	16			88	1.19	-1.4	76	$
1st Half	3	7	35	35	4.11	1.34	4.44	1.50	104	87	4.1	14%	24%	10%	8%	9.9%	96.5	48	17	35	27%	72%	13%	19%	0	17			78	1.30	0.7	54	$
2nd Half	0	7	34	41	4.76	1.41	4.34	1.33	104	100	4.1	11%	28%	16%	7%	12.4%	97.0	38	18	44	33%	68%	11%	18%	0	16			100	1.08	-2.1	99	-$
Proj	**3**	**2**	**65**	**70**	**4.03**	**1.39**	**4.55**	**1.42**	**107**	**95**	**4.3**	**12%**	**26%**	**13%**	**8%**	**11.4%**	**96.5**	**39**	**20**	**41**	**30%**	**75%**	**12%**	**15%**	**0**						**3.4**	**75**	**-$**

Rodón,Carlos

Health	F	LIMA Plan	C
PT/Exp	C	Rand Var	-4
Consist	F	MM	3403

Age: 29 Th: L Role: SP
Ht: 6' 3" Wt: 250 Type: Pwr/FB

Finally, the big season we knew he had in him. Filthy raw stuff enjoyed full conversion into skills thanks to 2.5 mph gain with four-seam fastball, which helped him double whiff rate with that pitch. Problem is, chronic shoulder issues came back late in season, so you can't trust him as a centerpiece yet... UP: 240 K; DN: 2018

Yr Tm	W	Sv	IP	K	ERA	WHIP	xERA	xWHIP	vL+	vR+	BF/G	BB%	K%	K-BB%	xBB%	SwK	Vel	G	L	F	H%	S%	HR/F	xHR/F	GS	APC	DOM%	DIS%	Sv%	LI	RAR	BPX	R$
17 CHW	2	0	69	76	4.15	1.37	4.06	1.35	99	105	24.8	10%	26%	15%	10%	10.9%	93.1	44	22	34	30%	76%	19%	13%	12	98	33%	25%			1.7	109	-$
18 CHW	6	0	121	90	4.18	1.26	5.00	1.51	118	91	25.6	11%	18%	7%	11%	9.4%	93.0	41	16	43	25%	70%	10%	10%	20	98	30%	30%			-0.4	33	$
19 CHW	3	0	35	46	5.19	1.44	4.26	1.31	49	101	22.6	11%	29%	18%	9%	12.6%	91.5	43	19	38	36%	65%	11%	13%	7	99	29%	14%			-2.9	127	-$
20 CHW	0	0	8	6	8.22	1.57	5.95	1.45	161	118	8.8	9%	17%	9%	7%	10.5%	92.9	28	24	48	34%	45%	8%	13%	2	33	0%	100%	0	1.90	-3.6	43	-$
21 CHW	13	0	133	185	2.37	0.96	3.20	1.02	82	73	22.3	7%	35%	28%	6%	15.7%	95.4	38	17	45	29%	81%	10%	12%	24	92	42%	21%			30.9	193	$2
1st Half	6	0	84	122	2.37	0.94	3.02	1.02	66	74	24.0	8%	36%	29%	6%	16.6%	95.9	39	18	43	29%	79%	9%	12%	14	101	50%	14%			19.6	195	$2
2nd Half	7	0	49	63	2.39	0.98	3.49	1.00	92	76	19.8	5%	32%	27%	6%	14.3%	94.7	36	17	48	30%	83%	10%	12%	10	81	30%	30%			11.3	189	$1
Proj	**13**	**0**	**145**	**174**	**3.35**	**1.10**	**3.63**	**1.16**	**89**	**84**	**21.2**	**8%**	**31%**	**22%**	**8%**	**13.1%**	**93.8**	**40**	**18**	**42**	**29%**	**74%**	**12%**	**12%**	**27**						**19.7**	**150**	**$1**

Rodriguez,Eduardo

Health	F	LIMA Plan	B+
PT/Exp	B	Rand Var	+4
Consist	A	MM	2303

Age: 29 Th: L Role: SP
Ht: 6' 2" Wt: 231 Type: Pwr

Results don't show it, but this was his best season yet. As SwK keeps inching upward, foundation is there to push K rate up even further. And those gains have been paired with two-year reduction in ball rate, validating K-BB% spike. Inflated hit rate was the only reason his ERA stayed above 4.00. Profit plays don't get much better than this one. UP: 3.50 ERA

Yr Tm	W	Sv	IP	K	ERA	WHIP	xERA	xWHIP	vL+	vR+	BF/G	BB%	K%	K-BB%	xBB%	SwK	Vel	G	L	F	H%	S%	HR/F	xHR/F	GS	APC	DOM%	DIS%	Sv%	LI	RAR	BPX	R$
17 BOS	6	0	137	150	4.19	1.28	4.26	1.28	107	97	23.3	9%	26%	17%	8%	11.9%	93.3	35	22	43	31%	71%	12%	13%	24	98	17%	21%	0	0.77	2.8	122	$
18 BOS	13	0	130	146	3.82	1.26	3.97	1.22	94	95	20.5	8%	26%	18%	8%	11.5%	93.3	39	20	41	32%	74%	11%	13%	23	86	30%	26%	0	0.81	5.3	132	$
19 BOS	19	0	203	213	3.81	1.33	4.10	1.30	103	93	25.3	9%	25%	16%	8%	12.1%	93.1	48	19	33	32%	75%	13%	15%	34	103	29%	21%			17.5	116	$1
20																																	
21 BOS	13	0	158	185	4.74	1.39	3.70	1.15	102	103	21.1	7%	27%	20%	7%	12.1%	92.6	43	22	34	37%	68%	13%	13%	31	85	13%	23%	0	0.79	-9.2	152	$
1st Half	6	0	85	99	5.42	1.35	3.63	1.11	91	108	22.6	6%	27%	22%	7%	11.5%	92.6	43	22	35	37%	62%	14%	13%	16	90	13%	25%			-12.1	165	$
2nd Half	7	0	73	86	3.95	1.44	3.78	1.20	101	101	19.6	8%	27%	19%	7%	12.8%	92.6	44	23	34	38%	74%	10%	14%	15	80	13%	20%	0	0.80	2.9	139	$
Proj	**13**	**0**	**174**	**192**	**3.80**	**1.29**	**3.87**	**1.22**	**99**	**94**	**20.9**	**8%**	**27%**	**19%**	**8%**	**12.0%**	**92.9**	**43**	**21**	**36**	**33%**	**74%**	**12%**	**14%**	**34**						**14.1**	**134**	**$1**

Rodriguez,Grayson

Health	A	LIMA Plan	C+
PT/Exp	F	Rand Var	0
Consist	F	MM	1200

Age: 22 Th: R Role: RP
Ht: 6' 5" Wt: 220 Type: Pwr

Scouts like him as a future SP2, and after a 121/22 K/BB in 79 IP at AA Bowie, it's easy to see why. High-90s fastball, plus slider, and diving change-up give him rotation-anchor arsenal. He'll be a candidate for a 2022 call-up to BAL after he gets some more seasoning in minors. A keeper league gem.

Yr Tm	W	Sv	IP	K	ERA	WHIP	xERA	xWHIP	vL+	vR+	BF/G	BB%	K%	K-BB%	xBB%	SwK	Vel	G	L	F	H%	S%	HR/F	xHR/F	GS	APC	DOM%	DIS%	Sv%	LI	RAR	BPX	R$
17																																	
18																																	
19																																	
20																																	
21 aa	6	0	81	100	2.71	0.87	1.94				16.7	7%	33%	27%							25%	74%									15.6	176	$1
1st Half	3	0	31	32	1.84	0.83	1.80				19.0	5%	28%	23%							22%	86%									9.4	167	$
2nd Half	3	0	50	68	3.25	0.90	2.02				15.5	8%	37%	29%							26%	68%									6.3	183	$1
Proj	**4**	**0**	**51**	**50**	**3.88**	**1.35**	**4.30**	**1.29**			**18.9**	**8%**	**24%**	**15%**				**40**	**22**	**38**	**32%**	**76%**	**13%**	**12%**	**10**						**3.6**	**108**	**-$**

Rodríguez,Joely

Health	D	LIMA Plan	C
PT/Exp	D	Rand Var	+4
Consist	B	MM	3210

Age: 30 Th: L Role: RP
Ht: 6' 1" Wt: 200 Type: Pwr/xGB

Recent stats won't send anyone his way. Still, this is the kind of guy you stash at the end of your pitching staff and see what happens. He's got one of the better change-ups in the game (40.9% SwK), and he pairs it with a sinker that also misses bats. That's a unique combo that can play well in short stints. With improvement against RH bats... UP: 20 Sv

Yr Tm	W	Sv	IP	K	ERA	WHIP	xERA	xWHIP	vL+	vR+	BF/G	BB%	K%	K-BB%	xBB%	SwK	Vel	G	L	F	H%	S%	HR/F	xHR/F	GS	APC	DOM%	DIS%	Sv%	LI	RAR	BPX	R$
17 PHI *	3	0	54	34	7.22	2.03	7.79	1.74	123	125	5.5	13%	13%	0%		9.0%	93.1	59	18	23	35%	67%	18%	9%	0	19			0	1.04	-19.0	-14	-$1
18 aaa	5	3	77	64	5.19	1.63	4.77				5.8	11%	19%	8%							36%	66%									-9.9	77	-$
19 for	3	1	60	73	2.05	1.04	2.50				3.6	7%	32%	24%							29%	85%									18.2	157	$
20 TEX	0	0	13	17	2.13	1.03	3.03	1.16	67	66	4.3	10%	33%	23%	7%	10.7%	94.6	52	24	24	30%	77%	0%	17%	0	20			0	0.76	3.6	171	-$
21 2AL	2	1	46	47	4.66	1.53	3.70	1.30	77	110	4.0	9%	23%	14%	7%	13.9%	94.1	58	20	21	37%	70%	14%	15%	0	15			33	1.12	-2.3	116	-$
1st Half	1	1	23	24	6.26	1.39	2.95	1.20	61	114	4.1	7%	24%	17%	6%	13.8%	94.0	70	17	13	35%	55%	33%	26%	0	16			50	1.18	-5.7	157	-$
2nd Half	1	0	23	23	3.09	1.67	4.44	1.40	86	109	3.9	11%	22%	12%	8%	14.1%	94.2	46	24	30	39%	82%	5%	10%	0	14			0	1.06	3.4	76	-$
Proj	**3**	**1**	**58**	**57**	**3.72**	**1.31**	**3.77**	**1.36**	**68**	**91**	**4.0**	**10%**	**24%**	**13%**	**8%**	**14.0%**	**94.1**	**56**	**21**	**23**	**30%**	**73%**	**13%**	**16%**	**0**						**5.2**	**102**	**-$**

Rodríguez,Manuel

Health	B	LIMA Plan	D+
PT/Exp	F	Rand Var	0
Consist	F	MM	1210

Age: 25 Th: R Role: RP
Ht: 5' 11" Wt: 205 Type: Pwr

3-3, 6.11 ERA in 18 IP at CHC. Futures Game participant struggled to find plate in first taste of majors, a continuation of the control demons that plagued him at nearly every stop in minors. Even with decent stuff and ability to keep the ball on the ground, chronic wildness means you need to watch him from afar.

Yr Tm	W	Sv	IP	K	ERA	WHIP	xERA	xWHIP	vL+	vR+	BF/G	BB%	K%	K-BB%	xBB%	SwK	Vel	G	L	F	H%	S%	HR/F	xHR/F	GS	APC	DOM%	DIS%	Sv%	LI	RAR	BPX	R$
17																																	
18																																	
19																																	
20																																	
21 CHC *	4	6	40	38	3.47	1.46	4.14	1.55	154	61	4.3	14%	22%	8%	10%	10.7%	97.2	54	17	30	29%	79%	19%	18%	0	15			75	1.13	3.9	72	$
1st Half	1	5	16	17	1.88	1.34	3.07				4.5	15%	25%	10%							27%	89%	0%		0	0					4.7	98	$
2nd Half	3	1	24	21	4.54	1.54	4.86	1.57	146	63	4.1	14%	20%	7%	10%	10.7%	97.2	54	17	30	30%	73%	19%	18%	0	15			100	1.13	-0.8	54	-$
Proj	**3**	**2**	**58**	**55**	**4.02**	**1.46**	**4.51**	**1.56**	**136**	**58**	**4.3**	**14%**	**22%**	**8%**	**10%**	**10.7%**	**97.2**	**54**	**17**	**30**	**29%**	**74%**	**14%**	**16%**	**0**						**3.1**	**45**	**-$**

STEPHEN NICKRAND

Rodriguez,Richard

Age: 32	Th: R	Role	RP	Health	B	LIMA Plan	C+
Ht: 6' 4"	Wt: 218	Type	Con/xFB	PT/Exp	C	Rand Var	-5
				Consist	F	MM	1110

On the surface, a solid follow-up to 2020. But K and swinging strike rates plummeted, which coincided with a big drop in slider usage—the same pattern we saw in his down 2019. Issues with a sore arm, perhaps? Regardless, only a further dip in walks and a favorable hit rate saved him, as xERA shows. There's risk in bidding on a repeat. DN: 5.00 ERA

Yr Tm	W	Sv	IP	K	ERA	WHIP	xERA	xWHIP	vL+	vR+	BF/G	BB%	K%	K-BB%	xBB%	SwK	Vel	G	L	F	H%	S%	HR/F	xHR/F	GS	APC	DOM%	DIS%	Sv%	LI	RAR	BPX	R$
17 BAL *	4	10	76	68	4.30	1.46	5.03	1.33	29	269	6.9	8%	21%	13%		6.7%	93.8	46	13	42	34%	74%	40%	36%	0	24			83	0.27	0.5	77	$3
18 PIT	4	0	69	88	2.47	1.07	3.38	1.07	60	102	4.4	7%	32%	25%	6%	14.5%	92.9	38	15	48	32%	80%	7%	9%	0	18			0	0.81	14.4	178	$7
19 PIT	4	1	65	63	3.72	1.35	4.91	1.34	119	85	4.0	8%	22%	14%	7%	11.3%	93.2	42	15	43	30%	82%	17%	12%	0	16			20	0.97	6.3	99	$1
20 PIT	3	4	23	34	2.70	0.86	2.86	0.94	67	78	3.9	5%	37%	32%	7%	15.3%	93.0	39	22	39	27%	76%	15%	15%	0	16			80	1.01	5.0	227	$14
21 2 NL	5	14	64	42	2.94	0.93	5.02	1.24	94	74	3.9	4%	17%	13%	5%	10.4%	93.1	31	15	54	23%	75%	7%	14%	0	15			82	1.14	10.5	84	$12
1st Half	3	10	31	27	2.59	0.80	4.34	1.07	63	64	3.9	3%	23%	21%	5%	11.3%	93.1	28	15	57	25%	67%	2%	9%	0	15			83	1.31	6.5	134	$11
2nd Half	2	4	33	15	3.27	1.06	5.73	1.40	117	84	3.9	5%	11%	6%	6%	9.5%	93.1	34	15	52	21%	82%	12%	19%	0	15			80	0.98	4.0	37	$12
Proj	**4**	**7**	**65**	**55**	**3.44**	**1.14**	**4.61**	**1.25**	**103**	**89**	**4.1**	**6%**	**21%**	**15%**	**6%**	**11.4%**	**93.1**	**35**	**15**	**51**	**27%**	**77%**	**11%**	**13%**	**0**						**8.2**	**103**	**$6**

Rogers,Josh

Age: 27	Th: L	Role	RP	Health	D	LIMA Plan	D+
Ht: 6' 3"	Wt: 220	Type	Con/FB	PT/Exp	D	Rand Var	-2
				Consist	F	MM	0001

1-2, 3.28 ERA in 36 IP at WAS. Flashy MLB ERA suppressed by a fortunate hit rate. Overall season numbers, which include Triple-A MLEs, are more indicative of his current level. Unless he finds a new offering for RH batters, extreme splits (.343 career OPS vL, .943 vR) will likely doom him to specialist duty for the long term.

Yr Tm	W	Sv	IP	K	ERA	WHIP	xERA	xWHIP	vL+	vR+	BF/G	BB%	K%	K-BB%	xBB%	SwK	Vel	G	L	F	H%	S%	HR/F	xHR/F	GS	APC	DOM%	DIS%	Sv%	LI	RAR	BPX	R$
17 aa	4	0	39	25	6.62	1.35	5.30				23.3	6%	15%	10%							30%	53%									-10.9	47	-$5
18 BAL *	9	0	153	87	4.99	1.55	5.93	1.41	94	144	24.8	7%	13%	6%	8%	6.1%	89.5	38	20	42	33%	71%	11%	16%	3	71	0%	67%			-15.8	28	-$10
19 BAL *	2	0	69	31	10.13	1.97	10.47	1.51	73	180	20.8	5%	9%	4%	11%	5.3%	89.5	24	20	56	36%	54%	23%	20%	0	53			0	0.27	-48.1	-74	-$24
20																																	
21 WAS *	9	0	127	70	5.11	1.55	6.33	1.46	47	125	23.1	7%	13%	5%	8%	8.6%	90.5	30	21	50	31%	73%	13%	15%	6	89	17%	50%			-13.2	9	-$9
1st Half																																	
2nd Half	9	0	127	70	5.11	1.55	6.33	1.46	47	125	23.1	8%	20%	12%	8%	8.6%	90.5	30	21	50	31%	73%	13%	15%	6	89	17%	50%			-13.2	9	-$9
Proj	**5**	**0**	**73**	**40**	**5.19**	**1.41**	**5.57**	**1.40**	**62**	**162**	**7.2**	**6%**	**13%**	**7%**	**8%**	**8.6%**	**90.5**	**30**	**21**	**50**	**30%**	**69%**	**14%**	**13%**	**7**						**-6.6**	**43**	**-$6**

Rogers,Taylor

Age: 31	Th: L	Role	RP	Health	D	LIMA Plan	A
Ht: 6' 3"	Wt: 190	Type	Pwr	PT/Exp	B	Rand Var	+4
				Consist	C	MM	5420

Missed the last two months with a finger sprain. Before that, skills had rebounded to vintage 2019 level—and beyond—with slight upticks in velocity and whiffs leading the way. And he wasn't chopped liver in "down" 2020. As a lefty, his grasp on the closer's job has always been a bit tenuous, but he's got the goods. With opportunity... UP: 30+ Saves

Yr Tm	W	Sv	IP	K	ERA	WHIP	xERA	xWHIP	vL+	vR+	BF/G	BB%	K%	K-BB%	xBB%	SwK	Vel	G	L	F	H%	S%	HR/F	xHR/F	GS	APC	DOM%	DIS%	Sv%	LI	RAR	BPX	R$
17 MIN	7	0	56	49	3.07	1.31	4.27	1.38	74	104	3.4	9%	21%	12%	7%	9.0%	93.2	45	24	31	30%	81%	12%	15%	0	13			0	1.23	8.8	89	$3
18 MIN	1	2	68	75	2.63	0.95	2.98	1.09	58	90	3.6	6%	29%	23%	6%	11.6%	93.4	45	26	30	28%	73%	6%	11%	0	14			50	1.04	12.8	166	$7
19 MIN	2	30	69	90	2.61	1.00	2.85	0.97	88	82	4.6	4%	33%	29%	5%	11.3%	94.8	51	18	31	32%	80%	15%	15%	0	18			83	1.50	16.1	220	$21
20 MIN	2	9	20	24	4.05	1.50	3.73	1.08	89	111	4.3	4%	26%	22%	4%	11.5%	94.6	42	29	29	43%	75%	11%	16%	0	17			82	1.15	1.0	187	$9
21 MIN	2	9	40	59	3.35	1.14	2.59	0.93	73	95	4.2	5%	36%	31%	4%	13.6%	95.8	50	20	30	38%	74%	14%	14%	0	16			69	1.55	4.6	238	$4
1st Half	2	7	33	44	2.73	1.12	2.72	0.96	78	93	4.2	5%	33%	29%	4%	14.2%	95.7	52	19	30	36%	79%	13%	13%	0	16			78	1.65	6.3	222	$6
2nd Half	0	2	7	15	6.14	1.23	2.04	0.81	0	107	4.0	6%	47%	41%	5%	11.3%	96.2	40	27	33	51%	50%	20%	17%	0	18			50	1.12	-1.7	311	$5
Proj	**4**	**15**	**65**	**78**	**2.75**	**1.09**	**3.06**	**1.06**	**77**	**90**	**3.9**	**6%**	**30%**	**25%**	**5%**	**11.9%**	**94.5**	**49**	**21**	**30**	**32%**	**79%**	**12%**	**14%**	**0**						**13.7**	**187**	**$12**

Rogers,Trevor

Age: 24	Th: L	Role	SP	Health	A	LIMA Plan	C+
Ht: 6' 5"	Wt: 217	Type	Pwr	PT/Exp	C	Rand Var	-4
				Consist	C	MM	3403

Missed August with a family emergency, but was terrific otherwise in his first full big-league season, flashing a nasty fastball/change-up combo. And, given light 2020 workload, the month break may have helped him on the mound: After sagging a bit in July, he posted his best skills month in Sept. Still just 24, this is a young arm in which to invest.

Yr Tm	W	Sv	IP	K	ERA	WHIP	xERA	xWHIP	vL+	vR+	BF/G	BB%	K%	K-BB%	xBB%	SwK	Vel	G	L	F	H%	S%	HR/F	xHR/F	GS	APC	DOM%	DIS%	Sv%	LI	RAR	BPX	R$
17																																	
18																																	
19 aa	1	0	26	24	6.99	1.64	5.96				23.2	9%	21%	12%							37%	58%									-8.0	60	-$7
20 MIA	1	0	28	39	6.11	1.61	3.80	1.23	108	120	18.6	10%	30%	20%	8%	13.2%	93.6	47	21	32	40%	65%	21%	11%	7	81	0%	14%			-5.7	156	-$8
21 MIA	7	0	133	157	2.64	1.15	3.63	1.18	92	79	22.0	8%	29%	20%	6%	14.7%	94.6	40	24	36	32%	78%	5%	12%	25	87	40%	16%			26.7	137	$16
1st Half	7	0	92	110	2.14	1.04	3.40	1.17	80	76	22.9	9%	30%	22%	6%	16.3%	94.6	42	22	35	28%	81%	7%	13%	16	88	44%	0%			24.2	142	$27
2nd Half	0	0	41	47	3.76	1.40	4.16	1.21	100	88	20.3	8%	26%	18%	7%	11.9%	94.6	36	28	36	38%	71%	2%	10%	9	85	33%	44%			2.5	129	$19
Proj	**12**	**0**	**174**	**204**	**3.22**	**1.17**	**3.65**	**1.19**	**90**	**83**	**22.3**	**9%**	**29%**	**21%**	**7%**	**13.4%**	**94.6**	**40**	**24**	**37**	**31%**	**74%**	**8%**	**11%**	**31**						**26.5**	**140**	**$20**

Rogers,Tyler

Age: 31	Th: R	Role	RP	Health	A	LIMA Plan	C
Ht: 6' 3"	Wt: 181	Type	Con/xGB	PT/Exp	C	Rand Var	-5
				Consist	B	MM	2011

Well, it's clear he and twin brother Taylor aren't exactly identical. This workhorse reliever continues to baffle with a fastball that barely breaks glass. The low walk rate helps, as does a strong groundball tilt. But sleek 2021 ERA also benefitted from a fortunate 1st-half strand rate. With his stuff, he'll never own a 9th, but with his control, he's unlikely to hurt you.

Yr Tm	W	Sv	IP	K	ERA	WHIP	xERA	xWHIP	vL+	vR+	BF/G	BB%	K%	K-BB%	xBB%	SwK	Vel	G	L	F	H%	S%	HR/F	xHR/F	GS	APC	DOM%	DIS%	Sv%	LI	RAR	BPX	R$
17 aaa	4	10	76	34	3.03	1.47	3.95				5.9	10%	10%	1%							30%	78%									12.5	49	$4
18 aaa	3	3	69	46	2.35	1.19	2.93				5.4	9%	17%	8%							27%	81%									15.4	82	$5
19 SF *	6	5	80	56	4.75	1.57	4.91	1.52	50	70	5.3	10%	16%	6%	4%	8.2%	82.4	69	16	14	33%	70%	0%	4%	0	15			56	1.17	-2.4	52	-$2
20 SF	3	3	28	27	4.50	1.32	3.58	1.16	100	93	4.2	5%	22%	17%	6%	10.9%	82.5	55	22	22	36%	66%	11%	6%	0	16			50	1.33	-0.2	155	$4
21 SF	7	13	81	55	2.22	1.07	3.77	1.22	63	99	4.1	4%	17%	13%	4%	7.8%	82.7	58	16	26	28%	82%	8%	5%	0	14			68	1.26	20.4	117	$16
1st Half	1	9	40	23	1.36	0.93	3.56	1.25	37	101	4.1	4%	15%	11%	5%	6.6%	82.4	65	13	21	25%	89%	8%	1%	0	15			69	1.42	14.2	110	$11
2nd Half	6	4	41	32	3.05	1.21	3.95	1.19	84	98	4.0	4%	19%	15%	4%	8.9%	83.1	50	19	30	32%	77%	8%	8%	0	14			67	1.11	6.2	124	$14
Proj	**6**	**9**	**73**	**48**	**3.41**	**1.17**	**3.98**	**1.27**	**70**	**102**	**4.2**	**5%**	**17%**	**12%**	**4%**	**8.0%**	**82.8**	**56**	**17**	**27**	**30%**	**71%**	**7%**	**5%**	**0**						**9.4**	**107**	**$7**

Romano,Jordan

Age: 29	Th: R	Role	RP	Health	C	LIMA Plan	C+
Ht: 6' 5"	Wt: 225	Type	Pwr/FB	PT/Exp	C	Rand Var	-5
				Consist	F	MM	3431

Went back to a more traditional pitch mix between still-improving upper-90s heat and his trademark versatile slider, but it didn't hurt his results. Sure, strand-rate fortune helped, but he bails himself out of a lot of those jams. Late flyball and HR spike a bit troubling, but K-BB% gains offset it. In short, this late bloomer should keep getting plenty of save opps.

Yr Tm	W	Sv	IP	K	ERA	WHIP	xERA	xWHIP	vL+	vR+	BF/G	BB%	K%	K-BB%	xBB%	SwK	Vel	G	L	F	H%	S%	HR/F	xHR/F	GS	APC	DOM%	DIS%	Sv%	LI	RAR	BPX	R$
17																																	
18 a/a	12	0	143	103	5.55	1.44	4.96				23.5	8%	17%	9%							32%	63%									-24.7	54	-$7
19 TOR *	2	5	55	63	7.42	1.63	6.72	1.32	86	141	5.9	10%	26%	16%	10%	13.8%	94.6	53	20	28	36%	59%	36%	29%	0	18			100	0.70	-19.6	46	-$8
20 TOR	2	2	15	21	1.23	0.89	2.54	1.06	51	84	3.8	9%	37%	28%	8%	20.7%	96.6	58	16	26	23%	100%	25%	24%	0	16			67	1.80	5.8	209	$7
21 TOR	7	23	63	85	2.14	1.05	3.28	1.15	60	90	4.1	10%	34%	24%	7%	15.2%	97.6	47	13	40	27%	86%	13%	13%	0	17			96	1.14	16.5	161	$20
1st Half	4	6	31	38	1.76	1.14	3.62	1.33	58	74	4.1	13%	30%	17%	10%	14.4%	97.3	54	11	35	28%	83%	0%	5%	0	17			86	1.19	9.5	117	$9
2nd Half	3	17	32	47	2.51	0.96	3.00	0.99	58	108	4.1	7%	37%	30%	5%	16.1%	97.9	39	16	45	25%	92%	23%	20%	0	17			100	1.09	7.0	203	$17
Proj	**6**	**30**	**73**	**87**	**2.92**	**1.12**	**3.57**	**1.16**	**68**	**107**	**5.1**	**8%**	**30%**	**22%**	**6%**	**15.4%**	**97.7**	**45**	**14**	**41**	**28%**	**82%**	**16%**	**14%**	**0**						**13.8**	**155**	**$21**

Romo,Sergio

Age: 39	Th: R	Role	RP	Health	B	LIMA Plan	C
Ht: 5' 11"	Wt: 185	Type	Pwr/FB	PT/Exp	C	Rand Var	0
				Consist	A	MM	2210

The "gentle decline" we noted in last year's book continues, with further skills erosion and a negative R$ earned for the first time in over a decade. Sure, he may be able to continue to stave off Father Time for another little while. But that said, there's no upside here anymore, and there are so many better relief options on which to speculate.

Yr Tm	W	Sv	IP	K	ERA	WHIP	xERA	xWHIP	vL+	vR+	BF/G	BB%	K%	K-BB%	xBB%	SwK	Vel	G	L	F	H%	S%	HR/F	xHR/F	GS	APC	DOM%	DIS%	Sv%	LI	RAR	BPX	R$
17 2 TM	3	0	56	59	3.56	1.10	4.04	1.26	97	86	4.1	8%	26%	18%	8%	15.2%	86.1	37	20	43	25%	75%	15%	12%	0	17			0	0.88	5.5	125	$3
18 TAM	3	25	67	75	4.14	1.26	3.96	1.17	97	101	3.9	7%	27%	20%	8%	13.9%	86.3	36	20	44	32%	73%	14%	14%	5	15	0%	40%	76	1.29	0.0	141	$10
19 2 TM	2	20	60	60	3.43	1.11	4.54	1.26	86	86	3.8	7%	24%	17%	6%	14.6%	86.4	36	19	45	28%	73%	9%	11%	0	15			87	1.05	8.0	116	$11
20 MIN	1	5	20	23	4.05	1.15	4.51	1.23	83	95	3.6	8%	26%	18%	8%	12.6%	85.6	31	20	48	28%	70%	12%	10%	0	15			83	1.35	1.0	125	$5
21 OAK	1	3	62	60	4.67	1.25	4.53	1.28	98	94	3.9	8%	23%	15%	8%	12.4%	85.5	38	18	44	29%	66%	12%	12%	0	16			43	0.90	-3.1	100	-$3
1st Half	0	0	29	29	4.60	1.19	4.32	1.24	84	90	3.7	7%	24%	16%	8%	13.0%	85.2	34	23	43	31%	61%	6%	9%	0	14			0	0.67	-1.2	107	-$6
2nd Half	1	3	32	31	4.73	1.30	4.72	1.32	102	100	4.2	9%	23%	14%	10%	11.9%	85.8	40	14	46	28%	71%	16%	14%	0	17			43	1.12	-1.9	92	-$4
Proj	**2**	**2**	**58**	**59**	**4.52**	**1.21**	**4.25**	**1.25**	**96**	**93**	**3.8**	**8%**	**25%**	**17%**	**8%**	**12.5%**	**85.9**	**37**	**18**	**44**	**29%**	**67%**	**13%**	**12%**	**0**						**-0.5**	**115**	**-$2**

ROD TRUESDELL

Rosenthal,Trevor

					Health	F	LIMA Plan	B+
Age: 32	Th: R	Role	RP		PT/Exp	D	Rand Var	0
Ht: 6' 2"	Wt: 230	Type	Pwr		Consist	F	MM	5520

Combination of thoracic outlet syndrome and a torn hip labrum resulted in two surgeries and a missed 2021 season. Before that, had put up quite the abbreviated 2020, boasting the top strikeout-to-walk ratio of his career. With health—no given, as he hasn't reached even 25 IP in MLB since 2017—he could be an under-the-radar steal. UP: 30 Sv

Yr	Tm	W	Sv	IP	K	ERA	WHIP	xERA	xWHIP	vL+	vR+	BF/G	BB%	K%	K-BB%	xBB%	SwK	Vel	G	L	F	H%	S%	HR/F	xHR/F	GS	APC	DOM%	DIS%	Sv%	LI	RAR	BPX	R$
17	STL	3	11	48	76	3.40	1.20	2.82	1.10	76	77	4.0	10%	38%	28%	6%	16.4%	98.4	41	28	31	37%	72%	9%	8%	0	18			85	1.33	5.6	211	$7
18																																		
19	2 TM *	0	0	33	32	12.72	2.43	7.79	2.39	96	94	4.4	26%	19%	-8%	12%	10.1%	98.0	43	22	35	32%	45%	0%	12%	0	18			0	0.77	-33.1	20	-$19
20	2 TM	1	11	24	38	1.90	0.85	2.84	0.98	54	90	4.0	9%	42%	33%	7%	17.1%	98.0	40	12	49	26%	83%	10%	13%	0	17			92	1.32	7.4	221	$21
21																																		
1st Half																																		
2nd Half																																		
Proj		2	12	44	58	3.58	1.15	3.19	1.21	82	79	3.5	11%	34%	23%	6%	15.4%	98.4	41	28	31	30%	69%	11%	7%	0						4.7	146	$5

Ross,Joe

					Health	F	LIMA Plan	B+
Age: 29	Th: R	Role	SP		PT/Exp	D	Rand Var	0
Ht: 6' 4"	Wt: 220	Type	Con		Consist	D	MM	1101

Missed the last seven weeks with a partially torn ulnar collateral ligament in his throwing elbow. Having already undergone Tommy John surgery in 2017, rest and rehab was the medical path chosen this time. Before the elbow woes, he had taken a nice skills step up across the board. But wow... with yet another elbow issue, can you stomach the risk?

Yr	Tm	W	Sv	IP	K	ERA	WHIP	xERA	xWHIP	vL+	vR+	BF/G	BB%	K%	K-BB%	xBB%	SwK	Vel	G	L	F	H%	S%	HR/F	xHR/F	GS	APC	DOM%	DIS%	Sv%	LI	RAR	BPX	R$
17	WAS *	7	0	101	86	5.34	1.54	6.05	1.30	122	109	24.5	6%	19%	13%	6%	10.5%	91.4	38	25	38	35%	70%	19%	14%	13	93	31%	46%			-12.3	62	-$5
18	WAS *	2	0	34	15	4.80	1.31	4.53	1.42	101	143	23.6	6%	11%	5%	6%	9.2%	93.1	36	22	42	29%	66%	13%	14%	3	83	0%	33%			-2.7	33	-$5
19	WAS *	6	0	104	82	5.38	1.66	5.59	1.46	119	102	13.3	9%	18%	9%	10%	10.5%	94.1	44	24	31	37%	68%	11%	17%	9	42	0%	33%	0	0.81	-11.3	59	-$8
20																																		
21	WAS	5	0	108	109	4.17	1.22	4.07	1.23	112	81	23.0	7%	24%	16%	7%	11.2%	93.5	43	20	36	29%	71%	15%	17%	19	85	26%	26%	0	0.79	1.3	118	$2
1st Half		5	0	81	80	4.02	1.21	4.16	1.27	106	84	22.7	8%	23%	15%	7%	11.6%	93.5	44	18	38	28%	74%	17%	17%	15	85	27%	33%			2.5	108	$7
2nd Half		0	0	27	29	4.61	1.24	3.80	1.13	105	79	23.8	5%	24%	19%	7%	10.2%	93.7	41	27	32	34%	65%	12%	16%	4	85	25%	0%	0	0.76	-1.2	151	-$9
Proj		5	0	109	92	4.49	1.32	4.36	1.29	112	87	21.3	7%	20%	13%	8%	10.7%	93.3	42	24	35	31%	69%	12%	16%	21						-0.5	99	-$1

Ruiz,José

					Health	A	LIMA Plan	B
Age: 27	Th: R	Role	RP		PT/Exp	D	Rand Var	-5
Ht: 6' 1"	Wt: 250	Type	Pwr		Consist	F	MM	1200

PRO: Climbing fastball velocity and SwK; controlled RH batters; curbed the walks a bit. CON: Couldn't turn those pros into even league-average command ratios; xERA shows benefit of favorable hit rate. Excluding those 4 IP in 2020, he's consistently posted skills at or below league average. Upper-90s heat gives him upside, but make him show it first.

Yr	Tm	W	Sv	IP	K	ERA	WHIP	xERA	xWHIP	vL+	vR+	BF/G	BB%	K%	K-BB%	xBB%	SwK	Vel	G	L	F	H%	S%	HR/F	xHR/F	GS	APC	DOM%	DIS%	Sv%	LI	RAR	BPX	R$
17	SD	0	0	1	1	0.00	1.00	5.60		44		4.0	25%	25%	0%		6.7%	95.3	50	0	50	0%	0%	0%	0%	0	15			0	0.09	0.5	-64	-$5
18	CHW *	3	14	50	53	4.36	1.41	3.88		73	131	5.5	12%	25%	13%		16.9%	96.2	42	25	33	32%	69%	25%	3%	0	15			88	0.45	-1.3	101	$3
19	CHW *	1	7	55	48	4.48	1.78	5.91	1.60	94	138	5.0	12%	19%	7%	8%	10.6%	96.4	37	22	40	36%	77%	11%	13%	1	19	0%	100%	78	0.55	0.2	48	-$4
20	CHW	0	0	4	5	2.25	0.50	3.08		99	38	2.8	0%	36%	36%		10.0%	96.8	33	11	56	14%	0%	20%	16%	0	12			0	1.41	1.1	241	-$4
21	CHW	1	0	65	63	3.05	1.17	4.35	1.32	104	76	4.6	9%	23%	14%	7%	11.2%	97.0	42	20	38	26%	79%	12%	16%	0	18			0	0.43	9.8	92	$1
1st Half		0	0	32	31	3.13	1.07	4.31	1.22	100	70	4.5	7%	24%	17%	6%	10.9%	96.8	34	23	42	26%	77%	11%	14%	0	17			0	0.32	4.4	112	-$2
2nd Half		1	0	33	32	2.97	1.26	4.39	1.42	97	83	4.7	11%	23%	11%	8%	11.5%	97.2	49	17	34	26%	82%	13%	18%	0	18			0	0.55	5.3	72	-$3
Proj		2	0	58	56	3.56	1.35	4.53	1.40	97	91	4.7	11%	23%	12%	7%	11.1%	96.9	42	20	38	30%	77%	11%	16%	0						6.4	76	-$2

Ryan,Joe

					Health	A	LIMA Plan	B+
Age: 26	Th: R	Role	RP		PT/Exp	F	Rand Var	+3
Ht: 6' 1"	Wt: 185	Type	Pwr/FB		Consist	F	MM	2303

2-1, 4.05 ERA in 27 IP at MIN. Rookie made quite the September splash after a successful stint with Team USA in the Olympics, notching a dazzling 30/5 K-to-BB ratio and four straight PQS 3 or 4 starts before a tough final outing. His only issue at higher levels has been the long ball, but a high K-BB% keeps that damage minimal. He seems ready now.

Yr	Tm	W	Sv	IP	K	ERA	WHIP	xERA	xWHIP	vL+	vR+	BF/G	BB%	K%	K-BB%	xBB%	SwK	Vel	G	L	F	H%	S%	HR/F	xHR/F	GS	APC	DOM%	DIS%	Sv%	LI	RAR	BPX	R$
17																																		
18																																		
19																																		
20																																		
21	MIN *	6	0	93	105	4.22	0.89	2.62	1.04	83	69	18.1	5%	31%	25%	4%	12.1%	91.3	28	19	53	24%	57%	12%	16%	5	82	40%	20%			0.5	172	$9
1st Half		3	0	46	50	5.17	1.02	3.28				17.7	6%	28%	23%							28%	51%	0%		0	0					-5.2	148	$0
2nd Half		3	0	47	55	3.29	0.75	1.98	0.98	78	70	18.5	5%	33%	28%	4%	12.1%	91.3	28	19	53	20%	65%	12%	16%	5	82	40%	20%			5.6	200	$11
Proj		7	0	131	139	4.69	1.17	3.95	1.17	115	104	19.7	7%	27%	20%	4%	12.1%	91.3	33	21	46	30%	63%	14%	15%	28						-3.8	135	$4

Ryu,Hyun-Jin

					Health	F	LIMA Plan	B+
Age: 35	Th: L	Role	SP		PT/Exp	A	Rand Var	0
Ht: 6' 3"	Wt: 255	Type			Consist	A	MM	3203

Now entering his age-35 season, note the multi-year decline in skills, as highlighted by xERA. The latter took a more notable jump in 2021, reflecting the lowest K rate he's managed since his first MLB season. On the other hand, he's mostly been healthy recently, and BPX shows he's still better than most. But if trends continue... DN: 4.75 ERA

Yr	Tm	W	Sv	IP	K	ERA	WHIP	xERA	xWHIP	vL+	vR+	BF/G	BB%	K%	K-BB%	xBB%	SwK	Vel	G	L	F	H%	S%	HR/F	xHR/F	GS	APC	DOM%	DIS%	Sv%	LI	RAR	BPX	R$
17	LA	5	1	127	116	3.77	1.37	4.23	1.34	127	99	21.6	8%	21%	13%	8%	11.4%	90.3	45	23	32	31%	79%	19%	17%	24	85	13%	33%	100	0.76	9.3	102	$4
18	LA	7	0	82	89	1.97	1.01	3.23	1.06	98	83	21.6	5%	27%	23%	6%	12.3%	90.2	46	19	35	29%	88%	12%	13%	15	83	40%	20%			22.2	178	$13
19	LA	14	0	183	163	2.32	1.01	3.47	1.13	71	87	24.9	3%	23%	19%	6%	11.8%	90.6	50	24	25	29%	82%	13%	12%	29	93	45%	7%			49.3	153	$31
20	TOR	5	0	67	72	2.69	1.15	3.49	1.15	79	87	22.9	6%	26%	20%	8%	12.3%	89.6	51	21	28	32%	80%	12%	10%	12	94	17%	17%			14.6	160	$21
21	TOR	14	0	169	143	4.37	1.22	4.09	1.21	95	99	22.6	5%	20%	15%	6%	10.1%	90.0	47	20	33	30%	68%	14%	17%	31	87	32%	29%			-2.1	119	$8
1st Half		7	0	94	74	3.65	1.15	4.11	1.24	89	97	23.8	6%	19%	14%	6%	9.8%	89.4	48	19	33	28%	74%	15%	15%	16	91	31%	25%			7.1	109	$14
2nd Half		7	0	75	69	5.26	1.31	4.06	1.18	91	106	21.3	5%	22%	17%	6%	10.4%	90.6	45	21	34	34%	62%	13%	20%	15	82	33%	33%			-9.2	132	$2
Proj		11	0	145	136	3.89	1.20	3.75	1.19	91	95	22.1	6%	23%	17%	6%	11.1%	90.1	48	21	31	31%	71%	14%	15%	26						10.1	136	$10

Sadler,Casey

					Health	F	LIMA Plan	B+
Age: 31	Th: R	Role	RP		PT/Exp	D	Rand Var	-5
Ht: 6' 3"	Wt: 205	Type	Con/xGB		Consist	C	MM	4100

Unheralded journeyman returned from 1st-half shoulder woes and just kept putting up zeroes. In fact, he didn't allow a single ER after July 25th, a streak reaching 29 appearances. Now, he clearly isn't THAT good—for example, that ridiculous 2nd-half hit rate will never repeat. But the extreme GB% is nice, and he can help a deep-league staff.

Yr	Tm	W	Sv	IP	K	ERA	WHIP	xERA	xWHIP	vL+	vR+	BF/G	BB%	K%	K-BB%	xBB%	SwK	Vel	G	L	F	H%	S%	HR/F	xHR/F	GS	APC	DOM%	DIS%	Sv%	LI	RAR	BPX	R$
17	a/a	3	0	67	39	6.66	1.70	6.35				15.1	4%	13%	9%							39%	60%									-18.9	73	-$12
18	PIT *	6	1	81	48	4.61	1.73	6.09		204	82	12.8	9%	13%	4%		7.0%	92.1	68	16	16	36%	75%	0%	24%	0	43			100	0.42	-4.7	32	-$8
19	2 TM *	5	3	87	71	2.89	1.23	4.20	1.25	94	82	7.6	5%	20%	15%	8%	9.6%	93.5	52	18	30	30%	83%	12%	10%	1	21	0%	100%	60	0.45	17.2	96	$7
20	2 TM	1	0	19	21	5.12	1.40	4.89	1.52	90	104	5.1	14%	24%	10%	10%	12.9%	92.9	40	27	33	26%	67%	18%	9%	0	20			0	0.81	-1.6	49	-$5
21	SEA	0	0	40	37	0.67	0.72	2.93	1.18	61	51	3.5	7%	26%	19%	7%	10.2%	93.1	63	11	26	19%	93%	4%	9%	0	14			0	1.09	17.9	142	$6
1st Half		0	0	11	10	1.64	1.27	5.10	1.52	83	77	4.2	13%	22%	9%	8%	12.5%	93.0	43	10	47	28%	86%	0%	7%	0	18			0	0.90	3.6	40	-$6
2nd Half		0	0	29	27	0.31	0.51	2.17	1.03	48	40	3.2	4%	27%	23%	6%	8.9%	93.1	72	12	16	15%	100%	9%	11%	0	12			0	1.15	14.3	182	$7
Proj		2	0	58	52	3.09	1.18	3.25	1.18	112	85	6.3	5%	23%	17%	7%	10.7%	93.3	64	15	22	31%	76%	13%	11%	0						9.8	153	$1

Sale,Chris

					Health	F	LIMA Plan	C
Age: 33	Th: L	Role	SP		PT/Exp	D	Rand Var	-2
Ht: 6' 6"	Wt: 183	Type	Pwr		Consist	C	MM	5503

Skills were well short of vintage; as we would expect ~18 months post-Tommy John surgery (with a September bout of COVID thrown in). Only two things we know for sure: 1) Rehab went very smoothly. 2) Velocity came back relatively intact; ticked even higher in postseason. That's not enough for full confidence, but it does bring into play... UP: Cy Young

Yr	Tm	W	Sv	IP	K	ERA	WHIP	xERA	xWHIP	vL+	vR+	BF/G	BB%	K%	K-BB%	xBB%	SwK	Vel	G	L	F	H%	S%	HR/F	xHR/F	GS	APC	DOM%	DIS%	Sv%	LI	RAR	BPX	R$
17	BOS	17	0	214	308	2.90	0.97	2.86	0.95	70	83	26.6	5%	36%	31%	5%	15.5%	94.4	39	20	41	32%	76%	12%	12%	32	107	69%	3%			38.6	241	$40
18	BOS	12	0	158	237	2.11	0.86	2.40	0.90	58	77	22.9	6%	38%	33%	5%	16.4%	94.7	44	20	36	30%	79%	9%	14%	27	94	63%	11%			39.8	245	$34
19	BOS	6	0	147	218	4.40	1.09	2.98	1.00	88	94	24.5	6%	36%	30%	6%	14.6%	93.2	43	21	36	33%	65%	20%	18%	25	99	32%	16%			2.0	218	$12
20																																		
21	BOS *	6	0	62	74	2.77	1.29	4.21	1.12	48	110	19.6	7%	29%	22%	6%	13.0%	93.6	47	21	32	35%	84%	17%	13%	9	82	0%	22%			11.5	136	$4
1st Half																																		
2nd Half		6	0	62	74	2.77	1.29	4.21	1.12	45	112	19.6	7%	29%	22%	6%	13.0%	93.6	47	21	32	35%	84%	17%	13%	9	82	0%	22%			11.5	136	$13
Proj		12	0	174	231	3.38	1.12	3.07	1.05	65	92	21.9	7%	34%	27%	6%	13.8%	93.9	44	21	36	33%	74%	14%	14%	31						23.1	193	$2

ROD TRUESDELL

Sánchez,Sixto

Age: 23 Th: R Role SP | Health F | LIMA Plan B
Ht: 6' 0" Wt: 234 Type Con/GB | PT/Exp D | Rand Var 0
Consist A | MM 3101

Bum shoulder kept him out all year, with July surgery to repair a small tear in the posterior capsule shutting things down for good. Before that, he seemed poised to become a rotation fixture at the tender age of 22. Now, the hope is he'll be ready for 2022 spring training. But given his low IP totals over two seasons, he'll surely be handled with kid gloves.

Yr	Tm	W	Sv	IP	K	ERA	WHIP	xERA	xWHIP	vL+	vR+	BF/G	BB%	K%	K-BB%	xBB%	SwK	Vel	G	L	F	H%	S%	HR/F	xHR/F	GS	APC	DOM%	DIS%	Sv%	LI	RAR	BPX	R$
17																																		
18																																		
19	aa	8	0	103	85	3.90	1.29	3.89				23.5	5%	20%	15%							34%	70%									7.8	121	$4
20	MIA	3	0	39	33	3.46	1.21	3.89	1.28	73	99	22.6	7%	21%	14%	6%	12.9%	97.6	58	13	29	30%	73%	9%	11%	7	80	43%	43%			4.8	118	$6
21																																		
1st Half																																		
2nd Half																																		
Proj		8	0	102	85	3.65	1.24	3.74	1.25	84	112	22.9	6%	21%	14%	6%	12.9%	97.6	58	13	29	32%	71%	9%	10%	18						10.1	125	$5

Sandoval,Patrick

Age: 25 Th: L Role RP | Health D | LIMA Plan B+
Ht: 6' 3" Wt: 190 Type Pwr/GB | PT/Exp C | Rand Var 0
Consist B | MM 3303

A stress fracture in his back ended this breakout-ish season in August. We say "ish" because there's still work to be done: mainly, the walk rate remains higher than you like. But a big step up in strikeout rate while maintaining his groundball tilt is very encouraging. Prospect growth can be uneven, but if he builds on this... UP 3.20 ERA, 180 K

Yr	Tm	W	Sv	IP	K	ERA	WHIP	xERA	xWHIP	vL+	vR+	BF/G	BB%	K%	K-BB%	xBB%	SwK	Vel	G	L	F	H%	S%	HR/F	xHR/F	GS	APC	DOM%	DIS%	Sv%	LI	RAR	BPX	R$
17																																		
18	aa	1	0	21	24	1.58	1.02	1.49				20.4	10%	29%	20%							28%	83%									6.7	163	-$1
19	LAA *	4	0	120	127	5.70	1.67	5.61	1.43	135	89	18.0	11%	24%	12%	11%	13.7%	93.0	47	26	27	37%	67%	21%	17%	9	71	11%	56%	0	0.72	-17.8	71	-$11
20	LAA	1	0	37	33	5.65	1.34	4.21	1.30	117	107	17.7	8%	21%	13%	8%	12.9%	92.8	55	18	27	28%	67%	32%	25%	6	66	0%	83%	0	0.87	-5.4	112	-$6
21	LAA	3	1	87	94	3.62	1.21	3.73	1.29	71	93	21.4	10%	26%	16%	9%	15.2%	93.3	51	19	30	28%	74%	16%	14%	14	85	21%	29%	100	0.75	6.9	114	$3
1st Half		2	1	44	46	3.89	1.25	3.72	1.28	90	100	18.3	9%	25%	16%	9%	16.5%	93.5	52	19	30	28%	77%	23%	18%	7	73	0%	29%	100	0.73	2.1	116	$0
2nd Half		1	0	43	48	3.35	1.16	3.74	1.31	51	90	25.7	11%	27%	16%	8%	13.9%	93.0	50	18	31	28%	72%	9%	9%	7	103	43%	29%			4.9	112	$0
Proj		8	0	145	151	4.16	1.27	3.81	1.32	92	95	19.2	10%	25%	15%	9%	14.3%	93.1	51	20	29	29%	72%	19%	16%	28						5.3	112	$5

Sanmartin,Reiver

Age: 26 Th: L Role SP | Health A | LIMA Plan B+
Ht: 6' 2" Wt: 160 Type Con | PT/Exp D | Rand Var -2
Consist D | MM 2101

2-0, 1.54 ERA in 12 IP at CIN. Reiver the Reliever? Not if his flashy two late starts (12/2 K/BB) carry any weight. Ah, but given his string-bean build, carrying weight is an issue. Given that and dominance against lefties, he may indeed eventually move to the 'pen. Doesn't throw hard, but has shown excellent command in the minors. Worth watching.

Yr	Tm	W	Sv	IP	K	ERA	WHIP	xERA	xWHIP	vL+	vR+	BF/G	BB%	K%	K-BB%	xBB%	SwK	Vel	G	L	F	H%	S%	HR/F	xHR/F	GS	APC	DOM%	DIS%	Sv%	LI	RAR	BPX	R$
17																																		
18																																		
19	aa	2	0	58	48	5.84	1.60	5.92				21.4	7%	19%	11%							36%	65%									-9.5	59	-$8
20																																		
21	CIN *	12	0	113	107	3.99	1.35	4.15	1.24	64	106	17.4	7%	23%	16%	7%	11.0%	89.4	47	21	32	35%	71%	0%	5%	2	91	50%	0%			3.8	111	$5
1st Half																																		
2nd Half		9	0	72	64	3.99	1.41	4.55	1.25	61	108	17.9	7%	21%	14%	7%	11.1%	89.4	47	21	32	36%	72%	0%	5%	2	91	50%	0%			2.5	104	$8
Proj		5	0	87	75	4.14	1.26	4.25	1.29			20.2	7%	21%	14%				45	20	35	30%	70%	11%	10%	18						3.4	103	$1

Santillan,Tony

Age: 25 Th: R Role RP | Health A | LIMA Plan B+
Ht: 6' 3" Wt: 240 Type Pwr/FB | PT/Exp D | Rand Var -4
Consist F | MM 1311

1-3, 2.91 ERA in 43 IP at CIN. Rode the Cincinnati-Louisville shuttle plenty in 2021, but 2nd-half switch to the bullpen seemed to suit him well, as skills show across the board. Teams are often hesitant to make that switch permanent with younger pitchers. But with his fastball/slider combo, this one could stick—and if it does, he's a saves sleeper. UP: 20 Sv

Yr	Tm	W	Sv	IP	K	ERA	WHIP	xERA	xWHIP	vL+	vR+	BF/G	BB%	K%	K-BB%	xBB%	SwK	Vel	G	L	F	H%	S%	HR/F	xHR/F	GS	APC	DOM%	DIS%	Sv%	LI	RAR	BPX	R$
17																																		
18	aa	4	0	63	55	4.54	1.46	5.56				24.6	6%	20%	14%							35%	74%									-3.0	78	-$4
19	aa	2	0	103	84	6.32	1.84	6.19				22.9	12%	17%	5%							37%	65%									-23.1	43	-$17
20																																		
21	CIN *	2	2	81	101	2.84	1.25	3.96	1.26	108	92	8.5	11%	31%	19%	10%	12.6%	95.0	33	24	43	28%	86%	16%	14%	4	29	0%	50%	100	0.76	14.3	99	$5
1st Half		2	0	51	61	3.31	1.38	4.87	1.29	115	121	19.4	11%	29%	18%	12%	10.9%	94.3	30	24	46	31%	85%	14%	19%	4	82	0%	50%			6.0	84	$0
2nd Half		0	2	33	40	1.92	0.96	2.06	1.23	90	78	4.4	11%	32%	21%	9%	13.9%	95.6	35	25	40	20%	89%	17%	9%	0	20			100	0.76	9.5	125	$4
Proj		2	5	73	82	3.56	1.34	4.30	1.31	113	96	7.7	10%	27%	17%	10%	12.6%	95.1	33	24	42	31%	79%	13%	13%	0						8.0	102	$2

Sawamura,Hirokazu

Age: 34 Th: R Role RP | Health C | LIMA Plan D+
Ht: 6' 0" Wt: 212 Type Pwr/xGB | PT/Exp C | Rand Var -4
Consist A | MM 1300

Japanese import spent 25 days on the IL (triceps, COVID). PRO: Excellent swing-and-miss stuff, xGB lean make him tough to hit; no big platoon split. CON: Offset whiffs with a walk rate among worst in majors; strand rate suppressed ERA. History, age suggest poor command isn't likely to change, so he's unlikely to hold much value for you.

Yr	Tm	W	Sv	IP	K	ERA	WHIP	xERA	xWHIP	vL+	vR+	BF/G	BB%	K%	K-BB%	xBB%	SwK	Vel	G	L	F	H%	S%	HR/F	xHR/F	GS	APC	DOM%	DIS%	Sv%	LI	RAR	BPX	R$
17																																		
18	for	1	0	52	51	5.80	1.78	5.90				4.9	14%	21%	7%							35%	69%									-10.6	56	-$11
19	for	2	1	48	52	3.26	1.33	3.84				4.6	11%	26%	16%							31%	79%									7.4	98	$0
20	for	1	1	34	38	4.27	1.41	4.16				4.1	15%	26%	11%							26%	74%									0.8	78	-$1
21	BOS	5	0	53	61	3.06	1.45	4.29	1.45	107	101	4.2	14%	26%	13%	12%	15.8%	96.1	52	13	35	29%	87%	19%	21%	0	17			0	0.86	7.9	77	$0
1st Half		4	0	33	40	2.48	1.32	4.15	1.37	88	103	4.5	13%	28%	16%	10%	16.0%	95.9	43	20	38	27%	92%	19%	26%	0	19			0	0.88	7.2	94	$3
2nd Half		1	0	20	21	3.98	1.67	4.49	1.59	125	103	3.8	15%	23%	8%	12%	15.4%	96.4	65	4	31	32%	81%	18%	12%	0	15			0	0.85	0.7	48	-$10
Proj		2	0	44	48	4.18	1.49	4.34	1.49	113	99	4.2	14%	25%	11%	12%	15.6%	96.2	56	10	34	30%	76%	16%	18%	0						1.5	75	-$4

Sborz,Josh

Age: 28 Th: R Role RP | Health A | LIMA Plan C
Ht: 6' 3" Wt: 215 Type Pwr | PT/Exp D | Rand Var -1
Consist B | MM 1310

Hard-thrower had his moments, but also struggled with walks, gopherballs. That said, xBB% shows the control issues might regress a little. And any hurler with his growing ability to miss bats gets our attention. If he can trim walks down to pre-2021 levels AND keep the whiffs up, there's some sneaky upside here... UP: 15 Sv

Yr	Tm	W	Sv	IP	K	ERA	WHIP	xERA	xWHIP	vL+	vR+	BF/G	BB%	K%	K-BB%	xBB%	SwK	Vel	G	L	F	H%	S%	HR/F	xHR/F	GS	APC	DOM%	DIS%	Sv%	LI	RAR	BPX	R$
17	aa	8	0	117	68	4.61	1.50	4.45				21.0	10%	13%	3%							30%	69%									-3.6	47	-$3
18	a/a	4	6	54	59	4.29	1.38	3.60				4.9	8%	26%	18%							37%	66%									-0.9	139	$0
19	LA *	4	3	59	62	5.67	1.55	5.10	1.24	165	89	4.9	7%	24%	17%	6%	10.3%	95.3	38	28	34	40%	62%	20%	22%	0	26			38	0.37	-8.5	116	-$4
20	LA	0	0	4	2	2.08	0.69	5.52		69	86	4.0	6%	13%	6%		13.6%	95.9	38	8	54	9%	100%	14%	18%	0	11			0	0.26	1.3	39	-$5
21	TEX	4	1	59	69	3.97	1.42	4.35	1.39	116	84	4.1	12%	27%	14%	9%	15.3%	96.8	42	21	37	32%	75%	12%	13%	0	17			25	0.88	2.2	85	-$2
1st Half		3	1	31	42	4.65	1.32	3.73	1.25	118	75	4.1	11%	31%	20%	8%	15.9%	96.5	44	21	36	33%	68%	14%	17%	0	17			25	1.14	-1.5	136	-$2
2nd Half		1	0	28	27	3.21	1.54	5.09	1.55	101	98	4.1	14%	22%	8%	11%	14.7%	97.1	40	21	39	31%	83%	10%	10%	0	18			0	0.58	3.6	30	-$8
Proj		4	2	58	63	4.19	1.37	4.28	1.35	116	88	4.6	11%	26%	15%	9%	15.1%	96.9	42	21	38	31%	73%	13%	13%	0						1.9	97	-$1

Scherzer,Max

Age: 37 Th: R Role SP | Health D | LIMA Plan D+
Ht: 6' 3" Wt: 215 Type Pwr/FB | PT/Exp A | Rand Var -4
Consist B | MM 4503

Groin strain cut into IP—and at his age, that kind of injury is perhaps more likely than not. But make no mistake, this was a full rebound to his glorious pre-2020 levels. Sure, the career-low ERA is highly unlikely to repeat, so factor that into your bid. And use 170 IP as your baseline now. Otherwise, even as he hits 37, this is the skill set of a true ace.

Yr	Tm	W	Sv	IP	K	ERA	WHIP	xERA	xWHIP	vL+	vR+	BF/G	BB%	K%	K-BB%	xBB%	SwK	Vel	G	L	F	H%	S%	HR/F	xHR/F	GS	APC	DOM%	DIS%	Sv%	LI	RAR	BPX	R$
17	WAS	16	0	201	268	2.51	0.90	3.21	1.05	91	57	25.2	7%	35%	27%	5%	16.3%	94.1	37	17	47	26%	79%	11%	9%	31	100	65%	3%			45.7	198	$41
18	WAS	18	0	221	300	2.53	0.91	3.10	0.98	83	76	26.2	6%	35%	29%	5%	16.7%	94.4	34	18	48	28%	78%	10%	11%	33	106	67%	6%			44.1	203	$44
19	WAS	11	0	172	243	2.92	1.03	3.04	0.97	100	70	25.7	5%	35%	30%	5%	17.1%	94.9	41	21	38	34%	76%	12%	11%	27	103	52%	7%			33.6	219	$27
20	WAS	5	0	67	92	3.74	1.38	3.86	1.13	119	82	24.6	8%	31%	23%	7%	15.3%	94.7	33	27	40	38%	78%	14%	16%	12	101	25%	33%			5.9	169	$12
21	2 NL	15	0	179	236	2.46	0.86	3.22	0.97	83	72	23.1	5%	34%	29%	6%	16.6%	94.3	34	18	48	26%	80%	12%	14%	30	94	57%	7%			40.0	192	$39
1st Half		7	0	94	127	2.10	0.85	3.20	0.97	61	89	22.4	6%	36%	30%	7%	17.4%	94.1	31	17	52	25%	87%	13%	14%	16	94	56%	6%			25.2	190	$34
2nd Half		8	0	85	109	2.86	0.88	3.25	0.97	94	55	23.9	4%	33%	28%	6%	15.6%	94.6	36	19	45	28%	74%	11%	14%	14	94	57%	7%			14.7	197	$34
Proj		14	0	174	223	2.95	1.09	3.43	1.06	101	76	23.7	7%	33%	26%	6%	16.3%	94.5	35	20	45	31%	79%	12%	13%	29						32.4	179	$26

ROD TRUESDELL

Schmidt,Clarke

Age: 26	Th: R	Role SP	Health F	LIMA Plan C	
Ht: 6' 1"	Wt: 200	Type Pwr	PT/Exp F	Rand Var -4	
			Consist D	MM 1200	

0-0, 5.68 ERA in 6 IP at NYY. Missed a big chunk of the season with an elbow strain, which continues a troubling trend for him of shoulder and elbow woes. When healthy, he's shown an effective three-pitch mix as a starter, and paired with his deceptive delivery, still owns SP2 upside. But he'll be on a short IP leash in 2022 given the injuries. Keep on radar.

Yr Tm	W	Sv	IP	K	ERA	WHIP	xERA	xWHIP	vL+	vR+	BF/G	BB%	K%	K-BB%	xBB%	SwK	Vel	G	L	F	H%	S%	HR/F	xHR/F	GS	APC	DOM%	DIS%	Sv%	LI	RAR	BPX	R$
17																																	
18																																	
19 aa	2	0	19	16	3.21	0.96	2.65				23.9	1%	22%	21%							30%	68%									3.0	373	-$
20 NYY	0	0	6	7	7.11	1.89	5.89	1.66	100	109	11.0	15%	21%	6%	12%	9.5%	95.0	44	17	39	39%	58%	0%	19%	1	42	0%	100%	0	1.18	-2.1	10	-$
21 NYY *	0	0	41	37	3.32	1.53	6.01	1.35	189	76	17.7	9%	21%	12%	8%	9.1%	93.0	60	20	20	33%	87%	20%	15%	1	72	0%	100%	0	0.48	4.7	46	-$
1st Half																																	
2nd Half	0	0	41	37	3.32	1.53	6.01	1.35	179	77	17.7	9%	21%	12%	8%	9.1%	93.0	60	20	20	33%	87%	20%	15%	1	72	0%	100%	0	0.48	4.7	46	-$
Proj	3	0	58	55	4.07	1.31	4.28	1.31			20.2	9%	23%	15%				43	20	37	29%	76%	17%	0%	9						2.7	102	-$

Scott,Tanner

Age: 27	Th: L	Role RP	Health C	LIMA Plan C	
Ht: 6' 2"	Wt: 220	Type Pwr/GB	PT/Exp D	Rand Var +4	
			Consist B	MM 3410	

Not as big a step back as ERA would have you believe. But still a step back, centered around a terrible walk rate and some untimely long-balls. Given GB lean, the latter shouldn't be a huge issue most years, but the walks? That's a real problem. xBB% says it's not quite as bad as it looked, and SwK remains terrific. So there's still hope.

Yr Tm	W	Sv	IP	K	ERA	WHIP	xERA	xWHIP	vL+	vR+	BF/G	BB%	K%	K-BB%	xBB%	SwK	Vel	G	L	F	H%	S%	HR/F	xHR/F	GS	APC	DOM%	DIS%	Sv%	LI	RAR	BPX	R$
17 BAL *	0	0	71	79	2.92	1.52	3.30		0	158	11.8	17%	26%	8%		10.8%	98.0	20	60	20	30%	80%	0%	0%	0	19			0	0.02	12.5	114	-$
18 BAL	3	0	53	76	5.40	1.56	3.26	1.26	87	122	4.5	12%	32%	20%	8%	17.5%	97.1	47	27	25	40%	66%	18%	15%	0	18			0	0.87	-8.2	148	-$
19 BAL *	4	7	72	82	4.03	1.44	4.16	1.37	90	133	5.3	11%	27%	15%	12%	15.1%	95.9	50	27	23	34%	73%	27%	21%	0	17			58	0.56	4.2	99	$
20 BAL	0	1	21	23	1.31	1.06	3.53	1.35	79	61	3.4	12%	27%	15%	12%	13.9%	96.5	58	18	24	24%	90%	8%	12%	0	14			50	1.77	8.0	112	$
21 BAL	5	0	54	70	5.17	1.57	4.02	1.46	81	103	4.0	15%	28%	13%	11%	15.7%	96.8	51	23	26	34%	68%	17%	18%	0	17			0	1.17	-6.0	80	-$
1st Half	3	0	31	48	2.87	1.50	3.74	1.50	92	70	3.8	18%	34%	16%	12%	16.1%	97.0	51	22	28	33%	80%	6%	14%	0	16			0	1.28	5.4	83	$
2nd Half	2	0	23	22	8.34	1.68	4.43	1.41	57	147	4.4	10%	20%	10%	9%	15.1%	96.4	51	25	24	34%	52%	29%	23%	0	17			0	1.01	-11.4	75	-$1
Proj	4	2	58	71	4.16	1.31	3.56	1.34	66	99	4.3	13%	30%	17%	10%	16.0%	96.8	50	25	25	30%	71%	19%	18%	0						2.1	113	$

Senzatela,Antonio

Age: 27	Th: R	Role SP	Health D	LIMA Plan D+	
Ht: 6' 1"	Wt: 236	Type Con/GB	PT/Exp B	Rand Var 0	
			Consist C	MM 1003	

Missed a month between the COVID list and a groin strain. Otherwise, some baby-steps of progress. Managed to whittle down the walks once again while boosting K metrics a bit as well, and maintained solid GB rate. If he can manage to stay off the IL, he projects as the archetypal low-ceiling/low-floor innings-eater.

Yr Tm	W	Sv	IP	K	ERA	WHIP	xERA	xWHIP	vL+	vR+	BF/G	BB%	K%	K-BB%	xBB%	SwK	Vel	G	L	F	H%	S%	HR/F	xHR/F	GS	APC	DOM%	DIS%	Sv%	LI	RAR	BPX	R$
17 COL	10	0	135	102	4.68	1.30	4.31	1.40	99	104	15.7	8%	18%	10%	9%	7.3%	94.3	50	22	28	28%	67%	16%	12%	20	62	10%	50%	0	0.64	-5.3	79	$
18 COL *	9	0	130	102	3.77	1.30	3.88	1.34	95	114	17.2	8%	19%	11%	9%	8.8%	93.7	46	21	33	30%	73%	11%	12%	13	66	15%	38%	0	0.73	6.1	85	$
19 COL *	12	0	160	85	6.61	1.74	6.66	1.59	124	113	22.8	9%	12%	2%	11%	7.7%	93.7	54	22	24	34%	64%	18%	19%	25	89	8%	68%			-41.5	2	-$1
20 COL	5	0	73	41	3.44	1.21	4.76	1.38	100	94	25.3	6%	14%	8%	8%	8.4%	94.4	51	20	29	27%	76%	13%	14%	12	95	25%	50%			9.2	68	$1
21 COL	4	0	157	105	4.42	1.34	4.27	1.27	108	96	23.9	5%	16%	11%	7%	9.2%	94.6	51	22	27	33%	67%	9%	15%	28	86	14%	39%			-3.1	96	-$
1st Half	2	0	88	60	4.58	1.40	4.30	1.29	100	113	24.3	5%	16%	10%	8%	8.7%	94.5	53	22	26	33%	69%	12%	14%	16	87	13%	50%			-3.5	94	-$
2nd Half	2	0	68	45	4.21	1.26	4.22	1.25	105	79	23.5	4%	16%	12%	6%	9.8%	94.8	49	23	29	32%	65%	5%	15%	12	85	17%	25%			0.4	100	-$
Proj	9	0	174	112	4.47	1.36	4.50	1.35	107	97	22.1	6%	15%	9%	8%	8.7%	94.4	51	22	28	31%	68%	11%	15%	33						-0.3	79	-$

Severino,Luis

Age: 28	Th: R	Role SP	Health F	LIMA Plan C+	
Ht: 6' 2"	Wt: 218	Type Pwr	PT/Exp F	Rand Var -5	
			Consist C	MM 4403	

That was one long road back. But late Sept stint in bullpen was a sight for sore eyes—and thankfully, without the sore shoulder, groin and elbow that all delayed return from early 2020 TJ surgery. And results were excellent, even if the fastball wasn't quite as peppy as pre-injury. Even if healthy (clearly, a big if), he'll be brought along slowly in 2022.

Yr Tm	W	Sv	IP	K	ERA	WHIP	xERA	xWHIP	vL+	vR+	BF/G	BB%	K%	K-BB%	xBB%	SwK	Vel	G	L	F	H%	S%	HR/F	xHR/F	GS	APC	DOM%	DIS%	Sv%	LI	RAR	BPX	R$
17 NYY	14	0	193	230	2.98	1.04	3.12	1.11	88	74	25.3	7%	30%	23%	6%	13.4%	97.6	51	19	31	29%	76%	14%	12%	31	99	65%	13%			32.9	189	$3
18 NYY	19	0	191	220	3.39	1.14	3.30	1.10	94	90	24.4	6%	28%	22%	6%	12.8%	97.6	41	26	33	33%	74%	11%	15%	32	99	41%	9%			18.0	169	$2
19 NYY	1	0	12	17	1.50	1.00	3.59	1.26	61	53	16.0	13%	35%	23%	6%	11.4%	96.1	42	13	46	26%	83%	0%	4%	3	73	33%	0%			4.4	139	-$
20																																	
21 NYY	1	0	6	8	0.00	0.50	2.58		161	23	5.5	5%	36%	32%		13.3%	95.3	42	17	42	18%	100%	0%	3%	0	25			0	0.63	3.2	214	-$
1st Half																																	
2nd Half	1	0	6	8	0.00	0.50	2.58		153	23	5.5	5%	36%	32%	11%	13.3%	95.3	42	17	42	18%	100%	0%	3%	0	25			0	0.63	3.2	214	-$
Proj	10	0	145	169	3.53	1.10	3.25	1.09	93	81	23.8	6%	30%	23%	6%	13.0%	97.6	45	23	32	31%	71%	13%	14%	24						16.5	172	$1

Sewald,Paul

Age: 32	Th: R	Role RP	Health A	LIMA Plan C+	
Ht: 6' 3"	Wt: 207	Type Pwr/xFB	PT/Exp D	Rand Var -2	
			Consist F	MM 4520	

Not just a late bloom, this is a late explosion. Lowering arm angle and working up in zone with the fastball turned it into a lethal pitch, and paired with wipe-out slider resulted in the fifth-best K rate among pitchers with at least 50 IP. It also meant the occasional gopherball—which was about all that hurt him. Assuming this all sticks... UP: 30 Sv

Yr Tm	W	Sv	IP	K	ERA	WHIP	xERA	xWHIP	vL+	vR+	BF/G	BB%	K%	K-BB%	xBB%	SwK	Vel	G	L	F	H%	S%	HR/F	xHR/F	GS	APC	DOM%	DIS%	Sv%	LI	RAR	BPX	R$
17 NYM	0	0	65	69	4.55	1.21	4.32	1.25	109	85	4.8	8%	25%	18%	7%	12.1%	91.4	32	22	46	30%	65%	10%	9%	0	20			0	0.89	-1.5	124	-$
18 NYM	0	2	56	58	6.07	1.51	4.84	1.33	118	110	5.5	9%	23%	14%	6%	9.8%	90.3	30	23	46	35%	61%	10%	9%	0	23			50	0.97	-13.4	87	-$
19 NYM *	4	4	71	63	4.51	1.57	5.85	1.34	80	103	5.3	6%	20%	14%	7%	9.7%	91.1	17	21	62	37%	75%	9%	9%	0	19			100	0.61	0.0	73	-$
20 NYM	0	0	6	2	13.50	2.67	8.99	1.84	207	117	7.0	11%	6%	-6%	12%	6.2%	91.8	32	39	29	42%	47%	13%	12%	0	26			0	0.56	-6.7	-111	-$1
21 SEA	10	11	65	104	3.06	1.02	3.28	1.03	90	73	4.3	9%	40%	30%	6%	17.2%	92.4	26	21	53	29%	79%	14%	17%	0	18			69	1.60	9.6	191	$1
1st Half	5	1	22	38	1.66	1.02	2.98	1.09	47	68	4.2	12%	43%	30%	5%	15.6%	92.4	28	26	46	32%	82%	0%	14%	0	19			50	1.24	7.0	183	$
2nd Half	5	10	43	66	3.77	1.02	3.43	1.00	106	77	4.3	7%	38%	30%	6%	18.1%	92.3	25	19	56	28%	76%	19%	18%	0	17			71	1.79	2.6	196	$1
Proj	6	15	65	95	3.33	1.09	3.38	1.09	94	79	4.4	9%	37%	28%	6%	14.5%	91.8	28	22	50	30%	76%	13%	13%	0						9.0	175	$1

Shaw,Bryan

Age: 34	Th: R	Role RP	Health B	LIMA Plan B	
Ht: 6' 1"	Wt: 226	Type Pwr	PT/Exp D	Rand Var -2	
			Consist F	MM 1100	

Big ERA drop! New pitch? New delivery? New routine of only eating chicken on game days? (Hey, it's worked for some.) Nah, nothing like that. As BPX and xERA clearly show, this is the same-old same-old he's been throwing out there for a while now. Strand rate and 1st-half hit rate just gussied it up a little. Ignore once again, and thank us later.

Yr Tm	W	Sv	IP	K	ERA	WHIP	xERA	xWHIP	vL+	vR+	BF/G	BB%	K%	K-BB%	xBB%	SwK	Vel	G	L	F	H%	S%	HR/F	xHR/F	GS	APC	DOM%	DIS%	Sv%	LI	RAR	BPX	R$
17 CLE	4	3	77	73	3.52	1.21	3.37	1.24	78	94	3.9	7%	23%	16%	7%	12.5%		56	22	22	32%	72%	11%	7%	0	15			50	1.07	7.9	142	$
18 COL	4	0	55	54	5.93	1.79	4.61	1.44	106	137	4.2	11%	21%	10%	11%	12.1%	94.5	49	21	30	38%	70%	17%	17%	0	17			0	0.87	-12.0	72	-$1
19 COL	3	1	72	58	5.38	1.36	4.80	1.45	81	126	4.4	9%	19%	9%	11%	11.2%	93.0	49	20	31	28%	64%	18%	15%	0	17			17	0.85	-7.7	65	-$
20 SEA	1	0	6	4	18.00	3.17	8.92	1.93	116	206	6.3	16%	11%	-5%	12%	6.5%		56	19	26	48%	39%	14%	17%	0	26			0	0.86	-10.0	-114	-$1
21 CLE	6	2	77	71	3.49	1.38	4.56	1.45	89	104	4.1	11%	21%	10%	9%	11.8%	94.9	46	24	31	29%	79%	15%	15%	0	17			25	1.09	7.4	57	$
1st Half	2	1	33	42	3.24	1.38	4.44	1.62	66	95	4.2	18%	29%	10%	11%	14.2%	93.8	48	22	30	24%	79%	13%	8%	0	18			33	1.18	4.2	37	-$
2nd Half	4	1	44	29	3.68	1.39	4.67	1.33	101	112	4.1	6%	16%	10%	8%	9.8%	95.2	44	25	31	31%	80%	16%	19%	0	16			20	1.02	3.2	75	-$
Proj	4	0	65	59	4.37	1.44	4.46	1.42	91	114	4.1	11%	21%	11%	9%	11.7%	84.8	48	22	30	31%	73%	16%	14%	0						0.7	72	-$

Sheffield,Justus

Age: 26	Th: L	Role SP	Health D	LIMA Plan D+	
Ht: 5' 10"	Wt: 195	Type	PT/Exp C	Rand Var +5	
			Consist C	MM 1101	

A season to forget. Missed two months with forearm, oblique injuries. But even when healthy, he was simply awful, and skills show it was well-earned. Still walking too many, but maybe that's Pavlovian—pitches were swatted on the nose when they did find the plate. Still owns pedigree, but needs 2018 velocity, and that seems to have disappeared.

Yr Tm	W	Sv	IP	K	ERA	WHIP	xERA	xWHIP	vL+	vR+	BF/G	BB%	K%	K-BB%	xBB%	SwK	Vel	G	L	F	H%	S%	HR/F	xHR/F	GS	APC	DOM%	DIS%	Sv%	LI	RAR	BPX	R$
17 aa	7	0	93	73	4.43	1.61	6.43				24.3	8%	18%	9%							33%	81%									-0.8	23	-$
18 NYY *	7	0	119	108	3.33	1.31	3.25		96	233	17.5	11%	22%	11%		1.8%	94.4	55	18	27	29%	75%	33%	26%	0	19			0	0.14	12.0	98	$
19 SEA *	7	0	169	155	5.20	1.56	5.30	1.46	109	120	22.5	11%	21%	10%	9%	13.1%	92.8	52	18	30	34%	69%	16%	15%	7	84	0%	43%	0	0.73	-14.5	57	-$
20 SEA	4	0	55	48	3.58	1.30	4.25	1.35	55	93	23.2	9%	21%	12%	9%	8.4%	92.0	51	21	28	32%	71%	4%	9%	10	88	20%	20%			6.0	92	$
21 SEA	7	0	80	63	6.83	1.84	5.52	1.54	107	127	18.3	11%	16%	5%	10%	8.6%	92.4	46	22	31	36%	65%	16%	25%	15	70	0%	53%	0	0.82	-25.5	23	-$1
1st Half	5	0	72	57	5.88	1.71	5.13	1.46	104	124	23.9	10%	17%	7%	9%	9.0%	92.3	46	23	31	35%	69%	18%	25%	14	91	0%	50%			-14.3	48	-$1
2nd Half	2	0	8	6	15.12	3.00	9.93	2.24	87	179	7.1	22%	12%	-10%	12%	5.9%	92.6	50	16	34	43%	46%	9%	24%	1	29	0%	100%	0	0.88	-11.2	-193	-$1
Proj	5	0	87	74	4.63	1.51	4.60	1.43	89	108	21.8	10%	20%	10%	9%	9.9%	92.3	49	21	30	33%	72%	13%	18%	17						-1.9	69	-$

ROD TRUESDELL

Sims,Lucas

Age: 28	Th: R	Role RP	Health	D	LIMA Plan	A
Ht: 6' 2"	Wt: 225	Type Pwr/xFB	PT/Exp	C	Rand Var	+4
			Consist	B	MM	3520

Missed 7 weeks mid-season with a right elbow strain. But note the velocity and K% trends, which improved even more after the injury. Only unlucky S% and normalized HR/F made this look worse than 2020; BPX confirms this was another big step up. HR will always be an issue, but elite K-BB% now helps offset that. UP: sub-3.00 ERA, 30 Saves

Yr Tm	W	Sv	IP	K	ERA	WHIP	xERA	xWHIP	vL+	vR+	BF/G	BB%	K%	K-BB%	xBB%	SwK	Vel	G	L	F	H%	S%	HR/F	xHR/F	GS	APC	DOM%	DIS%	Sv%	LI	RAR	BPX	R$
17 ATL *	10	0	173	161	5.01	1.37	4.78	1.34	121	112	21.3	9%	22%	14%	8%	8.9%	91.8	38	23	39	31%	68%	13%	11%	10	70	10%	60%	0	0.74	-14.0	74	$1
18 2 NL *	4	0	118	114	4.42	1.47	4.88	1.41	112	115	17.4	11%	23%	12%	12%	11.5%	92.5	37	22	41	32%	74%	16%	13%	0	35			0	0.52	-3.9	69	-$4
19 CIN *	7	0	122	145	5.56	1.44	4.80	1.39	88	99	13.0	12%	28%	16%	8%	15.6%	93.6	25	19	57	33%	65%	15%	11%	4	31	25%	50%	0	0.66	-15.9	82	-$4
20 CIN	3	0	26	34	2.45	0.94	3.62	1.21	75	77	5.2	11%	33%	22%	12%	13.1%	94.0	42	13	45	21%	81%	12%	5%	0	23			0	1.20	6.3	147	$9
21 CIN	5	7	47	76	4.40	1.11	3.12	1.03	101	81	4.1	9%	39%	30%	8%	15.3%	95.1	26	26	47	33%	63%	13%	12%	0	17			70	1.47	-0.8	190	$4
1st Half	4	7	29	44	5.02	1.33	3.66	1.21	105	89	4.5	12%	35%	23%	9%	15.2%	94.9	23	33	44	35%	63%	11%	13%	0	19			78	1.72	-2.7	135	$3
2nd Half	1	0	18	32	3.44	0.76	2.41	0.76	79	69	3.6	4%	46%	42%	7%	15.5%	95.4	32	15	53	29%	64%	17%	12%	0	16			0	1.11	1.9	278	-$3
Proj	**4**	**14**	**65**	**88**	**3.70**	**1.21**	**3.75**	**1.15**	**105**	**92**	**6.3**	**9%**	**34%**	**24%**	**8%**	**14.1%**	**94.2**	**30**	**22**	**49**	**32%**	**75%**	**13%**	**12%**	**0**						**6.1**	**153**	**$8**

Singer,Brady

Age: 25	Th: R	Role SP	Health	C	LIMA Plan	C
Ht: 6' 5"	Wt: 210	Type /GB	PT/Exp	B	Rand Var	+3
			Consist	B	MM	2203

Missed about a month between COVID list and minor arm ailments. Otherwise, as BPX tells us, he's about as average as they come. But only now 25, there's room for more here: gets his share of GB and whiffs with a small platoon split. Without elite stuff, watch walk rate: If he can keep it around 8% as in 2nd half, ERA could dip below 4.00.

Yr Tm	W	Sv	IP	K	ERA	WHIP	xERA	xWHIP	vL+	vR+	BF/G	BB%	K%	K-BB%	xBB%	SwK	Vel	G	L	F	H%	S%	HR/F	xHR/F	GS	APC	DOM%	DIS%	Sv%	LI	RAR	BPX	R$
17																																	
18																																	
19 aa	7	0	92	70	4.75	1.46	4.87				24.7	7%	18%	11%							34%	69%									-2.7	68	-$2
20 KC	4	0	64	61	4.06	1.17	3.98	1.31	93	83	21.9	9%	23%	14%	7%	9.8%	93.4	53	17	30	27%	69%	15%	15%	12	89	33%	50%			3.1	110	$11
21 KC	5	0	128	131	4.91	1.55	4.17	1.32	112	97	21.7	9%	22%	13%	8%	10.5%	93.7	50	22	28	36%	70%	13%	17%	27	85	22%	37%			-10.2	102	-$9
1st Half	3	0	80	85	4.74	1.52	4.15	1.33	105	96	21.5	10%	23%	14%	8%	10.8%	93.7	50	21	29	36%	70%	12%	15%	17	85	12%	41%			-4.7	104	-$5
2nd Half	2	0	49	46	5.18	1.60	4.21	1.32	108	104	22.1	8%	21%	13%	8%	9.9%	93.9	49	25	26	37%	69%	15%	20%	10	84	40%	30%			-5.5	99	-$11
Proj	**7**	**0**	**145**	**136**	**4.52**	**1.35**	**4.00**	**1.31**	**100**	**90**	**21.2**	**9%**	**22%**	**14%**	**8%**	**10.2%**	**93.7**	**50**	**22**	**28**	**32%**	**69%**	**14%**	**17%**	**29**						**-1.1**	**106**	**$0**

Skubal,Tarik

Age: 25	Th: L	Role SP	Health	A	LIMA Plan	A
Ht: 6' 3"	Wt: 215	Type Pwr/FB	PT/Exp	C	Rand Var	+2
			Consist	C	MM	2403

4 reasons he'll take another step up: 1) Improving vR; 2) walk rate trending down, velocity staying up; 3) started to level out G/F ratio, potentially making HR less of an issue; 4) 2nd-half gains a solid indicator in first full MLB season. Still solving fastball location/hard-hit ball issues, but he's starting to turn raw stuff into pitchability. UP: 15 W, 3.50 ERA

Yr Tm	W	Sv	IP	K	ERA	WHIP	xERA	xWHIP	vL+	vR+	BF/G	BB%	K%	K-BB%	xBB%	SwK	Vel	G	L	F	H%	S%	HR/F	xHR/F	GS	APC	DOM%	DIS%	Sv%	LI	RAR	BPX	R$
17																																	
18																																	
19 aa	2	0	43	67	3.09	1.19	2.67				19.2	12%	39%	27%							35%	75%									7.5	165	$1
20 DET	1	0	32	37	5.63	1.22	4.58	1.22	48	120	16.8	8%	28%	19%	8%	13.4%	94.5	28	18	54	26%	63%	20%	17%	7	74	14%	43%	0	0.80	-4.6	124	-$4
21 DET	8	0	149	164	4.34	1.26	4.11	1.20	93	107	20.5	7%	26%	18%	7%	12.1%	94.4	39	20	41	29%	76%	20%	23%	29	82	17%	31%	0	0.76	-1.4	129	$5
1st Half	5	0	83	100	4.35	1.39	4.34	1.28	93	111	21.3	10%	28%	17%	8%	13.0%	94.2	33	22	44	31%	77%	18%	18%	15	88	13%	20%	0	0.77	-0.9	108	$3
2nd Half	3	0	67	64	4.32	1.10	3.83	1.09	83	107	19.4	4%	24%	20%	5%	10.7%	94.7	44	18	38	27%	75%	24%	30%	14	75	21%	43%			-0.4	155	$5
Proj	**8**	**0**	**174**	**205**	**4.09**	**1.22**	**3.87**	**1.18**	**78**	**104**	**20.8**	**8%**	**29%**	**21%**	**7%**	**12.2%**	**94.5**	**37**	**19**	**44**	**29%**	**76%**	**19%**	**23%**	**34**						**7.7**	**144**	**$10**

Smith,Caleb

Age: 30	Th: L	Role RP	Health	D	LIMA Plan	D+
Ht: 6' 0"	Wt: 206	Type Pwr/xFB	PT/Exp	B	Rand Var	0
			Consist	C	MM	0300

Strong start fueled by lots of luck, which all ran out late as he was demoted to bullpen. Big drop in fastball effectiveness, and with it SwK rate; that puts his one previously reliable asset—strikeouts—at risk. Given shoddy control and HR propensity, he'll need that elite K rate back to have any value; as xERA history shows, you won't get any ERA help.

Yr Tm	W	Sv	IP	K	ERA	WHIP	xERA	xWHIP	vL+	vR+	BF/G	BB%	K%	K-BB%	xBB%	SwK	Vel	G	L	F	H%	S%	HR/F	xHR/F	GS	APC	DOM%	DIS%	Sv%	LI	RAR	BPX	R$
17 NYY *	9	0	119	101	4.22	1.40	4.60	1.42	118	113	18.0	9%	20%	11%		13.5%	94.0	28	29	43	31%	74%	16%	15%	2	38	0%	100%	0	0.35	2.1	67	$2
18 MIA	5	0	77	88	4.19	1.24	4.36	1.29	98	96	20.4	10%	27%	17%	8%	12.3%	92.8	28	21	51	29%	70%	10%	14%	16	87	19%	25%			-0.4	100	$1
19 MIA	10	0	153	168	4.52	1.23	4.89	1.33	82	106	23.1	9%	26%	17%	7%	13.4%	91.6	26	21	52	26%	72%	16%	16%	28	95	25%	36%			-0.3	94	$8
20 2 NL	0	0	14	15	2.57	1.29	6.39	1.82	77	83	12.0	20%	25%	5%	10%	15.0%	92.1	28	6	66	11%	93%	14%	17%	4	53	0%	50%	0	0.65	3.2	-32	-$3
21 ARI	4	0	114	124	4.83	1.37	5.16	1.45	110	93	11.1	13%	25%	12%	8%	11.7%	91.4	28	20	52	27%	70%	13%	12%	13	46	8%	46%	0	0.72	-7.9	53	-$4
1st Half	2	0	64	75	3.08	1.27	4.58	1.37	89	89	11.2	12%	27%	15%	8%	11.4%	91.5	28	24	48	28%	80%	9%	13%	7	46	0%	43%	0	0.66	9.4	77	$5
2nd Half	2	0	49	49	7.11	1.50	5.94	1.55	118	103	11.1	14%	22%	9%	9%	12.1%	91.3	28	14	58	26%	57%	16%	12%	6	46	17%	50%	0	0.79	-17.3	21	-$15
Proj	**3**	**0**	**58**	**62**	**4.91**	**1.34**	**4.91**	**1.41**	**106**	**97**	**13.8**	**12%**	**26%**	**14%**	**8%**	**12.2%**	**91.7**	**28**	**19**	**53**	**28%**	**69%**	**13%**	**13%**	**7**						**-3.3**	**68**	**-$4**

Smith,Riley

Age: 27	Th: R	Role RP	Health	A	LIMA Plan	D+
Ht: 6' 1"	Wt: 175	Type Con	PT/Exp	D	Rand Var	+3
			Consist	F	MM	0000

1-4, 6.01 ERA in 67 IP at ARI. Took to swingman role like a duck to an oil slick—as in, things got messy. Even with elite control, he needs some kind of strikeout pitch to keep hitters honest. His 2020 K% was better, but SwK shows that was likely a short-sample mirage. As long as the whiffs remain this low, there's no reason to speculate here.

Yr Tm	W	Sv	IP	K	ERA	WHIP	xERA	xWHIP	vL+	vR+	BF/G	BB%	K%	K-BB%	xBB%	SwK	Vel	G	L	F	H%	S%	HR/F	xHR/F	GS	APC	DOM%	DIS%	Sv%	LI	RAR	BPX	R$
17																																	
18																																	
19 a/a	6	0	136	90	4.99	1.52	5.64				23.7	6%	15%	9%							34%	70%									-8.2	47	-$6
20 ARI	2	0	18	18	1.47	1.09	3.62	1.20	59	90	11.7	7%	26%	19%	6%	5.2%	93.4	48	20	33	29%	89%	7%	8%	0	42			0	0.48	6.7	134	$4
21 ARI *	1	1	84	46	6.17	1.50	5.97	1.36	111	122	13.0	5%	13%	7%	6%	6.4%	92.9	43	21	36	33%	60%	11%	15%	6	45	0%	100%	100	0.63	-19.8	36	-$14
1st Half	1	1	61	33	6.02	1.53	5.43	1.38	110	125	13.7	5%	12%	7%	6%	6.4%	92.9	42	21	36	33%	63%	13%	16%	6	48	0%	100%	100	0.72	-13.2	53	-$14
2nd Half	0	0	23	13	6.59	1.41	5.46		66	116	12.2	4%	13%	9%	6%	6.7%	93.0	52	17	30	34%	53%	0%	1%	0	26			0	0.21	-6.6	76	-$15
Proj	**0**	**0**	**29**	**17**	**5.43**	**1.49**	**5.00**	**1.35**	**121**	**131**	**14.3**	**5%**	**13%**	**8%**	**6%**	**6.4%**	**92.9**	**42**	**21**	**36**	**33%**	**66%**	**12%**	**15%**	**4**						**-3.5**	**69**	**-$7**

Smith,Will

Age: 32	Th: L	Role RP	Health	D	LIMA Plan	C+
Ht: 6' 5"	Wt: 255	Type Pwr/FB	PT/Exp	B	Rand Var	-2
			Consist	B	MM	3430

Post-season hero righted what was a legitimately shaky 2nd half with 11 scoreless IP in the playoffs. In fairness, xBB% shows the late walk spike wasn't as bad as it looked, and SwK did revert toward previous elite levels. In short, while those sensational 2018-19 skills may not return, what's left is still good enough to keep harvesting bushels of saves.

Yr Tm	W	Sv	IP	K	ERA	WHIP	xERA	xWHIP	vL+	vR+	BF/G	BB%	K%	K-BB%	xBB%	SwK	Vel	G	L	F	H%	S%	HR/F	xHR/F	GS	APC	DOM%	DIS%	Sv%	LI	RAR	BPX	R$
17																																	
18 SF	2	14	53	71	2.55	0.98	2.99	1.05	60	81	3.9	7%	34%	27%	5%	15.1%	92.7	42	20	38	30%	76%	7%	9%	0	15			78	1.44	10.5	194	$10
19 SF	6	34	65	96	2.76	1.03	2.95	1.05	52	95	4.1	8%	37%	29%	6%	15.8%	92.7	42	22	36	29%	82%	20%	16%	0	17			89	1.58	14.1	196	$24
20 ATL	2	0	16	18	4.50	0.94	4.12	1.13	102	109	3.4	6%	29%	23%	10%	17.5%	92.6	30	18	53	13%	88%	33%	25%	0	14			0	1.24	-0.1	146	$1
21 ATL	3	37	68	87	3.44	1.13	3.94	1.21	97	92	4.0	10%	31%	21%	7%	14.7%	92.8	31	21	47	27%	77%	14%	12%	0	15			86	1.33	6.9	127	$20
1st Half	2	17	35	46	3.63	1.13	3.79	1.13	72	94	3.9	8%	32%	24%	7%	14.0%	92.9	26	26	48	31%	71%	10%	8%	0	15			89	1.44	2.7	148	$11
2nd Half	1	20	33	41	3.24	1.14	4.10	1.30	113	93	4.1	12%	29%	18%	8%	15.6%	92.7	37	16	47	22%	84%	19%	16%	0	15			83	1.21	4.2	107	$18
Proj	**3**	**32**	**65**	**78**	**3.38**	**1.08**	**3.63**	**1.15**	**85**	**93**	**3.8**	**8%**	**31%**	**23%**	**6%**	**15.1%**	**92.8**	**36**	**21**	**43**	**28%**	**75%**	**14%**	**13%**	**0**						**8.7**	**150**	**$18**

Smyly,Drew

Age: 33	Th: L	Role RP	Health	F	LIMA Plan	B+
Ht: 6' 2"	Wt: 188	Type Pwr	PT/Exp	B	Rand Var	+1
			Consist	D	MM	1203

Regressed from eye-catching 2020. Never exceeded 6 IP in a start, with only one such outing after June. That paired with longball issues eventually landed him in 'pen. Look, he's gone from utterly valueless for years to a marginally useful pitcher, so that's progress. But the injuries have taken their toll. The exciting skills he had at 25 are not coming back.

Yr Tm	W	Sv	IP	K	ERA	WHIP	xERA	xWHIP	vL+	vR+	BF/G	BB%	K%	K-BB%	xBB%	SwK	Vel	G	L	F	H%	S%	HR/F	xHR/F	GS	APC	DOM%	DIS%	Sv%	LI	RAR	BPX	R$
17																																	
18																																	
19 2 TM	4	1	114	120	6.24	1.59	5.31	1.44	142	116	20.6	11%	23%	13%	9%	11.0%	91.2	33	22	45	32%	68%	21%	20%	21	85	19%	48%	100	0.73	-24.3	70	-$11
20 SF	0	0	26	42	3.42	1.10	2.97	1.03	37	96	15.9	8%	38%	30%	6%	15.1%	93.8	42	23	35	36%	70%	10%	18%	5	69	20%	20%	0	0.74	3.4	221	$1
21 ATL	11	0	127	117	4.48	1.37	4.55	1.28	117	105	18.8	8%	22%	14%	6%	12.1%	92.1	39	22	39	31%	76%	18%	19%	23	74	4%	26%	0	0.74	-3.3	97	$1
1st Half	6	0	73	64	4.42	1.28	4.83	1.33	103	101	22.2	8%	21%	13%	7%	11.2%	92.5	38	17	45	27%	73%	15%	17%	14	89	7%	29%			-1.4	82	$4
2nd Half	5	0	53	53	4.56	1.50	4.16	1.23	120	115	15.7	7%	23%	16%	5%	13.3%	91.2	40	28	31	35%	78%	24%	22%	9	59	0%	22%	0	0.69	-1.9	117	-$2
Proj	**10**	**0**	**131**	**127**	**4.52**	**1.40**	**4.46**	**1.31**	**121**	**106**	**17.7**	**8%**	**23%**	**15%**	**6%**	**12.1%**	**91.6**	**38**	**23**	**39**	**30%**	**77%**	**21%**	**20%**	**24**						**-1.1**	**98**	**$1**

ROD TRUESDELL

Snell,Blake

Age: 29 | Th: L | Role: SP | Ht: 6' 4" | Wt: 225 | Type: Pwr
Health: D | PT/Exp: B | Consist: A
LIMA Plan: B+ | Rand Var: 0 | MM: 3503

Some bad luck played a role in 1st half struggles, but he surged late with 1.83 ERA and 39% K% in last eight starts before September groin injury. Still, SwK wasn't as high as usual, BB% issues resurfaced, and averaged less than 5 IP per start for third consecutive season. Ratios should improve, but that's a lot of yellow flags for a rotation foundation piece.

Yr	Tm	W	Sv	IP	K	ERA	WHIP	xERA	xWHIP	vL+	vR+	BF/G	BB%	K%	K-BB%	xBB%	SwK	Vel	G	L	F	H%	S%	HR/F	xHR/F	GS	APC	DOM%	DIS%	Sv%	LI	RAR	BPX	R$
17	TAM *	10	0	173	171	3.95	1.40	4.31	1.39	65	100	23.6	10%	23%	13%	11%	11.0%	94.3	44	18	38	31%	75%	11%	11%	24	95	17%	29%			8.7	86	$7
18	TAM	21	0	181	221	1.89	0.97	3.17	1.16	56	82	22.6	9%	32%	22%	9%	15.3%	95.8	45	19	36	25%	86%	11%	14%	31	94	55%	19%			50.3	156	$39
19	TAM	6	0	107	147	4.29	1.27	3.49	1.16	118	89	19.2	9%	33%	24%	8%	18.2%	95.6	39	25	36	35%	70%	15%	11%	23	82	26%	48%			2.8	162	$5
20	TAM	4	0	50	63	3.24	1.20	3.27	1.17	96	98	18.5	9%	31%	22%	9%	15.6%	95.1	49	23	28	29%	84%	29%	22%	11	79	9%	27%			7.5	162	$13
21	SD	7	0	129	170	4.20	1.32	3.85	1.31	63	101	20.4	13%	31%	18%	10%	13.4%	95.2	40	23	37	31%	71%	14%	23%	27	87	26%	37%			1.1	112	$4
1st Half		3	0	66	90	5.29	1.55	3.97	1.36	68	117	20.1	13%	30%	17%	12%	12.8%	95.5	44	25	31	35%	69%	19%	29%	15	85	20%	47%			-8.4	104	-$6
2nd Half		4	0	62	80	3.03	1.07	3.73	1.25	49	88	20.7	12%	32%	21%	8%	14.1%	94.9	34	20	46	25%	75%	10%	17%	12	90	33%	25%			9.5	118	$14
Proj		**9**	**0**	**145**	**186**	**3.83**	**1.26**	**3.64**	**1.24**	**78**	**97**	**20.6**	**11%**	**32%**	**21%**	**9%**	**14.7%**	**95.2**	**41**	**22**	**37**	**31%**	**74%**	**16%**	**19%**	**29**						**11.1**	**136**	**$9**

Snyder,Nick

Age: 26 | Th: R | Role: RP | Ht: 6' 4" | Wt: 190 | Type: Pwr
Health: C | PT/Exp: F | Consist: F
LIMA Plan: B+ | Rand Var: -3 | MM: 2210

0-0, 4.91 ERA in 4 IP at TEX. September shoulder injury ended season soon after his call-up, but in 33 minor league innings across three levels, both his K% (38%) and BB% (4%) took major steps forward. Plus fastball has top-tier velocity, and if he's back to full strength, could jump into late-inning mix if he can show an effective secondary pitch.

Yr	Tm	W	Sv	IP	K	ERA	WHIP	xERA	xWHIP	vL+	vR+	BF/G	BB%	K%	K-BB%	xBB%	SwK	Vel	G	L	F	H%	S%	HR/F	xHR/F	GS	APC	DOM%	DIS%	Sv%	LI	RAR	BPX	R$
17																																		
18																																		
19																																		
20																																		
21	TEX *	1	1	26	25	3.28	1.01	2.73		23	150	4.5	5%	25%	20%		10.2%	98.7	55	27	18	28%	70%	0%	0%	0	15			50	0.42	3.2	154	-$1
1st Half		0	0	7	8	1.67	0.70	2.30				5.0	0%	32%	32%							24%	97%	0%		0	0					2.3	0	-$6
2nd Half		1	1	19	17	3.93	1.14	2.97		22	153	4.4	7%	23%	16%		10.2%	98.7	55	27	18	30%	65%	0%	0%	0	15			50	0.42	0.8	121	-$6
Proj		**2**	**6**	**51**	**51**	**3.98**	**1.30**	**4.06**	**1.23**			**5.1**	**7%**	**25%**	**17%**				**44**	**18**	**38**	**33%**	**73%**	**12%**	**10%**	**0**						**2.9**	**129**	**$1**

Soroka,Michael

Age: 24 | Th: R | Role: SP | Ht: 6' 5" | Wt: 225 | Type: Con
Health: F | PT/Exp: C | Consist: B
LIMA Plan: B+ | Rand Var: 0 | MM: 3101

Faced plenty of obstacles in return from 2020 Achilles surgery—shoulder injury in April, another Achilles procedure in May, and completely tore it again in June. Results outpaced the skills in 2019, he's barely pitched in two seasons and is set to miss a good chunk of 2022. Could deliver late-season value, but even if healthy by then, workload will be light.

Yr	Tm	W	Sv	IP	K	ERA	WHIP	xERA	xWHIP	vL+	vR+	BF/G	BB%	K%	K-BB%	xBB%	SwK	Vel	G	L	F	H%	S%	HR/F	xHR/F	GS	APC	DOM%	DIS%	Sv%	LI	RAR	BPX	R$
17	aa	11	0	154	117	3.75	1.28	3.80				24.2	6%	19%	13%							32%	72%									11.4	105	$10
18	ATL *	4	0	53	48	2.91	1.23	3.15	1.21	86	120	21.3	6%	22%	16%	8%	10.6%	92.6	44	32	24	34%	75%	5%	13%	5	81	20%	40%			8.1	146	$2
19	ATL	13	0	175	142	2.68	1.11	3.87	1.27	99	72	24.2	6%	20%	14%	7%	10.7%	92.5	51	23	25	28%	79%	11%	12%	29	88	34%	17%			39.3	113	$23
20	ATL	0	0	14	8	3.95	1.32	4.60	1.64	100	55	19.0	12%	14%	2%	9%	10.6%	92.1	61	24	15	26%	67%	0%	12%	3	66	0%	33%			0.8	11	-$6
21																																		
1st Half																																		
2nd Half																																		
Proj		**5**	**0**	**73**	**60**	**3.76**	**1.24**	**3.74**	**1.24**	**122**	**86**	**23.4**	**6%**	**20%**	**15%**	**7%**	**10.7%**	**92.5**	**51**	**23**	**25**	**32%**	**70%**	**9%**	**11%**	**13**						**6.2**	**120**	**$2**

Soto,Gregory

Age: 27 | Th: L | Role: RP | Ht: 6' 1" | Wt: 236 | Type: Pwr
Health: B | PT/Exp: C | Consist: D
LIMA Plan: B | Rand Var: -2 | MM: 2320

Held at least a share of closer role for much of the season, and though K% dipped slightly, increased slider usage led to SwK surge. High BB% is the major weakness, one he'll need to improve upon to take step from just dominant vL to reliable closer. Not the safest option, but one with velocity and upside, and if 2nd half xBB% is any indication... UP: 30 Sv.

Yr	Tm	W	Sv	IP	K	ERA	WHIP	xERA	xWHIP	vL+	vR+	BF/G	BB%	K%	K-BB%	xBB%	SwK	Vel	G	L	F	H%	S%	HR/F	xHR/F	GS	APC	DOM%	DIS%	Sv%	LI	RAR	BPX	R$
17																																		
18																																		
19	DET *	0	0	96	78	6.28	1.77	6.30	1.58	89	129	10.5	12%	18%	6%	9%	8.5%	95.4	48	19	34	35%	66%	14%	18%	7	34	0%	86%	0	0.67	-21.0	33	-$16
20	DET	0	2	23	29	4.30	1.26	3.62	1.37	54	90	3.6	13%	30%	16%	11%	11.4%	97.3	54	20	26	28%	67%	14%	13%	0	15			67	0.69	0.4	112	-$1
21	DET	6	18	64	76	3.39	1.35	4.35	1.46	68	93	4.5	14%	28%	13%	8%	13.5%	98.3	45	18	37	27%	78%	12%	14%	0	18			95	1.49	6.9	70	$10
1st Half		4	6	33	38	2.18	1.24	4.00	1.43	69	81	3.9	14%	28%	14%	10%	12.7%	97.8	52	14	34	27%	85%	7%	9%	0	17			100	1.43	8.5	84	$8
2nd Half		2	12	31	38	4.70	1.47	4.72	1.50	58	106	5.1	15%	28%	12%	7%	14.5%	98.7	38	22	40	28%	73%	16%	17%	0	20			92	1.56	-1.6	55	$5
Proj		**4**	**20**	**65**	**75**	**3.79**	**1.32**	**4.15**	**1.40**	**66**	**97**	**5.0**	**13%**	**28%**	**15%**	**8%**	**12.3%**	**97.6**	**44**	**19**	**37**	**28%**	**75%**	**14%**	**15%**	**0**						**5.4**	**89**	**$9**

Springs,Jeffrey

Age: 29 | Th: L | Role: RP | Ht: 6' 3" | Wt: 218 | Type: Pwr/FB
Health: F | PT/Exp: D | Consist: D
LIMA Plan: A | Rand Var: +1 | MM: 3510

Excelled in high-leverage role before knee injury ended season in July. Showed that small-sample 2020 SwK gains were no fluke, and this time he wasn't done in by terrible luck. Track record of success is short and homers have been an issue, but with added velocity and 38% K% vR, wouldn't be surprising to see some Sv chances in his future.

Yr	Tm	W	Sv	IP	K	ERA	WHIP	xERA	xWHIP	vL+	vR+	BF/G	BB%	K%	K-BB%	xBB%	SwK	Vel	G	L	F	H%	S%	HR/F	xHR/F	GS	APC	DOM%	DIS%	Sv%	LI	RAR	BPX	R$
17																																		
18	TEX *	5	2	90	107	4.71	1.47	4.40	1.24	116	98	7.6	9%	28%	18%	9%	11.7%	91.3	32	24	44	38%	68%	10%	10%	2	31	0%	0%	33	0.68	-6.3	122	-$3
19	TEX	4	0	32	32	6.40	1.89	6.56	1.70	120	116	6.2	15%	21%	6%	9%	12.6%	92.1	23	31	45	36%	67%	9%	8%	0	27			0	0.49	-7.6	-13	-$7
20	BOS	0	0	20	28	7.08	1.82	4.18	1.16	122	138	6.2	7%	28%	21%	7%	17.0%	92.1	35	29	35	46%	66%	23%	25%	0	25			0	0.75	-6.6	172	-$12
21	TAM	5	2	45	63	3.43	1.10	3.22	1.05	117	87	4.2	8%	35%	27%	8%	16.5%	93.4	34	23	42	29%	80%	21%	18%	0	17			50	1.07	4.6	180	$3
1st Half		4	2	35	48	3.82	1.16	3.33	1.08	106	100	4.2	8%	33%	26%	8%	15.4%	93.5	35	25	40	30%	79%	24%	18%	0	18			50	1.15	1.9	173	$4
2nd Half		1	0	9	15	1.93	0.86	2.82	0.95	140	49	3.9	9%	43%	34%	6%	21.4%	93.4	31	13	56	26%	86%	11%	18%	0	16			0	0.80	2.7	210	-$6
Proj		**6**	**2**	**58**	**75**	**3.88**	**1.20**	**3.68**	**1.17**	**102**	**90**	**5.0**	**9%**	**32%**	**23%**	**8%**	**16.8%**	**92.5**	**31**	**27**	**42**	**30%**	**74%**	**16%**	**13%**	**0**						**4.1**	**146**	**$3**

Stammen,Craig

Age: 38 | Th: R | Role: RP | Ht: 6' 2" | Wt: 228 | Type: Con/GB
Health: B | PT/Exp: C | Consist: A
LIMA Plan: B+ | Rand Var: 0 | MM: 4201

Showed that 2020 struggles were due mostly to bad luck, as H%/S% corrected and he tossed most IP since 2012. Uptick in SwK was nice but K% still mediocre, as it's the heavy GB tilt and low BB% that continue to drive his success. Getting up there in age, but could be good for at least one more year of good volume and helpful ERA and WHIP.

Yr	Tm	W	Sv	IP	K	ERA	WHIP	xERA	xWHIP	vL+	vR+	BF/G	BB%	K%	K-BB%	xBB%	SwK	Vel	G	L	F	H%	S%	HR/F	xHR/F	GS	APC	DOM%	DIS%	Sv%	LI	RAR	BPX	R$
17	SD	2	0	80	74	3.14	1.20	3.90	1.32	106	80	5.5	9%	22%	14%	8%	11.8%	91.5	52	17	31	27%	81%	17%	16%	0	21			0	1.18	12.1	114	$4
18	SD	8	0	79	88	2.73	1.04	3.06	1.08	90	73	4.3	5%	28%	22%	5%	14.4%	91.7	49	21	30	32%	73%	5%	9%	0	16			0	1.33	13.8	179	$10
19	SD	8	4	82	73	3.29	1.16	3.94	1.19	80	109	4.5	4%	22%	17%	7%	9.4%	92.8	51	19	30	30%	79%	18%	13%	0	16			31	1.36	12.3	140	$9
20	SD	4	0	24	20	5.63	1.29	3.64	1.18	83	104	4.4	4%	19%	15%	7%	9.8%	92.2	59	20	20	34%	55%	13%	10%	0	16			0	0.66	-3.5	149	$0
21	SD	6	1	88	83	3.06	1.04	3.36	1.09	91	86	5.3	4%	23%	20%	7%	10.9%	92.3	55	16	29	28%	78%	18%	17%	4	20	0%	100%	50	0.83	13.2	164	$9
1st Half		3	1	48	49	2.83	0.99	3.13	1.05	92	76	5.4	4%	26%	22%	7%	11.1%	92.0	52	18	30	28%	80%	18%	21%	1	20	0%	100%	50	0.83	8.4	177	$8
2nd Half		3	0	41	34	3.32	1.11	3.63	1.14	76	99	5.2	4%	20%	17%	6%	10.7%	92.7	58	14	29	29%	77%	17%	14%	3	19	0%	100%	0	0.83	4.7	149	$2
Proj		**6**	**0**	**73**	**69**	**3.45**	**1.16**	**3.48**	**1.13**	**94**	**94**	**4.8**	**5%**	**24%**	**19%**	**6%**	**11.0%**	**92.3**	**53**	**17**	**30**	**31%**	**75%**	**15%**	**14%**	**0**						**8.9**	**158**	**$4**

Stanek,Ryne

Age: 30 | Th: R | Role: RP | Ht: 6' 4" | Wt: 226 | Type: Pwr/xFB
Health: A | PT/Exp: D | Consist: D
LIMA Plan: B+ | Rand Var: -3 | MM: 1400

Looked good at the start (1.65 ERA in first 16 appearances) and end, but hit rough patch from mid-May through June where he had 5.45 ERA, 16% BB%. Should continue to be solid strikeout source out of pen, but BB% and FB% put ratios at risk and will prevent anything more than occasional save. Plenty others like him with better shot at 9th-inning gig.

Yr	Tm	W	Sv	IP	K	ERA	WHIP	xERA	xWHIP	vL+	vR+	BF/G	BB%	K%	K-BB%	xBB%	SwK	Vel	G	L	F	H%	S%	HR/F	xHR/F	GS	APC	DOM%	DIS%	Sv%	LI	RAR	BPX	R$
17	TAM *	3	8	65	79	2.99	1.39	3.90	1.31	81	172	4.7	11%	29%	18%		15.6%	98.2	35	22	43	34%	82%	26%	18%	0	20			89	0.82	10.9	121	$5
18	TAM	2	0	66	81	2.98	1.09	3.86	1.22	70	95	4.5	10%	31%	21%	9%	16.3%	98.0	33	15	52	26%	78%	10%	13%	29	18	3%	48%	0	0.89	9.5	127	$4
19	2 TM	0	1	77	89	3.97	1.30	4.77	1.41	94	90	5.2	12%	27%	15%	10%	15.7%	97.6	32	23	46	28%	74%	12%	15%	27	21	0%	19%	20	0.96	5.0	81	$0
20	MIA	0	0	10	11	7.20	1.90	6.47	1.69	226	95	5.3	17%	23%	6%	12%	15.9%	96.0	36	11	54	32%	69%	20%	18%	0	21			0	0.36	-3.4	-2	-$10
21	HOU	3	2	68	83	3.42	1.21	4.37	1.37	113	64	4.0	13%	29%	16%	10%	14.5%	97.7	34	20	47	26%	76%	11%	16%	0	16			50	1.15	7.1	85	$3
1st Half		1	1	35	44	4.33	1.33	4.74	1.44	104	88	4.2	14%	28%	14%	10%	14.7%	97.5	32	16	52	25%	73%	14%	19%	0	17			33	1.27	-0.3	66	-$4
2nd Half		2	1	33	39	2.45	1.09	3.97	1.29	111	41	3.9	11%	29%	18%	9%	14.3%	97.8	36	23	41	26%	79%	6%	11%	0	16			100	1.02	7.4	104	$3
Proj		**2**	**0**	**65**	**78**	**3.85**	**1.30**	**4.37**	**1.37**	**115**	**80**	**4.3**	**13%**	**29%**	**17%**	**9%**	**15.1%**	**97.7**	**33**	**20**	**47**	**28%**	**76%**	**13%**	**14%**	**0**						**4.8**	**90**	**-$1**

BRIAN RUDD

Staumont,Josh				Health	B	LIMA Plan	B
Age: 28	Th: R	Role	RP	PT/Exp	D	Rand Var	-5
Ht: 6' 3"	Wt: 205	Type	Pwr/FB	Consist	A	MM	2310

On the surface, it looks like short-season success carried over, and he even earned some Sv chances. But dips in K%, velocity, SwK say this wasn't the same guy, even during hot 2nd half that was driven more by trifecta of good fortune (H%, S%, HR/F). This isn't a sub-3.00 ERA pitcher once luck factors correct, so use xERA to set expectations.

Yr Tm	W	Sv	IP	K	ERA	WHIP	xERA	xWHIP	vL+	vR+	BF/G	BB%	K%	K-BB%	xBB%	SwK	Vel	G	L	F	H%	S%	HR/F	xHR/F	GS	APC	DOM%	DIS%	Sv%	LI	RAR	BPX	R$
17 a/a	6	0	125	111	7.45	1.86	5.87				22.5	17%	19%	2%							32%	60%									-47.6	40	-$23
18 aaa	2	1	75	81	4.45	1.68	4.51				8.2	16%	24%	8%							34%	73%									-2.8	91	-$7
19 KC *	1	2	71	72	3.81	1.51	4.17	1.67	101	130	6.4	16%	23%	7%	11%	9.2%	95.9	34	24	42	28%	78%	15%	16%	0	20			33	0.45	6.1	70	-$2
20 KC	2	0	26	37	2.45	1.40	4.40	1.37	109	68	4.3	14%	33%	19%	8%	15.7%	98.1	29	20	52	34%	85%	7%	7%	0	18			0	0.77	6.3	101	$3
21 KC	4	5	66	72	2.88	1.07	4.13	1.29	85	71	4.1	10%	27%	17%	9%	11.0%	96.6	38	17	45	25%	77%	8%	14%	0	17			100	1.00	11.2	103	$8
1st Half	0	5	33	36	3.82	1.30	4.82	1.40	99	84	4.7	12%	25%	13%	12%	11.2%	96.6	38	11	51	28%	74%	9%	13%	0	19			100	0.59	1.8	74	-$2
2nd Half	4	0	33	36	1.93	0.83	3.45	1.16	54	61	3.6	8%	30%	21%	7%	10.9%	96.7	38	24	38	21%	80%	7%	15%	0	15			0	1.37	9.4	132	$9
Proj	3	5	58	64	3.73	1.23	4.25	1.34	96	85	5.3	11%	27%	16%	8%	11.0%	96.7	38	19	43	27%	74%	12%	14%	0						5.2	96	$2

Steckenrider,Drew				Health	F	LIMA Plan	C+
Age: 31	Th: R	Role	RP	PT/Exp	D	Rand Var	-5
Ht: 6' 4"	Wt: 217	Type	Pwr/FB	Consist	C	MM	2210

This sure looked a lot like dominant 2017 campaign as far as ERA/WHIP are concerned, but skills were nowhere close. Though he delivered saves and strong ratios in 2nd half, he struggled to miss bats while H%/S% and HR/F deserved much of the credit. Even if health complies, he won't come close to a repeat, and a good chance he won't even be a ratio asset.

Yr Tm	W	Sv	IP	K	ERA	WHIP	xERA	xWHIP	vL+	vR+	BF/G	BB%	K%	K-BB%	xBB%	SwK	Vel	G	L	F	H%	S%	HR/F	xHR/F	GS	APC	DOM%	DIS%	Sv%	LI	RAR	BPX	R$
17 MIA *	1	6	68	90	2.18	1.15	2.95	1.19	92	89	4.3	10%	33%	23%	6%	14.3%	95.3	42	20	38	30%	87%	13%	11%	0	19			86	1.27	18.3	152	$9
18 MIA	4	5	65	74	3.90	1.27	4.06	1.28	110	76	3.8	10%	27%	17%	6%	11.5%	94.7	34	24	42	31%	72%	10%	10%	0	16			50	1.09	2.0	110	$2
19 MIA	0	0	14	14	6.28	0.98	5.26	1.34	78	124	3.9	9%	24%	16%	9%	9.3%	94.8	32	3	66	10%	50%	24%	24%	0	16			0	0.97	-3.1	91	-$5
20																																	
21 SEA	5	14	68	58	2.00	1.02	4.18	1.23	71	91	4.3	6%	22%	15%	6%	9.6%	94.1	37	22	41	26%	84%	7%	9%	0	16			82	1.18	18.9	102	$15
1st Half	2	2	30	31	2.40	1.03	3.85	1.27	51	89	4.5	9%	26%	17%	8%	10.4%	93.3	41	21	37	26%	77%	4%	11%	0	18			50	0.99	6.9	107	$3
2nd Half	3	12	38	27	1.67	1.01	4.44	1.21	77	96	4.1	4%	18%	14%	4%	9.0%	94.7	35	22	43	26%	91%	8%	8%	0	15			92	1.32	12.0	99	$18
Proj	4	2	65	65	3.77	1.22	4.14	1.24	93	100	4.2	8%	25%	17%	6%	11.2%	94.5	38	22	40	30%	74%	12%	10%	0						5.5	117	$2

Steele,Justin				Health	D	LIMA Plan	B+
Age: 26	Th: L	Role	RP	PT/Exp	F	Rand Var	0
Ht: 6' 2"	Wt: 205	Type	Pwr	Consist	F	MM	2201

4-4, 4.26 ERA in 57 IP at CHC. Solid in early-season relief role prior to May hamstring strain, but when he returned as starter, skills nosedived. While both samples were small, a 25% K-BB% as RP vs. 9% as SP provides a pretty good hint at where any potential value lies. Monitor his role, and consider scratching him off your cheat sheet if he cracks rotation.

Yr Tm	W	Sv	IP	K	ERA	WHIP	xERA	xWHIP	vL+	vR+	BF/G	BB%	K%	K-BB%	xBB%	SwK	Vel	G	L	F	H%	S%	HR/F	xHR/F	GS	APC	DOM%	DIS%	Sv%	LI	RAR	BPX	R$
17																																	
18																																	
19 aa	0	0	40	35	7.70	1.99	6.92				17.6	12%	18%	6%							40%	60%									-15.8	44	-$13
20																																	
21 CHC *	6	0	85	82	3.33	1.25	3.84	1.41	65	112	11.9	12%	24%	12%	9%	11.8%	93.1	50	20	30	25%	80%	26%	17%	9	48	11%	67%	0	0.90	9.9	71	$4
1st Half	2	0	17	22	2.14	0.99	2.45	1.30	73	82	4.7	14%	33%	20%	11%	15.5%	94.0	73	12	15	16%	92%	50%	11%	0	21			0	1.00	4.6	108	-$1
2nd Half	4	0	68	60	3.63	1.32	4.19	1.43	52	120	18.7	11%	21%	10%	9%	10.7%	92.9	46	21	33	27%	78%	24%	17%	9	81	11%	67%			5.3	62	$5
Proj	6	0	102	101	4.14	1.34	4.20	1.40	56	111	10.1	11%	24%	13%	9%	10.7%	92.9	46	21	33	29%	74%	18%	16%	1						4.0	82	$1

Stephan,Trevor				Health	A	LIMA Plan	C
Age: 26	Th: R	Role	RP	PT/Exp	D	Rand Var	0
Ht: 6' 5"	Wt: 225	Type	Pwr/FB	Consist	D	MM	1300

Transition to bullpen in first taste of majors was a mixed bag. Dished out too many free passes, while high FB% and all that hard contact (xHR/F) led to trouble with the long ball. Did show encouraging signs in 2nd half as BB%, SwK, and velocity all improved. This is one to watch from a distance for now, but most likely outcome is mediocre ratios in middle relief.

Yr Tm	W	Sv	IP	K	ERA	WHIP	xERA	xWHIP	vL+	vR+	BF/G	BB%	K%	K-BB%	xBB%	SwK	Vel	G	L	F	H%	S%	HR/F	xHR/F	GS	APC	DOM%	DIS%	Sv%	LI	RAR	BPX	R$
17																																	
18 aa	3	0	84	79	5.99	1.52	4.90				21.5	8%	22%	13%							36%	60%									-19.1	90	-$10
19 aa	2	0	47	48	7.13	1.92	6.51				18.6	12%	21%	9%							41%	62%									-15.3	62	-$11
20																																	
21 CLE	3	1	63	75	4.41	1.41	4.60	1.33	103	111	6.6	11%	27%	16%	9%	13.4%	96.2	33	22	45	29%	78%	19%	21%	0	28			100	0.57	-1.1	92	-$3
1st Half	1	0	31	37	4.31	1.56	5.19	1.42	92	125	6.6	12%	26%	13%	10%	12.2%	95.9	30	20	50	31%	83%	18%	21%	0	28			0	0.36	-0.2	65	-$7
2nd Half	2	1	32	38	4.50	1.25	4.05	1.25	102	100	6.5	9%	28%	18%	8%	14.7%	96.6	37	24	39	28%	73%	21%	20%	0	28			100	0.80	-0.9	119	-$3
Proj	3	0	58	64	4.49	1.43	4.60	1.37	102	106	8.6	11%	26%	15%	9%	13.6%	96.3	34	22	44	31%	74%	15%	21%	0						-0.2	86	-$4

Stephenson,Robert				Health	D	LIMA Plan	C
Age: 29	Th: R	Role	RP	PT/Exp	D	Rand Var	-3
Ht: 6' 3"	Wt: 205	Type	Pwr	Consist	A	MM	2300

Velocity took huge step forward, but cutting down significantly on slider usage led to huge dip in SwK. First half BB% spike may have been injury-related, as he issued 7 BB in 4 IP leading up to June IL stint (back strain). Ratios were superb upon return, but he can thank S% and HR/F for that. Without the return of his slider, value will be very limited.

Yr Tm	W	Sv	IP	K	ERA	WHIP	xERA	xWHIP	vL+	vR+	BF/G	BB%	K%	K-BB%	xBB%	SwK	Vel	G	L	F	H%	S%	HR/F	xHR/F	GS	APC	DOM%	DIS%	Sv%	LI	RAR	BPX	R$
17 CIN *	6	1	125	125	4.73	1.44	4.74	1.49	104	111	16.1	13%	23%	11%	11%	13.3%	93.7	38	22	41	29%	73%	13%	14%	11	59	0%	36%	100	0.63	-5.7	62	-$1
18 CIN *	11	0	125	124	4.27	1.46	4.45	1.53	163	126	22.2	14%	23%	9%	12%	11.3%	93.2	33	28	40	28%	75%	13%	15%	3	62	0%	67%	0	0.57	-1.8	67	$1
19 CIN	3	0	65	81	3.76	1.04	4.03	1.22	100	72	4.6	9%	31%	22%	6%	19.6%	95.0	32	22	46	25%	69%	13%	8%	0	18			0	0.96	6.0	134	$4
20 CIN	0	0	10	13	9.90	1.40	4.54	1.13	170	168	4.3	7%	30%	23%	6%	18.8%	94.8	23	15	62	16%	50%	50%	27%	0	18			0	0.45	-6.7	157	-$10
21 COL	2	1	46	52	3.13	1.30	4.10	1.26	102	94	4.0	9%	27%	17%	7%	12.3%	96.5	38	24	38	32%	80%	11%	15%	0	16			50	0.76	6.4	114	-$1
1st Half	0	0	24	27	4.56	1.56	4.84	1.41	106	106	4.0	12%	25%	13%	8%	13.2%	96.6	36	24	40	33%	76%	15%	20%	0	16			0	0.69	-0.9	72	-$9
2nd Half	2	1	22	25	1.61	1.03	3.36	1.08	84	85	4.0	6%	28%	23%	5%	11.1%	96.5	41	23	36	31%	86%	5%	9%	0	16			50	0.84	7.3	160	$1
Proj	3	0	58	65	4.10	1.26	4.14	1.31	102	92	4.8	10%	27%	17%	7%	12.8%	95.6	37	23	40	30%	71%	12%	12%	0						2.6	105	-$1

Strasburg,Stephen				Health	F	LIMA Plan	C
Age: 33	Th: R	Role	SP	PT/Exp	C	Rand Var	-2
Ht: 6' 5"	Wt: 235	Type	Pwr	Consist	F	MM	3301

A 2nd straight season basically lost to injury—this time it was calf issue in March, shoulder in April, and season-ending neck strain in June. Looked like an ace in last decent-sized sample, but that was a couple years and a handful of injuries ago. Monitor in spring, but no matter how positive the news is, be sure to factor in quite a bit of missed time.

Yr Tm	W	Sv	IP	K	ERA	WHIP	xERA	xWHIP	vL+	vR+	BF/G	BB%	K%	K-BB%	xBB%	SwK	Vel	G	L	F	H%	S%	HR/F	xHR/F	GS	APC	DOM%	DIS%	Sv%	LI	RAR	BPX	R$
17 WAS	15	0	175	204	2.52	1.02	3.27	1.13	76	80	25.0	7%	29%	22%	6%	13.4%	95.6	47	19	34	29%	78%	9%	11%	28	98	46%	11%			39.9	178	$31
18 WAS	10	0	130	156	3.74	1.20	3.34	1.13	99	97	24.7	7%	29%	22%	8%	12.5%	94.5	44	22	34	32%	74%	16%	18%	22	98	36%	5%			6.6	167	$10
19 WAS	18	0	209	251	3.32	1.04	3.18	1.12	77	86	25.5	7%	30%	23%	7%	13.9%	93.9	51	20	29	29%	73%	16%	14%	33	103	52%	9%			30.7	173	$31
20 WAS	0	0	5	2	10.80	1.80	6.24		152	107	11.5	4%	9%	4%		10.6%	91.7	37	26	37	37%	38%	14%	6%	2	43	0%	100%			-3.9	35	-$10
21 WAS	1	0	22	21	4.57	1.38	5.17	1.59	122	78	19.0	15%	22%	7%	12%	10.2%	91.9	36	27	37	23%	73%	18%	21%	5	72	20%	20%			-0.8	15	-$5
1st Half	1	0	22	21	4.57	1.38	5.17	1.59	116	79	19.0	15%	22%	7%	12%	10.2%	91.9	36	27	37	23%	73%	18%	21%	5	72	20%	20%			-0.8	15	-$7
2nd Half																																	
Proj	8	0	116	124	3.68	1.10	3.63	1.21	94	79	21.1	8%	27%	19%	9%	12.2%	93.7	43	23	34	27%	70%	14%	16%	22						11.1	133	$10

Stratton,Chris				Health	C	LIMA Plan	B
Age: 31	Th: R	Role	RP	PT/Exp	C	Rand Var	-1
Ht: 6' 2"	Wt: 210	Type	Pwr	Consist	B	MM	2311

Unable to sustain short-season SwK gains, especially in 1st half, but got some assistance from S% and HR/F to provide useful early ratios. Not as lucky in 2nd half, but whiffs rebounded to some extent and he was even handed ninth-inning duties at end of year. His xERA history shows these aren't closer-worthy skills; his impact will likely be minimal.

Yr Tm	W	Sv	IP	K	ERA	WHIP	xERA	xWHIP	vL+	vR+	BF/G	BB%	K%	K-BB%	xBB%	SwK	Vel	G	L	F	H%	S%	HR/F	xHR/F	GS	APC	DOM%	DIS%	Sv%	LI	RAR	BPX	R$
17 SF *	8	1	138	107	5.32	1.65	5.65	1.43	107	91	22.0	8%	17%	9%	9%	9.3%	91.6	43	28	29	36%	69%	10%	11%	10	80	20%	30%	50	0.68	-16.3	59	-$9
18 SF *	13	0	169	130	4.85	1.45	4.90	1.40	114	103	22.5	9%	18%	9%	8%	9.0%	91.1	43	25	32	32%	69%	13%	17%	26	88	23%	38%	0	0.80	-14.6	59	-$3
19 2 TM	1	0	76	69	5.57	1.66	5.16	1.44	117	115	9.8	10%	20%	10%	8%	10.8%	92.2	40	26	34	36%	70%	16%	10%	5	39	0%	60%	0	0.53	-9.9	65	-$9
20 PIT	2	0	30	39	3.90	1.30	3.76	1.24	82	93	4.9	10%	30%	20%	8%	15.7%	93.3	47	22	32	34%	72%	12%	16%	0	20			0	1.28	2.0	147	$2
21 PIT	7	8	79	86	3.63	1.30	4.20	1.30	103	82	5.0	10%	26%	16%	8%	12.7%	93.0	41	21	38	31%	76%	11%	14%	0	20			62	0.90	6.2	103	$7
1st Half	2	1	45	41	3.02	1.21	4.14	1.31	98	75	5.4	9%	22%	14%	8%	11.8%	92.9	46	21	33	29%	78%	10%	13%	0	21			50	0.74	6.8	95	$2
2nd Half	5	7	35	45	4.41	1.41	4.27	1.28	97	95	4.5	11%	29%	18%	8%	13.8%	93.2	34	21	44	34%	73%	13%	14%	0	19			64	1.06	-0.6	114	$6
Proj	6	8	73	79	4.17	1.35	4.15	1.32	100	91	5.7	10%	26%	16%	8%	12.7%	92.7	41	23	36	31%	72%	13%	14%	0						2.5	104	$4

BRIAN RUDD

Stripling,Ross

Age: 32 Th: R Role RP	Health F	LIMA Plan C	Shook off April forearm scare and pitched fine through June... then fell apart. July brought K% dip and HR/F surge, while August and Sept were ruined by an oblique injury. Still owns pre-2020 skills, but given age, Health grade, and fringy xERA/xWHIP of late, the likelihood of those returning is slim. Place your end game gamble elsewhere.
Ht: 6' 3" Wt: 220 Type	PT/Exp B	Rand Var +1	
	Consist C	MM 1101	

Yr Tm	W	Sv	IP	K	ERA	WHIP	xERA	xWHIP	vL+	vR+	BF/G	BB%	K%	K-BB%	xBB%	SwK	Vel	G	L	F	H%	S%	HR/F	xHR/F	GS	APC	DOM%	DIS%	Sv%	LI	RAR	BPX	R$
17 LA	3	2	74	74	3.75	1.18	3.56	1.20	73	108	6.2	6%	25%	18%	7%	12.0%	92.9	49	22	29	30%	73%	17%	13%	2	24	50%	0%	40	0.86	5.5	152	$4
18 LA	8	0	122	136	3.02	1.19	3.27	1.06	90	110	15.2	4%	27%	23%	6%	11.7%	91.7	45	22	33	34%	82%	16%	13%	21	61	29%	19%	0	0.83	16.9	184	$11
19 LA	4	0	91	93	3.47	1.15	3.66	1.16	93	92	11.6	5%	25%	20%	6%	10.6%	90.5	50	19	31	31%	74%	14%	14%	15	45	13%	27%	0	0.73	11.5	153	$6
20 2 TM	3	1	49	40	5.84	1.50	5.20	1.39	102	137	18.3	8%	18%	10%	7%	7.5%	91.7	40	24	36	30%	69%	23%	23%	9	68	11%	78%	100	0.69	-8.4	69	-$6
21 TOR	5	0	101	94	4.80	1.27	4.66	1.26	102	110	18.0	7%	22%	15%	8%	10.5%	91.9	36	20	45	28%	71%	17%	17%	19	70	11%	37%	0	0.73	-6.6	101	-$2
1st Half	3	0	71	73	4.06	1.21	4.29	1.21	77	109	21.3	7%	24%	17%	8%	10.3%	92.1	38	18	44	29%	74%	15%	16%	13	82	8%	31%	0	0.74	1.8	121	$4
2nd Half	2	0	30	21	6.53	1.42	5.55	1.37	131	122	13.3	7%	16%	9%	8%	10.9%	91.5	31	24	45	27%	64%	22%	19%	6	54	17%	50%	0	0.71	-8.5	54	-$12
Proj	5	0	87	77	4.43	1.31	4.40	1.27	105	114	13.8	7%	22%	15%	7%	10.2%	91.6	39	22	39	29%	75%	20%	17%	10						0.2	105	-$1

Stroman,Marcus

Age: 31 Th: R Role SP	Health D	LIMA Plan C	Didn't miss a beat after 2020 calf injury and COVID opt-out, delivering his best overall season. It was driven by career-best K%/SwK with improved control and elite GB%. Consistent 2nd half is encouraging given the high workload after layoff. Not a rotation anchor, but solid floor and good volume make him a nice SP2.
Ht: 5' 7" Wt: 180 Type Con/GB	PT/Exp B	Rand Var -1	
	Consist A	MM 3103	

Yr Tm	W	Sv	IP	K	ERA	WHIP	xERA	xWHIP	vL+	vR+	BF/G	BB%	K%	K-BB%	xBB%	SwK	Vel	G	L	F	H%	S%	HR/F	xHR/F	GS	APC	DOM%	DIS%	Sv%	LI	RAR	BPX	R$
17 TOR	13	0	201	164	3.09	1.31	3.58	1.32	86	104	25.3	7%	20%	12%	8%	10.2%	93.3	62	18	20	31%	80%	18%	17%	33	95	39%	27%			31.5	117	$17
18 TOR	4	0	102	77	5.54	1.48	3.93	1.38	102	108	23.6	8%	17%	9%	9%	9.3%	92.4	62	18	20	33%	62%	14%	19%	19	90	16%	42%			-17.6	88	-$9
19 2 TM	10	0	184	159	3.22	1.31	4.14	1.33	102	82	24.2	8%	21%	13%	9%	10.6%	92.5	54	20	26	31%	78%	13%	12%	32	95	25%	28%			29.2	104	$14
20																																	
21 NYM	10	0	179	158	3.02	1.15	3.65	1.21	89	88	22.1	6%	22%	16%	7%	11.9%	92.0	51	23	26	29%	77%	13%	19%	33	83	36%	30%			27.6	123	$19
1st Half	6	0	89	78	2.44	1.12	3.61	1.24	72	90	21.2	7%	22%	15%	6%	12.3%	92.3	53	22	25	28%	83%	15%	22%	17	78	35%	29%			20.0	119	$19
2nd Half	4	0	90	80	3.59	1.17	3.68	1.19	97	90	23.1	5%	22%	16%	7%	11.6%	91.6	48	24	28	31%	71%	11%	17%	16	89	38%	31%			7.6	127	$13
Proj	10	0	174	147	3.62	1.23	3.78	1.28	95	90	22.6	7%	21%	14%	8%	10.9%	92.3	55	21	25	30%	73%	13%	17%	31						17.8	114	$11

Suarez,José

Age: 24 Th: L Role SP	Health B	LIMA Plan B+	Excellent in relief during 1st half, but shakier as SP in 2nd. Upon move to rotation, S% regression brought surface stats more in line with xERA/xWHIP, while K-BB% dropoff rendered skills mediocre. Change-up is his best weapon (20% SwK, 50% GB%) but without plus offering to pair it with, he's just a back-end starter. Pay for that; anything else is a bonus.
Ht: 5' 10" Wt: 225 Type	PT/Exp D	Rand Var -1	
	Consist F	MM 1103	

Yr Tm	W	Sv	IP	K	ERA	WHIP	xERA	xWHIP	vL+	vR+	BF/G	BB%	K%	K-BB%	xBB%	SwK	Vel	G	L	F	H%	S%	HR/F	xHR/F	GS	APC	DOM%	DIS%	Sv%	LI	RAR	BPX	R$
17																																	
18 a/a	3	0	110	113	4.00	1.41	3.99				19.4	8%	24%	16%							36%	70%									2.0	123	-$2
19 LAA *	4	0	114	100	5.93	1.49	5.82	1.46	87	140	18.9	10%	20%	11%	9%	11.2%	91.8	35	22	43	30%	66%	21%	14%	15	78	7%	60%	0	0.81	-20.0	33	-$9
20 LAA	0	0	2	2	38.57	6.43	19.69		254	199	11.5	22%	9%	-13%		13.6%	93.3	53	33	13	66%	36%	50%	84%	2	44	0%	100%			-9.8	-396	-$17
21 LAA	8	0	98	85	3.75	1.23	4.30	1.35	133	79	18.0	9%	21%	12%	8%	11.5%	92.7	48	19	33	28%	73%	12%	12%	14	72	7%	50%	0	0.79	6.2	85	$5
1st Half	3	0	27	26	1.98	1.10	3.80	1.27	138	56	12.1	8%	24%	16%	8%	12.6%	92.7	51	16	33	26%	89%	13%	11%	0	49			0	0.80	7.7	113	$2
2nd Half	5	0	71	59	4.44	1.28	4.50	1.38	118	88	21.7	9%	20%	11%	8%	11.1%	92.7	47	20	33	28%	67%	12%	12%	14	87	7%	50%			-1.5	74	$3
Proj	7	0	131	119	4.31	1.33	4.42	1.37	119	90	20.6	10%	22%	12%	8%	11.5%	92.5	45	20	35	30%	71%	12%	12%	26						2.4	84	$1

Suárez,Ranger

Age: 26 Th: L Role SP	Health A	LIMA Plan D+	Unheralded and simply terrific, he garnered saves in July and rotation success in Aug/Sept. Skills were good, too: tons of GB; burgeoning combo of K%, SwK, and velocity; and adequate control. Perfect storm of H%/S%, HR/F drove 2-run xERA/ERA gap and will regress. And this: 10 of his 12 starts were vs ARI (2), BAL, CHC, COL, MIA (2), NYM, PIT and WAS.
Ht: 6' 1" Wt: 217 Type /GB	PT/Exp D	Rand Var -5	
	Consist F	MM 3203	

Yr Tm	W	Sv	IP	K	ERA	WHIP	xERA	xWHIP	vL+	vR+	BF/G	BB%	K%	K-BB%	xBB%	SwK	Vel	G	L	F	H%	S%	HR/F	xHR/F	GS	APC	DOM%	DIS%	Sv%	LI	RAR	BPX	R$
17																																	
18 PHI *	7	0	140	87	3.46	1.35	4.00	1.39	78	157	23.4	7%	15%	8%	8%	8.0%	91.8	51	18	31	31%	75%	19%	17%	3	56	0%	67%	0	0.58	12.0	72	$3
19 PHI *	8	0	87	70	4.69	1.40	5.37	1.29	75	110	8.3	6%	19%	13%	9%	10.0%	92.4	55	22	22	32%	72%	18%	17%	0	21			0	1.00	-2.0	64	$0
20 PHI	0	0	4	1	20.25	3.50	11.55		152	187	8.7	15%	4%	-12%		8.5%	91.2	45	20	35	47%	38%	14%	13%	0	31			0	0.64	-7.8	-203	-$15
21 PHI	8	4	106	107	1.36	1.00	3.21	1.21	43	80	10.7	8%	26%	18%	8%	11.7%	93.2	59	15	26	26%	88%	6%	7%	12	41	42%	8%	57	1.01	38.0	137	$23
1st Half	4	1	32	29	0.85	0.69	2.91	1.18	43	65	6.3	7%	24%	18%	8%	11.3%	92.8	65	12	23	17%	95%	11%	10%	0	23			33	1.03	13.3	143	$11
2nd Half	4	3	74	78	1.57	1.13	3.33	1.22	39	87	15.0	8%	26%	18%	8%	11.9%	93.4	57	16	27	30%	87%	4%	6%	12	59	42%	8%	75	1.00	24.7	135	$25
Proj	10	0	138	133	3.50	1.24	3.55	1.25	62	101	21.1	8%	24%	16%	8%	11.2%	92.9	55	21	24	31%	73%	11%	10%	23						16.2	128	$10

Sulser,Cole

Age: 32 Th: R Role RP	Health A	LIMA Plan B	Once again started as bullpen depth and finished as closer, but this time with some sparkling stats. He shook off previous control issues to rediscover excellent K-BB% (22% career in AA/AAA), but also benefitted from good S% and HR/F fortune (especially considering his home park). A good-not-great closing option if high-leverage finds him again.
Ht: 6' 1" Wt: 190 Type Pwr/FB	PT/Exp C	Rand Var -4	
	Consist F	MM 2321	

Yr Tm	W	Sv	IP	K	ERA	WHIP	xERA	xWHIP	vL+	vR+	BF/G	BB%	K%	K-BB%	xBB%	SwK	Vel	G	L	F	H%	S%	HR/F	xHR/F	GS	APC	DOM%	DIS%	Sv%	LI	RAR	BPX	R$
17 a/a	3	3	63	49	3.91	1.79	5.90				6.5	12%	17%	4%							35%	81%									3.5	43	-$4
18 a/a	8	2	62	72	5.52	1.51	4.98				5.7	7%	27%	19%							40%	63%									-10.5	126	-$3
19 TAM *	6	2	73	78	4.00	1.40	3.88		49	74	5.5	10%	25%	15%	7%	11.5%	93.4	38	13	50	34%	72%	0%	3%	0	19			100	0.12	4.6	106	$2
20 BAL	1	5	23	19	5.56	1.50	6.22	1.80	64	127	5.3	17%	19%	2%	11%	13.9%	93.8	38	20	43	25%	63%	8%	10%	0	22			63	1.29	-3.1	-34	-$1
21 BAL	5	8	63	73	2.70	1.12	3.82	1.21	75	86	4.3	9%	29%	20%	7%	14.8%	93.3	41	19	40	29%	79%	8%	11%	0	18			73	1.18	12.2	129	$9
1st Half	2	3	31	43	2.05	1.08	3.21	1.13	59	89	4.6	10%	35%	25%	6%	16.4%	93.3	41	21	38	30%	84%	8%	13%	0	20			100	0.79	8.4	166	$5
2nd Half	3	5	33	30	3.31	1.16	4.42	1.30	82	86	4.1	8%	23%	14%	8%	13.2%	93.3	41	17	41	28%	74%	8%	9%	0	16			63	1.50	3.9	95	$5
Proj	6	11	73	78	3.70	1.33	4.18	1.29	89	100	4.9	9%	26%	17%	7%	14.5%	93.3	41	19	40	33%	74%	8%	11%	0						6.8	114	$7

Suter,Brent

Age: 32 Th: L Role RP	Health F	LIMA Plan B	Crafty soft-tossing southpaw vultured plenty of relief wins to return value despite WHIP pullback. Underneath, however, both K% and BB% faltered, consistent with SwK and xBB%, and S% luck pulled ERA a run lower than deserved. BPX supports continued success, but expectations should be downgraded from "non-closing ace" to "won't hurt you."
Ht: 6' 4" Wt: 213 Type	PT/Exp D	Rand Var -3	
	Consist D	MM 3201	

Yr Tm	W	Sv	IP	K	ERA	WHIP	xERA	xWHIP	vL+	vR+	BF/G	BB%	K%	K-BB%	xBB%	SwK	Vel	G	L	F	H%	S%	HR/F	xHR/F	GS	APC	DOM%	DIS%	Sv%	LI	RAR	BPX	R$
17 MIL *	6	0	118	93	3.94	1.38	4.68	1.30	72	102	15.5	6%	19%	13%	5%	9.4%	85.8	45	24	31	33%	75%	10%	8%	14	58	21%	43%	0	0.67	6.1	88	$2
18 MIL	8	0	101	84	4.44	1.19	4.22	1.19	93	108	21.2	5%	20%	16%	6%	10.4%	86.7	33	29	38	29%	69%	16%	15%	18	82	22%	22%	0	0.83	-3.6	115	$3
19 MIL *	4	0	35	31	0.26	0.59	0.07	1.10	85	48	7.8	4%	26%	22%	5%	14.2%	87.5	52	15	33	18%	100%	6%	7%	0	26			0	0.84	18.1	224	$7
20 MIL	2	0	32	38	3.13	1.11	2.94	1.01	99	81	8.1	4%	29%	26%	8%	14.1%	85.6	51	24	25	34%	77%	19%	19%	4	32	25%	0%	0	0.83	5.2	209	$6
21 MIL	12	1	73	69	3.07	1.31	3.95	1.27	91	99	5.1	8%	22%	14%	7%	9.3%	87.4	53	19	29	31%	82%	15%	15%	1	20	0%	100%	11	0.99	10.8	114	$7
1st Half	8	0	41	41	3.48	1.35	3.80	1.26	89	104	5.6	8%	23%	15%	6%	9.4%	87.8	59	13	28	32%	80%	18%	15%	1	21	0%	100%	0	1.06	4.0	126	$6
2nd Half	4	1	32	28	2.53	1.25	4.13	1.29	82	97	4.6	8%	21%	14%	8%	9.2%	87.1	45	26	30	30%	84%	11%	17%	0	19			20	0.90	6.8	97	$3
Proj	6	0	73	69	3.38	1.20	3.79	1.23	85	91	6.4	7%	24%	17%	7%	10.5%	86.7	46	23	30	30%	76%	13%	15%	0						9.6	125	$4

Syndergaard,Noah

Age: 29 Th: R Role SP	Health F	LIMA Plan C+	A May setback in rehab from Tommy John surgery cost the season. Last time we saw him he owned excellent BPX built from above-average K%, SwK, and GB%, with good control. Take that as a baseline, expect bumps and a bit of rust along the way, and amortize it over a (likely) limited workload to set a prudent valuation... and don't overpay for name.
Ht: 6' 6" Wt: 242 Type /GB	PT/Exp C	Rand Var +5	
	Consist A	MM 4301	

Yr Tm	W	Sv	IP	K	ERA	WHIP	xERA	xWHIP	vL+	vR+	BF/G	BB%	K%	K-BB%	xBB%	SwK	Vel	G	L	F	H%	S%	HR/F	xHR/F	GS	APC	DOM%	DIS%	Sv%	LI	RAR	BPX	R$
17 NYM	1	0	30	34	2.97	1.05	2.75	0.99	65	89	17.7	2%	28%	25%	6%	14.2%	98.3	58	19	24	36%	69%	0%	11%	7	66	43%	29%			5.2	232	$0
18 NYM	13	0	154	155	3.03	1.21	3.40	1.17	90	90	25.8	6%	24%	18%	6%	14.0%	97.4	49	24	27	33%	76%	8%	7%	25	96	36%	16%			21.3	148	$16
19 NYM	10	0	198	202	4.28	1.23	3.90	1.20	99	91	25.8	6%	25%	19%	5%	12.9%	97.7	48	20	32	32%	68%	13%	12%	32	97	41%	16%			5.5	142	$11
20																																	
21 NYM	0	0	2	2	9.00	1.50	4.08		138	186	4.0	0%	25%	25%		11.5%	94.7	17	33	50	35%	50%	33%	33%	2	13	0%	50%			-1.2	172	-$6
1st Half																																	
2nd Half	0	0	2	2	9.00	1.50	4.08		131	190	4.0	0%	25%	25%		11.5%	94.7	17	33	50	35%	50%	33%	33%	2	13	0%	50%			-1.2	172	-$13
Proj	7	0	116	121	3.81	1.21	3.42	1.15	92	91	22.5	6%	26%	20%	6%	13.5%	97.8	51	21	28	33%	70%	11%	10%	21						9.2	158	$6

ALAIN DE LEONARDIS

Taillon,Jameson

Age: 30	Th: R	Role SP	Health F	LIMA Plan B
Ht: 6' 5"	Wt: 230	Type	PT/Exp C	Rand Var 0
			Consist A	MM 2203

Respectable showing after Tommy John surgery cost him all of 2020. K% and SwK reached new heights, but FB% spike led to career-worst 1.5 HR/9 and late ankle issue led to October surgery. Opening Day is in question, but with another year removed from Tommy John, he should be ready to take a step forward if ankle is healthy.

Yr Tm	W	Sv	IP	K	ERA	WHIP	xERA	xWHIP	vL+	vR+	BF/G	BB%	K%	K-BB%	xBB%	SwK	Vel	G	L	F	H%	S%	HR/F	xHR/F	GS	APC	DOM%	DIS%	Sv%	LI	RAR	BPX	R$
17 PIT	8	0	134	125	4.44	1.48	4.11	1.32	110	102	23.5	8%	21%	13%	8%	9.1%	95.3	47	25	28	36%	71%	10%	10%	25	93	16%	32%			-1.4	112	$0
18 PIT	14	0	191	179	3.20	1.18	3.66	1.19	101	86	24.5	6%	23%	17%	6%	11.0%	95.2	46	22	31	31%	77%	12%	12%	32	93	25%	16%			22.3	135	$19
19 PIT	2	0	37	30	4.10	1.13	4.17	1.26	88	93	22.6	5%	19%	14%	5%	12.1%	94.8	50	23	27	28%	66%	13%	16%	7	79	14%	29%			1.9	116	-$1
20																																	
21 NYY	8	0	144	140	4.30	1.21	4.60	1.25	101	95	20.8	7%	23%	16%	6%	12.9%	94.0	33	19	48	28%	70%	12%	13%	29	82	17%	28%			-0.7	103	$6
1st Half	3	0	70	73	5.43	1.36	4.52	1.21	115	102	20.2	7%	24%	17%	6%	13.2%	93.9	32	22	46	33%	65%	15%	15%	15	80	20%	33%			-10.0	117	-$5
2nd Half	5	0	75	67	3.25	1.06	4.67	1.28	72	92	21.4	8%	22%	15%	8%	12.5%	94.1	34	15	51	24%	75%	10%	10%	14	84	14%	21%			9.3	91	$16
Proj	9	0	145	137	3.97	1.20	4.11	1.23	98	93	21.3	7%	24%	17%	6%	12.7%	94.5	41	21	39	30%	71%	12%	13%	27						8.7	119	$8

Tate,Dillon

Age: 28	Th: R	Role RP	Health D	LIMA Plan C
Ht: 6' 2"	Wt: 195	Type Con/xGB	PT/Exp D	Rand Var 0
			Consist A	MM 2000

Took heavy ground ball tilt one step further with increased sinker usage. But even with another velocity bump, the pitch mix change had negative impact on already weak K%, and career 21/20 K/BB vL further highlights his limitations. Tough to find a path to meaningful value for a low-strikeout reliever with subpar ratios.

Yr Tm	W	Sv	IP	K	ERA	WHIP	xERA	xWHIP	vL+	vR+	BF/G	BB%	K%	K-BB%	xBB%	SwK	Vel	G	L	F	H%	S%	HR/F	xHR/F	GS	APC	DOM%	DIS%	Sv%	LI	RAR	BPX	R$
17 aa	1	0	25	15	4.65	1.55	5.78				27.3	9%	14%	5%							30%	76%									-0.9	12	-$5
18 aa	7	0	124	77	4.80	1.33	4.26				23.4	7%	15%	8%							31%	64%									-9.9	65	-$3
19 BAL *	4	7	65	49	4.82	1.24	4.10	1.37	100	96	7.2	8%	18%	11%	9%	8.3%	93.7	59	14	27	28%	64%	19%	14%	0	22			88	1.03	-2.5	64	$2
20 BAL	1	0	17	14	3.24	0.84	3.65	1.29	125	37	5.3	8%	22%	14%	12%	9.8%	94.4	51	22	27	20%	62%	9%	16%	0	24			0	0.98	2.5	104	$1
21 BAL	0	3	68	49	4.39	1.24	4.12	1.38	106	91	4.6	8%	17%	9%	7%	10.0%	95.5	60	15	25	28%	66%	13%	17%	0	17			60	1.10	-1.0	80	-$3
1st Half	0	1	34	29	4.28	1.16	3.94	1.30	91	88	5.4	8%	21%	13%	8%	10.2%	95.0	56	13	31	27%	64%	10%	11%	0	20			100	0.78	0.0	104	-$4
2nd Half	0	2	34	20	4.50	1.32	4.32	1.45	110	98	4.1	8%	14%	5%	6%	9.8%	96.0	63	17	20	28%	68%	18%	24%	0	15			50	1.33	-1.0	55	-$8
Proj	2	1	65	45	4.57	1.27	4.13	1.39	109	95	5.7	8%	17%	9%	7%	9.9%	95.6	60	15	25	28%	66%	15%	19%	0						-0.9	83	-$3

Taylor,Josh

Age: 29	Th: L	Role RP	Health D	LIMA Plan C
Ht: 6' 5"	Wt: 245	Type Pwr	PT/Exp D	Rand Var 0
			Consist F	MM 2300

Wipeout slider got plenty of whiffs and he's been dominant vL, but the rest of this package needs refinement: bad fastball gets knocked around, walks have been an area of concern, and he allowed a ton of hard contact (11th percentile HardHit%). With ERA likely heading north, there are probably better dart throws to fill out the end of your roster.

Yr Tm	W	Sv	IP	K	ERA	WHIP	xERA	xWHIP	vL+	vR+	BF/G	BB%	K%	K-BB%	xBB%	SwK	Vel	G	L	F	H%	S%	HR/F	xHR/F	GS	APC	DOM%	DIS%	Sv%	LI	RAR	BPX	R$
17 aa	4	1	97	75	6.98	2.00	7.01				14.2	11%	16%	5%							40%	64%									-31.4	41	-$20
18 a/a	2	8	39	31	4.78	1.88	6.01				5.4	10%	17%	7%							40%	73%									-3.1	67	-$5
19 BOS *	3	3	71	87	3.27	1.28	3.67	1.24	74	94	4.1	10%	30%	20%	9%	15.6%	94.9	44	21	35	33%	78%	13%	11%	1	16	0%	100%	60	1.00	10.9	119	$4
20 BOS	1	0	7	7	9.82	1.64	6.02	1.63	93	128	4.5	14%	19%	6%	11%	12.3%	93.6	43	17	39	27%	40%	22%	22%	0	18			0	0.70	-4.9	11	-$8
21 BOS	1	1	48	60	3.40	1.43	3.75	1.29	53	118	3.4	11%	29%	18%	8%	16.1%	94.6	43	26	30	37%	76%	5%	15%	0	13			100	1.09	5.1	118	-$3
1st Half	0	0	29	36	2.83	1.40	3.66	1.23	58	110	3.6	10%	29%	19%	9%	16.0%	94.4	38	32	30	38%	79%	5%	12%	0	14			0	1.01	5.1	129	-$4
2nd Half	1	1	19	24	4.26	1.47	3.87	1.38	37	136	3.1	13%	28%	15%	6%	16.1%	94.9	52	17	31	35%	70%	7%	20%	0	12			100	1.21	0.0	103	-$8
Proj	2	0	58	64	4.00	1.38	4.14	1.37	55	119	3.9	12%	26%	15%	8%	14.9%	94.7	44	23	34	32%	72%	10%	15%	0						3.2	95	-$2

Thielbar,Caleb

Age: 35	Th: L	Role RP	Health B	LIMA Plan B+
Ht: 6' 0"	Wt: 205	Type /xFB	PT/Exp D	Rand Var -2
			Consist B	MM 1200

Luck drove 2020 success, but solid follow-up came with a little more skill support, most notably the drop in BB%. But he was again fortunate that huge FB% didn't lead to many homers, and while velocity spiked late in the year, SwK and K% each took turns for the worse. He's a decent end-gamer in deep leagues, but likely to fall short of repeat.

Yr Tm	W	Sv	IP	K	ERA	WHIP	xERA	xWHIP	vL+	vR+	BF/G	BB%	K%	K-BB%	xBB%	SwK	Vel	G	L	F	H%	S%	HR/F	xHR/F	GS	APC	DOM%	DIS%	Sv%	LI	RAR	BPX	R$
17																																	
18 a/a	7	0	57	35	3.10	1.27	4.22				6.0	3%	15%	12%							33%	77%									7.4	154	$2
19 aaa	2	5	79	68	4.79	1.55	5.63				6.8	5%	20%	14%							38%	71%									-2.8	89	-$4
20 MIN	2	0	20	22	2.25	1.15	4.63	1.35	52	74	4.8	11%	27%	16%	7%	13.5%	89.8	27	27	47	29%	78%	0%	6%	0	22			0	0.88	5.4	83	$3
21 MIN	7	0	64	77	3.23	1.17	4.01	1.15	89	96	4.5	8%	29%	21%	6%	12.3%	91.3	32	19	49	31%	78%	10%	16%	0	19			0	1.00	8.1	141	$5
1st Half	2	0	30	40	3.26	1.15	3.73	1.08	90	89	4.6	7%	32%	25%	6%	13.1%	90.8	31	18	51	34%	75%	8%	16%	0	20			0	0.76	3.7	165	$0
2nd Half	5	0	34	37	3.21	1.19	4.28	1.21	79	106	4.4	8%	26%	18%	6%	11.6%	91.8	33	20	47	29%	80%	12%	17%	0	18			0	1.21	4.4	120	$4
Proj	5	0	58	59	3.99	1.22	4.34	1.19	95	106	4.9	6%	25%	19%	6%	12.2%	91.4	32	19	49	31%	72%	11%	16%	0						3.3	126	$1

Thompson,Keegan

Age: 27	Th: R	Role RP	Health B	LIMA Plan D+
Ht: 6' 2"	Wt: 210	Type Pwr	PT/Exp F	Rand Var -5
			Consist F	MM 1201

3-3, 3.38 ERA in 53 IP at CHC. Initially worked out of the 'pen with some success, albeit with the help of sky-high 1st half S%. He got brief look in the rotation, but failed to impress with 7.11 ERA in five starts before September shoulder injury ended season. Marginal SwK, high BB% are signs that ERA will surely rise, and ceiling appears low in any role.

Yr Tm	W	Sv	IP	K	ERA	WHIP	xERA	xWHIP	vL+	vR+	BF/G	BB%	K%	K-BB%	xBB%	SwK	Vel	G	L	F	H%	S%	HR/F	xHR/F	GS	APC	DOM%	DIS%	Sv%	LI	RAR	BPX	R$
17																																	
18 aa	6	0	62	46	5.15	1.62	5.22				21.2	8%	17%	8%							37%	67%									-7.6	70	-$7
19																																	
20																																	
21 CHC *	3	1	70	68	2.59	1.29	3.73	1.45	111	92	7.9	13%	24%	11%	9%	10.7%	93.9	43	22	35	26%	86%	17%	20%	6	30	0%	50%	50	0.94	14.4	75	$3
1st Half	3	0	29	32	1.86	1.38	4.41	1.46	108	80	6.6	14%	26%	12%	9%	11.2%	94.6	43	23	34	28%	94%	16%	21%	1	25	0%	0%	0	1.09	8.6	63	$1
2nd Half	0	1	41	36	3.11	1.23	3.48	1.45	103	109	9.7	12%	22%	10%	9%	10.1%	93.4	43	21	36	25%	80%	18%	20%	5	37	0%	60%	100	0.72	5.8	72	-$2
Proj	5	0	87	80	3.95	1.38	4.66	1.46	100	89	11.0	11%	22%	10%	9%	10.5%	93.9	43	22	35	28%	76%	14%	20%	3						5.4	60	$0

Toussaint,Touki

Age: 26	Th: R	Role RP	Health F	LIMA Plan D+
Ht: 6' 3"	Wt: 215	Type Pwr	PT/Exp D	Rand Var +1
			Consist C	MM 1201

3-3, 4.50 ERA in 50 IP at ATL. Missed 1st half with shoulder injury, then returned with better, yet still mediocre results. His K% remained decent, but velocity and SwK dipped, BB% and homers are ongoing concerns, and he boasts awful 4% career K-BB% vL. Young enough to turn things around, but not much reason for short-term optimism.

Yr Tm	W	Sv	IP	K	ERA	WHIP	xERA	xWHIP	vL+	vR+	BF/G	BB%	K%	K-BB%	xBB%	SwK	Vel	G	L	F	H%	S%	HR/F	xHR/F	GS	APC	DOM%	DIS%	Sv%	LI	RAR	BPX	R$
17 aa	3	0	40	40	4.42	1.54	4.27				24.7	14%	23%	9%							32%	72%									-0.3	85	-$3
18 ATL *	11	0	166	171	3.14	1.25	2.99	1.34	70	98	21.8	11%	25%	15%	12%	9.9%	93.2	48	28	24	30%	75%	6%	14%	5	68	20%	0%	0	0.67	20.8	117	$14
19 ATL *	5	0	83	81	7.49	1.93	6.61	1.64	159	78	11.6	14%	21%	7%	12%	12.3%	93.5	44	17	39	38%	61%	11%	12%	1	33	0%	100%	0	1.24	-30.6	47	-$17
20 ATL	0	0	24	30	8.88	1.77	4.86	1.48	133	126	17.1	13%	25%	12%	11%	12.6%	94.0	39	30	31	34%	53%	33%	29%	5	70	20%	60%	0	0.72	-13.3	64	-$17
21 ATL *	5	0	77	74	4.46	1.24	3.83	1.42	110	102	16.6	12%	24%	12%	11%	10.4%	92.8	47	18	35	24%	69%	23%	20%	10	75	30%	50%	0	0.72	-1.9	69	$0
1st Half	0	0	11	9	8.44	1.50	2.80				16.5	20%	18%	-2%							24%	37%	0%		0	0					-5.9	86	-$12
2nd Half	5	0	66	65	3.77	1.20	4.00	1.33	104	104	16.6	10%	24%	14%	11%	10.4%	92.8	47	18	35	25%	77%	23%	20%	10	75	30%	50%	0	0.72	4.0	71	$8
Proj	6	0	87	87	4.70	1.46	4.64	1.46	129	91	16.5	12%	23%	11%	12%	11.2%	93.1	46	18	36	30%	72%	16%	17%	15						-2.6	66	-$3

Treinen,Blake

Age: 34	Th: R	Role RP	Health B	LIMA Plan B
Ht: 6' 5"	Wt: 225	Type Pwr/GB	PT/Exp C	Rand Var -5
			Consist C	MM 4320

While not quite as elite as 2018's peak, he was back to being a dominant bullpen force. Threw more sliders than ever, induced whiffs and ground balls at high rates, and completely shut down both LHB and RHB. The strong ERA/WHIP combo with healthy dose of strikeouts gives him value in setup role, with potential for much more... UP: 35 Sv.

Yr Tm	W	Sv	IP	K	ERA	WHIP	xERA	xWHIP	vL+	vR+	BF/G	BB%	K%	K-BB%	xBB%	SwK	Vel	G	L	F	H%	S%	HR/F	xHR/F	GS	APC	DOM%	DIS%	Sv%	LI	RAR	BPX	R$
17 2 TM	3	16	76	74	3.93	1.39	3.53	1.28	116	84	4.5	8%	23%	15%	8%	13.5%	97.2	58	19	23	35%	73%	12%	14%	0	17			76	1.30	4.0	137	$7
18 OAK	9	38	80	100	0.78	0.83	2.61	1.06	63	52	4.6	7%	32%	25%	5%	18.6%	97.4	52	24	24	26%	92%	4%	7%	0	17			88	1.60	33.3	194	$36
19 OAK	6	16	59	59	4.91	1.62	5.26	1.59	104	103	4.7	14%	22%	8%	8%	12.6%	96.7	43	24	33	32%	73%	16%	16%	0	18			76	1.40	-2.9	33	$3
20 LA	3	1	26	22	3.86	1.21	3.43	1.29	92	79	4.0	7%	21%	13%	6%	11.4%	96.9	64	21	15	30%	67%	9%	8%	0	15			50	1.25	1.9	119	$4
21 LA	6	7	72	85	1.99	0.98	3.16	1.17	69	70	4.0	9%	30%	21%	7%	13.4%	97.5	53	17	30	26%	83%	10%	8%	0	15			64	1.41	20.3	151	$15
1st Half	2	3	33	38	3.03	1.16	3.17	1.15	100	71	4.1	7%	28%	21%	7%	14.5%	97.5	56	17	27	32%	77%	13%	10%	0	15			50	1.45	5.0	162	$2
2nd Half	4	4	40	47	1.13	0.83	3.16	1.20	37	71	3.8	10%	31%	21%	7%	12.5%	97.4	49	17	33	20%	90%	7%	7%	0	15			80	1.38	15.3	140	$18
Proj	6	10	65	74	3.03	1.07	3.27	1.19	79	73	4.1	9%	29%	20%	7%	13.7%	97.3	51	20	29	28%	74%	11%	10%	0						11.5	148	$11

BRIAN RUDD

Trivino,Lou

Age: 30	Th: R	Role: RP	Health: A	LIMA Plan: C
Ht: 6' 5"	Wt: 235	Type: Pwr	PT/Exp: C	Rand Var: -3
			Consist: B	MM: 1210

Gave up as many ER (13) during five-game stretch in Aug-Sept as rest of season combined, which booted him from closer role. Skills say 1st half results were over his head anyway, as H%/S% combo wasn't going to hold all year and xERA stayed consistently mediocre throughout. Lack of whiffs and Ks cast further doubt he can reclaim back-end gig.

Yr Tm	W	Sv	IP	K	ERA	WHIP	xERA	xWHIP	vL+	vR+	BF/G	BB%	K%	K-BB%	xBB%	SwK	Vel	G	L	F	H%	S%	HR/F	xHR/F	GS	APC	DOM%	DIS%	Sv%	LI	RAR	BPX	R$
17 a/a	8	5	68	52	3.57	1.38	3.54				6.0	7%	18%	11%							34%	71%									6.7	112	$4
18 OAK	8	4	74	82	2.92	1.14	3.50	1.29	88	79	4.3	10%	28%	17%	8%	14.9%	97.6	47	23	31	26%	79%	14%	13%	1	16	0%	0%	44	1.18	11.2	118	$9
19 OAK	4	0	60	57	5.25	1.53	5.21	1.51	105	102	4.4	12%	21%	10%	8%	12.7%	97.5	45	16	39	32%	67%	10%	8%	0	16			0	1.08	-5.5	56	-$5
20 OAK	0	0	23	26	3.86	1.11	4.07	1.31	106	65	4.7	11%	28%	17%	10%	12.4%	95.5	40	21	39	25%	70%	14%	17%	0	19			0	0.39	1.7	107	-$2
21 OAK	7	22	74	67	3.18	1.25	4.36	1.43	111	66	4.4	11%	22%	11%	9%	10.5%	95.8	48	19	33	27%	76%	8%	17%	0	17			85	1.22	9.9	67	$14
1st Half	3	13	40	37	2.01	1.17	4.10	1.41	102	64	4.1	11%	23%	12%	9%	9.1%	96.1	49	19	32	25%	86%	9%	15%	0	16			87	1.16	11.2	73	$13
2nd Half	4	9	33	30	4.59	1.35	4.67	1.45	113	69	4.7	11%	21%	10%	8%	12.2%	95.5	47	20	33	30%	65%	6%	20%	0	17			82	1.31	-1.3	60	$14
Proj	4	5	65	61	3.77	1.31	4.36	1.41	108	76	4.4	11%	23%	12%	8%	12.1%	96.5	47	19	34	29%	72%	8%	15%	0						5.5	77	$2

Turnbull,Spencer

Age: 29	Th: R	Role: SP	Health: F	LIMA Plan: B+
Ht: 6' 3"	Wt: 211	Type: /GB	PT/Exp: B	Rand Var: -4
			Consist: B	MM: 2100

Made the most of his nine starts (including a no-hitter!) before "forearm strain" became a torn UCL that needed Tommy John surgery in July. Minuscule ERA was mostly driven by HR/F good fortune, but he kept elite GB% in check with improved control that was backed by xBB%. Rehab timeline should bleed well into season though, so check back in 2023.

Yr Tm	W	Sv	IP	K	ERA	WHIP	xERA	xWHIP	vL+	vR+	BF/G	BB%	K%	K-BB%	xBB%	SwK	Vel	G	L	F	H%	S%	HR/F	xHR/F	GS	APC	DOM%	DIS%	Sv%	LI	RAR	BPX	R$
17 aa	0	0	20	17	8.04	1.74	5.60				23.2	10%	18%	9%							39%	50%									-9.2	77	-$8
18 DET *	5	0	131	110	5.76	1.50	4.43	1.39	89	94	22.6	9%	19%	10%	7%	9.9%	94.1	46	28	26	35%	59%	8%	15%	3	71	0%	33%	0	0.89	-25.9	87	-$12
19 DET	3	0	148	146	4.61	1.44	4.46	1.36	107	95	21.9	9%	22%	13%	10%	11.1%	93.8	48	19	32	34%	69%	10%	14%	30	89	7%	33%			-1.9	97	-$2
20 DET	4	0	57	51	3.97	1.34	4.59	1.49	90	90	22.0	12%	21%	9%	12%	11.8%	94.1	50	22	28	29%	69%	5%	17%	11	88	18%	18%			3.4	56	$6
21 DET	4	0	50	44	2.88	0.98	3.47	1.20	74	77	22.3	6%	22%	16%	8%	11.2%	94.2	57	15	28	27%	70%	5%	13%	9	86	33%	11%			8.5	131	$4
1st Half	4	0	50	44	2.88	0.98	3.47	1.20	70	78	22.3	6%	22%	16%	8%	11.2%	94.2	57	15	28	27%	70%	5%	13%	9	86	33%	11%			8.5	131	$8
2nd Half																																	
Proj	2	0	29	26	4.08	1.27	4.02	1.34	92	89	21.5	9%	22%	13%	9%	11.4%	94.1	53	18	29	31%	67%	6%	14%	6						1.3	98	-$3

Underwood Jr.,Duane

Age: 27	Th: R	Role: RP	Health: C	LIMA Plan: D+
Ht: 6' 2"	Wt: 210	Type:	PT/Exp: D	Rand Var: 0
			Consist: C	MM: 1110

Career-best ERA by a wide margin in multi-inning relief role, but couldn't hold most of 2020's tiny-sample skill gains. Whiffs evaporated, particularly in 2nd half as change-up effectiveness waned, which derailed K% and pushed xERA/BPX below average. Late injuries (hip in July, shoulder discomfort in Sept) further cloud outlook. An easy pass.

Yr Tm	W	Sv	IP	K	ERA	WHIP	xERA	xWHIP	vL+	vR+	BF/G	BB%	K%	K-BB%	xBB%	SwK	Vel	G	L	F	H%	S%	HR/F	xHR/F	GS	APC	DOM%	DIS%	Sv%	LI	RAR	BPX	R$
17 aa	13	0	138	85	5.85	1.53	5.04				24.0	9%	14%	5%							32%	62%									-25.4	40	-$7
18 CHC *	4	0	124	90	4.98	1.50	4.82		34	152	19.1	8%	17%	9%		5.2%	92.4	50	10	40	34%	66%	25%	26%	1	77	0%	100%			-12.7	71	-$9
19 CHC *	3	0	95	90	6.36	1.73	5.91	1.49	170	91	9.6	11%	21%	9%	8%	12.3%	94.8	55	18	27	37%	64%	22%	18%	0	18			0	0.48	-21.7	57	-$13
20 CHC	1	0	21	27	5.66	1.50	3.73	1.10	134	121	5.2	7%	31%	24%	7%	15.5%	94.6	39	20	41	39%	69%	23%	19%	0	20			0	0.38	-3.1	179	-$6
21 PIT	2	0	73	65	4.33	1.43	4.47	1.34	124	91	7.4	8%	20%	12%	8%	10.5%	94.0	44	26	31	33%	73%	13%	16%	0	27			0	0.69	-0.6	83	-$5
1st Half	2	0	49	47	3.67	1.33	4.22	1.33	99	87	7.5	9%	22%	13%	8%	11.5%	93.8	43	26	31	32%	73%	7%	13%	0	27			0	0.79	3.6	91	-$1
2nd Half	0	0	24	18	5.70	1.65	5.00	1.37	159	100	7.3	7%	16%	9%	8%	8.5%	94.3	44	26	30	34%	73%	24%	23%	0	27			0	0.49	-4.2	69	-$4
Proj	2	2	51	41	5.30	1.56	4.78	1.41	134	95	9.5	9%	19%	10%	8%	9.6%	94.1	44	26	31	34%	68%	14%	19%	0						-5.3	68	-$7

Ureña,José

Age: 30	Th: R	Role: SP	Health: F	LIMA Plan: D+
Ht: 6' 2"	Wt: 208	Type: Con/GB	PT/Exp: C	Rand Var: +2
			Consist: B	MM: 0001

Semi-rosterable with 3.60 ERA through seven starts, then injuries struck yet again (forearm, groin) and finished season as reliever. Elite GB% still isn't enough to garner interest, as velocity and SwK% sunk, resulting in second straight single-digit K-BB% and 5.00+ xERA. Those aren't traits you want anywhere near your rotation, even in a streaming capacity.

Yr Tm	W	Sv	IP	K	ERA	WHIP	xERA	xWHIP	vL+	vR+	BF/G	BB%	K%	K-BB%	xBB%	SwK	Vel	G	L	F	H%	S%	HR/F	xHR/F	GS	APC	DOM%	DIS%	Sv%	LI	RAR	BPX	R$
17 MIA	14	0	170	113	3.82	1.27	5.06	1.49	100	97	21.3	9%	16%	7%	10%	8.5%	95.5	43	19	38	26%	76%	13%	13%	28	85	7%	46%	0	0.73	11.3	45	$11
18 MIA	9	0	174	130	3.98	1.18	4.10	1.33	100	89	23.0	7%	18%	11%	9%	9.2%	95.8	50	18	32	27%	69%	12%	12%	31	90	16%	26%			3.6	90	$8
19 MIA	4	3	85	62	5.21	1.48	4.78	1.39	120	98	15.4	7%	17%	10%	8%	10.1%	95.9	50	21	29	33%	68%	16%	16%	13	57	8%	38%	60	1.03	-7.3	78	-$4
20 MIA	0	0	23	15	5.40	1.50	5.91	1.67	171	71	20.8	13%	14%	2%	9%	11.9%	95.5	47	18	36	26%	68%	15%	20%	5	79	20%	40%			-2.7	-7	-$9
21 DET	4	0	101	67	5.81	1.60	5.06	1.48	130	98	17.5	9%	15%	5%	10%	9.1%	94.0	52	20	28	33%	65%	15%	22%	18	65	11%	56%	0	0.80	-19.2	40	-$14
1st Half	2	0	72	47	6.22	1.66	5.33	1.53	125	103	22.2	10%	14%	4%	10%	7.9%	93.8	51	20	29	33%	64%	15%	21%	15	83	13%	53%			-17.4	26	-$17
2nd Half	2	0	28	20	4.76	1.45	4.38	1.37	121	92	11.2	7%	16%	9%	9%	12.5%	94.4	55	20	25	33%	68%	13%	26%	3	41	0%	67%	0	0.83	-1.7	77	-$15
Proj	5	0	102	66	4.89	1.47	4.93	1.49	120	96	21.3	9%	15%	6%	9%	10.0%	95.0	51	20	29	31%	69%	14%	19%	20						-5.5	45	-$7

Urías,Julio

Age: 25	Th: L	Role: SP	Health: D	LIMA Plan: D
Ht: 6' 0"	Wt: 225	Type: /FB	PT/Exp: A	Rand Var: -2
			Consist: C	MM: 2205

Eschewed concerns over volume and became MLB's only 20-game winner. Pinpoint control came with best xBB% in majors (min. 100 IP), but if we're to nitpick: xERA, HR/F question another sub-3.00 ERA; SwK% hints the jump in Ks might be temporary. Health is less of a concern now and ratios should be stout, but you're rostering him after a career year.

Yr Tm	W	Sv	IP	K	ERA	WHIP	xERA	xWHIP	vL+	vR+	BF/G	BB%	K%	K-BB%	xBB%	SwK	Vel	G	L	F	H%	S%	HR/F	xHR/F	GS	APC	DOM%	DIS%	Sv%	LI	RAR	BPX	R$
17 LA *	3	0	55	39	3.91	1.31	2.97	1.59	178	77	20.5	12%	17%	5%		9.2%	93.1	40	28	32	27%	69%	4%	5%	5	82	20%	40%			3.0	84	-$1
18 LA	0	0	4	7	0.00	0.25	1.23		0	28	4.3	0%	54%	54%		22.4%	93.1	50	17	33	19%	0%	0%	1%	0	19			0	0.00	2.0	359	-$3
19 LA	4	4	80	85	2.49	1.08	4.14	1.27	89	76	8.8	8%	26%	18%	8%	14.4%	95.2	39	22	39	27%	81%	9%	9%	8	36	38%	25%	80	0.96	19.9	117	$10
20 LA	3	0	55	45	3.27	1.15	5.04	1.36	68	86	20.4	8%	20%	12%	6%	12.5%	94.2	33	22	46	27%	74%	7%	10%	10	80	10%	20%	0	0.74	8.0	72	$10
21 LA	20	0	186	195	2.96	1.02	3.73	1.10	88	80	23.3	5%	26%	21%	4%	11.9%	94.1	40	19	41	29%	75%	9%	12%	32	87	34%	19%			30.0	152	$32
1st Half	10	0	99	110	3.81	1.07	3.60	1.08	87	91	23.6	5%	28%	22%	4%	13.0%	94.2	40	21	39	29%	70%	14%	16%	17	87	35%	29%			5.6	160	$22
2nd Half	10	0	86	85	1.98	0.96	3.89	1.12	83	71	22.9	5%	25%	20%	5%	10.6%	94.0	41	16	44	28%	82%	5%	8%	15	87	33%	7%			24.3	143	$29
Proj	15	0	189	176	3.24	1.12	4.11	1.21	95	87	23.1	6%	24%	17%	5%	12.4%	94.3	38	20	42	28%	76%	11%	11%	32						28.3	121	$23

Urquidy,José

Age: 27	Th: R	Role: SP	Health: D	LIMA Plan: C+
Ht: 6' 0"	Wt: 217	Type: Con/xFB	PT/Exp: C	Rand Var: -3
			Consist: B	MM: 1101

Battled shoulder problems with May, July IL stints; ERA predictably rose as H%/S% came back to earth. PRO: Uptick in slider usage (16% SwK) drove K% growth; he did it without sacrificing elite control. CON: xERA, xWHIP hint luck factor correction isn't finished; injury history raises volume concerns. A step forward, but take the under (again) on a ratio repeat.

Yr Tm	W	Sv	IP	K	ERA	WHIP	xERA	xWHIP	vL+	vR+	BF/G	BB%	K%	K-BB%	xBB%	SwK	Vel	G	L	F	H%	S%	HR/F	xHR/F	GS	APC	DOM%	DIS%	Sv%	LI	RAR	BPX	R$
17																																	
18																																	
19 HOU *	9	0	144	153	5.20	1.26	4.76	1.15	70	110	20.2	5%	26%	21%	8%	12.3%	93.3	37	18	45	33%	63%	12%	14%	7	77	29%	29%	0	0.93	-12.4	130	$3
20 HOU	1	0	30	17	2.73	1.01	5.15	1.42	52	114	23.2	7%	15%	8%	5%	10.0%	93.1	36	23	41	21%	81%	11%	12%	5	86	20%	60%			6.3	47	$3
21 HOU	8	0	107	90	3.62	0.99	4.35	1.17	79	97	21.2	5%	21%	17%	5%	12.5%	92.6	32	22	46	25%	71%	12%	14%	20	82	35%	25%			8.6	113	$11
1st Half	6	0	77	66	3.38	0.96	4.27	1.15	70	96	21.6	4%	22%	18%	4%	12.7%	92.5	32	23	46	24%	73%	12%	13%	14	83	43%	21%			8.5	117	$16
2nd Half	2	0	30	24	4.25	1.08	4.56	1.21	87	104	20.0	5%	20%	15%	7%	12.0%	92.7	34	20	45	26%	67%	13%	15%	6	79	17%	33%			0.1	103	$12
Proj	8	0	116	98	4.22	1.09	4.31	1.20	84	106	20.9	5%	22%	17%	6%	12.3%	92.8	34	21	45	27%	67%	13%	14%	22						3.3	116	$7

Valdez,Framber

Age: 28	Th: L	Role: SP	Health: D	LIMA Plan: C+
Ht: 5' 11"	Wt: 239	Type: Pwr/xGB	PT/Exp: B	Rand Var: +1
			Consist: B	MM: 4203

Broken finger in March initially threatened season, but avoided surgery and returned in May. Couldn't hold 2020's control gains, Ks fell more in line with SwK, and H%/S% combo won't repeat, but posting an MLB-best 70% GB% sure helped prevent runs anyway. A solid mid-rotation arm, but with middling K-BB% baseline, he's not likely to take that next step.

Yr Tm	W	Sv	IP	K	ERA	WHIP	xERA	xWHIP	vL+	vR+	BF/G	BB%	K%	K-BB%	xBB%	SwK	Vel	G	L	F	H%	S%	HR/F	xHR/F	GS	APC	DOM%	DIS%	Sv%	LI	RAR	BPX	R$
17 aa	5	0	49	46	7.38	1.93	6.75				19.4	10%	20%	10%							42%	61%									-18.3	64	-$11
18 HOU *	10	1	142	140	3.95	1.35	3.83	1.31	58	91	19.8	9%	24%	14%	12%	8.5%	92.0	70	13	16	32%	71%	20%	15%	5	79	0%	20%	50	0.93	3.5	104	$5
19 HOU *	9	1	116	124	5.05	1.47	4.31	1.44	87	112	13.8	12%	25%	12%	11%	10.8%	93.0	62	21	17	32%	67%	26%	19%	8	45	25%	50%	100	0.46	-7.7	83	-$1
20 HOU	5	0	71	76	3.57	1.12	2.96	1.11	85	85	26.2	6%	26%	21%	7%	10.5%	93.1	60	21	19	32%	69%	14%	23%	10	95	50%	10%	0	0.77	7.7	178	$18
21 HOU	11	0	135	125	3.14	1.25	3.31	1.37	99	83	26.0	10%	22%	12%	10%	10.7%	92.5	70	15	15	28%	78%	21%	24%	22	95	36%	23%			18.7	103	$12
1st Half	5	0	45	41	2.18	1.04	2.97	1.26	68	79	26.1	8%	23%	15%	9%	11.4%	92.2	71	14	15	25%	84%	21%	13%	7	95	43%	14%			11.6	132	$10
2nd Half	6	0	89	84	3.63	1.35	3.49	1.43	104	86	25.9	11%	22%	10%	11%	10.3%	92.7	70	15	15	29%	75%	22%	30%	15	95	33%	27%			7.0	89	$11
Proj	14	0	174	171	3.34	1.27	3.33	1.30	88	90	21.3	9%	24%	15%	10%	10.5%	92.6	65	17	18	30%	76%	17%	22%	33						23.9	125	$15

RYAN BLOOMFIELD

Velasquez,Vincent

Age: 30 | Th: R | Role: RP | Ht: 6' 3" | Wt: 212 | Type: Pwr/FB
Health: D | PT/Exp: B | Consist: B | LIMA Plan: C | Rand Var: +5 | MM: 1301

We used to complain about his maddening inconsistency; DOM%/DIS% tells us he's now just consistently bad. Flyballs (and homers) returned, which in tandem with brutal BB% led to August DFA; issues persisted in four Sept starts with SD. Damaging R$ history says what you get in Ks isn't worth the pain everywhere else, and that's unlikely to change.

Yr Tm	W	Sv	IP	K	ERA	WHIP	xERA	xWHIP	vL+	vR+	BF/G	BB%	K%	K-BB%	xBB%	SwK	Vel	G	L	F	H%	S%	HR/F	xHR/F	GS	APC	DOM%	DIS%	Sv%	LI	RAR	BPX	R$
17 PHI	2	0	72	68	5.13	1.50	4.63	1.45	116	112	21.0	11%	22%	11%	7%	9.6%	93.9	43	23	35	30%	72%	21%	17%	15	85	7%	40%			-6.8	71	-$5
18 PHI	9	0	147	161	4.85	1.34	4.11	1.28	122	85	20.3	9%	26%	16%	8%	12.2%	93.8	38	21	41	33%	65%	10%	9%	30	80	27%	30%	0	0.83	-12.6	111	$0
19 PHI	7	0	117	130	4.91	1.39	4.65	1.29	109	112	15.6	8%	25%	17%	8%	11.8%	94.1	34	22	44	32%	72%	18%	16%	23	64	4%	35%	0	0.85	-5.8	112	$0
20 PHI	1	0	34	46	5.56	1.56	4.08	1.28	125	98	17.1	11%	30%	19%	8%	12.0%	93.7	40	24	36	38%	67%	16%	17%	7	72	0%	14%	0	0.63	-4.6	131	-$7
21 2 NL	3	0	94	101	6.30	1.48	4.99	1.42	130	110	16.7	12%	24%	13%	9%	12.5%	93.1	31	22	47	29%	63%	19%	19%	21	70	5%	52%	0	0.71	-23.6	62	-$12
1st Half	3	0	64	71	4.22	1.28	4.59	1.39	98	95	16.9	12%	26%	14%	10%	12.5%	93.3	34	21	45	26%	72%	14%	15%	12	71	8%	33%	0	0.68	0.4	73	$1
2nd Half	0	0	30	30	10.68	1.91	5.82	1.46	174	143	16.2	11%	21%	10%	8%	12.3%	92.9	26	25	49	34%	49%	28%	25%	9	68	0%	78%			-24.0	40	-$28
Proj	**2**	**0**	**73**	**81**	**5.52**	**1.50**	**4.67**	**1.37**	**126**	**104**	**16.3**	**11%**	**26%**	**15%**	**8%**	**12.1%**	**93.5**	**34**	**23**	**43**	**33%**	**68%**	**16%**	**18%**	**12**						**-9.5**	**85**	**-$8**

Verlander,Justin

Age: 39 | Th: R | Role: SP | Ht: 6' 5" | Wt: 235 | Type: Pwr/xFB
Health: F | PT/Exp: C | Consist: A | LIMA Plan: B | Rand Var: 0 | MM: 3301

Will be 18 months removed from Tommy John surgery by Opening Day—well past the typical rehab window. A quick look at 2018-19 BPX, R$ shows the upside that's possible here, but concerns over volume and post-injury skills at his age are well-warranted. The ultimate risk/reward play; just don't rule out a Hall of Fame player doing Hall of Fame things.

Yr Tm	W	Sv	IP	K	ERA	WHIP	xERA	xWHIP	vL+	vR+	BF/G	BB%	K%	K-BB%	xBB%	SwK	Vel	G	L	F	H%	S%	HR/F	xHR/F	GS	APC	DOM%	DIS%	Sv%	LI	RAR	BPX	R$
17 2 AL	15	0	206	219	3.36	1.17	4.19	1.27	94	83	25.7	8%	26%	17%	6%	11.0%	95.2	33	24	43	28%	77%	11%	12%	33	107	55%	15%			25.3	118	$24
18 HOU	16	0	214	290	2.52	0.90	3.16	0.93	80	86	24.5	4%	35%	30%	5%	15.3%	95.1	29	20	51	29%	81%	11%	9%	34	101	62%	3%			42.9	212	$42
19 HOU	21	0	223	300	2.58	0.80	3.18	0.98	74	80	24.9	5%	35%	30%	5%	16.8%	94.7	36	19	45	23%	80%	16%	13%	34	101	59%	6%			52.9	203	$50
20 HOU	1	0	6	7	3.00	0.67	2.73		83	95	21.0	5%	33%	29%		12.3%	94.9	62	0	38	9%	100%	40%	31%	1	73	0%	0%			1.1	213	-$2
21																																	
1st Half																																	
2nd Half																																	
Proj	**8**	**0**	**116**	**130**	**3.30**	**1.03**	**3.71**	**1.09**	**90**	**89**	**24.6**	**6%**	**29%**	**23%**	**5%**	**14.8%**	**94.9**	**33**	**20**	**46**	**28%**	**75%**	**12%**	**12%**	**18**						**16.5**	**158**	**$13**

Voth,Austin

Age: 30 | Th: R | Role: RP | Ht: 6' 2" | Wt: 210 | Type: Pwr/FB
Health: D | PT/Exp: C | Consist: B | LIMA Plan: D+ | Rand Var: +2 | MM: 0201

Decent start in transition to bullpen, but broke his nose on a HBP in June and skills tanked the rest of the way. Velocity uptick was likely related to shorter stints, and while it drove SwK and K% gains, loss of control quickly washed those away. Unlikely to ascend as RP, and without a league-average BPX on this page, returning to rotation likely won't work either.

Yr Tm	W	Sv	IP	K	ERA	WHIP	xERA	xWHIP	vL+	vR+	BF/G	BB%	K%	K-BB%	xBB%	SwK	Vel	G	L	F	H%	S%	HR/F	xHR/F	GS	APC	DOM%	DIS%	Sv%	LI	RAR	BPX	R$
17 a/a	4	0	121	70	7.57	1.92	7.66				24.9	9%	12%	3%							37%	62%									-47.8	-6	-$26
18 WAS *	7	0	140	103	6.04	1.53	5.50	1.41	100	114	21.7	8%	17%	9%	8%	7.9%	91.4	43	14	43	33%	62%	19%	7%	2	54	0%	50%	0	0.44	-32.5	48	-$14
19 WAS *	6	0	118	105	5.11	1.43	5.04	1.30	101	79	20.9	6%	21%	15%	8%	13.0%	92.8	35	24	41	35%	66%	11%	11%	8	76	25%	13%	0	0.74	-8.8	85	-$3
20 WAS	2	0	50	44	6.34	1.51	5.65	1.37	122	127	20.5	8%	20%	12%	8%	9.6%	92.1	29	22	49	31%	66%	18%	16%	11	81	18%	73%			-11.6	71	-$11
21 WAS	4	0	57	59	5.34	1.48	4.59	1.40	120	103	5.1	11%	24%	13%	8%	11.7%	94.2	38	24	38	31%	68%	17%	21%	1	21	0%	0%	0	0.94	-7.6	70	-$6
1st Half	2	0	37	37	3.65	1.16	3.80	1.29	119	63	5.4	10%	26%	16%	8%	11.4%	94.1	45	22	34	26%	74%	16%	20%	1	21	0%	0%	0	0.70	2.8	102	$0
2nd Half	2	0	20	22	8.41	2.07	6.07	1.57	105	167	4.6	14%	22%	8%	9%	12.0%	94.4	28	28	44	39%	62%	18%	22%	0	20			0	1.25	-10.4	15	-$17
Proj	**5**	**0**	**80**	**75**	**4.92**	**1.45**	**4.82**	**1.36**	**113**	**118**	**7.4**	**9%**	**22%**	**13%**	**8%**	**11.6%**	**93.5**	**34**	**24**	**42**	**31%**	**72%**	**16%**	**18%**	**0**						**-4.6**	**78**	**-$5**

Wacha,Michael

Age: 31 | Th: R | Role: RP | Ht: 6' 6" | Wt: 215 | Type:
Health: D | PT/Exp: B | Consist: A | LIMA Plan: C | Rand Var: +3 | MM: 2201

Bid to become latest TAM reclamation project didn't come to fruition, but some promising 2nd half signs if we squint: upticks in velocity, SwK spurred late K% growth; he did so with excellent control and xBB% support; BPX/xERA took off. Health and track record say it's a long shot, but if HR/F ever comes back to earth, he's a potentially lucrative dart throw.

Yr Tm	W	Sv	IP	K	ERA	WHIP	xERA	xWHIP	vL+	vR+	BF/G	BB%	K%	K-BB%	xBB%	SwK	Vel	G	L	F	H%	S%	HR/F	xHR/F	GS	APC	DOM%	DIS%	Sv%	LI	RAR	BPX	R$
17 STL	12	0	166	158	4.13	1.36	3.99	1.30	96	101	23.4	8%	23%	15%	7%	10.0%	95.1	48	21	31	33%	72%	12%	12%	30	90	27%	30%			4.7	120	$8
18 STL	8	0	84	71	3.20	1.23	4.24	1.42	80	99	23.7	10%	20%	10%	10%	10.2%	93.5	43	29	27	26%	78%	14%	17%	15	95	40%	33%			9.9	62	$5
19 STL	6	0	127	104	4.76	1.56	4.99	1.48	107	120	19.4	10%	19%	9%	9%	10.1%	93.1	48	22	30	32%	76%	22%	22%	24	76	8%	58%	0	0.80	-4.0	58	-$5
20 NYM	1	0	34	37	6.62	1.56	4.53	1.14	112	143	19.5	4%	24%	19%	7%	12.0%	93.6	36	23	41	39%	64%	20%	15%	7	76	0%	71%	0	0.70	-9.1	158	-$11
21 TAM	3	0	125	121	5.05	1.31	4.09	1.19	99	110	18.2	6%	23%	17%	5%	11.8%	93.8	39	25	35	32%	66%	18%	22%	23	68	22%	39%	0	0.76	-12.1	125	-$5
1st Half	1	0	51	44	5.26	1.40	4.58	1.30	108	110	15.6	7%	20%	13%	6%	10.1%	93.4	37	27	37	32%	67%	16%	22%	9	58	22%	44%	0	0.77	-6.3	85	-$8
2nd Half	2	0	73	77	4.91	1.24	3.76	1.11	85	113	20.7	5%	25%	20%	5%	12.9%	94.1	42	24	34	32%	66%	19%	22%	14	78	21%	36%	0	0.76	-5.8	154	-$1
Proj	**5**	**0**	**102**	**97**	**4.56**	**1.33**	**4.13**	**1.24**	**95**	**109**	**18.5**	**7%**	**23%**	**16%**	**7%**	**11.3%**	**93.7**	**41**	**25**	**35**	**32%**	**71%**	**16%**	**20%**	**19**						**-1.3**	**118**	**-$1**

Wainwright,Adam

Age: 40 | Th: R | Role: SP | Ht: 6' 7" | Wt: 230 | Type: Con
Health: F | PT/Exp: A | Consist: A | LIMA Plan: D+ | Rand Var: -3 | MM: 2103

Logged the most IP of any 39+ year-old since 2007 and did it with a second straight sub-3.20 ERA. Another fortunate H% made ratios look much better than their xERA/xWHIP counterparts, as SwK was the lowest of any qualified starter. There's value in his BB%/GB% combo and volume (even at his age); just don't expect anything close to 2020-21.

Yr Tm	W	Sv	IP	K	ERA	WHIP	xERA	xWHIP	vL+	vR+	BF/G	BB%	K%	K-BB%	xBB%	SwK	Vel	G	L	F	H%	S%	HR/F	xHR/F	GS	APC	DOM%	DIS%	Sv%	LI	RAR	BPX	R$
17 STL	12	0	123	96	5.11	1.50	4.58	1.41	109	104	22.8	8%	18%	9%	8%	7.8%	89.7	47	25	28	33%	67%	13%	11%	23	90	30%	39%	0	0.74	-11.4	75	-$2
18 STL *	4	0	59	54	3.03	1.34	3.94	1.33	102	105	19.0	9%	22%	13%	10%	9.3%	89.3	49	18	33	32%	80%	13%	15%	8	92	25%	38%			8.2	94	$1
19 STL	14	0	172	153	4.19	1.43	4.48	1.38	116	94	24.0	9%	21%	12%	9%	8.0%	89.9	49	22	29	32%	74%	15%	14%	31	93	16%	39%			6.6	88	$6
20 STL	5	0	66	54	3.15	1.05	4.21	1.24	92	82	26.2	6%	21%	15%	6%	11.0%	89.3	43	22	34	26%	77%	14%	15%	10	93	40%	20%			10.5	112	$19
21 STL	17	0	206	174	3.05	1.06	3.85	1.23	91	79	25.9	6%	21%	15%	7%	8.5%	89.1	47	22	30	26%	75%	12%	13%	32	96	41%	28%			30.9	113	$29
1st Half	6	0	101	96	3.49	1.10	3.64	1.20	83	92	25.8	7%	23%	17%	8%	8.7%	89.6	48	24	29	27%	73%	16%	14%	16	98	38%	25%			9.7	126	$17
2nd Half	11	0	106	78	2.64	1.01	4.04	1.25	88	68	26.0	6%	19%	13%	6%	8.4%	88.6	47	21	32	26%	77%	8%	13%	16	94	44%	31%			21.2	101	$37
Proj	**13**	**0**	**174**	**142**	**3.57**	**1.16**	**4.01**	**1.26**	**98**	**86**	**23.9**	**6%**	**21%**	**14%**	**7%**	**8.9%**	**89.3**	**47**	**22**	**31**	**28%**	**73%**	**13%**	**14%**	**29**						**19.0**	**109**	**$16**

Walker,Taijuan

Age: 29 | Th: R | Role: SP | Ht: 6' 4" | Wt: 235 | Type:
Health: F | PT/Exp: B | Consist: A | LIMA Plan: B+ | Rand Var: -1 | MM: 1103

Picked up where he left off in 2020, then BAM... it all unraveled as Ks vanished and S%, HR/F flipped in 2nd half. There were some positives—highest IP, best velocity since 2015—but didn't rack up many whiffs and xERA was in lockstep with ERA once dust settled. In fact, xERA has consistently shown his true skills level—a mid-4s ERA—since 2016.

Yr Tm	W	Sv	IP	K	ERA	WHIP	xERA	xWHIP	vL+	vR+	BF/G	BB%	K%	K-BB%	xBB%	SwK	Vel	G	L	F	H%	S%	HR/F	xHR/F	GS	APC	DOM%	DIS%	Sv%	LI	RAR	BPX	R$
17 ARI	9	0	157	146	3.49	1.33	4.29	1.36	96	100	24.4	9%	22%	13%	8%	9.3%	93.8	49	18	33	31%	77%	11%	13%	28	98	18%	32%			16.9	100	$10
18 ARI	0	0	13	9	3.46	1.54	4.72	1.45	132	73	18.7	9%	16%	7%	8%	6.7%	93.7	43	28	30	34%	79%	8%	21%	3	75	0%	67%			1.1	46	-$5
19 ARI	0	0	1	1	0.00	1.00	4.79		0	201	4.0	0%	25%	25%		13.3%	93.3	33	0	67	35%	0%	0%	10%	1	15	0%	100%			0.6	188	-$5
20 2 AL	4	0	53	50	2.70	1.16	4.65	1.33	120	68	20.5	8%	22%	14%	9%	8.1%	93.2	39	21	40	26%	85%	13%	15%	11	80	27%	36%			11.5	93	$14
21 NYM	7	0	159	146	4.47	1.18	4.40	1.31	89	98	21.8	8%	22%	14%	7%	10.1%	94.2	42	17	41	26%	67%	14%	17%	29	85	21%	28%	0	0.77	-4.0	93	$5
1st Half	7	0	90	93	2.61	1.04	3.84	1.20	69	81	22.4	8%	26%	18%	7%	10.0%	94.0	38	24	38	27%	77%	7%	12%	15	87	33%	13%	0	0.79	18.3	122	$23
2nd Half	0	0	69	53	6.88	1.37	5.17	1.44	103	123	21.1	9%	18%	8%	8%	10.3%	94.5	46	10	45	25%	56%	21%	22%	14	82	7%	43%			-22.4	54	-$18
Proj	**7**	**0**	**152**	**137**	**4.30**	**1.28**	**4.43**	**1.32**	**103**	**100**	**21.3**	**8%**	**22%**	**14%**	**8%**	**9.6%**	**94.0**	**43**	**17**	**40**	**29%**	**72%**	**15%**	**16%**	**29**						**2.9**	**96**	**$3**

Warren,Art

Age: 29 | Th: R | Role: RP | Ht: 6' 3" | Wt: 230 | Type: Pwr/FB
Health: D | PT/Exp: F | Consist: A | LIMA Plan: A | Rand Var: +2 | MM: 4510

3-0, 1.29 ERA in 21 IP at CIN. IL stint (oblique) knocked out most of July-Aug, but AAA dominance translated seamlessly to majors. Knockout slider (28% SwK) was his primary pitch and it took K% to elite heights. Career 10% BB% in minors and lack of volume are drawbacks, but among vast crowd of long-shot closer specs, he's one worth flagging.

Yr Tm	W	Sv	IP	K	ERA	WHIP	xERA	xWHIP	vL+	vR+	BF/G	BB%	K%	K-BB%	xBB%	SwK	Vel	G	L	F	H%	S%	HR/F	xHR/F	GS	APC	DOM%	DIS%	Sv%	LI	RAR	BPX	R$
17																																	
18 aa	1	2	17	19	1.91	1.54	2.91				5.4	20%	25%	5%							28%	86%									4.8	117	-$3
19 SEA *	3	15	39	39	2.22	1.32	3.17		75	19	4.6	11%	24%	13%		11.7%	95.1	29	36	36	31%	84%	0%	1%	0	13			88	0.34	10.9	108	$7
20																																	
21 CIN *	4	2	37	58	3.83	1.32	3.63	1.05	76	59	3.7	9%	38%	29%	8%	19.5%	95.2	35	19	46	41%	71%	6%	5%	0	13			67	0.50	2.0	175	$0
1st Half	1	2	24	38	4.29	1.30	3.24	1.08	100	53	4.3	10%	38%	28%	8%	20.6%	95.4	33	17	50	41%	65%	8%	6%	0	16			67	0.34	-0.1	178	-$3
2nd Half	3	0	15	20	2.51	1.14	3.24	1.04	13	71	3.4	7%	33%	26%	6%	17.7%	94.9	38	23	38	34%	82%	0%	5%	0	10			0	0.69	3.3	172	-$2
Proj	**4**	**2**	**58**	**76**	**3.50**	**1.15**	**3.48**	**1.14**			**3.8**	**9%**	**33%**	**24%**				**38**	**20**	**42**	**31%**	**72%**	**10%**	**0%**	**0**						**6.8**	**161**	**$4**

RYAN BLOOMFIELD

Weathers,Ryan

Age: 22	Th: L	Role RP	Health	A	LIMA Plan	D+
Ht: 6' 1"	Wt: 230	Type Con	PT/Exp	D	Rand Var	+2
			Consist	F	MM	0001

A prime example of the havoc luck factors can wreak on ratios as H%, S%, and HR/F all pulled a 180 from 1st to 2nd half. Skills-wise, xERA/xWHIP were subpar throughout, but he'd never pitched above Single-A before this season. Pedigree points to mid-rotation ceiling, but unless he can miss bats or regain control (5% BB% in minors), it'll take time.

Yr Tm	W	Sv	IP	K	ERA	WHIP	xERA	xWHIP	vL+	vR+	BF/G	BB%	K%	K-BB%	xBB%	SwK	Vel	G	L	F	H%	S%	HR/F	xHR/F	GS	APC	DOM%	DIS%	Sv%	LI	RAR	BPX	R$
17																																	
18																																	
19																																	
20																																	
21 SD	4	1	95	72	5.32	1.38	4.72	1.35	106	115	13.4	8%	18%	11%	8%	7.8%	94.0	44	19	37	29%	68%	19%	17%	18	54	6%	56%	100	0.64	-12.4	75	-$7
1st Half	3	1	51	39	2.63	1.11	4.44	1.36	61	101	13.7	8%	19%	11%	9%	8.0%	93.9	45	17	38	24%	82%	11%	13%	9	58	11%	33%	100	0.67	10.4	72	$7
2nd Half	1	0	43	33	8.52	1.71	5.06	1.33	145	134	13.1	7%	17%	10%	8%	7.5%	94.1	43	20	37	35%	55%	26%	22%	9	50	0%	78%	0	0.62	-22.7	78	-$24
Proj	3	0	87	66	4.82	1.41	4.79	1.36	109	110	13.0	7%	18%	11%	8%	7.7%	94.0	44	19	37	31%	71%	16%	18%	9						-3.9	78	-$5

Weaver,Luke

Age: 28	Th: R	Role SP	Health	F	LIMA Plan	C
Ht: 6' 2"	Wt: 185	Type /FB	PT/Exp	C	Rand Var	0
			Consist	C	MM	2201

Shoulder strain shelved him from mid-May through August, as ERA/WHIP gains from 2020 were just a H%/S% correction. Skills look stagnant, as SwK and K-BB% continued to hang near league average, making 2019 look like an outlier. A reasonable floor when healthy, but with volume concerns and declining BPX, not much of a ceiling either.

Yr Tm	W	Sv	IP	K	ERA	WHIP	xERA	xWHIP	vL+	vR+	BF/G	BB%	K%	K-BB%	xBB%	SwK	Vel	G	L	F	H%	S%	HR/F	xHR/F	GS	APC	DOM%	DIS%	Sv%	LI	RAR	BPX	R$
17 STL *	17	0	138	132	3.47	1.23	3.47	1.22	76	107	20.0	6%	24%	17%	6%	9.9%	93.2	49	24	27	32%	73%	16%	15%	10	80	40%	30%	0	0.64	15.2	135	$15
18 STL	7	0	136	121	4.95	1.50	4.63	1.37	115	101	20.3	9%	20%	11%	8%	10.1%	93.7	42	22	36	33%	70%	13%	14%	25	80	16%	40%	0	0.69	-13.5	78	-$7
19 ARI	4	0	64	69	2.94	1.07	3.83	1.14	80	91	21.7	5%	27%	21%	8%	11.8%	93.9	41	22	38	30%	76%	9%	13%	12	88	42%	25%			12.4	152	$5
20 ARI	1	0	52	55	6.58	1.56	5.17	1.28	133	105	19.7	8%	23%	16%	8%	11.3%	94.1	32	19	48	37%	61%	13%	13%	12	81	25%	25%			-13.6	110	-$14
21 ARI	3	0	66	62	4.25	1.19	4.35	1.25	116	94	21.2	7%	23%	15%	6%	11.5%	93.7	38	22	40	28%	70%	15%	18%	13	85	15%	31%			0.1	104	-$1
1st Half	2	0	40	38	4.50	1.20	4.31	1.27	100	102	20.9	8%	23%	15%	6%	11.4%	93.4	38	24	38	28%	67%	14%	22%	8	84	25%	38%			-1.2	100	-$3
2nd Half	1	0	26	24	3.86	1.17	4.42	1.23	123	85	21.6	7%	23%	16%	5%	11.5%	94.1	39	19	43	27%	76%	16%	14%	5	87	0%	20%			1.3	112	-$6
Proj	6	0	116	114	4.25	1.24	4.21	1.25	111	93	21.7	7%	24%	17%	6%	11.3%	93.8	38	21	41	30%	71%	14%	15%	22						2.9	116	$3

Webb,Logan

Age: 25	Th: R	Role SP	Health	D	LIMA Plan	C+
Ht: 6' 1"	Wt: 220	Type /xGB	PT/Exp	B	Rand Var	0
			Consist	B	MM	4203

Missed six weeks (shoulder) late in 1st half, which did little stop to this breakout. It checks all the boxes, too: ditched four-seamer for more sliders (22% SwK) to drive K% growth, more sinkers (69% GB%) to keep ball on ground, and he did it with BB%/xBB% gains. Regression has to be a concern, but the tangible changes and skill growth eases that quite a bit.

Yr Tm	W	Sv	IP	K	ERA	WHIP	xERA	xWHIP	vL+	vR+	BF/G	BB%	K%	K-BB%	xBB%	SwK	Vel	G	L	F	H%	S%	HR/F	xHR/F	GS	APC	DOM%	DIS%	Sv%	LI	RAR	BPX	R$
17																																	
18 aa	1	0	32	22	4.38	1.40	4.61				22.7	8%	16%	8%							31%	71%									-0.9	58	-$5
19 SF *	3	0	89	82	3.82	1.45	4.65	1.29	92	123	22.3	7%	22%	14%	9%	9.8%	92.9	49	28	23	36%	75%	18%	19%	8	85	13%	38%			7.5	97	-$1
20 SF	3	0	54	46	5.47	1.56	4.49	1.44	109	110	18.9	10%	19%	9%	10%	9.3%	92.7	52	26	22	35%	64%	11%	15%	11	77	9%	55%	0	0.82	-6.8	68	-$7
21 SF	11	0	148	158	3.03	1.11	2.81	1.12	94	75	22.1	6%	27%	21%	7%	12.8%	92.9	61	21	19	31%	74%	13%	16%	26	82	46%	23%	0	0.79	22.5	167	$19
1st Half	4	0	49	54	3.86	1.29	3.06	1.21	110	74	20.7	8%	26%	18%	9%	12.2%	92.6	58	25	17	33%	71%	18%	16%	9	78	22%	22%	0	0.81	2.5	143	$2
2nd Half	7	0	99	104	2.63	1.02	2.69	1.07	78	79	22.9	5%	27%	22%	6%	13.1%	93.1	62	18	19	30%	75%	10%	16%	17	84	59%	24%			20.1	180	$33
Proj	12	0	160	157	3.42	1.15	3.25	1.21	90	84	20.2	7%	25%	18%	8%	11.3%	92.9	56	23	20	30%	72%	14%	16%	31						20.4	141	$16

Wells,Tyler

Age: 27	Th: R	Role RP	Health	C	LIMA Plan	B+
Ht: 6' 8"	Wt: 265	Type /xFB	PT/Exp	D	Rand Var	0
			Consist	F	MM	1210

Appeared as reliever in first game action since 2018 (Tommy John surgery) with some positive signs beneath mediocre ERA. July wrist injury diluted 2nd half sample, but he produced whiffs and Ks galore, limited the free pass, and even snagged some September saves. Extreme FB% does open him up to HR risk, but color us interested as a closer flyer.

Yr Tm	W	Sv	IP	K	ERA	WHIP	xERA	xWHIP	vL+	vR+	BF/G	BB%	K%	K-BB%	xBB%	SwK	Vel	G	L	F	H%	S%	HR/F	xHR/F	GS	APC	DOM%	DIS%	Sv%	LI	RAR	BPX	R$
17																																	
18 aa	2	1	34	31	1.97	1.21	2.69				23.0	10%	22%	12%							29%	84%									9.2	112	$1
19																																	
20																																	
21 BAL	2	4	57	65	4.11	0.91	4.08	1.07	65	90	5.1	5%	29%	24%	5%	14.4%	95.2	21	22	57	24%	60%	11%	14%	0	20			57	0.85	1.1	145	$4
1st Half	2	0	38	46	3.58	0.96	3.71	1.03	72	91	6.2	5%	31%	26%	5%	14.9%	94.7	23	26	51	27%	70%	13%	15%	0	24			0	0.73	3.2	162	$3
2nd Half	0	4	19	19	5.12	0.83	4.81	1.14	41	92	3.8	5%	25%	20%	4%	13.6%	96.1	19	15	66	20%	38%	9%	12%	0	16			67	1.00	-2.0	116	-$4
Proj	2	5	65	68	3.91	1.19	4.48	1.19	73	112	5.7	6%	26%	19%	4%	14.1%	95.6	23	21	55	30%	73%	10%	13%	0						4.4	121	$2

Wheeler,Zack

Age: 32	Th: R	Role SP	Health	B	LIMA Plan	D+
Ht: 6' 4"	Wt: 195	Type	PT/Exp	A	Rand Var	-1
			Consist	B	MM	4205

Led majors in IP, 2nd in Ks as he delivered league-winning type of breakout. Repeat odds are mixed: he's never shown this level of skill before, yet everything in 2021—from the uptick in whiffs and climbing velocity to the pinpoint BB% and GB% lean—give this plenty of support. Hard to pay up coming off career year, but it just might be worth it.

Yr Tm	W	Sv	IP	K	ERA	WHIP	xERA	xWHIP	vL+	vR+	BF/G	BB%	K%	K-BB%	xBB%	SwK	Vel	G	L	F	H%	S%	HR/F	xHR/F	GS	APC	DOM%	DIS%	Sv%	LI	RAR	BPX	R$
17 NYM	3	0	86	81	5.21	1.59	4.50	1.43	114	109	22.7	10%	21%	11%	8%	9.7%	94.6	47	23	30	34%	71%	19%	17%	17	92	18%	47%			-9.1	77	-$7
18 NYM	12	0	182	179	3.31	1.12	3.74	1.23	93	77	25.7	7%	24%	17%	6%	11.3%	95.9	44	20	35	29%	72%	8%	10%	29	99	45%	28%			18.9	124	$19
19 NYM	11	0	195	195	3.96	1.26	4.22	1.22	102	85	26.7	6%	24%	18%	6%	11.0%	96.7	43	21	35	33%	71%	11%	12%	31	102	45%	19%			13.1	131	$13
20 PHI	4	0	71	53	2.92	1.17	3.67	1.26	90	90	26.2	6%	18%	13%	6%	11.1%	96.9	56	25	19	30%	75%	8%	12%	11	98	27%	18%			13.5	113	$16
21 PHI	14	0	213	247	2.78	1.01	2.98	1.06	82	77	26.5	5%	29%	24%	5%	12.9%	97.1	50	23	28	30%	75%	11%	12%	32	100	63%	6%			39.0	179	$35
1st Half	6	0	114	139	2.05	0.94	2.85	1.03	71	72	26.1	6%	32%	26%	6%	13.5%	97.2	49	21	30	29%	81%	9%	11%	17	101	71%	6%			31.1	188	$36
2nd Half	8	0	99	108	3.62	1.09	3.14	1.09	84	87	27.0	5%	27%	22%	5%	12.3%	97.0	50	24	25	31%	69%	13%	14%	15	100	53%	7%			7.9	168	$25
Proj	13	0	196	199	3.27	1.13	3.40	1.16	90	84	25.4	6%	26%	20%	6%	11.9%	96.7	49	23	28	31%	73%	11%	12%	30						28.7	150	$22

White,Mitch

Age: 27	Th: R	Role RP	Health	A	LIMA Plan	B+
Ht: 6' 3"	Wt: 210	Type	PT/Exp	D	Rand Var	-2
			Consist	C	MM	2201

1-3, 3.66 ERA in 47 IP at LA. Tough to find much rhythm when you're recalled from AAA 11 separate times. Role fluctuated as well in limited sample, but 2nd half skills surged with more sliders (22% SwK), more strikes (xBB%), and more GBs. Middling prospect pedigree and xERA history say to give him short leash, but he's dart-throw-worthy with a rotation gig.

Yr Tm	W	Sv	IP	K	ERA	WHIP	xERA	xWHIP	vL+	vR+	BF/G	BB%	K%	K-BB%	xBB%	SwK	Vel	G	L	F	H%	S%	HR/F	xHR/F	GS	APC	DOM%	DIS%	Sv%	LI	RAR	BPX	R$
17 aa	1	0	28	27	3.01	1.11	2.47				15.7	11%	25%	14%							25%	75%									4.7	112	-$1
18 aa	6	0	106	74	4.84	1.47	5.12				20.7	7%	16%	9%							34%	69%									-9.0	62	-$6
19 a/a	4	0	95	87	6.09	1.45	5.55				17.7	7%	21%	14%							33%	61%									-18.6	60	-$7
20 LA	1	0	3	2	0.00	0.67	5.96		23	53	5.5	9%	18%	9%		11.4%	93.6	13	13	75	13%	100%	0%	0%	0	22			0	0.03	1.6	20	-$3
21 LA *	2	0	79	80	2.90	1.24	3.54	1.26	94	79	10.3	9%	25%	16%	6%	10.8%	94.5	48	18	34	31%	80%	14%	11%	4	36	0%	25%	0	0.69	13.3	107	$3
1st Half	0	0	22	23	3.27	1.54	4.59	1.49	80	106	5.7	13%	24%	10%	8%	8.1%	94.9	43	17	39	33%	81%	6%	9%	0	24			0	0.86	2.8	79	-$7
2nd Half	2	0	56	57	2.75	1.12	3.12	1.17	93	67	15.9	7%	26%	19%	5%	12.4%	94.3	50	19	31	30%	79%	19%	13%	4	53	0%	25%	0	0.47	10.5	128	$8
Proj	4	0	87	81	3.83	1.26	3.97	1.29	122	85	11.1	8%	23%	15%	5%	11.4%	94.3	47	20	33	30%	73%	14%	12%	6						6.7	110	$1

Whitlock,Garrett

Age: 26	Th: R	Role RP	Health	B	LIMA Plan	B
Ht: 6' 5"	Wt: 190	Type	PT/Exp	D	Rand Var	-5
			Consist	D	MM	3211

Rapid ascent from Rule 5 in 2020 to dominant reliever in 2021. Impressive array of skills mostly support it, as elite fastball drove SwK, K% gains; xBB% lent credence to plus control; GB% tilt shielded him from HR damage. Looming S%, xERA correction says he won't be THIS good again, and talk of rotation move clouds projection. If still in pen... UP: 30 Sv.

Yr Tm	W	Sv	IP	K	ERA	WHIP	xERA	xWHIP	vL+	vR+	BF/G	BB%	K%	K-BB%	xBB%	SwK	Vel	G	L	F	H%	S%	HR/F	xHR/F	GS	APC	DOM%	DIS%	Sv%	LI	RAR	BPX	R$
17																																	
18																																	
19 aa	3	0	71	49	4.12	1.53	5.16				22.1	6%	16%	9%							35%	74%									3.4	66	-$4
20																																	
21 BOS	8	2	73	81	1.96	1.10	3.30	1.10	114	69	6.5	6%	27%	21%	5%	13.2%	96.0	50	20	30	32%	87%	10%	9%	0	25			40	1.20	20.8	165	$12
1st Half	3	1	40	43	1.58	1.13	3.26	1.15	103	74	7.0	7%	27%	20%	6%	11.7%	95.7	52	22	26	30%	93%	14%	12%	0	28			50	1.06	13.3	151	$7
2nd Half	5	1	33	38	2.43	1.08	3.34	1.04	114	67	5.9	4%	28%	24%	4%	15.2%	96.3	47	18	36	33%	79%	6%	8%	0	22			33	1.33	7.5	182	$8
Proj	8	5	116	117	3.23	1.14	3.53	1.15	117	71	7.4	6%	25%	20%	5%	13.7%	96.0	49	19	32	31%	73%	9%	9%	0						17.5	152	$13

RYAN BLOOMFIELD

Wick,Rowan

Age: 29	Th: R	Role: RP	Health: F	LIMA Plan: C	
Ht: 6' 3"	Wt: 234	Type: Pwr	PT/Exp: D	Rand Var: -2	
			Consist: B	MM: 2320	

Recent sample size is small, as oblique strain cut 2020 short and similar issue delayed 2021 debut until August. Didn't take long to get saves chances once he returned, but SwK didn't support K% jump, and three HR in 82 career IP is unsustainable. May be just good enough to hold closer gig if it's handed to him, but skills are nothing special.

Yr Tm	W	Sv	IP	K	ERA	WHIP	xERA	xWHIP	vL+	vR+	BF/G	BB%	K%	K-BB%	xBB%	SwK	Vel	G	L	F	H%	S%	HR/F	xHR/F	GS	APC	DOM%	DIS%	Sv%	LI	RAR	BPX	R$
17 a/a	2	6	38	26	4.58	1.52	4.49				5.5	11%	16%	4%							30%	71%									-1.0	53	-$2
18 SD *	4	14	65	59	3.38	1.38	3.61	1.47	99	158	4.6	12%	22%	10%	4%	11.3%	94.6	39	14	46	30%	76%	8%	12%	0	13			88	0.76	6.1	90	$6
19 CHC *	3	8	68	69	2.44	1.18	2.72	1.32	84	59	4.7	10%	25%	16%	8%	12.1%	95.9	54	15	31	29%	81%	0%	12%	0	19			100	0.98	17.4	116	$9
20 CHC	0	4	17	20	3.12	1.38	4.10	1.22	103	92	3.9	8%	27%	19%	7%	11.5%	95.0	38	27	35	37%	78%	6%	15%	0	16			100	1.23	2.9	134	$1
21 CHC	0	5	23	29	4.30	1.35	4.26	1.41	67	91	4.5	14%	29%	15%	10%	11.8%	94.7	35	27	38	31%	67%	5%	10%	0	18			63	1.14	-0.1	76	-$3
1st Half																																	
2nd Half	0	5	23	29	4.30	1.35	4.26	1.41	63	92	4.5	14%	29%	15%	10%	11.8%	94.7	35	27	38	31%	67%	5%	10%	0	18			63	1.14	-0.1	76	-$4
Proj	2	14	58	62	4.00	1.29	4.15	1.36	81	98	4.6	11%	26%	15%	9%	11.9%	95.1	42	22	35	30%	71%	10%	11%	0						3.2	93	$4

Widener,Taylor

Age: 27	Th: R	Role: RP	Health: F	LIMA Plan: D+	
Ht: 6' 0"	Wt: 230	Type: Pwr/xFB	PT/Exp: D	Rand Var: -1	
			Consist: B	MM: 0201	

Ratios looked good before he went down with May groin injury, but that was due to some major help from H% and S%. Skills have been a mess now for three years running, as BB% is troubling, high FB% leaves him homer-prone, and both his velocity and SwK went the wrong way in 2021. Doesn't look like there's any reason to have him on your radar.

Yr Tm	W	Sv	IP	K	ERA	WHIP	xERA	xWHIP	vL+	vR+	BF/G	BB%	K%	K-BB%	xBB%	SwK	Vel	G	L	F	H%	S%	HR/F	xHR/F	GS	APC	DOM%	DIS%	Sv%	LI	RAR	BPX	R$
17																																	
18 aa	5	0	138	146	3.34	1.16	3.13				21.1	8%	27%	19%							30%	74%									13.9	128	$10
19 aaa	6	0	101	88	7.66	1.76	7.04				20.1	8%	19%	11%							38%	58%									-39.3	35	-$18
20 ARI	0	0	20	22	4.50	1.30	5.13	1.50	135	82	7.3	14%	25%	11%	9%	12.1%	94.5	37	14	49	21%	76%	20%	16%	0	30			0	0.27	-0.1	54	-$5
21 ARI	2	0	70	73	4.35	1.45	5.13	1.44	122	96	13.9	12%	23%	11%	9%	10.6%	92.6	34	19	47	29%	77%	15%	19%	13	53	0%	31%	0	0.69	-0.7	57	-$5
1st Half	1	0	24	20	2.63	1.17	4.96	1.34	99	87	20.8	8%	20%	12%	7%	10.3%	93.0	33	21	46	25%	88%	13%	21%	5	77	0%	20%			4.9	71	-$3
2nd Half	1	0	46	53	5.24	1.60	5.21	1.49	123	104	11.9	14%	25%	11%	10%	10.7%	92.4	35	18	47	31%	73%	17%	18%	8	46	0%	38%	0	0.66	-5.6	50	-$12
Proj	3	0	73	72	4.69	1.43	4.90	1.39	122	98	15.7	10%	23%	13%	8%	10.6%	92.7	34	19	47	31%	73%	14%	19%	11						-2.1	74	-$5

Williams,Devin

Age: 27	Th: R	Role: RP	Health: B	LIMA Plan: B+	
Ht: 6' 2"	Wt: 200	Type: Pwr	PT/Exp: D	Rand Var: -3	
			Consist: D	MM: 5510	

Not surprisingly, a step back from other-worldly 2020, but still with elite-level stuff. His 2nd half SwK, K%, and xERA show he was getting stronger as season wore on, until he broke hand punching a wall. The excellent ratios, strikeouts, and high-leverage role already give him mixed-league value, and he'd be a top-tier closer if he ever got the chance.

Yr Tm	W	Sv	IP	K	ERA	WHIP	xERA	xWHIP	vL+	vR+	BF/G	BB%	K%	K-BB%	xBB%	SwK	Vel	G	L	F	H%	S%	HR/F	xHR/F	GS	APC	DOM%	DIS%	Sv%	LI	RAR	BPX	R$
17																																	
18																																	
19 MIL *	7	4	73	83	3.13	1.41	3.77	1.43	107	129	6.6	13%	27%	14%	9%	10.7%	96.2	41	23	36	32%	80%	13%	12%	0	21			100	0.32	12.4	99	$6
20 MIL	4	0	27	53	0.33	0.63	1.40	0.80	48	43	4.5	9%	54%	44%	9%	22.3%	96.5	61	11	28	23%	100%	10%	18%	0	20			0	1.16	13.7	312	$21
21 MIL	8	3	54	87	2.50	1.19	2.99	1.16	93	66	3.9	12%	39%	26%	8%	19.0%	95.4	45	18	37	32%	83%	13%	11%	0	17			50	1.36	11.8	173	$8
1st Half	5	0	31	49	3.19	1.39	3.46	1.30	116	62	4.0	15%	37%	22%	9%	17.7%	95.2	44	19	38	33%	82%	17%	17%	0	17			0	1.35	4.1	133	$3
2nd Half	3	3	23	38	1.57	0.91	2.43	0.97	47	74	3.8	9%	42%	33%	8%	21.0%	95.8	48	16	36	31%	85%	6%	3%	0	17			100	1.38	7.7	229	$7
Proj	7	5	65	101	2.43	1.13	2.88	1.11	83	72	4.1	11%	39%	28%	8%	19.6%	95.6	46	17	37	33%	82%	11%	9%	0						16.3	192	$11

Wilson,Bryse

Age: 24	Th: R	Role: SP	Health: B	LIMA Plan: D+	
Ht: 6' 2"	Wt: 225	Type: Con	PT/Exp: D	Rand Var: 0	
			Consist: D	MM: 0001	

3-7, 5.35 ERA in 74 IP at ATL/PIT. Bounced around between AAA and majors prior to trade deadline without much success in either place. Given a chance to stick in rotation after trade to PIT, but subpar SwK and K% dipped further and he dealt with arm and hamstring issues. Still young, but there's a lot of work to do before he is worth an investment.

Yr Tm	W	Sv	IP	K	ERA	WHIP	xERA	xWHIP	vL+	vR+	BF/G	BB%	K%	K-BB%	xBB%	SwK	Vel	G	L	F	H%	S%	HR/F	xHR/F	GS	APC	DOM%	DIS%	Sv%	LI	RAR	BPX	R$
17																																	
18 ATL *	7	0	106	107	5.35	1.44	4.73	1.24	118	124	19.7	8%	24%	16%	9%	15.6%	95.0	29	48	24	36%	63%	0%	16%	1	45	0%	0%	0	0.35	-15.7	107	-$6
19 ATL *	11	0	141	116	4.77	1.44	5.14	1.32	149	130	22.2	6%	19%	13%	6%	9.0%	94.7	31	26	43	35%	69%	18%	17%	4	59	0%	50%	0	0.58	-4.6	79	$0
20 ATL	1	1	16	15	4.02	1.72	5.42	1.53	139	99	12.2	12%	21%	8%	8%	9.3%	94.0	42	23	35	35%	80%	12%	24%	2	52	50%	50%	100	0.26	0.8	40	-$5
21 2 NL *	8	0	130	80	5.33	1.51	6.07	1.40	116	113	21.7	7%	14%	7%	6%	9.2%	93.0	37	25	38	32%	69%	16%	19%	16	71	6%	63%			-17.1	24	-$10
1st Half	6	0	75	51	5.10	1.55	6.30	1.35	124	116	23.3	6%	16%	9%	5%	10.5%	93.2	41	21	37	34%	72%	20%	23%	6	70	0%	67%			-7.7	33	-$5
2nd Half	2	0	55	29	5.63	1.46	5.76	1.46	102	114	19.7	7%	12%	5%	6%	8.4%	92.9	34	27	39	30%	65%	14%	16%	10	72	10%	60%			-9.3	13	-$13
Proj	5	0	87	63	5.28	1.47	5.05	1.36	115	114	21.0	7%	17%	10%	6%	9.2%	93.0	37	25	38	32%	69%	15%	19%	18						-8.9	69	-$7

Wittgren,Nick

Age: 31	Th: R	Role: RP	Health: B	LIMA Plan: C	
Ht: 6' 2"	Wt: 216	Type:	PT/Exp: C	Rand Var: +5	
			Consist: A	MM: 2210	

Appeared to be in ninth-inning mix when season started—even earned team's first save—but 6 ER in first six outings moved him down in the pecking order. Though xERA says not much changed, K% and SwK slipped, got knocked around vL, and xHR/F shows that HR/F wasn't all bad luck. Looks like an uphill battle to get closing chances again.

Yr Tm	W	Sv	IP	K	ERA	WHIP	xERA	xWHIP	vL+	vR+	BF/G	BB%	K%	K-BB%	xBB%	SwK	Vel	G	L	F	H%	S%	HR/F	xHR/F	GS	APC	DOM%	DIS%	Sv%	LI	RAR	BPX	R$
17 MIA	3	0	42	43	4.68	1.39	4.50	1.26	121	97	4.8	7%	24%	16%	8%	11.7%	92.4	33	24	43	35%	69%	9%	11%	0	20			0	0.74	-1.7	121	-$3
18 MIA *	2	2	66	59	4.74	1.51	5.08	1.34	82	92	4.8	8%	21%	12%	8%	10.0%	92.1	46	17	37	35%	70%	3%	11%	0	19			33	0.65	-4.8	78	-$5
19 CLE	5	4	58	60	2.81	1.08	4.05	1.20	101	83	4.2	6%	26%	19%	7%	9.7%	92.3	38	23	39	27%	85%	17%	18%	0	18			67	1.08	12.1	132	$7
20 CLE	2	0	24	28	3.42	1.01	3.64	1.10	77	115	3.9	6%	29%	23%	8%	13.8%	92.9	33	28	40	27%	75%	17%	20%	0	15			0	1.56	3.0	159	$4
21 CLE	2	1	62	61	5.05	1.25	3.76	1.20	139	86	4.3	7%	24%	17%	8%	11.9%	92.5	45	24	30	29%	66%	25%	26%	1	17	0%	100%	100	0.75	-6.1	126	-$4
1st Half	2	1	29	31	4.66	1.07	3.31	1.09	126	70	3.9	5%	27%	22%	6%	12.3%	92.8	42	29	30	27%	64%	26%	24%	0	16			100	0.61	-1.4	156	-$2
2nd Half	0	0	33	30	5.40	1.41	4.17	1.29	137	102	4.6	8%	21%	13%	9%	11.5%	92.2	48	21	30	31%	68%	23%	28%	1	18	0%	100%	0	0.89	-4.7	101	-$12
Proj	3	1	65	63	3.99	1.23	3.97	1.24	118	89	4.3	7%	24%	17%	8%	11.0%	92.4	43	23	34	29%	74%	18%	20%	0						3.8	121	$0

Wood,Alex

Age: 31	Th: L	Role: SP	Health: F	LIMA Plan: B	
Ht: 6' 4"	Wt: 215	Type:	PT/Exp: C	Rand Var: 0	
			Consist: C	MM: 3203	

Opened year on IL with back injury after missing most of previous two seasons, but showed no rust upon return. Velocity, K%, GB%, and xERA were mirror images of breakout 2017 campaign. Spotty health history can't be dismissed, and realistic IP ceiling is probably around 150, but a good bet to deliver strong numbers on a per-game basis.

Yr Tm	W	Sv	IP	K	ERA	WHIP	xERA	xWHIP	vL+	vR+	BF/G	BB%	K%	K-BB%	xBB%	SwK	Vel	G	L	F	H%	S%	HR/F	xHR/F	GS	APC	DOM%	DIS%	Sv%	LI	RAR	BPX	R$
17 LA	16	0	152	151	2.72	1.06	3.34	1.18	80	85	22.7	6%	25%	19%	6%	12.4%	91.8	53	20	27	28%	79%	14%	12%	25	84	44%	24%	0	0.78	30.8	157	$25
18 LA	9	0	152	135	3.68	1.21	3.75	1.24	81	97	19.3	6%	21%	15%	6%	11.3%	89.9	49	22	29	31%	72%	11%	11%	27	74	19%	26%	0	0.81	8.8	123	$9
19 CIN	1	0	36	30	5.80	1.40	4.65	1.30	120	124	21.9	6%	20%	14%	8%	11.4%	90.0	38	28	34	30%	69%	30%	21%	7	84	14%	43%			-5.7	99	-$6
20 LA	0	0	13	15	6.39	1.82	5.29	1.34	106	133	7.2	9%	23%	14%	9%	12.8%	91.2	39	17	44	42%	67%	11%	10%	2	31	0%	100%	0	0.68	-3.0	106	-$10
21 SF	10	0	139	152	3.83	1.18	3.34	1.16	93	91	22.5	7%	26%	19%	6%	13.0%	91.8	51	22	27	32%	70%	14%	17%	26	84	31%	23%			7.5	152	$10
1st Half	7	0	76	81	3.89	1.19	3.39	1.21	99	90	22.7	8%	25%	18%	6%	13.1%	91.7	55	18	27	30%	71%	17%	19%	14	89	29%	29%			3.5	138	$11
2nd Half	3	0	62	71	3.75	1.17	3.27	1.09	74	95	22.3	5%	27%	21%	5%	13.0%	91.9	46	27	27	34%	69%	11%	14%	12	79	33%	17%			3.9	169	$6
Proj	8	0	138	138	3.88	1.22	3.60	1.18	91	96	20.7	6%	25%	18%	6%	12.6%	91.1	47	24	29	32%	71%	15%	16%	27						9.8	141	$8

Woodford,Jake

Age: 25	Th: R	Role: RP	Health: A	LIMA Plan: D+	
Ht: 6' 4"	Wt: 215	Type: Con	PT/Exp: D	Rand Var: -2	
			Consist: A	MM: 0001	

3-4, 3.99 ERA in 68 IP at STL. Shuttled back and forth between AAA and MLB for much of year and had some late success (8 ER in 29 IP after September recall), but without skills support. Upside is non-existent given inability to miss bats, especially since he doesn't have stellar BB% or GB lean to fall back on. Likely to keep seat warm on that shuttle.

Yr Tm	W	Sv	IP	K	ERA	WHIP	xERA	xWHIP	vL+	vR+	BF/G	BB%	K%	K-BB%	xBB%	SwK	Vel	G	L	F	H%	S%	HR/F	xHR/F	GS	APC	DOM%	DIS%	Sv%	LI	RAR	BPX	R$
17																																	
18 a/a	8	0	145	85	5.22	1.56	5.34				22.7	9%	13%	4%							32%	68%									-19.1	33	-$11
19 aaa	9	0	153	109	4.75	1.38	4.40				24.8	11%	17%	6%							27%	69%									-4.6	41	$0
20 STL	1	0	21	16	5.57	1.19	4.58	1.28	74	142	7.1	6%	19%	13%	9%	8.3%	92.9	45	17	38	23%	67%	29%	25%	1	30	0%	0%	0	0.41	-2.9	100	-$5
21 STL *	5	0	102	70	4.16	1.43	4.76	1.42	120	83	13.1	8%	16%	8%	10%	8.4%	91.7	41	24	35	31%	73%	10%	10%	8	44	13%	50%	0	0.68	1.3	55	-$3
1st Half	1	0	27	23	5.60	1.58	5.74	1.55	142	81	6.7	12%	19%	7%	12%	9.3%	92.2	45	23	32	30%	69%	21%	18%	0	28			0	0.64	-4.5	31	-$10
2nd Half	4	0	74	47	3.63	1.38	4.40	1.38	96	86	20.8	7%	15%	8%	9%	7.8%	91.4	39	24	37	32%	75%	4%	6%	8	76	13%	50%	0	0.76	5.8	67	$2
Proj	6	0	109	75	4.42	1.41	5.06	1.46	127	87	13.7	9%	16%	7%	10%	8.4%	91.7	42	24	35	30%	71%	11%	11%	13						0.5	44	-$3

BRIAN RUDD

Woodruff,Brandon

Age: 29	Th: R	Role	SP	PT/Exp	A	Rand Var	-2
Ht: 6' 4"	Wt: 243	Type	Pwr	Consist	A	MM	4305
				Health	B	LIMA Plan	D+

Put any lingering volume concerns to bed with a comparable encore to 2020's breakout. Tough to find a weakness here: K% remains steadily elite, supported by growing SwK; walk rate looks pristine; and he's been consistently dominant (DOM%/DIS%) since 2019. Unlikely to run into 1st half stretch of luck again, but he's an ace you can build around.

Yr Tm	W	Sv	IP	K	ERA	WHIP	xERA	xWHIP	vL+	vR+	BF/G	BB%	K%	K-BB%	xBB%	SwK	Vel	G	L	F	H%	S%	HR/F	xHR/F	GS	APC	DOM%	DIS%	Sv%	LI	RAR	BPX	R$
17 MIL *	8	0	118	91	4.66	1.40	4.62	1.37	115	77	20.8	8%	18%	11%	6%	9.4%	94.3	47	19	34	32%	69%	11%	8%	8	90	38%	63%			-4.3	72	$0
18 MIL *	6	1	114	103	3.95	1.34	4.11	1.36	85	92	13.2	9%	22%	12%	8%	11.1%	95.3	53	18	29	31%	73%	12%	16%	4	39	0%	50%	100	0.51	2.7	84	$2
19 MIL	11	0	122	143	3.62	1.14	3.43	1.12	100	74	22.4	6%	29%	23%	6%	12.4%	96.3	45	23	32	33%	71%	12%	12%	22	90	32%	9%			13.2	167	$13
20 MIL	3	0	74	91	3.05	0.99	3.22	1.06	82	83	22.5	6%	31%	25%	6%	13.1%	96.5	49	15	36	28%	75%	14%	15%	13	93	31%	0%			12.7	189	$23
21 MIL	9	0	179	211	2.56	0.96	3.18	1.07	75	80	23.6	6%	30%	24%	5%	13.6%	96.5	41	26	32	28%	79%	13%	14%	30	94	47%	10%			37.7	166	$30
1st Half	7	0	101	119	1.87	0.78	2.93	1.06	55	72	23.9	6%	31%	25%	6%	13.0%	96.6	46	22	31	22%	83%	12%	12%	16	95	56%	6%			29.8	173	$38
2nd Half	2	0	78	92	3.45	1.20	3.48	1.09	92	93	23.2	6%	28%	23%	5%	14.3%	96.2	36	30	33	34%	75%	13%	16%	14	93	36%	14%			7.9	160	$10
Proj	13	0	189	215	3.19	1.09	3.33	1.12	88	83	20.7	7%	29%	22%	6%	12.9%	96.2	44	23	33	30%	75%	13%	14%	36						29.4	163	$24

Yarbrough,Ryan

Age: 30	Th: L	Role	SP	PT/Exp	B	Rand Var	+2
Ht: 6' 5"	Wt: 205	Type	Con	Consist	B	MM	1003
				Health	B	LIMA Plan	C

You drafted him for strong ratios knowing you wouldn't get many Ks. The latter held true (not good) and the former fell apart (also not good). Low S% was partially to blame and BB% was still elite, but another year of velocity decline with SwK collapse and FB% spike raises red flags. ERA should improve, but not to the point where it masks other deficiencies.

Yr Tm	W	Sv	IP	K	ERA	WHIP	xERA	xWHIP	vL+	vR+	BF/G	BB%	K%	K-BB%	xBB%	SwK	Vel	G	L	F	H%	S%	HR/F	xHR/F	GS	APC	DOM%	DIS%	Sv%	LI	RAR	BPX	R$
17 aaa	13	0	157	131	4.87	1.47	5.38				25.9	7%	19%	13%							34%	71%									-9.9	72	$0
18 TAM	16	0	147	128	3.91	1.29	4.41	1.33	89	106	16.5	8%	20%	12%	7%	9.2%	89.4	38	25	37	30%	73%	11%	12%	6	63	0%	50%	0	1.21	4.4	86	$9
19 TAM *	13	0	168	146	4.25	1.04	3.11	1.14	93	84	19.6	4%	23%	19%	6%	10.6%	88.2	44	20	36	29%	61%	10%	10%	14	73	50%	29%	0	0.90	5.2	171	$16
20 TAM	1	0	56	44	3.56	1.19	4.23	1.24	95	92	21.3	5%	19%	14%	5%	13.7%	87.4	42	29	29	30%	72%	10%	13%	9	76	33%	33%	0	0.84	6.2	108	$5
21 TAM	9	0	155	117	5.11	1.23	4.61	1.21	86	106	21.8	4%	18%	14%	6%	9.6%	86.5	36	24	40	30%	62%	13%	13%	21	83	14%	29%	0	0.77	-16.1	103	$0
1st Half	4	0	86	70	4.48	1.19	4.31	1.19	88	104	22.7	4%	19%	15%	6%	10.1%	86.7	37	26	37	30%	67%	13%	12%	11	84	18%	18%	0	0.72	-2.3	115	$4
2nd Half	5	0	69	47	5.90	1.27	4.99	1.25	73	114	20.7	4%	16%	12%	6%	9.1%	86.2	34	23	43	30%	56%	12%	14%	10	82	10%	40%	0	0.83	-13.8	88	-$4
Proj	9	0	145	114	4.34	1.21	4.33	1.23	91	102	20.0	5%	19%	15%	6%	10.5%	87.3	39	24	37	30%	68%	12%	12%	21						2.1	108	$5

Yates,Kirby

Age: 35	Th: R	Role	RP	PT/Exp	C	Rand Var	0
Ht: 5' 10"	Wt: 205	Type	Pwr/FB	Consist	F	MM	4510
				Health	F	LIMA Plan	C+

Off-season elbow concerns turned out to be quite valid. Season was over before it began with Tommy John surgery in March. Run of top-notch production from 2017-19 has to keep him on periphery, but 2022 return is questionable and he's not at an age where skills just snap right back. A speculative candidate for 50-round draft&holds.

Yr Tm	W	Sv	IP	K	ERA	WHIP	xERA	xWHIP	vL+	vR+	BF/G	BB%	K%	K-BB%	xBB%	SwK	Vel	G	L	F	H%	S%	HR/F	xHR/F	GS	APC	DOM%	DIS%	Sv%	LI	RAR	BPX	R$
17 2 TM	4	1	57	88	3.97	1.11	3.36	1.04	111	80	3.7	8%	38%	30%	6%	18.0%	94.0	29	15	56	31%	75%	18%	16%	0	16			25	0.85	2.7	213	$4
18 SD	5	12	63	90	2.14	0.92	2.72	0.99	91	58	3.8	7%	36%	29%	6%	17.1%	94.0	43	20	37	29%	83%	12%	17%	0	16			92	1.37	15.6	215	$15
19 SD	0	41	61	101	1.19	0.89	2.31	0.87	75	60	4.1	5%	42%	36%	6%	16.2%	93.5	48	17	35	36%	88%	5%	9%	0	17			93	1.60	24.8	265	$28
20 SD	0	2	4	8	12.46	2.54	4.86		157	86	4.2	16%	32%	16%	9%	18.8%	93.7	38	31	31	59%	50%	25%	23%	0	17			100	0.80	-4.3	103	-$8
21																																	
1st Half																																	
2nd Half																																	
Proj	1	1	15	19	3.41	1.09	3.47	1.19	94	67	3.8	10%	33%	23%	6%	16.9%	93.8	42	18	41	28%	72%	11%	13%	0						1.9	150	-$3

Ynoa,Huascar

Age: 24	Th: R	Role	SP	PT/Exp	C	Rand Var	+2
Ht: 6' 2"	Wt: 220	Type	Pwr	Consist	D	MM	3301
				Health	F	LIMA Plan	A

Broke his hand in May punching a dugout bench (the hand never wins), didn't return until August. An otherwise strong performance: he missed tons of bats, racked up Ks, and held plus GB%... all with improved control. Some hurdles—change-up needs to be usable third pitch, hasn't gone 100+ IP since 2018—but if BB% gains hold... UP: sub-3.50 ERA.

Yr Tm	W	Sv	IP	K	ERA	WHIP	xERA	xWHIP	vL+	vR+	BF/G	BB%	K%	K-BB%	xBB%	SwK	Vel	G	L	F	H%	S%	HR/F	xHR/F	GS	APC	DOM%	DIS%	Sv%	LI	RAR	BPX	R$
17																																	
18																																	
19 ATL *	4	1	92	83	7.66	1.82	7.39		148	163	17.1	10%	19%	10%		10.6%	97.6	42	33	25	37%	61%	33%	33%	0	33			50	0.03	-36.0	22	-$18
20 ATL	0	0	22	17	5.82	1.66	5.37	1.63	92	117	11.1	13%	17%	4%	9%	11.6%	94.9	54	18	28	32%	65%	11%	13%	5	44	20%	40%	0	0.62	-3.6	15	-$11
21 ATL	4	0	91	100	4.05	1.11	3.46	1.15	92	97	20.7	7%	27%	20%	7%	13.5%	96.5	47	21	32	28%	69%	18%	21%	17	82	24%	12%	0	0.73	2.4	149	$4
1st Half	4	0	45	50	3.02	1.05	3.30	1.11	64	109	19.9	6%	28%	22%	7%	13.7%	96.7	47	22	31	28%	80%	19%	26%	8	78	25%	0%	0	0.68	6.8	160	$7
2nd Half	0	0	46	50	5.05	1.17	3.61	1.18	107	89	21.4	7%	26%	19%	7%	13.3%	96.3	48	20	33	29%	60%	18%	17%	9	87	22%	22%			-4.5	140	-$6
Proj	5	0	123	132	3.86	1.24	3.65	1.20	99	100	20.4	8%	26%	19%	7%	13.5%	96.5	47	21	32	31%	73%	15%	20%	25						9.0	141	$5

Young,Alex

Age: 28	Th: L	Role	RP	PT/Exp	C	Rand Var	+5
Ht: 6' 3"	Wt: 220	Type		Consist	C	MM	0100
				Health	A	LIMA Plan	D+

Tumultuous season featured bullpen demotion, numerous trips to AAA, July DFA. Whiff rate ticked up thanks to change-up (20% SwK) and slider (17%), but it didn't translate to Ks. BB% collapsed and he was smashed equally vL and vR. Luck factors didn't help, but with four 5.00+ xERAs on this page, he needs a lot more than just better fortune to be usable.

Yr Tm	W	Sv	IP	K	ERA	WHIP	xERA	xWHIP	vL+	vR+	BF/G	BB%	K%	K-BB%	xBB%	SwK	Vel	G	L	F	H%	S%	HR/F	xHR/F	GS	APC	DOM%	DIS%	Sv%	LI	RAR	BPX	R$
17 aa	9	0	137	85	5.13	1.60	5.27				22.4	10%	14%	4%							32%	69%									-13.0	34	-$7
18 a/a	10	0	132	88	5.41	1.52	5.29				19.8	7%	15%	9%							35%	65%									-20.6	60	-$9
19 ARI *	11	0	140	121	4.46	1.40	4.66	1.40	74	103	15.9	9%	21%	12%	8%	12.9%	89.3	48	17	35	31%	72%	16%	16%	15	78	13%	47%	0	0.76	0.8	66	$3
20 ARI	2	0	46	39	5.44	1.40	5.18	1.32	93	127	13.6	7%	19%	12%	8%	12.0%	91.0	37	21	42	30%	69%	18%	19%	7	53	0%	57%	0	0.68	-5.6	88	-$5
21 2 TM	2	0	52	43	6.58	1.77	5.35	1.51	121	127	6.2	11%	18%	7%	8%	13.0%	90.3	44	23	32	34%	68%	22%	21%	2	23	0%	100%	0	1.01	-14.8	33	-$13
1st Half	2	0	39	37	5.82	1.60	4.82	1.43	118	112	6.0	11%	21%	10%	8%	14.6%	90.1	42	26	32	33%	69%	21%	19%	2	24	0%	100%	0	1.07	-7.4	61	-$10
2nd Half	0	0	13	6	8.78	2.25	7.08	1.73	109	183	6.5	11%	8%	-3%	8%	8.4%	90.8	50	19	31	36%	65%	24%	24%	0	20			0	0.85	-7.4	-49	-$20
Proj	3	0	44	36	5.31	1.50	4.88	1.40	104	115	10.6	9%	19%	10%	8%	13.4%	90.2	42	22	36	32%	68%	15%	19%	1						-4.6	68	-$6

Zimmer,Kyle

Age: 30	Th: R	Role	RP	PT/Exp	D	Rand Var	0
Ht: 6' 3"	Wt: 225	Type	Pwr/GB	Consist	F	MM	1210
				Health	C	LIMA Plan	D+

Hit the IL in May (back) and Aug (neck), and while he seemed to be on 2020 repeat track early, most of that was luck-fueled before skills collapsed in 2nd half. Drop in whiffs was the lowlight as slider lost effectiveness, which in combination with awful walk rate, drove K-BB% to low depths. Given age and non-short-season BPX history, he's unlikely to ascend.

Yr Tm	W	Sv	IP	K	ERA	WHIP	xERA	xWHIP	vL+	vR+	BF/G	BB%	K%	K-BB%	xBB%	SwK	Vel	G	L	F	H%	S%	HR/F	xHR/F	GS	APC	DOM%	DIS%	Sv%	LI	RAR	BPX	R$
17 a/a	0	3	37	31	7.55	1.91	6.91				8.3	10%	18%	7%							40%	60%									-14.5	43	-$10
18																																	
19 KC *	2	1	72	56	6.92	1.96	6.39	1.83	100	154	6.6	16%	16%	0%	12%	11.7%	96.5	43	32	25	34%	65%	13%	17%	0	29			25	0.32	-21.6	30	-$16
20 KC	1	0	23	26	1.57	1.04	3.52	1.30	62	83	5.7	11%	29%	18%	7%	12.9%	94.1	50	22	28	26%	83%	0%	7%	1	23	0%	0%	0	0.36	8.2	119	$4
21 KC	4	2	54	46	5.00	1.41	4.72	1.56	75	116	4.3	13%	21%	7%	11%	10.9%	94.1	52	11	37	27%	67%	13%	18%	2	18	0%	0%	67	0.99	-4.9	36	-$4
1st Half	4	2	33	32	2.45	1.03	3.77	1.39	58	82	4.1	12%	26%	14%	9%	12.0%	94.3	55	7	39	22%	78%	7%	12%	2	18	0%	0%	100	1.11	7.4	87	$6
2nd Half	0	0	21	14	9.00	2.00	6.39	1.78	88	166	4.5	15%	14%	-1%	12%	9.4%	94.0	50	16	34	33%	57%	21%	25%	0	18			0	0.83	-12.3	-41	-$22
Proj	2	5	58	56	4.82	1.50	4.69	1.50	76	126	5.1	13%	23%	10%	12%	10.4%	94.1	52	12	36	30%	71%	15%	20%	0						-2.6	62	-$4

Zimmermann,Bruce

Age: 27	Th: L	Role	SP	PT/Exp	D	Rand Var	0
Ht: 6' 2"	Wt: 215	Type		Consist	C	MM	1101
				Health	F	LIMA Plan	C

4-5, 5.04 ERA in 64 IP at BAL. Cracked rotation out of camp, but was sent to AAA in May and missed most of 2nd half (biceps). Inflated HR/F and LD% didn't help, but subpar K% and xERA say it didn't matter much anyway. Did have a 15% SwK on three separate pitches, so maybe a pitch-mix tweak unlocks some growth; just don't pay much to find out.

Yr Tm	W	Sv	IP	K	ERA	WHIP	xERA	xWHIP	vL+	vR+	BF/G	BB%	K%	K-BB%	xBB%	SwK	Vel	G	L	F	H%	S%	HR/F	xHR/F	GS	APC	DOM%	DIS%	Sv%	LI	RAR	BPX	R$
17																																	
18 aa	4	0	50	34	4.50	1.63	5.36				20.2	11%	15%	4%							32%	74%									-2.2	39	-$6
19 a/a	7	0	142	108	4.11	1.51	4.96				24.7	9%	18%	8%							33%	75%									7.0	56	-$1
20 BAL	0	0	7	7	7.71	1.14	4.21	1.22	90	108	15.5	6%	23%	16%	6%	8.4%	91.5	50	10	40	24%	33%	25%	22%	1	54	0%	100%	0	0.43	-2.8	136	-$7
21 BAL *	5	0	82	70	4.85	1.45	5.74	1.33	127	109	18.5	8%	20%	12%	8%	11.2%	91.5	40	26	34	32%	73%	20%	24%	13	79	0%	69%	0	0.74	-5.9	47	-$5
1st Half	4	0	63	55	4.96	1.46	5.96	1.30	109	112	20.6	7%	21%	13%	8%	11.7%	91.6	41	26	32	32%	73%	20%	25%	11	84	0%	64%	0	0.73	-5.3	50	-$5
2nd Half	1	0	20	14	4.55	1.43	5.08		361	107	14.0	10%	17%	7%	8%	6.1%	90.6	33	17	50	29%	73%	22%	18%	2	49	0%	100%			-0.7	38	-$10
Proj	6	0	102	87	4.57	1.44	4.51	1.35	118	112	20.5	8%	20%	12%	8%	11.7%	91.6	44	20	36	32%	72%	15%	23%	21						-1.5	86	-$3

RYAN BLOOMFIELD

THE NEXT TIER

The preceding section provided player boxes and analysis for 406 pitchers. As we know, far more than 406 pitchers will play in the major leagues in 2022. Many of those additional pitchers are covered in the minor league section, but that still leaves a gap: established major leaguers who don't play enough, or well enough, to merit a player box.

This section looks to fill that gap. Here, you will find "The Next Tier" of pitchers who are mostly past their growth years, but who are likely to see some playing time in 2022. We are including their 2020-21 statlines here for reference for you to do your own analysis. (Years that include MLEs are marked by an asterisk.) This way, if Yimi García sniffs a bullpen role at some point in 2022, you can confirm that he had above-average skills seasons the past two years. Or if Julio Tehran makes a comeback, you can deftly wait for him to "prove it" before rushing to the waiver wire.

Pitcher	T	Yr	Age	W	Sv	IP	K	ERA	xERA	WHIP	vL+	vR+	BB%	K%	K-BB	xBB%	SwK	G/L/F	H%	S%	BPX
Adams, Austin L	R	20	30	0	0	4	7	4.50	2.84	1.25	236	45	12	41	29		16.2	50/13/38	32	75	215
		21	31	3	0	53	76	4.10	3.88	1.20	92	78	15	32	17	11	13.8	34/22/44	27	63	92
Anderson, Chase	R	20	33	1	0	34	38	7.22	4.44	1.63	140	131	6	25	18	10	12.1	37/27/37	37	64	142
		21*	34	3	0	81	56	6.51	6.52	1.60	88	149	10	16	6	9	10.2	36/19/44	31	64	8
Andriese, Matt	R	20	31	2	2	32	33	4.50	3.91	1.00	106	69	9	26	17	7	10.6	46/17/37	22	59	121
		21	32	2	1	48	50	5.21	4.19	1.61	121	116	6	23	17	8	9.9	44/22/33	40	70	136
Bleier, Richard	L	20	34	1	0	17	11	2.16	3.12	1.08	53	123	6	16	10	6	8.3	72/22/6	28	78	111
		21	35	3	0	58	44	2.95	2.86	0.98	65	96	3	20	17	4	10.9	65/20/15	28	72	154
Brothers, Rex	L	20	33	0	0	3	8	8.10	2.67	1.50	45	231	20	53	33		22.4	25/25/50	0	67	196
		21	34	3	1	53	75	5.26	4.21	1.43	92	109	15	32	17	12	14.1	35/21/44	30	67	90
Chacin, Jhoulys	R	20	33	1	0	5	3	7.20	7.76	1.80	88	135	13	13	0		-	17/33/50	31	63	-61
		21	34	3	0	64	47	4.34	4.79	1.26	93	100	10	17	7	9	9.9	46/22/32	25	68	40
Chargois, J.T.	R	21	31	6	0	54	53	2.52	3.94	1.08	77	94	9	25	15	9	12.2	45/18/37	25	81	101
Cishek, Steve	R	20	35	0	0	20	21	5.40	5.32	1.50	83	140	10	23	13	11	10.7	32/19/49	32	69	80
		21	36	0	0	68	64	3.42	4.89	1.49	90	92	13	21	7	10	8.1	50/17/33	31	76	37
Davis, Wade	R	20	35	0	2	4	3	20.77	8.43	2.77	122	322	12	12	0	10	6.7	42/16/42	39	22	-41
		21	36	0	2	43	38	6.75	5.25	1.48	116	104	10	20	10	10	10.8	35/21/44	30	56	54
Detwiler, Ross	L	20	35	1	0	20	15	3.20	4.04	1.22	59	121	6	19	12	8	13.5	58/15/27	30	77	110
		21	36	3	0	52	62	4.64	4.02	1.22	99	108	9	27	18	8	10.1	40/19/41	28	69	128
Doolittle, Sean	L	20	34	0	0	8	6	5.87	7.18	1.70	104	166	11	17	6	5	10.2	0/40/60	28	80	-25
		21	35	3	1	50	53	4.53	5.33	1.47	90	124	10	24	13	6	12.7	19/27/54	33	73	63
Fiers, Mike	R	20	36	6	0	59	37	4.58	5.65	1.37	99	111	6	14	8	8	6.7	35/22/43	30	71	55
		21	37	0	0	9	5	7.71	6.62	2.04	171	149	9	11	2	8	4.6	42/17/42	34	73	3
Fry, Paul	L	20	28	1	0	22	29	2.45	3.40	1.41	110	88	9	30	20	11	11.7	58/15/27	37	89	170
		21	29	4	2	47	60	6.08	4.25	1.52	101	77	16	28	12	12	9.7	50/21/29	32	58	59
García, Yimi	R	20	30	3	1	15	19	0.60	3.40	0.93	85	45	8	32	23	8	12.4	42/25/33	28	93	163
		21	31	4	15	58	60	4.21	3.90	1.16	114	81	8	25	18	6	13.0	40/25/35	29	68	121
Gsellman, Robert	R	20	27	0	0	14	9	9.64	6.91	2.14	154	150	11	13	1	12	7.2	42/23/36	37	58	-17
		21	28	0	0	29	17	3.77	4.39	1.19	95	94	6	14	8	8	10.3	49/23/27	27	71	70
Guerra, Junior	R	20	36	1	0	24	21	3.04	4.74	1.35	111	70	15	20	6	10	12.6	51/27/22	26	77	21
		21	37	5	0	65	61	6.06	5.46	1.73	125	90	15	20	5	12	11.1	47/21/32	33	64	6
Harris, Will	R	20	36	0	1	18	21	3.06	4.61	1.70	117	102	11	25	14	8	13.8	42/27/31	38	89	100
		21	37	0	0	6	9	9.00	4.12	1.67	52	148	10	30	20	9	11.9	33/33/33	43	44	145
Hembree, Heath	R	20	32	3	0	19	20	9.00	5.61	1.79	152	163	9	22	13	8	12.9	32/17/52	34	60	88
		21	33	2	9	58	83	5.59	3.88	1.19	126	81	10	34	24	7	13.1	26/20/54	29	58	148
Holland, Derek	L	20	34	1	0	41	45	6.86	4.47	1.40	51	137	8	25	17	10	11.1	37/23/40	30	58	118
		21	35	3	0	50	51	5.07	4.40	1.57	97	119	9	23	14	6	11.3	45/22/32	37	69	100
Hudson, Daniel	R	20	34	3	10	21	28	6.10	4.75	1.26	92	122	12	30	18	6	16.4	18/24/57	23	60	97
		21	35	5	0	52	75	3.31	3.47	1.08	96	89	8	36	28	7	16.6	30/19/51	31	77	184
Hutchison, Drew	R	21*	31	11	0	110	72	5.00	5.76	1.70	90	96	12	14	3	12	10.6	49/13/38	33	72	31
Jiménez, Joe	R	20	26	1	5	23	22	7.15	4.69	1.37	139	120	6	22	16	6	13.1	31/26/43	30	54	115
		21	27	6	1	45	57	5.96	5.26	1.52	104	103	17	27	10	10	14.3	34/13/53	28	62	31
Kelly, Joe	R	20	33	0	0	10	9	1.80	4.59	1.50	79	102	17	21	5	12	10.5	58/23/19	29	87	13
		21	34	2	2	44	50	2.86	3.02	0.98	75	74	8	27	19	8	11.7	59/20/21	25	73	152
LeBlanc, Wade	L	20	36	1	0	22	13	8.06	6.18	1.57	84	129	8	13	5	8	10.9	35/26/39	30	52	23
		21*	37	3	0	85	53	4.13	4.74	1.34	118	112	8	15	7	8	9.3	36/24/40	28	74	39
Leone, Dominic	R	20	29	0	0	10	16	8.38	3.74	1.97	143	138	11	34	23	9	17.8	31/38/31	49	63	171
		21	30	4	2	54	50	1.51	4.25	1.10	68	80	10	23	13	9	13.4	48/14/38	26	88	85

THE NEXT TIER   Pitchers

Pitcher	T	Yr	Age	W	Sv	IP	K	ERA	xERA	WHIP	vL+	vR+	BB%	K%	K-BB	xBB%	SwK	G/L/F	H%	S%	BPX
McFarland, T.J.	L	20	32	2	0	21	9	4.35	5.06	1.50	131	115	5	10	4	10	6.9	60/17/23	30	81	56
		21*	33	6	2	70	45	3.70	3.57	1.18	67	102	6	16	10	8	8.2	64/14/22	29	70	84
Miller, Andrew	L	20	36	1	4	13	16	2.77	3.40	1.08	58	81	9	29	20	9	13.7	58/6/35	30	71	160
		21	37	0	0	36	40	4.75	4.35	1.58	74	159	10	24	15	7	11.1	44/19/38	37	73	103
Minter, A.J.	L	20	27	1	0	22	24	0.83	3.71	1.11	87	82	11	28	18	8	13.9	49/18/33	27	96	119
		21	28	3	0	52	57	3.78	3.91	1.22	74	100	9	26	17	6	14.8	45/21/34	32	68	117
Misiewicz, Anthony	L	20	26	0	0	20	25	4.05	3.81	1.30	68	135	7	30	23	10	14.3	28/32/40	36	71	153
		21	27	5	0	55	53	4.61	4.18	1.39	91	114	6	22	16	6	13.2	42/23/35	35	70	121
Newcomb, Sean	L	20	28	0	0	14	10	11.20	6.41	1.90	155	127	9	14	6	12	7.3	36/24/40	36	41	29
		21*	29	5	5	51	64	3.77	3.29	1.41	93	102	15	30	15	12	11.6	39/27/34	32	73	121
Parker, Blake	R	20	36	3	0	16	25	2.81	3.51	1.31	103	80	13	36	23	11	12.4	37/29/34	33	84	148
		21	37	2	0	44	37	3.09	4.66	1.31	80	119	8	20	12	8	10.4	39/22/39	31	81	84
Plutko, Adam	R	20	29	2	1	28	15	4.88	5.87	1.34	85	135	6	13	7	6	11.2	24/30/46	28	69	32
		21	30	1	1	56	44	6.71	6.05	1.63	141	132	11	17	7	12	10.9	30/18/52	29	67	20
Quintana, José	L	20	32	0	0	10	12	4.50	3.28	1.30	147	82	7	29	22	12	10.9	42/35/23	36	67	160
		21	33	0	0	63	85	6.43	4.06	1.73	70	138	12	29	17	10	12.5	47/21/32	40	66	119
Raley, Brooks	L	20	33	0	1	20	27	4.95	3.27	0.95	55	113	7	32	25	7	14.3	39/24/37	25	50	184
		21	34	2	2	49	65	4.78	3.06	1.20	65	110	8	32	24	8	14.9	45/26/29	34	62	174
Santana, Edgar	R	21	30	3	0	43	33	3.59	4.17	1.15	62	111	7	19	12	6	13.0	50/20/30	26	76	93
Santiago, Hector	L	21	34	1	0	26	30	3.42	4.29	1.44	114	91	9	26	16	7	13.0	45/17/38	36	78	116
Shoemaker, Matt	R	20	34	0	0	29	26	4.71	4.15	1.08	97	106	8	23	15	7	12.6	48/18/34	20	70	109
		21*	35	8	0	131	92	6.08	5.61	1.48	135	112	8	16	8	8	10.4	45/21/34	31	61	37
Shreve, Chasen	L	20	30	1	0	25	34	3.96	3.68	1.16	68	103	12	33	22	10	17.5	42/18/40	26	72	140
		21	31	3	0	56	45	3.20	5.13	1.26	86	99	12	19	7	9	11.2	38/21/41	24	80	27
Smith, Burch	R	20	31	2	1	12	13	2.25	3.73	0.67	70	60	2	30	27	5	14.4	30/17/53	22	71	184
		21	32	1	0	43	28	5.40	5.28	1.38	121	96	6	15	9	7	8.1	36/23/41	32	62	63
Smith, Joe	R	21	38	4	0	40	34	4.99	4.13	1.39	74	123	5	20	15	5	9.2	44/26/30	35	66	123
Soria, Joakim	R	20	37	2	2	22	24	2.82	5.16	1.25	49	92	10	25	15	8	10.3	27/21/52	30	78	79
		21	38	1	6	37	40	5.06	4.30	1.37	130	101	8	25	18	6	12.7	32/26/42	34	67	116
Strickland, Hunter	R	20	32	0	0	3	4	8.10	3.58	1.80	53	173	6	25	19		13.1	55/27/18	48	50	175
		21	33	3	0	59	58	2.61	4.58	1.16	91	92	9	24	15	7	12.7	35/17/48	26	85	90
Suero, Wander	R	20	29	2	0	24	28	3.80	4.15	1.27	66	109	10	27	18	7	16.3	37/25/38	33	69	117
		21	30	2	0	43	44	6.33	4.71	1.41	118	116	8	23	15	7	11.8	33/22/45	31	61	102
Taylor, Blake	L	20	25	2	1	21	17	2.18	5.20	1.21	72	83	14	20	6	11	8.5	51/12/37	21	87	24
		21	26	4	0	43	41	3.16	5.14	1.41	64	122	12	22	10	12	10.4	41/15/45	29	83	54
Teheran, Julio	R	20	30	0	0	31	20	10.05	6.60	1.76	151	127	11	13	3	9	6.5	35/25/40	28	47	-9
		21	31	1	0	5	3	1.80	5.83	1.40	123	69	15	15	0		6.7	36/21/43	21	100	-38
Tepera, Ryan	R	20	33	0	0	21	31	3.92	3.34	1.40	86	99	13	35	21	12	19.5	40/36/24	35	74	135
		21	34	0	2	61	74	2.79	3.42	0.88	59	77	8	31	23	8	16.9	44/13/43	24	70	156
Thornton, Trent	R	20	27	0	0	6	6	11.12	6.82	3.18	132	185	9	18	9	7	9.9	29/33/38	60	61	56
		21	28	1	0	49	52	4.78	4.21	1.43	100	130	7	24	17	8	10.2	40/23/37	33	76	121
Tomlin, Josh	R	20	36	2	0	40	36	4.76	4.40	1.21	89	110	5	22	17	6	10.6	38/21/41	31	64	129
		21	37	4	0	49	37	6.57	4.98	1.50	107	133	2	17	15	5	12.5	33/24/43	37	59	118
Valdez, César	R	20	36	1	3	14	12	1.26	3.54	0.70	81	38	6	23	17	8	13.6	53/18/29	20	80	131
		21	37	2	8	46	45	5.87	4.13	1.65	104	136	7	21	15	5	14.7	48/25/27	39	68	121
Valdez, Phillips	R	20	29	1	0	30	30	3.26	4.68	1.62	79	124	12	22	10	12	10.8	47/25/28	35	83	64
		21*	30	3	2	56	50	5.75	4.77	1.56	103	91	14	20	6	11	9.4	58/17/25	30	64	57
Watson, Tony	L	20	36	1	2	18	15	2.50	4.01	0.89	76	79	4	21	16	6	12.9	50/17/33	22	85	138
		21	37	7	0	57	44	3.92	4.27	1.01	74	74	8	20	12	8	12.0	46/19/35	23	61	79
Wendelken, J.B.	R	20	28	1	0	25	31	1.80	4.00	1.12	89	65	10	30	19	9	11.5	46/14/40	28	88	133
		21	29	4	2	44	39	4.33	4.91	1.51	109	89	11	20	9	9	10.8	45/22/33	32	73	50
Williams, Trevor	R	20	29	2	0	55	49	6.18	4.99	1.57	101	154	8	19	11	9	10.9	45/20/35	32	68	84
		21*	30	6	0	110	102	3.85	4.60	1.38	106	115	7	22	15	6	10.7	46/23/31	34	75	92
Winkler, Daniel	R	20	31	0	0	18	18	2.95	4.76	1.20	62	96	14	24	9	10	12.7	42/22/36	19	84	38
		21	32	1	0	40	40	5.22	5.40	1.56	94	109	16	21	5	12	11.8	45/20/35	27	68	3
Wisler, Matthew	R	20	28	0	1	25	35	1.07	4.62	1.14	60	88	13	33	20	7	15.0	24/13/64	26	96	103
		21	29	3	1	49	62	3.70	3.68	1.07	95	90	6	32	26	7	14.0	25/26/50	32	70	169

2022 CHEATER'S BOOKMARK

PLAYER NOTES

BATTING STATISTICS / BENCHMARKS

Abbrv	Term	Formula / Desc.	BAD UNDER	'21 LG AVG AL	'21 LG AVG NL	BEST OVER
Avg	Batting Average	h/ab	225	246	249	275
xBA	Expected Batting Average	*See glossary*		251	254	
OB	On Base Average	(h+bb)/(ab+bb)	285	311	319	330
Slg	Slugging Average	total bases/ab	350	416	420	450
OPS	On Base plus Slugging	OB+Slg	650	727	739	800
bb%	Walk Rate	bb/(ab+bb)	6%	9%	9%	10%
ct%	Contact Rate	(ab-k) / ab	73%	74%	75%	83%
Eye	Batting Eye	bb/k	0.30	0.37	0.41	0.50
PX	Power Index	Normalized power skills	80	100	100	120
Spd	Speed Score	Normalized speed skills	80	100	100	120
SBA	Stolen Base Attempt Rate %	(sb+cs)/(singles+bb+hbp)		7%	7%	
G	Ground Ball Per Cent	gb / balls in play		42%	43%	
L	Line Drive Per Cent	ld / balls in play		21%	21%	
F	Fly Ball Per Cent	fb / balls in play		37%	36%	
HR/F	Home runs per fly ball	HR/FB		13%	14%	
Brl%	Barrel rate	barrels/batted ball event		8.3%	7.5%	
RAR	Runs Above Replacement	*See glossary*	0.0			10.0

Batting statistics do not include pitchers' batting statistics

PITCHING STATISTICS / BENCHMARKS

Abbrv	Term	Formula / Desc.	BAD OVER	'21 LG AVG AL	'21 LG AVG NL	BEST UNDER
ERA	Earned Run Average	er*9/ip	5.00	4.33	4.21	3.50
xERA	Expected ERA	*See glossary*		3.90	3.83	
WHIP	Baserunners per Inning	(h+bb)/ip	1.45	1.30	1.29	1.15
PC	Pitch Counts per Start		100	83	82	
H%	BatAvg on balls in play	(h-hr)/((ip*2.82)+h-k-hr)		29%	29%	
BB%	Walk percentage	BB/total batters faced	11%	9%	9%	7%
Ball%	Ball%	Balls/total pitches	38%	36%	36%	34%
HR/F	Homerun per Fly ball	HR/FB		13%	14%	
S%	Strand Rate	(h+bb-er)/(h+bb-hr)		71%	71%	
DIS%	PQS Disaster Rate	% GS that are PQS 0/1	36%	35%		15%

Abbrv	Term	Formula / Desc.	BAD UNDER	'21 LG AVG AL	'21 LG AVG NL	BEST OVER
RAR	Runs Above Replacement	*See glossary*	-0.0			+10
K%	Strikeout percentage	K/total batters faced	20%	23%	23%	28%
K-BB%	K rate minus BB rate	K%-BB%	10%	15%	14%	18%
SwK	Swinging Strike Percentage	swinging strikes/pitches		11.8%	11.7%	13.0%
DOM%	PQS Dominance Rate	% GS that are PQS 4/5		20%	22%	50%
Sv%	Saves Conversion Rate	(saves / save opps)		62%	60%	80%

Five-Year Injury Log

The following chart details the injured list stints for all players during the past five years. Use this as a supplement to our health grades in the player profile boxes as well as the "Risk Management" charts that start on page 271. It's also where to turn when in April you want to check whether, say, Andrelton Simmons' L ankle injury should be concerning (tip: it is), or where you might realize that 2021 was Nathan Eovaldi's first non-IL season in the past five.

For each injury, the number of days the player missed during the season is listed. A few IL stints are for fewer than 10 days; these are either cases when a player was placed on the IL prior to Opening Day or less than 10 days before the end of the season (only in-season time lost is listed) or when players went on the temporary "COVID-related" list for contact tracing or vaccination side effects.

Abbreviations:
Lt, L = left
Rt, R = right
fx = fractured
R/C = rotator cuff
str = strained
surg = surgery
TJS = Tommy John surgery (ulnar collateral ligament reconstruction)
x 2 = two occurrences of the same injury
x 3 = three occurrences of the same injury

Throughout the spring and all season long, BaseballHQ.com has comprehensive injury coverage.

FIVE-YEAR INJURY LOG — Hitters

Batter	Yr	Days	Injury
Abreu, Jose	18	20	Surg to repair ABD muscle
Acuña, Ronald	18	32	L knee & ACL strain
	20	11	Strn L wrist
	21	68	Torn ACL R knee
Adames, Willy	21	12	Strn L quad
Adams, Matt	18	15	Fractured L index finger
	19	18	L shoulder strain
	20	12	Strn L hamstring
	21	49	Bruised R shin; Strn R elbow
Adell, Jo	21	2	Strn lower back
Adrianza, Ehire	17	48	R oblique muscle; ab muscle
	18	11	Strn L hamstring
	19	11	Strn ab muscle
	21	7	COVID-related
Aguilar, Jesús	21	9	Inflammation L knee
Ahmed, Nick	17	95	Fractured R hand
	21	26	Inflam R knee; inflam R shoulder
Akiyama, Shogo	21	37	Strn R hamstring; strn L hamstring
Alberto, Hanser	17	182	Tightness R shoulder
	18	11	R hamstring strain
Albies, Ozzie	20	35	Wrist
Alfaro, Jorge	19	8	Concussion
	20	29	COVID-19
	21	34	Strn L hamstring
Alford, Anthony	20	20	Fractured R elbow, Covid-19
	21	9	Strn lower back
Almonte, Abraham	17	66	Strn R biceps; L hammy
Almora, Albert	21	39	Bruised L shoulder
Alonso, Pete	21	13	Sprained R hand
Altuve, Jose	18	24	R knee discomfort
	19	39	Strn L hamstring
	20	12	Sprained R knee
	21	13	COVID-19
Alvarez, Yordan	20	67	Surg repair ligament dam R knee
	21	8	COVID-related
Amburgey, Trey	21	31	Strn R hamstring
Anderson, Brian	19	38	Fx L finger
	21	88	Strn L oblique; sublux L shoulder
Anderson, Tim	19	34	Sprained R ankle
	20	11	Strn R groin
	21	25	Strn L hamstring x2

FIVE-YEAR INJURY LOG — Hitters

Batter	Yr	Days	Injury
Andrus, Elvis	18	67	Fractured R elbow
	19	11	Strn R hamstring
	20	30	Strn lower back
Andújar, Miguel	19	175	Surg repair torn labrum R shoulder
	21	97	Strn L wrist
Apostel, Sherten	20	4	Tightness lower back
Aquino, Aristides	21	59	Fractured hamate bone L hand
Araúz, Jonathan	21	13	COVID-19
Arenado, Nolan	20	9	Bone bruise L shoulder
Arozarena, Randy	20	39	COVID-19
	21	4	COVID-related
Arraez, Luis	20	19	Tendinitis L knee
	21	39	Concuss; inflam R shldr; R knee
Arroyo, Christian	18	30	Strn L oblique
	19	109	Strn R forearm
	20	2	COVID-related
	21	91	COVID-19; R knee contusion
Astudillo, Williams	19	82	Strn R hamstring
	20	20	COVID-19
Avila, Alex	18	11	Strn R hamstring
	19	51	Strn L calf
	20	12	Tightness lower back
	21	67	COVID-related; bilateral calf strains
Baddoo, Akil	21	13	Concussion
Bader, Harrison	19	11	Strn R hamstring
	21	68	Strn R forearm; fx R side rib
Báez, Javier	21	11	Strn lower back
Barnes, Austin	19	11	Strn L groin
Barnhart, Tucker	19	32	Strn R oblique
Barrera, Luis	19	22	R shoulder surgery
Barreto, Franklin	20	25	Subluxation L shoulder, Covid-19
	21	169	Strn R elbow
Basabe, Luis	20	6	Strn L hamstring
Beaty, Matt	19	11	Strn L hip flexor
Bell, Josh	18	12	Strn L oblique
	21	11	COVID-19
Bellinger, Cody	17	10	Sprained R ankle
	21	63	L hamstring strain; fx L fibula
Belt, Brandon	17	57	Concussion
	18	35	Appendectomy; hyperexnd R knee
	20	9	Tendinitis R Achilles
	21	57	Str L oblique;R knee infl;Fx L thumb
Bemboom, Anthony	19	61	Sprained L knee

FIVE-YEAR INJURY LOG — Hitters

Batter	Yr	Days	Injury
Benintendi,Andrew	20	47	Strn R ribcage muscle
	21	21	Fx R rib
Berti,Jon	19	72	Strn L oblique
	20	11	Laceration R index finger
	21	56	Concussion
Betts,Mookie	18	11	Pulled abdominal muscle
	21	24	Inflammation R hip x2
Bichette,Bo	20	28	Sprained R knee
Biggio,Cavan	21	66	Sprain cervical spine;midback tight
Bird,Greg	17	116	Bruised R ankle
	18	59	R ankle surgery
	19	168	Torn plantar fascia L foot
	20	8	Strn R calf
Bishop,Braden	19	89	Lacerated spleen
Blackmon,Charlie	19	12	Strn R calf
Blandino,Alex	18	73	Torn ACL - R knee
	21	108	COVID-related; fx R hand
Bogaerts,Xander	18	19	Stress fracture L ankle
	21	10	COVID-19
Bohm,Alec	21	13	COVID-19
Bote,David	21	69	Dislocate L shldr; sprain R ankle
Bradley,Bobby	21	21	Strn L knee
Bradley,Jackie	17	20	Sprained R knee; L thumb
Brantley,Michael	17	61	Sprained R ankle x2
	18	9	Recovery R ankle surgery
	20	8	Strn R quad
	21	17	Tightness R ham; sore R knee
Bregman,Alex	20	20	Sore R hamstring
	21	77	COVID-related; L quad strain
Brinson,Lewis	18	60	L hip inflammation
	20	12	Bone bruise R hip
	21	17	Sprained index finger L hand
Brosseau,Michael	21	13	Strn R oblique
Brown,Seth	21	15	COVID-19
Bruce,Jay	18	66	Sore R hip
	19	47	Strn R oblique muscle
	20	23	Sprained flexor tendon L elbow
Bryant,Kris	18	54	L shoulder inflammation x 2
	20	14	Sprained ring finger L hand
Buxton,Byron	17	17	Strn L groin
	18	57	Fractured great L toe; migraines
	19	73	Concus;L shldr sublux;brse R wrist
	20	12	Inflammation L shoulder
	21	111	Strn R hip; fx L hand
Cabrera,Asdrubal	17	21	Sprained L thumb x 2
	21	38	Strn R hamstring
Cabrera,Miguel	17	10	Strn R groin
	18	140	R ham. strn; Rup L biceps tendon
	21	15	Strn L biceps
Cain,Lorenzo	18	13	L groin strain
	21	77	Strn R hamstring; Strn L quad
Calhoun,Kole	18	17	R oblique strain
	21	119	Torn menisc R knee; str L hamst x2
Calhoun,Willie	19	27	Strn L quadriceps
	20	27	Strn L hamstring
	21	98	Strn L groin; fx ulna L forearm
Camargo,Johan	17	27	Bruised R knee
	18	21	Strn R oblique
	19	18	Fx shin R lower leg
Cameron,Daz	20	48	COVID-19
	21	46	Sprained R big toe
Campusano,Luis	20	16	Sprained L wrist

FIVE-YEAR INJURY LOG — Hitters

Batter	Yr	Days	Injury
Candelario,Jeimer	18	12	L wrist tendinitis
	19	71	Sprained L thumb; L shldr inflam
	21	4	COVID-related
Canha,Mark	19	16	Sprain R wrist
	21	23	Strn L hip
Canó,Robinson	17	12	Strn R quadriceps
	18	93	Fractured R hand
	19	52	Strn L quadriceps
	20	11	Strn L adductor muscle
Caratini,Victor	19	35	Fx hamate bone L hand
Carlson,Dylan	21	10	Sprained R wrist
Carpenter,Matt	19	33	Bruised R foot
Casali,Curt	19	40	Sprained R knee
	21	12	Strn L wrist
Castellanos,Nick	21	14	Sprained R wrist
Castillo,Welington	17	24	Tendinitis R should; testicular inj
	18	11	R shoulder inflammation
	19	37	Concussion; Strn L oblique
Castro,Harold	20	31	Strn L hamstring
Castro,Jason	17	11	Concussion
	18	149	Torn meniscus - R knee
	21	37	Sore R Achilles; sore R knee
Castro,Starlin	17	52	Strn R ham x2
	20	46	Fx R wrist
Castro,Willi	20	1	Sore R shoulder
Cave,Jake	21	71	Strn lower back
Cervelli,Francisco	17	59	Concuss x2; L wrist inflam; L quad
	18	30	Concussion
	19	90	Concussion
	20	37	Concussion
Céspedes,Yoenis	17	79	Strn L ham; Strn R ham
	18	136	Strn R hip; heel calcifications
	19	187	Recovery from L and R heel injuries
Chapman,Matt	17	11	L knee cellulitis
	18	18	R hand soreness
	20	17	Strn R hip, COVID-19
Chavis,Michael	19	49	Sprained AC joint L shoulder
	21	19	Strn R elbow
Chirinos,Robinson	20	14	Sprained R ankle
Chisholm,Jazz	21	38	COVID-related; Strn L hamstring
Choi,Ji-Man	19	11	Sprained L ankle
	20	16	Strn L hamstring
	21	73	Surge R knee; Strn groin; str L ham
Choo,Shin-Soo	20	19	Sprained R hand
Clement,Ernie	21	22	COVID-19
Conforto,Michael	17	48	Bruised L hand; Disloc L shoulder
	18	8	Recovery from L shoulder surgery
	19	10	Concussion
	20	5	Tightness L hamstring
	21	38	Strn R hamstring
Contreras,Willson	17	32	Strn R hamstring
	19	42	Strn R foot; Strn R hamstring
	21	24	Sprained R knee
	21	26	Sprained R knee; inflam R hip
Cooper,Garrett	17	46	L hamstring tendinitis
	18	163	R wrist contusion
	19	42	Strn L calf
	20	34	COVID-19
	21	79	COVID-rel; sprain L elbow; lumbar strn
Cordero,Franchy	18	140	L abductor strain; bone spur R elb
	19	176	Sprained R elb; stress reax R elbow
	20	46	Fractured hamate bone R wrist

FIVE-YEAR INJURY LOG — Hitters

Batter	Yr	Days	Injury
Correa,Carlos	17	47	Torn ligament L thumb
	18	43	Lower back soreness
	19	87	Fx ribs; lower back strain
	21	7	COVID-19
Cozart,Zack	17	21	Strn R quad; L quad
	18	109	Sprained L ankle
	19	141	Strn neck; L shoulder inflam
Crawford,Brandon	17	12	Strn R groin
	21	11	Strn L oblique
Crawford,J.P.	18	91	Strn R elbow
	19	17	Sprained L ankle
Cron,C.J.	17	15	Bruised L foot
	19	25	R thumb inflammation
	20	49	Sprained L knee
	21	12	Strn lower back
Cruz,Nelson	18	12	Sprained R ankle
	19	29	L wrist sprain
	21	2	COVID-related
Cuevas,Noel	19	42	Strn L quadriceps
Culberson,Charlie	19	13	Fx R cheekbone
	21	13	COVID-19
Cuthbert,Cheslor	17	41	Sprained L wrist
	18	136	Lower back strain
Dahl,David	17	108	Stress reaction ribcage
	18	123	Fractured R foot
	19	10	Strn abdominal
	20	42	Sore lower back, strnd R shoulder
	21	37	Bruised L rib cage
d'Arnaud,Travis	17	19	Bone bruise R wrist
	18	174	TJS
	19	11	TJS
	20	6	COVID-related
	21	102	Sprained L thumb
Davidson,Matthew	17	18	Bruised R wrist
	18	8	Back spasms
	20	7	COVID-related
Davis,Chris	17	29	Strn R oblique
	19	10	L hip flexor inflammation
	20	34	Patellar tendinitis L knee x2
	21	169	Strn lower back
Davis,J.D.	21	84	Bruised & sprained R hand
Davis,Jaylin	21	155	L patellar tendonitis; Strn L ham.
Davis,Jonathan	19	28	Sprained R ankle
	20	11	Sprained R ankle
Davis,Khris	18	9	Strn R groin
	19	11	L hip contusion
	21	38	Strn L quad
Daza,Yonathan	18	28	Strn L shoulder
	21	40	COVID-19; laceration L thumb
Dean,Austin	20	44	Strn R elbow, COVID-19
DeJong,Paul	18	50	Fractured L hand
	20	20	COVID-19
	21	30	Fx rib R side
Delmonico,Nick	17	11	Sprained R wrist
	18	63	Fractured R hand
Descalso,Daniel	19	40	Sprained L ankle
	20	68	Sprained L ankle
DeShields,Delino	18	48	Fx R fing; concussion; Fx L hamate
	20	15	COVID-19
Desmond,Ian	17	72	Fx L hand; Strn R calf x 2
Devers,José	21	95	Impingement R shoulder
Devers,Rafael	18	40	L should. inflam; Strn L ham.

FIVE-YEAR INJURY LOG — Hitters

Batter	Yr	Days	Injury
Díaz,Aledmys	18	25	Sprained L ankle
	19	67	Dizziness; Strn L hamstring
	20	36	Strn R groin
	21	51	Fx L hand
Díaz,Elias	19	25	Viral infection
Díaz,Isan	20	14	Strn L groin
	21	3	COVID-related
Díaz,Yandy	19	91	Strn R ham; bruised L foot
	20	28	Strn R hamstring
Dickerson,Alex	17	182	Herniated disc
	18	187	TJS
	19	28	Strn R oblique muscle; strn R wrist
	21	37	Impinge R shldr;up back;R hamstr
Dickerson,Corey	18	8	Strn L hamstring
	19	80	Strn R shoulder; Fx L foot
	21	50	Bruised L foot
Dietrich,Derek	19	20	L shoulder inflammation
Donaldson,Josh	17	42	Strn R calf
	18	125	R shoulder inflam; tight L calf x 2
	20	27	Strn R calf
	21	12	Strn R hamstring
Dozier,Hunter	17	60	Strn L oblique
	19	22	Bruised chest
	20	18	COVID-19
	21	15	Concussion
Drury,Brandon	18	94	Migraines; fractured L hand
Duffy,Matt	17	182	Recovery surgery L Achilles
	18	11	Strn R hamstring
	19	118	Tightness L hamstring
	21	66	Strn lower back; COVID-related
Duggar,Steven	18	34	Torn labrum - L shoulder
	19	67	Strn low back;sprn AC joint L shldr
Duran,Jarren	21	15	COVID-19
Dyson,Jarrod	17	13	Strn R groin
	18	89	Strn R groin
Eaton,Adam	17	155	Torn ACL L knee
	18	60	Bone bruise - L ankle
	20	12	Fractured L index finger
Encarnación,Edwin	18	11	L biceps inflammation
	19	32	Fx R wrist
Engel,Adam	20	3	COVID-related
	21	119	Strn R hamstring
Escobar,Eduardo	21	12	Strn R hamstring
Espinal,Santiago	21	19	Strn R hip flexor
Espinoza,Anderson	20	68	TJS
Estrada,Thairo	19	22	Strn R hamstring
Evans,Phillip	18	61	Fractured L tibia
	20	51	Fractured jaw, concussion
	21	38	Concussion; Strn L hamstring
Fairchild,Stuart	21	20	COVID-19
Fargas,Johneshwy	21	51	Sprained A/C joint L shoulder
Farmer,Kyle	19	27	Strn L oblique; concussion
Fisher,Derek	18	15	Gastrointestinal discomfort
	20	34	Strn L quad, bruised R knee
	21	78	Strn L hamstring
Flaherty,Ryan	17	88	Strn R shoulder
Fletcher,David	20	13	Sprained L ankle
Flores,Wilmer	17	12	Infection R knee
	18	19	Lower back soreness
	19	59	Fx R foot
	21	22	Strn R hamstring
Flowers,Tyler	17	10	Bruised L wrist
	18	29	L oblique strain
	20	7	COVID-related

FIVE-YEAR INJURY LOG — Hitters

Batter	Yr	Days	Injury
Forsythe,Logan	17	34	Fractured R big toe
	18	31	R shoulder inflammation
	20	32	Strn R oblique
Fowler,Dexter	17	25	Spur R heel; L forearm
	18	59	Fractured L foot
	20	20	COVID-19
	21	160	Sprained L knee
Fowler,Dustin	17	93	Ruptured patella tendon R knee
Fraley,Jake	20	6	Strn R quad
	21	89	COVID-19; Strn L hamstr;inflam R shldr
France,Ty	21	10	Inflammation L wrist
Franco,Maikel	21	17	Sprained R ankle
Franco,Wander	21	6	Tightness R hamstring
Frazier,Adam	17	29	Strn L ham x 2
Frazier,Clint	17	33	Strn L oblique
	18	113	Concussion
	19	12	Sprained L ankle
	21	78	Medical Illness
Frazier,Todd	18	54	Strnd L hammy; strnd L rib cage
	19	26	Strn L oblique
Freeman,Freddie	17	47	Fractured L wrist
Freese,David	17	13	Strn R hamstring
	19	56	Strn L hamstring
Gallagher,Cameron	19	25	Strn L oblique
	20	11	COVID-19
	21	54	Concussion; R shldr imping; L knee
Gallo,Joey	17	7	Concussion
	19	92	Strn L oblique
Galvis,Freddy	21	59	Strn R quad
Gamel,Ben	20	10	Strn L quad
	21	11	Strn R hamstring
Garcia,Aramis	20	68	Torn labrum L hip
	21	10	Viral enteritis
García,Avisaíl	17	13	Sprained R thumb
	18	72	Strn R hamstring x 2
	19	11	Strn R oblique muscle
García,Leury	17	70	Sprained L finger; R thumb
	18	75	Strn L hamstring x 2; spr. L knee
	20	49	Sprained L thumb
	21	12	Concussion
García,Luis (WAS)	21	3	Strn oblique
García,Robel	21	7	COVID-related
Gardner,Brett	19	12	L knee inflammation
Garlick,Kyle	20	13	Strn R oblique
	21	110	Sports hernia; COVID-19
Garver,Mitch	19	19	High ankle sprain L ankle
	20	30	Strn R intercostal muscle
	21	69	Surgery groin; lower back tightness
Gennett,Scooter	19	93	Strn R groin
Giménez,Andrés	20	7	Tight R oblique
Gittens,Chris	21	20	Sprained R ankle
Gomes,Yan	21	24	COVID-related; Strn L oblique
González,Erik	19	105	Fx L clavicle
	21	37	Strn R oblique
González,Luis	21	45	R shoulder surgery
Gonzalez,Marwin	19	11	Strn R hamstring
	21	22	Strn R hamstring
Goodrum,Niko	19	38	Strn L groin
	20	11	Strn R oblique
	21	67	Spr L hand; bruised L calf; groin
Goodwin,Brian	17	46	Strn L groin
	18	109	L wrist contusion; groin strain
	19	14	Bruised R wrist

FIVE-YEAR INJURY LOG — Hitters

Batter	Yr	Days	Injury
Gordon,Dee	18	10	Fractured R great toe
	19	41	Strn L quad; bruised R wrist
Gordon,Nick	20	68	COVID-19
Grandal,Yasmani	21	53	Torn tendon L knee
Graterol,Juan	19	44	Concussion
Green,Zach	19	24	L hip impingement
Gregorius,Didi	17	26	Strn R shoulder
	18	18	Bruised L heel
	19	72	TJS
	21	52	COVID-related; impingement R elbow
Greiner,Grayson	19	70	Strn lower back
	21	38	Strn L hamstring
Grichuk,Randal	17	11	Strn lower back
	18	32	R knee sprain
Grisham,Trent	21	29	Strn R hamstring; bruised L heel
Grossman,Robbie	17	18	Fractured L thumb
	18	14	Strn R hamstring
Guillorme,Luis	21	75	Strn R oblique; Strn L hamstring
Gurriel,Lourdes	18	32	Concussion; sprained L knee/ankle
	19	43	Appendectomy; Strn L quad
	21	3	COVID-related
Gurriel,Yulieski	18	11	Recov hamate surgery, L hand
	21	12	Strn neck
Gutierrez,Kelvin	19	19	Fx toe R foot
	20	52	Strn R elbow
Guzmán,Ronald	18	8	Concussion
	19	32	Strn R hamstring
	21	157	Torn lateral meniscus R knee
Gyorko,Jedd	17	16	Strn R hamstring
	18	29	Ham strain; R shoulder impinge
	19	81	Strn back; Strn L calf
Haase,Eric	21	12	Strn abdominal muscle
Haggerty,Sam	20	22	Strn L forearm
	21	116	Inflamed R shoulder
Hamilton,Billy	17	12	Fractured L thumb
	21	73	Strn L hamstring; Strn R oblique x2
Haniger,Mitch	17	66	Strn R oblique; face laceration
	19	116	Ruptured testicle
	20	67	Strn ab muscle
Happ,Ian	21	12	Bruised ribs
Harper,Bryce	17	44	Hyperextended L knee
	21	14	Bruised L forearm
Harrison,Josh	17	28	Fractured metacarpal L hand
	18	35	Fractured metacarpal - L hand
	19	91	Strn L ham tendon; L shldr inflam
	21	11	COVID-19
Haseley,Adam	19	23	Strn L groin
	20	10	Sprained R wrist
	21	55	COVID-19
Hayes,Ke'Bryan	21	61	Sore L wrist
Hays,Austin	18	8	Sprained R ankle
	20	31	Non-displaced fx rib L side
	21	35	Strn R & L hamstring
Healy,Ryon	18	18	Sprained R ankle
	19	133	Lower back inflammation
Heath,Nick	20	24	Strn L hamstring
Hechavarria,Adeiny	17	59	Strn IL oblique; L ham
	18	30	Strn R hamstring
Hedges,Austin	17	12	Concussion
	21	7	Concussion
Heim,Jonah	21	7	COVID-related
Heineman,Scott	19	98	Recovery from surgery L shoulder
Heredia,Guillermo	21	16	Inflammation R hamstring

FIVE-YEAR INJURY LOG — Hitters

Batter	Yr	Days	Injury
Hermosillo, Michael	19	187	Abdominal muscle injury
	21	26	Strn L forearm
Hernández, César	17	36	Strn L oblique
Hernández, Enrique	19	23	Sprained L hand
	21	24	COVID-19; Strn R hamstring
Hernández, Marco	17	150	L shoulder subluxation
	18	187	Recovery from L shoulder surgery
	19	29	Recovery from L shoulder surgery
Hernández, Teoscar	17	18	Bruised L knee
	20	10	Strn L oblique
	21	22	COVID-19
Herrera, Odúbel	17	17	Strn L hamstring
	19	16	Strn R hamstring
	21	14	Tendinitis L ankle
Heyward, Jason	17	24	Sprn R finger; lacerated R hand
	18	28	Concussion; R hamstring tightness
	21	30	Concus;str L ham;infl L index fing
Hicks, Aaron	17	68	Strn R oblique; L oblique
	18	14	R intercostal muscle strain
	19	105	Strn L lower back
	21	127	Sprained L wrist
Hicks, John	18	55	Strn R groin
Higashioka, Kyle	20	25	Strn R oblique
	21	12	COVID-19
Higgins, P.J.	21	98	Strn R forearm
Hill, Aaron	17	32	Strn R forearm
Hill, Derek	21	31	Sprain R shldr; bruised ribs; L knee
Hiura, Keston	19	12	Strn L hamstring
	21	15	COVID-19
Hoerner, Nico	21	101	Str L forearm;str L ham;str R obliq
Holt, Brock	17	86	Vertigo
	18	12	Strn L hamstring
	19	52	Scratched cornea R eye
	21	51	COVID-19; Strn R hamstring
Hoskins, Rhys	18	10	Facial injury
	20	16	Strn L elbow
	21	38	Strn L groin; ab surgery
Hosmer, Eric	20	20	Gastritis, fx index finger L hand
	21	7	COVID-related
Huff, Sam	21	108	Strn L hamstring
Hundley, Nick	19	46	Back spasms
Iannetta, Chris	17	7	Concussion
	19	19	Strn R lat muscle
Ibáñez, Andy	21	19	Strn L hamstring
Iglesias, José	17	7	Concussion
	18	33	Lower abdominal strain
	20	12	Strn L quad
	21	11	Strn L hamstring
Inciarte, Ender	19	109	Strn lumbar region; str. R hammy
	21	34	Strn L hamstring; COVID-19
India, Jonathan	21	2	COVID-related
Jackson, Alex	19	26	Sprained L knee
	21	81	Strn L hamstring
Jankowski, Travis	17	102	Bone bruise R foot
	19	117	Fx L wrist
	21	16	COVID-related; bruised R foot
Jansen, Danny	21	67	Strn R hamstring
Jay, Jon	19	121	Sore L shoulder
Jiménez, Eloy	19	36	Bruise uln nerve R elb;R ankle sprn
	21	117	Surgery - torn L pectoral tendon
Joe, Connor	21	13	Strn R hamstring

FIVE-YEAR INJURY LOG — Hitters

Batter	Yr	Days	Injury
Jones, JaCoby	17	15	Lacerated lip
	18	15	R hamstring strain
	19	82	Sprn R shldr; strn back; Fx L wrist
	20	27	Fractured L hand
Jones, Taylor	21	19	COVID-19
Joyce, Matt	18	74	Lumbar strain x 2
	20	12	COVID-19
	21	102	Strn R calf; Strn lower back
Judge, Aaron	18	50	Chip fracture, R wrist
	19	62	Strn L oblique
	20	34	Strn R calf x2
	21	12	COVID-19
Kang, Jung Ho	19	26	Strn L oblique
Kelly, Carson	18	10	R hamstring strain
	21	52	Fx L big toe; fx R wrist
Kemp, Matt	17	31	Strn R hamstring x 2
	19	12	Fx L rib
Kendrick, Howie	17	62	Strn R Ab; L ham
	18	135	Torn R Achilles
	19	20	Strn L hamstring
	20	20	Strn L hamstring
Kepler, Max	20	10	Strn L adductor muscle
	21	30	COVID-19; Strn L hamstring
Kieboom, Carter	20	7	Contusion L wrist
Kieboom, Spencer	19	23	R elbow inflammation
Kiermaier, Kevin	17	70	Fractured R hip
	18	65	Torn ligament R rhumb
	19	11	Sprained L thumb
	21	23	Strn L quad; COVID-related; spr R wrist
Kiner-Falefa, Isiah	19	44	Sprained ligament R middle finger
Kingery, Scott	19	30	Strn R hamstring
	20	15	Back spasms
	21	22	Concussion
Kinsler, Ian	17	10	Strn L hamstring
	18	27	L adductor strain; Strn L ham.
	19	49	Herniated cervical disc low region
Kipnis, Jason	17	72	R shoulder inflam; R ham x2
	19	19	Strn R calf
Kirilloff, Alex	21	77	Torn ligament R wrist
Kirk, Alejandro	21	80	Strn L hip flexor
Knapp, Andrew	17	37	Fractured R hand
	21	25	COVID-19; concussion
Kramer, Kevin	20	67	Recovery from R hip surgery
Kratz, Erik	19	9	Strn L hamstring
Lagares, Juan	17	66	Strn L oblique; L thumb
	18	137	L toe surgery
	21	18	Strn R calf
LaMarre, Ryan	21	28	Strn R hamstring
Lamb, Jake	18	113	Sprained L AC joint
	19	83	Strn L quad
	21	40	Strn R quad muscle
LaStella, Tommy	19	87	Fx tibia L leg
	21	93	Strn L hamstring
Laureano, Ramon	19	38	R lower leg stress reaction
	21	19	Strn R hip
LeMahieu, D.J.	18	40	Strn R ham; L thumb; L oblique
	20	14	Sprained L thumb, COVID-19
	21	3	Sports hernia
Lewis, Kyle	21	128	Bone brs R knee;torn menisc R kn
Lin, Tzu-Wei	19	150	Sprained L knee
Lindor, Francisco	19	24	Strn R calf
	21	39	Strn R oblique
Lobaton, Jose	21	79	Strn R shoulder
Locastro, Tim	21	78	Torn ACL R knee

FIVE-YEAR INJURY LOG — Hitters

Batter	Yr	Days	Injury
Long,Shed	20	20	Stress fracture L tibia
	21	114	Stress Fx R shin
Longoria,Evan	18	42	Fractured L hand
	19	21	Plantar fasciitis L foot
	20	9	Strn R oblique
	21	83	Sprain R shldr; brse R hand; COVID-rel
Lopes,Timmy	19	12	Concussion
	21	61	Strn R oblique
Lowe,Brandon	19	83	Bone bruise R shin
Lowrie,Jed	19	164	Sprained L knee capsule
	20	68	Capsule injury L knee
Lucroy,Jonathan	19	23	Concussion
Luplow,Jordan	19	28	Strn R hamstring
	21	76	Sprained L ankle
Lux,Gavin	21	41	Strn L hamstring; sore R wrist
Madrigal,Nick	20	23	Separated L shoulder
	21	98	Surgery R hamstring
Maile,Luke	17	59	Inflam R knee
	19	53	L oblique strain
	20	68	Fractured R index finger
Maldonado,Martin	21	6	COVID-related
Mancini,Trey	20	67	Recovery from colon cancer
Margot,Manuel	17	31	Strn R calf
	18	11	Bruised ribs
	21	21	Strn L hamstring
Marisnick,Jake	17	7	Concussion
	18	22	L groin discomfort
	20	39	Strn L hamstring
	21	29	Strn R hamstring
Markakis,Nick	19	49	Fractured L wrist
	20	7	COVID-related
Marte,Ketel	20	14	Inflammation L wrist
	21	77	Strn R & L hamstrings
Marte,Starling	18	9	Strn R oblique
	19	11	Bruised abdominal wall
	21	39	Fx rib
Martin,Jason	19	28	Dislocated L shoulder
	20	8	Strn upper back
Martin,Leonys	18	83	Strnd L ham x2; bacterial infection
Martin,Richie	20	68	Fractured R wrist
	21	64	Fx L wrist
Martin,Russell	17	45	Nerve irritation L shldr; L oblique
	19	18	Lower back inflam
Martinez,J.D.	17	42	Sprained ligament R foot
	21	1	COVID-related
Martínez,José	17	22	Strn L groin
	19	21	Sprained AC joint R shoulder
	21	169	Torn meniscus L knee
Martini,Nick	19	62	Sprained R knee
Mateo,Jorge	20	22	COVID-19
	21	26	Strn lower back; COVID-related
Mathias,Mark	21	169	Torn labrum R shoulder
Mathis,Jeff	17	38	Fractured R hand
Maybin,Cameron	17	27	Strn L oblique; MCL R knee
	19	35	Strn L calf
	20	15	Strn R quad
Mazara,Nomar	18	28	Sprained R thumb
	19	13	Strn L oblique
	20	12	COVID-19
	21	25	Strn L ab muscle
McCann,Brian	17	17	Concussion; sore R knee
	18	72	Strn R knee
	19	23	L knee spasm; L ham strain

FIVE-YEAR INJURY LOG — Hitters

Batter	Yr	Days	Injury
McCann,James	17	14	Laceration on L hand
	21	19	Strn lower back
McCormick,Chas	21	12	Sore L hand
McCutchen,Andrew	19	119	Torn ACL L knee
	21	11	Inflammation L knee
McKinney,Billy	18	55	L AC shoulder sprain
	21	24	R hip impingement
McKinstry,Zach	21	38	Strn R oblique
McMahon,Ryan	19	13	Sprained L elbow
McNeil,Jeff	19	29	Strn L ham; Fx R wrist
	21	36	Strn L hamstring
Meadows,Austin	19	20	Sprained R thumb
	20	24	Strn L oblique, COVID-19
Mejía,Francisco	19	41	Strn R oblique muscle; sore L knee
	20	31	Thumb
	21	10	L intercostal injury
Mercer,Jordy	18	14	Strn L calf
	19	73	Strn R quad
	21	75	COVID-related; Strn R quad; str L calf
Miller,Brad	17	44	Strn L ab; L groin
	18	12	Groin strain
	19	12	Strn R hip flexor
Molina,Yadier	18	31	Pelvic injury
	19	48	Strn tendon R thumb
	20	17	COVID-19
	21	12	Strn tendon R foot
Moncada,Yoán	17	11	Bone bruise R shin
	18	10	Tight L hamstring
	19	23	Strn R hamstring
Mondesi,Adalberto	18	33	R shoulder impingement syndrome
	19	61	Strn R groin
	21	140	Strn R oblique; L ham; L oblique
Moore,Dylan	19	12	Bruised R wrist
	20	22	Concussion, sprained R wrist
	21	25	Strn L calf
Morales,Kendrys	18	11	Strn R hamstring
	19	110	Strn L calf
Moran,Colin	17	56	Facial fractures
	20	5	Concussion
	21	69	Strn L groin; fx L wrist
Moreland,Mitch	19	59	Strn R quad
	21	47	Inflam cartilage L rib; L wrist
Moroff,Max	21	113	L shoulder subluxation
Morrison,Logan	18	63	L hip impingement
Mountcastle,Ryan	21	11	Concussion
Moustakas,Mike	20	15	Bruised L quad, COVID-related
	21	91	Non-COVID illness; bruised R heel
Muncy,Max	19	16	Fx R wrist
	21	11	Strn R oblique
Muñoz,Yairo	18	12	Sprained R wrist
	20	11	Lower back strain
	21	16	COVID-19
Murphy,Tom	17	74	Fractured R forearm
	20	68	Fractured metatarsal L foot
Myers,Wil	18	81	Nerve irrit;bone bruise L Ft;L obliq
	20	2	Recovery from bone spur surgery
	21	12	COVID-19
Naquin,Tyler	18	101	R hip strain; Strn L ham.
	19	53	Torn ACL R knee; Strn L calf
	20	18	Hairline fx L big toe
Narváez,Omar	21	13	Strn L hamstring
Naylor,Josh	21	81	Fx R ankle
Newman,Kevin	19	24	Lacerated R middle finger
	20	9	Bruised peroneal nerve L knee

FIVE-YEAR INJURY LOG — Hitters

Batter	Yr	Days	Injury
Nido,Tomás	19	9	Concussion
	20	35	COVID-19
	21	42	Bruised R wrist; sprained L thumb x2
Nimmo,Brandon	17	64	Strn R ham; collapsed lung
	18	9	Bruised L index finger
	19	132	Stiff neck
	21	72	Bruised L index fing; Strn R hamstr
Nogowski,John	21	29	Bone bruise L hand
Nola,Austin	21	88	Fx L middle finger; sprained L knee
Nottingham,Jacob	21	22	Sprained L thumb
Núñez,Eduardo	17	21	Strn hamstring
	19	17	Strn lower back
	20	60	Knee
Núñez,Renato	18	19	Strn L hamstring
O'Brien,Peter	19	143	Bruised L rib
	20	25	Undisclosed injury
Odor,Rougned	18	32	Strn L hamstring
	19	14	Sprained R knee
	20	10	Infection R eye
	21	14	COVID-related; sprained L knee
O'Hearn,Ryan	20	6	COVID-related
Ohtani,Shohei	18	26	Sprained UCL, R elbow
	19	41	Recovery from TJS
Olson,Matt	19	41	R hand surgery
Oña,Jorge	21	169	Strn R elbow
O'Neill,Tyler	18	22	Inflammation groin area
	19	41	Ulnar nerve subluxation R elbow
	21	24	Strn R groin; fx L middle finger
Owings,Chris	17	62	Fractured R middle finger
	20	40	Strn L hamstring
	21	134	Spr L thumb;mallet fing inj L thumb
Ozuna,Marcell	18	11	R shoulder inflammation
	19	94	Fx middle finger on R hand
	21	108	Fx L index finger
Pache,Cristian	21	31	Strn L groin; inflammation R ham
Panik,Joe	17	10	Concussion
	18	59	Sprnd L thumb; L groin strain
	21	37	COVID-19
Paredes,Isaac	20	17	COVID-19
	21	30	Strn R hip
Parra,Gerardo	17	30	Strn R quadriceps
	21	12	Inflammation R knee
Pearce,Steven	17	32	Strn R calf
	18	50	L oblique strain
	19	129	Strn lower back; L calf muscle
Pederson,Joc	17	32	Strn R groin; concussion
	21	12	Tendinitis L wrist
Pedroia,Dustin	17	45	Sprained L wrist; L knee inflam
	18	180	L knee surgery (meniscus)
	19	178	Recovery from L knee surgery
	20	68	Recovery from knee surgery
Pence,Hunter	17	20	Strn L hamstring
	18	44	Sprained R thumb
	19	68	Strn R groin; Strn low back
Peralta,David	19	70	R shoulder AC joint inflammation
Peralta,Jhonny	17	29	Upper respiratory ailment
Peraza,José	21	58	Fx R middle finger
Perdomo,Luis	20	8	R forearm inflam
Perez,Michael	18	32	L hamstring strain
	19	34	Strn R oblique
Pérez,Roberto	20	21	Strn R shoulder
	21	102	Inflam R shldr; fx finger R hand

Batter	Yr	Days	Injury
Perez,Salvador	17	16	Strn R intercostal
	18	27	Sprained R MCL
	19	187	Recovery from TJS
	20	25	CSC L eye
Peterson,Jace	21	40	COVID-related; sprained L thumb
Pham,Tommy	18	14	Fractured R foot
	20	33	Fractured hamate bone R hand
Phegley,Josh	17	44	Concussion; L oblique
	18	24	Fractured R hand
	19	17	L thumb contusion
Phillips,Brett	20	8	COVID-related
	21	23	Strn L hamstring; sprained R ankle
Pillar,Kevin	18	20	Sprained R shoulder
	21	14	Multiple facial fractures
Piña,Manny	18	22	R calf strain; L biceps strain
	19	17	Strn R hamstring
	20	32	Torn meniscus R knee
	21	25	Strn L oblique; fx big toe L foot
Pinder,Chad	17	37	Strn L hamstring
	18	20	Hyperext. L knee; L elb laceration
	20	15	Strn R hamstring
	21	85	Sprained L knee; Strn R hamstring
Pirela,José	19	90	Strn L oblique
Piscotty,Stephen	17	32	Strn R ham; R groin
	19	68	Sprained R knee; R ankle
	21	46	Sprained L wrist x2
Plawecki,Kevin	18	46	Hairline fracture - L hand
	21	19	Strn L hamstring
Polanco,Gregory	17	45	Strn L ham x 3
	18	14	Surgery to stabilize L shoulder
	19	127	L shoulder inflammation
	20	7	COVID-19
	21	20	COVID-related; sore R shoulder
Pollock,A.J.	17	50	Strn R groin
	18	49	Fractured L thumb
	19	74	R elbow inflammation
	21	32	L hamstring; R hamstring
Profar,Jurickson	21	22	COVID-19
Puello,César	19	57	Strn L hip flexor
Pujols,Albert	18	44	L knee surgery
Quinn,Roman	19	181	Strn R groin; Strn R oblique muscle
	21	133	COVID-related: torn L Achilles
Ramirez,Harold	20	64	Strn L hamstring, COVID-19
	21	21	Strn R hamstring
Ramírez,José	19	31	Fx hamate bone R hand
Ramos,Wilson	17	85	Surg R knee to repair torn ACL
	18	29	Strn L hamstring
	21	51	Torn ACL L knee;
Rasmus,Colby	17	51	Recov surgery on hip; hip tend
	18	76	L hip flexor strain
Ravelo,Rangel	20	29	COVID-19
Realmuto,J.T.	18	20	Lower back bruise
	21	14	COVID-related; bone bruise L wrist
Reddick,Josh	17	7	Concussion
	18	15	Leg infection
Refsnyder,Rob	21	61	Concussion; Strn L hamstr; R elbow
Rendon,Anthony	18	13	L toe contusion
	19	11	Bruised L elbow
	21	98	Groin strain;L ham strn;L knee brse
Renfroe,Hunter	17	10	Strn neck
	18	38	R elbow inflammation
Rengifo,Luis	19	13	Fx hamate bone L hand
	20	9	Strn R hamstring
Reyes,Franmil	21	41	Strn abdominal muscle

FIVE-YEAR INJURY LOG — Hitters

Batter	Yr	Days	Injury
Reyes,Victor	21	37	Strn intercostal; Strn R groin
Rickard,Joey	17	19	Sprnd L pinky fing & middle fing
	20	29	Inflammation L elbow
Riddle,J.T.	17	68	L biceps tendinitis
	18	36	Recovery from L shoulder surgery
	19	75	Strn R forearm
	20	14	Strn ab muscle
Riley,Austin	19	33	Torn LCL R knee
Ríos,Edwin	20	16	Strn L hamstring
	21	135	Partially torn R rotator cuff
Rivera,Emmanuel	21	36	Fx hamate bone R hand
Rivera,René	18	88	R knee inflammation
	20	58	Hyperextended L elbow
	21	46	Bruised R elbow
Rivera,T.J.	17	65	Partially torn UCL R elbow
	18	187	TJS
Rizzo,Anthony	18	9	Lower back tightness
	21	11	COVID-19
Robert,Luis	21	101	COVID-related; torn flexor tendon R hip
Robertson,Daniel	17	35	Neck spasms
	18	71	Sprnd L thumb; strnd L hamstring
	19	39	Recov R knee surgery (meniscus)
	21	26	Concussion
Robles,Victor	21	12	Sprained R ankle
Rodgers,Brendan	19	98	R shoulder impingement
	20	29	Strn capsule R shoulder
	21	51	Strn R hamstring
Rodríguez,Manuel	20	3	Strn R biceps
Rodríguez,Sean	17	106	Recovery from L shoulder surgery
	18	42	Strn R quad; Strn L abdom
	19	15	Strn R abdominal muscle
Rogers,Jake	21	31	Strn pronator R arm
Rojas,Josh	20	7	Lower back inflammation
	21	20	Dislocated R pinkie finger
Rojas,Miguel	17	70	Fractured R thumb
	19	26	Strn R hamstring
	20	17	COVID-19
	21	22	Dislocation index finger L hand
Romine,Austin	21	123	Sprain R knee;spr L wrist; undisc
Rooker,Brent	20	16	Fx R forearm
	21	14	Strn neck
Rosario,Eddie	19	19	Sprained L ankle
	21	52	Strn abdominal muscle
Rua,Ryan	18	45	Back spasms
Ruf,Darin	21	26	Strn R hamstring
Rutledge,Josh	17	127	Strn L ham: concussion
Saladino,Tyler	17	48	Back spasms
	18	37	Sprained L ankle
Sánchez,Gary	17	27	Strn R biceps
	18	65	R groin strain
	19	32	Strn L groin
	21	13	COVID-19
Sánchez,Jesús	21	52	COVID-19; Strn R groin
Sandoval,Pablo	17	59	Sprained R knee; ear infection
	18	63	R hamstring strain
	19	50	R elbow inflammation
Sanó,Miguel	17	39	Stress reaction L shin
	18	24	Strn L hamstring
	19	49	Laceration on R heel
	21	15	Strn R hamstring
Santana,Danny	17	54	Bacterial infection; Strn L quad
	20	48	Strn R forearm
	21	64	COVID-19; L groin strain; L quad strain
Santana,Domingo	19	30	Inflammation R elbow

FIVE-YEAR INJURY LOG — Hitters

Batter	Yr	Days	Injury
Santander,Anthony	17	136	R elbow inflammation
	20	24	Strn R oblique
	21	41	COVID-related; sprained R knee
Schebler,Scott	17	17	Strn L shoulder
	18	51	R ulnar nerve bruise; sprn R A/C
	20	2	COVID-related
Schoop,Jonathan	18	25	R oblique strain
	20	16	Sprained R wrist
Schrock,Max	21	38	Strn L calf
Schwarber,Kyle	21	50	COVID-related; Strn R hamstring
Seager,Corey	18	154	UCL strain - R elbow
	19	29	Strn L hamstring
	21	76	Fx R hand
Seager,Kyle	19	58	Recovery from surgery L hand
Segura,Jean	17	33	Strn R ham; high R ankle sprain
	19	11	Strn L hamstring
	21	30	Strn R quad; Strn L groin
Semien,Marcus	17	81	Bruised R wrist
Senzel,Nick	20	27	COVID-19
	21	87	Inflammation & surgery L knee
Shaw,Travis	19	21	Strn R wrist
	21	66	Dislocated L shoulder
Sierra,Magneuris	20	32	Strn R hamstring
Simmons,Andrelton	18	11	Grade 2 R ankle sprain
	19	60	Sprained L ankle
	20	25	Sprained L ankle
	21	13	COVID-19
Slater,Austin	17	59	Strn R groin
	20	14	Strn L groin
	21	7	Concussion
Smith Jr.,Dwight	19	38	Concussion; Strn L calf
Smith,Dominic	19	62	Stress reaction L foot
Smith,Kevan	18	24	Sprained L ankle
	19	55	Concuss; sprn L hand; back spasms
	20	2	COVID-related
Smith,Mallex	17	13	Strn R hamstring
	18	10	Viral infection
Smith,Pavin	21	5	COVID-related
Smith,Will	20	24	Neck inflammation
Smoak,Justin	19	11	Strn L quadriceps
Sogard,Eric	17	16	Strn L ankle
	21	11	Bruised L thumb
Solano,Donovan	21	50	COVID-19; Strn R calf
Soler,Jorge	17	34	Strn L oblique
	18	107	Fractured L toe
	20	15	Strn R oblique
Sosa,Edmundo	20	24	COVID-19
Soto,Geovany	17	154	R elbow inflam
Soto,Juan	19	11	Back spasms
	20	12	COVID-19
	21	15	Strn L shoulder
Souza,Steven	18	81	Strn R pectoral muscle
	19	186	Recovery from torn ACL, PCL & LCL
	20	16	Strn R hamstring
Springer,George	17	12	L quadriceps injury
	18	12	Sprained L thumb
	19	31	Strn L hamstring
	21	95	Strn L oblique;str R quad;spr L knee
Stallings,Jacob	20	1	Concussion
Stanton,Giancarlo	19	164	Sprained PCL R knee
	20	38	Strn L hamstring
	21	15	Strn L quad

FIVE-YEAR INJURY LOG — Hitters

Batter	Yr	Days	Injury
Stassi,Max	17	10	L hand inflammation
	19	27	Sore L knee
	20	17	Strn R quad
	21	43	Concussion; sprained L thumb
Stevenson,Andrew	19	16	Back spasms
	21	33	Strn oblique muscle
Stewart,Christin	19	45	Concussion; Strn R quad
Stewart,D.J.	19	50	Concussion; sprained R ankle
	21	10	R Knee osteochondral defect
Stokes,Troy	20	51	Fx bone R hand
Story,Trevor	17	12	Strn L shoulder
	19	13	Sprained R thumb
	21	14	Inflammation R elbow
Suárez,Eugenio	18	18	Fractured R thumb
Susac,Andrew	17	28	Strn trap x 2
Swanson,Dansby	18	16	L wrist inflammation
	19	34	Bruised R heel
Swihart,Blake	18	12	Strn R hamstring
	19	68	Strn R oblique
Tapia,Raimel	19	11	Bruised L hand
	21	21	Sprained big toe R foot
Tatis Jr.,Fernando	19	86	Strn L ham; stress reax low back
	21	36	COVID-19; L shoulder subluxation x2
Tauchman,Mike	19	22	Strn L calf
	21	17	Sprained R knee
Taylor,Chris	19	37	Fx L forearm
Taylor,Michael	17	37	Strn R oblique muscle
	19	12	Sprained L knee
Taylor,Tyrone	21	39	Strn R oblique; Strn R shoulder
Tellez,Rowdy	20	21	Knee
	21	30	Strn patella tendon R knee
Thames,Eric	18	58	Strn R hamstring
Thomas,Lane	19	34	Fx R wrist
	20	23	COVID-19
Tillo,Daniel	20	68	TJS L elbow surg 8/20
Tom,Ka'Ai	21	92	COVID-rel; brse L wrist; low back strain
Torrens,Luis	20	2	Back spasms-lumbar area
Torres,Gleyber	18	22	Strn R hip
	20	16	Strn L quad, L hamstring
	21	33	COVID-19; sprained L thumb
Torreyes,Ronald	21	30	COVID-19
Trevino,Jose	20	16	Sprained L wrist
	21	25	Bruised R forearm
Tromp,Chadwick	20	7	Strn R shoulder
Trout,Mike	17	46	Torn ligament L thumb
	18	15	R wrist inflammation
	21	122	Strn R calf muscle
Tsutsugo,Yoshitomo	21	31	Strn R calf
Tucker,Cole	20	12	Concussion
Tucker,Kyle	21	19	COVID-19
Turner,Justin	17	21	Strn R hamstring
	18	59	Recover fr fx L wrist; groin strain
	20	18	Strn L hamstring
Turner,Trea	17	71	Strn R ham; fractured R wrist
	19	45	Fx R index finger
	21	10	COVID-19
Upton,Justin	18	10	L index finger laceration
	19	82	Turf toe L foot
	21	42	Strn lower back
Urías,Luis	20	20	COVID-19
Urshela,Giovanny	18	37	Strn R hamstring
	19	11	Tightness L groin
	20	12	Bone spur R elbow
	21	35	COVID-related; Strn L hamstring

FIVE-YEAR INJURY LOG — Hitters

Batter	Yr	Days	Injury
Vargas,Ildemaro	20	8	Strn R hamstring
Vaughn,Andrew	21	113	Strn lower back; COVID-related
Vázquez,Christian	18	56	R fifth finger fx
Verdugo,Alex	19	56	Strn R oblique muscle
Villanueva,Christian	18	40	Fractured R middle finger
Villar,Jonathan	17	17	Strn lower back
	18	19	Sprained R thumb
	21	13	Strn R calf
Vogelbach,Dan	21	71	Strn L hamstring
Vogt,Stephen	17	31	Sprained L knee
	18	187	R shoulder strain
	21	24	R hip inflammation
Voit,Luke	19	45	Strn ab muscle; sports hernia
	21	96	Torn menisc L knee; Strn R oblique
Votto,Joey	18	14	R lower leg contusion
	19	13	Lower back strain
	21	34	Sprained L thumb
Wade,LaMonte	19	57	Dislocated R thumb
	21	30	Strn L oblique
Walker,Christian	18	3	Sinus bone fracture
	21	50	Strn R oblique x2
Walker,Neil	17	44	Strn L hamstring
	19	12	Sprained R index finger
Wallach,Chad	19	132	Concussion
	20	26	COVID-19
Walls,Taylor	21	11	R wrist tendonitis
Walsh,Jared	21	16	Intercostal strain
Ward,Taylor	21	3	Strn adductor R groin
Wendle,Joe	17	28	Strn R shoulder
	19	98	Strn L hamstring; Fx L wrist
White,Eli	21	44	Strn R elbow
White,Evan	21	125	Strn L hip
White,Tyler	19	49	Strn R trapezius muscle
Wieters,Matt	18	70	Strn L oblique; Strn L ham
	20	16	Bruised L big toe
Wilkerson,Steve	18	50	L oblique strain
Williams,Justin	19	187	Fx second metacarpal R hand
	21	16	Strn neck
Williams,Lucas	21	21	COVID-19
Winker,Jesse	17	19	Strn L hip flexor
	18	68	R shoulder subluxation
	19	43	Strn cervical spine
	21	32	Intercostal ligament strain
Wolters,Tony	17	13	Concussion
Wong,Kolten	17	37	Strn L elbow; R triceps
	18	21	L knee inflammation
	21	44	Strn R calf; Strn L oblique
Wynns,Austin	19	21	Strn L oblique
Yastrzemski,Mike	21	21	Strn L oblique; sprained R thumb
Yelich,Christian	18	10	Strn R oblique
	21	47	COVID-19; Strn lower back
Zagunis,Mark	18	28	R shoulder inflammation
Zimmer,Bradley	18	18	L rib contusion
	19	156	Recovery from surgery (July 2018)
Zimmerman,Ryan	18	71	Strn R oblique
	19	106	Plantar fasciitis R foot
Zobrist,Ben	17	15	L wrist inflammation
	18	8	Back tightness
Zunino,Mike	18	39	Strn L oblique
	19	22	Strn L quadriceps
	20	23	Strn L oblique, COVID-19

FIVE-YEAR INJURY LOG — Pitchers

Pitchers	Yr	Days	Injury
Abreu,Bryan	21	39	Strained R calf
Adam,Jason	21	3	COVID-related
Adams,Austin	19	60	Strained R shoulder
	20	60	Strained L hamstring
	21	10	Strained R elbow
Adams,Chance	20	16	Post surg recov bone spur R elbow
Agrazal,Dario	20	64	Strained R forearm
Akin,Keegan	21	12	COVID-19
Alaniz,Ruben	21	25	Strained R calf
Alcala,Jorge	21	19	Tendinitis R biceps
Alcantara,Sandy	18	35	R axillary/armpit infection
	20	27	COVID-19
Alexander,Scott	17	29	Strained R hamstring
	19	115	L forearm inflam
	21	123	Inflammation L shoulder x2
Almonte,Yency	21	32	COVID-19; bruised R hand
Altavilla,Dan	18	95	R AC joint inflam; R UCL sprain
	19	58	Strained R forearm
	21	168	Strained R calf; inflam R elbow
Alvarado,José	19	75	Strained R oblique muscle
	20	45	Inflammation L shoulder
	21	27	COVID-related; impingement L shldr
Álvarez,José	20	16	Testicular contusion
	21	11	Sprained R ankle
Alzolay,Adbert	21	33	Strn L hamstring; blist R index fing
Anderson,Brett	17	80	Strn lower back
	18	68	Strn L shoulder
	20	10	Blister L index finger
	21	46	Strn R ham; bruised R knee; L shldr
Anderson,Chase	17	52	Strn L oblique muscle
	18	9	Food poisoning
	19	17	Lacerated R middle finger
	20	17	Strn R oblique
	21	60	COVID-19; tendinitis R triceps
Anderson,Drew	21	23	COVID-19
Anderson,Ian	21	48	Inflammation R shoulder
Anderson,Justin	19	30	Strn trap upper R back
	20	68	TJS
Anderson,Nick	20	16	Inflam R forearm
	21	165	Sprained R elbow; Strn lower back
Anderson,Shaun	19	17	Blister on R middle finger
	21	28	Strn L quad; blister R hand
Anderson,Tanner	21	3	Bruised R foot
Anderson,Tyler	17	99	L knee inflammation x2
	19	148	Recovery from L knee surgery
Andriese,Matt	17	87	Strnd groin; stress reaction R hip
	19	23	L foot contusion
	21	39	Strn R hamstring
Antone,Tejay	21	99	Inflam R forearm; surgery R elbow
Arano,Víctor	18	18	Strn R rotator cuff
	19	165	R elbow inflammation
Araújo,Pedro	18	113	Sprained UCL - R elbow
Archer,Chris	18	35	L abdominal strain
	19	60	R thumb inflammation
	20	67	Recovery from neck surgery
	21	140	Strn R forearm; Strn L hip
Arihara,Kohei	21	116	Recovery from surgery R shoulder
Armenteros,Rogelio	20	68	TJS
Armstrong,Shawn	19	27	Strn R forearm
	20	25	Inflm S.I. joint R shldr; sore low back
	21	2	COVID-related
Arrieta,Jake	19	48	Bone spur R elbow
	20	13	Strn R hamstring
	21	51	Strn L hamstring; abrasion R thumb

FIVE-YEAR INJURY LOG — Pitchers

Pitchers	Yr	Days	Injury
Avilán,Luis	17	15	L triceps soreness
	19	60	Sore L elbow
	20	8	Inflammation L shoulder
	21	154	Tommy John surgery
Axford,John	21	45	R elbow pain
Bacus,Dakota	20	22	Strn flexor muscle R forearm
Baez,Michel	21	169	Tommy John surgery
Baez,Pedro	17	12	Bruised R wrist
	18	42	R biceps tendinitis
	20	24	Strn R groin
	21	149	Sore R shoulder
Bailey,Brandon	21	169	Tommy John surgery recovery
Bailey,Homer	17	86	Bone spurs R elbow
	18	53	R knee inflammation
	20	52	Tendinitis R biceps
Banda,Anthony	19	180	TJS
	21	2	COVID-related
Bañuelos,Manny	19	86	Strn L shoulder
Baragar,Caleb	21	14	Inflammation L elbow
Bard,Luke	19	12	Bruised R triceps
	21	169	Inflammation R hip
Barlow,Joe	21	11	Blister R middle finger
Barnes,Matt	17	10	Strn lower back
	21	20	COVID-19
Barnette,Tony	17	16	Sprained R ring finger
	18	115	Low back strain; R shldr inflam
	19	88	R shoulder inflammation
Barraclough,Kyle	17	20	R shoulder impingement
	18	15	Lower back stiffness
	19	25	R radial nerve irritation
Barrett,Aaron	20	8	Strn R triceps
Bashlor,Tyler	20	19	Inflammation lower back
Bass,Anthony	18	34	Viral illness; R mid-thoracic strain
Bassitt,Chris	17	115	Recovery from TJS
	19	19	R lower leg contusion
	21	30	Head injury
Bauer,Trevor	18	39	Stress fracture, R fibula
Bautista,Gerson	19	70	Strn R pectoral muscle
	20	68	Sprained UCL R elbow
Bazardo,Edward	21	71	Strn lower back
Beasley,Jeremy	20	44	Strn R shoulder
Bednar,David	21	12	Strn R oblique
Bedrosian,Cam	17	56	Strn R groin
	19	33	Strn R forearm
	20	28	Strn R adductor muscle
Beede,Tyler	20	67	TJS
	21	128	Tommy John surgery
Beeks,Jalen	20	34	Sprained L elbow
	21	169	Tommy John surgery
Bergen,Travis	19	81	Strn L shoulder
	21	24	Impingement L shoulder
Betances,Dellin	19	184	R shldr impinge; torn Achilles ten
	20	25	Tight R lat muscle
	21	162	Impingement R shoulder
Biagini,Joe	18	11	Strn L oblique
	20	19	Sore R shoulder
Biddle,Jesse	19	96	L shoulder fatigue
	20	30	Impingement L shoulder
Bieber,Shane	21	95	Strn subscapularis R shoulder
Black,Ray	20	54	Strn R rotator cuff
Blackburn,Paul	17	37	Bruised R forearm
	18	157	Strn R forearm

FIVE-YEAR INJURY LOG — Pitchers

Pitchers	Yr	Days	Injury
Bleier,Richard	18	109	Torn upper lat; L shoulder surg
	19	36	L shoulder tendinitis
	20	14	Strn L triceps muscle
Bolaños,Ronald	21	94	Strn flexor R forearm
Borucki,Ryan	19	182	Surg remove bone spur R elbow
	21	69	COVID-rel; Strn flexor tendon L forearm
Bourque,James	20	8	Strn R elbow
Bowden,Ben	21	17	Strn L shoulder
Bowman,Matthew	18	45	Blisters pitching hand
	20	60	Sprained R elbow
Boxberger,Brad	17	89	Strn R flexor
Boyd,Matt	21	84	Tendinitis L triceps; Strn L elbow
Brach,Brad	20	20	COVID-19
	21	29	R shoulder impingement
Bracho,Silvino	19	186	Recovery from TJS
	20	64	TJS
Bradford,Chasen	19	135	R shoulder inflam; strn R forearm
Bradley,Archie	21	38	Strn L & R oblique
Brasier,Ryan	21	154	Strn L calf muscle
Brault,Steven	19	32	Strn L shoulder
	21	132	Strn L lat x2
Brebbia,John	20	67	TJS
	21	81	Tommy John surgery
Brennan,Brandon	19	73	Inflammation R shoulder
	20	50	Strn L oblique
Brentz,Jake	21	10	Impingement R shoulder
Brewer,Colten	18	37	Strn L oblique
	20	26	Strn finger R hand
Brice,Austin	17	59	Ulnar neuritis R elb; R lat strain
	18	11	Mid-back strain
	19	79	Gastroenteritis
	20	20	Strn R Lat muscle
Brigham,Jeff	20	56	R Biceps injury
	21	169	COVID-19
Britton,Zack	17	76	Strn L forearm x2
	18	75	Ruptured R Achilles
	20	13	Strn L hamstring
	21	104	Bone spur L elbow; Strn L hamstring
Brogdon,Connor	21	21	COVID-19
	21	37	COVID-rel; tend. R elbow; str R groin
Brubaker,JT	21	23	Bilateral adductor strain, R hip
Buchter,Ryan	18	60	Strn L shoulder
Buehler,Walker	18	32	R rib microfracture
	20	23	Blister R hand
Bukauskas,J.B.	21	48	Strn R flexor
Bumgarner,Madison	17	85	Bruised ribs, sprained L shoulder
	18	69	Fractured L hand
	20	26	Mid-back strain
	21	44	Inflammation L shoulder
Bummer,Aaron	20	48	Strn L biceps
	21	18	Strn R hamstring
Bundy,Dylan	18	11	L ankle sprain
	19	11	R knee tendinitis
	21	23	Strn R ankle
Burdi,Nick	18	157	TJS
	19	161	Sore R elbow
	20	54	Strn R forearm
Burke,Brock	20	67	Torn L labrum surgery
	21	24	Recovery from L shoulder surgery
Burnes,Corbin	19	17	R shoulder irritation
	21	15	COVID-19
Burr,Ryan	19	141	R shldr AC joint inflam; str R elbow
Bush,Matt	21	162	Inflamed R shoulder

FIVE-YEAR INJURY LOG — Pitchers

Pitchers	Yr	Days	Injury
Cahill,Trevor	17	85	Strn back; R shldr; R Shldr impinge
	18	37	R elbow impingement
	19	21	R elbow inflammation
	20	21	Torn fingernail R hand, L hip inflam
	21	119	Strn L calf
Campbell,Paul	21	3	COVID-related
Canning,Griffin	19	55	Inflammation R elbow
Carle,Shane	18	25	R shoulder inflammation
Carpenter,Ryan	18	56	Strn R oblique
Carrasco,Carlos	18	20	R elbow contusion
	19	89	Leukemia
	21	121	Strn R hamstring
Cashner,Andrew	17	25	Tendinitis R biceps; L oblique
	18	21	Lower back strain; Strn neck
Castano,Daniel	21	74	Impingement L shoulder
Castillo,Diego	19	19	R shoulder inflam/impingement surg
	21	28	COVID-rel; inflam R shldr; tight R groin
Castillo,Jose	18	22	R hamstring strain
	19	187	Torn L finger tendon
	20	68	Strn lat muscle
	21	169	Tommy John surgery
Castro,Anthony	21	73	Strn R forearm; ulnar nerve irritation
Castro,Miguel	21	2	COVID-related
Cease,Dylan	21	3	COVID-related
Cederlind,Blake	21	169	Tommy John surgery
Cessa,Luis	17	47	Ribcage injury
	18	64	L oblique strain
	20	15	COVID-19
Chacin,Jhoulys	19	84	Strn lower back; oblique
	21	13	COVID-19
Chafin,Andrew	20	32	Sprained finger L hand
Chapman,Aroldis	17	35	L rotator cuff injury
	18	29	L knee tendinitis
	20	26	COVID-19
	21	13	Impingement L elbow
Chargois,J.T.	17	26	R elbow surg
	18	35	Nerve irritation neck
Chatwood,Tyler	17	10	Strn R calf
	18	12	L hip tightness
	20	39	Strn lower back
	21	63	Strn cervical spine
Chavez,Jesse	19	49	Strn R groin
	20	15	Sprained L big toe
Chirinos,Yonny	18	35	R forearm strain
	19	48	R middle finger inflammation
	20	54	TJS
	21	169	Tommy John surgery
Cishek,Steve	19	10	L hip inflammation
Cisnero,Jose	21	21	Laceration R elbow
Civale,Aaron	21	76	Sprained finger R hand
Clarke,Taylor	19	17	Lower L back inflammation
	21	52	Strn teres major muscle R shoulder
Claudio,Alexander	18	7	Sprained L ankle
Cleavinger,Garrett	21	72	L forearm inflam; R oblique strain
Clevinger,Mike	19	81	Strn R upper back; sprained R ankle
	21	169	Tommy John surgery
Clippard,Tyler	21	119	COVID-related; Strn R shoulder
Cobb,Alex	17	15	Turf toe R big toe
	19	176	Strn R groin; R hip impinge surg
	20	9	COVID-related
	21	65	Inflammation R wrist; blister R hand
Cody,Kyle	21	146	Inflamed R shoulder

FIVE-YEAR INJURY LOG — Pitchers

Pitchers	Yr	Days	Injury
Cole,A.J.	18	13	L neck strain
	19	52	R shoulder impingement
	21	110	Cervical spine inflammation
Cole,Gerrit	21	14	COVID-19
Cole,Taylor	17	10	Fractured R toe
	19	12	Strn R shoulder
Colina,Edwar	21	169	Inflammation R elbow
Conley,Adam	20	27	COVID-19
Coonrod,Sam	20	27	Strn R lat muscle
	21	61	Tendinitis R forearm
Corbin,Patrick	21	6	COVID-related
Cordero,Jimmy	21	169	Tommy John surgery
Cortes,Nestor	20	45	Impingement L elbow
	21	10	COVID-19
Cousins,Jake	21	11	COVID-19
Covey,Dylan	17	80	Strn L oblique
	19	53	Inflammation R shoulder
Crick,Kyle	19	30	Tight R triceps; surg R index fing
	20	50	Strn R shoulder, lat muscle
	21	26	COVID-related; Strn R triceps
Crochet,Garrett	21	12	Strn lower back
Cueto,Johnny	17	48	Blisters on R hand
	18	133	Spr R ankle; R elbow inflam x 3; TJS
	19	167	TJS
	21	59	COVID-rel; Strn lat muscle; str. R elbow
Curtiss,John	21	51	Torn UCL R elbow
Darvish,Yu	17	10	Lower back tightness
	18	138	Viral infection; R triceps tendinitis
	21	25	Inflammation L hip; Strn lower back
Davidson,Tucker	21	93	Inflammation L forearm
Davies,Zach	18	106	R rotator cuff inflammation
	19	57	Back spasms
Davis,Austin	18	17	Lower back tightness
	21	67	Tommy John surgery
Davis,Wade	19	17	Strn L oblique
	20	42	Strn R shoulder
	21	26	Strn R forearm; R shoulder inflam
Dayton,Grant	17	90	Strn L intercostal; stiff neck x 2
	18	187	TJS
	19	67	Fractured R big toe
	21	115	L shoulder inflam; L quad inflam.
De León,José	18	187	TJS
	19	98	TJS
	20	13	Strn R groin
deGrom,Jacob	18	8	Hyperextended R elbow
	19	11	Sore R elbow
	21	77	Low back tightness; tight R forearm
DeJong,Chase	21	16	Inflammation L knee
Delaplane,Sam	21	108	Tommy John surgery
DelPozo,Miguel	21	30	COVID-19
DeSclafani,Anthony	17	182	Sprained UCL R elbow
	18	69	L oblique strain
	20	11	Strn R teres major muscle
	21	21	Fatigue R shldr;R ankle inflam
Detmers,Reid	21	23	COVID-19
Devenski,Chris	18	27	L hamstring tightness
	20	57	Elbow/undisclosed
	21	125	Sprained UCL R elbow
Díaz,Jairo	17	48	Recovery surg R elbow
Díaz,Miguel	17	67	Strn R forearm
	19	162	Recov R knee surgery (meniscus)
Díaz,Yennsy	20	68	Strn R lat muscle
Diekman,Jake	17	156	Colitis
Dobnak,Randy	21	82	Strn R index finger

FIVE-YEAR INJURY LOG — Pitchers

Pitchers	Yr	Days	Injury
Dolis,Rafael	21	29	Strn R calf; sprained finger R hand
Domínguez,Seranthon	19	117	Torn UCL R elbow
	20	67	TJS
	21	154	Tommy John surgery
Doolittle,Sean	17	38	Strn L shoulder
	18	60	L toe inflammation
	19	15	Tendonitis R knee
	20	31	Inflammation R knee, str R oblique
Drake,Oliver	20	38	Tendinitis R biceps
	21	169	Strn flexor tendon in R elbow
Duffy,Danny	17	57	Strn L oblique; L elbow imping
	18	11	L shoulder impingement
	19	59	L shoulder impinge; strn L ham
	21	100	Strn flexor L forearm
Dugger,Robert	20	26	COVID-19
	21	2	COVID-related
Dull,Ryan	17	68	Strn R knee
	18	17	Strn R shoulder
Dunn,Justin	21	100	Inflamed R shoulder x2
Dunning,Dane	21	28	COVID-19; impingement R ankle
Duplantier,Jon	19	38	R shoulder inflammation
	21	44	Sprained R middle finger
Dyson,Sam	17	11	Bruised R hand
	19	10	R biceps tendinitis
Eaton,Adam	21	23	Strn R hamstring x2; inflam L shldr
Edwards,C.J.	21	75	Strn L oblique
Edwards,Carl	18	38	R shoulder fatigue
	19	89	Strn R shoulder
	20	50	Strn R forearm
Eflin,Zach	17	50	Rec surg pat tend 2 knees; R shldr
	18	9	Blister - R middle finger
	19	11	Tightness lower back
	21	59	COVID-19; patellar tendinitis R knee
Eickhoff,Jerad	17	50	Strnd upper back; nerve irrit R hand
	18	159	R lat strain
	19	106	R biceps tendinitis
Elías,Roenis	17	138	R intercostal injury
	18	20	Strn L triceps
	19	27	Strn R hamstring
	20	67	Strn L flexor tendon, COVID-19
Emanuel,Kent	21	114	Sore L elbow
Eovaldi,Nathan	17	183	Rec. Tommy John surg
	18	63	Loose bodies R elbow
	19	92	R elbow surg remove loose bodies
	20	14	Strn R calf
Erlin,Robbie	17	182	TJS L elbow
Estévez,Carlos	18	109	Strn L oblique
	21	23	Strn R middle finger
Evans,Demarcus	21	24	Strn R lat muscle
Fairbanks,Pete	21	57	Strn R/C R shoulder
Falter,Bailey	21	32	COVID-19
Familia,Jeurys	17	106	Blood clot R shoulder
	18	10	Sore R shoulder
	19	27	Bennett lesion R shoulder
	21	12	Impingement R hip
Faria,Jake	17	26	Strn L abdominal
	18	71	Strn L oblique
Farmer,Buck	20	10	Strn L groin
Farrell,Luke	19	150	Fractured jaw
	20	49	COVID-19
	21	75	Strn R oblique
Fedde,Erick	17	27	Strn flexor R forearm
	18	62	R shoulder inflammation
	21	38	COVID-19; Strn oblique muscle

FIVE-YEAR INJURY LOG — Pitchers

Pitchers	Yr	Days	Injury
Feliz,Michael	17	38	R shoulder injury
	18	14	R shoulder inflammation
	20	58	Strn R forearm
	21	99	COVID-related; sprained R elbow
Ferguson,Caleb	19	19	Strn L oblique
	20	13	Torn UCL L elbow
	21	169	L elbow TJS
Fernández,Junior	20	24	COVID-19
	21	15	Torn lat muscle R shoulder area
Feyereisen,J.P.	21	41	Discomfort R shoulder
Fiers,Michael	18	11	R lumbar strain
	21	159	Strn lower back; Strn R elbow
File,Dylan	21	99	Surgery R elbow
Finnegan,Kyle	21	17	Strn L hamstring
Flaherty,Jack	21	97	Strn L oblique; Strn R shoulder
Fleming,Josh	21	12	Strn R calf
Floro,Dylan	19	25	Neck inflam; strn L intercostal lig
Flynn,Brian	17	123	Strn L groin
	19	59	Sprained UCL pitching elbow
Foltynewicz,Mike	18	10	R triceps tightness
	19	31	Bone spur R elbow
	21	25	COVID-19
Font,Wilmer	18	94	R lat strain
	20	16	Bruised R shin
Frankoff,Seth	21	104	Strn R forearm x2
Freeland,Kyle	17	10	Strn L groin
	19	40	Blister L middle finger
	21	55	Strn L shoulder
Freeman,Sam	18	21	L shoulder inflammation
	20	47	Strn L flexor muscle
Fried,Max	18	43	Blister L index finger; L groin strain
	19	12	Blister on L index finger
	20	12	Back spasms-lumbar area
	21	34	Blist L index fing;Strn R index fing
Fry,Jace	19	11	Sore L shoulder
	20	11	Back spasms-lumbar area
	21	87	Strn lower back
Fuentes,Steven	21	77	Strn R shoulder
Fulmer,Carson	19	30	Strn R hamstring
Fulmer,Michael	17	11	Ulnar neuritis R elbow
	18	47	Strn L oblique; torn meniscs R knee
	19	187	Recovery from TJS
	21	43	Strn cervical spine
Gallegos,Giovanny	20	16	Strn R groin x2
Gallen,Zac	21	67	Fx R forearm;sprn R elb;strn R ham
Gant,John	17	47	Strn R groin
	20	3	Tightness R groin
	21	15	Strn L ab muscle; str R groin
García,Jarlín	17	10	Strn L biceps
	18	12	R ankle contusion
	20	18	COVID-19
	21	14	Strn L groin
Garcia,Luis	18	36	Strn R wrist
Garcia,Rico	21	169	Tommy John surgery
Garcia,Rony	21	115	Strn L ab muscle; sprained L knee
Garcia,Yimi	18	49	R forearm inflammation
	20	25	COVID-19
Garrett,Amir	17	10	R hip inflammation
	18	13	Strn L Achilles
	19	17	Strn lat L shoulder
Gausman,Kevin	19	50	R foot plant fasc;tendinitis R shldr
	21	9	COVID-related
Germán,Domingo	19	26	Strn L hip flexor
	21	47	Inflamed R shoulder

FIVE-YEAR INJURY LOG — Pitchers

Pitchers	Yr	Days	Injury
Gibson,Kyle	19	10	Ulcerative colitis
	21	14	Strn R groin
Gilbert,Tyler	21	20	Inflammation L elbow
Giles,Ken	19	9	Inflammation R elbow
	20	55	Strn R forearm x2
	21	169	Tommy John surgery
Ginkel,Kevin	21	19	Inflammation R elbow
Giolito,Lucas	19	32	Strn L hammy; strn R muscle
	21	13	Strn R hamstring
Givens,Mychal	21	20	Strn lower back
Glasnow,Tyler	19	121	Strn R forearm
	21	94	Sprained UCL in R elbow
Godley,Zack	20	22	Strn flexor mass R elbow
	21	13	Bruised R index finger
Gomber,Austin	20	7	COVID-related
	21	45	L forearm tight stress fx lower back
Gómez,Yoendrys	21	51	COVID-19; Strn lower back
Gonsolin,Anthony	21	111	R shoulder inflammation
Gonzales,Marco	18	16	Cervical neck muscle strain
	21	34	Strn L forearm
González,Chi Chi	17	182	TJS July 2017
	20	23	Tendinitis R biceps
	21	31	COVID-19; Strn R oblique
González,Gio	19	50	L arm fatigue
	20	13	Strn R groin
González,Victor	21	30	Plant fasciitis L foot; inflam R knee
Goody,Nick	18	152	R elbow inflammation
	20	15	Lower back spasms
Gott,Trevor	19	47	Strn R elbow
	20	16	Inflammation R elbow
Graterol,Brusdar	21	56	R forearm strain
Graveman,Kendall	17	76	Strn R shoulder x2
	18	31	TJS
	19	187	Recovery from TJS
	20	29	Neck spasms
	21	20	COVID-19
Gray,Jon	17	77	Stress fracture L foot
	19	41	Fractured L foot
	20	27	Inflammation R shoulder
	21	29	Strn R flexor
Gray,Sonny	17	30	Strn lat muscle R shoulder
	20	10	Strn back
	21	52	Strn back; Strn R groin; str rib cage
Greene,Shane	18	12	R shoulder strain
Gregerson,Luke	18	142	R shldr impinge x 2; torn meniscs
	19	38	R shoulder impingement
Greinke,Zack	21	15	COVID-19
Griffin,Foster	20	63	Strn L forearm
Grimm,Justin	17	14	Infection R index finger
	18	61	Back stiffness; R shoulder impinge
	20	15	Laceration R index finger
Gsellman,Robert	17	48	Strn L hamstring
	19	48	Tightness R tightness
	20	35	Fractured rib L side
	21	89	Strn lower back
Guduan,Reymin	21	29	Sprained L thumb; Strn R groin
Guenther,Sean	21	1	Strn upper back
Guerra,Javier	20	16	COVID-19
	21	169	Sprained UCL R elbow
Guerra,Javy	20	27	Strn L hamstring
Guerra,Junior	17	63	Strn R calf; bruised R shin
	18	11	R forearm tightness
	21	12	Strn R groin; Strn L forearm

FIVE-YEAR INJURY LOG — Pitchers

Pitchers	Yr	Days	Injury
Guerrero,Tayron	18	27	Strn L lumbar spine
	19	44	Blister R middle finger
Guilbeau,Taylor	20	39	Strn L shoulder
Gustave,Jandel	17	164	Tightness R forearm
	18	187	TJS
	21	36	COVID-19
Guzman,Jorge	21	133	Strn R elbow
Hader,Josh	21	11	COVID-19
Hahn,Jesse	17	10	Strn R triceps
	18	187	Sprained R UCL
	19	160	Recovery from TJS
	21	158	Inflammation R shoulder
Hale,David	19	60	Strn lumbar spine
	21	3	COVID-related
Hamels,Cole	17	54	Strn R oblique
	19	35	Strn L oblique
	20	67	Tend. L triceps, fatigue L shoulder
	21	32	Strn L rotator cuff
Hamilton,Ian	19	8	R shoulder inflammation
	20	35	Sore R shoulder
Hammer,JD	21	8	COVID-related
Hancock,Justin	18	98	R shoulder inflammation
Hand,Brad	21	4	COVID-related
Hanhold,Eric	18	7	Strnd L oblique; R shoulder inflam
Happ,J.A.	17	42	L elbow inflammation
	18	8	Viral infection
Hardy,Blaine	18	15	L elbow tendinitis
	19	73	Strn L flexor tendon
Harris,Will	17	41	R shoulder inflam x2
	20	14	Strn R groin
	21	151	Blood clot R arm; TOS surgery
Hart,Kyle	20	27	Impingement L hip
Hartman,Ryan	21	17	COVID-19
Harvey,Hunter	20	39	Strn R elbow
	21	143	Strn R triceps
Harvey,Joe	20	39	Strn R elbow
Harvey,Matt	17	79	Stress fracture R scapula
	19	50	Upper back strain
	20	13	Strn R lat muscle
	21	25	Strn R triceps
Hatch,Thomas	21	97	Impingement R elbow x2
Heaney,Andrew	17	130	Recovery surg UCL L elbow
	18	16	L elbow inflammation
	19	83	L elbow inflam; L shoulder inflam
Hearn,Taylor	19	158	Tightness L elbow
Heller,Ben	18	183	Bone spurs - R elbow
	19	167	TJS
	20	7	Nerve injury R biceps
Helsley,Ryan	19	21	R shoulder impingement
	20	21	COVID-19
	21	31	Stress reaction R elbow
Hembree,Heath	19	74	Strn R elbow extensor
	20	8	Strn R elbow
Hendricks,Kyle	17	46	R hand tendinitis
	19	17	R shoulder inflammation
Hendriks,Liam	18	53	R groin strain
Hernandez,Darwinzon	20	48	Sprained A/C joint L shldr, Covid-19
	21	43	Strn R oblique
Hernandez,David	18	30	R shoulder inflammation
	19	13	R shoulder fatigue
Hernandez,Elieser	18	55	Finger blister; dental surg
	20	27	Strn R late
	21	133	Inflammation R biceps
Hernández,Jonathan	21	169	Tommy John surgery

FIVE-YEAR INJURY LOG — Pitchers

Pitchers	Yr	Days	Injury
Hicks,Jordan	19	98	Torn UCL R elbow
	21	136	Inflammation R elbow
Hill,Cam	21	119	Surgery R wrist
Hill,Rich	17	39	Blister L middle finger x 2
	18	52	Blisters L hand x 2
	19	117	Strn L forearm; sprained L knee
	20	16	Shoulder fatigue L shoulder
	21	2	COVID-related
Hirano,Yoshihisa	19	23	R elbow inflammation
	20	30	COVID-19
Hoffman,Jeff	21	56	R shoulder impingement
Holder,Jonathan	19	52	R shoulder inflammation
	21	169	Strn R shoulder
Holland,Derek	19	22	Bruise L wrist; bruise L index fing
	21	50	Strn L shoulder; inflam L shldr
Holland,Greg	18	25	R hip impingement
	21	28	COVID-related; impingement R shlder
Holloway,Jordan	20	56	COVID-19
	21	118	Strn R groin
Holmes,Clay	19	31	R triceps inflammation
	20	63	Strn R forearm
	21	13	COVID-19
Houser,Adrian	21	16	COVID-19
Howard,Sam	21	61	Tendinitis R knee; Strn R oblique
Howard,Spencer	20	12	Stiffness R shoulder
	21	12	COVID-19
Hudson,Dakota	20	11	Strn R forearm
	21	169	Tommy John surgery
Hudson,Daniel	18	49	R forearm tightness
	21	43	COVID-19; inflammation R elbow
Hughes,Jared	20	11	COVID-19
Hunter,Tommy	17	32	Strn R calf
	18	25	Strn R hamstring
	19	172	R forearm surgery
	21	121	Strn lower back
Iglesias,Raisel	18	8	Strn L biceps
Ivey,Tyler	21	46	Inflammation R elbow
Jackson,Edwin	19	27	Lower back strain
Jackson,Jay	21	2	COVID-related
Jackson,Luke	17	13	Strn R shoulder
James,Josh	19	41	Inflammation R shoulder
	20	19	Sore L hip
	21	123	L hip surgery
Jansen,Kenley	18	11	Irregular heartbeat
Jeffress,Jeremy	17	12	Strn lower back
	19	57	R shoulder inflammation
Jiménez,Joe	21	10	COVID-19
Johnson,Brian	17	21	L shoulder impingement
	18	8	L hip inflammation
	19	108	L elbow inflam; undisclosed issue
Johnson,D.J.	21	38	Sprained R shoulder
Johnson,Pierce	21	26	Strn R groin; inflam R triceps tendon
Jones,Nate	17	150	R elbow neuritis
	18	90	Strn pronator muscle - R arm
	19	157	Recovery from surgery R shoulder
Junis,Jake	18	14	Lower back inflammation
	20	26	Lower back spasms/COVID-19
	21	16	Impingement R shoulder
Kahnle,Tommy	18	39	R shoulder tendinitis
	20	59	TJS
	21	169	Tommy John surgery
Kaprielian,James	21	9	Impingement R shoulder
Kay,Anthony	21	22	COVID-19; blister L hand

FIVE-YEAR INJURY LOG — Pitchers

Pitchers	Yr	Days	Injury
Kela,Keone	17	60	Sore R shoulder x2
	19	79	Shoulder and elbow inflammation
	20	54	Tight R forearm, COVID-19
	21	143	Inflammation R shoulder; R forearm
Keller,Brad	20	14	COVID-19
	21	21	Strn R Lat
Keller,Mitch	20	44	Strn L oblique
	21	3	COVID-related
Kelly,Joe	17	21	Strn L hamstring
	20	32	Inflammation R shoulder
	21	52	R shoulder inflammation x2
Kelly,Merrill	20	36	Impingement R shoulder
	21	36	COVID-19; undisclosed inj
Kennedy,Ian	17	16	Strn R hamstring
	18	68	Strn L oblique
	20	29	Strn L calf
	21	10	Strn L hamstring
Kershaw,Clayton	17	39	Strn lower back
	18	49	L biceps tendinitis; low back strain
	19	19	L shoulder inflammation
	20	11	Lower back stiffness
	21	69	L forearm inflammation x2
Keuchel,Dallas	17	61	Pinched nerve neck; Strn neck
	20	13	Back spasms
Kikuchi,Yusei	21	2	COVID-related
Kilome,Franklyn	20	14	Torn fingernail R hand
Kim,Kwang-hyun	20	13	Kidney ailment
	21	43	Tight lower back; inflam L elbow
Kimbrel,Craig	19	30	R knee inflam; R elbow inflam
King,John	21	72	Inflamed L shoulder
King,Michael	21	68	Bruised R middle finger
Kintzler,Brandon	18	16	Flexor muscle strain - R arm
	19	10	R pectoral muscle inflammation
	21	24	Strn neck
Kittredge,Andrew	20	48	Sprained UCL R elbow
Kluber,Corey	17	29	Strn lower back
	19	151	Fractured ulna R forearm
	20	63	Torn teres major muscle R shoulder
	21	97	Strn R shoulder
Knebel,Corey	18	34	L hamstring strain
	19	187	Recovery from TJS
	20	20	Strn L hamstring
	21	109	Strn R Lat
Kopech,Michael	18	24	TJS
	19	187	Recovery from TJS
	21	34	Strn L hamstring
Kuhl,Chad	18	95	Strn R forearm
	19	187	TJS
	21	59	COVID-19; sore R shoulder
Lakins,Travis	21	79	Stress Fx R elbow
Lambert,Jimmy	20	62	Strn R forearm
Lambert,Peter	20	68	TJS
	21	169	Tommy John surgery
Lamet,Dinelson	18	187	Recovery from TJS
	19	99	Recovery from TJS
	21	101	Strn UCL R elbow; Strn R forearm
Lange,Alex	21	23	Strn R shoulder
Lauer,Eric	18	32	L forearm strain
	20	3	COVID-related
	21	12	COVID-19
Law,Derek	21	62	Impingement R shoulder

FIVE-YEAR INJURY LOG — Pitchers

Pitchers	Yr	Days	Injury
LeBlanc,Wade	17	14	Strn L quadriceps
	19	35	Strn R oblique
	20	35	Stress reaction L elbow
	21	35	L elbow inflammation
Leclerc,José	17	25	Bruised R index finger
	20	60	Strn teres major muscle R shldr
	21	169	Tommy John surgery
Leibrandt,Brandon	20	22	Ulnar neuritis L elbow
Leone,Dominic	18	114	R upper arm nerve irritation
Lester,Jon	17	15	L shoulder fatigue
	19	17	Strn L hamstring
	21	26	COVID-19
Lindblom,Josh	17	35	L side injury
	21	20	R knee effusion
Lindgren,Jacob	18	187	TJS
Littell,Zack	20	30	Strn L elbow, inflam R elbow
Loaisiga,Jonathan	19	93	Strn R shoulder
	20	14	Undisclosed medical condition
	21	26	COVID-19; Strn R/C R shoulder
Lockett,Walker	20	20	Sore lower back
Long,Sam	21	24	Strn lower back
López,Jorge	20	6	COVID-related
	21	10	Sprained R ankle
López,Pablo	18	31	R shoulder strain
	19	69	Strn R shoulder
	21	65	Strn R rotator cuff
López,Reynaldo	17	13	Strn back
	20	27	Strn R shoulder
Lorenzen,Michael	18	56	R shoulder strain
	21	120	Strn R shoulder; Strn R hamstring
Loup,Aaron	18	34	Strn L forearm
	19	176	Strn L elbow
Lovelady,Richard	21	19	Sprained UCL L elbow
Lucas,Josh	19	19	Inflammation/strain R shoulder
Lucchesi,Joey	18	37	R hip strain
	21	90	Inflammation L elbow; surgery
Luciano,Elvis	19	92	Sprained R elbow
	20	67	COVID-19
Lugo,Seth	17	82	Part torn UCL R elb; R shldr imping
	19	12	R shoulder tendinitis
	21	61	Recovery from R elbow surgery
Luzardo,Jesus	21	29	Fx L hand
Lyles,Jordan	18	36	R elbow inflammation
	19	29	Strn L ham; Strn L oblique
Lynn,Lance	21	27	Strn R trap muscle; inflam R knee
Lyons,Tyler	17	42	Rec surg R knee; R intercostal
	18	52	Mid-back strain; sprained L elbow
Maeda,Kenta	17	14	Hamstring tightness
	18	15	R hip strain
	19	10	Bruised L adductor muscle
	21	49	Strn R adductor; tightness R forearm
Magill,Matt	19	30	R shoulder tendinitis
	20	32	Strn R shoulder
Mahle,Tyler	19	32	Strn L hamstring
Manaea,Sean	17	15	Strn L shoulder
	18	37	L shoulder impingement
	19	158	R shoulder surgery rehab
Manoah,Alek	21	16	Strn lower back
Mantiply,Joe	21	17	COVID-19
Maples,Dillon	21	70	Strn R biceps; blist R index finger
Margevicius,Nick	21	144	Inflamed L shoulder
Márquez,Germán	19	39	R arm inflammation

FIVE-YEAR INJURY LOG — Pitchers

Pitchers	Yr	Days	Injury
Marshall,Evan	17	88	Strn R hamstring
	18	50	R elbow inflammation
	20	11	Inflammation R shoulder
	21	79	Strn R flexor pronator muscle
Marte,José	21	26	COVID-19
Martes,Francis	19	45	recovery from TJS
Martin,Brett	20	26	RC inflam L shoulder, COVID-19
	21	9	Strn lower back
Martin,Chris	18	54	R forearm irrit;str R calf;str L groin
	20	14	Esophageal constriction
	21	51	Inflam R shoulder; R elbow inflam
Martin,Corbin	20	68	TJS
Martínez,Carlos	18	59	R lat strain; R oblique strain
	19	51	Strn R shoulder cuff
	20	41	Strn L oblique
	21	85	Sprn R ankle; torn ligament R thumb
Maton,Phil	18	40	R lat strain
Matz,Steven	17	109	L elbow inflam; Ulnar nerve irrit
	18	14	L flexor pronator strain
	19	10	Sore L elbow
	20	15	Impingement L shoulder
	21	18	COVID-19
May,Dustin	21	138	Tommy John surgery
May,Trevor	17	182	TJS R elbow
	18	71	TJS
Mayers,Mike	18	17	R shoulder inflammation
	19	99	Strn lat R shoulder
	21	3	COVID-related
Mayza,Tim	19	26	Ulnar neuritis L 4arm; TJS
	21	13	Inflammation L elbow
Mazza,Chris	21	132	Inflamed R shoulder
McClanahan,Shane	21	10	Strn lower back
McCullers,Lance	17	49	Sore lower back x2
	18	51	R elbow discomfort
	19	187	Recovery from TJS
	20	10	Neck irritation
	21	24	Sore R shoulder
McFarland,T.J.	17	11	Bruised L ankle
	18	12	L neck strain
	19	34	Inflammation L shoulder
McGee,Jake	17	10	Strn mid-back
	19	46	Sprained L knee
	21	18	COVID-related; Strn R oblique
McGowin,Kyle	21	57	Strn R biceps; sprained UCL R elbow
McHugh,Collin	17	114	Hypertrophy R arm
	19	66	R elbow pain
	21	33	COVID-rel;Strn low back;R arm fatigue
McKay,Brendan	20	19	Sore L shoulder, COVID-19
McKenzie,Triston	21	10	Fatigue R shoulder
Means,John	19	26	Strn L biceps; Strn L shldr
	20	14	COVID-related, L shoulder fatigue
	21	45	Strn L shoulder
Megill,Trevor	21	34	Strn R forearm
Mejía,Adalberto	17	36	Brachialis strain L arm
	18	53	Strn L wrist
	19	62	Strn R calf
Melancon,Mark	17	56	R elbow tendinitis x 2
	18	65	R elbow flexor strain
Mella,Keury	18	28	L oblique strain
Mengden,Daniel	17	48	Fractured R foot
	18	18	L shoulder impingement
	20	19	COVID-19
Merryweather,Julian	20	8	Tendinitis R elbow
	21	148	Strn L oblique

FIVE-YEAR INJURY LOG — Pitchers

Pitchers	Yr	Days	Injury
Middleton,Keynan	18	151	R elbow inflammation
	19	153	Recovery from TJS
	21	17	Strn R biceps tendon
Mikolas,Miles	20	63	Strn flexor tendon R forearm
	21	142	Rec fr TJS; tightness R forearm
Miley,Wade	17	10	Medical
	18	101	Strn R oblique x 2
	20	40	Strn L groin, Strn L shoulder
	21	11	Sprained L foot
Miller,Andrew	17	39	Patella tendinitis R knee x2
	18	99	L shldr; R knee inflam x2; str L ham
	20	13	Fatigue L shoulder
	21	46	Blist big toe; ulnar nerve irrit R elb
Miller,Justin	19	88	Low back strain; strn AC R shldr
	21	25	Ulnar nerve irritation R elbow
Miller,Shelby	17	160	R elbow inflammation
	18	169	Recovery from TJS - R elbow
	21	35	Strn lower back
Miller,Tyson	21	35	COVID-19
Mills,Alec	21	24	Strn lower back
Milner,Hoby	19	20	Bruised cervical nerve
	20	10	Lower back spasms
Milone,Tom	17	87	Sprained L knee
	18	14	L shoulder soreness
	20	19	Inflammation L elbow
	21	101	Inflamed L shoulder
Minaya,Juan	17	24	Strn R Ab
Minor,Mike	21	19	Impingement R shoulder
Minter,A.J.	19	26	L shoulder inflammation x2
Misiewicz,Anthony	21	18	COVID-related; Strn L forearm
Montero,Rafael	18	187	TJS
	20	16	Tendinitis R elbow
	21	38	Discomfort R shoulder
Montgomery,Jordan	18	151	TJS
	19	172	TJS
	21	15	COVID-19
Montgomery,Mike	18	14	L shoulder inflammation
	19	33	Inflammation L shoulder
	20	58	Strn lat muscle
Moore,Matt	18	12	R knee soreness
	19	178	Recovery meniscus surgery R knee
	21	42	Strn lower back; COVID-19
Moran,Brian	20	43	Patellar tendinitis R knee
Morejon,Adrian	19	55	L shoulder impingement
	21	158	Strn L forearm
Morgan,Adam	18	11	Back strain
	19	85	Strn L forearm
	20	12	Fatigue L shoulder
Morin,Mike	17	36	Stiff neck
	20	47	Torn UCL R elbow
Moronta,Reyes	19	27	Torn labrum R shoulder
	20	68	Recov labrum surgery R shldr
	21	134	Strn R flexor mass
Morton,Charlie	17	40	Strn R lat muscle
	18	11	R shoulder discomfort
	20	24	Inflammation R shoulder
Mujica,José	18	29	R forearm strain
Muñoz,Andrés	20	68	TJS
	21	169	Tommy John surgery
Murphy,Patrick	21	77	Sprained A/C joint R shoulder
Musgrave,Harrison	18	11	R hip flexor strain
	19	75	Strn flexor L elbow

FIVE-YEAR INJURY LOG — Pitchers

Pitchers	Yr	Days	Injury
Musgrove,Joe	17	13	R shoulder injury
	18	62	Strnd R shldr; infected R index fing
	20	23	Inflam R triceps
Nance,Tommy	21	3	COVID-related
Neidert,Nick	20	41	COVID-19
	21	33	Inflammation R biceps
Nelson,Jimmy	17	17	Strn rotator cuff R shoulder
	18	187	Recovery from R rotator cuff surg
	19	126	Labrum surg R shldr; effusion R elb
	20	68	Recovery from lower back surgery
	21	85	Inflam R forearm;Low back strn; TJS
Neverauskas,Dovydas	19	20	Strn L oblique
Newberry,Jake	19	19	R shoulder inflammation
Newcomb,Sean	19	7	Concussion
	21	13	COVID-19
Newsome,Ljay	21	133	Inflamed R elbow
Nicasio,Juan	18	71	R knee effusion
	19	45	Strn L groin; tendinitis R/C R shldr
Nogosek,Steve	21	48	Impingement R shoulder
Nola,Aaron	17	27	Strn lower back
	21	9	COVID-related
Norris,Daniel	17	57	Strn L groin
	18	125	L groin strain
	20	11	COVID-19
Norwood,James	20	58	Inflammation R shoulder
Nova,Ivan	18	14	Sprained R ring finger
	20	45	Tendinitis R triceps
Nuñez,Darien	21	8	Undisclosed arm injury
Nuñez,Dedniel	21	169	Sprained R elbow
Oberg,Scott	18	18	Back strain
	19	45	Blood clot R arm
	20	68	Strnd low back, blood clot R arm
	21	169	Blood clots R arm
O'Day,Darren	17	14	Strn R shoulder
	18	129	Hyperext R elbow; str L hamstring
	19	162	Strn R forearm
	21	133	Strn rotator cuff R shoulder
Odorizzi,Jake	17	30	Strn L ham; lower back
	19	11	Blister R index finger
	20	55	Strnd R intercost;brsed chest;R fing
	21	37	Strn R pronator; sore R foot
Ohtani,Shohei	18	26	Sprained UCL, R elbow
	19	41	Recovery from TJS
Olson,Tyler	18	25	Strn L lat muscle
	19	60	Shingles
Osich,Josh	18	14	Strn R hip
Osuna,Roberto	17	10	Cervical spasms
	20	58	Sore R elbow
Oswalt,Corey	20	23	Tendinitis R biceps
	21	74	Inflammation R knee
Ottavino,Adam	17	10	R shoulder inflammation
	18	18	L oblique strain
Oviedo,Johan	20	7	COVID-related
Oviedo,Luis	21	47	Strn L quad
Paddack,Chris	21	46	Strn L oblique; inflam R elbow
Pagan,Emilio	20	11	Tendinitis R biceps
Palumbo,Joe	20	53	Ulcerative colitis, Covid-19
Paredes,Enoli	21	121	Strn R shoulder; R oblique
Patiño,Luis	21	12	laceration R middle finger
Paxton,James	17	61	Strn L forearm; L pec muscle
	18	36	Low back inflam; L forearm bruise
	19	26	L knee inflammation
	20	39	Strn flexor muscle L forearm
	21	163	Strn L forearm

FIVE-YEAR INJURY LOG — Pitchers

Pitchers	Yr	Days	Injury
Payamps,Joel	21	3	COVID-related
Peacock,Brad	19	78	Sore R shoulder
	20	56	Strn R shoulder
Pearson,Nate	20	37	Strn flexor tendon R elbow
	21	29	Strn R adductor muscle
Peña,Félix	19	58	Torn ACL R knee
	21	36	Strn R hamstring
Peralta,Freddy	19	17	Sore AC joint R shoulder
	21	16	Inflammation R shoulder
Peralta,Wandy	19	28	Strn R hip flexor
	21	27	COVID-19; Strn lower back
Peralta,Wily	17	32	Strn R calf
	21	11	Blister index finger R hand
Perdomo,Angel	21	70	Strn lower back
Perdomo,Luis	17	12	R shoulder inflammation
	18	38	R shoulder strain
Pérez,Martín	17	10	Fractured R thumb
	18	84	R elbow discomfort
	21	16	COVID-19
Peters,Dillon	20	42	COVID-19
	21	11	Strn lower back
Peterson,David	20	11	Fatigued R shoulder
	21	78	Sore R side
Pfeifer,Philip	20	68	Bone bruise L elbow
Phelps,David	17	54	R elbow imping x2
	18	187	TJS
	19	82	Recovery from TJS
	21	134	Strn R lat muscle
Phillips,Evan	20	6	Inflammation R elbow
	21	11	Strn R quad
Pineda,Michael	17	79	Torn UCL R elbow
	18	187	TJS
	19	25	R knee tendinitis; strn R triceps
	21	59	Abscess leg;R elbow infl;Str L oblige
Pivetta,Nick	21	10	COVID-19
Plesac,Zach	21	45	Fx R thumb
Poche,Colin	20	68	Torn UCL L elbow
	21	169	Recovery from surgery L elbow
Pomeranz,Drew	17	12	Strn flexor L forearm
	18	73	L forearm strain; L biceps tendinitis
	19	11	Strn L Lat
	20	13	Strn L shoulder
	21	99	Tight L lat; inflammation L forearm
Ponce,Cody	21	18	Tightness R forearm
Poncedeleon,Daniel	21	68	Inflamed R shoulder
Pop,Zach	21	18	Inflammation index finger R hand
Poppen,Sean	19	30	R elbow contusion
Poteet,Cody	21	98	Sprained R knee; Strn R MCL
Poyner,Bobby	18	11	Strn L hamstring
Pressly,Ryan	19	41	Sore R knee
Price,David	17	106	Strn L elbow; L elbow inflam
	19	46	TFCC cyst L wrist; L elb tendinitis
	21	22	Strn R hamstring
Pruitt,Austin	20	68	Sore R elbow
	21	107	Recovery from surgery on R elbow
Puk,A.J.	20	68	Strn L shoulder
	21	51	Strn L biceps
Quijada,Jose	20	32	COVID-19
Quintana,Jose	20	57	Laceration R thumb, Strn L lat
	21	22	Inflamed L shoulder
Rainey,Tanner	20	17	Strn flexor muscle R forearm
	21	40	COVID-related; stress reaction R tibia
Raley,Brooks	21	71	COVID-19

FIVE-YEAR INJURY LOG — Pitchers

Pitchers	Yr	Days	Injury
Ramírez,Erasmo	18	129	R shldr/lat strn; R teres major strn
	20	1	Tightness R groin
	21	56	Strn R pectoral muscle
Ramírez,J.C.	17	41	Strn R forearm
	18	177	R elbow surg
	19	125	Recovery from TJS
Ramírez,Neil	18	11	Lower back spasms
Ramirez,Nick	21	19	Inflamed R/C L shoulder
Ramírez,Noé	19	19	Viral infection
	21	21	COVID-19
Ramírez,Yefry	19	11	Strn R calf
Ramos,A.J.	18	127	R shoulder surg
Ramos,Edubray	18	33	R shldr imping; R pat tend; fing blst
	19	94	Stiff R shldr; R shldr impingement
Ray,Robbie	17	26	Concussion
	18	59	Strn R oblique
	19	10	Lower R back spasms
	21	12	Bruised R elbow
Reed,Cody	20	12	Laceration L index finger
	21	136	sprained L thumb
Reed,Jake	21	27	Strn R forearm
Reid-Foley,Sean	21	78	Inflammation R elbow
Reyes,Alex	17	182	Surg on R elbow
	18	187	Recovery from TJS; back surg
Rhame,Jacob	19	58	Ulnar nerve transp surg R elb
Richards,Garrett	17	151	Strn R biceps
	18	103	Strn L hamstring; TJS
	19	173	Recovery from TJS
Riddle,J.T.	21	9	COVID-related
Rios,Yacksel	20	45	Inflammation L shoulder
Robertson,David	19	169	Strn R shoulder
	20	68	TJS
Robles,Hansel	18	29	Sprained R knee
Rodgers,Brady	17	29	TJS
	18	107	TJS
Rodón,Carlos	17	95	Bursitis L biceps; L shoulder inflam
	18	73	Surg on L shoulder
	19	152	L elbow inflammation
	20	52	Sore L shoulder
	21	19	L shoulder fatigue
Rodriguez,Chris	21	29	Inflammation R shoulder
Rodríguez,Dereck	18	8	Strn R hamstring
Rodríguez,Eduardo	17	45	R knee subluxation
	18	90	Recov fr R knee surg.; spr. R ankle
	20	68	Covid-19, myocarditis
	21	10	Inflammation L elbow
Rodriguez,Jefry	19	98	Strn R shoulder
	20	20	Strnd R shldr, strnd L hamstring
Rodríguez,Joely	20	37	Strn L lat, str L hamstring
	21	16	Sprained L ankle
Rodríguez,Richard	18	11	R shoulder discomfort
	19	11	R shoulder inflammation
Rodríguez,Sean	20	43	COVID-19
Roe,Chaz	17	85	Strn R lat muscle
	18	38	R groin strain
	19	9	Strn R flexor
	20	40	Sore R elbow
	21	164	Strn R shoulder
Rogers,Josh	19	96	Sprained L elbow
	21	3	Strn R hamstring
Rogers,Taylor	21	52	Sprained index finger L hand
Rogers,Trevor	21	13	Strn lower Back; COVID-related
Romano,Jordan	20	31	Strn R middle finger
	21	10	Ulnar neuritis R elbow

FIVE-YEAR INJURY LOG — Pitchers

Pitchers	Yr	Days	Injury
Romero,JoJo	21	134	Strn L elbow
Romero,Seth	20	36	Fractured R hand
Romo,Sergio	17	10	Sprained L ankle
Rosario,Randy	20	30	Tightness L forearm
Rosenthal,Trevor	17	56	Strn R lat; R elbow irritation
	19	44	Viral infection
	21	169	Inflamed R shoulder
Ross,Joe	17	79	TJS
	18	160	TJS
	21	56	Inflammation R elbow; torn UCL
Ross,Tyson	17	94	Rec surg TOS; blister index finger
	19	142	Ulnar neuritis R elbow
Ruiz,José	20	18	COVID-19
Rusin,Chris	17	10	Strn R oblique muscle
	18	27	R intercostal strn; L plant fasciitis
	19	65	Strn lower back
Ryu,Hyun-Jin	17	30	Bruised L hip; bruised L foot
	18	105	L groin strain
	19	23	Strn L groin; neck stiffness
	21	20	Strn R glute; tightness neck
Sadler,Casey	21	84	Inflamed R shoulder
Sadzeck,Connor	19	119	R elbow inflammation
Sale,Chris	18	38	Inflamed L shoulder x 2
	19	44	L elbow inflammation
	20	67	TJS
	21	143	COVID-19; recovery from TJS
Samardzija,Jeff	18	141	Strnd R pec muscle; R shldr tight
	20	52	Impingement R shoulder
Sampson,Adrian	19	14	Lower back spasms
Sanchez,Aaron	17	146	Laceration/blister R middle fing x2
	18	64	R index finger contusion
	19	41	Stained R pectoral muscle
	21	86	Tightness R biceps
Sánchez,Anibal	17	14	Strn L hamstring
	18	42	R hamstring strain
	19	13	Strn L hamstring
Sánchez,Ricardo	20	54	Sore L elbow, Covid-19
Sandlin,Nick	21	36	Strn R shoulder
Sandoval,Patrick	21	33	Strn lower back
Santana,Dennis	18	116	Strn R rotator cuff
	21	3	COVID-related
Santana,Edgar	19	187	TJS
	21	6	Strn R intercostal lig
Santana,Ervin	18	163	Surg on R middle finger
Santiago,Héctor	17	107	Strn L shoulder
Sawamura,Hirokazu	21	25	COVID-19; inflammation R triceps
Sborz,Josh	19	11	Sore lower back
Sceroler,Mac	21	56	Tendinitis R shoulder
Scherzer,Max	17	10	Neck inflammation
	19	42	Inflamed bursa sac back/shoulder
	21	11	Strn R groin
Schmidt,Clarke	21	133	Strn extensor R elbow
Scott,Tanner	21	14	Sprained R knee
Scrubb,Andre	21	91	Sore R shoulder; R shoulder strain
Senzatela,Antonio	18	24	Finger blister; R shoulder inflam
	19	19	Infected blister on R heel
	21	33	COVID-19; Strn R groin
Severino,Luis	19	174	Inflammation R/C R shoulder
	20	67	TJS
	21	169	Tommy John surgery
Shaw,Bryan	18	18	R calf strain
Sheffield,Jordan	21	92	Strn R lat muscle
Sheffield,Justus	21	57	L forearm strain
Sherfy,Jimmie	21	55	Inflammation R elbow

FIVE-YEAR INJURY LOG — Pitchers

Pitchers	Yr	Days	Injury
Sherriff,Ryan	18	27	R big toe fracture
Shoemaker,Matt	17	106	Strn R forearm
	18	154	R forearm strain
	19	163	Torn ACL L knee
	20	31	Strnd R lat, inflam R shldr
Sims,Lucas	21	47	Sprained R elbow
Singer,Brady	21	35	COVID-rel; R shldr fatigue; R biceps inj
Skoglund,Eric	18	102	Sprained L UCL
Slegers,Aaron	18	75	R shoulder inflammation
Smeltzer,Devin	21	128	Inflammation L elbow
Smith,Burch	20	44	Strn R forearm
	21	35	Strn R groin
Smith,Caleb	17	15	Viral infection
	18	99	L lat surg
	19	30	L hip inflammation
	20	39	COVID-19
Smith,Drew	19	187	TJS
	21	59	Impingement R shoulder
Smith,Joe	17	33	R shoulder inflammation
	18	24	R elbow soreness
	19	107	Recovery surgery L Achilles
	21	29	Sore R elbow
Smith,Josh	20	5	Torn fingernail
Smith,Riley	21	7	COVID-related
Smith,Will	17	182	Surg on L elbow
	18	34	TJS
	19	11	Concussion
	20	15	COVID-19
Smyly,Drew	17	182	Strn flexor L arm
	18	187	Recovery from L elbow surg
	19	16	Tightness L arm
	20	40	Strn L index finger
	21	10	Inflammation L forearm
Snell,Blake	18	13	L shoulder fatigue
	19	69	Fx R big toe; loose bodies L elbow
	21	19	Gastroenteritis x2; Strn L adductor
Snyder,Nick	21	13	R shoulder fatigue
Sobotka,Chad	19	27	Strn L ab muscle
Soria,Joakim	17	29	Strn L oblique
	18	15	R thigh strain
	21	53	COVID-19; sprained R middle finger
Soriano,José	21	169	Tommy John surgery
Soroka,Michael	18	130	R shoulder strain
	20	56	Torn R Achilles tendon
	21	169	Recovery from R Achilles injury
Sparkman,Glenn	17	88	Fractured R thumb
	20	54	Strn R forearm
Springs,Jeffrey	19	77	L biceps tendinitis
	21	47	Sprained R knee
Stanek,Ryne	19	17	Bruised R hip
	20	32	COVID-19
Stashak,Cody	20	25	Lower back inflammation
	21	101	Strn lower back
Staumont,Josh	21	15	COVID-19
Steckenrider,Drew	19	147	R elbow inflammation
	20	68	Tendinitis R triceps
	21	16	COVID-19
Steele,Justin	21	49	Strn R hamstring
Stephenson,Robert	17	10	Bruised R shoulder
	18	33	R shoulder tendinitis
	19	17	Strn cervical spine
	20	28	Strn mid-back
	21	38	Strn lower back

FIVE-YEAR INJURY LOG — Pitchers

Pitchers	Yr	Days	Injury
Stewart,Brock	17	66	R shoulder tendinitis
	18	30	R oblique strain
Stewart,Kohl	21	73	Inflammation R elbow
Stock,Robert	19	77	Inflammation R biceps
	21	58	Strn R hamstring
Strahm,Matthew	18	40	Torn L patellar tendon
	19	9	Strn L rib ligament
	20	10	Inflammation R knee
	20	10	Inflammation R knee
	21	155	Rec fr patellar tendon surg R knee
Strasburg,Stephen	17	23	R elbow nerve impingement
	18	71	R shoulder inflammation
	20	45	Carpal tunnel syndrome R hand
	21	144	Inflamed R shoulder; TOS surgery
Stratton,Chris	17	10	Dislocated/sprained R ankle
	19	45	Inflammation R ribcage
Strickland,Hunter	18	61	Fractured R hand
	19	121	Strn R lat muscle
	21	10	COVID-19
Stripling,Ross	18	35	Low back inflam; R big toe inflam.
	19	39	R biceps tendinitis
	21	48	Strn flexor R forearm; Strn L oblique
Stroman,Marcus	18	60	R shldr fatigue; fing blisters
	20	19	Strn L calf
Strop,Pedro	19	36	Strn L hamstring; neck tightness
	20	16	Strn R groin
Stumpf,Daniel	18	34	L ulnar nerve irritation
	19	15	Strn L elbow
Suarez,José	20	20	COVID-19
Suárez,Ranger	20	40	COVID-19
Suero,Wander	20	13	COVID-19
	21	25	Strn L oblique
Suter,Brent	17	19	Strn L rotator cuff
	18	80	Torn UCL - TJS
	19	158	Recovery from TJS
Swanson,Erik	20	29	Strn R forearm
	21	40	Strn R groin
Swarzak,Anthony	18	100	Strn L oblique; R shldr inflam
	19	20	R shoulder inflammation
Syndergaard,Noah	17	145	Torn R lat muscle
	18	57	Strn R index finger; viral infect
	19	15	Strn R hamstring
	20	68	TJS
	21	188	COVID-19; recovery from TJS
Taillon,Jameson	17	37	Ttesticular cancer
	19	150	Strn flexor R elbow
	20	68	TJS
	21	10	Tendon injury R ankle
Tanaka,Masahiro	17	10	R shoulder inflam
	18	32	Strn R and L hamstrings
	20	10	Concussion
Tarpley,Stephen	19	33	L shoulder impingement
	20	33	Strn R oblique
Tate,Dillon	20	34	Bruised R elbow, sprained R finger
	21	20	Strn L hamstring
Taylor,Blake	20	12	Sore L elbow
	21	45	Sprained R ankle
Taylor,Josh	20	43	Tendinitis L shldr, Covid-19
	21	10	COVID-19
Teheran,Julio	18	12	R thumb contusion
	20	14	COVID-19
	21	163	Strn R shoulder

FIVE-YEAR INJURY LOG — Pitchers

Pitchers	Yr	Days	Injury
Tepera,Ryan	18	16	R elbow inflammation
	19	126	R elbow inflammation
	21	17	Laceration R index finger
Thielbar,Caleb	21	19	COVID-related; Strn L groin
Thompson,Keegan	21	14	Inflammation R shoulder
Thompson,Ryan	21	79	Inflamed R shoulder
Thornburg,Tyler	17	182	R shoulder impingement
	18	98	recovery from R shoulder surg
	19	49	R hip impingement
	20	17	Sprained R elbow
Thornton,Trent	19	11	Inflammation R elbow
	20	51	Inflammation R elbow
Thorpe,Lewis	21	29	Impingement L shoulder
Tillo,Daniel	21	137	Tommy John surgery
Tomlin,Josh	17	32	Strn L hamstring
	18	45	Strn R hamstring
	21	19	Strn neck
Topa,Justin	21	146	Strn R elbow
Toussaint,Touki	21	107	Strn R shoulder
Treinen,Blake	19	12	Strn R shoulder
Triggs,Andrew	17	113	Strn L hip
	18	137	Blood clot, L calf
	20	15	R radial nerve irritation
Tropeano,Nicholas	17	182	Surg on R elbow to repair UCL
	18	105	R shoulder inflammation
	19	63	Strn R shoulder
Tuivailala,Sam	18	77	L knee strain; Strn R Achilles
	19	110	Surgery on R Achilles
Turley,Nik	18	96	Sprained L elbow
Turnbull,Spencer	19	34	Strn upper back; R shoulder fatigue
	21	125	COVID-19; Strn R forearm
Uceta,Edwin	21	53	Strn R lower back
Underwood,Duane	21	23	Sore R oblique; inflam R shoulder
Urena,Jose	18	13	R shoulder impingement
	19	86	Strn L lower back
	20	44	COVID-19
	21	53	Strn R forearm; Strn R groin
Urías,Julio	18	150	Recovery from L shoulder surg
	21	11	Contusion L calf
Urquidy,José	20	45	COVID-19
	21	80	Sore R shoulder x2
Valdez,César	17	54	R shoulder impingement
	21	14	Strn lower back
Valdez,Framber	21	58	Fractured L index finger
Váldez,José	18	133	R elbow inflammation
Valdez,Phillips	21	22	COVID-19
Vargas,Jason	18	65	Fractured R hand; Strn calf
	19	20	Strn L hamstring
Velasquez,Vincent	17	99	Strnd flexr R elbow;R index fing str
	18	11	Bruised R forearm
	19	18	Strn R forearm
	21	43	Blister R middle finger
Velázquez,Hector	18	11	Lower back strain
	19	31	Strn lower back
Venditte,Pat	20	41	Strn R oblique
Venters,Jonny	18	31	Strn R hamstring
	19	111	Strn L shoulder
VerHagen,Drew	18	20	Fractured nose
	19	11	Strn R forearm
Verlander,Justin	20	64	Strn R forearm/TJS
	21	169	Tommy John surgery
Vesia,Alex	20	26	COVID-19
Vest,Will	21	8	COVID-related

FIVE-YEAR INJURY LOG — Pitchers

Pitchers	Yr	Days	Injury
Vincent,Nick	18	27	Strn R groin
	19	62	Strn R pectoral muscle
Vizcaíno,Arodys	17	14	Strn R index finger
	18	73	R shoulder inflammation
	19	173	Surgery to repair torn labrum
Vólquez,Edinson	17	96	Blister R thumb; L knee tendinitis
	19	150	Sprained R elbow
	20	46	Strn R oblique
Voth,Austin	19	43	Sprained AC joint R shoulder
	21	37	COVID-19; broken nose
Wacha,Michael	18	103	L oblique strain
	19	11	Patellar tendinitis L knee
	20	19	Inflammation R shoulder
	21	20	Strn R hamstring
Waddell,Brandon	21	30	COVID-19
Waguespack,Jacob	19	36	Strn R shoulder
	20	12	Strn lower back
Wahl,Bobby	17	130	Strn R shoulder
	18	46	Strn R hamstring
	19	187	Torn ACL R knee
	21	61	Strn R oblique
Wainwright,Adam	17	44	Tight mid-back; R elbow imping
	18	150	R elbow inflam x 2; str L hamstring
	19	10	Strn L hamstring
	21	4	COVID-related
Walker,Jeremy	20	67	Impingement R shoulder
Walker,Taijuan	17	24	Blister on R index finger
	18	170	R elbow surg
	19	186	Recovery from TJS
	21	11	Tightness L oblique
Warren,Art	21	67	Stained L oblique
Warren,Austin	21	23	COVID-19
Watson,Tony	19	16	Fx L wrist
	21	11	Strn L calf
Weathers,Ryan	21	12	Fx R ankle
Weaver,Luke	19	118	Tightness R forearm
	21	107	Strn R shoulder
Webb,Jacob	19	65	R elbow impingement
	20	48	Shoulder
Webb,Logan	21	54	Strn R shoulder
Weber,Ryan	17	122	Strn R biceps
Webster,Allen	19	143	Radial nerve inflammation R arm
Weems,Jordan	20	11	Shoulder
Wells,Tyler	21	24	Inflammation R shoulder
Wendelken,J.B.	20	5	Undisclosed medical condition
	21	59	Strn L oblique
Wheeler,Zack	17	83	R biceps tend; stress react R arm
	19	15	R shoulder fatigue
White,Mitchell	21	3	COVID-related
Whitley,Kodi	20	50	COVID-19
	21	46	Strn lower back
Whitlock,Garrett	21	2	R pectoral strain
Wick,Rowan	20	12	Strn L oblique
	21	132	Strn L oblique
Widener,Taylor	20	20	Strn R ribcage muscle
	21	80	COVID-related; Strn R groin x2
Wieck,Brad	20	65	Strn R hamstring
	21	72	Irregular heartbeat
Williams,Austen	19	165	Strn L hamstring
Williams,Devin	21	11	Strn R elbow
Williams,Taylor	18	11	R elbow soreness
	21	140	Inflammation R knee
Williams,Trevor	19	34	Strn R side
	21	40	Appendix surgery

FIVE-YEAR INJURY LOG — Pitchers

Pitchers	Yr	Days	Injury
Wilson,Alex	18	32	Strn L plantar fascia
Wilson,Bryse	21	11	Fatigue R arm; Strn R hamstring
Wilson,Justin	19	67	Sore R elbow
	21	42	Inflam L shldr; Strn R hamstring
Wingenter,Trey	19	15	Strn R shoulder
	20	68	TJS
	21	169	Tommy John surgery
Winkler,Daniel	17	141	Recovery surg fractured R elbow
	21	18	COVID-related; R triceps tendinitis
Wisler,Matt	21	32	Inflamed R middle finger
Wittgren,Nick	17	65	Strn R elbow
	18	21	Bruised middle finger - R hand
Wood,Alex	17	24	SC joint inflam L shoulder x 2
	18	11	L wrist inflammation
	19	123	Lower back strain
	20	36	Inflammation R shoulder
	21	36	COVID-19; Strn lower back
Wood,Hunter	19	17	R shoulder inflammation
	21	117	Sprained UCL R elbow
Woodruff,Brandon	17	41	Strn R hamstring
	19	58	Strn L oblique
Workman,Brandon	21	6	COVID-related
Wright,Steven	17	153	Surg on L knee
	18	68	Recovery from L knee surg
	19	78	Bruised R big toe
Yajure,Miguel	21	84	Sore R forearm
Yamamoto,Jordan	19	25	Strn R forearm
	21	116	Sore R shoulder
Yarbrough,Ryan	20	10	Tightness L groin
	21	11	COVID-19
Yardley,Eric	21	26	Strn R shoulder
Yates,Kirby	18	12	R ankle tendinitis
	20	45	Bone chips R elbow
	21	169	Tommy John surgery
Ynoa,Gabriel	17	16	Strn R hamstring
	18	187	Stress reaction R shin
Ynoa,Huascar	21	93	Fx R Hand
Zeuch,T.J.	21	12	Tendinitis R shoulder
Zimmer,Kyle	20	6	Neuritis R elbow
	21	38	Strn lower back; Strn neck
Zimmermann,Bruce	21	91	Tendinitis L biceps tendon
Zimmermann,Jordan	18	40	R shoulder impingement
	19	68	Sprained UCL R elbow
	20	50	Strn R forearm

Top 75 Impact Prospects for 2022

1	Bobby Witt, Jr. (SS, KC)	21	Cristian Pache (OF, ATL)
2	Shane Baz (RHP, TAM)	22	Sixto Sánchez (RHP, MIA)
3	Julio Rodríguez (OF, SEA)	23	CJ Abrams (SS, SD)
4	Riley Greene (OF, DET)	24	Luis Campusano (C, SD)
5	Josh Jung (3B, TEX)	25	Jordan Groshans (SS, TOR)
6	Vidal Bruján (2B/OF, TAM)	26	Austin Martin (SS/OF, MIN)
7	Jarren Duran (OF, BOS)	27	MJ Melendez (C, KC)
8	Josh Lowe (OF, TAM)	28	Joe Ryan (RHP, MIN)
9	Spencer Torkelson (3B, DET)	29	Jake Burger (3B, CHW)
10	Kyle Isbel (OF, KC)	30	Brett Baty (3B, NYM)
11	Nick Pratto (1B, KC)	31	Brennan Davis (OF, CHC)
12	Adley Rutschman (C, BAL)	32	Aaron Ashby (LHP, MIL)
13	Joey Bart (C, SF)	33	Reid Detmers (LHP, LAA)
14	Triston Casas (1B, BOS)	34	Max Meyer (RHP, MIA)
15	Oneil Cruz (SS, PIT)	35	Luis Gil (RHP, NYY)
16	Nolan Gorman (2B, STL)	36	Hunter Greene (RHP, CIN)
17	Jake McCarthy (OF, ARI)	37	Gerardo Perdomo (SS, ARI)
18	Kahlil Lee (OF, NYM)	38	Matt Brash (RHP, SEA)
19	Alek Thomas (OF, ARI)	39	Edward Cabrera (RHP, MIA)
20	Seth Beer (1B, ARI)	40	Roansy Contreras (RHP, PIT)

A.J. Alexy (RHP, TEX)	Emerson Hancock (RHP, SEA)	Jeremy Peña (SS, HOU)
Logan T. Allen (LHP, CLE)	Sam Huff (C, TEX)	Oswald Peraza (SS, NYY)
Gabriel Arias (SS, CLE)	Drey Jameson (RHP, ARI)	Grayson Rodriguez (RHP, BAL)
JJ Bleday (OF, MIA)	Nolan Jones (3B/OF, CLE)	Clarke Schmidt (RHP, NYY)
Michael Busch (2B, LA)	George Kirby (RHP, SEA)	Ethan Small (LHP, MIL)
Cade Cavalli (RHP, WAS)	Royce Lewis (SS, MIN)	Bryson Stott (SS, PHI)
Tucker Davidson (LHP, ATL)	Matthew Liberatore (LHP, STL)	Spencer Strider (RHP, ATL)
Jeter Downs (SS, BOS)	Nick Lodolo (LHP, CIN)	Anthony Volpe (SS, NYY)
Tyler Freeman (SS, CLE)	Ronny Mauricio (SS, NYM)	Drew Waters (OF, ATL)
Nick Gonzales (2B, PIT)	Jose Miranda (IF, MIN)	Brandon Williamson (RHP, SEA)
MacKenzie Gore (LHP, SD)	Garrett Mitchell (OF, MIL)	Cole Winn (RHP, TEX)
DL Hall (LHP, BAL)	Gabriel Moreno (C, TOR)	

by Chris Blessing, Rob Gordon and Jeremy Deloney

Let's be honest, you've come to this part of the *Forecaster* to grab a sneak peek at the rookies you'll be spending most of your FAAB on this year. As in past years, in the following pages you'll find skills and narrative profiles of the 75 rookie-eligible prospects most likely to have an impact in 2022.

Above, we've ranked the Top 40 prospects in terms of projected 2022 Rotisserie value via our figures elsewhere in the book. Beyond those 40, we list 35 more, presented in alphabetical order, who could see time in the majors in 2022, but whose raw skill might be less polished or a step below others in terms of potential 2022 impact. Keep in mind, this is just a pre-season snapshot.

Prospects develop at different paces and making that one adjustment or finding opportunity when one doesn't seem to exist can make all the difference.

Starting on the next page, each of the 75 has his own narrative capsule, presented in alphabetical order. It's a primer on each player's strengths and weaknesses that attempts to balance raw skill, readiness for the majors and likelihood of 2022 playing time.

For even more detail, including profiles of over 900 prospects, statistics and our overall HQ100 top prospect list, see our sister publication, the *2022 Minor League Baseball Analyst*—as well as the weekly scouting reports and minor league information at BaseballHQ.com. Happy Prospecting!

CJ Abrams (SS, SD) quickly established himself as a top prospect after his draft-year success in 2019. He followed up with a solid performance in 2021, but suffered a fractured tibia and a sprained MCL that shut down his season in July. Abrams should be 100% by next spring. His elite speed, contact skills, and average over power make him an old-school leadoff hitter and his improvements on defense should get him to the majors in short order.

A.J. Alexy (RHP, TEX) made his 2021 MLB debut after a strong showing split between high minor affiliates, where he carried a 1.66 ERA and a 10.5 K/9 despite less than average overall stuff. His numbers crashed upon his MLB debut. Alexy's best pitch is his four-seam FB. He mixes a SL, CB and CU as well. He currently lacks an out pitch necessary to be rosterable in a standard format.

Logan T. Allen (LHP, CLE) is a close-to-ready performer, utilizing a rising four-seam FB out of a lower 3/4s slot to create significant deception. He rounds out his arsenal with two solid secondary offerings he commands well in and out of the zone. Despite below-average velocity, Allen piles up strikeouts with a low ERA.

Gabriel Arias (SS, CLE) slashed .284/.348/.454 with 13 HR at Triple-A. Arias has a solid hit tool, near plus bat speed, solid launch angles off of his bat and has above-average raw power. Unfortunately, over-aggressiveness has not been his friend. He's curtailed some of it but it's something MLB pitchers could exploit, which could cause problems for his short-term BA and OBP.

Aaron Ashby (LHP, MIL) has a five-pitch mix including a wipeout slider, but his most notable characterisic is a deceptive, moving-parts delivery. He commands the zone amazingly well, finished strong in a 32-inning MLB stint in 2021, which sets him up well for a 2022 role to be determined on Brewers' staff. As a starter, he has middle-of-the rotation upside.

Joey Bart (C, SF) is primed to take over as the Giants' primary backstop. In 68 Triple-A games, Bart slashed .294/.358/.472 in 2021, missing time due to quad injury. He has dealt with his share of injuries since being drafted in 2018 out of Georgia Tech. Bart is at his best offensively, getting to hard contact and lifting the ball out of the park. He does have swing-and-miss in his profile, which will affect his overall BA impact, especially as a rookie starter in 2022.

Brett Baty (3B, NYM) was the 12th overall pick in the 2019 draft and continues to show improvement in all facets of the game. Though listed as a 3B, the 22-year-old saw action in LF, a trial that should result in big league time in the very near future. Despite groundball tendencies and only 12 HR in 2021, the left-handed hitter projects to hit for a high BA with good contact skills and the chance to pop 25+ HR once he realizes his power potential.

Shane Baz (RHP, TAM) flourished at the two highest levels of the minors before showcasing his plus repertoire in three starts with the Rays to end the regular season and in the playoff rotation. Not only does he bring the heat with a high-90s FB, he locates it with precision. The enhancement in his command along with the combination of velocity and pitch movement make him very difficult to make hard contact again. He has ace potential.

Seth Beer (1B, ARI) would be the ideal benefactor should the National League adopt the designated hitter. He may not be ready for spring training due to shoulder surgery in September 2021, but his bat is too good to ignore. Beer is a career .292/.392/.509 hitter with a high of 26 HR in 2019. He has poor speed and subpar defensive abilities, but can hit for both BA and power while being a menace to left-handed pitching.

JJ Bleday (OF, MIA) has struggled to find his footing as a professional after a standout career at Vanderbilt. He still has plus raw power and a discerning eye at the plate (14% BB% rate in 2021), but his bat speed is a tick slower, his leg kick causes him to drift, and too often he is late on fastballs in the zone. Bleday made some adjustments in the Arizona Fall League, but questions remain. Despite the struggles, he has too much raw talent to give up on and he could be poised for a breakout in 2022.

Vidal Bruján (2B/OF, TAM) had a weird 2021 season, which included a HR barrage in May, a slump in June and his MLB debut later in the summer. While his MLB debut was forgettable, Brujan slashed .262/.345/.440 with 12 HR, 31 2B and 44 SB in Triple-A. The switch-hitter is at his best as a slasher, working holes and shooting gaps and utilizing his foot speed. Even in an up-down scenario, will have SB value.

Matt Brash (RHP, SEA) is an under-the-radar prospect who, while not blessed with tremendous size, reaches the high 90s with a plus fastball and can wipe out hitters with a devastating SL that he locates well. If he can polish and enhance his change-up, he looks like a #2-3 type starter for many years to come.

Jake Burger (3B, CHW) overcame two Achilles tendon tears to post productive returns in his first action since 2017. He slashed .274/.332/.513 with 18 HR in 82 Triple-A games, plus logged an .807 OPS in 42 MLB plate appearances. It's a power-over-hit profile, though he does well game-planning his at-bats. That helps him maximize his hard-hit tendencies which will lead to HR.

Michael Busch (2B, LA) consistently comes to the plate with a reasonable plan and uses his disciplined eye, short stroke and picturesque swing to make easy, hard contact. He performed very well in 2021, hitting .267/.386/.484 with 20 HR in Double-A. He saw action at 1B, though 2B is his best spot. If his power continues to develop, then he has a chance to be a potential impact bat in the middle of the Dodgers lineup.

Edward Cabrera (RHP, MIA) is a strong bet to begin the 2022 campaign ensconced in the middle of the Marlins rotation. He started seven games for Miami in 2021 and though his control and command failed him, he showed dynamic swing-and-miss stuff. Blessed with a fastball that sits in the high-90s, he also has improved the shape of his hard slider to complement his above average change-up.

Luis Campusano (C, SD) spent most of the season in Triple-A after initially struggling in MLB; he had a .906 OPS and hit 15 HR in the minors but missed out on a late-season promotion due to an oblique injury. The hit tool carries the overall profile, as Campusano is adept at hitting balls to the gaps. Like every rookie catcher, expect some struggles with the bat early on.

Triston Casas (1B, BOS) enjoyed a spectacular season between Double-A and Triple-A in 2021, hitting .279/.394/.484 with 14 HR. He benefited from an increased walk rate and combined his seasoned approach with massive raw power. Though his swing can get long, he understands the strike zone innately and can reach the seats in any ballpark with a flick of the bat thanks to his natural strength and elite bat speed.

Cade Cavalli (RHP, WAS) is a power pitcher who emerged as one of the top pitching prospects in baseball last year, piling up 175 strikeouts in 123.1 innings. Cavalli throws four pitches and varies between a four-seam FB with incredible ride, and a two-seam FB with sink. His best secondary offering is a plus curveball with plus downward break. Command concerns cloud immediate impact potential, but he should get the call for Washington this year.

Roansy Contreras (RHP, PIT) worked hard to reshape his body during the lockdown and came into the season noticeably stronger, more athletic, and with better velocity. Despite his small frame, Contreras blows away hitters with a plus 95-97 mph fastball and his secondary offerings are good enough to keep hitters off-balance. There is some effort to his delivery, but he tunnels his pitches well and was impressive in his one start in Pittsburgh. He should get an extended look as a rotation candidate and is an excellent sleeper prospect.

Oneil Cruz (SS, PIT) made his major league debut in 2021 after establishing career highs in HR (17) and SB (19) along with the ability to stick at shortstop. Many evaluators foresee a move to a corner outfield position because of his 6'-6" size and double-plus arm strength, but he can handle the infield. His raw power is unmatched in the system and he will be counted on to provide offensive oomph and electricity in a rather moribund lineup.

Tucker Davidson (LHP, ATL) has a solid four-pitch mix headlined by a fastball that is a tick above-average from the LH-side, sitting at 92-94 and topping at 96. With the Braves starting rotation in flux following their World Series win, Davidson should get a chance at a rotation spot at some point in 2022, but realistically profiles as a back-end starter.

Brennen Davis (OF, CHC) spent time at three levels last season, doing most of his damage in Double-A, where he slashed .252/.367/.474. Overall, he hit 19 HR and stole 8 bases. He struggles some with his hit tool, due to his long levers that create plate coverage holes, and spin recognition issues. The could result in weak BA returns early, but the power carries the profile, both over the short and long terms.

Reid Detmers (LHP, LAA) posted a dominant 3.19 ERA with 108 strikeouts in just 62 innings in the minors, but was roughed up in his MLB debut. He features an average low-90s fastball that maxes out at 98 but has low spin, which puts pressure on his other offerings. Fortunately Detmers also packs a plus 12-6 curve, a

slider, and a serviceable changeup. He will get an extended look in 2022, and projects as a solid mid-rotation starter.

Jeter Downs' (SS, BOS) hit tool absolutely cratered in 2021, as he slashed .190/.272/.333 and wasn't on base enough to utilize his run tool (18 SB in 21 attempts). He's regained some promise with a strong Arizona Fall League, though he still shows problems reacting to spin. He's likely a source of SB and occasional HR if he finds MLB playing time in 2022.

Jarren Duran's (OF, BOS) speed has always carried his profile. However, a swing transformation allowed for more power to develop in 2021. In Triple-A, he slashed .258/.357/.516 with 16 HR and 16 SB in 60 games. He struggled mightily in MLB, as pitchers exposed his hit tool and uber-aggressiveness. It remains to be seen if Duran makes the proper adjustments to get back to hard contact.

Tyler Freeman (INF, CLE) is one of the best pure hitters in the minors and now owns a career .319 batting average over four seasons. A labrum tear in July resulted in shoulder surgery that limited him to just 164 AB, but he should be 100% by spring. Freeman has a line-drive, contact-oriented approach and excellent bat-to-ball skills that have held up as he's advanced. The lack of power (just 9 career HR) could force him into a super utility role once he reaches the majors.

Luis Gil (RHP, NYY) made his MLB debut and pitched well despite below-average command. His 3.07 ERA and 11.7 K/9 were better than command measures indicated. At his best, Gil overpowers with a high-riding, high-velocity FB. His SL is also solid and capable of getting whiffs. But command improvement is key to reaching his ceiling.

Nick Gonzales (2B, PIT) showed better than anticipated power, notching 45 XBH and a .302 average in 324 AB in his pro debut. He shows an advanced ability to square up the baseball, but did have more swing-and-miss as he hunted for pitches he could drive. Drafted as a SS, he was quickly moved to 2B where he is unlikely to be more than an average defender. Though speed is not part of his game, his advanced bat and improved power profile give him plenty of value.

MacKenzie Gore (LHP, SD) struggled mightily, as his stuff and command backed up in 2021—so much that he's no longer in the conversation as the minors' top pitching prospect. His fastball was back up to the mid-90s in the Arizona Fall League and he's trying to recapture the feel of his CB but the results haven't been good. It remains to be seen what sort of impact he has moving forward.

Nolan Gorman (2B, STL) has some of the best raw power in the minors and smoked 25 home runs as a 21-year-old in 2021. He can be overly aggressive at the plate, but his K% fell from 32% in 2019 to less than 20% once he moved up to Triple-A Memphis. The position change from 3B to 2B and his production at Triple-A gives him a clear path to full-time ABs, where his 30+ HR potential is hard to find.

Hunter Greene (RHP, CIN) finally got back on track after not pitching competitively since 2018 due to Tommy John surgery.

His plus fastball sits in the upper-90s and tops out at 102 mph; a cutter and a plus slider gives him elite swing-and-miss stuff (11.8 K/9). Greene works up in the zone, making him susceptible to the long ball, but he has the stuff to be a future ace and should be ready to make his MLB debut in 2022.

Riley Greene (OF, DET) continued to showcase an advanced hit tool for age/level, dominating the two top minor league levels in 2021, as he slashed .301/.387/.524 with 24 HR and 16 SB. He struck out an alarming 153 times, but when he makes contact, it's usually hard contact sprayed to all fields. Greene has found some over-the-fence pull power, but may struggle to get to high HR numbers early due to the swing-and-miss.

Jordan Groshans (SS, TOR) hardly missed a beat after missing most of 2019 with a foot injury, hitting .291/.367/.450 with 23 doubles and 7 HR at Double-A. He is as smooth of a hitter as there is in the system and the Blue Jays will look to get his natural bat into the lineup at some point in 2022. Most see an eventual move to 3B – where he got ample reps this season – and his hitting prowess should more than suffice.

D.L. Hall (LHP, BAL) is a short lefty who ended his season in early June due to a stress reaction in his elbow. Fortunately, there are no structural concerns and he is expected to be fully healthy for spring training. He has dynamic stuff, highlighted by an electric fastball with both velocity and movement. He operates with two breaking balls, both help in achieving very high strikeout rates. With better command, Hall could be a #2 starter.

Emerson Hancock (RHP, SEA) is one among many arms that should compete for time in Seattle's rotation in 2022. The tall and strong righty certainly delivered in his first pro experience in 2021 with a 2.62 ERA and 8.7 K/9 in 12 starts between High-A and Double-A. Though he missed time with shoulder tenderness, he is a smart and savvy pitcher with a solid fastball and slider.

Sam Huff (C, TEX) returned in late June from a knee injury and he assaulted minor league pitching with his tremendous all-fields power. He is considered a favorite to win a big league job in 2022 and should, at the very least, inject double-plus pop into the lineup. He will also likely stick behind the plate long-term due to advances in his receiving and blocking.

Kyle Isbel (OF, KC) showed enough in his MLB debut to be in contention for the starting RF job next spring. Isbel is a bit undersized and has a wiry, athletic frame with above-average speed and enough pop to hit 15-20 HR at peak. Isbel will need to tap into that power more consistently to develop into an everyday regular. Speed is his best asset and he can play all three OF spots, giving him positional flexibility.

Drey Jameson (RHP, ARI) is undersized and undervalued, but took a huge step forward in 2021, posting a 3.98 ERA and striking out 145 in 110.2 IP between High-A and Double-A. He has a compact, repeatable delivery with plus arm speed that generates mid-90s velocity on his heater, topping at 100 mph. Jameson mixes in a pair of above-average breaking balls and an improved change-up. He tends to work away from hitters and struggles with command at times so he could play well in relief.

Nolan Jones (3B/OF, CLE) is willing to draw walks as he waits for pitches he can drive. At times, he has been criticized for being too selective and falling behind in too many ABs, raising concerns about his ability to fully tap into his plus power at the next level. He will need that power as he is a below-average defender at 3B; the club had him split time in RF before a season-ending ankle injury in September.

Josh Jung (3B, TEX) has plus bat-to-ball skills and rarely chases balls out of the zone—a rare feat for a player with plus power. Jung was limited to just 304 AB, but he still managed 42 XBH and a .592 SLG%. Jung is an above-average defender at 3B with a decent range, good hands, and a strong arm. The retooling Rangers should be able to make room for Jung to take over at 3B in 2022 and his career line of .322/.394/.538 is plenty to get excited about.

George Kirby (RHP, SEA) more than held his own during stints at High-A and Double-A, striking out 80 while walking just 15 in 67.2 IP. Kirby doesn't light up the radar gun, but instead keeps hitters off-balance with a plus four-pitch mix. His fastball sits at 91-94 with good spin and arm-side run and his slider, curveball, and change-up all flash as above-average to plus. What separates Kirby from others is his plus command of all four offerings.

Khalil Lee (OF, NYM) slashed .274/.451/.500 with 14 HR in 102 Triple-A games, all career highs, and limited his K-rate significantly. Unfortunately, he was exposed in his big league debut, striking out 13 times in 18 plate appearances. His inflated 2019 stolen base totals dropped dramatically; he'll have value due to his speed, but this is likely a fourth outfielder profile.

Royce Lewis (SS, MIN) missed last year due to ACL surgery, but when healthy, is a power/speed performer who struggles with whiffs due to a great deal of moving parts in his swing. The power is mostly to the pull side and his plus speed plays in games. He has 20 HR/20 SB potential and the athleticism to play anywhere.

Matthew Liberatore (LHP, STL) is a sum-of-all-his-pitches type of prospect. A velocity spike late in the season helped salvage a rather lackluster Triple-A campaign where he posted a 4.04 ERA and struck out just less than a batter an inning. His tools are close to projection, likely a back-end SP long term with limited strikeout potential.

Nick Lodolo (LHP, CIN) added velocity to his command/control arsenal, increasing his strikeout profile and elevating his upside from a back-end SP to a potential mid-rotation SP. Lodolo utilizes a lower 3/4s slot and can achieve some ride on his FB. His best secondary is a sweeping CB he can utilize against both lefties and righties. His command should allow Lodolo to compete against MLB hitters out of the gate.

Josh Lowe (OF, TAM) has a lot of competition for playing time in the deep Rays system. He hit .291/.381/.535 with 22 HR and 26 SB in Triple-A and even earned a promotion to the majors. Despite his first round pedigree, he doesn't often get the spotlight he has earned, but he has quietly been terrific with both the bat and glove. As a true centerfielder, his glovework may give him a leg up for a big league spot.

Austin Martin (SS/OF, MIN) is a hit-over-power tool hitter lauded for his ability to go to the opposite field. He had an odd .270/.414/.382 slash line; he must make an adjustment in his lower half to enable him to lift the ball in the air to the pull side for power. He's extremely disciplined and has advanced contact skills. Martin may also have multi-positional eligibility (2B, SS, 3B & OF) with some SB potential sprinkled in.

Ronny Mauricio (SS, NYM) is a lean, projectable, switch-hitting shortstop who is just starting to tap into his full potential. An aggressive approach and lengthy swing results in too much swing-and-miss and not enough walks (5% BB% and 25% K%), which his offensive production—though he did swat a career-high 20 home runs. Mauricio shows good instincts, soft hands, and a strong arm, but he could outgrow the position as he matures and fills out his 6'3", 165 frame.

Jake McCarthy (OF, ARI) has solid tools and an opportunity to get meaningful at-bats in the Arizona outfield in 2022. The left-handed hitter only hit .220/.333/.373 in 59 AB in the majors, but he has 20+ HR potential to complement his disciplined approach. With above-average speed and shrewd instincts, he should steal bases as well.

MJ Melendez (C, KC) retooled his swing at the Royals alternate training site and had a monster season, crushing 41 home runs between Double and Triple-A. Melendez does have some swing-and-miss as he chases power, but a more disciplined approach (14% BB% and 22% K%) fueled the breakout. He has a plus arm and athleticism to stick at catcher, but also saw some action at 3B at Triple-A given the presence of Salvador Perez. But the Royals will need to find a way to get his bat into their lineup on a regular basis.

Max Meyer (RHP, MIA) enjoyed a splendid pro debut; he finished the year with a 2.27 ERA and 10.5 K/9 in 22 starts. It's likely he'll pitch meaningful innings with the Marlins at some point in 2022 whether as a starter or reliever. He owns two plus offerings in his 93-97 mph fastball and hard slider. Both are legitimate out pitches in any role.

Jose Miranda (IF, MIN) broke out in a big way in 2021, slashing .344/.401/.572 with 30 HR split between upper minor affiliates and showcasing versatility to play across the IF. Miranda has reworked his approach and swing, which has enabled him to get to hard contact frequently while not losing his plus contact ability. He could be in line for playing time in 2022.

Garrett Mitchell (OF, MIL) had some of the best all-around tools in the 2020 draft class, but concerns about his Type 1 diabetes caused him to slide to the Brewers at #20. At the plate, he uses a compact, contact-oriented approach to shoot line drives to the pull side and questions remain about his long-term power development. Mitchell has plus speed, a strong arm, and gold glove caliber defense in CF. If he can learn to tap into his raw power, he has the other tools to be an All-Star caliber player.

Gabriel Moreno (C, TOR) is unlikely to contend for an Opening Day role with the Blue Jays as currently constituted, though Moreno had one of the best seasons in all of minor league baseball in 2021 and his time will come soon. Moreno should hit for a very high BA to go along with 20 HR while being an above average backstop. He does not strike out often and is a career .308 hitter. The Blue Jays could really use those ingredients in 2022.

Cristian Pache (OF, ATL) did not live up to the billing early in 2021 when he hit .111/.152/.206 in 63 at-bats. The 22-year-old will make his case for another shot in 2022, given the openings in Atlanta's outfield. He has the potential to be an elite defender in CF with double-plus speed. Offensively, there is a lot of upside with bat speed and pitch recognition.

Jeremy Peña (SS, HOU) missed most of 2021 recovering from a fractured wrist, but was surprisingly productive when he returned to action, belting a career-high 10 home runs in just 145 AB. He is a plus defender with good range, hands, and a strong, accurate arm and has the potential to be a 20 HR/20 SB shortstop down the road, and could contend for the starting SS job in the spring if it's open.

Oswald Peraza (SS, NYY) has the best bat-to-ball skills in the Yankees system and a tweak in his approach allowed him to get more balls in the air and to tap into his plus raw power. Peraza is a plus runner and swiped 38 bags to go along with 26 doubles and 18 home runs across three different levels. An above-average to plus defender at short, he shows good instincts and a strong arm. An exciting player who put it all together in 2021.

Geraldo Perdomo (SS, ARI) saw his normally reliable hit tool disappear early and reemerge after a stint working out at Arizona's complex mid-season. Afterwards, Perdomo slashed .329/.414/.521 in Double-A, earning a late season call-up. If Perdomo is able to maintain his swing adjustment, he could be a source of BA and OBP returns as a rookie.

Nick Pratto (1B, KC) casually went out and hit .265/.385/.602 with 28 doubles and 36 HR between Double-A and Triple-A after an awful 2019 season. He cleaned up his swing, modified his approach and started to tap into his natural bat speed and leverage. The left-handed hitter finished 2nd in the minors in HR and should battle for the starting first base job in spring training. Given his above-average glovework, he could even challenge for Rookie of the Year honors.

Grayson Rodriguez (RHP, BAL) has established himself as the top pitching prospect in baseball. He used an elite four-pitch mix to overpower hitters en route to a 2.36 ERA and a 14.1 K% between High-A and Double-A. Rodriguez works off a plus fastball that sits at 94-97, up to 99 mph with excellent spin and command. He complements the fastball with a plus slider, a 12-6 curveball, and a plus change-up with late fade and sink. When he's on—which was most of 2021—his stuff can be unhittable (just 58 hits allowed in 103 IP) and has the potential to be a legitimate staff ace.

Julio Rodríguez (OF, SEA) is a consensus top-three prospect in all of baseball and has the skills and pedigree to be a cornerstone player for years to come. Despite being only 20, the right-handed hitter makes the game look easy with both the bat and glove. He hit .347/.441/.560 with 13 HR and 21 SB between High-A and

Double-A in 2021 and is a career .331 hitter. While there may be other players in front of him on the depth chart, there is little doubt he will make a big impact in 2022, possibly early in the year.

Adley Rutschman (C, BAL) was the first overall selection in 2019 and the big question revolves around service time. His bat is certainly ready—he went.285/.397/.502 with 23 HR between Double-A and Triple-A in 2021. He makes incredibly consistent contact and works deep counts. There is some work he needs to do behind the plate, but the bat is more than special.

Joe Ryan (RHP, MIN) is a unique pitcher, a product of today's emphasis on riding FBs and biomechanical coaching techniques. He creates double-plus deception with his FB by flicking his wrist forward late in his delivery from a high 3/4s angle. This plays up his low-90s riding FB to elite levels, and he throws it nearly 70% of the time. His secondaries, grouped together, are rather ordinary. It remains to be seen the role Ryan is best suited for, but he'll pile strikeouts wherever he's at.

Sixto Sánchez (RHP, MIA) did not pitch in 2021 (shoulder surgery), which comes on the heels of seven starts in 2020 that gave a glimpse of his enormous upside. Though he should be ready for spring training, it may take time to get back into a rhythm. He operates with exceptional velocity and a change-up that may rank among the best in baseball. He's still only 23 and has the goods to be a top-of-the-rotation stud in short order.

Clarke Schmidt (RHP, NYY) may have missed most of the season with an elbow strain, but he was able to make his way back to the majors in 2021. He has been beset by a variety of ailments over the years, but can toy with hitters by appropriately sequencing his above-average 95 mph fastball with an outstanding, tight curveball that he uses as his wipeout pitch. He could contend for a starting spot in spring training.

Ethan Small (LHP, MIL) comes after hitters with a slight hesitation and straight over-the-top arm slot and gets surprising carry up in the zone on his 89-92 mph fastball. He pairs the fastball with a 12-6 curveball and above-average change-up, and relies on disrupting hitters' timing and changing speeds rather than elite stuff. He also gets a surprising amount of weak contact, but struggles with control could create challenges at the next level.

Bryson Stott (SS, PHI) has an opportunity to win a job with the Phillies in spring training after an eye-opening campaign at three levels of the minors in 2021 and the Arizona Fall League. He has gotten stronger over the last two years which has culminated in more power than anticipated and a mature approach to use all fields. Though strikeouts can be an issue, he should hit for a moderately high BA with possible 20+ HR power and above-average defensive skills.

Spencer Strider's (RHP, ATL) fastball now sits in the mid-90s, topping out at 99 mph with excellent late life up in the zone. He has a max-effort delivery that leads to below-average command which is offset some by his 14.9 K%. The lack of secondary offerings likely means a permanent move to relief, where he has the stuff to pitch in high-leverage situations.

Alek Thomas (OF, ARI) exploded when bumped up to Triple-A Reno, slashing .369/.434/.658 in 149 AB there. He has a busy approach at the plate but keeps his weight back as he drives into the zone with a quick bat and smooth LH stroke. Thomas roasted RHP (1.133 OPS) but handles LHP well and so is not a likely platoon candidate. Plus speed gives him Thomas the potential to be a 20 HR/20 SB threat at peak and he should be able to stick in CF.

Spencer Torkelson (1B/3B, DET) combines plus power with a discerning eye at the plate and plus bat-to-ball skills. He saw extended action at 3B in his pro debut and while he improved defensively, the Tigers had him playing 1B exclusively when he moved up to Triple-A Toledo. Torkelson has elite offensive tools and the potential to post .300/.400/.500 slash lines on a regular basis. He should be considered a top AL Rookie of the Year candidate in 2022.

Anthony Volpe (SS, NYY) was always considered an advanced hitter with above-average speed, but he was noticeably stronger and the uptick in power put him on the verge of a 30 HR/30 SB season as a 20-year-old in 2021. Volpe uses a compact RH stroke and an advanced understanding of the strike zone to hunt for pitches he can punish. At 5-11, 180 he will need to prove that 2021 was no fluke, but a SS with a 1.027 OPS is someone to keep an eye on.

Drew Waters (OF, ATL) struggled in 2021, slashing .240/.329/.381 in Triple-A. The switch-hitter has curtailed some of his aggressiveness but his whiff rate has climbed exponentially and his hard hit percentage has fallen. He's much better as a left-handed hitter and could be a candidate to give up hitting right-handed, like Cedric Mullins did. He could have some 2022 SB impact.

Brandon Williamson (RHP, SEA) has among the top strikeout rates in a pitching-rich farm system. He was very effective between High-A and Double-A in his first full pro season and that could translate to higher levels. His deceptively quick delivery and fastball give hitters fits and he has a slider that misses bats with tremendous break.

Cole Winn (RHP, TEX) ascended top prospect charts with a dominant 2021 and will have a reasonable chance to pitch in the big leagues in 2022. He held hitters to a .145 oppBA while posting a 32.2% strikeout rate in 21 total starts (mostly at Double-A). With a plus 93-97 mph fastball and above-average slider, he could evolve into a #2 or #3 starter in the near-term.

Bobby Witt, Jr. (SS, KC) emerged as one of the two top prospects in baseball last season. The second-generation player did nearly identical damage at the two top minor league levels, slashing a combined .290/.361/.575 with 33 HR and 29 SB. High strikeout potential complicates his true BA upside. However, in 2021, Witt did better to adjust his bat path to get to balls lower in the zone. Power and speed carry the profile as a rookie.

Top Players from East Asia for 2022 and Beyond

by Tom Mulhall

Despite some optimism about free agents from East Asia in 2021, events caused it to be one of the more disappointing in years. Several top stars were posted but only a few lesser talents were signed. The biggest letdown was the lack of interest in Tomoyuki Sugano, one of the premier starting pitchers in Japan.

Not only are MLB teams offering less money, Japanese teams are starting to offer their free agent stars better contracts with opt-out provisions. This means that MLB teams can no longer simply out-bid the Japanese teams. With labor issues looming and COVID-19 still a factor, we may see another slow signing season for players from East Asia.

But the talent is still there, as shown by Japan's Olympic Gold Medal run where they went undefeated, including two wins over Silver Medal Team USA. This could mean an opportunity for you if your opponents decide to write off these players, especially if you have a large farm or reserve team.

NOTES: For more background, see the Encyclopedia article about East Asia baseball regarding style of play and the posting systems beginning on page 50. The Sawamura Award for starting pitchers is roughly equivalent to the Cy Young Award but is not given every year. It emphasizes complete games and wins over other stats. Names are sometimes difficult to translate so the official NPB or KBO designation is used.

Jung-Hoo Lee (OF, Kiwoom Heroes) is a young hitting machine who won the KBO batting title with a .360 BA nearly 30 years after his father won the same title. In five seasons he has a career .341 BA and .404 OBP. Lee doesn't have much power but plays good defense and has some speed. He probably projects as an average fourth OF if he makes it to MLB. Just 23, Lee is a few years away from being posted, but Ha-seong Kim showed that Korean teams will post their younger stars.
Possible ETA: 2023

Raidel Martínez (RHP, Chunichi Dragons) is a 6'-3", 205 pound Cuban who has played in Japan the past four seasons and could be available to interested MLB teams. Closers coming from Japan have a decent track record when making the move to MLB, and the 25-year-old righty could continue that trend. He's logged seasons with ERAs of 2.66 and 1.13, and in 2021 had a 2.06 ERA and 0.75 WHIP with 59 strikeouts in 48 IP.
Possible ETA: 2022

Hiroya Miyagi (LHP, Orix Buffaloes) has the misfortune of being overshadowed by his amazing teammate, Yoshinobu Yamamoto, who is the best young pitcher in the NPB. Although still many years away from free agency, you have to start tracking a pitcher who made the All-Star team and finished second in the Pacific League in ERA in just his second year. For those of you who have a long-term farm club and missed out on Yamamoto, Miyagi may be a nice consolation prize.
Possible ETA: 2025

Sung-Bum Na, also rendered as **Seong-Beom Na (OF, NC Dinos)** has a strong desire to play in MLB and signed with Scott Boras to make that happen. However, at age 33, he has probably missed his window of opportunity after drawing no interest in 2021. That's unfortunate since the lefty has a solid batting eye, raw power and plays good defense.
Barely possible ETA: 2022

Haruki Nishikawa (OF, Nippon Ham Fighters) drew no interest from MLB teams when posted last season. The speedster has won the SB title three times, but slumped again in 2021 as he did in 2019, so consistency is an issue. Nishikawa is a good defender with a lifetime .380 OBP but at age 29, he may have run out of time.
Possible ETA: 2022

Koudai Senga (RHP, SoftBank Hawks) has finally earned domestic free agency rights and is just a year away from international free agency, which is usually when a team decides to post them. However, the Hawks are a notoriously conservative team that almost never posts, so Senga may have to wait one more year. The wait could be worth it as he is major league ready, with a 98-mph fastball and an excellent forkball/splitter. When his control is on, he is almost unhittable. In the last three seasons, he has had an ERA of 2.79, 2.16 and 2.66, giving him a lifetime ERA of 2.69. Senga is an elite pitcher in Japan and projects to be a solid mid-level starting pitcher in MLB.
Probable ETA: 2023

Robert Suarez (RHP, Hanshin Tigers) is a 30-year-old Venezuelan who originally started in the Mexican League and has pitched in Japan the last five years, where he has developed into a dependable closer. After a solid 2020 season, he finished 2021 with an impressive 42 saves, 58 strikeouts, 1.16 ERA and 0.77 WHIP in 62.1 IP. Now a free agent, he will probably try his luck in MLB if Hanshin doesn't make a decent offer.
Possible ETA: 2022

Tomoyuki Sugano (RHP, Yomiuri Giants) almost incomprehensibly failed to attract sufficient offers from any MLB team when he was posted in 2021, despite only asking for a contract similar to the one signed by Yusei Kikuchi. He now has full free agent rights, which means he can sign without a MLB team having to pay a posting fee. Sugano has plus command of up to seven pitches including a deadly slider and curveball, which complement an average fastball in the low to mid-90s. Sugano had one of the best seasons in his storied career in 2020 and still managed a 3.19 ERA in 2021 while battling minor ailments. Of all the pitchers in Japan who have reached free agency, he would have the biggest immediate impact and projects to a solid mid-level starting pitcher in MLB.
Probable ETA: 2022

Seiya Suzuki (OF, Hiroshima Carp) now has six consecutive seasons with 25 or more HR, capped off with a spectacular 2021 campaign with 38 HR and a Central League Batting Championship. Suzuki is a solid defender who should have no

defensive issues in MLB. He has an excellent plate discipline, with a career .414 OBP. Almost certain to sign with a MLB team at some point soon, perhaps even this year, Suzuki may prove whether Ohtani's power production is a fluke. This is the hitter to take a chance on.
Almost definite ETA: 2022

Masahiro Tanaka (RHP, Tohoku Rakuten Golden Eagles) needs no introduction and is listed here just so we don't forget about him. While he signed a two-year contract in 2021, there could be an opt-out after one season. Although he went 4-9 during his return to Japan, he had a solid 3.01 ERA and 1.03 WHIP. Does he have enough left at his age to justify a reserve pick?
Possible ETA: 2022

Yoshinobu Yamamoto (RHP, Orix Buffaloes) put up three solid seasons before breaking out this season to become perhaps the best pitcher in Japan. After leading the league in 2019 with a 1.95 ERA and following it up with an astonishing 2.20 ERA in 2020, Yamamoto dominated the league in 2021 with a minuscule 1.39 ERA and 0.848 WHIP. Yamamoto has a fastball in the mid-90s, complemented with a splitter and a knee-buckling curveball. Yamamoto is just 5'8" so there will be questions about his durability, but he pitched 193.2 innings in 2021. If you have a large and long-term farm team, this is the guy you want.
Possible ETA: 2024

Conclusion

If you have an early draft before free agent signings, the two players to take for 2022 are Sugano and Suzuki. The long-term target would be Senga, and the very long-term target is clearly Yamamoto.

Other players previously covered who may be taken off your watch list: Former MLB player Shin-Soo Choo (impressive 20/20 year in Korea but now age 39); shortstop Ryosuke Kikuchi (long-term contract); pitcher Takahiro Norimoto (long-term contract); shortstop Hayato Sakamoto (age 32); infielder Tetsuto Yamada (long-term contract); former closer Yasuaki Yamasaki (two subpar years in a row); and outfielder Yuki Yanagita (six years remaining on long-term contract after which he will "finish"). Note that a new trend in Japan is to sign a long-term contract that includes an opt-out provision, so don't completely give up on those players.

In his 1985 *Baseball Abstract*, Bill James introduced the concept of major league equivalencies. His assertion was that, with the proper adjustments, a minor leaguer's statistics could be converted to an equivalent major league level performance with a great deal of accuracy.

Because of wide variations in the level of play among different minor leagues, it is difficult to get a true reading on a player's potential. For instance, a .300 batting average achieved in the high-offense Pacific Coast League is not nearly as much of an accomplishment as a similar level in the Eastern League. MLEs normalize these types of variances, for all statistical categories.

The actual MLEs are not projections. They represent how a player's previous performance might look at the major league level. However, the MLE stat line can be used in forecasting future performance in just the same way as a major league stat line would.

The model we use contains a few variations to James' version and updates all of the minor league and ballpark factors. In addition, we designed a module to convert pitching statistics, which is something James did not originally do.

Players are listed if they spent at least part of 2019 or 2021 in Triple-A or Double-A (R.I.P. Minor League Baseball in 2020) and had at least 100 AB or 30 IP within those two levels (players who split a season at both levels are indicated as a/a). Major league and Single-A (and lower) stats are excluded. Each player is listed in the organization with which they finished the season. Some players over age 30 with major-league experience have been omitted for space.

These charts also provide the unique perspective of looking at two seasons' worth of data—even when the span is over three years. These are only short-term trends, for sure. But even here we can find small indications of players improving their skills, or struggling, as they rise through more difficult levels of competition. Since players—especially those with any modicum of talent —are promoted rapidly through major league systems, a two-season scan is often all we get to spot any trends. Five-year trends do appear in the *Minor League Baseball Analyst*.

Used correctly, MLEs are excellent indicators of potential. But, just like we cannot take traditional major league statistics at face value, the same goes for MLEs. The underlying measures of base skill—contact rates, pitching command ratios, BPV, etc.—are far more accurate in evaluating future talent than raw home runs, batting averages or ERAs. This chart format focuses more on those underlying gauges.

Here are some things to look for as you scan these charts:

Target players who...
- had a full season's worth of playing time in AA and then another full year in AAA
- had consistent playing time from one year to the next
- improved their base skills as they were promoted

Raise the warning flag for players who...
- were stuck at the same level both years, or regressed
- displayed marked changes in playing time from one year to the next
- showed large drops in BPIs from one year to the next

BATTER	yr	b	age	pos	lvl	org	ab	hr	sb	ba	bb%	ct%	px	sx	bpv
Abrams,CJ	21	L	21	SS	aa	SD	162	1	10	259	7	76	78	97	10
Abreu,Willie	19	L	24	RF	aa	COL	159	2	5	223	10	69	87	128	-3
	21	L	26	LF	aa	COL	228	5	3	197	4	65	90	41	-44
Adams,Riley	19	R	23	C	aa	TOR	287	11	3	252	10	61	155	140	23
	21	R	25	C	aaa	WAS	120	5	0	202	10	56	146	50	-20
Adell,Jo	19	R	20	RF	a/a	LAA	280	7	6	257	8	67	141	116	29
	21	R	22	CF	aaa	LAA	311	14	5	229	4	63	132	95	-4
Adolfo,Micker	19	R	23	DH	aa	CHW	78	0	0	192	15	48	129	10	-84
	21	R	25	RF	a/a	CHW	367	19	3	202	6	55	167	70	-12
Adolph,Ross	21	L	25	LF	aa	HOU	216	8	2	204	8	58	117	90	-31
Aguilar,Ryan	19	L	25	1B	aa	MIL	72	3	2	228	10	62	129	92	-7
	21	L	27	CF	aa	MIL	213	4	6	115	11	48	69	105	-99
Alcantara,Arisme	19	B	28	2B	a/a	NYM	403	12	17	227	8	64	119	212	29
	21	B	30	SS	aaa	SF	232	9	1	199	5	53	135	101	-36
Alexander,C.J.	21	L	25	3B	aa	ATL	304	8	12	174	6	61	111	131	-13
Alford,Anthony	19	R	25	RF	aaa	TOR	282	6	18	232	8	62	119	178	11
	21	R	27	CF	aaa	PIT	189	9	6	242	11	51	171	63	-18
Allen,Austin	19	L	25	C	aaa	SD	270	13	0	262	5	75	167	48	61
	21	L	27	C	aaa	OAK	281	12	0	240	3	75	100	27	-3
Allen,Greg	19	B	26	CF	aaa	CLE	198	4	8	232	7	74	87	170	30
	21	B	28	LF	aaa	NYY	215	4	19	257	8	73	69	134	7
Allen,Nick	21	R	23	SS	a/a	OAK	339	4	8	241	6	74	60	85	-15
Almora,Albert	19	R	25	CF	aaa	CHC	49	0	2	197	6	84	64	165	48
	21	R	27	CF	aaa	NYM	152	4	1	195	5	84	53	53	8
Alonso,Lazaro	19	L	25	1B	aa	MIA	34	1	0	135	11	63	56	129	-48
	21	L	27	1B	aa	MIA	198	4	1	173	14	48	89	31	-100
Alu,Jake	21	L	24	3B	aa	WAS	197	4	4	233	5	76	79	75	0
Alvarez,Armando	21	R	27	3B	aaa	NYY	360	8	1	187	7	76	75	44	-7
Amaral,Daniel	21	R	24	CF	aa	PIT	220	5	6	182	7	69	79	77	-21
Amaya,Jacob	21	R	23	SS	aa	LA	417	9	3	177	8	72	59	68	-27
Amburgey,Trey	19	R	25	RF	aaa	NYY	470	20	5	236	5	72	135	115	43
	21	R	27	RF	aaa	NYY	257	6	1	220	7	61	120	64	-26
Angulo,Andres	21	R	24	C	aa	SF	163	3	2	175	9	65	60	67	-50
Antonini,Aaron	21	L	23	C	a/a	STL	115	2	0	135	9	61	60	20	-82
Apostel,Sherten	21	R	22	3B	a/a	TEX	226	6	0	201	8	60	97	28	-58
Aranda,Jonathan	21	L	23	1B	a/a	TAM	274	8	3	280	8	73	106	102	26
Arauz,Jonathan	19	S	21	2B	aa	HOU	108	3	1	225	8	81	79	129	39
	21	B	23	2B	aaa	BOS	233	4	2	221	9	79	58	63	1
Arcia,Orlando	21	R	27	SS	aaa	ATL	287	12	4	233	7	84	93	62	47
Arias,Diosbel	21	R	25	1B	aa	TEX	379	4	2	230	7	78	47	42	-21
Arias,Gabriel	21	R	21	SS	aaa	CLE	436	10	4	250	6	72	92	75	-2
Arteaga,Humbert	19	R	25	SS	aaa	KC	284	3	8	255	3	86	48	104	27
	21	R	27	SS	a/a	WAS	244	2	1	148	3	68	37	53	-77
Ascanio,Rayder	19	R	23	SS	aa	STL	267	5	3	240	5	78	84	70	13
	21	R	25	3B	aaa	STL	184	5	1	172	6	75	57	42	-28
Asuaje,Carlos	19	L	28	2B	aaa	ARI	159	3	1	173	7	75	71	122	6
	21	L	30	2B	aaa	LA	261	1	4	177	7	81	39	92	-3
Avans,Drew	19	L	23	LF	aa	LA	220	6	15	263	7	67	90	151	-1
	21	L	25	CF	aaa	LA	233	3	13	217	10	70	79	132	4
Avelino,Abiatal	19	R	24	SS	aaa	SF	473	8	13	249	4	80	85	190	57
	21	R	26	SS	aaa	CHC	380	4	10	212	7	78	51	88	-5
Aviles Jr.,Luis	19	R	24	SS	aa	MIL	300	2	28	248	10	67	75	151	-13
	21	R	26	2B	a/a	LAA	269	9	8	176	4	67	100	104	-12
Azocar,Jose	19	R	23	RF	aa	DET	504	10	10	276	4	73	84	149	14
	21	R	25	CF	a/a	SD	491	5	21	219	5	72	64	130	-10
Bae,Ji-Hwan	21	L	22	2B	aa	PIT	320	5	15	244	8	72	64	126	-3
Baker,Luken	21	R	24	1B	a/a	STL	353	16	0	193	6	66	120	19	-20
Baldwin,Roldani	21	R	25	3B	aa	BOS	150	3	1	211	6	53	111	64	-66
Banks,Nick	19	L	25	RF	aa	WAS	156	1	6	269	8	70	99	164	24
	21	L	27	LF	a/a	WAS	335	6	0	187	6	61	72	19	-77
Bannon,Rylan	19	R	23	3B	a/a	BAL	470	10	7	239	8	80	95	107	43
	21	R	25	3B	aaa	BAL	289	12	7	149	11	73	91	74	10
Banuelos,David	21	R	25	C	a/a	MIN	144	2	0	171	4	58	87	87	-63
Barefoot,Matthev	21	R	24	RF	aa	HOU	137	3	3	147	4	58	77	71	-75
Barrera,Luis	19	L	24	CF	aa	OAK	224	3	8	294	4	76	106	165	50
	21	L	26	CF	aaa	OAK	341	2	6	213	7	76	52	103	-8
Barrera,Tres	19	R	25	C	aa	WAS	357	8	1	233	8	78	96	44	17
	21	R	27	C	aaa	WAS	169	2	0	166	9	70	44	12	-61
Barrero,Jose	21	R	23	SS	a/a	CIN	330	17	13	274	8	70	130	93	31
Bart,Joey	19	R	23	C	aa	SF	79	3	0	302	8	72	143	97	44
	21	R	25	C	aaa	SF	252	6	0	230	5	61	93	26	-61
Basabe,Luis Aleja	21	B	25	3B	aa	ARI	283	6	5	181	6	56	97	94	-56
Basabe,Olivier	21	R	24	3B	aa	SD	215	3	2	159	7	75	41	85	-27
Batten,Matt	21	R	26	SS	a/a	SD	440	4	18	224	7	65	44	103	-57
Baty,Brett	21	L	22	3B	aa	NYM	153	4	1	219	9	65	81	35	-45
Bautista,Rafael	19	R	26	LF	aa	WAS	35	0	2	131	9	77	0	90	-50
	21	R	28	CF	aaa	WAS	236	4	2	192	3	76	53	48	-31
Beaty,Matt	19	L	26	3B	aaa	LA	121	2	0	244	5	88	70	67	39
Bec,Chris	21	R	26	C	aaa	TOR	166	1	7	142	7	67	24	88	-72
Bechina,Marty	21	R	25	LF	a/a	OAK	261	6	3	161	3	54	109	85	-63
Bechtold,Andrew	21	R	25	3B	aa	MIN	351	12	1	198	8	57	133	36	-37
Beer,Seth	19	L	23	1B	aa	ARI	322	16	0	258	9	72	136	42	24
	21	L	25	1B	aaa	ARI	362	8	0	209	6	74	91	33	-7
Bell,Brantley	19	R	25	2B	aa	CIN	359	6	9	216	7	79	72	84	11
	21	R	27	1B	aaa	CIN	236	1	6	163	7	68	41	101	-47
Bell,Chad	21	L	24	3B	aa	NYY	107	4	1	153	7	56	84	46	-78
Beltre,Michael	19	S	24	RF	aa	CIN	231	3	3	213	10	71	57	116	-22
	21	L	26	CF	aa	NYY	398	13	28	211	9	67	105	156	17
Benson,Will	21	L	23	LF	a/a	CLE	355	13	10	177	14	54	141	125	-7
Berman,Stevie	21	R	27	C	a/a	MIN	143	1	0	140	9	77	48	13	-31
Bernard,Wynton	19	R	29	LF	a/a	CHC	126	1	6	228	9	75	99	168	45
	21	R	31	CF	aaa	COL	319	4	12	195	4	71	61	145	-13

BATTER	yr	b	age	pos	lvl	org	ab	hr	sb	ba	bb%	ct%	px	sx	bpv
Bethancourt,Chris	21	R	30	C	aaa	PIT	331	8	3	209	5	72	78	57	-19
Bewley,Brhet	21	R	24	2B	aa	KC	204	4	1	202	5	71	65	69	-30
Biggers,Jax	21	L	24	2B	a/a	TEX	303	3	11	183	6	79	45	94	-7
Bird,Corey	19	L	24	CF	aa	MIA	298	3	16	216	7	81	39	157	15
	21	L	26	RF	aaa	MIA	280	4	12	194	9	71	74	123	2
Bird,Gregory	21	L	29	1B	aaa	COL	393	16	0	204	8	67	111	26	-17
Bishop,Braden	19	R	26	CF	aaa	SEA	185	6	1	217	8	70	125	52	9
	21	R	28	LF	aaa	SF	305	7	6	237	5	75	83	110	11
Bissonette,Josh	21	R	25	3B	aa	PIT	231	1	1	188	7	75	36	41	-43
Blanco,Dairon	19	R	26	CF	aa	KC	427	5	28	239	7	64	112	200	20
	21	R	28	CF	a/a	KC	422	9	28	220	5	73	68	138	3
Blankenhorn,Trav	19	L	23	2B	aa	MIN	388	17	10	266	4	75	126	148	55
	21	L	25	2B	aaa	NYM	195	6	2	185	9	58	108	37	-51
Bleday,J.J.	21	L	24	RF	aa	MIA	397	9	4	180	12	71	83	76	-1
Boldt,Ryan	21	L	27	LF	aaa	TAM	300	9	10	214	8	59	121	103	-18
Bolt,Skye	19	B	25	RF	aaa	OAK	305	8	5	224	8	64	124	147	13
	21	B	27	CF	aaa	OAK	163	6	3	299	11	66	123	98	17
Bonifacio,Jorge	19	R	26	LF	aaa	KC	451	13	4	183	6	69	103	138	14
	21	R	28	RF	a/a	PHI	325	12	3	202	9	68	118	71	6
Booker,Joel	19	R	26	LF	a/a	CHW	351	4	16	209	5	69	54	143	-24
	21	R	28	CF	a/a	CHW	197	4	12	168	1	53	74	123	-88
Bouchard,Sean	21	R	25	LF	aa	COL	342	10	5	235	6	68	132	95	20
Bour,Justin	19	L	31	1B	aaa	LAA	187	10	1	221	11	66	162	65	30
	21	L	33	1B	aaa	SF	108	3	0	147	10	64	84	39	-44
Boyd,B.J.	21	L	28	LF	a/a	MIN	351	11	8	231	5	73	83	108	5
Brantly,Rob	19	L	30	C	aaa	PHI	236	5	0	239	9	83	73	69	25
	21	L	32	C	aaa	NYY	228	7	1	220	6	76	67	51	-12
Breaux,Josh	21	R	24	C	aa	NYY	100	5	1	205	3	70	138	53	14
Brennan,Will	21	L	23	CF	aa	CLE	150	2	2	249	9	78	45	61	-14
Briceno,Jose	19	R	27	C	aaa	LAA	79	3	1	155	2	68	91	48	-30
	21	R	29	C	aaa	COL	101	3	1	165	3	71	95	43	-17
Bride,Jonah	21	R	26	1B	aa	OAK	264	6	1	211	13	74	69	62	-2
Brigman,Bryson	19	R	24	SS	aa	MIA	312	2	2	236	11	78	62	62	-5
	21	R	26	SS	aaa	MIA	376	4	8	232	9	78	54	98	5
Brito,Daniel	21	L	23	2B	a/a	PHI	276	6	2	267	6	78	78	79	12
Brito,Socrates	19	L	27	LF	aaa	TOR	394	13	9	243	5	71	143	167	59
	21	L	29	RF	aaa	NYY	375	7	16	191	6	67	61	114	-35
Brodey,Quinn	19	L	24	CF	aa	NYM	247	5	5	224	8	71	95	66	-7
	21	L	26	RF	a/a	NYM	222	2	9	132	6	50	60	126	-102
Brooks,Trenton	19	L	24	RF	aa	CLE	241	8	1	260	7	83	145	101	90
	21	L	26	1B	a/a	CLE	360	9	2	208	9	71	92	61	-2
Brosseau,Michae	19	R	25	3B	aaa	TAM	270	12	2	255	9	74	149	87	54
	21	R	27	3B	aaa	TAM	170	6	2	179	10	63	78	78	-39
Broxton,Keon	21	R	31	CF	aaa	MIL	257	5	7	123	7	30	114	90	-146
Brujan,Vidal	19	S	21	2B	aa	TAM	207	3	22	256	9	81	77	202	61
	21	R	23	2B	aaa	TAM	389	10	38	234	10	80	95	137	58
Burcham,Scott	19	R	26	SS	aa	COL	220	3	5	199	10	69	89	88	-14
	21	R	28	2B	aaa	COL	124	1	0	183	3	57	53	64	-101
Burdick,Peyton	21	R	24	CF	aa	MIA	401	18	7	190	14	58	133	87	-4
Burger,Jake	21	R	25	3B	aaa	CHW	310	12	0	218	5	64	112	44	-28
Burleson,Alec	21	L	23	RF	a/a	STL	414	11	1	214	5	77	66	34	-18
Burt,D.J.	19	R	24	LF	aa	KC	257	2	23	210	9	72	53	146	-10
	21	R	26	2B	aa	MIN	215	2	14	244	9	68	64	103	-27
Burt,Max	19	R	23	3B	aa	NYY	72	0	0	232	5	71	39	39	-62
	21	R	25	3B	a/a	NYY	269	5	5	182	7	68	74	84	-30
Busch,Michael	21	L	24	2B	aa	LA	409	14	1	217	10	63	117	49	-17
Byrd,Grayson	21	L	25	1B	aa	CHC	184	1	1	184	7	63	58	38	-75
Cabbage,Trey	21	L	24	RF	aa	MIN	244	13	1	222	9	48	171	61	-32
Cabrera,Leobaldo	21	R	23	LF	aa	MIN	170	8	4	203	10	57	136	102	-8
Cabrera,Oswaldo	21	B	22	2B	a/a	NYY	467	25	17	243	7	70	139	97	35
Calabuig,Chase	19	L	24	LF	aa	OAK	403	3	6	250	12	72	56	115	-19
	21	L	26	LF	aa	OAK	323	3	1	167	8	77	38	45	-29
Calixte,Orlando	19	R	27	3B	aaa	SEA	97	1	2	215	5	68	45	66	-61
	21	R	29	3B	aaa	NYM	196	1	8	160	6	69	41	87	-53
Call,Alex	19	R	25	CF	aa	CLE	293	5	4	190	6	64	90	117	-23
	21	R	27	CF	a/a	CLE	386	10	10	209	9	79	75	81	22
Camargo,Johan	19	B	26	3B	aaa	ATL	58	2	0	423	7	76	138	37	37
	21	B	28	1B	aaa	ATL	386	14	0	265	8	77	100	54	23
Cameron,Daz	19	R	22	CF	aaa	DET	448	12	15	204	11	65	122	182	28
	21	R	24	CF	aaa	DET	162	5	6	269	7	74	108	128	38
Campusano,Luis	21	R	23	C	aaa	SD	292	9	1	229	6	74	99	59	5
Cancel,Gabriel	19	R	23	2B	aa	KC	464	15	13	232	6	67	135	131	29
	21	R	25	2B	aaa	KC	206	9	8	194	6	63	130	111	6
Canelo,Malquin	19	R	25	SS	aaa	PHI	423	2	6	218	5	60	78	100	-55
	21	R	27	2B	a/a	BAL	123	3	1	181	5	62	81	82	-49
Canning,Gage	21	L	24	RF	aa	WAS	158	0	1	223	6	69	53	46	-55
Cantu,Michael	21	R	26	C	aaa	SD	145	2	0	132	7	53	34	20	-137
Canzone,Dominic	21	L	24	LF	aa	ARI	130	5	1	296	7	75	103	69	19
Capel,Conner	19	L	22	LF	a/a	STL	371	9	8	222	5	74	85	103	7
	21	L	24	RF	a/a	STL	369	8	4	201	7	75	70	75	-6
Capra,Vinny	19	R	23	2B	aa	TOR	388	3	14	224	7	77	67	147	19
	21	R	25	3B	aaa	TOR	256	8	3	274	7	65	124	96	5
Cardenas,Ruben	21	R	24	LF	aa	TAM	290	11	2	219	3	65	96	88	-27
Carpenter,Kerry	21	L	24	LF	aa	DET	416	11	4	227	5	76	84	58	-1
Carpio,Luis	19	R	22	2B	aa	NYM	243	3	2	245	10	77	75	40	-4
	21	R	24	2B	aa	NYM	305	5	4	195	7	64	77	52	-50
Carrasco,Dennich	21	R	26	3B	aa	KC	151	3	0	177	6	52	98	32	-89
Casas,Triston	21	L	21	1B	a/a	BOS	310	10	6	257	13	75	99	94	35
Casey,Donovan	19	R	23	CF	aa	LA	94	3	2	195	6	60	114	102	-28
	21	R	25	CF	a/a	WAS	484	13	16	233	5	60	101	99	-36
Castellano,Angel	19	R	24	1B	aa	KC	217	4	5	201	8	72	77	96	-9
	21	R	26	2B	a/a	KC	297	6	6	190	5	71	52	70	-40

BATTER	yr	b	age	pos	lvl	org	ab	hr	sb	ba	bb%	ct%	px	sx	bpv
Castellanos,Pedr	21	R	24	LF	aa	BOS	325	9	1	251	7	78	79	76	13
Castillo,Ali	19	R	30	2B	a/a	PHI	466	7	4	252	5	81	71	98	22
	21	R	32	2B	a/a	WAS	216	0	3	165	3	81	13	76	-33
Castillo,Diego	21	R	24	2B	a/a	PIT	388	13	6	234	8	84	86	68	42
Castillo,Erick	19	R	26	C	a/a	CHC	84	0	0	206	5	75	32	57	-46
	21	R	28	C	a/a	CHC	172	1	0	150	7	76	24	23	-54
Castillo,Ivan	19	B	24	2B	aa	SD	432	6	13	277	4	85	86	162	68
	21	B	26	2B	aaa	SD	404	2	7	210	4	77	33	74	-35
Castro,Luis	19	R	24	1B	aa	COL	59	2	1	226	17	72	85	94	3
	21	R	26	1B	a/a	MIL	237	6	2	170	7	52	110	68	-68
Castro,Rodolfo	21	B	22	3B	a/a	PIT	320	10	5	215	5	72	98	78	3
Cecchini,Gavin	19	R	26	2B	a/a	NYM	145	2	3	200	8	70	56	62	-43
	21	R	28	SS	a/a	LAA	344	3	4	187	3	77	46	54	-32
Cedrola,Lorenzo	21	R	23	CF	a/a	CIN	441	9	8	284	4	86	64	102	35
Celestino,Gilbertc	21	R	22	CF	a/a	MIN	267	5	3	250	10	73	86	50	-5
Cervenka,Martin	19	R	27	C	a/a	BAL	203	3	2	200	7	62	53	49	-83
	21	R	29	C	aaa	NYM	186	4	1	123	7	61	68	48	-71
Chatham,C.J.	19	R	25	SS	a/a	BOS	436	4	6	278	4	78	87	105	25
	21	R	27	SS	aaa	PHI	155	2	0	227	5	78	47	44	-24
Chavez,Santiago	19	R	24	C	aa	MIA	248	1	0	164	7	62	31	46	-99
	21	R	26	C	a/a	MIA	164	1	1	133	5	57	43	59	-105
Chavis,Michael	19	R	24	2B	aaa	BOS	70	6	0	236	8	68	220	28	68
	21	R	26	1B	aaa	PIT	192	9	1	216	5	66	113	61	-15
Chester,Carl	19	R	24	LF	aa	TAM	121	2	5	241	4	70	99	172	23
	21	R	26	RF	aaa	TEX	338	5	4	148	4	56	66	105	-82
Chinea,Chris	19	R	25	1B	a/a	STL	294	7	0	235	4	68	99	45	-25
	21	R	27	1B	a/a	MIA	157	4	0	198	6	73	64	20	-36
Cintron,Jancarlos	21	R	27	2B	a/a	ARI	309	4	7	173	4	78	39	77	-25
Citta,Brendt	21	R	25	DH	aa	PIT	160	1	0	244	4	74	62	53	-26
Clemens,Kody	19	L	23	2B	aa	DET	47	1	0	163	11	60	96	50	-52
	21	L	25	2B	aaa	DET	369	14	3	220	7	72	105	117	25
Clement,Ernie	19	R	23	SS	a/a	CLE	405	1	15	254	6	91	40	125	45
	21	R	25	3B	a/a	CLE	131	1	1	203	5	77	81	65	5
Clementina,Hendı	21	R	24	C	aa	ATL	141	7	0	184	6	62	105	24	-48
Cluff,Jackson	21	L	25	SS	aa	WAS	126	2	2	163	5	65	55	66	-65
Collins,Gavin	21	R	26	C	aaa	CLE	148	3	1	143	8	64	55	36	-71
Conine,Griffin	21	L	24	RF	aa	MIA	159	10	0	148	6	41	201	26	-52
Conley,Jack	19	R	22	C	aa	PHI	22	1	1	259	20	64	145	80	15
	21	R	24	C	a/a	PHI	160	3	1	128	7	59	76	76	-62
Contreras,Mark	19	L	24	LF	aa	MIN	281	9	8	197	7	64	125	148	14
	21	L	26	RF	a/a	MIN	410	14	11	209	7	60	136	106	-3
Contreras,Williarr	19	R	22	C	aa	ATL	191	3	0	253	8	79	74	65	6
	21	R	24	C	aaa	ATL	155	7	0	256	6	74	109	30	6
Cordell,Ryan	19	R	27	RF	aaa	CHW	51	1	1	219	5	58	150	157	12
	21	R	29	RF	aaa	PHI	197	8	5	157	7	43	142	73	-77
Cordero,Franchy	19	L	25	CF	aaa	SD	46	2	0	169	5	52	169	130	-5
	21	L	27	LF	aaa	BOS	287	9	9	253	10	61	144	105	10
Cordoba,Allen Oc	21	R	26	3B	aa	SD	251	3	4	238	8	80	72	59	12
Corredor,Aldrem	21	L	26	1B	aa	WAS	323	7	1	217	7	72	80	34	-24
Cortes,Carlos	21	L	24	LF	aa	NYM	307	10	1	204	7	66	117	51	-10
Costes,Marty	21	R	26	RF	a/a	HOU	330	4	8	243	10	74	59	79	-11
Coulter,Clint	21	R	28	RF	aaa	STL	128	5	0	169	5	56	98	26	-79
Cowan,Jordan	19	L	24	2B	aa	SEA	440	2	17	246	11	78	34	105	-16
	21	L	26	SS	aa	SEA	295	3	13	207	11	70	55	108	-19
Craig,Will	19	R	25	1B	aaa	PIT	494	17	2	214	7	67	115	48	-13
	21	R	27	1B	aaa	PIT	122	5	0	226	7	73	112	30	6
Cribbs,Galli	19	L	27	2B	aa	ARI	245	2	2	186	8	54	95	145	-53
	21	L	29	SS	a/a	MIA	168	1	3	144	4	50	58	91	-116
Crim,Blaine	21	R	24	DH	aa	TEX	139	7	0	254	4	71	116	35	-1
Crook,Narciso	19	R	24	LF	a/a	CIN	346	10	9	254	6	65	145	176	42
	21	R	26	RF	a/a	CIN	295	12	6	206	10	59	131	59	-18
Cruz,Michael	21	L	25	C	aa	LAA	179	6	0	176	8	60	90	31	-61
Cruz,Oneil	19	L	21	SS	aa	PIT	119	1	3	269	11	70	114	151	32
	21	L	23	SS	a/a	PIT	271	12	14	267	7	72	126	142	48
Cuadrado,Romer	21	R	24	RF	aa	LA	278	7	0	183	6	51	66	21	-122
Cumana,Grenny	19	R	24	RF	a/a	PHI	186	2	1	266	3	86	55	99	27
	21	R	26	RF	aa	PHI	147	1	0	215	5	87	31	22	-10
Cumberland,Brett	19	S	24	C	aa	BAL	125	4	0	225	14	71	115	55	7
	21	B	26	C	aaa	BAL	267	8	1	154	10	55	88	41	-78
Curry,Michael	21	R	24	DH	aa	SD	252	5	2	188	10	62	73	40	-59
Cuthbert,Cheslor	19	R	27	1B	aaa	KC	197	5	0	254	6	72	130	66	26
	21	R	29	1B	aaa	NYM	302	9	1	151	8	69	77	48	-29
Czinege,Todd	21	R	27	RF	aa	COL	123	3	1	154	6	49	87	25	-112
Dahl,David	21	L	27	RF	a/a	MIL	144	3	1	275	5	79	93	76	26
Daniel,Clayton	19	R	24	SS	aa	CHC	79	0	0	285	6	87	42	122	32
	21	R	26	DH	a/a	LA	169	1	1	178	6	76	31	47	-45
Daschbach,Andre	21	R	24	1B	aa	BAL	102	6	0	182	8	53	154	31	-37
Davidson,Logan	21	B	24	SS	aa	OAK	448	5	3	174	9	61	67	53	-68
Davidson,Matthev	19	R	28	1B	aaa	TEX	469	24	1	214	6	62	157	47	0
	21	R	30	1B	aaa	LA	313	18	0	213	6	62	151	24	-11
Davis,Brendon	19	R	22	LF	aa	TEX	346	3	0	204	11	67	64	57	-49
	21	R	24	SS	a/a	LAA	230	11	5	239	8	67	123	104	15
Davis,Brennen	21	R	22	CF	a/a	CHC	323	12	4	221	10	62	132	59	-6
Davis,Jaylin	19	R	25	RF	a/a	SF	468	25	9	265	11	67	166	113	47
	21	R	27	RF	aaa	SF	161	6	2	170	6	55	126	118	-30
Davis,Jonah	21	L	24	CF	aa	PIT	190	5	3	175	9	45	130	106	-65
Davis,Zach	19	S	25	LF	aa	CHC	75	0	10	207	12	79	24	249	25
	21	B	27	LF	a/a	CHC	166	1	12	184	7	67	36	103	-57
Dawkins,Ian	21	R	26	LF	aa	CHW	209	4	9	212	5	67	65	116	-33
Dawson,Ronnie	19	L	24	CF	a/a	HOU	426	13	10	172	8	59	125	123	-15
	21	L	26	CF	aaa	HOU	353	5	10	190	8	71	62	85	-25

BATTER	yr	b	age	pos	lvl	org	ab	hr	sb	ba	bb%	ct%	px	sx	bpv
De Goti,Alex	19	R	25	2B	aaa	HOU	481	10	3	217	7	73	90	89	5
	21	R	27	SS	aaa	HOU	383	3	4	172	7	65	62	99	-47
De La Cruz,Bryaı	19	R	23	LF	aa	HOU	269	4	6	256	7	75	81	168	28
	21	R	25	RF	aaa	HOU	272	9	1	257	4	73	88	43	-13
De La Guerra,Ch	19	L	27	SS	aaa	BOS	226	10	1	251	7	67	163	74	36
	21	L	29	3B	aaa	BOS	152	2	4	159	9	53	108	105	-48
De La Trinidad,Eı	19	L	23	LF	aa	MIN	122	2	0	196	11	72	52	58	-37
	21	L	25	RF	aa	MIN	289	6	3	222	5	67	74	70	-39
De Leon,Michael	19	B	22	SS	aa	TEX	477	3	3	261	6	87	41	58	10
	21	B	24	3B	a/a	CIN	294	7	0	229	5	71	80	20	-34
Dean,Justin	21	R	25	CF	aa	ATL	363	6	24	210	9	60	79	144	-33
DeCarlo,Joe	19	R	26	C	aa	SEA	171	1	0	146	10	54	42	57	-118
	21	R	28	1B	a/a	CHW	162	2	0	152	8	58	40	31	-106
Dedelow,Craig	21	L	27	RF	aa	CHW	366	14	2	185	9	54	132	61	-41
Deglan,Kellin	19	L	27	C	a/a	NYY	249	8	1	216	6	62	122	85	-18
	21	L	29	C	aaa	TOR	109	3	1	174	9	55	99	41	-70
Deichmann,Greg	19	L	24	RF	aa	OAK	301	9	16	194	9	62	106	169	-4
	21	L	26	RF	aaa	CHC	329	5	7	220	11	65	88	106	-15
DeLoach,Zach	21	L	23	RF	aa	SEA	185	4	1	193	11	63	90	74	-31
DeLuzio,Ben	19	R	25	CF	a/a	ARI	374	3	13	247	8	70	90	170	17
	21	R	27	CF	a/a	ARI	241	2	9	214	4	68	79	144	-14
Demeritte,Travis	19	R	25	LF	aaa	ATL	339	16	3	250	11	65	184	112	54
	21	R	27	RF	aaa	ATL	266	15	5	232	8	55	171	71	-1
DeShields Jr.,Del	19	R	27	CF	aaa	TEX	66	2	5	213	8	70	102	103	7
	21	R	29	LF	aaa	BOS	309	4	15	201	12	65	63	109	-30
Devanney,Cam	21	R	24	2B	aa	MIL	291	4	1	148	8	62	55	28	-81
Diaz,Brent	21	R	25	C	a/a	MIL	182	4	1	168	5	54	78	49	-93
Diaz,Edwin	19	R	24	3B	a/a	OAK	471	10	2	202	8	63	144	152	25
	21	R	26	3B	a/a	OAK	198	6	1	159	6	51	100	35	-92
Diaz,Isan	19	L	23	2B	aaa	MIA	377	21	5	270	11	71	159	136	68
	21	L	25	3B	aaa	MIA	103	4	0	200	8	66	128	76	6
Diaz,Lewin	19	L	23	1B	aa	MIA	241	14	0	240	8	77	186	69	90
	21	L	25	1B	aaa	MIA	278	15	2	204	7	75	116	64	26
Diaz,Yusniel	19	R	23	RF	aa	BAL	286	11	0	243	9	75	134	102	53
	21	R	25	RF	a/a	BAL	230	4	1	132	5	61	59	62	-78
Didder,Ray-Patric	19	R	25	SS	aa	ATL	340	4	29	196	13	62	77	158	-29
	21	R	27	SS	aa	LAA	329	3	11	187	7	68	72	121	-16
Dietrich,Derek	21	L	32	2B	aaa	WAS	239	6	0	127	10	49	83	27	-106
Dingler,Dillon	21	R	23	C	aa	DET	188	3	1	181	3	66	56	105	-52
Donovan,Brendar	21	L	24	3B	a/a	STL	296	6	8	243	8	76	66	78	-3
Dorow,Ryan	19	R	24	3B	aa	TEX	183	4	3	210	9	62	86	155	-22
	21	R	26	SS	a/a	TEX	369	11	2	209	8	64	116	72	-12
Dorrian,Patrick	21	L	25	3B	a/a	BAL	414	17	3	202	11	62	121	63	-15
Downs,Jeter	19	R	21	SS	aa	LA	48	5	1	319	10	77	206	114	122
	21	R	23	SS	aaa	BOS	357	10	14	170	8	60	81	83	-54
Drury,Brandon	21	R	29	3B	aaa	NYM	214	5	0	177	5	69	80	23	-43
Duarte,Osvaldo	19	R	23	SS	aa	HOU	458	11	19	211	5	64	94	187	-2
	21	R	25	2B	aa	WAS	217	1	4	162	5	56	64	116	-79
Dubon,Mauricio	19	R	25	SS	aaa	SF	503	13	8	257	4	85	83	88	42
	21	R	27	SS	aaa	SF	247	5	6	253	7	81	63	82	14
Dunand,Joe	19	R	24	SS	aa	MIA	462	5	2	228	8	71	74	82	-17
	21	R	26	3B	aaa	MIA	204	6	0	162	6	59	94	39	-63
Dungan,Clay	21	L	25	2B	aa	KC	444	6	21	250	6	82	52	114	19
Dunlap,Alex	21	R	27	C	a/a	WAS	149	2	1	149	5	61	67	53	-74
Dunn,Nick	21	L	24	2B	aa	STL	324	3	2	199	6	79	42	43	-23
Duran,Jarren	19	L	23	CF	aa	BOS	320	1	25	247	6	73	59	207	12
	21	L	25	CF	aaa	BOS	244	11	12	223	9	69	122	120	28
Duran,Rodolfo	21	R	23	C	a/a	PHI	129	5	0	176	3	75	95	14	-11
Duzenack,Camde	19	R	24	SS	aa	ARI	68	2	2	136	16	73	61	72	-21
	21	R	26	2B	a/a	ARI	221	5	2	189	3	61	90	91	-47
Edgeworth,Danny	21	L	26	3B	a/a	COL	119	2	0	131	5	58	64	23	-98
Edwards,Xavier	21	R	22	2B	aa	TAM	291	0	15	264	9	83	36	103	13
Eierman,Jeremy	21	R	25	3B	aa	OAK	223	7	6	200	6	52	131	93	-46
Ellis,Drew	19	R	24	3B	aa	ARI	379	13	0	217	14	68	124	32	-1
	21	R	26	3B	aaa	ARI	296	10	1	212	8	63	138	72	3
Encarnacion,Jera	21	R	24	RF	aa	MIA	230	7	4	189	8	51	124	70	-59
Engelmann,Jonat	21	R	25	1B	aa	CLE	198	5	1	188	8	61	94	63	-45
Erceg,Lucas	19	L	24	3B	aaa	MIL	357	12	1	187	8	67	114	78	-5
	21	L	26	DH	aa	MIL	103	2	2	183	5	74	82	62	-9
Ervin,Phillip	19	R	27	CF	aaa	CIN	145	5	5	245	10	70	123	117	29
	21	R	29	LF	aaa	ATL	229	6	8	150	10	62	68	87	-49
Escarra,J.C.	21	L	26	1B	a/a	BAL	310	6	3	180	9	72	65	81	-16
Estevez,Omar	19	R	21	2B	aa	LA	299	6	0	272	8	74	112	25	8
	21	R	23	SS	aaa	LA	361	6	0	163	7	67	56	34	-62
Estrada,Thairo	19	R	23	SS	aaa	NYY	241	7	2	236	5	77	116	126	49
	21	R	25	SS	aaa	SF	210	5	4	265	6	80	82	73	21
Evans,Phillip	19	R	27	3B	aaa	CHC	466	13	1	236	9	81	100	75	40
	21	R	29	1B	aaa	PIT	127	0	0	191	7	72	56	31	-42
Fabian,Sandro	21	R	23	RF	aa	SF	296	11	0	227	3	78	85	41	2
Fairchild,Stuart	19	R	23	CF	aa	CIN	153	4	3	257	10	83	114	113	70
	21	R	25	RF	aaa	ARI	156	5	4	222	7	70	95	108	3
Fargas,Johneshw	19	R	25	CF	aa	SF	413	4	46	231	7	75	52	195	13
	21	R	27	CF	a/a	CHC	128	2	11	191	5	64	69	148	-30
Feduccia,Hunter	21	L	24	C	aa	LA	284	7	0	205	8	75	61	37	-24
Feliciano,Mario	21	R	23	C	aaa	MIL	105	2	1	170	3	71	45	49	-58
Ferguson,Jaylen	21	R	24	CF	aa	BAL	100	2	3	123	6	51	110	124	-54
Fermin,Freddy	19	R	24	C	aa	KC	107	2	0	232	2	77	66	39	-18
	21	R	26	DH	a/a	KC	282	6	1	228	7	78	71	54	0
Fermin,Jose	21	R	22	3B	a/a	CLE	306	5	3	231	6	85	62	69	22
Fernandez,Juan	21	R	22	C	aa	SD	257	6	2	193	8	74	64	60	-15
Fernandez,Vince	19	L	24	LF	aa	COL	230	16	1	269	11	62	251	133	105
	21	L	26	LF	aa	SF	249	9	2	186	8	53	133	117	-27

BATTER	yr	b	age	pos	lvl	org	ab	hr	sb	ba	bb%	ct%	px	sx	bpv
Fernandez,Xavier	19	R	24	C	a/a	KC	183	5	1	223	7	81	75	50	12
	21	R	26	C	aa	CHW	195	7	0	241	8	73	77	23	-22
Figuera,Edwin	21	R	24	SS	a/a	CHC	108	1	0	193	3	70	32	37	-76
Filia,Eric	19	L	27	RF	aaa	SEA	121	1	0	257	13	84	92	53	41
	21	L	29	LF	aaa	SEA	149	2	3	190	12	77	54	65	-4
Fisher,Jameson	21	L	28	1B	aa	CHW	328	10	2	234	8	68	93	73	-16
Fitch,Colby	21	L	26	C	aa	PHI	102	1	3	142	15	50	101	110	-56
Fitzgerald,Ryan	21	L	27	SS	a/a	BOS	365	11	3	224	7	73	121	75	25
Fletcher,Dominic	21	L	24	RF	aa	ARI	402	10	2	219	4	69	84	85	-22
Flores,Jecksson	19	R	26	SS	aaa	KC	410	5	12	206	7	79	52	104	2
	21	R	28	SS	a/a	WAS	215	1	1	188	9	79	54	48	-7
Florial,Estevan	21	L	24	CF	a/a	NYY	347	14	10	186	10	60	123	100	-11
Forbes,Tl'Quan	21	R	25	1B	a/a	CHW	303	5	5	222	5	64	72	92	-45
Ford,Mike	19	L	27	1B	aaa	NYY	294	20	0	252	11	77	164	34	65
	21	L	29	1B	aaa	WAS	268	10	1	168	8	63	99	41	-40
Fortes,Nick	21	R	25	C	a/a	MIA	330	5	5	205	7	81	56	68	5
Fowler,Dustin	19	L	25	CF	aaa	OAK	556	17	8	230	5	70	107	163	25
	21	L	27	RF	aaa	MIA	142	6	2	233	6	58	124	93	-30
Fox,Lucius	19	B	22	SS	a/a	TAM	407	3	35	205	12	71	70	220	22
	21	B	24	2B	aaa	KC	215	3	13	204	10	69	72	107	-12
Foyle,Devin	21	L	25	LF	aa	OAK	362	8	6	210	7	71	78	109	-6
Fraizer,Matt	21	L	23	CF	aa	PIT	132	2	1	250	7	72	111	89	19
Franco,Wander	21	B	20	SS	aaa	TAM	163	6	5	302	7	86	123	125	96
Freeman,Cole	21	R	27	CF	aa	WAS	397	4	10	220	4	86	35	79	5
Freeman,Isaac	21	R	23	2B	aa	CLE	122	1	0	165	8	60	43	57	-89
Freeman,Tyler	21	R	22	SS	aa	CLE	164	2	3	295	4	86	79	93	43
Frick,Patrick	21	R	24	SS	aa	SEA	137	2	1	202	8	77	31	53	-32
Friedl,T.J.	21	L	26	CF	aaa	CIN	386	10	10	224	8	79	71	97	21
Friis,Tyler	19	S	23	2B	aa	CLE	72	1	4	242	11	82	59	102	21
	21	B	25	2B	aa	MIL	105	0	6	224	7	77	38	125	-7
Fry,David	21	R	26	3B	a/a	MIL	314	9	1	203	8	65	100	61	-24
Fuentes,Josh	19	R	26	3B	aaa	COL	402	12	1	213	4	67	118	92	2
	21	R	28	3B	aaa	COL	193	6	1	213	3	74	95	66	-1
Gamboa,Arquime	19	S	22	SS	aa	PHI	356	3	19	177	13	64	62	169	-26
	21	B	24	SS	a/a	PHI	324	8	7	202	11	66	76	76	-28
Garcia,Aramis	19	R	26	C	aaa	SF	332	10	0	224	7	60	139	84	-10
	21	R	28	C	aaa	OAK	112	1	0	197	5	69	68	27	-49
Garcia,Dermis	21	R	23	1B	aa	NYY	385	26	8	185	10	51	178	79	-8
Garcia,Gabriel	21	R	24	3B	aa	MIL	115	3	0	186	6	55	125	38	-55
Garcia,Luis	19	L	19	SS	aa	WAS	525	4	11	268	3	84	58	159	40
	21	L	21	SS	aaa	WAS	142	11	1	283	8	81	123	34	48
Garcia,Robel	19	B	26	3B	a/a	CHC	338	22	3	246	10	58	208	102	45
	21	B	28	2B	aaa	HOU	117	4	0	117	8	51	114	15	-81
Garcia,Wilson	19	B	25	1B	aa	CLE	257	9	0	250	5	85	131	35	66
	21	B	27	DH	aa	CIN	400	14	0	238	3	75	83	14	-21
Garrett,Stone	19	R	24	LF	aa	MIA	412	13	16	228	4	66	126	191	34
	21	R	26	LF	a/a	ARI	412	14	10	206	3	65	94	82	-34
Gatewood,Jacob	19	R	24	3B	aa	MIL	353	14	3	185	7	56	138	147	-10
	21	R	26	CF	aaa	LAA	450	16	3	162	4	53	118	65	-65
George,Max	21	R	25	C	aa	COL	199	7	7	168	11	52	117	113	-43
Gettys,Michael	19	R	24	CF	aaa	SD	507	20	9	205	4	62	146	160	24
	21	R	26	RF	aaa	BOS	149	3	5	171	6	53	102	101	-63
Giambrone,Trent	19	R	26	2B	aaa	CHC	431	18	13	203	7	64	146	107	19
	21	R	28	2B	aaa	CHC	235	2	3	131	8	59	46	71	-89
Gilliam,Isiah	19	S	23	RF	aa	NYY	161	9	0	172	7	59	168	35	-7
	21	B	25	RF	aa	NYY	328	9	20	195	10	58	112	91	-28
Gimenez,Andres	19	L	21	SS	aa	NYM	432	9	28	235	5	74	94	181	36
	21	L	23	SS	aaa	CLE	209	7	6	245	4	70	108	81	-1
Gittens,Chris	19	R	25	1B	aa	NYY	398	23	0	256	14	60	169	42	4
	21	R	27	1B	a/a	NYY	154	12	0	248	15	61	178	31	29
Godoy,Jose	19	L	25	C	a/a	STL	239	5	0	233	7	78	91	39	10
	21	L	27	C	aaa	SEA	298	5	1	218	4	75	57	55	-28
Goins,Ryan	19	L	31	2B	aaa	CHW	273	7	2	246	9	62	138	94	2
	21	L	33	SS	aaa	ATL	300	4	2	181	7	58	55	47	-94
Golden,Casey	21	R	27	RF	aa	COL	140	4	1	198	5	43	178	71	-50
Gomez,Jose	19	R	23	2B	aa	PHI	292	3	4	233	6	71	61	110	-22
	21	R	25	SS	a/a	COL	303	3	4	199	4	67	55	76	-57
Gomez,Moises	21	R	23	RF	aa	TAM	269	6	4	142	7	51	97	69	-83
Gonzalez,Luis	19	L	24	CF	aa	CHW	473	9	16	231	9	79	73	145	30
	21	L	26	CF	aaa	CHW	137	5	6	187	10	63	82	81	-36
Gonzalez,Luis	19	R	25	2B	a/a	CIN	84	0	0	263	7	77	83	151	32
Gonzalez,Marcos	21	R	22	1B	aa	CLE	205	6	0	202	6	60	104	35	-53
Gonzalez,Norel	21	L	27	1B	a/a	HOU	316	11	3	213	7	73	92	45	-4
Gonzalez,Oscar	19	R	21	LF	aa	CLE	96	1	0	187	3	81	66	45	3
	21	R	23	RF	a/a	CLE	478	24	1	255	3	73	115	36	4
Gonzalez,Romy	21	R	25	SS	a/a	CHW	357	18	19	235	9	62	130	87	-2
Gonzalez,Yariel	19	S	25	3B	a/a	STL	237	10	2	220	6	81	104	46	33
	21	B	27	3B	a/a	DET	315	13	1	228	7	69	91	49	-21
Gorman,Nolan	21	L	21	2B	a/a	STL	480	16	5	230	5	74	81	62	-9
Govern,Jimmy	21	R	25	3B	a/a	KC	170	5	2	187	5	76	83	56	-1
Gozzo,Sal	21	B	23	2B	a/a	PHI	129	0	0	124	6	61	13	44	-116
Granberg,Devlin	21	R	26	RF	aa	BOS	263	7	3	242	3	76	87	83	5
Granite,Zack	19	L	27	LF	aaa	TEX	504	2	17	243	4	90	43	140	47
	21	L	29	CF	aa	CHW	195	4	6	179	12	68	68	110	-17
Gray,Tristan	19	L	23	1B	aa	TAM	418	15	2	209	12	75	110	101	33
	21	L	25	SS	aaa	TAM	248	6	1	213	7	61	109	96	-24
Green,Zach	19	R	25	3B	aaa	SF	252	16	1	233	11	55	248	83	57
	21	R	27	3B	aaa	MIL	327	10	0	160	7	42	140	21	-96
Greene,Riley	21	L	21	CF	a/a	DET	485	20	13	284	10	68	128	137	36
Greiner,Grayson	19	R	27	C	aaa	DET	48	2	0	211	6	62	93	72	-44
	21	R	29	C	aaa	DET	119	1	0	161	7	51	63	17	-123
Grenier,Cadyn	21	R	25	SS	a/a	BAL	389	7	9	183	9	60	77	80	-54

BATTER	yr	b	age	pos	lvl	org	ab	hr	sb	ba	bb%	ct%	px	sx	bpv
Groshans,Jordan	21	R	22	SS	aa	TOR	278	6	0	255	8	76	92	30	4
Grullon,Deivy	19	R	23	C	aaa	PHI	407	19	1	249	8	61	159	42	-1
	21	R	25	C	aaa	CHW	143	7	0	153	6	50	137	28	-65
Gushue,Taylor	19	B	26	C	aaa	WAS	263	8	0	260	5	71	123	50	11
	21	B	28	C	aaa	CHC	247	5	0	168	6	59	85	21	-77
Guthrie,Dalton	21	R	26	SS	a/a	PHI	295	4	3	221	4	70	67	65	-36
Gutierrez,Kelvin	19	R	25	3B	aaa	KC	286	6	9	244	8	72	75	143	5
	21	R	27	3B	aaa	BAL	126	3	1	206	3	74	79	52	-16
Guzman,Jeison	21	L	23	SS	aa	KC	125	1	2	194	4	66	78	74	-43
Hager,Jake	19	R	26	1B	aaa	MIL	327	9	4	198	6	60	114	114	-21
	21	R	28	SS	aaa	ARI	308	7	3	161	5	67	86	62	-33
Hairston,Devin	21	R	25	2B	a/a	MIA	205	3	3	162	6	61	62	87	-65
Haley,Jim	19	R	24	3B	aa	TAM	133	7	8	261	4	80	139	236	112
	21	R	26	3B	a/a	TAM	340	10	14	165	5	57	109	132	-33
Hall,Darick	19	L	24	1B	aa	PHI	456	20	4	213	10	65	173	104	45
	21	L	26	1B	aaa	PHI	400	11	0	193	9	69	89	16	-27
Hamilton,Caleb	19	R	24	C	a/a	MIN	335	6	6	206	9	69	93	117	-3
	21	R	26	C	a/a	MIN	232	6	3	148	12	55	93	62	-63
Hamilton,David	21	L	24	SS	aa	MIL	133	2	8	213	8	72	76	132	5
Hampson,Garrett	19	R	25	2B	aaa	COL	109	1	4	230	3	75	105	141	37
Hannah,Jameson	21	L	24	CF	aa	COL	302	2	7	228	6	65	67	101	-41
Hanson,Alen	19	B	27	2B	aaa	TOR	166	2	5	158	4	72	48	147	-17
	21	B	29	2B	aaa	SEA	138	1	3	202	6	73	62	129	-4
Harris,Trey	19	R	23	RF	aa	ATL	146	2	1	283	3	76	90	136	30
	21	R	25	RF	aa	ATL	364	6	3	219	6	78	56	55	-15
Harrison,KJ	21	R	25	1B	aa	WAS	300	11	0	210	6	62	126	21	-30
Harrison,Monte	19	R	24	CF	aaa	MIA	215	7	18	239	9	61	114	215	14
	21	R	26	CF	aaa	MIA	269	11	19	196	8	46	134	129	-51
Haseley,Adam	19	L	23	CF	a/a	PHI	233	9	4	248	9	75	129	117	54
	21	L	25	CF	aaa	PHI	156	2	5	197	5	75	30	67	-44
Hatch,LJ	21	R	27	2B	a/a	COL	124	1	1	200	4	53	81	95	-84
Hearn,Matt	21	L	25	CF	aa	COL	245	0	18	172	6	74	19	100	-46
Heath,Nick	19	L	26	CF	a/a	KC	408	6	47	222	10	60	91	221	-5
	21	L	28	CF	aaa	ARI	196	2	9	175	6	50	89	140	-74
Heineman,Tyler	19	B	28	C	aaa	MIA	244	9	3	270	7	82	121	147	81
	21	B	30	C	aaa	PHI	129	0	0	208	7	70	30	26	-71
Henry,Payton	21	R	24	C	a/a	MIA	241	5	0	228	8	64	70	36	-58
Hensley,David	21	R	25	2B	aa	HOU	396	7	8	244	8	69	81	84	-18
Heredia,Guillermo	19	R	28	CF	aaa	TAM	28	1	0	166	3	54	99	60	-77
Hermosillo,Michael	19	R	24	CF	aaa	LAA	259	10	4	188	6	60	123	126	-13
	21	R	26	CF	aaa	CHC	147	7	5	245	11	61	144	98	12
Hernandez,Elier	19	R	25	LF	aaa	KC	396	7	6	207	5	67	71	108	-30
	21	R	27	RF	a/a	TEX	385	11	4	185	5	62	86	55	-56
Hernandez,Marco	19	L	27	2B	aaa	BOS	137	1	2	251	3	73	105	96	17
	21	L	29	2B	aaa	CHW	334	3	1	193	2	76	48	50	-37
Hernandez,Ronald	21	R	24	C	a/a	BOS	365	11	0	250	2	76	112	35	12
Hernandez,Yonny	19	S	21	2B	aa	TEX	170	0	15	283	15	85	39	188	46
	21	B	23	SS	aaa	TEX	192	1	16	214	16	74	39	117	-1
Herrera,Dilson	19	R	25	2B	aaa	NYM	407	19	10	203	8	62	166	116	29
	21	R	27	2B	aaa	TOR	174	9	0	184	8	58	129	58	-30
Herrera,Ivan	21	R	21	C	a/a	STL	367	11	1	186	10	72	71	30	-26
Herrera,Jose	21	B	24	C	a/a	ARI	306	6	2	203	9	69	67	72	-28
Heyward,Jacob	19	R	24	LF	a/a	SF	388	8	9	188	16	58	106	62	-48
	21	R	26	LF	aa	SF	202	8	2	165	11	58	129	54	-23
Hicklen,Brewer	21	R	25	LF	aa	KC	362	11	31	209	10	60	104	149	-10
Hicks,John	21	R	32	C	aaa	TEX	248	8	5	216	4	59	124	72	-35
Hill,Darius	21	L	24	LF	aa	CHC	249	4	1	239	6	79	34	48	-30
Hill,Derek	19	R	24	CF	aa	DET	470	13	20	231	7	67	112	200	31
	21	R	26	CF	aaa	DET	125	3	3	282	6	65	99	117	-11
Hilliard,Sam	19	L	25	RF	aaa	COL	500	25	14	227	7	64	176	191	67
	21	L	27	CF	aaa	COL	188	9	3	193	7	63	146	95	12
Hinojosa,C.J.	19	R	25	2B	aa	MIL	415	9	3	268	9	83	86	72	37
	21	R	27	2B	aaa	HOU	414	7	3	239	3	76	78	53	-8
Hiura,Keston	19	R	23	2B	aaa	MIL	213	16	5	292	8	65	229	117	93
	21	R	25	1B	aaa	MIL	172	5	1	202	10	51	139	33	-54
Hoese,Kody	21	R	24	3B	aa	LA	229	1	1	150	4	72	31	57	-59
Holder,Kyle	19	L	25	SS	aa	NYY	412	9	6	236	8	82	87	119	46
	21	L	27	SS	aaa	NYY	250	1	1	171	7	67	36	50	-73
Honeyman,Bobby	21	L	25	1B	aa	SEA	304	3	2	196	8	76	50	46	-26
Hopkins,T.J.	21	R	24	LF	aa	CIN	257	4	2	235	8	67	92	112	-8
Hudgins,Chris	21	R	25	C	a/a	BAL	216	7	1	161	7	55	116	61	-53
Huff,Samuel	21	R	23	1B	a/a	TEX	195	10	0	210	7	51	147	22	-56
Hulsizer,Niko	21	R	24	RF	aa	TAM	173	6	1	201	8	46	151	91	-49
Hummel,Cooper	19	S	25	LF	aa	MIL	342	18	4	241	16	67	147	137	43
	21	B	27	LF	aaa	ARI	293	6	2	223	10	73	87	95	14
Hunter Jr.,Torii	21	R	26	CF	a/a	LAA	309	5	8	175	6	54	76	77	-86
Hurst,Scott	19	L	23	RF	aa	STL	141	1	1	168	9	65	76	82	-41
	21	L	25	CF	aaa	STL	266	2	3	157	7	59	57	78	-77
Ibanez,Andy	19	R	26	3B	aaa	TEX	467	15	5	255	8	78	109	83	37
	21	R	28	3B	aaa	TEX	114	5	1	267	7	80	122	61	51
Isabel,Ibandel	19	R	24	1B	aa	CIN	334	25	0	225	7	46	270	77	37
	21	R	26	DH	aa	LAA	219	9	0	155	7	47	135	42	-75
Isbel,Kyle	21	L	24	CF	aaa	KC	394	10	16	225	7	75	76	108	10
Jackson,Alex	19	R	24	C	aaa	ATL	306	22	1	201	5	58	200	82	27
	21	R	26	C	aaa	ATL	108	8	1	242	7	62	218	76	62
Jackson,Drew	19	R	26	2B	aaa	LA	273	4	6	164	7	59	74	107	-59
	21	R	28	2B	aaa	NYM	243	5	15	177	12	57	82	105	-50
Jarrett,Zach	19	R	25	LF	aa	BAL	92	0	1	182	4	70	49	32	-59
	21	R	27	CF	a/a	BAL	346	7	8	184	8	59	81	83	-58
Jenista,Greyson	19	L	23	LF	aa	ATL	222	5	2	244	11	65	72	60	-50
	21	L	25	1B	aa	ATL	273	15	6	189	13	51	158	93	-12

BATTER	yr	b	age	pos	lvl	org	ab	hr	sb	ba	bb%	ct%	px	sx	bpv
Johnson Jr.,Danie	19	L	24	RF	a/a	CLE	483	17	10	269	8	73	145	131	60
	21	L	26	RF	aaa	CLE	279	9	5	176	8	54	130	84	-38
Johnson,Bryce	19	S	24	RF	aa	SF	210	2	8	229	10	72	94	122	13
	21	B	26	CF	aaa	SF	353	5	20	222	8	63	70	138	-33
Jones,JaCoby	19	R	27	CF	aaa	DET	21	0	0	375	4	67	97	140	0
	21	R	29	CF	aaa	DET	269	5	1	184	7	55	88	35	-85
Jones,Jahmai	19	R	22	2B	aa	LAA	482	5	8	218	9	75	65	103	-2
	21	R	24	2B	aaa	BAL	255	9	8	211	9	71	90	96	6
Jones,Nolan	19	L	21	3B	aa	CLE	178	8	2	252	14	63	171	147	49
	21	L	23	3B	aaa	CLE	341	9	7	201	11	59	122	83	-17
Jones,Ryder	21	L	27	1B	a/a	ARI	251	6	1	210	4	70	94	50	-21
Jones,Taylor	19	R	26	1B	aaa	HOU	447	15	0	225	9	69	115	46	-5
	21	R	28	1B	aaa	HOU	178	7	0	247	10	68	117	30	-3
Jones,Travis	19	R	24	1B	aa	KC	195	2	14	243	9	67	75	153	-10
	21	R	26	3B	a/a	KC	195	3	4	177	12	63	60	99	-45
Jordan,Levi	21	R	26	3B	a/a	CHC	247	5	1	202	6	63	85	41	-54
Julks,Corey	19	R	23	LF	aa	HOU	37	0	0	145	9	52	0	47	-165
	21	R	25	LF	aa	HOU	338	11	11	239	7	70	105	112	14
Jung,Josh	21	R	23	3B	a/a	TEX	304	15	2	288	7	72	136	50	28
Justus,Connor	19	R	25	SS	aa	LAA	347	2	6	161	9	69	57	91	-37
	21	R	27	3B	a/a	MIA	282	1	2	161	8	62	42	57	-82
Kaiser,Connor	21	R	25	SS	a/a	PIT	158	3	0	154	8	67	69	43	-45
Katoh,Gosuke	19	L	25	2B	a/a	NYY	359	10	9	235	11	65	95	98	-21
	21	L	27	2B	aaa	SD	350	4	5	220	7	69	77	80	-20
Kelenic,Jarred	19	L	20	CF	aa	SEA	83	6	3	255	9	78	185	144	117
	21	L	22	LF	aaa	SEA	125	7	5	274	9	79	128	104	69
Kelley,Christian	19	R	26	C	aaa	PIT	252	4	0	150	6	65	69	73	-52
	21	R	28	C	aaa	MIL	127	1	0	197	9	62	52	20	-86
Kelly,Dalton	19	L	25	1B	a/a	TAM	420	8	10	242	12	66	86	104	-20
	21	L	27	1B	aaa	TAM	377	21	14	200	11	57	156	87	4
Kendall,Jeren	21	L	25	CF	aa	LA	201	7	10	165	7	46	128	103	-66
Kennedy,Buddy	21	R	23	3B	aa	ARI	237	11	5	235	10	65	110	96	0
Kerrigan,Jimmy	19	R	25	CF	a/a	MIN	347	13	13	196	4	69	116	129	18
	21	R	27	RF	a/a	MIN	362	13	7	210	6	54	126	101	-39
Kessinger,Grae	21	R	24	SS	aa	HOU	297	7	10	176	6	69	62	92	-34
Kieboom,Carter	19	R	22	SS	aaa	WAS	412	13	4	274	11	73	115	111	34
	21	R	24	3B	aaa	WAS	148	4	1	209	12	77	75	46	6
Kirwer,Tanner	21	R	25	LF	aa	TOR	159	4	13	169	9	63	67	116	-40
Knight,Nash	19	S	27	3B	a/a	TOR	361	6	3	216	11	70	96	58	-10
	21	B	29	3B	aaa	TOR	212	6	1	151	12	56	96	60	-57
Kohlwey,Taylor	19	L	25	LF	a/a	SD	226	3	5	230	10	70	74	137	-5
	21	L	27	1B	a/a	SD	409	5	7	233	8	70	62	74	-32
Kolozsvary,Mark	21	R	26	C	a/a	CIN	204	6	0	185	8	54	131	73	-40
Kopach,Connor	19	R	25	2B	aaa	SEA	56	1	1	232	5	49	91	75	-97
	21	R	27	SS	aa	SEA	147	3	6	116	10	33	95	103	-141
Koperniak,Matt	21	L	23	RF	aa	STL	133	2	1	213	4	83	50	46	-4
Kozma,Pete	19	R	31	2B	aaa	DET	278	5	2	211	8	79	85	127	34
	21	R	33	SS	aaa	OAK	454	2	3	173	4	72	46	76	-41
Kramer,Kevin	19	L	26	2B	aaa	PIT	393	7	3	221	8	66	115	62	-11
	21	L	28	SS	aaa	MIL	232	2	0	151	8	60	51	52	-86
Kreidler,Ryan	21	R	24	SS	a/a	DET	482	17	12	237	8	65	103	83	-15
Krieger,Tyler	19	B	25	3B	a/a	CLE	207	3	8	188	8	71	68	136	-7
	21	B	27	2B	aaa	CLE	172	1	1	129	4	59	44	50	-103
Kroon,Matt	21	R	25	CF	aa	PHI	163	4	4	258	5	67	75	85	-36
Kruger,Jack	19	R	25	C	aa	LAA	346	3	2	210	6	77	48	60	-24
	21	R	27	C	aaa	TEX	161	2	1	210	4	74	52	54	-35
Kwan,Steven	21	L	24	CF	a/a	CLE	296	9	4	281	8	88	77	93	59
Lagrange,Wagner	21	R	26	RF	a/a	NYM	284	5	2	200	4	72	59	46	-42
LaMarre,Ryan	19	R	31	CF	aaa	ATL	405	6	14	248	6	64	104	156	-3
	21	R	33	LF	aaa	NYY	206	4	10	209	8	60	93	96	-36
Langeliers,Shea	21	R	24	C	a/a	ATL	340	18	1	227	9	66	126	45	-1
Lara,Gilbert	21	R	24	SS	a/a	WAS	241	4	1	212	3	72	82	29	-31
Large,Cullen	19	S	23	3B	aa	TOR	94	0	2	230	1	65	74	157	-26
	21	B	25	RF	aaa	TOR	403	7	3	230	10	71	79	66	-11
Larsen,Jack	21	L	26	CF	aa	SEA	173	8	1	224	11	66	107	68	-5
Lavastida,Bryan	21	R	23	C	a/a	CLE	122	3	2	235	8	64	99	74	-23
Leblanc,Charles	19	R	23	3B	aa	TEX	479	7	3	263	8	76	63	115	1
	21	R	25	3B	aaa	TEX	332	12	4	187	8	54	130	87	-36
Lee,Braxton	19	L	26	CF	a/a	NYM	384	2	8	224	8	67	64	99	-37
	21	L	28	LF	a/a	CIN	263	0	2	179	7	66	43	76	-64
Lee,Khalil	19	L	21	RF	aa	KC	470	7	49	259	12	67	89	189	9
	21	L	23	RF	aaa	NYM	292	9	6	216	14	52	137	83	-26
Lee,Korey	21	R	23	C	a/a	HOU	220	6	2	209	6	77	82	63	6
Leon,Pedro	21	R	23	SS	a/a	HOU	246	7	12	183	10	58	88	97	-45
Lester,Josh	19	L	25	1B	a/a	DET	466	17	0	203	8	70	127	63	13
	21	L	27	1B	a/a	DET	395	24	2	219	6	63	163	99	26
Leyba,Domingo	19	B	24	SS	aaa	ARI	457	11	0	237	4	80	104	89	42
	21	B	26	2B	aaa	TEX	208	9	1	253	3	82	97	59	31
Liberato,Luis	19	L	24	CF	a/a	SEA	198	2	3	210	6	71	66	130	-13
	21	L	26	CF	aaa	SEA	298	5	2	218	7	66	72	100	-33
Lien,Connor	19	R	25	CF	a/a	ATL	213	9	5	192	11	41	241	176	25
	21	R	27	CF	aa	SEA	147	3	1	116	11	27	142	111	-120
Lipcius,Andre	21	R	23	3B	aa	DET	341	7	3	207	8	75	74	80	0
Lipka,Matthew	19	R	27	CF	a/a	NYY	294	4	15	218	5	69	82	157	1
	21	R	29	CF	a/a	MIL	361	7	20	218	5	62	81	129	-38
Listi,Austin	19	R	26	1B	a/a	PHI	468	17	1	213	9	72	113	56	8
	21	R	28	3B	aaa	PHI	190	1	0	180	6	69	31	16	-79
Lockridge,Brando	21	R	24	CF	aa	NYY	174	8	10	285	6	61	136	97	-5
Loehr,Trace	19	L	24	2B	aaa	OAK	36	1	0	284	4	77	116	131	54
	21	L	26	2B	a/a	TEX	163	0	1	202	4	65	53	76	-64
Longhi,Nick	19	R	24	1B	aaa	CIN	389	11	0	255	6	69	133	80	18
	21	R	26	LF	aaa	COL	219	3	0	196	7	65	63	21	-65

BATTER	yr	b	age	pos	lvl	org	ab	hr	sb	ba	bb%	ct%	px	sx	bpv
Longo,Mitch	19	L	24	LF	aa	CLE	327	5	10	234	8	75	85	164	32
	21	L	26	LF	a/a	MIL	318	9	15	229	6	70	89	135	4
Lopes,Christian	19	R	27	2B	a/a	TEX	446	10	11	229	10	73	102	99	20
	21	R	29	2B	aaa	ARI	181	4	2	181	7	55	102	74	-58
Lopes,Tim	19	R	25	2B	aaa	SEA	374	7	19	244	7	76	102	126	36
	21	R	27	3B	aaa	MIL	327	7	6	170	6	64	81	102	-34
Lopez,Alejo	21	B	25	2B	a/a	CIN	356	5	7	276	9	89	66	75	52
Lopez,Irving	19	L	24	2B	a/a	STL	362	8	1	226	6	76	93	135	32
	21	L	26	3B	a/a	STL	232	2	1	174	4	71	47	72	-48
Lopez,Jack	19	R	27	3B	aaa	ATL	359	9	7	229	4	70	87	125	0
	21	R	29	2B	a/a	BOS	242	3	10	227	6	70	76	101	-17
Lopez,Jason	21	R	23	C	a/a	NYY	173	4	6	176	11	59	75	85	-54
Lopez,Otto	21	R	23	2B	a/a	TOR	451	4	18	283	7	78	74	125	25
Lowe,Josh	19	L	21	CF	aa	TAM	448	17	29	241	12	67	136	184	48
	21	L	23	CF	aaa	TAM	402	19	23	262	12	65	145	125	37
Lugbauer,Drew	21	L	25	1B	aa	ATL	300	15	0	196	10	51	163	35	-34
Lukes,Nathan	19	L	25	CF	aaa	TAM	260	3	6	184	7	74	56	132	-7
	21	L	27	RF	aaa	TAM	294	3	2	249	5	82	83	69	30
Lund,Brennon	19	L	25	CF	aaa	LAA	352	5	4	214	6	68	98	120	-1
	21	L	27	CF	aaa	LAA	286	6	2	157	3	62	82	60	-61
Lutz,Tristen	21	R	23	RF	aa	MIL	240	6	2	189	6	59	96	53	-58
Machin,Vimael	19	L	26	SS	a/a	CHC	447	6	7	257	12	84	71	97	37
	21	L	28	3B	aaa	OAK	336	7	1	219	8	73	74	84	-7
Macias,Fabricio	21	R	23	RF	aaa	PIT	102	1	1	208	3	71	37	61	-60
MacIver,Willie	21	R	25	C	a/a	COL	196	3	6	136	5	64	48	78	-70
MacKinnon,David	21	R	27	1B	aa	LAA	366	9	1	223	9	72	96	35	-6
Madris,Bligh	19	L	23	RF	aa	PIT	457	7	3	250	8	77	86	73	13
	21	L	25	RF	a/a	PIT	360	6	1	220	9	76	76	39	-4
Mahan,Riley	19	L	23	2B	aa	MIA	207	6	0	213	4	67	116	95	2
	21	L	26	2B	aa	MIA	275	4	1	166	6	55	79	50	-89
Maile,Luke	21	R	30	C	aaa	MIL	129	1	1	159	9	48	78	48	-112
Maldonado,Nelson	21	R	25	DH	aa	CHC	245	4	1	254	6	76	83	66	6
Manea,Scott	21	R	26	C	aa	HOU	210	7	0	233	12	70	87	22	-19
Mangum,Jake	21	B	25	CF	aa	NYM	305	5	10	231	3	76	73	117	6
Mann,Devin	21	R	24	1B	aa	LA	369	10	4	197	8	68	100	54	-12
Marabell,Connor	19	L	25	RF	a/a	CLE	485	8	7	239	5	87	69	95	43
	21	L	27	LF	aaa	CLE	337	5	3	228	3	76	70	57	-15
Marcano,Tucupita	21	L	22	2B	aaa	PIT	355	5	9	218	10	82	45	91	15
Marchan,Rafael	21	B	22	C	a/a	PHI	242	0	1	184	6	79	22	44	-40
Maris,Peter	19	L	26	3B	a/a	SF	170	1	2	165	5	75	55	146	-2
	21	L	28	2B	a/a	SF	180	5	1	215	6	64	95	74	-34
Marmolejos,Jose	19	L	26	1B	a/a	WAS	391	15	1	274	6	74	141	85	47
	21	L	28	1B	aaa	SEA	293	17	0	256	11	68	137	45	20
Marte,Hamlet	19	R	25	C	aa	SF	187	2	2	173	7	61	56	74	-75
	21	R	27	C	a/a	LA	131	2	1	154	5	47	79	66	-115
Martin,Austin	21	R	22	CF	aa	MIN	330	4	10	240	12	72	66	100	-1
Martin,Jason	19	L	24	CF	aaa	PIT	370	6	7	231	6	77	99	135	39
	21	L	26	LF	aaa	TEX	129	7	1	199	13	69	119	83	23
Martin,Mason	21	L	22	1B	a/a	PIT	439	17	0	210	6	59	145	43	-22
Martin,Richie	21	R	27	SS	a/a	BAL	111	1	5	171	9	71	62	114	-14
Martin,Rudy	19	L	23	CF	aaa	KC	42	1	5	187	5	69	111	141	21
	21	L	25	RF	a/a	KC	277	7	15	225	12	61	88	106	-28
Martinez,J.P.	21	L	25	CF	aa	TEX	285	4	16	209	11	55	86	144	-46
Martinez,Orlando	21	L	23	LF	aa	LAA	400	12	4	219	6	66	101	71	-21
Martinez,Renae	19	R	25	C	aa	ARI	90	0	0	202	7	75	40	54	-39
	21	R	27	C	a/a	ARI	140	3	1	150	7	56	104	75	-54
Martini,Nick	19	L	29	LF	aaa	OAK	274	5	0	251	11	76	85	59	4
	21	L	31	RF	aaa	CHC	270	7	1	197	9	67	72	81	-32
Martorano,Brando	21	R	23	C	a/a	SF	120	5	1	149	11	59	101	45	-44
Masters,Dave	21	R	28	SS	a/a	SEA	123	5	1	159	7	54	106	38	-72
Mastrobuoni,Miles	19	L	24	LF	a/a	TAM	392	3	13	261	9	74	51	155	-3
	21	L	26	SS	a/a	TAM	382	4	6	244	9	70	71	94	-13
Matheny,Shane	21	L	25	SS	aa	SF	174	3	2	172	13	56	93	82	-51
Matheny,Tate	19	R	25	RF	a/a	BOS	341	6	10	217	4	64	97	110	-20
	21	R	27	CF	a/a	BOS	240	7	6	200	8	54	135	106	-27
Mathisen,Wyatt	19	R	26	3B	aaa	ARI	283	13	1	212	8	64	158	111	29
	21	R	28	3B	aaa	SF	237	5	0	155	8	63	82	37	-53
Matijevic,J.J.	19	L	24	1B	aa	HOU	281	8	7	216	8	60	145	148	15
	21	L	26	1B	a/a	HOU	402	18	4	201	8	59	136	82	-12
Maton,Nick	19	L	22	2B	aa	PHI	62	2	1	197	12	74	103	36	6
	21	L	24	SS	aaa	PHI	207	4	2	173	11	66	79	71	-28
Mazeika,Patrick	19	L	26	C	aa	NYM	413	14	1	209	8	74	115	79	23
	21	L	28	C	aaa	NYM	157	4	0	199	6	84	66	21	8
McAfee,Quincy	21	R	24	2B	aa	CIN	122	2	4	206	13	69	61	96	-21
McBroom,Ryan	19	R	27	1B	aaa	NYY	413	22	1	261	10	70	158	57	39
	21	R	29	DH	aaa	KC	433	19	2	195	6	69	95	64	-12
McCann,Kyle	21	L	24	C	aa	OAK	320	5	1	135	9	51	75	41	-103
McCarthy,Jake	21	L	24	CF	a/a	ARI	328	9	17	205	6	67	102	152	8
McCarthy,Joe	19	L	25	RF	aaa	SF	227	4	1	156	11	58	99	136	-31
	21	L	27	1B	aaa	SF	275	8	3	230	7	72	95	63	0
McCoy,Mason	19	R	24	SS	aa	BAL	429	2	9	242	7	79	44	179	17
	21	R	26	SS	aaa	BAL	408	7	9	181	7	63	82	108	-34
McDonald,Mickey	19	S	24	CF	aa	OAK	156	0	3	216	7	65	41	66	-73
	21	L	26	CF	a/a	OAK	364	1	12	240	8	70	48	123	-25
McDowell,Max	19	R	25	C	aa	MIL	258	4	2	205	12	74	84	81	4
	21	R	27	C	a/a	NYY	143	1	2	171	11	63	52	83	-58
McGovern,Keega	21	L	26	RF	aa	SEA	143	3	4	150	12	41	87	111	-109
McKay,Brendan	19	L	24	DH	a/a	TAM	145	4	1	174	9	59	93	65	-57
McKenna,Alex	21	R	24	CF	aa	HOU	131	2	1	173	9	52	71	59	-100
McKenna,Ryan	19	R	22	CF	aa	BAL	488	9	23	218	10	74	90	186	40
	21	R	24	CF	aaa	BAL	101	9	5	271	14	64	188	102	68

BATTER	yr	b	age	pos	lvl	org	ab	hr	sb	ba	bb%	ct%	px	sx	bpv
McKinstry,Zach	19	L	24	2B	a/a	LA	430	15	6	259	7	75	120	110	42
	21	L	26	SS	aaa	LA	147	5	3	211	8	78	88	113	35
McLaughlin,Matt	21	R	25	3B	aa	COL	279	2	1	183	6	75	44	45	-35
Mejia,Erick	19	B	25	SS	aaa	KC	495	5	14	232	7	77	66	172	24
	21	B	27	3B	aaa	KC	203	4	1	194	7	77	67	43	-11
Mejias-Brean,Set	19	R	28	SS	aaa	SD	411	6	3	236	5	76	64	93	-6
	21	R	30	LF	a/a	BAL	218	6	5	176	7	68	73	68	-32
Melean,Kelvin	21	R	23	2B	a/a	SD	136	1	1	133	6	80	20	46	-35
Melendez Jr.,MJ	21	L	23	C	a/a	KC	448	29	2	251	11	73	143	63	49
Melendez,Manuel	19	L	22	CF	aa	COL	500	7	18	277	4	89	67	142	62
	21	L	24	RF	aa	COL	266	4	3	176	6	74	64	44	-26
Mendoza,Drew	21	L	24	1B	aa	WAS	106	3	1	141	9	53	123	40	-56
Mendoza,Evan	19	R	23	3B	a/a	STL	222	1	4	222	6	77	43	108	-11
	21	R	25	SS	aaa	STL	396	1	10	189	5	69	29	83	-62
Meneses,Joey	21	R	29	RF	a/a	BOS	334	9	0	227	5	72	121	50	12
Mercado,Oscar	19	R	25	CF	aaa	CLE	119	3	11	262	10	69	142	172	57
	21	R	27	CF	aaa	CLE	171	3	6	168	8	77	81	106	22
Mercedes,Yermir	19	R	26	C	a/a	CHW	334	20	2	274	9	76	152	57	55
	21	R	28	DH	aaa	CHW	222	7	2	205	3	77	67	65	-10
Merrell,Kevin	19	L	24	SS	aa	KC	455	2	19	228	5	75	63	195	22
	21	L	26	2B	a/a	KC	150	2	5	163	7	64	57	85	-55
Meyer,Nick	21	R	24	C	a/a	NYM	220	2	4	198	7	74	34	60	-41
Meyers,Jake	21	R	25	CF	aaa	HOU	271	11	7	274	6	73	109	86	19
Mieses,Johan	19	R	24	RF	a/a	STL	386	17	5	199	7	72	108	101	18
	21	R	26	DH	a/a	BOS	283	13	2	194	7	65	118	70	-6
Miller,Anderson	19	L	25	LF	aa	KC	307	4	9	226	5	69	62	140	-19
	21	L	27	RF	aaa	KC	219	7	6	166	7	65	79	80	-38
Miller,Brian	19	L	24	LF	aa	MIA	449	2	23	251	8	80	64	176	37
	21	L	26	CF	aaa	MIA	396	1	28	220	6	73	38	127	-24
Miller,Ian	19	L	27	CF	aaa	MIN	450	9	27	225	8	77	100	188	57
	21	L	29	CF	aaa	CHC	368	2	12	195	6	74	39	107	-26
Miller,Jalen	19	R	23	2B	aa	SF	491	9	27	207	9	77	73	147	25
	21	R	25	2B	aa	ATL	229	7	2	177	7	63	108	60	-27
Miller,Luke	21	R	25	1B	aa	PHI	277	9	0	178	5	58	109	20	-64
Miller,Owen	19	R	23	SS	aa	SD	507	10	4	261	7	81	83	91	32
	21	R	25	2B	aaa	CLE	182	5	0	244	7	66	102	33	-29
Milone,Thomas	19	L	24	RF	aa	TAM	84	1	6	193	12	74	51	102	-19
	21	L	26	LF	a/a	NYY	311	8	12	230	10	63	94	92	-24
Miranda,Jose	21	R	23	3B	a/a	MIN	535	23	2	306	6	84	98	33	40
Miroglio,Dominic	19	R	24	C	aa	ARI	146	2	0	216	10	80	67	40	2
	21	R	26	C	aa	ARI	296	7	1	195	8	67	84	65	-27
Mitchell,Calvin	21	L	22	RF	a/a	PIT	402	8	4	244	4	80	67	45	-2
Mitchell,Garrett	21	L	23	CF	aa	MIL	129	2	4	161	10	64	40	70	-71
Monasterio,Andru	19	R	22	2B	aa	CLE	249	1	5	213	8	76	31	52	-43
	21	R	24	3B	a/a	CLE	376	6	5	245	9	65	93	95	-18
Mondou,Nate	19	L	24	2B	aa	OAK	427	4	6	221	10	75	55	99	-10
	21	L	26	2B	aaa	OAK	308	5	0	218	8	78	68	42	-3
Moniak,Mickey	19	L	21	CF	aa	PHI	465	11	14	241	6	73	126	199	66
	21	L	23	CF	aaa	PHI	366	12	4	218	6	68	98	91	-7
Montero,Elehuris	19	R	21	3B	aa	STL	224	6	0	170	5	65	88	47	-42
	21	R	23	3B	a/a	COL	431	20	0	248	8	73	113	35	10
Montes,Coco	21	R	25	2B	aa	COL	431	10	2	227	5	70	112	60	-2
Morales,Jonathar	19	R	24	C	a/a	ATL	275	2	0	225	8	81	52	43	-9
	21	R	26	C	aaa	ATL	152	1	0	121	1	78	37	25	-46
Morales,Roy	21	R	26	1B	aa	MIN	333	1	3	251	7	83	32	53	-10
Morel,Christopher	21	R	22	CF	a/a	CHC	404	14	13	197	8	64	107	128	-2
Moreno,Gabriel	21	R	21	C	a/a	TOR	135	7	1	332	8	81	128	67	63
Morgan,Josh	21	R	26	C	aa	SEA	232	7	1	197	10	69	73	29	-34
Motter,Taylor	19	R	30	3B	aa	OAK	248	6	3	160	9	66	78	101	-28
	21	R	32	3B	aaa	BOS	259	16	0	246	13	69	156	41	40
Mottice,Kyle	21	L	25	2B	aa	SF	110	0	5	215	8	80	37	93	-5
Mount,Drew	21	L	25	RF	a/a	CIN	205	9	1	236	6	65	105	71	-22
Mulrine,Anthony	21	R	23	C	a/a	LAA	183	3	0	165	7	69	56	24	-56
Muno,JJ	21	L	28	3B	aa	CHW	186	5	11	170	8	57	82	142	-48
Munoz,Yairo	21	R	26	3B	aaa	BOS	351	6	13	264	3	82	62	107	19
Myers,Connor	19	R	25	CF	aa	CHC	338	3	14	238	5	63	102	192	2
	21	R	27	CF	aa	CHC	113	1	5	176	4	44	86	120	-110
Navarreto,Brian	19	R	25	C	aa	NYY	160	6	0	158	4	78	87	12	-3
	21	R	27	C	a/a	MIA	183	6	0	156	5	69	83	52	-28
Nay,Mitch	19	R	26	1B	a/a	CIN	353	15	1	243	8	74	145	105	57
	21	R	28	3B	aa	LAA	367	15	1	180	10	61	120	35	-28
Naylor,Bo	21	L	21	C	aa	CLE	313	8	8	171	9	61	90	96	-36
Neslony,Tyler	19	L	25	RF	aa	ATL	192	5	4	281	10	76	108	176	56
	21	L	27	LF	aa	CHW	176	7	1	245	11	63	153	63	18
Neuse,Sheldon	19	R	25	3B	aaa	OAK	498	19	2	265	8	69	138	91	26
	21	R	27	2B	aaa	LA	314	9	4	223	5	66	81	89	-30
Neustrom,Robert	21	L	25	LF	a/a	BAL	453	13	8	215	8	74	94	81	12
Nevin,Tyler	19	R	22	1B	aa	COL	466	14	6	271	12	81	114	111	65
	21	R	24	1B	aaa	BAL	401	13	1	196	7	75	81	27	-9
Nishioka,Tanner	21	R	27	2B	aa	BOS	150	4	1	205	4	64	81	58	-54
Noda,Ryan	21	L	25	1B	aa	LA	384	20	2	199	11	61	130	53	-14
Nogowski,John	19	R	26	1B	aaa	STL	380	11	1	241	12	83	88	64	39
	21	R	28	1B	aaa	SF	209	3	4	152	8	74	45	61	-31
Nola,Austin	19	R	30	C	aaa	SEA	196	5	3	240	9	72	104	99	14
Nolan,Nate	19	R	25	C	a/a	CHW	165	4	0	157	6	51	123	83	-61
	21	R	27	C	aaa	CHW	154	4	0	115	5	35	132	44	-132
Noll,Jake	19	R	25	3B	aaa	WAS	456	8	4	242	4	77	74	81	4
	21	R	27	2B	aaa	WAS	438	13	3	251	4	80	88	61	19
Nootbaar,Lars	19	L	22	LF	aa	STL	93	0	1	245	12	75	27	104	-32
	21	L	24	RF	aaa	STL	117	4	1	249	9	75	65	60	-9
Nunez,Malcom	21	R	20	3B	aa	STL	202	4	1	212	6	77	44	43	-31
Nunez,Renato	21	R	27	1B	aaa	MIL	332	14	1	204	7	64	112	65	-20

BATTER	yr	b	age	pos	lvl	org	ab	hr	sb	ba	bb%	ct%	px	sx	bpv
O Grady,Brian	19	L	27	1B	aaa	CIN	429	24	16	238	9	60	201	117	49
	21	L	29	RF	aaa	SD	285	8	5	191	7	61	112	92	-25
Ockimey,Josh	19	L	24	1B	aaa	BOS	377	20	0	188	15	60	177	75	23
	21	L	26	1B	aaa	BOS	293	10	0	189	14	53	117	12	-61
O'Keefe,Brian	21	R	28	C	a/a	SEA	406	16	3	204	8	57	107	50	-54
Okey,Chris	19	R	25	C	a/a	CIN	182	6	0	186	8	57	133	89	-25
	21	R	27	C	aaa	CIN	169	4	0	196	9	65	80	43	-44
Oliva,Jared	19	R	24	CF	aa	PIT	447	5	32	262	8	75	85	204	43
	21	R	26	CF	aaa	PIT	225	1	7	201	6	66	64	112	-40
Olivares,Edward	19	R	23	RF	aa	SD	488	14	30	254	7	78	98	158	51
	21	R	25	CF	aaa	KC	256	10	8	260	7	80	92	109	43
Orimoloye,Demi	21	R	24	RF	aa	TOR	283	5	9	197	3	62	81	98	-50
Ortega,Dennis	21	R	24	C	aaa	STL	160	1	0	183	6	65	47	27	-79
Outman,James	21	L	24	CF	aa	LA	166	6	1	236	7	64	115	83	-12
Overstreet,Kyle	19	R	26	1B	aa	SD	367	5	1	218	6	74	56	68	-25
	21	R	28	1B	aa	SD	361	3	1	182	10	70	40	31	-60
Owen,Hunter	19	R	26	3B	a/a	PIT	357	15	1	226	6	62	152	89	9
	21	R	28	3B	aaa	PIT	328	12	1	178	6	54	108	49	-69
Pabst,Arden	19	R	24	C	aa	PIT	250	3	0	181	4	69	81	93	-21
	21	R	26	C	aa	PIT	206	4	0	154	2	59	71	28	-91
Pache,Cristian	19	R	21	CF	a/a	ATL	487	11	8	273	8	74	131	138	57
	21	R	23	CF	aaa	ATL	321	9	7	238	7	67	87	68	-26
Padlo,Kevin	19	R	23	3B	a/a	TAM	351	18	11	236	15	61	206	121	64
	21	R	25	3B	aaa	SEA	357	14	4	177	8	60	106	89	-30
Palacios,Jermain	19	R	23	2B	aa	TAM	123	2	8	181	10	75	55	170	9
	21	R	25	SS	aa	MIN	410	13	12	214	8	69	85	73	-17
Palacios,Richard	21	L	24	2B	a/a	CLE	357	5	15	254	11	77	94	118	42
Palensky,Aaron	21	R	23	LF	aa	NYY	111	2	0	186	13	61	102	69	-24
Palka,Daniel	19	L	28	RF	aaa	CHW	395	21	1	207	11	65	156	79	23
	21	L	30	RF	aaa	WAS	357	13	3	200	10	68	102	71	-3
Palma,Alexander	21	R	26	DH	aa	MIL	320	10	0	205	4	77	75	20	-17
Palmeiro,Preston	19	L	24	1B	aa	BAL	350	5	2	214	6	74	79	109	3
	21	L	26	1B	aaa	LAA	399	8	3	175	4	71	63	57	-39
Palomaki,Jake	21	B	26	SS	aa	TAM	217	0	10	158	11	72	22	109	-40
Papierski,Michael	21	B	25	C	aaa	HOU	333	5	1	192	11	69	64	36	-37
Paredes,Isaac	19	R	20	3B	aa	DET	478	13	5	286	10	87	86	86	59
	21	R	22	3B	aaa	DET	253	9	0	249	16	81	87	49	42
Park,Hoy Jun	19	L	23	2B	aa	NYY	416	3	18	252	11	76	66	157	18
	21	L	25	SS	a/a	PIT	224	7	8	238	16	71	88	85	16
Pasquantino,Vinn	21	L	24	1B	aa	KC	200	8	2	273	11	86	110	46	69
Paul,Ethan	21	L	25	2B	a/a	PIT	150	1	3	168	10	56	35	60	-108
Payne,Tyler	19	R	27	C	aa	CHC	73	1	0	213	6	77	78	59	2
	21	R	29	C	aa	CHC	213	3	1	175	5	61	79	62	-64
Payton,Mark	19	L	28	LF	aaa	OAK	395	20	5	262	7	76	154	114	73
	21	L	30	CF	aaa	NYM	290	5	4	201	6	76	65	73	-9
Pearson,Jacob	21	L	23	LF	aa	ATL	152	3	3	157	9	70	56	96	-28
Pena,Jeremy	21	R	24	SS	aaa	HOU	122	7	3	234	3	66	132	111	11
Peraza,Oswald	21	R	21	SS	a/a	NYY	354	11	18	266	6	73	86	102	4
Perdomo,Geraldo	21	B	22	SS	a/a	ARI	298	4	5	197	9	69	53	104	-28
Pereda,Jhonny	19	R	23	C	aa	CHC	344	2	2	227	12	83	49	41	-3
	21	R	25	C	a/a	BOS	203	0	1	215	10	85	52	48	17
Perez,Carlos	19	R	29	C	a/a	BAL	374	11	0	192	4	82	90	28	19
	21	R	31	C	aaa	OAK	376	18	0	190	5	78	99	25	11
Perez,Carlos	21	R	25	C	a/a	CHW	422	10	1	214	5	87	63	40	22
Perez,Cristian	21	R	23	3B	a/a	NYY	160	1	6	189	8	79	32	98	-10
Perez,Delvin	21	R	23	SS	aa	STL	389	2	15	209	4	72	31	113	-44
Perez,Joe	21	R	22	3B	aa	HOU	281	7	2	235	6	68	93	41	-26
Perkins,Blake	19	S	23	LF	aa	KC	110	2	4	209	7	71	66	152	-2
	21	B	25	CF	aa	KC	238	5	7	172	11	63	70	92	-40
Peters,DJ	19	R	24	CF	a/a	LA	457	19	2	213	9	57	146	86	-14
	21	R	26	CF	aaa	LA	180	3	1	179	6	61	73	67	-63
Peterson,Cole	19	L	24	SS	a/a	DET	151	0	3	202	2	77	37	128	-14
	21	L	26	SS	a/a	DET	184	0	5	183	6	82	44	138	18
Peterson,Dustin	19	R	25	1B	aaa	DET	301	9	1	253	4	71	97	34	-15
	21	R	27	LF	aaa	MIL	291	6	0	205	6	81	59	28	-8
Pinto,Rene	19	R	23	C	aa	TAM	260	5	1	215	8	70	92	35	-23
	21	R	25	C	a/a	TAM	354	15	3	228	5	61	127	51	-28
Pita,Matt	21	R	24	LF	a/a	NYY	181	7	9	192	5	64	120	108	-2
Plummer,Nick	21	L	25	LF	a/a	STL	386	9	8	216	10	62	92	97	-28
Podkul,Nick	21	R	24	1B	aa	TOR	181	5	3	170	8	68	90	78	-14
Podorsky,Robbie	21	R	26	CF	a/a	SD	119	1	8	212	6	75	53	144	2
Polcovich,Kaden	21	B	22	2B	aa	SEA	128	2	3	113	9	63	47	74	-66
Policelli,Brady	21	R	26	C	a/a	DET	268	6	9	162	7	66	83	80	-32
Pompey,Dalton	19	B	27	LF	aaa	TOR	27	0	0	219	15	69	0	0	-107
	21	B	29	LF	a/a	LAA	127	3	1	196	7	70	66	80	-29
Pompey,Tristan	21	B	24	LF	a/a	MIA	164	1	0	167	13	54	44	71	-99
Potts,Hudson	19	R	21	3B	aa	SD	409	13	3	209	7	67	125	101	10
	21	R	23	3B	aa	BOS	282	8	0	192	4	61	116	26	-47
Pozo,Yohel	21	R	24	C	aaa	TEX	315	17	0	286	2	85	109	32	40
Pratto,Nick	21	L	23	1B	a/a	KC	445	25	9	232	12	63	173	120	52
Proctor,Ford	21	L	25	C	aa	TAM	308	9	3	198	13	61	91	81	-33
Procyshen,Jordan	19	L	26	C	aa	LA	79	2	0	141	6	78	58	96	-3
	21	L	28	C	aa	TEX	132	4	1	158	10	61	77	52	-56
Pruitt,Reggie	21	R	24	LF	a/a	TOR	200	2	10	147	7	49	74	138	-88
Puello,Cesar	19	R	28	CF	aaa	MIA	149	5	2	219	11	66	109	73	-10
	21	R	30	RF	aaa	NYM	117	1	5	143	6	65	36	93	-70
Querecuto,Juniel	19	B	27	SS	aaa	ARI	386	5	4	216	2	78	70	122	13
	21	B	29	SS	aaa	ARI	362	6	4	206	4	77	58	95	-6
Quiroz,Esteban	19	L	27	2B	aaa	SD	306	11	2	203	10	67	143	75	19
	21	L	29	2B	aaa	TAM	213	9	1	209	13	65	139	55	18
Rabago,Chris	19	R	26	C	a/a	COL	199	3	6	199	10	71	85	53	-16
	21	R	28	C	aaa	COL	154	2	2	181	7	67	45	50	-64

BATTER	yr	b	age	pos	lvl	org	ab	hr	sb	ba	bb%	ct%	px	sx	bpv
Raleigh, Cal	19	S	23	C	aa	SEA	145	7	0	217	9	63	147	33	-6
	21	R	25	C	aaa	SEA	176	6	2	260	5	82	125	78	64
Raley, Luke	19	L	25	RF	aaa	MIN	126	6	3	267	4	63	148	135	20
	21	L	27	RF	aaa	LA	272	13	5	225	6	66	120	90	0
Ramos, Heliot	19	R	20	CF	aa	SF	95	3	2	244	10	65	145	148	35
	21	R	22	CF	a/a	SF	449	9	11	218	7	66	88	106	-18
Ramos, Henry	19	B	27	RF	aaa	SF	335	7	2	217	5	74	94	73	4
	21	B	29	RF	aaa	ARI	256	6	2	256	5	74	73	62	-13
Ramos, Jefrey	21	R	22	LF	aa	ATL	197	5	3	171	6	65	80	112	-28
Randolph, Corneliu	19	L	22	LF	aa	PHI	348	10	8	234	9	67	114	143	15
	21	L	24	RF	aaa	PHI	145	4	4	207	8	60	91	75	-47
Raposo, Nick	21	R	23	C	aa	STL	116	1	1	211	8	74	40	80	-30
Ray, Corey	19	L	25	CF	a/a	MIL	247	6	5	177	8	51	125	76	-59
	21	L	27	CF	aaa	MIL	146	4	1	208	4	60	119	77	-30
Redmond, Chandle	21	L	24	1B	aa	STL	122	3	0	235	5	52	121	19	-76
Reed, Tyreque	21	R	24	LF	aa	BOS	138	2	0	209	9	56	101	29	-68
Reetz, Jakson	21	R	25	C	a/a	WAS	259	5	1	163	7	63	83	48	-50
Reinheimer, Jack	19	R	27	SS	aaa	BAL	342	3	9	197	8	74	54	112	-15
	21	R	29	SS	aaa	SEA	327	3	12	175	6	65	44	105	-60
Reks, Zach	19	L	26	LF	a/a	LA	444	22	2	241	9	64	150	92	18
	21	L	28	LF	aaa	LA	321	12	0	209	8	57	139	49	-29
Remillard, Zach	19	R	25	SS	aa	CHW	95	2	2	212	11	56	87	106	-60
	21	R	27	SS	a/a	CHW	313	9	10	163	8	63	79	104	-34
Rengifo, Luis	19	R	22	SS	aaa	LAA	110	4	2	220	6	75	90	81	9
	21	R	24	SS	aaa	LAA	207	5	8	253	5	81	87	117	41
Rey, Brian	21	R	23	2B	a/a	CIN	256	3	3	233	7	77	39	48	-31
Reyes, Pablo	19	R	26	LF	aaa	PIT	175	7	4	242	6	76	148	54	50
	21	R	28	2B	aaa	MIL	132	3	1	167	7	76	61	66	-11
Reynolds, Matt	19	R	29	SS	aaa	WAS	376	11	6	229	10	68	130	122	27
	21	R	31	SS	aaa	CHW	309	3	3	192	10	59	71	63	-66
Riddle, J.T.	19	L	28	SS	aaa	MIA	121	3	2	189	4	79	107	184	69
	21	L	30	SS	aaa	MIN	317	5	2	157	5	75	54	78	-21
Rijo, Wendell	19	R	24	2B	a/a	NYY	324	12	3	224	7	72	127	95	30
	21	R	26	2B	aa	ATL	322	12	7	204	8	70	99	74	0
Rincon, Carlos	19	R	22	RF	aa	LA	254	9	1	202	6	64	123	57	-16
	21	R	24	RF	aa	NYM	383	15	4	207	6	64	110	66	-24
Rincones, Diego	21	R	22	RF	aa	SF	186	7	1	257	7	78	92	67	21
Ripken, Ryan	19	L	26	1B	aa	BAL	103	1	0	246	3	74	64	59	-25
	21	L	28	1B	aaa	BAL	150	1	1	130	5	60	41	59	-98
Ritchie, Jamie	19	R	26	C	aaa	HOU	252	3	1	206	10	72	86	82	-3
	21	R	28	C	aaa	ARI	284	2	0	220	7	76	49	53	-25
Rivas III, Alfonso	19	L	23	1B	aaa	OAK	32	1	0	362	5	75	125	76	35
	21	L	25	1B	aaa	CHC	197	3	0	232	11	71	70	17	-31
Rivas, Leonardo	21	B	24	2B	aa	CIN	190	0	7	237	12	71	35	108	-28
Rivera, Emmanue	19	R	23	3B	aa	KC	496	6	5	245	4	84	55	117	25
	21	R	25	3B	a/a	KC	270	13	2	240	6	75	123	83	36
Rivera, Jeremy	19	B	24	SS	aa	BOS	339	5	11	226	5	78	64	130	14
	21	B	26	LF	a/a	BOS	217	1	3	190	8	72	44	72	-38
Rivera, Laz	19	R	25	SS	aa	CHW	424	2	9	225	4	78	54	94	-6
	21	R	27	3B	a/a	CHW	218	5	7	219	4	68	77	96	-27
Rivera, Mike	21	R	26	C	a/a	CLE	160	2	0	156	6	68	51	22	-68
Rivera, T.J.	19	R	31	1B	aa	WAS	38	0	0	200	6	74	68	55	-21
	21	R	33	2B	aaa	PHI	279	6	1	211	4	72	72	31	-33
Rivero, Sebastian	21	R	23	C	aaa	KC	150	2	1	225	5	68	66	73	-42
Rizer, Johnny	21	L	25	CF	aa	BAL	312	8	7	203	4	69	70	99	-28
Rizzo, Joe	21	L	23	3B	aa	SEA	380	9	3	216	8	67	79	54	-32
Robertson, Krame	19	R	25	SS	a/a	STL	373	8	11	193	12	74	74	108	4
	21	R	27	2B	aaa	STL	391	7	7	189	9	75	66	99	2
Robinson, Chuckie	19	R	25	C	aa	HOU	374	6	8	186	5	63	81	104	-39
	21	R	27	C	aa	CIN	210	6	1	202	9	72	74	57	-15
Robinson, Errol	19	R	25	SS	a/a	LA	346	4	7	219	8	73	57	69	-30
	21	R	27	SS	a/a	CIN	191	1	5	157	11	55	47	90	-89
Robson, Jake	19	L	25	LF	aaa	DET	409	8	21	237	9	65	99	154	-2
	21	L	27	LF	a/a	DET	305	5	14	248	12	53	115	122	-32
Rocchio, Brayan	21	B	20	SS	aa	CLE	184	5	6	275	6	76	110	128	43
Rodgers, Brendan	19	R	23	2B	aaa	COL	143	7	0	315	6	80	145	100	78
Rodriguez, Aderlin	19	R	28	1B	aaa	SD	265	11	0	238	3	78	143	64	56
	21	R	30	1B	aaa	DET	434	21	1	232	6	65	137	60	1
Rodriguez, Alfredo	19	R	25	SS	a/a	CIN	486	1	14	235	5	81	44	113	6
	21	R	27	2B	aaa	CIN	410	2	2	234	5	76	40	42	-41
Rodriguez, David	19	R	23	C	aa	TAM	262	6	4	209	10	70	94	159	18
	21	R	25	C	a/a	NYM	164	4	1	185	8	66	71	28	-54
Rodriguez, Julio	19	R	22	C	aa	STL	45	1	0	201	4	65	59	3	-82
	21	R	24	C	aa	STL	107	2	1	148	4	76	35	37	-49
Rodriguez, Julio	21	R	21	RF	aa	SEA	174	6	13	325	12	75	95	87	29
Rodriguez, Manny	21	R	25	SS	aa	NYM	224	4	1	159	4	52	74	58	-105
Rodriguez, Yorma	21	R	24	1B	a/a	SD	148	4	0	236	3	79	68	26	-16
Rojas, Jose	19	L	26	2B	aaa	LAA	515	21	2	219	6	68	145	93	29
	21	L	28	3B	aaa	LAA	216	4	2	179	6	77	60	62	-13
Roller, Chris	21	R	25	LF	aa	CLE	246	1	11	172	7	66	51	110	-48
Roman, Mitch	19	R	24	2B	aa	CHW	121	1	1	154	11	65	51	130	-44
	21	R	26	2B	aa	CHW	218	1	13	175	10	56	37	116	-88
Romero, Yoel	21	R	23	2B	aa	NYM	231	3	0	204	6	63	70	25	-72
Rooker, Brent	19	R	25	LF	aaa	MIN	228	11	2	248	11	53	214	71	20
	21	R	27	LF	aaa	MIN	220	14	1	201	12	56	168	52	0
Rortvedt, Ben	19	L	22	C	aa	MIN	197	5	0	232	10	73	84	28	-17
	21	L	24	C	aaa	MIN	122	4	0	223	6	68	94	30	-31
Rosa, Dylan	19	R	23	RF	aa	DET	43	1	1	134	4	52	90	164	-60
	21	R	25	RF	a/a	DET	207	6	1	201	3	59	128	86	-27
Rosario, Eguy	21	R	22	SS	aa	SD	420	9	23	243	9	71	94	104	11
Rosario, Jeisson	21	L	22	CF	aa	BOS	346	2	8	212	10	65	56	75	-52
Rosoff, Jon	21	L	27	C	a/a	DET	160	0	3	154	8	67	29	62	-70

BATTER	yr	b	age	pos	lvl	org	ab	hr	sb	ba	bb%	ct%	px	sx	bpv
Ruiz, Agustin	21	L	22	RF	aa	SD	134	4	0	164	4	66	72	44	-56
Ruiz, Esteury	21	R	22	LF	aa	SD	309	7	28	214	7	74	78	138	15
Ruiz, Keibert	19	R	21	C	a/a	LA	314	5	0	236	7	92	45	47	32
	21	R	23	C	aaa	WAS	284	17	0	282	8	87	135	21	80
Ruiz, Rio	19	L	25	3B	a/a	BAL	22	1	0	199	4	80	64	-19	-24
	21	L	27	2B	aaa	COL	224	4	2	245	5	80	90	62	22
Ruta, Ben	19	L	25	LF	aa	NYY	442	8	22	232	9	78	86	156	41
	21	L	27	LF	a/a	SD	270	3	4	129	7	69	58	65	-42
Rutherford, Blake	19	L	22	RF	aa	CHW	438	7	9	258	8	71	77	142	0
	21	L	24	LF	aaa	CHW	448	8	3	201	3	68	81	79	-29
Rutschman, Adley	21	R	23	C	a/a	BAL	452	19	2	249	12	79	100	55	36
Sagdal, Ian	19	L	26	3B	aa	WAS	447	7	1	247	8	77	95	91	27
	21	L	28	3B	aa	WAS	110	3	0	183	6	62	62	20	-80
Salazar, Cesar	21	L	25	C	a/a	HOU	111	6	1	212	5	74	127	61	29
Sanchez, Ali	19	R	22	C	a/a	NYM	326	1	1	234	7	78	49	52	-20
	21	R	24	C	aaa	STL	251	3	0	220	4	79	40	20	-37
Sanchez, Jesus	19	L	22	RF	a/a	MIA	415	12	5	245	9	74	86	100	8
	21	L	24	RF	aaa	MIA	141	8	1	303	7	76	124	85	44
Sanchez, Yolbert	21	R	24	2B	aa	CHW	143	3	3	307	3	87	58	51	18
Sanchez, Yolmer	21	B	29	2B	aaa	ATL	310	6	4	170	7	65	64	79	-49
Sands, Donny	21	R	25	C	a/a	NYY	341	15	2	219	7	80	88	39	19
Santana, Cristian	19	R	22	3B	aa	LA	399	9	0	282	2	76	95	53	5
	21	R	24	3B	aaa	LA	331	6	0	254	2	76	67	24	-30
Santos, Jhonny	21	R	25	CF	aa	OAK	322	9	1	196	7	69	83	36	-29
Schebler, Scott	19	L	29	CF	aaa	CIN	194	4	0	173	5	65	72	31	-61
	21	L	31	RF	aaa	LAA	255	6	2	142	3	55	87	48	-88
Scheiner, Jake	21	R	26	1B	aa	SEA	395	13	1	203	8	57	113	75	-39
Schreiber, Scott	21	R	26	1B	aa	HOU	140	5	1	215	4	72	99	51	-7
Schrock, Max	19	L	25	3B	aaa	STL	265	1	9	230	9	79	71	129	25
	21	L	27	2B	aaa	CIN	128	5	0	240	4	75	79	13	-22
Schuemann, Max	21	R	24	2B	a/a	OAK	245	1	12	255	7	75	56	112	-6
Schuyler, Jay	21	R	24	C	a/a	CIN	127	2	0	157	7	52	79	18	-107
Schwarz, JJ	21	R	25	C	aa	OAK	254	4	0	194	9	68	64	34	-45
Schwindel, Frank	19	R	27	1B	a/a	DET	354	13	0	229	5	81	102	50	32
	21	R	29	1B	aaa	CHC	226	10	0	221	4	75	103	31	-1
Seagle, Chandler	21	R	25	C	aa	SD	158	1	0	152	3	67	51	71	-62
Senger, Hayden	21	R	24	C	aa	NYM	181	2	0	199	6	58	85	48	-72
Sepulveda, Carlos	21	L	25	2B	aa	CHC	264	2	1	179	9	75	41	48	-31
Serven, Brian	19	R	24	C	aa	COL	242	10	1	210	8	74	125	69	32
	21	R	26	C	aaa	COL	252	10	1	205	4	73	104	53	-1
Sharpe, Chris	19	R	23	LF	aa	PIT	231	10	2	206	7	70	149	152	56
	21	R	25	CF	aaa	PIT	317	3	4	161	8	61	90	66	-46
Shaver, Colton	19	R	24	3B	aa	HOU	188	13	0	199	14	56	202	88	27
	21	R	26	1B	a/a	HOU	216	9	0	142	10	43	138	19	-92
Sheets, Gavin	19	L	23	1B	aa	CHW	464	17	3	256	10	76	99	79	22
	21	L	25	1B	aaa	CHW	227	8	1	235	7	70	99	37	-12
Shewmake, Brade	19	L	22	SS	aa	ATL	46	0	2	224	9	76	0	133	-44
	21	L	24	SS	aa	ATL	324	10	3	206	4	74	86	86	3
Short, Zack	19	R	24	SS	a/a	CHC	197	5	2	203	12	62	134	131	8
	21	R	26	SS	aaa	DET	157	7	1	202	14	67	112	45	0
Sierra, Miguelange	21	R	24	2B	aaa	HOU	207	7	2	153	6	54	106	113	-51
Sims, Demetrius	21	R	26	SS	aa	MIA	276	3	13	159	8	51	58	91	-102
Siri, Jose	19	R	24	CF	a/a	CIN	468	10	22	214	7	58	103	140	-30
	21	R	26	CF	aaa	HOU	362	11	16	246	4	58	131	128	-15
Sisco, Chance	19	L	24	C	aaa	BAL	168	8	0	252	9	71	142	53	27
	21	L	26	C	aaa	NYM	150	4	0	145	7	64	89	52	-42
Smith, Dwight	19	L	27	LF	aaa	BAL	45	2	0	254	5	79	118	65	42
	21	L	29	LF	aaa	CIN	127	1	1	173	11	64	42	21	-79
Smith, Josh	21	L	24	SS	aa	TEX	102	2	6	260	13	78	70	62	13
Smith, Kevin	19	R	23	SS	aa	TOR	430	18	11	205	6	62	159	120	25
	21	R	25	SS	aaa	TOR	355	19	16	259	10	69	161	126	64
Smith-Njigba, Can	21	L	22	LF	a/a	PIT	240	4	10	225	13	67	70	76	-26
Snyder, Taylor	21	R	27	RF	a/a	COL	432	20	7	204	6	67	127	83	8
Sosa, Lenyn	21	R	21	SS	aa	CHW	117	1	0	198	2	74	45	43	-51
Souza, Steven	21	R	32	RF	aaa	LA	186	8	2	197	9	57	143	77	-15
Spanberger, Chad	19	L	24	RF	aa	TOR	431	12	4	227	8	70	129	71	19
	21	L	26	RF	a/a	MIL	302	9	1	160	7	53	114	61	-65
Stankiewicz, Drew	19	L	26	2B	aa	CLE	22	0	1	82	29	69	0	103	-70
	21	B	28	2B	aaa	MIN	146	1	1	206	9	68	85	68	-20
Steer, Spencer	21	R	24	3B	aa	MIN	249	10	3	204	6	67	109	97	-4
Stefanic, Michael	21	R	25	2B	a/a	LAA	491	11	4	265	7	81	64	42	2
Stephen, Josh	19	L	22	LF	aa	PHI	362	12	6	256	9	65	169	140	53
	21	L	24	LF	a/a	PHI	325	6	3	176	8	68	68	62	-36
Stevenson, Cal	21	L	25	CF	aa	TAM	295	6	12	206	12	68	76	95	-13
Stewart, Christin	19	L	26	LF	aaa	DET	83	3	1	250	15	66	103	54	-20
	21	L	28	RF	aaa	DET	303	16	2	212	7	62	145	96	9
Stokes Jr., Troy	19	R	23	LF	aaa	MIL	322	7	11	203	10	69	109	107	10
	21	R	25	RF	aaa	MIL	207	3	6	147	8	67	55	115	-35
Stokes, Madison	21	R	25	1B	aa	PHI	342	8	1	201	6	63	89	52	-47
Stott, Bryson	21	L	24	SS	a/a	PHI	345	8	4	265	8	71	87	63	-12
Stowers, Josh	21	R	24	RF	aa	TEX	305	16	17	193	9	61	135	139	14
Stowers, Kyle	21	L	23	RF	a/a	BAL	318	16	4	245	10	61	142	46	-8
Strange-Gordon, I	21	L	33	SS	aaa	PIT	229	3	4	184	3	81	50	90	-2
Strumpf, Chase	21	R	23	3B	aa	CHC	214	5	1	180	12	67	98	30	-20
Stubbs, Garrett	19	L	26	C	aaa	HOU	204	5	8	183	7	77	78	111	17
	21	L	28	C	aaa	HOU	113	1	2	194	14	67	49	67	-44
Suddleson, Jake	21	R	24	RF	aa	OAK	236	5	1	206	7	73	54	63	-30
Sugilio, Andy	21	L	25	RF	aa	SF	152	1	4	209	5	69	33	68	-66
Sullivan, Brett	19	L	25	LF	aa	TAM	364	9	20	250	8	84	102	194	90
	21	L	27	C	aaa	TAM	309	7	6	182	7	78	75	77	13
Susnara, Tim	21	L	25	C	aa	CHC	112	2	0	201	9	52	86	41	-92
Suwinski, Jack	21	L	23	RF	aa	PIT	367	13	8	223	13	63	113	87	-5

BATTER	yr	b	age	pos	lvl	org	ab	hr	sb	ba	bb%	ct%	px	sx	bpv
Swihart,Blake	19	B	27	RF	aaa	ARI	106	3	0	138	8	65	88	128	-20
	21	B	29	C	aaa	WAS	178	4	1	155	9	64	69	80	-46
Szczur,Matthew	19	R	30	RF	aaa	ARI	149	4	0	227	7	76	110	80	29
	21	R	32	CF	aaa	STL	102	3	0	129	4	64	73	31	-67
Talley,L.J.	21	L	24	1B	aa	TOR	296	6	2	206	7	75	72	64	-8
Tanielu,Nick	19	R	27	3B	aaa	HOU	454	13	1	221	6	76	115	68	28
	21	R	29	3B	aaa	SD	318	7	1	156	5	71	63	52	-38
Tatum,McCarthy	21	R	25	3B	aa	PHI	193	5	2	151	5	54	93	66	-77
Tauchman,Mike	19	L	29	CF	aaa	NYY	95	2	3	211	11	78	121	202	86
	21	L	31	LF	aaa	SF	128	2	1	190	9	63	84	99	-31
Taveras,Leody	19	B	21	CF	aa	TEX	264	3	10	273	8	77	82	157	36
	21	B	23	CF	aaa	TEX	322	13	10	209	10	67	117	95	12
Taylor,Chandler	21	L	25	RF	a/a	HOU	199	6	5	120	10	40	99	65	-120
Taylor,Samad	21	R	23	2B	aa	TOR	319	12	22	254	9	61	122	112	-5
Tejada,Ruben	19	R	30	3B	a/a	NYM	285	5	2	257	8	74	91	97	10
	21	R	32	3B	aaa	CHW	253	1	1	167	8	69	18	40	-78
Tejeda,Anderson	21	B	23	SS	a/a	TEX	274	9	8	158	7	48	120	90	-69
Telis,Tomas	19	B	28	C	aaa	MIN	306	6	0	275	4	87	85	83	53
	21	B	30	1B	aaa	MIN	423	8	3	231	4	82	47	63	-3
Tenerowicz,Robb	19	R	24	1B	aa	TAM	255	4	7	194	8	72	62	95	-22
	21	R	26	3B	aa	CIN	303	11	2	221	6	63	118	66	-18
Terry,Curtis	21	R	25	1B	aaa	TEX	364	16	2	226	5	70	122	63	8
Thaiss,Matt	19	L	24	3B	aaa	LAA	310	10	1	212	11	75	99	89	21
	21	L	26	C	aaa	LAA	379	10	1	203	8	69	86	61	-17
Theroux,Collin	19	R	25	C	a/a	OAK	324	9	0	149	10	33	195	55	-82
	21	R	27	C	a/a	OAK	192	3	0	100	6	42	67	36	-154
Thomas,Alek	21	L	21	CF	a/a	ARI	435	11	8	266	7	75	106	107	31
Thomas,Cody	19	L	25	RF	aa	LA	474	20	4	207	7	65	132	140	19
	21	L	27	LF	aaa	OAK	218	11	0	221	7	56	197	79	19
Thomas,Dillon	19	L	27	RF	aa	MIL	449	13	21	245	8	65	135	181	36
	21	L	29	RF	aaa	SEA	335	8	8	196	7	52	104	101	-61
Thomas,Lane	19	R	24	CF	aaa	STL	265	7	9	228	8	66	123	128	15
	21	R	26	CF	aaa	WAS	126	4	2	236	6	66	102	96	-12
Thompson,Bubba	21	R	23	CF	aa	TEX	429	13	21	248	5	69	110	150	21
Thompson,David	19	R	26	1B	a/a	NYM	405	7	11	179	7	69	86	146	2
	21	R	28	1B	aaa	NYM	219	8	6	160	6	59	105	98	-39
Thompson,Trayc	19	R	28	LF	aaa	CLE	334	18	6	181	7	51	187	131	6
	21	R	30	CF	aaa	CHC	323	12	2	171	8	52	126	55	-54
Thompson-Williar	19	L	24	CF	aa	SEA	432	12	15	218	7	59	136	172	10
	21	L	26	RF	aa	SEA	190	4	3	146	6	53	83	49	-91
Tilson,Charlie	19	L	27	LF	aaa	CHW	236	2	3	231	6	77	64	110	5
	21	L	29	CF	aaa	PHI	203	1	8	235	5	70	56	132	-25
Tocci,Carlos	19	R	24	CF	aaa	TEX	328	3	3	215	6	79	39	53	-25
	21	R	26	CF	a/a	WAS	120	1	0	168	6	75	34	13	-56
Toerner,Justin	19	L	23	RF	aa	STL	166	6	8	186	12	64	99	118	-13
	21	L	25	CF	a/a	STL	271	5	2	162	8	61	69	58	-64
Toffey,Will	21	L	26	3B	a/a	SF	175	5	5	168	11	41	110	86	-98
Toglia,Michael	21	B	23	1B	aa	COL	143	4	2	199	10	63	121	72	-8
Tolman,Mitchell	19	L	25	2B	a/a	PIT	434	5	8	229	9	73	72	141	5
	21	L	27	3B	a/a	SF	296	6	3	202	6	67	84	93	-22
Tomscha,Damek	19	R	28	1B	a/a	CHW	346	10	2	196	6	67	103	63	-19
	21	R	30	3B	a/a	MIN	290	6	1	184	5	65	81	53	-48
Torkelson,Spenc	21	R	22	1B	a/a	DET	322	21	2	230	12	73	145	68	52
Torres,Bryan	21	L	24	C	aa	SF	132	0	5	242	4	73	46	105	-29
Tostado,Frankie	21	L	23	1B	aa	SF	366	10	1	216	6	72	87	64	-10
Tovar,Wilfredo	19	R	28	SS	aaa	LAA	327	3	2	228	3	82	54	91	8
	21	R	30	SS	aaa	NYM	355	4	8	189	7	82	39	66	-5
Trammell,Taylor	19	L	22	LF	aa	SD	436	8	17	214	12	70	70	149	-3
	21	L	24	CF	aaa	SEA	274	9	6	213	10	67	95	74	-13
Travis,Sam	19	R	26	LF	aaa	BOS	236	5	4	246	9	71	108	109	15
	21	R	28	1B	aaa	SEA	277	7	1	190	5	58	105	48	-59
Trejo,Alan	19	R	23	SS	aa	COL	437	16	5	255	5	76	115	55	25
	21	R	25	SS	aaa	COL	334	11	1	238	4	74	140	87	45
Tromp,Chadwick	21	R	26	C	aaa	ATL	209	4	0	185	3	71	78	29	-35
Tsutsugo,Yoshitc	21	L	30	LF	aaa	LA	148	6	0	185	9	72	96	26	-9
Tucker,Cole	19	B	23	SS	aaa	PIT	310	6	9	237	9	75	91	168	37
	21	B	25	SS	aaa	PIT	220	4	6	182	12	70	73	91	-8
Turang,Brice	21	L	22	SS	a/a	MIL	431	5	15	222	9	78	54	90	3
Turchin,Doran	21	R	24	RF	aa	BAL	161	6	3	155	8	55	118	61	-51
Twine,Justin	19	R	24	2B	aa	MIA	359	1	6	227	7	71	49	138	-22
	21	R	26	2B	a/a	MIA	237	4	9	184	2	51	92	169	-67
Unroe,Riley	19	B	24	3B	a/a	ATL	311	5	9	253	9	75	75	120	9
	21	B	26	2B	a/a	ATL	121	2	2	176	7	74	48	97	-20
Urena,Richard	19	B	23	SS	aaa	TOR	369	5	3	255	5	75	82	114	11
	21	B	25	2B	aaa	TOR	324	8	2	245	4	72	105	58	-2
Valente,John	21	R	26	DH	aa	DET	229	3	7	254	6	83	68	98	30
Valera,Breyvic	19	B	27	SS	aaa	NYY	379	12	7	250	9	86	89	68	48
	21	B	29	LF	aaa	TOR	150	3	6	259	11	84	73	95	48
Vargas,Ildemaro	19	B	28	SS	aaa	ARI	124	1	1	306	5	95	71	116	83
	21	B	30	SS	aaa	ARI	249	5	1	208	3	85	67	56	20
Vargas,Miguel	21	R	22	3B	aa	LA	327	12	5	275	7	80	86	75	28
Vasquez,Jeremy	19	L	23	1B	aa	NYM	39	0	0	210	13	82	21	42	-25
	21	L	25	1B	aa	NYM	105	1	0	129	9	62	40	27	-94
Vavra,Terrin	21	L	24	2B	aa	BAL	149	4	4	207	12	69	96	92	7
Velazquez,Andre	19	B	25	CF	aaa	CLE	174	3	2	235	4	74	110	118	33
	21	B	27	SS	aaa	NYY	264	5	21	217	10	59	108	132	-17
Velazquez,Nelsor	21	R	23	RF	aa	CHC	124	6	4	253	6	69	149	97	36
Vicuna,Kevin	21	R	23	SS	a/a	TOR	290	2	10	217	4	73	48	78	-36
Vientos,Mark	21	R	22	3B	a/a	NYM	312	17	0	227	7	62	147	25	-12
Vierling,Matt	21	R	25	RF	a/a	PHI	294	8	7	238	8	73	73	78	-7
Vigil,Rodrigo	19	R	26	C	a/a	MIA	156	1	3	166	5	77	25	80	-34
	21	R	28	C	a/a	TOR	102	0	0	219	3	70	22	39	-85
Vilade,Ryan	21	R	22	LF	aaa	COL	468	5	8	255	5	80	67	100	14
Villar,David	21	R	24	3B	aa	SF	385	14	4	233	9	67	124	67	5
Viloria,Meibrys	19	L	22	C	aa	KC	220	1	2	256	9	72	66	61	-28
	21	L	24	C	a/a	KC	281	5	2	208	12	62	84	52	-45
Vinsky,David	21	R	23	LF	aa	STL	210	2	2	163	9	58	47	82	-88
Vizcaino,Vance	19	L	25	LF	aa	COL	304	7	30	272	9	68	119	206	43
	21	L	27	RF	a/a	CHC	132	2	3	184	7	63	51	53	-78
Vosler,Jason	19	L	26	3B	aaa	SD	375	12	0	224	7	67	115	94	2
	21	L	28	3B	aaa	SF	261	8	0	216	8	78	81	41	7
Wagner,Brandon	19	L	24	1B	a/a	NYY	396	8	1	159	9	58	81	96	-62
	21	L	26	1B	a/a	NYY	155	3	1	137	12	42	68	39	-138
Walding,Mitch	19	L	27	3B	aaa	PHI	282	9	1	165	14	40	165	93	-64
	21	L	29	3B	aaa	LAA	122	3	1	159	6	29	197	47	-98
Walker,Steele	21	L	25	RF	a/a	TEX	423	11	8	202	6	75	73	82	-2
Wall,Forrest	19	L	24	CF	a/a	TOR	462	10	12	251	9	71	116	153	35
	21	L	26	CF	aaa	TOR	297	1	30	234	8	66	62	166	-19
Wallach,Chad	21	R	30	C	aaa	LAA	254	8	0	140	8	57	85	25	-77
Walls,Taylor	19	S	23	SS	aa	TAM	211	5	14	252	11	72	142	206	79
	21	B	25	SS	aaa	TAM	178	7	8	213	16	61	116	110	3
Walton,Donnie	19	L	25	SS	aa	SEA	480	11	10	275	11	82	78	97	36
	21	L	27	SS	aaa	SEA	283	9	1	233	8	83	83	46	31
Ward,Drew	19	L	25	3B	a/a	WAS	296	14	1	243	5	54	205	86	16
	21	L	27	1B	aa	DET	275	11	1	194	8	56	118	60	-45
Warmoth,Logan	19	R	24	2B	aa	TOR	220	0	11	193	8	63	76	189	-17
	21	R	26	CF	aaa	TOR	342	8	14	201	12	54	99	108	-48
Waters,Drew	19	S	21	LF	a/a	ATL	527	6	16	306	7	68	124	192	41
	21	R	23	LF	aaa	ATL	404	9	23	216	9	62	93	113	-26
Watson,Zach	21	R	24	CF	aa	BAL	183	9	4	207	3	66	123	78	-7
Weber,Andy	21	L	24	SS	aa	CHC	131	0	0	182	7	56	97	64	-65
Welk,Toby	21	R	24	1B	aa	BAL	249	8	2	171	6	69	99	86	-6
Wendzel,Davis	21	R	24	SS	a/a	TEX	187	5	1	201	9	69	89	43	-20
Westbrook,Jamie	19	R	24	LF	a/a	ARI	448	12	1	236	8	79	91	70	23
	21	R	26	2B	a/a	MIL	320	9	3	225	6	79	74	79	13
Westburg,Jordan	21	R	22	SS	aa	BAL	112	3	2	202	8	70	97	96	5
Whalen,Seaver	21	R	26	1B	aa	TAM	187	4	4	168	3	72	82	89	-11
Whatley,Matt	21	R	25	C	aa	TEX	227	3	6	173	11	60	50	57	-81
White,Tyler	21	R	31	1B	aaa	TOR	353	11	2	238	15	74	99	31	16
Whitefield,Aaron	19	R	23	CF	aa	MIN	102	0	5	132	3	62	35	204	-53
	21	R	25	CF	aa	MIN	397	4	25	214	7	67	49	124	-39
Whiteman,Simon	21	R	24	2B	aa	SF	267	2	13	201	10	63	77	105	-35
Whitley,Garrett	21	R	24	LF	a/a	TAM	293	10	9	195	9	59	130	136	0
Wilkerson,Stevie	21	B	29	CF	aaa	BAL	123	1	0	188	10	61	60	25	-76
Williams,Grant	21	L	26	2B	a/a	BOS	282	1	7	228	3	90	32	108	25
Williams,Luke	19	R	23	2B	aa	PHI	441	11	27	219	9	70	118	187	46
	21	R	25	2B	aaa	PHI	126	0	5	236	6	73	36	113	-33
Williams,Mason	19	L	28	RF	aaa	BAL	442	14	3	245	7	76	82	52	0
	21	L	30	LF	aaa	NYM	210	3	4	192	5	66	63	74	-52
Williams,Nick	19	L	26	LF	aaa	PHI	190	8	1	263	5	65	170	117	44
	21	L	28	RF	aaa	CHW	126	3	3	194	4	63	81	83	-50
Williams-Sutton,[	21	R	24	LF	aa	SD	114	3	4	157	13	55	73	77	-69
Wilson,Cody	21	R	25	CF	a/a	WAS	154	0	5	105	8	62	26	109	-81
Wilson,Izzy	21	L	23	RF	aa	LAA	296	16	19	209	9	61	121	95	-13
Wilson,Jacob	19	R	29	3B	aaa	WAS	197	10	1	241	9	72	148	83	46
	21	R	31	3B	aaa	HOU	259	9	0	181	7	68	105	45	-15
Wilson,Marcus	19	R	23	RF	aa	BOS	240	9	8	221	11	59	177	154	38
	21	R	25	RF	aaa	SEA	363	10	11	190	12	50	114	104	-52
Wilson,Weston	19	R	25	3B	aa	MIL	445	21	12	224	12	71	135	159	57
	21	R	27	1B	aaa	MIL	217	10	5	203	8	66	120	72	0
Wilson,William	21	R	23	SS	aa	SF	196	3	1	161	8	54	79	40	-89
Winaker,Matt	21	L	26	1B	a/a	NYM	189	1	1	189	10	67	50	63	-51
Wiseman,Rhett	19	L	25	RF	aa	WAS	335	14	6	201	9	59	161	103	9
	21	L	27	RF	aa	WAS	286	7	1	179	4	55	108	51	-69
Witt Jr.,Bobby	21	R	21	SS	a/a	KC	497	24	23	263	7	73	138	123	55
Witte,Jantzen	19	R	29	3B	a/a	BOS	413	7	6	230	6	74	79	64	-10
	21	R	31	3B	aaa	SEA	405	12	2	217	6	72	76	45	-21
Wolters,Tony	21	L	29	C	aaa	LA	208	4	1	173	7	67	66	47	-50
Wong,Connor	19	R	23	C	aa	LA	149	8	2	323	6	62	191	67	34
	21	R	25	C	aaa	BOS	199	6	5	224	3	67	108	69	-18
Wong,Kean	19	L	24	2B	aaa	TAM	453	8	5	265	7	70	101	150	20
	21	L	26	2B	aaa	LAA	189	2	6	250	4	78	54	89	-7
Woodrow,Danny	19	L	24	LF	aaa	DET	376	1	20	250	8	75	47	197	9
	21	L	26	CF	aaa	DET	117	0	1	149	3	68	33	89	-68
Wrenn,Stephen	19	R	25	RF	a/a	HOU	390	6	19	204	8	66	100	199	16
	21	R	27	LF	aa	SEA	308	5	17	191	7	55	77	124	-66
Yangui,Yoel	21	L	25	1B	aa	CIN	272	6	3	200	9	63	71	80	-48
Yepez,Juan	19	R	21	LF	aa	STL	52	2	0	210	7	72	94	67	-5
	21	R	23	1B	a/a	STL	367	17	1	228	8	75	122	31	24
Young,Andy	19	R	25	2B	a/a	ARI	462	20	2	227	6	70	142	139	47
	21	R	27	2B	aaa	ARI	194	5	1	215	5	49	169	93	-30
Young,Chavez	21	B	24	CF	aa	TOR	279	5	14	222	8	67	80	108	-19
Young,Jared	19	L	24	1B	aa	CHC	455	4	4	217	6	74	63	90	-13
	21	L	26	1B	a/a	CHC	256	6	3	234	7	74	81	78	2
Yurchak,Justin	21	L	25	1B	aa	LA	115	1	0	311	7	77	66	28	-17
Zavala,Seby	19	R	26	C	aaa	CHW	297	16	1	182	6	53	185	66	-9
	21	R	28	C	aaa	CHW	154	5	0	123	8	39	131	33	-113
Zehner,Zack	19	R	27	LF	a/a	NYY	363	11	2	190	8	63	107	105	-20
	21	R	29	LF	a/a	MIA	225	3	4	187	11	56	76	88	-65

PITCHER	yr	t	age	lvl	org	ip	era	whip	bf/g	k%	bb%	k-bb	hr/9	h%	s%	bpv
Abbott, Cory	19	R	24	aa	CHC	148	4.26	1.36	23.9	22%	10%	13%	1.2	30	62	70
	21	R	26	aaa	CHC	96	6.57	1.72	23.0	23%	13%	11%	1.9	35	65	38
Acevedo, Domingo	19	R	25	a/a	NYY	53	5.60	1.27	6.8	20%	7%	13%	2.6	26	36	82
	21	R	27	aaa	OAK	34	2.42	0.88	4.2	32%	5%	28%	0.7	28	76	207
Adames, Jose	21	R	28	a/a	BOS	37	5.05	1.61	4.7	21%	13%	8%	0.8	33	69	62
Adams, Derrick	21	L	24	aa	KC	51	10.14	2.34	12.0	14%	13%	1%	1.8	41	57	-11
Adams, Mike	21	R	27	aaa	PHI	37	4.39	1.68	5.6	14%	12%	2%	0.3	34	72	47
Aguilar, Miguel	19	L	28	aa	ARI	31	3.25	1.15	4.8	20%	4%	16%	0.4	32	67	107
	21	L	30	aaa	ARI	42	4.54	1.59	4.3	18%	8%	10%	1.2	35	75	46
Alaniz, Ruben	19	R	28	aaa	CIN	41	5.62	1.91	5.6	22%	11%	11%	1.3	41	65	61
	21	R	30	aaa	CIN	39	5.07	2.01	5.7	19%	11%	7%	0.3	43	73	60
Alexy, A.J.	21	R	23	a/a	TEX	67	1.86	1.05	16.3	25%	10%	14%	0.8	23	88	94
Alldred, Cam	21	L	25	a/a	PIT	68	2.30	1.18	8.3	17%	11%	6%	0.9	23	85	57
Allgeyer, Nick	21	L	25	aaa	TOR	90	7.50	1.98	19.6	15%	13%	2%	2.0	35	65	-8
Almeida, Adrian	19	L	24	aa	LAA	28	7.89	2.85	5.3	16%	23%	-6%	0.4	44	69	-147
	21	L	26	aa	LAA	32	5.30	1.83	6.2	22%	24%	-1%	0.6	27	70	72
Almengo, Diogenes	21	R	26	a/a	BAL	50	4.09	1.47	5.3	20%	10%	11%	1.7	31	79	40
Alvarez, Manuel	21	R	26	a/a	CLE	45	8.34	2.03	6.1	22%	21%	1%	0.9	34	57	55
Alvarez, R.J.	19	R	28	aaa	MIA	55	6.50	1.69	5.0	20%	13%	7%	2.3	31	50	20
	21	R	30	aaa	MIL	36	4.61	1.67	4.3	21%	12%	9%	0.8	36	73	60
Amaya, Luis	21	L	23	aa	SF	54	6.29	1.66	7.3	24%	13%	11%	1.4	34	64	57
Anderson, Drew	19	R	25	aaa	PHI	49	6.80	1.71	20.2	16%	12%	3%	2.0	30	49	-6
	21	R	27	aaa	TEX	72	3.56	1.33	20.0	22%	10%	12%	1.1	29	77	70
Anderson, Jack	19	R	25	aa	SEA	54	2.33	1.64	5.9	18%	8%	10%	0.2	38	84	63
	21	R	27	aa	SEA	53	6.83	1.79	6.8	11%	13%	-2%	0.7	32	60	18
Anderson, Tanner	19	R	26	aaa	OAK	96	7.19	1.93	21.7	10%	9%	1%	2.0	35	53	-9
	21	R	28	aaa	PIT	53	4.53	1.65	8.2	9%	12%	-3%	0.8	30	74	9
Angulo, Argenis	19	R	25	a/a	CLE	64	4.79	1.53	5.8	26%	16%	10%	1.3	29	62	34
	21	R	27	aaa	OAK	43	7.48	2.05	6.3	17%	13%	5%	2.1	37	67	-1
Appel, Mark	21	R	30	a/a	PHI	74	7.12	1.83	15.1	13%	16%	-2%	1.8	29	64	-5
Arano, Victor	21	R	26	aaa	ATL	36	3.31	1.32	4.7	24%	11%	13%	0.9	29	78	81
Arias, Skylar	21	L	24	aa	CLE	41	8.26	1.87	5.4	23%	19%	5%	0.5	35	52	73
Armenteros, Roge	19	R	25	aaa	HOU	85	5.51	1.59	19.7	19%	8%	10%	1.6	34	57	63
	21	R	27	aaa	WAS	40	7.96	2.06	19.5	17%	14%	3%	2.6	35	66	-20
Armstrong, Shawn	21	R	31	aaa	TAM	31	4.15	1.57	4.7	23%	7%	16%	1.5	38	79	73
Arredondo, Edgar	19	R	22	aa	TEX	102	6.06	1.75	23.3	13%	7%	6%	1.4	37	58	40
	21	R	24	a/a	ARI	53	3.58	1.26	7.8	16%	10%	6%	0.9	26	75	49
Ashby, Aaron	21	L	23	aaa	MIL	64	4.36	1.36	12.8	33%	11%	22%	0.5	37	67	127
Ashcraft, Graham	21	R	23	aa	CIN	73	4.05	1.27	21.3	22%	8%	14%	0.6	31	68	92
Assad, Javier	21	R	24	aa	CHC	94	5.98	1.69	19.3	15%	8%	7%	1.2	36	66	30
Avila, Pedro	21	R	24	a/a	SD	76	3.96	1.34	8.8	21%	11%	11%	0.5	30	70	83
Aybar, Yoan	21	L	24	aa	COL	47	7.58	1.99	4.6	18%	15%	3%	1.9	35	65	9
Bacon, Troy	21	R	25	aa	ATL	40	3.73	1.62	5.8	19%	11%	8%	0.3	36	76	71
Bacus, Dakota	19	R	28	a/a	WAS	57	5.01	1.73	5.5	15%	12%	3%	0.6	34	66	-5
	21	R	30	aaa	WAS	52	4.54	1.64	6.5	15%	10%	5%	1.2	33	75	30
Bahr, Jason	19	R	24	aa	TEX	64	4.93	1.34	22.2	20%	11%	9%	0.4	30	58	42
	21	R	26	aaa	TEX	33	10.47	2.24	7.9	18%	18%	0%	2.3	36	54	-8
Bain, Jeff	19	R	23	aa	ARI	15	5.21	1.72	22.7	12%	10%	2%	1.5	33	63	-2
	21	R	25	a/a	ARI	63	4.97	1.54	9.8	18%	7%	11%	0.9	36	69	61
Baker, Bryan	19	R	25	a/a	TOR	54	4.58	1.58	4.8	24%	17%	7%	0.7	30	66	10
	21	R	27	aaa	TOR	42	1.90	1.03	4.2	23%	12%	11%	0.3	22	82	100
Baker, Dylan	21	R	29	a/a	CIN	51	7.98	2.29	16.4	11%	11%	0%	1.5	41	66	-12
Balazovic, Jordan	21	R	23	aa	MIN	97	3.96	1.50	21.0	21%	9%	12%	0.8	35	75	70
Baldonado, Alberto	21	L	28	a/a	WAS	42	3.69	1.21	5.0	21%	6%	15%	0.6	31	70	106
Banda, Anthony	19	L	26	aaa	TAM	29	7.45	1.58	14.2	18%	9%	8%	2.4	31	37	43
	21	L	28	aaa	NYM	51	6.32	1.69	17.8	18%	8%	10%	1.4	37	64	39
Banks, Tanner	19	L	28	a/a	CHW	128	6.05	1.62	19.0	12%	4%	8%	1.2	36	55	57
	21	L	30	aaa	CHW	61	5.35	1.63	10.9	19%	5%	14%	1.6	38	71	66
Barbato, John	21	R	29	aa	TOR	71	5.22	1.62	18.6	16%	8%	7%	0.7	35	68	49
Barker, Brandon	21	R	29	aaa	KC	52	9.56	2.19	17.4	12%	8%	5%	2.3	42	58	-23
Barker, Luke	19	R	27	a/a	MIL	61	1.92	0.80	5.5	24%	8%	16%	0.6	19	71	89
	21	R	29	aaa	MIL	62	2.65	0.92	4.4	26%	5%	21%	1.4	24	82	140
Barnes, Charlie	19	L	24	a/a	MIN	95	5.74	1.80	24.4	16%	9%	8%	0.6	39	63	44
	21	L	26	aaa	MIN	76	4.88	1.53	20.7	15%	8%	7%	1.0	33	69	41
Barraclough, Kyle	19	R	29	a/a	SF	18	6.69	1.48	5.7	21%	17%	4%	0.0	28	50	-12
	21	R	31	aaa	MIN	40	3.75	1.30	5.2	28%	15%	12%	1.7	22	79	65
Barria, Jaime	19	R	23	aaa	LAA	49	8.43	1.65	21.9	17%	4%	13%	2.6	37	31	100
	21	R	25	aaa	LAA	49	3.99	1.27	20.0	14%	4%	10%	1.5	30	75	67
Bartow, Frankie	21	R	24	aa	WAS	33	6.26	1.56	5.0	17%	9%	8%	1.0	34	60	49
Bashlor, Tyler	19	R	26	aaa	NYM	37	4.26	1.38	4.7	20%	10%	10%	0.8	30	63	48
	21	R	28	aaa	PIT	39	2.67	1.44	4.5	20%	12%	8%	1.1	29	87	51
Bass, Blake	19	R	26	aa	TEX	72	7.36	1.73	9.6	17%	11%	6%	0.6	36	51	20
	21	R	28	a/a	TEX	38	4.28	1.82	5.9	15%	19%	-5%	1.1	27	79	25
Bass, Brad	21	R	25	a/a	DET	60	5.49	1.39	8.16	20%	8%	13%	1.2	32	62	64
Bates, Nathan	21	R	27	aa	LAA	43	4.56	1.42	6.53	17%	11%	6%	1.6	27	73	28
Battenfield, Blake	19	R	25	aa	CHW	97	6.89	1.77	23.5	13%	6%	6%	1.8	36	51	42
	21	R	27	aa	CHW	106	6.92	1.83	21.4	13%	5%	8%	1.7	39	64	20
Battenfield, Peyton	21	R	24	aa	CLE	72	3.65	0.98	19.5	25%	5%	20%	1.3	26	68	128
Baumann, Mike	21	R	26	a/a	BAL	67	4.34	1.30	17.3	18%	12%	6%	1.0	26	69	53
Bautista, Felix	21	R	26	a/a	BAL	33	1.95	1.08	4.47	29%	16%	13%	0.3	20	83	116
Baz, Shane	21	R	22	a/a	TAM	80	2.27	0.84	17.3	35%	4%	30%	1.0	27	81	224
Beckman, Cody	21	L	27	aa	MIL	48	7.90	1.99	7.74	18%	14%	4%	1.4	38	61	26
Beede, Tyler	19	R	26	aaa	SF	36	2.89	1.24	21	26%	10%	16%	0.7	29	72	86
	21	R	28	aaa	SF	50	6.98	2.05	15.3	16%	19%	-3%	1.1	33	66	23
Beggs, Dustin	19	R	26	a/a	MIA	85	6.84	1.86	25	12%	9%	3%	1.8	36	54	9
	21	R	28	aa	NYM	48	4.34	1.38	20.1	11%	7%	4%	1.0	29	71	27
Belen, Carlos	19	R	23	aa	SD	25	5.89	1.57	7.31	21%	7%	15%	1.2	38	54	99
	21	R	25	aa	SD	55	4.67	1.60	6.26	13%	7%	7%	0.3	36	69	56

PITCHER	yr	t	age	lvl	org	ip	era	whip	bf/g	k%	bb%	k-bb	hr/9	h%	s%	bpv
Bellatti, Andrew	19	R	28	aa	NYY	32	7.59	1.70	6.9	22%	10%	13%	1.8	35	44	48
	21	R	30	a/a	MIA	35	1.78	1.00	4.5	23%	13%	11%	0.6	22	86	95
Bello, Brayan	21	R	22	aa	BOS	65	5.09	1.46	18.6	20%	7%	13%	0.7	38	65	110
Benjamin, Wes	19	L	26	aaa	TEX	136	6.89	1.80	23.3	32%	5%	28%	1.9	35	52	17
	21	L	28	aaa	TEX	48	9.76	2.38	16.7	21%	13%	8%	1.2	44	58	0
Bennett, Nick	21	L	24	aa	MIL	47	5.51	1.44	20.1	14%	13%	1%	2.2	25	69	15
Bermudez, Jonath	21	L	26	a/a	HOU	113	3.55	1.24	18.4	14%	12%	2%	0.9	32	74	109
Bettinger, Alec	19	R	24	aa	MIL	147	5.68	1.41	23.9	20%	4%	16%	1.3	34	50	96
	21	R	26	aaa	MIL	98	4.99	1.45	20.0	18%	8%	10%	1.4	34	69	65
Biagini, Joe	21	R	31	aaa	CHC	93	6.51	1.83	19.7	22%	11%	11%	1.5	35	66	11
Bice, Dylan	21	R	24	aa	MIA	56	3.82	1.27	6.4	19%	11%	7%	1.2	25	75	48
Biddle, Jesse	21	L	30	aaa	ATL	35	3.67	1.60	4.9	25%	10%	14%	1.0	36	80	77
Bido, Osvaldo	21	R	26	a/a	PIT	104	5.77	1.53	19.7	17%	11%	6%	1.2	33	64	40
Biegalski, Boomer	21	R	27	a/a	LAA	53	5.04	1.42	13.3	15%	13%	2%	1.9	31	71	46
Bilous, Jason	21	R	24	aa	CHW	65	8.88	1.86	17.9	16%	23%	-6%	1.3	40	51	50
Bird, Jake	21	R	26	a/a	COL	60	4.00	1.53	6.7	22%	24%	-1%	0.7	32	75	52
Bishop, Cameron	21	L	25	aa	BAL	49	3.52	1.33	17.0	20%	10%	11%	0.8	30	76	73
Black, Grant	21	R	27	a/a	STL	60	4.90	1.65	8.9	22%	21%	1%	0.6	34	70	53
Blackburn, Paul	19	R	26	aaa	OAK	134	5.14	1.43	23.8	20%	13%	7%	1.2	31	56	43
	21	R	28	aaa	OAK	90	5.10	1.73	24.1	21%	12%	9%	0.7	39	71	50
Blackwood, Nolan	19	R	24	a/a	DET	70	3.66	1.45	6.8	24%	13%	11%	0.7	30	70	24
	21	R	26	aaa	DET	61	6.84	1.71	7.5	16%	12%	3%	0.9	35	59	30
Blair, Aaron	21	R	29	aa	SF	35	5.69	1.73	17.8	22%	10%	12%	1.1	29	68	10
Blanco, Ronel	19	R	26	a/a	HOU	46	6.48	1.81	7.7	18%	8%	10%	1.7	36	56	30
	21	R	28	aaa	HOU	45	3.70	1.10	4.2	11%	13%	-2%	1.5	24	74	80
Blewett, Scott	19	R	23	a/a	KC	108	9.15	2.00	22.7	10%	9%	1%	2.3	37	42	2
	21	R	25	aaa	KC	69	7.18	1.76	13.7	9%	12%	-3%	2.3	33	64	-5
Bolanos, Ronald	19	R	23	aa	SD	78	5.21	1.47	22.4	26%	16%	10%	0.9	34	58	73
	21	R	25	a/a	KC	46	7.38	1.93	16.9	17%	13%	5%	2.3	30	66	-16
Bonnell, Bryan	19	R	26	a/a	WAS	64	4.66	1.35	7.0	13%	16%	-2%	1.6	31	56	82
	21	R	28	aaa	WAS	65	5.75	1.61	8.0	24%	11%	13%	0.9	36	64	46
Bosiokovic, Jacob	21	R	28	a/a	STL	58	3.92	1.28	6.3	23%	19%	5%	0.5	30	69	98
Bostick, Akeem	19	R	24	aaa	HOU	81	8.17	1.87	18.1	19%	8%	10%	2.2	35	44	17
	21	R	26	a/a	NYM	59	4.48	1.50	14.2	17%	14%	3%	1.2	29	73	30
Boushley, Caleb	21	R	28	a/a	SD	117	5.38	1.62	21.7	23%	7%	16%	1.8	35	72	31
Boyle, Sean	21	R	25	a/a	NYY	41	1.33	0.98	15.7	13%	7%	6%	0.3	28	87	147
Bracewell, Ben	19	R	29	a/a	OAK	76	4.03	1.82	8.2	16%	10%	6%	0.5	35	74	-13
	21	R	31	aaa	OAK	61	4.29	1.77	5.7	33%	11%	22%	1.4	37	80	23
Bracho, Silvino	21	R	29	aaa	SF	50	4.59	1.78	4.7	22%	8%	14%	1.6	40	79	46
Bradford, Cody	21	L	23	aa	TEX	36	4.63	1.44	22.0	15%	8%	7%	0.3	41	66	212
Bradish, Kyle	21	R	25	a/a	BAL	103	4.20	1.46	18.5	21%	11%	11%	1.0	33	74	73
Brash, Matt	21	R	23	aa	SEA	55	2.39	1.06	21.3	18%	15%	3%	0.5	28	79	140
Braymer, Ben	19	L	25	a/a	WAS	139	6.14	1.66	24.0	19%	11%	8%	2.1	32	53	22
	21	L	27	aaa	WAS	101	7.46	1.80	18.7	15%	12%	3%	2.2	29	62	-16
Bremer, Noah	21	R	25	aa	TEX	69	5.73	1.53	13.7	15%	10%	5%	1.2	33	64	43
Brennan, Brandon	21	R	30	aaa	BOS	39	8.03	1.94	5.8	20%	11%	9%	0.8	40	57	31
Brettell, Michael	21	R	24	aa	STL	70	7.06	1.70	13.7	18%	18%	0%	1.5	36	59	24
Brice, Austin	21	R	29	aaa	BOS	33	4.53	1.48	5.5	12%	10%	2%	1.3	29	73	39
Brickhouse, Bryar	19	R	27	a/a	KC	30	9.40	1.75	6.6	18%	7%	11%	2.0	22	31	-108
	21	R	29	aa	LA	60	3.84	1.26	12.9	24%	17%	7%	1.0	29	72	60
Brieske, Beau	21	R	23	aa	DET	44	3.19	1.12	21.7	23%	12%	11%	0.4	30	71	118
Briggs, Austin	21	L	26	aa	OAK	55	7.00	1.68	6.0	11%	11%	0%	1.1	32	58	19
Brink, Jordan	21	R	28	aa	TAM	57	5.26	1.47	7.6	21%	9%	12%	0.8	34	64	67
Bristo, Braden	19	R	25	aa	NYY	24	5.30	1.60	7.6	21%	6%	15%	1.1	35	60	63
	21	R	27	aaa	NYY	50	6.17	1.65	5.9	18%	9%	8%	1.5	31	65	40
Brito, Jhony	21	R	23	aa	NYY	48	5.74	1.37	25.3	18%	8%	10%	1.7	33	62	78
Brnovich, Kyle	21	R	24	aa	BAL	62	4.16	1.20	16.7	12%	4%	8%	1.6	30	72	94
Broom, Robert	19	R	23	aa	CLE	38	1.37	1.04	5.9	19%	5%	14%	0.6	21	84	43
	21	R	25	aaa	CLE	50	5.80	1.47	4.8	16%	8%	7%	1.6	30	64	39
Brown, Aaron	19	L	27	aa	PHI	66	5.51	1.77	6.7	12%	8%	5%	1.2	36	62	33
	21	L	29	a/a	OAK	65	3.39	1.47	5.5	24%	8%	16%	0.4	29	77	52
Brown, Hunter	21	R	23	a/a	HOU	101	4.20	1.44	17.9	26%	5%	21%	1.1	34	74	82
Bruihl, Justin	21	L	24	a/a	LA	39	2.50	1.00	5.8	16%	9%	8%	0.6	29	78	151
Bueno, Hever	21	R	27	aa	TEX	49	5.70	1.74	7.0	15%	8%	7%	0.7	37	66	56
Bugg, Parker	19	R	25	a/a	MIA	61	8.01	1.52	6.5	21%	17%	4%	2.1	30	31	57
	21	R	27	aaa	MIA	68	5.67	1.63	9.5	28%	15%	12%	1.5	28	68	43
Bullock, Justin	21	R	22	aa	MIL	35	7.40	1.64	19.6	17%	4%	13%	2.2	34	59	14
Burdi, Zack	19	R	24	aa	CHW	21	9.01	2.17	6.2	14%	4%	10%	3.1	38	45	6
	21	R	26	aaa	BAL	30	7.83	1.55	4.9	17%	9%	8%	3.3	26	58	6
Burke, Brock	19	L	23	a/a	TEX	54	5.04	1.37	20.6	20%	10%	10%	0.6	33	57	80
	21	L	25	aaa	TEX	79	6.34	1.49	16.3	20%	12%	8%	1.5	34	59	60
Burrows, Beau	19	R	23	a/a	DET	71	7.06	1.72	20.2	17%	11%	6%	2.0	32	48	14
	21	R	25	aaa	MIN	66	6.34	1.55	13.1	15%	19%	-5%	2.1	30	65	14
Burrows, Thomas	19	L	25	a/a	ATL	57	6.77	1.57	5.82	20%	8%	13%	1.0	34	48	44
	21	L	27	aaa	ATL	49	3.47	1.51	6.09	17%	11%	6%	0.9	27	80	72
Bush, Nick	21	L	25	aa	COL	35	6.83	2.12	24.7	13%	6%	6%	1.3	43	69	12
Butler, Eddie	21	R	30	aaa	KC	80	7.39	1.97	14.2	13%	5%	8%	1.6	36	64	-15
Butto, Jose	21	R	23	aa	NYM	41	2.90	1.01	19.7	25%	5%	20%	1.1	29	77	153
Byrne, Michael	21	R	24	a/a	CIN	51	4.03	1.40	6.35	18%	12%	6%	0.4	28	71	56
Cabrera, Edward	19	R	21	aa	MIA	40	3.78	1.26	20.5	29%	16%	13%	1.7	27	61	82
	21	R	23	a/a	MIA	56	3.89	1.30	21	35%	4%	30%	1.2	31	74	97
Camarena, Daniel	19	L	27	aaa	NYY	104	8.11	1.75	26.4	18%	14%	4%	2.6	37	38	75
	21	L	29	aaa	SD	84	4.53	1.46	16.3	26%	10%	16%	1.0	30	71	31
Campos, Yeizo	19	R	23	aa	NYM	16	6.96	1.35	8.45	16%	19%	-3%	2.0	30	31	75
	21	R	25	a/a	NYM	59	3.51	1.28	7.82	12%	9%	3%	0.9	29	75	63
Cano, Yennier	21	R	27	a/a	MIN	71	3.95	1.60	7.49	11%	7%	4%	0.7	34	76	67
Carlton, Drew	19	R	24	aa	DET	68	2.20	1.21	6.23	21%	7%	15%	0.6	29	79	70
	21	R	26	aaa	DET	53	4.05	1.32	6.66	13%	7%	7%	1.1	32	72	75

PITCHER	yr	t	age	lvl	org	ip	era	whip	bf/g	k%	bb%	k-bb	hr/9	h%	s%	bpv
Carr,Tyler	21	R	25	aa	PHI	52	5.92	1.63	7.02	16%	9%	7%	1.5	33	66	24
Carrera,Faustino	21	L	22	aa	TAM	49	3.25	1.08	12	15%	7%	8%	0.7	25	72	67
Carrillo,Gerardo	21	R	23	aa	WAS	97	5.63	1.56	18.5	21%	12%	9%	1.5	32	67	44
Carroll,Cody	21	R	29	a/a	MIA	31	6.42	1.76	4.9	23%	11%	12%	2.1	37	68	32
Carter,Will	19	R	26	a/a	NYY	69	7.21	1.93	8.65	10%	14%	-4%	0.9	33	56	-69
	21	R	28	aaa	CHW	39	5.65	1.87	4.97	19%	14%	5%	0.2	38	67	65
Case,Brad	21	R	25	aa	PIT	67	5.74	1.66	10.7	15%	7%	8%	1.6	35	69	22
Castano,Daniel	19	L	25	aa	MIA	86	5.53	1.54	20.8	16%	5%	11%	0.3	38	59	76
	21	L	27	aaa	MIA	79	5.04	1.31	23.4	13%	5%	8%	2.0	27	69	17
Castellani,Ryan	19	R	23	aaa	COL	44	8.84	1.99	21.2	18%	14%	4%	3.1	34	40	-3
	21	R	25	aaa	COL	95	7.04	1.84	18.4	15%	16%	-1%	1.7	29	64	5
Castellanos,Humb	21	R	23	aaa	ARI	59	3.91	1.08	19.3	22%	5%	17%	1.5	27	71	99
Castillo,Jesus	19	R	24	aa	LAA	101	3.64	1.51	11.5	15%	7%	9%	0.5	35	72	57
	21	R	26	a/a	MIL	107	5.61	1.51	17.9	13%	5%	8%	1.7	33	67	26
Castillo,Luis	21	R	26	a/a	ARI	35	4.44	1.89	5.71	17%	11%	6%	0.9	39	78	39
Castillo,Maximo	21	R	22	aa	TOR	102	5.06	1.41	20.6	18%	7%	10%	1.1	32	66	58
Castro,Kervin	21	R	22	aaa	SF	44	2.73	1.16	5.83	30%	11%	18%	0.5	29	77	120
Cate,Tim	21	L	24	aa	WAS	98	6.35	1.73	21.3	15%	8%	6%	1.3	36	65	25
Cavalli,Cade	21	R	23	a/a	WAS	84	4.86	1.55	21.7	24%	13%	11%	0.5	34	68	82
Chalmers,Dakota	21	R	25	a/a	CHC	72	6.73	1.65	15.4	19%	16%	3%	1.8	27	62	25
Chentouf,Yaya	21	R	24	aa	DET	45	4.89	1.61	7.98	17%	11%	6%	1.5	32	74	24
Clarkin,Ian	21	L	26	a/a	COL	70	9.36	2.09	16.4	7%	12%	-5%	2.2	34	57	-50
Clemmer,Dakody	21	R	25	aa	CLE	51	4.16	1.42	6.2	24%	16%	8%	0.4	28	70	87
Cobb,Trey	21	R	27	a/a	NYM	45	8.20	2.04	8.12	13%	10%	3%	2.3	38	63	-24
Coleman,Dylan	21	R	25	a/a	KC	59	3.78	1.13	5.19	31%	10%	21%	0.6	30	67	128
Conine,Brett	19	R	23	aa	HOU	18	2.88	1.77	20.6	15%	8%	7%	0.7	38	81	38
	21	R	25	aaa	HOU	100	5.67	1.53	17.5	16%	9%	7%	1.8	31	68	18
Conley,Adam	21	L	31	aaa	TAM	31	6.23	1.47	4.92	20%	16%	4%	1.5	24	59	38
Conley,Bryce	21	R	27	aa	OAK	95	4.88	1.44	14	17%	11%	6%	0.6	30	65	58
Conn,Devin	21	R	24	aa	HOU	35	2.96	1.09	6.56	19%	7%	12%	1.4	24	82	64
Contreras,Roansy	21	R	22	a/a	PIT	60	2.61	0.92	17.4	30%	5%	25%	0.7	28	74	173
Coshow,Cale	19	R	27	aaa	NYY	16	6.55	1.94	5.48	22%	15%	8%	2.3	36	57	22
	21	R	29	aa	DET	48	5.63	1.89	6.86	18%	8%	9%	0.7	42	70	55
Cotton,Jharel	19	R	27	aaa	OAK	20	8.72	1.90	6.81	20%	11%	9%	2.3	37	41	41
	21	R	29	aaa	TEX	42	3.73	1.39	7.38	24%	11%	13%	0.7	32	75	85
Cox,Austin	21	L	24	a/a	KC	68	4.76	1.50	17.3	16%	10%	6%	1.4	30	72	29
Cozart,Logan	19	R	26	a/a	COL	56	4.96	1.71	5.92	15%	8%	7%	2.0	34	63	38
	21	R	28	aaa	COL	52	4.36	1.61	4.28	17%	12%	5%	1.0	32	75	38
Crawford,Kutter	19	R	23	aa	BOS	20	5.83	1.99	19.4	19%	17%	3%	1.1	36	65	-24
	21	R	25	a/a	BOS	96	5.16	1.22	19.5	27%	5%	22%	1.2	34	59	136
Crawford,Leo	19	L	22	aa	LA	31	2.96	1.39	21.8	19%	5%	14%	0.7	35	75	93
	21	L	24	aa	MIL	64	5.92	1.51	11.1	21%	10%	11%	1.6	32	64	44
Criswell,Cooper	21	R	25	a/a	LAA	120	4.88	1.30	22.5	22%	4%	18%	1.2	34	65	128
Crouse,Hans	21	R	23	a/a	PHI	87	3.40	1.07	17	25%	10%	16%	1.0	24	72	94
Cruz,Jesus	19	R	24	a/a	STL	64	6.95	1.65	5.54	25%	16%	9%	1.2	32	49	28
	21	R	26	aaa	STL	36	3.05	1.55	4.26	19%	15%	3%	0.2	30	79	71
Cruz,Omar	21	L	22	aa	PIT	72	3.46	1.31	21.3	17%	7%	10%	0.7	31	75	70
Cuas,Jose	21	R	27	a/a	KC	38	2.04	1.28	6.25	17%	5%	12%	0.2	33	84	96
Cuello,Edward	21	R	23	a/a	LA	30	7.20	1.56	6.64	12%	8%	3%	2.2	29	58	-14
Curlis,Connor	21	L	25	aa	CIN	99	6.35	1.60	21.9	17%	12%	5%	2.4	28	67	0
Curtis,Keegan	21	R	26	a/a	ARI	30	3.70	1.34	5.07	22%	9%	13%	0.2	33	71	98
Custodio,Claudio	19	R	29	aa	ATL	80	4.95	1.54	11.3	14%	9%	5%	0.4	34	63	24
	21	R	31	a/a	BAL	51	4.81	1.65	8.15	12%	9%	3%	1.1	33	73	16
Cyr,Tyler	19	R	26	a/a	SF	51	2.76	1.37	5.64	21%	12%	9%	0.2	30	77	39
	21	R	28	aaa	SF	38	5.10	1.25	4.86	24%	14%	10%	0.8	25	59	81
Damron,Ty	21	L	27	aa	OAK	90	6.61	1.81	18.9	16%	7%	9%	1.1	39	64	39
Daniel,Davis	21	R	24	a/a	LAA	68	5.01	1.37	20.4	27%	5%	22%	1.3	38	66	140
Daniels,Brett	21	R	25	aa	HOU	91	7.70	1.76	19	22%	12%	11%	1.3	37	56	49
Danish,Tyler	19	R	25	aaa	SEA	17	21.43	3.40	17.9	8%	8%	0%	4.8	50	17	-28
	21	R	27	a/a	LAA	71	4.03	1.35	9.27	21%	5%	16%	1.2	34	74	97
De Horta,Adrian	19	R	24	a/a	LAA	50	5.86	1.49	13.5	27%	15%	13%	2.2	27	48	56
	21	R	26	a/a	TAM	55	7.00	1.68	9.9	21%	13%	8%	2.3	31	63	15
De Jesus,Angel	21	R	24	a/a	DET	66	4.18	1.26	6.14	23%	14%	9%	1.1	23	70	69
De Jesus,Enmanı	21	L	25	a/a	BOS	64	4.83	1.73	13.2	21%	10%	11%	0.6	40	72	71
De La Cruz,Jasse	19	R	22	aa	ATL	87	6.30	1.57	22.5	16%	11%	5%	1.0	32	52	15
	21	R	24	aaa	ATL	57	8.81	1.92	13.5	17%	13%	4%	1.4	36	53	19
De La Cruz,Osca	19	R	24	aa	CHC	82	5.81	1.41	11.2	21%	10%	11%	1.1	31	50	63
	21	R	26	a/a	NYM	72	7.92	1.82	16	18%	9%	9%	0.7	40	54	53
Deal,Hayden	21	L	27	aa	ATL	89	5.42	1.62	17.2	14%	10%	4%	0.6	34	66	40
DeJuneas,Tommy	19	R	24	aa	HOU	31	11.90	2.56	7.27	19%	22%	-3%	2.0	39	43	-109
	21	R	26	aa	HOU	30	8.63	1.98	8.54	11%	19%	-9%	0.7	30	54	19
Del Pozo,Miguel	19	L	27	aaa	LAA	50	4.66	1.56	5.5	25%	9%	15%	1.0	37	64	94
	21	L	29	aaa	DET	39	4.16	1.25	4.68	24%	12%	12%	1.9	23	76	51
Del Rosario,Yefri	21	R	22	aa	KC	72	6.89	1.71	12.6	20%	11%	9%	1.5	36	61	37
Demurias,Eddy	21	R	24	a/a	CIN	44	3.36	1.27	5.65	20%	13%	7%	0.5	25	74	76
Dennis,Matt	19	R	24	aa	COL	82	5.72	1.85	27.3	12%	7%	5%	2.1	37	61	33
	21	R	26	aa	COL	96	7.52	1.77	19.2	14%	5%	9%	1.5	38	58	31
Derby,Bubba	19	R	25	aaa	MIL	116	5.81	1.60	19	17%	10%	7%	1.8	32	54	34
	21	R	27	a/a	MIL	48	8.62	1.78	8.82	18%	10%	8%	1.9	36	52	18
Detmers,Reid	21	L	22	a/a	LAA	62	3.05	1.13	17.5	39%	7%	32%	1.2	36	80	172
Diaz,Alexis	21	R	25	aa	CIN	43	4.78	1.35	5.14	33%	12%	21%	0.5	35	63	126
Diaz,Jhonathan	21	L	25	a/a	LAA	77	4.04	1.16	19.2	25%	6%	19%	0.5	32	65	128
Diehl,Phillip	19	L	25	a/a	COL	60	7.01	1.57	5.28	19%	8%	11%	3.3	30	35	70
	21	L	27	aaa	CIN	56	3.32	1.14	3.84	26%	6%	20%	2.0	27	84	91
Dobzanski,Bryan	19	R	24	a/a	STL	38	4.57	1.65	6.33	20%	12%	9%	1.5	34	66	40
	21	R	26	aa	WAS	48	4.26	1.37	6.12	18%	12%	6%	0.9	27	71	52
Dohy,Kyle	19	L	23	a/a	PHI	69	6.40	1.86	6.89	29%	19%	11%	0.7	39	60	27
	21	L	25	a/a	PHI	44	3.16	1.17	5.51	31%	16%	15%	0.7	23	75	111

PITCHER	yr	t	age	lvl	org	ip	era	whip	bf/g	k%	bb%	k-bb	hr/9	h%	s%	bpv
Dominguez,Johar	21	R	25	a/a	CHW	42	7.34	1.61	20.7	16%	9%	7%	1.9	38	56	62
Donato,Chad	19	R	24	aa	HOU	53	5.24	1.38	20.3	15%	7%	8%	1.6	32	52	96
	21	R	26	a/a	HOU	56	5.03	1.35	15.6	21%	12%	9%	1.4	31	66	58
Doval,Camilo	21	R	24	aaa	SF	32	4.71	1.61	5.09	23%	11%	12%	0.7	33	71	82
Dowdy,Kyle	19	R	26	a/a	CLE	43	5.16	1.75	12.3	10%	14%	-4%	0.6	35	66	-4
	21	R	28	aaa	CLE	60	5.71	1.81	7.13	19%	14%	5%	1.5	32	71	23
Drury,Austin	21	L	24	aa	LA	45	4.36	1.23	9.15	15%	7%	8%	1.1	30	67	90
Dubin,Shawn	21	R	26	aaa	HOU	51	3.47	1.11	12.6	16%	5%	11%	0.7	28	70	115
Dugger,Robert	19	R	24	a/a	MIA	126	7.31	1.66	24.6	13%	5%	8%	1.5	36	46	67
	21	R	26	aaa	SEA	70	6.67	1.55	20.4	18%	14%	4%	1.5	34	58	38
Duncan,Frank	21	R	29	a/a	COL	124	4.53	1.51	22.4	15%	16%	-1%	1.1	34	73	44
Dunshee,Parker	19	R	24	a/a	OAK	130	5.32	1.38	21	22%	5%	17%	1.6	29	51	55
	21	R	26	aaa	OAK	44	6.52	1.54	19.2	15%	7%	9%	1.3	33	58	34
DuRapau,Montan	19	R	27	aaa	PIT	47	2.85	0.90	4.74	13%	5%	8%	0.7	21	62	84
	21	R	29	aa	OAK	55	4.60	1.28	6.1	17%	11%	6%	0.7	28	64	49
Duron,Nick	21	R	25	a/a	SEA	44	4.79	1.34	4.85	18%	7%	10%	1.2	25	67	52
Dye,Josh	21	L	25	a/a	KC	67	3.01	1.28	6.88	30%	11%	18%	0.8	31	79	86
Eastman,Colton	19	R	23	aa	PHI	34	3.84	1.25	23.2	15%	8%	6%	1.1	27	62	55
	21	R	25	a/a	PHI	54	3.70	1.30	14.8	24%	13%	11%	0.9	27	74	57
Eckelman,Matt	19	R	26	a/a	PIT	53	5.32	1.83	5.16	19%	16%	3%	0.6	36	66	-3
	21	R	28	aaa	PIT	66	5.72	1.70	8.28	17%	11%	6%	1.6	37	70	26
Eder,Jacob	21	L	23	aa	MIA	72	2.15	1.08	18.7	7%	12%	-5%	0.4	28	81	131
Effross,Scott	19	R	26	aa	CHC	35	8.41	1.77	9.52	24%	16%	8%	1.0	36	44	5
	21	R	28	a/a	CHC	62	3.99	1.12	7.91	13%	10%	3%	1.2	26	69	78
Eickhoff,Jerad	19	R	29	a/a	PHI	26	8.19	1.55	19.1	31%	10%	21%	2.5	27	29	7
	21	R	31	aaa	NYM	81	4.93	1.37	21.3	15%	8%	7%	1.7	31	70	51
Elder,Bryce	21	R	22	a/a	ATL	94	3.49	1.10	23.1	16%	9%	7%	0.9	24	71	86
Elledge,Seth	19	R	23	a/a	STL	69	4.95	1.47	6.32	20%	16%	4%	0.8	33	60	54
	21	R	25	aaa	STL	37	6.28	1.80	5.74	17%	11%	6%	0.6	39	64	66
Ellenbest,Mike	21	R	27	aa	TOR	36	6.37	1.48	6.19	19%	7%	12%	1.4	34	58	60
Elliott,Jake	21	R	26	aa	CHW	57	5.15	1.50	8.24	30%	5%	25%	1.6	30	70	23
Ellis,Chris	19	R	27	aaa	STL	79	9.03	2.14	9.8	22%	15%	8%	1.6	40	49	-5
	21	R	29	aaa	TAM	57	8.93	2.00	18.3	18%	8%	9%	2.8	35	60	-24
Endersby,Jimmy	21	R	23	aa	HOU	68	3.89	1.49	18.3	20%	11%	9%	0.7	30	75	61
Engler,Scott	21	R	25	a/a	TEX	56	4.25	1.38	6.41	24%	11%	13%	1.1	30	72	67
Enns,Dietrich	19	L	28	aaa	SD	137	7.38	1.97	23.4	16%	10%	6%	2.3	37	52	8
	21	L	30	aaa	TAM	73	3.69	1.14	15.2	15%	8%	7%	1.3	27	73	90
Enright,Nic	21	R	24	aa	CLE	41	5.05	1.04	6.92	17%	12%	5%	1.2	28	53	134
Eppler,Tyler	21	R	28	aaa	WAS	72	10.39	2.14	18.8	19%	17%	3%	3.1	36	55	-63
Erceg,Lucas	21	R	26	aa	MIL	49	6.42	1.70	10.1	27%	5%	22%	1.1	28	62	34
Erwin,Tyler	19	L	25	a/a	BAL	45	4.22	1.59	5.4	19%	5%	14%	0.3	35	70	32
	21	L	27	aa	BAL	32	5.64	1.86	5	21%	10%	11%	2.0	36	75	-1
Erwin,Zack	19	L	25	aa	OAK	60	4.18	1.72	7.02	22%	4%	18%	1.0	41	71	102
	21	L	27	a/a	OAK	63	4.27	1.51	5.57	25%	10%	16%	0.5	35	71	73
Escobar,Edgar	21	R	24	aa	STL	42	5.11	1.11	6.62	25%	16%	9%	1.9	25	60	79
Eshelman,Tom	19	R	25	a/a	BAL	95	6.02	1.62	24.9	19%	15%	3%	1.6	36	54	71
	21	R	27	aaa	BAL	30	9.99	1.84	9.32	17%	7%	10%	2.3	38	46	22
Espinal,Raynel	19	R	28	aaa	NYY	75	5.75	1.58	18.3	17%	5%	12%	1.7	34	54	67
	21	R	30	aaa	BOS	119	4.75	1.38	21.8	12%	8%	3%	1.1	28	68	46
Eveld,Tommy	19	R	26	a/a	MIA	50	7.58	1.54	5.2	17%	12%	5%	2.6	31	32	77
	21	R	28	aaa	MIA	46	4.67	1.44	5.47	22%	9%	13%	1.8	31	74	44
Falter,Bailey	19	L	22	aa	PHI	78	4.94	1.44	23.8	14%	9%	5%	1.4	34	57	87
	21	L	24	aaa	PHI	32	1.89	1.05	15.6	12%	9%	3%	1.0	30	89	145
Faria,Jake	19	R	26	aaa	MIL	68	4.59	1.57	10.3	21%	12%	9%	1.4	34	64	62
	21	R	28	aaa	LAA	38	5.23	1.54	23.8	24%	14%	10%	1.4	35	69	56
Faucher,Calvin	21	R	26	a/a	TAM	57	5.39	1.72	8.12	16%	7%	9%	1.2	36	71	56
Feigl,Brady	21	R	26	a/a	OAK	123	4.89	1.41	20.9	27%	5%	22%	1.2	31	68	53
	19	L	29	aaa	TEX	21	4.60	1.34	6.24	22%	12%	11%	1.7	33	56	109
Feltman,Durbin	19	R	22	aa	BOS	52	7.35	1.62	5.38	8%	8%	0%	1.7	29	43	7
	21	R	24	a/a	BOS	53	3.45	1.16	5.43	21%	5%	16%	1.4	29	77	94
Feltner,Ryan	21	R	25	a/a	COL	78	3.83	1.39	23.6	27%	15%	13%	1.2	32	77	59
Fenter,Gray	21	R	25	aa	BAL	78	6.12	1.64	16.6	21%	13%	8%	1.6	31	65	31
Fernander,Chave	21	R	24	aa	DET	40	4.40	1.36	7.59	23%	14%	9%	1.2	27	71	44
Fernandez,Julian	21	R	26	a/a	COL	44	2.97	1.33	4.17	21%	10%	11%	1.0	28	82	52
Ferrell,Riley	19	R	26	a/a	HOU	25	4.76	1.49	6.04	16%	11%	5%	0.4	27	63	-15
	21	R	28	aaa	HOU	40	3.18	1.46	4.5	17%	13%	4%	0.7	27	80	70
Figueroa,Miquel	21	R	24	aa	CIN	40	6.72	1.97	6.61	21%	10%	11%	1.9	42	70	46
File,Dylan	19	R	23	aa	MIL	82	4.45	1.42	24.9	18%	9%	9%	0.9	35	63	91
	21	R	25	aaa	MIL	44	5.31	1.57	21.6	14%	10%	4%	1.4	35	69	41
Fillmyer,Heath	19	R	25	aaa	KC	50	6.09	1.67	11.8	19%	22%	-3%	1.4	32	55	16
	21	R	27	aaa	CLE	83	7.19	1.67	17.7	11%	19%	-9%	2.0	32	60	11
Finnegan,Brandoı	19	L	26	aa	CIN	15	9.44	1.99	5.56	25%	9%	15%	0.9	37	45	-18
	21	L	28	aaa	CIN	56	7.72	2.13	6.95	24%	12%	12%	1.8	37	66	3
Fishman,Jake	19	L	24	aa	TOR	64	5.09	1.55	6.69	20%	11%	9%	0.8	38	62	96
	21	L	26	aaa	MIA	57	4.62	1.26	6.86	20%	13%	7%	1.2	28	66	54
Flaa,Jay	19	R	27	a/a	BAL	71	6.50	1.78	8.17	12%	7%	5%	1.5	35	55	15
	21	R	29	aaa	ATL	37	8.57	2.25	5.9	14%	5%	9%	1.2	37	61	23
Fletcher,Aaron	19	L	23	aa	SEA	20	5.33	1.62	6.38	17%	10%	7%	0.0	43	63	121
	21	L	25	aaa	SEA	50	3.69	1.45	5.49	18%	10%	8%	1.0	34	78	66
Flores Jr.,Bernar	19	L	24	aa	CHW	79	5.01	1.44	22.4	39%	7%	32%	1.7	33	56	87
	21	L	26	aaa	COL	43	6.48	2.03	19	33%	12%	21%	1.9	35	72	-16
Foley,Jason	21	R	26	aaa	DET	36	5.94	1.78	5.2	25%	6%	19%	1.6	33	70	16
Fox,Mason	21	R	24	a/a	SD	34	9.80	2.21	7.19	19%	8%	11%	1.7	43	55	26
France,J.P.	21	R	26	a/a	HOU	116	4.15	1.38	19.5	26%	6%	20%	1.2	32	73	81
Francis,Bowden	19	R	23	aa	MIL	130	6.40	1.58	22.9	20%	12%	9%	1.5	34	50	67
	21	R	25	a/a	TOR	134	4.84	1.26	21.9	18%	12%	6%	1.9	25	69	41
Frias,Luis	21	R	23	a/a	ARI	103	4.71	1.21	19.9	29%	19%	11%	1.2	28	64	77

PITCHER	yr	t	age	lvl	org	ip	era	whip	bf/g	k%	bb%	k-bb	hr/9	h%	s%	bpv
Friedrichs, Kyle	21	R	29	a/a	OAK	106	5.03	1.43	19.6	12%	6%	6%	1.0	32	66	37
Frisbee, Matt	21	R	25	a/a	SF	114	6.05	1.46	22.2	18%	6%	13%	1.8	33	63	51
Fry, Jace	21	L	28	aaa	CHW	40	3.43	1.19	4.72	29%	13%	16%	0.7	26	73	106
Fulmer, Carson	19	R	26	aaa	CHW	34	5.95	1.75	6.48	27%	14%	13%	0.6	39	61	59
	21	R	28	aaa	CIN	41	6.53	2.02	5.36	21%	15%	6%	1.2	39	69	38
Gaddis, Will	21	R	25	aa	COL	67	7.48	1.85	8.45	12%	7%	5%	2.1	36	63	-10
Gadea, Kevin	21	R	27	a/a	NYY	42	3.28	1.46	6.43	26%	14%	11%	0.5	31	78	90
Gage, Matt	21	L	28	a/a	ARI	47	4.02	1.35	4.69	22%	6%	16%	1.3	33	75	83
Gamez, Juan	21	R	27	a/a	CHC	34	7.43	1.95	6.02	16%	13%	3%	0.6	38	60	42
Garabito, Gerson	19	R	24	aa	KC	141	5.34	1.80	25.1	14%	10%	4%	1.0	36	65	7
	21	R	26	a/a	SF	86	5.04	1.68	15.5	16%	11%	6%	0.9	34	71	40
Garcia, Deivi	19	R	20	a/a	NYY	95	5.37	1.46	18.5	29%	11%	18%	1.2	35	55	101
	21	R	22	aaa	NYY	92	7.70	1.96	18.4	19%	15%	4%	2.2	34	65	4
Garcia, Edgar	19	R	23	aaa	PHI	29	2.85	0.85	4.26	32%	7%	25%	1.5	20	54	142
	21	R	25	aaa	MIN	45	4.03	1.45	5.2	21%	17%	4%	0.2	27	70	80
Garcia, Jason	19	R	27	aa	TAM	51	7.42	2.07	25	11%	10%	1%	0.7	40	59	-11
	21	R	29	a/a	MIN	46	6.10	2.01	13.2	14%	13%	1%	1.1	37	71	15
Garcia, Julian	19	R	24	aa	PHI	30	8.06	1.87	23.6	16%	8%	8%	0.8	41	50	54
	21	R	26	a/a	PHI	53	9.78	2.15	13.2	16%	13%	3%	2.5	37	57	-23
Garcia, Junior	19	L	24	aa	ARI	18	3.69	1.64	5.35	22%	16%	6%	0.0	33	75	1
	21	L	26	a/a	ARI	37	3.26	1.62	5	18%	10%	8%	0.8	35	82	54
Garcia, Robert	21	L	25	aa	KC	48	7.04	1.73	6.61	21%	11%	10%	1.4	37	60	46
Garcia, Ruben	21	R	25	aa	DET	41	6.03	1.83	7.33	21%	15%	5%	1.0	35	67	49
Gardner, Will	21	R	25	aa	PIT	42	8.45	1.71	5.77	18%	15%	2%	1.4	30	50	28
Garrett, Braxton	21	L	24	aaa	MIA	87	4.66	1.36	20.3	20%	9%	11%	1.1	30	68	61
Gatto, Joe	19	R	24	aa	LAA	55	6.46	1.98	8.26	18%	12%	7%	0.4	41	63	23
	21	R	26	a/a	TEX	61	4.00	1.23	7.09	22%	8%	14%	1.0	29	70	82
Gavin, Grant	19	R	24	aa	KC	53	5.05	1.55	5.66	25%	12%	13%	1.2	34	60	69
	21	R	26	aaa	KC	75	4.95	1.38	6.58	22%	11%	11%	1.3	29	67	60
German, Frank	21	R	24	aa	BOS	85	5.91	1.68	16	16%	8%	8%	1.3	36	66	33
Gibaut, Ian	19	R	26	aaa	TEX	16	6.35	2.10	4.63	21%	20%	2%	0.0	39	66	-47
	21	R	28	aaa	MIN	45	9.15	2.09	6.9	19%	11%	7%	1.2	42	55	33
Gil, Luis	21	R	23	a/a	NYY	82	4.49	1.37	17.3	29%	13%	16%	1.1	30	70	90
Gilbert, Tyler	19	L	26	aaa	PHI	49	3.36	1.25	5.56	19%	7%	12%	0.9	29	67	73
	21	L	28	aaa	ARI	53	3.03	1.23	19.6	18%	8%	10%	0.5	29	76	75
Gillies, Darin	19	R	27	a/a	SEA	63	8.26	1.84	7.37	20%	9%	12%	2.1	39	43	73
	21	R	29	a/a	SEA	47	3.27	1.30	4.88	21%	12%	9%	1.0	26	79	63
Godley, Zack	21	R	31	aaa	NYM	99	4.51	1.56	20.7	15%	12%	3%	1.1	30	74	31
Gold, Brandon	19	R	25	aa	COL	144	6.32	1.84	25.8	13%	4%	9%	1.7	40	58	71
	21	R	27	aaa	COL	87	7.17	1.68	21.8	14%	6%	8%	1.5	36	58	28
Gomez, Michael	21	R	25	aa	NYY	49	3.85	1.23	6.39	21%	8%	13%	0.9	29	71	84
Gomez, Moises	21	R	24	a/a	SEA	48	3.08	1.24	5.45	19%	6%	14%	0.7	31	77	96
Gomez, Ofreidy	19	R	24	a/a	KC	131	5.49	1.67	21.1	16%	10%	6%	1.0	34	61	22
	21	R	26	a/a	CHW	53	5.91	1.41	7.3	21%	15%	6%	0.6	27	56	73
Gomez, Rio	21	L	27	aa	BOS	40	4.18	1.44	6.57	23%	7%	15%	0.7	36	72	93
Gonsalves, Steph	21	L	27	aaa	BOS	73	6.19	1.90	15.7	23%	16%	7%	1.8	35	71	33
Gonzalez, Brian	19	L	24	aa	BAL	43	5.87	1.24	9.76	16%	7%	9%	2.5	24	32	55
	21	L	26	a/a	COL	46	5.23	1.87	5.69	23%	14%	10%	1.4	38	75	46
Goody, Nicholas	19	R	28	aaa	CLE	25	10.81	2.09	5.87	21%	13%	8%	3.9	37	28	36
	21	R	30	aaa	NYY	49	5.90	1.41	5.34	21%	10%	11%	1.9	29	63	40
Gordon, Cole	21	R	26	aa	NYM	83	3.71	1.04	16	22%	10%	12%	1.1	21	69	75
Gose, Anthony	19	L	29	aa	CLE	18	5.79	2.47	4.33	17%	27%	-10%	0.0	35	74	-182
	21	L	31	aaa	CLE	33	4.37	1.69	5.31	25%	21%	4%	1.2	27	77	61
Gossett, Daniel	21	R	29	aaa	BOS	98	5.84	1.80	22.6	13%	12%	2%	1.5	33	70	5
Gott, Trevor	21	R	29	aaa	SF	43	4.38	1.39	4.23	22%	9%	13%	0.7	33	69	80
Goudeau, Ashton	19	R	27	aa	COL	79	3.79	1.33	20.5	20%	5%	16%	0.8	34	66	107
	21	R	29	aaa	COL	39	6.25	1.77	16.3	10%	9%	1%	2.0	33	69	-22
Gray, Josiah	21	R	24	aaa	LA	17	2.58	0.59	14.7	31%	3%	28%	1.5	16	71	262
Green, Josh	19	R	24	aa	ARI	49	6.22	1.79	28.3	12%	4%	8%	0.5	40	60	59
	21	R	26	aaa	ARI	100	6.23	1.75	17.6	11%	6%	5%	1.4	36	66	10
Green, Nick	19	R	24	aa	NYY	70	9.57	2.09	23	12%	11%	1%	0.6	40	48	-16
	21	R	26	a/a	NYY	73	4.61	1.64	10.5	16%	15%	1%	0.7	30	72	43
Greene, Hunter	21	R	22	a/a	CIN	107	4.00	1.30	21	29%	9%	20%	1.3	32	74	96
Greene, Zach	21	R	25	aa	NYY	40	4.43	1.32	6.65	29%	8%	21%	1.1	35	69	110
Grey, Connor	19	R	25	a/a	ARI	48	5.67	1.84	13.2	13%	11%	2%	1.3	35	63	-9
	21	R	27	aa	NYM	33	4.46	1.21	19.1	23%	4%	18%	0.7	33	63	138
Griffin, Foster	19	L	24	aaa	KC	132	6.13	1.66	23.7	15%	11%	4%	1.3	32	55	7
	21	L	26	a/a	KC	39	4.16	1.56	19.1	14%	7%	7%	0.2	36	72	61
Grove, Michael	21	R	25	aa	LA	71	8.00	1.82	15.7	22%	11%	11%	2.3	36	60	18
Gudino, Norwith	21	R	26	a/a	SF	60	4.37	1.28	7.69	28%	9%	18%	1.2	31	69	95
Guduan, Reymin	19	L	27	aaa	HOU	28	3.10	1.92	5.79	19%	14%	5%	0.4	39	82	0
	21	L	29	aaa	OAK	32	5.41	1.85	4.99	17%	9%	7%	0.5	40	70	52
Guenther, Sean	21	L	26	a/a	MIA	43	3.75	1.08	6.52	25%	4%	21%	0.7	31	66	159
Guerrero, Alberto	21	R	24	a/a	MIA	45	3.69	1.18	6.26	21%	7%	13%	1.1	28	73	79
Guerrero, Jordan	21	R	25	aaa	SD	41	3.47	1.46	6.51	18%	9%	9%	1.3	31	82	45
	19	L	25	a/a	MIA	85	9.53	2.44	16.5	14%	13%	1%	2.5	42	51	-25
Guerrieri, Taylor	19	R	27	aaa	TEX	37	4.36	1.66	7.23	18%	10%	7%	0.3	36	70	34
	21	R	29	aaa	PHI	37	6.08	1.83	5.97	17%	10%	7%	1.2	38	68	32
Guillen, Alexander	19	R	24	aa	COL	78	2.60	1.22	8.55	23%	8%	14%	0.8	30	75	86
	21	R	26	a/a	MIA	49	4.72	1.55	7.69	13%	8%	5%	1.2	32	73	23
Haberer, Jake	19	R	24	a/a	SEA	29	7.02	1.70	6	22%	17%	6%	1.1	31	51	-2
	21	R	26	aa	SEA	33	6.83	2.01	6.15	14%	16%	-3%	1.4	33	68	5
Hackimer, Tom	19	R	25	aa	MIN	42	4.73	1.44	6.64	21%	12%	9%	0.3	32	63	40
	21	R	27	a/a	NYM	43	4.37	1.45	5.44	24%	18%	6%	0.5	26	69	82
Hagenman, Justin	21	R	25	aa	LA	64	3.42	1.16	6.72	25%	6%	18%	0.8	31	73	118
Hall, DL	21	L	23	aa	BAL	33	3.23	0.98	18	36%	12%	24%	1.2	21	73	126
Hall, Matt	19	L	26	aaa	DET	88	7.31	1.87	16.5	20%	8%	11%	2.1	40	50	73
	21	L	28	aaa	BOS	38	9.55	2.44	7.18	14%	14%	0%	1.1	43	59	8

PITCHER	yr	t	age	lvl	org	ip	era	whip	bf/g	k%	bb%	k-bb	hr/9	h%	s%	bpv
Hamilton, Ian	19	R	24	aaa	CHW	17	11.34	2.07	5.23	12%	6%	6%	2.4	47	30	137
	21	R	26	aaa	MIN	59	5.30	1.70	7.01	18%	6%	13%	0.9	34	69	73
Hardy, Matt	21	R	26	aa	MIL	43	4.71	1.46	6.83	29%	13%	16%	2.0	30	75	42
Harris, Hobie	21	R	28	aaa	TOR	45	5.72	1.45	4.59	27%	14%	13%	2.3	25	68	16
Harris, Jon	21	R	28	a/a	TOR	44	4.88	1.36	6.15	21%	15%	6%	1.8	27	71	16
Harris, Nate	21	R	27	aa	COL	70	11.22	2.32	15	12%	7%	5%	3.3	38	55	-67
Hart, Kyle	19	L	27	a/a	BOS	158	5.25	1.49	25.3	26%	14%	11%	0.8	32	58	33
	21	L	29	aaa	BOS	108	5.75	1.71	21.3	22%	6%	16%	1.9	31	71	-1
Hartman, Ryan	19	L	25	aaa	HOU	117	6.66	1.71	21.3	16%	13%	3%	2.2	35	49	58
	21	L	27	aaa	BAL	100	5.99	1.46	18.6	14%	10%	4%	2.1	31	65	25
Hatch, Thomas	19	R	25	aa	TOR	136	6.23	1.59	22.2	16%	11%	6%	1.7	34	51	60
	21	R	27	aaa	TOR	66	5.83	1.49	19	29%	11%	18%	1.9	32	66	35
Hauschild, Mike	19	R	29	aaa	STL	38	10.26	2.23	19.3	19%	15%	4%	1.3	36	45	-85
	21	R	31	aaa	CHC	55	8.26	2.05	20.6	32%	7%	25%	4.2	30	72	-101
Head, Louis	19	R	29	a/a	LA	24	7.41	1.99	7.77	21%	17%	4%	1.4	43	55	62
	21	R	31	aaa	TAM	30	2.98	1.28	4.77	11%	10%	1%	0.8	30	79	85
Heasley, Jon	21	R	24	aa	KC	106	4.05	1.38	20.3	14%	13%	1%	1.5	31	77	59
Henderson, Layne	21	R	25	aa	HOU	51	4.36	1.48	8.47	16%	8%	8%	1.0	30	73	66
Hendrickson, Josh	21	L	24	a/a	PHI	78	4.00	1.24	21.2	16%	13%	3%	1.5	26	74	45
Hennigan, Jonatha	19	L	25	aa	PHI	47	6.08	1.99	7.31	22%	16%	6%	0.5	38	65	-20
	21	L	27	aa	PHI	39	7.72	2.04	5.94	18%	10%	8%	0.8	39	61	38
Henriquez, Ronny	21	R	21	aa	TEX	71	5.94	1.27	18.2	21%	11%	10%	2.1	30	59	75
Henry, Henry	21	R	23	aa	SD	67	4.12	1.38	7.4	21%	15%	5%	0.4	30	69	69
Henry, Thomas	21	L	24	aa	ARI	117	5.41	1.51	22	18%	15%	2%	1.7	32	69	47
Herb, Tyler	19	R	27	a/a	BAL	134	7.89	1.99	24.9	20%	9%	11%	2.2	36	50	-1
	21	R	29	a/a	SEA	90	5.53	1.57	22	18%	12%	7%	1.4	37	68	75
Herget, Jimmy	19	R	26	aaa	CIN	60	3.87	1.55	5.48	22%	8%	14%	1.4	27	69	5
	21	R	28	aaa	LAA	43	3.63	1.22	5.62	25%	12%	13%	1.1	29	74	86
Herget, Kevin	21	R	30	aaa	CLE	81	5.47	1.57	12.7	22%	11%	11%	2.2	33	73	21
Hernandez, Aaron	21	R	25	aa	LAA	45	8.11	2.03	19.9	16%	8%	8%	1.4	40	60	37
Hernandez, Dayst	21	R	25	a/a	ATL	45	4.78	1.39	5.31	21%	20%	2%	0.9	29	67	76
Hernandez, Jakob	19	L	23	aa	PHI	71	2.18	1.13	5.99	19%	11%	7%	0.7	26	77	70
	21	L	25	a/a	PHI	54	5.17	1.43	5.48	29%	13%	16%	0.9	35	65	89
Hernandez, Kenny	21	L	23	a/a	ARI	62	5.22	1.51	19.2	19%	7%	12%	1.2	33	68	33
Hernandez, Nick	19	R	25	aa	HOU	25	4.82	1.58	6.17	18%	8%	10%	1.0	31	64	7
	21	R	27	a/a	HOU	56	1.84	1.15	6.73	20%	9%	12%	0.9	21	90	83
Hernandez, Osval	21	L	23	aa	SD	101	5.36	1.53	20	21%	12%	9%	1.6	35	69	45
Hess, David	19	R	26	aaa	BAL	42	5.65	1.49	14	15%	12%	3%	1.8	33	51	83
	21	R	28	aaa	TAM	46	4.86	1.38	9.67	13%	4%	9%	2.6	30	77	40
Higgins, Connor	21	L	25	a/a	LAA	44	4.78	1.87	5.43	14%	6%	8%	0.7	36	75	50
Highberger, Nick	21	R	28	aa	OAK	40	7.20	2.01	6.05	21%	8%	13%	1.4	36	65	4
Hill, Adam	21	R	24	aa	SEA	61	7.28	1.74	19.9	19%	6%	14%	2.1	35	62	22
Hill, David	21	R	27	aa	COL	75	6.80	1.76	21.5	16%	10%	6%	2.6	35	68	-10
Hillman, Juan	21	L	24	a/a	CLE	111	4.47	1.48	21.7	21%	15%	6%	1.4	32	74	37
Hintzen, J.T.	21	R	25	aa	MIL	58	4.76	1.35	6.72	23%	7%	15%	2.0	32	73	79
Hitt, Robbie	21	R	25	aa	MIL	43	3.59	1.40	5.05	23%	16%	7%	1.0	30	77	67
Hjelle, Sean	19	R	22	aa	SF	26	8.55	2.21	26.3	16%	7%	9%	0.4	45	56	35
	21	R	24	a/a	SF	121	4.54	1.53	22	23%	14%	10%	0.9	33	72	48
Hock, Colton	21	R	25	a/a	MIA	53	4.27	1.36	5.07	21%	13%	8%	0.9	33	70	78
Holder, Heath	19	R	27	a/a	COL	101	4.11	1.39	13.7	21%	10%	11%	1.2	31	64	64
	21	R	29	aaa	COL	47	11.99	2.46	6.72	22%	10%	12%	2.1	39	51	-26
Holloway, Jordan	21	R	25	aaa	MIA	32	5.94	1.54	17.5	17%	27%	-10%	1.5	31	64	28
Holmes, Grant	19	R	23	a/a	OAK	89	3.73	1.30	16	25%	21%	4%	1.0	30	65	67
	21	R	25	aaa	OAK	67	7.73	2.11	9.2	13%	12%	2%	1.3	42	64	24
Holton, Tyler	21	L	25	a/a	ARI	65	6.24	1.57	11	22%	9%	13%	0.8	40	59	97
Honeywell, Brent	21	R	26	aaa	TAM	83	5.15	1.42	11.4	20%	5%	16%	1.7	30	69	29
Hovis, Reilly	21	R	28	aa	TOR	51	7.74	1.90	20.1	10%	9%	1%	3.2	35	68	-50
Howard, Brian	19	R	24	a/a	OAK	145	5.22	1.66	24.1	31%	3%	28%	0.7	38	63	62
	21	R	26	aaa	OAK	112	5.77	1.55	20.4	12%	4%	8%	1.6	33	66	26
Howard, Nick	21	R	28	a/a	CIN	44	6.24	1.89	4.93	11%	6%	5%	1.4	29	69	33
Hudson, Bryan	21	L	24	a/a	CHC	60	5.10	1.37	7.2	12%	11%	1%	0.7	28	62	58
Hughes, Brandon	21	L	26	aa	CHC	32	1.98	1.31	7.39	16%	15%	1%	0.9	31	90	89
Hutchison, Drew	19	R	29	aaa	LAA	132	5.29	1.62	23.5	29%	9%	20%	1.4	34	60	42
	21	R	31	aaa	DET	89	5.69	1.76	21.5	29%	8%	21%	1.1	34	69	26
Jackson, Andre	21	R	25	a/a	LA	91	3.80	1.13	17.2	13%	11%	2%	1.7	25	75	71
Jackson, Zach	19	R	25	aaa	TOR	68	5.41	1.57	6.49	23%	4%	18%	1.7	30	57	18
	21	R	27	a/a	OAK	30	2.54	1.10	4.75	15%	11%	4%	0.3	28	76	133
Jacques, Joe	21	L	26	aaa	PIT	48	4.81	1.57	5.7	14%	7%	7%	0.9	35	70	58
Jameson, Drey	21	R	24	aa	ARI	47	4.22	1.24	23.9	22%	11%	11%	1.0	32	69	110
Jankins, Thomas	19	R	24	a/a	MIL	136	5.65	1.59	24	28%	9%	18%	1.5	34	56	52
	21	R	26	aaa	MIL	84	6.52	1.62	14.9	19%	14%	5%	1.4	33	61	19
Jarvis, Bryce	21	R	24	aa	ARI	35	5.95	1.46	18.7	17%	9%	7%	1.9	30	64	41
Javier, Odalvi	21	R	25	aa	ATL	76	4.44	1.39	13.3	25%	4%	21%	0.7	30	69	68
Jax, Griffin	19	R	25	a/a	MIN	128	4.06	1.40	23.5	21%	7%	13%	0.6	33	66	56
	21	R	27	aaa	MIN	42	4.77	1.53	23	18%	9%	9%	0.5	33	68	52
Jefferies, Daulton	19	R	24	aa	OAK	64	4.76	1.31	12.6	14%	13%	1%	1.1	36	55	141
	21	R	26	aaa	OAK	77	4.90	1.40	21.7	18%	10%	7%	1.4	34	68	99
Jennings, Steven	21	R	23	aa	PIT	31	6.66	1.72	10.9	17%	10%	7%	1.0	35	61	19
Jewell, Jake	19	R	26	aaa	LAA	39	4.76	1.53	5.02	23%	8%	14%	0.7	35	64	56
	21	R	28	aaa	SF	45	3.68	1.32	5.65	13%	8%	5%	0.7	29	73	73
Jimenez, Dany	19	R	26	aa	TOR	35	2.82	1.25	5.74	22%	17%	6%	1.5	28	71	89
	21	R	28	aaa	TOR	46	3.24	1.49	5.1	14%	16%	-3%	1.4	30	85	71
Johnson, Brian	19	L	29	a/a	BOS	22	8.34	2.11	12.2	21%	12%	9%	1.1	41	53	11
	21	L	31	aaa	LAA	62	5.65	1.49	19.1	24%	18%	6%	1.0	31	63	30
Johnson, Chase	19	R	27	a/a	SF	79	6.94	2.04	10.7	25%	6%	18%	0.6	39	61	-20
	21	R	29	aaa	SD	30	10.39	2.53	8.44	36%	12%	24%	0.7	42	56	-1
Johnston, Kyle	21	R	25	a/a	TOR	71	1.88	1.27	8.34	20%	8%	11%	0.5	27	87	60

PITCHER	yr	t	age	lvl	org	ip	era	whip	bf/g	k%	bb%	k-bb	hr/9	h%	s%	bpv
Johnstone,Connoı	21	R	27	aaa	ATL	75	6.49	1.37	9.53	12%	4%	8%	2.2	30	57	27
Jones,Connor	19	R	25	a/a	STL	51	5.46	1.95	5.67	16%	15%	2%	0.9	36	67	-24
	21	R	27	aaa	STL	57	6.08	1.96	5.81	14%	11%	3%	0.4	39	67	38
Jones,Damon	19	L	25	a/a	PHI	56	5.57	1.44	19.9	23%	16%	7%	0.8	27	54	16
	21	L	27	aaa	PHI	42	6.42	2.02	5.99	23%	19%	4%	0.8	37	68	59
Joyner,Tyler	21	R	25	a/a	BAL	46	7.06	1.66	9.46	13%	9%	4%	2.3	31	62	-11
Junk,Janson	21	R	25	aa	LAA	93	3.26	1.23	19.8	21%	7%	14%	1.1	29	78	80
Kalish,Jake	19	L	28	a/a	KC	129	6.77	1.63	21.3	13%	5%	8%	2.1	34	46	55
	21	L	30	aaa	KC	96	8.61	1.84	14.9	17%	9%	8%	3.0	35	59	-20
Katz,Alex	21	L	27	aa	CHC	35	7.12	2.19	13.6	14%	12%	1%	1.7	39	70	-7
Kauffmann,Karl	21	R	24	aa	COL	82	9.11	2.30	22.1	12%	10%	2%	2.5	41	64	-38
Keel,Jerry	19	L	26	aaa	SD	152	7.11	1.90	24.8	12%	8%	4%	1.5	38	55	18
	21	L	28	a/a	SD	97	6.48	1.90	18.3	12%	9%	4%	1.6	37	69	-2
Keller,Brian	19	R	25	a/a	NYY	72	5.27	1.42	25.5	16%	7%	9%	0.7	33	56	54
	21	R	27	aaa	NYY	56	3.46	1.85	10.1	20%	19%	0%	0.6	32	82	58
Kelley,Trevor	19	R	26	aaa	BOS	66	2.52	1.35	5.3	18%	8%	9%	1.4	29	77	52
	21	R	28	aaa	ATL	42	2.07	1.32	4.71	20%	12%	8%	0.5	28	86	74
Kellogg,Ryan	21	L	27	a/a	CHC	67	5.17	1.64	15	11%	6%	4%	1.1	34	70	18
Kelly,Michael	21	R	29	a/a	HOU	52	3.08	1.39	5.38	21%	9%	13%	1.0	32	82	72
Kelly,Zack	19	R	24	aa	LAA	76	5.16	1.67	17.1	21%	9%	11%	0.8	38	64	65
	21	R	26	a/a	BOS	48	2.56	1.17	5.36	28%	10%	19%	0.4	30	79	122
Kennedy,Brett	21	R	27	a/a	SD	44	9.83	2.27	16	14%	11%	3%	1.4	42	56	2
Kennedy,Nick	21	L	25	aa	COL	44	8.28	1.99	5.43	21%	11%	10%	2.4	40	62	12
Kent,Matt	19	L	27	a/a	BOS	153	7.65	1.91	25.8	10%	9%	2%	0.9	38	53	-1
	21	L	29	a/a	BOS	75	5.11	1.49	12.1	13%	5%	8%	0.7	35	65	56
Kent,Zak	21	R	23	aa	TEX	30	6.29	1.62	22.4	25%	7%	18%	3.0	36	72	35
Kerr,Ray	21	L	27	a/a	SEA	41	3.59	1.16	4.55	30%	10%	20%	0.5	30	68	126
Kilian,Caleb	21	R	24	aa	CHC	80	3.06	1.08	20.9	21%	4%	17%	0.6	30	73	145
Kilome,Franklyn	21	R	26	aaa	NYM	46	3.74	1.36	9.16	17%	14%	4%	0.8	25	74	53
Kingham,Nolan	19	R	23	aa	ATL	37	6.10	1.48	26.7	13%	7%	6%	1.7	30	47	32
	21	R	25	a/a	ATL	95	6.09	1.58	22	12%	6%	6%	1.3	34	63	21
Kirby,Chance	21	R	26	aa	DET	48	6.93	1.50	18.9	13%	10%	3%	2.2	27	58	-5
Kirby,Nathan	21	L	28	aa	PIT	38	4.99	1.77	5.13	24%	17%	6%	0.5	35	71	77
Klimek,Steven	19	R	25	aa	BAL	22	2.34	1.54	7.42	18%	15%	3%	0.0	30	83	-17
	21	R	27	aa	BAL	54	5.29	1.49	6.5	22%	10%	13%	1.6	33	69	53
Klobosits,Gabe	21	R	26	a/a	WAS	39	2.05	1.26	5.15	23%	9%	13%	0.3	31	84	100
Knehr,Reiss	21	R	25	a/a	SD	77	3.42	1.16	16.2	17%	10%	8%	0.7	25	72	67
Knight,Blaine	21	R	25	a/a	BAL	70	7.07	1.64	17.4	14%	9%	5%	1.3	33	57	19
Knight,Dusten	21	R	31	aaa	BAL	39	4.06	1.35	4.66	17%	9%	8%	1.9	27	79	25
Kober,Collin	21	R	27	aa	SEA	41	4.01	1.52	5.59	22%	12%	10%	0.7	33	75	72
Koch,Matt	19	R	29	aaa	ARI	100	7.71	1.86	22.3	13%	7%	6%	1.7	38	48	39
	21	R	31	aaa	CLE	64	7.09	1.70	8.53	13%	11%	2%	1.7	31	61	1
Koenig,Jared	21	L	27	aa	OAK	122	3.64	1.38	21.4	15%	9%	7%	1.0	29	77	42
Koerner,Brody	19	R	26	a/a	NYY	140	6.69	1.86	24.3	13%	9%	4%	1.6	37	56	17
	21	R	28	aaa	NYY	77	4.40	1.57	13	15%	8%	7%	1.2	34	75	35
Komar,Brandon	21	R	22	aa	SD	51	5.11	1.53	11.7	21%	12%	9%	0.9	32	67	59
Kowar,Jackson	19	R	23	aa	KC	75	4.83	1.51	25	20%	7%	13%	1.1	35	61	82
	21	R	25	aaa	KC	82	3.81	1.32	20	26%	10%	16%	0.7	32	72	98
Kranick,Max	21	R	24	a/a	PIT	72	4.26	1.26	19.7	17%	6%	11%	0.9	30	68	69
Krauth,Ben	19	L	25	a/a	CLE	57	6.51	1.82	7.57	16%	15%	1%	1.9	31	55	-30
	21	L	27	a/a	CLE	38	5.23	1.46	6.51	22%	12%	11%	1.3	30	67	56
Krehbiel,Joey	19	R	27	aaa	ARI	65	7.59	1.91	6.04	17%	14%	2%	1.9	33	50	-19
	21	R	29	aaa	TAM	43	5.92	1.42	4.14	22%	6%	16%	2.1	33	64	64
Kremer,Dean	19	R	23	a/a	BAL	106	5.06	1.49	24.1	19%	8%	12%	1.1	34	59	74
	21	R	25	aaa	BAL	63	5.94	1.47	15.9	20%	8%	12%	1.6	33	63	51
Kriske,Brooks	19	R	25	aa	NYY	50	3.54	1.29	5.73	25%	13%	13%	0.8	27	67	60
	21	R	27	aaa	BAL	30	4.59	1.12	4.74	27%	13%	14%	0.8	23	59	99
Krook,Matt	19	L	25	aa	TAM	50	6.50	1.89	7.37	19%	16%	3%	0.7	36	60	-17
	21	L	27	a/a	NYY	108	3.61	1.37	18.9	23%	15%	8%	0.5	27	74	83
Kubat,Kyle	19	L	27	a/a	CHW	105	5.87	1.54	22.9	12%	6%	6%	1.1	34	54	41
	21	L	29	a/a	CHW	61	6.52	1.72	10.3	17%	7%	10%	1.6	37	64	33
Kuzia,Nick	19	R	23	aa	SD	15	12.65	2.10	8.32	9%	11%	-2%	3.8	32	16	-45
	21	R	25	a/a	SD	54	3.25	1.17	5.28	27%	12%	15%	0.7	26	74	99
Labosky,Jack	21	R	25	aa	TAM	80	4.63	1.20	11.5	20%	5%	15%	1.7	29	68	81
Lackney,Nick	21	L	24	a/a	PHI	36	4.32	1.56	7.92	15%	16%	-1%	1.1	25	75	29
Ladwig,A.J.	21	R	29	a/a	DET	109	6.38	1.47	19.5	13%	4%	9%	2.5	31	63	12
Lail,Brady	19	R	26	a/a	NYY	48	4.80	1.32	7.99	26%	9%	17%	1.1	33	56	105
	21	R	28	aaa	PHI	46	6.74	1.73	5.98	19%	14%	5%	2.2	30	66	8
Lambert,Jimmy	19	R	25	aa	CHW	60	6.96	1.89	25.8	21%	11%	10%	2.5	37	52	50
	21	R	27	aaa	CHW	65	5.38	1.39	14.4	24%	12%	12%	1.6	28	65	57
Latcham,Will	19	R	23	aa	STL	42	8.36	2.01	6.58	13%	10%	3%	2.0	37	48	3
	21	R	25	aa	ATL	40	5.59	1.61	5.94	18%	12%	6%	0.8	33	65	49
Latz,Jake	21	L	25	a/a	TEX	97	5.17	1.51	19.1	23%	11%	12%	1.4	33	69	56
Lau,Adam	19	R	25	a/a	BOS	63	5.15	1.63	7.04	20%	13%	6%	1.1	32	62	16
	21	R	27	aa	MIN	43	5.71	1.45	6.36	17%	11%	7%	1.8	28	65	23
Lawrence,Justin	19	R	25	a/a	COL	39	11.37	2.32	5.32	12%	16%	-4%	1.3	38	42	-80
	21	R	27	aaa	COL	33	5.43	1.53	4.65	15%	9%	7%	1.0	33	65	41
Lawson,Brandon	19	R	25	aa	SF	129	5.74	1.85	25.1	11%	9%	2%	0.7	37	64	-4
	21	R	27	aa	HOU	96	5.08	1.43	16.3	15%	7%	7%	0.6	32	63	56
Leahy,Kyle	21	R	24	aa	STL	88	7.14	1.89	16.6	12%	9%	3%	1.3	37	63	7
Leasher,Aaron	21	L	25	a/a	SD	66	3.59	1.36	17.3	18%	9%	9%	0.7	30	75	66
Leban,Zack	21	R	25	a/a	MIA	48	4.48	1.43	6.4	19%	8%	10%	1.0	32	71	60
Lebron,David	21	R	28	a/a	BAL	76	4.29	1.58	12.5	23%	14%	9%	2.2	29	83	27
Ledo,Luis	21	R	26	aa	CHW	41	5.94	1.66	5.4	23%	12%	11%	0.6	37	63	77
Lee,Andrew	19	R	26	aa	WAS	40	3.93	1.42	15.5	14%	12%	2%	1.0	27	67	-8
	21	R	28	a/a	WAS	68	7.03	1.65	11.7	18%	11%	7%	1.7	32	60	24
Lee,Dylan	19	L	25	a/a	MIA	60	4.19	1.50	5.79	18%	9%	8%	1.3	32	66	44
	21	L	27	aaa	ATL	48	2.02	0.90	5.13	23%	4%	19%	0.9	25	84	164

PITCHER	yr	t	age	lvl	org	ip	era	whip	bf/g	k%	bb%	k-bb	hr/9	h%	s%	bpv
Lee,Zach	19	R	28	a/a	NYM	124	7.09	1.87	24.3	12%	4%	8%	1.0	40	55	47
	21	R	30	aaa	CIN	82	8.98	2.11	16.9	16%	15%	2%	2.7	37	61	-43
Leeper,Ben	21	R	24	a/a	CHC	37	1.33	0.80	5	14%	11%	3%	0.5	19	87	146
Leibrandt,Brandoı	21	L	29	a/a	MIA	90	7.72	1.88	20.2	23%	16%	7%	1.9	36	61	-6
Leiter,Mark	21	R	30	a/a	DET	116	5.39	1.38	19.5	23%	19%	4%	1.4	32	64	64
Lemieux,Mack	21	L	25	a/a	ARI	47	3.05	1.42	5.56	13%	9%	4%	0.2	32	77	95
Lemoine,Jake	19	R	26	a/a	TEX	56	6.07	1.89	6.02	21%	7%	14%	1.1	38	62	19
	21	R	28	aaa	TEX	58	3.38	1.39	5.45	13%	5%	8%	0.9	25	78	35
Lescher,Billy	21	R	26	aa	DET	32	5.73	1.46	5.09	17%	9%	8%	1.6	33	64	56
Leverett,Adam	21	R	23	a/a	PHI	45	5.54	1.45	19.2	14%	12%	1%	1.5	32	65	53
Lewis,Justin	21	R	26	aa	ARI	34	10.46	1.79	6.53	12%	10%	2%	2.3	35	41	16
Leyer,Robinson	19	R	26	a/a	BOS	55	6.51	1.95	7.12	12%	8%	4%	0.6	38	61	-1
	21	R	28	aaa	MIN	46	9.19	1.98	6.32	12%	9%	4%	2.6	31	57	-14
Liberatore,Matthe	21	L	22	aaa	STL	126	3.75	1.20	23.1	16%	7%	9%	1.1	30	73	93
Lindgren,Jeff	21	R	25	aa	MIA	106	4.90	1.47	22.7	20%	19%	0%	1.6	31	72	29
Little,Brendon	21	L	25	a/a	CHC	43	3.51	1.47	7.14	18%	8%	9%	0.8	34	79	76
Llovera,Mauricio	19	R	23	aa	PHI	66	5.96	1.54	20.6	20%	12%	8%	1.3	34	53	67
	21	R	25	aaa	PHI	52	3.98	1.38	6.82	11%	6%	4%	1.0	28	74	53
LoBrutto,Dominic	21	L	25	aa	BOS	40	6.12	1.77	5.6	21%	9%	13%	0.7	40	64	55
Lodolo,Nicholas	21	L	23	a/a	CIN	52	2.79	1.08	15.7	21%	9%	11%	0.6	35	76	187
Logue,Zach	19	L	23	a/a	TOR	105	5.71	1.54	22.9	28%	10%	19%	1.6	32	53	37
	21	L	25	a/a	TOR	127	4.49	1.27	20.8	14%	11%	3%	1.3	32	68	101
Long,Sam	21	L	26	a/a	SF	42	2.63	1.07	10.9	21%	11%	10%	0.4	28	76	123
Lopez,Diomar	21	R	25	a/a	CIN	46	3.04	1.25	6.95	10%	9%	2%	1.2	24	82	52
Lopez,Reynaldo	21	R	27	aaa	CHW	39	8.72	2.15	19.4	13%	5%	8%	1.4	44	59	34
Lopez,Yoan	21	R	28	aaa	ATL	37	4.36	1.54	4.64	25%	7%	18%	1.2	32	75	45
Lovegrove,Kieran	19	R	25	aa	BAL	21	11.60	1.78	6.51	30%	10%	20%	1.8	28	19	-56
	21	R	27	aa	LAA	40	8.73	2.27	8.14	21%	4%	17%	2.4	33	65	-5
Lowther,Zac	19	L	23	aa	BAL	148	3.53	1.31	23.5	17%	14%	4%	0.6	28	68	44
	21	L	25	a/a	BAL	35	6.63	1.74	17.8	13%	7%	6%	1.2	36	63	37
Luciano,Elvis	21	R	21	aa	TOR	37	3.26	1.43	13.1	12%	6%	6%	1.0	30	81	56
Lugo,Luis	19	L	25	aa	CHC	61	4.95	1.67	21.1	13%	10%	3%	1.3	35	64	45
	21	L	27	a/a	CHC	97	5.75	1.67	17.5	24%	17%	6%	1.5	32	68	27
Lujan,Hector	19	R	25	aa	MIN	18	5.86	2.23	7.62	18%	15%	3%	0.7	45	70	31
	21	R	27	aa	MIN	33	4.21	1.20	7.39	22%	10%	13%	2.3	24	78	34
Luna,Carlos	21	R	25	aa	MIL	30	3.67	1.20	20.2	23%	9%	13%	1.4	30	76	108
Lynch,Daniel	21	L	25	aaa	KC	57	6.56	1.79	21.9	17%	10%	8%	1.5	40	65	44
MacGregor,Travi	21	R	24	aa	PIT	92	6.59	1.53	18.3	14%	9%	5%	1.2	32	57	42
Madero,Luis	19	R	22	aa	LAA	91	7.36	1.80	21.1	17%	9%	8%	1.4	39	50	67
	21	R	24	aaa	MIA	57	3.47	1.38	14.1	22%	12%	10%	0.7	31	76	72
Manning,Matt	19	R	21	aa	DET	135	3.63	1.15	22.4	13%	7%	6%	0.6	29	63	95
	21	R	23	aaa	DET	33	10.41	1.77	21.7	13%	11%	2%	3.6	35	44	-14
Marciano,Joey	21	L	26	aa	SF	48	3.64	1.29	5.08	15%	9%	7%	0.7	32	73	95
Marconi,Brian	21	L	24	a/a	PHI	49	3.58	1.43	5.51	13%	9%	4%	1.0	30	78	71
Marinaccio,Ron	21	R	26	a/a	NYY	69	2.43	1.03	6.69	15%	8%	7%	0.6	25	79	128
Markel,Parker	19	R	29	a/a	PIT	44	2.48	1.19	5.74	21%	12%	9%	0.8	19	75	41
	21	R	31	aaa	SD	57	4.30	1.55	6.07	20%	7%	13%	0.9	28	74	80
Marte,Jose	21	R	25	a/a	LAA	35	4.14	1.57	5.35	26%	10%	16%	0.0	37	71	104
Marte,Yunior	19	R	24	a/a	KC	61	4.57	1.54	5.79	17%	6%	11%	0.8	34	65	57
	21	R	26	aaa	SF	58	3.52	1.52	5.87	16%	15%	1%	0.5	35	77	75
Martinez,Adrian	21	R	25	a/a	SD	127	3.25	1.26	20	22%	12%	11%	0.6	30	75	81
Martinez,Henry	19	R	25	a/a	CLE	61	6.07	1.67	5.85	17%	14%	2%	0.8	32	57	-10
	21	R	27	a/a	DET	57	7.09	1.64	6.73	22%	6%	16%	1.0	36	56	51
Martinez,Joan	21	R	25	aa	BOS	37	2.88	1.27	4.6	19%	8%	12%	0.0	30	75	117
Martinez,Jose	21	R	22	aa	LA	34	6.79	2.01	18.4	20%	8%	12%	1.7	40	69	-1
Martinez,Marcelo	21	L	25	a/a	KC	114	5.97	1.47	19.6	25%	13%	13%	2.0	31	65	29
Martinez,Seth	19	R	25	aa	OAK	30	1.58	1.18	7.55	27%	13%	14%	0.0	31	85	84
	21	R	27	aaa	HOU	59	2.91	1.00	6.28	19%	16%	3%	0.8	25	74	116
Martinson,Jordan	21	L	24	a/a	LA	42	8.01	1.63	6.49	23%	15%	8%	1.6	30	51	21
Marvel,James	19	R	26	a/a	PIT	165	4.13	1.34	24.6	12%	6%	6%	0.7	30	64	43
	21	R	28	aaa	PIT	133	6.06	1.74	24.3	17%	7%	10%	1.4	33	67	5
Mason,Ryan	19	R	25	aa	MIN	23	3.46	1.44	6.54	9%	11%	-2%	0.0	40	73	127
	21	R	27	a/a	MIN	56	3.20	1.53	6.45	27%	12%	15%	0.7	32	81	62
Matson,Zach	21	L	26	aa	COL	33	7.41	1.54	4.11	20%	5%	15%	2.1	35	55	62
McArthur,James	21	R	25	aa	PHI	75	4.75	1.39	16.7	15%	16%	-1%	1.2	33	69	73
McCambley,Zach	21	R	22	aa	MIA	40	6.24	1.67	20	13%	4%	9%	2.6	33	71	18
McCarthy,Kevin	19	R	27	aaa	KC	18	4.37	1.58	6.17	26%	9%	17%	0.0	37	69	46
	21	R	29	aaa	CHW	43	8.53	1.99	5.92	19%	14%	5%	1.6	43	57	38
McCarthy,Shane	21	R	25	aa	CLE	30	5.92	1.32	17.9	21%	11%	10%	1.4	26	57	45
McCarty,Kirk	21	L	26	aaa	CLE	124	5.70	1.45	22.1	24%	12%	12%	1.9	29	66	19
McCaughan,Darrı	19	R	23	a/a	SEA	146	5.34	1.41	23.8	13%	10%	3%	1.7	34	51	105
	21	R	25	a/a	SEA	123	4.92	1.22	23.7	18%	12%	6%	1.5	30	63	107
McClain,Reggie	19	R	27	a/a	SEA	58	3.55	1.19	10.2	23%	11%	12%	0.6	25	65	37
	21	R	29	aaa	NYY	56	2.35	1.39	6.56	20%	13%	6%	0.2	29	83	74
McClure,Kade	21	R	25	a/a	CHW	106	5.93	1.57	19.4	17%	11%	7%	1.5	35	65	52
McGee,Easton	21	R	24	a/a	TAM	86	4.40	1.22	17.4	12%	16%	-4%	1.1	31	66	114
McGough,Trey	21	L	23	aa	PIT	95	3.58	1.22	21.3	15%	9%	7%	0.6	30	71	86
McGrath,Kyle	19	L	27	a/a	SD	64	9.13	1.89	11.6	11%	9%	2%	2.4	36	37	20
	21	L	29	aaa	SD	42	7.61	2.02	7.84	15%	7%	7%	1.2	38	62	-7
McIntyre,Aiden	21	R	26	aa	OAK	31	4.11	1.58	6.54	12%	9%	3%	0.8	37	76	70
McInvale,Andrew	21	R	25	aa	MIA	45	5.12	1.58	5.83	18%	9%	9%	1.3	31	70	66
McKee,Colin	19	R	25	a/a	HOU	64	3.12	1.35	6.67	19%	8%	10%	1.4	21	71	11
	21	R	27	a/a	HOU	48	5.52	1.63	6.34	23%	14%	9%	1.4	34	69	54
McKinney,Ian	19	L	25	aa	SEA	15	7.45	1.55	21.9	23%	12%	11%	4.3	29	23	107
	21	L	27	a/a	SEA	88	5.27	1.52	22.5	14%	12%	2%	1.3	31	68	51
McLaughlin,Sean	21	R	27	aa	ATL	36	7.61	1.99	5.97	18%	11%	7%	1.3	42	62	32
McMahan,Pearsc	21	R	25	a/a	WAS	48	5.38	1.55	6.56	18%	9%	8%	0.7	27	65	40

PITCHER	yr	t	age	lvl	org	ip	era	whip	bf/g	k%	bb%	k-bb	hr/9	h%	s%	bpv
McRae, Alex	21	R	28	aaa	CHW	90	6.19	1.86	16.2	16%	11%	5%	1.2	37	68	24
McWilliams, Sam	19	R	24	a/a	TAM	133	5.30	1.76	23.5	16%	8%	7%	0.8	38	65	41
	21	R	26	a/a	SD	51	7.89	1.88	6.7	18%	20%	-2%	1.2	29	57	36
Medeiros, Kodi	19	L	23	aa	CHW	83	7.58	1.91	14	17%	14%	2%	1.7	34	51	-20
	21	L	25	aaa	CHW	30	5.90	1.72	4.55	23%	18%	4%	1.5	29	68	45
Medina, Adonis	19	R	23	aa	PHI	107	6.46	1.57	21.4	16%	9%	6%	1.3	32	50	31
	21	R	25	aaa	PHI	69	5.69	1.56	17.8	15%	9%	7%	1.5	32	67	23
Medina, Luis	21	R	22	aa	NYY	75	4.16	1.51	21.7	22%	13%	10%	0.9	32	74	66
Megill, Tylor	21	R	26	a/a	NYM	41	3.22	1.11	20.2	31%	7%	24%	0.6	32	72	150
Meisinger, Ryan	19	R	25	aaa	STL	35	3.72	1.49	7.19	22%	7%	16%	1.3	36	69	103
	21	R	27	aaa	LA	41	3.46	1.41	5.11	28%	11%	17%	1.8	32	84	71
Mejia, Humberto	21	R	24	a/a	ARI	105	4.65	1.38	21	19%	7%	11%	1.2	32	69	61
Mekkes, Dakota	19	R	25	aaa	CHC	50	6.80	1.83	5.42	21%	16%	5%	1.3	34	55	-6
	21	R	27	a/a	CHC	42	5.01	1.56	6.37	16%	14%	2%	0.7	29	68	47
Melendez, Cristofe	21	R	24	aa	PIT	34	4.51	1.19	4.91	23%	13%	10%	0.5	25	61	88
Mella, Keury	19	R	26	aaa	CIN	144	6.81	1.85	24.9	13%	10%	3%	1.9	35	54	6
	21	R	28	aaa	PIT	48	6.34	1.64	5.95	18%	11%	7%	1.1	34	62	41
Mendez, Sal	21	L	26	a/a	TEX	66	5.89	1.44	10.1	18%	11%	7%	0.9	30	59	51
Menez, Conner	19	L	24	a/a	SF	123	5.08	1.42	22.7	24%	10%	13%	1.3	32	56	75
	21	L	26	aaa	SF	44	6.74	2.03	8.24	17%	13%	4%	1.2	39	67	24
Meyer, Max	21	R	22	a/a	MIA	111	2.70	1.30	20.8	25%	9%	16%	0.7	32	82	98
Miednik, Jake	21	L	25	aa	CLE	44	3.80	1.50	5.96	24%	11%	13%	1.4	33	80	61
Mikolajchak, Nick	21	R	24	aa	CLE	41	3.72	1.19	5.51	29%	6%	24%	1.7	32	78	126
Milburn, Matt	19	R	26	aa	OAK	152	6.59	1.75	26.8	10%	6%	4%	1.2	36	55	26
	21	R	28	a/a	OAK	93	6.53	1.61	17.2	10%	3%	7%	2.0	35	64	29
Miller, Evan	19	R	24	a/a	SD	33	6.11	1.61	6.41	19%	10%	10%	1.0	35	54	55
	21	R	26	aaa	SD	79	4.70	1.53	8.4	20%	7%	12%	0.5	37	68	81
Miller, Troy	21	R	24	aa	NYM	31	6.14	1.43	22	18%	6%	12%	1.5	33	59	54
Miller, Tyson	19	R	24	a/a	CHC	138	5.81	1.53	23.1	17%	8%	9%	1.5	33	53	53
	21	R	26	aaa	TEX	62	3.71	1.33	11.2	20%	10%	10%	1.1	29	76	61
Mills, Wyatt	19	R	24	aa	SEA	54	6.31	1.40	5.58	25%	9%	17%	0.5	36	48	102
	21	R	26	aaa	SEA	30	3.29	0.95	4.95	38%	6%	31%	0.6	32	66	202
Milner, Hoby	19	L	28	aaa	TAM	63	3.96	1.18	5.06	28%	6%	22%	1.1	33	58	143
	21	L	30	aaa	MIL	32	1.95	0.79	3.85	32%	2%	30%	0.6	28	79	417
Mitchell, Andrew	21	L	27	a/a	NYM	40	3.82	1.29	7.5	21%	7%	14%	0.8	32	72	87
Mitchell, Bryan	19	R	28	aaa	SD	44	10.37	2.40	17.7	11%	13%	-2%	1.7	41	48	-48
	21	R	30	aaa	MIA	59	5.87	1.73	8.7	16%	13%	3%	0.9	34	66	34
Moats, Dalton	19	L	24	aa	TAM	66	4.62	1.55	6.88	19%	9%	9%	1.3	33	63	51
	21	L	26	a/a	TAM	30	6.58	1.82	6.99	19%	7%	12%	1.3	41	65	52
Molina, Cristopher	21	R	24	aa	LAA	41	3.99	1.11	20.2	21%	9%	12%	0.9	25	66	81
Moll, Sam	19	L	27	a/a	SF	51	3.32	1.63	5.57	18%	12%	6%	0.2	35	77	21
	21	L	29	aaa	OAK	36	4.79	1.55	4.79	22%	13%	9%	1.2	32	72	56
Morales, Francisco	21	R	22	a/a	PHI	93	6.45	1.61	17.2	25%	15%	10%	1.1	32	60	67
Moran, Jovani	19	L	22	aa	MIN	35	6.75	1.64	7.83	27%	16%	11%	1.0	34	51	43
	21	L	24	a/a	MIN	70	2.70	0.93	7.55	34%	13%	22%	0.8	19	75	129
Moreno, Gerson	21	R	26	a/a	DET	51	5.87	1.48	5.97	25%	14%	11%	1.9	28	65	46
Moreta, Dauri	21	R	25	a/a	CIN	55	1.27	0.86	4.85	24%	5%	20%	1.0	23	97	138
Morgan, Reid	21	R	24	a/a	SEA	35	5.35	1.21	7.46	20%	5%	15%	1.5	29	59	86
Morimando, Shawn	19	L	27	aaa	TOR	71	8.46	1.96	21.2	17%	11%	6%	2.1	37	45	25
	21	L	29	aaa	MIA	91	5.78	1.68	22.8	16%	9%	7%	2.0	34	71	9
Morris, Akeel	21	R	29	a/a	SF	76	6.67	1.63	22.5	19%	8%	11%	1.6	36	61	43
Morris, Cody	21	R	25	a/a	CLE	58	1.82	1.11	16.3	29%	8%	21%	0.3	31	85	137
Moseley, Ryan	19	R	25	aa	LA	51	4.33	1.54	7.4	16%	9%	6%	0.9	32	67	29
	21	R	27	aaa	LA	49	7.70	2.02	5.96	13%	12%	1%	1.3	37	62	5
Mota, Juan	21	R	25	a/a	CLE	51	5.99	1.67	5.75	27%	15%	11%	0.9	35	64	76
Moyers, Steven	21	L	28	aa	SEA	54	3.54	1.25	10.5	18%	7%	11%	0.6	30	72	79
Muckenhirn, Zach	19	L	24	a/a	BAL	59	5.13	1.48	6.23	23%	12%	11%	0.8	33	59	56
	21	L	26	aa	CHW	42	2.43	1.43	5.98	19%	12%	7%	0.8	29	87	59
Mujica, Jose	21	R	25	aaa	COL	92	9.79	1.87	18	15%	6%	9%	3.0	37	51	-16
Muller, Kyle	19	L	22	aa	ATL	113	5.11	1.64	23	20%	15%	5%	0.6	32	64	-4
	21	L	24	aaa	ATL	81	4.22	1.51	20.7	22%	12%	9%	1.1	31	75	58
Murfee, Penn	21	R	27	a/a	SEA	80	4.88	1.52	13.4	23%	11%	12%	1.3	34	71	61
Murphy, Chris	21	L	23	aa	BOS	33	6.22	1.40	19.9	29%	9%	20%	1.1	36	55	102
Murray, Jayden	21	R	24	aa	TAM	39	3.01	0.77	17.5	26%	5%	22%	1.3	19	70	146
Murray, Shea	21	R	28	aa	PIT	45	4.66	1.99	5.88	17%	19%	-2%	0.6	34	77	46
Mushinski, Parker	21	L	26	a/a	HOU	67	3.88	1.46	12.5	24%	8%	16%	0.9	36	75	89
Myers, Tobias	21	R	23	a/a	TAM	119	4.42	1.18	19.1	27%	6%	21%	1.5	31	68	117
Naile, James	19	R	26	a/a	OAK	142	6.86	1.86	24.6	11%	8%	3%	1.1	37	56	11
	21	R	28	aaa	OAK	63	4.17	1.62	5.49	14%	5%	9%	0.9	37	76	49
Naughton, Packy	19	L	23	aa	CIN	107	4.85	1.50	24.4	16%	6%	9%	0.9	35	62	63
	21	L	25	a/a	LAA	62	4.85	1.53	19.4	17%	5%	12%	1.2	36	71	67
Naughton, Tim	21	R	26	aa	BAL	45	5.97	1.87	5.89	21%	19%	2%	0.9	33	68	52
Navas, Carlos	19	R	27	a/a	SF	86	4.86	1.39	10.4	17%	7%	10%	1.2	31	57	64
	21	R	29	a/a	WAS	45	9.25	1.94	5.96	16%	10%	6%	3.7	34	60	-48
Navilhon, Joe	19	R	26	a/a	DET	50	6.92	1.55	7.57	20%	7%	13%	1.7	35	43	88
	21	R	28	a/a	DET	65	4.43	1.51	7.44	19%	7%	12%	0.7	36	71	74
Neff, Zach	21	L	25	aa	MIN	54	5.31	1.23	7.08	20%	9%	11%	1.5	26	60	52
Neidert, Nick	19	R	23	aaa	MIA	41	6.45	1.86	21.3	16%	12%	4%	0.9	37	59	6
	21	R	25	aaa	MIA	70	4.48	1.53	21.8	14%	7%	7%	1.1	33	73	35
Nelson, Nick	19	R	24	a/a	NYY	86	3.80	1.49	21.8	24%	12%	12%	0.9	33	70	58
	21	R	26	aaa	NYY	52	4.73	1.76	8.22	21%	13%	8%	1.2	36	76	46
Nelson, Ryne	21	R	23	aa	ARI	77	3.61	1.23	22.3	28%	8%	20%	1.4	31	77	103
Newberry, Jake	19	R	25	aaa	KC	28	4.67	1.74	5.81	18%	11%	7%	1.0	36	68	28
	21	R	27	aaa	KC	61	5.87	1.70	6.27	20%	8%	12%	0.9	39	65	67
Nicolas, Kyle	21	R	22	aa	MIA	40	2.97	1.28	20.6	26%	15%	11%	0.7	25	79	92
Nittoli, Vinny	19	R	29	a/a	TOR	62	8.47	1.71	8.3	16%	7%	8%	1.5	37	39	53
	21	R	31	aaa	MIN	41	7.03	1.56	5.99	21%	7%	14%	2.2	35	59	42
Nogosek, Stephen	21	R	26	aaa	NYM	35	4.91	1.48	5.57	16%	11%	5%	0.4	39	65	117
Norwood, James	19	R	26	aaa	CHC	59	5.47	1.44	5.61	16%	8%	7%	1.6	28	52	49
	21	R	28	aaa	SD	46	4.03	1.38	4.51	18%	20%	-2%	0.5	35	70	109
Nunez, Andres	21	R	26	a/a	KC	76	4.71	1.42	6.88	17%	14%	2%	0.9	33	68	68
Nunez, Darien	21	L	28	a/a	LA	53	2.57	1.05	6.41	23%	18%	4%	0.7	28	79	130
Nunez, Oddy	21	L	25	aa	PIT	45	8.96	2.02	7.8	16%	9%	6%	0.9	36	54	38
Nunn, Chris	19	L	29	a/a	LA	52	6.87	1.98	6.59	15%	9%	7%	1.3	42	58	53
	21	L	31	a/a	MIN	46	5.15	1.62	5.88	22%	13%	10%	0.9	25	69	53
O Brien, Riley	21	R	26	aaa	CIN	114	6.08	1.58	21.8	31%	7%	24%	1.7	30	65	33
Ochsenbein, Aaro	21	R	25	aa	LA	57	3.37	1.22	6.05	22%	7%	16%	2.3	25	87	53
Ogando, Cristofer	21	R	28	a/a	TAM	41	4.44	1.27	7.7	28%	11%	17%	1.2	27	68	77
Ogle, Braeden	21	L	24	aaa	PHI	52	6.22	1.76	5.44	19%	7%	11%	1.4	33	67	42
Olczak, Jon	19	R	26	a/a	MIL	50	5.57	1.72	6.53	21%	16%	5%	1.2	38	61	67
	21	R	28	a/a	HOU	50	3.13	1.01	5.36	16%	14%	2%	0.6	27	70	120
Oller, Adam	21	R	27	a/a	NYM	120	3.46	1.22	21.1	23%	13%	10%	0.6	29	72	95
Olson, J.B.	21	R	26	aa	CHW	43	8.94	1.87	6.72	13%	10%	3%	1.3	41	51	45
O'Reilly, John	21	R	26	a/a	PIT	69	6.39	1.76	8.34	18%	11%	7%	0.5	38	62	27
Ort, Kaleb	19	R	27	a/a	NYY	48	4.92	1.72	6.62	18%	11%	7%	0.5	38	67	47
	21	R	29	aaa	BOS	46	4.05	1.64	4.89	24%	10%	13%	0.9	36	77	66
Ortega, Oliver	19	R	23	aa	LAA	18	10.56	2.01	17.6	17%	13%	4%	0.0	42	42	10
	21	R	25	a/a	LAA	44	5.38	1.46	5.57	25%	9%	16%	0.9	37	64	96
Ortiz, Luis	19	R	24	aaa	BAL	67	7.60	1.81	22.2	24%	11%	13%	2.3	32	46	-6
	21	R	26	aaa	TEX	43	5.36	1.60	6.79	29%	6%	24%	1.5	34	70	35
Orze, Eric	21	R	24	a/a	NYM	31	2.17	0.85	5.46	10%	6%	4%	0.7	25	79	164
Osnowitz, Mitchel	19	R	28	aa	STL	26	6.12	1.57	5.73	10%	3%	7%	1.6	32	51	42
	21	R	30	a/a	MIN	38	8.68	2.36	7.38	19%	10%	10%	1.9	36	65	-11
Otero, Andy	21	L	29	a/a	MIL	74	4.93	1.31	13.3	20%	7%	12%	1.3	32	65	88
Otto Jr., Glenn	21	R	25	a/a	TEX	97	3.81	1.14	22.6	18%	6%	12%	0.6	32	67	142
Overton, Connor	19	R	26	aa	SF	28	5.58	2.07	9.82	17%	8%	9%	1.2	41	68	16
	21	R	28	aaa	PIT	60	2.26	1.23	11.1	20%	10%	10%	0.4	31	83	90
Oviedo, Johan	19	R	21	aa	STL	113	6.73	1.74	22.4	25%	9%	17%	0.7	38	55	43
	21	R	23	aaa	STL	55	5.79	1.48	19.8	38%	6%	31%	0.9	32	61	62
Ozuna, Fernery	21	R	26	aa	TEX	47	6.81	1.50	6.37	28%	6%	22%	2.5	30	61	15
Pallante, Neil	21	R	23	a/a	STL	100	3.44	1.48	18.7	32%	2%	30%	0.6	33	77	59
Pannone, Thomas	19	L	25	aaa	TOR	35	4.17	1.35	18.4	21%	7%	14%	1.3	28	62	59
	21	L	27	aaa	LAA	119	6.64	1.75	22.7	11%	13%	-2%	1.5	36	64	8
Paredes, Enoli	19	R	24	aa	HOU	50	5.55	1.22	16.8	16%	13%	3%	0.2	30	48	92
	21	R	26	a/a	HOU	33	3.95	1.60	4.88	19%	9%	9%	2.0	31	85	43
Parke, John	19	L	24	aa	CHW	77	3.90	1.43	23.4	19%	7%	12%	0.9	31	68	31
	21	L	26	a/a	CHW	114	5.14	1.44	19.5	21%	9%	12%	1.1	31	66	38
Parkinson, David	19	L	24	aa	PHI	119	5.53	1.46	23.2	18%	12%	6%	1.0	34	54	73
	21	L	26	a/a	PHI	82	8.58	1.88	18.4	22%	13%	9%	2.0	39	56	8
Parrish, Drew	21	L	24	aa	KC	83	4.12	1.23	18.7	25%	15%	10%	0.9	30	68	88
Parsons, Tommy	19	R	24	a/a	STL	89	6.62	1.45	25.4	27%	16%	11%	3.0	32	34	100
	21	R	26	aaa	STL	75	5.86	1.52	13.6	34%	13%	22%	2.0	32	67	26
Passantino, Jeffre	19	R	24	a/a	CHC	19	3.84	1.42	20.1	25%	14%	11%	0.6	41	69	152
	21	R	26	aa	PIT	76	5.17	1.43	18	24%	5%	20%	1.4	33	67	54
Patino, Luis	21	R	22	aaa	TAM	30	3.64	1.24	17.5	20%	5%	15%	0.6	33	72	124
Paulino, David	19	R	25	aaa	TOR	30	4.46	1.63	19.2	17%	11%	6%	0.7	36	68	40
	21	R	27	a/a	PHI	82	4.83	1.51	11.1	16%	9%	7%	1.2	32	70	50
Paulino, Felix	19	R	24	aa	CHW	35	5.86	1.76	26.7	19%	8%	11%	1.9	35	58	34
	21	R	26	a/a	CHW	46	8.99	1.64	9.86	29%	8%	21%	2.2	32	46	13
Payano, Pedro	19	R	25	a/a	TEX	86	6.59	1.66	20.3	16%	9%	6%	1.5	31	51	6
	21	R	27	a/a	DET	124	6.36	1.70	22.4	13%	12%	1%	1.3	31	64	23
Pazos, James	19	L	28	aaa	COL	52	10.00	2.42	5.93	27%	15%	11%	1.7	42	50	-29
	21	L	30	aaa	LA	46	4.14	1.75	4.38	18%	7%	11%	1.4	37	81	45
Pearson, Nate	19	R	23	a/a	TOR	82	3.65	1.11	17	23%	12%	11%	0.8	26	60	82
	21	R	25	aaa	TOR	32	5.94	1.27	11	19%	12%	7%	1.5	28	56	76
Peguero, Joel	21	R	24	a/a	TAM	58	4.90	1.44	6.19	15%	6%	9%	0.3	33	64	75
Pelaez, Ivan	19	L	25	aa	TAM	57	6.15	1.60	7.01	20%	15%	5%	1.4	35	53	49
	21	L	27	aa	TAM	56	6.14	1.54	6.63	22%	12%	9%	1.3	36	62	59
Pena, Felix	21	R	31	aaa	LAA	69	7.95	1.73	10.1	23%	11%	12%	1.6	35	55	11
Pena, Ronald	19	R	28	a/a	WAS	49	8.77	2.18	6.45	29%	9%	20%	1.5	41	52	1
	21	R	30	aaa	WAS	40	6.83	1.74	5.92	26%	5%	22%	1.2	33	61	13
Pepiot, Ryan	21	R	24	a/a	LA	104	4.44	1.24	16.3	17%	19%	-2%	1.5	27	70	72
Peralta, Ofelky	21	R	24	a/a	BAL	96	5.27	1.53	18.2	24%	8%	16%	1.1	31	67	47
Perez, Andrew	21	L	24	aa	CHW	45	4.61	1.39	6.13	27%	6%	21%	1.5	35	71	96
Perez, Cionel	19	L	23	aaa	HOU	47	5.95	1.74	16.5	11%	8%	3%	1.2	35	59	26
	21	L	25	aaa	CIN	31	4.22	1.50	4.34	14%	5%	9%	0.4	37	71	102
Perez, Francisco	21	L	24	a/a	CLE	53	2.15	1.15	7.01	16%	6%	9%	0.4	27	82	130
Perez, Hector	19	R	23	aa	TOR	122	6.77	1.97	22.5	17%	5%	12%	0.9	39	60	2
	21	R	25	a/a	CIN	40	7.53	2.29	6.25	21%	19%	2%	0.6	34	65	57
Perkins, Jack	21	R	24	a/a	PHI	85	4.94	1.54	20.6	17%	7%	10%	1.5	34	72	39
Peters, Dillon	19	L	27	aaa	LAA	57	6.24	1.68	19.7	16%	10%	6%	1.7	37	54	72
	21	L	29	aaa	PIT	54	4.36	1.54	18.1	20%	7%	13%	2.4	31	83	17
Peterson, Tim	19	R	28	aaa	NYM	55	3.85	1.23	5.43	19%	7%	12%	1.3	29	61	81
	21	R	30	aaa	LAA	48	4.48	1.43	4.76	20%	9%	11%	1.3	31	73	45
Pfaadt, Brandon	21	R	23	aa	ARI	34	4.62	1.35	23.7	16%	12%	4%	2.8	30	81	58
Pfeifer, Philip	19	L	27	a/a	ATL	42	3.76	1.59	13.3	14%	7%	7%	0.9	33	72	31
	21	L	29	a/a	SF	36	8.36	2.31	13.2	24%	12%	12%	1.4	42	64	11
Phillips, Alex	19	R	25	aa	MIN	33	6.43	1.63	6.68	21%	13%	8%	1.5	33	51	26
	21	R	27	aa	MIN	51	6.29	1.47	7.32	28%	8%	20%	1.7	33	60	50
Phillips, Tyler	19	R	22	aa	TEX	94	6.86	1.51	22.6	18%	11%	7%	2.0	32	41	65
	21	R	24	a/a	PHI	38	6.91	1.69	12.3	20%	8%	12%	2.1	32	63	18
Pidich, Matt	21	R	27	a/a	CIN	51	9.29	2.01	7.49	26%	15%	11%	1.6	44	53	36
Pike, Tyler	21	L	27	aa	STL	70	4.48	1.42	19.8	16%	7%	8%	0.5	36	68	94
Pilkington, Konnor	21	L	24	aa	CLE	102	3.64	1.09	18.2	21%	7%	14%	1.1	24	71	90
Pimentel, Chester	21	R	26	a/a	ARI	52	4.15	1.48	5.61	22%	13%	8%	1.0	32	75	62

PITCHER	yr	t	age	lvl	org	ip	era	whip	bf/g	k%	bb%	k-bb	hr/9	h%	s%	bpv
Pinto,Aaron	21	R	25	aa	CLE	43	2.86	1.18	6.87	32%	8%	24%	1.2	32	82	128
Pinto,Julio	21	R	26	aa	CIN	34	3.42	1.54	5.14	20%	20%	0%	1.0	22	81	56
Pinto,Ricardo	19	R	25	a/a	TAM	126	5.51	1.61	20	17%	11%	6%	1.7	31	57	25
	21	R	27	a/a	DET	125	5.80	1.67	23.4	14%	9%	5%	1.3	34	67	20
Pinto,Wladimir	19	R	21	aa	DET	28	3.69	1.67	7.86	25%	13%	13%	0.9	38	74	65
	21	R	23	a/a	DET	54	5.42	1.51	6.18	21%	15%	6%	1.7	26	69	35
Plassmeyer,Mich:	21	L	25	aa	SF	110	5.56	1.47	20.5	21%	5%	16%	1.2	37	63	98
Politi,Andrew	21	R	25	aa	BOS	75	7.56	1.71	16.2	21%	11%	10%	1.3	36	56	47
Ponce,Cody	19	R	25	a/a	PIT	65	5.60	1.39	8.09	20%	8%	12%	1.0	32	51	71
	21	R	27	aaa	PIT	58	5.29	1.43	16.5	18%	8%	10%	1.2	32	65	53
Ponticelli,Thomas	21	R	24	aa	CLE	88	3.73	1.35	13.6	18%	9%	9%	0.9	29	75	57
Poppen,Sean	19	R	25	a/a	MIN	91	5.56	1.69	20.6	21%	12%	9%	0.5	37	62	39
	21	R	27	aaa	ARI	36	1.74	1.14	5.98	20%	8%	12%	0.4	28	86	93
Powers,Alex	19	R	27	a/a	CIN	50	2.31	1.32	5.18	26%	10%	16%	0.8	32	79	90
	21	R	29	aaa	SD	49	5.11	1.48	6.04	21%	10%	11%	1.2	33	68	59
Puckett,A.J.	21	R	26	aa	ATL	35	4.36	1.61	19.4	16%	11%	5%	0.3	34	71	57
Puk,A.J.	19	L	24	a/a	OAK	20	5.46	1.23	5.44	29%	7%	22%	2.3	29	38	138
	21	L	26	aaa	OAK	50	5.90	1.67	7.78	20%	8%	12%	1.9	37	70	37
Quezada,Jose	21	R	26	a/a	SD	52	4.82	1.39	4.78	24%	10%	13%	0.7	32	65	85
Quijada,Jose	19	L	24	aaa	MIA	30	5.46	1.51	5.93	23%	10%	13%	1.6	33	55	72
	21	L	26	aaa	LAA	30	1.38	0.92	5.12	27%	9%	18%	0.5	23	89	122
Quinones,Luis	21	R	24	aa	TOR	37	5.53	1.41	19.6	27%	16%	11%	1.0	27	61	80
Rackoski,Sean	21	R	26	aa	TOR	31	5.26	1.57	5.44	12%	4%	8%	0.6	36	66	59
Ragans,Cole	21	L	24	aa	TEX	37	7.07	1.82	19.1	16%	12%	4%	2.2	33	66	-6
Ramirez,Roel	19	R	24	a/a	STL	76	5.74	1.56	7.75	21%	9%	12%	0.7	36	57	70
	21	R	26	aaa	NYM	42	5.32	1.52	5.7	22%	10%	12%	0.9	35	65	71
Ramirez,Yefry	19	R	26	aaa	PIT	63	5.51	1.72	15	22%	15%	7%	1.1	34	62	19
	21	R	28	aaa	LA	113	5.40	1.58	19.9	18%	10%	8%	1.1	33	67	44
Ramsey,Lane	21	R	25	a/a	CHW	38	6.07	1.70	5.08	21%	12%	9%	0.5	37	62	68
Rangel,Alan	21	R	24	aa	ATL	34	6.12	1.18	19.4	25%	4%	21%	1.0	33	46	159
Rea,Colin	19	R	29	aaa	CHC	148	5.64	1.78	26.2	13%	11%	2%	1.3	34	62	-4
	21	R	31	aaa	MIL	37	2.51	1.19	21.3	18%	3%	15%	0.5	33	80	154
Record,Joe	21	R	26	aa	HOU	63	3.95	1.42	14.1	16%	14%	2%	0.8	26	74	46
Reed,Jake	19	R	27	aaa	MIN	75	8.12	1.83	7.75	20%	11%	9%	1.1	38	47	40
	21	R	29	aaa	NYM	31	5.03	1.48	5.15	21%	7%	14%	0.8	37	66	87
Reeves,James	19	L	26	aa	NYY	56	2.55	1.25	8.46	22%	11%	11%	1.0	27	75	55
	21	L	28	a/a	SD	53	5.64	1.45	5.69	25%	16%	9%	1.2	27	62	67
Remy,Peyton	21	R	25	aa	CHC	35	7.45	1.71	19.8	13%	7%	6%	1.6	35	58	12
Rennie,Luc	19	R	25	aa	NYM	24	7.05	1.29	24.8	20%	9%	11%	2.4	24	23	58
	21	R	27	aa	NYM	50	9.82	1.93	18.3	17%	7%	10%	2.3	40	50	7
Requena,Alejandr	21	R	25	aa	SEA	90	6.68	1.84	18.2	15%	10%	5%	1.0	37	64	29
Reyes,Denyi	19	R	23	aa	BOS	152	5.99	1.44	24.9	15%	6%	9%	1.0	33	50	56
	21	R	25	aa	BOS	59	4.88	1.45	12.6	20%	4%	16%	1.5	36	71	90
Reyes,Jesus	19	R	26	aaa	CIN	77	6.85	2.04	8.7	14%	17%	-2%	1.8	33	59	-65
	21	R	28	aaa	NYM	118	5.33	1.69	21.3	16%	11%	5%	1.2	34	70	28
Reyes,Luis	21	R	27	a/a	WAS	128	6.68	1.72	23.3	14%	11%	3%	1.7	32	64	7
Reyes,Marcus	21	L	26	a/a	TOR	30	4.20	1.43	6.38	19%	11%	9%	1.8	28	79	31
Rheault,Dylan	21	R	29	aa	SD	34	7.94	2.51	7.9	10%	18%	-8%	0.8	39	67	1
Roach,Dalton	21	R	25	aa	STL	116	5.05	1.52	21	19%	8%	11%	1.6	33	72	42
Roberts,Ethan	21	R	24	a/a	CHC	54	3.30	1.04	5.34	28%	8%	20%	0.3	28	67	136
Robertson,Nick	21	R	23	aa	LA	60	3.36	1.19	6.19	22%	6%	16%	0.7	31	73	110
Robinson,Jared	19	R	25	a/a	CLE	48	4.78	1.54	8.08	24%	15%	9%	1.2	29	62	26
	21	R	27	aa	NYM	49	3.76	1.41	7.17	28%	9%	19%	1.8	33	82	76
Robles,Domingo	19	L	21	aa	PIT	103	5.69	1.57	25.1	14%	5%	9%	1.4	35	55	67
	21	L	23	aa	STL	93	5.20	1.42	17.2	16%	5%	11%	1.3	33	66	62
Rodning,Brody	21	L	25	aa	TOR	41	6.07	1.82	5.97	18%	9%	9%	0.5	41	65	63
Rodriguez,Dereck	19	R	27	aaa	SF	31	4.57	1.40	22	16%	8%	8%	1.2	30	60	42
	21	R	29	aaa	COL	87	8.13	1.98	19	15%	8%	7%	2.2	39	62	-6
Rodriguez,Elvin	21	R	23	a/a	DET	79	7.00	1.40	17.6	20%	9%	11%	2.3	28	55	25
Rodriguez,Graysc	21	R	22	aa	BAL	81	2.71	0.87	16.7	33%	7%	27%	0.9	25	74	161
Rodriguez,Jefry	19	R	26	a/a	CLE	28	5.06	1.28	16.6	13%	11%	2%	0.9	24	52	-6
	21	R	28	aaa	WAS	47	6.40	1.69	17.7	16%	13%	4%	1.0	33	62	35
Rodriguez,Jesus	21	R	23	aa	DET	71	6.83	1.59	19.6	15%	7%	8%	1.9	33	60	16
Rodriguez,Jose	19	R	24	a/a	LAA	63	6.96	1.70	12.4	20%	10%	11%	1.4	37	50	61
	21	R	26	a/a	ATL	102	6.03	1.48	19.1	17%	6%	10%	1.8	32	63	33
Rodriguez,Nivaldo	21	R	24	aaa	DET	62	7.24	1.92	12.8	12%	10%	2%	1.9	35	65	-16
Rodriguez,Yerry	21	R	24	a/a	TEX	83	5.39	1.44	13.1	23%	9%	14%	0.9	34	63	79
Rogalla,Keith	21	R	26	a/a	LAA	46	3.64	1.35	6.21	18%	7%	11%	0.4	33	72	86
Rogers,Josh	19	L	25	aaa	BAL	55	10.48	2.05	24.4	10%	4%	6%	3.5	39	30	48
	21	L	27	aaa	WAS	91	5.82	1.65	22.6	12%	6%	5%	1.8	34	69	4
Rolison,Ryan	21	L	24	a/a	COL	63	5.79	1.41	20.6	19%	7%	12%	1.3	33	61	60
Rom,Drew	21	L	22	aa	BAL	40	4.06	1.15	17.6	25%	5%	19%	1.4	30	70	113
Romano,Sal	19	R	26	aaa	CIN	70	5.78	1.73	7.41	20%	9%	11%	1.1	38	60	62
	21	R	28	aaa	NYY	31	4.51	1.64	5.55	14%	4%	10%	0.4	39	71	82
Romero,Jhon	21	R	26	a/a	WAS	57	3.20	1.27	6.17	23%	5%	18%	1.2	33	80	113
Romero,Miguel	19	R	25	aaa	OAK	74	4.55	1.50	7.13	20%	11%	9%	1.3	31	63	43
	21	R	27	aaa	OAK	76	6.27	1.68	12.2	12%	10%	3%	1.6	32	66	2
Romero,Tommy	21	R	24	a/a	TAM	111	3.04	1.05	18.7	29%	7%	22%	0.8	29	75	132
Rondon,Angel	19	R	22	aa	STL	115	3.85	1.33	23.9	20%	8%	11%	0.9	31	65	66
	21	R	24	aaa	STL	78	4.39	1.39	17.3	17%	6%	11%	1.4	32	73	52
Roney,Bradley	19	R	27	aa	ATL	28	5.27	1.55	6.14	26%	11%	15%	1.0	36	59	82
	21	R	29	a/a	NYM	44	5.79	1.56	5.35	27%	16%	10%	0.6	32	61	90
Rooney,John	21	L	24	aa	LA	30	3.86	1.48	16.2	27%	14%	13%	0.8	32	76	85
Rosado,Cesar	21	R	25	aa	HOU	55	8.09	1.88	16.2	21%	11%	10%	1.7	39	58	34
Rosenberg,Kenny	19	L	24	a/a	TAM	139	4.49	1.53	23.3	16%	11%	6%	0.8	32	65	22
	21	L	26	a/a	TAM	37	2.96	1.36	9.71	26%	10%	16%	1.3	31	85	79
Ross,Austin	21	R	27	a/a	PHI	51	5.28	1.52	6.55	22%	15%	7%	1.2	28	67	53
Rosso,Ramon	19	R	23	a/a	PHI	125	5.39	1.42	22.2	20%	9%	11%	1.9	30	51	62
Rosso,Ramon	21	R	25	aaa	PHI	30	5.16	1.71	6.5	32%	8%	24%	0.7	33	70	47
Royalty,Alex	21	R	24	aa	CLE	40	6.02	1.50	19.2	20%	20%	0%	1.0	34	60	55
Rubio,Frank	21	R	26	aa	SF	43	4.34	1.31	4.8	17%	11%	6%	0.8	32	68	84
Rucker,Michael	19	R	25	a/a	CHC	81	5.66	1.59	9.95	14%	9%	5%	1.4	37	56	83
	21	R	27	aaa	CHC	40	5.36	1.52	9.16	25%	13%	13%	1.8	36	70	72
Ruotolo,Patrick	21	R	26	aa	SF	37	3.27	0.79	3.42	21%	15%	6%	1.2	23	65	200
Russ,Addison	19	R	25	aa	PHI	58	3.42	1.40	4.46	21%	5%	16%	1.1	36	70	120
	21	R	27	a/a	NYY	45	4.59	1.62	5.73	21%	11%	10%	1.2	31	75	51
Ryan,Joe	21	R	25	aaa	MIN	66	4.29	0.93	17.7	20%	8%	12%	1.4	25	58	153
Ryan,Ryder	19	R	24	aa	NYM	45	4.26	1.49	7.79	18%	8%	10%	0.5	30	67	5
	21	R	26	aaa	TEX	45	6.52	1.68	5.33	18%	9%	9%	1.5	37	63	49
Ryan,Zac	19	R	25	a/a	LAA	56	4.07	1.37	6.22	21%	12%	9%	0.7	28	65	37
	21	R	27	aaa	LAA	31	6.58	1.97	6.45	20%	8%	12%	1.5	38	68	33
Sadzeck,Connor	21	R	30	aaa	MIL	46	5.40	1.67	5.19	26%	10%	16%	1.1	31	69	40
Salinas,Ricky	21	R	25	aa	CIN	77	5.93	1.74	20.7	21%	10%	11%	1.8	37	70	38
Salow,Logan	19	L	25	aa	LA	20	5.48	2.08	6.16	16%	11%	5%	0.0	34	71	-99
	21	L	27	aaa	LA	41	3.93	1.62	4.79	29%	7%	22%	0.4	30	75	68
Sammons,Bryan	19	L	24	aa	MIN	82	6.01	1.53	21	20%	8%	12%	1.6	30	51	35
	21	L	26	a/a	MIN	109	7.87	1.79	18.7	24%	10%	13%	2.2	31	59	-5
Sampson,Adrian	21	R	30	aaa	CHC	83	5.86	1.81	24.1	23%	10%	13%	2.2	33	74	-23
Sanabria,Carlos	19	R	22	aa	HOU	55	4.39	1.51	6.44	27%	9%	18%	0.9	30	66	30
	21	R	24	a/a	KC	59	4.41	1.36	6.5	27%	16%	11%	0.7	25	68	61
Sanchez,Cristopt	21	L	25	aaa	PHI	73	5.39	1.58	16.9	12%	4%	8%	0.6	32	65	77
Sanchez,Mario	19	R	25	a/a	WAS	130	5.04	1.34	20.1	16%	12%	4%	1.7	31	51	91
	21	R	27	a/a	WAS	116	5.35	1.33	20.1	21%	9%	12%	1.6	31	64	66
Sanders,Cam	21	R	25	aa	CHC	91	6.06	1.44	21.6	22%	10%	12%	1.6	29	61	46
Sanders,Phoenix	19	R	24	a/a	TAM	63	2.42	1.29	5.78	22%	15%	7%	0.8	29	78	61
	21	R	26	aaa	TAM	64	4.46	1.12	5.04	18%	10%	8%	1.3	30	64	128
Sands,Cole	21	R	24	aa	MIN	81	2.73	1.26	17.4	21%	12%	9%	0.7	29	81	90
Sanmartin,Reiver	19	L	23	aa	CIN	58	5.84	1.60	21.4	25%	4%	21%	1.3	36	56	74
	21	L	25	a/a	CIN	101	4.27	1.37	16.9	13%	11%	2%	0.7	35	69	96
Santillan,Tony	19	R	22	aa	CIN	103	6.32	1.84	22.9	18%	3%	15%	0.9	37	60	12
	21	R	24	aaa	CIN	38	2.77	1.23	11.8	16%	14%	2%	1.5	28	87	86
Santos,Antonio	19	R	23	aa	COL	47	8.10	1.62	26.2	20%	11%	9%	1.0	38	40	77
	21	R	25	aaa	COL	46	8.79	1.93	6.44	21%	7%	14%	2.2	32	57	-28
Santos,Ramon	21	R	27	a/a	STL	67	3.32	1.27	8.09	22%	11%	11%	0.8	26	76	96
Santos,Victor	21	R	21	aa	BOS	66	3.02	1.13	18.6	25%	16%	9%	0.9	30	77	136
Sceroler,Mac	21	R	26	a/a	CIN	42	11.87	2.00	17	13%	7%	6%	2.5	42	40	15
Scheetz,Kit	19	L	25	a/a	HOU	53	6.64	1.72	7.77	20%	9%	11%	1.7	38	52	79
	21	L	27	aaa	HOU	55	4.18	1.58	6.37	17%	7%	10%	1.0	30	76	30
Schilling,Garrett	21	R	26	aa	COL	52	7.15	1.96	22.7	15%	10%	5%	1.8	40	66	7
Schlichtholz,Fred	21	L	26	aa	SD	31	6.51	1.72	6.15	15%	6%	9%	0.8	33	61	30
Schmidt,Clarke	19	R	23	aa	NYY	19	3.21	0.96	23.9	20%	4%	16%	0.7	30	60	142
	21	R	25	a/a	NYY	34	2.89	1.34	17.9	14%	17%	-2%	1.8	30	90	55
Scholtens,Jesse	19	R	25	aa	SD	125	7.09	1.77	23.9	16%	11%	5%	1.2	39	52	67
	21	R	27	aaa	SD	103	4.57	1.38	20.6	14%	11%	3%	1.0	32	69	63
Schreiber,John	19	R	25	a/a	DET	67	3.32	1.22	5.12	19%	11%	9%	0.9	28	67	77
	21	R	27	aaa	BOS	67	3.54	1.57	8.92	10%	18%	-8%	0.5	35	77	62
Schryver,Hunter	19	L	24	a/a	CHW	65	5.16	1.65	7.14	19%	8%	11%	0.7	35	64	35
	21	L	26	aaa	CHW	44	5.49	1.73	5.02	28%	8%	20%	1.4	33	71	34
Schulfer,Austin	21	R	26	aa	MIN	110	5.06	1.63	20.4	22%	6%	16%	0.6	35	68	53
Schwaab,Andrew	19	R	26	aa	BOS	18	8.48	1.93	8.56	24%	15%	9%	0.0	36	51	-45
	21	R	28	a/a	LA	67	3.76	1.30	6.3	28%	9%	19%	1.1	28	75	68
Scioneaux,Tate	19	R	27	aa	COL	41	11.35	2.02	6.03	14%	5%	9%	3.2	41	24	89
	21	R	29	a/a	COL	56	7.06	1.61	5.44	16%	5%	11%	2.9	31	64	-16
Scott,Adam	19	L	24	aa	CLE	76	5.78	1.50	23.5	18%	9%	9%	1.5	34	52	71
	21	L	26	a/a	CLE	61	4.78	1.47	18.7	16%	8%	8%	1.1	32	70	63
Seabold,Connor	19	R	23	aa	PHI	40	2.98	1.32	23.7	15%	8%	7%	0.6	33	74	85
	21	R	25	aaa	BOS	54	4.43	1.33	20.4	20%	9%	11%	1.1	29	69	59
Sears,JP	21	L	25	a/a	NYY	106	4.15	1.25	17.3	33%	7%	27%	1.1	32	70	106
Sedlock,Cody	19	R	24	aa	BAL	34	5.22	1.76	17.3	13%	11%	2%	1.1	33	65	-11
	21	R	26	a/a	BAL	95	5.33	1.64	17.7	16%	13%	4%	1.9	32	73	19
Seelinger,Matt	21	R	26	aa	SF	41	3.75	1.70	5.14	15%	7%	8%	1.3	33	82	68
Semple,Shawn	19	R	24	a/a	NYY	40	8.15	1.95	23.9	20%	10%	11%	2.1	35	47	-5
	21	R	26	a/a	NYY	71	5.69	1.45	16.9	17%	6%	10%	1.1	31	61	58
Severino,Andersc	21	L	27	a/a	CHW	47	2.93	1.48	5.07	12%	10%	2%	0.0	28	78	88
Sharp,Sterling	19	R	24	aa	WAS	51	5.91	1.74	26	23%	9%	14%	0.3	40	62	61
	21	R	26	a/a	WAS	88	5.45	1.71	21.1	18%	7%	11%	1.5	30	72	0
Shepherd,Chandl	19	R	27	aaa	BAL	102	7.95	1.98	22.2	10%	4%	6%	2.1	39	49	39
	21	R	29	aaa	MIN	106	7.23	1.97	19.6	12%	6%	5%	1.9	38	66	-20
Shore,Logan	19	R	25	aa	DET	97	5.30	1.70	19.1	19%	7%	12%	1.1	32	63	-17
	21	R	27	aaa	DET	73	5.67	1.63	20.3	25%	5%	19%	1.0	33	66	32
Short,Wyatt	19	L	25	a/a	CHC	60	3.91	1.54	6.11	20%	9%	11%	0.6	34	71	42
	21	L	27	aa	CHC	41	6.38	1.61	6.99	14%	4%	10%	1.9	30	65	23
Singer,Jeff	19	L	26	aa	PHI	63	3.22	1.19	6.03	23%	5%	18%	0.6	28	68	82
	21	L	28	aaa	PHI	53	5.85	1.71	5.46	20%	11%	9%	0.4	38	64	77
Sisk,Evan	21	L	24	aa	MIN	41	4.65	1.79	6.53	12%	10%	3%	0.9	36	75	60
Sittinger,Brandyn	21	R	27	a/a	ARI	40	3.97	1.19	4.59	29%	7%	22%	0.8	28	68	98
Slegers,Aaron	19	R	27	aaa	TAM	113	6.50	1.71	19.7	20%	8%	11%	2.0	35	52	45
	21	R	29	aaa	TAM	36	9.19	2.25	10.1	17%	6%	11%	3.5	39	66	-84
Small,Ethan	21	L	24	a/a	MIL	77	2.19	1.30	18.7	26%	11%	15%	0.5	28	85	92
Smith,Chad	19	R	24	aa	MIA	19	6.85	1.90	6.45	27%	16%	10%	1.9	38	55	45
	21	R	26	aaa	COL	34	3.34	1.33	3.93	27%	14%	13%	0.3	26	74	78
Smith,Kevin	19	L	22	aa	NYM	32	4.59	1.45	22.8	21%	11%	10%	0.3	31	64	24
	21	L	24	a/a	BAL	83	5.24	1.71	17.1	16%	11%	6%	1.9	31	75	31
Smith,Ryan	21	L	24	a/a	LAA	58	5.68	1.57	23.3	26%	10%	16%	1.5	36	67	50
Snead,Kirby	19	L	25	a/a	TOR	64	4.87	1.49	5.54	22%	15%	7%	1.3	34	60	77
	21	L	27	aaa	TOR	40	2.33	1.16	4.42	20%	9%	11%	0.3	28	80	116

PITCHER	yr	t	age	lvl	org	ip	era	whip	bf/g	k%	bb%	k-bb	hr/9	h%	s%	bpv
Snider,Collin	21	R	26	a/a	KC	67	5.35	1.66	6.27	16%	9%	7%	1.1	35	69	37
Sobotka,Chad	19	R	26	aaa	ATL	22	6.19	1.52	5.67	26%	5%	21%	1.4	41	49	152
	21	R	28	aaa	MIL	39	5.41	1.57	3.98	13%	14%	0%	0.5	29	64	42
Solbach,Markus	19	R	28	aa	LA	42	3.74	1.39	22.1	17%	5%	12%	0.3	35	69	83
	21	R	30	a/a	LA	54	8.33	1.86	14.1	13%	7%	6%	0.7	39	52	33
Solomon,Peter	21	R	25	aaa	HOU	99	4.71	1.37	19.8	22%	9%	13%	1.4	30	70	61
Sotillet,Andres	19	R	22	aa	KC	76	4.51	1.49	9.65	16%	9%	7%	0.8	32	64	31
	21	R	24	a/a	KC	47	6.19	1.82	6.45	18%	13%	5%	0.7	36	65	47
Sousa,Bennett	21	L	26	a/a	CHW	50	4.25	1.31	5.09	28%	10%	18%	1.4	31	73	84
Speier,Gabe	21	L	26	aaa	KC	46	3.36	1.33	4.25	23%	5%	18%	0.9	35	78	119
Spitzbarth,Shea	19	R	25	a/a	LA	66	4.97	1.41	5.37	26%	9%	18%	1.1	35	57	108
	21	R	27	aaa	PIT	48	2.34	1.31	4.74	16%	11%	4%	0.7	26	85	51
Spraker,Graham	21	R	26	a/a	TOR	46	3.22	1.34	6.2	27%	13%	14%	1.2	29	81	80
St. John,Locke	19	L	26	a/a	TEX	52	5.78	1.51	5.83	22%	12%	9%	1.4	30	53	41
	21	L	28	aaa	DET	60	3.74	1.66	7.48	20%	11%	10%	0.8	36	79	61
Stadler,Fitz	21	R	24	a/a	TOR	50	6.55	1.58	5.67	26%	16%	10%	1.5	30	60	59
Stephens,Jordan	19	R	27	a/a	CLE	90	10.54	2.15	18.7	14%	9%	5%	2.8	40	37	27
	21	R	29	aaa	CLE	49	5.57	1.82	6.17	16%	9%	6%	2.0	36	75	3
Stevens,Tyler	19	R	23	a/a	MIA	57	4.01	1.22	6.42	22%	9%	13%	1.1	28	59	76
	21	R	25	aa	MIA	33	4.17	1.47	6.2	21%	11%	10%	2.4	27	84	21
Stewart,Will	21	L	24	aa	MIA	101	5.36	1.52	22	16%	9%	7%	0.9	33	65	47
Stiever,Jonathan	21	R	24	aaa	CHW	74	6.27	1.56	19	23%	8%	15%	1.5	36	62	63
Stratton,Hunter	21	R	25	a/a	PIT	51	2.49	1.30	5.56	26%	12%	14%	0.5	30	82	100
Strider,Spencer	21	R	23	a/a	ATL	64	5.97	1.38	17.9	30%	11%	19%	1.0	34	56	103
Strotman,Drew	21	R	25	aaa	MIN	113	6.61	1.83	21	16%	13%	3%	1.1	35	64	28
Stryffeler,Michael	21	R	25	aa	SEA	43	2.45	1.21	4.23	35%	21%	14%	0.7	17	82	125
Strzelecki,Peter	21	R	27	a/a	MIL	52	4.08	1.42	5.51	26%	9%	17%	1.2	35	75	89
Stumpo,Mitchell	21	R	25	a/a	ARI	31	2.18	1.02	4.98	24%	8%	16%	0.7	25	83	106
Sulser,Beau	19	R	25	aa	PIT	96	4.14	1.59	12.8	12%	9%	3%	0.5	33	70	10
	21	R	27	aaa	PIT	124	6.36	1.86	22.4	13%	10%	4%	1.5	36	68	6
Swarmer,Matt	19	R	26	aaa	CHC	152	7.50	1.82	26.1	15%	7%	8%	2.5	36	46	54
	21	R	28	a/a	CHC	114	5.67	1.45	20.3	19%	8%	10%	1.9	31	60	34
Sweet,Devin	21	R	25	aa	SEA	81	5.45	1.52	14.1	23%	8%	14%	2.1	34	71	44
Szapucki,Thomas	21	L	25	aaa	NYM	43	3.70	1.59	19.1	18%	13%	5%	0.9	31	79	50
Tabor,Matt	21	R	23	a/a	ARI	84	5.99	1.35	19.5	18%	8%	9%	1.8	28	60	32
Tago,Peter	21	R	29	a/a	CHW	58	4.15	1.44	7.08	22%	10%	11%	0.7	33	72	75
Takahashi,Rodrig	19	R	22	aa	ARI	120	5.20	1.46	23.4	17%	8%	9%	1.1	32	57	52
	21	R	24	aaa	CIN	89	5.77	1.51	21.4	20%	9%	11%	1.8	32	66	38
Tapani,Ryan	21	R	27	aa	WAS	48	5.34	1.39	8.44	19%	10%	9%	2.1	26	69	23
Tarnok,Freddy	21	R	23	aa	ATL	45	3.46	1.29	20.6	28%	9%	19%	0.5	35	73	120
Taylor,Curtis	19	R	24	aa	TAM	19	3.97	1.21	5.17	18%	7%	11%	0.0	30	64	64
	21	R	26	a/a	TOR	36	6.95	1.70	5.46	20%	11%	9%	1.5	35	61	36
Teel,Carson	21	L	26	a/a	WAS	92	5.47	1.49	12.1	15%	7%	8%	2.1	31	70	16
Tejada,Felipe	21	R	23	aa	HOU	37	5.24	1.52	5.95	25%	7%	17%	1.3	38	68	85
Tetreault,Jackson	19	R	23	aa	WAS	87	6.95	1.95	23.1	13%	11%	2%	1.2	37	58	-7
	21	R	25	a/a	WAS	67	4.52	1.52	24.3	15%	8%	7%	1.5	32	75	28
Thomas,Connor	21	L	23	a/a	STL	124	3.03	1.30	19.7	19%	5%	13%	0.9	32	80	86
Thomas,Tyler	21	L	26	a/a	TEX	46	5.09	1.59	7.24	20%	10%	10%	1.1	35	70	56
Thompson,Zack	21	L	24	aaa	STL	93	6.91	1.83	19.7	15%	12%	4%	1.5	35	64	15
Tinoco,Jesus	19	R	24	aaa	COL	34	4.39	1.60	5.19	12%	12%	0%	1.2	29	67	-22
	21	R	26	aaa	COL	54	6.90	1.92	7.1	17%	11%	6%	1.2	39	64	31
Todd,Reagan	21	L	26	a/a	COL	53	5.35	1.58	4.78	22%	10%	12%	1.7	34	71	46
Toplikar,Trent	21	R	25	aa	SF	95	5.76	1.72	19.6	16%	9%	8%	1.3	36	68	33
Toribio,Noe	21	R	22	aa	PIT	50	4.45	1.22	14.4	17%	6%	10%	0.8	29	64	73
Torres-Costa,Qui	21	L	27	aaa	MIL	37	7.12	2.01	5.14	22%	21%	1%	0.5	35	62	69
Tropeano,Nichola	19	R	29	aaa	LAA	81	5.81	1.63	21.3	18%	9%	9%	1.3	35	56	53
	21	R	31	aaa	LA	47	4.04	1.61	12.3	18%	11%	7%	1.0	33	77	45
Tully,Tanner	19	L	25	a/a	CLE	146	6.22	1.71	25.5	11%	5%	6%	0.9	37	57	43
	21	L	27	a/a	CLE	113	4.30	1.62	19.3	15%	7%	9%	0.9	36	75	49
Tyler,Kyle	21	R	25	a/a	LAA	86	3.72	1.33	17.9	21%	7%	15%	0.8	33	74	90
Uceta,Edwin	19	R	21	aa	LA	73	4.06	1.43	19.4	22%	10%	12%	0.7	32	66	62
	21	R	23	aaa	LA	30	4.32	1.29	12.4	26%	9%	17%	1.1	31	69	93
Uelmen,Erich	19	R	23	aa	CHC	29	10.89	2.16	24.1	15%	15%	0%	1.9	37	38	-39
	21	R	25	a/a	CHC	93	6.27	1.49	13	18%	10%	7%	1.6	30	60	31
Uvila,Cole	21	R	27	a/a	TEX	55	6.60	1.88	6.65	18%	12%	6%	0.7	38	64	45
Valdez,Jefry	21	R	26	aa	NYY	31	4.74	1.29	7.98	16%	8%	8%	1.0	28	65	51
Vallimont,Chris	21	R	24	aa	MIN	91	6.74	1.80	20	26%	15%	11%	1.5	37	64	54
Valverde,Alex	21	R	25	aa	TAM	72	5.43	1.48	10.3	25%	9%	16%	0.7	36	63	92
Vargas,Emilio	19	R	23	aa	ARI	87	5.37	1.37	21.5	16%	7%	9%	1.3	30	51	54
	21	R	25	a/a	CHW	85	3.97	1.39	17.1	23%	9%	14%	1.2	33	75	74
Varland,Gus	21	R	25	aa	LA	36	5.56	1.43	9.61	12%	10%	1%	1.7	26	65	3
Vasquez,Andrew	19	L	26	a/a	MIN	36	7.87	2.18	6.24	19%	21%	-2%	0.3	37	59	-85
	21	L	28	aaa	LA	49	3.75	1.09	4.93	32%	12%	20%	0.9	25	68	113
Vennaro,Zach	21	R	25	aa	MIL	38	8.96	2.09	5.07	22%	13%	10%	2.2	41	59	18
Verrett,Logan	19	R	29	aa	OAK	35	5.59	1.29	20.6	17%	3%	14%	1.3	32	46	99
	21	R	31	aaa	SEA	114	5.67	1.48	25.8	14%	4%	10%	1.9	33	67	48
Vespi,Nick	21	L	26	a/a	BAL	40	4.84	1.35	5.59	23%	10%	13%	1.6	28	69	57
Vieaux,Cam	19	L	26	a/a	PIT	141	4.93	1.54	23.7	15%	11%	4%	1.6	29	60	10
	21	L	28	a/a	PIT	74	6.10	1.72	13.4	16%	12%	4%	1.3	33	66	23
Villines,Stephen	19	R	24	a/a	NYM	61	3.45	1.51	6.45	18%	9%	9%	0.8	34	73	49
	21	R	26	a/a	TEX	44	4.04	1.38	7.13	18%	6%	12%	0.9	33	73	74
Vines,Jace	19	R	25	aa	KC	51	7.92	2.14	23	12%	9%	3%	1.1	41	56	4
	21	R	27	aaa	KC	68	4.81	1.55	6.75	17%	12%	4%	0.3	32	67	62
Viza,Tyler	19	R	25	a/a	PHI	76	9.43	2.09	18.7	16%	7%	9%	2.8	42	41	66
	21	R	27	aa	SD	30	5.14	1.84	28.2	12%	6%	5%	1.5	38	76	9
Vizcaino,Raffi	19	R	24	aa	SF	48	5.39	1.73	6.86	16%	14%	2%	0.6	33	64	-19
	21	R	26	aa	SF	40	6.59	1.82	5.46	19%	14%	5%	0.9	36	63	47
Vodnik,Victor	21	R	22	aa	ATL	35	6.67	1.72	14.5	22%	14%	8%	1.5	33	63	42

PITCHER	yr	t	age	lvl	org	ip	era	whip	bf/g	k%	bb%	k-bb	hr/9	h%	s%	bpv
Wade,Konner	19	R	28	a/a	BOS	101	4.13	1.51	24.3	16%	9%	7%	0.6	35	68	50
	21	R	30	aaa	BAL	73	4.01	1.30	15.1	26%	5%	21%	1.8	26	78	9
Waguespack,Jac	19	R	26	aaa	TOR	54	7.16	1.85	21.1	13%	14%	0%	1.9	35	52	17
	21	R	28	aaa	TOR	70	4.27	1.57	12.8	17%	5%	12%	0.6	37	73	69
Waldichuk,Ken	21	L	23	aa	NYY	80	4.91	1.39	21.1	13%	7%	6%	1.6	31	70	70
Waldron,Matt	21	R	25	aa	SD	32	7.10	1.74	20.9	22%	9%	13%	0.5	36	57	53
Walker,Josh	21	L	27	a/a	NYM	96	3.94	1.10	22.2	16%	9%	7%	0.7	26	65	77
Wantz,Andrew	19	R	24	aa	LAA	48	9.72	2.12	18.2	18%	13%	5%	3.1	39	39	27
	21	R	26	aaa	LAA	31	1.60	0.91	9.68	28%	10%	18%	0.5	25	85	134
Warner,Austin	19	L	25	a/a	STL	143	5.69	1.67	24.7	23%	5%	18%	1.7	35	57	52
	21	L	27	aaa	STL	74	3.42	1.14	7.17	26%	9%	18%	0.9	27	73	81
Warren,Austin	21	R	25	aaa	LAA	37	5.48	1.59	7.44	16%	11%	4%	1.0	37	66	70
Warren,Zach	21	L	25	a/a	PHI	47	4.65	1.64	5.4	27%	13%	14%	1.1	33	74	80
Warzek,Bryan	21	L	24	aa	LA	46	5.65	1.92	7.04	22%	12%	9%	2.2	32	77	10
Washington,Mark	21	R	25	aa	LA	63	2.04	1.15	6.76	20%	11%	10%	1.4	24	93	63
Watkins,Spenser	19	R	27	a/a	DET	121	9.92	1.98	24.3	26%	16%	10%	2.6	38	35	37
	21	R	29	aaa	BAL	37	4.54	1.31	19.2	14%	9%	5%	1.9	25	74	13
Watson,Cyrillo	21	R	24	a/a	LA	44	6.05	1.64	5.63	16%	9%	6%	1.5	31	66	34
Watson,Nolan	21	R	24	aa	KC	69	7.02	1.92	13.1	22%	9%	13%	1.6	35	65	-14
Webb,Braden	19	R	24	aa	MIL	15	14.93	2.57	13.5	21%	11%	10%	1.9	36	30	-155
	21	R	26	aa	MIL	49	5.76	1.65	5.34	16%	9%	7%	1.5	33	68	54
Weber,Ryan	19	R	29	aaa	BOS	78	6.85	1.90	23	23%	8%	15%	1.4	38	56	21
	21	R	31	aaa	SEA	104	4.96	1.34	22.8	26%	12%	14%	1.4	34	66	113
Weigel,Patrick	19	R	25	a/a	ATL	81	4.07	1.39	12.2	30%	11%	19%	1.3	24	64	-9
	21	R	27	aaa	MIL	44	7.79	2.09	6.01	16%	13%	3%	1.3	36	63	26
Weiman,Blake	19	L	24	a/a	PIT	33	3.71	1.12	5.47	35%	21%	14%	1.3	26	58	87
	21	L	26	aaa	PIT	46	5.22	1.19	5.28	26%	9%	17%	2.0	25	63	44
Weisenburger,Ja	21	R	24	aa	OAK	38	4.72	1.85	6.36	24%	8%	16%	1.1	34	77	51
Weiss,Ryan	21	R	25	a/a	ARI	79	4.28	1.21	9.38	12%	9%	3%	1.1	28	68	77
Weiss,Zack	19	R	27	a/a	MIN	30	9.57	2.19	9.53	13%	10%	4%	2.0	40	46	0
	21	R	29	aaa	SEA	41	4.90	1.63	6.12	15%	7%	8%	1.1	33	72	62
Weissert,Greg	19	R	24	aa	NYY	24	2.59	1.13	6.77	19%	8%	10%	0.0	22	74	28
	21	R	26	a/a	NYY	52	1.93	1.23	5.31	23%	8%	14%	0.4	25	86	89
Wells,Alex	19	L	22	aa	BAL	138	3.97	1.26	23.5	18%	13%	5%	0.8	31	62	76
	21	L	24	aaa	BAL	56	3.84	1.14	17.1	18%	8%	9%	1.1	29	70	118
Wells,Nick	21	L	25	a/a	WAS	49	6.19	1.87	7.18	22%	10%	11%	0.7	37	66	44
Wentz,Joey	19	L	22	aa	DET	130	6.02	1.46	22.3	17%	8%	9%	1.5	31	48	62
	21	L	24	aa	DET	54	4.48	1.50	18	20%	9%	11%	1.3	27	74	43
Wesneski,Hayden	21	R	24	a/a	NYY	94	4.71	1.36	21.8	19%	10%	9%	1.2	33	68	81
White,Brandon	21	R	27	aa	ATL	40	3.24	1.49	5.42	28%	9%	19%	0.3	32	78	73
White,Mitchell	19	R	25	a/a	LA	95	6.09	1.45	17.7	18%	7%	11%	1.7	33	46	88
	21	R	27	aaa	LA	32	1.78	1.33	13.3	20%	11%	9%	0.3	34	87	105
Wiles,Collin	19	R	25	aa	TEX	31	8.59	1.69	15.5	15%	7%	8%	2.2	33	34	22
	21	R	27	aaa	TEX	86	4.98	1.45	16	25%	7%	17%	1.4	34	69	58
Willeman,Zach	21	R	25	aa	LA	49	3.72	1.34	6.2	13%	11%	2%	0.7	31	73	87
Williams,Garrett	19	L	25	aa	SF	110	5.59	1.72	17.2	15%	8%	7%	0.6	33	63	-14
	21	L	27	a/a	STL	53	5.20	1.59	6.34	19%	5%	13%	0.6	29	66	65
Williams,Ronnie	19	R	23	aa	STL	34	5.19	1.70	6.15	20%	10%	10%	1.7	32	62	12
	21	R	25	a/a	SF	80	2.95	1.18	11.1	15%	12%	4%	0.7	24	77	64
Williamson,Brand	21	L	23	aa	SEA	68	3.86	1.34	21.8	12%	12%	0%	0.9	37	74	120
Wilson,Brooks	21	R	25	a/a	ATL	50	3.14	1.25	5.22	17%	11%	6%	0.6	34	77	132
Wilson,Bryse	19	R	22	aaa	ATL	121	4.37	1.38	24.2	22%	10%	12%	1.0	35	62	99
	21	R	24	aaa	ATL	56	5.30	1.59	24.8	16%	9%	8%	1.4	34	70	25
Wilson,Steven	19	R	25	aaa	SD	35	4.24	1.42	5.93	17%	6%	10%	1.1	27	64	26
	21	R	27	aaa	SD	40	3.09	0.91	5.35	22%	21%	1%	1.2	22	73	126
Winckowski,Josh	21	R	23	a/a	BOS	117	4.69	1.38	20.5	18%	9%	9%	0.8	33	67	68
Winder,Josh	21	R	25	a/a	MIN	74	3.05	1.05	20.6	18%	11%	7%	1.2	27	77	118
Winn,Cole	21	R	22	a/a	TEX	86	2.74	0.90	15.3	11%	5%	6%	0.8	21	73	122
Withrow,Matt	21	R	28	aa	ATL	51	4.19	1.58	8.98	15%	7%	9%	0.5	29	73	58
Woodford,Jake	19	R	23	aaa	STL	153	4.75	1.38	24.8	21%	7%	15%	1.3	27	57	19
	21	R	25	aaa	STL	34	4.50	1.61	21.5	22%	10%	12%	0.9	35	74	35
Woods Richardso	21	R	21	aa	MIN	54	6.19	1.55	15.8	26%	9%	17%	0.8	35	59	91
Woods,Stephen	21	R	26	aa	KC	48	9.33	2.50	11.6	15%	15%	0%	1.0	40	61	12
Workman,Blake	21	R	24	aa	ARI	31	8.24	1.61	6.87	18%	10%	7%	2.7	39	53	71
Wright,Kyle	19	R	24	aaa	ATL	113	5.51	1.48	23.2	18%	12%	6%	1.2	34	55	74
	21	R	26	aaa	ATL	137	4.01	1.42	24.2	16%	8%	8%	0.7	33	73	68
Wright,Mike	19	R	29	aaa	SEA	58	6.39	1.62	17.2	26%	15%	11%	0.7	37	54	62
	21	R	31	aaa	CHW	96	4.09	1.25	24.4	25%	9%	16%	1.1	27	71	56
Wynkoop,Jack	19	L	26	aa	COL	149	6.46	1.71	28.1	16%	7%	9%	2.0	36	52	53
	21	L	28	aaa	COL	30	3.22	1.51	10.9	23%	9%	14%	0.7	30	81	32
Wynne,Randy	21	R	28	aa	CIN	90	6.65	1.65	16.1	12%	10%	1%	1.7	37	62	53
Yacabonis,Jimmy	19	R	27	aaa	BAL	24	5.79	2.03	6.85	19%	21%	-2%	0.9	37	67	-37
	21	R	29	aaa	SEA	38	2.51	1.18	5.08	32%	12%	20%	0.7	28	82	83
Yajure,Miguel	21	R	23	aaa	PIT	45	3.12	1.06	19.5	22%	13%	10%	1.1	24	76	74
Yardley,Eric	19	R	29	aaa	SD	65	3.11	1.32	6.28	17%	3%	14%	0.4	32	73	58
	21	R	31	aaa	MIL	37	3.64	1.47	4.08	14%	4%	10%	0.5	34	75	62
Young,Danny	19	L	25	a/a	TOR	51	3.81	1.59	5.96	23%	10%	13%	0.7	31	72	-12
	21	L	27	aaa	CLE	53	5.13	1.66	5.95	15%	11%	4%	1.6	33	74	31
Zambrano,Jesus	19	R	23	aa	OAK	46	1.49	1.34	6.87	16%	12%	4%	0.2	32	87	43
	21	R	25	a/a	OAK	55	5.67	1.44	7.36	18%	9%	9%	1.3	29	63	39
Zamora,Daniel	19	L	26	aaa	NYM	30	5.25	1.30	4.26	18%	6%	12%	0.3	36	54	120
	21	L	28	aaa	SEA	45	7.36	1.89	6.66	12%	9%	3%	1.6	37	63	29
Zarbnisky,Braden	21	R	25	a/a	PHI	46	4.74	1.02	6.59	17%	12%	4%	2.2	22	63	66
Zastryzny,Rob	19	L	27	a/a	LA	115	6.94	1.82	23.3	16%	7%	9%	1.6	38	53	50
	21	L	29	aaa	MIA	30	4.89	1.84	5.84	12%	6%	5%	2.5	35	83	12
Zavolas,Noah	21	R	25	aa	MIL	122	5.34	1.36	23.2	16%	14%	2%	1.5	32	65	64
Zerpa,Angel	21	L	22	a/a	KC	48	6.85	1.60	15.2	19%	14%	5%	1.4	36	58	54
Zeuch,T.J.	21	R	26	aaa	STL	97	4.45	1.41	19.5	15%	6%	8%	1.1	31	71	45
Zuber,Tyler	19	R	24	aa	KC	26	3.44	1.09	4.62	24%	5%	18%	0.8	29	62	116
	21	R	26	aaa	KC	30	3.07	1.11	4.25	27%	14%	14%	0.8	22	76	96
Zuniga,Guillermo	21	R	23	aa	LA	36	2.92	1.02	5.55	30%	8%	22%	1.2	26	78	122

LEADERBOARDS & INSIGHTS

This section provides rankings of projected skills indicators for 2022. Rather than take shots in the dark predicting league leaders in the exact number of home runs, or stolen bases, or strikeouts, the Forecaster's Leaderboards focus on the component elements of each skill.

For batters, we've ranked the top players in terms of pure power, speed, and batting average skill, breaking each down in a number of different ways. For pitchers, we rank some of the key base skills, differentiating between starters and relievers, and provide a few interesting cuts that might uncover some late round sleepers.

In addition, the section examines some potential gainers/faders for 2022 based on 2021 results and supporting skills (or lack thereof), and a few format-specific leaderboards for Head-to-Head and DFS play.

These are clearly not exhaustive lists of sorts and filters—drop us a note if you see something we should consider for next year's book. Also, the database at BaseballHQ.com allows you to construct your own custom sorts and filters. Finally, remember that these are just tools. Some players will appear on multiple lists—even mutually exclusive lists—so you have to assess what makes most sense and make decisions for your specific application.

Power

Top PX, 400+ AB: Top power skills among projected full-time players.

Top PX, –300 AB: Top power skills among projected part-time players; possible end-game options are here.

Position Scarcity: See which positions have deepest power options.

Top PX, ct% over 75%: Top power skills among the top contact hitters. Best pure power options here.

Top PX, ct% under 70%: Top power skills among the worst contact hitters; free-swingers who might be prone to streakiness and lower BAs.

Top PX, FB% over 40%: Top power skills among the most extreme fly ball hitters. Most likely to convert their power into home runs.

Top PX, FB% under 35%: Top power skills among those with lesser fly ball tendencies. There may be more downside to their home run potential.

Speed

Top Spd, 400+ AB: Top speed skills among projected full-time players.

Top Spd, -300 AB: Top speed skills among projected part-time players; possible end-game options here.

Position Scarcity: See which positions have deepest speed options.

Top Spd, OB% .330 and above: Top speed skills among those who get on base most often. Best opportunities for stolen bases here.

Top Spd, OB% under .300: Top speed skills among those who have trouble getting on base; worth watching if they can improve OB%.

Top Spd, SBA% over 15%: Top speed skills among those who get the green light most often. Most likely to convert their speed into stolen bases.

Top Spd, SBA% under 10%: Top speed skills among those who are currently not running; sleeper SBs here if given more opportunities.

Batting Average

Top ct%, 400+ AB: Top contact skills among projected full-time players. Contact is strongly correlated to higher BAs.

Top ct%, -300 AB: Top contact skills among projected part-time players; possible end-gamers here.

Low ct%, 400+ AB: The poorest contact skills among projected full-time players. Potential BA killers.

Top ct%, bb% over 9%: Top contact skills among the most patient hitters. Best batting average upside here.

Top ct%, bb% under 6%: Top contact skills among the least patient hitters; free-swingers who might be prone to streakiness or lower BAs.

Top ct%, GB% over 50%: Top contact skills among the most extreme ground ball hitters. A ground ball has a higher chance of becoming a hit than a non-HR fly ball so there may be some batting average upside here.

Top ct%, GB% under 40%: Top contact skills from those with lesser ground ball tendencies. These players make contact but hit more fly balls, which tend to convert to hits at a lower rate than GB.

Potential Skills Gainers/Faders
Expected Stats vs. Actual

These charts look to identify upcoming changes in performance by highlighting 2021 results that were in conflict with their corresponding skill indicators as well as our own set of expected statistics (xBA, xHR, xSB for hitters; xW, xERA, xWHIP for pitchers). Use these as a check on recency bias, as players here could compile stats in the upcoming season that look every different than the one just completed. Additional details are provided on the page in which the charts appear.

Pitching Skills

Top K-BB%: Leaders in projected K-BB% rates.

Top BB%: Leaders in fewest projected walks allowed.

Top K%: Leaders in projected strikeout rate.

Top Ground Ball Rate: GB pitchers tend to have lower ERAs (and higher WHIP) than fly ball pitchers.

Top Fly Ball Rate: FB pitchers tend to have higher ERAs (and lower WHIP) than ground ball pitchers.

High GB, Low K%: GB pitchers tend to have lower K rates, but these are the most extreme examples.

High GB, High K%: The best at dominating hitters and keeping the ball down. These are the pitchers who keep runners off the bases and batted balls in the park, a skills combination that is the most valuable a pitcher can own.

Lowest xERA: Leaders in projected skills-based ERA.

Top BPX: Two lists of top skilled pitchers. For starters, those projected to be rotation regulars (160+ IP) and fringe starters with skill (<120 IP). For relievers, those projected to be frontline closers (10+ saves) and high-skilled bullpen fillers (<10 saves).

Risk Management

These lists include players who've accumulated the most days on the injured list over the past five years (Grade "F" in Health) and whose performance was the most consistent over the past three years. Also listed are the most reliable batters and pitchers overall, with a focus on positional and skills reliability. As a reminder, reliability in this context is not tied to skill level; it is a gauge of which players manage to accumulate playing time and post consistent output from year to year, whether that output is good or bad.

Head-to-Head Tools

2021 Usable Weeks for hitters and Aggregate Consistency Score for pitchers. For more detail, see the accompanying articles on pages 81-82.

Daily Fantasy Indicators

Players splits, teams and park factors designed to give you an edge in DFS.

BATTER SKILLS RANKINGS — Power

TOP PX, 400+ AB

NAME	POS	PX
Dalbec,Bobby	3	200
Gallo,Joey	7 9	198
Hoskins,Rhys	3	191
Sanó,Miguel	3	189
Tatis Jr.,Fernando	6 9	186
Trout,Mike	8	185
Harper,Bryce	9	184
Acuña,Ronald	9	174
Ohtani,Shohei	0	170
Alvarez,Yordan	0 7	167
Lowe,Brandon	4	167
Buxton,Byron	8	164
Judge,Aaron	0 8 9	162
Schwarber,Kyle	7	161
Duvall,Adam	7 8 9	158
Bradley,Bobby	3	158
Suárez,Eugenio	5 6	157
Devers,Rafael	5	153
Reyes,Franmil	0	153
Hernández,Teoscar	7 9	152
Alonso,Pete	3	151
Wisdom,Patrick	5	150
Springer,George	0 8	150
Muncy,Max	3 4	150
Chapman,Matt	5	150
Soler,Jorge	0 9	149
Renfroe,Hunter	9	148
Castellanos,Nick	9	147
O Neill,Tyler	7	147
Happ,Ian	7 8	146
Stanton,Giancarlo	0 0	145
Martinez,J.D.	0 7	145
Smith,Will	2	145
Grandal,Yasmani	2	145
Ramirez,Jose	5	145
Cron,C.J.	3	144
Voit,Luke	3	144
Olson,Matt	3	143
Story,Trevor	6	143
Tucker,Kyle	9	142

TOP PX, 300 or fewer AB

NAME	POS	PX
Aquino,Aristides	7 9	161
Pratto,Nick	3	158
Ruf,Darin	3 7	152
Nuñez,Dom	2	150
Ríos,Edwin	3	149
Hiura,Keston	3	146
Luplow,Jordan	8	144
Phillips,Brett	8 9	140
Siri,Jose	0	139
Miller,Brad	3 0	138
Rooker,Brent	7	137
Garlick,Kyle	0	136
Alford,Anthony	7	133
Rogers,Jake	2	132
Guzmán,Ronald	3	129
Frazier,Clint	7 9	128
Sheets,Gavin	0	127
Odor,Rougned	4 5	124
Díaz,Lewin	3	123
Taylor,Tyrone	7 9	120
Davis,Brennen	0	120
Pinder,Chad	9	120
Cruz,Oneil	6	119

POSITIONAL SCARCITY

NAME	POS	PX
Ohtani,Shohei	DH	170
Alvarez,Yordan	2	167
Judge,Aaron	3	162
Reyes,Franmil	4	153
Springer,George	5	150
Soler,Jorge	6	149
Garver,Mitch	CA	153
Nuñez,Dom	2	150
Smith,Will	3	145
Grandal,Yasmani	4	145
Haase,Eric	5	143
Jeffers,Ryan	6	142
Perez,Salvador	7	139
Sánchez,Gary	8	138
Dalbec,Bobby	1B	200
Hoskins,Rhys	2	191
Sanó,Miguel	3	189
Belt,Brandon	4	163
Bradley,Bobby	5	158
Pratto,Nick	6	158
Ruf,Darin	7	152
Alonso,Pete	8	151
Muncy,Max	9	150
Ríos,Edwin	10	149
Lowe,Brandon	2B	167
Muncy,Max	2	150
Báez,Javier	3	138
Taylor,Chris	4	128
McMahon,Ryan	5	127
Semien,Marcus	6	125
Odor,Rougned	7	124
Albies,Ozzie	8	123
Suárez,Eugenio	3B	157
Devers,Rafael	2	153
Wisdom,Patrick	3	150
Chapman,Matt	4	150
Ramirez,Jose	5	145
Donaldson,Josh	6	138
Riley,Austin	7	138
Moustakas,Mike	8	127
McMahon,Ryan	9	127
Odor,Rougned	10	124
Tatis Jr.,Fernando	SS	186
Suárez,Eugenio	2	157
Story,Trevor	3	143
Adames,Willy	4	141
Báez,Javier	5	138
Taylor,Chris	6	128
Semien,Marcus	7	125
Swanson,Dansby	8	124
Gallo,Joey	OF	198
Tatis Jr.,Fernando	2	186
Trout,Mike	3	185
Harper,Bryce	4	184
Acuña,Ronald	5	174
Alvarez,Yordan	6	167
Hilliard,Sam	7	165
Buxton,Byron	8	164
Judge,Aaron	9	162
Aquino,Aristides	10	161
Schwarber,Kyle	11	161
Duvall,Adam	12	158
Ruf,Darin	13	152
Hernández,Teoscar	14	152
Springer,George	15	150
Soler,Jorge	16	149

TOP PX, ct% over 75%

NAME	ct%	PX
Devers,Rafael	76	153
Springer,George	76	150
Castellanos,Nick	75	147
Ramirez,Jose	84	145
Olson,Matt	76	143
Tucker,Kyle	79	142
Perez,Salvador	75	139
Soto,Juan	80	138
Winker,Jesse	80	138
Pollock,A.J.	78	134
Freeman,Freddie	82	132
Abreu,José	76	132
Guerrero Jr.,Vladimir	83	127
Goldschmidt,Paul	76	127
Moustakas,Mike	76	127
Jansen,Danny	78	126
Betts,Mookie	83	125
Semien,Marcus	79	125
Reynolds,Bryan	77	125
Meadows,Austin	75	124
Albies,Ozzie	79	123
Rendon,Anthony	83	123
Longoria,Evan	76	122
Gurriel Jr.,Lourdes	78	122
Ozuna,Marcell	77	121
Seager,Kyle	77	121
Tellez,Rowdy	78	120
Taylor,Tyrone	76	120
Bichette,Bo	78	120
Santander,Anthony	78	119
Dickerson,Alex	75	119
Machado,Manny	82	118
Marte,Ketel	84	117
Seager,Corey	81	116
Kirilloff,Alex	77	116
Bell,Josh	77	116
Grichuk,Randal	76	116
Hernández,Kiké	79	115
Arenado,Nolan	84	115
Wade Jr.,LaMonte	77	115

TOP PX, ct% under 70%

NAME	ct%	PX
Dalbec,Bobby	63	200
Gallo,Joey	57	198
Sanó,Miguel	58	189
Tatis Jr.,Fernando	69	186
Acuña,Ronald	70	174
Ohtani,Shohei	67	170
Lowe,Brandon	68	167
Hilliard,Sam	62	165
Judge,Aaron	68	162
Aquino,Aristides	62	161
Schwarber,Kyle	68	161
Duvall,Adam	68	158
Bradley,Bobby	62	158
Pratto,Nick	63	158
Suárez,Eugenio	67	157
Garver,Mitch	70	153
Reyes,Franmil	66	153
Hernández,Teoscar	70	152
Wisdom,Patrick	58	150
Nuñez,Dom	65	150
Chapman,Matt	65	150
Soler,Jorge	69	149
Brown,Seth	67	149

TOP PX, FB% over 40%

NAME	FB%	PX
Dalbec,Bobby	44	200
Gallo,Joey	52	198
Hoskins,Rhys	51	191
Sanó,Miguel	42	189
Trout,Mike	44	185
Harper,Bryce	40	184
Acuña,Ronald	43	174
Lowe,Brandon	43	167
Buxton,Byron	41	164
Belt,Brandon	48	163
Aquino,Aristides	51	161
Schwarber,Kyle	40	161
Duvall,Adam	53	158
Pratto,Nick	44	158
Suárez,Eugenio	45	157
Garver,Mitch	44	153
Alonso,Pete	43	151
Wisdom,Patrick	45	150
Nuñez,Dom	51	150
Springer,George	43	150
Muncy,Max	41	150
Chapman,Matt	49	150
Soler,Jorge	41	149
Brown,Seth	48	149
Ríos,Edwin	48	149
Renfroe,Hunter	45	148
O Neill,Tyler	41	147
Hiura,Keston	41	146
Martinez,J.D.	41	145
Smith,Will	49	145
Grandal,Yasmani	40	145
Ramirez,Jose	46	145
Luplow,Jordan	49	144
Cron,C.J.	42	144
Haase,Eric	42	143
Olson,Matt	44	143
Story,Trevor	45	143
Tucker,Kyle	44	142
Phillips,Brett	42	140
Siri,Jose	42	139

TOP PX, FB% under 35%

NAME	FB%	PX
Reyes,Franmil	34	153
Ruf,Darin	31	152
Stanton,Giancarlo	34	145
Báez,Javier	33	138
Soto,Juan	31	138
Winker,Jesse	32	138
Jiménez,Eloy	30	135
Walsh,Jared	32	133
Freeman,Freddie	34	132
Abreu,José	34	132
Sánchez,Jesús	33	130
Guzmán,Ronald	31	129
Arozarena,Randy	33	127
Guerrero Jr.,Vladimir	34	127
Contreras,Willson	33	126
Laureano,Ramón	35	123
Davis,J.D.	30	121
Pinder,Chad	33	120
Bichette,Bo	32	120
Candelario,Jeimer	35	119
Ward,Taylor	34	117
Mancini,Trey	31	117
Marte,Ketel	33	117

BATTER SKILLS RANKINGS — Speed

TOP Spd, 400+ AB

NAME	POS	Spd
Hampson,Garrett	4 8	151
Tapia,Raimel	7	149
Turner,Trea	4 6	147
Rosario,Amed	6	143
Chisholm Jr.,Jazz	4 6	139
Lux,Gavin	4 6	139
Smith,Pavin	3 7 8 9	139
Franco,Wander	6	139
Straw,Myles	8	138
Mullins,Cedric	8	133
Anderson,Tim	6	132
Mondesi,Adalberto	5	131
Baddoo,Akil	7 8	131
Story,Trevor	6	131
Lopez,Nicky	6	130
Albies,Ozzie	4	130
Taveras,Leody	8	130
Marte,Starling	8	129
Arozarena,Randy	7 9	129
Betts,Mookie	8 9	128
Solak,Nick	4	128
Ohtani,Shohei	0	127
Nimmo,Brandon	8	127
Reynolds,Bryan	8	124
Canha,Mark	7 8 9	124
Bader,Harrison	8	123
Dozier,Hunter	5 9	123
Thomas,Lane	8	122
Taylor,Chris	4 6 7 8	122
Newman,Kevin	6	121
Kiner-Falefa,Isiah	6	120
Wendle,Joe	5 6	119
Merrifield,Whit	4 0	119
Hays,Austin	7 9	119
Marsh,Brandon	8	118
Tatis Jr.,Fernando	6 9	118
Gamel,Ben	7 8	118
Sánchez,Jesús	7 9	117
Arraez,Luis	4 5 7	117
Bryant,Kris	5 7 9	117

TOP Spd, 300 or fewer AB

NAME	POS	Spd
Hill,Derek	8	172
Quinn,Roman	8	165
McCarthy,Jake	0	165
Perdomo,Geraldo	6	161
Sierra,Magneuris	8	160
Thomas,Alek	8	151
Alcantara,Sergio	4 6	146
Cruz,Oneil	6	144
Wade,Tyler	5 6 0	143
Phillips,Brett	8 9	139
Siri,Jose	0	137
Difo,Wilmer	4	137
Clement,Ernie	4	136
Martin,Richie	6	136
Park,Hoy Jun	4	136
Alford,Anthony	7	134
Williams,Luke	0	133
Cameron,Daz	0	133
Hernandez,Yonny	5	130
Burger,Jake	5	129
Jones,Jahmai	4	129
Ibáñez,Andy	4	128
Duggar,Steven	8	127

POSITIONAL SCARCITY

NAME	POS	Spd
Ohtani,Shohei	DH	127
Mountcastle,Ryan	2	108
Haniger,Mitch	3	108
Springer,George	4	107
Calhoun,Willie	5	104
Casas,Triston	6	104
Varsho,Daulton	CA	116
Melendez,MJ	2	114
Rogers,Jake	3	114
Realmuto,J.T.	4	108
Adams,Riley	5	108
Contreras,William	6	104
Nuñez,Dom	7	103
Jackson,Alex	8	102
Smith,Pavin	1B	139
Pratto,Nick	2	120
Cronenworth,Jake	3	116
Miller,Brad	4	114
Chang,Yu	5	108
Mountcastle,Ryan	6	108
Wade Jr.,LaMonte	7	107
Fuentes,Joshua	8	105
Jones,Taylor	9	105
LeMahieu,DJ	10	104
Castro,Willi	2B	155
Sosa,Edmundo	2	155
Hampson,Garrett	3	151
Madrigal,Nick	4	148
Turner,Trea	5	147
Alcantara,Sergio	6	146
Giménez,Andrés	7	141
Chisholm Jr.,Jazz	8	139
Wade,Tyler	3B	143
Mondesi,Adalberto	2	131
Hernandez,Yonny	3	130
Burger,Jake	4	129
Gutierrez,Kelvin	5	126
Dozier,Hunter	6	123
Torreyes,Ronald	7	122
Espinal,Santiago	8	121
Wendle,Joe	9	119
Arraez,Luis	10	117
Perdomo,Geraldo	SS	161
Castro,Willi	2	155
Sosa,Edmundo	3	155
Turner,Trea	4	147
Alcantara,Sergio	5	146
Cruz,Oneil	6	144
Wade,Tyler	7	143
Rosario,Amed	8	143
Hill,Derek	OF	172
Quinn,Roman	2	165
McCarthy,Jake	3	165
Sierra,Magneuris	4	160
Reyes,Victor	5	152
Hampson,Garrett	6	151
Thomas,Alek	7	151
Tapia,Raimel	8	149
Gordon,Nick	9	147
Kiermaier,Kevin	10	144
Ortega,Rafael	11	144
Mateo,Jorge	12	144
De La Cruz,Bryan	13	144
Wade,Tyler	14	143
Duran,Jarren	15	140
Phillips,Brett	16	139

TOP Spd, .330+ OBP

NAME	OBP	Spd
Sosa,Edmundo	331	155
Madrigal,Nick	364	148
Turner,Trea	358	147
Smith,Pavin	341	139
Franco,Wander	356	139
Straw,Myles	338	138
Greene,Riley	334	137
Park,Hoy Jun	336	136
Mullins,Cedric	335	133
Story,Trevor	346	131
Lopez,Nicky	335	130
Hernandez,Yonny	352	130
Marte,Starling	353	129
Arozarena,Randy	352	129
Barrero,Jose	345	129
Betts,Mookie	377	128
Ohtani,Shohei	352	127
Nimmo,Brandon	382	127
Reynolds,Bryan	371	124
Canha,Mark	363	124
Taylor,Chris	340	122
Martin,Austin	346	122
Espinal,Santiago	349	121
Urías,Ramón	344	120
Tatis Jr.,Fernando	361	118
Gamel,Ben	337	118
Arraez,Luis	359	117
Gardner,Brett	334	117
Bryant,Kris	357	117
Kemp,Tony	346	117
Verdugo,Alex	354	117
Cronenworth,Jake	349	116
Robert,Luis	330	116
Ward,Taylor	344	116
Melendez,MJ	339	114
Crawford,J.P.	337	114
Tucker,Kyle	345	114
Rojas,Josh	330	113
Berti,Jon	341	113
Bellinger,Cody	339	113

TOP Spd, OBP under .300

NAME	OBP	Spd
Hill,Derek	289	172
Quinn,Roman	298	165
McCarthy,Jake	295	165
Perdomo,Geraldo	295	161
Sierra,Magneuris	291	160
Castro,Willi	289	155
Hampson,Garrett	297	151
Gordon,Nick	299	147
Mateo,Jorge	291	144
Duran,Jarren	277	140
Phillips,Brett	289	139
Clement,Ernie	278	136
Martin,Richie	269	136
Williams,Luke	285	133
Mondesi,Adalberto	289	131
Burger,Jake	282	129
Jones,Jahmai	296	129
Tucker,Cole	283	126
Gutierrez,Kelvin	288	126
Kingery,Scott	286	125
Hilliard,Sam	297	122
Torreyes,Ronald	277	122
Newman,Kevin	287	121

TOP Spd, SBA% over 15%

NAME	SBA%	Spd
Hill,Derek	18%	172
Quinn,Roman	38%	165
McCarthy,Jake	29%	165
Sierra,Magneuris	18%	160
Castro,Willi	15%	155
Reyes,Victor	16%	152
Hampson,Garrett	20%	151
Thomas,Alek	17%	151
Tapia,Raimel	17%	149
Gordon,Nick	22%	147
Turner,Trea	18%	147
Ortega,Rafael	17%	144
Cruz,Oneil	21%	144
Mateo,Jorge	23%	144
Wade,Tyler	40%	143
Giménez,Andrés	21%	141
Duran,Jarren	20%	140
Chisholm Jr.,Jazz	22%	139
Phillips,Brett	22%	139
Straw,Myles	16%	138
Siri,Jose	23%	137
Martin,Richie	20%	136
Alford,Anthony	21%	134
Margot,Manuel	16%	133
Mullins,Cedric	18%	133
Williams,Luke	16%	133
Cameron,Daz	19%	133
Anderson,Tim	15%	132
Mondesi,Adalberto	55%	131
Baddoo,Akil	16%	131
Story,Trevor	16%	131
Hernandez,Yonny	26%	130
Albies,Ozzie	15%	130
Taveras,Leody	21%	130
Marte,Starling	25%	129
Arozarena,Randy	16%	129

TOP Spd, SBA% under 10%

NAME	SBA%	Spd
Madrigal,Nick	8%	148
Alcantara,Sergio	8%	146
De La Cruz,Bryan	9%	144
Lux,Gavin	7%	139
Smith,Pavin	5%	139
Difo,Wilmer	5%	137
Clement,Ernie	8%	136
Burger,Jake	4%	129
Solak,Nick	9%	128
Ibáñez,Andy	5%	128
Nimmo,Brandon	8%	127
Gutierrez,Kelvin	7%	126
Reynolds,Bryan	6%	124
Canha,Mark	9%	124
Dozier,Hunter	9%	123
Taylor,Chris	9%	122
Torreyes,Ronald	6%	122
Newman,Kevin	7%	121
Espinal,Santiago	9%	121
Urías,Ramón	7%	120
Castro,Harold	5%	120
Hays,Austin	7%	119
Marsh,Brandon	9%	118
Gamel,Ben	8%	118
Aquino,Aristides	9%	118
Sánchez,Jesús	5%	117
Arraez,Luis	5%	117

BATTER SKILLS RANKINGS— Batting Average

TOP ct%, 400+ AB

NAME	ct%	BA
Arraez,Luis	90	302
Fletcher,David	90	275
Newman,Kevin	89	243
Brantley,Michael	88	303
Gurriel,Yuli	87	286
Franco,Wander	87	301
Frazier,Adam	86	276
Rojas,Miguel	86	276
Bregman,Alex	86	264
LeMahieu,DJ	86	278
McNeil,Jeff	86	279
Simmons,Andrelton	85	245
Kiner-Falefa,Isiah	85	266
Marte,Ketel	84	300
Lopez,Nicky	84	270
Arenado,Nolan	84	262
Merrifield,Whit	84	284
Rosario,Eddie	84	265
Segura,Jean	84	278
Ramirez,Jose	84	273
Altuve,Jose	84	280
Rendon,Anthony	83	284
Harrison,Josh	83	265
Rizzo,Anthony	83	260
Guerrero Jr.,Vladimir	83	300
Betts,Mookie	83	286
Cronenworth,Jake	82	275
Naylor,Josh	82	257
Tapia,Raimel	82	279
Edman,Tommy	82	262
Machado,Manny	82	281
Verdugo,Alex	82	295
Turner,Trea	82	303
Turner,Justin	82	273
Freeman,Freddie	82	304
Santana,Carlos	81	235
Seager,Corey	81	297
Blackmon,Charlie	81	290
García,Luis	81	265
Polanco,Jorge	81	273
Schwindel,Frank	81	266
Lindor,Francisco	81	255
Vázquez,Christian	81	262
Winker,Jesse	80	288
Marte,Starling	80	290
Smith,Pavin	80	271
Toro,Abraham	80	245
Soto,Juan	80	315
Benintendi,Andrew	79	276
Peralta,David	79	265
France,Ty	79	287
Albies,Ozzie	79	267
Bogaerts,Xander	79	291
Mullins,Cedric	79	269
Semien,Marcus	79	255
Tucker,Kyle	79	279
Hosmer,Eric	79	275
Crawford,J.P.	79	261
Kepler,Max	79	230
Hernández,Kiké	79	251
Urshela,Gio	79	273
Escobar,Eduardo	78	250
Bichette,Bo	78	288
Rodgers,Brendan	78	274
Straw,Myles	78	264
Gurriel Jr.,Lourdes	78	281

LOW ct%, 400+ AB

NAME	ct%	BA
Gallo,Joey	57	214
Wisdom,Patrick	58	218
Sanó,Miguel	58	224
Bradley,Bobby	62	210
Dalbec,Bobby	63	241
Chapman,Matt	65	225
Marsh,Brandon	65	241
Goodrum,Niko	65	228
O Neill,Tyler	65	257
Happ,Ian	66	247
Adell,Jo	66	248
Reyes,Franmil	66	259
Ohtani,Shohei	67	251
Báez,Javier	67	264
Chisholm Jr.,Jazz	67	251
Adames,Willy	67	263
García,Adolis	67	227
Suárez,Eugenio	67	226
Myers,Wil	68	260
Taylor,Chris	68	258
Mondesi,Adalberto	68	254
Taylor,Michael A.	68	232
Dozier,Hunter	68	231
Lowe,Brandon	68	261
Schwarber,Kyle	68	256
Judge,Aaron	68	278
Duvall,Adam	68	236
Voit,Luke	68	253
Moncada,Yoán	69	268
Tatis Jr.,Fernando	69	286
Thomas,Lane	69	242
Contreras,Willson	69	247
Stanton,Giancarlo	69	262
Gamel,Ben	69	249
Soler,Jorge	69	237
Acuña,Ronald	70	275

TOP ct%, 300 or fewer AB

NAME	ct%	BA
Astudillo,Willians	95	252
Alberto,Hanser	89	275
La Stella,Tommy	88	256
Torreyes,Ronald	86	241
Espinal,Santiago	85	291
Kirk,Alejandro	85	262
Canó,Robinson	85	286
Kemp,Tony	85	253
Ibáñez,Andy	84	273
Pujols,Albert	84	241
Clement,Ernie	83	223
Profar,Jurickson	83	240
Andújar,Miguel	83	251
Daza,Yonathan	82	268
Franco,Maikel	82	221
Paredes,Isaac	82	253
Díaz,Aledmys	82	256
Schrock,Max	82	251
Estrada,Thairo	81	264
Dickerson,Corey	80	276
Beaty,Matt	80	265
Ramos,Wilson	80	252
Bruján,Vidal	80	247
Knizner,Andrew	79	217
Dubón,Mauricio	79	258
Duffy,Matt	79	279
Mejía,Francisco	79	260

TOP ct%, bb% over 9%

NAME	bb%	ct%
Bregman,Alex	13	86
LeMahieu,DJ	9	86
Kirk,Alejandro	10	85
Kemp,Tony	11	85
Ramirez,Jose	12	84
Rendon,Anthony	13	83
Profar,Jurickson	10	83
Rizzo,Anthony	10	83
Guerrero Jr.,Vladimir	10	83
Betts,Mookie	12	83
Cronenworth,Jake	9	82
Nola,Austin	9	82
Machado,Manny	10	82
Paredes,Isaac	12	82
Turner,Justin	10	82
Freeman,Freddie	13	82
Díaz,Yandy	13	82
Posey,Buster	11	81
Santana,Carlos	15	81
Seager,Corey	10	81
Lindor,Francisco	10	81
Cain,Lorenzo	9	81
Winker,Jesse	12	80
Smith,Pavin	9	80
Toro,Abraham	9	80
Heyward,Jason	10	80
Soto,Juan	21	80
Bogaerts,Xander	10	79
Semien,Marcus	10	79
Crawford,J.P.	9	79
Kepler,Max	11	79
Hernández,Kiké	10	79
Rutschman,Adley	11	78
Jansen,Danny	10	78
Stephenson,Tyler	10	78
Straw,Myles	10	78
Senzel,Nick	9	78
Hernandez,Yonny	14	78
Akiyama,Shogo	10	78
Lowrie,Jed	10	78

TOP ct%, bb% under 6%

NAME	bb%	ct%
Astudillo,Willians	2	95
Madrigal,Nick	5	93
Fletcher,David	6	90
Newman,Kevin	5	89
Alberto,Hanser	2	89
Torreyes,Ronald	5	86
Calhoun,Willie	6	85
Iglesias,José	4	85
Kiner-Falefa,Isiah	6	85
Merrifield,Whit	6	84
Molina,Yadier	5	84
Clement,Ernie	5	83
Harrison,Josh	6	83
Andújar,Miguel	4	83
Daza,Yonathan	5	82
Edman,Tommy	6	82
Schrock,Max	6	82
Ramirez,Harold	4	81
García,Luis	5	81
Trevino,Jose	4	81
Estrada,Thairo	6	81
Schwindel,Frank	5	81
Ramos,Wilson	6	80

TOP ct%, GB% over 50%

NAME	GB%	ct%
Madrigal,Nick	58	93
LeMahieu,DJ	52	86
Simmons,Andrelton	54	85
Kiner-Falefa,Isiah	54	85
Lopez,Nicky	57	84
Segura,Jean	51	84
Daza,Yonathan	56	82
Naylor,Josh	51	82
Tapia,Raimel	60	82
Hoerner,Nico	50	82
Díaz,Yandy	54	82
Ramirez,Harold	54	81
García,Luis	54	81
Estrada,Thairo	52	81
Cain,Lorenzo	51	81
Marte,Starling	53	80
Ramos,Wilson	55	80
Soto,Juan	50	80
Knizner,Andrew	55	79
Duffy,Matt	51	79
Peralta,David	53	79
Hosmer,Eric	54	79
Rodgers,Brendan	50	78
Hernandez,Yonny	52	78
Akiyama,Shogo	56	78
Rosario,Amed	52	78
Sosa,Edmundo	51	78
Bell,Josh	52	77
Solak,Nick	54	77
Sierra,Magneuris	52	77
Rengifo,Luis	50	77
Anderson,Tim	53	77
Ruiz,Rio	51	76
García,Leury	54	76
Gordon,Nick	53	76
Caratini,Victor	52	76
Arroyo,Christian	50	74
Berti,Jon	62	74
Hernandez,Yadiel	54	74
Pham,Tommy	50	74

TOP ct%, GB% under 40%

NAME	GB%	ct%
Bregman,Alex	36	86
Flores,Wilmer	36	86
Espinal,Santiago	40	85
Kemp,Tony	37	85
Arenado,Nolan	34	84
Merrifield,Whit	40	84
Rosario,Eddie	36	84
Ramirez,Jose	34	84
Gregorius,Didi	37	84
Ibáñez,Andy	37	84
Clement,Ernie	38	83
Rendon,Anthony	33	83
Harrison,Josh	39	83
Betts,Mookie	34	83
Machado,Manny	39	82
Paredes,Isaac	39	82
Turner,Justin	35	82
Freeman,Freddie	39	82
Schrock,Max	31	82
Polanco,Jorge	33	81
Solano,Donovan	39	81
Lindor,Francisco	39	81
Dubón,Mauricio	40	79

POTENTIAL SKILLS GAINERS AND FADERS — Batters

Power Gainers

Batters whose 2021 Power Index (PX) fell significantly short of their underlying power skill (xPX). If they show the same xPX skill in 2022, they are good candidates for more power output.

Power Faders

Batters whose 2021 Power Index (PX) noticeably outpaced their underlying power skill (xPX). If they show the same xPX skill in 2022, they are good candidates for less power output.

BA Gainers

Batters who had strong Hard Contact Index levels in 2021, but lower hit rates (h%). Since base hits come most often on hard contact, if these batters can make hard contact at the same strong rate again in 2022, they may get better results in terms of hit rate, resulting in a batting average improvement.

BA Faders

Batters who had weak Hard Contact Index levels in 2021, but higher hit rates (h%). Since base hits come most often on hard contact, if these batters only make hard contact at the same weak rate again in 2022, they may get worse results in terms of hit rate, resulting in a batting average decline.

PX GAINERS

NAME	PX	xPX
Carpenter,Matt	85	161
Lowrie,Jed	96	150
Calhoun,Kole	85	145
Hampson,Garrett	88	139
Casali,Curtis	99	136
Benintendi,Andrew	95	133
Short,Zack	95	133
Nido,Tomas	66	132
Gamel,Ben	95	129
Perez,Michael	95	124
Marsh,Brandon	81	122
Lagares,Juan	89	119
Gomes,Yan	95	118
Bote,David	76	117
Pham,Tommy	96	117
Heim,Jonah	94	117
Polanco,Gregory	91	116
Biggio,Cavan	86	111
Bellinger,Cody	82	110
Molina,Yadier	68	110
Farmer,Kyle	86	109
Cabrera,Miguel	76	107
Smith,Dominic	75	107
Reddick,Josh	77	106
Alberto,Hanser	79	101
Maldonado,Martin	83	101

PX FADERS

NAME	PX	xPX
Acuna,Ronald	187	139
Schwarber,Kyle	176	136
Lowe,Brandon	172	137
Hilliard,Sam	168	123
Jansen,Danny	147	117
Cron,C.J.	146	115
Sheets,Gavin	145	110
Stanton,Giancarlo	145	113
Schwindel,Frank	144	107
Haase,Eric	142	105
Riley,Austin	139	111
Sanchez,Gary	132	103
Abreu,Jose	127	99
Chang,Yu	124	82
Arozarena,Randy	124	89
Arroyo,Christian	120	84
Davis,J.D.	119	95
Slater,Austin	114	88
Chisholm,Jazz	111	88
D Arnaud,Travis	107	80
Ramos,Wilson	105	66
Moustakas,Mike	105	64
Garcia,Luis	101	67
Brinson,Lewis	94	62
Reyes,Victor	94	65
Schoop,Jonathan	90	66
Culberson,Charlie	90	62
Mejia,Francisco	90	71
Stephenson,Tyler	89	66
Marte,Starling	88	69
Mateo,Jorge	87	61
Gregorius,Didi	86	65
Franco,Maikel	85	65

BA GAINERS

NAME	h%	HctX
Ramirez,Jose	26	136
Pujols,Albert	23	129
Donaldson,Josh	27	124
Grandal,Yasmani	25	122
Muncy,Max	26	122
Sheets,Gavin	27	121
Bote,David	24	121
Calhoun,Willie	27	120
Diaz,Elias	25	118
Heim,Jonah	21	116
Arenado,Nolan	25	115
Kirk,Alejandro	24	115
Santana,Carlos	23	115
Kepler,Max	23	113
Ramos,Wilson	21	112
Soler,Jorge	25	111
Seager,Kyle	23	110
Meadows,Austin	25	110
McCutchen,Andrew	25	108
Rizzo,Anthony	26	108
Flores,Wilmer	27	108
Higashioka,Kyle	20	107
Grichuk,Randal	27	107
Garcia,Luis	27	105
Peters,DJ	24	104
Jansen,Danny	23	103
McKinstry,Zach	27	103
Lindor,Francisco	25	103
Polanco,Gregory	27	103
La Stella,Tommy	26	103
Hoskins,Rhys	27	101
DeJong,Paul	22	100
Moreland,Mitch	26	100
Murphy,Tom	27	100
Rojas,Jose	26	99
Pina,Manny	16	99

BA FADERS

NAME	h%	HctX
Escobar,Alcides	34	70
Straw,Myles	34	70
Davis,J.D.	43	78
Difo,Wilmer	34	78
Duggar,Steven	35	81
Larnach,Trevor	34	82
Kiermaier,Kevin	35	82
Daza,Yonathan	35	82
Myers,Wil	34	83
Garcia,Leury	34	83
Duffy,Matt	35	83
Carlson,Dylan	34	84
Ortega,Rafael	35	86
Frazier,Adam	34	86
Espinal,Santiago	35	86
Rojas,Josh	35	87
Lopez,Nicky	35	87
Arozarena,Randy	37	88
Baddoo,Akil	34	90
Castro,Harold	36	91
McCormick,Chas	36	93
Rosario,Amed	34	93
Baez,Javier	36	95
Alfaro,Jorge	35	95
Stephenson,Tyler	34	96
Cooper,Garrett	38	96
Marsh,Brandon	41	99
Posey,Buster	35	100
De La Cruz,Bryan	38	100
Castro,Starlin	34	101
Crawford,Brandon	34	102
Lowe,Nate	34	103
Riley,Austin	38	104
Marte,Starling	37	106
Nimmo,Brandon	37	106
Anderson,Tim	37	107

EXPECTED STATS vs. ACTUAL — Batters

BA Underperformers (min. 250 AB)

NAME	BA	xBA	Diff
Bradley,Jackie	163	205	-42
Heim,Jonah	196	238	-42
Bellinger,Cody	165	203	-38
Kepler,Max	211	247	-36
Franco,Maikel	210	245	-35
Kelenic,Jarred	181	215	-34
Heyward,Jason	214	244	-30
Gregorius,Didi	209	238	-29
McCutchen,Andrew	222	251	-29
Newman,Kevin	226	255	-29
Suarez,Eugenio	198	227	-29
Zunino,Mike	216	245	-29
McKinney,Billy	192	220	-28
Muncy,Max	249	277	-28
Gonzalez,Marwin	199	226	-27
Maldonado,Martin	172	198	-26
Seager,Kyle	212	238	-26
Diaz,Elias	246	270	-24
Hedges,Austin	178	202	-24
DeJong,Paul	197	220	-23
Eaton,Adam	201	224	-23

HR Underperformers

NAME	HR	xHR	Diff
Goldschmidt,Paul	31	49	-18
Alvarez,Yordan	33	46	-13
Dalbec,Bobby	25	38	-13
Ohtani,Shohei	46	59	-13
Freeman,Freddie	31	43	-12
Lowrie,Jed	14	26	-12
Reynolds,Bryan	24	35	-11
Candelario,Jeimer	16	26	-10
Donaldson,Josh	26	36	-10
Harper,Bryce	35	45	-10
Martinez,J.D.	28	38	-10
Soler,Jorge	27	37	-10
Benintendi,Andrew	17	26	-9
Cabrera,Miguel	15	24	-9
Carpenter,Matt	3	12	-9
Crawford,Brandon	24	33	-9
Devers,Rafael	38	47	-9
Hoskins,Rhys	27	36	-9
Muncy,Max	36	45	-9
O Neill,Tyler	34	43	-9
Torres,Gleyber	9	18	-9

SB Underperformers

NAME	SB	xSB	Diff
Straw,Myles	30	52	-22
Fraley,Jake	10	25	-15
Hamilton,Billy	9	22	-13
Crawford,J.P.	3	15	-12
Margot,Manuel	13	25	-12
Villar,Jonathan	14	26	-12
Alford,Anthony	5	16	-11
Carlson,Dylan	2	11	-9
Ramirez,Harold	3	12	-9
Soto,Juan	9	18	-9
Betts,Mookie	10	18	-8
Bogaerts,Xander	5	13	-8
Haniger,Mitch	1	9	-8
Smith,Pavin	1	9	-8
Cronenworth,Jake	4	11	-7
Altuve,Jose	5	11	-6
Benintendi,Andrew	8	14	-6
Brantley,Michael	1	7	-6
Gardner,Brett	4	10	-6
Gurriel,Lourdes	1	7	-6
Heredia,Guillermo	0	6	-6

BA Overperformers (min. 250 AB)

NAME	BA	xBA	Diff
Baez,Javier	265	235	30
Hernandez,Teoscar	296	266	30
Taylor,Chris	254	224	30
Myers,Wil	256	228	28
Rosario,Amed	282	254	28
Baddoo,Akil	259	232	27
Bichette,Bo	298	271	27
Bogaerts,Xander	295	268	27
Kemp,Anthony	279	252	27
Lowe,Nate	264	237	27
Posey,Buster	304	277	27
Schoop,Jonathan	278	251	27
Taylor,Michael	244	217	27
Goldschmidt,Paul	294	268	26
France,Ty	291	266	25
Marte,Ketel	318	293	25
Sosa,Edmundo	271	246	25
Torres,Gleyber	259	234	25
Duggar,Steven	257	233	24
Seager,Corey	306	282	24
Alfaro,Jorge	244	221	23

HR Overperformers

NAME	HR	xHR	Diff
Semien,Marcus	45	37	8
Altuve,Jose	31	24	7
Arenado,Nolan	34	27	7
Gregorius,Didi	13	8	5
Hedges,Austin	10	6	4
Torreyes,Ronald	7	3	4
Walsh,Jared	29	25	4
Diaz,Elias	18	15	3
Flores,Wilmer	18	15	3
Fuentes,Josh	7	4	3
Kemp,Anthony	8	5	3
Nunez,Renato	4	1	3
Pillar,Kevin	15	12	3
Schwindel,Frank	14	11	3
Trammell,Taylor	8	5	3
Wisdom,Patrick	28	25	3
Astudillo,Willians	7	5	2
Barnes,Austin	6	4	2
Beaty,Matt	7	5	2
Engel,Adam	7	5	2
Farmer,Kyle	16	14	2

SB Overperformers

NAME	SB	xSB	Diff
Marte,Starling	47	20	27
Edman,Tommy	30	11	19
Merrifield,Whit	40	24	16
Garcia,Adolis	16	3	13
Baddoo,Akil	18	7	11
Cain,Lorenzo	13	2	11
Taylor,Michael	14	3	11
Torres,Gleyber	14	3	11
Wade,Tyler	17	7	10
Baez,Javier	18	9	9
Laureano,Ramon	12	3	9
Ramirez,Jose	27	18	9
Tatis Jr.,Fernando	25	16	9
Acuna,Ronald	17	9	8
Hernandez,Yonny	11	3	8
Lopez,Nicky	22	14	8
Albies,Ozzie	20	13	7
Bryant,Kris	10	3	7
Fletcher,David	15	8	7
Goldschmidt,Paul	12	5	7
Gordon,Nick	10	3	7

PITCHER SKILLS RANKINGS — Starting Pitchers

Top K-BB%

NAME	K-BB%
deGrom,Jacob	30
Cole,Gerrit	29
Baz,Shane	28
Burnes,Corbin	28
Glasnow,Tyler	27
Sale,Chris	27
Scherzer,Max	26
Bieber,Shane	25
Nola,Aaron	25
Kershaw,Clayton	24
Darvish,Yu	24
May,Dustin	24
Severino,Luis	23
Verlander,Justin	23
Ray,Robbie	23
Paxton,James	23
Detmers,Reid	23
Gausman,Kevin	23
Bauer,Trevor	22
Woodruff,Brandon	22
Kopech,Michael	22
Rodón,Carlos	22
Musgrove,Joe	22
Morton,Charlie	22
Ohtani,Shohei	22
Maeda,Kenta	22
Peralta,Freddy	22
Buehler,Walker	21
Skubal,Tarik	21
McClanahan,Shane	21
Eovaldi,Nathan	21

Top BB%

NAME	BB%
Kershaw,Clayton	4
Mikolas,Miles	5
Paddack,Chris	5
Pineda,Michael	5
Greinke,Zack	5
Means,John	5
Urquidy,José	5
Yarbrough,Ryan	5
Baz,Shane	5
Hendricks,Kyle	5
Manaea,Sean	5
Plesac,Zach	5
Eflin,Zach	6
Irvin,Cole	6
Verlander,Justin	6
Ober,Bailey	6
Ryu,Hyun-Jin	6
Eovaldi,Nathan	6
Soroka,Michael	6
Syndergaard,Noah	6
Kirby,George	6
Bieber,Shane	6
Civale,Aaron	6
Wheeler,Zack	6
Senzatela,Antonio	6
Kelly,Merrill	6
Nola,Aaron	6
Sánchez,Sixto	6
deGrom,Jacob	6
Barria,Jaime	6
Wainwright,Adam	6

Top K%

NAME	K%
Glasnow,Tyler	37
deGrom,Jacob	36
Cole,Gerrit	35
Burnes,Corbin	35
Sale,Chris	34
Baz,Shane	33
Scherzer,Max	33
Ray,Robbie	33
Kopech,Michael	32
Peralta,Freddy	32
Bieber,Shane	32
Snell,Blake	32
Bauer,Trevor	32
Nola,Aaron	31
Detmers,Reid	31
Darvish,Yu	31
Paxton,James	31
May,Dustin	31
Rodón,Carlos	31
Ohtani,Shohei	30
Gil,Luis	30
Lamet,Dinelson	30
Severino,Luis	30
Morton,Charlie	29
Gausman,Kevin	29
Rogers,Trevor	29
Cease,Dylan	29
Skubal,Tarik	29
Verlander,Justin	29
Woodruff,Brandon	29
Manoah,Alek	29

Top Ground Ball Rate

NAME	GB%
Valdez,Framber	65
Sánchez,Sixto	58
Houser,Adrian	57
McCullers,Lance	57
Dobnak,Randy	57
Hudson,Dakota	57
Anderson,Brett	57
Webb,Logan	56
Castillo,Luis	56
Fleming,Josh	56
Keuchel,Dallas	56
Suárez,Ranger	55
Stroman,Marcus	55
Turnbull,Spencer	53
May,Dustin	53
Fried,Max	52
Dunning,Dane	52
Gibson,Kyle	51
Fedde,Erick	51
Soroka,Michael	51
Sandoval,Patrick	51
Ureña,José	51
Syndergaard,Noah	51
Cobb,Alex	51
Senzatela,Antonio	51
Singer,Brady	50
Mills,Alec	50
Alcantara,Sandy	50
Kershaw,Clayton	50
Miley,Wade	50
Márquez,Germán	50

Top Fly Ball Rate

NAME	FB%
Gray,Josiah	54
Jax,Griffin	53
Gil,Luis	52
Dunn,Justin	49
McKenzie,Triston	49
Patino,Luis	49
Kremer,Dean	48
Morgan,Elijah	48
Means,John	47
Kaprielian,James	47
Hernandez,Elieser	47
Peralta,Freddy	47
Garcia,Deivi	47
Ryan,Joe	46
Verlander,Justin	46
Gilbert,Logan	46
Ober,Bailey	46
Odorizzi,Jake	46
Detmers,Reid	46
Urquidy,José	45
Gonsolin,Tony	45
Scherzer,Max	45
Ray,Robbie	44
Skubal,Tarik	44
López,Reynaldo	44
Archer,Chris	44
Boyd,Matthew	44
Velasquez,Vincent	43
Duffy,Danny	43
Kopech,Michael	43
Akin,Keegan	43

High GB, Low K%

NAME	GB%	K%
Sánchez,Sixto	58	21
Houser,Adrian	57	19
Dobnak,Randy	57	15
Hudson,Dakota	57	20
Anderson,Brett	57	14
Fleming,Josh	56	16
Keuchel,Dallas	56	16
Stroman,Marcus	55	21
Turnbull,Spencer	53	22
Gibson,Kyle	51	21
Fedde,Erick	51	19
Soroka,Michael	51	20
Ureña,José	51	15
Cobb,Alex	51	20
Senzatela,Antonio	51	15
Mills,Alec	50	18
Miley,Wade	50	18
Keller,Brad	50	19
Sheffield,Justus	49	20
Mikolas,Miles	49	17
Kim,Kwang-Hyun	49	18
Arrieta,Jake	48	18
Freeland,Kyle	47	18
Wainwright,Adam	47	21
Bubic,Kris	47	21
Mize,Casey	47	19
Oviedo,Johan	46	20
Manning,Matt	46	18
Suarez,José	45	22
Allen,Logan	45	19
Greinke,Zack	45	21

High GB, High K%

NAME	GB%	K%
McCullers,Lance	57	27
Castillo,Luis	56	27
May,Dustin	53	31
Kershaw,Clayton	50	28
Gray,Sonny	49	28
Burnes,Corbin	47	35
Ynoa,Huascar	47	26
Morton,Charlie	47	29
Bieber,Shane	46	32
Glasnow,Tyler	46	37
McClanahan,Shane	45	28
Nola,Aaron	45	31
Contreras,Roansy	45	27
Severino,Luis	45	30
Musgrove,Joe	45	29
Woodruff,Brandon	44	29
deGrom,Jacob	44	36
Sale,Chris	44	34
Eovaldi,Nathan	44	27
Carrasco,Carlos	44	27
Ohtani,Shohei	44	30
Strasburg,Stephen	43	27
Buehler,Walker	43	28
Gallen,Zac	43	27
Brash,Matt	43	29
Montas,Frankie	43	28
Rodriguez,Eduardo	43	27
Flaherty,Jack	43	29
Pivetta,Nick	42	26
Pearson,Nate	42	28
Megill,Tylor	42	28

Lowest xERA

NAME	xERA
Burnes,Corbin	2.81
deGrom,Jacob	2.82
May,Dustin	2.86
Cole,Gerrit	3.07
Sale,Chris	3.07
Bieber,Shane	3.08
Kershaw,Clayton	3.09
Glasnow,Tyler	3.12
Nola,Aaron	3.19
Baz,Shane	3.20
Webb,Logan	3.25
Severino,Luis	3.25
Morton,Charlie	3.31
Valdez,Framber	3.33
Woodruff,Brandon	3.33
Musgrove,Joe	3.39
Wheeler,Zack	3.40
McCullers,Lance	3.41
McClanahan,Shane	3.41
Darvish,Yu	3.42
Syndergaard,Noah	3.42
Scherzer,Max	3.43
Castillo,Luis	3.43
Gausman,Kevin	3.44
Buehler,Walker	3.46
Ohtani,Shohei	3.47
Fried,Max	3.54
Gray,Sonny	3.54
Paxton,James	3.54
Suárez,Ranger	3.55
Otto Jr.,Glenn	3.55

Top BPX, 160+ IP

NAME	BPX
Burnes,Corbin	178
Cole,Gerrit	178
Sale,Chris	170
Bieber,Shane	167
Nola,Aaron	161
Scherzer,Max	158
Woodruff,Brandon	143
Gausman,Kevin	142
Musgrove,Joe	141
Eovaldi,Nathan	138
Buehler,Walker	133
Wheeler,Zack	132
Ray,Robbie	132
Manaea,Sean	132
Montas,Frankie	130
Skubal,Tarik	127
Rogers,Trevor	123
Giolito,Lucas	122
Castillo,Luis	121
Lynn,Lance	119
Rodriguez,Eduardo	118
Fried,Max	117
Means,John	115
Márquez,Germán	113
Alcantara,Sandy	113
Garcia,Luis	112
Mahle,Tyler	111
Berríos,José	111
Valdez,Framber	110
Urías,Julio	106
Gallen,Zac	106

Top BPX, <120 IP

NAME	BPX
May,Dustin	159
Glasnow,Tyler	153
Paxton,James	142
Syndergaard,Noah	139
Verlander,Justin	139
Maeda,Kenta	135
Bauer,Trevor	132
Contreras,Roansy	125
Heaney,Andrew	120
McKay,Brendan	118
Strasburg,Stephen	117
Lamet,Dinelson	111
Kluber,Corey	110
Sánchez,Sixto	110
Otto Jr.,Glenn	108
Brash,Matt	106
Soroka,Michael	105
Liberatore,Matthew	104
Wacha,Michael	104
Kirby,George	103
Urquidy,José	102
Weaver,Luke	102
Archer,Chris	98
Boyd,Matthew	96
Mikolas,Miles	95
Greene,Hunter	93
Rodriguez,Grayson	93
Meyer,Max	92
Beeks,Jalen	91
Sanmartin,Reiver	91
Pearson,Nate	91

PITCHER SKILLS RANKINGS — Relief Pitchers

Top K-BB%

NAME	K-BB%
Hader,Josh	36
Hendriks,Liam	33
Kimbrel,Craig	32
Williams,Devin	28
Iglesias,Raisel	28
Sewald,Paul	28
Díaz,Edwin	28
Poche,Colin	28
Green,Chad	27
Chapman,Aroldis	27
Pressly,Ryan	27
Neris,Héctor	25
Knebel,Corey	25
Kahnle,Tommy	25
Giles,Ken	25
Rogers,Taylor	25
Gallegos,Giovanny	24
Sims,Lucas	24
Warren,Art	24
Barnes,Matt	24
Bednar,David	24
Fairbanks,Peter	23
Jansen,Kenley	23
Castillo,Diego	23
Springs,Jeffrey	23
Alcala,Jorge	23
Yates,Kirby	23
Smith,Will	23
Rosenthal,Trevor	23
McHugh,Collin	22
Ashby,Aaron	22

Top BB%

NAME	BB%
Martin,Christopher	3
Petit,Yusmeiro	4
Stammen,Craig	5
Rogers,Tyler	5
Hendriks,Liam	5
Smith,Riley	5
Luetge,Lucas	5
Sadler,Casey	5
Alexander,Tyler	6
Clase,Emmanuel	6
King,John	6
Rogers,Josh	6
McGee,Jake	6
Rogers,Taylor	6
Payamps,Joel	6
Whitlock,Garrett	6
Green,Chad	6
Alcala,Jorge	6
Falter,Bailey	6
Rodríguez,Richard	6
Kittredge,Andrew	6
Martin,Brett	6
Thielbar,Caleb	6
Gallegos,Giovanny	6
Pressly,Ryan	6
Wells,Tyler	6
Pagan,Emilio	7
Iglesias,Raisel	7
Cimber,Adam	7
Garcia,Jarlin	7
McHugh,Collin	7

Top K%

NAME	K%
Hader,Josh	46
Kimbrel,Craig	42
Chapman,Aroldis	41
Williams,Devin	39
Hendriks,Liam	38
Sewald,Paul	37
Díaz,Edwin	37
Poche,Colin	36
Barnes,Matt	36
Knebel,Corey	35
Kahnle,Tommy	35
Iglesias,Raisel	35
Rainey,Tanner	34
Leclerc,José	34
Fairbanks,Peter	34
Neris,Héctor	34
Rosenthal,Trevor	34
Cousins,Jake	34
Giles,Ken	34
Sims,Lucas	34
Pressly,Ryan	33
Green,Chad	33
Warren,Art	33
Yates,Kirby	33
Karinchak,James	33
Jansen,Kenley	32
Ashby,Aaron	32
Springs,Jeffrey	32
Diekman,Jake	32
Bednar,David	32
Doval,Camilo	31

Top Ground Ball Rate

NAME	GB%
Bummer,Aaron	73
Clase,Emmanuel	67
Holmes,Clay	66
Sadler,Casey	64
Ashby,Aaron	61
Hicks,Jordan	61
Tate,Dillon	60
Peacock,Matt	60
Hill,Tim	60
King,John	58
Graterol,Brusdar	58
Pop,Zach	57
Martin,Brett	57
Rogers,Tyler	56
Sawamura,Hirokazu	56
Melancon,Mark	56
Rodríguez,Joely	56
Cimber,Adam	55
Alvarado,José	55
Peralta,Wandy	55
Loaisiga,Jonathan	54
Graveman,Kendall	54
Mayza,Tim	54
Coonrod,Sam	54
Pressly,Ryan	54
Rodríguez,Manuel	54
Funkhouser,Kyle	53
Stammen,Craig	53
Jackson,Luke	53
Kittredge,Andrew	52
Zimmer,Kyle	52

Top Fly Ball Rate

NAME	FB%
Poche,Colin	62
Pagan,Emilio	57
Clippard,Tyler	55
Wells,Tyler	55
Smith,Caleb	53
Rodríguez,Richard	51
Feyereisen,J.P.	50
Rainey,Tanner	50
Rogers,Josh	50
Sewald,Paul	50
Guerra,Deolis	50
Hader,Josh	49
Thielbar,Caleb	49
Kennedy,Ian	49
Sims,Lucas	49
Green,Chad	49
Foster,Matt	49
Javier,Cristian	48
Hendriks,Liam	48
May,Trevor	48
Gallegos,Giovanny	47
Kimbrel,Craig	47
Barlow,Joe	47
Leclerc,José	47
Stanek,Ryne	47
Widener,Taylor	47
Cortes,Nestor	47
James,Josh	46
Richards,Trevor	46
Falter,Bailey	46
Petit,Yusmeiro	45

High GB, Low K%

NAME	GB%	K%
Tate,Dillon	60	17
Peacock,Matt	60	13
Hill,Tim	60	21
King,John	58	19
Graterol,Brusdar	58	21
Pop,Zach	57	22
Martin,Brett	57	19
Rogers,Tyler	56	17
Cimber,Adam	55	18
Peralta,Wandy	55	19
Rodríguez,Manuel	54	19
Funkhouser,Kyle	53	20
Crismatt,Nabil	51	21
De Geus,Brett	51	17
López,Jorge	49	19
Cessa,Luis	49	21
Alvarez,Jose	48	19
Finnegan,Kyle	48	22
Mejía,Jean Carlos	48	21
Harvey,Hunter	48	20
Shaw,Bryan	48	21
Lorenzen,Michael	48	20
Gant,John	47	20
Peralta,Wily	47	16
Bass,Anthony	46	21
Richards,Garrett	46	22
Montero,Rafael	45	22
Bielak,Brandon	44	21
Beede,Tyler	44	19
Weathers,Ryan	44	18
Heuer,Codi	44	18

High GB, High K%

NAME	GB%	K%
Bummer,Aaron	73	27
Clase,Emmanuel	67	26
Holmes,Clay	66	27
Ashby,Aaron	61	32
Alvarado,José	55	28
Mayza,Tim	54	27
Pressly,Ryan	54	33
Jackson,Luke	53	28
Kittredge,Andrew	52	28
Abreu,Bryan	51	27
Treinen,Blake	51	29
Loup,Aaron	51	26
Castillo,Diego	50	31
Scott,Tanner	50	30
Bender,Anthony	50	29
Familia,Jeurys	50	27
Brentz,Jake	49	29
Garrett,Amir	49	29
Rogers,Taylor	49	30
Doval,Camilo	48	31
Antone,Tejay	48	29
Bickford,Phil	47	29
Houck,Tanner	47	30
Kahnle,Tommy	47	35
Williams,Devin	46	39
Chafin,Andrew	46	27
Robertson,David	46	31
Barnes,Matt	46	36
Alcala,Jorge	45	29
Cousins,Jake	45	34
Romano,Jordan	45	30

Lowest xERA

NAME	xERA
Hader,Josh	2.64
Clase,Emmanuel	2.72
Pressly,Ryan	2.72
Bummer,Aaron	2.86
Williams,Devin	2.88
Ashby,Aaron	2.92
Holmes,Clay	2.93
Kimbrel,Craig	2.94
Chapman,Aroldis	2.96
Hendriks,Liam	2.96
Kahnle,Tommy	3.04
Rogers,Taylor	3.06
Iglesias,Raisel	3.09
Díaz,Edwin	3.15
Knebel,Corey	3.16
Kittredge,Andrew	3.18
Rosenthal,Trevor	3.19
Castillo,Diego	3.20
Bender,Anthony	3.24
Sadler,Casey	3.25
Houck,Tanner	3.27
Treinen,Blake	3.27
Neris,Héctor	3.29
Giles,Ken	3.33
Barnes,Matt	3.33
Alcala,Jorge	3.34
Fairbanks,Peter	3.36
Doval,Camilo	3.37
Sewald,Paul	3.38
Cousins,Jake	3.40
Loaisiga,Jonathan	3.41

Top BPX, 10+ Saves

NAME	BPX
Hendriks,Liam	198
Hader,Josh	189
Pressly,Ryan	178
Kimbrel,Craig	173
Iglesias,Raisel	170
Rogers,Taylor	164
Díaz,Edwin	162
Clase,Emmanuel	156
Neris,Héctor	154
Giles,Ken	154
Sewald,Paul	154
Kittredge,Andrew	153
Chapman,Aroldis	148
Castillo,Diego	147
Barnes,Matt	146
Bednar,David	144
Gallegos,Giovanny	140
Romano,Jordan	137
Sims,Lucas	134
Jansen,Kenley	132
Smith,Will	132
Loaisiga,Jonathan	131
Treinen,Blake	130
Rosenthal,Trevor	128
Doval,Camilo	119
Barlow,Scott	114
McGee,Jake	108
Fulmer,Michael	104
Melancon,Mark	103
Sulser,Cole	100
Kennedy,Ian	99

Top BPX, <10 Saves

NAME	BPX
Williams,Devin	169
Green,Chad	158
Kahnle,Tommy	155
Ashby,Aaron	149
Knebel,Corey	148
Poche,Colin	146
Warren,Art	142
Houck,Tanner	139
Stammen,Craig	139
Fairbanks,Peter	138
Martin,Christopher	137
Holmes,Clay	137
McHugh,Collin	137
Bender,Anthony	136
Lugo,Seth	136
Sadler,Casey	135
Robertson,David	134
Whitlock,Garrett	133
Yates,Kirby	132
Luetge,Lucas	126
Bummer,Aaron	124
Mayza,Tim	124
Boxberger,Brad	124
Bickford,Phil	124
Maton,Phil	121
Pagan,Emilio	120
Chafin,Andrew	120
Cousins,Jake	118
Loup,Aaron	116
Hernández,Jonathan	115
May,Trevor	114

POTENTIAL SKILLS GAINERS AND FADERS — Pitchers

K% Gainers

From a pitcher's swinging-strike rate (SwK), we can establish a typical range in which we would expect to find their K%. The pitchers on this list posted a 2021 K% that was in the bottom of the expected range based on their SwK. The names above the break line are in the bottom 10% of that range, and are the strongest candidates for K% gains. The names below the break line are in the bottom 25%, and are also good candidates for K% gains.

K% Faders

From a pitcher's swinging-strike rate (SwK), we can establish a typical range in which we would expect to find their K%. The pitchers on this list posted a 2021 K% that was in the top of that expected range based on their SwK. The names above the break line are in the top 10% of that range, and are the strongest candidates for a K% fade. The names below the break line are in the top 25%, and are also good candidates for a K% fade.

BB% Gainers

A pitcher's xBB% is a skills-based representation of what their BB% should be. Assuming the same underlying skills across seasons, a pitcher's actual BB% should move in the direction of their xBB%. Therefore, by ordering pitchers with the biggest gap between actual BB% and xBB% in 2021 in the chart below, we can identify those whose walk rates should improve (Gainers) in 2022.

BB% Faders

A pitcher's xBB% is a skills-based representation of what their BB% should be. Assuming the same underlying skills across seasons, a pitcher's actual BB% should move in the direction of their xBB%. Therefore, by ordering pitchers with the biggest gap between xBB% and actual BB% in 2021 in the chart below, we can identify those whose walk rates should get worse (Faders) in 2022.

K% GAINERS

NAME	SwK	K%
Plesac, Zach	12	16.7
Crismatt, Nabil	12	20.2
Anderson, Tyler	12	19.1
Corbin, Patrick	12	19.0
Lyles, Jordan	11	19.0
Miley, Wade	11	18.1
Kittredge, Andrew	16	27.3
Smyly, Drew	12	21.4
Urquidy, Jose	13	21.3
Thompson, Zach	12	21.0
Suarez, Jose	12	20.6
Pineda, Michael	11	19.2
Gutierrez, Vladimir	10	17.7
Patino, Luis	12	22.2
Stroman, Marcus	12	21.6
Paddack, Chris	12	21.6
Shaw, Bryan	12	21.3
Boyd, Matthew	11	19.9
Richards, Garrett	10	18.6
Cimber, Adam	10	17.8
Gray, Josiah	15	24.8
German, Domingo	15	23.9
Castillo, Luis	13	23.9
Kinley, Tyler	14	23.1
Luzardo, Jesus	14	22.4
Barlow, Scott	16	29.7
Kershaw, Clayton	17	29.5
Sandoval, Patrick	15	25.9

K% FADERS

NAME	SwK	K%
Wheeler, Zack	13	29.1
Cortes, Nestor	11	27.5
Gallen, Zac	10	26.6
Berrios, Jose	10	26.1
Bassitt, Chris	11	25.0
Suter, Brent	9	22.0
Wainwright, Adam	9	21.0
Darvish, Yu	12	29.2
Morton, Charlie	13	28.6
Mahle, Tyler	12	27.7
Lopez, Pablo	13	27.5
Lynn, Lance	12	27.5
Rodriguez, Eduardo	12	27.4
McCullers Jr., Lance	12	27.0
Gray, Sonny	11	27.0
Pivetta, Nick	11	26.5
Urias, Julio	12	26.2
Cobb, Alex	11	24.9
Stammen, Craig	11	23.4
Fedde, Erick	9	21.7
Espino, Paolo	9	20.2
Lopez, Jorge	9	20.2
Freeland, Kyle	9	20.4
Bauer, Trevor	13	31.7
Cole, Gerrit	15	33.5
Snell, Blake	13	30.9
Javier, Cristian	14	30.7
Nola, Aaron	13	29.8
Keller, Mitch	9	19.6
Perez, Martin	9	19.1
Happ, J.A.	9	18.2

BB% GAINERS

NAME	xBB%	BB%
Reyes, Alex	11.6	16.4
Smith, Caleb	8.3	12.6
Castro, Miguel	10.5	14.2
McKenzie, Triston	8.3	11.7
Gray, Josiah	7.6	10.7
Neris, Hector	7.2	10.3
Moore, Matt	8.3	11.4
Velasquez, Vince	8.7	11.8
Snell, Blake	9.6	12.5
Hoffman, Jeff	10.5	13.4
Widener, Taylor	8.7	11.6
Gant, John	11.6	14.5
Shaw, Bryan	8.7	11.4
Pivetta, Nick	7.2	9.8
Hill, Rich	5.9	8.3
Martinez, Carlos	7.6	9.9
Trivino, Lou	8.7	11.0
Rogers, Trevor	6.1	8.4
Stratton, Chris	7.6	9.8
Akin, Keegan	7.2	9.4
Richards, Garrett	7.6	9.7
Kikuchi, Yusei	7.2	9.3
Kluber, Corey	7.6	9.7
Price, David	5.9	8.0
Javier, Cristian	10.5	12.5
Hearn, Taylor	7.6	9.5
Bubic, Kris	8.7	10.6
Hernandez, Carlos	9.6	11.5
Glasnow, Tyler	6.1	7.9
Boyd, Matthew	5.0	6.8
Castillo, Luis	7.6	9.3
Keller, Mitch	8.7	10.4

BB% FADERS

NAME	xBB%	BB%
Anderson, Brett	11.6	6.8
Luetge, Lucas	8.7	5.0
Stammen, Craig	7.2	3.7
Hendriks, Liam	5.9	2.6
Means, John	7.2	4.4
Greinke, Zack	7.6	5.2
Senzatela, Antonio	7.2	4.8
Petit, Yusmeiro	6.1	3.8
Gilbert, Logan	7.6	5.6
Flexen, Chris	7.2	5.4
Yarbrough, Ryan	5.9	4.1
Espino, Paolo	7.2	5.5
Mize, Casey	8.3	6.7
Kershaw, Clayton	5.9	4.3
Flaherty, Jack	9.6	8.1
Fedde, Erick	9.6	8.1
Crismatt, Nabil	8.3	6.8

EXPECTED STATS vs. ACTUAL — Pitchers

ERA Underperformers (min. 70 IP)

NAME	ERA	xERA	Diff
Heaney,Andrew	5.83	4.19	1.64
Luzardo,Jesus	6.61	4.98	1.63
Lopez,Jorge	6.07	4.51	1.56
Bundy,Dylan	6.06	4.64	1.42
Martinez,Carlos	6.23	4.85	1.38
Brubaker,Jonathan	5.36	4.03	1.33
Corbin,Patrick	5.82	4.50	1.32
Velasquez,Vincent	6.30	4.99	1.31
Fedde,Erick	5.47	4.21	1.26
Nola,Aaron	4.63	3.48	1.15
Rodriguez,Eduardo	4.74	3.70	1.04
Wacha,Michael	5.05	4.09	0.96
Paddack,Chris	5.07	4.12	0.95
Alzolay,Adbert	4.58	3.74	0.84
Singer,Brady	4.91	4.17	0.74
Allard,Kolby	5.41	4.70	0.71
Minor,Mike	5.05	4.37	0.68
Mills,Alec	5.07	4.40	0.67
Keller,Brad	5.39	4.74	0.65
Marquez,German	4.40	3.76	0.64
Holmes,Clay	3.60	2.96	0.64

WHIP Underperformers (min. 70 IP)

NAME	WHIP	xWHIP	Diff
Keller,Mitch	1.79	1.45	0.34
Arrieta,Jake	1.77	1.43	0.34
Rodriguez,Eduardo	1.39	1.15	0.24
Singer,Brady	1.55	1.32	0.23
Keller,Brad	1.66	1.44	0.22
Williams,Trevor	1.49	1.27	0.22
Lopez,Jorge	1.63	1.41	0.22
Harvey,Matt	1.54	1.33	0.21
Luzardo,Jesus	1.62	1.41	0.21
Perez,Martin	1.51	1.31	0.20
Richards,Garrett	1.60	1.43	0.17
Akin,Keegan	1.58	1.41	0.17
Dunning,Dane	1.44	1.30	0.14
Happ,J.A.	1.48	1.34	0.14
Heaney,Andrew	1.32	1.18	0.14
Eflin,Zach	1.25	1.11	0.14
Fedde,Erick	1.44	1.30	0.14
Crowe,Wil	1.57	1.43	0.14
Peacock,Matt	1.56	1.43	0.13
Freeland,Kyle	1.42	1.30	0.12
Corbin,Patrick	1.47	1.35	0.12

Wins Underperformers (SP)

NAME	W	xW	Diff
Woodruff,Brandon	9	16	-7
Castillo,Luis	8	14	-6
Montgomery,Jordan	6	12	-6
Senzatela,Antonio	4	10	-6
Alcantara,Sandy	9	14	-5
Anderson,Brett	4	9	-5
Mize,Casey	7	12	-5
Ober,Bailey	3	8	-5
Rogers,Trevor	7	12	-5
Anderson,Tyler	7	11	-4
Burnes,Corbin	11	15	-4
Gallen,Zac	4	8	-4
Gray,Sonny	7	11	-4
Lopez,Pablo	5	9	-4
Lynn,Lance	11	15	-4
Means,John	6	10	-4
Ray,Robbie	13	17	-4
Stroman,Marcus	10	14	-4

ERA Overperformers (min. 70 IP)

NAME	ERA	xERA	Diff
Peralta,Wily	3.07	4.98	-1.91
Suarez,Ranger	1.36	3.21	-1.85
Cimber,Adam	2.26	3.89	-1.63
Rogers,Tyler	2.22	3.77	-1.55
Quantrill,Cal	2.89	4.36	-1.47
Whitlock,Garrett	1.96	3.30	-1.34
Thompson,Zach	3.24	4.57	-1.33
Reyes,Alex	3.24	4.57	-1.33
Petit,Yusmeiro	3.92	5.20	-1.28
Barlow,Scott	2.42	3.68	-1.26
Cortes,Nestor	2.90	4.16	-1.26
Kim,Kwang-Hyun	3.46	4.68	-1.22
Lynn,Lance	2.69	3.89	-1.20
Hernandez,Carlos	3.68	4.87	-1.19
Kittredge,Andrew	1.88	3.06	-1.18
Trivino,Lou	3.18	4.36	-1.18
Treinen,Blake	1.99	3.16	-1.17
Lauer,Eric	3.19	4.32	-1.13
Bauer,Trevor	2.59	3.70	-1.11
Buehler,Walker	2.47	3.56	-1.09
Shaw,Bryan	3.49	4.56	-1.07

WHIP Overperformers (min. 70 IP)

NAME	WHIP	xWHIP	Diff
Petit,Yusmeiro	1.04	1.32	-0.28
Suarez,Ranger	1.00	1.21	-0.21
Houser,Adrian	1.28	1.49	-0.21
Castro,Miguel	1.29	1.49	-0.20
Cimber,Adam	1.07	1.27	-0.20
Gallegos,Giovanny	0.88	1.07	-0.19
Treinen,Blake	0.98	1.17	-0.19
Hernandez,Carlos	1.28	1.47	-0.19
deGrom,Jacob	0.55	0.74	-0.19
Buehler,Walker	0.97	1.15	-0.18
Rasmussen,Drew	1.08	1.26	-0.18
Urquidy,Jose	0.99	1.17	-0.18
Peralta,Freddy	0.97	1.14	-0.17
Trivino,Lou	1.25	1.42	-0.17
Peralta,Wily	1.33	1.50	-0.17
McKenzie,Triston	1.18	1.35	-0.17
Wainwright,Adam	1.06	1.23	-0.17
Gonzales,Marco	1.17	1.33	-0.16
Manoah,Alek	1.05	1.21	-0.16
Reyes,Alex	1.35	1.50	-0.15
Flaherty,Jack	1.06	1.21	-0.15

Wins Overperformers (SP)

NAME	W	xW	Diff
Civale,Aaron	12	8	4
Urias,Julio	20	16	4
Cole,Gerrit	16	13	3
Hendricks,Kyle	14	11	3
Happ,J.A.	10	8	2
Wainwright,Adam	17	15	2
Cobb,Alex	8	7	1
Flexen,Chris	14	13	1
Gomber,Austin	9	8	1
Gutierrez,Vladimir	9	8	1
Keller,Brad	8	7	1
Matz,Steven	14	13	1
Plesac,Zach	10	9	1
Ryu,Hyun-Jin	14	13	1
Sale,Chris	5	4	1

RISK MANAGEMENT

GRADE "F" in HEALTH

Pitchers

Ivarado,Jose	Sale,Chris
nderson,Brett	Samardzija,Jeff
nderson,Tyler	Severino,Luis
rcher,Chris	Shoemaker,Matt
ailey,Homer	Smith,Caleb
assitt,Chris	Smyly,Drew
etances,Dellin	Soroka,Michael
ritton,Zack	Strasburg,Stephen
umgarner,Madison	Suter,Brent
ahill,Trevor	Syndergaard,Noah
arrasco,Carlos	Taillon,Jameson
obb,Alex	Tepera,Ryan
ueto,Johnny	Tropeano,Nick
arvish,Yu	Urena,Jose
avies,Zachary	Wacha,Michael
eSclafani,Anthony	Walker,Taijuan
oolittle,Sean	Weaver,Luke
uffy,Danny	Wheeler,Zack
uplantier,Jon	Whitley,Forrest
ovaldi,Nathan	Wood,Alex
ulmer,Michael	Zimmer,Kyle
lasnow,Tyler	Zimmermann,Jordan
raveman,Kendall	
ray,Jonathan	**Batters**
amels,Cole	Andújar,Miguel
eaney,Andrew	Arroyo,Christian
earn,Taylor	Berti,Jon
ill,Rich	Buxton,Byron
oneywell,Brent	Calhoun,Kole
unter,Tommy	Cooper,Garrett
ela,Keone	Cordero,Franchy
ennedy,Ian	D Arnaud,Travis
ershaw,Clayton	Dickerson,Alex
luber,Corey	Duffy,Matt
nebel,Corey	Engel,Adam
opech,Michael	Frazier,Clint
uhl,Chad	Garlick,Kyle
amet,Dinelson	Guzmán,Ronald
Manaea,Sean	Hicks,Aaron
Marshall,Evan	Jiménez,Eloy
Martinez,Carlos	La Stella,Tommy
Matz,Steven	Lewis,Kyle
Mayers,Mike	Long Jr.,Shed
McCullers,Lance	Longoria,Evan
McHugh,Collin	Lowrie,Jed
Miley,Wade	Mondesi,Adalberto
Miller,Andrew	Nimmo,Brandon
Montero,Rafael	Ozuna,Marcell
Montgomery,Jordan	Perez,Salvador
elson,Jimmy	Pollock,A.J.
lorris,Daniel	Quinn,Roman
berg,Scott	Rendon,Anthony
Odorizzi,Jake	Ríos,Edwin
axton,James	Seager,Corey
eacock,Brad	Senzel,Nick
ineda,Michael	Springer,George
rice,David	Stanton,Giancarlo
eyes,Alex	Trout,Mike
ichards,Garrett	Upton,Justin
odón,Carlos	Voit,Luke
odriguez,Eduardo	White,Evan

Highest Reliability-Health/Experience/Consistency (Min. Grade BBB)

CA	POS	Rel
Realmuto,J.T.	2	AAA
Severino,Pedro	2	AAA
Maldonado,Martín	2	AAB
Vázquez,Christian	2	AAB
Barnhart,Tucker	2	ABA
Stallings,Jacob	2	ABA
Caratini,Victor	2	ABB
Murphy,Sean	2	ABB
Contreras,Willson	2	BAB
Alfaro,Jorge	27	BBA
Gomes,Yan	2	BBB

1B/DH	POS	Rel
Cronenworth,Jake	346	AAA
France,Ty	034	AAA
Lowe,Nate	3	AAA
Schoop,Jonathan	34	AAA
Smith,Pavin	3789	AAA
Alonso,Pete	3	AAB
Goldschmidt,Paul	3	AAB
Miller,Brad	3	ABA
Sheets,Gavin	0	ABA
Brantley,Michael	07	BAA
Reyes,Franmil	0	BAA
Aguilar,Jesús	3	BAB
Cron,C.J.	3	BAB
Díaz,Yandy	35	BAB
Soler,Jorge	09	BAB
Walker,Christian	3	BAB
Ruf,Darin	37	BBA
Tsutsugo,Yoshitomo	39	BBB

2B	POS	Rel
Schoop,Jonathan	34	AAA
Cronenworth,Jake	346	AAA
Hernandez,Cesar	4	AAA
India,Jonathan	4	AAA
Merrifield,Whit	4	AAA
Hampson,Garrett	48	AAA
Taylor,Chris	4678	AAA
Albies,Ozzie	4	AAB
Solak,Nick	4	AAB
Edman,Tommy	49	AAB
McMahon,Ryan	45	AAB
Kim,Ha-Seong	456	AAB
García,Luis	4	ABA
Dubón,Mauricio	468	ABA
Miller,Owen	4	ABB
Kemp,Tony	47	ABB
Giménez,Andrés	46	ABB
Segura,Jean	4	BAA
Arraez,Luis	457	BAA
Lowe,Brandon	4	BAB
Odor,Rougned	45	BAB
Hernández,Kiké	48	BAB
Alberto,Hanser	45	BBA
Gonzalez,Marwin	4	BBB

SS	POS	Rel
Cronenworth,Jake	346	AAA
Taylor,Chris	4678	AAA
Adames,Willy	6	AAA
Bichette,Bo	6	AAA
Bogaerts,Xander	6	AAA
Farmer,Kyle	6	AAA
Kiner-Falefa,Isiah	6	AAA
Kim,Ha-Seong	456	AAB
Story,Trevor	6	AAB
Swanson,Dansby	6	AAB
Dubón,Mauricio	468	ABA
Giménez,Andrés	46	ABB
Escobar,Alcides	6	ABB
Anderson,Tim	6	BAA
Crawford,J.P.	6	BAA
DeJong,Paul	6	BAA
Urshela,Gio	56	BAB
Ahmed,Nick	6	BAB
Andrus,Elvis	6	BAB
Lindor,Francisco	6	BAB
Torres,Gleyber	6	BAB

3B	POS	Rel
Kim,Ha-Seong	456	AAB
McMahon,Ryan	45	AAB
Gosselin,Phil	357	ABA
Arraez,Luis	457	BAA
Seager,Kyle	5	BAA
Turner,Justin	5	BAA
Urshela,Gio	56	BAB
Odor,Rougned	45	BAB
Díaz,Yandy	35	BAB
Chapman,Matt	5	BAB
Alberto,Hanser	45	BBA

OF	POS	Rel
Acuna,Ronald	89	AAB
Biggio,Cavan	459	AAA
Bradley,Jackie	8	AAB
Calhoun,Kole	9	AAB
Castellanos,Nick	9	AAB
Choo,Shin-Soo	7	BAB
Grichuk,Randal	8	AAB
Happ,Ian	78	ABB
Harper,Bryce	9	AAB
Heyward,Jason	9	BBB
Margot,Manuel	789	ABA
Markakis,Nick	9	BBB
Marte,Starling	8	AAB
McNeil,Jeff	47	ABB
Merrifield,Whit	489	AAB
Pillar,Kevin	89	AAB
Reddick,Josh	9	BBA
Rosario,Eddie	7	AAA
Solak,Nick	478	ABB
Tapia,Raimel	7	ABB
Taylor,Chris	467	BBB

SP	Rel
Alcantara,Sandy	AAB
Bauer,Trevor	BAB
Berríos,José	AAA
Buehler,Walker	BAA
Castillo,Luis	AAB
Cole,Gerrit	BAB
Corbin,Patrick	AAB
Gibson,Kyle	BAA
Happ,J.A.	BAB
Hendricks,Kyle	BAB
Houser,Adrian	BBA
Kikuchi,Yusei	AAB
López,Jorge	BBA
Mahle,Tyler	BAA
Márquez,Germán	BAA
Montas,Frankie	AAB
Nola,Aaron	BAB
Peralta,Freddy	BBB
Wheeler,Zack	BAB
Woodruff,Brandon	BAA
Yarbrough,Ryan	BBB

RP	Rel
Colome,Alex	ABB
Diaz,Edwin	AAB
Greene,Shane	BBA
Hader,Joshua	ABB
Hand,Brad	AAA
Iglesias,Raisel	BBB
Jansen,Kenley	BAA

RISK MANAGEMENT

GRADE "A" in CONSISTENCY

Pitchers (min 70 IP)	Batters (min 350 AB)
Anderson,Brett	Alberto,Hanser
Archer,Chris	Alfaro,Jorge
Bassitt,Chris	Alford,Anthony
Berríos,José	Bruján,Vidal
Brubaker,Jonathan	Carpenter,Matt
Bubic,Kris	Choi,Ji-Man
Buehler,Walker	Clement,Ernie
Cabrera,Edward	Cooper,Garrett
Carrasco,Carlos	Cordero,Franchy
Civale,Aaron	Cruz,Oneil
Cueto,Johnny	Daza,Yonathan
Dunning,Dane	De La Cruz,Bryan
Flaherty,Jack	Díaz,Aledmys
Fried,Max	Dubón,Mauricio
Gausman,Kevin	Duran,Jarren
Germán,Domingo	Galvis,Freddy
Gibson,Kyle	Gonzalez,Erik
Giolito,Lucas	Gosselin,Phil
Gomber,Austin	Hedges,Austin
Gray,Sonny	Ibáñez,Andy
Greinke,Zack	Jansen,Danny
Heaney,Andrew	Kiermaier,Kevin
Hearn,Taylor	Martin,Richie
Houser,Adrian	McKinstry,Zach
Johnson,Pierce	Mendick,Danny
Kershaw,Clayton	Miller,Brad
Keuchel,Dallas	Nootbaar,Lars
Kim,Kwang-Hyun	Nuñez,Dom
Kowar,Jackson	Park,Hoy Jun
Kuhl,Chad	Peterson,Jace
Lester,Jon	Phillips,Brett
Lugo,Seth	Pinder,Chad
Lynn,Lance	Piscotty,Stephen
Mahle,Tyler	Pujols,Albert
Márquez,Germán	Reyes,Victor
Matz,Steven	Ruf,Darin
McCullers,Lance	Ruiz,Rio
McKenzie,Triston	Sheets,Gavin
Mikolas,Miles	Sierra,Magneuris
Minor,Mike	Sosa,Edmundo
Montgomery,Jordan	Stewart,D.J.
Odorizzi,Jake	Taylor,Tyrone
Paddack,Chris	Torrens,Luis
Pérez,Martin	Trammell,Taylor
Petit,Yusmeiro	Tucker,Cole
Pineda,Michael	Vogelbach,Daniel
Quantrill,Cal	Ward,Taylor
Richards,Garrett	Williams,Luke
Rodriguez,Eduardo	Zimmerman,Ryan
Ryu,Hyun-Jin	
Sánchez,Sixto	
Snell,Blake	
Stammen,Craig	
Stroman,Marcus	
Syndergaard,Noah	
Taillon,Jameson	
Verlander,Justin	
Wacha,Michael	
Wainwright,Adam	
Walker,Taijuan	
Wilson,Bryse	
Woodford,Jake	
Woodruff,Brandon	

TOP COMBINATION OF SKILLS AND RELIABILITY
Maximum of one "C" in Reliability Grade

BATTING POWER (Min. 350 AB)

PX 115+	PX	Rel
Hoskins,Rhys	191	CAA
Sanó,Miguel	189	CAB
Tatis Jr.,Fernando	186	CAB
Harper,Bryce	184	BAC
Zunino,Mike	174	BBC
Lowe,Brandon	167	BAB
Hilliard,Sam	165	ABA
Judge,Aaron	162	CAB
Duvall,Adam	158	AAA
Suárez,Eugenio	157	AAC
Devers,Rafael	153	AAC
Reyes,Franmil	153	BAA
Ruf,Darin	152	BBA
Hernández,Teoscar	152	AAC
Alonso,Pete	151	AAB
Chapman,Matt	150	BAB
Soler,Jorge	149	BAB
Happ,Ian	146	AAB
Cron,C.J.	144	BAB
Story,Trevor	143	AAB
Tucker,Kyle	142	AAC
Adames,Willy	141	AAA
Phillips,Brett	140	ACA
Siri,Jose	139	ABB
Miller,Brad	138	ABA
Donaldson,Josh	138	CAA
Mountcastle,Ryan	138	AAC
Riley,Austin	138	AAC
Votto,Joey	137	CAB
Haniger,Mitch	131	CAA
Murphy,Sean	131	ABB
Taylor,Chris	128	AAA
Sheets,Gavin	127	ABA
Guerrero Jr.,Vladimir	127	AAC
Goldschmidt,Paul	127	AAB
McMahon,Ryan	127	AAB
Contreras,Willson	126	BAB
Betts,Mookie	125	BAB
Odor,Rougned	124	BAB
Cruz,Nelson	124	AAC
Swanson,Dansby	124	AAB
Pederson,Joc	124	AAC
Albies,Ozzie	123	AAB
Laureano,Ramón	123	BAC
Stewart,D.J.	123	BCA
Gurriel Jr.,Lourdes	122	BAC
Seager,Kyle	121	BAA
Bichette,Bo	120	AAA
Candelario,Jeimer	119	BAC
Carpenter,Matt	117	BCA
Ward,Taylor	117	ACA
Dozier,Hunter	117	BAC
McKinstry,Zach	116	BCA
Grichuk,Randal	116	AAB
Hernández,Kiké	115	BAB
Kepler,Max	115	BAA

RUNNER SPEED (Min. 350 AB)

Spd 110+	Spd	Rel
Sierra,Magneuris	160	ACA
Sosa,Edmundo	155	ACA
Reyes,Victor	152	BCA
Hampson,Garrett	151	AAA
Tapia,Raimel	149	BAB
Turner,Trea	147	AAC
Alcantara,Sergio	146	ACB
Kiermaier,Kevin	144	CAA
Ortega,Rafael	144	ACB
De La Cruz,Bryan	144	ACA
Rosario,Amed	143	AAC
Giménez,Andrés	141	ABB
Duran,Jarren	140	ACA
Phillips,Brett	139	ACA
Smith,Pavin	139	AAA
Siri,Jose	137	ABB
Park,Hoy Jun	136	ACA
Margot,Manuel	133	BAA
Anderson,Tim	132	BAA
Story,Trevor	131	AAB
Albies,Ozzie	130	AAB
Taveras,Leody	130	ABB
Marte,Starling	129	BAB
Betts,Mookie	128	BAB
Solak,Nick	128	AAB
Ibáñez,Andy	128	ACA
Tucker,Cole	126	ACA
Dubón,Mauricio	126	ABA
Canha,Mark	124	BAB
Olivares,Edward	124	ABB
Bader,Harrison	123	CBA
Dozier,Hunter	123	BAC
Hilliard,Sam	122	ABA
Taylor,Chris	122	AAA
Newman,Kevin	121	AAC
Espinal,Santiago	121	ACB
Kiner-Falefa,Isiah	120	AAA
Lee,Khalil	120	ACB
Wendle,Joe	119	CAB
Merrifield,Whit	119	AAA
Hays,Austin	119	BAA
Tatis Jr.,Fernando	118	CAB
Gamel,Ben	118	ABA
Arraez,Luis	117	BAA
Gardner,Brett	117	AAB
Kemp,Tony	117	ABB
Verdugo,Alex	117	BAB
García,Leury	117	CAB
Cronenworth,Jake	116	AAA
Goodrum,Niko	116	CBB
Ward,Taylor	116	ACA
Miller,Brad	114	ABA
Crawford,J.P.	114	BAA
Tucker,Kyle	114	AAC
Pillar,Kevin	113	BAC
Edman,Tommy	113	AAB
Anderson,Brian	112	CBA
McNeil,Jeff	112	BAC
Hernandez,Cesar	112	AAA
Bichette,Bo	111	AAA
Fletcher,David	111	AAC
McCormick,Chas	111	ACB
Bruján,Vidal	110	ACA
Daza,Yonathan	110	BCA
Frazier,Adam	110	AAC

OVERALL PITCHING SKILL

BPX 100+	BPX	Rel
Hendriks,Liam	225	BAA
Hader,Josh	214	AAB
Pressly,Ryan	203	CBB
Cole,Gerrit	202	BAB
Kimbrel,Craig	197	BCB
Iglesias,Raisel	193	ABB
Díaz,Edwin	184	ABB
Nola,Aaron	183	BAB
Green,Chad	180	ACA
Neris,Héctor	175	ABC
Chapman,Aroldis	169	CBB
Barnes,Matt	166	CBB
Woodruff,Brandon	163	BAA
Gallegos,Giovanny	160	ACB
Stammen,Craig	158	BCA
Morton,Charlie	158	CAB
Buehler,Walker	152	BAA
Jansen,Kenley	151	AAA
Wheeler,Zack	150	BAB
Bauer,Trevor	150	BAB
Montas,Frankie	148	AAB
Giolito,Lucas	139	CAA
Castillo,Luis	138	AAB
Pagan,Emilio	137	ACB
Lynn,Lance	135	CAA
Peralta,Freddy	132	BBB
Barlow,Scott	130	ACB
Márquez,Germán	129	BAA
Alcantara,Sandy	128	AAB
Greinke,Zack	127	CAA
Garcia,Luis	127	ACB
Mahle,Tyler	127	BAA
Berríos,José	126	AAA
Wittgren,Nick	121	BCA
Minor,Mike	119	CAA
Cease,Dylan	119	ABC
Pivetta,Nick	117	ACB
Romo,Sergio	115	BCA
Corbin,Patrick	114	AAB
Floro,Dylan	109	BCB
Hendricks,Kyle	108	BAB
Yarbrough,Ryan	108	BBB
Kikuchi,Yusei	108	AAB
Rogers,Tyler	107	ACB
Colomé,Alex	107	ABA
Singer,Brady	106	CBB
Bard,Daniel	105	ACA
Dunning,Dane	103	BCA

HEAD-TO-HEAD TOOLS

2021 USABLE WEEKS

NAME	R	RBI	SB	BA	HR	TOT
Shohei Ohtani	13	13	13	11	12	62
Vladimir Guerrero	15	13	4	16	13	61
Jose Ramirez	14	11	11	13	9	58
Bo Bichette	15	11	13	12	6	57
Rafael Devers	15	14	4	12	9	54
Marcus Semien	13	9	10	11	10	53
Ozzie Albies	14	10	10	12	7	53
Freddie Freeman	13	11	8	11	8	51
Cedric Mullins	13	5	14	14	5	51
Paul Goldschmidt	11	11	10	12	6	50
Jorge Polanco	10	10	8	14	8	50
Trea Turner	12	5	13	14	5	49
Fernando Tatis	12	9	11	8	9	49
Teoscar Hernandez	10	13	8	11	7	49
Chris Taylor	12	10	11	12	4	49
Salvador Perez	10	13	1	12	12	48
Whit Merrifield	10	7	18	10	3	48
Matt Olson	13	12	4	8	10	47
Bryce Harper	11	6	7	13	8	45
Austin Riley	8	11	0	14	12	45
Jose Abreu	11	14	1	11	8	45
Kris Bryant	12	6	8	11	8	45
Juan Soto	13	10	4	13	4	44
Nick Castellanos	12	11	2	12	7	44
Aaron Judge	11	9	4	13	7	44
Bryan Reynolds	8	12	3	14	6	43
Nolan Arenado	10	15	2	10	6	43
Adolis Garcia	10	11	8	7	7	43
Tim Anderson	12	6	11	11	3	43
Manny Machado	8	11	8	10	5	42
Brandon Crawford	6	10	10	12	4	42
Jonathan India	11	7	8	11	5	42
Mitch Haniger	14	10	1	8	8	41
Tommy Edman	9	5	16	11	0	41
Jesse Winker	11	10	1	14	5	41
Jose Altuve	12	10	3	9	6	40
Javier Baez	9	9	9	6	7	40
Adam Duvall	7	12	4	9	8	40
Yordan Alvarez	10	11	1	11	6	39
Pete Alonso	8	11	3	10	7	39
Randy Arozarena	8	7	9	11	4	39
Trevor Story	8	9	11	7	4	39
Austin Meadows	9	12	3	9	6	39
Dansby Swanson	8	8	8	8	7	39
Tyler O'Neill	8	6	8	11	5	38
Brandon Lowe	10	9	5	4	10	38
Xander Bogaerts	8	9	4	11	6	38
Nelson Cruz	7	9	2	11	9	38
Jake Cronenworth	11	7	4	11	5	38
Kyle Tucker	6	8	8	10	5	37
Starling Marte	7	4	13	10	3	37
Ronald Acuna	10	5	9	5	8	37
Max Muncy	11	8	2	7	8	36
Jared Walsh	7	11	1	9	8	36
Ryan Mountcastle	7	10	4	6	9	36
Robbie Grossman	10	6	10	6	4	36
Carlos Correa	10	9	0	12	4	35
Joey Votto	8	10	1	8	8	35
Hunter Renfroe	11	10	0	8	6	35
Justin Turner	10	8	1	12	4	35
Avisail Garcia	6	11	5	9	4	35
Kyle Seager	6	10	3	6	10	35
J.D. Martinez	9	9	0	11	5	34
C.J. Cron	5	8	1	11	9	34
Josh Bell	7	12	0	10	5	34
Willy Adames	6	8	5	12	3	34
Ty France	9	6	0	15	4	34
Jonathan Schoop	9	7	1	12	4	33
Eduardo Escobar	7	10	1	8	7	33
Andrew McCutchen	9	7	5	5	7	33
Will Smith	8	9	3	8	5	33
Luis Urias	7	8	4	9	5	33
Isiah Kiner-Falefa	8	2	10	12	1	33
Matt Chapman	9	8	3	5	8	33
Yuli Gurriel	7	8	1	13	3	32
Ryan McMahon	6	7	4	11	4	32
Mookie Betts	10	4	7	7	4	32
Franmil Reyes	4	9	4	7	8	32
Mark Canha	9	3	9	8	3	32
Kyle Schwarber	7	5	1	10	8	31
AJ Pollock	3	8	5	12	3	31
Myles Straw	7	2	13	9	0	31
Jean Segura	8	6	5	11	1	31
Giancarlo Stanton	5	10	0	9	6	30
Alex Verdugo	9	3	5	12	1	30
Jazz Chisholm	6	6	10	5	3	30
Trent Grisham	5	5	8	9	3	30
Joey Gallo	8	5	6	4	6	29
Anthony Rizzo	6	5	6	8	4	29
Dylan Carlson	8	4	2	11	4	29
Nathaniel Lowe	3	7	5	11	2	28
J.T. Realmuto	4	6	6	10	2	28
Trey Mancini	7	5	0	12	4	28
Charlie Blackmon	5	7	2	10	3	27
Eugenio Suarez	7	8	0	4	8	27
Yoan Moncada	5	6	3	11	1	26
Lourdes Gurriel	2	6	1	11	5	25
Andrew Benintendi	5	4	6	6	2	23
Austin Hays	6	5	3	6	3	23
Francisco Lindor	7	4	9	2	1	23

2021 AGGREGATE CONSISTENCY SCORE

NAME	ACS	NAME	ACS
Bauer, Trevor	100	Brubaker, Jonathan	55
Berrios, Jose	100	Civale, Aaron	55
Buehler, Walker	95	Maeda, Kenta	55
Cole, Gerrit	95	Ross, Joe	55
Rogers, Trevor	95	Skubal, Tarik	55
Wheeler, Zack	95	Hendricks, Kyle	50
Alcantara, Sandy	90	Kaprielian, James	50
Burnes, Corbin	90	Kelly, Merrill	50
Manoah, Alek	90	Marquez, German	50
Montas, Frankie	90	McCullers, Lance	50
Bassitt, Chris	85	Means, John	50
Garcia, Luis	85	Mize, Casey	50
Giolito, Lucas	85	Rodriguez, Eduardo	50
Nola, Aaron	85	Yarbrough, Ryan	50
Ohtani, Shohei	85	Corbin, Patrick	45
Ray, Robbie	85	Greinke, Zack	45
Scherzer, Max	85	Gutierrez, Vladimir	45
Urias, Julio	85	Irvin, Cole	45
Woodruff, Brandon	85	Matz, Steven	45
Cease, Dylan	80	Pivetta, Nick	45
Eovaldi, Nathan	80	Singer, Brady	45
Gausman, Kevin	80	Walker, Taijuan	45
Gilbert, Logan	80	Crowe, Wil	40
Gray, Sonny	80	Foltynewicz, Mike	40
Lauer, Eric	80	Gallen, Zac	40
Lynn, Lance	80	Gonzales, Marco	40
Morton, Charlie	80	Happ, J.A.	40
Peralta, Freddy	80	Lyles, Jordan	40
Wainwright, Adam	80	Montgomery, Jordan	40
Castillo, Luis	75	Snell, Blake	40
Darvish, Yu	75	Taillon, Jameson	40
Gibson, Kyle	75	Anderson, Tyler	35
Kershaw, Clayton	75	Bumgarner, Madison	35
McClanahan, Shane	75	Freeland, Kyle	35
Rodon, Carlos	75	Gray, Jonathan	35
Fried, Max	70	Houser, Adrian	35
Kikuchi, Yusei	70	Keller, Brad	35
Manaea, Sean	70	Keuchel, Dallas	35
Valdez, Framber	70	Paddack, Chris	35
Webb, Logan	70	Senzatela, Antonio	35
DeSclafani, Anthony	65	Cueto, Johnny	30
Lopez, Pablo	65	Fedde, Erick	30
Mahle, Tyler	65	Keller, Mitch	30
Minor, Mike	65	Lester, Jon T	30
Stroman, Marcus	65	Plesac, Zach	30
Anderson, Ian	60	Davies, Zachary	25
Eflin, Zach	60	Harvey, Matt	25
Flexen, Chris	60	Pineda, Michael	25
Gomber, Austin	60	Hill, Rich	20
Miley, Wade	60		
Musgrove, Joe	60		
Ryu, Hyun-Jin	60		
Urquidy, Jose	60		
Wood, Alex	60		

DAILY FANTASY INDICATORS

Top OPS v LHP, 2020-21

Hitter	OPS
Turner, Trea	1160
Marte, Ketel	1148
Zunino, Mike	1134
Hernandez, Teoscar	1090
Goldschmidt, Paul	1056
Robert, Luis	1052
Cruz, Nelson	1027
Anderson, Tim	1017
Hoskins, Rhys	1013
Ramirez, Jose	1009
Grandal, Yasmani	1006
McCutchen, Andrew	1005
Story, Trevor	996
Longoria, Evan	995
Acuna, Ronald	992
Rojas, Miguel	990
Judge, Aaron	981
Ozuna, Marcell	974
Arozarena, Randy	971
Perez, Salvador	968
Pollock, A.J.	966
Cron, C.J.	948
Abreu, Jose	943
Soto, Juan	939
Bichette, Bo	935
Guerrero Jr., Vladimir	930
Gurriel, Yulieski	915
Garcia, Avisail	913
Olson, Matt	911
Tatis Jr., Fernando	910
Donaldson, Josh	907
Muncy, Max	906
Gomes, Yan	904
Dalbec, Bobby	901
Myers, Wil	899
Castellanos, Nick	899
Schoop, Jonathan	897
Bryant, Kris	893
O Neill, Tyler	893
Springer, George	893
Alvarez, Yordan	892

450+ PA, 2020-2021

Top OPS v RHP, 2020-21

Hitter	OPS
Harper, Bryce	1097
Soto, Juan	1097
Belt, Brandon	1042
Winker, Jesse	1035
Freeman, Freddie	1028
Walsh, Jared	1006
Acuna, Ronald	988
Votto, Joey	984
Tatis Jr., Fernando	981
Guerrero Jr., Vladimir	954
Devers, Rafael	953
Seager, Corey	943
Smith, Will	939
Brantley, Michael	925
Lowe, Brandon	923
Crawford, Brandon	922
Betts, Mookie	918
Tucker, Kyle	916
Springer, George	908
Schwarber, Kyle	906
Mullins II, Cedric	902
Nimmo, Brandon	896
Castellanos, Nick	891
Verdugo, Alex	889
Cron, C.J.	888
Judge, Aaron	885
Ramirez, Jose	883
Riley, Austin	883
Machado, Manny	877
Yastrzemski, Mike	876
Voit, Luke	874
Stanton, Giancarlo	873
Alvarez, Yordan	870
Bogaerts, Xander	862
Ozuna, Marcell	857
Abreu, Jose	854
Turner, Trea	854
Turner, Justin	853
Pollock, A.J.	853
Perez, Salvador	852
Alonso, Pete	850

Top L-R Splits, 2020-21

Hitter	OPS vL-vR
Zunino, Mike	483
Marte, Ketel	428
McCutchen, Andrew	345
Rojas, Miguel	341
Turner, Trea	306
Longoria, Evan	285
Hernandez, Teoscar	274
Goodrum, Niko	273
Pujols, Albert	267
Robert, Luis	253
Anderson, Tim	249
Gomes, Yan	244
Story, Trevor	240
Kelly, Carson	229
McCann, James	223
Cruz, Nelson	219
Goldschmidt, Paul	218
Fletcher, David	215
Arozarena, Randy	213

Top R-L Splits, 2020-21

Hitter	OPS vR-vL
Walsh, Jared	408
Naquin, Tyler	387
Winker, Jesse	381
Kepler, Max	356
Brantley, Michael	335
Meadows, Austin	316
Narvaez, Omar	302
Choi, Ji-Man	298
Belt, Brandon	295
Votto, Joey	289
Freeman, Freddie	280
Eaton, Adam	279
Miller, Bradley	276
Verdugo, Alex	266
Harper, Bryce	253
Devers, Rafael	239
La Stella, Tommy	238
Lux, Gavin	224
Moran, Colin	220

Best Parks - LH HR

Ballpark	Factor
CHW	48%
TOR	38%
CIN	37%
BAL	35%
LAA	23%
COL	15%
PHI	13%
ATL	11%
NYY	10%

Worst Parks - LH HR

Ballpark	Factor
DET	-25%
KC	-24%
OAK	-19%
TAM	-19%
PIT	-19%
MIA	-19%
STL	-18%

Best Parks - Runs

Ballpark	Factor
COL	34%
CIN	16%
BOS	12%
KC	11%

Worst Parks - Runs

Ballpark	Factor
TAM	-16%
OAK	-14%
SD	-12%
NYM	-12%
STL	-11%
SEA	-10%

Best Parks - BB

Ballpark	Factor
PIT	9%
SF	8%

Best Parks - RH HR

Ballpark	Factor
LAA	44%
BAL	32%
CIN	28%
CHW	22%
MIL	15%
COL	13%
PHI	11%

Worst Parks-RH HR

Ballpark	Factor
ARI	-22%
KC	-21%
SF	-18%
STL	-18%
OAK	-17%
PIT	-16%
MIA	-16%
TAM	-15%
MIN	-12%
TEX	-11%

Best Parks - Ks

Ballpark	Factor
TAM	9%
NYM	9%
SEA	8%
MIL	7%

Worst Parks - Ks

Ballpark	Factor
COL	-15%
KC	-12%
STL	-8%
DET	-6%

Worst Parks - BB

Ballpark	Factor
LAA	-12%
KC	-10%
TOR	-10%

Note: for Runs, the best parks for hitters are also the worst for pitchers and vice versa

Consistent Hi-PQS SP

Pitcher	QC*
deGrom, Jacob	119
Bauer, Trevor	100
Bieber, Shane	86
Burnes, Corbin	81
Wheeler, Zack	70
Glasnow, Tyler	64
Woodruff, Brandon	56
Cole, Gerrit	52
Scherzer, Max	38
Kershaw, Clayton	31
Buehler, Walker	29
Gausman, Kevin	28
Darvish, Yu	24
Bassitt, Chris	16
Alcantara, Sandy	10
Valdez, Framber	6
Lynn, Lance	5
Eovaldi, Nathan	5

20+ Starts, 2020-2021

*Quality-Consistency score

Consistent Low-PQS SP

Pitcher	QC*
Gonzalez, Chi Chi	(273)
Arrieta, Jake	(255)
Lester, Jon	(240)
Anderson, Brett	(218)
Gant, John	(210)
Keuchel, Dallas	(200)
Peterson, David	(183)
Urena, Jose	(183)
Richards, Garrett	(181)
Harvey, Matt	(181)
Martinez, Carlos	(181)
Mills, Alec	(181)
Stripling, Ross	(179)
Canning, Griffin	(175)
Lopez, Jorge	(174)
Houser, Adrian	(173)
Keller, Mitch	(171)
Velasquez, Vincent	(164)
Happ, J.A.	(159)
Davies, Zachary	(155)

Most DOMinant SP

Pitcher	DOM
deGrom, Jacob	67%
Bauer, Trevor	57%
Wheeler, Zack	53%
Kershaw, Clayton	53%
Burnes, Corbin	51%
Bieber, Shane	50%
Glasnow, Tyler	48%
Scherzer, Max	48%
Alcantara, Sandy	45%
Buehler, Walker	44%
Gausman, Kevin	42%
Woodruff, Brandon	42%
Valdez, Framber	41%
Wainwright, Adam	40%
Darvish, Yu	40%
Cole, Gerrit	40%
Bassitt, Chris	39%
Lopez, Pablo	39%
Rodon, Carlos	38%
Manaea, Sean	37%

Most DISastrous SP

Pitcher	DIS
Gonzalez, Chi Chi	68%
Arrieta, Jake	67%
Lester, Jon	63%
Anderson, Brett	59%
Keuchel, Dallas	54%
Martinez, Carlos	52%
Gant, John	52%
Urena, Jose	52%
Canning, Griffin	50%
Stripling, Ross	50%
Peterson, David	50%
Houser, Adrian	49%
Lopez, Jorge	48%
Mills, Alec	48%
Corbin, Patrick	48%
Richards, Garrett	47%
Harvey, Matt	47%
Wacha, Michael	47%
Keller, Mitch	46%
Lyles, Jordan	46%

Universal Draft Grid

Most publications and websites provide cheat sheets with ranked player lists for different fantasy draft formats. The biggest problem with these tools is that they perpetrate the myth that players can be ranked in a linear fashion.

Since rankings are based on highly variable projections, it is foolhardy to draw conclusions that a $24 player is better than a $23 player is better than a $22 player. Yes, a first round pick is better than a 10th round pick, but within most rounds, all players are pretty much interchangeable commodities.

But typical cheat sheets don't reflect that reality. Auction sheets rank players by dollar value. Snake draft sheets rank players within round, accounting for position and categorical scarcity. But just as ADPs have a ridiculously low success rate, these cheat sheets are similarly flawed.

We have a tool at BaseballHQ.com called the Rotisserie Grid. It is a chart—that can be customized to your league parameters—which organizes players into pockets of skill, by position. It is one of the most popular tools on the site. One of the best features of this grid is that its design provides immediate insight into position scarcity.

So in the *Forecaster*, we have transitioned to this format as a sort of Universal Draft Grid.

How to use the chart

Across the top of the grid, players are sorted by position. First and third base, and second and shortstop are presented side-by-side for easy reference when considering corner and middle infielders, respectively.

The vertical axis separates each group of players into tiers based on potential fantasy impact. At the top are the Elite players; at the bottom are the Fringe players.

Auction leagues: The tiers in the grid represent rough break-points for dollar values. Elite players could be considered those that are purchased for $30 and up. Each subsequent tier is a step down of approximately $5.

Snake drafters: Tiers can be used to rank players similarly, though most tiers will encompass more than one round. Any focus on position scarcity will bump some players up a bit. In recent years, Catcher has been the only position to exhibit any real positional scarcity effect. As such, one might opt to draft Will Smith (from the Stars tier) before the Gold level Myles Straw.

To build the best foundation, try to stay balanced in the first 10 rounds of your draft: 2 MI, 2 CI, 3 OF, and 3 SP (likely one closer) is a foundation target that will set you up for maximum flexibility in the mid- and end-games.

The players are listed at the position where they both qualify and provide the most fantasy value. Additional position eligibility (10 games) is listed in parentheses. (NOTE: check out our new Multiposition Eligiblity Chart on page 282 for additional eligibility detail.) Listings in bold are players with high reliability grades (minimum "B" across the board).

Each player is presented with his 7-character Mayberry score. The first four digits (all on a 0-5 scale) represent skill: power, speed, batting average and playing time for batters; ERA, dominance, saves potential and playing time for pitchers. The last three alpha characters are the reliability grade (A-F): health, experience and consistency.

Within each tier, players are sorted by the first character of their Mayberry score. This means that batters are sorted by power; pitchers by ERA potential. If you need to prospect for the best skill sets among players in a given tier, target those with 4s and 5s in whatever skill you need.

CAVEATS and DISCLAIMERS

The placement of players in tiers does not represent average draft positions (ADP) or average auction values (AAV). It represents where each player's true value may lie. It is the variance between this true value and the ADP/AAV market values—or better, the value that your league-mates place on each player—where you will find your potential for profit or loss.

That means *you cannot take this chart right into your draft with you*. You have to compare these rankings with your ADPs and AAVs, and build your draft list from there. In other words, if we project Paul Goldschmidt as a "Elite" level pick but you know the other owners (or your ADPs) see him as a third-rounder, you can probably wait to pick him up in round two. If you are in an auction league with owners who overvalue young award-winning players and Jazz Chisholm (projected at $27) gets bid past $30, you will likely take a loss should you decide to chase the bidding, especially given the depth of shortstops in in that tier for 2022.

Finally, this chart is intended as a preliminary look based on current factors. For Draft Day, you will need to make your own adjustments based upon many different criteria that will impact the world between now and then. Daily updates appear online at BaseballHQ.com. A free projections update is available in March at **http://www.baseballhq.com/bf2022**

Simulation League Cheat Sheet   Using Runs Above Replacement creates a more real-world ranking of player value, which serves simulation gamers well. Batters and pitchers are integrated, and value break-points are delineated.

Multi-Position Eligiblity Chart   The default position eligibility requirements throughout this book is 20 games in the previous season. This chart serves those who play in leagues where the eligiblity requirements are 10 or 5 games at a position in the preceeding year.

Universal Draft Grid

TIER	FIRST BASE	THIRD BASE	SECOND BASE	SHORTSTOP
Elite	**Goldschmidt,Paul** (4345 AAB) Freeman,Freddie (4255 AAF) Guerrero Jr.,Vladimir (4155 AAC)	Devers,Rafael (4155 AAC) Ramirez,Jose (4455 AAD) Machado,Manny (3245 AAD)	**Albies,Ozzie** (4535 AAB) **Merrifield,Whit (o)** (1545 AAA)	**Tatis Jr.,Fernando (o)** (5445 CAB) **Story,Trevor** (4525 AAB) **Anderson,Tim** (3545 BAA) Bichette,Bo (3455 AAA) Turner,Trea (4) (3555 AAC)
Gold	Abreu,José (4145 AAD) Olson,Matt (4245 AAD)	Mondesi,Adalberto (3503 FDA)	**Lowe,Brandon** (5335 BAB) **India,Jonathan** (3335 AAA) Marte,Ketel (o) (3355 CAF) Altuve,Jose (2245 BAD)	**Báez,Javier (4)** (4425 BAD) Semien,Marcus (4) (4335 AAD) Bogaerts,Xander (3345 AAA) Chisholm Jr.,Jazz (4) (3515 ADF) Franco,Wander (3355 ADF) Polanco,Jorge (4) (3245 AAD)
Stars	**Hoskins,Rhys** (5155 CAA) Alonso,Pete (4235 AAB) Mountcastle,Ryan (o) (4235 AAD) Walsh,Jared (4135 BAD) Bell,Josh (3145 AAD) Rizzo,Anthony (2145 AAC) Gurriel,Yuli (1135 BAD)	Bryant,Kris (o) (4425 AAD) Rendon,Anthony (4245 FBD) Riley,Austin (4035 AAC) Arenado,Nolan (3245 AAD) Bregman,Alex (3245 CAC) Moncada,Yoán (3225 AAD)	**McMahon,Ryan (5)** (4225 AAB) **Muncy,Max (3)** (4135 BAD) **France,Ty (3)** (2045 AAA) **Edman,Tommy (o)** (1435 BAD) Segura,Jean (1245 BAA) LeMahieu,DJ (53) (1255 AAF)	**Adames,Willy** (4225 AAA) **Swanson,Dansby** (4325 AAB) **Lindor,Francisco** (3335 BAB) **Correa,Carlos** (3335 CAD) **Crawford,Brandon** (3235 AAC) **Seager,Corey** (3255 FAB) Cronenworth,Jake (43) (2345 AAA) Torres,Gleyber (2225 BAB) Rosario,Amed (1525 AAC) Kiner-Falefa,Isiah (0435 AAA)
Regulars	**Belt,Brandon** (5143 DAF) **Dalbec,Bobby** (5235 AAD) **Cron,C.J.** (4135 BAB) Voit,Luke (4025 FCC) Votto,Joey (4245 CAB) Aguilar,Jesús (3025 BAB) Kirilloff,Alex (o) (3135 DDA) Mancini,Trey (3135 AAD) Lowe,Nate (2325 AAA) Hosmer,Eric (2135 AAC) Schwindel,Frank (2135 ACD)	**Longoria,Evan** (4133 FBB) Turner,Justin (3335 BAA) Candelario,Jeimer (3135 BAC) Hayes,Ke'Bryan (3345 CBF) Jung,Josh (3015 ADF) Anderson,Brian (2415 CBA)	**Hernández,Kiké (o)** (3235 BAB) **Escobar,Eduardo (5)** (3235 BAD) **Hampson,Garrett (o)** (2515 AAA) **Schoop,Jonathan (3)** (2225 AAA) **Toro,Abraham (5)** (2225 ABF) **Wong,Kolten** (2335 CAB) Arraez,Luis (5o) (1255 BAA) García,Luis (1145 ABA) Solak,Nick (1325 AAB) Madrigal,Nick (1353 DDA) McNeil,Jeff (o) (1245 BAC)	**Taylor,Chris (4o)** (4425 AAA) **Suárez,Eugenio (5)** (4125 AAC) Witt Jr.,Bobby (4423 ABF) Barrero,Jose (3503 ADF) Urias,Luis (45) (3235 AAC) Lux,Gavin (4) (2425 BBD) Rodgers,Brendan (4) (2135 DCF) Rojas,Josh (4o) (2225 AAF) Wendle,Joe (2335 CAB) Crawford,J.P. (1225 BAA) Rojas,Miguel (1345 BAD) Fletcher,David (4) (0345 AAC) Lopez,Nicky (0435 AAD)
Mid-Level	**Sanó,Miguel** (5015 CAB) **Ruf,Darin (o)** (4253 BBA) **Tellez,Rowdy** (4045 BCC) Walker,Christian (3223 BAB) Wade Jr.,LaMonte (o) (3333 CCC) Smith,Pavin (o) (2435 AAC) Moran,Colin (2025 CBA) Torkelson,Spencer (2223 ADF) Cabrera,Miguel (1125 CAA)	**Chapman,Matt** (4105 BAB) **Seager,Kyle** (4125 BAA) **Donaldson,Josh** (4125 CAA) Wisdom,Patrick (4205 ACF) Dozier,Hunter (o) (3305 BAC) Bohm,Alec (2223 ABD) Díaz,Yandy (3) (1133 BAB)	Hernandez,Cesar (2315 AAA) Bruján,Vidal (o) (2523 ACA) Flores,Wilmer (53) (2343 CAA) Moore,Dylan (o) (2403 BBD) Berti,Jon (5) (1413 FCB) Frazier,Adam (1245 AAC) García,Leury (o) (1423 CAB) Harrison,Josh (5o) (1235 DAB) Hoerner,Nico (0223 DDC)	**DeJong,Paul** (3203 BAA) **Goodrum,Niko** (3405 CBB) **Giménez,Andrés (4)** (2513 ABB) **Kim,Ha-Seong (45)** (2413 AAB) **Urshela,Gio (5)** (2335 BAB) Castro,Willi (4) (2523 ABF) Iglesias,José (2253 BAF) Urías,Ramón (4) (2233 ACF) Villar,Jonathan (5) (2313 BAC) Andrus,Elvis (1333 BAB) Gregorius,Didi (1223 DBD) Sosa,Edmundo (4) (1323 ACA) Wade,Tyler (5o) (1501 ADB)
Bench	**Miller,Brad (o)** (4313 ABA) **Bradley,Bobby** (4015 ACC) Choi,Ji-Man (4023 CCA) Díaz,Lewin (4211 ACD) Pratto,Nick (4313 ABF) Ríos,Edwin (4001 FFF) Zimmerman,Ryan (4131 DDA) Tsutsugo,Yoshi (o) (3003 BBB) Santana,Carlos (2225 AAC) Profar,Jurickson (o) (1333 AAC)	Davis,J.D. (4313 DCC) Moustakas,Mike (4135 DCB) Biggio,Cavan (3303 CBB) Díaz,Aledmys (2133 DCA) Gorman,Nolan (2313 ABF) Astudillo,Willians (3) (1041 BDB) Espinal,Santiago (1331 ACB) Kieboom,Carter (1115 ACC) Hernandez,Yonny (0521 ADD)	**Odor,Rougned (5)** (4001 BAB) **Arroyo,Christian** (3231 FFB) **Brosseau,Mike (5)** (3301 ACF) Chavis,Michael (3201 CCB) Lowrie,Jed (3033 FBD) VanMeter,Josh (5) (3213 ACF) Bote,David (5) (2213 CBB) Canó,Robinson (2051 CFD) Ibáñez,Andy (2233 ACA) Alberto,Hanser (5) (1341 BBA) Kemp,Tony (o) (1323 ABB) Difo,Wilmer (1311 ADD) Duffy,Matt (5) (1331 FDB) Jones,Jahmai (1403 ACF) La Stella,Tommy (1143 FCB) Paredes,Isaac (1223 BBD) Peterson,Jace (3o) (1313 BCA) Solano,Donovan (1233 CBB)	**Cruz,Oneil** (3521 AFA) **Estrada,Thairo** (3241 ADD) **Ahmed,Nick** (2325 BAD) **Dubón,Mauricio (4o)** (2331 ABA) Farmer,Kyle (2123 AAA) Galvis,Freddy (2223 CAA) Escobar,Alcides (1223 ABB) Alcantara,Sergio (4) (1503 ACB) Walls,Taylor (1301 ADB) Castro,Harold (4) (0133 ACD) Newman,Kevin (0335 AAC)
Fringe	**Guzmán,Ronald** (4131 FFC) Hiura,Keston (4201 ABD) Vogelbach,Daniel (3001 CCA) Pujols,Albert (2221 BBA) Beaty,Matt (o) (2131 ADC) Jones,Taylor (2001 ACB) O'Hearn,Ryan (o) (2301 ACB) White,Evan (2103 FDD) Bauers,Jake (o) (1301 ACB)	**Burger,Jake** (3001 BFF) Chang,Yu (3) (3211 ADC) Franco,Maikel (2221 ABC) Fuentes,Joshua (3) (2101 ABD) Mayfield,Jack (2201 ACC) Welker,Colton (2221 AFC) Gosselin,Phil (3o) (1101 ABA) Baty,Brett (1301 AFF) Gonzalez,Erik (1111 DDA) Gutierrez,Kelvin (1303 ACD)	**Carpenter,Matt** (3301 BCA) **McKinstry,Zach (o)** (3111 BCA) Gonzalez,Marwin (2001 BBB) Ruiz,Rio (2111 ACA) Miller,Owen (1213 ABB) Clement,Ernie (1233 ADA) Díaz,Isan (5) (1101 ACD) Park,Hoy Jun (1401 ACA)	Groshans,Jordan (5) (3011 ADF) Abrams,CJ (2431 BFF) Martin,Austin (o) (1411 ADF) Martin,Richie (1401 CDA) Mendick,Danny (4) (1101 ACA) Perdomo,Geraldo (1401 AFF) Rengifo,Luis (1311 ACC) Tucker,Cole (1401 ACA) Simmons,Andrelton (0215 CAB) Torreyes,Ronald (5) (0321 BDC)

Universal Draft Grid

TIER	CATCHER		DH		OUTFIELD			
Elite			Ohtani,Shohei	(5435 BAD)	Harper,Bryce	(5355 BAC)	Hernández,Teoscar	(4335 AAC)
					Judge,Aaron	(5135 CAB)	Soto,Juan	(4255 AAF)
					Trout,Mike	(5355 FCD)	Tucker,Kyle	(4445 AAC)
					Betts,Mookie	(4445 BAB)	Marte,Starling	(2545 BAB)
					Castellanos,Nick	(4155 AAD)		
Gold	Perez,Salvador	(4045 FAD)			Acuña,Ronald	(5335 DAA)	Robert,Luis	(4435 DCD)
					Alvarez,Yordan	(5145 AAD)	Springer,George	(4345 FAB)
					Buxton,Byron	(5445 FDC)	Baddoo,Akil	(3515 ACF)
					Arozarena,Randy	(4425 AAD)	Mullins,Cedric	(3525 AAD)
					O Neill,Tyler	(4315 BAD)	Straw,Myles	(0515 AAD)
					Reynolds,Bryan	(4345 AAF)		
Stars	Smith,Will	(4435 AAD)	Reyes,Franmil	(4125 BAA)	Schwarber,Kyle	(5135 BAD)	Winker,Jesse	(4155 DAB)
			Cruz,Nelson	(4225 AAC)	Bellinger,Cody	(4425 CAF)	García,Avisaíl	(3135 BAD)
					Conforto,Michael	(4135 BAD)	Kelenic,Jarred	(3215 ACD)
					Gurriel Jr.,Lourdes	(4145 BAC)	Rosario,Eddie	(3345 CAA)
					Haniger,Mitch	(4325 CAA)	Yelich,Christian	(3435 CAF)
					Jiménez,Eloy	(4045 FCC)	Blackmon,Charlie	(2245 AAB)
					Martinez,J.D.	(4245 AAF)	Verdugo,Alex	(2445 BAB)
					Myers,Wil	(4325 BAD)	Benintendi,Andrew	(2235 BAF)
					Pollock,A.J.	(4243 FAB)	Brantley,Michael	(1355 BAA)
					Renfroe,Hunter	(4125 AAD)	Tapia,Raimel	(1545 BAB)
					Stanton,Giancarlo	(4135 FAA)		
Regulars	Contreras,Willson	(4125 BAB)			Gallo,Joey	(5205 BAD)	Kepler,Max	(3335 BAA)
	Garver,Mitch	(4133 DDF)			Duvall,Adam	(4315 AAA)	Adell,Jo	(3305 BBD)
	Grandal,Yasmani	(4125 CAC)			Happ,Ian	(4225 AAB)	Bader,Harrison	(3315 CBA)
	Realmuto,J.T.	(3325 AAA)			Soler,Jorge	(4125 BAB)	Carlson,Dylan	(3225 AAD)
	Varsho,Daulton (o)	(3425 ABD)			Laureano,Ramón	(4223 BAC)	Greene,Riley	(3503 ABF)
					McCutchen,Andrew	(4235 DAA)	Naquin,Tyler	(3235 DBD)
					Meadows,Austin	(4125 AAD)	Nimmo,Brandon	(3335 FCB)
					Sánchez,Jesús	(4235 BCF)	Rodríguez,Julio	(3323 AFF)
					Yastrzemski,Mike	(4225 AAD)	Santander,Anthony	(3035 CAC)
					Canha,Mark	(3425 BAB)	Meyers,Jake	(2313 ADD)
					Grisham,Trent	(3225 BAB)	Pham,Tommy	(2325 AAC)
					Grossman,Robbie	(3325 AAB)	Cain,Lorenzo	(1433 DCD)
					Hays,Austin	(3235 BAA)		
Mid-Level	Zunino,Mike	(5203 BBC)			Hilliard,Sam	(5413 ABA)	Herrera,Odúbel	(2233 ABB)
	Murphy,Sean	(4025 ABB)			Siri,Jose	(4503 ABB)	Olivares,Edward	(2333 ABB)
	Haase,Eric (o)	(4203 ACD)			Alford,Anthony	(4403 BDA)	Peralta,David	(2335 BAA)
	Jansen,Danny	(4143 CDA)			Brown,Seth	(4213 ACF)	Robles,Victor	(2313 AAB)
	Gomes,Yan	(3333 BBB)			García,Adolis	(4305 AAF)	Taveras,Leody	(2505 ABB)
	Kirk,Alejandro	(3043 CFF)			Lewis,Kyle	(4413 FCB)	Taylor,Michael A.	(2205 AAA)
	Kelly,Carson	(2025 BBC)			Ozuna,Marcell	(4233 FBF)	Dickerson,Corey	(2333 DBB)
	McCann,James	(2115 AAC)			Pederson,Joc	(4125 AAC)	Duran,Jarren	(2503 ACA)
	Nola,Austin	(2033 DDB)			Taylor,Tyrone	(4423 BDA)	Heyward,Jason	(2333 CAD)
	Posey,Buster	(2043 BAD)			Gamel,Ben	(3125 ABA)	Kiermaier,Kevin	(2523 CAA)
	Ruiz,Keibert	(2033 ACC)			Grichuk,Randal	(3123 AAB)	Marsh,Brandon	(2405 ACC)
	Stephenson,Tyler (3)	(2043 ABD)			Calhoun,Kole	(3125 FBB)	Mateo,Jorge	(2503 ACD)
	Vázquez,Christian	(1125 AAB)			Cameron,Daz	(3513 BCC)	Mercado,Oscar	(2413 ABD)
					Cooper,Garrett	(3043 FCA)	Naylor,Josh	(2035 DCB)
					Engel,Adam	(3413 FDC)	Ortega,Rafael	(2523 ACB)
					Hicks,Aaron	(3213 FDB)	Reyes,Victor	(2533 BCA)
					Joe,Connor	(3135 BDD)	Vaughn,Andrew	(2025 ACF)
					Lowe,Josh	(3401 ABC)	Margot,Manuel	(1423 BAA)
					McCormick,Chas	(3313 ACB)	De La Cruz,Bryan	(1213 ACA)
					Slater,Austin	(3433 ACD)	Gordon,Nick	(1533 ADB)
					Smith,Dominic	(3035 BAD)	Ramirez,Harold	(1133 ABF)
					Thomas,Lane	(3305 ACD)	Senzel,Nick	(1223 FFB)
Bench	Jeffers,Ryan	(4003 ADB)	Sheets,Gavin	(4011 ABA)	Frazier,Clint	(4311 FCF)	Brinson,Lewis	(2313 BCA)
	Raleigh,Cal	(4113 ADA)	Casas,Triston	(3211 ADF)	Luplow,Jordan	(4111 DDD)	Calhoun,Willie	(2033 DCD)
	Sánchez,Gary	(4003 CAD)			Phillips,Brett	(4501 ACA)	Dahl,David	(2221 DCD)
	D Arnaud,Travis	(3123 FCF)			Rooker,Brent	(4103 ACC)	Hill,Derek	(2501 BCF)
	Díaz,Elias	(3033 ACA)			Stewart,D.J.	(4103 BCA)	Isbel,Kyle	(2403 ADF)
	Mejía,Francisco	(3233 BDF)			Peters,DJ	(3203 ABB)	Lee,Khalil	(2301 ACB)
	Murphy,Tom	(3103 BCD)			Cordero,Franchy	(3301 FDA)	Piscotty,Stephen	(2313 DDA)
	Torrens,Luis	(3123 ACA)			Dickerson,Alex	(3223 FCD)	Thomas,Alek	(2311 ACF)
	Alfaro,Jorge (o)	(2303 BBA)			Duggar,Steven	(3403 BCD)	Zimmer,Bradley	(2403 DDC)
	Barnhart,Tucker	(2013 ABA)			Fraley,Jake	(3301 CDD)	Hernandez,Yadiel	(1223 ACC)
	Severino,Pedro	(2213 AAA)			McCarthy,Jake	(3501 ADF)	Larnach,Trevor	(1303 BDD)
	Heim,Jonah	(2123 ACC)			Pillar,Kevin	(3331 BAC)	Quinn,Roman	(1501 FFB)
	Ramos,Wilson	(2111 DCB)			Polanco,Gregory	(3301 DCD)	Schrock,Max	(1211 BDC)
	Rutschman,Adley	(2123 ABF)			Upton,Justin	(3103 FBB)	Daza,Yonathan	(0211 BCA)
	Stallings,Jacob	(1015 ABA)			Ward,Taylor	(3321 ACA)	Sierra,Magneuris	(0511 ACA)
	Molina,Yadier	(1123 CAA)			Gardner,Brett	(2313 AAB)		
	Narváez,Omar	(1025 AAD)			Andújar,Miguel	(2231 FFC)		
					Bradley,Jackie	(2301 ACA)		
Fringe	Nuñez,Dom	(4201 ADA)	Beer,Seth	(3021 BCC)	Aquino,Aristides	(5301 BDD)		
	Rogers,Jake	(4401 BFC)	Mercedes,Yermín	(1201 ABF)	Davis,Brennen	(4201 ADF)		
	Adams,Riley	(3303 ADB)			Garlick,Kyle	(4301 FFF)		
	Contreras,William	(3011 ADF)			Rojas,Jose	(3221 ABB)		
	Melendez,MJ	(3111 ABF)			Trammell,Taylor	(3201 ABA)		
	Stassi,Max	(3003 CCF)			Goodwin,Brian	(3211 CBB)		
	Maldonado,Martín	(2003 AAB)			Martin,Jason	(3211 ADD)		
	Bart,Joey	(2001 AFC)			McKinney,Billy	(3201 BCF)		
	Collins,Zack	(2101 ADF)			Pinder,Chad	(3221 DDA)		
	Hedges,Austin	(2201 ACA)			Kingery,Scott	(2401 DDC)		
	Jackson,Alex	(2403 DDB)			Long Jr.,Shed	(2201 FDB)		
	Caratini,Victor	(1101 ABB)			Pache,Cristian	(2201 BBC)		
	Campusano,Luis	(1301 BFF)			White,Eli	(2301 CCB)		
	Knizner,Andrew	(1101 ADB)			Eaton,Adam	(1421 CBB)		
	McGuire,Reese	(1221 AAC)			Nootbaar,Lars	(1201 AFA)		
	Nido,Tomás	(1411 BFF)			Stevenson,Andrew	(1201 BDF)		
	Trevino,Jose	(1133 BDB)			Williams,Luke	(1401 ADA)		
					Akiyama,Shogo	(0231 CCC)		

Universal Draft Grid

TIER	STARTING PITCHERS				RELIEF PITCHERS			
Elite	Cole,Gerrit	(5505 BAB)						
Gold	Burnes,Corbin	(5503 BBF)	Scherzer,Max	(4503 DAB)				
	Buehler,Walker	(4305 BAA)						
Stars	Bieber,Shane	(5403 FAB)	Woodruff,Brandon	(4305 BAA)	Clase,Emmanuel	(5230 ADB)		
	deGrom,Jacob	(5503 FAB)	Alcantara,Sandy	(3205 AAB)	Hader,Josh	(5530 AAB)		
	Nola,Aaron	(5405 BAB)	Fried,Max	(3205 DAA)	Hendriks,Liam	(5530 BAA)		
	Sale,Chris	(5503 FDC)	Lynn,Lance	(3305 CAA)	Iglesias,Raisel	(5530 ABB)		
	Musgrove,Joe	(4305 DAB)	Urías,Julio	(2205 DAC)	Romano,Jordan	(3431 CCF)		
	Wheeler,Zack	(4205 BAB)						
Regulars	Baz,Shane	(5403 AFF)	Flaherty,Jack	(3303 FBA)	Chapman,Aroldis	(5530 CBB)		
	Kershaw,Clayton	(5303 FAA)	Giolito,Lucas	(3305 CAA)	Díaz,Edwin	(5530 ABB)		
	Gausman,Kevin	(4305 DAA)	Montas,Frankie	(3305 AAB)	Kimbrel,Craig	(5520 BCB)		
	McClanahan,Shane	(4303 ADF)	Ray,Robbie	(3505 DAF)	Pressly,Ryan	(5430 CBB)		
	Morton,Charlie	(4403 CAB)	Rodón,Carlos	(3403 FCF)	Gallegos,Giovanny	(3420 ACB)		
	Ohtani,Shohei	(4403 CDF)	Rogers,Trevor	(3403 ACC)	Jansen,Kenley	(3430 AAA)		
	Severino,Luis	(4403 FFC)	Berríos,José	(2205 AAA)	Smith,Will	(3430 DBB)		
	Valdez,Framber	(4203 DBB)	Peralta,Freddy	(2403 BBB)				
	Webb,Logan	(4203 DBB)	Wainwright,Adam	(2103 FAA)				
Mid-Level	Castillo,Luis	(4305 AAB)	Verlander,Justin	(3301 FCA)	Castillo,Diego	(5420 CCB)	Barlow,Scott	(2421 ACB)
	Darvish,Yu	(4403 FAB)	Anderson,Ian	(2303 DCB)	Kittredge,Andrew	(5320 DDC)	Floro,Dylan	(2220 BCB)
	McCullers,Lance	(4303 FBA)	Bassitt,Chris	(2203 DAA)	Rogers,Taylor	(5420 DBC)	Fulmer,Michael	(2221 FDF)
	Eovaldi,Nathan	(3303 DBB)	Cease,Dylan	(2403 ABC)	Williams,Devin	(5510 BDD)		
	Gray,Sonny	(3303 DAA)	Clevinger,Mike	(2303 FCB)	Bednar,David	(4420 BDF)		
	López,Pablo	(3203 FBB)	Garcia,Luis	(2303 ACB)	Doval,Camilo	(4521 AFF)		
	Manaea,Sean	(3203 FBB)	Mahle,Tyler	(2303 BAA)	Green,Chad	(4410 ACA)		
	Manoah,Alek	(3303 BFF)	McKenzie,Triston	(2303 BDA)	Houck,Tanner	(4403 ADC)		
	Márquez,Germán	(3205 BAA)	Means,John	(2203 DBB)	Sewald,Paul	(4520 ADF)		
	Strasburg,Stephen	(3301 FCF)	Rodriguez,Eduardo	(2303 FBA)	Treinen,Blake	(4320 BCC)		
	Stroman,Marcus	(3103 DBA)	Plesac,Zach	(1003 DBB)	Melancon,Mark	(3220 DBB)		
	Suárez,Ranger	(3203 ADF)			Whitlock,Garrett	(3211 BDD)		
Bench	Syndergaard,Noah	(4301 FCA)	Matz,Steven	(2203 DBA)	Holmes,Clay	(5311 CDC)	Soto,Gregory	(2320 BCD)
	Carrasco,Carlos	(3303 FBA)	Montgomery,Jordan	(2203 FCA)	Knebel,Corey	(5510 FDF)	Sulser,Cole	(2321 ACF)
	Kopech,Michael	(3503 FDF)	Ober,Bailey	(2303 AFF)	Rosenthal,Trevor	(5520 FDF)	Kennedy,Ian	(1320 DCC)
	Megill,Tylor	(3303 AFF)	Paddack,Chris	(2103 DBA)	Alcala,Jorge	(4310 BDC)	Quantrill,Cal	(1103 ACA)
	Otto Jr.,Glenn	(3201 CFF)	Pineda,Michael	(2103 FBA)	Barnes,Matt	(4520 CBB)	Rodríguez,Richard	(1110 BCF)
	Ryu,Hyun-Jin	(3203 FAA)	Skubal,Tarik	(2403 ACC)	Giles,Ken	(4520 FDF)		
	Sánchez,Sixto	(3101 FDA)	Taillon,Jameson	(2203 FCA)	Loaisiga,Jonathan	(4320 FDB)		
	Sandoval,Patrick	(3303 DCB)	Civale,Aaron	(1103 DBA)	Neris,Héctor	(4521 ABC)		
	Snell,Blake	(3503 DBA)	DeSclafani,Anthony	(1103 FAD)	Duffey,Tyler	(3310 ADB)		
	Wood,Alex	(3203 FCC)	Flexen,Chris	(1103 AAF)	Karinchak,James	(3510 ADB)		
	Cobb,Alex	(2103 FCB)	Gilbert,Tyler	(1001 BFB)	McHugh,Collin	(3310 FDC)		
	Gallen,Zac	(2303 DBB)	Gonzales,Marco	(1103 CAC)	Sims,Lucas	(3520 DCB)		
	Germán,Domingo	(2301 DCA)	Lauer,Eric	(1203 BCF)	Colomé,Alex	(2220 ABA)		
	Gilbert,Logan	(2303 ADC)	Mize,Casey	(1003 ACC)	Javier,Cristian	(2401 ACD)		
	Greinke,Zack	(2103 CAA)	Patino,Luis	(1303 ADF)	May,Trevor	(2411 DCB)		
	Hendricks,Kyle	(2005 BAB)	Urquidy,José	(1101 DCB)	McGee,Jake	(2120 DCF)		
	Kelly,Merrill	(2103 DAB)	Yarbrough,Ryan	(1003 BBB)	Rogers,Tyler	(2011 ACB)		
Fringe	Detmers,Reid	(3503 CFF)	Weaver,Luke	(2201 FCC)	Ashby,Aaron	(5501 AFF)	Givens,Mychal	(2310 BCB)
	Maeda,Kenta	(3301 FAC)	Anderson,Tyler	(1103 FBB)	Bummer,Aaron	(5300 DDA)	Hernández,Jonathan	(2210 FDF)
	Paxton,James	(3400 FCF)	Bumgarner,Madison	(1103 FAC)	Kahnle,Tommy	(5500 FDF)	Johnson,Pierce	(2411 CDA)
	Soroka,Michael	(3101 FCB)	Gil,Luis	(1401 AFF)	Bender,Anthony	(4310 ADF)	Leclerc,José	(2510 FDD)
	Ynoa,Huascar	(3301 FCD)	Gomber,Austin	(1201 DCA)	Cousins,Jake	(4510 BFF)	Littell,Zack	(2300 BDF)
	Alzolay,Adbert	(2203 CCB)	Gonsolin,Tony	(1301 FCY)	Fairbanks,Peter	(4510 DDC)	Martínez,Carlos	(2201 FCD)
	Brubaker,Jonathan	(2203 CCA)	Gray,Josiah	(1203 BFD)	King,John	(4000 FDC)	Matzek,Tyler	(2410 ADF)
	Dunning,Dane	(2203 BCA)	Hearn,Taylor	(1103 FDA)	Mayza,Tim	(4311 BDC)	Mayers,Mike	(2310 DCD)
	Eflin,Zach	(2201 FAB)	Hernandez,Elieser	(1203 FDB)	Robertson,David	(4410 FFF)	Ottavino,Adam	(2410 BCA)
	Gibson,Kyle	(2103 BAA)	Hill,Rich	(1201 FBB)	Sadler,Casey	(4100 FDC)	Price,David	(2201 DCB)
	Gray,Josh	(2203 FBD)	Hudson,Dakota	(1103 FCD)	Stammen,Craig	(4201 DCA)	Rainey,Tanner	(2510 DDF)
	Heaney,Andrew	(2301 DBA)	Kaprielian,James	(1203 CDF)	Warren,Art	(4510 DFA)	Rasmussen,Drew	(2301 ADB)
	Houser,Adrian	(2003 BBA)	Luzardo,Jesús	(1201 BCD)	Bickford,Phil	(3310 AFA)	Snyder,Nick	(2210 CFF)
	Kikuchi,Yusei	(2203 AAB)	Miley,Wade	(1003 FBB)	Boxberger,Brad	(3410 BDC)	Staumont,Josh	(2310 BDA)
	Kluber,Corey	(2301 FDB)	Odorizzi,Jake	(1203 FBA)	Brentz,Jake	(3410 ADD)	Steckenrider,Drew	(2210 FDC)
	Meyer,Max	(2301 AFF)	Peterson,David	(1201 FCB)	Chafin,Andrew	(3310 CDB)	Steele,Justin	(2201 DFF)
	Mikolas,Miles	(2001 FCA)	Smyly,Drew	(1203 FBD)	Graterol,Brusdar	(3110 DDB)	Stratton,Chris	(2311 CCB)
	Minor,Mike	(2203 CAA)	Suarez,José	(1103 BDF)	Graveman,Kendall	(3210 FDD)	White,Mitch	(2201 ADC)
	Pivetta,Nick	(2303 ACB)	Walker,Taijuan	(1103 FBA)	Jackson,Luke	(3300 ACD)	Wick,Rowan	(2320 FDB)
	Ryan,Joe	(2303 AFF)	Hernández,Carlos	(0103 ADC)	Loup,Aaron	(3300 FDB)	Wittgren,Nick	(2210 BCA)
	Sanmartin,Reiver	(2101 ADD)	Irvin,Cole	(0003 ACB)	Lugo,Seth	(3311 FCA)	Barlow,Joe	(1220 AFD)
	Singer,Brady	(2203 CBB)			Martin,Christopher	(3110 FDB)	Cabréra,Genesis	(1211 ACC)
					Poche,Colin	(3500 FFF)	Cortes,Nestor	(1203 DDF)
					Scott,Tanner	(3410 CDB)	Estevez,Carlos	(1210 DCB)
					Springs,Jeffrey	(3510 FDD)	Finnegan,Kyle	(1210 BDA)
					Suter,Brent	(3201 FDD)	Heuer,Codi	(1010 ADB)
					Bard,Daniel	(2410 ACA)	Petit,Yusmeiro	(1011 ACA)
					Bradley,Archie	(2210 DCB)	Reyes,Alex	(1411 DCC)
					Brogdon,Connor	(2210 CDB)	Richards,Trevor	(1311 ACC)
					Cessa,Luis	(2110 CCB)	Santillan,Tony	(1311 ADF)
					Crochet,Garrett	(2400 BDD)	Thielbar,Caleb	(1200 BDB)
					Diekman,Jake	(2510 BCC)	Trivino,Lou	(1210 ACB)
					Falter,Bailey	(2201 CFD)	Wells,Tyler	(1210 CDF)
					Garcia,Jarlin	(2110 BDA)		

Universal Draft Grid

TIER	STARTING PITCHERS				RELIEF PITCHERS			
Below Fringe	Glasnow,Tyler	(5500 FBA)	Keuchel,Dallas	(1003 CAA)	Yates,Kirby	(4510 FCF)	Mejía,Jean Carlos	(1100 AFF)
	May,Dustin	(5400 FCC)	Kim,Kwang-Hyun	(1001 DBA)	Antone,Tejay	(3300 FDD)	Merryweather,Julian	(1110 FFB)
	Bauer,Trevor	**(3400 BAB)**	Kowar,Jackson	(1201 ADA)	Coonrod,Sam	(3300 DDC)	Montero,Rafael	(1100 FCB)
	Contreras,Roansy	(3300 BFF)	Kuhl,Chad	(1203 FCA)	Hicks,Jordan	(3210 FDD)	Norris,Daniel	(1200 DCB)
	Beeks,Jalen	(2200 FDD)	Manning,Matt	(1001 ADF)	Rodríguez,Joely	(3210 DDB)	Pagan,Emilio	(1300 ACB)
	Brash,Matt	(2400 AFF)	Mills,Alec	(1003 BBC)	Abreu,Bryan	(2300 CDF)	Patton,Spencer	(1310 ACC)
	Cabrera,Edward	(2311 AFA)	Pérez,Martin	(1101 DAA)	Alvarado,José	(2410 DDB)	Payamps,Joel	(1000 ADF)
	Corbin,Patrick	**(2203 AAB)**	Ross,Joe	(1101 FDD)	Anderson,Nick	(2310 FDF)	Peacock,Matt	(1010 ADA)
	Kirby,George	(2100 AFF)	Schmidt,Clarke	(1200 FFD)	Cimber,Adam	(2000 ADC)	Peralta,Wandy	(1100 CDA)
	Lamet,Dinelson	(2400 FCB)	Senzatela,Antonio	(1003 DBC)	Crismatt,Nabil	(2101 ADC)	Richards,Garrett	(1201 FCA)
	Liberatore,Matthew	(2200 AFF)	Sheffield,Justus	(1101 DCC)	Familia,Jeurys	(2400 CCB)	Robles,Hansel	(1310 BCC)
	McKay,Brendan	(2300 FFF)	Toussaint,Touki	(1201 FDC)	Garrett,Amir	(2410 BDC)	Rodríguez,Manuel	(1110 BFF)
	Pearson,Nate	(2301 DDF)	Velasquez,Vincent	(1301 DBB)	Hill,Tim	(2100 ADA)	Ruiz,José	(1200 ADF)
	Rodríguez,Grayson	(2200 AFF)	Zimmermann,Bruce	(1101 FDC)	James,Josh	(2400 FDF)	Sawamura,Hirokazu	(1300 CCA)
	Turnbull,Spencer	(2100 FBB)	Akin,Keegan	(0103 BCC)	King,Michael	(2300 DDB)	Sborz,Josh	(1310 ADB)
	Wacha,Michael	(2201 DBA)	Allen,Logan	(0100 ADA)	Luetge,Lucas	(2200 ADB)	Shaw,Bryan	(1100 BDF)
	Anderson,Brett	(1001 FBA)	Arrieta,Jake	(0100 FBA)	Martin,Brett	(2010 BDF)	Stanek,Ryne	(1400 ADD)
	Archer,Chris	(1301 FDA)	Barria,Jaime	(0001 ACC)	Maton,Phil	(2400 BDC)	Stephan,Trevor	(1300 ADD)
	Arihara,Kohei	(1001 FAC)	Bukauskas,J.B.	(0110 DFC)	Pomeranz,Drew	(2300 FCA)	Stripling,Ross	(1101 FBC)
	Boyd,Matthew	(1201 FAB)	Crowe,Wil	(0103 ACF)	Pop,Zach	(2100 BFF)	Thompson,Keegan	(1201 BFF)
	Bubic,Kris	(1103 ACA)	Davies,Zachary	(0003 CAC)	Puk,A.J.	(2300 FFF)	Underwood Jr.,Duane	(1110 CDC)
	Bundy,Dylan	(1201 DAB)	Dunn,Justin	(0200 FCB)	Romo,Sergio	(2210 BCA)	Zimmer,Kyle	(1210 CDF)
	Canning,Griffin	(1201 CCB)	Garcia,Deivi	(0200 ADC)	Stephenson,Robert	(2300 DDA)	Allard,Kolby	(0101 ACB)
	Cavalli,Cade	(1300 AFF)	González,Chi Chi	(0001 FCB)	Tate,Dillon	(2000 DDA)	Beede,Tyler	(0101 FDD)
	Cueto,Johnny	(1101 FBA)	Gutierrez,Vladimir	(0101 ADF)	Taylor,Josh	(2300 DDF)	Clippard,Tyler	(0210 FDB)
	Dobnak,Randy	(1001 FCC)	Harvey,Matt	(0001 FCB)	Alexander,Tyler	(1101 ACD)	De Geus,Brett	(0000 AFF)
	Duffy,Danny	(1200 FBA)	Jax,Griffin	(0001 ADB)	Alvarez,Jose	(1000 CDA)	Espino,Paolo	(0001 ADD)
	Fedde,Erick	(1103 DBB)	Kremer,Dean	(0101 ADB)	Bass,Anthony	(1111 BCB)	Feyereisen,J.P.	(0200 CDC)
	Fleming,Josh	(1001 ACC)	Lester,Jon	(0003 DAA)	Bielak,Brandon	(1100 ADD)	Funkhouser,Kyle	(0100 ADC)
	Foltynewicz,Mike	(1101 DCF)	López,Reynaldo	(0201 BCB)	Castro,Miguel	(1200 ACC)	Gant,John	(0101 BCD)
	Freeland,Kyle	(1003 DBC)	Lyles,Jordan	(0101 CAC)	Cisnero,José	(1210 BCB)	Helsley,Ryan	(0100 DDD)
	Greene,Hunter	(1301 AFF)	Lynch,Daniel	(0101 AFF)	Foster,Matt	(1200 ADB)	Holloway,Jordan	(0100 CFF)
	Hancock,Emerson	(1000 CFF)	Morgan,Elijah	(0101 ADB)	Guerra,Deolis	(1200 ADB)	Moore,Matt	(0100 FCD)
	Happ,J.A.	**(1101 BAB)**	Oviedo,Johan	(0100 ADA)	**Hand,Brad**	**(1210 ABB)**	Peralta,Wily	(0001 BDC)
	Howard,Spencer	(1201 BDD)	Ureña,José	(0001 FCB)	Harvey,Hunter	(1100 FDB)	Rogers,Josh	(0001 DDF)
	Keller,Brad	(1103 CAB)	Widener,Taylor	(0201 FDB)	Hentges,Sam	(1201 ADF)	Smith,Caleb	(0300 DBC)
	Keller,Mitch	(1203 CDB)	Wilson,Bryse	(0001 BDA)	Hoffman,Jeff	(1300 DDC)	Smith,Riley	(0000 ADF)
					Holland,Greg	(1210 DCD)	Voth,Austin	(0201 DCB)
					Junis,Jakob	(1200 DCB)	Weathers,Ryan	(0001 ADF)
					Kinley,Tyler	(1200 ADB)	Woodford,Jake	(0001 ADA)
					López,Jorge	**(1100 BBA)**	Young,Alex	(0100 ACA)
					Lorenzen,Michael	(1110 FCA)		

SIMULATION LEAGUE DRAFT　　　　　　　　TOP 500+

NAME	POS	RAR	NAME	POS	RAR	NAME	POS	RAR	NAME	POS	RAR
Soto,Juan	9	75.5	Realmuto,J.T.	2	23.1	Suárez,Ranger	P	16.2	Arozarena,Randy	79	11.6
Trout,Mike	8	65.3	Polanco,Jorge	46	22.9	Varsho,Daulton	28	16.1	Treinen,Blake	P	11.5
Harper,Bryce	9	62.1	Robert,Luis	8	22.8	Garcia,Luis	P	16.1	Márquez,Germán	P	11.5
Freeman,Freddie	3	55.6	Altuve,Jose	4	22.7	Contreras,Willson	2	16.1	Mancini,Trey	3	11.4
Guerrero Jr.,Vladimir	3	48.2	Anderson,Tim	6	22.5	Cruz,Nelson	0	16.0	Knebel,Corey	P	11.3
Ramirez,Jose	5	45.3	Musgrove,Joe	P	22.4	France,Ty	34	16.0	Lewis,Kyle	8	11.3
Tatis Jr.,Fernando	69	44.3	Verdugo,Alex	789	22.3	Gallo,Joey	79	15.9	Flores,Wilmer	345	11.3
Reynolds,Bryan	8	40.6	Donaldson,Josh	5	22.1	McCullers,Lance	P	15.8	Gallegos,Giovanny	P	11.2
Judge,Aaron	89	40.2	Montas,Frankie	P	21.7	Kirk,Alejandro	2	15.8	Jackson,Luke	P	11.2
Marte,Ketel	48	40.2	Pollock,A.J.	7	21.5	Morton,Charlie	P	15.6	Snell,Blake	P	11.1
Goldschmidt,Paul	3	39.2	Bell,Josh	3	21.5	Happ,Ian	78	15.6	Renfroe,Hunter	9	11.1
Turner,Trea	46	38.7	Correa,Carlos	6	21.4	Gallen,Zac	P	15.4	Strasburg,Stephen	P	11.1
Springer,George	8	38.2	Nola,Aaron	P	21.4	Stephenson,Tyler	23	15.3	Witt Jr.,Bobby	6	11.1
Betts,Mookie	89	38.1	Bregman,Alex	5	21.3	Baddoo,Akil	78	15.2	Lowe,Nate	3	11.1
Acuña,Ronald	9	36.3	Cron,C.J.	3	21.1	Haniger,Mitch	9	15.2	Bednar,David	P	11.0
Winker,Jesse	7	35.7	Bellinger,Cody	8	21.0	Nola,Austin	2	14.8	Kimbrel,Craig	P	11.0
Bogaerts,Xander	6	35.6	Arenado,Nolan	5	21.0	O Neill,Tyler	7	14.8	Rosario,Eddie	7	11.0
Smith,Will	2	35.3	Gausman,Kevin	P	20.9	Reyes,Franmil	0	14.8	Slater,Austin	789	11.0
Tucker,Kyle	9	35.3	Mullins,Cedric	8	20.7	Merrifield,Whit	40	14.7	Segura,Jean	4	10.9
Castellanos,Nick	9	35.1	Ohtani,Shohei	P	20.7	Jiménez,Eloy	7	14.7	Fulmer,Michael	P	10.8
Devers,Rafael	5	34.8	Webb,Logan	P	20.4	Bassitt,Chris	P	14.6	Zunino,Mike	2	10.5
Lowe,Brandon	4	33.8	Yelich,Christian	7	20.3	Gray,Sonny	P	14.6	Gurriel,Yuli	3	10.5
Olson,Matt	3	33.6	Ruf,Darin	37	20.2	LeMahieu,DJ	345	14.5	Rodgers,Brendan	46	10.5
Seager,Corey	6	33.3	Peralta,Freddy	P	20.1	Díaz,Elias	2	14.1	Rutschman,Adley	2	10.4
Franco,Wander	6	33.3	Cronenworth,Jake	346	20.1	Rodriguez,Eduardo	P	14.1	Kittredge,Andrew	P	10.4
Machado,Manny	5	33.3	Blackmon,Charlie	9	19.9	Walsh,Jared	3	14.0	Kopech,Michael	P	10.4
Alvarez,Yordan	7	32.9	Bryant,Kris	579	19.8	Rizzo,Anthony	3	14.0	Holmes,Clay	P	10.4
Burnes,Corbin	P	32.8	Adames,Willy	6	19.7	Iglesias,Raisel	P	13.9	Chapman,Aroldis	P	10.4
Rendon,Anthony	5	32.6	Abreu,José	3	19.7	Yastrzemski,Mike	89	13.9	Montgomery,Jordan	P	10.4
Scherzer,Max	P	32.4	Rodón,Carlos	P	19.7	Romano,Jordan	P	13.8	Rasmussen,Drew	P	10.4
Cole,Gerrit	P	32.3	McClanahan,Shane	P	19.4	Rogers,Taylor	P	13.7	Floro,Dylan	P	10.2
Hoskins,Rhys	3	31.8	Nimmo,Brandon	8	19.4	Swanson,Dansby	6	13.7	Castillo,Diego	P	10.2
Grandal,Yasmani	2	31.3	Gurriel Jr.,Lourdes	7	19.3	Madrigal,Nick	4	13.6	McNeil,Jeff	47	10.2
Alonso,Pete	3	31.1	Wainwright,Adam	P	19.0	Flaherty,Jack	P	13.4	Mejía,Francisco	2	10.2
Buehler,Walker	P	30.3	Brantley,Michael	7	19.0	Clevinger,Mike	P	13.4	Narváez,Omar	2	10.2
Bichette,Bo	6	30.1	Posey,Buster	2	19.0	Manaea,Sean	P	13.4	Quantrill,Cal	P	10.2
Belt,Brandon	3	30.1	Turner,Justin	5	18.9	Mahle,Tyler	P	13.4	Loup,Aaron	P	10.2
Schwarber,Kyle	7	29.6	Crawford,Brandon	6	18.9	Ozuna,Marcell	7	13.4	Ryu,Hyun-Jin	P	10.1
Story,Trevor	6	29.6	Giolito,Lucas	P	18.7	Eovaldi,Nathan	P	13.3	Melancon,Mark	P	10.1
Woodruff,Brandon	P	29.4	Berríos,José	P	18.6	Myers,Wil	9	13.0	Meyer,Max	P	10.1
Riley,Austin	5	29.2	Candelario,Jeimer	5	18.5	Hendriks,Liam	P	13.0	Sánchez,Sixto	P	10.1
Wheeler,Zack	P	28.7	Ray,Robbie	P	18.3	Cobb,Alex	P	12.9	Darvish,Yu	P	9.9
Alcantara,Sandy	P	28.6	Castillo,Luis	P	18.2	Manoah,Alek	P	12.9	Longoria,Evan	5	9.9
Votto,Joey	3	28.6	Cease,Dylan	P	18.2	Mountcastle,Ryan	37	12.9	Lowrie,Jed	4	9.9
Perez,Salvador	2	28.4	Clase,Emmanuel	P	18.1	McCutchen,Andrew	7	12.7	Greene,Riley	0	9.8
Urías,Julio	P	28.3	Stroman,Marcus	P	17.8	Pressly,Ryan	P	12.7	Pineda,Michael	P	9.8
deGrom,Jacob	P	28.3	Anderson,Ian	P	17.7	McHugh,Collin	P	12.5	Wood,Alex	P	9.8
Martinez,J.D.	7	27.8	Stanton,Giancarlo	0	17.7	Urías,Luis	456	12.5	Sadler,Casey	P	9.8
Muncy,Max	34	27.6	Kershaw,Clayton	P	17.6	Ruiz,Keibert	2	12.5	Arraez,Luis	457	9.6
Hernández,Teoscar	79	27.5	Whitlock,Garrett	P	17.5	Hayes,Ke'Bryan	5	12.5	Green,Chad	P	9.6
India,Jonathan	4	26.5	Moncada,Yoán	5	17.5	Grisham,Trent	8	12.3	Suter,Brent	P	9.6
Rogers,Trevor	P	26.5	Taylor,Chris	4678	17.0	Benintendi,Andrew	7	12.2	Naquin,Tyler	789	9.5
Garver,Mitch	2	26.3	Houck,Tanner	P	17.0	Voit,Luke	3	12.2	Miley,Wade	P	9.5
Buxton,Byron	8	25.7	López,Pablo	P	17.0	Bummer,Aaron	P	12.1	Kelenic,Jarred	8	9.4
Bieber,Shane	P	25.6	Hader,Josh	P	16.6	Sánchez,Jesús	79	12.1	Neris,Héctor	P	9.4
Semien,Marcus	46	24.4	Baz,Shane	P	16.6	Aguilar,Jesús	3	12.1	Matzek,Tyler	P	9.4
Fried,Max	P	24.4	Lindor,Francisco	6	16.5	Soler,Jorge	9	12.1	Suárez,Eugenio	56	9.4
Lynn,Lance	P	24.3	Verlander,Justin	P	16.5	Jansen,Danny	2	11.7	Rogers,Tyler	P	9.4
Valdez,Framber	P	23.9	Severino,Luis	P	16.5	Dalbec,Bobby	3	11.7	García,Avisaíl	9	9.3
Ohtani,Shohei	0	23.7	Hernández,Kiké	48	16.4	Means,John	P	11.7	Syndergaard,Noah	P	9.2
Albies,Ozzie	4	23.4	Murphy,Sean	2	16.3	Báez,Javier	46	11.7	Graveman,Kendall	P	9.2
Marte,Starling	8	23.3	Williams,Devin	P	16.3	Torres,Gleyber	6	11.6	Kelly,Carson	2	9.1
Sale,Chris	P	23.1	Conforto,Michael	9	16.2	McMahon,Ryan	45	11.6	Matz,Steven	P	9.1

SIMULATION LEAGUE DRAFT TOP 500+

NAME	POS	RAR	NAME	POS	RAR	NAME	POS	RAR	NAME	POS	RAR
Houser,Adrian	P	9.0	Stallings,Jacob	2	6.6	Rosenthal,Trevor	P	4.7	Thielbar,Caleb	P	3.3
Sewald,Paul	P	9.0	Mize,Casey	P	6.4	Choi,Ji-Man	3	4.7	Kennedy,Ian	P	3.3
Ynoa,Huascar	P	9.0	Bickford,Phil	P	6.4	Cabréra,Genesis	P	4.6	Duffy,Danny	P	3.3
Hendricks,Kyle	P	9.0	Ruiz,José	P	6.4	Luetge,Lucas	P	4.6	McKay,Brendan	P	3.2
Stammen,Craig	P	8.9	May,Trevor	P	6.2	Gilbert,Logan	P	4.6	Wick,Rowan	P	3.2
Gomes,Yan	2	8.9	Laureano,Ramón	8	6.2	Sánchez,Gary	2	4.6	Taylor,Josh	P	3.2
Grossman,Robbie	79	8.9	Soroka,Michael	P	6.2	Kaprielian,James	P	4.5	Hicks,Jordan	P	3.2
Díaz,Edwin	P	8.9	Ashby,Aaron	P	6.2	Littell,Zack	P	4.5	Biggio,Cavan	5	3.2
Lugo,Seth	P	8.9	Civale,Aaron	P	6.2	Poche,Colin	P	4.4	Calhoun,Willie	7	3.2
Bader,Harrison	8	8.7	Garcia,Jarlin	P	6.2	Peralta,David	7	4.4	Beaty,Matt	379	3.2
Tellez,Rowdy	3	8.7	Jansen,Kenley	P	6.2	Wells,Tyler	P	4.4	Diekman,Jake	P	3.1
Taillon,Jameson	P	8.7	Smith,Pavin	3789	6.2	Kirby,George	P	4.4	Mikolas,Miles	P	3.1
Cessa,Luis	P	8.7	Ibáñez,Andy	4	6.1	McGee,Jake	P	4.4	Cisnero,José	P	3.0
Cousins,Jake	P	8.7	Chafin,Andrew	P	6.1	Graterol,Brusdar	P	4.3	Rogers,Jake	2	3.0
Loaisiga,Jonathan	P	8.7	Sims,Lucas	P	6.1	Karinchak,James	P	4.3	Hill,Rich	P	3.0
Escobar,Eduardo	45	8.7	Canha,Mark	789	6.1	Alvarez,Jose	P	4.3	Colomé,Alex	P	3.0
Smith,Will	P	8.7	Sanó,Miguel	3	6.1	Schoop,Jonathan	34	4.2	Brash,Matt	P	3.0
Ober,Bailey	P	8.5	Gilbert,Tyler	P	6.1	Hill,Tim	P	4.2	Snyder,Nick	P	2.9
McKenzie,Triston	P	8.4	Martin,Christopher	P	6.0	Richards,Trevor	P	4.2	Dickerson,Alex	7	2.9
Hudson,Dakota	P	8.4	Rodríguez,Julio	9	5.9	Kahnle,Tommy	P	4.1	Weaver,Luke	P	2.9
Plesac,Zach	P	8.3	Doval,Camilo	P	5.9	Barlow,Joe	P	4.1	Miller,Brad	30	2.9
Alcala,Jorge	P	8.2	Duvall,Adam	789	5.9	Brogdon,Connor	P	4.1	Walker,Taijuan	P	2.9
Rodríguez,Richard	P	8.2	Giles,Ken	P	5.9	Contreras,William	2	4.1	Espinal,Santiago	5	2.9
Cain,Lorenzo	8	8.1	D Arnaud,Travis	2	5.8	Springs,Jeffrey	P	4.1	Gray,Josiah	P	2.9
Canó,Robinson	4	8.1	Brentz,Jake	P	5.8	Rodriguez,Grayson	P	4.1	Estevez,Carlos	P	2.8
Flexen,Chris	P	8.1	Patino,Luis	P	5.8	Petit,Yusmeiro	P	4.1	Paxton,James	P	2.8
Santillan,Tony	P	8.0	Otto Jr.,Glenn	P	5.8	Peterson,David	P	4.1	Iglesias,José	6	2.8
Solano,Donovan	4	8.0	Price,David	P	5.8	Severino,Pedro	2	4.0	Kepler,Max	89	2.8
Bender,Anthony	P	7.9	Melendez,MJ	2	5.7	Alvarado,José	P	4.0	Finnegan,Kyle	P	2.8
Hosmer,Eric	3	7.9	Greinke,Zack	P	5.7	Givens,Mychal	P	4.0	Bohm,Alec	5	2.7
Wong,Kolten	4	7.9	Urías,Ramón	46	5.6	Steele,Justin	P	4.0	Hays,Austin	79	2.7
Hilliard,Sam	8	7.9	Steckenrider,Drew	P	5.5	Ramos,Wilson	2	3.9	Schmidt,Clarke	P	2.7
Hernandez,Elieser	P	7.8	Trivino,Lou	P	5.5	Ward,Taylor	9	3.9	Beeks,Jalen	P	2.7
Hicks,Aaron	8	7.8	Dunning,Dane	P	5.5	Bass,Anthony	P	3.9	La Stella,Tommy	4	2.7
Skubal,Tarik	P	7.7	Heuer,Codi	P	5.5	Crismatt,Nabil	P	3.9	Peralta,Wandy	P	2.7
Crochet,Garrett	P	7.7	Germán,Domingo	P	5.5	Coonrod,Sam	P	3.9	Edman,Tommy	49	2.6
Gonzales,Marco	P	7.7	Frazier,Adam	4	5.5	Murphy,Tom	2	3.9	Casas,Triston	0	2.6
Barlow,Scott	P	7.6	Thompson,Keegan	P	5.4	Megill,Tylor	P	3.8	Cueto,Johnny	P	2.6
Javier,Cristian	P	7.6	Soto,Gregory	P	5.4	Rojas,Josh	469	3.8	Barnhart,Tucker	2	2.6
Cooper,Garrett	9	7.5	Boxberger,Brad	P	5.3	Reyes,Alex	P	3.8	Gomber,Austin	P	2.6
Mayza,Tim	P	7.4	Sandoval,Patrick	P	5.3	Wittgren,Nick	P	3.8	Moustakas,Mike	5	2.6
DeSclafani,Anthony	P	7.4	Rodríguez,Joely	P	5.2	Pederson,Joc	789	3.8	Stephenson,Robert	P	2.6
Urshela,Gio	56	7.4	Luplow,Jordan	8	5.2	Kluber,Corey	P	3.8	Ottavino,Adam	P	2.6
Davis,J.D.	5	7.3	Haase,Eric	27	5.2	Pomeranz,Drew	P	3.7	Stratton,Chris	P	2.5
Hernández,Carlos	P	7.2	Staumont,Josh	P	5.2	Guerra,Deolis	P	3.7	Contreras,Roansy	P	2.5
Eflin,Zach	P	7.2	Wade Jr.,LaMonte	379	5.2	Castro,Miguel	P	3.6	Herrera,Odúbel	78	2.5
Gonsolin,Tony	P	7.2	Anderson,Brian	5	5.2	Alzolay,Adbert	P	3.6	Grichuk,Randal	89	2.4
Robertson,David	P	7.2	Fairbanks,Peter	P	5.1	Cimber,Adam	P	3.6	Rosario,Amed	6	2.4
Lauer,Eric	P	7.1	Rainey,Tanner	P	5.1	Anderson,Nick	P	3.5	Martin,Brett	P	2.4
Joe,Connor	7	7.1	Johnson,Pierce	P	5.0	Maeda,Kenta	P	3.5	Brubaker,Jonathan	P	2.4
Rojas,Miguel	6	7.1	Lowe,Josh	O	4.9	Hernández,Jonathan	P	3.5	Suarez,José	P	2.4
Cortes,Nestor	P	7.0	May,Dustin	P	4.9	Bradley,Archie	P	3.5	Kim,Kwang-Hyun	P	2.4
Duffey,Tyler	P	6.9	Dickerson,Corey	7	4.9	Paredes,Isaac	4	3.5	Heaney,Andrew	P	2.4
Warren,Art	P	6.8	Nuñez,Dom	2	4.9	Taylor,Tyrone	79	3.5	Leclerc,José	P	2.3
Chisholm Jr.,Jazz	46	6.8	Mayers,Mike	P	4.9	Robles,Hansel	P	3.4	Tapia,Raimel	7	2.3
Sulser,Cole	P	6.8	Stassi,Max	2	4.9	Bauer,Trevor	P	3.4	Lamet,Dinelson	P	2.2
King,John	P	6.8	Seager,Kyle	5	4.9	García,Leury	4789	3.4	Scott,Tanner	P	2.1
Kirilloff,Alex	39	6.7	Gibson,Kyle	P	4.8	Toro,Abraham	45	3.4	Barnes,Matt	P	2.1
Díaz,Yandy	35	6.7	Barrero,Jose	6	4.8	Sanmartin,Reiver	P	3.4	Yarbrough,Ryan	P	2.1
Carlson,Dylan	89	6.7	Stanek,Ryne	P	4.8	Estrada,Thairo	6	3.3	Glasnow,Tyler	P	2.1
White,Mitch	P	6.7	Chapman,Matt	5	4.8	Urquidy,José	P	3.3	Familia,Jeurys	P	2.0
Meadows,Austin	7	6.7	McCann,James	2	4.8	Carrasco,Carlos	P	3.3	Zimmerman,Ryan	3	2.0
Kelly,Merrill	P	6.7	Smith,Dominic	7	4.7	Ríos,Edwin	3	3.3	Martínez,Carlos	P	2.0

MULTI-POSITION ELIGIBLITY

*Position player eligibility for leagues that use 5 games, 10 games and 20 games as their requirements. *Qualified based on the position played the most.*

NAME	5-Gm	10-Gm	20-Gm	NAME	5-Gm	10-Gm	20-Gm	NAME	5-Gm	10-Gm	20-Gm
Adrianza,Ehire	2B 3B SS OF	3B OF	OF	Gonzalez,Marwin	1B 2B 3B SS OF	1B 2B 3B SS OF	2B	Polanco,Jorge	2B SS	2B SS	2B SS
Alcantara,Sergio	2B SS	2B SS	2B SS	Goodrum,Niko	2B SS OF	SS	SS	Profar,Jurickson	1B 2B OF	1B 2B OF	1B OF
Alfaro,Jorge	CA OF	CA OF	CA OF	Gosselin,Phil	1B 3B OF	1B 3B OF	1B 3B OF	Realmuto,JT	CA 1B	CA 1B	CA
Arauz,Jonathan	2B SS	2B SS	SS *	Grandal,Yasmani	CA 1B	CA	CA	Rengifo,Luis	3B SS OF	3B SS OF	SS
Arcia,Orlando	SS OF	OF	OF*	Guillorme,Luis	2B 3B SS	2B 3B SS	3B	Riley,Austin	1B 3B	1B 3B	3B
Arraez,Luis	2B 3B OF	2B 3B OF	2B 3B OF	Gurriel,Lourdes	1B OF	1B OF	OF	Rios,Edwin	1B 3B	1B	1B *
Astudillo,Willians	CA 1B 3B	CA 1B 3B	1B 3B	Haase,Eric	CA OF	CA OF	CA OF	Rivas III,Alfonso	1B OF	OF*	OF*
Baez,Javier	2B SS	2B SS	2B SS	Hampson,Garrett	2B SS OF	2B OF	2B OF	Robertson,Daniel	2B 3B SS	3B	3B
Barnes,Austin	CA 2B	CA	CA	Hernandez,Enrique	2B SS OF	2B OF	2B OF	Rodgers,Brendan	2B SS	2B SS	2B SS
Barrero,Jose	SS OF	SS *	SS *	Hernandez,Yonny	2B 3B SS	3B	3B	Rojas,Jose	2B 3B OF	2B 3B OF	OF
Bauers,Jake	1B OF	1B OF	1B OF	Hiura,Keston	1B 2B	1B	1B	Rojas,Josh	2B 3B SS OF	2B 3B SS OF	2B SS OF
Beaty,Matt	1B 3B OF	1B OF	1B OF	Hoerner,Nico	2B SS OF	2B SS	2B	Rondon,Jose	3B OF	OF	OF*
Bell,Josh	1B OF	1B	1B	Ibanez,Andy	1B 2B 3B	1B 2B 3B	2B	Rosario,Amed	SS OF	SS OF	SS
Berti,Jon	2B 3B OF	2B 3B	2B 3B	Iglesias,Jose	2B SS	2B SS	SS	Ruf,Darin	1B OF	1B OF	1B OF
Biggio,Cavan	1B 2B 3B OF	3B OF	3B	Joe,Connor	1B OF	1B OF	OF	Ruiz,Rio	2B 3B	2B 3B	2B
Blandino,Alex	1B 2B 3B	1B	1B *	Kemp,Anthony	2B OF	2B OF	2B OF	Sano,Miguel	1B 3B	1B	1B
Bohm,Alec	1B 3B	3B	3B	Kim,Ha-Seong	2B 3B SS	2B 3B SS	2B 3B SS	Santana,Danny	1B OF	1B OF	OF*
Bote,David	2B 3B	2B 3B	2B 3B	Kirilloff,Alex	1B OF	1B OF	1B OF	Schoop,Jonathan	1B 2B	1B 2B	1B 2B
Brosseau,Michael	1B 2B 3B	1B 2B 3B	2B 3B	Knapp,Andrew	CA 1B	CA	CA	Schrock,Max	1B 2B 3B OF	OF	OF
Brown,Seth	1B OF	OF	OF	La Stella,Tommy	2B 3B	2B	2B	Schwarber,Kyle	1B OF	1B OF	OF
Cabrera,Asdrubal	1B 3B	1B 3B	3B	Lamb,Jake	3B OF	3B OF	OF	Semien,Marcus	2B SS	2B SS	2B SS
Carpenter,Matt	1B 2B 3B	1B 2B	2B	LeMahieu,DJ	1B 2B 3B	1B 2B 3B	1B 2B 3B	Senzel,Nick	2B OF	OF	OF
Castro,Harold	1B 2B 3B SS OF	1B 2B 3B SS	2B SS	Long,Shed	2B OF	2B OF	OF	Sheets,Gavin	1B OF	1B OF	OF*
Castro,Rodolfo	2B 3B	2B	2B	Lowe,Brandon	2B OF	2B OF	2B	Smith,Pavin	1B OF	1B OF	1B OF
Chang,Yu	1B 2B 3B SS	1B 3B	1B 3B	Luplow,Jordan	1B OF	1B OF	OF	Sogard,Eric	2B 3B	2B 3B	2B
Chavis,Michael	1B 2B	2B	2B	Lux,Gavin	2B SS OF	2B SS OF	2B SS	Stephenson,Tyler	CA 1B	CA 1B	CA 1B
Chisholm,Jazz	2B SS	2B SS	2B SS	Marcano,Tucupita	2B OF	2B *	2B *	Suarez,Eugenio	3B SS	3B SS	3B SS
Clement,Ernie	2B 3B	2B 3B	2B	Marmolejos,Jose	1B OF	1B OF	1B *	Taylor,Chris	2B 3B SS OF	2B 3B SS OF	2B SS OF
Cooper,Garrett	1B OF	1B OF	OF	Mateo,Jorge	2B 3B SS OF	2B SS OF	OF	Toro,Abraham	2B 3B	2B 3B	2B 3B
Cordero,Franchy	1B OF	1B OF	OF	Maton,Nick	2B SS	2B SS	2B SS	Torrens,Luis	CA 1B	CA	CA
Cronenworth,Jake	1B 2B SS	1B 2B SS	1B 2B SS	Mayfield,Jack	2B 3B SS	3B SS	3B	Torres,Gleyber	2B SS	2B SS	SS
Culberson,Charlie	3B OF	3B	3B	McCann,James	CA 1B	CA	CA	Torreyes,Ronald	2B 3B SS	2B 3B SS	3B SS
Dalbec,Bobby	1B 3B	1B 3B	1B	McKinney,Billy	1B OF	1B OF	OF	Trejo,Alan	2B SS	2B	2B *
Devers,Jose	2B SS	2B	2B *	McMahon,Ryan	2B 3B	2B 3B	2B 3B	Tucker,Cole	2B SS OF	SS OF	SS *
Diaz,Aledmys	1B 2B 3B SS OF	1B 2B 3B OF	3B	Mendick,Danny	2B SS OF	2B SS	2B SS	Turner,Trea	2B SS	2B SS	2B SS
Diaz,Isan	2B 3B	2B 3B	2B 3B	Mercer,Jordy	2B 3B SS	2B 3B	2B	Urias,Luis	2B 3B SS	2B 3B SS	2B 3B SS
Diaz,Yandy	1B 3B	1B 3B	1B 3B	Merrifield,Whit	2B OF	2B OF	2B OF	Urias,Ramon	2B 3B SS	2B 3B SS	2B SS
Difo,Wilmer	2B 3B OF	2B 3B	2B	Miller,Bradley	1B 2B 3B OF	1B 2B OF	1B OF	Urshela,Giovanny	3B SS	3B SS	3B SS
Dozier,Hunter	1B 3B OF	1B 3B OF	3B OF	Miller,Owen	1B 2B 3B	1B 2B	2B	Valaika,Pat	1B 2B SS	2B SS	2B
Drury,Brandon	3B OF	OF	OF*	Moore,Dylan	2B 3B OF	2B 3B OF	2B OF	Valera,Breyvic	2B 3B	2B 3B	3B
Dubon,Mauricio	2B 3B SS OF	2B 3B SS OF	2B SS OF	Mountcastle,Ryan	1B OF	1B OF	1B OF	VanMeter,Josh	2B 3B	2B 3B	2B 3B
Edman,Tommy	2B OF	2B OF	2B OF	Moustakas,Mike	1B 3B	1B 3B	3B	Vargas,Ildemaro	2B 3B SS	3B	3B *
Escobar,Alcides	2B SS	2B SS	SS	Muncy,Max	1B 2B 3B	1B 2B	1B 2B	Varsho,Daulton	CA OF	CA OF	CA OF
Escobar,Eduardo	1B 2B 3B	1B 2B 3B	2B 3B	Naylor,Josh	1B OF	1B OF	OF	Vaughn,Andrew	1B OF	1B OF	OF
Estrada,Thairo	2B SS OF	2B SS	SS *	Neuse,Sheldon	2B 3B OF	2B	2B *	Vierling,Matt	1B OF	OF	OF*
Evans,Phillip	1B 3B OF	1B 3B OF	1B OF	Newman,Kevin	2B SS	2B SS	SS	Villar,Jonathan	2B 3B SS	3B SS	3B SS
Franco,Wander	3B SS	SS	SS	O'Hearn,Ryan	1B OF	1B OF	1B OF	Wade,LaMonte	1B OF	1B OF	1B OF
Frazier,Adam	2B OF	2B OF	2B	Odor,Rougned	2B 3B	2B 3B	2B 3B	Wade,Tyler	2B 3B SS OF	2B 3B SS OF	3B SS OF
Fuentes,Josh	1B 3B	1B 3B	1B 3B	Panik,Joe	1B 2B 3B	2B 3B	2B 3B	Walsh,Jared	1B OF	1B OF	1B
Galvis,Freddy	3B SS	3B SS	SS	Paredes,Isaac	2B 3B SS	2B	2B *	Walton,Donnie	2B OF	2B	2B *
Garcia,Leury	2B 3B SS OF	2B 3B SS OF	2B OF	Park,Hoy Jun	2B 3B SS OF	2B	2B *	Wendle,Joe	2B 3B SS	2B 3B SS	3B SS
Garcia,Luis	2B SS	2B	2B	Peraza,Jose	2B 3B	2B	2B	Williams,Luke	1B 2B 3B SS OF	OF	OF
Garcia,Robel	2B 3B SS	3B SS	3B *	Peterson,Jace	1B 2B 3B OF	1B 2B 3B OF	1B 2B OF	Wisdom,Patrick	1B 3B OF	1B 3B OF	3B
Gonzalez,Erik	1B 3B SS	1B 3B SS	3B	Pinder,Chad	2B 3B SS OF	OF	OF				

Get Forecaster Insights Every Single Day.

The **Baseball Forecaster** provides the core concepts in player evaluation and gaming strategy. You can maintain that edge all season long.

From spring training to the season's last pitch, **BaseballHQ.com** covers all aspects of what's happening on and off the field—all with the most powerful fantasy slant on the Internet:

- Nationally-renowned baseball analysts.
- MLB news analysis; including anticipating the **next** move.
- Dedicated columns on starting pitching, relievers, batters, and our popular Fact or Fluke? player profiles.
- Minor-league coverage beyond just scouting and lists.
- FAAB targets, starting pitcher reports, strategy articles, daily game resources, call-up profiles and more!

Plus, **BaseballHQ.com** gets personal, with customizable tools and valuable resources:

- Team Stat Tracker and Power Search tools
- Custom Draft Guide for YOUR league's parameters
- Sortable and downloadable stats and projection files
- Subscriber forums, the friendliest on the baseball Internet

Visit **www.baseballhq.com/subscribe**
to lock down your path to a 2022 championship!

Full Season subscription $89
(prorated at the time of order; auto-renews each October)

Draft Prep subscription $39
(complete access from January through April 30, 2022)

Please read our Terms of service at www.baseballhq.com/terms.html

Baseball Forecaster & BaseballHQ.com: Your season-long championship lineup.

Save the date!

March 4-6, 2022

Interactive sessions • Player analysis

Injury updates • Current ADP feedback

Gaming strategies • Live drafts

Spring training games

Plus the LABR experts drafts in-person

.... and a whole lot more!

Details: www.baseballhq.com/first-pitch-florida

BONUS DATE: First Pitch Arizona at the Arizona Fall League • November 3-6, 2022

Where else to find Ron Shandler these days